THE NEW BOOK OF KNOWLEDGE

THE NEW BOOK OF KNOWLEDGE

Scholastic Library Publishing, Inc.
Danbury, Connecticut

VOLUME 1

A

Library of Congress Cataloging-in-Publication Data

The new book of knowledge.
p. cm.
Includes bibliographical references and index.
ISBN 0-7172-0539-8 (set: alk. paper)
1. Children's encyclopedias and dictionaries. I. Scholastic Library Publishing.
AG5.N273 2005
031—dc22

2004008685

ISBN 0-7172-0539-8 (set)

PRINTED AND MANUFACTURED IN THE UNITED STATES OF AMERICA

The publishers wish to thank the following for permission to use copyrighted material:
Little, Brown and Company for excerpt from *Little Women* by Louisa May Alcott.
Harcourt, Brace & World, Inc., and Alfred J. Bedard for "The Emperor's New Clothes" from *It's Perfectly True and Other Stories* by Hans Christian Andersen, translated by Paul Leyssac, copyright 1938 by Paul Leyssac.
David McKay Company, Inc., for excerpts from *Arabian Nights,* edited by Andrew Lang, new edition 1946, copyright 1898, 1946, Longmans Green and Company, Inc., now David McKay Company, Inc.
Harcourt Brace Jovanovich, Inc., for excerpt on measuring star distances from *Space in Your Future* by Leo Schneider, copyright 1961 by Leo Schneider.

PREFACE

The mission of *The New Book of Knowledge* is simply stated: to provide authoritative, up-to-date content tailored to the needs and interests of younger readers. Today, on the threshold of a new millenium, this mission is more challenging—and more important—than ever before. Children and teens must filter an explosion of information unlike that of any previous generation. To help them in this task, editors of young people's reference materials must present balanced and appropriate coverage, while remaining sensitive to a young person's ability to absorb complex information.

We at *The New Book of Knowledge* are committed to meeting these goals for our encyclopedia. In its pages, elementary- and middle-school students will find information on a wealth of topics, clearly presented and beautifully illustrated, that helps them understand the constantly changing realities of the world they live in. More than two thousand advisers and contributors, together with a staff of editors, artists, and other specialists, have worked to create and sustain *The New Book of Knowledge*—an encyclopedia designed for the young people of the 21st century.

SCOPE

The New Book of Knowledge is designed for the library and the classroom as well as for practical and educational use at home. It is useful to a wide range of readers, from very young children to students ready for an adult encyclopedia. The content of the encyclopedia was selected by educators who analyzed the curriculum requirements of school systems across the nation, by librarians familiar with the research needs of children and young adults, and by cultural specialists who considered the interests and needs of the set's users beyond school and library settings. Students will find a wealth of information and concepts that will be important and useful in their schoolwork. In addition, the articles have been enriched by many informative projects, experiments, and colorful illustrations.

For children, and the young child in all of us, there are carefully selected illustrations, games, and activities, as well as selections from well-known and much-loved stories, myths, fables, and other classic works of literature. Parents will find much material to use with and read aloud to their children, both for enjoyment and as answers to their questions. These materials will provide important additions to every child's growing-up experiences. They will also help children learn the value of books as sources of information, imagination, and pleasure.

AUTHORITY

The articles in *The New Book of Knowledge* are written or reviewed by experts eminent in their fields who understand how to address and write about their subjects in a way that is both informative and interesting to our readership. Nearly all the articles are signed, and the contributor's or reviewer's name and affiliation are displayed at the end of an article. Many are signed not only by an author but also by a reviewer. A complete list of authors, reviewers, and contributors appears in Volume 20.

ACCURACY

Every article, map, drawing, photograph, diagram, chart, and fact box is checked by skilled researchers to ensure that the information provided is correct and current. Where authorities disagree or information is unknown, the reader is so informed. Editorial policy is to present fact, not opinion.

READABILITY

Reading consultants to the encyclopedia have helped the staff design a set that is comprehensible, informative, and interesting. Articles whose subjects appeal to younger children are at lower levels of comprehension, whereas other articles, especially those with a technical vocabulary, are at higher levels. The editors put information in context, providing the background material necessary to ensure a complete understanding of a topic. They realize that for information to become knowledge, it must be understood so well that its seekers can both use it correctly and communicate it to others. The editors also make sure to present information in an engaging style that will capture the reader's interest. To further ensure an enjoyable reading experience, the set is printed in a typeface that was chosen after careful research in typeface legibility.

ARRANGEMENT and AVAILABILITY of INFORMATION

The New Book of Knowledge is organized alphabetically in unit letter volumes. Each volume contains an Index that is cross-referenced to the entire contents of the set. Blue paper is used for the Index pages so that they can be easily identified. Articles and Index entries are arranged in alphabetical order, letter by letter to the comma, ignoring hierarchical orders. In addition, there is extensive use of *See also* references following articles.

The encyclopedia also includes standing cross-references. These are printed in the same type as article headings and refer the reader to the article or articles where the subject is covered. Other devices that assist the search for information include placing word guides at the bottom of each page close to the page number; placing a page number on every page or, where this is not possible, on one out of every double spread of pages; organizing long articles into shorter units through the use of boldface headings; and presenting information in concise forms such as fact summaries, chronologies, charts, graphs, and lists. Wonder Questions, which have been a part of the set since the original 1911 edition, along with many other special features, appeal to a child's curiosity and provide concise information about a wide range of topics.

MAPS

The New Book of Knowledge presents a map program planned especially to meet the needs of its readers. Maps are prepared by skilled cartographers in collaboration with geographers and subject editors. The maps are clear, accurate, informative, attractive, and easy to understand. Information of various kinds is presented on different but related maps, not crowded onto one map. Pictorial symbols, decorative insets, and rich color make the maps appealing to the eye and also provide additional information. There are more than one thousand maps of all kinds in the encyclopedia.

ILLUSTRATIONS

The New Book of Knowledge is printed on a full-color press so that color can be available throughout. There are more than twenty-five thousand color illustrations in the set. All the photographs, illustrations, and maps were selected to complement and add information to the text and were as carefully checked for accuracy as the text itself. The illustrations appear near the information they illustrate, and they are large enough to show details clearly. Most of the artwork was commissioned especially for this publication.

BIBLIOGRAPHY

A comprehensive bibliography in the Home and School Reading and Study Guides points the way to further reading on more than thirteen hundred topics. The recommended readings are grouped by general levels—primary, intermediate, and advanced. These references emphasize that *The New Book of Knowledge* is a springboard to learning that will stimulate the curiosity of its readers and lead them to further study.

The Editors

THE NEW BOOK OF KNOWLEDGE STAFF

EDITORIAL

Vice President and Publisher, Reference
Mark Cummings

Editor in Chief
Virginia Quinn McCarthy

Executive Editor
Elaine C. Henderson

Managing Editor
Doris E. Lechner

Editors
Alison Ousey Cantone
Kim C. Fitzsimons
Matthew Ziem

Copy Editor
Sara A. Boak

Contributing Editors
Cynthia Berger
James E. Churchill
Elaine Pascoe
William E. Shapiro

Editorial Assistant
Rosemarie Kent

Art and Design
Nancy Hamlen, *Director of Design*
Elizabeth DeBella, *Senior Designer*
Mary Ellen Casey, *Designer*
Barbara Cottingham, *Designer*

Photo Research
Cindy Joyce, *Director of Photo Research*
Susan Petruzzi, *Photo Researcher*

Picture Library
Jane H. Carruth, *Manager, Picture Library*
Emma P. Smith, *Assistant*

Indexer
Lighthouse Indexing Plus

Production Editor
Carolyn F. Reil

Proofreader
Donna M. Lusardi

Associate Editors
Patricia Bayer
Patricia A. Behan
Deirdre Casey
Joseph M. Castagno
Brian Feinberg
Fern Mamberg
Scott Monje
Susan Randel
Ronald B. Roth
Veronica F. Towers
Barbara Winard

Financial Manager
Joseph Cantone

Publishing Technology
Cyndie Cooper, *Director*
Emilia Urra Smith, *Senior Content Analyst/Programmer*
Linda K. Dillon, *Senior Publishing Systems Analyst*
Stephanie Grant, *Publishing Application Development Specialist*
Meghan O'Reilly Fiero, *Editorial Systems Analyst*
Raymond Casey, *Senior Programmer*

MANUFACTURING

Vice President, Manufacturing
Valerie Plue

Director, Reference, International, and Children's Publishing
Christine L. Matta

Production Managers
Elizabeth Kovats-Steger
Teresa K. Ahearn

FIRST EDITION STAFF

Martha Glauber Shapp, M.A.
Editor in Chief

Cathleen FitzGerald, B.A., H. Dip. Ed.
Managing Editor

Ben Feder
Designer and Graphic Arts Consultant

Lowell A. Martin, Ph.D.
Vice President and Editorial Director, Grolier, Inc.

EDITORIAL

SOCIAL STUDIES

Chief Editor: Dorothy W. Furman, B.S.

Senior Editors: Sue Brandt, B.A.; F. Richard Hsu, M.A.; Mary B. Irving, B.A.; Jerome Z. Neibrief, B.S.; John Ratti, M.A.; Eugenio C. Villicaña, M.A.

Associate Editors: Jay Bennett; Joyce Berry, B.A.; Claudia H. Cohl, B.A.; Mary-Stuart Garden, B.A.; Carol Z. Rothkopf, M.A.

Assistant Editors: Lorraine Abelson Abraham, B.A.; Marcus Anton Cohen, B.A.; Ellen Gendell, B.A.; Bryna Mandel, B.A.; Paul Schmel, B.A.; Amy Small, B.A.; Annette Stiefbold, M.A.

Editorial Assistants: Cecilia H. Bustos; Judith Glickman, B.A.; Mada Levine, B.A.; Barbara Mathes, B.A.

LANGUAGE AND LITERATURE

Senior Editor: James E. Jarnagin, M.A.

Associate Editors: Marcia B. Marks, B.A.; Janet Stone, B.A.

Assistant Editors: Carol Smith Bundy, B.A.; Lis Shabecoff, B.A.

TECHNOLOGY

Senior Editor: Peter R. Limburg, B.S.F.S., M.A.

Associate Editor: Sara L. Hannum, B.A.

Assistant Editors: Marion Bowman; Arthur G. Hudgins, M.A., Winifred B. Luhrmann, B.A.; Anthony M. Quintavalla, B.A.

EDITORIAL COORDINATOR

Lois C. Schwartz, B.A.

SCIENCE AND MATHEMATICS

Chief Editor: Patricia G. Lauber, B.A.

Senior Editor: Herbert Kondo, M.A.

Administrative Assistant: Anita Sedler

Associate Editors: John S. Bowman, B.A.; Barbara Land, M.S.; Rebecca Marcus, B.A.; Elizabeth Shepherd, B.A.

Assistant Editors: Chica Minnerly, B.A.; Steven Moll, B.A.; Harvey M. Weiss, M.A.

Editorial Assistants: Larry Baker, B.A.; Larry Blaser, M.A.; Stephen Kreitzman, B.A.; Ruth Plager, B.A.

MUSIC AND ART

Senior Music Editor: David L. Buckley, B.A.

Senior Art Editor: David Jacobs, B.F.A.

Associate Editor: Gwendolyn E. Reed, B.A. (Art)

Assistant Editors: Sara Friedman, B.A. (Art); Barbara Kaye, B.A. (Art); Joseph H. Markham, B.A. (Music); Robert Porter, B.F.A. (Art)

SPORTS AND LEISURE; HEALTH, HOME, AND COMMUNITY

Senior Editor: Helen Hull Jacobs

Associate Editors: Eleanor Felder, M.S.; Virginia Gurnee; Sylvia Rosenthal, B.A.

Assistant Editor: Noemie Emery, M.A.

STAFF EDITORS

Elisabeth Freidel Earley, M.A.; Susan Elliott, B.A.; Rosalyn Heith, B.A.; Fay Leviero; Sarah Lee McSweeney, B.A.

COPY EDITORS

Chief Copy Editor: Patricia Ellsworth, B.A.

Senior Copy Editors: Paule H. Jones, M.A.; Sandra L. Russell, B.A.; Damsey Wilson

Staff Members: Philip G. Anthony; Marcy Benstock, B.A.; Jeane Pavelle Garment, B.A.; Philip C. Johnson, B.A.; Naomi Kassabian, M.A.; Marian Klein, B.A.; Martin S. Mitchell, B.A.; Thomas W. Wyckoff

RESEARCHERS

Chief Researcher: Marshall Tulloch, B.A.

Senior Researcher: Thomas Cuddihy, B.A.

Staff Members: Margaret Anderson, B.A.; Lydia Cohen, B.A.; Helen McVey Colvin, B.A.; Margaret Covode, B.A.; Susan Day, B.A.; David Diao, B.A.; Edward Diaz, B.A.; Stephen Elliott, B.A.; Imre Horvath, M.A.; Rita Horvath, B.A.; Leland Lowther, M.A.; Susan Nergaard, B.F.A.; Peter Scarlet, B.A.; Ralph Slayton, B.S.; Camilla Turnbull, B.A.; Sally Valentine, B.A.

PROOFREADERS

Chief Proofreader: Martha L. Moffett, B.S.

Staff Members: Elizabeth M. Elkind, B.A.; Patricia M. Godfrey, B.A.; Susan F. Heimann, M.A.; Louise Oblan-Shor, B.A.

INDEXERS

Chief Indexer: Ruth Hines, M.L.S.

Consulting Indexer: Sarita Robinson, M.A.

Dictionary Index Editor: Sybil Rhoads, B.S.

Staff Members: Diane Gilroy, M.A.; Janet Hadley; Zohreh Kerendian, B.S.; Brenda Kurz, B.A.; Martin S. Mitchell, B.A.; Barbara Paskell, B.A.; Margaret Reed; Carole Schindeler, M.A.; Toni Strauss, B.S.; Barbra Wood, B.A.

MAPS

Map Designer: George Buctel, B.A.

Editor: Linda Keim, B.A.

Assistant Editors: Emily Wood Corbin, A.A.; Margo Dryden, A.A.; Cyril Edoho, M.A.; Arlene Zuckerman, B.A.

OFFICE MANAGER

Joanne Burns

STAFF ASSISTANTS

Kiki Barroso; Rose Ann Bonetti; Sheridan Cogan; Willie May Elcock; Louisa Folta; Anne Hegarty; Ruth Heim; Aline Moyler; Mitzi L. Sanchez; Dorothy Schatten; Minna Sedler; Stephanie Shaffer

ART AND PRODUCTION

Art and Production Director: Verne Bowman, B.F.A.

Production Manager: Charles Behre, B.A.

Assistant Art Director: Chester Prosinski, B.F.A.

Art Coordinator: Rita Maduro, B.S.

Typography Manager: Barbara Effron, B.S.

Typography Coordinators
Tema Harris, B.F.A.; Geraldine Felder Smith

Layout Designers
Susan Colton, B.A.; Ronald Cooper, A.A.S.; Sue Crooks; Nancy Ferguson, B.A.; Mary Ann Joulwan; Sidney Miller; Miriam Troner, B.A.

Staff Artist
Irmgard Lochner

PHOTO EDITORS

Chief Editor: Isabelle Rubin, M.A.

Administrative Assistant: Susan Lewis West, B.A.

Staff Members: Anne Alpert, B.A.; Carol Baker, B.A.; Beverly Bayne, B.A., B.S.; Laura Bustard; Lois Davis, M.A.; Wesley Day, B.A.; Monika Dillon, B.A.; Iris Eaton; Ada Fridman, M.D.; Richard Green, B.A.; Elizabeth Heskett, M.A.; Gloria Hoffman, B.A.; Dorothy Kalins, B.A.; Jane Latta; Diana Lee, B.A.; Alice Lundoff, M.S.; Ivy Minely, B.A.; Barbara Nagelsmith, B.S.; Marjorie Goreff Neuwirth, B.A.; Joan Scafarello, B.A.; Lisl Steiner, B.A.; Patricia Walsh, M.A.

STAFF ASSISTANTS

Linda Bokor; Nancy Hammalian, B.A.; Michael Harvest; Lynn Jacobs, B.S.; Laura Johnson, B.A.; Franklin Schmidt; Marcy Waxman, B.A.; Marjorie Williams

MANUFACTURING

Director: Ed McKenna

Staff: Raymond Labott; Walter Stork

ADVISORS AND CONSULTANTS

Russell L. Adams, Ph.D.
Chairman, Afro-American Studies Department
College of Arts and Sciences
Howard University

Jeremy Black, Ph.D.
Professor of History
University of Exeter
Author, *European Warfare: 1600–1815; War for America; Culloden and the '45; Eighteenth Century Europe*

Alfred B. Bortz, Ph.D.
Author, science books for children

Hugh C. Brooks, Ph.D.
Director, Center for African Studies
St. John's University (New York)

Jeanne S. Chall, Ph.D.
Professor of Education and
Director of the Reading Laboratory
Graduate School of Education
Harvard University

Suzanne H. Chapin, Ed.D., Ed.M.
Assistant Professor of Mathematics
School of Education
Boston University

Peter Conn, Ph.D.
Professor of English
University of Pennsylvania
Author, *Literature in America: An Illustrated History*

Robert I. Crane, Ph.D.
Ford-Maxwell Professor of South Asian History
Syracuse University

Kathryn Cullen-DuPont
Author, *Encyclopedia of Women's History in America*

Bernice E. Cullinan, Ph.D.
Professor of Reading
New York University
Author, *Literature and the Child,* 3rd ed.; *Read to Me: Raising Kids Who Love to Read*

Lawrence S. Finkel, Ed.D.
Superintendent, Chester Township (New Jersey) Public Schools

Arthur W. Foshay, Ed.D.
Professor Emeritus Research and Field Services
Teachers College
Columbia University

M. L. Frankel, Ph.D.
Member, National Task Force on Economic Education

Christine B. Gilbert, B.L.S., M.A.
Coeditor, *Best Books for Children*
Former Librarian and Adjunct Associate
Professor of Library Science
Long Island University
C. W. Post Center

John T. Gillespie, M.L.S.
Professor Emeritus
Palmer Graduate Library School
Long Island University
C. W. Post Center

Colonel C. V. Glines, M.B.A.
Former Assistant Secretary of Defense (Public Affairs)
U.S. Department of Defense

Maria Guglielmino, M.S., R.D.
Registered Dietitian and Exercise Physiologist

William A. Gutsch, Jr.
Former Chairman, The American Museum—Hayden Planetarium

John Jarolimek, Ph.D.
Professor Emeritus
Department of Education
University of Washington

Bryan H. King, M.D.
Professor of Psychiatry and Pediatrics
Director of Child and Adolescent Psychiatry
Dartmouth—Hitchcock Medical Center

Heidi King, M.A.
Department of Primitive Art
The Metropolitan Museum of Art

Nancy Larrick, Ed.D.
Author, *A Parent's Guide to Children's Reading*

Vincent H. Malmstrom, Ph.D.
Professor Emeritus of Geography
Dartmouth College

John H. McDowell
Chair, Folklore Institute
Indiana University

Patricia McKissack, M.A.
Fredrick McKissack, B.S.
Authors, *The History of the Civil Rights Movement in America from 1865 to the Present; African-American Heroes*

Alexander Melamid, Ph.D.
Professor of Economics
New York University

H. Michael Mogil, M.S.
Meteorologist/Educator
How the Weatherworks

Charles Moritz, M.A.
Former Editor, *Current Biography*

Holly Pittman, Ph.D.
Curator of the Near East Section
Museum of Archaeology and Anthropology
Chair, Graduate Group in Art and Archaeology of the Mediterranean World
University of Pennsylvania

Carol Mattson Porth, Ph.D.
Physiologist, School of Nursing
University of Wisconsin (Milwaukee)

Daniel Roselle, Ph.D.
Former Editor, *Social Education* magazine
Former Director of Publications
National Council for the Social Studies

Herman Schneider
Author, Health Science series

Philip Sherlock, Ph.D.
Former Secretary-General
Association of Caribbean Universities and Research Institutes

Robert Shogan
National Political Correspondent
The Los Angeles Times, Washington Bureau
Author, *The Double-Edged Sword: How Character Makes and Ruins Presidents, from Washington to Clinton*; *War Without End: Cultural Conflict and the Struggle for America's Political Future*

Cynthia V. Sommer, Ph.D.
Professor of Microbiology
Department of Biological Sciences
University of Wisconsin (Milwaukee)

Isidore Starr, Ph.D., LL.B., J.S.D.
Professor Emeritus of Education
City University of New York
Queens College

Monsignor George E. Tiffany, Ph.D.
Editor in Chief, *The Contemporary Church*

Kenneth E. Wing, Ph.D.
President
College of Agriculture and Technology
State University of New York (Cobleskill)

Virginia A. Zellner, M.A.
Teacher, Science Curriculum Chairperson
Sherman School (Connecticut)

A, the first letter of the English alphabet, was also the first letter of the Phoenician, Hebrew, and Greek alphabets. The Hebrews called it *aleph* and the Greeks changed it slightly, calling it *alpha.* The word "alphabet" itself comes from joining the Greek names for the first two letters—*alpha* (A) and *beta* (B). Thus the first two letters have come to stand for all the rest, just as "learning your ABC's" really means learning your DEFGHIJ's as well.

The shape of the letter A has changed slightly from time to time. The legs have been shorter or longer, the crossbar more crooked. But even the earliest traces of the letter look familiar to us. The Phoenician picture symbol for A was probably an ox's head with two long horns. It looked like this: . The later Greek forms stand up straight. By the time the Romans had adapted the Greek alphabet, the A looked very much as it does today.

A is a vowel. It stands for different sounds. Pronounce these words: *fate, bare, am, farm, grass.* You will notice that each A has a different sound. The most common sounds are the long A, as in *fate*; the short A, as in *am*; and the broad A, as in *farm.*

A is a word in itself. It is found before the name of a thing to show that this thing is one of a particular class or kind: a tree, a bird, a worm.

In Phoenician, Hebrew, and Greek, the letter A also meant the number 1. In English too, A has come to mean the first or best. Some schools give A as the highest grade. Grade-A milk and grade-A eggs mean top quality.

In music A is a note; in chemistry A sometimes stands for the element argon. Two of our most common abbreviations employ the A—A.D., for the Latin *anno Domini*, is used with dates and means "in the year of our Lord"; A.M., for *ante meridiem*, is used with times and means "before noon."

Reviewed by MARIO PEI
Author, *The Story of Language*

See also ALPHABET.

AARON, HENRY (Hank). See ALABAMA (Famous People); BASEBALL (Great Players).

SOME WAYS TO REPRESENT A:

Aa *Aa*

The **manuscript** or printed forms of the letter (left) are highly readable. The **cursive** letters (right) are formed from slanted flowing strokes joining one letter to the next.

The **Manual Alphabet** (left) enables a deaf person to communicate by forming letters with the fingers of one hand. **Braille** (right) is a system by which a blind person can use fingertips to "read" raised dots that stand for letters.

The **International Code of Signals** is a special group of flags used to send and receive messages at sea. Each letter is represented by a different flag.

International Morse Code is used to send messages by radio signals. Each letter is expressed as a combination of dots (•) and dashes (––).

Many Asian children learn to operate an abacus in primary school. The best known of the many forms of this instrument is the Chinese *suan p'an* which has a dividing bar across the frame. Beads above the bar count 5 and those below it count 1.

ABACUS

The abacus is a simple calculating machine that is used for doing arithmetic. A modern abacus is made of beads, rods, and a frame. The rods are fastened in the frame, and each stands for a place in the decimal system. One rod stands for units, one for 10's, one for 100's, and so on. The beads are counters. Numbers are added or subtracted by moving the beads on the rods.

The abacus was invented thousands of years ago. It provided a way of doing arithmetic without using written numerals. The numerals of ancient times were very awkward for doing arithmetic. The trouble was that they did not express zero or place value.

For example, compare our numerals with the Roman ones. Our numeral 5 can stand for 5, 50, or 500, depending on the place it is given. In the number 555, each 5 has a different value. The Romans used letters as numerals and expressed place by using a different letter. The numbers 5, 50, and 500 were written as V, L, and D. Without the idea of zero and place, there was no way to make the same numeral stand for more than one number. That is, V could not be made to stand for any number except 5.

This system of numerals made written arithmetic very difficult. So the Romans, like other ancient peoples, used the abacus. The idea of place was built into the abacus. One counter could be made to express 1, 10, or 100, according to its place on the abacus.

The abacus offered an easy way of adding and subtracting and could also be used for multiplication and division.

The abacus was first made by placing pebbles in grooves drawn in soft dirt or sand. Later, the Romans and Arabs learned to make a portable abacus. It was usually a flat piece of wood or metal with grooves or slots for the counters.

The abacus is still widely used today in China, Japan, India, and other countries. Some people can add on an abacus as fast as a person using an electronic calculator. Shortly after World War II a Japanese bank clerk using an abacus was matched against an American soldier using a desk calculator. The two men were given identical sets of business figures that needed addition, subtraction, multiplication, and division. The Japanese clerk, with the abacus, won every time.

Multiplication can be done by adding equal groups. For example, to multiply 12 x 4, you would set up the number 12 on the abacus (one bead in the 10's row and two beads in the 1's row). Then add 12 three more times. Your abacus should show the answer: 48. Division can be done on the abacus by subtracting equal groups.

Reviewed by Forrest M. Mims, III
Author, *Number Machines*

The drawings on the opposite page show you how to do simple addition and subtraction, as well as addition and subtraction that require exchanging 5 counters for 1.

See also Numbers and Number Systems.

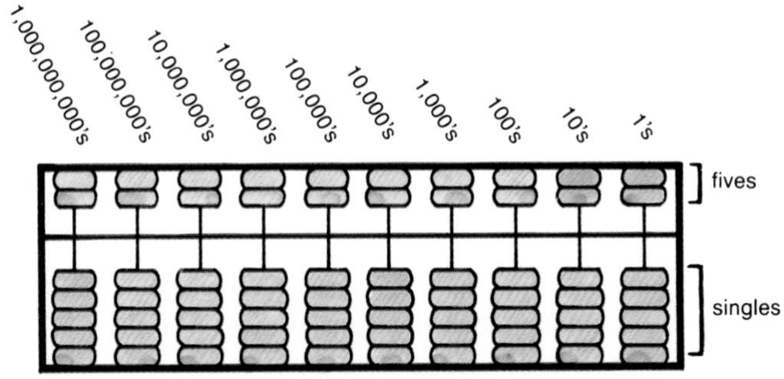

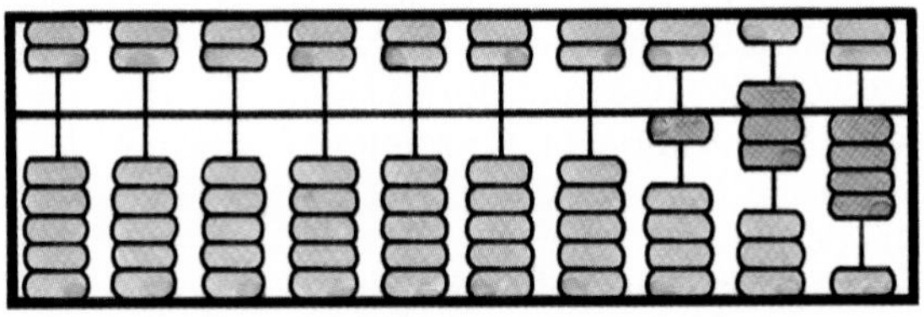

THE CHINESE ABACUS

In a Chinese abacus, each of the five counters below the horizontal divider bar stands for a single decimal unit. A single counter below the bar on the 1's wire represents 1. A single counter below the bar on the 10's wire represents 10, on the 100's wire 100, and so on.

Each counter above the divider bar equals five single decimal units. Therefore a counter above the bar on the 1's wire stands for 5. A counter above the bar on the 10's wire stands for 50, on the 100's wire 500, and so on.

To operate the abacus, counters are moved toward the divider bar. The number 174 is set out at left. Think of the number as 100-70-4. The four counters up against the bar on the 1's wire represent the 4. The 70 is represented by one counter from the top of the 10's wire, which stands for 50, plus two counters from underneath the bar on the 10's wire, which represent 10 apiece. The 50 and the two 10's make a total of 70. The 100 is represented by a single counter from below the bar on the 100's wire.

Simple Addition: 823 + 126

First set out 823
3 on the 1's wire
2 on the 10's wire
8 on the 100's wire

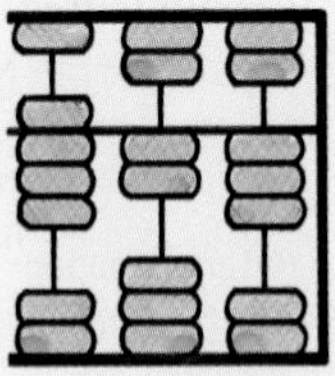

Then move in 126
6 on the 1's wire
2 on the 10's wire
1 on the 100's wire

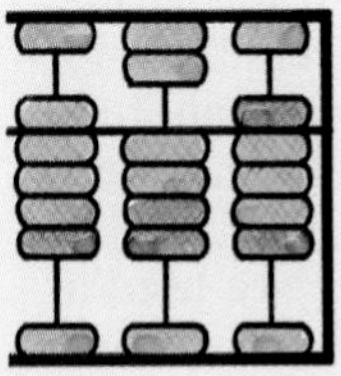

Read the number shown on the abacus for the answer: 949

Addition with Carrying: 76 + 98

First set out 76
6 on the 1's wire
7 on the 10's wire

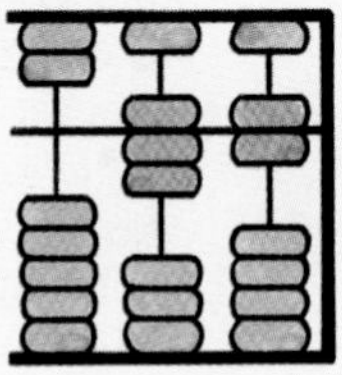

Then move in 98
8 on the 1's wire
(This now makes 14 1's, which must be expressed as one 10 and four 1's — so move the two 5's off the top of the 1's wire and move one 10 up on the 10's wire.)

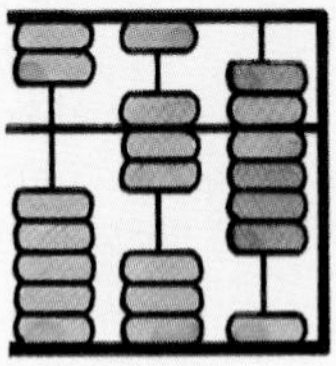

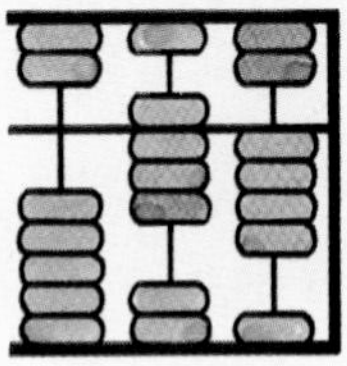

9 on the 10's wire
(Adding nine 10's to the 10's that are already shown on the 10's wire would make 17 10's — there are not enough counters to do that. To express 90, move one 100 counter up on the 100's wire, and remove one 10 counter from the bottom of the 10's wire.)

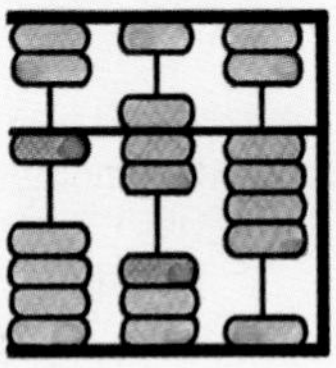

Read the number shown on the abacus for the answer: 174

Simple Subtraction: 137 – 26

Set up 137
7 on the 1's wire
3 on the 10's wire
1 on the 100's wire

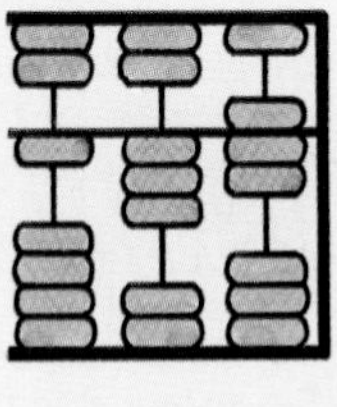

Move away 26
Move away 6 from the 1's wire
Move away 2 from the 10's wire

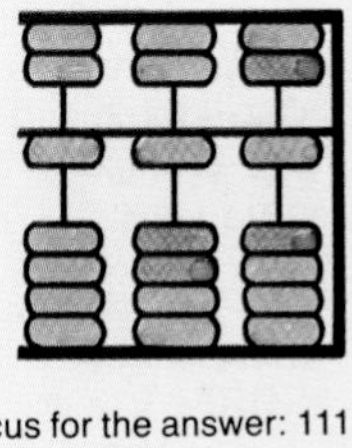

Read the number shown on the abacus for the answer: 111

Subtraction with Borrowing: 44 – 28

Set up 44
4 on the 1's wire
4 on the 10's wire

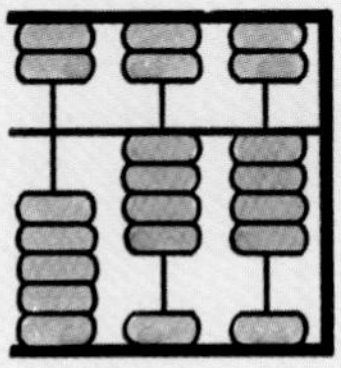

Move away 28
Move 8 away from the 1's wire
(Take away one counter from the 10's wire and *add* 2 counters to the 1's wire for a net loss of 8.)

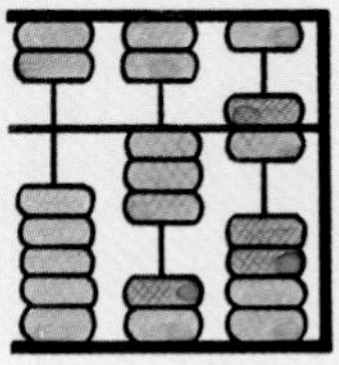

Move 2 away from the 10's wire

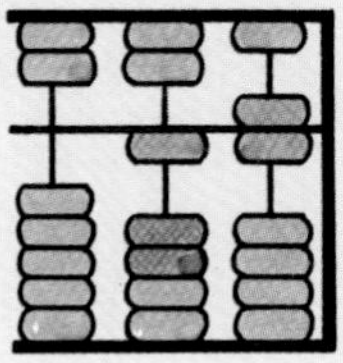

Read the number shown on the abacus for the answer: 16

the counters being used	the counters being moved	the counters unused

What the Colors Mean

ABBOTT, SIR JOHN JOSEPH CALDWELL.
See CANADA, GOVERNMENT OF (Profiles).

ABBREVIATIONS

Abbreviations are shortened forms of words and phrases. In the past, when all writing was done by hand, abbreviations saved time and space. Today, although most of what we read is printed, so much information is available that we need abbreviations for much the same reasons.

There are various ways of abbreviating words. A part of the whole word followed by a period may be used. It is often the first syllable or letters, as in Mon. for Monday, Jan. for January, co. for company or county. Some words are shortened to the first and last letters: pr. for pair, yr. for year, Mr. for Mister. In other cases key letters are selected: TV for *t*ele*v*ision, pkg. for package. Modern abbreviations often use initials, and many omit periods (CB, mpg, UFO).

Initials for many Latin phrases are used as abbreviations. Here the period is retained. For example, the letters i.e. stand for the Latin *id est*, which means "that is." No., meaning number, goes back to *numero*, the Latin word meaning "by number."

People often make up their own abbreviations, and some of these, like VIP (*v*ery *i*mportant *p*erson), come into general usage. Your notebook may contain abbreviations that you have made up yourself.

An **acronym** is a word formed from the initial letters in a phrase or title. It is pronounced as a single word, not as a series of letters. OPEC, one such form, stands for the name *O*rganization of *P*etroleum *E*xporting *C*ountries. This acronym, like many others, omits periods.

Some common abbreviations and acronyms are listed below. Others may be found in the dictionary, in the regular alphabetical order of words or in a special appendix.

ISABELLE FORST
Former Assistant Superintendent of Schools
New York City

See also CHEMISTRY for abbreviations of chemical elements; POSTAL SERVICE for abbreviations of state names; articles on letters of the alphabet for abbreviations beginning with those letters.

AAA—American Automobile Association
A.A.U.—Amateur Athletic Union
ABC—American Broadcasting Company
AC—alternating current
ACLU—American Civil Liberties Union
A.D., A.D.—*anno Domini* (Latin, "in the year of our Lord")
ad, advt.—advertisement
adj.—adjective
aka—also known as
ALA—American Library Association
alt.—altitude
A.M., a.m.—*ante meridiem* (Latin, "before noon")
AMA—American Medical Association
anon.—anonymous (giving no name)
AP—Associated Press
assn., assoc.—association
asst.—assistant
att., atty.—attorney
attn.—attention
ATV—all-terrain vehicle
Ave., Av.—Avenue
AWOL—absent without leave
b.—born
B.A., A.B.—Bachelor of Arts
BBC—British Broadcasting Corporation
B.C., B.C.—before Christ
B.C.E.—before (the) common era
bldg.—building
Blvd.—Boulevard
B.S., B.Sc.—Bachelor of Science
C—Celsius
c., ca.—*circa* (Latin, "about")
cap.—capital
Capt.—Captain
CB—citizens band (radio frequency)
CBC—Canadian Broadcasting Corporation
CBS—Columbia Broadcasting System
CD—certificate of deposit; compact disc
cf.—*confer* (Latin, "compare")
chap.—chapter
CO—Commanding Officer
co.—company; county
c/o.—care of
Col.—Colonel
col.—college; column
cop., ©—copyright
CORE—Congress of Racial Equality
corp.—corporation; corporal
C.P.A.—certified public accountant
CPR—cardiopulmonary resuscitation
CPU—central processing unit
CST—central standard time
d.—died; day
D.A.—District Attorney
D.A.R.—Daughters of the American Revolution
DC—direct current
D.D.—Doctor of Divinity
D.D.S.—Doctor of Dental Surgery
dec.—deceased
Dem.—Democrat
dept.—department
dia., diam.—diameter
DNA—deoxyribonucleic acid (chemical carrying genetic information)
Dr.—Doctor
DST—daylight saving time
e.g.—*exempli gratia* (Latin, "for example")
EKG—electrocardiogram
elev.—elevation
EPA—Environmental Protection Agency
ERA—Equal Rights Amendment
Esq.—Esquire
est.—established; estimated
EST—eastern standard time
ETA—estimated time of arrival
et al.—*et alii* (Latin, "and other")
etc.—*et cetera* (Latin, "and the rest")
F—Fahrenheit
FBI—Federal Bureau of Investigation
FCC—Federal Communications Commission
fed.—federal

ff.—following (pages)
FHA—Federal Housing Administration
Fig.—Figure
Gen.—General
GI—government issue
GNP—gross national product
G.O.P.—Grand Old Party, nickname for present Republican Party in the United States
Gov.—Governor
H.M.S.—His (or Her) Majesty's Service; His (or Her) Majesty's Ship
Hon.—Honorable
hosp.—hospital
H.P., HP, h.p.—horsepower
hr.—hour(s)
H.R.H.—His (or Her) Royal Highness
ht.—height
ibid.—*ibidem* (Latin, "in the same place")
ICBM—intercontinental ballistic missile
i.e.—*id est* (Latin, "that is")
ill., illus.—illustrated; illustration
inc.—incorporated; including
I.N.R.I.—*Iesus Nazarenus Rex Iudaeorum* (Latin, "Jesus of Nazareth, King of the Jews")
intro.—introduction
IOU—I owe you
IQ—intelligence quotient
IRA—individual retirement account
I.R.A.—Irish Republican Army
IRS—Internal Revenue Service
J.P.—justice of the peace
Jr.—Junior
KO—knockout
kwhr., kwh.—kilowatt-hour(s)
l., ll.—line, lines
lab—laboratory
Lat.—Latin
lat.—latitude
Lieut., Lt.—Lieutenant
lit.—literary
lon., long.—longitude
L.P.N.—licensed practical nurse
Ltd.—limited
m.—married, meter
M.A., A.M.—Master of Arts
Maj.—Major
max.—maximum
M.B.A.—Master of Business Administration
M.D.—Doctor of Medicine
med.—medical; medicine
mfg., manuf.—manufacturing
mgr.—manager
MIA—missing in action
min.—minimum; minute(s)
misc.—miscellaneous
mo.—month(s)
M.O.—*modus operandi* (Latin, "method of operation"); mail order
MP—military police
M.P.—member of Parliament
mpg—miles per gallon
mph—miles per hour
Mr.—Mister
Mrs.—Mistress (the original term for a married or unmarried woman)
M.S.—Master of Science
Ms.—Miss or Mrs.
MS, ms; MSS, mss—manuscript; manuscripts
MST—mountain standard time
Mt., mt.—mount; mountain
n.—noun
NAACP—National Association for the Advancement of Colored People
NASA—National Aeronautics and Space Administration
natl.—national
NATO—North Atlantic Treaty Organization
N.B.—*nota bene* (Latin, "note well")
NBC—National Broadcasting Company
NFL—National Football League
NOW—National Organization for Women
OAS—Organization of American States
op. cit.—*opere citato* (Latin, "in the work cited")
OPEC—Organization of Petroleum Exporting Countries
p., pp.—page; pages
P.A.—physician's assistant
par.—paragraph; parallel
PBS—Public Broadcasting Service
PC—personal computer
pd.—paid
Pfc.—Private, First Class
Ph.D.—Doctor of Philosophy
pkg.—package
pl.—plural
P.M.—Prime Minister
P.M., p.m.—*post meridiem* (Latin, "after noon")
P.O.—Post Office
pop.—population
POW—prisoner of war
pr.—pair
pres.—president
prof.—professor
pron.—pronoun
pro tem.—*pro tempore* (Latin, "for the time being"; "temporarily")
P.S.—postscript; Public School
pseud.—pseudonym
PST—Pacific standard time
PTA—Parent-Teacher Association
pub.—public; publisher; published
Q.E.D.—*quod erat demonstrandum* (Latin, "which was to be shown or proved")
q.v.—*quod vide* (Latin, "which see")
RAF—Royal Air Force
rd.—road
RDA—recommended dietary allowance
recd.—received
Rep.—Republican; Representative
Rev.—Reverend
rev.—revenue; revised
R.N.—Registered Nurse
RNA—ribonucleic acid (in cells, chemical used to build protein)
R.O.T.C.—Reserve Officers' Training Corps
rpm—revolutions per minute
R.R.—railroad; rural route
R.S.V.P.—*Répondez, s'il vous plaît* (French, "please reply")
RV—recreational vehicle
SEC—Securities and Exchange Commission
sec.—second
sec., secy.—secretary
Sen.—Senator
sing.—singular
soc.—society
SPCA—Society for the Prevention of Cruelty to Animals
SPCC—Society for the Prevention of Cruelty to Children
sq.—square
Sr.—Senior
SST—supersonic transport
St.—Saint; Street
Ste.—Sainte (French, feminine of Saint)
subj.—subject
supt.—superintendent
syn.—synonym
tbs., T—tablespoon(s)
temp.—temperature
tr.—translation; transpose
treas.—treasury; treasurer
tsp., t—teaspoon(s)
U., univ.—university
UFO—unidentified flying object
UHF—ultrahigh frequency
U.N.—United Nations
UPI—United Press International
USPS—United States Postal Service
U.S.S.—United States Ship
v.—verb; verse
VA—Veterans Administration
VAT—value-added tax
VCR—videocassette recorder
VFW—Veterans of Foreign Wars
VHF—very high frequency
vid.—*vide* (Latin, "see"; used to direct attention, as *vide p. 40*)
VISTA—Volunteers in Service to America
viz.—*videlicet* (Latin, "namely")
v.p.—vice president
vs.—*versus* (Latin, "against")
wk.—week
wt.—weight
yr.—year

ABELARD, PETER. See MIDDLE AGES (Profiles).

ABERNATHY, RALPH DAVID. See ALABAMA (Famous People).

ABNAKI INDIANS. See INDIANS, AMERICAN (The Algonkians).

ABOLITION MOVEMENT

The abolition movement in United States history was a two-hundred-year campaign to free American blacks from the practice of slavery, or forced labor. The movement, which began in the late 1600's, evolved through several increasingly militant stages before the Civil War (1861–65) brought the issue to a climax. After four years of bloodshed, the victory of the Union forces made possible the ratification of the 13th Amendment (1865), which finally declared slavery illegal in the United States.

Early Activities and Accomplishments

The first recorded abolition meeting took place in 1688 in Germantown, Pennsylvania, among a group of Quakers and Mennonites, whose religious beliefs equated slavery with sin. "What thing in the world," they inquired of other colonists, "can be done worse toward us, than if men should rob or steal us away and sell us for slaves to strange countries?" For the next one hundred years, individuals continued to speak out against forced servitude, but no formal antislavery organization was founded until Benjamin Franklin helped organize the Pennsylvania Society for Promoting the Abolition of Slavery in Philadelphia in 1775. Dozens of similar protest organizations soon sprang up in other Northern states, gaining members beyond religious circles.

The three primary goals of these pioneer antislavery societies were to improve the living conditions of the black population, both slave and free; to challenge suspected false claims of slave ownership; and to petition legislative bodies to emancipate, or free, slaves within their jurisdictions. These initial movements were highly successful, and by 1804 slavery had been abolished in Rhode Island,

At Boston's Tremont Temple in 1860, police and a hostile mob broke up an abolitionist meeting held in memory of the first anniversary of John Brown's execution.

Vermont, Pennsylvania, Massachusetts, New Hampshire, Connecticut, and New Jersey. In addition, the importation of slaves from Africa ended in 1808, according to the terms of the U.S. Constitution.

Militant Abolitionism

A more militant stage of the antislavery movement began in 1829 with the publication of *An Appeal to the Colored People of the World*. Written by David Walker, a freeborn black, the *Appeal* called for a slave revolt in the United States similar to the violent uprisings that had freed Haitian slaves from French colonial rule in the late 1700's. Legislators in Georgia and North Carolina enacted laws to censor what they termed incendiary, or explosive, publications, and African Americans in the South were arrested for distributing copies of Walker's pamphlet.

In 1831, a young white abolitionist from Massachusetts named William Lloyd Garrison published the first issue of his antislavery newspaper, *The Liberator*. The following year he helped organize the New England Anti-Slavery Society in Boston.

In 1833 representatives from eleven states met in Philadelphia to form a national organization, the American

This moving emblem of a man in chains became the unofficial symbol of the abolition movement. It was used to illustrate a wide variety of antislavery publications.

Frederick Douglass

John Brown

Profiles

John Brown (1800–59), born in Torrington, Conn., was the most radical of the militant white abolitionists and a hero to the slaves. A biography of John Brown appears in Volume B.

Frederick Douglass (Frederick Augustus Washington Bailey) (1817–95), born a slave in Tuckahoe, Md., escaped to the North in 1838. An orator and editor of the antislavery newspaper the *North Star*, he was the most influential of the black abolitionists. A biography of Frederick Douglass appears in Volume D.

James Forten (1766–1842), a free black, born in Philadelphia, Pa., was a major financial contributor to the abolition movement. As a teenager, he served on an American ship during the Revolutionary War and was taken prisoner by the British. After the war, he returned to Philadelphia and became an apprentice to a sailmaker. By 1798 he owned the business and had become quite wealthy. Forten was opposed to the movement to colonize American blacks in Africa. He assisted blacks escaping from the South and became a major financial backer of William Lloyd Garrison's newspaper, *The Liberator*.

Henry Highland Garnet (1815–82), born a slave in Kent County, Md., escaped to New York in 1824 and later became a Presbyterian minister and professional speaker with the American Anti-Slavery Society. At an 1843 National Convention of Free Colored People, he called upon slaves to rise up and "strike for your lives and liberties!" Garnet was the first African American to address the U.S. House of Representatives (1865).

William Lloyd Garrison (1805–79), born in Newburyport, Mass., was perhaps the most outspoken white champion of the abolitionist cause. In the first edition (1831) of his newspaper, *The Liberator*, Garrison declared slavery an abomination in God's sight. He demanded immediate emancipation, vowing never to be silenced. "I am in earnest—I will not equivocate—I will not excuse—I will not retreat a single inch; and I will be heard!" He cofounded the American Anti-Slavery Society in 1833. For additional information, see the article MASSACHUSETTS (Famous People) in Volume M.

Elijah Parish Lovejoy (1802–37), born in Albion, Me., was a white Presbyterian minister and abolitionist. Opposition to his views in St. Louis, Mo., forced Lovejoy to abandon his position there as editor of a religious newspaper. In 1837 he relocated to Alton, Ill., where he began publishing the *Alton Observer* and tried to establish a chapter of the American Anti-Slavery Society. Within the year, Lovejoy was killed by a mob that came to seize his printing press. He became a martyr to the abolitionist cause.

Robert Purvis (1810–98), a freeborn South Carolinian of a well-to-do family, moved to Philadelphia and became an antislavery activist. He was one of three African Americans who helped organize the American Anti-Slavery Society (1833). Purvis also headed (1838–44) the Philadelphia Vigilance Committee, which assisted hundreds of fugitive slaves on the Underground Railroad. "Slavery," he said, "will be abolished in this land, and with it, that twin relic of barbarism—prejudice against color."

John Brown Russwurm (1799–1851), born in Port Antonio, Jamaica, was a cofounder of *Freedom's Journal*, the first newspaper owned and operated by African Americans. The first issue was published in New York on March 16, 1827. Seeking freedom for slaves, Russwurm favored the back-to-Africa movement of the day, for which he was burned in effigy by activists opposed to colonization. In 1829 he moved to Liberia, in West Africa.

Harriet Beecher Stowe (1811–96), born in Litchfield, Ct., gained international renown for her novel *Uncle Tom's Cabin*. Published in 1852 in reaction to the Fugitive Slave Law, the book increased popular support for ending slavery. A biography of Harriet Beecher Stowe appears in Volume S.

Sojourner Truth (Isabella Van Wagener) (1797?–1883), born a slave in Ulster County, N.Y., became the most famous antislavery spokeswoman. In 1843 she said that God called upon her to "travel up and down the land" and preach his word. She changed her name to Sojourner (meaning traveler) Truth and set out on a lecture tour to speak out about religion, slavery, and women's issues. Although she could neither read nor write, she was a captivating orator. Truth touched her audiences with such declarations as, "I have borne 13 children and seen them most all sold off into slavery, and when I cried out with a mother's grief, none but Jesus heard!"

David Walker (1785–1830), a free black, born in Wilmington, N.C. , settled in Boston in 1827. He became a charter member of the Massachusetts Colored General Association and contributed to *Freedom's Journal*. In 1829, Walker published a 76-page pamphlet, *An Appeal to the Colored People of the World*, urging slaves to rise up against their oppressors, convinced that violence was the only sure way to gain freedom. Walker's *Appeal* outraged slaveholders. He died mysteriously in 1830. Most abolitionists believed he had been poisoned.

William Lloyd Garrison

Harriet Beecher Stowe

William Lloyd Garrison's *The Liberator* was the most militant antislavery publication. Founded in 1831, it was published until emancipation was achieved in 1865.

Anti-Slavery Society. Three African Americans took part in the proceedings, making it the nation's first interracial public advocacy group. Most of its members believed that persistent "moral persuasion" would eventually convince slaveholders of the immorality of slavery, and that the practice would gradually disappear. Others, however, insisted on taking political action and called for the creation of an abolitionist political party.

Political Abolitionism

In 1840 the Liberty Party was organized in Albany, New York. The new party nominated a reformed ex-slaveholder, James G. Birney, for president. Despite the tens of thousands of Americans who called themselves abolitionists, only 7,000 cast their vote for Birney. Even fewer voted for him in 1844.

In 1846, as Congress was preparing to administer the transfer of territory from Mexico, David Wilmot, a U.S. representative from Pennsylvania, offered a provision that would prohibit slavery in land added to the Union.

WONDER QUESTION

What were the Gag Rules?

By 1836, the U.S. Congress had been overwhelmed by the number of petitions from citizens requesting that slavery not be extended into new U.S. territories. Because the reading of these petitions took up so much time, that year the House of Representatives passed a series of resolutions, known as the Gag Rules, to prevent further discussion of the issue. Opponents, led by House member and former president John Quincy Adams, argued that the Gag Rules violated the citizens' First Amendment right to petition the federal government for "redress of grievances." The measures were repealed in 1844.

This Wilmot Proviso became the basis of the new Free Soil Party, which attracted former Liberty Party members as well as antislavery Democrats, known as the Barnburners.

In 1848 the Free Soil Party endorsed former president Martin Van Buren under the slogan "Free Soil, Free Speech, Free Labor, and Free Men." However, when Van Buren drew only slightly more than 10 percent of the vote, support for the Free Soil Party dwindled. By 1856 most of its members had joined the Republican Party, which was organized in 1854 in opposition to the Kansas-Nebraska Act.

The Kansas-Nebraska Act (1854), which overturned the Missouri Compromise of 1820, allowed settlers to vote for or against slavery in their own territories. Nebraskans voted no, but Kansans voted yes. The growing number of "free staters" were enraged, notably John Brown, whose subsequent attacks on Kansas slaveholders gave rise to the name Bleeding Kansas.

Abolitionists already were embittered by the passage of the Fugitive Slave Act (1850) that had made it illegal for any American to assist fugitive slaves. Outrage over this law actually increased support for the Underground Railroad, a secret network of people dedicated to helping slaves escape to the North. Abolitionists were further outraged when the U.S. Supreme Court ruled in 1857, in the Dred Scott Decision, that the Constitution protected slave property throughout the United States. Each of these actions propelled the North and South toward a civil war, which began in April 1861.

On September 22, 1862, as a military measure, U.S. president Abraham Lincoln issued his Emancipation Proclamation, declaring that as of January 1, 1863, any slave residing in a Confederate state would be "forever free." Enforcement of this policy, however, depended upon which side won the war.

On April 9, 1865, the Confederates surrendered to the Union forces and the Civil War came to an end. Eight months later, on December 18, 1865, abolition was assured with the ratification of the 13th Amendment to the Constitution.

RUSSELL L. ADAMS
Chair, Department of Afro-American Studies
Howard University

See also EMANCIPATION PROCLAMATION; UNDERGROUND RAILROAD.

ABORIGINES, AUSTRALIAN

The Australian Aborigines were the earliest known inhabitants of Australia and today are regarded as the native people of that continent. The term "aborigine," which comes from the Latin words *ab origine*, means "from the beginning" and can be applied to the native peoples of any region.

It is believed that Australia's first Aborigines migrated from Southeast Asia more than 75,000 years ago. They probably crossed the Indian Ocean and the various seas in between by raft or dugout canoe.

In Australia's Aboriginal societies, adult males are the principal guardians of sacred rites and culture. Ritual dances and body painting are two forms of expression that create a spiritual connection to ancestral origins.

TRADITIONAL WAY OF LIFE

Traditionally the Aborigines were divided into about 500 tribal groups, each with its own language or dialect. Each tribe claimed its own territory and moved from place to place within that area to hunt, fish, and gather food.

Each tribe was an extended family made up of several clans. Clan members lived in family groups of thirty to forty people. Each clan had an emblem called a totem—perhaps an animal or a plant. The totem was honored as a clan member and served as a reminder of the clan's common ancestry. The Aborigines believed that all things—people, animals, plants, and even rocks—were important parts of nature and of the spirit world.

The Aborigines survived by adapting to Australia's often harsh conditions. They were one of the few early peoples to use the lever, as part of a woomera (spear-thrower). They also used several types of boomerangs, flat, curved throwing sticks made of hardwood. One type, the returning boomerang, was used for sport. When thrown properly, this kind spins through the air and returns to the thrower in a perfect arc. The Aborigines also used non-returning boomerang-type weapons for hunting, fighting, and other purposes, but they were not the only early culture to use such a tool. The Aborigines also left a rich heritage of artwork in the form of rock carvings and bark and cave paintings.

In 1788, when the first European settlers came to Australia, there were perhaps more than 300,000 Aborigines living there. As the Europeans spread out, many natives were driven from their lands into remote areas. Many others died from foreign diseases.

ABORIGINES IN MODERN AUSTRALIA

Today there are about 265,000 Aboriginal peoples in Australia. About one-third of them are considered full-blooded. The remainder are of mixed Aboriginal-European ancestry.

All together, Aborigines make up only about 1.5 percent of Australia's population. Most live in cities and towns, although a few are trying to preserve some form of the old, nomadic way of life.

The standard of living for most Aborigines lags far behind that of other Australian citizens. In the past few decades, the government has sponsored a number of programs to help the Aborigines compete for jobs and housing opportunities.

In recent years, efforts also have been made on the part of the Aborigines to regain title to their ancestral lands. They have been successful in regaining ownership of some parts of the Northern Territory and of South Australia. Since 1980, these lands have been administered by the Aboriginal Development Commission. In 1992 the Australian High Court ruled that the Aborigines owned Australia before European settlement began, and in 1994 they were given the right to claim land under "native" title.

CAROL PERKINS
Author, *The Sound of Boomerangs*

See also AUSTRALIA (The Aborigines).

ABORTION

Abortion is the ending of a pregnancy before the fetus (unborn child) has developed and grown enough to live outside the mother. If abortion happens naturally, before the 20th week of pregnancy, it is called a spontaneous abortion, or miscarriage. If it happens naturally after the 20th week, it is termed a late fetal death or a stillbirth.

If abortion is caused by artificial means, generally by medical procedure, it is called an induced abortion. Most induced abortions in the United States are performed in the first trimester of the pregnancy.

In the United States, a debate rages over the ethical and legal aspects of induced abortion. Members of the right-to-life movement believe that abortion is morally wrong and should be restricted or prohibited because it ends the life of a human being. They have influenced a number of states to vote on bills that would outlaw abortion except for pregnancies caused by criminal acts, or when the mother's life is at risk. People who refer to themselves as pro-choice may also believe that abortion is morally wrong. But they believe that the law should protect the woman's right to medical privacy and the right to choose for herself whether to have an abortion. They also argue that statistics show fewer pregnancy-related deaths wherever abortion is legal.

In 1973, in the *Roe* v. *Wade* case, the U.S. Supreme Court ruled that a woman could not be prevented from having an induced abortion during her first trimester. Prevention, the Court said, would violate the woman's right to privacy. States could, however, restrict second trimester abortions and prohibit third trimester abortions. In 1992 the Court allowed additional restrictions. Some states may now require a 24-hour waiting period or permission from the parents of a pregnant teenager or the father of the fetus. The abortion-inducing drug RU-486 was approved for use in the United States in 2000.

ANN E. WEISS
Author, *Bioethics: Dilemmas in Modern Medicine*

ABRAHAM

Abraham is called the father of the Jews and is considered the founder of the Jewish religion. He was the first to believe in one all-powerful God instead of many gods.

Abraham's story is found in the book of Genesis, the first book of the Bible. When Abraham was 75 years old, God commanded him to leave Haran in search of a new home. God promised that a great nation would arise in the new land. Abraham set out with his wife, Sarah, his nephew Lot, and some followers. They traveled into the land of Canaan. God told Abraham that this was the land he would give to Abraham's descendants. Abraham journeyed on toward the south, building altars to God wherever he went. When a famine came, he went into Egypt. He grew rich in cattle, silver, and gold.

When Abraham and his followers left Egypt, both Abraham and Lot grew very prosperous. They acquired so many sheep that their shepherds quarreled over grazing land. Abraham and Lot agreed to separate and live in different places.

The story of Abraham is told in Genesis, the first book of the Bible. Here Abraham is shown receiving a message from God, promising him a son.

Abraham settled in Hebron. Lot and his family settled in Sodom. When Sodom was attacked by the armies of four great kings, Lot was taken captive. Abraham went to his rescue with 318 men and brought Lot and all his goods back to Sodom.

The people of Sodom and neighboring Gomorrah grew very wicked. God told Abraham that he would destroy both cities because no righteous people could be found in them. But God warned Lot to escape with his wife and two daughters, forbidding them to look behind as they fled. Lot's wife looked back, and she became a pillar of salt.

When Abraham and Sarah had grown very old and were still childless, God promised them a son. God also said that Abraham would have as many descendants as there were stars in the sky and that one day they would dwell in the Promised Land. In time, a son was born to Abraham and Sarah and was named Isaac. God told Abraham that he would keep his promise with Isaac and his descendants.

While Isaac was still a boy, God tested Abraham again. He told Abraham to take Isaac to the top of a mountain and sacrifice him. Abraham loved his son, but he could not disobey God's command. At the place of sacrifice, Isaac asked, "Where is the lamb for a burnt offering?" Abraham answered that God would provide it. Then he built an altar, bound up Isaac, and laid him on top of the altar. Just as he was about to put the knife to his son, God stopped him. God said, "Lay not thine hand upon the lad, neither do thou any thing unto him: for now I know that thou fearest God, seeing thou hast not withheld thy son, thine only son, from me." Abraham looked up and saw a ram caught in a thicket. He offered the ram in sacrifice. God blessed Abraham for his obedience.

When Sarah and Abraham died, they were buried in the cave of Machpelah in Hebron. After Abraham's death, God blessed Isaac.

Christians and Muslims also honor Abraham and trace their belief in one God back to him. The Arabs claim descent from Ishmael, who was Abraham's son by Hagar, Sarah's handmaiden. Sarah had given Hagar to Abraham when she thought she herself would have no children.

Abraham's life is regarded as an example of the proving of faith through trial. Because Abraham listened to God, he is called the Friend of God. His unquestioning obedience to God's commands is taken as proof of genuine righteousness.

Reviewed by MORTIMER J. COHEN
Author, *Pathways Through the Bible*

ACCIDENTS. See FIRST AID; SAFETY.

ACCOUNTING. See BOOKKEEPING AND ACCOUNTING.

ACHAEMENIDS. See PERSIA, ANCIENT.

ACHILLES. See GREEK MYTHOLOGY.

ACID RAIN

Acid rain is a general term for rain or other precipitation that has been polluted by chemicals called acids. This environmental problem can pollute lakes, rivers, and streams; damage metals and other construction materials; and even pose a health risk to people.

Acid rain forms when certain pollutants, such as sulfur oxides and nitrogen oxides, mix with tiny droplets of water vapor in the atmosphere. Power plants are the main source of pollutants causing acid rain. Smoke from factories, exhaust fumes from automobiles and trucks, and even gases given off by chemical fertilizers also put pollutants into the air. The pollutants change the clean, fresh water to droplets of acid. These acids fall to the ground as rain, snow, or sleet. Even fog can contain acids.

Rain normally contains some naturally occurring acids, which are not considered a problem. However, sulfuric and nitric acids in rain are a problem. Acid rain soaks the ground and can make soil, lakes, and rivers abnormally acidic. In badly affected regions, plants and many types of aquatic animals are harmed. Entire lakes and some forest trees can be affected. Even buildings and statues can be damaged by acid rain.

Pollution That Causes Acid Rain. When fossil fuels—oil, coal, and gas—are burned, in industrial plants or automobile engines, for example, sulfur oxides and nitrogen oxides are released into the air.

Nitrogen oxides and other acid-forming chemicals also enter the air from the breakdown of agricultural fertilizers. Hydrochloric acid often comes directly from smokestacks.

Acid rain weakened these trees (*above*), leaving them unable to survive a deadly insect infestation. Sculptures (*right*) that existed intact for centuries are decaying at an alarming rate due to acid rain and other pollution.

Carbon monoxide and carbon dioxide are produced by motor vehicles.

Because pollutants can travel over hundreds and even thousands of miles, acid rain often affects areas that are far from power plants and heavy automobile exhaust. Pollutants in smoke enter the air high above the ground through tall smokestacks and are carried by winds for great distances. Pollutants from the midwestern United States are regularly carried to New York, New England, and southeastern Canada. Similarly, pollution from Canada is carried by winds into the United States. Norway and Sweden have received acid rain created by pollutants from England, Germany, Italy, France, and Austria.

The Effects of Acid Rain. Millions of tons of acids fall in rain on the United States and Canada each year. The concentrations of these acids are too weak to cause burns, but they do produce other less severe effects.

When acid rain falls on metal objects, the objects can be damaged. Shiny objects become dull and, if the process continues for many years, the metal objects can corrode and lose strength or crumble. Acid rain also affects the surfaces of stone statues and stone or brick buildings.

The way in which acid rain reacts with aluminum can cause serious ecological problems. Aluminum is normally present in soil. If acid rain causes soil acidification, the aluminum in the soil may dissolve in water and be absorbed by plants, where it can damage root cells. Animal cells are also very sensitive to aluminum. In lakes and streams, it can kill the eggs of many kinds of fish and the embryos of salamanders and other amphibians. Aluminum affects mature fish by causing the gills to clog with mucus, preventing breathing. It also disrupts eggshell formation in birds.

Human beings may also be at risk from the effects of acid rain. In moist air, high levels of pollutants from acidic aerosols have been found to affect lung function in experimental studies. People who suffer from asthma, emphysema, and chronic bronchitis are more sensitive to acid environments.

Stopping Acid Rain. In 1990, the United States passed the Clean Air Act Amendments. This was a law that required significant annual reductions in air pollution. One measure to fight acid rain is to remove from the air those sulfur and nitrogen compounds that become acids. Some of these compounds can be taken out of fuel before the fuel is burned. Or the pollutants can be removed from smoke before the smoke enters the air. Each individual also can play a role in reducing air pollution by conserving energy through such activities as cutting back on the use of electricity and carpooling or using public transportation.

Reviewed by Patricia M. Irving
Director, National Acid Precipitation
Assessment Program

ACIDS. See Chemistry.

ACNE. See Diseases (Descriptions of Some Diseases).

ACOUSTICS. See Sound and Ultrasonics.

ADAMS, ANSEL. See PHOTOGRAPHY (Great Photographers).

ADAMS, CHARLES FRANCIS (1807–1886)

Charles Francis Adams was an American historian and diplomat. The son of President John Quincy Adams and the grandson of President John Adams, he was born in Boston, Massachusetts, on August 18, 1807. He graduated from Harvard in 1825, became a lawyer, and later entered politics, serving in the Massachusetts state legislature (1840–45) as a Whig. Adams, who opposed slavery, switched over to the Free Soil Party and ran unsuccessfully as its vice-presidential candidate in 1848. Later he served in the U.S. House of Representatives as a Republican (1859–61).

Adams performed his most important work during the U.S. Civil War as ambassador to Great Britain (1861–68). Britain had declared itself neutral in the American conflict, yet many Britons openly supported the Confederacy. Adams persuaded the British government not to intervene diplomatically on the Confederate side and to officially ban further shipbuilding for the Confederates (although several ships continued to slip through on the black market).

In 1872 Adams represented the United States on an international committee that settled the so-called *Alabama* claims for damages caused by British-built Confederate ships during the Civil War. The committee assessed Great Britain $15.5 million in damages for violating international neutrality laws.

Adams edited many letters, papers, and diaries of his famous parents and grandparents. Among the most notable is his 12-volume *Memoirs of John Quincy Adams* (1864–67). He died in Boston on November 21, 1886.

MICHAEL WINSHIP
Cornell University

ADAMS, HENRY (1838–1918)

In 1919, a year after Henry Adams' death, *The Education of Henry Adams* was awarded a Pulitzer Prize. It is still considered a classic among autobiographies.

Henry Brooks Adams—historian, novelist, and philosopher—was born on February 16, 1838, in Boston, Massachusetts. Adams came from a distinguished family. His grandfather, John Quincy Adams, and his great grandfather, John Adams, both were former presidents of the United States; his father, Charles Francis Adams, was a historian, diplomat, and politician. Not surprisingly, Henry Adams grew up assuming that he, too, would be an important person one day.

When Adams graduated from Harvard in 1858, he entered a world in which he felt he did not belong. He tried a number of careers, first as his father's private secretary (1861–68). He later became a journalist, and then for seven years he taught history at Harvard.

Finally in 1877, Adams settled down in Washington, D.C. There he suffered a great personal tragedy in 1885 when his beloved wife Marian committed suicide. Adams devoted himself to writing books. In his *Mont-Saint-Michel and Chartres: A Story of 13th Century Unity* (1913), he described the Middle Ages as a time of beauty and spiritual unity, very much unlike the chaotic times in which he felt he lived. It seemed to him that America was a harsh place where only the most brutal and energetic people could succeed, not the most intelligent and idealistic. In *The Education of Henry Adams* (1918), he explored this observation, trying to understand how the world had changed and why he could not adapt to the new society.

Among Adams' other works were two novels, *Democracy, an American Novel* (1880), a political satire; and *Esther* (1884), the story of a woman's search for religious truth. His most important historical work was the multi-volume *History of the United States during the Administrations of Jefferson and Madison* (1884–91). Adams died in Washington, D.C., on March 27, 1918.

MICHAEL WINSHIP
Cornell University

JOHN ADAMS (1735-1826)

2nd President of the United States

FACTS ABOUT JOHN ADAMS

Birthplace: Braintree (now Quincy), Massachusetts *(below)*
Religion: Unitarian
College Attended: Harvard College, Cambridge, Massachusetts
Occupation: Lawyer
Married: Abigail Smith
Children: Abigail, John Quincy, Susanna, Charles, Thomas
Political Party: Federalist
Office Held Before Becoming President: Vice President
President Who Preceded Him: George Washington
Age on Becoming President: 61
Years in the Presidency: 1797–1801
Vice President: Thomas Jefferson
President Who Succeeded Him: Thomas Jefferson
Age at Death: 90
Burial Place: First Unitarian Church, Quincy, Massachusetts

DURING JOHN ADAMS' PRESIDENCY

The first cast-iron plow was patented by Charles Newbold (1797). *Below:* Disputes between the United States and France led to an undeclared naval war between the two nations and the creation of the Navy Department (1798). *Left:* The U.S. Marine Corps was established as a permanent service by Congress (1798). The Mississippi Territory, including what is now Mississippi and Alabama, was created (1798). The Indiana Territory, including all or parts of present-day Indiana, Wisconsin, Illinois, Michigan, and Minnesota, was created (1800). The capital was moved from Philadelphia to Washington, D.C. (1800).

ADAMS, JOHN. Of all the early presidents of the United States, John Adams has been the least understood and appreciated. His reputation, both during his lifetime and after, has suffered from this lack of understanding. Yet he was a remarkable man who contributed greatly to the creation of the United States during the American Revolution and in its formative years.

EARLY YEARS

Adams was born on October 30, 1735, in Braintree (now Quincy), Massachusetts. His great-grandfather Henry Adams had emigrated from England. But both his grandfather Joseph Adams and his father, John Adams, had been born in Braintree. His mother, Susanna Boylston Adams, came from the nearby city of Boston.

Adams grew up on his father's farm, doing the usual country chores, including feeding the horses, milking the cows, and chopping wood. In 1751, at the age of 16, he entered Harvard, then a small college, and graduated four years later. He then taught school during the day and studied law at night. In 1758 he became a lawyer. Perhaps his most famous case, which showed Adams' characteristic courage, was his successful defense of the British soldiers who were arrested after the Boston Massacre in 1770.

In 1764, Adams married Abigail Smith. She was an intelligent and sprightly woman whose letters are still a source of interesting information. The marriage was happy and successful. It lasted 54 years, until Abigail Adams' death in 1818. Their eldest son, John Quincy, later became the sixth president.

POLITICAL BEGINNINGS

Altogether, Adams spent about 25 years in public life. He became interested in politics quite early in his career as a lawyer. In 1765 a crisis arose when the British Government passed the Stamp Act. This was an unpopular tax on public documents, newspapers, licenses, insurance policies, and even playing cards. Adams wrote powerful articles against the tax in the Boston *Gazette*. These articles

Abigail Adams was the wife of one president, John Adams, and the mother of a second, John Quincy Adams. She was the first First Lady to occupy the White House.

helped to establish his reputation as a political thinker, as an opponent of Britain's colonial policies in America, and as a champion of individual liberties.

The Continental Congress. Adams served as a delegate from Massachusetts to the First Continental Congress in Philadelphia in 1774 and to the Second Continental Congress, which met in 1775. With brilliance and persistence, he argued for American independence from Britain. When the fighting broke out in 1775 that marked the beginning of the Revolutionary War, Adams proposed George Washington as the commander of American military forces.

Adams was a member of the committee that drafted the Declaration of Independence. Although the Declaration was written chiefly by Thomas Jefferson, Adams bore the burden of defending it on the floor of the Continental Congress. It was adopted on July 4, 1776.

Diplomatic Service. Adams' diplomatic career began in 1778 when he was sent to France to help negotiate a treaty of alliance. In 1780 he returned to Europe as minister to arrange for loans and trade agreements in France and the Netherlands. Two years later Adams, together with Benjamin Franklin and John Jay, signed the preliminary peace treaty with Britain. The treaty, known as the Treaty of Paris, was finally concluded in 1783. It ended the Revolutionary War and crowned Adams' long struggle for American independence.

In 1785, Adams was appointed the first U.S. minister to Britain. He tried to win British friendship and economic co-operation, but without success. One reason was that he was too outspoken in defense of American interests. He was happy to return home in 1788, after having spent some ten years abroad.

Vice President. In the first presidential election in the United States, in 1788, George Washington won all the electoral votes cast for president. Adams became vice president. Both men were re-elected in 1792.

In spite of his general agreement with Washington's policies, Adams was impatient with his position as vice president. Adams was eager to lead and to act. Instead, he had to confine himself to the largely ceremonial job of presiding over the U.S. Senate.

PRESIDENT

Adams' frustration was ended by his victory in the presidential election of 1796. Running as the Federalist candidate, he edged out Thomas Jefferson, leader of the Democratic-Republicans (also called the Republicans). According to the laws of the time, Jefferson thus became vice president. As a result, the new president and vice president belonged to opposing political parties.

John Adams was the first president to occupy the White House. He and Abigail moved in near the end of his term, in the fall of 1800. The President's Palace, as it was then known, was still unfinished and littered with debris.

Adams' one term as president was marked by troubles, both international and domestic. The foreign affairs crisis involved American neutrality at a time when Britain and France were at war. French attacks on American ships stirred up a warlike atmosphere in the United States, even inside Adams' own Cabinet. The situation was aggravated by the so-called XYZ Affair.

The XYZ Affair. Adams had sent a diplomatic mission to France to arrange a treaty. There the diplomats were visited by three agents of the French foreign minister Talleyrand. These agents, known as X, Y, and Z, asked for a bribe of $240,000. When news of this XYZ Affair reached America, it caused an uproar and led to an undeclared war between the United States and France. But despite immense pressure, including that of members of his own Federalist Party, President Adams knew that the United States was not strong enough to fight the French Empire. He persisted in his efforts for peace, which was finally achieved by the Convention of 1800. Adams considered it his great accomplishment. He said, "I desire no other inscription over my gravestone than: 'Here lies John Adams, who took upon himself the responsibility of the peace with France in the year 1800.' "

Adams' courageous but unpopular peace policy and his stubborn independence in other political matters cost him the support of his own party. The leading Federalists, including the powerful Alexander Hamilton, turned bitterly against him. This led to a hopeless split in their party.

The Alien and Sedition Acts. President Adams' unpopularity was aggravated by the Alien and Sedition Acts. These acts were a direct result of the excitement over the trouble with France. The country was divided into pro-French and pro-British groups. Adams' Federalist Party was strongly anti-French. The opposition Democratic-Republican Party, led by Jefferson, was just as strongly anti-British.

The Federalists were convinced that opposition against them was aroused by the French and Irish living in America. They were sure that the country swarmed with French spies. The Federalists controlled Congress. In 1798 they decided to crush the opposition through legislation that came to be known as the Alien and Sedition Acts.

The Alien Act contained three provisions. One required that the period of naturalization for foreigners be changed from 5 to 14 years. The second authorized the president to deport all aliens considered dangerous to the peace and security of the country. The third gave the president the power to imprison or banish citizens of an enemy country in time of war.

More serious was the Sedition Act, which was aimed at American opponents of the government. This act made it a crime to oppose the administration directly or indirectly. Even those who voiced criticism in print were made subject to harsh penalties.

The Sedition Act resulted in the prosecution of 25 persons and the conviction of 10 of them. All were prominent Democratic-Republicans.

These acts were violently unpopular. They were considered an attack on the basic liberties of the American people. President Adams was not personally responsible for them, but they were passed by his party and he signed them. Therefore the blame fell upon him. In the election of 1800, Adams and his party suffered disastrous defeat. The Federalist Party never recovered.

On March 4, 1801, after the inauguration of President Jefferson, Adams retired from public life. He returned to Braintree and devoted the remaining 25 years of his life to

Final plans for the White House (*below*) were drawn up by Irish architect James Hoban. Construction began in 1792, and the Adams family became its first occupants in 1800.

John Adams (*standing, in rust-colored suit*) and the four other members of the drafting committee present the Declaration of Independence to the Second Continental Congress.

intellectual pursuits, mainly reading (philosophy, religion, political thought, science) and letter writing. He resumed his friendship and correspondence with Thomas Jefferson in 1812. The two men had been separated for 12 years because of political differences. On July 4, 1826—the 50th anniversary of the Declaration of Independence—John Adams died at Quincy. That same day Jefferson died at Monticello, Virginia.

HIS POLITICAL PHILOSOPHY

Adams expressed his ideas in a number of essays and books, as well as in his letters. There are three main elements in his philosophy. One is Adams' view of human nature. Another is his conception of inequality. The third is his idea of government.

IMPORTANT DATES IN THE LIFE OF JOHN ADAMS

1735	Born at Braintree (now Quincy), Massachusetts, October 30.
1755	Graduated from Harvard College.
1758	Began practicing law.
1764	Married Abigail Smith.
1765	Attacked the Stamp Act in articles in the Boston *Gazette*.
1774–1777	Served in the Continental Congress.
1780	Minister to the Netherlands.
1782	Went to Paris (with John Jay and Benjamin Franklin) to arrange peace treaty with Great Britain ending the Revolutionary War. Treaty of Paris concluded 1783.
1785–1788	Minister to Great Britain.
1789–1797	Vice-president of the United States.
1797–1801	2nd president of the United States.
1826	Died at Quincy, Massachusetts, July 4.

Adams did not agree with democrats like Jefferson that human beings were naturally good and decent. On the contrary, he believed that people were basically selfish and only good because of necessity.

Adams also denied the democratic idea of equality. He pointed out that among all nations the people were "naturally divided into two sorts, the gentlemen and the simple men." The gentlemen, being superior in abilities, education, and other advantages, were therefore qualified to rule.

These views underlay Adams' philosophy of government. Since human beings were greedy and selfish, it was necessary for society to keep them in check. The average person, he felt, could not be entrusted with power.

Adams believed in liberty and was opposed to tyranny. Though he was sometimes accused of being a monarchist, he actually preferred a republic. But instead of a Jefferson-type democracy, Adams favored a republican government run by an aristocracy of talented men.

Such views, expressed with his typical bluntness, gained Adams unpopularity and even hostility among the American people. But he was not one to seek popular favor. He died as he had lived, an independent, tough-minded, somewhat opinionated and irritable Yankee—but always a courageous patriot and scholar.

SAUL K. PADOVER
Editor, *The World of the Founding Fathers*

JOHN QUINCY ADAMS (1767-1848)

6th President of the United States

FACTS ABOUT JOHN QUINCY ADAMS

Birthplace: Braintree (now Quincy), Massachusetts *(center)*

Religion: Unitarian
College Attended: Harvard College, Cambridge, Massachusetts
Occupation: Lawyer
Married: Louisa Catherine Johnson
Children: George, John, Charles Francis, Louisa Catherine
Political Party: Federalist, Democratic-Republican (National Republican), Whig
Nickname: "Old Man Eloquent"
Office Held Before Becoming President: Secretary of State
President Who Preceded Him: James Monroe
Age on Becoming President: 57
Years in the Presidency: 1825-1829
Vice President: John C. Calhoun
President Who Succeeded Him: Andrew Jackson
Age at Death: 80
Burial Place: Quincy, Massachusetts

DURING JOHN QUINCY ADAMS' PRESIDENCY

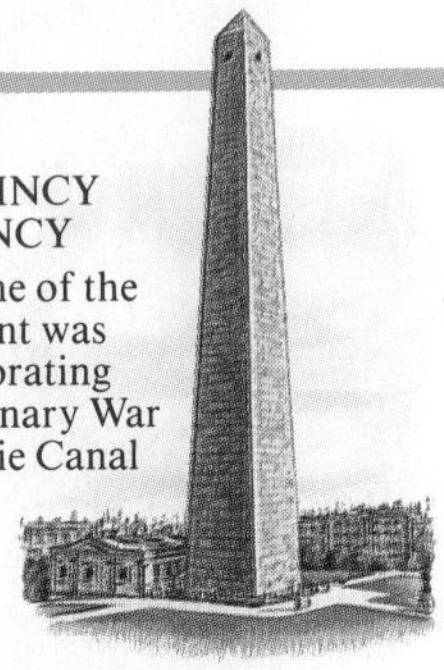

Right: The cornerstone of the Bunker Hill Monument was laid (1825), commemorating the famous Revolutionary War battle. *Below:* The Erie Canal was opened (1825), linking New York with Lake Erie and the other Great Lakes and increasing trade with and settlement of the growing Midwest. The first iron vessel, built of sheet iron, in the United States, the steamboat *Codorus,* was tested (1825) on the Susquehanna River. Construction of the Baltimore and Ohio Railroad, the first commercial passenger and freight railroad in the United States, was begun (1828).

ADAMS, JOHN QUINCY. Many Americans have sought the office of president of the United States and have deliberately shaped their lives to that end. John Quincy Adams' parents prepared him for the presidency from boyhood. But although Adams achieved his goal of becoming president, his term in the White House was overshadowed by his two other political careers—as America's greatest diplomat and as its greatest defender of human freedom in the U.S. House of Representatives.

▸AN UNUSUAL CHILDHOOD

John Quincy Adams was born on July 11, 1767, in Braintree (now Quincy), Massachusetts. His father was John Adams, who would later become the second president of the United States. His mother, Abigail Smith Adams, was the most accomplished American woman of her time. Young Adams grew up as a child of the American Revolution, which began when he was 7 years old.

John Quincy's education began in the village school and continued under his mother's guidance. His education was inspired by letters from his father, who had been serving in the Continental Congress in Philadelphia since 1774.

During the Revolutionary War, John Quincy accompanied his father on two diplomatic missions to Europe. In 1781, at the age of 14, he acted as French interpreter to his father on a mission to Russia. In 1783, John Quincy served as his father's secretary when the elder Adams was minister to France. Young Adams was present at the signing of the Treaty of Paris in 1783, which ended the Revolutionary War.

In Paris, John Quincy Adams began his famous diary. He was to continue it for over 60 years. On the title page of the first volume was the proverb that ruled his life: "Sweet is indolence [laziness] and cruel its consequences." Adams never had a lazy day.

Young Adams returned to Massachusetts in 1785 to complete his education at Harvard College. He graduated in 1787 and then studied law.

HIS EARLY DIPLOMATIC CAREER

He had barely developed a law practice when the French Revolution broke out. Articles Adams wrote for a Boston newspaper attracted the attention of President George Washington. In 1794 Washington appointed the 28-year-old John Quincy Adams minister to the Netherlands. Adams' official dispatches and his letters from the Dutch capital at The Hague convinced the President that this young man would one day stand at the head of the American diplomatic corps.

In 1797, while on a mission from the Netherlands to England, Adams married Louisa Catherine Johnson, daughter of the American consul in London.

From The Hague Adams (whose father was now president) was assigned to the Court of Prussia. There he negotiated a treaty of friendship and commerce. He continued his letters and dispatches about the war of the French Revolution. Because of political reasons, John Adams recalled him after Thomas Jefferson was elected president in 1800.

Adams' experiences had convinced him that the United States must never be caught in the "vortex" of European rivalries and wars. This lesson guided him through his later diplomatic career and influenced United States policy for a century afterwards.

A SHORT TERM IN THE SENATE

When he returned to Boston, Adams found the practice of law frustrating. He had a strong desire to enter politics. In 1803 the Massachusetts legislature elected him to the United States Senate. Though elected as a Federalist, Adams felt that party politics stopped at the ocean's edge. To the disgust of Massachusetts Federalists, he voted for President Jefferson's Embargo of 1807. The embargo was aimed at protecting United States neutrality in the wars between England and France. It stopped all American trade with the two countries. Adams' vote in favor of the embargo cost him his Senate seat. The legislature held a special election ahead of time to replace him with a more faithful Federalist.

DIPLOMAT AGAIN

In 1809 President James Madison appointed Adams the first American minister to Russia. Adams was in Russia when the War of 1812 broke out between the United States and Great Britain. He served on the delegation that brought about the Peace of Ghent in 1814. The following year he became minister to Great Britain, where he served until 1817.

By now Adams was in his 50th year. He was without question the most experienced man in the United States diplomatic service. Because of his European experience, Adams had become a confirmed isolationist. He felt that the future of the United States lay in expansion across the North American continent rather than in European alliances.

SECRETARY OF STATE

In 1817 President James Monroe called Adams home to become secretary of state. The most important achievements of Secretary Adams were the treaties he negotiated, which brought much of the Far West under American control. The famous Transcontinental Treaty of 1819 (ratified 1821) with Spain gave the United States access to the Pacific Ocean. This was the greatest diplomatic triumph ever achieved by one man in the history of the United States. Adams was also responsible for treaties with the newly independent countries of Latin America.

The Monroe Doctrine

John Quincy Adams had a major role in forming the Monroe Doctrine. Adams' words in that famous document made it clear that the United States would not tolerate any new European colonization in the Americas. The doctrine properly bears President Monroe's name. For it was Monroe who in 1823 first declared its principles to the world as American foreign policy.

The Election of 1824

Adams was never a dynamic politician. But his accomplishments brought him before the people in the national election of 1824. There was no real party contest. The old political parties had disappeared during the so-called Era of Good Feeling of Monroe's administration. It was a contest of leaders.

General Andrew Jackson, the hero of the battle of New Orleans during the War of 1812, received a majority of the popular vote. But no candidate received the necessary ma-

The 79-year-old Adams sat for this photograph in 1847, a year before he died.

This portrait of Louisa Catherine Adams, the President's wife, dates from the 1820's. The harp and book symbolize her love of music and literature.

jority in the electoral college. Jackson had 99 electoral votes; Adams, 84; William H. Crawford of Georgia, 41; and Henry Clay of Kentucky, 37. Under the Constitution the election had to be decided by the House of Representatives. The voting there was by states and was limited to the first three candidates. On February 9, 1825, Adams was elected president by a bare majority of states.

John Adams, then 90 years old, was delighted at his son's victory. But Abigail Adams did not live to see the presidency come to rest on her son's shoulders. She had died in 1818.

HIS TERM AS PRESIDENT

President John Quincy Adams appointed Henry Clay secretary of state. Clay had thrown the votes of his supporters in the House of Representatives to Adams rather than Jackson. At once Jackson and his followers raised the cry of "corrupt bargain." That there was a political deal seems fairly certain. But there is nothing to show that it was dishonest.

The charge of corrupt bargain was the beginning of a quarrel with Jackson that marred Adams' administration. Jackson had strong support among the voters of the newly admitted states. Adams, after all, had not received a majority of the popular vote. The Jacksonians were out to get rid of Adams and seize office themselves.

The 4 years of Adams' presidency were prosperous and generally happy years for the United States. Adams' ambition was to govern "as a man of the whole nation," not as the leader of a political party. He believed in liberty with power. He favored more power for the federal government in the disposal of public lands and in building new roads and canals to keep up with the westward movement. He supported federal control and protection of the Indian groups against invasion of their lands by the states.

This program hit at the narrow interpretation of the Constitution under the old Jeffersonian concept of states' rights. It thus aroused Adams' opponents. In the election of 1828, Andrew Jackson was elected president by an overwhelming majority.

With his term as president over, Adams' career seemed finished. He returned sadly to

Quincy, Massachusetts. However, he was still willing to serve his country in any office, large or small. In 1830 he was elected to the House of Representatives. Nothing could have been more pleasing to Adams, for the ghost of the presidency still haunted him. He hoped for the nomination again. But these hopes soon faded.

"OLD MAN ELOQUENT"

During Adams' years in the House of Representatives, the stormy issue of slavery faced the United States. At heart Adams was an abolitionist: he wished to do away completely with slavery. But he was politically prudent, and did not say so publicly. He became a leader of the antislavery forces in Congress but limited his efforts to constitutional means. He sought to abolish slavery in the District of Columbia. He opposed its expansion into the territories of the United States. And he championed the right of petition to Congress for abolition of slavery.

As secretary of state and as president, Adams had tried to obtain Texas from Mexico. But in Congress he resisted to the last the movement for annexation of Texas. By that time the entry of Texas into the Union would have meant the creation of one or more new slave states. On the other hand, he championed the annexation of Oregon, where slavery did not exist. "I want the country for our Western pioneers," he said.

Adams was a patron and supporter in Congress of scientific activities, especially in the fields of weights and measures, and astronomy. He led the movement for establishment of the Smithsonian Institution, in Washington, D.C., one of the nation's foremost centers of learning.

Adams' long career of public service ended in the U.S. House of Representatives. He was elected to Congress in 1830 and died there on February 23, 1848.

"Old Man Eloquent," as Adams was called, opposed the war with Mexico that followed the annexation of Texas in 1845. He considered it an unjust war. On February 21, 1848, while protesting the award of swords of honor to the American generals who had won the war, Adams collapsed on the floor of the House of Representatives. He died two days later in the Capitol.

During most of his early career as a diplomat, Adams was little known throughout the country. His term as president was unpopular. Always a reserved man, he seemed cold and aloof to the people. His career in the House of Representatives made him a violently controversial figure. It was not until the final years of his life that Adams won esteem and almost affection, especially in the hearts and minds of the millions who hated slavery. Representatives of both political parties journeyed to Quincy, Massachusetts, for his funeral. In death, John Quincy Adams seemed at last to belong to the whole nation.

SAMUEL FLAGG BEMIS
Yale University
Author, *John Quincy Adams and the Union*

See also MONROE DOCTRINE.

IMPORTANT DATES IN THE LIFE OF JOHN QUINCY ADAMS

1767	Born at Braintree (later Quincy), Massachusetts, July 11.
1787	Graduated from Harvard College.
1794	Appointed minister to the Netherlands.
1797	Married Louisa Catherine Johnson.
1797–1801	Minister to Prussia.
1803–1808	Served in the United States Senate.
1809–1814	Minister to Russia.
1814	Headed American delegation that negotiated the Peace of Ghent, ending the War of 1812.
1815–1817	Minister to Great Britain.
1817–1825	Secretary of state.
1825–1829	6th president of the United States.
1831–1848	Served in the U.S. House of Representatives.
1848	Died at Washington, D.C., February 23.

ADAMS, SAMUEL (1722–1803)

Samuel Adams was an American patriot whose skills as an orator and organizer did much to arouse the American colonists against British rule and helped bring about the revolution that created the United States.

Early Years. Adams was born in Boston, Massachusetts, on September 27, 1722. He was a cousin of John Adams, who was to become the second president of the United States. He attended the Boston Grammar School and graduated from Harvard College in 1740. He later returned to Harvard to earn his master's degree. His father was a well-to-do businessman who wanted him to follow a similar career, but Samuel had no talent for business. He studied law but gave it up to devote his time to politics.

Orator and Organizer. In 1765, Adams was elected to the Massachusetts legislature, where he soon became a leader of the radical (anti-British) party. He spoke out against and wrote many angry articles protesting unpopular British laws such as the Stamp Act, which required the purchase of a tax stamp for use on business and legal documents and newspapers. Adams' argument was that the people could not be taxed without their consent. When the British Parliament was forced to repeal the Stamp Act but introduced new taxes under the Townshend Acts in 1767, he delivered fiery speeches against them.

In 1772, Adams organized a committee of correspondence to spread the news of events in Boston and to coordinate the activities of other patriots. By 1773 dozens of such committees had been formed. Eventually extending from Massachusetts to Georgia, they played a vital role in the revolutionary cause.

Boston Tea Party. The British tried to quiet the unrest by repealing most of the unpopular taxes, but they retained a tax on tea. The fact that a British company was given a monopoly on the tea trade, at the expense of American merchants, made the situation even worse.

Matters came to a crisis on the night of December 16, 1773. Adams had demanded the departure from Boston of three British ships carrying tea. When the royal governor of Massachusetts refused, a group of Bostonians, on Adams' prearranged signal and disguised as Indians, boarded the ships and dumped their cargoes into the harbor. The action was celebrated as the Boston Tea Party. But it provoked the British Parliament into passage, in 1774, of what were known as the Intolerable Acts, which closed the port of Boston and restricted colonial liberties.

Independence and After. Events moved rapidly. Adams approved the Suffolk Resolves, calling for a boycott on trade with Britain, and was elected to the First Continental Congress. Named to the Second Continental Congress in 1775, he narrowly escaped arrest by British troops, who fired the shots at Lexington that touched off the Revolutionary War. In 1776, he proudly signed his name to the Declaration of Independence.

Adams' work as an organizer of the revolution was now complete. He played a minor role as a member of the Continental Congress during the war. When peace came in 1783, many people thought he was too much of a firebrand for the new nation and too gruff and critical of opposition. But Adams did serve as lieutenant governor and as governor of Massachusetts before retiring in 1797. He died in Boston on October 2, 1803.

Reviewed by Richard B. Morris
Columbia University
Editor, *Encyclopedia of American History*

ADDAMS, JANE (1860–1935)

Jane Addams founded Hull House, one of the first settlement houses (centers for social welfare) in the United States. All of her life she crusaded for social reforms, equal rights for women, and world peace.

Born in Cedarville, Illinois, on September 6, 1860, Addams came from a large and moderately wealthy family. At an early age, she decided to do something important with her life. She attended Rockford College in Illinois and later was forced to drop out of medical school due to poor health.

While traveling in London, Addams became impressed with Toynbee Hall, a settlement house founded in 1884, and she decided to attempt a similar project in Chicago. In 1889, with the help of Ellen Gates Starr, a former college classmate, Addams founded Hull House in a run-down mansion to help the immigrants crowded into the poor sections of the city.

By 1907, Hull House had expanded to 13 buildings and was providing important social services, such as child care and adult education. Meanwhile, Addams led successful campaigns against child labor and fought for better housing and an eight-hour working law for women. She also campaigned vigorously to obtain for women the right to vote. Addams lectured all over the country on behalf of social reform and published many books and articles, among them *Twenty Years at Hull House* (1920).

Recognizing that private charitable donations could not adequately address the problems of the poor, Jane Addams founded Hull House in Chicago to help the needy.

After World War I broke out in 1914, Addams, an ardent pacifist, served as president (1915–29) of the Women's International League for Peace and Freedom. In 1931 she was awarded a Nobel Peace Prize. When Addams died on May 21, 1935, she was mourned by thousands.

ALLEN F. DAVIS
Author, *American Heroine: The Life and Legend of Jane Addams*

ADDITION. See ARITHMETIC.

ADDRESS, FORMS OF

If you were to meet a governor, a rabbi, or the president of the United States, how would you address that person? If you wanted to write a letter to one of them, how would you start your letter?

Forms of address are ways of addressing people in speech or in writing. Some are used in everyday life. For example, Mr., Mrs., Miss, and Ms. are used as courtesy titles for men and women. The term Mr. applies to all men, Mrs. to all married women, and Miss to unmarried women and girls. Some women prefer to be addressed as Ms., whether they are married or not. A physician is addressed as Dr., as are people in the academic world who hold doctorate degrees.

Other forms of address are needed for speaking or writing to persons who hold special positions or offices. For example, Excellency serves as a title for certain high dignitaries of state (as a governor or ambassador) and church (as a Roman Catholic archbishop or bishop). The courtesy title Honorable, given to many government officials, is used in written address and in formal introductions but never in conversation.

Esquire was long used as a form of address for gentlemen. Placed after a name—Ernest Johnson, Esq.—it takes the place of Mr. It is sometimes used today as a form of address for lawyers.

Military personnel are addressed in writing by their title and full name: General George Thompson; Sergeant Marjorie Hall; Commander Virgil Beasley.

Courtesy demands that we use the proper forms of address in speech and writing. The chart on the following page shows how to address various government officials and religious dignitaries.

ISABELLE FORST
Former Assistant Superintendent of Schools
New York City

See also ETIQUETTE; LETTER WRITING.

PERSON	ADDRESS IN WRITING	SALUTATION OF LETTER	SPEAKING TO
The President of the United States	The President The White House	Dear Mr. (*or* Madam) President:	Mr. (*or* Madam) President *or* Sir (*or* Madam)
The Vice President of the United States	The Vice President The United States Senate	Dear Mr. (*or* Madam) Vice President:	Mr. (*or* Madam) Vice President *or* Sir (*or* Madam)
The Chief Justice of the United States	The Chief Justice The Supreme Court	Dear Chief Justice:	Chief Justice *or* Sir (*or* Madam)
Associate Justice of the Supreme Court	Justice Holmes The Supreme Court	Dear Justice Holmes:	Justice Holmes *or* Sir (*or* Madam)
United States Senator (*or* State Senator)	The Honorable Stephen A. Douglas United States Senate	Dear Senator Douglas:	Senator *or* Senator Douglas
United States Representative (*or* State Representative)	The Honorable Charles A. Halleck United States House of Representatives	Dear Mr. (*or* Mrs.) Halleck:	Mr. (*or* Mrs.) Halleck
Governor	The Honorable Ella Grasso Governor of Connecticut	Dear Governor Grasso:	Governor Grasso
Mayor	The Honorable Fiorello La Guardia Mayor of New York	Dear Mayor La Guardia:	Mayor La Guardia *or* Mr. (*or* Madam) Mayor
Federal Judge	The Honorable Learned Hand Judge of the 2nd U.S. Circuit Court of Appeals	Dear Judge Hand:	Judge Hand *or* Mr. (*or* Madam) Justice
Ambassador of the United States	The Honorable Dwight Whitney Morrow The Ambassador of the United States	Dear Mr. (*or* Madam) Ambassador	Mr. (*or* Madam) Ambassador *or* Sir (*or* Madam)
Foreign Ambassador to the United States	His Excellency, Rubens Ricupero The Ambassador of Brazil	Dear Mr. (*or* Madam) Ambassador:	Mr. (*or* Madam) Ambassador *or* Sir (*or* Madam) *or* Excellency
The Prime Minister of Canada	The Right Honourable Lester Pearson, P.C., M.P.[1] Prime Minister of Canada	Dear Mr. (*or* Madam) Prime Minister *or* Dear Sir (*or* Madam):	Mr. (*or* Madam) Prime Minister *or* Sir (*or* Madam)
Premier of a Canadian Province	The Honourable William A. C. Bennett, M.L.A.[2] Premier of the Province of British Columbia	Dear Mr. (*or* Mrs.) Bennett *or* Dear Sir (*or* Madam):	Mr. (*or* Madam) Premier *or* Mr. (*or* Mrs.) Bennett
Rabbi without (*or* with) a Doctor of Divinity Degree	Rabbi Stephen Samuel Wise (D.D. *and/or* LL.D., if held) The Free Synagogue of New York	Dear Rabbi (*or* Dr.) Wise *or* Dear Sir:	Rabbi (*or* Dr.) Wise
Episcopal Bishop	The Right Reverend Samuel Seabury, D.D, LL.D.	Dear Bishop Seabury *or* Right Reverend Sir:	Bishop Seabury
Protestant Minister without (*or* with) a Doctor's Degree	The Reverend Henry Ward Beecher (D.D. *and/or* LL.D., if held) Plymouth Church of the Pilgrims	Dear Mr. (*or* Mrs.) (*or* Dr.) Beecher *or* Dear Sir (*or* Madam):	Mr. (*or* Mrs.) (*or* Dr.) Beecher
The Pope	His Holiness Pope John Paul II *or* His Holiness the Pope	Your Holiness *or* Most Holy Father:	Your Holiness *or* Most Holy Father
Cardinal	His Eminence, Cardinal Francis Joseph Spellman Archbishop of New York	Dear Cardinal Spellman *or* Your Eminence:	Your Eminence *or* Cardinal Spellman
Roman Catholic Bishop (*or* Archbishop)	The Most Reverend Fulton John Sheen Bishop (*or* Archbishop) of Rochester	Dear Bishop (*or* Archbishop) Sheen *or* Your Excellency:	Your Excellency *or* Bishop (*or* Archbishop) Sheen:
Roman Catholic Priest	The Reverend Joseph Damien de Veuster, SS.CC.[3]	Dear Father Damien *or* Reverend Father:	Father Damien *or* Father

[1] P.C.—Privy Council, M.P.—Member of Parliament. [2] M.L.A.—Member of the Legislative Assembly. [3] Letters addressed to members of religious orders include the initials or abbreviation of the order.

ADEN. See Yemen.

ADENA INDIANS. See Indians, American (Empires and Other Extended Groups).

ADHD

Attention-Deficit Hyperactivity Disorder (ADHD) is a commonly diagnosed behavioral disorder in children. Children with ADHD have great difficulty with tasks that involve sitting still and paying attention. The symptoms of ADHD are divided into two behavioral categories, inattention and hyperactivity or impulsiveness. Some children have symptoms of both types while other children have mostly one type and not the other. Individuals with symptoms of inattention have trouble concentrating and finishing school assignments, are easily distracted, and are often forgetful. Children with symptoms of hyperactivity fidget, talk excessively, and have trouble awaiting their turn.

To distinguish ADHD symptoms from normal childhood energy, the behaviors must be extreme compared with other children of the same age. The behaviors must also cause significant problems at home and at school. A rating scale completed by the child's parents and teachers is often used to evaluate the child's behavior. A diagnosis is made after an examination by a psychiatrist, pediatrician, or psychologist.

Prevalence of ADHD. About 3 to 5 percent of school-age children in the United States are thought to have ADHD. This means for a classroom of 20 to 30 students, on average there is one child with ADHD. Boys are four times more likely than girls to be diagnosed with ADHD.

Causes and Treatments of ADHD. Scientists do not know exactly what causes ADHD. The condition often runs in families, which suggests that genes play a role. Also, magnetic resonance imaging (MRI) studies show that certain brain regions involved in regulating attention tend to be smaller in children with ADHD than in children without ADHD. This suggests a biological basis for the condition, but more research is needed before MRI or other brain imaging methods can be used for diagnosis or evaluating treatments of ADHD.

The most widely used methods for treating ADHD are stimulant medications and behavioral therapy. The stimulant drug Ritalin (methylphenidate) is the most commonly prescribed medication for ADHD. Scientists believe that some of the symptoms of ADHD may be caused by lower than normal levels of the neurotransmitter dopamine (a brain chemical) in regions of the brain important for concentration. Ritalin and other stimulant medications act on the brain to increase the levels of dopamine and other brain chemicals in certain brain regions.

Stimulant medications are often effective in reducing the symptoms of ADHD. When taken orally at low doses, they have been shown to be safe and have few side effects. However, when injected or sniffed or used at inappropriately high doses, they can be addictive. Many parents are concerned about giving their children potentially addictive drugs, and this has led to controversy about the treatment of ADHD.

Behavioral therapies are also effective for the treatment of ADHD symptoms. Typically, behavioral modification is based on reward systems to encourage suitable behavior at home and at school. For example, points are awarded in the classroom for staying on task, interacting appropriately with others, and completing work on time. Points are lost for getting out of one's seat, talking without permission, and so forth. Earned points are used to gain access to desirable activities such as playing computer games, spending individual time with teachers, and being at the head of the line at school.

Combined treatment using both medication and behavioral therapy may be the most effective and leads to a slightly greater decrease in symptoms than medication alone. Many other treatments for ADHD have been proposed, including dietary changes, herbal remedies, and biofeedback, but they have not yet been shown to be effective.

There is no known cure for ADHD. Coping strategies can be learned and used to deal with the disorder, and certain symptoms may decrease with age, but the condition continues into adulthood in some cases. Research on the effects of long-term medication and treatment of ADHD is ongoing.

James M. Swanson
University of California, Irvine
Sackler Institute, Cornell University

ADHESIVES. See Glue and Other Adhesives.

ADJECTIVE. See Parts of Speech.

ADOLESCENCE

The time between childhood and adulthood is known as adolescence. It is a period of physical growth. But it is also a time that the mind and behavior mature. The length of time for this period of development varies. Adolescence can start at 9 and end at 18. It can start at 14 and end at 25.

Young people may grow quickly in some ways and slowly in others. This is why children who may be only 9, 10, or 11 years old may be adolescents in some ways already, while teenagers of 13 or 14 may just be reaching adolescence.

Making friends and being a friend take on special importance during adolescence. Friendships are often formed with those who have similar interests and ideas.

For example, 11-year-old Sue is already 5 feet 4 inches (163 centimeters) tall. Her body is fully developed. But sometimes she acts very babyish. She has not yet learned to concentrate, so her schoolwork is far below that of others in her class.

On the other hand, Ricky, at 14, looks much younger than he is. But he is the brightest boy in his class. He is editor of his school newspaper, and his teachers and friends know that he is reliable and capable.

Sue is an adolescent because of her physical growth, and Ricky is one because he is mature in his thinking and behavior. When they "catch up with themselves," they will be well on the way to adulthood.

During adolescence, young people begin to find out about themselves and what they want to do, and what kind of people they want to be. It can be a time of self-expression, curiosity, and exploration, a time of discovery and adventure. Slowly but surely, boys and girls accept more and more responsibility for their own behavior.

THE BODY BEGINS TO CHANGE

Only a short time ago, the adolescent boy or girl had the body of a child. Now many physical changes begin to take place. Girls begin to develop breasts and have more of a waistline. They also begin to grow pubic hair and hair under their arms. Boys may notice that their voices are becoming deeper and that they are growing hair on their faces and other parts of their bodies. This period of dramatic physical development is called puberty.

Before, during, or after some of these changes, girls will begin to menstruate and boys will begin to mature sexually. These are normal glandular changes. They show that the organs of reproduction are being prepared for the part they will someday play.

Both boys and girls may feel that their arms and legs are growing too fast for the rest of their bodies. They may feel clumsy and awkward. Glandular changes sometimes cause acne, a skin disturbance. The skin may become oily, and pimples may appear. It is natural for young people to feel strange and uncomfortable about these physical changes. But part of growing during adolescence is getting acquainted with the new self that is appearing and gradually accepting the changes that are taking place.

FEELINGS ARE CHANGING, TOO

These body changes affect feelings as well as appearance. The glands and hormones that are bringing about external physical changes are also working toward a new internal balance. This is hard work for the body. There are times when adolescents feel very tired and seem to need a lot of sleep. At times they may feel happy and lively, at other times gloomy and depressed. Ups and downs are natural during adolescence, but eventually boys and girls begin to have more control over their feelings.

Adolescents still feel unsure of themselves, so they are annoyed at anything that makes them feel exceptional or different, whether it is wearing glasses or braces or having many freckles. As young people mature and gain self-confidence, they begin to accept themselves as they are.

▶ ADOLESCENTS CAN HELP THEMSELVES

There are many ways boys and girls can help themselves handle the changes of adolescence. If they are tired, they can get extra sleep and relaxation. If they feel full of energy, they can participate in sports or go dancing. They can eat sensibly and take proper care of their bodies.

They can also help themselves by seeking information and advice about any questions and worries. They are often concerned about their role as adults, and about their future careers and adult relationships. Many adolescents are also troubled by their new feelings about sex. It is quite normal for people at this age to begin to feel strong physical desires.

Both boys and girls need reassurance and information. They can get information from reading. Or they can talk to their parents. But sometimes it is hard to talk freely and openly with parents because the relationship is so close. Then an understanding adult who is not part of the family may be able to help. It may be easier to confide in a favorite teacher or camp counselor. The person whose advice an adolescent seeks should be someone whom she or he trusts and who has enough background and experience to be of help.

If boys and girls feel guilty and unhappy about some of their thoughts and keep all their fears and confusions to themselves, they will make this an unnecessarily difficult time.

▶ GROWING UP WITH OTHERS

This is a time that will influence a boy's or girl's choice of adult companions, of a vocation, and even of a marriage partner.

Friends

Making friends and learning how to be a friend take on special importance during adolescence. It is the time that the center of their social world changes from their home environment to their peer group environment. At first the most important thing is popularity. Boys and girls want to be well liked. They want to do what their friends want to do, and be what their friends want to be. This is all part of feeling unsure.

Later on, young people become more selective about their friends. They begin to choose those who have the same ideas and interests or those who are interesting because they have different backgrounds. As boys and girls develop their own standards, popularity becomes less important to them than the genuine affection of individuals they admire.

Young people often need to make friends among those of their own sex before they feel ready for relationships with the opposite sex. It is natural to feel more at ease with those who are having the same experiences and feelings. Later, girl-boy friendships may begin and become more intense and personal. At this time a young person may face some important issues and decisions.

Dating is one of these issues. Many girls and boys hope that they will be attractive and appealing to members of the opposite sex, but feel confused and uncertain about just how this can be accomplished. Also, they may wonder whether they should date only one person because it makes them feel safe and popular or because everyone else in the crowd is dating only one person. Or should they go out with many different kinds of people in order to learn more about themselves, to find out what relationships give them the most satisfaction?

The intimacy that develops between a girl and a boy who go out only with each other can create a problem. How far should an adolescent girl and boy permit this intimacy to lead them? Girls and boys are often very curious about sex and their sexual drive can be very strong. It is a powerful and sometimes disturbing feeling. They have certain worries and fears about it, too.

As boys and girls mature they try to understand their feelings about sex. They try to find answers to their questions so that they can set standards for their own behavior. The more responsible and mature they become, the more they think about long-range goals. They are willing to give up immediate satisfactions for something that is more important to them in the future. The more they care about their own feelings and needs, the more sensitive they are to other people. They understand the need for making choices seriously, rather than on a sudden impulse, to avoid hurting themselves and others.

Family

All adolescents have mixed feelings about their families. There are times when boys and girls feel that they could manage very well if only their parents would leave them alone. At other times young people feel uncertain and confused. They wish their parents would take over and tell them what to do.

Many conflicts with parents come up over social relationships. Teenagers are often so eager to belong to a group that they do not always use good judgment in making friends. Then their parents have to step in and help them by keeping some control over their activities. This is especially true when matters of health and safety are concerned. But when boys and girls show signs of greater maturity and sounder judgment, parents usually have more confidence in them and allow them to make more decisions and choices.

Family chores and responsibilities are other common causes of conflict. Teenagers sometimes forget that as members of the family group they have certain obligations. At times they feel they are being nagged about everything. Their rooms are untidy, their clothes are not neat, they sleep too late, they talk on the phone too much, they go to bed too late, they are careless with money, they do not allow enough time for homework. At times teenagers feel overwhelmed with criticism. But at other times they may sense that all their parents' comments are really signs of loving and caring.

Sometimes younger brothers and sisters seem to be a nuisance. Teenagers resent baby-sitting. It interferes with their privacy and cuts into their free time. Older sisters and brothers may tease teenagers, and this makes them feel young and foolish. But all this is only one side of the picture. Adolescents still need their families and the love a family gives, and their families still need them.

Some rebellion against adult authority is healthy—within limits. An adolescent wants to become a strong and independent person, and that is right. But this is not accomplished by fighting against adults. Being cooperative is much more effective.

But adolescents cannot grow up alone. They need the help and understanding of the adults who are closest to them. Parents can help their teenagers as they mature. One of the best ways is simply by acting as parents. This means being strong and firm when necessary. Children may call their parents old-fashioned. They may say, "You don't understand me." But wise parents overlook such expressions. They know that many times teenagers ask for permission to do something they are not ready for. They ask because the whole crowd is asking, and they do not want to be different. But secretly the teenagers want their parents to say "No," to set limits for them. They need to feel that their parents have authority and will use this authority wisely. Teenagers also need to know that their parents will not take a firm stand one day and then give in the next day. They want their parents to be consistent.

Being firm, of course, does not mean being too strict, and being consistent does not mean being stubborn. Understanding parents also give their teenagers love and encouragement and let them feel that they are free to grow.

▶ LOOKING AHEAD

A young child finds it hard to imagine being grown up. Adulthood seems so far away and strange. To a child what happens each day matters most. The child is not really interested in what will happen next month, next year, or in the next ten years.

During adolescence all that changes. The subjects boys and girls study in school and the marks they get have a great deal to do with their plans for a vocation. Their friendships with other boys and girls and their dating have a clear relationship to adult love and the choice of a marriage partner.

One of the most exciting things about adolescence is that it suddenly brings the future so much closer. That is what makes adolescence such a special time.

EDA J. LESHAN
Author, *You and Your Feelings*

See also FAMILY.

ADOPTION

Adoption is a way for children who cannot be cared for by their birth parents to become members of another family. Certain laws and procedures create the same legal relation between adoptive parents and a child as the biological one that exists between birth parents and a child. Adoption ends the child's ties to his former parents. After adoption the child has a new and permanent home.

▶ WHY CHILDREN NEED ADOPTION

In most countries children are brought up in families that are made up of a father, a mother, and the children born to them. Some birth parents, however, cannot give the love and care that every child needs. They are often very young and unmarried. They did not think ahead of time about the responsibilities of being parents. These parents may decide, after much sorrow, to give up their child for adoption. They want the child to have a chance to grow up in a family that can provide love and the potential to fulfill the child's needs for security and permanence.

Other children may lose their parents by death, accident, illness, war, or some other disaster. Sometimes parents with serious personal problems neglect or abandon a child. Children may be left for a long time in temporary foster homes or institutions. Then it may become clear that their parents will never be able to take them home. In all these cases someone other than the parents has to decide that adoption will be best for the child.

Families have to be found for children who no longer have parents to care for them. There are many childless people who wish to adopt. They have a desire to love and raise a child and to have a child who loves them. Also, some parents who already have children want to share their love and family life with another child who needs parents.

▶ WHO IS ADOPTED

The children who are adopted in the United States are mostly white babies. They go into their new homes shortly after birth. It has usually been difficult to find families for older, handicapped, or nonwhite children. Recently, however, a greater number of these children—especially African American, Native American, and Asian children—are being adopted.

The total number of children adopted each year in the United States is almost 130,000. About half are adopted by a stepparent, by grandparents, or by other relatives. The others are adopted by unrelated people.

▶ HOW ADOPTION TAKES PLACE

Children needing families and people seeking children may be brought together in several ways. The majority of the adoptions by nonrelatives now take place through recognized social agencies.

Physicians, lawyers, clergymen, and other well-meaning individuals have frequently arranged adoptions. Sometimes a dishonest person tries to make money by finding a child for someone willing to pay a high price. Such transactions are illegal.

Arrangements by individuals have in some cases been harmful to a child, to birth parents, or to adoptive parents. An individual cannot usually give the time, help, or protections needed in adoption. Many difficulties are prevented when social agencies are responsible for planning an adoption and selecting adoptive parents.

Social agencies are established and supported by concerned people in a community or by state governments. Some agencies have been given the duty by law to protect children and to provide adoption and other social services. Such agencies are known as child-welfare agencies, children's aid societies, or family and children's services.

▶ ADOPTION SERVICES

The purpose of an adoption service is to help children, birth parents, and adoptive parents. Social workers, who have special training and experience, provide the service. They know how to study children and find out what may be best for each child. They work with physicians, psychologists, and lawyers. They use the advice of other experts in selecting suitable parents for a particular child. Then they help adoptive parents take the necessary steps to complete a legal adoption. Agencies usually charge a fee for this service, based on ability to pay.

Parents and older children especially may need continuing help as they become a family. Most problems that occur are the usual ones that all parents and children have. Some of the problems have to do with adoption. For example, adoptive parents are encouraged to help a child understand, as soon as the child is able, what it means to be adopted. It is not easy to explain about adoption. Many adoptive parents would like to keep it a secret. Sooner or later, however, adopted children discover that they have not been born to their parents. Many become upset about it. They wonder why their birth parents gave them up. They may imagine that they would have been happier with those other parents, and they are curious about their heredity.

It takes time for children to feel comfortable about being adopted. They have to learn that true parents are the people who help a child grow up and feel loved. They have to know why their birth parents made an adoption plan for them. Usually it is because they care about the child and want him or her to have a better family life than they could ever provide.

LEGAL PROCESS

An adoption must take place according to law. In each state and in most countries, laws have been passed that say how the relationship of parent and child can be ended and a new one created. The laws require certain procedures to be followed. These are designed to protect the various people, and especially the child, involved in an adoption.

The parent-child relation is very important in our society. The law requires that a judge must decide whether it should be broken. A judge must also grant an adoption decree to make the adoption legal and final.

After the adoption has been arranged, either by agreement between the biological and adoptive parents or through an agency, the adoptive parents must go to court and ask that lasting family ties between the child and them be established. They must first wait until the child has lived with them for a set period of time. Then the judge has to make sure that the adoption is likely to benefit the child.

The judge considers all the facts obtained in a study of the case and talks with a child if he or she is old enough to understand. In most states, after the decree is granted all court records are sealed. No one can see these without a court order. Then a new birth certificate for the child is issued with the names of the adoptive parents. Lawyers are used in an adoption to see that all legal procedures are properly carried out.

TRENDS IN ADOPTION

Formerly, the purpose of adoption was to enhance the family unit by providing a childless family with an heir to inherit property or to continue a family name. It was not until 1851, in Massachusetts, that the first adoption law to protect children was passed. Since then people have become more concerned about the child's welfare in adoption.

Gradually ideas about adoption have changed. Adoption is now considered a way to find families for children. Communities and social agencies are trying to give more children the benefits of adoption. One reason is the belief that every child has a right to a caring and supportive family.

Social agencies are using new methods to find families to care for an older child, a sibling group, or a child with handicaps. Legislation has been passed to help families who choose to adopt children with special needs. The adoptive parents of such children are given allowances to help meet the costs of including the child in their family.

People who are members of minority groups are being encouraged to adopt children. Also, in some states, the law allows single persons to adopt children.

Various organizations are engaged in research to find out how to make adoption as satisfactory as possible for children and their biological and adoptive families.

Recently, there has been a trend toward the re-establishment of a relationship, later in life, between adoptees and their birth parents. A few states have passed "open records" legislation that allows the examination of certain adoption records. This makes it easier for adult adoptees and their birth parents to secure the information needed to conduct a search for each other. Some states have adoption registries that take information from, and provide information to, any person engaged in such a search.

Zitha R. Turitz
Former Director, Standards Development
Child Welfare League of America, Inc.
Reviewed by Beverly Stubbee
Child Welfare Specialist

Magazine advertisements, such as this one for crayons, must be eye-catching in order to attract the attention of the parents and children who will buy the product.

ADVERTISING

Advertising is part of our daily lives. To realize this fact, simply count the television and radio commercials you see and hear in one day, or leaf through the pages of a magazine or newspaper. Most people receive hundreds of advertising messages every day.

▶ WHAT IS ADVERTISING?

Advertising is the difficult business of bringing information to great numbers of people. The purpose of an advertisement is to make people respond—to make them react to an idea, such as helping to prevent forest fires, or to affect their attitudes toward a certain product or service.

At the beginning of the 1900's, advertising was described as salesmanship in print. If this definition were expanded to include television and radio, it would still stand today. The most effective way to sell something is through person-to-person contact. But the cost of person-to-person selling is high. Because it takes a great deal of time, it increases the cost of the product or service. Advertising distributes the selling message to many people at one time.

▶ THE MEDIA

To bring their messages to the public, advertisers must use carriers, such as television, radio, magazines and newspapers, and direct mail. The carrier of a message is called a **medium** of communication, or simply a medium. The five media (plural of medium) just mentioned are the ones most commonly used. Other media include billboards, posters, printed bulletins, and, especially in Europe, films. Unusual methods that have been used to attract attention include skywriting and messages painted on the sails of boats or trailed from high-flying kites.

When advertisers select a medium or a group of media to carry a message, they must think of the kind of product they are selling and the kind of people who are most likely to buy it. They must figure out how to reach the largest possible number of these people at the lowest possible cost. The cost of reaching a thousand people—the cost per thousand—is different in each medium. In print media such as newspapers and magazines, advertisers buy **space** (pages or parts of pages) in which to display their messages. In the broadcast media—radio and television—they buy **time** in which to present them.

Most magazines, newspapers, and radio and television stations in the United States depend on advertising for their support. Without advertising, newspapers and magazines would have to charge much higher rates to their readers and therefore risk losing business. Radio and television would have to charge their listeners and viewers directly or be supported by the government. Public radio and television stations carry no advertising and depend primarily on listener and viewer support—often through pledge drives—and on donations from businesses and foundations. Cable television offers commercial-free movie channels, but viewers must pay a monthly fee.

Magazines

Magazines cover a wide range of audiences. There are general magazines that reach several million people with varied interests. And there are hundreds of magazines for readers with special interests. They offer the advertiser a good way to reach a particular group of likely customers. An advertiser who is trying to sell washing machines, for example, would select a magazine for homemakers rather than one for hunters or boat owners. And an advertisement for tennis rackets would be placed in a tennis or sports magazine rather than in a general magazine or a newsmagazine.

Newspapers

Newspapers carry news, and good advertising is a kind of news. Most newspapers reach an audience that is concentrated in one geographical area—a town, a city, or a county. Most are published daily or weekly. For these reasons, newspapers have several advantages for advertisers. Ads placed in newspapers often bring quick results. And advertising can be placed in newspapers on very short notice. Usually ads can be placed for a specific day—to announce a sale, for example. If the ad had to be published a week or a month in advance, many people would forget about the sale before it took place. An advertiser can also choose to place an ad in a special section of the newspaper, such as the sports section, or in the classified pages, where ads of similar kinds are grouped together.

Local businesses depend on newspapers to reach customers in their neighborhoods or metropolitan areas. Newspapers also carry a great deal of advertising for nationally sold products. These ads will often list the names and addresses of all of the local dealers carrying the product.

In recent years, transmission of editorial material by satellites has brought us to an age where newspapers can be distributed across the entire country. This has helped to make the newspaper medium increasingly important for national advertisers.

An advertising campaign will often use a famous person to promote a product. Here comedian Bill Cosby and his young friends are enjoying some pudding in a television ad.

Above: Billboards are advertisements made to be read from a distance. They feature large illustrations and short messages. **Below:** Advertisements that promote ideas for the common good are called public service ads.

Radio and Television

Nothing has had more effect on advertising than the development of the broadcast media—radio and television. Radio took words off the printed page and gave them a voice and a sound of urgency. Radio lacks the advantage of a visual image, but it reaches places that other media do not because it is portable. Radios can be found in automobiles or can be carried with you wherever you go. Television is the most dramatic of the media. Because it combines sight, sound, and motion, it gives advertisers many ways of catching customers' attention.

Radio and television use every dramatic device possible to get advertisers' messages across. Commercials may be presented as short plays that tell how a new detergent can make doing the laundry pleasant or how a headache remedy can transform someone who is grouchy and ill-tempered into a cheerful, lovable person. Jingles help plant the name of the advertiser's product in the listener's mind. In radio, tones of voice and sound effects—like breaking glass or slamming doors—attract the listener's attention. In addition to the devices used by radio, television uses elaborate sets, picturesque costumes, and cartoons or other types of animation to help put the message across. Filming commercials has become a business in itself.

To attract listeners on a nationwide or regional basis, an advertiser or a group of advertisers sometimes **sponsors** a program—that is, pays for the time and the costs of producing the program. An advertiser may purchase **spot announcements** between or during programs. Today a minute's time on television may cost advertisers several hundred thousand, or even as much as a million, dollars. The cost of radio and television advertisements depends on the time of broadcast and whether they are aired across the entire nation, in certain regions of the country only, or in just one community.

Outdoor Advertising

Outdoor advertising is one of the oldest media. It is usually colorful and strong on illustration, and it has short selling messages. Billboards are placed in locations where surveys have shown that they will be seen by large numbers of people. They range from

In direct mail advertising, a business mails an advertisement or catalog to the consumer who is then able to order the product directly from the advertiser.

lithographed paper sheets pasted together to the more permanent and more expensive **painted bulletin** (painted on the billboard or on the side of a building) and the very costly **spectacular**, which uses flashing lights to attract attention. By flashing the lights in proper sequence, the spectacular can create the effect of motion, such as a coffee cup being filled. Spectaculars are sometimes controlled by computers.

Posters are often placed in train stations and in buses and railroad trains. This is called **transit advertising**.

Electronic Media

Rapidly advancing technology is creating new ways and places to advertise. Space satellites have helped create new TV networks, and the number of programs one can choose to watch has grown dramatically.

We can now use the television set in many different ways. It can be used as part of a personal computer or to play video games. Television sets are appearing in places like shopping malls and hotels to provide information on an interactive, or two-way, basis. For example, suppose you are visiting a strange city and want to find a Chinese restaurant near your hotel that has prices in a particular range. You may, if your hotel subscribes to an interactive database service, get the information by asking the television set. The television set is connected to a computer that is programmed to answer certain types of questions.

The use of video cassette recorders has advertisers concerned because TV viewers who have the machines are able to watch the programs at their convenience, thus shifting the time of day when they view commercials. They may also completely eliminate commercials when they watch a recorded program.

Direct Marketing

Direct response is defined as any form of advertising that elicits a measurable response. That is, it encourages people to contact the advertiser directly. It uses all forms of media—direct mail (including catalogs), magazines, newspapers, radio, television, the telephone (toll-free numbers), and the new electronic media.

Direct marketing, particularly direct mail, allows advertisers to target their advertising to very specific audiences, those who would most likely be interested in buying a particular product or service. It is a very personal method of selling.

The computer is an important advertising tool in direct marketing. It is used to build databases that record the purchasing habits of various groups of people.

▶ NATIONAL AND RETAIL ADVERTISING

From the marketing, or selling, point of view, advertising has two main divisions.

National advertising is used to promote products or services that are sold all over the country or over large areas. Examples are products such as automobiles, soft drinks, household appliances, and such services as insurance and air travel. Such products and services are advertised in magazines with nationwide circulation and on nationwide radio and television programs.

Retail advertising is used by local businesses. Unlike most national advertising, retail advertisements give specific prices and dealers' addresses. Department stores, drugstores, automobile dealers, and banks are typical retail advertisers. Most retail advertisements are carried by newspapers, direct mail, and local broadcasting stations. They are usually prepared by the business that is doing the advertising or by a local agency. Some large businesses have special departments to handle retail advertising.

In the United States, about 45 percent of advertising money is spent on retail advertising and 55 percent on national advertising. Of the two types, national advertising has a more direct influence on the products and services the consumer buys. The rest of this article will deal with national advertising. For simplicity's sake, services will be considered products.

THE AGENCY

In most cases, manufacturers and other national advertisers do not produce their own advertising. Instead, they rely on specialists—the advertising agencies. These agencies bring together a number of people with specialized talents in various fields.

The advertising agency is a service company. It is appointed by a client to perform certain functions—planning, creating, researching, producing, and placing printed advertisements and broadcast commercials for that client.

Large agencies employ a variety of specialists, including writers, artists, photographers, film production specialists, musicians, actors, producers, and directors. Experts in economics, law, accounting, marketing, media, management, and research are also involved in the advertising business.

Each client of the agency is served by an account team representing most of these specialties. The team's job is to create the client's advertising. Everything the team does must be approved by the client—the kind of advertising chosen, the media used, and the amount of money spent. The person in charge of the team, called the account manager or account executive, meets often with the client to discuss these matters and to determine how well the advertising has been working.

Creating Advertising

The first step in preparing an advertising campaign is to conduct research on the possibilities of the product. The members of the agency team must come to understand consumers' attitudes toward the product and its competitors, and what qualities of the product, practical or emotional, are most likely to appeal to the buying public. The team finds out the age, sex, occupation, income, personality, and special interests of the product's best or prospective customers—the target group for the sales message. They learn where and how the product is sold and consider such factors as climate and season, which have a bearing on sales. For instance, cold remedies sell best in cold weather, soft drinks in warm weather.

After studying this information, the team's writers and artists, working with the creative director, explore different advertising approaches. They arrive at a good, interesting, and persuasive idea about the product—one that will make it stand out from competing products.

The idea alone is not yet advertising. What is needed now is a way of expressing or dramatizing the idea that will produce in the consumer the thoughts and feelings about the product the advertiser wants to convey. This is not always easy to do because a reader, or a viewer, may get a different message from the one that was intended. A number of different messages may be explored to determine which one communicates most effectively. Layouts are made for printed media such as newspapers, magazines, and posters. Scripts are prepared for radio commercials. A storyboard—a series of pictures with captions for spoken dialogue or written messages—is prepared for each television commercial. Writers and artists work together in developing this material. Today computer-generated graphics are sometimes used in the preparation of storyboards and layouts.

When the rough draft is ready, it is presented to the client for approval. Usually the team designs one ad or commercial as the recommendation. The preliminary draft of a print ad is called a **comp**, or **comprehensive**.

When the client has approved the advertisement, it is put into final form. The agency commissions specialists to prepare finished art or photography, and type is set for printed advertisements. Then the material goes on to an engraver or a printer. Filmed and taped commercials for the broadcast media are also produced outside the agency, by specialists who are hired to do this work.

Meanwhile, media planners at the agency decide on the most efficient way to reach the target group. They also determine the size, color, and dates for printed advertisements; the time periods for broadcast commercials; and the costs in each case. These media recommendations must also be approved by the client. The materials for the completed advertisement are then shipped to the media with authorization for their use on specific dates or for specific periods of time at agreed-upon rates or prices.

The agency checks to make sure that each advertisement or commercial actually appears. If everything is satisfactory, the agency then bills the client. The total cost includes the agency commission; when the agency pays the media, the agency's commission for its service is deducted. Some agencies work for flat fees rather than commissions, and the client pays the agency a sum of money in addition to the cost of producing the advertising.

What Makes Customers Buy?

Advertisers and their agencies have spent great amounts of time, money, and effort trying to determine what makes potential customers want a product. There is no single answer. To find the special quality of a product that will cause people to buy, advertisers often turn to research.

Several kinds of research are employed in advertising. **Marketing research** explores sales patterns, sales problems, and sales possibilities for a product. **Product research** is designed to discover how the public feels about a product. **Copy research** discovers how well an advertisement gets its message across. **Motivational research** unearths the reasons people behave as they do.

A consumer may buy a certain brand of face soap because it is used by a glamorous movie star or sports figure. When selecting a new refrigerator, that same consumer may be attracted to a sleek or colorful style. Or perhaps that consumer is most concerned with how much food the refrigerator will hold and how efficiently a particular model uses energy.

Some advertisements appeal to logic through straightforward presentation of facts about a product. Others appeal more to the emotions. Most advertisements combine logical and emotional approaches. Advertisements offer consumers an opportunity to make their purchasing decisions from among a wide range of choices. One of the important roles of advertising is to provide the consumer with a free and abundant choice.

ADVERTISING AS A CAREER

Advertising is a big business—and a fascinating business. It combines writing, art, show business, and science.

The average advertising agency has a need for people with many different kinds of experience and talent. But opportunities are limited. Some estimates suggest that there are probably not more than a few thousand places for newcomers in advertising each year.

Most advertising jobs require the ability to use language with skill. Other important qualities are curiosity and the ability to use imagination in analyzing situations. Retail selling experience is excellent preparation for a career in advertising. The American Association of Advertising Agencies, in New York City, offers information about careers in advertising.

HISTORY

Advertising is very old. It can be traced back as far as the public criers of ancient Greece—who, for a fee, shouted out messages about their clients' wares. It first became important in the late 1400's, when the merchants of the rapidly growing cities and towns needed a way to tell people where their goods could be bought.

The first printed advertisement in the English language appeared in 1478. This early ad was the work of William Caxton, England's first printer, who used it to advertise religious books from his own workshop. Caxton posted small printed notices along London's main streets. Besides advertising his product, he identified his shop with a red-striped shield so that customers could find it easily.

This same sort of simple, informational advertising is still used. Examples are the roadside signs that tell travelers that they can buy eggs or take flying lessons just down the road.

The Industrial Revolution, in the 1700's and 1800's, brought a new kind of advertising. Large factories took the place of small workshops, and goods were produced in large quantities. Manufacturers used the newly built railroads to distribute their products over wide areas. They had to find many thousands of customers in order to stay in business. They

This early advertisement is a simple listing of the products and services available from Paul Revere's foundry. Compare it to today's advertisements.

could not simply tell people where shoes or cloth or tea could be bought—they had to learn how to make people want to buy a specific product. Thus modern advertising was born. Advertising created new markets and helped to raise standards of living as people came to feel that they had a right to new and better products.

Advertising agencies began to develop in the United States just after the Civil War. At first these agencies merely sold space in the various media, mainly newspapers and magazines. But they soon added the service of writing and producing advertisements. From these beginnings, advertising has developed into a highly specialized profession.

PROS AND CONS OF ADVERTISING

Advertising has received a great deal of criticism from various sources. Its critics say that it appeals to unworthy motives like vanity, snobbery, and the fear of being "left out." And they say that high-pressure advertising makes people buy some things that they do not really need and cannot afford. Another common criticism is that some advertising is deceitful.

Most people who work in advertising feel that it can certainly help shape attitudes toward products. But they know from experience that it is not possible to sell a poor product more than once. People may try a product because they are attracted by the advertising, but if they do not like it they simply will not buy it again. Consumers make the choices, and because of advertising they may have many more products from which to choose and are more informed about their choices.

Advertising agencies and the media work against deceptive practices by setting standards within the industry. In the United States there is also some government regulation. Consumers are protected by such agencies as the Federal Trade Commission, the Federal Communications Commission, and the U.S. Postal Service. State and local agencies, as well as private organizations, work to prevent false or misleading advertising.

Advertising is used for public service messages as well as for commercial ones. Smokey the Bear, who for many years warned the public against the dangers of forest fires, was a creation of the advertising industry. Advertising agencies produce the campaigns for organizations such as the Red Cross, helping them to gather money. And advertising is an efficient way of telling large numbers of people about new ideas, useful inventions, and scientific discoveries. Defenders of advertising say that it stimulates the economy by helping to keep production and employment high.

Advertising is an important part of life in a complex society. Often a word or phrase from an advertisement will enter the language, at least for a time. Songs written for use in advertising may become popular apart from their original use. A character seen or heard in advertising may become a favorite with the public. These are some of the ways advertising becomes part of popular culture.

Advertising has been described as the news of the marketplace. Partly because of the influence of advertising, people have learned to want ever better products and services, to take better care of their health, and to improve their way of living. Advertising is an important economic and social force.

DON JOHNSTON
Chairman and Chief Executive Officer
J. Walter Thompson Company

See also MAIL ORDER; SALES AND MARKETING.

AENEID

The most famous work in Latin literature is the *Aeneid*, an epic poem about the hero Aeneas. (An epic is a long narrative poem, written in a noble, complex style, that tells a story of heroic deeds.) Publius Vergilius Maro, whom we call Vergil, began the *Aeneid* about 29 B.C. at the request of the emperor Augustus. Vergil worked on it for over ten years. He meant to spend three more years revising the poem, but he died in 19 B.C. before he could complete it. On his deathbed he asked for his manuscript, intending to burn it because he felt it was imperfect, but his friends refused to give it to him. It was published as Vergil left it.

The twelve parts (called books) of the *Aeneid* tell the story of Aeneas, a legendary ancestor of Augustus. At the end of the Trojan War, when his native city, Troy, was destroyed by the Greeks, Aeneas escaped with his father, Anchises; his son, Ascanius; and a band of followers. He intended to build a new Troy, and searched long for a site. After founding several settlements (which failed) and having many adventures, he and his party were shipwrecked in North Africa and were given shelter in the city of Carthage.

Carthage was ruled by the beautiful Queen Dido, who fell in love with Aeneas and wanted him to marry her. But the gods had chosen him to go on to Italy, where his descendants would found the Roman nation. The messenger of the gods, Mercury, came to Aeneas and reminded him of his destiny. So Aeneas left Dido, who then killed herself in despair.

Aeneas and his men sailed across the Mediterranean and landed at Cumae, in Italy. There he met the sibyl, a prophetess who guided him to the underworld so that he could consult the spirit of his father. Anchises told his son that he was to establish a city in central Italy and that his descendants were to be the founders and citizens of Rome. Then he showed him the souls of the great Romans of the future, waiting for their time to be born; among them was Vergil's own friend and patron, the emperor Augustus.

The last six books of the *Aeneid* tell of the settlement in Italy and the warfare between the Trojans and some of the Italians, who rise against the invaders. The poem ends with a fierce duel between Aeneas and his chief enemy, Turnus. Turnus is killed, and Aeneas' triumph is assured.

Tales of Aeneas and Rome had been told by the older Roman poets Naevius and Ennius. Vergil owes something to them. He also owes a debt to Homer, from whose *Iliad* and *Odyssey* he borrowed freely, intending to create a Roman epic that would rival Homer's work. The wanderings of Aeneas in the first six books are like the wanderings of Odysseus in the *Odyssey*; the fighting in the last six books of the *Aeneid* is like the savage battles of the *Iliad*.

Vergil also follows Homer in using gods as characters in the story. The gods struggle against one another to help or hinder Aeneas. This means that he was not merely a wanderer, but a man with a great mission. Even with a spiteful goddess opposing him, he succeeded, and worked out the will of fate.

The *Aeneid* is a proudly national epic, showing Rome as the chief carrier of civilization. Its poetry is magnificent. It has many fine phrases, such as the opening line, "Arms and the man I sing," the warning, "I fear the Greeks even when they bring gifts," and the advice to Rome, "Spare the conquered and crush the proud." Its scenes and symbols stir our imagination: the golden bough that opens the path to the underworld, the shield of Aeneas decorated with the battles and the champions of future Rome, the description of the fall of Troy, and the mystical vision of heaven filled with noble and happy souls.

The *Aeneid* was the greatest achievement in the golden age of Latin literature, and it has continued to influence poets through the centuries. Dante Alighieri, the greatest Italian poet of the Middle Ages, called Vergil his master and his model. English poetry also has been shaped by Vergil. Shakespeare read him at school, and quotes him several times in his works. Chaucer, Spenser, Milton, and Tennyson all imitated him, each in his own way. Poets in French, German, Spanish, and other European languages also felt his power and tried to equal his artistry. Despite the fact that he himself had imitated Homer, Vergil was one of the great creators of Western literature.

GILBERT HIGHET
Author, *The Speeches in Vergil's Aeneid*

See also VERGIL.

Some aspects of the aerodynamics of flight can be studied by observing models of airplanes in wind and water tunnels. This model of the supersonic airplane Concorde was photographed in a water tunnel. Colored dyes ejected from the top surfaces of its wings into a slow-moving water current show the path of air flowing over the plane at low speeds and how the vortex, or corkscrew of air, gives the wings their lift.

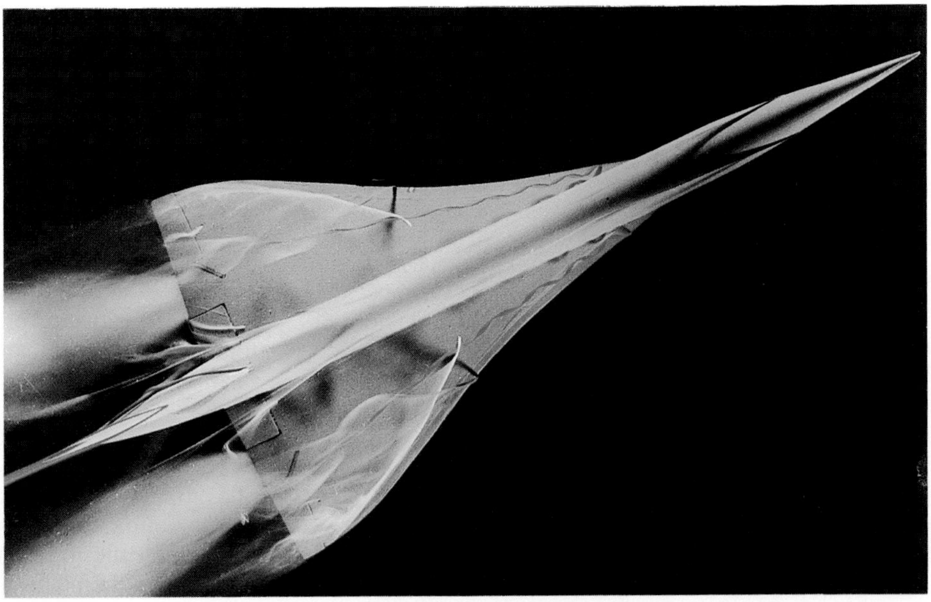

AERODYNAMICS

Aerodynamics is the science that examines what happens when air, or any other gas, is in motion. Its name comes from two Greek words meaning "air" and "power." Aerodynamics sometimes deals with air moving against an object—like wind filling the sails of a boat. Sometimes it deals with an object moving through air—like an airplane flying through the sky. The same laws apply in both cases.

PUTTING AIR TO WORK

Long before anything was known about aerodynamics, people noticed that moving air pushed things. The wind scattered leaves and bent tree branches. Strong winds could uproot trees and knock down houses. Hunters could run faster and throw spears farther when the wind was behind them.

In time people learned how to put the wind to work. They built sailboats and windmills. Today we still use the wind in these ways. But an understanding of aerodynamics has opened up many other ways of using the power of moving air. For example, it is an understanding of aerodynamics that has made possible all heavier-than-air craft. This includes spacecraft, airplanes, helicopters, hovercraft—in fact, all aircraft except balloons, which are lighter than air and float in it.

The Dream of Human Flight

People have always envied the ability of birds to fly through the air, and the first flying machines made it possible for people to make their dream of flight come true. Since ancient times there have been myths and legends about people who could fly like birds. Perhaps the best-known story tells of Daedalus, the Greek craftsman who was imprisoned with his son Icarus. Using wax and birds' feathers, Daedalus made two pairs of wings. When he and Icarus put the wings on, they were able to fly away from the prison. But Icarus flew so close to the sun that the wax in his wings melted. The feathers dropped out, and Icarus fell into the sea and drowned.

The flight of Daedalus and Icarus was only a story, but the idea of flying like a bird seemed possible to people for hundreds of years. It was a long time before anyone realized that the human body is simply not built in a way to allow birdlike flight.

Powered flight in a heavier-than-air craft had to await several things. One was an understanding of aerodynamics, which began in the 1700's with a discovery made by a Swiss mathematician who was studying not flight but the flow of water in pipes.

BERNOULLI'S PRINCIPLE

The Swiss was Daniel Bernoulli, who came from a family of famous mathematicians and scientists. In the 1730's, Bernoulli began to investigate what happened to water flowing through pipes that were partially blocked. He experimented by putting obstacles of different sizes in pipes and keeping track of differences in the speed and pressure with which the water flowed.

The first thing Bernoulli discovered was that the water flowed faster as it went past an obstacle. Then he discovered that wherever the water flowed faster, it lost some of its normal pressure. On the far side of the obstacle, the flow of water slowed down again and pressure returned to normal.

The explanation is that steadily flowing water has a constant amount of energy. This energy depends on both the speed and the pressure of the water. If more of the energy goes into speed, then there is less for pressure; if less goes into speed, then there is more for pressure. To put it another way, where the speed is great, the pressure is small. This idea is known as Bernoulli's principle.

Other scientists became interested in what Bernoulli had discovered. They began to experiment with what happened inside pipes of different shapes. One of the first to do this was an Italian scientist named Giovanni Venturi. Later, a pipe invented for such experiments was named the venturi tube in his honor.

THE VENTURI TUBE

The venturi tube consists of a short narrow section of pipe called the throat that gradually tapers outward, or grows wider, at each end. Experiments with it revealed an important fact: Air passing through the tube behaves the same as water. When air passes through the tube's narrow throat, it moves faster. When the air moves faster, its pressure decreases. When the air moves beyond the throat into a wider section of the tube, it moves more slowly again and its pressure increases.

A venturi tube can be used to measure the flow rate of a liquid. As a liquid is poured into one end of a venturi tube, recording devices called manometers attached to the throat and to the two wide sections at each end can measure the drop in air pressure at the throat and then calculate the liquid's overall flow rate through the entire tube.

The venturi tube can also be used in many practical ways. A paint sprayer and an automobile carburetor are two devices that depend on it. In each, a liquid is driven forward by an airstream affected by a difference in air pressures. In an automobile carburetor, for example, gasoline is made into a fine spray by being drawn through a small jet attached to the throat of a venturi tube. It is then pulled through the throat and into the tube where it mixes with the air that is being drawn through the tube and into the automobile's engine. The gasoline is sucked through the jet and into the tube because the air pressure outside the venturi tube is greater than the air pressure inside its throat.

WHAT KEEPS A PLANE UP IN THE AIR?

The principle of the venturi tube also applies to an airplane in flight.

The bottom of an airplane wing is flat. This means that the top surface is longer than the bottom. As the plane wing rushes through the air, the particles of air are separated. They move over or under the wing and meet again behind the wing. The air that passes over the wing has a longer way to go, so it must move faster to join the air that passes under the wing. As we saw, more speed means less pressure. So the pressure above the wing is lower than the pressure beneath the wing. The wing, and the plane it is attached to, are forced upward by the higher pressure under the wing. The upward force is called **lift**, and it offsets the downward force of **gravity**. As a plane's speed increases, so does the lift of the plane's wings.

A wing develops lift in a second way. The wing is set into the plane at a slight angle. Air that hits the bottom of the wing is deflected

Because air has a longer distance to travel when it flows over the curved surface of an airplane wing than when it flows under its flat bottom, the air above the wing must move faster. This causes air pressure above the wing to be lower than it is below it, resulting in a force called lift. The angle of the wing also helps develop lift. Air hitting the bottom of an angled wing is deflected downward. The effect of this is to push the wing upward.

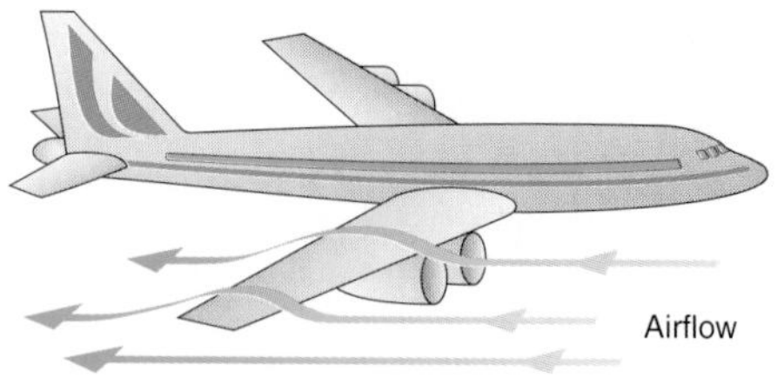

downward, pushing the wing upward. The major part of a wing's lift comes from its curved top, and the rest of the lift comes from the bottom.

Other Forces That Act on a Plane

Besides working against gravity, an airplane must work against the resistance of air. Air resists the movement of any object through it. This resistance is called **drag**. The faster an airplane flies through the air, the more drag there is.

An airplane opposes drag with **thrust**. A jet or rocket engine forces a powerful blast of hot air out of the back of the engine to move the plane forward against the air's resistance.

In propeller-driven planes, thrust is provided in another way. The engine turns a propeller rapidly. The propeller pulls its way through air somewhat as a wood screw pulls itself through wood.

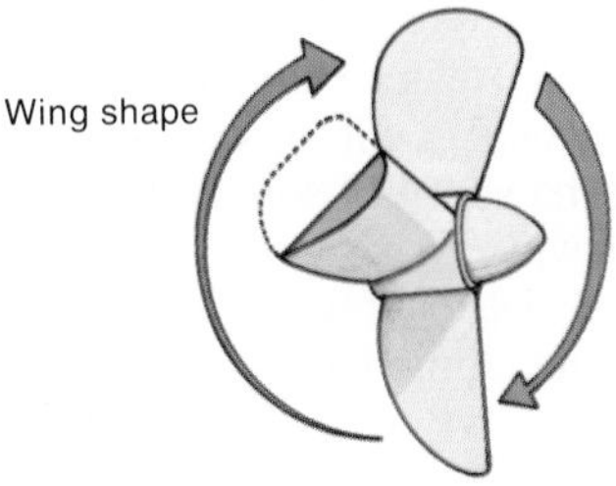

A propeller blade is shaped like an airplane wing—flat on the back side and curved on the front side. As a blade revolves, air passes over the two sides. The air speed is greater when it passes over the curved side so the pressure is less. This means that there is less pressure in front of the propeller than behind it. The propeller moves forward, pulling the rest of the plane with it.

Stalling Speed and Turbulence

There is a certain minimum speed that an airplane must have if the amount of lift is to be greater than the force of gravity. This minimum speed is called the airplane's stalling speed. A plane must be moving faster than its stalling speed to take off, and it cannot stay up in the air if it flies slower than its stalling speed.

An airplane also loses lift if the smooth flow of air over its wings is disturbed. This disturbance is called turbulence. Turbulent air swirls in eddies above the wings.

▸STREAMLINING

Drag is a special problem for designers of high-speed planes because drag increases much faster than speed does. If a plane is to fly at 125 miles (200 kilometers) an hour, the thrust of its engines must overcome a certain amount of drag. But at twice that speed the drag is four times as great, and at three times that speed the drag is nine times as great.

To reduce drag as much as possible, all parts of an airplane exposed to the air are streamlined. Streamlining helps to make the air flow over an airplane as smoothly as possible. A scientist thinks of streamlines as imaginary lines along which particles of air flow smoothly. Streamlines can be made visible in a wind tunnel by letting small tubes blow thin lines of smoke into the airstream. If the

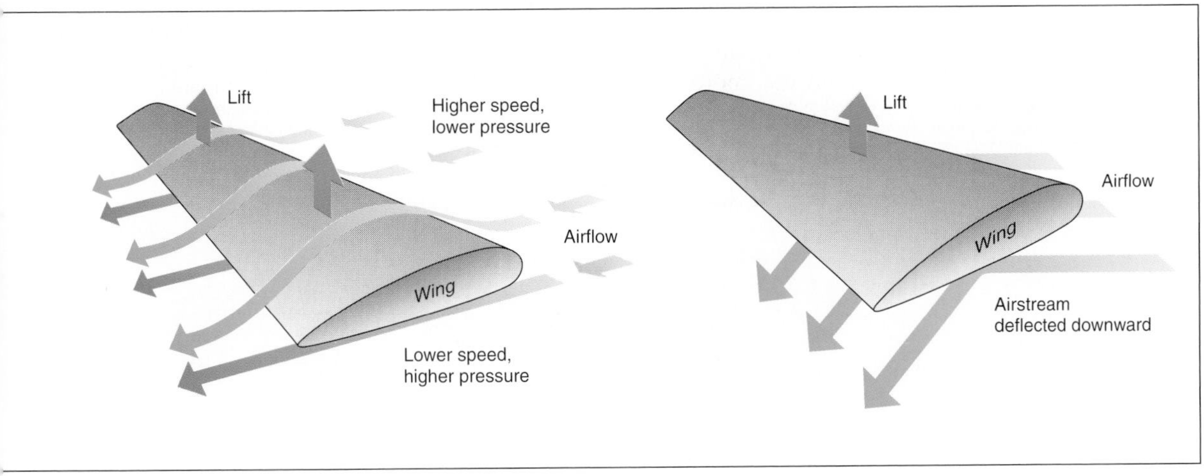

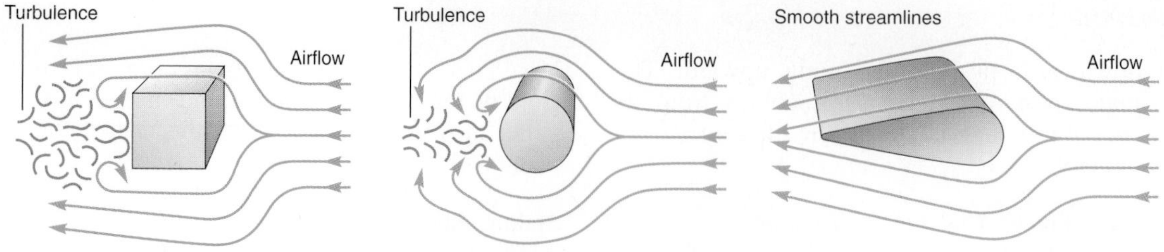

Square shape: high turbulence and drag **Round shape:** some turbulence and drag **Teardrop shape:** laminar airflow

The shape of an object determines how smoothly air is able to flow around it. A square shape causes a great deal of drag. As the streamlines break up around it, they cause turbulence. A round shape allows air to flow around it more smoothly. The ideal streamlined shape, however, is the teardrop shape on which the airplane wing is based.

streamlines are smooth, gentle curves, the airflow is called **laminar**. Laminar airflow causes the least amount of drag. If the streamlines break up and become irregular, then turbulence results.

The perfect streamlined shape is neither round like a ball nor pointed like an arrowhead. The shape that causes the least amount of drag is that of a teardrop. However, a perfect, horizontal teardrop shape does not make a good wing. This is because there is no difference in pressure between air flowing above and underneath it. As a result there is no lift. Most airplane wings are shaped like half teardrops. This shape provides the most lift with the least drag.

THE SOUND BARRIER

The designers of modern high-speed planes must also take into account what happens when a plane passes the speed of sound. At sea level the speed of sound is about 760 miles (1,225 kilometers) an hour. At higher altitudes the particles of air are farther apart and the speed of sound is less. As it reaches the speed of sound, an airplane is said to meet the sound barrier.

Air flows smoothly past the wing of a plane flying at less than the speed of sound. But at the speed of sound, the wing produces a thin wave of compressed air, called a **shock wave**. This shock wave increases drag, destroys lift, and, when it moves relative to the wing, shakes the plane violently. A plane must be specially designed to go through the sound barrier safely. Even so, pilots try to go through it as quickly as possible into the smooth flight of **supersonic** (faster than sound) speeds.

Shock waves occur at supersonic speeds as well as at the speed of sound. But the effect of the shock waves on a plane is most severe at or near the speed of sound. The effect is reduced at supersonic speeds.

A shock wave spreads out like the wave formed by the bow of a ship. Just as the ship's waves strike the shore, the plane's shock wave may sweep along the ground below the plane. It causes a thunderlike noise called a **sonic boom**. If a plane is flying low enough, the boom may shake houses and break windows.

Speeds of fast-moving planes are measured in units called **Mach numbers**. The numbers are named after Ernst Mach (1838–1916), an Austrian scientist. A plane traveling at the

A moving airplane causes waves in the air that move ahead of the plane at the speed of sound. When the plane reaches the speed of sound, the waves begin to pile up, forming a sort of wall called a shock wave. When the airplane moves at supersonic speed, the wall bends ahead of the airplane, leaving shock waves behind and causing a sonic boom on the ground.

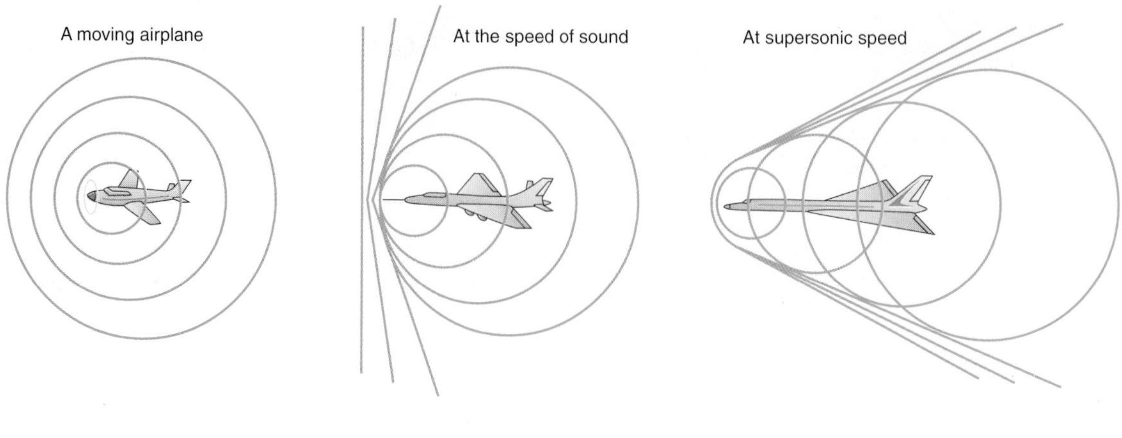

The aerodynamics of the wing is also used in vehicles that do not fly. A racing car (*above*) uses an inverted wing at its rear to provide a downward force on its tires for greater road traction. A submarine (*right*) uses winglike structures called diving planes to help guide it underwater.

speed of sound is said to fly at Mach 1. For a plane flying at twice that speed, the Mach number is 2. A spacecraft re-entering the Earth's atmosphere may travel at Mach 20 or higher.

OTHER CRAFT

The principles of aerodynamics apply to several kinds of craft.

Lighter-Than-Air Craft. The lighter-than-air craft such as dirigibles and balloons do not require forward motion to produce lift. They rise because they are filled with a gas that is lighter than air. However, their design must take drag into account, and for controlled, forward motion, thrust must be provided.

Gliders. Gliders have no engines and so have no thrust. For launching they must be pulled forward or shot into the air to overcome gravity. But once in the air, glider pilots use the changing currents to gain lift. By controlling the relationship between lift and drag, glider pilots can keep their craft aloft for many hours. Gliders are sometimes compared to birds. But in many ways birds are more like airplanes, since they create thrust. Only when birds soar can their motion be compared to that of a glider.

Helicopters. Helicopters also use the basic aerodynamic forces. Helicopters have no recognizable wings. But the rotating blades—called rotors—are a combination of wings and propeller. As they revolve, the rotors act like wings by creating lift. By using the controls to tip the rotors slightly, the pilot can make the helicopter travel forward and backward, as well as go up and down and hover, or stand still, in the air.

VTOL Aircraft. VTOL (*v*ertical *t*ake*o*ff and *l*anding) aircraft have the advantages of both standard airplanes and helicopters. They can fly through the air like propeller or jet airplanes at speeds greater than those of a helicopter. These experimental aircraft can also take off and land like helicopters. Engine thrust is used for a straight-up takeoff and for forward movement.

Hovercraft. A hovercraft is meant not to fly high but to hover just above the surface of water or land. The propeller is on the bottom of the craft. When the propeller turns, it pushes air down, against the surface. A "skirt" around the edge of the craft helps to confine the air, allowing the hovercraft to ride a short distance above the surface. A second source of thrust moves the craft forward. Instead of using the lift of a wing, the hovercraft rides on a cushion of air.

IRA M. FREEMAN
Rutgers, The State University of New Jersey

Reviewed by Chuen-Yen Chow
Coauthor, *Foundations of Aerodynamics*

See also AVIATION; BALLOONS AND BALLOONING; BERNOULLI FAMILY; GLIDERS; HELICOPTERS; SUPERSONIC FLIGHT.

AERONAUTICS. See AVIATION.

AESOP. See FABLES; SLAVERY (Profiles).

AFGHANISTAN

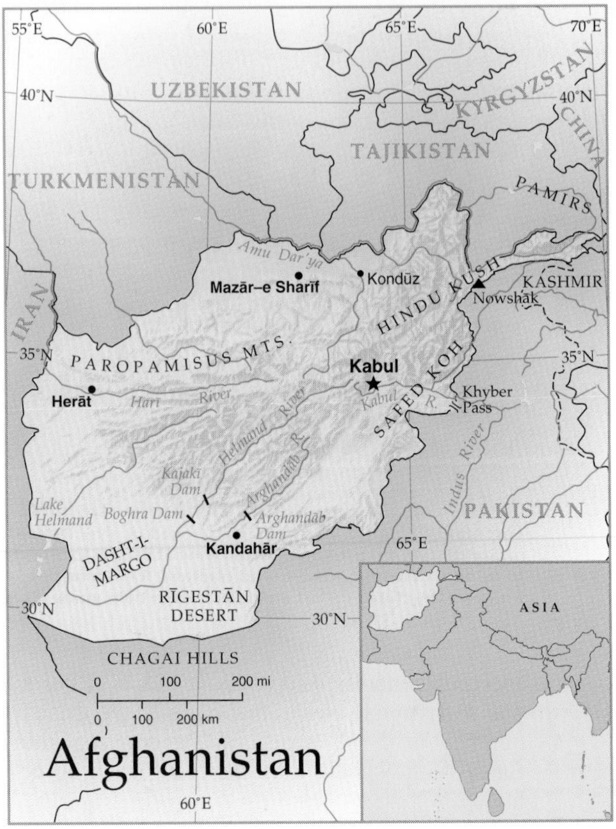

Afghanistan is a rugged, landlocked nation in west central Asia. Historically, the area has been a crossroads, connecting China, Central Asia, South Asia, and the Middle East.

Many centuries of regional migration, trade, and continuous invasions by outsiders produced a proud and independent society of many races, tribal groups, and languages. But years of political upheaval and war brought little but enduring hardship, starvation, and poverty for the majority of Afghan civilians. In the late 1900's, occupation by the Soviet Union (1979–89) and civil wars among various Afghan tribal groups weakened the central government. Neighboring countries, particularly Pakistan and Iran, became more influential in Afghanistan's internal affairs.

In 1996, the Taliban, a radical Islamic group supported by Pakistan, gained control over most of Afghanistan. But in 2001, the United States and its allies went to war against the Taliban for harboring members of the terrorist group responsible for the September 11 attacks on the World Trade Center and the Pentagon. Afghanistan has since been ruled by a temporary interim government supported by the United Nations.

PEOPLE

Afghanistan has more than a dozen different tribal groups. The Pashtuns, the largest group, make up nearly 40 percent of the population. Most live across southern Afghanistan. The Tajiks, the second largest group, are

Below: The Blue Mosque in Mazār-e Sharīf is revered by Muslims as the burial site of Hazrat Ali, son-in-law of Mohammed. _Right:_ Pashtuns form the largest group among Afghanistan's many tribes.

an Indo-Iranian people (related to the Tajiks found in Tajikistan). They live mainly in the northeast. The Hazaras, believed to be descendants of the Mongols, inhabit the central mountain region. Uzbeks, Turkomans, and others live on the northern plains.

Language. The Pashtuns speak Pashto, an Indo-Iranian-based language. The Tajiks speak Dari, which is an Afghan form of Persian, also known as Farsi. Other Persian/Farsi dialects are spoken by the Hazaras. The Uzbeks and Turkomans speak languages related to Turkish.

Religion. Although Afghanistan is not an Arab country, most Afghans belong to the Sunni branch of Islam. About 15 percent are members of the Shi'a sect. Afghanistan also has small communities of Hindus, Sikhs, and Jews.

Education. Under the rule of the Taliban, education was supervised by religious leaders. Boys learned to read and write the language of the Koran (Qur'an), but they did not learn mathematics, history, or science. Girls were not allowed to attend formal school past the age of 8. Some parents risked jail and other forms of punishment in order to educate their daughters in secret. When the Taliban government fell, boys and girls of all ages eagerly returned to school.

Way of Life. Although some Afghans still live a traditional nomadic life, most are now settled farmers, plowing their small fields with wooden plows drawn by oxen or cutting their wheat crops by hand with sickles.

In the countryside, a typical Afghan house is built of mud or mud brick and has three or four rooms, furnished with rugs and pillows. Round flat bread and rice are staple foods, together with mutton (sheep), goat meat, chicken, yogurt, and fruit. Traditional clothing for men consists of a turban wound around either a skullcap or a karakul cap (made out of lambskin), and a long shirt worn outside the trousers. Village women wear long dresses over trousers and large scarves over their hair.

LAND

Afghanistan is bordered by Iran to the west; Turkmenistan, Uzbekistan, Tajikistan, and China to the north; and Pakistan to the south and east.

Land Regions. The three major land regions of Afghanistan are the dry and dusty Northern Plains; the Central Highlands, which cover approximately two-thirds of the land; and the desert Southwestern Lowlands. The country's most fertile areas are in the east and southwest.

Farmers with oxen plow their fields in the Bāmiān valley in northeastern Afghanistan. The Hindu Kush mountains rise in the background.

The towering, snowcapped Hindu Kush range rises in the northeast, reaching heights greater than 20,000 feet (6,100 meters). It contains Mount Nowshāk, the country's highest peak, rising 24,551 feet (7,483 meters) above sea level. The twisting Khyber Pass, which cuts through the Safed Koh range in the east, links Afghanistan with Pakistan in the southeast.

Rivers. Because much of Afghanistan is arid (dry), farmers depend on the rivers to provide irrigation for growing crops. Afghani-

FACTS and figures

TRANSITIONAL ISLAMIC STATE OF AFGHANISTAN is the official name of the country.

LOCATION: South central Asia.

AREA: 250,000 sq mi (647,500 km^2).

POPULATION: 27,800,000 (estimate).

CAPITAL AND LARGEST CITY: Kabul.

MAJOR LANGUAGES: Pashto, Dari.

MAJOR RELIGIOUS GROUP: Muslim.

GOVERNMENT: Republic. **Head of state and government**—president. A Transitional Authority, established by a *loya jirga* (grand council), will rule Afghanistan until a new constitution is approved.

CHIEF PRODUCTS: Agricultural—wheat, rice, and other grains; cotton; fruits; nuts; karakul pelts; wool; mutton. **Manufactured**—textiles, processed foods. **Mineral**—natural gas, petroleum, coal, iron ore, copper, chromium.

MONETARY UNIT: Afghani (1 afghani = 100 puls).

stan has several rivers. But only the Amu Dar'ya can be used by ships. Other major rivers include the Helmand, Harī, Arghandāb, and Kabul rivers.

Climate. Afghanistan's climate is generally marked by extremes—very cold, snowy winters and hot, dry summers. Precipitation is slight, ranging from 2 to 9 inches (50 to 230 millimeters) per year.

Natural Resources. Most of Afghanistan's known resources have not been developed. Minerals include natural gas, coal, iron ore, copper, chromium, petroleum, and small amounts of gold and silver. Lapis lazuli, emeralds, and rubies are also found.

ECONOMY

Afghanistan was once one of the few developing nations that was self-sufficient, with its own food supply. But after the wars began in the 1970's, trade was interrupted. Nearly one-third of the population eventually fled the country, causing severe labor shortages. Farmlands were bombarded and laced with landmines. Agriculture was further damaged by several years of drought.

MAJOR CITIES

Kabul, Afghanistan's capital and largest city, has a population of more than 1 million. For the past 200 years, Kabul has been the commercial, cultural, political, and educational center of the country. But in recent years the city was almost completely destroyed. A priority of the transitional government was to restore Kabul to its previous stature.

Kandahār, situated in a fertile valley in the southeast, has long been a trading center for Pakistan and Iran. With a population of about 190,000, it is Afghanistan's second largest city. It formerly served as headquarters for the Taliban regime.

CULTURAL HERITAGE

Because Afghanistan is situated at the crossroads of many different lands, many cultural similarities can be found with Iranians, Pakistanis, and other peoples of Central Asia. The national dance is called the *attan*. Intense and warlike, the *attan* reminds Afghans of their long and hard fight for freedom and independence.

HISTORY AND GOVERNMENT

Afghanistan has known many conquerors and many rulers. With each invasion came new peoples and new influences. Great cities were built, and a prosperous agricultural economy based on irrigation was developed. But these achievements were destroyed by invading Mongols in the 1200's and 1300's.

Independence. In 1747 the Pashtun tribes made Afghanistan an independent kingdom. But the Afghans, situated between the expanding superpowers of the region, Russia and Great Britain, struggled hard to keep their independence. They fought two wars against the British before Great Britain took control of Afghanistan's foreign affairs in the late 1800's. In 1919, after World War I (1914–18), Afghanistan successfully asserted its full independence again.

After World War II (1939–45), Afghanistan and Pakistan disagreed over their border. Pakistan sometimes refused to allow imported goods to reach Afghanistan. This forced Afghanistan to approach the Soviet Union, which sent imports through its country.

A Communist Government. Afghanistan remained a kingdom until 1973, when a military coup toppled the monarchy. The leader of the coup, General Mohammed Daoud Khan, was named president and prime minister. Daoud was killed during another coup in 1978, and the government was taken over by a leftist group, which signed a treaty of peace and friendship with the Soviet Union. But most Afghans opposed the new government, and a revolt, led in part by tribal, civilian, and religious leaders, erupted. In 1979, thousands of Soviet troops were sent in to stop the spread of Afghan resistance to the Soviet-supported government.

The Struggle for Control. Between 1979 and 1989, more than 100,000 Soviet troops were engaged in Afghanistan, battling Afghan resistance forces called *mujahideen*, who were fighting for independence. The economy was devastated, and more than 5 million Afghans fled the country, most settling in refugee camps in neighboring Pakistan and Iran.

After the Soviets withdrew in 1989, a struggle for control began between the *mujahideen* and the Communists, led by President Najibullah. In 1992, Kabul was occupied by *mujahideen* forces, and Afghanistan was declared an Islamic state. In 1996 a *mujahideen* faction called the Taliban captured Kabul, executed Najibullah, and imposed strict laws in the name of Islam. These laws offended most mainstream Muslim people. Most foreign governments refused to recognize the Taliban's government, citing its harsh treatment of women, its destruction of non-Muslim art treasures, and its harboring of international terrorists.

On September 11, 2001, terrorists attacked the United States, killing thousands of people. The attackers were linked to Osama bin Laden, a Muslim militant living in Afghanistan under the Taliban's protection. After the crisis, U.S. president George W. Bush declared a global war on terrorists and warned the Taliban that if they did not turn over bin Laden to the proper international authorities, they would risk the same fate as the terrorists themselves.

When the Taliban failed to respond by October 7, U.S. and British forces initiated air strikes against them and bin Laden. The regime finally collapsed on December 7, although bin Laden and Taliban leader Mullah Omar had not yet been captured. With the support of various anti-Taliban Afghan leaders, a *loya jirga* (grand council) elected Pashtun tribal leader Hamid Karzai to serve as interim president until a new constitution was written.

Karzai's first priorities were to settle internal differences, distribute humanitarian aid, accommodate returning refugees, and rebuild Afghanistan's devastated economy. Security for the new government was tightened after an attempt was made on President Karzai's life and three other top government officials, including the vice president, were assassinated. In early 2003, Taliban loyalists reemerged as a force in the south. The United States encouraged Pakistan to intensify its efforts to catch outlaws trying to escape over the border.

To help speed reconstruction of the wartorn country, the United States formally announced an end to major combat operations on May 1, 2003. In January 2004, Karzai signed a new constitution that provided for a president and vice president and the creation of two houses of congress, paving the way for presidential and parliamentary elections later in the year. The presidential election was scheduled for October 2004. But the parliamentary elections were postponed until 2005 due to organizational problems and security concerns.

After the Taliban regime collapsed in 2001 during the war on terrorism, Muslim women were free to lift the veils of their burkas for the first time in five years.

Reviewed by ALAM PAYIND
JENNIFER NICHOLS
Middle East Studies Center
The Ohio State University

See also TERRORISM, WAR ON.

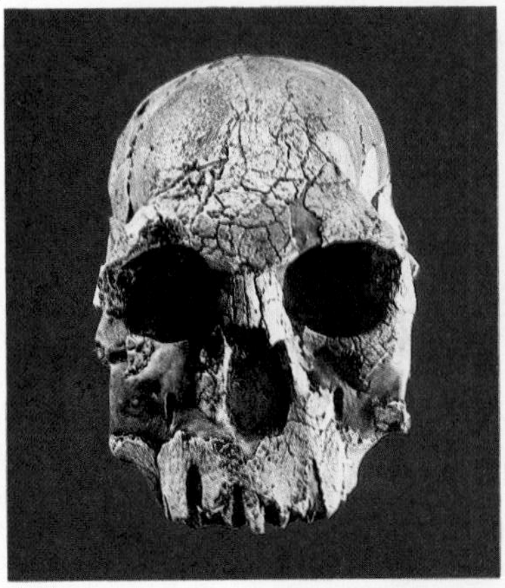

AFRICA

Africa is the world's second largest continent in area, after Asia. It ranks second in population, after Asia. Africa is separated from Europe on the north by the Mediterranean Sea. On the northeast, the Suez Canal serves as its traditional dividing line with Asia. The Atlantic Ocean borders Africa on the west, while the Red Sea and the Indian Ocean wash its eastern shores.

Africa lies astride the equator, which divides it almost evenly in half, and is the most tropical of the continents. It is, nevertheless, a continent of great diversity, of broad plateaus and snowcapped mountain peaks, barren deserts and lush rain forests, and enormous rivers and lakes. Africa has the world's longest river, the Nile, and its largest desert, the awesome Sahara.

Africa has been called the probable cradle of humanity because of the many fossils of human ancestors found there. It was the site of one of the world's earliest civilizations, that of ancient Egypt, which flourished in the valley of the Nile thousands of years ago. Numerous African kingdoms, some of great wealth and culture, existed there before the arrival of Europeans, who came first as explorers and then as missionaries and colonists. For much of its modern history, Africa was under the political and economic domination of European powers. It was only in relatively recent

A panorama of Africa. *Opposite page:* The sands of the Sahara, the world's largest desert; a fossil skull of one of the earliest human ancestors; zebras at a waterhole; Mount Kilimanjaro, highest point on the continent; and the awesome Victoria Falls. *Above and right:* Night scene of Cairo, Africa's most populous city; a West African dignitary; and the great pyramids at Giza.

times that the present-day African nations gained their independence and were recognized as an important force in world affairs.

See articles on African art and architecture, literature, and music following this article.

THE LAND

A map of Africa shows the familiar western bulge, the hornlike projection of land in the east (the Horn of Africa), and the land tapering toward the south. Topographically, most of the continent consists of a vast plateau, or tableland, which drops sharply to a narrow coastal belt. The plateau varies in elevation from about 500 to 2,000 feet (150 to 500 meters) in the north and west to more than 3,000 feet (900 meters) in the east and south. In the north, the Sahara separates the Mediterranean coastal plain from the savanna (grasslands) and rain forests to the south. Two smaller but equally forbidding deserts, the Kalahari and Namib, lie at the continent's southern end.

Africa's coastline is more regular than that of most other continents, with fewer bays and other inlets, and as a result, it has relatively fewer good harbors. A number of offshore islands are considered part of the continent. The largest of these, the island nation of Madagascar, lies off the southeastern coast.

Divisions of the Landscape

Mountains and Rivers. The African landscape is broken by modest-size mountain ranges. Among the larger ranges are the Atlas in the northwest, the Ruwenzori in east central Africa, the Cameroon in the west, and the Drakensberg in the southeast. Mount Kilimanjaro, in Tanzania, in eastern Africa, is the highest point on the continent.

In the northeast, in the midst of the barren desert, the Nile has carved out a fertile valley that is one of the most densely populated regions on earth. The continent's second great river, the Congo, drains a vast area in the heart of central Africa. Separate articles on the Congo and Nile rivers can be found in volumes C and N.

Other major waterways include the Niger, which irrigates much of western Africa before emptying into the Atlantic Ocean; and the Zambezi and Orange rivers of southern Africa. The Zambezi flows into the Indian Ocean, and the Orange, which rises in the Drakensberg range, empties into the Atlantic. Africa's rivers generally form rapids and waterfalls as they near the coast, which makes navigation difficult and which long hampered European penetration of the interior. The most spectacular waterfall, Victoria Falls, is located on the Zambezi, at the border of Zambia and Zimbabwe, and drops some 400 feet (120 meters).

Great Rift Valley and Chief Lakes. The Great Rift Valley is one of the continent's most distinctive landforms. Created by ancient volcanic activity and the sinking of the earth's crust, it consists of an enormous trench running along the eastern part of Africa and into southwestern Asia. Within or along the two branches of the valley lie many of Africa's greatest lakes—Victoria (the world's third largest lake), Tanganyika, Malawi (also called Nyasa), Turkana (or Rudolf), Albert, Kivu, and Edward. Lake Chad, which lies at the southern edge of the Sahara, is the continent's largest lake with interior drainage.

For more information on Africa's lakes, see the article LAKES (Africa) in Volume L. An article on the SAHARA appears in Volume S.

The Atlas Mountains of northwestern Africa (*above*) separate the Mediterranean coastal plain from the desert to the south. The waters of the Nile (*left*), the world's longest river, have carved out a fertile valley that is one of Africa's most densely populated regions.

Climate

The climate is largely tropical, except at the northern and southern edges of the continent and in the eastern highlands, which are more temperate. Away from the elevated areas, temperatures remain high throughout the year. The world's highest temperature, 138° F (58° C), was recorded at Azizia, in Libya.

Rainfall varies widely. More than half the continent receives less than 20 inches (500 millimeters) a year, with desert areas receiving much less. It is heaviest in the central equatorial region and along parts of the Atlantic coast, where 100 inches (2,500 millimeters) or more may fall in a year. For much of Africa, the year is marked by alternating dry and wet seasons.

Natural Resources

Minerals. Africa is rich in a variety of mineral resources, including diamonds, gold, cobalt, petroleum, bauxite (aluminum ore), copper, iron ore, chromite (chromium ore), manganese, uranium, and phosphate rock. Much of its mineral wealth, however, still remains to be developed.

Africa is the most tropical of the world's continents. Its central equatorial region consists of thick rain forests, with alternating wet and dry seasons.

FACTS and figures

LOCATION AND SIZE: Mainland Africa extends from: **Latitude**—37°21′ N to 34°50′ S. **Longitude**—51°24′ E to 17°32′ W. **Area**—approximately 11,708,000 sq mi (30,324,000 km²). **Highest Point**—Mount Kilimanjaro (Kibo Peak), Tanzania, 19,341 ft (5,895 m). **Lowest Point**—Qattara Depression, Egypt, 440 ft (134 m) below sea level.

POPULATION: 823,000,000 (estimate).

PRINCIPAL LAKES: Victoria, Tanganyika, Malawi (Nyasa), Chad, Turkana (Rudolf), Albert, Kivu, Edward.

PRINCIPAL RIVERS: Nile, Congo, Niger, Zambezi, Orange.

PRINCIPAL MOUNTAIN RANGES: Kilimanjaro (Kibo Peak, Mawenzi); Kenya; Meru; Elgon; Cameroon; **Ruwenzori**—Margherita, Alexandra; **Simen**—Ras Dashan; **Virunga**—Karisimbi, Mikeno; **Atlas**—Djebel Toubkal, Bou Naceur; **Drakensberg**—Thabana Ntlenyana; **Tibesti Massif**—Emi Koussi; **Ahaggar**—Tahat.

PRINCIPAL DESERTS: Sahara (including the Eastern and Libyan deserts), Kalahari, Nubian, Namib.

The discovery of petroleum deposits in the Sahara in the mid-1950's turned Algeria and Libya into major oil-producing countries. Nigeria, Angola, and Gabon are also among the continent's chief oil producers. Much of the world's diamond supply comes from such African countries as Botswana, South Africa, and Namibia. South Africa, which has the continent's most extensive mineral deposits, leads the world in gold production. It is an important exporter of chromite, copper, iron and manganese ore, and uranium, and has most of Africa's limited coal deposits as well.

Zambia and the Democratic Republic of Congo have extensive deposits of copper, and the latter is the world's major producer of cobalt (used to harden steel). Ghana, once known as the Gold Coast, still produces that mineral. Guinea ranks among the world's leading producers of bauxite, while Morocco is one of the leading producers of phosphate rock (used in making fertilizer).

Scattered across the barren desert areas of northern Africa are fertile oases, watered by underground streams. This oasis is in Morocco.

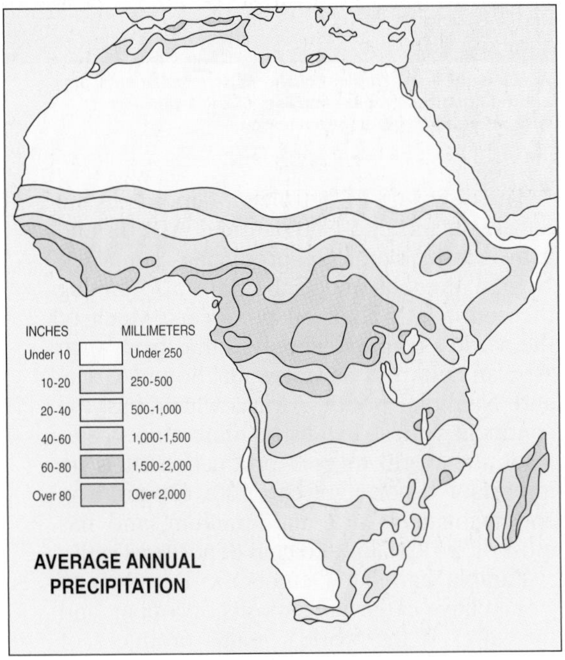

INDEX TO AFRICA PHYSICAL MAP

Aden, Gulf of F3
Agulhas, Cape D8
Ahaggar Mountains C2
Albert, Lake E4
Ankaratra Highlands F6
Arabian Desert E2
Atlas Mountains B1
Bab el Mandeb F3
Bauchi Plateau C4
Benue River C4
Blue Nile River E3
Bié Plateau C6
Bodélé Depression D3
Canary Islands A1
Chad, Lake C3
Chari River D3
Congo Basin D4
Congo River D4
Drakensberg E7
Edward, Lake E4
Elgon, Mt. E4
Emi Koussi D2
Erg Iguidi B2
Ethiopian Highlands E4
Fouta Djallon A3
Gibralter, Strait of B1
Great Karroo D8
Great Rift Valley E4
Good Hope, Cape of D8
Gough Island B8
Guardafui, Cape F3
Guinea, Gulf of B4
Kalahari Desert D7
Kariba, Lake E6
Kasai River D5
Kenya, Mt. E5
Kilimanjaro, Mt. E5
Kivu, Lake E5
Libyan Desert D2
Limpopo River E7
Mediterranean Sea D1
Molopo River D7
Mozambique Channel F6
Mweru, Lake E5
Namib Desert C7
Nasser, Lake E2
Niger River B3
Nile River E3
Nubian Desert E2
Nyasa, Lake E6
Okavango Basin D7
Okavango River D6
Orange River D7
Prince Edward Islands . . . E8
Qattara Depression D2
Ras Dashan E3
Red Sea E2
Ruwenzori E4
Senegal River A3
Serengeti Plain E5
Shebeli River F4
Sidra, Gulf of D1
Sinai Peninsula E2
Suez Canal E1
Tahat C2
Tana, Lake E3
Tanganyika, Lake E5
Tibesti Massif D2
Turkana, Lake E4
Uele River D4
Vaal River D7
Victoria Falls D6
Victoria, Lake E5
Volta River B4
White Nile River E4
Zambezi River E6

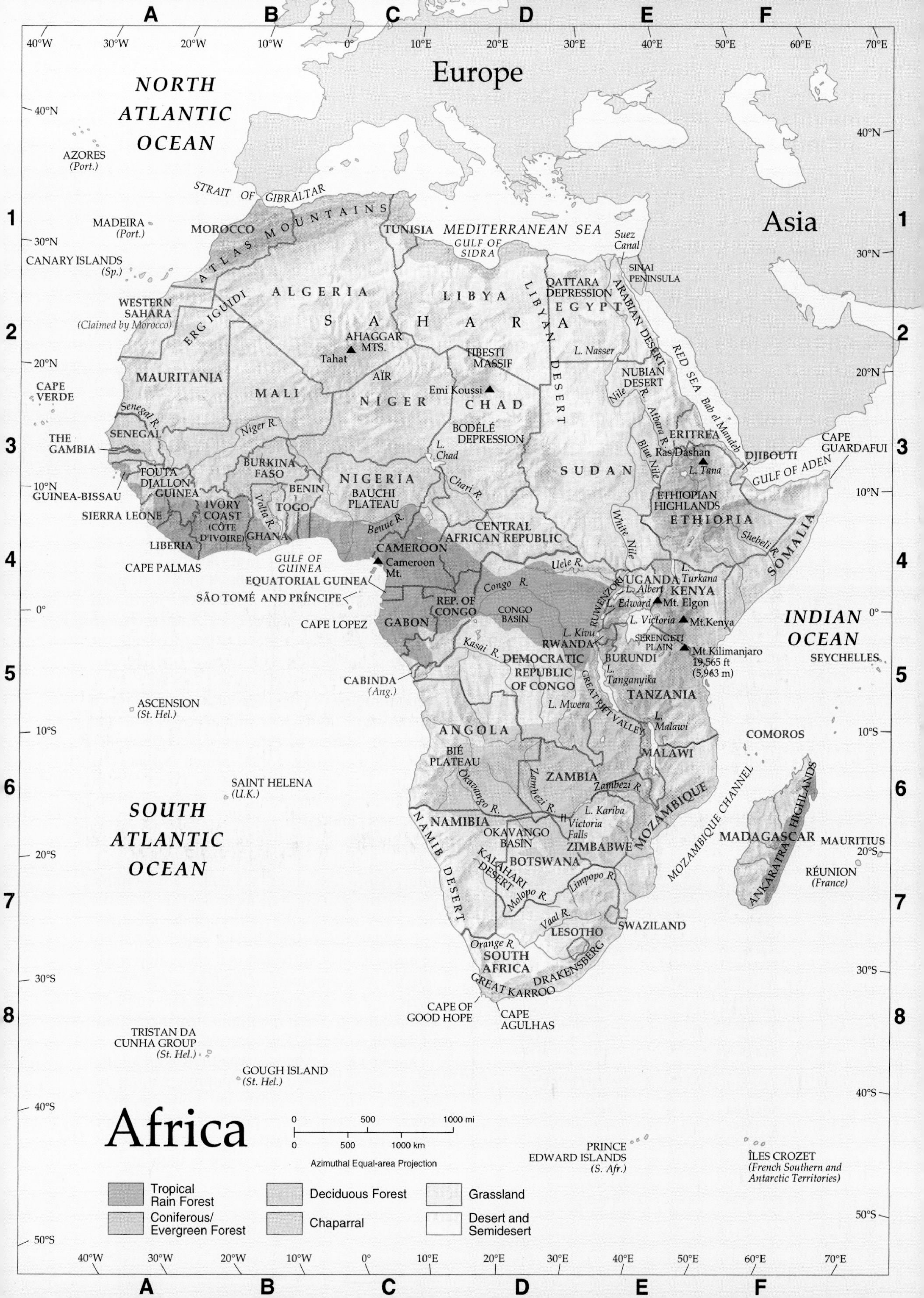
Africa
Europe
Asia
NORTH ATLANTIC OCEAN
SOUTH ATLANTIC OCEAN
INDIAN OCEAN
AZORES (Port.)
MADEIRA (Port.)
CANARY ISLANDS (Sp.)
CAPE VERDE
STRAIT OF GIBRALTAR
ATLAS MOUNTAINS
MOROCCO
TUNISIA
MEDITERRANEAN SEA
GULF OF SIDRA
Suez Canal
SINAI PENINSULA
WESTERN SAHARA (Claimed by Morocco)
ERG IGUIDI
ALGERIA
LIBYA
LIBYAN DESERT
QATTARA DEPRESSION
EGYPT
ARABIAN DESERT
RED SEA
S A H A R A
AHAGGAR MTS.
Tahat
TIBESTI MASSIF
Emi Koussi
L. Nasser
NUBIAN DESERT
Nile R.
AÏR
MAURITANIA
MALI
NIGER
CHAD
Senegal R.
SENEGAL
THE GAMBIA
Niger R.
BODÉLÉ DEPRESSION
L. Chad
Atbara R.
Bab el Mandeb
ERITREA
Ras Dashan
L. Tana
DJIBOUTI
CAPE GUARDAFUI
GULF OF ADEN
Blue Nile
SUDAN
FOUTA DJALLON
GUINEA
GUINEA-BISSAU
SIERRA LEONE
LIBERIA
BURKINA FASO
IVORY COAST (CÔTE D'IVOIRE)
GHANA
Volta R.
TOGO
BENIN
NIGERIA
BAUCHI PLATEAU
Chari R.
Benue R.
ETHIOPIAN HIGHLANDS
ETHIOPIA
White Nile
Shebeli R.
SOMALIA
CENTRAL AFRICAN REPUBLIC
CAMEROON
Cameroon Mt.
CAPE PALMAS
GULF OF GUINEA
EQUATORIAL GUINEA
SÃO TOMÉ AND PRÍNCIPE
CAPE LOPEZ
GABON
REP. OF CONGO
Congo R.
Uele R.
CONGO BASIN
RUWENZORI
UGANDA
L. Albert
L. Edward
Mt. Elgon
L. Turkana
KENYA
L. Victoria
Mt.Kenya
L. Kivu
RWANDA
SERENGETI PLAIN
Mt.Kilimanjaro 19,565 ft (5,963 m)
Kasai R.
DEMOCRATIC REPUBLIC OF CONGO
BURUNDI
L. Tanganyika
TANZANIA
SEYCHELLES
CABINDA (Ang.)
L. Mwera
GREAT RIFT VALLEY
L. Malawi
ASCENSION (St. Hel.)
ANGOLA
BIÉ PLATEAU
MALAWI
COMOROS
ZAMBIA
Zambezi R.
Okavango R.
SAINT HELENA (U.K.)
MOZAMBIQUE
MOZAMBIQUE CHANNEL
L. Kariba
Victoria Falls
NAMIBIA
OKAVANGO BASIN
ZIMBABWE
MADAGASCAR
ANKARATRA HIGHLANDS
MAURITIUS
RÉUNION (France)
NAMIB DESERT
KALAHARI DESERT
BOTSWANA
Limpopo R.
Molopo R.
Vaal R.
LESOTHO
SWAZILAND
Orange R.
SOUTH AFRICA
DRAKENSBERG
GREAT KARROO
CAPE OF GOOD HOPE
CAPE AGULHAS
TRISTAN DA CUNHA GROUP (St. Hel.)
GOUGH ISLAND (St. Hel.)
PRINCE EDWARD ISLANDS (S. Afr.)
ÎLES CROZET (French Southern and Antarctic Territories)
0 500 1000 mi
0 500 1000 km
Azimuthal Equal-area Projection
Tropical Rain Forest
Coniferous/ Evergreen Forest
Deciduous Forest
Chaparral
Grassland
Desert and Semidesert
40°W 30°W 20°W 10°W 0° 10°E 20°E 30°E 40°E 50°E 60°E 70°E
40°N 30°N 20°N 10°N 0° 10°S 20°S 30°S 40°S 50°S
A B C D E F
1 2 3 4 5 6 7 8

COUNTRIES OF AFRICA

COUNTRY	CAPITAL
Algeria	Algiers
Angola	Luanda
Benin	Porto-Novo
Botswana	Gaborone
Burkina Faso	Ouagadougou
Burundi	Bujumbúra
Cameroon	Yaoundé
Cape Verde	Praia
Central African Republic	Bangui
Chad	N'Djamena
Comoros	Moroni
Congo	Brazzaville
Dem. Rep. of Congo	Kinshasa
Djibouti	Djibouti
Egypt	Cairo
Equatorial Guinea	Malabo
Eritrea	Asmara
Ethiopia	Addis Ababa
Gabon	Libreville
Gambia, The	Banjul
Ghana	Accra
Guinea	Conakry
Guinea-Bissau	Bissau
Ivory Coast	Yamoussoukro
Kenya	Nairobi
Lesotho	Maseru
Liberia	Monrovia
Libya	Tripoli
Madagascar	Antananarivo
Malawi	Lilongwe
Mali	Bamako
Mauritania	Nouakchott
Mauritius	Port Louis
Morocco	Rabat
Mozambique	Maputo
Namibia	Windhoek
Niger	Niamey
Nigeria	Abuja
Rwanda	Kigali
São Tomé and Príncipe	São Tomé
Senegal	Dakar
Seychelles	Victoria
Sierra Leone	Freetown
Somalia	Mogadishu
South Africa	Pretoria (administrative) Cape Town (legislative) Bloemfontein (judicial)
Sudan	Khartoum
Swaziland	Mbabane
Tanzania	Dar es Salaam
Togo	Lomé
Tunisia	Tunis
Uganda	Kampala
Zambia	Lusaka
Zimbabwe	Harare

Vegetation and Soils. Vegetation zones vary with the climate. Central Africa, with its heavy rainfall, is a region of dense tropical forests. As the climate grows drier north and south of the equator, there is a gradual change from rain forest to a broad belt of savanna, or grassy plains dotted with trees. With decreasing rainfall, the savanna gives way to a drier, steppe region of shorter grasses and thorn bushes with only occasional trees. In the north, the steppe merges into a semidesert region known as the Sahel, which borders the Sahara. The Mediterranean-type vegetation of the northern coast includes such trees as pine, cork, oak, and olive.

In spite of their lush growth, the rain forests have soil that is of limited value for agriculture, while the drier savannas are suitable chiefly for grazing livestock. The most fertile areas are found in the valleys of the great rivers, which have rich alluvial soils. A variety of crops can be cultivated in the Mediterranean coastal zone and parts of eastern and southern Africa. But in general, Africa has nothing comparable to the large grain-growing regions of North America, Europe, and Asia.

Animal Life. Africa's wealth of wild animal life is one of its most important natural resources. The rain forests are home to monkeys, chimpanzees, gorillas, and okapis (shorter-necked relatives of the giraffe), snakes such as the large rock python and the

A broad belt of savanna, or plains dotted with trees (*opposite page*), covers much of the African landscape. It is home to such wildlife as the sable antelope (*left*) and the African lion (*bottom*). The mountain gorilla, by contrast, lives in upland areas.

poisonous African cobra and black mamba, and numerous kinds of birds. Crocodiles inhabit many African rivers. Herds of zebra and antelope graze on the savannas, serving as prey for lions, cheetahs, leopards, and scavenging hyenas. Among the larger African mammals are elephants, two species of rhinoceroses (white and black), and giraffes. Gazelles, foxes, and hares are some of the animals that have adapted to the harsh environment of the deserts. Lemurs (monkeylike primates) are found mainly on the island of Madagascar.

Some of Africa's animals are endangered and others close to extinction, due to population growth, the destruction of their natural habitat, and illegal or excessive hunting. The most threatened species are the black rhinoceros and the mountain gorilla. Elephants, hunted for their ivory, have also greatly diminished in numbers. Several African countries have passed strict laws to protect their wildlife, and game reserves have been established in various parts of the continent. Among the largest are Serengeti National Park in Tanzania, Kruger National Park in South Africa, and Tsavo Park in Kenya.

An article on endangered species appears in Volume E.

THE PEOPLE

Of all the world's continents, Africa has the most rapidly growing population. By 2000, it exceeded Europe as the second most populous continent. The people of Africa are very unevenly distributed across the land, however.

Since much of Africa consists of desert or semidesert land, mountains, and dense rain forests, large areas of the continent are only sparsely inhabited. Other areas, by contrast, are thickly crowded with people. Millions of people live in the valley and delta area of the Nile, where the soil is fertile, and water is available. Parts of the northern, or Mediterranean, coast are also well populated. This region has a generally pleasant climate and, historically, is well situated for trade and other contacts with Europe.

Some of the earliest large African kingdoms originated in western Africa south of the Sahara, and the well-watered parts of this region, chiefly along the Gulf of Guinea, are still home to great numbers of people. The eastern highlands and the southeastern coast of the continent, with their temperate climates, can also support sizable populations.

Although Africa has a number of large cities, the great majority of its people live in rural areas, as they have traditionally for centuries. Only about one-third of Africans live in urban areas, or cities— less than any of the other inhabited continents. But the rate of urban growth is very high, as rising indus-

trialization, cultural changes, the hope for a better life in the cities, and other factors attract growing numbers of people from the countryside. Often this strains the abilities of the cities to provide jobs, housing, and services for all who need them.

Racial and Ethnic Groups

Africa is home to a variety of peoples, languages, and cultures. Africans are usually divided into two major racial groups—the Negroid, or black, and the Caucasoid, or white. Black Africans are by far the more numerous, inhabiting a region from just south of the Sahara to the southern part of the continent. Generally considered as related groups are the Nilotic peoples of eastern Africa and the pygmies of central Africa, distinguished by their small stature. The San and Khoikhoi of southern Africa may be the most ancient people of the continent. Few in numbers, most live in the deserts.

The major Caucasoid groups are the Arabs and Berbers of northern Africa. There are also relatively small numbers of Africans of European origin. The largest of these are the whites of South Africa, descendants of early, mainly Dutch, settlers. The others are remnants of the European colonial period. In addition to the Europeans, Asians, mostly from India, have settled in eastern Africa and parts of South Africa. The intermingling of many of the various peoples over the course of history has created the Africans of today.

The faces of Africa. *Opposite page:* A South African railway inspector; an Ethiopian university student; three Senegalese schoolgirls; and a Berber boy from Morocco holding a Koran, or Muslim holy book. *Right and below:* A Nigerian couple in traditional wedding dress; a Masai girl in beaded finery; and a Sudanese warrior.

Africa's varied people speak a multitude of languages. Arabic is the language of these fishermen from northern Africa; the boys on camelback, from Niger, speak Fulani, a major language of western Africa.

Languages

Africa has a multitude of languages, estimated at 1,000 or more, spread across the continent. Some are spoken by large numbers of people; others by relatively few. Languages are often a more accurate way of defining the continent's ethnic groups. They are generally classified into several broad categories.

Afro-Asian and Nilo-Saharan. Afro-Asian languages are spoken mainly in northern and northeastern Africa. They include Arabic, the dominant language of northern Africa; Berber, spoken by the people who inhabited the region before the arrival of the Arabs; and the various languages of Ethiopia, Eritrea, and Somalia. The group also includes ancient Egyptian and its more modern relative, Coptic, as well as Hausa, spoken in northern Nigeria and adjacent areas.

The Nilo-Saharan language family is found in the central Sahara and just south of it, the basin of the Nile, and parts of eastern Africa. It is spoken by people in an area stretching from Mali in the west, through southern Sudan, to parts of Uganda, Kenya, and Tanzania in the east. Its major languages include Dendi, Kanuri, Dinka, Nuer, and Masai.

Niger-Kordofanian and Khoisan. The large Niger-Kordofanian family makes up a majority of the continent's languages and is spoken in most of Africa below the Sahara. In western Africa, its major language branches include Mande, Fulani, and Kwa. The hundreds of languages of the Bantu subfamily are found in central and southern and large areas of eastern Africa. One of the most widespread of the Bantu-based languages, Swahili, which was influenced by Arabic-speaking traders, became a common language of communication for much of the east African coastal region.

The San and Khoikhoi of southern Africa speak languages belonging to the small Khoisan family. They are sometimes referred to as click languages, because of the distinctive sound made in speaking them.

European Languages and Others. European languages were introduced by settlers and colonizers. French is still often used in former French territories in nothern, western, and central Africa, as well as in the Democratic Republic of Congo, once a Belgian colony. English continues to be spoken in former British colonies in western, eastern, and southern Africa, while Portuguese remains the official language of Angola and Mozambique. The descendants of the original white settlers of South Africa speak Afrikaans, based on a mixture of Dutch and Bantu languages.

Another distinctive language of the continent, Malagasy, spoken on Madagascar, is of Malayo-Polynesian origin.

Religions

Africa has three main religious faiths—Islam, Christianity, and traditional religions. Islam, the Muslim religion, arrived in northern Africa with conquering Arab armies. It became the predominant faith of the region, displacing Christianity, and quickly spread into areas immediately south of the Sahara. Christianity survived in Ethiopia and parts of Egypt and, centuries later, was reintroduced to other regions of Africa by European and American missionaries.

A great variety of traditional religions has existed in Africa since earliest times. As a particular society developed, it evolved its own beliefs, which were handed down from

A Catholic priest blesses a Ugandan boy; Muslims in Nigeria pray before a mosque; and a practitioner of traditional religion surveys his artifacts. Islam, Christianity, and traditional religions are Africa's main faiths.

In a rapidly changing Africa, the old and the new frequently meet. Here, in Niger, a skyscraper looms over traditional beehive-shaped thatched homes.

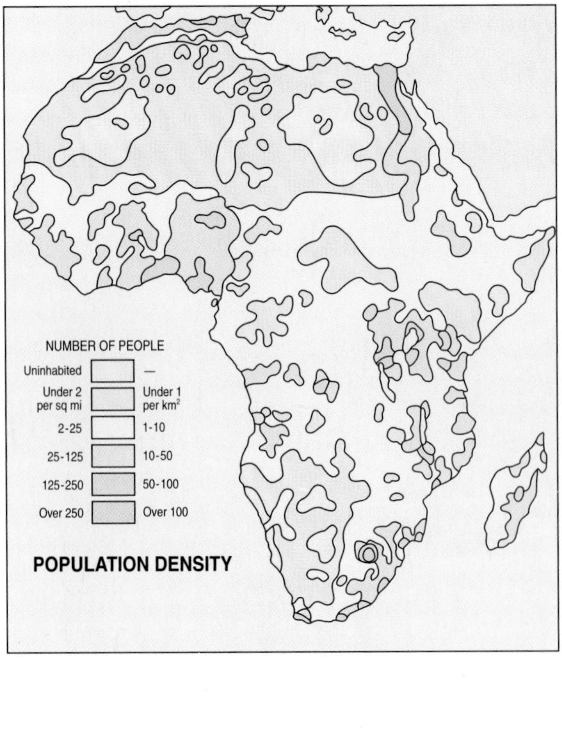

INDEX TO AFRICA POLITICAL MAP

Abidjan B4
Abuja C4
Accra B4
Addis Ababa E4
Agadez C3
Al Aiún A2
Algiers B1
Alexandria E1
Annaba C1
Antananarivo F6
Arusha E5
Asmara E3
Aswan E2
Atbara E3
Bamako A3
Bangui D4
Banjul A3
Bata C4
Beida D1
Benghazi D1
Benguela C6
Berbera F3
Bissau A3
Bizerte C1
Bloemfontein D7
Brazzaville C5
Bujumbúra E5
Bulawayo E6
Cairo E1
Cape Town D8
Casablanca B1
Conakry A3
Constantine C1
Dakar A3
Dakhla A2
Dar es Salaam E5
Djibouti F3
Dodoma E5
Douala C4
Durban E7
El Obeid E3
Entebbe E4
Freetown A4
Gaborone D7
Gondar E3
Harar F3
Harare E6
Hargeisa F3
Ibadan B4
Johannesburg D7
Juba E4
Kaédi A3
Kabwe E6
Kampala E4
Kananga D5
Kankan A4
Kano C3
Kaolack A3
Kayes A3
Khartoum E3
Kigali E5
Kimberley D7
Kinshasa C5
Kisangani D4
Kismayu F4
Kisumu E4
Kufra Oasis D2
Lagos B4
Lambaréné C4
Libreville C4
Livingstone D6
Lilongwe E6
Lobito C6
Lomé B4
Luanda C5
Lubumbashi D6
Lusaka D6
Luxor E2
Malabo C4
Maputo E7
Marrakesh B1
Maseru D7
Mbabane E7
Merca F4
Mogadishu F4
Mombasa F5
Monrovia A4
Moroni F6
Nairobi E5
Nakuru E4
N'Djamena C3
Ndola D6
Niamey B3
Nouadhibou A2
Nouakchott A3
Omdurman E3
Oran B1
Ouagadougou B3
Pemba F6
Pointe-Noire C5
Port Elizabeth D8
Port-Gentil C5
Port Harcourt C4
Port Louis F7
Porto Novo B4
Port Said E1
Port Sudan E2
Praia A3
Pretoria D7
Rabat B1
Sá de Bandeira C6
São Tomé C4
Ségou B3
Sekondi-Takoradi A4
Sfax C1
Sidi-bel-Abbès B1
Sofala E6
Tabora E5
Tanga E5
Tangier B1
Timbuktu B3
Tripoli C1
Tunis C1
Victoria F5
Windhoek D7
Yamoussoukro B4
Yaoundé C4
Zomba E6

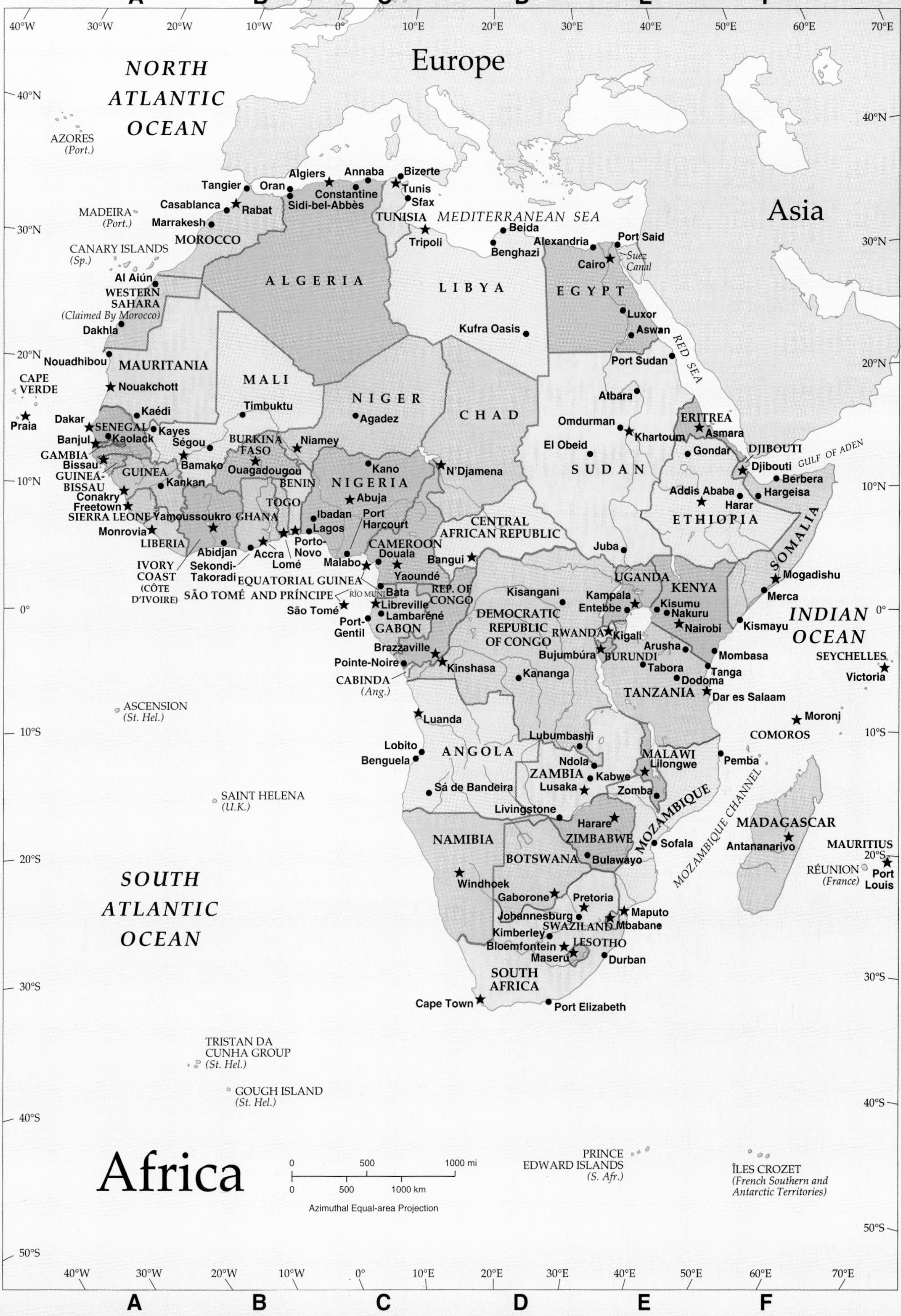
Africa
Europe
Asia
NORTH ATLANTIC OCEAN
SOUTH ATLANTIC OCEAN
INDIAN OCEAN
MEDITERRANEAN SEA
RED SEA
GULF OF ADEN
MOZAMBIQUE CHANNEL
Suez Canal
AZORES (Port.)
MADEIRA (Port.)
CANARY ISLANDS (Sp.)
CAPE VERDE
Praia
ASCENSION (St. Hel.)
SAINT HELENA (U.K.)
TRISTAN DA CUNHA GROUP (St. Hel.)
GOUGH ISLAND (St. Hel.)
PRINCE EDWARD ISLANDS (S. Afr.)
ÎLES CROZET (French Southern and Antarctic Territories)
SEYCHELLES
Victoria
COMOROS
Moroni
MAURITIUS
Port Louis
RÉUNION (France)
MOROCCO
Tangier
Casablanca
Rabat
Marrakesh
WESTERN SAHARA (Claimed By Morocco)
Al Aiún
Dakhla
ALGERIA
Algiers
Oran
Sidi-bel-Abbès
Constantine
Annaba
TUNISIA
Bizerte
Tunis
Sfax
LIBYA
Tripoli
Beida
Benghazi
Kufra Oasis
EGYPT
Alexandria
Port Said
Cairo
Luxor
Aswan
MAURITANIA
Nouadhibou
Nouakchott
Kaédi
MALI
Timbuktu
Kayes
Ségou
Bamako
NIGER
Agadez
Niamey
CHAD
N'Djamena
SUDAN
Port Sudan
Atbara
Omdurman
Khartoum
El Obeid
Juba
ERITREA
Asmara
DJIBOUTI
Djibouti
ETHIOPIA
Gondar
Addis Ababa
Harar
SOMALIA
Berbera
Hargeisa
Mogadishu
Merca
Kismayu
SENEGAL
Dakar
Kaolack
GAMBIA
Banjul
GUINEA-BISSAU
Bissau
GUINEA
Conakry
Kankan
SIERRA LEONE
Freetown
LIBERIA
Monrovia
IVORY COAST (CÔTE D'IVOIRE)
Yamoussoukro
Abidjan
BURKINA FASO
Ouagadougou
GHANA
Sekondi-Takoradi
Accra
TOGO
Lomé
BENIN
Porto-Novo
NIGERIA
Kano
Abuja
Ibadan
Lagos
Port Harcourt
CAMEROON
Douala
Yaoundé
Malabo
EQUATORIAL GUINEA
RÍO MUNI
Bata
SÃO TOMÉ AND PRÍNCIPE
São Tomé
GABON
Libreville
Lambaréné
Port-Gentil
REP. OF CONGO
Brazzaville
Pointe-Noire
CENTRAL AFRICAN REPUBLIC
Bangui
DEMOCRATIC REPUBLIC OF CONGO
Kisangani
Kinshasa
Kananga
Lubumbashi
CABINDA (Ang.)
UGANDA
Kampala
Entebbe
KENYA
Kisumu
Nakuru
Nairobi
Mombasa
RWANDA
Kigali
BURUNDI
Bujumbúra
TANZANIA
Arusha
Tabora
Dodoma
Tanga
Dar es Salaam
ANGOLA
Luanda
Lobito
Benguela
Sá de Bandeira
ZAMBIA
Ndola
Kabwe
Lusaka
Livingstone
MALAWI
Lilongwe
Zomba
MOZAMBIQUE
Pemba
Sofala
Maputo
ZIMBABWE
Harare
Bulawayo
NAMIBIA
Windhoek
BOTSWANA
Gaborone
SOUTH AFRICA
Pretoria
Johannesburg
Kimberley
Bloemfontein
Durban
Cape Town
Port Elizabeth
SWAZILAND
Mbabane
LESOTHO
Maseru
MADAGASCAR
Antananarivo
0 500 1000 mi
0 500 1000 km
Azimuthal Equal-area Projection
A B C D E F
1 2 3 4 5 6 7 8
40°W 30°W 20°W 10°W 0° 10°E 20°E 30°E 40°E 50°E 60°E 70°E
40°N 30°N 20°N 10°N 0° 10°S 20°S 30°S 40°S 50°S

generation to generation, reflecting its cultural as well as its spiritual ideas. Most have as a basic element a belief in spirits, which are thought to exist in such things as trees and mountains, and a reverence for or worship of one's ancestors. Magic is also an important ingredient of many traditional religions and is often used in healing. Although most traditional religions do not deny the existence of many minor gods, most recognize the existence of a supreme creator.

Africa also has small numbers of Hindus and Jews. Hinduism is practiced by the Indian communities living mainly in South Africa and in parts of eastern Africa. Most Jews live in the north and in South Africa.

Education

Along with improvements in health care and economic conditions, the expansion of education has been one of the chief aims of African countries since independence. This has been a major undertaking. The adult literacy rate (the percentage able to read and write), although it varies widely, still averages only about 25 percent for most of Africa. In addition, with nearly half the African population under 15 years of age, the cost of educating its young people represents an enormous strain on the economies of the continent's poorer countries.

Society

Traditional Society: The Tribe. For centuries much of traditional African society has revolved around the tribe. People of the same tribe usually speak the same language and observe the same customs. They share a similar way of life and a distinctive culture. Although some tribes are small, more commonly they consist of large populations, in some cases numbering millions of people. Most of the

Traditional African society revolved around the tribe, whose members shared a common language, culture, and way of life (*left*). But traditional life is undergoing rapid change, due in part to the movement of people from rural areas to the cities. Tribal conflicts have also caused the large-scale dislocation of peoples. These Rwandan refugees (*top*) fled their homeland because of fighting between the country's two main ethnic groups.

large African tribes, in fact, would be considered nations or nationalities if they lived in Europe.

Tribal society, traditionally, was the center of an individual's life. It offered social and economic security and regulated conduct through tribal laws and customs. It took care of its members in time of need and protected them from hostile outsiders. In return, members gave their services to the tribe. A tribe was usually ruled by a chieftain or a tribal council or, sometimes, by both. In some areas, tribes with similar cultural backgrounds banded together under a paramount chief.

One of the values basic to virtually all traditional African life was the strong attachment to the land. Probably this was because most Africans have always lived off the land. It was considered to belong to all, and not only to the living but to one's ancestors and to future generations as well.

National and Tribal Conflicts. But tribal boundaries do not always correspond to the political realities of modern African countries. The border between Togo and Ghana, for example, cuts through the traditional homeland of the Ewe people. This and similar situations came about because most of Africa's present-day borders were drawn by colonial powers, who divided vast territories among themselves without regard for traditional boundary lines. In a number of instances this has been the cause of conflict and outright civil war. Eventually, it is hoped that as the ties of traditional society lessen, Africans will feel a greater loyalty to their national governments than to their tribes.

Social Change. The traditional ways of life are rapidly changing. Some 200 years of European influence have profoundly affected the thinking and life of many Africans. Improved transportation and communications have brought the outside world even closer to the rural villages. Although many Africans have been reluctant to leave their traditional homelands and the security they represent, each year increasing numbers move to the cities in search of greater opportunities. In spite of improvements in health and standards of living in general, governments often cannot cope with the rapid urban growth or satisfy the people's demands. Economic and social dislocation are frequently the result, often aggravated by civil strife.

WONDER QUESTION

What and where are the Mountains of the Moon?

One of the mysteries of Africa that had perplexed historians and explorers from earliest times was the source, or origin, of the Nile—the mighty river whose life-giving waters enabled the ancient Egyptians to create a great civilization in an otherwise barren land. The Greek geographer Ptolemy (A.D. 90–168) conjectured that the river originated in the heart of Africa, in a vague region that he called the Mountains of the Moon. It was not until the 1870's that the true source of the White Nile, its main tributary, was discovered, chiefly in lakes Victoria, Edward, and Albert. As for the Mountains of the Moon, they are generally, although not always, identified today with the Ruwenzori range, on the border between Uganda and the Democratic Republic of Congo. Ptolemy may not have been entirely wrong, however, for the melting snows of the Ruwenzori do contribute to the waters that ultimately feed into the Nile.

Cape Town (*left*), the legislative capital of South Africa, lies on the southernmost tip of the continent. Nairobi (*above*) is Kenya's capital and largest city and one of the chief cities of eastern Africa.

CITIES

In spite of a largely rural population, Africa also has a considerable culture based on urban life. Cairo, the capital of Egypt, is the continent's largest city and continues to attract increasing numbers of people from the countryside. Alexandria, Egypt's chief port, is an ancient center of learning and commerce, named for Alexander the Great. Other important cities of the north are Casablanca, Morocco's principal city and port; and Algiers and Tunis, the capitals, respectively, of Algeria and Tunisia.

Southern Africa's major cities include Cape Town, located at the southernmost tip of the continent, and Johannesburg, both in South Africa. Lagos, Nigeria's largest city and chief port, and Abidjan, capital of Ivory Coast, are western Africa's largest urban centers. Dakar, Senegal's capital, is a leading port situated on Africa's most westerly point of land.

Eastern Africa has several major cities. Dar es Salaam, Tanzania's capital and largest city, is one of the region's leading ports. Nairobi is Kenya's chief city and capital, and Addis Ababa is the largest city, commercial center, and capital of Ethiopia. Central Africa's largest city, Kinshasa, is the capital of the Democratic Republic of Congo.

THE ECONOMY

Although rich in terms of its natural resources, most of Africa is in the developing stage, economically. The continent has emerged in only relatively recent times from the colonial period, when it served mainly as a source of raw materials for Europe's industry and as a market for its manufactured goods. Aside from South Africa, the most highly industrialized of the African countries, the continent in general has only begun to develop a modern industrial economy. Agriculture and the mining of its mineral wealth are still the main sources of Africa's income.

Agriculture

Most Africans earn their livelihood from the soil. The great majority practice subsistence farming, growing basic food crops for their own use, generally on small plots of land. Commercial crops, intended for export, are often grown on large plantations. Ordinarily, a variety of crops can be grown in some regions of the continent. In others, the thinness of the soil, the arid climate, and frequent drought make farming difficult.

Northern and Western Regions. Wheat, barley, and grapes flourish on the Mediterranean coast. Date palms, fig trees, and wheat, cotton, and vegetables can be grown in the scattered oases, or watered areas, of the desert regions. In the rainy, tropical areas of western Africa, the main food crops are yams, cassava (a starchy root), and rice. Commercial crops grown here include cacao (from which chocolate is made), coffee, rubber, and palm oil. Ivory Coast is the world's leading producer of cacao, while Nigeria is a major producer of coffee and natural rubber. In the drier savanna, important crops include such grains as millet, sorghum, and corn, peanuts, and cotton.

Eastern and Southern Regions. Corn and wheat, along with millet, cassava, and vegetables, are the major food crops of eastern Africa. Commercial crops include sisal (a fiber from which cord and twine are made), cotton, coffee, tea, and pyrethrum (used in making insecticides). Winter wheat, wine grapes, and other fruits are grown in South Africa's southern Cape province, which has a Mediterranean-type climate. Sugarcane is an important crop in the coastal region of Mozambique and along the eastern coast of South Africa.

Livestock Raising. Livestock raising is an important element of African agriculture, particularly in the savanna and steppe regions. Goats are grazed in the arid Sahel, while farther north, in the Sahara itself, semi-nomadic peoples regularly migrate, seeking pasture for their herds of camels and sheep. Eastern Africa has a distinctive cattle culture, especially among the Masai of Kenya and Tanzania, where ownership of cattle is a sign of wealth and prestige. Smaller domestic livestock, such as pigs and chickens, are kept as part of the traditional subsistance farming. Large-scale commercial cattle- and sheep-raising is carried out in South Africa.

Livestock raising (*left*) is an important part of African agriculture, particularly in regions of limited rainfall. In more fertile areas, such as the Nile Valley (*below*), a variety of crops can be grown.

Mining and Manufacturing

Mining accounts for about half of Africa's total exports and is the major source of income for a number of African countries. For detailed information on Africa's mineral resources and where they are found, see the section Mineral Resources.

While South Africa has a variety of heavy industry, including the production of iron and steel, most African industry consists of light manufacturing. The bulk of the labor force is employed in the processing of foods and other agricultural products and the production of textiles, clothing, and chemicals. Manufacturing is usually concentrated in the larger cities, but many of the newer industries are located near rivers to take advantage of the continent's considerable hydroelectric power potential.

Forestry and Fishing

Forests cover about one-quarter of the continent. But the commercially valuable trees, such as mahogany and other hardwoods, are often widely scattered and transportation is frequently inadequate. Usable areas of forest lie mainly in west central Africa.

Africa is rich in mineral resources. Libya is one of the world's major oil producers (*above*) and Zambia ranks among the leading producers of copper (*below*).

Freshwater fish obtained from Africa's rivers and lakes partially make up for the lack of meat in the diet of most Africans. The major commercial fishing grounds are found off the southwestern coast, where the cold Benguela Current attracts large schools of fish; in the Mediterranean; and in the Gulf of Guinea. Much of the catch is processed for export as fish meal and fish oil.

Transportation

Africa's often difficult terrain and severe climate have combined to hinder transportation over much of the continent. Most of its system of roads and railroads was built during the colonial period to connect the interior with the coastal ports, and its further development has been slow and painstaking. South Africa and the Mediterranean area have the most extensive road and rail networks.

Historically, Africa's rivers and lakes have served as a natural transportation system, although limited by the numerous rapids and falls. Air transportation is now of major importance in areas difficult to reach by other means and in connecting major cities, as well as by linking Africa with the rest of the world.

HISTORY

Africa is believed to have been the home of the earliest humans. Scientists have discovered the remains of humanlike ancestors in eastern Africa who are estimated to have lived more than 3 million years ago. Africa, which has been incorrectly called the continent without a history, may well have the longest human history of all the continents. For more information on this subject, see the articles FOSSILS in Volume F and PREHISTORIC PEOPLE in Volume P.

Northern Africa

Early peoples in the valley of the Nile developed a form of agriculture based on the cultivation of cereal grains, irrigated by the yearly flooding of the great river. In about 3200 B.C., the northern and southern states of the region were united, marking the beginning of Egyptian civilization. A later kingdom, that of Kush (or Nubia), arose just to the south, while in the Horn of Africa, in what is now Ethiopia, the kingdom of Aksum eventually grew out of contacts with southwestern Asia.

The Phoenicians, a people from the eastern Mediterranean, and their successors, the Carthaginians, established themselves on the coast of northern Africa. Their most famous settlement, the city-state of Carthage, was founded in the 800's B.C. The Carthaginians were displaced by the Romans, who by the A.D. 100's had gained control of the entire northern coast of Africa from Morocco to Egypt.

Between the A.D. 600's and 1000's, Arab armies from southwestern Asia swept across northern Africa, bringing with them the Islamic religion and Arabic language that still prevails over most of the region. Islam gradually spread southward, and Arabs later traded and settled along the coast of eastern Africa.

West African Kingdoms

Several ancient African kingdoms flourished in the valley of the Niger River in western Africa. They engaged in trade with the Arabs of the north and became wealthy centers of learning and culture.

The earliest of the great kingdoms of the region, Ghana, originated in the A.D. 300's and reached its height in the A.D. 1000's. It

A European map of 1375 depicts the king of Mali, Mansa Musa, on his throne. Mali was one of the early empires and kingdoms that flourished in western Africa.

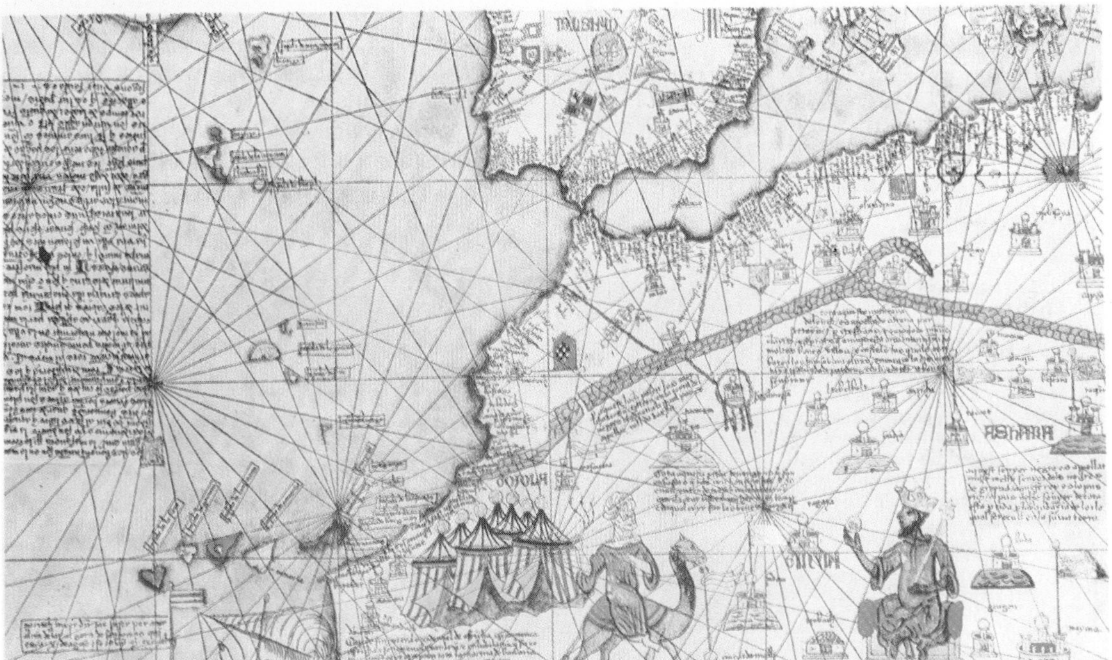

was succeeded by the empire of Mali, one of whose chief cities was the fabled Timbuktu. Mali held sway until it was replaced, in turn, as the most powerful western state by Songhai, which at its height during the early 1500's stretched from the Atlantic coast to northern Nigeria. Two modern African nations, Ghana and Mali, have taken their names from these old kingdoms.

European Exploration

European exploration along the coast of Africa began with the Portuguese, who were looking for a convenient water route to India. Bartholomeu Dias rounded the Cape of Good Hope at the southern tip of Africa in 1488. Another Portuguese explorer, Vasco da Gama, visited the eastern coast and reached India in 1498. Soon afterward, the Portuguese established coastal settlements and began trading in gold, spices, ivory, and slaves.

Other European powers began to compete with the Portuguese, establishing forts and trading posts along the coast. But the dense rain forests, disease, and hostility by Africans long kept Europeans from penetrating to the inland areas.

European exploration of the interior of Africa first began in the second half of the 1700's, with the discoveries of two Scots—James Bruce, who explored the region of the Blue Nile; and Mungo Park, who traveled down the Niger River. The Scottish missionary and doctor David Livingstone made extensive discoveries in central Africa and the lake region of southeastern Africa in the mid-1800's. He was joined by Henry Morton Stanley, who later explored the vast Congo region. Sir Richard Burton and John Speke both sought the source of the Nile.

See EXPLORATION AND DISCOVERY (Exploring Africa) in Volume E. An article on Stanley and Livingstone appears in Volume S. An article on Sir Richard Burton appears in Volume B.

The Slave Trade

The slave trade was a by-product of the opening of Africa. Arabs had long been established in the trade in slaves in eastern Africa. By the 1600's and 1700's, the Portuguese, British, Dutch, and French had joined them. Millions of black Africans were to become its victims before the trade was banned by most European countries in the 1800's. For more information on the slave trade, see the article SLAVERY (The African Slave Trade and other sections) in Volume S.

Top: **The British explorer Richard Burton (1821–90) spent years searching for the source of the Nile. His discoveries included Lake Tanganyika.** ***Right:*** **The slave trade was one of the tragic episodes of African history, lasting from the 1600's until it was abolished by most European countries in the 1800's.**

IMPORTANT DATES

About 3200 B.C. Egypt united under King Menes.

About 2000 B.C. Rise of kingdom of Kush (Nubia).

814 B.C. Phoenicians settle the colony of Carthage in northern Africa.

About 600 B.C. Greeks replace Phoenicians in trade and exploration of Africa.

264–146 B.C. Punic Wars involve Rome and Carthage in a struggle for control of the Mediterranean. Victorious Roman armies destroy Carthage.

168 B.C. Romans conquer Egypt.

A.D. 300's–1000's Kingdom of Ghana flourishes in western Africa.

300's Kingdom of Aksum (in northern Ethiopia) converted to Christianity.

429–439 Vandals conquer northern Africa, which had been part of the Roman Empire.

About 500 Decline of Vandals; northern Africa becomes part of the Byzantine Empire.

640–710 Period of the Arab conquest of northern Africa; introduction of Islam and the Arabic language.

1000's Mali empire conquers Ghana.

1415 Prince Henry the Navigator sends Portuguese expeditions down the western coast of Africa.

1487–88 Bartholomeu Dias of Portugal discovers Cape of Good Hope.

1497–98 Portugal's Vasco da Gama sails around the Cape of Good Hope to India.

1500's Songhai kingdom overthrows Mali.

1517 Ottoman Turks conquer Egypt.

1520–26 Francisco Alvarez of Portugal explores Ethiopia.

1535 Spain conquers Tunis.

1595 First Dutch settlement established on the Guinea coast.

1626 French settle in Senegal.

1652 Cape Town founded by the Dutch.

1660 Rise of the Bambara kingdoms on the upper Niger.

1697 France completes conquest of Senegal.

1768–73 James Bruce explores the Blue Nile.

1787 Home for freed African slaves set up in Sierra Leone.

1792 Denmark becomes the first country to abolish the slave trade.

1795, 1805 Mungo Park explores the Niger River.

1807, 1811 Britain abolishes slave trade.

1814 Cape Colony becomes a British possession.

1815 France, Spain, and Portugal abolish slave trade.

1821 Freed American slaves arrive in Liberia.

1830–47 France conquers Algeria.

1834 Britain frees all slaves in its colonies.

1836–40 Great Trek of Boers (descendants of Dutch settlers) to interior of what is now South Africa.

1841 David Livingstone begins exploration of Africa.

1847 Liberia becomes the first independent black republic.

1849 The French establish a home for freed slaves at Libreville in Gabon.

1850's Richard Burton and John Hanning Speke explore source of the Nile.

1866 Diamonds are found in South Africa.

1869 Suez Canal opens.

1871 Henry M. Stanley's search for Livingstone ends successfully in Tanganyika.

1871 Cecil Rhodes starts building his fortune and empire in southern Africa.

1884 Germany annexes South-West Africa, gains control of Togoland and the Cameroons.

1885 King Leopold II of Belgium establishes the Congo Free State as his personal property. Germany acquires Tanganyika.

1886 Gold discovered in South Africa—gold rush begins.

1898 Fashoda Crisis on the upper Nile brings Britain and France to the brink of war.

1899–1902 Boer War: Britain's defeat of Boers gives it control of South Africa.

1908 Congo Free State is turned over to the Belgian government and renamed the Belgian Congo.

1910 The British colonies in South Africa are united to form the Union of South Africa.

1922 Egypt gains independence from Britain.

1935 Italy invades Ethiopia.

1941–43 North African campaign of World War II fought.

1948 South Africa formally adopts policy of apartheid, or racial separation.

1951 Libya gains independence.

1954–62 Period of Algerian war of independence.

1956 Tunisia, Morocco, Sudan gain independence. Egypt nationalizes the Suez Canal, touching off a Middle East war.

1957 Ghana gains independence.

1958 Guinea gains independence.

1960 Belgian Congo, Cameroon, Central African Republic, Chad, Congo, Dahomey (now Benin), Gabon, Ivory Coast, Malagasy Republic (now Madagascar), Mali, Mauritania, Niger, Nigeria, Senegal, Somalia, Togo, and Upper Volta (now Burkina Faso) gain independence.

1961 Sierra Leone and Tanganyika gain independence. South Africa becomes a republic.

1962 Algeria, Burundi, Rwanda, and Uganda gain independence.

1963 African leaders form the Organization of African Unity (OAU). Zanzibar and Kenya gain independence.

1964 Zanzibar and Tanganyika united as Tanzania. Malawi and Zambia gain independence.

1965 The Gambia gains independence. Rhodesia unilaterally declares independence.

1966 Botswana and Lesotho gain independence.

1967–70 Civil war rages in Nigeria.

1968 Equatorial Guinea, Mauritius, and Swaziland gain independence.

1971 Egypt's Aswan Dam formally opened.

1974 Guinea-Bissau gains independence.

1975 Comoros, Mozambique, São Tomé and Príncipe, Angola, and Cape Verde gain independence.

1976 Seychelles gains independence.

1977 Djibouti gains independence.

1980 Zimbabwe (former Rhodesia) gains independence under black majority rule.

1990 Namibia gains independence.

1993 Eritrea wins independence from Ethiopia.

1994 Inauguration of Nelson Mandela as first black president of South Africa.

1998 Civil war resumes in the Democratic Republic of Congo (formerly Zaïre).

2001 OAU is dissolved to make way for a new African Union.

The Colonial Era

The "scramble for Africa," as the rivalry for African possessions was called, began in the mid-1800's. During the next 50 years, the continent came almost completely under European domination. France and Britain were the main colonial powers, but Portugal, Germany, Spain, Italy, and Belgium also carved out large African empires that were often many times larger than the European countries themselves. By the beginning of the 1900's, the only African states that were still independent were Ethiopia and Liberia. Ethiopia had successfully resisted colonization, while Liberia had been founded, in the early 1800's, as a refuge for freed American slaves.

The March Toward Independence

The end of World War II in 1945 saw the rise of African nationalism as a mass movement. The great march toward independence began in the late 1950's and proceeded swiftly. In 1960 alone, 17 nations won independence. By 1970 most of the continent had freed itself from colonial rule. Independence was generally gained peacefully, although in a few cases it was preceded by years of guerrilla war.

The transfer of authority was usually orderly. In several instances, however, independence was followed by civil war, either immediately or some years later. In some countries, separatists sought to break away

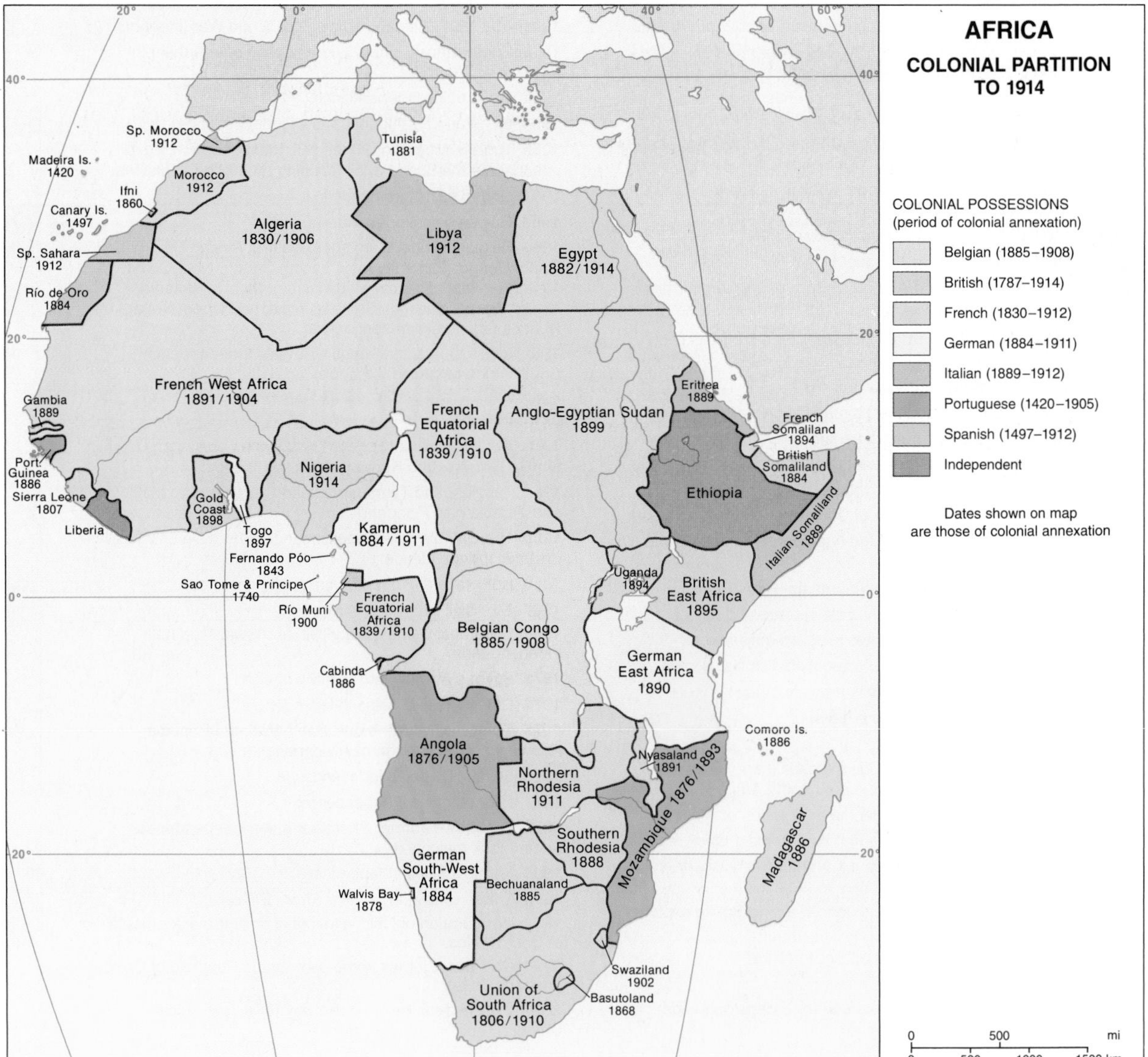

The inauguration of Nelson Mandela as South Africa's first black president in 1994 was an event of globally historic importance.

and form their own nations. This occurred in the Belgian Congo in 1960 and in Nigeria in 1967. When Angola and Mozambique won independence from Portugal in the 1970's, civil war erupted as opposing political factions fought for power.

Nevertheless, progress toward complete independence continued. Zimbabwe finally gained independence under black-majority rule in 1980. The last of the great African colonies, Namibia (a former German territory administered by South Africa) gained its independence in 1990. Africa's newest nation, Eritrea, won independence from Ethiopia in 1993, after years of fighting. In South Africa the inauguration, in 1994, of Nelson Mandela as its first black president marked a historic turning point in a country where a white minority had long been dominant.

The Future

Much remains to be done, however. Average incomes for most Africans are very low. There are still not enough schools or teachers and relatively few hospitals and doctors compared to Africa's vast size and numbers of people. Traditional ways of life have been disrupted by the migration of people from the countryside to the cities. Tribal and ethnic loyalties that sometimes cross the old European-drawn boundaries have also led to violent conflict in several regions.

Most African nations are dependent on one or two primary exports, chiefly agricultural or mineral products, for much of their income. Their economies are thus subject to changes in world prices for these products. Falling prices, together with increases in the cost of vital imports, have forced many countries to reduce needed social and economic programs. Drought has caused widespread crop failure. Famines in Ethiopia, Zimbabwe, Malawi, and Zambia, combined with brutal civil wars in Liberia, Sierra Leone, Sudan, the Democratic Republic of Congo, Somalia, Angola, Rwanda, and Burundi, have caused the death of millions and created serious refugee problems. AIDS has also had a devastating impact on the continent.

Africans now make up more than one-quarter of the member nations of the United Nations and have an increasingly important voice in world affairs. In 2002, the Organization of African Unity (OAU) was replaced by the African Union. It was hoped that this new organization, modeled on the European Union, would increase Africa's importance as a regional economic bloc. That same year, in a program called the New Partnership for Africa's Development, the world's leading industrial nations pledged billions of dollars to aid any African country that successfully reformed its economy and government.

DONALD J. BALLAS
Indiana University of Pennsylvania

Reviewed by HUGH C. BROOKS
St. John's University (New York)

L. GRAY COWAN
Columbia University

See also articles on individual African countries.

AFRICA, ART AND ARCHITECTURE OF

African art has developed from ancient traditions. Generations before the United States and the nations of Europe became great powers, Africa had known the rise and fall of many great kingdoms. The organization, discipline, laws, and religions of these ancient kingdoms show that Africa has been civilized for thousands of years.

The continent of Africa is often divided into two parts. To the north of the Sahara desert are the peoples known as Arabs, living in such countries as Morocco, Algeria, and Egypt. The articles EGYPTIAN ART AND ARCHITECTURE and ISLAMIC ART AND ARCHITECTURE contain information on the arts of these peoples. This article discusses the arts of the peoples living south of the Sahara.

Prehistoric rock paintings by the San people of southern Africa are the earliest existing examples of African art south of the Sahara desert.

The land varies greatly across sub-Saharan Africa. Victoria Falls, in Zimbabwe, and snowcapped mountains such as Kilimanjaro are in sharp contrast to dry plains and tropical rain forests. The differences in physical environment produced many different cultures, each with a distinct artistic tradition.

▶ THE FUNCTIONS OF AFRICAN ART

Much of the world's art was made for religious reasons, and African art is no exception. Ancestor worship, spirits, magic, and other aspects of the religion of African peoples are reflected in their art. Art was also created for marriage ceremonies, for funerals, for honoring leaders, and for celebrations.

Nearly all African art has a function. Statues are carved to honor ancestors, kings, and gods. Masks are used in rituals surrounding boys' and girls' coming-of-age ceremonies, at funerals, and for entertainment. Jewelry, clothing, hairstyles, and body painting are sometimes used to signify wealth, power, and social status.

Carved figures are used to guard containers filled with sacred relics of ancestors. Combs, spoons, bowls, stools, and other useful items are elaborately carved and decorated. Objects are made with taste and skill, regardless of their function.

African art is not anonymous, but very few African artists are known by name. Most worked alone or in a workshop composed of a master and one or more apprentices. Because their work often consisted of replacing existing objects that had deteriorated, artists were obliged to conform to the ancient artistic laws. Yet despite these restrictions, African artists managed to express individual imagination and to employ new materials and techniques. If these innovations proved to make the art more effective, they became part of an ever-growing tradition.

▶ BEGINNINGS

In prehistoric times, the nomadic San people of southern Africa left many paintings and engravings in caves and on rock faces. These works portray human figures and animals (especially antelopes) as well as mythological symbols. They show men and women hunting, fishing, gathering food, dancing, and performing ritual activities.

Other early works of art are those of the Nok culture, which flourished in northern Nigeria from about 500 B.C. to A.D. 200. The human and animal figures made of terra cotta (fired clay) that have been found in the region are the earliest known sculptures of

Artists of the ancient kingdom of Ifé used cast-metal techniques to create life-like sculpture that, in its naturalism, differs greatly from most other African art.

sub-Saharan Africa. The heads of the figures are several times larger than the heads of real human beings. This is a stylistic convention that, with slight variations, can be observed in the art of most African peoples. Although we do not know why this convention was used in the Nok culture 2,000 years ago, in most African sculpture the head is emphasized because it is the most vital part of the body.

SCULPTURE

Sculpture is Africa's greatest art. Wood is used far more than any other material. This means that much African art did not last, because wood is more easily destroyed than stone or metal. Because of this, there are some gaps in our knowledge of African art history.

An Early Tradition: Ifé and Benin

In the midwestern part of what is now Nigeria, two ancient kingdoms existed, Ifé and Benin. Artists in Ifé were casting metal sculpture by the A.D. 1000's. Archaeological evidence suggests that artists in Benin were casting metal as early as the 1300's; their earliest metal sculptures date from the 1400's.

This cast-metal plaque is characteristic of the art of the kingdom of Benin. There, too, artists followed a tradition of naturalism, often depicting events at the royal court.

The cast-metal sculpture of Ifé and Benin was naturalistic; that is, the work of art resembled the actual object it was meant to represent. For subject matter the artists used animals, birds, people, and events at the royal court. Benin artists depicted Portuguese soldiers, merchants, and other foreigners who visited the kingdom. Artists also worked in ivory, especially at Benin, where elephant tusks were carved to honor deceased kings.

Ifé and Benin sculpture represents a very different tradition from that of most other African art. In its naturalism, it is closer than any other type of art in Africa to classical Western art.

Regional Styles

Most African sculpture originated in western and central Africa, a vast area containing three main cultural regions: the Western Sudan, the Guinea Coast, and Central Africa. Figure carving is rare in eastern and southern Africa, except among a few peoples in Kenya, Tanzania, and Madagascar.

Many different styles of sculpture exist in western and central Africa, and even within each cultural region. Some stylistic characteristics, however, are common to all the regions. In addition to the "head-heavy" proportions described above, these characteristics are simplified forms, balanced and symmetrical design, and unemotional facial expression. Although the form of a face or figure may be minimal, details are both precise and abundant. For example, figures may have intricately designed hairstyles and body adornments such as necklaces and bracelets.

Western Sudan. This region extends from Senegal through Chad, ranging from semi-desert to grassland to wooded savanna. Sculpted figures tend to be angular and elongated, and the facial features are only suggested. Many of these figures are used in religious rituals; they usually have dull or encrusted surfaces

from ceremonial offerings of millet gruel or other liquid substances that have been poured over them.

Guinea Coast. This region extends along the Atlantic Ocean from Guinea-Bissau through central Nigeria and Cameroon. It includes coastal rain forests and inland wooded grasslands. Sculpted figures from this cultural region tend to be shorter and more rounded than those from the Western Sudan region. Figures often have smooth, luminous surfaces. Much art from the central part of the region, including that of the Akan people—the Baule of Ivory Coast and the Asante of Ghana—and the Yoruba people of southwestern Nigeria, was made to honor leaders. Here gold and ivory as well as wood were used to make objects of value.

The royal arts of the small kingdoms in the grasslands area of central Cameroon are bold and expressive. Colorful beadwork is used to embellish carved wood thrones and figures. The face, hands, and feet of some sculpted figures are covered with molded sheet brass.

Central Africa is an enormous area that extends down the Atlantic coast from Equatorial Guinea to northern Angola and eastward through the Democratic Republic of Congo.

In the Ogowe River basin region of Gabon, sculpted guardian figures are placed atop containers holding the sacred relics of deceased ancestors. Among the Kota people, guardian figures are flat metal-sheathed heads with minimal facial features set on lozenge-shaped bases. In contrast, those of the Fang people are single heads or complete figures that are more naturalistic in appearance.

The Kongo people predominate in the Lower Congo River basin. Their art displays a greater degree of naturalism than most African sculpture. Gesture and emotion are subtly indicated. Many figures depict a mother with a child on her lap. Because the Kongo were once part of a powerful kingdom, much of their art consists of items made for royalty.

Most African sculpture has simplified forms and a balanced design. ***Top:*** **A terra cotta figure of a horse and rider from Mali has an elongated shape typical of sculpture from the Western Sudan region.** ***Far left:*** **A wood sculpture of a mother and child was made by the Yoruba people of Nigeria.** ***Left:*** **Much African art serves a practical purpose: In this Luba wood sculpture from the Democratic Republic of Congo, "twin" female figures form the support for a headrest.**

The Kuba and the Hemba are only two peoples among hundreds in the Democratic Republic of Congo who have important sculptural traditions. Kuba figure sculpture portrays ancestral kings seated cross-legged. Standing Hemba figures are rounded naturalistic forms that serve to commemorate ancestors.

Eastern and Southern Africa. This cultural region extends south along the southern Atlantic coast and around South Africa to Ethiopia. Here, in Botswana and Namibia, are found the ancient rock paintings attributed to the San people of the Kalahari Desert. Figure carving is rare in this region. Instead, the arts of personal adornment, including body painting, and of decorating useful objects, such as headrests, spoons, and stools, are very highly developed. In Ethiopia, the art of the highlands reflects the influence of Christianity, which was introduced there in the A.D. 300's. Non-Christian Ethiopians created figurative carvings for use in their own religious worship.

MASKS

Masks are supports for spirits, which according to traditional beliefs are found in nature and in humans and animals. Some spirits are gods. Masks perform a variety of functions: They may be used in rites marking the transition from childhood to adulthood, to enforce the laws of society, to cause rain to fall during periods of drought, and to celebrate gods and ancestors.

Masks are usually worn as disguises, along with a full costume of leaves or cloth, but they are sometimes used for display. They are used in masquerades, which may be performed publicly or secretly. Generally music and dance are part of the event. Although masks may represent male or female spirits, they are almost always worn by men. During the performance, a masked dancer is no longer himself, but the spirit the mask represents.

Face masks are only one type of mask. There are also helmet, or "bucket," masks,

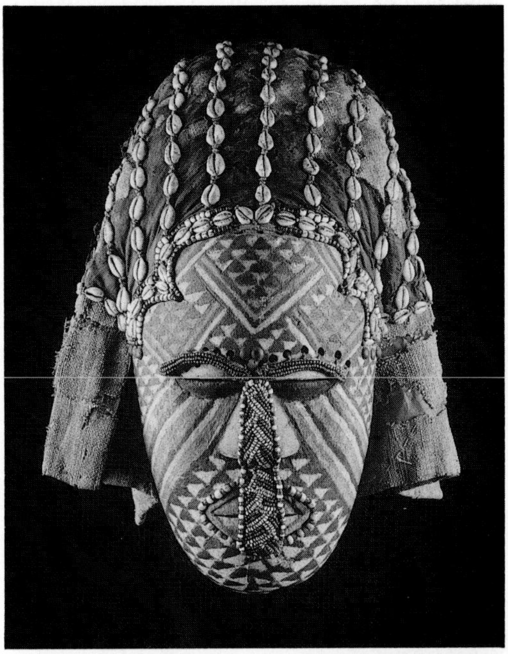

Masks serve a variety of important functions in African society, and distinctive styles of mask making have arisen in different regions. *Left:* A two-faced mask of painted wood was made by the Fang people of Gabon. *Above:* A painted-wood and fiber mask made by the Kuba people of the Democratic Republic of Congo is decorated with paint, beads, and shells. *Right:* A wooden mask made by the Songe people of the Democratic Republic of Congo is covered with a pattern of finely cut lines.

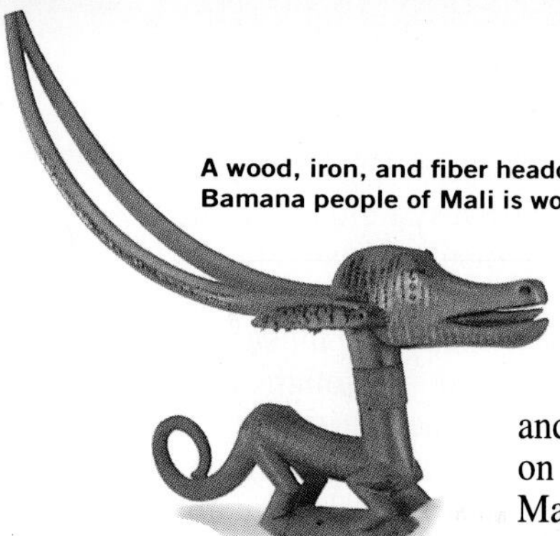

A wood, iron, and fiber headdress made by the Bamana people of Mali is worn on top of the head.

covering all or half of the head, and crest masks, worn on top of the head. Masks are made from a variety of materials. They may be carved of wood and painted with pigments made from plants or minerals. They may be decorated with animal skins, feathers, or beads. Artists also make masks out of paint fibers, tree bark, metal, or other materials.

DECORATIVE ARTS

Goldwork

For centuries, African goldsmiths have used different techniques to create gold objects. They can cast solid forms, hammer gold into shapes, or press thin pieces of gold (gold leaf) onto ready-made objects.

Goldwork prevailed in areas of Africa where gold was mined and used for trade. Gold mines were located in the modern nations of Senegal, Mali, Ivory Coast, and Ghana. Ghana was so famous for its gold that it was once called the Gold Coast. A rare and expensive material, gold was used as currency and worn by kings and important religious and political officials. It was also used to make jewelry and other body ornaments, as well as to decorate weapons.

The Akan people of Ivory Coast and Ghana used metal counterweights to weigh gold dust, which was the local currency from the 1400's to the mid-1800's. Called goldweights, the counterweights were actually miniature sculptures made of cast bronze or brass. They depict animals, plants, human beings, objects, and scenes from everyday life.

Jewelry

Men, women, and children wear jewelry to decorate their bodies or as a badge of distinction. Jewelry includes a variety of objects: hair ornaments, necklaces, earrings, bracelets, rings, and anklets. Artists make jewelry from many different materials. These include gold, silver, brass, iron, and copper, carved ivory, and beads made of glass, amber, stone, or shells.

Textiles

Textiles are woven on looms by both men and women. Locally grown cotton, raffia palm, and a woody fiber called bast are the most commonly used fibers, but silk and wool are also woven.

Among the Kuba of the Democratic Republic of Congo, men and women work together to make cloth. First, men weave raffia into square or rectangular pieces. Next, the women embroider designs on the cloth with raffia thread. They can also create a cut-pile effect that resembles velvet. Although Africans commonly wear Western-style clothing, traditional apparel made from locally woven cloth is the proud national dress. Thus weaving remains a vital occupation in many parts of Africa.

Above: In gold-mining areas of western Africa, small weights such as this were used to weigh gold dust. *Right:* A carved ivory bracelet from the court of Benin.

The skill of African artisans can be seen in the beauty of everyday objects. *Far left:* A woven cotton rug from Sierra Leone has a geometric design. Textiles are woven by both men and women. *Left:* A terra cotta vessel from central Africa. Most African pottery is made by women.

Textile artists create patterns on textiles using various techniques, including weaving, dyeing, stamping, painting, embroidery, and appliqué. Patterns may be plain or extremely intricate, consisting of geometric forms or figures such as animals and birds. Materials such as metallic or glossy threads may be incorporated to enhance the design. Natural or imported dyes are used to color the cloth.

Pottery

Pottery is usually crafted by women, who have made vessels in different sizes and shapes for cooking, storing, and serving food and drink since time beyond memory. The smooth, symmetrical vessels are hand-formed; the mechanical potter's wheel has been introduced only recently.

Potters create designs on the surface of the vessel by burnishing it with a smooth pebble, by cutting lines in with a blade, or by making impressions with combs and other objects. The surface may also be decorated with slip, a thin wash of clay, in a different color than the clay of the vessel. The vessels are fired in the open and may be dipped in a vegetable solution to seal them. Because they are fired at low temperatures, African vessels made by traditional methods do not shatter when used over an open fire.

Some vessels are used for religious rituals or for display as works of art. Such vessels are decorated with modeled figures and are usually made by especially skilled potters.

Basketry

Like pottery and weaving, basketry is a very old craft that is practiced by both men and women. Baskets are essential household objects, used for storage, for preparing or serving food, and for carrying objects.

The techniques and materials used to make baskets are determined by how the basket will be used. There are three basic techniques: coiling, twining, and plaiting (braiding). Vegetable fibers, such as grasses and raffia, are the main materials used. Leather, wood, or other materials may be added for both decoration and strengthening.

▶PAINTING

Although easel painting was introduced only at the beginning of the 1900's, Africans have always painted. The most ancient evidence is in the prehistoric San rock paintings in southern Africa. In Christian Ethiopia, artists illustrated Bible stories in books, on scrolls, and later on canvas.

African artists have always used paint to decorate surfaces. People painted their bodies when they participated in religious or social rituals and ceremonies, or simply to make themselves more attractive. They have traditionally painted the internal and external walls of their houses and places of worship. Sculpted figures and masks were also painted.

Until European paints were introduced, artists obtained their colors from natural sources, including clay, plant leaves and roots, stones, and minerals.

ARCHITECTURE

A wide range of architectural forms can be found in Africa. The simplest houses are the beehive-shaped houses of the Pygmies of central Africa. The frames of such houses are constructed with flexible branches that are covered with large, fresh leaves. This type of temporary housing suits the Pygmies' nomadic way of life. Agricultural people, in contrast, require sturdy, permanent houses.

Houses may be built with thick mud walls or with sturdy bamboo frames. Roofs may be thatched or covered with corrugated metal. The spacious Islamic mosques in Mali are perhaps the most dramatic example of mud architecture. The royal palaces of the Cameroon grassfields, some of which reach heights of more than 25 feet, are outstanding examples of bamboo-frame structures.

The most noteworthy stone architecture is the complex of buildings constructed during the 1100's to the 1400's at the ancient city of Great Zimbabwe in southern Africa. It is remarkable because of its great size and because the stone walls were assembled without mortar.

Important buildings are ornamented with carved and painted doors, door frames, and posts to support the veranda roofs. Kings and other sponsors of elaborate architecture often brought specially skilled sculptors from great distances to work for them.

A wide variety of architecture can be found in Africa. The Ndebele people of southern Africa have traditionally painted the clay walls of their houses with striking geometric designs. Inside walls may also be decorated with painted designs.

CONTEMPORARY TRENDS

The traditional art of Africa has had a great impact on modern art. In the early 1900's, European artists came into increased contact with the art of Africa. Artists such as Pablo Picasso and Henri Matisse incorporated elements of African art into their works.

Contemporary Africans create art in a variety of styles. In some societies, traditional religion and social practices have prevailed (usually with modern modifications), and there is a need for sculptors to create masks for initiations and sculptures for shrines, much as their predecessors did. However, they may use modern innovations such as imported paints. Sign painters, graphic artists, photographers, and textile and fashion designers also are part of the contemporary visual art scene.

Some artists are like their counterparts in Europe and America. They are self-taught or trained at universities and art schools. They display their art at exhibitions in art galleries and museums at home and abroad, and have local and foreign patrons. The content of their art may be African or not; it may be realistic or non-representational—the choice is theirs. The African art that caused a revolution in Western art early in the 1900's continues to inspire artists all over the world, including those born in Africa.

ROSLYN WALKER
Curator, National Museum of African Art

Storytellers play a key role in traditional African society. The stories they perform dramatize important truths, teach moral lessons, and transmit the history of the community. For many years, these stories were not written down but were passed on from one generation to the next by word of mouth. This oral tradition is a vital part of African literature.

AFRICA, LITERATURE OF

This article concerns both the oral traditions and the written literature of the peoples of Africa. While literature is generally considered to be a written body of work, it can also be defined more broadly. This fact is of special significance when discussing the nonwritten oral tradition by which Africans transmit history, culture, and duty from one generation to the next.

THE ORAL TRADITION (ORATURE)

In many parts of Africa, the spoken word is considered to be much more powerful than the written word. For centuries, a great deal of the traditional literature of Africa was not written down. It was performed, and passed on by word of mouth. That is why an African philosopher once said, "Whenever an old man dies, it is as though a library had been burned to the ground."

(It should be noted, however, that not all of Africa's literature was of the oral tradition alone. Throughout the many dynasties and civilizations along the Nile River, written literature flourished for centuries and continues to be written in Ethiopia today.)

In recent years, a major debate has taken place among scholars of African literature as to whether the term "literature" should be used to define the oral tradition. The term **orature** emerged from the debate, giving the spoken tradition its own name. African orature serves an important social, religious, and educational purpose. The truths by which the people have always lived are dramatized, providing valuable lessons for social behavior.

The performer or storyteller relies on common experience and shared tradition. As he tells the story to his audience, he also acts out the narrative by means of gestures, facial expressions, body movement, mime, voice modulation, song, and dance. The members of the audience understand according to their ages and social circumstances. A story may mean one thing to the teller, another to the adults, and still another to the children. Everyone learns something from the performance. The good storyteller makes certain that learning takes place by punctuating his performance with proverbs that underscore the social value of the story.

In Africa the spoken word is an art and a celebration of life, to be shared by all who live in the community. Like life, this art constantly changes. When a story is repeated, it will be different because it will have been adapted to the changes in society. The ancestral wisdom, however, is not lost in the changed version. It, too, will have been adapted to the circumstances of the changed times. The actively participating audience, joining in singing and clapping, will be different, too. Each listener will be older and wiser than the last time. In this way, the past and the present remain harmoniously linked in a balanced expression of culture and duty.

Although most people in African society are capable of storytelling, not everyone becomes an expert performer in public. Those who do must be specially trained in the art of eloquence and must learn to sing and play one or more musical instruments because of the importance of music to the oral tradition.

FORMS OF THE ORAL TRADITION

Although there are many different forms of orature in Africa, they all share certain themes. Universal traits of human behavior—honesty and dishonesty, charity and greed, bravery and cowardice, wisdom and foolishness—are exposed and examined. The main forms of orature are proverbs, riddles, folktales, poetry, and epics.

Proverbs and Riddles. Proverbs are extremely popular and are used in almost every kind of situation. They are short and witty and are treasured by Africans for the traditional wisdom and universal truths contained in them.

Riddles are commonly used to set the mood for performances and are especially popular with children, who are encouraged to use them to sharpen their wits. Like proverbs, riddles are usually short. Their language is poetic and indirect, relying on metaphor (a way of suggesting a likeness between two objects or ideas) as well as on subtleties of sound, rhythm, and tone. Some examples of African proverbs and riddles are given below.

Proverbs

Sierra Leone: If you climb up a tree, you must climb down the same tree.

Ghana: Only when you have crossed the river can you say the crocodile has a lump on his snout.

Ashanti: The ruin of a nation begins in the homes of its people.

Ethiopia: A fool and water go the way they are diverted.

Riddles

What talks a lot when going, but is silent when coming back? Answer: water gourds. Empty gourds rattle together—"talk"—on the way to be filled. Full gourds do not rattle.

What darts about all day and rests behind a gate of straw at night? Answer: the eye. The straw refers to the eyelashes.

Folktales. Short oral narratives commonly referred to as folktales are told in nearly all societies in Africa. They are used to teach moral lessons, expose trickery, promote heroic behavior, and tell about how or why things came to be. Or they may present a dilemma, challenging the listener to make a choice between two or more equally deserving arguments. Folktales can be purely fictional, or they can be based on real events of the past.

The main characters in fictional folktales are usually **tricksters**—small and normally weak characters endowed with cleverness, cunning, and resourcefulness, which they use to outwit their adversaries. Because they are always motivated by greed and selfishness, tricksters sometimes become the victims of their own excesses.

Trickster characters are usually animals but are sometimes human or part human. Gods may also be used as trickster characters. For example, among the Yoruba people of Nigeria, the god Elegba is the trickster. In Sudan, the clever hare is the subject of these stories. Anansi the spider is the greedy trickster from Ghana, Liberia, and Sierra Leone. In Nigeria and Cameroon, the tortoise is the mischievous hero. The Ethiopian tricksters are Totta the monkey and Koora the crow.

Some of the trickster characters were brought to the Americas by Africans. Anansi stories are still popular in Jamaica, Belize, and Suriname, and the clever hare has become Brer Rabbit in the United States.

Poetry. Poetry is one of the oldest, most highly developed, and most widespread of African oral traditions. It has many forms and is used for a variety of purposes—for religious and sacred practices as well as for such secular (nonreligious) events as birth and marriage celebrations. There is also lyric poetry, political poetry, satirical poetry, and drum poetry.

The practice of poetry requires formal training in the language, history, culture, and music of the society. Performers of poetry are usually identified with a specific social group. In Mali, these performers are called *djeli*; in eastern Democratic Republic of Congo, they are called *karisi*. The Zulu of South Africa call them *imbongi*. The bards, or heroic singers, of Cameroon and Gabon bear the same name as the instrument they play and the type of tale they recite: *mvet*. In Ethiopia, storytellers are called *amina*.

Epics. The epic, a major part of Africa's oral tradition, is found mainly in western and central Africa and, to a lesser extent, in eastern and southern Africa. An epic is a long poem that tells about the fantastic deeds of a legendary hero. Often it weaves the ideals and traditions of a people into the story. It is usually narrated to a musical accompaniment.

Sundiata is the national epic of the Malinke people of Mali. It honors the founder of the Mali empire. *Lianja* tells the fabulous story of the epic hero of the Mongo people of the Democratic Republic of Congo. Liyongo, the spear lord, gives his name to an epic sung in the languages of eastern and central Africa. These are only three of the many epics of Africa.

The famous storyteller (*djeli*, or griot) of Mali, *Djeli* Mamoudou Kouyate, describes his position and role in society just before recounting the great *Sundiata* epic:

I am a griot. It is I, *Djeli* Mamoudou Kouyate, son of Bintu Kouyate and *Djeli* Kedian Kouyate, master in the art of eloquence. Since time immemorial the Kouyates have been in the service of the Keita princes of Mali; we are vessels of speech, we are the repositories which harbour secrets many centuries old. The art of eloquence has no secrets for us; without us the names of kings would vanish into oblivion, we are the memory of mankind. I teach kings the history of their ancestors so that the lives of the ancients might serve them as an example, for the world is old, but the future springs from the past. My word is pure and free of all untruth; it is the word of my father; it is the word of my father's father. . . .

AFRICAN LITERATURE IN EUROPEAN LANGUAGES

During the colonial period, beginning in the 1700's, Europeans introduced their own written languages as tools of power, education, and government. Different peoples with different languages and cultures were grouped together in the various colonial territories. When these territories became independent, choosing one official African language proved difficult. Thus most of the new African states retained the language of their former colonizers as their official language.

The written translation of orature into these foreign languages was natural and inevitable. And as it gains recognition and popularity, orature is being written and translated into more of the major languages of the world. This rapid shift from the oral to the written tradition carries with it the danger that young Africans may choose not to become performers of orature. The risk of losing the tradition, under these circumstances, is quite real.

Learning to write the European languages also produced a new literature: short stories, poems, and novels that were never meant to be recited and plays that were meant to be performed on a stage rather than in a traditional African setting.

Some of these literary forms have been explored by African writers in their own languages. But those who write in English, French, or Portuguese can expect to have more readers. For this reason most recent African literature has been written in these languages. Ethiopia is an exception; written literature in the Ge'ez script has been practiced there for centuries, together with an oral tradition. An example is the epic story of Solomon and Mequeda, Queen of Sheba, which has also been translated into European languages.

African writing in French developed primarily in the regions of western and central Africa once occupied by the French. African literature in English comes from countries in eastern, western, and southern Africa where, for a time, English-speaking people ruled. Portuguese is used in Mozambique and Angola, former colonies of Portugal.

The Negritude Movement. Beginning in the 1930's, some African writers writing in French launched a literary movement known as negritude. Aimé Césaire, a West Indian from the island of Martinique, was the first to use the word. Césaire had been influenced by the African American literary movement of the 1920's known as the Harlem Renaissance. In his greatest poem, *Return to My Native Land* (1939), he defined negritude as a celebration of blackness.

Césaire's friend Léopold Sédar Senghor became the president of Senegal and one of the major writers of his generation. Senghor defined negritude as the cultural heritage, values, and spirit of black African civilization.

The negritude movement also expressed anger. It attacked the white world for racism, for concern with wealth and material things, and for pretending one thing but being another. This anger may be seen in the novels of Ferdinand Oyono from Cameroon, especially in *Houseboy*, the story of an African servant in a white household.

Other writers of the negritude movement include poet Tchicaya U Tam'si of the Congo and novelist Camara Laye of Guinea.

Other Views. Wole Soyinka, a Nobel Prize-winning Nigerian playwright, expressed a different view. Soyinka wrote *A Dance of the Forests* for the celebration of Nigerian independence in 1960. This play is a fantasy in which traditional gods and spirits call up a group of ancestors to accuse them of participating in the European slave trade. "Do not romanticize old Africa," the play is saying.

This no-nonsense attitude is shared by Ezekiel Mphahlele, a South African writer, and by most Africans writing in English. To them, Senghor's idea of traditional African life is unrealistic.

The Nigerian novelist Chinua Achebe has recorded the strife within the traditional African community. He says it is useless to deny social change; the problem is how to meet it. His novels *Things Fall Apart* (1958) and *Arrow of God* (1964) ask whether modern Nigerian leaders can develop the strength of character of certain old chiefs and priests who resisted European ways.

The terrible experience under colonialism and the struggle for independence provided substantial material for African novelists and poets of the new literature. In South Africa, in particular, the new literature played an extremely important role in expressing the Africans' feelings in their struggle against apartheid. But censorship and persecution forced many black writers, such as the poet Dennis Brutus, to flee the country.

White South African writers, too, voiced their objections to apartheid. Alan Paton wrote about racial conflict in *Cry, the Beloved Country* (1948) and other novels. Athol Fugard dramatized the plight of black South Africans in many plays, notably *The Blood Knot* (1961), *A Lesson from Aloes* (1978), and *The Road to Mecca* (1984). The novels and short stories of Nadine Gordimer, winner of the 1991 Nobel Prize for literature, explore these same social and political themes.

Women in African Literature. Traditionally, the position of women in orature was secondary to that of men. The early stages of the new African literature also tended to be male-dominated. Recently, however, many women novelists and poets, as well as feminist scholars and literary critics, have emerged. Notable women writers include Ama Ata Aidoo of Ghana, Buchi Emecheta of Nigeria, Martha Mvungi of Tanzania, Grace Ogot of Kenya, Bessie Head of South Africa, and Kebedech Tekleab of Ethiopia.

FILM

Filmmaking came to Africa after independence in the 1960's. Film, more than written literature, was ideally suited to accommodate the performance aspects of orature. As filmmaking in Africa gained momentum, so did the search for stories suitable for film. Both filmmakers and writers soon turned to the rich oral tradition for their material. As a result, many of the leading African films are patterned after the traditional epics and other forms of orature.

For these reasons, and because they are seen by a great number of people, African films play an important role in keeping the oral tradition alive in modern times.

The number of African filmmakers is growing steadily, along with that of novelists, poets, and playwrights. The work of all these artists constitutes a major contribution to the richness of world literature. African orature and modern literature tell about a world many people of the West have never visited, or even imagined correctly. It is a world that is well worth getting to know.

Abiyi R. Ford
School of Communications
Howard University

The traditional music of Africa is celebrated for its richness and diversity. ***Clockwise from upper left:*** Percussion instruments such as drums and xylophones are the most common African instruments. However, traditional instruments also include wind instruments such as this wooden horn as well as a variety of stringed instruments.

AFRICA, MUSIC OF

Africans perform and listen to all types of music—popular, classical, and traditional. Traditional music has its roots in the soil of Africa and is extremely diverse: There are more than 700 different languages and ethnic groups in Africa, and each is associated with a particular kind of music.

At one time, scholars assumed that all African music was the same and that it rarely changed. We now know that traditional African music has been changing for centuries. Many changes occurred even before Europeans and other outsiders visited Africa. When people come in contact with each other, through trade, war, or other circumstances, musical ideas are often exchanged. For example, the Asante people of Ghana in western Africa adopted the *donno*, a type of talking drum, from people who lived north of them.

The physical environment, occupation, and social structure of the people also affect their music making. For example, the Khoisan people of southern Africa used to be nomadic—that is, they were constantly moving from place to place to hunt and gather foods. Clans of twenty to fifty people lived together as equals, with no political leaders. The Khoisan used few musical instruments; singing was their main form of music making. While the women and girls sang and clapped their hands, the men danced and played drums.

The music of the Baganda people of Uganda, on the other hand, developed in a very different way. In earlier times, their kingdom was one of the largest in eastern Africa. The king's court included several musicians, who played a variety of instruments—drums, trumpets, flutes, harps, lyres, drum-chimes, and xylophones—for the king's private enjoyment and for official activities. Other musicians performed at community events and ceremonies.

MUSIC IN AFRICAN LIFE

Africans perform music when they come together for leisure and recreation. They also use music at religious ceremonies, festivals, and work. Music plays an important role at birth, initiation, wedding, and funeral ceremonies. Songs performed at some events help people remember their history and customs.

In many parts of Africa, adults take their children to special camps for initiation ceremonies. There the elders teach the girls and boys what they need to know about adulthood. The girls learn lullabies as part of child-care training. The boys learn historical songs to teach them the customs of their society. Through music, children may also learn about numbers and language, as well as singing and dancing techniques.

Some musicians in Africa are specialists who receive formal training from a family member or a professional musician. But music is a vital part of everyday life for all Africans. Everyone participates in a performance by dancing, singing, handclapping, or playing a musical instrument. Mothers train their children when they are infants by rocking them to music and singing songs. Among the Fon people in western Africa, children who lose their first tooth have to sing a special song to commemorate the event. Children also learn music by playing games and telling stories.

In many African communities, musicians are admired and respected for the service they perform for the community. But some people believe musicians are lazy because they spend all their time making music. Also, through their music, musicians sometimes warn and criticize people about unacceptable behavior, and this can make them unpopular. However, most people believe that musicians play an important role in society.

The Talking Drum

Some of the most interesting African drums are known as talking drums because they imitate the tones of African languages. One type of talking drum is the hourglass pressure drum, such as the *dùndún* played by the Yoruba people of Nigeria. It consists of two drum heads connected by cords on an hourglass-shaped frame. The drum is held at the performer's side under the arm. When the cords are pressed by the arm, the drum heads are stretched and the pitch of the drum is raised. Changing the pressure on the cords changes the pitch of the sound produced when the drum head is struck.

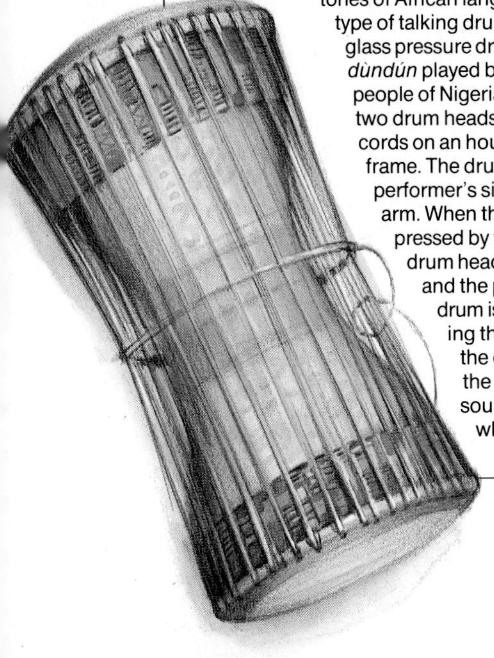

▶ INSTRUMENTS

Africans perform music on a wide variety of percussion, stringed, and wind instruments.

Percussion Instruments are the most common instruments in Africa. Societies that do not use drums may perform on rattles, bells, sticks, clappers, and stamping tubes.

Percussion instruments are mainly used for rhythm, but some also play melodies. For example, the xylophone has wooden keys of various sizes, which produce different tones when struck with a stick. The Chopi people of eastern Africa include as many as 13 xylophones in ensembles that also include drums, rattles, and whistles. While some of the xylophone musicians play the main melody, others play a supporting repetitive part.

Drums come in a variety of sizes and shapes. Some are small and held in the hand; others are large and are placed on the ground when played. To produce a sound, musicians strike the drum head with sticks, hands, or both. Sometimes the musician scrapes or rubs the drum head with a stick to produce a sound. The Akan-speaking people of Ghana play a drum called *etwie* in honor of their king. The drum is made of wood and covered with the skin of a leopard. When the drum head is rubbed with a stick, the sound that is produced imitates the sound of the leopard. By reproducing the sound of a feared and powerful animal, *etwie* music symbolizes and praises the might and majesty of the king.

Stringed Instruments include musical bows, harps, zithers, lyres, and lutes. The musical bow is the most common stringed instrument in Africa. It has only one string, which is plucked or struck. Harps and zithers are common in eastern and central Africa; eastern Africa is also the primary location for lyres. The lute is found in societies influenced by Arab culture. Lutes can be bowed like a fiddle or plucked like a banjo. The *kora*, a 21-string harp lute, is prominent among the Mandinka people. The *kora* looks like a lute but is played like a harp.

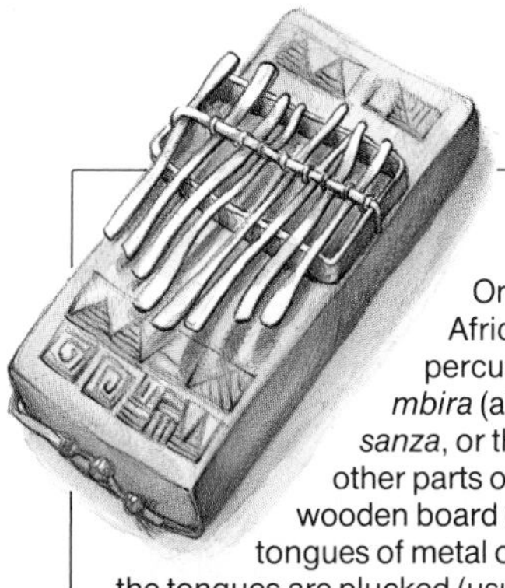

The Mbira

One of the most distinctive African instruments is a small percussion instrument called the *mbira* (also known as the *kalimba*, *sanza*, or thumb piano). Rarely found in other parts of the world, it consists of a wooden board or box over which several tongues of metal or bamboo are fastened. When the tongues are plucked (usually with the thumbs), soft sounds are produced. The sound can be modified by wrapping wire around the tongues to produce a buzzing effect, or by attaching a hollow gourd to make the sound resonate (vibrate and grow louder). Many African musicians play the *mbira* as a solo instrument or to accompany singing. Several *mbira* can also be played together in an ensemble, with singing and rattle accompaniment.

Wind Instruments include flutes, reed pipes, horns, and trumpets. The flute is the most widespread. Flutes can be made of wood, bamboo, clay, or other materials and can have as many as seven finger holes. They are played vertically or horizonally. The reed pipe, like the lute, is located in areas influenced by Arab culture. Horns and trumpets are made of animal horns and tusks, wood, gourd, or bamboo and can be either end-blown or side-blown.

▸ CHARACTERISTICS

Singing is the most characteristic way of performing African music. Although people sing solos, singing in a group is more common. Often, one person leads a song and a group of singers responds by repeating the same theme or a variation. This arrangement is sometimes called call and response.

Language or speech serves as the basis for most African melodies and rhythms. Many African languages are **tone languages**, meaning that the pitch on which a word or a syllable is spoken determines its meaning. The high and low sounds of the rhythms played on African talking drums correspond closely to speech. In earlier times, such "talking" instruments informed African people about current events.

In an African performance, music, dance, song, and drama are all important. Although musicians include a variety of musical sounds in their ensembles, percussion is essential. The Ewe people of Ghana include singing, handclapping, rattles, bells, and four or five drums in their ensembles. The bell players perform a repetitive rhythm that serves as the base for all other parts. Some of the drummers and other musicians perform a different repetitive pattern. The leader of the group, playing the largest drum or drums, does not play a repetitive rhythm but **improvises**—spontaneously creates different but related music. When everyone performs the various rhythms and melodies together, this is called **polyphony**. African music is interesting not because of the individual parts that each person plays. Rather, Africans enjoy hearing how the parts interrelate and communicate with each other.

▸ INFLUENCES

Much of today's popular music contains African elements. This is because African Americans have greatly influenced music throughout the world. When Europeans took Africans as slaves to the Americas, Africans remembered much about the music they performed in Africa. Those in the West Indies and various parts of Central and South America continued to worship African gods and play African instruments.

In the United States, most slaves could not openly practice their African traditions. Slaveowners outlawed drums and other loud instruments when they discovered that slaves could use them to communicate. Instead of playing drums, slaves patted different parts of the body or used handclapping or foot-stomping to make music. When they sang songs, they performed them differently from European Americans. They used a different vocal quality and added bends and slurs to the melody. Also, they created their own songs and styles of music. Spirituals, blues, jazz, gospel, and other forms of popular music come from the integration of African and European elements.

Music from the United States, Europe, and Asia has influenced musicians in modern Africa. Highlife, juju, and soukous are a few of the new forms of popular music that one can hear in dance halls and nightclubs in Africa. Musicians now create new hymns for the church. Also, Africans have begun to compose their own style of classical music. Along with traditional music, each of these types of music plays an important role among the people who live in various cities, towns, and villages throughout Africa.

JACQUELINE COGDELL DJEDJE
University of California, Los Angeles

From left to right: Kathy E. Morris Wilkerson, New Orleans' first female firefighter. NBA All-Star Kevin Johnson takes time out to play with a group of young friends. Dr. James W. Mitchell, Director of Analytical Chemistry at AT&T Bell Laboratories. Farmworkers pick peppers near Atchafalaya, Louisiana.

AFRICAN AMERICANS

African Americans are citizens of the United States who trace at least part of their ancestry to the continent of Africa. Although some are recent immigrants, most are descended from Africans who were brought in slavery to the American colonies and states between the years 1619 and 1808. Today, African Americans number about 34.6 million, or 12.3 percent of the total United States population. The largest communities reside in the states in the Deep South, followed by those in the Northeast, Midwest, and West.

Over the centuries, African Americans have been known by a succession of names. Many of these name changes reflected the African Americans' desire to establish a distinctive identity and to express pride in their racial heritage. Until the early 1800's, the preferred name was African. Later the terms black, colored, and Negro (the Spanish word for "black") came into use. After the 1960's, the terms Negro and colored were largely abandoned in favor of black and Afro-American. Since the late 1980's, the term African American has been preferred.

The African heritage in North America, which dates as far back as any other except Native American, has greatly influenced the American culture through the centuries. African roots are evident in the distinctive African American styles of clothing and adornment, in cooking, and in modern dance. They also are found in African American literature and in orature, or oral history, passed down through the generations, that tell the stories of the African American experience.

Perhaps the strongest influence, however, is found in music, an art form that has always been central to the daily lives of most Africans. African roots can be found in nearly every American music form, from the early spirituals and the gospel singing of religious celebration to rhythm and blues, soul, rock and roll, rap, and the most uniquely American music form of all—jazz.

Today, in music as well as all other forms of mass popular culture, African Americans are more influential than ever. The better part of black creative expression has been directed toward widening the nation's perceptions and understanding of African Americans and their values.

▶ OVERVIEW

For three hundred years, European colonists brought Africans to the New World as slaves

to clear vast tracts of land for the cultivation of sugar, rice, cotton, and tobacco. The black community in what is now the United States began in 1619 at Jamestown, Virginia, where 20 Africans were traded for water and supplies by Dutch seamen on their way from New York to Suriname, South America. Historians are divided on the issue of whether or not these particular immigrants were slaves or indentured servants (people who were contracted to work for a specific period of time in exchange for voyage costs, food, and lodging). One thing is certain: At least 1 million Africans became unwilling travelers to North America before the United States outlawed the importation of slaves in 1808.

Much of African American history is based on the blacks' struggle to achieve the equality and unalienable rights promised by the founders of a democratic government. In 1776, Thomas Jefferson wrote in the Declaration of Independence, "We hold these truths to be self-evident, that all men are created equal, that they are endowed by their Creator with certain unalienable Rights, that among these are Life, Liberty, and the pursuit of Happiness." Frederick Douglass, an ex-slave and the most prominent black abolitionist of the mid-1800's, challenged this notion of democracy when he declared to the white community, "The rich inheritance of justice, liberty, prosperity, and independence, bequeathed by your fathers, is shared by you, not by me."

A strong antislavery movement helped set the stage for the United States Civil War (1861–65) between the free states in the North and the slave states in the South. Emancipation, or freedom, for the slaves was assured in 1865 by the 13th Amendment to the U.S. Constitution after the North defeated the South. But it was not until the ratification of the 14th Amendment (1868) that African Americans were declared citizens in the land of their birth. The 15th Amendment (1870) assured African American men their right to vote.

Slavery had encouraged a false assumption that blacks were inferior to whites. Despite emancipation, discrimination against blacks continued to deprive African Americans of their legal rights well into the 1900's. Fundamental democratic privileges, such as the right to vote, were routinely denied them, and they were set apart from mainstream society by laws designed to keep the races socially separate and politically unequal. Their frustrations finally erupted in a civil rights movement in the 1950's and 1960's, when African Americans began demanding their proper and equal place in society.

The modern-day historian John Hope Franklin has noted, "With an optimism born in hope when only despair was in view," African Americans struggled for equal status "in the land that [African American author] James Weldon Johnson reminded them was theirs by right of birth and by right of toil."

AFRICAN AMERICAN FIRSTS

1624 William Tucker, born in Jamestown, Virginia, is believed to have been the first African American born in what is now the United States.

1770 Crispus Attucks, an American patriot, was killed by British troops in the Boston Massacre. He was the first-known African American to die in the American revolutionary movement.

1821 Thomas L. Jennings, a New York tailor, was the first black to receive a U.S. patent, for inventing a dry-cleaning process.

1827 *Freedom's Journal*, the first African American newspaper, was published by coeditors John B. Russwurm and Charles B. Ray, in New York City.

1842 Lenox Remond of Boston was hired by the American Anti-Slavery Society as the first of many black professional anti-slavery lecturers.

1853 *Clotel: A Tale of the Southern States*, written by William Wells Brown, was the first-known novel written by an African American.

1865 John S. Rock became the first African American allowed to practice law in the U.S. Supreme Court.

1868 John Willis Menard, the first African American elected to the U.S. Congress, was not permitted to take his seat in the U.S. House of Representatives.

1870 Hiram Rhoades Revels became the first African American to serve in the U.S. Senate; Joseph Hayne Rainey was the first to win election and be seated in the U.S. House of Representatives.

1872 Pinckney Benton Stewart Pinchback, the lieutenant governor of Louisiana, became the first African American elevated to the position of governor.

1893 Dr. Daniel Hale Williams performed the world's first successful heart operation.

1903 Maggie Walker founded the St. Luke Penny Thrift Savings Bank in Richmond, Va., becoming the first African American woman to head a bank.

1940 Benjamin O. Davis, Sr., became the first black brigadier general in the U.S. Army; Hattie McDaniel became the first African American to win an Academy Award for her supporting role in *Gone With the Wind*.

1947 Jackie Robinson of the Brooklyn Dodgers was the first African American to join a major league baseball team.

1950 Gwendolyn Brooks became the first African American to win a Pulitzer Prize, for her volume of poetry *Annie Allen*; Ralph Bunche became the first African American to win the Nobel Peace Prize.

1955 Marian Anderson became the first African American soloist to perform with the Metropolitan Opera in New York City.

1957 Althea Gibson became the first African American tennis player to win a singles championship at Wimbledon, in England.

1963 Sidney Poitier became the first African American to win the Academy Award for best actor.

1966 Constance Baker Motley became the first African American woman to serve as a federal judge; Robert C. Weaver became the first African American appointed to a cabinet position, as secretary of the Department of Housing and Urban Development; Edward W. Brooke, a Republican from Massachusetts, became the first African American elected to the U.S. Senate since the Reconstruction period.

1967 Thurgood Marshall became the first African American appointed to the U.S. Supreme Court; Carl Stokes, a Democrat, was elected mayor of Cleveland, the first African American to govern a major city.

1968 Shirley Chisholm, a Democrat from New York, became the first African American woman elected to the U.S. House of Representatives.

1975 Daniel "Chappie" James became the first African American four-star general (in the U.S. Air Force); Virginia Hamilton became the first African American to win a Newbery Medal, for her novel *M.C. Higgins, the Great* (1974).

1977 Patricia R. Harris became the first African American woman appointed to a president's cabinet, as secretary of Housing and Urban Development.

1983 Guion S. Bluford, Jr., became the first African American astronaut to make a space flight.

1989 The Reverend Barbara L. Harris, an African American Episcopalian priest, became the first female bishop consecrated by the worldwide Anglican community.

1990 L. Douglas Wilder, a Democrat, became the first African American elected governor of a state (Virginia).

1992 Mae C. Jemison, M.D., became the first African American woman to make a space flight; Carole Moseley Braun, a Democrat from Illinois, became the first African American woman elected to the U.S. Senate.

1993 Toni Morrison became the first African American to win the Nobel Prize for literature.

2001 General Colin L. Powell was the first African American named secretary of state, the nation's highest cabinet office.

2002 Halle Berry was the first African American to win the Academy Award for best actress.

Many African American families are active members of their churches. The church has long been a source of comfort, strength, and leadership in black communities.

THE ROLE OF THE CHURCH

When Africans were first brought to America, they were forced to abandon their native religions and were taught Christianity. Many embraced the new faith, finding spiritual comfort and hope. In the late 1700's, black churches started to form, and many became centers of African American community life. Their music—spirituals and rousing gospel songs—has since become part of the American musical tradition.

Many black churches led the fight against discrimination, and throughout their history, African Americans have often chosen their leaders from the ranks of the church.

In the 1960's the Nation of Islam challenged the black churches, claiming that Islam is the true religion of African peoples. But most worshipers have remained with the Christian churches, which continue to play an important role in many African American communities.

THE AFRICAN PAST

From the ancient civilization of Egypt of 3000 B.C. to the fall of Timbuktu in the A.D. 1600's, the African continent was the site of a succession of great inland societies, whose names still carry hints of mystery and grandeur—Meroe, Napata, Axum, and Kush. In western Africa along the Niger River, three massive societies rose and fell: ancient Ghana (A.D. 800–1200); Melle (or Mali) (1000–1400); and Songhai (1200–1600). Through trade, commerce, and warfare, these societies grew from small village kingdoms into complex empires, ruled by great kings and covering thousands of square miles. No coastal African society ever matched these inland empires in terms of size, governmental organization, and military power.

In the 1500's, gold and slaves were traded out of Timbuktu, the legendary city of Africa's Songhai Empire.

Long before Europeans appeared on Africa's Atlantic coast, traditional African societies had traded people for goods. African communities recognized ownership claims to people not belonging to their family or clan. In traditional African exchange systems, claims to the rights of individual slaves were bought and sold along with tangible goods, such as gold and ivory.

The hardships endured by slaves in Africa were softened somewhat by the cultural traditions they shared with their African slaveholders, such as religion and respect for ancestors. By contrast, the European treatment of enslaved Africans from the late 1400's on was influenced by myths of black inferiority and the promise of wealth that could be gained by using slave labor. Few Europeans had any interest in or knowledge of Africa's true history or greatness.

PLANTATION BONDAGE ERA (1619–1865)

Over a period of about 350 years, from the early 1500's to the mid-1800's, approximately 12 million Africans were forcibly transported across the Atlantic Ocean to the Americas. Of this number, about 8 percent, or approximately 1 million, were brought to North America (after 1619), with the rest going to the islands of the Caribbean and the shores of Central and South America. Collected by European slave traders working out of western Africa, millions of Africans were taken in exchange for guns, iron, beads, silks, brocades, and other cloths, knives, basins, mirrors, and the like. They were then sold as slaves to colonial plantation owners in the Americas.

The Slave Trade

The business of trading goods for people, and then selling those people as slaves for a financial profit, was initiated and funded by European royalty and merchants. They fi-

This article traces the history of African Americans, from their African roots to the present day. For more information, refer to the following articles in the appropriate volumes in *The New Book of Knowledge*: ABOLITION MOVEMENT; AFRICA; AFRICA, ART AND ARCHITECTURE OF; AFRICA, LITERATURE OF; AFRICA, MUSIC OF; AMERICAN LITERATURE; CIVIL RIGHTS; CIVIL RIGHTS MOVEMENT; CIVIL WAR, UNITED STATES; COMPROMISE OF 1850; DRED SCOTT DECISION; EMANCIPATION PROCLAMATION; HYMNS (Spiritual and Other Folk Hymns); JAZZ; KANSAS-NEBRASKA ACT; LINCOLN, ABRAHAM (The Lincoln-Douglas Debates); MISSOURI COMPROMISE; RACISM; RECONSTRUCTION PERIOD; SEGREGATION; SLAVERY; SPINGARN MEDAL; UNDERGROUND RAILROAD; UNITED STATES, HISTORY OF THE; the history sections of individual state articles; and biographies and profiles of notable individuals.

1526–39 The first Africans arrived in the Americas in the company of Spanish and Portuguese explorers.

1539 Estevanico (Little Stephen), a Moroccan slave who had escaped his Spanish captors, led the first expedition of explorers into the Southwest as far as present-day New Mexico and Arizona.

1565 Africans helped establish North America's oldest European settlement, St. Augustine, Florida.

1619 North America's first slaves were brought to Jamestown, Virginia.

1688 The first formal protest against slavery was made in Germantown, Pennsylvania.

1775–81 At least 5,000 blacks fought in the Revolutionary War, notably at the battles of Bunker Hill, Lexington, Brandywine, White Plains, Concord, and Saratoga. Two of them, Prince Whipple and Oliver Cromwell, crossed the Delaware River with George Washington on Christmas Day, 1776.

From 1619 to 1808, about 1 million black Africans were sold into slavery and shipped across the Atlantic Ocean to what is now the United States.

nanced the trading companies that outfitted ships and their crews and maintained agents on both sides of the Atlantic Ocean.

Over the years, thousands of European ships crisscrossed the Atlantic on this triangular, or three-legged, business route between Europe, Africa, and the Americas. On the journey's second leg, known as the Middle Passage, each ship carried between 200 and 300 Africans to America. During a journey lasting four to six months, the slaves traveled most of the way lying down because there was no room for standing or sitting. They were branded with hot irons, separated by gender, and fed a diet of beans, yams, and corn mush. Some were under 10 years of age. The tightly packed conditions promoted contagious diseases that killed an estimated 20 percent of the blacks as well as many of the white crew members. From the diaries of Africa-based trading company agents, scholars calculate that an additional 2 to 4 percent of the slaves died before they ever reached the ships. These losses increased the value of the slaves who survived the rigorous crossing.

On arrival in the colonies, slaves were evaluated for their strength and potential work capabilities and put up for sale on the auction block. Most slaves in North America were bought by well-to-do plantation owners living in the Southern colonies, with open areas suitable for commercial agriculture. About 10,000 planters made up the Southern ruling class, each owning 50 or more slaves. Virginia planters George Washington and Thomas Jefferson each held at least 250 slaves, even as they debated the morality of slavery.

Slave Life

Slaves engaged in three basic categories of work—domestic, mechanical, and agricultural. Domestic slaves worked around the slaveholders' homes, cooking, cleaning, and raising the white children. Other slaves were skilled artisans, trained as carpenters, millwrights, masons, tailors, and shoemakers. Most slaves, however, were engaged in some form of farming. Those who were skilled in crop production were more valuable than unskilled farm laborers, or "field hands." As such, they were treated differently, often having better food, clothing, and shelter.

The typical day for a slave began in a lineup for task or group assignments. Except for a short break for a midday meal, work continued until nightfall. Generally the slaves were not required to work on Saturday afternoons or on Sundays, except during certain stages of rice and sugarcane cultivation, when they were required to work 16 to 18 hours a day, seven days a week. If the taskmaster felt it necessary, slaves could be worked to the very limit of their strength.

Weekly food rations were a peck (eight dry quarts) of corn, three or four pounds of bacon

In 1816 the Reverend Richard Allen of Philadelphia was consecrated the first bishop of the African Methodist Episcopal (A.M.E.) Church, the first independent black religious denomination.

1777 Vermont became the first state to abolish slavery.

1787 The Free African Society was founded by Richard Allen and Absalom Jones in Philadelphia.

1817 James Forten presided over the first interstate convention of African Americans. More than 3,000 attended to protest a proposal by the American Colonization Society to deport free blacks to Africa.

1822 Denmark Vesey organized 6,000 slaves in South Carolina in a failed effort to overthrow slavery.

1826 The Massachusetts Colored General Association, established in Boston, became the nation's first African American political group.

1830 A national meeting of African American leaders in Philadelphia was the first time black leaders met to review the problems and status of black Americans.

or salt pork, and perhaps some yams and molasses. This was supplemented with vegetables and salad greens raised by the slaves themselves on patches of ground allowed them near their one-room cabins. Leisure time was enjoyed after the fall harvest season and during major holidays.

Although many slaves were not intentionally mistreated, most slaves lived in constant fear. At the word of any person in authority, a slave could be punished, physically abused, or even sold away from his or her family. Although some considerate buyers made an effort to keep family members together, often children were sold apart from their mothers, and husbands and wives were taken to separate plantations. This disregard for the slaves' emotional needs weakened the foundations of many black families. In spite of such inhumane treatment, there were relatively few slave uprisings in North America, perhaps because there were at least four times as many whites as blacks, and blacks generally did not have access to weapons.

Forced to be submissive and obedient by day, slaves created a different style of life for themselves at night. Between sundown and sunup, they tried to maintain normal family traditions and relationships. Many found comfort in religion, and community gatherings often were centered on religious celebration. They sang hymns and other religious songs called spirituals to lift their burdens and to express their suffering. Songs such as "Nobody Knows the Trouble I've Seen" and "Swing Low, Sweet Chariot" were among the first created in America.

Free Blacks

Not all of the blacks in antebellum (pre–Civil War) America were slaves. "Free blacks" lived and worked in major cities throughout the nation. The rights of free blacks, however, were strictly limited, especially in the South, where so-called Black Codes dictated their behavior. Free blacks were not allowed to express any kind of social or political viewpoint, nor were they allowed to socialize with whites or to carry weapons. Therefore, not surprisingly, black leadership became centered in the North, where blacks enjoyed a greater measure of freedom.

Although Northerners made up only 15 percent of the nation's free-black population, they set the standard for the black community's social and religious values. Free blacks financed neighborhood elementary schools in New York and many other Northern cities. Even in the slaveholding South, where "compulsory ignorance" laws prohibited black education, many blacks taught their children how to read and write during the time permitted for religious instruction. They treasured literacy, even though they were forced to hide it.

The Abolitionist Movement

In the 30 years prior to the outbreak of the Civil War in 1861, free blacks in the North played a major role in the struggle to abolish slavery in the United States. They founded organizations, such as the American Society of Free People of Color, to protest racial prejudice in the North as well as slavery in the South. Free-black churches raised money to support antislavery lecturers and news-

Frederick Douglass was the most famous black abolitionist of his day. In 1845 an antislavery song was published describing his escape from slavery.

1831 Nat Turner led an unsuccessful slave revolt in Southampton County, Virginia. He and many others were hanged for the deaths of more than 50 whites. The uprising led to the nation's first public debate over the morality of slavery.

1840–61 Harriet Tubman, working through the Underground Railroad, rescued more than 300 slaves from the South. She later became a spy and a nurse for the Union Army.

1850 Enactment of the Fugitive Slave Law caused many African Americans and others to flee to Canada to join the abolitionist movement against slavery in the United States.

1857 In the Dred Scott Decision, the U.S. Supreme Court held that slaves, and also free blacks, were not citizens of the United States and therefore had no rights protected by the Constitution.

This tinted photo of black Union soldiers (Company E, 4th U.S. Infantry) was taken at Fort Lincoln, District of Columbia, in 1865.

papers, such as the *North Star*, published by Frederick Douglass. The free-black communities of the North supported these publications to the limit of their resources and were the main sponsors of *The Liberator*, edited by the militant white abolitionist William Lloyd Garrison. Blacks also were instrumental in the efforts of the Underground Railroad, a secret society of people who helped thousands of slaves escape from bondage in the South.

As the abolitionist movement rapidly gained followers in the 1840's and 1850's, bitter arguments over states' rights and the existence of slavery pushed the nation ever closer to war. When the Civil War began in 1861, abolitionists prayed for a Northern victory of pro-Union forces that would bring emancipation, or freedom, to the slaves.

In 1863, immigrants in New York City rioted when the U.S. government tried to draft them into the Union Army. Unwilling to fight to free the slaves, they expressed their outrage by lynching blacks in the city streets.

The Civil War and Emancipation

During the course of the Civil War (1861–65), nearly 200,000 African Americans, both slave and free, volunteered to fight for the Union against the slaveholding Confederate states in the South. Black servicemen took part in nearly every major military engagement, although until 1864 they were paid less than white soldiers. They also built fortifications, handled provisions, and served as lookouts. Some also served as spies.

The promise of emancipation was fulfilled when the Union forces won the war in 1865. By the end of that year, the 13th Amendment was ratified, abolishing slavery in the United States. In 1868 the 14th Amendment extended full legal citizenship to African Americans, and in 1870 the 15th Amendment guaranteed voting rights to black men. A profound national social revolution was set in motion.

▶RURAL EMANCIPATION ERA (1865–1915)

Between 1865 and 1915, many Americans left their farms and moved to a town or city, where new jobs were opening up. About 90 percent of the African Americans remained within the eleven ex-Confederate Southern states where they had been raised and where their families had lived for generations.

The Evolution of Black Education

The "social reconstruction" of former slaves began with basic education, the success of which was by far the most dramatic evidence of their new legal freedom. Tens of thousands of ex-slaves, so long forbidden to learn to read and write, now displayed a passion for knowledge so powerful that, in the words of one observer, "it was as if an entire race was trying to go to school."

The nation's first real "teacher corps" consisted of several thousand Northern-born white women who went South to instruct black students, braving the taunts and threats of white

1861–65 Of the 200,000 blacks who served in the Union forces during the Civil War, 72% were from the slave and border states and 28% were from the Northern free states. Nearly 30,000 lost their lives; 21 received the Medal of Honor.

1863 President Abraham Lincoln's Emancipation Proclamation declared the freedom of any slave residing in a state in rebellion against the Union.

▼ The announcement of a military draft prompted Irish American attacks on blacks in New York City, leaving 74 people dead.

1865 The urgent need for food and first aid and other services prompted the federal government to establish the Bureau of Freedmen, Refugees, and Abandoned Lands (later called the Freedmen's Bureau) to assist the 4 million African Americans making the transition from slavery to freedom.

Southerners who feared that blacks would be "overeducated for their places." Within a decade, these teachers were replaced in the classrooms by many of their older black pupils. The faculties of the earliest black colleges and universities remained more white than black for a much longer period, due to the shortage of college-trained blacks.

In 1890 the Morrill Land Grant Act established 17 institutions of higher learning. These tax-supported A & I (Agricultural and Industrial) and A & M (Agricultural and Mechanical) colleges reflected the doctrine of industrial education of the sort promoted by the educator Booker T. Washington at his Tuskegee Institute in Alabama. Washington's theories directly conflicted with those of another prominent black scholar of the era, W. E. B. Du Bois, who believed that blacks should study the liberal arts. This historic debate was but one example of the emerging conflict within the black community over the proper focus of black education.

The post-emancipation educational experience produced a small but highly educated group of African Americans who supported at least a dozen black-issue-oriented newspapers. In 1910, Du Bois, at his own expense, launched *Crisis*, black America's first race-relations journal, which is still published today. These publications, financed by their readers, boldly explored race relations.

Political Advances

Prior to 1868, John M. Langston had been the only black to hold elective office anywhere in the United States. He had been a city councilman in Brownhelm, Ohio, in 1856. Then between 1868 and 1898, 22 African Americans were elected to the U.S. Congress, including two to the U.S. Senate. At the state and local levels, nearly a thousand gained public office. Many had gained political experience working in the antislavery campaigns.

In 1905, W. E. B. Du Bois, a scholar and early civil rights leader, founded the Niagara Movement, a forerunner of the NAACP, to fight discrimination.

Discrimination and Violence

After the war, during the period known as Reconstruction, blacks in the South were protected by federal troops who occupied the former Confederate states. But when those troops were withdrawn in 1877, blacks found themselves at the mercy of the Ku Klux Klan and similar white-supremacist groups. Violence against blacks became so commonplace that approximately 100,000 fled from the Carolinas, Tennessee, Alabama, and Mississippi to the safer havens of Kansas, Missouri, and Illinois. By 1892, lynchings, or unlawful executions, of African Americans by terrorist groups in the South averaged one every two days.

Two U.S. Supreme Court decisions further undermined the new freedom of African Americans. In 1883, the Court declared that the 1875 Civil Rights Act, which forbade discrimination against blacks in public facilities, was unconstitutional and that local authorities could discriminate for a variety of reasons, including that of race. Most of the former

1865 The 13th Amendment to the Constitution abolished slavery in the United States. African American and white abolitionists celebrated the victory with church programs, speeches, and parades.

1865–70 Howard University, Bowie State University, Morehouse College, Talladega College, Morgan State University, and Fisk University were among the institutions of higher learning founded to educate African Americans.

1868 The 14th Amendment to the Constitution granted citizenship to "All persons born or naturalized in the United States," overturning the Dred Scott Decision (see 1857).

1870 The 15th Amendment to the Constitution affirmed that no citizen may be denied the right to vote due to their race or color.

1875 The U.S. Congress passed the Civil Rights Act of 1875, prohibiting discrimination of blacks in public facilities.

Beginning in the late 1800's, many poor black Southern sharecroppers (*left*) moved to the cities, hoping to find economic prosperity. The oppressive conditions they found in urban centers, however, prompted early civil rights marches, such as one in Harlem in 1912 (*below*).

Confederate states quickly passed "Jim Crow" laws (named for a minstrel show character) that segregated (separated) the races in all public facilities, including schools. The trend climaxed in 1896 with the infamous Supreme Court case *Plessy* v. *Ferguson*, which declared that segregation was constitutional as long as white and black facilities were equal. Seven Southern state legislatures used additional tactics to keep blacks from voting. They began charging blacks money to vote (a poll tax), which few could afford to pay. They also instituted "grandfather clause" voting rules, meaning that voters had to demonstrate their understanding of the federal and state constitutions unless they could prove that one of their grandfathers had voted before January 1, 1867. Since African Americans were not declared citizens until July 23, 1868, few could claim kinship to such an unusual relative. These discouragement tactics successfully eliminated most blacks from the voting process.

Migration to the Cities

After the Civil War, many blacks supported themselves by working as sharecroppers, cultivating sections of other people's land in exchange for a share of the crop as payment. But after a series of economic depressions, in 1872, 1884, and 1893, many found it difficult to feed their families. After each depression cycle, thousands of blacks, as well as whites, abandoned farming and moved to the nearest industrial town or city to look for jobs in manufacturing industries. Many of the blacks who remained in the farming communities joined protest organizations, such as the Colored Farmers' Alliance, which by the 1890's had gained a membership of more than 1 million in nine states. White resistance to this union climaxed in North Carolina, the state with the highest concentration of alliance members. In 1898, after the Southern Democrats who were hostile to black issues won control of the state legislature, a riot broke out in Wilmington, North Carolina. More than 40 people were killed over a period of several days.

1883 Jan Ernest Matzeliger revolutionized the shoe industry with his invention of the shoe lasting machine, which was capable of attaching soles of shoes to their upper parts.

1896 In the ruling *Plessy* v. *Ferguson*, the U.S. Supreme Court upheld the right of a state to establish separate but equal facilities for blacks and whites, encouraging racial segregation and discrimination.

1903 W. E. B. Du Bois became a national figure with the publication of *The Souls of Black Folk*.

1905 Du Bois and other early civil rights activists launched the Niagara Movement, calling for an immediate halt to segregation and racism.

1909 The National Association for the Advancement of Colored People (NAACP) was founded by a group of whites and blacks to favorably influence public opinion and to defend the legal rights of African Americans.

Soldiers of the all-black 369th Infantry distinguished themselves at the Battle of the Argonne Forest in World War I. The entire regiment was awarded the Croix de Guerre, France's highest medal for bravery.

▶URBANIZATION (1915–1945)

Following the terror of the Wilmington Riot, many Southern blacks headed north to settle in Boston, Newark, Philadelphia, Pittsburgh, Cleveland, Cincinnati, Detroit, Chicago, St. Louis, and Harlem, a section of New York City. Over the next two decades, hundreds of thousands of blacks moved into these urban centers. But on arrival, most discovered overcrowded facilities, inadequate housing, and dead-end jobs. As a result, concerned individuals of both races formed the National Association for the Advancement of Colored People (NAACP) in 1909 and the National Urban League (NUL) in 1911. The NAACP was devoted to the pursuit of civic justice and the NUL to economic fairness.

World War I

When the United States entered World War I in 1917, W. E. B. Du Bois, among others, urged blacks to support the war effort "shoulder to shoulder with our white fellow citizens." Of the 2.2 million African Americans who registered for the draft following the passage of the Selective Service Act in May 1917, a total of 367,000 were actually drafted and 42,000 went overseas to fight in France. More than 600 African Americans received commissions as officers of the U.S. Army to take command of segregated black military units.

During the war, tens of thousands of black men and women found employment as coal miners and in industrial centers where war supplies, such as ammunition, ships, and motor vehicles, were manufactured. These job opportunities brought economic prosperity to many black communities for the first time. Racism, however, continued to undermine the African American community, and competition between blacks and poor whites for limited job opportunities led to a violent cycle of race riots.

Meanwhile, the Ku Klux Klan was rapidly expanding northward and its membership grew to 4 million. Northern lampposts, as well as Southern oak trees, now served as lynching gallows. In 1919 at least 70 blacks were lynched, including 10 African American war veterans wearing full uniform.

The 1920's

This wave of racial hatred divided the African American community itself. The majority of middle-class blacks believed racism could end with full integration of the races, but many working-class blacks, who felt completely removed from white society, supported a new Back-to-Africa movement led by Marcus Garvey. For nearly a million individuals, Garvey was a prophet of black pride, independence, and separatism.

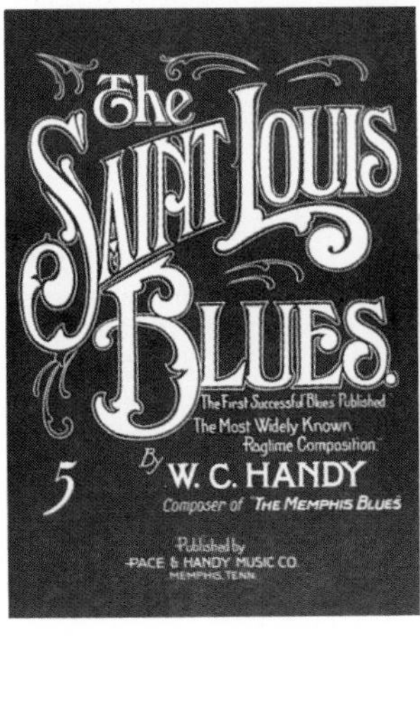

1911 The National Urban League (NUL) was founded to help African Americans find employment.

1914 W. C. Handy, known as the "father of the blues," popularized the blues style of music with the release of his classic "St. Louis Blues."

1918 Approximately 370,000 African Americans distinguished themselves in combat during World War I.

▼ Nearly 100 people lost their lives in hundreds of race riots that erupted in major U.S. cities, partly as a result of competition for jobs among returning soldiers.

About this time, the black middle class began producing a stunning collection of now-classic literary and artistic works. Because so many were created in Harlem, this period of the 1920's became known as the Harlem Renaissance. The works of Langston Hughes, Claude McKay, Countee Cullen, Jessie Fauset, and James Weldon Johnson were widely circulated. Also popular were "race movies," produced for black audiences by Oscar Micheaux.

Marcus Garvey attracted millions of followers with his Back-to-Africa movement in the 1920's.

dent's wife, Eleanor Roosevelt, formed what was known as the Black Cabinet to deal with governmental problems and policies affecting African Americans. The formation of the Committee for Industrial Organization (CIO) in 1935 extended union membership to blacks who found employment in the automobile, railroad, textile, and tobacco industries and in the building trades. Before this time, they had generally been limited to service jobs, such as janitors and cooks.

The Depression Years

Creative expression diminished during the Great Depression of the 1930's, as jobs became increasingly scarce and racial tensions once again exploded. A riot in Harlem in 1935 was directly connected to housing shortages and to a local unemployment rate that exceeded 50 percent. Blacks also were highly frustrated because they felt generally unprotected by the law. In cases involving blacks and whites, the law courts almost always ruled in favor of the whites.

On the positive side, however, the administration of President Franklin D. Roosevelt included blacks in its economic relief efforts. In 1936 the esteemed black educator Mary McLeod Bethune, an associate of the presi-

World War II

America's entry into World War II in 1941 renewed an old debate concerning the role African Americans should play in defense of the nation. Black service personnel were excluded by law from the United States Marines and by custom from the Air Force. Blacks in the Navy could only aspire to be cooks and kitchen helpers. Despite these barriers, more than 1 million patriotic African Americans joined the armed forces. Pressure from the NAACP and other African American leadership groups persuaded the Marine Corps to drop its policy of discrimination and the Air Force to set up pilot training operations for blacks in Tuskegee, Alabama. By mid-1942 approximately 200 African American officers had received commissions for duty, and by 1945 nearly 500,000 African Americans were serving overseas. It did not escape their notice, however, that while they were fighting for democracy overseas, many were still living in segregation in the United States.

World War II significantly affected the lives of African Americans. Employers in the military industries were ordered by the federal

Mary McLeod Bethune

1925 The first major African American labor union, the Brotherhood of Sleeping Car Porters, was organized by A. Philip Randolph. His work paved the way for the acceptance of blacks in the labor movement of the 1930's and 1940's.

1936 Mary McLeod Bethune helped organize the National Council of Black Federal Officials, known as the Black Cabinet, during the administration of President Franklin Roosevelt.

1939 Concert singer Marian Anderson performed before 75,000 people at the Lincoln Memorial, after the Daughters of the American Revolution (DAR) refused to allow her to appear at Constitution Hall.

BREAKING THE COLOR BARRIER

By the 1940's, blacks had made inroads into mainstream popular culture. Among those who rose to the top were (*clockwise from left*) singer Sarah Vaughan, known as "the Divine One"; Richard Wright, author of the acclaimed novel *Native Son*; jazz great Count Basie and his orchestra; Jackie Robinson, the first black major league player of the 1900's; and the esteemed artist W. H. Johnson.

1940 Richard Wright published *Native Son*, describing the hostile social and economic conditions that can lead blacks into crime.

1941 President Franklin Roosevelt issued Executive Order 8802, prohibiting discrimination in government and in defense industries.

1942 The Congress of Racial Equality (CORE), led by James Farmer, was founded in Chicago to seek nonviolent, direct action to combat discrimination.

1946 The U.S. Supreme Court ruled in *Morgan* v. *Virginia* that segregation in interstate bus travel was unconstitutional.

1948 President Harry S. Truman issued Executive Order 9981, abolishing segregation in the armed forces.

1953 Ralph Ellison won a National Book Award for *Invisible Man* (1952), a story of a black man's efforts to overcome society's stereotypes and assert his individuality.

Left: During World War II, African American artist Horace Pippin, a disabled World War I veteran, painted *Mr. Prejudice* (1943) to show that racial discrimination was weakening the war effort.

Right: "Colored Only" marks the front of a segregated store in Belle Glade, Florida, 1945.

Opposite page, left: Rosa Parks, who refused to yield her bus seat to a white man in 1955, is known as the mother of the modern civil rights movement.

government not to discriminate against blacks when hiring, stimulating another wave of migration to the major cities in the South, Northeast, and West. As their income and wages increased, more African Americans were able to afford to buy automobiles, radios, record players, ready-made clothing, and other luxury items.

▶ MODERNIZATION (1945–)

Under the administration of President Roosevelt, the executive branch had determined that blacks must be included in federal assistance programs. In addition, the Supreme Court had indicated that it was unconstitutional to exclude African Americans from due process of law. As a matter of record, between the years 1938 and 1948, the NAACP, with Thurgood Marshall as its chief counsel, successfully challenged racial discrimination in housing, interstate travel, graduate-level education, and voting requirements. Within the decade the number of blacks registered to vote rose from 100,000 to more than 1 million, setting the stage for political changes of an unforeseen magnitude.

The Civil Rights Movement

In 1954 the U.S. Supreme Court ruled in the case of *Brown* v. *Board of Education of Topeka* (Kansas) that racial segregation in public schools was unconstitutional, or unlawful. This victory unleashed a new era of civil rights activities, particularly in the South. For example, in 1955, Rosa Parks of Montgomery, Alabama, touched off a boycott of the city's transportation system after she was arrested for refusing to yield her bus seat to a white man. The boycott was led by a young minister named Martin Luther King, Jr., who came to symbolize the civil rights movement.

During the administration (1953–61) of President Dwight D. Eisenhower, the Civil Rights Commission and the Civil Rights Division were created in the Justice Department. This signaled to the nation that civil rights issues were a concern of the executive and legislative branches of the federal govern-

1954 In the ruling of *Brown* v. *Board of Education of Topeka* (Kansas), the U.S. Supreme Court overturned *Plessy* v. *Ferguson* (see 1896) and declared the segregation of public schools unconstitutional.

1955 Dr. Martin Luther King, Jr., led a yearlong boycott of the Montgomery, Alabama, bus system after Rosa Parks, a black seamstress, was arrested for not giving up her seat to a white person.

1956 As a result of the nonviolent Montgomery boycott, the U.S. Supreme Court ruled that segregation on public transportation was unconstitutional.

1957 President Eisenhower signed a civil rights bill and created a commission to investigate civil- and voting-rights violations.

▼ Federal troops were ordered to Little Rock, Arkansas,to ensure the safety of nine black students attempting to enroll in the all-white Central High School.

Right: **Most African American civil rights activists were dedicated to nonviolent protest and bore hostility and injustice with dignity and perseverance.**

ment. This commitment was put to the test in Arkansas in 1957, when President Eisenhower was compelled to send federal troops to Little Rock to enforce a federal court order to integrate Central High School.

In February 1960, in Greensboro, North Carolina, four young black college students were arrested for refusing to leave a drugstore lunch counter after they had been denied service. Such peaceful methods of protest, which became popular among college students, resulted in the founding of the Student Non-Violent Coordinating Committee (SNCC) in April 1960. Through freedom rides and sit-ins, boycotts and demonstrations, activists tried to evaluate the extent of continued segregation and communicate their findings to the media. Each group encountered violent resistance throughout the Deep South. Some of the most bitter confrontations took place in Alabama, Mississippi, and Georgia.

At the height of the movement, civil rights leaders planned a March on Washington. On August 28, 1963, huge crowds gathered at the Lincoln Memorial in Washington, D.C., to show their support for civil rights and to persuade Congress to pass a comprehensive civil rights bill. Before an audience of more than 200,000 people, Dr. King delivered his stirring speech, "I Have A Dream," in which he envisioned a day when discrimination and social injustice would no longer exist.

In 1964, after extensive debate and with the support of President Lyndon Johnson, Congress passed the Civil Rights Act, prohibiting all racial discrimination in public life. Building on this momentum, Johnson succeeded in getting Congress to pass the Voting Rights Act of 1965, which expanded the scope of the 15th Amendment. Many people then started to believe that because civil rights were now protected by law, further protest would seem excessive. But people continued to protest, venting their anger over the fact that racism and economic inequality remained characteristic of American society.

1960 In Greensboro, North Carolina, four black college students began sit-in demonstrations at an all-white lunch counter. This nonviolent protest method soon spread throughout the South.

1961 Bus loads of black and white youths from the North called freedom riders were organized by CORE to journey through the South to test the enforcement of desegregation laws on interstate transportation.

1962 Federal troops were ordered to Oxford, Mississippi, to protect James H. Meredith, the first African American to register at the University of Mississippi.

▾ President John F. Kennedy signed an executive order banning discrimination in federally funded housing.

1963 Civil rights demonstrations in Birmingham, Alabama, resulted in police brutality. Late in the year, four young black girls were killed in a church bombing.

Separratism, Militancy, and Black Power

During the civil rights era, a religious group called the Nation of Islam, or Black Muslims, began to grow in strength. The group, founded by Wali D. Farad (Fard) in the 1930's, required its followers to separate themselves from whites. In the 1960's, the two most visible Black Muslim leaders were Elijah Muhammad and Malcolm X. In 1964, however, Malcolm X moved away from the separatist doctrine and founded his own movement, the Organization of Afro-American Unity (OAAU). He was assassinated at a meeting in Harlem the following year.

Also prominent during this time was a group known as the Black Panther Party for Unity and Self-Defense, organized in California by Huey P. Newton and Bobby G. Seale. The Panthers brought attention to such problems as unfair rent evictions and police brutality. Soon they were teaching black history classes and informing people of their rights. "Black Power" became a popular slogan. It was meant to encourage blacks to gain economic and political power and, more importantly, to gain self-pride and dignity. Eventually, however, the Black Panthers grew increasingly militant. They started rejecting nonviolent protest methods and urged blacks to prepare for an armed struggle against the whites. Many people began to fear them.

The civil rights movement headed North and began addressing matters of economic inequality. In response to some police encounters, rioting broke out in black neighborhoods in Harlem, Newark, and the Watts section of Los Angeles. As black ghettos went up in flames, televised newscasts showed African

Top: **The dynamic Black Muslim leader Malcolm X was in the process of re-examining his theories of black separatism when he was killed by an assassin in 1965.**

Left: **In March 1965, blacks and whites marched together from Selma to Montgomery, Alabama, to protest racial discrimination in voting procedures.**

1963 On August 20, more than 200,000 blacks and whites participated in a March on Washington, D.C., to protest the lack of federal civil rights legislation. Dr. Martin Luther King, Jr., delivered an electrifying speech, "I Have a Dream."

1964 Malcolm X left the Black Muslim organization Nation of Islam and formed the Organization of Afro-American Unity (OAAU), stressing black nationalism and social action. He was assassinated the following year.

▼ The U.S. Congress passed the Civil Rights Act of 1964, prohibiting racial discrimination in public places and in employment and education.

▼ Dr. Martin Luther King, Jr., won the Nobel Peace Prize.

1965 White resistance to a black voter registration drive led to a Freedom March, from Selma to Montgomery, Alabama, to protest discrimination at the polls.

▼ Congress passed the Voting Rights Act.

Americans chanting threatening slogans like "Burn, Baby, Burn." Then on April 4, 1968, the African American community was dealt a crushing blow when Dr. King, the principal advocate of nonviolence and social justice, was assassinated by a white man in Memphis, Tennessee. The civil rights movement had lost its most respected leader.

Beyond Civil Rights

During the election campaigns of 1968, it became apparent that a conservative, anti-civil rights backlash had begun to take hold of the nation. George Wallace, the defiant, pro-segregationist governor of Alabama, became a popular third-party candidate for president of the United States.

Race relations worsened in the 1970's as national support for issues concerning African Americans diminished. Racial violence returned in the 1980's and 1990's in such communities as Forsyth, Georgia; Howard Beach and Crown Heights, New York; and Los Angeles, California.

Meanwhile, black separatists also attracted new followers. By 1978, Minister Louis Farrakhan, the most influential Black Muslim leader since Malcolm X, began addressing audiences of 8,000 to 10,000 African Americans, who were seeking solutions to social problems that included poverty, drug abuse, crime, and gang violence. By 1990, Farrakhan had become a controversial figure. Many applauded his preaching the virtues of decent and law-abiding behavior. However, many others, especially within the rising and prosperous black middle class, rejected Farrakhan's notion of black superiority and racist tendencies.

The Reverend Jesse Jackson founded the Rainbow Coalition in 1984 to carry on the fight for civil justice and to promote racial tolerance and understanding.

A more positive force within the African American community was the Reverend Jesse Jackson. In 1984, Jackson founded the Rainbow Coalition, a political organization dedicated to social, economic, judicial, and environmental reforms to enrich the lives of African Americans and other minorities. The popular support for Jackson's candidacy for president of the United States in 1984 and 1988 brought African American issues back into the national spotlight.

While two-thirds of the African American community thrived, at least one-third was living in poverty in areas with disproportionately high rates of crime, unemployment, and welfare dependency. Routine concerns of inner-city residents were quality of housing, personal safety, and inadequacy of services.

Despite persistent problems, by the end of the 20th century, the African Americans had also achieved many goals. The community was characterized by its diversity of income levels, occupations, religious affiliations, levels of education, and lifestyles. Increasingly they were represented in the various professions and at all levels of government.

In recent years, many inner-city school systems with large enrollments of African Americans have suffered from a lack of resources and adequate funding. Efforts have been made to raise the esteem and performance levels of

The New York Times

NEW YORK, FRIDAY, APRIL 5, 1968

RTIN LUTHER KING IS SLAIN IN MEMP
WHITE IS SUSPECTED; JOHNSON URGES

Hanoi Charges U.S. Raid Far North of 20th Parallel

DISMAY IN NATION — Negroes Urge Others to Carry on Spirit

PRESIDENT'S PLEA — On TV, He Deplores 'Brutal' Murder of Negro Leader

1968 The U.S. Senate passed a civil rights bill prohibiting racial discrimination in the sale or rental of most housing.

▼ Dr. Martin Luther King, Jr., was assassinated by a white man, touching off a new wave of violence in more than one hundred cities nationwide.

1971 African American members of the House of Representatives founded the Congressional Black Caucus to focus on legislative issues affecting blacks and other under-represented groups.

1986 For the first time, the birthday of Dr. Martin Luther King, Jr., was celebrated as a national holiday (on the third Monday of every January).

1995 The Million Man March on Washington called on black men to declare responsibility for their families and communities.

The civil rights movement, which began in the 1950's and reached its peak in the 1960's, helped free African Americans from traditional stereotypes and discrimination. Changes in social attitudes made it easier for them to pursue professional opportunities and win recognition for their accomplishments. Among today's most notable achievers are *(top, left to right)* Wynton Marsalis, award-winning jazz trumpeter; Toni Morrison, winner of the 1993 Nobel Prize for literature; Colin Powell, the nation's first African American secretary of state; and *(left)* Oprah Winfrey, talk-show host and publisher.

African American students by exposing them to more information relevant to the accomplishments of black people throughout the world. This approach, called afrocentrism, attempts to reclaim black culture. Toward this goal, Americans have observed **Black History Month** every February since 1976 to spotlight some of the achievements of African Americans that have long been overlooked in mainstream education—for example, that beautiful poetry once was written by a colonial slave named Phillis Wheatley; that a black engineer named Norbert Rillieux invented a sugar-refining process that is still used today; that black cowboys and the so-called "buffalo soldiers," as well as whites, helped settle the West; that black musicians invented the blues and developed jazz; that an African American explorer, Matthew Henson, reached the North Pole with Robert Peary; that an African American surgeon, Daniel Hale Williams, performed the first successful heart operation; and that African American officers led black soldiers into battle. Thousands of accomplishments such as these, great and small, have profoundly influenced the nation and contributed immeasurably to American culture.

RUSSELL L. ADAMS
Chair, Department of Afro-American Studies
Howard University

WONDER QUESTION

What is Kwanzaa?

Kwanzaa, meaning "first fruits" in Swahili, is an annual seven-day festival observed by some African Americans during the week of December 26 to January 1. Inspired by an African harvest festival, Kwanzaa was created in 1966 by an American activist named Maulana Karenga to increase awareness of African heritage and to encourage unity.

Kwanzaa teaches seven lessons, or *Nguzo Saba*, one for each day of the week. They are unity (*umoja*), self-determination (*kujichagulia*), cooperation (*ujima*), sharing (*ujamma*), creativity (*kuumba*), purpose (*nia*), and faith (*imani*). The observance includes lighting candles in a holder called a *kinara*, one for each lesson learned. Festivities also may include exchanging gifts and eating an African-style meal known as *karamu*.

AFRICAN UNION

The African Union (AU) officially succeeded the Organization of African Unity (OAU) in July 2002. Many of its goals remain the same—to unite all the peoples of Africa so they might work toward the common goals of peace, political stability, mutual cooperation, and economic development and integration. But the African Union also promotes democracy and good governance. Furthermore, it reserves the right to intervene in any member's affairs under such grave circumstances as war crimes or genocide (the extermination of a targeted group of people).

The treaty of the African Union is loosely modeled on that of the European Union. It calls for the creation of several new agencies, including a continental parliament, made up of members from every African nation; a continental court; and an African central bank, monetary fund, and investment bank. The treaty also calls for specialized committees to examine agriculture, industry, transportation, health, education, and the like.

The treaty was approved in July 2000 in Lomé, Togo, by 47 of the 53 member states of the OAU. In March 2001, Libya accelerated the process of formal ratification by sponsoring a special summit meeting.

The AU's highest decision-making authority is the Conference of the Union, an annual summit meeting of heads-of-state. Headquarters are located in Addis Ababa, Ethiopia, which had been the seat of the OAU since its creation in 1963. For a complete listing of member nations, see the article ORGANIZATION OF AFRICAN UNITY (OAU) in Volume O.

ROBERT MORTIMER
Haverford College

AGASSIZ, JEAN LOUIS RODOLPHE (1807–1873)

Louis Agassiz was a Swiss-born American naturalist who did pioneering work on the classification of fish and was the first to develop the idea of an ice age. Agassiz was born on May 28, 1807, in Môtier-en-Vully, Switzerland. As a boy he showed a strong interest in animals and plants. At 10, Louis was sent away to school. Later he studied at several universities. He completed a degree in medicine but became more interested in the natural sciences.

While studying at the University of Munich, Agassiz began work on the classification of fish, both living and fossil. His research soon drew the attention of scientists all over Europe. In 1832 he became a professor of natural history at the University of Neuchâtel in Switzerland.

Agassiz's interest in glaciers began in 1836 during a trip to the Swiss Alps. Over the next several years he carried out field studies of glaciers and eventually performed an experiment that demonstrated that glaciers move. Further observations convinced him that ice had played a major role in shaping the Earth's surface, and he introduced the theory that a large part of the Earth had once been covered with ice.

In 1846 Agassiz went to the United States to give a series of lectures. His lectures were well received and he settled there permanently, becoming a professor at Harvard University in 1848. His first wife had died and he married Elizabeth Cabot Cary, who later became a founder of Radcliffe College.

Agassiz was an extraordinary teacher. He believed his students should learn to gather facts rather than learn facts already gathered. The first summer school for studying animals in their natural environment was set up by Agassiz on an island in Buzzards Bay, Massachusetts. He also founded the first natural history museum in America. It is the Museum of Comparative Zoology at Harvard (often known as the Agassiz museum). Agassiz died on December 14, 1873.

PATRICIA G. LAUBER
Science Author and Editor

See also GLACIERS; ICE AGES.

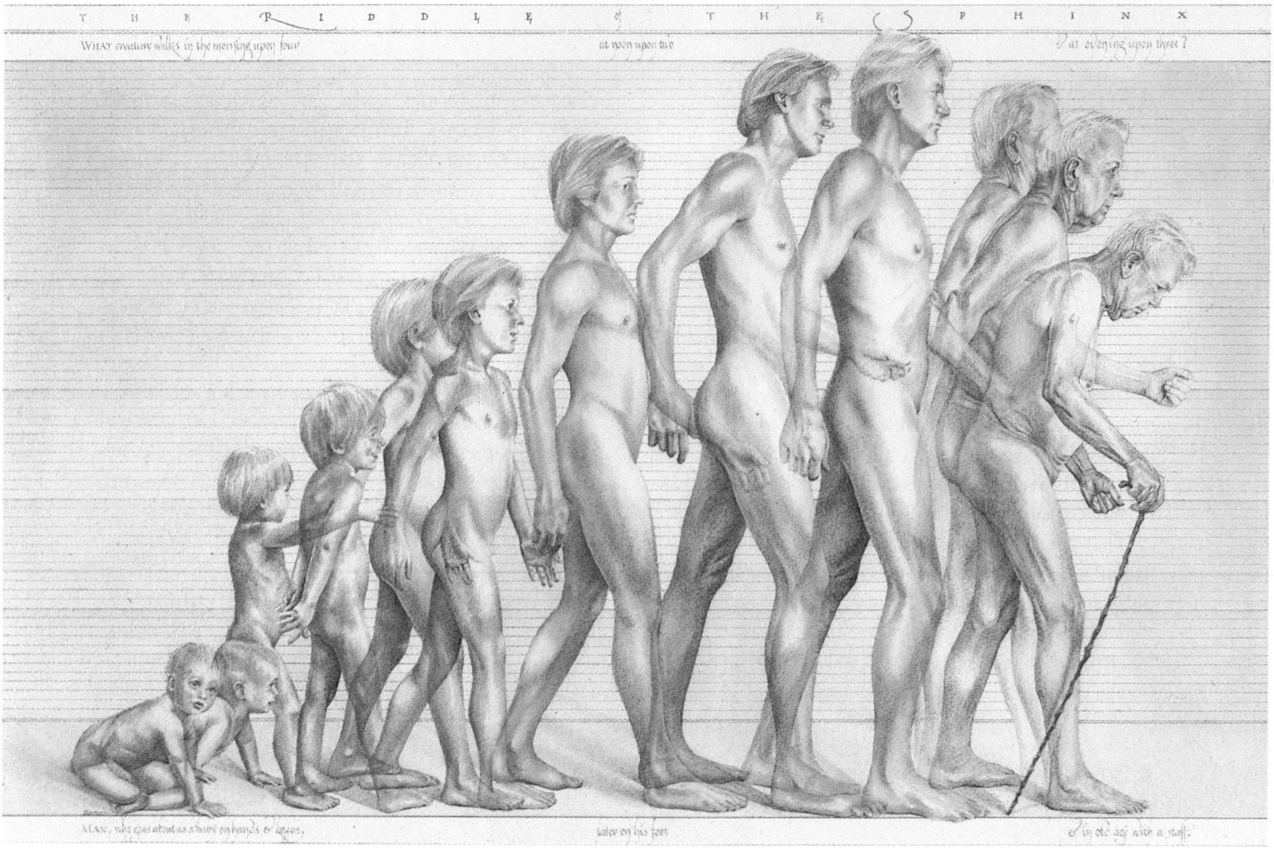

Aging is a normal part of life. It begins with a phase of growth and development which is followed by a gradual decrease in the body's size and ability to function efficiently.

AGING

Everybody knows that old people are more likely to die than young people. We know it from experience. We also can find the facts and figures in life insurance tables. For example, in an advanced country with a well-fed population only about one in every 1,000 children dies during his or her 12th year. But one in every 20 men aged 70 will die before his 71st birthday.

The risk we run of dying at any particular age is called the **force of mortality** for that age. The force of mortality has been carefully worked out for all ages of people—this is what life insurance rates are based on. Naturally, it grows steadily greater with age. If we kept all through life the same force of mortality that we had at 12—never becoming any more likely to die than we were then—we could all hope to live several hundred years, unless we were very unlucky or careless. The fact that people do not live several hundred years (and only rarely reach 100) is due to a process called **aging.**

We can recognize aging by the gray hair, weakened muscles, wrinkled skin, loss of hearing, and other signs that it produces. It also has a more important effect on us. It reduces our power of staying well and of getting better if we fall ill. A common cold may not be serious in a young person, but its complications may lead to death in an old person.

This loss of the power to stay healthy (and the increase in the likelihood of dying) happens at about the same rate in everybody. As we age, we tend to be like an old automobile—more and more things go wrong with us.

But old cars and radios do not repair themselves. When we are young, our bodies do. What seems to decline with age is the power of self-repair. There comes a time beyond which it is very difficult to stay alive at all. The least thing may be enough to finish us. This is the end of our **life span.**

LIFE SPANS IN HUMANS

People and other animals that age have fixed life spans, or characteristic ages of death. Some individuals may die sooner, while strong or lucky ones live longer. But most individuals of a species have about the same length of life. In countries with good food and medical services, the most common length of life in people is between 70 and 80 years. Where there is hunger or little medical care, many people die young. Often death among babies, called **infant mortality,** is very high. For those who survive, the expectation of life is low—perhaps 40 to 45 years.

Women, for reasons not clearly understood, live a little longer on the average than men. This could be because their genetic makeup (two X chromosomes instead of one) gives them a better chance of avoiding defective genes. Also, differences in hormone levels between men and women also appear to affect life span.

Some people, especially if they have come from long-lived families, live longer than others. Some are able to live as much as 20 years beyond the usual limit of life. For example, in England, Canada, and the United States, three out of every 100 babies born will live to be 90 years old. About one out of every 1,000 will live to be 100.

A few people live longer still, up to 107 or 108 years. There is a great deal of argument about the highest age ever reached by a person. Probably it is just short of 120 years. For instance, a man who said he was 117 and the last survivor of the Confederate Army died in Texas in 1959. People who have claimed to be older than 120 have never been able to prove it. Some old people are jokers who tell tremendous tales about their age. Other people are willing to believe these tales because they like the idea of living a long time.

▶LIFE SPANS IN ANIMALS

We are used to the idea that we will age. We are so used to this that it comes as a surprise to find that there may be some animals that do not age. Sea anemones are an example. Some have been kept for nearly a century without showing any signs of losing vigor. Some kinds of marine worm can even "grow backwards." If starved and kept in the dark, they get steadily smaller. They finally end as a ball of cells, looking rather like the egg from which they came. Under favorable conditions the ball will turn back to a worm and start growing again. They could probably keep growing and "un-growing" indefinitely.

An animal that does not age is not immortal. That is, it is not deathless. Some individuals will die by accident or from disease every year. But such animals do not get *more likely* to die with age. The force of mortality stays the same in them.

It is sometimes said that small wild animals and birds do not age. What really happens is that they do not have a chance to age. Nearly all die by accident before they have a chance to get really old. Few small birds in the wild survive more than a couple of years. But in a cage, protected from hunger and enemies, they can live as long as 20 years and then die of old age.

Most animals are like us in having fixed life spans. But the life spans of different kinds of animals vary greatly. Birds live longer than mammals of the same size. Fish and reptiles, which are cold blooded, live longer still.

Tortoises (land turtles) and sturgeon are probably the two longest-lived vertebrates (animals with backbones). Human beings are the longest-lived mammals. The elephant is the only other mammal that approaches our life span. In spite of what you read in some books, whales and elephants do not live for hundreds of years.

▶INVESTIGATIONS ON AGING

The study of aging is called **gerontology.** This name comes from the Greek word *gerōn,* which means "old man." The general aim of gerontology is to find out exactly how aging occurs and how, if possible, it can be altered. The ultimate object is to discover if the rate of aging in humans can be slowed down and, if so, by how much. If successful, gerontology could help people stay young and healthy longer.

What Happens During Aging?

We do not yet know why people and animals lose vigor with age. There seem to be three main possibilities.

First, aging might be due to the dying off of cells we cannot replace. The animals that do not age are mostly kinds that can replace all their cells. In people and other vertebrates, cells of the skin, blood, and liver are renewed. But this renewal slows down with age. Other cells, like those of the brain, cannot divide and are never renewed. We keep the same brain cells all our lives, but they get fewer as we get

Gray hair and wrinkled skin are two of the most common signs of aging. Changes such as these may be caused by the body's inability to replace old cells with healthy new ones.

older. Aging may be due simply to a loss of cells or structures that we cannot renew.

A second possibility has to do with cell formation. Aging may be due to a change in the cells that are newly produced throughout life. Perhaps the new cells formed by an old man are different from, and not so good as, new cells in a baby.

The third possibility is that aging is more complicated than this. It may be the result of development. Chemical changes in the body make us grow up. Perhaps these same chemical changes eventually damage the body in some way and make it grow old.

Those are only three of the theories that have been suggested to explain aging. Nobody yet knows for certain which, if any, of them is right.

DNA Repair and the Rate of Aging

Two important facts have been discovered, however, that help us better understand the aging process. The first concerns not the repair of cells but the repair of material inside the cells that makes it possible for them to grow and reproduce.

This material is made up of DNA (short for deoxyribonucleic acid). DNA forms long strands that carry instructions for everything the cell makes or does. (You can read more about DNA in the articles on BODY CHEMISTRY and GENETICS.) Breaks and alterations can form in these strands, but the cell has ways of snipping out errors and mending breaks.

Scientists have found that long-lived animals have cells that are better at making such repairs than cells in short-lived animals, such as mice. It could be that DNA repair is an important factor in remaining vigorous and healthy for a long time.

The second important discovery is that aging can be slowed down. This can be done by slowing growth and development. A great many animals (cockroaches, for example) have shorter lives if they are fed heavily and made to grow as fast as possible. They live longer if they eat less and grow more slowly. Dr. Clive M. McCay, at Cornell University, found that this was also true of rats.

In McCay's experiment, litters of young rats are divided at random into two groups.

One group is fed a normal rat diet; the other gets everything it needs except enough energy-giving food (calories) to grow. The fully fed rats grow up, become adult, live their lives, and die of old age. During the same period of time, the underfed rats stay apparently young. And they can be made to grow long after their fully fed brothers and sisters are dead of old age. This means that aging, then, is not simply a matter of passing weeks and months, but also of the rate of living. McCay's experiment does not mean, of course, that starving people will live longer than the well fed. Starvation in people is a shortage of everything. The rats were short only of enough energy foods for growth.

Aging and the Brain

Much research on slowing down aging is now concerned with the brain. Certain parts of the brain are known to act as the "clocks" that control growing up and becoming adult. There is much evidence that while many aging processes are going on in different parts of the body, it is the brain—in a region called the hypothalamus—that controls and organizes life span.

"Clocks" in the brain are able to determine which cells divide, what substances they make, and how they react to invading bacteria and other foreign substances. They may even control DNA repair. The difficulty for researchers is that because the body acts as a whole, changes in one part of the body affect many other parts. This makes it difficult to determine what exactly the "clocks" are controlling. There may even be many "clocks" in different parts of the body.

Aging and the Immune System

The body's immune system is responsible for repelling invaders, that is, disease-producing viruses and bacteria. Researchers know that old people do not resist infection very well. Studies have shown that this is partly due to changes in the white cells of the blood, an important part of the immune system.

These changes can be reversed, however. A great deal of research is directed at finding ways to do this and at understanding why the changes occur in the first place. Another research effort is aimed at discovering why the immune system sometimes damages the body by mistaking its own cells for enemies. Once

Disabilities or disease may limit the capabilities of some elderly people. However, most can still enjoy simple activities such as a trip through a garden with a friend (*above*) or benefit from the thoughtful attention of a caregiver (*below*).

A scientist studies cells in hopes of uncovering clues about the causes of aging and the factors that determine an organism's life span. Research such as this may one day help us to slow down or completely control the aging process.

we understand the immune system, we may be a lot closer to controlling the aging process.

RESEARCH ON LIFE SPANS

Another type of research on aging involves the collection of facts about ages and growth rates in animals. It is very hard to study the force of mortality in animals by keeping them for life and recording when they die, since many live half as long as we do ourselves.

What we need to find out is the force of mortality at different ages in populations of animals in captivity and in the wild. For the most part we must rely on research records, though the records are far from complete. In a few cases, however, we can tell the ages of animals by some structure on the animal's body that grows regularly. The shells, bones, or teeth of certain animals lay down a fixed number of marks or rings every year. We can tell the ages of these animals just as we can tell the age of a tree by counting its rings.

Life Spans of Organs and Cells

In addition to studying how long an entire animal or person lives, researchers are exploring the life spans of organs and cells.

Would our heart age if it were not joined to the rest of us? We know that when a healthy young heart is transplanted into an old person, it does not prevent the older person from aging. But would an older person's heart last longer in the body of a young person?

Scientists have tried to find answers to such questions by putting tissue from an old animal (a mouse, for example) in the body of a young animal. Unfortunately, the experiments have produced unclear results, so scientists have simplified their experiments and turned to studying individual cells.

When human cells are grown outside the body in a laboratory, they usually divide a limited number of times before the cell culture dies out. One reason appears to be that the tips of cell structures called chromosomes break off each time a cell divides. Eventually, these bits (called telomeres) wear down, leading to cell death. However, by injecting a substance called telomerase into cells, scientists have been able to protect the telomeres and thus create "immortal" cells that divide without limit. Telomerase also appears to enable many types of cancer cells to divide continuously, so its potential as an anti-aging medicine remains unclear.

Clearly there are still many puzzles to be solved before we have a complete picture of what controls the life span of cells, organs, or entire animals. The results of some experiments have raised more questions than they have answered.

Other experiments seem to provide valuable new information, but it cannot be safely used until we have a clearer understanding of the aging process.

THE DREAM OF A LONGER LIFE

Research on aging has raised many interesting questions about how the body works and how it changes over time. But one of the most important questions is whether the ultimate goal of gerontology—to make people live longer—is really a good idea.

People have never liked to think that they would get old or that their lives would end around a fixed age. So there have always been stories about miraculously long lives and about people who regained their youth. A Greek myth tells us of Eos (Aurora), goddess of the dawn, who prayed that her husband, Tithonus, be made immortal. The prayer was granted, but unfortunately she had forgotten to ask that he stay eternally young. So he grew older and older and more and more decrepit until he prayed to be allowed to die.

Poets in the Middle Ages wrote of a Fountain of Youth in which one could bathe and become young. The fountain was a fiction. But during that time, early chemists called alchemists tried to discover the elixir of life, which would make old people young.

The alchemists failed. But many scientists, backed by governments and universities, are now carrying out serious research on aging.

Certainly if we only made people live longer, like Tithonus—instead of preventing them from aging as well—it would not be a good thing. On the other hand, there are some people of 80 who are ill or crippled because of age, while others are healthy and active. If it were possible that we could all be healthy and useful at 80—even if we lived no longer in the end—it would be a great improvement both for individuals and for society. Now we spend nearly a third of our lives learning our jobs. If we lived longer, we could do more work in a lifetime and carry out more of our plans.

However, if we lived longer lives and if birth rates remained the same, the world's increasing population would grow even faster. Such an increase would have major impacts on our society and environment.

Already, the North American population has experienced what is known as the "baby boom"—an 18-year period of rapid population growth following the end of World War II, from 1946 to 1964. During this period, many more children were born (76 million in the United States alone) than in the same period before or after.

The legendary Fountain of Youth, sought by Ponce de León, was a magic spring that would restore youth to the aged. It is one of the many myths about eternal youth.

The children of this generation, often called baby boomers, brought about much prosperity as they grew up and entered the workforce. However, as the baby boomers age and enter their retirement years, they are predicted to place a mounting burden on the rest of society, which will have to care for them in their old age.

The possibility of lengthening life raises some difficult questions. At the moment we do not know for certain whether we can ever hope to change the rate of aging. Yet everyone should think about the problems because scientists are making a serious attempt to find the means of slowing aging. It seems reasonable to think they will succeed eventually—but when and by how much nobody can yet say.

ALEX COMFORT
Author, *A Good Age*

See also OLD AGE.

AGNEW, SPIRO T. See VICE PRESIDENCY OF THE UNITED STATES.

A combine gathers grain in one of the highly productive wheat fields of North America. Large machines capable of working vast farmlands are the basis of modern agriculture.

AGRICULTURE

When you think about agriculture, do you picture a farmer driving a large tractor across a huge field? If you do, you will be partly correct, for a farmer on a tractor certainly represents agriculture. But agriculture is also much more. It is the tank truck driver who carries loads of milk from farms to dairy-processing plants. It is the merchant who sells livestock feed to cattle ranchers. It is the worker who taps rubber trees or plants cotton, tobacco, or potatoes. It is the scientist researching better ways to grow grain, the operator of a grain elevator, the migrant worker picking apples, the worker in a modern chicken factory, and even the farm lobbyist trying to get a bill enacted into law. And agriculture is still more. Agriculture includes the raising of every kind of plant and animal that is useful to human beings—and all the people and services that help bring agricultural products to the world's markets.

MODERN AND TRADITIONAL AGRICULTURE

Big farm machines and large fields are common in the great agricultural regions of the United States and Canada. Most of the food consumed in these two countries comes from these large modern farms. These farms often produce only one or two products but in very large amounts. The farms are usually named for their chief product, for example, cattle ranches, wheat farms, and dairy farms.

There are other forms of agriculture, which use fewer and smaller machines. Almost half the people of the world are farmers. Most of them are part of "traditional" agriculture,

The article AGRICULTURE discusses the agricultural industry, types of agriculture, important agricultural products, agriculture around the world, general and specialized farming, land management, and agricultural education and history. If you want to read about the business of farming, farming methods, and farm machinery, see the article FARMS AND FARMING.

using animals and their own muscles for power and using the same tools and practices that have been used for centuries.

Traditional farmers grow much of their own food and the fiber for their clothing. They do not spend much for machinery, fertilizer, or other modern materials. Even in the "modern" United States, some people farm in the traditional way. Amish farmers, for example, use no machines, even in such jobs as scooping grain, pitching hay to cattle, milking cows, and hauling the cow manure to the fields to serve as fertilizer.

Many countries have a "dual agriculture," that is, traditional farms in some areas, modern farms in others. But traditional agriculture is losing out. Millions of traditional farmers are moving to crowded cities in search of an easier life. These people must be fed by the modern agriculture that replaces them. Other millions of small farmers have stayed on the farms but have adopted modern practices including the use of fertilizers and high-producing seeds and the efficient use of small machines. Some of these small modern farmers also have jobs off the farm, so they are called "part-time" farmers. Most U.S. farms are part-time farms—even some of the larger ones—because part of the farm family's income is earned off the farm.

Modern agriculture is changing. On future farms, there may be fewer big tractors, as scientists find ways to farm with less energy as well as less human labor. Agriculture is becoming more successful in producing food for all the world's people.

An Amish farmer in Pennsylvania cultivates a field with a team of horses. Traditional agricultural methods are still practiced by many peoples the world over.

IMPORTANT AGRICULTURAL PRODUCTS

The most important sources of human food are the grains or "cereals"—wheat, rice, corn, and others. Wheat is the most important grain in the United States, Canada, and many other western countries. But much of the world's wheat is grown and eaten in the large Asian nations of China and India. Wheat will grow well in most farming areas, even those with little rainfall, and those where the weather is cold most of the year, as in Siberia in the Russian Federation. Wheat is used to make bread, pasta (such as spaghetti and macaroni), cereals, and numerous other products. Wheat products are growing in popularity, and fortunately, farms are producing enough wheat to keep up with the demand.

Rice is grown in areas where the weather is warm throughout the year and rainfall is plentiful. Most rice is grown in wetlands or paddies that are flooded with water during the growing season. Rice is the main food of Asia, but it is a part of the diet in other lands as well. Rice requires more labor than wheat, but it yields more grain per acre.

Corn is the highest producer per acre. It is grown in temperate zones where rainfall is plentiful and summer days are long, such as in the midwestern United States. Corn was first raised by American Indian peoples, and corn *tortillas* ("little cakes") are a basic food in Central and South America.

Other important grains include rye, oats, barley, sorghum, and millet. Sorghum and millet are important foods in some parts of Africa and Asia.

Grains are seeds that usually grow at the top of the plant. But there are also many common

foods that grow underground as roots and tubers of plants. These include potatoes, the basic food of early Europe, and sweet potatoes, an important food in China and the Pacific. Many Africans rely on cassava, another root crop.

Most people eat several kinds of foods to make their diets more interesting and also because a single food is unlikely to provide all the nutrients a human body needs. Meat is a useful supplement to foods made from grains. And because meat comes from animals, it can be moved and stored "on the hoof." Canadian and U.S. agriculture produces meat mainly from cows (beef), pigs (pork), chicken, and turkeys. In other lands some other animals are used. For example, mutton (from sheep) is popular in many countries.

For many people in the world, meat is very expensive. So it may be eaten only on special occasions, and then only as a small part of the meal. As people become wealthier, they eat more meat. For this reason, the use of meat is increasing in the developing countries of Asia.

Eggs and dairy products such as milk and cheese are popular and nutritious foods. To assure that they are fresh and safe to eat, they must be carefully refrigerated, and dairy products must also be processed, that is, specially treated and prepared.

Legumes, such as beans, are another important food. A good source of protein, legumes can even take the place of meat and dairy products in the diet. Soybeans, in particular, are becoming a major source of protein in human diets.

Soybeans are also the source of soy oil, which is used as an ingredient in many prepared foods. Edible oils also come from sunflower seeds, olives, corn, cottonseed, and many other plants.

Because people everywhere enjoy sweets, there is a large world demand for sugar. Sugarcane is the principal export of many tropical lands, such as Cuba. In northern countries, sugar beets are the main source of sugar.

Among the fruits of the world, the banana is the most commonly eaten, and it is becom-

Some countries are especially known for particular agricultural products. Top: On a plantation in the Dominican Republic, a worker cuts sugarcane, the country's leading commercial crop. Left: A good grape harvest assures another fine year for France's world-famous wines.

A Dominican farmer inspects tobacco leaves that have been hung to dry. Though not a food, tobacco is a commercially important agricultural product.

ing even more popular. The second most popular fruit is the orange. Grapes, too, are widely grown because the juice of the grape, as wine, is a popular beverage.

Different countries have different choices of fresh vegetables. Peppers are a favorite among Spanish-speaking peoples. Cabbage is an important vegetable in areas with cold winters, such as Poland, because cabbage can withstand frost. Therefore it can be eaten fresh, after the season for other vegetables is past. The most popular vegetable in the world is the tomato, which is used in more than 100 countries. Another especially popular vegetable is the onion.

There is another group of products in great worldwide demand. These are the so-called ''stimulants'': tobacco, tea, coffee, and cocoa.

Agriculture produces not only food but also fibers. Cotton, flax (linen), and wool for clothing are among the important fibers produced. Rubber for industry is another important product from agriculture. Some medicines, too, are made from agricultural products.

AGRICULTURE AROUND THE WORLD

Many countries do not have to buy much food from others. They meet their food needs largely from their own agriculture. Even the world's most populous countries, China and India, can meet most of their food needs. Even so, there is a large and lively international trade in agricultural products.

Farmers in the United States supply the nation with hundreds of foods, including the basic foods such as wheat for bread, potatoes, milk, and meat. But bananas, coffee, and tea are grown more easily in the tropics, so these products are imported to the United States, mainly from Central and South America. Africa and Asia provide tropical products for Europe.

Many countries produce more farm products than they need. This surplus (overproduction) is traded for other goods. The United States sends grain and meat to Japan, which sends back radios, cars, and other manufactured goods. Some countries are famous for their farm exports, such as Brazil for its coffee, New Zealand for wool and lamb, and Canada and Australia for wheat.

Taxes on farm exports provide income for governments of developing countries. Governments may also control farm prices, hoping to assure inexpensive food for their own people. But if a government taxes farm products too much, or holds prices too low, farmers may protest.

Farmers have formed farm organizations. These organizations demand that government push farm prices higher, not lower. Farmers demand help in expanding their markets, both at home and outside the country. They also demand better roads, better storage facilities, water for irrigation, and useful agricultural research, all of which help make farmers more efficient and more competitive.

Responding to farmers' demands, some governments have contributed much to agricultural growth. With government help, agriculture in Canada, the United States, and Europe has grown so much that farmers can often produce far more than can be sold at a fair price. Food surpluses drive prices down. So too much growth may lead to hard times on the farms, in farm towns, and in industries that serve farmers. In the United States in the 1980's, for example, many efficient farmers went broke, and so did some banks and equipment companies that served them. Farming is a risky business, especially when it is rapidly changing.

There are countries where agriculture is not rapidly improving. One such country is Russia, a vast land that must import grain to meet its food needs. One reason for the slow agricultural growth is that much of Russian farmland is in cold places where crops often fail. To help provide more food, the Russians have planned engineering projects for capturing water from their rivers to be used for irrigating farmland.

On the continent of Africa, there is a shortage of food, and here, too, the natural environment is part of the problem. African geography offers both advantages and disadvantages for farming. The advantages are lots of unused land that could be made into farms and much water in rivers that could be captured for irrigation to help yield additional crops. The disadvantages are the lack of rainfall in some years and, in tropical Africa, no cold winter to kill off pests and diseases. Farm plants may be attacked by swarms of birds or locusts, by weeds, fungi, insects, and viruses. After the crops are harvested, rats may move in to eat them in the storage places. Diseases attack animals and human beings. Many African farmers suffer from malaria, dysentery, and parasites such as worms.

Agriculture faces many other problems in the developing countries of Africa and of

Around the world, agriculture takes many forms. Far left: Merino sheep in New Zealand are herded prior to shearing for their excellent wool. Center: In Indonesia, rice is grown in flooded paddies on terraced hillsides. Above: On a *kibbutz,* a collective farm in Israel, workers cultivate a peanut field. Below: A hand-powered machine separates coffee beans from their shells in Colombia.

Latin America as well. Some countries are losing forests and grasslands. People cut down too many trees for timber, causing forests to disappear. Animals eat grassy lands bare. When forests and grass are gone, rainwater washes away the topsoil. Beautiful lands turn into wastelands.

Agriculture in Asia sets a good example for the developing world. In most Asian countries, there is now more food per person than ever before, even though the number of people has grown larger than ever. Gains in food production have come about partly as a result of government policies and programs. Countries such as India and China are also overcoming the problems of unpredictable weather and tropical pests.

GENERAL AND SPECIALIZED FARMING

A farm where a variety of things are raised is called a general farm. On such a farm there may be a herd of dairy cows whose milk the farmer sells. There may also be hogs, sheep, or poultry to provide extra income and supply some of the family's needs. The farmer may raise some of the hay and grain for feeding the animals. There may be some "cash crop"

Specialized farming of beef cattle is a huge enterprise in western regions of the United States and Canada. The structures at the rear of the feedlot are for grain storage.

such as tobacco, soybeans, or vegetables. Cash crops, as the name indicates, are raised to be sold rather than for use on the farm.

General farms usually require constant labor and often cannot use new technologies. As a result, general farms are becoming few in number. In most countries with modern agriculture systems, specialized farming is predominant.

Specialized farms concentrate on one or two products. In North America, some specialized farms are clustered by region. Wheat farms stretch across the Prairie Provinces of Canada and the High Plains of the United States, from Montana and North Dakota through Colorado, Kansas, and Oklahoma.

Sometimes two products fit well together. The dry climate most suitable for wheat lands is also suitable for the grasslands that support beef cattle. The cattle can also graze on young wheat plants. So wheat and beef production often go together.

In the U.S. Midwestern region extending from Nebraska to Ohio, which has heavier rainfall than the High Plains, corn is the favored crop. Corn is a high-yielding crop, producing as much as 200 bushels per acre (500 bushels per hectare). Another important Midwestern crop is soybeans, which sell for high prices. Soybean and corn production go together because the same farm machinery can be used for both crops and because both thrive during the long humid summer days.

Cotton and soybeans often go together on specialized farms in the humid South—in Mississippi, Arkansas, and Tennessee. Cotton and wheat go together in the dry southern plains of Oklahoma, West Texas, and New Mexico. (Cotton can grow well in dry climates if there is enough irrigation.)

The irrigated valleys of California and other Western states provide fresh fruits and vegetables—even for millions of people living across the continent on the East Coast. In the East, Florida produces vegetables and provides orange juice for the whole nation. There are also other centers for fruit and vegetable production—Michigan, for example.

While some specialized farms, such as fruit and vegetable farms, are located far away from consumers, others, such as dairy farms, tend to be located on the edges of cities. Los Angeles County in California, for example, with one of the world's largest cities, is also one of the United States' major agricultural centers. Dairies located near Los Angeles, like other specialized farms, may do just one thing —in this case they just feed and milk the cows. Many other steps are done elsewhere. For example, the dairy cows were probably born and raised on other farms, to be purchased by the dairy farm just before they were ready to be milked.

Farmers are just one of many groups involved in agriculture. Others include feed and fertilizer suppliers, truckers and shippers, food processors and packagers, distributors, and grocers. There are some kinds of specialized agriculture, in fact, that have no farmers at all. For example, in the United States today, chickens and eggs are produced largely in factories. Not long ago almost every farm had some chickens, which provided eggs and meat for the farm family. Now, however, most chickens are raised in large buildings, which may be owned by grocery store chains or by large companies. Specialized farming has greatly changed the process of food production in highly developed countries. The term **agribusiness** is now used to describe the entire industry involved in the production, distribution, and sale of agricultural products.

LAND MANAGEMENT

Plants grow in the earth's thin skin of topsoil. Because such a small portion of the earth's surface can be used to produce crops, it is very important that farmers take care of the soil so that it does not become exhausted and is not eroded away by rain and wind. All over the world, much good farmland has been lost to erosion. For example, people seeking timber and food may cut down trees and other vegetation that hold the soil, and they may plow steep hillsides that soon become eroded and barren. (For more information, see the article EROSION in Volume E.)

In the United States alone, roughly 30 percent of all cropland is considered to be at high risk of being eroded. Several billion tons of soil on U.S. cropland are lost to wind and water erosion each year. However, there are a number of soil conservation methods that farmers can practice to control erosion. These ways include changing crops from year to year (rotating crops) so that high-profit crops are followed by soil-building crops. Or, different crops can be planted side by side in narrow bands (strip cropping). Water erosion can be slowed by cultivating across, rather than up and down, the sides of hills and by digging ridges (terraces) along the sides of hills, which keep water from rushing downhill and washing away the soil.

A new practice is "minimum till," in which plant residues (remains) are not plowed under after the harvest but instead are left on the surface to protect soil from wind and rain. Minimum till is easier than other methods, so this is a popular form of soil conservation.

There are other losses of farmland, but these losses are small by comparison to erosion. For example, some farmland is being used for roads, factories, and houses. Some

A modern "chicken factory" can accommodate flocks of more than 100,000 chickens at a time. The birds remain indoors and are fed and watered by machines.

To help prevent soil erosion, this farm uses strip cropping (planting different crops side by side in bands) and contour farming (cultivating across the sides of hills).

land is being polluted by salt and other chemicals carried in irrigation water.

Since our food comes from the soil, the loss of soil is a great concern. In the future, people will thank us if we are able to preserve most of our farmland and other natural resources.

AGRICULTURAL EDUCATION

Until the 19th century agricultural education was limited to whatever practical information and folklore a father might hand down to his son. England led the way in scientific agricultural education by establishing an experimental station in 1843 and an agricultural college in 1845. Other European countries soon followed suit. Agricultural education had a hard time winning acceptance. Many farmers were unwilling to change the methods they were used to, and many also disliked and distrusted ''book learning.''

One of the leaders in the movement to establish agricultural education in the United States was Senator Justin S. Morrill (1810–98), the son of a Vermont blacksmith. It was he who introduced the bill, signed by President Lincoln in 1862, that provided for the establishment of agricultural colleges in every state. Money for these colleges was to come from the sale of public lands granted to the states by the federal government. For this reason these agricultural colleges are known as ''land-grant'' colleges. Some of the leading universities in the United States began as small land-grant colleges.

Research stations that worked closely with the land-grant colleges were established soon after. They proved their value by the contributions they made to agricultural knowledge. They also were important in developing better types of animals and plants.

The county agents played an important part in bringing the knowledge of the agricultural colleges and research stations to the ordinary farmer. Their on-the-spot demonstrations probably did more than anything else to convince farmers that ''book learning'' was truly practical.

In Canada, agricultural education on the college level began in 1851 at the University of Toronto. The first agricultural college, St.

Anne's Agricultural School (now affiliated with Laval University), was opened at Ste. Anne de la Pocatière, Quebec, in 1859. The Ontario Agricultural College, founded at Guelph in 1874, was the first institution that succeeded in taking agricultural education to the farmer in much the same way that the county agents did in the United States. The success of the Ontario Agricultural College led to the founding of similar schools throughout Canada.

Typical subjects taught in agricultural colleges nowadays include plant and animal biology, genetics, soil conservation, soil chemistry and the use of fertilizers, bacteriology, entomology and pest control, agricultural engineering, and marketing.

HISTORY OF AGRICULTURE

Nobody knows exactly when or where agriculture began. But scientists now believe that it began 8,000 years ago or more when people discovered that the wild grass seeds that they ate as part of their diet would grow if they were placed in the ground at the right time of year. Not only did the seeds grow, but each one produced many more seeds to fill the stomachs of the tribe. This may seem like a small thing to modern people, but for primitive people it was a truly revolutionary discovery. Up until then they had depended for their lives on their luck in hunting and fishing and finding wild plants that they could eat. Being able to grow a part of their own food meant that starvation was no longer such a danger.

As early people learned about raising crops, they came to depend more and more on farming and less on hunting to keep themselves alive. In addition to wild grasses, from which our present-day grains are descended, these early people learned to grow many other plants, the ancestors of today's vegetables.

Permanent settlements grew up where the land was good for farming. As time passed and the population increased, some of these settlements grew into large towns and eventually cities. People who were especially skilled at making things, such as pots, cloth, or tools and weapons, began to work full-time at their specialties. This was the beginning of division of labor.

Agriculture was developed independently by different groups of people in widely separated parts of the world. The knowledge probably spread slowly from each little group of farmers to their neighbors. Today, historians look at the crops early people raised as a clue to how much contact they had with other areas and continents.

Two of the very earliest places where we know that agriculture was practiced were the valley of the Nile River, in northeastern Africa, and the region called Mesopotamia, along the Tigris and Euphrates rivers in southwestern Asia. The little farming settlements of the Nile Valley grew into the mighty civilization of Egypt. A whole series of countries, from Ur of the Chaldees to Babylonia, flourished in Mesopotamia.

Primitive farming methods were extremely crude. Seeds were planted in little holes in the ground made with a sharp stick. Grain was harvested with flint knives or flint-edged sickles or was sometimes pulled up by the roots. The invention of the spade and the hoe made it possible to cultivate the ground. This helped the crops by loosening the soil and keeping down weeds. At first the work in the fields seems to have been done by women, while the men watched the herds, hunted occasionally, and defended the village against its enemies.

Domestic animals were probably kept at first for hunting (such as dogs) or food (such as cows, sheep, and pigs). Eventually it was discovered that some of them could be used to carry loads or pull a plow. This was another great step forward. The first plows were little more than forked sticks pulled through the soil to stir it up. They were hard to pull and did not work very well by modern standards. Still, they made it possible to cultivate more land with less work than had ever been possible with only hand tools.

The Egyptians, the Mesopotamians, and the Chinese developed advanced systems of agriculture. They knew the value of fertilization, irrigation, and drainage. They developed

improved varieties of plants and animals by selective breeding. The Chinese, in particular, were skilled at getting the most possible use out of every piece of land. By comparison Europe lagged far behind. The Romans developed fairly advanced methods of farming around the beginning of the Christian Era, but most of their knowledge was lost when the Roman Empire fell apart during the 5th century A.D.

Farming methods in Europe during the Middle Ages were generally crude, wasteful, and inefficient. Very few farmers owned their own land. Most of the land was owned by nobles or the church. It was worked by tenant farmers who were little better off than slaves. On each estate, or **manor,** much of the land was kept as forest, where the nobles hunted for sport. The less fertile land was used as pasture. Hay was gathered from swampy meadows. The cultivated land was divided into three large sections. Crops were grown on two of these sections, while the third lay **fallow;** that is, nothing was grown on it This allowed the land to recover a little of its fertility. Each year a different section lay fallow. In the sections that were cultivated, each peasant was allotted a certain amount of land. The fields were usually long, narrow strips rather than squares because this shape made plowing easier. The plow did not need to be turned around so many times at the end of the furrow. The peasant's land strips were usually scattered in different parts of the big field. The average size of the individual allotments was as much as one peasant could plow in one day. Our word "acre" comes from the Latin word *ager,* meaning "field." So does the word "agriculture."

During the Middle Ages, most farm work was done by hand. Workers are shown harvesting grain with sickles and then tying the stalks into bundles.

Deep-rooted customs forced all the peasants on a manor to plant the same crops and do their plowing, planting, and harvesting together. Thus there was very little chance for trying out new crops or new farming methods.

Agricultural machinery was unknown, and all farm work except for plowing and harrowing was done by hand. The harrow of those days was an implement like a large rake. It was pulled over the ground after plowing to break up the clods and smooth the surface somewhat. Sometimes a large bundle of brush was used instead. Seeds for grain crops, the main food of the people, were **broadcast** (scattered by hand) over the ground. Since seeds were not covered, many were eaten by birds. Much grain was also lost by inefficient harvesting and storage. Domestic animals were usually small and scrawny from lack of food. The swamp meadows did not yield enough hay to support many animals over the winter; so most of them were slaughtered in the fall. The lack of domestic animals meant that there was never enough manure for the fields. This kept crop yields very low. Under these conditions starvation was never very far around the corner.

The revival of European agriculture really began in the Low Countries (now the Netherlands and Belgium) around the 16th century A.D. The Dutch and Flemish (Belgian) farmers had begun to cultivate two new "wonder crops"—clover and turnips. Clover enriched the soil by adding nitrogen and made very nutritious hay. Turnips made good winter feed for animals. They fitted in well with the primitive scheme of crop rotation. With plenty of feed the farmers could keep herds of animals over the winter. Furthermore, animals could be kept in farmyards during the rest of the year so that the manure could be easily collected. The manure was carefully put on the fields to maintain their fertility.

In America in the early 1800's, much farm work, such as gathering hay, was still done by hand. But agriculture would soon be changed by machines like the reaper.

With more and better food, the animals soon improved in size and quality. Historians call this discovery the Agricultural Revolution.

The new methods spread slowly. But more advances were made in 18th-century England. Pioneer experimenters developed horse-drawn farming machines, improved systems of crop rotation and fertilization, and better breeds of sheep and cattle.

Meanwhile, Europeans were exploring the New World. They returned home with crops previously unknown in Europe—white and sweet potatoes, corn, pumpkins, and tomatoes. Most of these remained little more than curiosities for many years. But one plant, the potato, was found to grow well in cold, damp climates and on poor soils. It soon became an important food item in northern Europe.

Similarly, crops and animals native to Europe and Asia were carried to North America by early explorers and colonists. Later, crops were exchanged between other lands. Coffee, a native of northern Africa, was taken to Brazil and Indonesia. Peanuts, native to South America, were carried to Africa.

As trade between the various countries of the world increased, there was a growing exchange not only of plants and animals but also of agricultural practices and technologies.

Scientific agriculture in the United States had its beginnings in the 1700's. Benjamin Franklin promoted the use of lime to improve acid soils. George Washington and Thomas Jefferson were leading experimenters in scientific farming. Their work was continued by a few wealthy landowners, who corresponded with one another and with like-minded people in Europe.

In the 1800's, the government began to become involved in helping farmers. Agricultural experiment stations were set up. The establishment of land-grant colleges and other institutions brought knowledge of scientific methods and improved techniques within reach of ordinary farmers.

Another advance during the 1800's was the discovery that chemicals could be used as fertilizers. These substances, produced cheaply and in large quantities, increased crop yields even on poor soil. The development of machines like the reaper, binder, and thresher also increased production. Steel plows replaced the less efficient cast-iron plows. The use of power, at first steam and then gasoline, took much of the physical labor out of agriculture.

In the 20th century the major advances have been in three areas—chemistry, breeding, and technology. Modern farming depends heavily on chemical fertilizers and insect-killers. Other chemicals fight plant diseases and kill weeds. Synthetically produced vitamins, hormones, and antibiotics speed the growth of livestock and chickens and control the tenderness of the meat and the amount of fat in it.

Plant and animal breeders, building on the discoveries of geneticists, developed improved breeds of plants and animals. Some plant breeds produce much higher yields per unit of land than earlier breeds. This has been particularly valuable in basic crops such as wheat, rice, and corn. Corn hybrids, for example, enable farmers of today to get three or four times more corn per acre of land than farmers of the early 1900's.

Power-driven machinery and the electrification of farms have also greatly increased pro-

An agricultural scientist records data on sunflower growth. Agricultural scientists work to improve the quality of crops and livestock and to increase food production.

duction. This has led to an increase in the size of farms and a decrease in the number of farm workers. One person operating large, efficient equipment can produce much more than a group of workers without machines.

Farm technology continues to improve. Already, modern agriculture is doing away with the plow, which caused soil erosion and used too much energy from humans, animals, and tractors. Using minimum-till or even no-till agricultural practices, farmers save time and money.

Agricultural scientists have done much to make agriculture more productive. They have found ways to control many plant and animal diseases. For example, Marek's disease, which harms chickens, can now be prevented with a vaccine. Agricultural scientists developed a type of ray gun that can check a plant's health, taking its temperature to determine if it is sick or thirsty for water. Also, new varieties of crops are constantly being developed to provide farmers in different parts of the world with plants that will grow best in their environments.

Scientific breakthroughs in the 1980's and 1990's have led to important changes in agricultural science. Scientists have learned to change living things by altering the genetic information in their cells. In a process called gene-splicing, nature can be changed quickly. For example, food plants can be improved to do a better job of fighting off insects and weeds, with less use of pesticides. Grains and other plant foods can be made more nutritious. These changes make farming easier and also help solve hunger problems in many parts of the world.

By the year 2000, many familiar food products were being made with ingredients that were genetically altered. Corn and soybeans are two examples. These foods are used to make cooking oils, margarine, and a variety of other products. Corn syrup is a common sweetener found in candies, cakes, and soft drinks.

Although genetically altered foods can provide important benefits, not everyone agrees with their use. Some people think that changing nature is not a good idea or that genetically altered foods may cause unknown problems in the future. Also, businesses that develop these foods want to protect their investments and prevent others from creating similar products.

These concerns must be studied, even as agricultural scientists continue to develop new ideas for improving food production. Their work has helped agriculture become one of the most progressive, efficient industries in the world.

Don F. Hadwiger
Iowa State University

See also Conservation; Erosion; Farms and Farming; Fertilizers; Genetics; Irrigation; Natural Resources; Plant Pests; Soils; names of products, such as Corn, Wheat; kinds of farming, such as Dairying and Dairy Products; and the agriculture sections of continent, country, and state articles.

AGRICULTURE, UNITED STATES DEPARTMENT OF

The Department of Agriculture (USDA) is one of the 15 executive departments of the United States government. Its purpose is to inspect and grade agricultural products—such as grain, livestock, and dairy products—to ensure the quality and safety of the nation's food supplies; to carry out soil and water conservation programs; to conduct research on crop production, nutrition, pest control, and animal and plant diseases; to grant federal loans to family-size farms and ranches; to aid the hungry and undernourished with supplementary food programs, such as food stamps and school lunches; to provide technical assistance and agricultural training in developing countries; to expand overseas markets for American produce; and to ensure fair prices for farmers as well as consumers.

Secretaries of Agriculture

Name	Took Office	Under President(s)
Norman J. Colman	1889	Cleveland
Jeremiah M. Rusk	1889	B. Harrison
Julius S. Morton	1893	Cleveland
James Wilson	1897	McKinley, T. Roosevelt, Taft
David F. Houston	1913	Wilson
Edwin T. Meredith	1920	Wilson
Henry C. Wallace	1921	Harding, Coolidge
Howard M. Gore	1924	Coolidge
William M. Jardine	1925	Coolidge
Arthur M. Hyde	1929	Hoover
*Henry A. Wallace	1933	F. D. Roosevelt
Claude R. Wickard	1940	F. D. Roosevelt
Clinton P. Anderson	1945	Truman
Charles F. Brannan	1948	Truman
Ezra Taft Benson	1953	Eisenhower
Orville L. Freeman	1961	Kennedy, L. B. Johnson
Clifford M. Hardin	1969	Nixon
Earl L. Butz	1971	Nixon, Ford
John A. Knebel	1976	Ford
Robert S. Bergland	1977	Carter
John R. Block	1981	Reagan
Richard E. Lyng	1986	Reagan
Clayton K. Yeutter	1989	G. Bush
Edward R. Madigan	1991	G. Bush
Mike Espy	1993	Clinton
Dan Glickman	1995	Clinton
Ann Veneman	2001	G. W. Bush

*Subject of a separate profile. Consult the Index.

Departmental Agencies

The Department of Agriculture is headed by the secretary of agriculture. The secretary is a member of the president's cabinet and is the president's principal adviser on agricultural matters. The secretary, who is assisted by a deputy secretary and various other agency administrators, is responsible for the overall planning and operations of the seven agencies listed below.

The undersecretary for **Rural Development** manages the Rural Utilities Service, the Rural Housing Service, the Office of Community Development, and the Rural Business-Cooperative Service.

The undersecretary for **Marketing and Regulatory Programs** manages the Agricultural Marketing Service; the Animal and Plant Health Inspection Service; and the Grain Inspection, Packers, and Stockyards Administration.

The undersecretary for **Food, Nutrition, and Consumer Services** manages the Food and Nutrition Service (including the Food Stamp Program) and the Center for Nutrition Policy and Promotion.

The undersecretary for **Farm and Foreign Agricultural Services** manages the Farm Service Agency (including the Farm Loans program), the Foreign Agricultural Service, and the Risk Management Agency.

The undersecretary for **Research, Education, and Economics** manages the Agricultural Research Service; the Cooperative State Research, Education, and Extension Service; the Economic Research Service; and the National Agricultural Statistics Service.

The undersecretary for **Natural Resources and Environment** manages the Forest Service (including the National Forest System) and the Natural Resources Conservation Service.

The undersecretary for **Food Safety** manages the Food Safety and Inspection Service.

As early as 1776, George Washington saw the need for a National Board of Agriculture, and in the 1820's both houses of Congress set up an Agriculture Committee. But the Department of Agriculture was not established until 1862. Its primary functions were to conduct experiments, collect statistics, and distribute seeds and plants. The USDA achieved cabinet-level status in 1889. Today the department's headquarters are located at 1400 Independence Avenue, S.W., Washington, D.C. 20250.

William Whyte
Public Information Specialist
United States Department of Agriculture

See also Food Regulations and Laws.

AIDS

In the mid-1970's, a new disease began to emerge—a disease that came to be called AIDS, or *a*cquired *i*mmune *d*eficiency *s*yndrome. Although not widely known at first, AIDS eventually became recognized as a major health threat. By the end of 2001, the disease had killed more than 25 million people. Over 40 million more were thought to be infected. Some parts of the world—sub-Saharan Africa, India, Thailand, the United States, and Brazil—have been more severely affected by AIDS than others. But the threat of AIDS is worldwide.

What Is AIDS? AIDS is a disease caused by a virus, the human immunodeficiency virus type 1 (HIV-1). Mainly, the virus attacks cells of the body's immune system (such as certain white blood cells) that help fight infection. When the virus attacks these cells, the immune system becomes weak, or deficient. (The name "acquired immune deficiency syndrome" describes the condition that results.) Once the immune system has been weakened by the virus, diseases of all kinds can easily take hold, including some that are rare and do not normally affect healthy people. Eventually, one of these diseases can kill the person with AIDS.

AIDS is a progressive disease. At first, a person infected with the virus shows no major signs. However, the person can spread the infection to others. Immune system cells begin waging a battle against the ever-multiplying virus. Over time, usually ten years or more, the immune system becomes weakened. Various symptoms may appear that can last a long time and may or may not be serious. Finally, the disease progresses to true AIDS. This end stage is characterized by certain life-threatening infections, such as pneumonia, and often by nervous disorders, cancers, and severe weight loss.

How AIDS Spreads. HIV is present in body fluids, and it can be spread only through an exchange of certain of those fluids. This means that it is difficult for most people to get AIDS. In fact, researchers think that HIV is spread mainly in the following ways: The virus can be transmitted from an infected person to another person during sexual intercourse. A woman who is infected with HIV can pass it to her unborn child through her blood or to her baby through breast milk. It can be transmitted by exposure to infected blood or blood products—as when drug abusers share hypodermic needles. Before 1985, when American blood banks began to screen for the virus, a number of people became infected when they received transfusions of infected blood.

The virus is rarely, if ever, transmitted by means other than those described above. As scientists have learned more about AIDS, they have been able to lay many unreasonable fears to rest. There is no need to avoid someone who has AIDS—you do not catch the disease by touching or being in a room with that person. The virus cannot be spread by sneezing or through eating utensils, drinking glasses, toilet seats, or swimming pools. And there is no evidence that it can be spread by insects such as mosquitoes.

You will not catch AIDS by donating blood because the needles used in this procedure are new. And screening tests for infected blood have dramatically reduced the chances of contracting the virus through a transfusion. The risk of becoming infected in a health-care setting is extremely small.

Searching for a Cure. Great progress has been made in understanding AIDS. Scientists have developed blood tests to find out if people have been infected with HIV. These tests look for HIV antibodies, substances that the body produces in an effort to fight the virus. But researchers have not yet discovered a cure for AIDS. Some drugs can slow the progress of the disease, and scientists are testing experimental vaccines that they hope will protect people from AIDS.

In 1999, researchers announced that the original source of the virus was a type of chimpanzee native to west Africa. The virus entered the human population when people who hunt the animals were exposed to infected blood. Scientists hoped to learn more about preventing AIDS by determining how infected chimpanzees resist disease.

For now, however, the best defense against AIDS lies in teaching people to avoid those behaviors that spread the disease.

Reviewed by MERVYN F. SILVERMAN, M.D.
President
American Foundation for AIDS Research

See also IMMUNE SYSTEM.

AIR. See AERODYNAMICS; ATMOSPHERE.

AIR CONDITIONING

Until the mid-1900's, summers were very uncomfortable for people living in the tropics and midlatitudes in much of the world. For example, the weather in Washington, D.C., was so hot and humid during the summer months that sessions of Congress were adjourned. Today air conditioning has made it possible to be comfortable even on the hottest, stickiest days of the year. You will almost certainly find air conditioning in the movie theaters you attend, in most of the stores and office buildings where your family shops and works, in the restaurants where you eat, perhaps even in your family's home and car.

Everyone knows that air conditioning makes you feel cool. But an air conditioning system is often used for more than just cooling. It keeps the temperature and humidity, or moisture content, of the air in an enclosed space at just the right level for the comfort of the people inside. It also circulates the air with fans and removes dust from the air with filters.

Many industries depend on air conditioning to keep the air in their plants clean, cool, and at the right moisture level. For example, textile fibers such as wool and cotton will stretch or shrink as the moisture content of the air changes. This causes variations in the quality of the cloth. Electronic products, such as computer chips, may require not only controlled temperature and humidity, but also special filters to remove dust from the air. And, because people work better when they are comfortable, air conditioning helps increase worker productivity.

▶ HISTORY OF AIR CONDITIONING

The earliest methods devised to cool buildings were based on evaporation of water. The ancient Egyptians and other desert dwellers hung woven mats soaked with water across the entrances to their houses. As the hot, dry air blew through the mats, the water evaporated, cooling the air. Modern devices based on the **evaporative cooling** method are still used in much of the American Southwest.

In more humid climates, another approach was needed. Evaporative cooling devices do not remove humidity from the air, and they do not work as well in humid conditions. For the best comfort, both temperature and relative humidity in a building must be lowered.

The first system of **mechanical air conditioning**, which keeps the humidity low and

How an Air Conditioner Works

This diagram shows how heat and humidity are removed from indoor air by an air conditioner, which then cools the air and blows it back indoors. A simple room air conditioner is shown, but all mechanical air conditioners work the same way.

1. Indoor air is cooled as it passes over an evaporator, a set of coils containing iiquid refrigerant. The moisture in the air forms droplets on the coils and trickles outside through a drain hole.

2. Heat from the air causes some of the refrigerant to evaporate, and it passes into the compressor as a vapor.

3. The compressor increases the pressure of the refrigerant vapor, making it hotter. It loses that heat to the outside air, becoming a warm high-pressure liquid in the condenser.

4. The warm liquid refrigerant sprays through the expansion valve back into the evaporator. As it expands, the refrigerant turns into a mixture of cold vapor and cold liquid, and the cycle is ready to begin again.

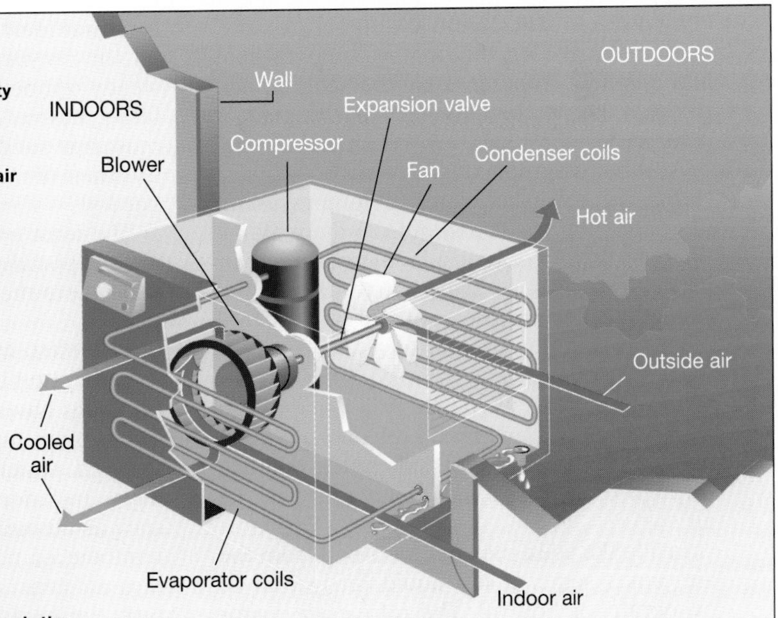

cools the air at the same time, was developed in 1902 by Willis H. Carrier. Carrier, who is often called the father of air conditioning, built this machine for a printing plant in Brooklyn, New York, that had trouble printing in color. Paper stretches when the air is damp and shrinks when the air is dry. Because each color had to be printed separately, printings of different colors on the same sheet of paper did not line up accurately because the paper changed size between printings. Carrier's system kept the humidity level constant by passing air over a network of small pipes that contained a refrigerated fluid. The cold surface of these pipes cooled the air and removed moisture from the air by condensation, the same principle that causes water droplets to form on the outside of a glass of ice water. The system removed excess humidity and reduced air temperature in a controlled way and thus enabled the different colors to line up accurately.

Carrier's patents are the basis of modern air conditioning. Air conditioning was soon being used in many factories, and by the 1920's, many American restaurants, theaters, and department stores were air conditioned. In the decades since then, air conditioned office buildings and homes have become increasingly common.

PRINCIPLES OF AIR CONDITIONING

Mechanical air conditioning removes heat and humidity from air using the same principle that keeps the inside of a refrigerator cold.

As the diagram on the previous page shows, a mechanical air conditioning system has parts both inside and outside the building or room that it cools. Inside, warm, humid air passes over a set of coils that contain a special fluid called a **refrigerant**. This coil of cold pipes—called the **evaporator**—absorbs heat from the air, making it quite cool. The cooler air cannot hold as much water vapor, so water droplets condense on the outside of the coils and trickle to the outside of the building through drain holes, thus dehumidifying the air.

Inside the coils, the heat absorbed from the air causes some of the liquid refrigerant to evaporate, or boil off. The refrigerant vapor then travels through pipes into a **compressor**, which is outside the cooled space. The pressure of the vapor builds up inside the compressor; as the pressure increases, the temperature of the vapor rises too.

From the compressor, the hot refrigerant vapor flows to a set of high-pressure coils called a **condenser**. Here the refrigerant cools and condenses back into a liquid. It can be liquid at a higher temperature in the condenser than in the evaporator because the high pressure in the condenser has raised its boiling point.

The refrigerant then passes back inside the cooled space through an **expansion valve**. The refrigerant sprays into the evaporator like deodorant from a pressure can, mostly liquid but with some vapor. It comes out cold, in part because some of it evaporates, and in part because expanding gases naturally get cooler. The cycle is ready to begin again.

HOME AIR CONDITIONERS

In homes, units known as window air conditioners are often used to cool individual rooms. They consume a lot of energy but are relatively inexpensive and easy to install. If you live in a warm, but not hot, climate and want air conditioning in only one room, window units are a good choice.

Central air conditioning requires less energy and is less costly than a whole house full of window units. The evaporator is placed in a central location, and a fan blows cool air to all the rooms through a system of ducts. A steady temperature is maintained by a regulating device called a **thermostat**. The thermostat is set at the desired temperature and switches the air conditioning on and off as needed.

The least expensive home cooling systems are evaporative coolers, but these only work well where the outdoor air is very dry.

COMMERCIAL AIR CONDITIONING

Office buildings, hospitals, and other large buildings have special air conditioning needs. They often have large banks of windows, through which solar heat flows on sunny days. In addition, lights, office equipment such as computers and copiers, and the large numbers of people gathered in these buildings all generate heat. In some large buildings, the heat sources are so numerous that the buildings must be air conditioned in the middle of winter.

A Central Air Conditioning System

Central air conditioning systems are used to filter and cool all the floors of large buildings at the same time. The arrows show the path of the air as it travels through the filters and supply ducts to each floor. The cool, filtered air comes out of vents on each floor and returns to the air conditioning system.

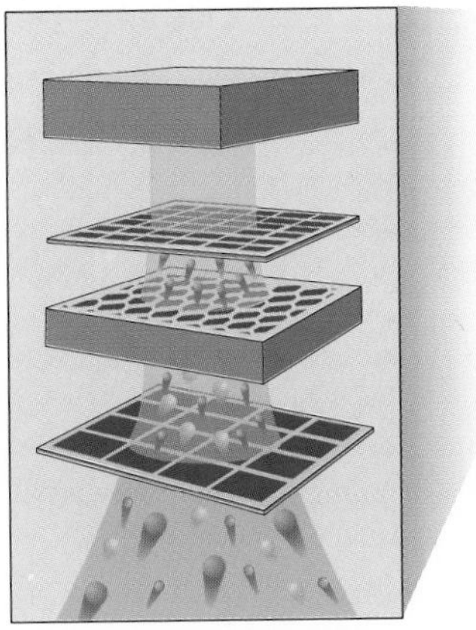

In a Filter

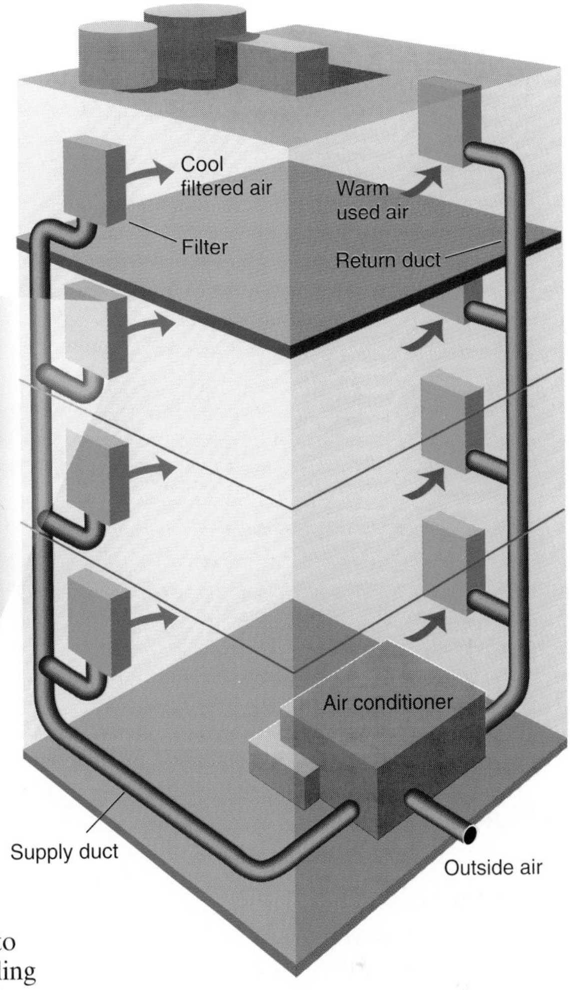

Commercial systems often use large, central pieces of equipment called **chillers**. Chillers produce cold water and pipe it around the building to cooling coils. Fans blow air across the cooling coils and distribute the cooled air to offices through insulated ductwork. Each working area has its own thermostat.

Commercial buildings are often very tightly sealed to prevent the loss of heated or cooled air. Many offices have windows that do not open. To keep the occupants healthy and productive, air conditioning systems for these buildings include ventilation to provide a constant supply of fresh air.

ENERGY CONSERVATION

Because energy is expensive, it is important for cooling systems to be efficient. During the 1990's, air conditioner manufacturers made great strides in improving efficiency. This improvement was needed to satisfy customers who needed to reduce costs and to meet new government efficiency standards. Today's best air conditioners use half the energy of those from the 1970's.

Improving buildings can also save energy. Adding insulation in walls, roofs, and floors keeps air cool longer. Better windows, especially those made from solar-reflecting glass, are also energy savers. Finally, improved control of air conditioning systems can save energy. Automatic thermostats that let building temperatures rise when a home or building is unoccupied can save great amounts of energy. In the future, new concepts for cooling and "intelligent controls" will result in greater comfort at lower cost.

JAN F. KREIDER
Professor and Founding Director
Joint Center for Energy Management
University of Colorado

See also HEAT; HEATING AND VENTILATING SYSTEMS; REFRIGERATION.

AIR FORCE. See CANADA, ARMED FORCES OF; UNITED STATES, ARMED FORCES OF THE.

A radio-controlled aerobatic (stunt) plane is readied for flight.

AIRPLANE MODELS

No one knows who built the first model airplane. Models of birds, carved from wood and able to fly like gliders, have been found in ancient Egyptian tombs. Early inventors such as Leonardo Da Vinci (1452–1519) built models of their concepts of "flying machines." But the modern hobby of model-airplane building did not really begin until after World War I. The war proved that the airplane was an exciting and practical way to transport people and products. The romance of air travel, together with a natural creative desire, led many people of all ages into the hobby of building miniature models of real airplanes.

▶ NON-FLYING MODELS

The easiest-to-build and least expensive model airplanes are constructed from plastic kits. They are made up of pre-molded plastic parts. The parts are very detailed. When they are glued together and painted, the result is a very realistic model of an airplane. They are simple to build, but serious modelers have been known to spend hundreds of hours in research and construction. They try to duplicate, as nearly as possible, an actual aircraft—perhaps one flown by a specific pilot in a particular battle. Many modelers go one step further. They build realistic settings, complete with trees and shrubs, buildings, and even miniature people, to create museumlike displays for their airplanes.

In the days before plastic kits, it was common practice to carve models from blocks of wood. That type of construction is mostly limited now to experienced modelers who wish to duplicate an airplane for which no kit is available. It is quite enjoyable to whittle an airplane from a piece of wood. And it is good practice for going on to the next step in model building.

▶ FLYING MODELS

This is the part of model-airplane building where the real excitement begins. An airplane is not truly an airplane unless it flies.

There is great variety in the types of models built for flight. They range from the simplest hand-launched glider to very complicated radio-controlled helicopters. Some are scale models of real airplanes. But others are special aircraft designed for contests in which the models are judged for flight duration, precision maneuvers, or speed.

Flying models are classified according to the way they are controlled in flight. The three categories of flying models are free flight, control line, and radio control.

Free Flight

The very early model airplanes were all free-flying. That is, once they were launched, there was no way to control their flight. Free flight remains a very popular activity today. To many modelers there is nothing quite so beautiful as the sight of a model drifting freely on a gentle breeze.

But it is not fun to lose a model if it flies too far. The wise free-flight flier sets the rudder on the airplane to produce a gentle turn. This keeps the model flying in circles overhead.

Free-flight models can be divided into three types—gliders, rubber-powered, and engine-powered. Gliders are relatively simple. They are launched into the air either by being thrown or by being towed on a string (like a kite) and then released for free flight. The towline is attached to a hook on the bottom of the glider. When it reaches altitude, the line is slackened, allowing it to slide off the hook. The glider is then free to soar like a bird.

Rubber-powered models have propellers that are turned by wound-up rubber bands. When the rubber unwinds, it turns the propeller, which causes the airplane to move forward through the air. Some rubber-powered models are very small, with wingspans of no more than 30 centimeters (12 inches). Others have wingspans of close to 2 meters (6 feet). A very special type of rubber-powered model is designed to be flown in large rooms indoors. These super-lightweight models can fly for almost an hour at a time.

Engine-powered models, sometimes called gas models, are powered by engines similar to those used in lawn mowers. But they are small enough to fit in the palm of your hand. These miniature engines produce a great deal of power for their small size. They can fly a model airplane to amazing heights. Once the model rises high enough, the motor is shut off by a timing mechanism, and the airplane is free to glide back to earth.

Free-flight models have one disadvantage. They require large open spaces in which to fly. This was one of the factors that led to the invention of a means of controlling the flight in a small area.

Control Line

Control-line airplanes are flown in circles at the end of two thin steel wires connected to a handle that is held by the pilot. The two wires are usually about 20 meters (65 feet) long. They are attached to a mechanism inside the airplane that controls the up-and-down direction of flight. By moving the handle, pilots can make the airplane do loops, figure eights, and other stunts. They can also control the takeoff and landing.

Control-line airplanes are all powered by miniature engines. There are contests for stunt flying, speed flying, and racing and for scale models.

Radio Control

Remote-control airplanes are the most realistic because they can be controlled in flight without wires or connections of any sort. Every maneuver that a real airplane makes can be duplicated by a radio-controlled model. Sometimes it is difficult to tell whether a model or a real plane is in the sky.

To understand how radio control works, think of your radio or television set. Somewhere outside your house there is a radio or television station transmitting radio waves through the air. You cannot see them or feel them or hear them. But your radio or television is designed to receive these waves and turn them into sound and pictures. Different kinds of radio waves are sent out on different channels, and you can tune your receiver to pick up these waves.

In a radio-control system for model airplanes, there is a transmitter, a receiver, and small electric motors (called servos) to move the airplane's controls. The pilot, using a handheld transmitter, moves various levers and buttons to transmit different signals on different channels. Inside the airplane, the receiver picks up these signals and activates the servos to move the controls that steer the plane.

On simple radio-controlled models, the only control is the rudder, which steers the airplane right or left. On the most complex models, all the controls of a real airplane are duplicated. These include retractable landing gear, engine throttle, sky-writing smoke in stunt planes, bomb-dropping in war planes, parachute drops, and just about anything else you can think of.

Radio-controlled models come in all types and sizes. There are gliders with wingspans of more than 3 meters (over 10 feet) that can soar for hours when the skillful pilot takes advantage of rising air currents. There are racing planes that fly at almost 200 kilometers (125 miles) per hour. Aerobatic airplanes can loop, roll, spin, and do everything a real air-show plane can do. And there are helicopters that hover and fly backward and sideways just like the real ones. In fact, radio-controlled models can be quite realistic in appearance and flight. Many have been used in motion pictures when it would have been too dangerous or expensive to use real aircraft.

Remember that flying models are not mere toys. Many of them are fast-moving objects that can fall and cause injury or damage. Care should be taken to fly them only under completely safe conditions.

ROCKETS

As the space age has developed, model rockets have become an exciting part of the modeling hobby. But model rockets are not strictly model airplanes. They are not toys, either. They are miniature missiles powered by real solid-fuel rocket motors.

Scale model rocket.

Model rockets are generally constructed of a basic cardboard tube for the body, with a balsa wood or plastic nose cone and balsa tail fins. There are many kits available, and it is best to start with a kit. They are properly designed and built to be completely safe in operation. A homemade rocket can be dangerous.

The rocket motor itself is a small cylinder that fits into the rear of the rocket body. Model-rocket motors are dangerous when they are not used properly. In certain places it is necessary to have a license to purchase them. For example, in California, in the United States, you must be at least 14 years of age to get a license. Your local hobby shop can give you full details on how to get a license.

Model-rocket motors are ignited by wires. These are attached at one end to the rocket and at the other end to an electric ignition device placed some distance away for safety. When electricity flows through the wires, the ignition wire in the rocket motor gets hot, just as the wires in a toaster do. This causes the rocket fuel to burn. When the fuel burns, the rocket does not go off like a firecracker. Instead, a hot, rapidly expanding gas is released. It shoots out through the motor nozzle at a very high speed and pushes the rocket up with a great deal of thrust (power).

A single rocket motor burns for just a few seconds. But it will push the model rocket to altitudes of more than 100 meters (over 325 feet). Multistage rockets use two or more motors, burning one after the other, to get to much greater heights.

Just before the motor burns out, the last little bit of gas pressure actually blows out through the front of the motor. This causes the nose cone of the rocket to pop off and release a parachute. The model rocket then comes down very gently on its parachute, ready for another blast-off.

As with airplanes, model rockets can be scale models of actual rockets and missiles. Or they can be original designs made up by the builder. Contests are often held on military bases, where the models can be tracked by radar to determine how high they fly.

YOU CAN DO IT, TOO

When the model-airplane hobby first started, very little equipment was available in

A model kit of the United States Air Force F-16 fighter jet. Engine-powered and radio-controlled, the finished model wil reach speeds of 125 miles (200 kilometers) per hour.

stores. Now, most cities and towns have well-stocked hobby shops, and construction kits are available for all types of airplanes.

The most common construction material is still lightweight balsa wood. But plastics are also popular, especially for complex shapes such as engine cowlings (housing for the engine) and wing tips. Some flying models are all plastic and are almost ready to fly right out of the box.

If you are just becoming interested in model airplanes, the best way to begin is with a well-proved kit of a simple airplane. It is not wise to start off with a big, complex model just because it looks exciting. Start with a model that is within your ability to build. You will soon progress to that big, fancy airplane. If at all possible, try to get advice from an experienced modeler. Read some of the model magazines that are available on newsstands and in hobby shops. If you wish to join a model-airplane club, your local hobby shop will know whether there are any clubs in your area. The Academy of Model Aeronautics in Washington, D.C., can give you information on flying-model contests.

Above all, be patient. Do not rush in building a model. If you follow the directions and work carefully and neatly, all your airplanes will fly like birds.

DON TYPOND
EDITOR, *Model Airplane News*

Airplanes influence many aspects of modern life. Airliners (*above*) carry tourists and business people around the world. Airplanes contribute to increased farm production by aerial spraying of fertilizer and pesticides (*left*). Military fighter planes (*top left*) are an important element in national security. And planes such as the small, slow-flying ultralight (*top right*) are flown just for fun.

AIRPLANES

The airplane has had a greater impact on our lives than any other modern invention. The ability to fly has dramatically increased the speed at which we can travel and decreased the time it takes to receive mail, food, and other goods from far-off places. It has brought us into closer contact with people in other parts of the world, and it has drastically changed the way we wage war.

Yet, until the beginning of the 20th century, the idea of a practical flying machine was only a dream. Balloons and gliders had been flown before 1900, but they were unreliable and could not carry a person over a long distance and land at a chosen destination. It was not until Orville and Wilbur Wright invented and successfully flew the first powered, controllable aircraft that the dream of flight became a reality. On December 17, 1903, the Wrights' plane, the *Flyer,* took off at Kitty Hawk, North Carolina, and flew 120 feet (37 meters).

The airplane has changed greatly since 1903. The wingspan of a modern jumbo jet is longer than the entire distance flown on the Wright brothers' first flight. That flight lasted only 12 seconds; in 1986 a plane named *Voyager* was flown around the world in nine days without stopping or refueling. Airplanes have been flown at more than 4,500 miles (7,300 kilometers) per hour and to altitudes of almost 70 miles (110 kilometers) above the earth. But no matter how fast, high, or far airplanes fly, they are still subject to the same basic principles of flight as the Wright *Flyer*.

HOW AN AIRPLANE FLIES

An airplane is a heavier-than-air craft that can fly only if air flows over its wings fast enough to produce an upward force called **lift.** The force of lift must be strong enough to overcome the force of **gravity,** the force that pulls objects toward the ground. A third force, called **thrust,** is required to move the plane through the air. Thrust is produced by the plane's engine. Thrust must be stronger than another force, called **drag.** Drag is the resistance of the air to anything moving through it. Lift, gravity, thrust, and drag are the four forces that act on every airplane.

The four forces can be experienced while riding a bicycle. The rider pedals, producing thrust by turning the rear wheel against the ground. The sensation of air pushing against the rider can be compared to the force of drag. If the rider holds out one hand with the palm down and slightly tilted to face the oncoming air, the hand will rise. This is similar to the way a wing reacts to one kind of lifting force. Gravity keeps the rider earthbound.

Of the four forces, lift is perhaps the least familiar. It is the result of physical laws that govern the way all liquids and gases behave when they are in motion. Air, a gas, moves faster when it flows past an obstacle. As it flows faster, its pressure is reduced. This law is known as Bernoulli's principle, and it is one of the basic laws of aerodynamics (the study of air, or any other gas, in motion). It is further explained in the article AERODYNAMICS, in this volume. Bernoulli's principle is used in the design of an airplane's wing to change the air pressure around the wing and produce lift.

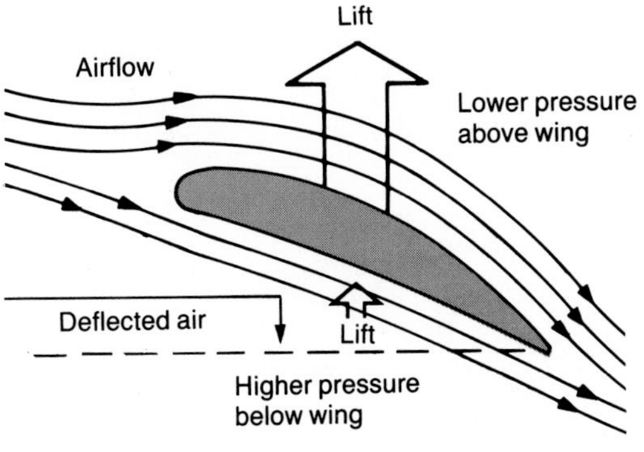

Air travels faster over the curved top of a wing than under its relatively flat bottom. As air moves faster, its pressure becomes lower. This lower pressure produces lift.

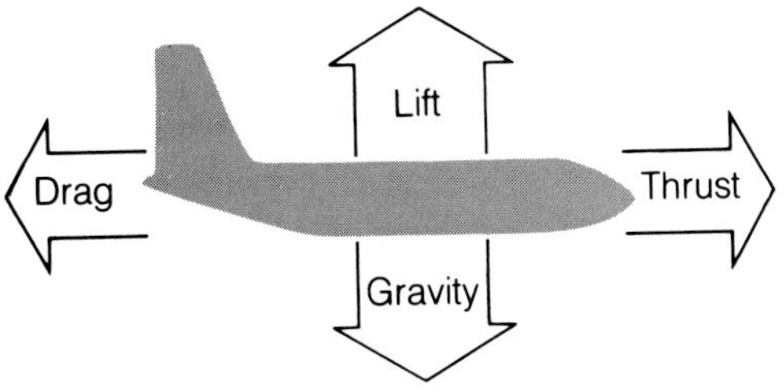

Four forces act on a plane. Thrust is produced by the engine to overcome the drag of air resistance. Air flowing over the wing creates lift, which overcomes gravity.

The airplane's wing is an **airfoil,** a surface that produces lift when air moves over it. A wing has a curved top surface and a relatively flat bottom surface. As the wing moves through the air, the particles of air are separated. They must move either over or under the wing and meet again behind the wing. Air passing over the curved top of the wing has a longer distance to travel and so moves faster than the air passing under the wing. Just as Bernoulli had proved, pressure is reduced in the faster-moving air over the wing. The lower pressure of the air above the wing pulls the wing up. This upward force is lift. As the airplane moves faster, the lift increases, until it is strong enough to overcome the force of gravity and lift the airplane's weight.

More lift is created as the result of another physical law. This is Newton's third law of motion, which states that for every action there is an equal and opposite reaction. In normal flight, the wing is slightly tilted, so the front is slightly higher than the back. When the bicyclist tilted an outstretched hand and felt it rise, that happened because air struck the bottom surface and was deflected, or turned, downward. According to Newton's law, the force of this deflected air exerts an equal force in the opposite direction, in this case, upward against the bottom of the wing or the bicyclist's palm, lifting them upward. This force may provide as much as 25 percent of the lift on a wing.

STRUCTURE

The design of modern airplanes is based on the same aerodynamic principles used by the Wright brothers. But modern airplanes are built with stronger materials and more powerful engines. They fly faster and carry heavy loads or many passengers. They may be single-engine (one-engine) or multi-engine airplanes. Some are owned by large airlines or corporations, while others are owned by individuals. Airplanes are used for business, pleasure, and sports, such as racing or aerobatics. Other airplanes are military fighters, bombers, or transports that carry soldiers, tanks, or other equipment.

All of these aircraft, as different as they may seem, work on the same aerodynamic principles and are made up of the same structural components (parts): the **fuselage;** the **wings;** the **tail assembly,** with **vertical** and **horizontal stabilizers;** and the **landing gear.** All of these components together are called the **airframe.** The other main component of an airplane is the engine, which provides the power.

Fuselage

The purpose of the fuselage, or body of the plane, is to carry the pilot, passengers, and cargo. The oldest fuselage design, the **truss type,** consists of a welded steel framework (truss) covered with tightly stretched fabric, metal, or composites which is painted to provide a smooth surface. The framework absorbs the stresses encountered in flight. The popular Piper Cub, first built in the 1930's and still flown today, has a fuselage of this type, as do many sport, recreational, and utility airplanes still being produced.

A second type of airplane fuselage is **monocoque.** Monocoque is a French word meaning "single shell." No truss is needed because the shell is made of metal or other strong material, such as composites (compounds) of plastic, fiberglass, and carbon fiber. These are strong enough to absorb the forces of normal flight. Small airplanes are often built with monocoque construction to save weight. But monocoque construction is not strong enough or rigid enough for large cargo planes or airliners. Therefore, most modern commercially built airline aircraft are manufactured using

It takes about four years from the first design of an airliner to reach the full-scale production stage shown here. These planes may be in use for 20 years.

The Boeing 747 is the largest airliner. It is 231 feet (70.5 meters) long and weighs 720,000 pounds (330,000 kilograms) when fully loaded. It can carry over 450 passengers. The 747 is used chiefly for long flights, such as from New York to San Francisco or London.

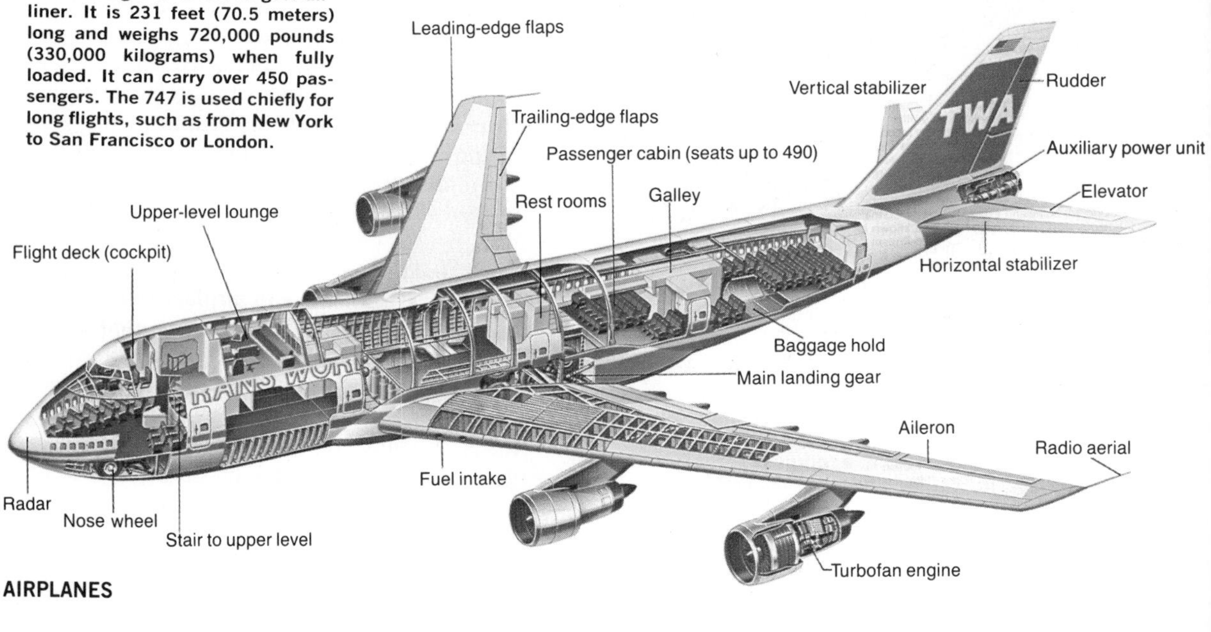

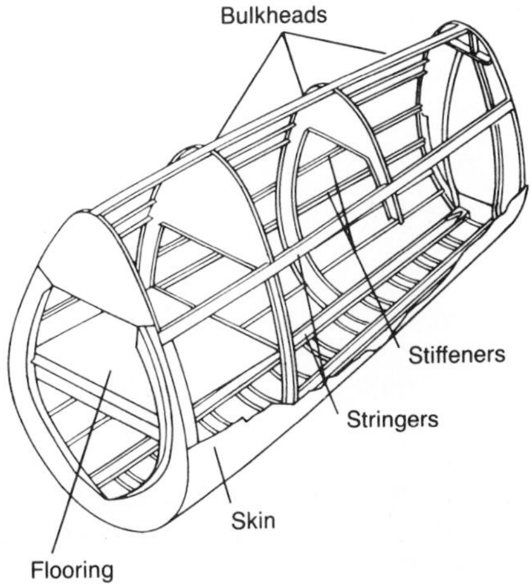

Semi-monocoque construction (*above*) is clearly visible in the fuselage of the airliner being built (*left*). The location of the windows indicates that the floor of the passenger compartment will be near the center of the fuselage. Cables provide temporary support during construction.

the **semi-monocoque** method, in which bracing and stiffeners of metal or other materials are added to the shell.

Modern airliners and military aircraft can fly at extremely high altitudes, where lower air pressure and oxygen content make breathing difficult. Also, the rapid changes in air pressure that occur when changing altitude can cause extreme physical discomfort. Therefore, the passenger cabin and cockpit of modern passenger jets are pressurized. Like the hull of a submarine, the fuselage of a pressurized aircraft is airtight. The air pressure inside the cabin and cockpit is increased by air compressors as the jet gains altitude. In this way, air pressure inside the plane is almost as high as pressure at ground level.

Wings

Airplane wings are designed to be very strong. Beneath the skin, or surface material, of the wing is a framework consisting of one or more **spars,** and **ribs, stringers,** and **formers.** The spars run from the wing root (the part of the wing attached to the fuselage) to the wing tip. Ribs run from the leading edge (front) of the wing to the trailing edge (back) of the wing. This framework provides the wing with its shape and its strength.

The distance from the leading edge to the trailing edge of the wing is called the **chord.** The distance from wing tip to wing tip is the **wingspan.**

Because the wing is an airfoil and thus produces lift, it is relatively flat on the bottom and curved on the top. This curve is called **camber.** Camber is the amount of curvature of the airfoil from the leading edge to the trailing edge of the wing. Thus a wing can have more or less camber, or curve, depending on the purpose for which it is designed.

The design and location of airplane wings vary according to the purpose of the airplane. Many modern airplanes have low wings—that is, wings attached near the bottom of the fuselage. Airplanes that operate out of rough, unpaved airfields often have wings attached near the top of the fuselage. High wings are less likely to hit the ground as the airplane bumps over the rough airfield. High-wing planes include the two-seat Piper Cub and the C-130, a large military plane that carries troops and equipment into grass or dirt air fields.

On most airplanes the wings are attached at a slight angle, so that when viewed from the front they form a shallow V. This angle is called the **dihedral,** and it reduces the plane's tendency to roll from side to side.

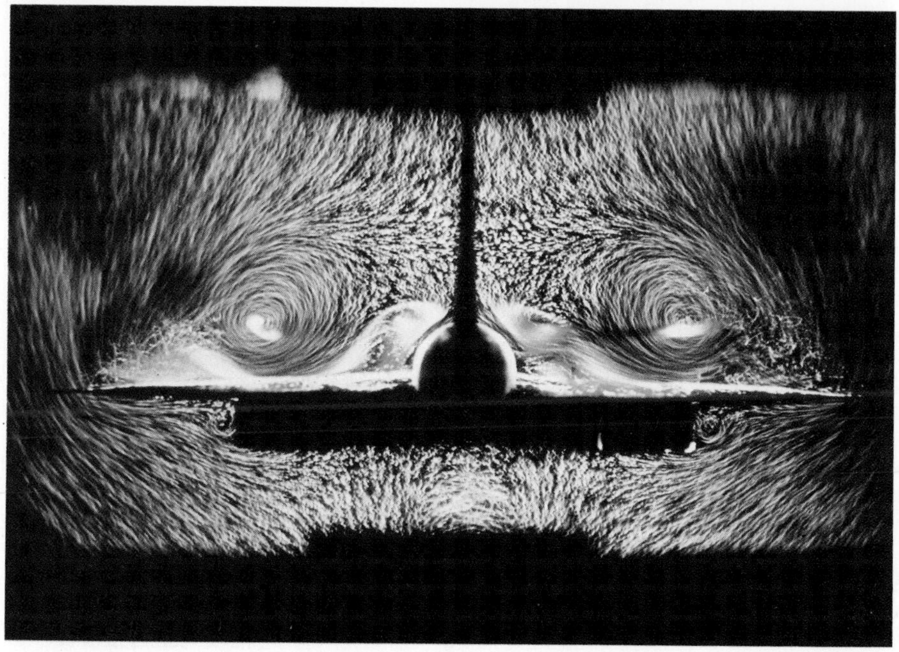

◀ A wind-tunnel test of a model of the supersonic Concorde shows how air flows over its wings when it flies at lower speeds. The pattern changes as airspeed increases. Water containing dyes is injected into the tunnel to make the airflow visible.

▶ The ribs of the small airplane wing (*right*) show the top curve that gives it an airfoil (lift-producing) shape. Ribs also curve the top of the large airliner wing (*far right*), seen here from a passenger window. The flaps have been lowered to increase the curve. This provides more lift at slow speeds during takeoff and landing.

The shape and thickness of the wing are determined by the speed at which the airplane will be flown. Slower-flying planes have wings that extend straight out from the fuselage, with a very visible curve on the top surface. This provides lift at slow speeds. Faster airplanes have thinner wings. Because the air flows faster over these wings, less curve is needed to create lift. On very high speed jet fighters, the wing appears almost flat on top and is shorter. Such wings are also very thin so they create less drag at high speeds.

Wings on high-speed planes are usually **swept** (angled back). On some planes the two swept wings together form a triangle called a **delta wing.**

Planes with thin, short, swept wings must land at much higher speeds than straight-wing airplanes in order to maintain lift until the plane is on the ground. The F-14 Tomcat, a jet fighter, has variable wings, which can be changed from straight to swept. This allows it to be more easily maneuvered at both low and high speeds.

On each wing of an airplane are hinged movable sections called **control surfaces** with which the pilot controls the movement of the plane. **Ailerons** are control surfaces located on the trailing edge of the wing, near the wing tip. The pilot controls the ailerons by moving the control stick or wheel of the airplane. If the pilot moves the stick or turns the wheel to the right, the right aileron moves up and the left aileron moves down. Air pushing against the upturned right aileron forces the right wing down, while, at the same time, air pushing against the downturned left aileron pushes the left wing up. This causes the airplane to turn and **bank,** (tilt) to the right. A left movement of the stick or wheel causes the ailerons to move in the opposite directions, and the airplane banks to the left.

Many airplanes also have other control surfaces on the wings, called **flaps.** Flaps are usually located on the trailing edge between the aileron and the wing root. Flaps move at the same time in the same direction. When the pilot puts the flaps down, the camber of the wings is increased, thus increasing lift and permitting the airplane to fly at slower speeds. Flaps are put down primarily when landing. Because having the flaps down also creates drag, they are put up for normal flight.

Tail Assembly

The tail assembly, or **empennage,** of an airplane has two purposes: to provide stability and to control direction.

In most situations, a pilot prefers to keep the plane stable, or steady, in straight and

level flight. In most aircraft, this stability is provided by surfaces called stabilizers. A fixed vertical stabilizer prevents the airplane from **yawing** (swinging from side to side). The horizontal stabilizer prevents **pitching** (up and down movement of the nose). On some planes the horizontal stabilizer is located near the nose. Then it is called a **canard.**

Directional control is provided by two control surfaces in the tail. These are the **rudder** and the **elevator.** The rudder is a hinged surface attached to the vertical stabilizer. The pilot moves the rudder by pushing foot pedals. When the pilot pushes the right rudder pedal, the rudder moves to the right. The pressure of the airflow against the rudder pushes the airplane's tail to the left. This, in turn, pushes the nose of the airplane to the right. When making a turn, the pilot uses both the ailerons and the rudder. This is called a co-ordinated turn.

Elevators are the movable control surfaces hinged to the horizontal stabilizer. When the pilot pushes the control stick or wheel forward, the elevators go down. The airflow pushes on the elevators, which makes the tail move up and the nose point down. Pulling the stick or wheel back puts the elevator up so the airflow pushes the tail down and the nose up. These movements are called changing the

A plane rotates around 3 lines, called axes. It rolls around an axis from nose to tail, yaws around an axis from top to bottom, and pitches around an axis from wing tip to wing tip.

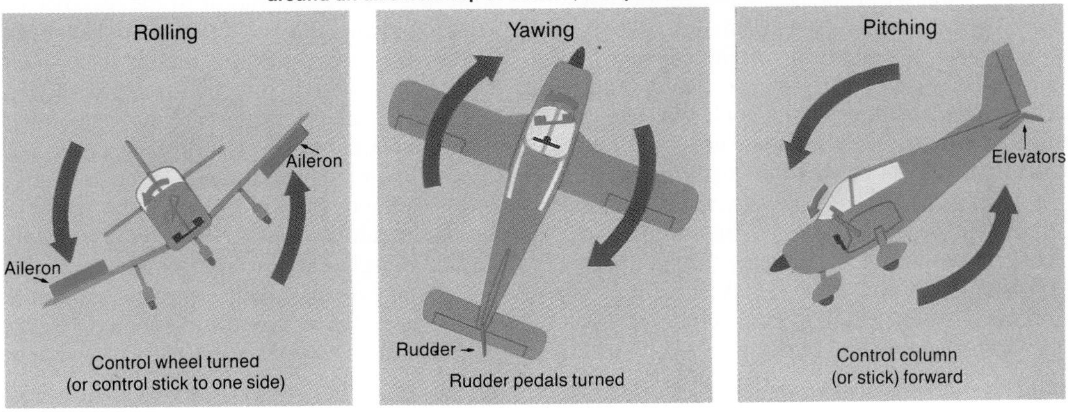

Planes equipped with special landing gear can land on surfaces other than runways. Planes with pontoons are able to land on water (*below*). Skis can be attached to landing gear (*right*) for winter flying in northern areas. Ski-planes and seaplanes are important means of transportation in remote areas of Canada and Alaska.

pitch of the airplane. On some airplanes, the function of the elevator is served by a horizontal stabilizer that can be moved up or down to control pitch. A horizontal stabilizer designed in this manner is called a **stabilator.**

Most airplanes also have **trim tabs**—small hinged sections of the elevator and rudder. These can be adjusted to stick out into the airflow to exert pressure on the control surface, causing it to move. In situations where a certain amount of pitch or yaw must be maintained for a period of time, the pilot can set the trim tab to hold the control surface in one position, such as a long, steady descent. Thus the pilot is better able to concentrate on other aspects of controlling the plane.

Landing Gear

In the early days of aviation, most airplanes had two wheels in front of the airplane's center of gravity (the point where the plane's weight is evenly balanced). A third, smaller wheel was located in the rear under the tail. Because this arrangement was used successfully for a long time, it is referred to as **conventional landing gear.** Newer aircraft often use **tricycle gear,** which consists of two wheels behind the center of gravity and a third wheel under the nose of the airplane. Aircraft with tricycle gear are easier to control on the ground than those with conventional landing gear. For this reason, tricycle gear aircraft are more popular with most of today's pilots.

All early airplanes were **fixed-gear** aircraft. The wheels remained in place whether the airplane was on the ground or in the air. Today, although many aircraft still have fixed gear, faster airplanes have **retractable gear**—the wheels are pulled up into the fuselage or wings of the airplane. Fixed gear causes a great deal of drag, which slows the airplane down and increases fuel consumption (amount of fuel used). Retracting the wheels into the wings or fuselage reduces drag.

Landing gear may consist of equipment other than wheels. For example, **seaplanes,** special aircraft that take off and land on water, have **pontoons** (floats) instead of wheels.

Flying boats have a boat-shaped hull on which they land. Seaplanes with retractable landing gear for use on land are called **amphibians.** There are also planes that are equipped with skis for landing on snow. Landing on either water or snow requires different piloting techniques from those used to land on pavement.

POWER AND PROPULSION

In order for an airplane to achieve flight, its wings must be pushed or pulled through the air fast enough to create lift. This function of propulsion is performed by the engine. There are three main types of airplane engines: **reciprocating** engines, **jet** engines, and **rocket** engines.

Reciprocating Engines

Reciprocating engines, or piston engines, used in airplanes are very similar to those used in automobiles. In a reciprocating engine, the expanding force of a burning fuel (gasoline) pushes pistons, which in turn rotate a crankshaft. In an airplane, the crankshaft turns the propeller. (You can learn more about how reciprocating engines work by consulting the article INTERNAL-COMBUSTION ENGINES in Volume I.

Reciprocating engines need cooling systems so they will not overheat. The first airplanes had liquid-cooled engines like those of many automobiles. Today, most reciprocating airplane engines are air cooled.

An air-cooled engine is lighter than a liquid-cooled engine because it does not have to carry hoses, radiators, cooling fluid, and circulation pumps. Air-cooled engines must be constructed so that the greatest possible area is exposed to the onrushing air. Air is forced into openings in the **cowling** (engine cover) behind the propeller and then flows over the engine to cool it. Because of their lightness, air-cooled engines replaced liquid-cooled engines for most uses by the 1930's. But liquid-cooled engines continued to be used very successfully for certain types of airplanes because they last longer than air-cooled engines and can produce more power. For example, some of the fastest piston-driven aircraft used during World War II (1939–45), such as the Spitfire and P-51 Mustang, had liquid-cooled engines. The *Voyager,* which in 1986 flew around the world without landing or refueling, used one air-cooled and one liquid-cooled engine.

Opened cowling (engine cover) reveals the four-cylinder engine of a small plane. A cone-shaped spinner reduces drag over the propeller hub.

Propellers. All reciprocating engines turn propellers. Some early airplanes, like the Wright *Flyer,* were pushed into the air by propellers at the rear, while most modern airplanes are pulled into the air by propellers at the front.

The propeller consists of a control **hub** at the center with two or more blades attached. The entire assembly is rotated by the engine, and the blades convert engine power into thrust. The propeller is a **rotating airfoil.** As the blade rotates through the air, lower pressure is created on its curved front surface, pulling the propeller and plane forward.

The angle at which the propeller blade strikes the air determines how much pulling or pushing power it produces. A flatter angle results in high pulling power but low forward speed. Early airplane propellers had fairly flat blade angles that could not be changed. This flatter blade angle was satisfactory as long as airplanes flew slowly, but it was not practical for high-speed aircraft. The problem was solved by **variable-pitch** propellers, invented in 1923. The blades of a variable-pitch propeller can be adjusted so that they have a flat angle for takeoff, when the most power is needed, and steep angles for normal flight, when speed is important. A more recent development is the **constant-speed** propeller, which automatically (without pilot input) adjusts the angle of the propeller blade to maintain a constant forward speed.

Jet Engines

Jet engines have fewer moving parts than reciprocating engines, but they burn a great deal more fuel. A jet engine burns its fuel in an enclosed space called a combustion chamber. The burning of fuel produces hot gases that rush out of the rear opening of the engine at high speed. This powerful jet exhaust pushes the engine (and the plane to which it is attached) forward.

Before leaving the engine, the gases race past a fanlike device called a **turbine,** making it turn. The turbine is mounted on a drive shaft. As the drive shaft turns, it turns another set of fans, called the **compressor,** at the front end of the engine. The spinning compressor packs enormous amounts of air into the combustion chamber, providing the oxygen needed for continuous burning of the fuel. This basic type of jet engine is called the **turbojet.** It powers some of the fastest high-altitude aircraft, such as military fighters and bombers.

The **turboprop** engine is very similar to the turbojet, but it uses the power of the jet exhaust to turn a propeller. Turboprops are used on planes that must use fuel more efficiently, but planes using them do not fly as fast.

Turbofans are jet engines with a second turbine that drives a fan near the front of the engine. This fan, which acts something like a propeller, forces air out through special openings at very high speed. The air passes around the outside of the engine and provides extra thrust without burning extra fuel. The rest of the air enters the engine. Turbofan engines are widely used in modern airliners because they burn less fuel and are usually quieter than turbojet engines used in earlier airliners.

More about how jet engines work can be found in the article JET PROPULSION in Volume J–K.

Rocket Engines

Rocket engines are used very rarely in aircraft today. Rockets require much more fuel than jet engines, so they would require much larger fuel tanks. Also, refueling a rocket is more complicated than putting jet fuel or aviation gas on an airplane. Unlike jet engines, rockets are closed at the forward end. As a solid or liquid fuel burns in the combustion chamber, hot gases rush rearward through a nozzle. Because every physical action results in an opposite reaction, the engine, and the aircraft attached to it, is pushed forward. Rocket engines have been used primarily on experimental types of aircraft such as the Bell X-1, which, in 1947, was the first plane to break the sound barrier. (Rocket engines are described in the article ROCKETS in Volume R.)

New Designs

Today, a great deal of research and development is being devoted to engines and propulsion. Because reciprocating engines are less expensive to operate than jet engines, and because jet engines often make a great deal of noise, many researchers are experimenting with high-performance propeller-driven engines. In the late 1980's, the National Aeronautics and Space Administration (NASA) and several private companies were experimenting

Most jet-powered passenger airplanes have turbofan engines similar to this one with its cowling removed for repairs (*left*). A new turboprop design (*right*) has two propellers, which move in opposite directions. It produces as much power as a turbofan at lower cost.

The *Solar Challenger* flew across the English Channel in 1981, powered only by sunlight. The black areas on the top of its wings are solar cells, which convert sunlight to electricity.

with curved propeller blades, which will be used on airliners of the future. The Beech Starship, which was developed by a private company, uses a rear-mounted **pusher prop,** which is almost as fast as a jet engine and more efficient than a propeller that pulls an airplane through the air.

There have been new developments in power for very light aircraft. Dr. Paul MacCready, an American inventor, built the *Gossamer Condor* in 1977 and the *Gossamer Albatross* in 1979. These were human-powered airplanes in which the pilot pedaled a bicycle-like mechanism that turns the propeller. A later MacCready design known as the *Solar Challenger* flew across the English Channel in 1981 entirely under solar power.

INSTRUMENTS

Aviation pioneers flew using very simple methods, such as looking for landmarks and other visual references. They also sensed the forces on the airplane through their bodies, so they said they "flew by the seat of their pants." But instruments have become more and more important in aviation. Generally, the larger the airplane, the greater the number of instruments. Even a relatively simple training airplane like a Cessna 152 contains enough instruments to confuse the nonflyer. But a highly complex airplane such as the Concorde, a supersonic airliner, contains many more instruments. As a result, the crew of the Concorde and some other large airliners includes a special crew member, the flight engineer, whose job is to monitor these instruments and make the necessary adjustments to the engines and other systems. The pilot and co-pilot fly the airplane and also give their attention to flight instruments and navigation instruments.

Engine Instruments

Each airplane, no matter how large or how small, has a number of instruments for each engine. A **tachometer** tells how many revolutions per minute the engine makes. The temperature and the pressure of the air entering the engine, the fuel pressure, the oil pressure, and the engine temperature are usually measured as well. Jet planes use gauges that measure the temperature of the exhaust gases as they exit the tail pipe. Although all aircraft also have fuel gauges, most pilots measure the amount of fuel at the beginning of the flight and mathematically compute their fuel consumption throughout the trip. They use the fuel gauge only as a backup to their own computations.

Flight Instruments

If a pilot is flying low and slow, he or she does not need many flight instruments. However, all pilots need to know four basic types of information. They must know the **heading** (the direction in which the airplane is flying), its altitude, its airspeed, and its **attitude** (pitch and bank in relation to the horizon).

The most basic of all flight instruments is the compass, which indicates the heading of the airplane. The magnetic compass can give a true heading in straight and level flight but has a tendency to be inaccurate when the airplane is turning. For this reason, many larger aircraft are equipped with instruments called **gyrocompasses,** which are not affected by the turns. (Gyrocompasses are described in the article GYROSCOPE in Volume G.)

Altimeters measure altitude. There are two types of altimeters. One measures the pressure of the outside air, which decreases at a fairly regular rate as the aircraft gains altitude. A pilot, however, must be careful with this type of altimeter because it is affected by changes in temperature and barometric pressure, which in turn are affected by the weather. The **radio altimeter** uses a radio beam to measure the distance to the ground.

The **airspeed indicator** measures the speed with which the airplane moves through the air. The air enters the instrument through a special tube called a **Pitot-static tube,** which is mounted on the outside of the airplane. The faster the plane moves, the more air rushes into the tube, moving a **diaphragm**—a flexible surface inside the instrument—that turns an indicator needle.

An airplane's **airspeed** (speed through the air) is seldom the same as its **ground speed** (speed in relation to the ground). For example, if a plane flies into the wind, this head wind reduces the plane's ground speed but does not affect its airspeed. If the plane is flying at the same airspeed but in the same direction as the wind is blowing, this tail wind increases the speed with which the plane moves over the ground. Ground speed may be calculated by measuring how long it takes to fly a known distance between two points. It also may be measured electronically with DME (Distance Measuring Equipment).

The attitude of the airplane in relation to the ground must be known when flying in clouds or fog. Three instruments can be used to determine the plane's attitude. The **rate-of-climb indicator** tells how many feet per minute the plane is climbing or descending. The **turn-and-bank indicator** shows how many degrees the plane is banked to the left or right. The artificial horizon shows the pitch of the nose above or below the horizon. All commercial aircraft have these instruments.

Navigation Instruments

Navigation is the science of getting to a destination in an airplane without getting lost. The oldest method of navigating an airplane is called **pilotage.** The pilot navigated by watching for landmarks on the ground and comparing them with a map. Pilotage works well at relatively low speeds and altitudes, when landmarks can be seen easily. However, when flying a plane higher, faster, or in clouds or fog, a pilot must be able to navigate without seeing the ground.

If a pilot knows the direction in which the aircraft is headed, its altitude and airspeed, the direction and speed of the wind, and the outside air temperature, he or she can compute, with the aid of a watch, the airplane's position on a flight map without seeing the ground. This is an excellent method of navigation called **dead reckoning.** However, the use of reliable electronic instruments has largely replaced dead reckoning for commercial flights.

The development of radio and electronic navigation has greatly simplified the task of navigating an aircraft. Many aircraft are equipped with automatic **radio compasses** that indicate the direction from which a radio signal is coming. If lost, the pilot simply tunes the radio compass to the frequency of an airport radio range transmitter. An indicator needle shows the way to the station. This is sometimes known as **homing in** on a radio station. The pilot can also pinpoint the airplane's position by tuning in two or three different stations and plotting the signals on a map. The airplane's position will be the point on the map where the directional lines cross. The locations and frequencies of these old-style radio range stations are still given on flight charts used by all pilots.

Radio ranges, however, are being replaced by more effective devices known as VOR's. VOR stands for Very-high-frequency Omnidirectional Range. A VOR radio station sends out 360 course signals spaced one degree apart, radiating like the spokes of a wheel from a radio transmitter. Pilots may select and fly on any of these courses. An indicator in the cockpit tells the pilot the position of the airplane in relationship to the VOR. As previously mentioned, a DME can be used for measuring the exact speed of the airplane. It also measures the exact distance of the airplane from the VOR transmitter.

Military pilots use a radio navigation system known as TACAN (TACtical Airborne Navigation). TACAN works like a combination of VOR and DME and has a longer range.

Several years ago, sailors began using a radio system called loran (*lo*ng-*ra*nge *n*avigation) aboard ships at sea and in the Great Lakes. Soon, private pilots discovered that loran signals can be transmitted long distances and that the system is extremely accurate. They began experimenting with Marine loran radio receivers. Today, loran plays an important role in aerial navigation across the United States for many types of aircraft.

Inertial Navigation. Today, most commercial aircraft and many military aircraft use inertial navigation. Inertial navigation is accomplished by a computer that uses a very precise program together with a memory, accelerometer (an instrument measuring all directions and rates of movement), and gyroscopes to measure the plane's precise position above the earth's surface in latitude and longitude. The latest developments in precision navigation make use of satellite technology.

Radar. Commercial aircraft and larger general aviation aircraft use radar to find and avoid storm systems. This is an important function because bad weather is the age-old enemy of the pilot. In fact, approximately 40 percent of all general aviation accidents are caused by bad weather. However, the type of radar used in civilian aircraft cannot help pilots detect other airplanes. Another, more complex type of radar is used for this purpose. It is found only in military aircraft, which must locate enemy planes even when they are too far away to see.

Most airplanes have duplicate instruments and flight controls for the captain, who sits on the left, and the co-pilot. The Boeing 747-400 has computer screens displaying flight, navigation, and engine information as well as traditional flight instruments.

Auto Pilot. Automatic pilots are standard equipment on most commercial aircraft, and increasing numbers of military and private aircraft have them as well. The simplest auto pilot is based on two gyroscopes, each of which is connected to the aircraft's controls. When an airplane deviates (strays) from straight and level flight, the gyroscopes detect the change. By means of electrical servomotors (much like those used on radio-controlled model airplanes), they move the controls slightly to return the airplane to straight and level flight. More sophisticated automatic pilots are used by aircraft that have computerized navigation systems. In these aircraft, the auto pilot may be set to fly a particular course at a certain airspeed and altitude. The auto pilot automatically updates its position through the navigation computers while monitoring its speed, altitude, and heading.

Until recently, the dozens, or sometimes hundreds, of instruments in an airplane's cockpit had analog displays; that is, they had clock-type faces with dials and hands. In today's most modern aircraft, these analog instruments have been replaced by digital instruments, which display information in the form of numbers. Also, high technology in the form of computerization and CRT's (Cathode-Ray Tubes) is changing the look of the modern aircraft cockpit. Some corporate aircraft such as the Beech Starship and the Gulfstream IV already have what have been nicknamed "glass cockpits." These areas display on video screens all of the important information needed to fly and navigate an airplane. Many military aircraft and commercial airliners are also beginning to use this highly developed technology.

AIRPLANE DESIGN

An airplane can fly at fast or slow speeds over long or short distances. It can carry hundreds of vacationers around the world or a single person from one side of a major city to the other. The designer of an airplane must keep in mind the task the airplane is to accomplish. Will the airplane fly great distances? If so, the designer will have to provide either very efficient power or the capacity to store a great amount of fuel. Should the airplane's structure be relatively light or heavy? That depends on the cargo it will carry. This might be two persons or a whole company of soldiers and equipment. A large airplane will mean more weight and more drag. As a result, larger engines and wings will be necessary to get it airborne. Crop dusters, aerobatic biplanes, personal transportation aircraft, and airliners all have different design requirements. The airplane designer has many choices to make, and modern technology can help with these decisions.

Recently, airplanes have been designed with the aid of computers. CAD-CAM (Computer-Aided Design and Computer-Aided Manufacturing) is becoming part of the industry. The *Voyager* was designed with the aid of a computer. The design required very light weight, large fuel capacity, relatively high horsepower for propulsion, and efficient engines. After determining these requirements,

The F-15E Eagle and its computer-drawn skeleton are examples of current aircraft design knowledge and technique.

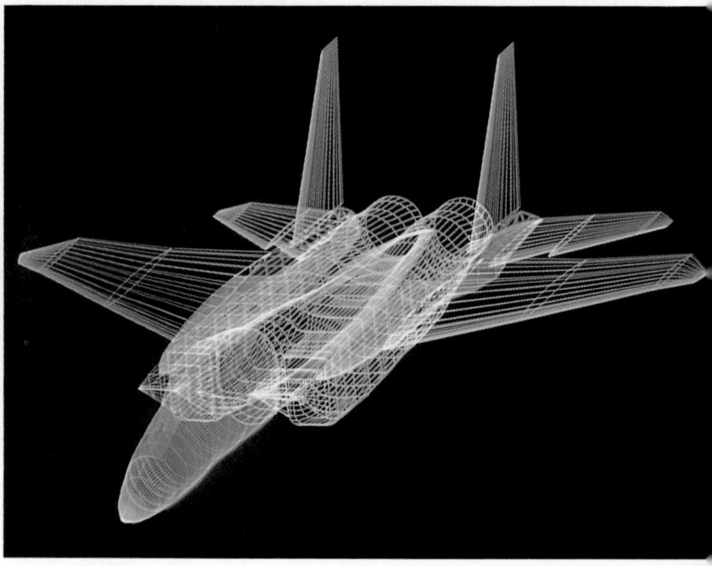

▲ A hypersonic plane similar to the one in this painting may be built in the near future. The orange areas indicate where heat would be created by friction with the air as it flies at about 10,000 miles (16,000 kilometers) per hour.

◄ The Bell XV-15 takes off and lands vertically like a helicopter. Once in flight, the engines rotate to a horizontal position and it flies like an airplane. It is designed to fly to and from the centers of cities.

the designers used computers to solve the complex mathematical problems encountered in designing aircraft.

▶THE FUTURE

Our future in the vast ocean of air above us is limited only by our imaginations. Today, composite materials similar to fiberglass are replacing some metal parts on many airplanes. These materials are stronger and lighter than those they replace. New engine and design technology will let aircraft fly higher and farther than ever before. Scientists are working on a hypersonic plane that will fly in the upper atmosphere at more than five times the speed of sound. It should cross the Pacific Ocean in only 2 hours instead of the 12 to 14 hours required by most commercial planes.

Other technological developments are bringing planes closer to home. Planes called VTOL's (Vertical Take Off and Landing) need very little space to take off and land, eliminating the need for long runways. One kind of VTOL, called a tilt rotor, has engines that can tilt to provide either horizontal or vertical thrust. The development of VTOL's allows planes to land at small airports closer to city centers.

At air shows around the world—Paris, France; Oshkosh, Wisconsin; Farnborough, England; Hanover, Germany; and Dayton, Ohio—engineers, designers, and developers all share information that will expand the future of flight.

PAUL H. POBEREZNY
President, Experimental Aircraft Association

See also AERODYNAMICS; AVIATION; GLIDERS; GYROSCOPE; INTERNAL-COMBUSTION ENGINES; JET PROPULSION; NAVIGATION; RADAR, SONAR, LORAN, AND SHORAN; ROCKETS.

Industrial plants pollute the air with smoke and gases that pour from their smokestacks.

AIR POLLUTION

Wherever you go—inside, outside, on top of a mountain, deep in a coal mine—you are always surrounded by a sea of gases. This sea is called the air, or the atmosphere.

The gases of the atmosphere cannot be seen, and we are rarely aware of them. But they are of the greatest importance. Without the atmosphere, people, animals, and plants could not live. Of almost equal importance is the quality of the atmosphere—whether it is pure or **polluted** (meaning impure).

The atmosphere is made up mainly of the gases nitrogen and oxygen, together with water vapor and smaller amounts of carbon dioxide and other gases. But all air contains some impurities. In rural areas, far removed from factories and heavy traffic, the air may contain pollen from plants, dust from the soil, and even bacteria. These impurities are usually in such small amounts that they are not important.

Air is said to be polluted when it contains enough harmful impurities to affect the health, safety, or comfort of living things. The impurities, or **pollutants**, could be tiny particles of matter or gases absent in clean air.

When people breathe, pollutants in the air may be deposited in the lungs or absorbed into the body. And polluted air can harm animals and plants as well as people. For this reason, our air supply should be closely watched and managed to assure its good quality.

▶ CAUSES OF AIR POLLUTION

There are two main types of air pollution: **gases**, which are mainly produced by the burning of fossil fuels such as oil and coal, and **particulates**, which are solid particles such as those found in the sooty debris released in the exhaust of automobiles.

Both types of pollution can have natural or human causes. Natural pollutants include windblown dust, pollen, and even the ash and gases from volcanic eruptions that can travel aound the world. Forest fires have blanketed huge areas of the United States with smoke so intense that air flights have to be canceled. Acts of nature such as these are often beyond human control.

The chief concern is perhaps a more serious source of air pollution—the pollution caused by human activity. Most of this pollution is produced by industry and by vehicles such as cars, trucks, and airplanes. It becomes worse as society becomes more industrialized—as more automobiles are produced and driven, new factories are built, and existing factories are expanded. It is most severe in cities, where people and industries are concentrated in large numbers.

The millions of people who live in cities need heat, hot water, and electric power. Much of the energy for these needs comes from furnaces and power plants burning fossil fuels. This produces large amounts of gases that enter the atmosphere. Another source of air pollution is the use of fossil fuels in transportation. Vehicles are the source of vast amounts of polluting gases and particulates. Sometimes factories produce waste chemicals that escape into the air. Smoke from cigarettes can pollute the air in a closed room. All kinds of surfaces grind against one another, sending tiny particles of dust into the air. Even ordinary wear and tear on brakes and tires produces dust, as do sanding, grinding, and drilling operations.

In a temperature inversion, cool air containing smoke and gases is trapped under warm air, keeping harmful pollutants close to the surface of the earth.

SOME MAJOR POLLUTANTS

Particulates are made up of tiny solid particles, which can also be covered by liquid (as in smog). Dust, produced either naturally or by human activity, is also made up of particles. Another example is fly ash, produced by the burning of fuels. In recent decades, government laws have limited two particulates especially; lead, once widely used in gasoline, and asbestos, which has been phased out in car brake linings, building insulation, and other uses.

Oxides of sulfur are gases. They are produced when sulfur-containing fuels, such as coal or oil, are burned. They are also produced in factories where sulfur is used in manufacturing processes. Oxides of sulfur irritate the breathing passages and can damage the lungs.

Carbon monoxide is a poisonous gas produced by the incomplete burning of the carbon in such fuels as gasoline, coal, and oil. Most of the carbon monoxide in the air comes from the exhausts of automobiles and other vehicles that burn gasoline.

Oxides of nitrogen are also produced by engines. Nitrogen makes up about 78 percent of the air, and oxygen, about 21 percent. Normally these gases do not combine chemically in the air. But in engines that run at high temperatures, such as those in automobiles, they combine to form gases called oxides of nitrogen.

Photochemical oxidants are formed when oxides of nitrogen combine with other substances present in automobile exhaust. Sunlight promotes the combining process. The photochemical oxidants are the main ingredient of smog, which irritates the eyes and breathing passages.

Some of these pollutants, such as exhaust from cars and trucks, are discharged into the air at street level. Others, such as smoke from power plants and factories, enter the atmosphere at higher levels. When smoke and other pollutants combine with fog, they form **smog** (from the words "smoke" and "fog"). An article on fog and smog is included in Volume F.

The amount of air pollution is affected by atmospheric conditions such as temperature and air pressure. Because the air near the earth's surface is normally warmer than the air at higher altitudes, air currents usually rise. The rising air currents carry pollutants to the upper atmosphere, where they are dispersed, or scattered. But sometimes the air above the earth's surface is warmer than the air at the surface. When this happens, the warm air stops the flow of rising air currents. This condition is called a **temperature inversion**. The pollutants are trapped close to the surface, where they do the most harm. Temperature inversions are common in large urban areas, such as Los Angeles and Mexico City.

High Cost of Air Pollution

The damage caused by air pollution is enormous. In money alone it represents a loss of billions of dollars each year. Many flower and vegetable crops suffer ill effects from car exhaust gases. Trees have been killed by pollution from power plants. Cattle have been poisoned by the fumes from smelters that recover aluminum from ore. Air pollution causes rubber tires on automobiles to crack and become porous. Fine buildings become shabby, their walls blackened with soot that has settled on them. Building surfaces may actually deteriorate because of air pollution.

But the high cost of air pollution is most strikingly illustrated in its damaging effects on the human body. Air pollution causes eye irritations, scratchy throats, and respiratory illnesses. It also contributes to a number of serious diseases. In both the United States and Europe, periods of high levels of air pollution were linked to an increased number of deaths.

Much direct harm is done by air pollution. Scientists are alarmed because the amounts of gases such as carbon dioxide, methane, and nitrous oxide in our atmosphere are increasing. These gases tend to trap the radiation that reaches the earth from the sun. Because the amount of radiation we receive from the sun tends to be constant, if less radiation escapes from our atmosphere, the atmosphere could become warmer. This process would eventually cause the temperature of the earth's surface to rise.

Scientists have been concerned, too, about the widespread use of a substance that may destroy the atmospheric layer that protects us from harmful kinds of solar energy. This substance belongs to a group of chemicals called **chlorofluorocarbons**. It is used as a refrigerant and a cleaner and was once widely used in spray cans.

Another concern is **acid rain**. This is rain or other precipitation that contains oxides of sulfur and nitrogen, along with other chemicals. Acid rain causes damage in lakes and rivers. It poisons the plants and animals that live in the water. Acid rain may also affect crops and other plants, stone buildings and monuments, and drinking water. More information on acid rain may be found in the article ACID RAIN in Volume A.

▶CONTROL OF AIR POLLUTION

There are three basic approaches to the control of air pollution—**preventive measures**, such as changing the raw materials used in industry or the ingredients of fuel; **dispersal measures**, such as raising the heights of smokestacks; and **collection measures**, such as designing equipment to trap pollutants before they escape into the atmosphere.

Smog has seriously affected more people than any other form of air pollution. It tends to collect over large industrialized cities. Other forms of air pollution are less visible than smog. At right, a government worker uses instruments to check air quality.

Top: Chemical pollutants in the air have eaten away the surface of stone statues of the 1600's that decorate the Palace of Versailles, near Paris. *Bottom:* Exhausts from jet planes create high levels of pollution near airports throughout the world.

Nearly all the highly industrialized countries of the world have some type of legislation to prevent and control air pollution. One difficulty is that pollutants may be carried by the wind from one country to another, often for distances of thousands of miles. The death of lakes in eastern Canada has been caused by acid rain that originated in the United States. Acids produced in Britain and France have caused damage in Sweden.

In the United States, control of air pollution is chiefly the responsibility of the state and local governments. All the states have air quality management programs, which are patterned after federal laws.

The basic federal law dealing with air pollution is the Clean Air Act of 1970. The act was last amended in 1990. Under this law, the federal Environmental Protection Agency set standards for air quality. The agency also placed limits on the amounts of pollutants that could be given off by cars, factories, and other sources of pollutants. The states and industries were expected to develop and carry out plans to meet these standards. Some of the federal deadlines could not be met, and they were extended several times.

Air quality programs have brought improvements in many areas. For example, burning low-sulfur coal and oil in factories and power plants has lowered pollution in many cities. To meet federal standards, automobile engines have been redesigned, and new cars have been equipped with devices such as the catalytic converter which changes pollutants into harmless substances. Because of these new devices, air pollution from car exhaust has also been reduced.

It is not easy to bring about the new developments needed to control air pollution. Many people—physicians, engineers, meteorologists, botanists, and others—are involved in research, seeking new ways. Permanent observatories have been established to measure gradual changes in the atmosphere over long periods of time. The first observatory of this type was established near Mauna Loa, in Hawaii.

Vast sums of money will have to be spent in the future to clean the air and to keep it clean. Often pollution control means higher prices—to cover the cost of control devices in emission systems of new cars, for example. But to most people, the cost is justified. Perhaps the day will come when people everywhere can breathe pure air in cities where the sunlight is no longer blocked by an umbrella of pollution.

FRED H. RENNER, JR.
Office of Regional Programs
U.S. Environmental Protection Agency

See also ACID RAIN; ENVIRONMENT.

In an airport's control tower, sophisticated electronic equipment and a clear view of the airfield below help air traffic controllers direct the takeoffs and landings of planes.

AIRPORTS

An airport is a place where airplanes land and take off. At an airport, passengers and cargo are picked up and dropped off, and airplanes are refueled and serviced.

The first airplanes were small and light and needed only an open, flat area to take off and land. For this reason, and because very few people traveled by air, an early "airport" often consisted of only an unpaved landing field and a **hangar**, a large building in which airplanes are housed and repaired.

Since those early days, flight has become an important means of transportation, and aviation is now a major industry. Today, there are some 36,000 airports of all sizes throughout the world (including nearly 20,000 private airfields). Airports, like airplanes, have become much larger and more complex. In fact, airports in major cities are often so large that they can almost qualify as cities themselves. These large **air carrier** airports handle thousands of flights every day, mainly those of scheduled airlines. They are especially well equipped to accommodate large, jet-engine airplanes.

The vast majority of airports, however, are not as large as the air carrier airports. For example, of the more than 5,300 public airports in the United States, only 8 percent are large enough to handle commercial flights. Most airports are equipped to handle mainly smaller, propeller-driven airplanes owned by businesses or private citizens. Airports that handle this type of airplane and not those of scheduled airlines are known as **general aviation** airports. If a small airport is located near a much larger airport, the small airport is likely to assume a large share of the area's small-airplane traffic and is known as a **reliever** airport.

Although smaller airports are more numerous than large ones, most air travelers—roughly 425 million per year in the United States alone—begin and end their journeys at a large airport.

A TRIP THROUGH A LARGE AIRPORT

Your first stop at the airport depends on the means of transportation you have used to get there. You can travel to some airports by train or bus, while others can be reached only by taxi or private car. If you have driven your own car, it must be parked in an airport lot or garage, which may have up to 20,000 parking spaces. From there you may have to board a shuttle bus to take you to your next destination, the terminal.

The Terminal. The terminal building or buildings are the largest at the airport and are the center of many services and activities. All passengers must pass through a terminal when boarding or leaving an airplane. When you arrive at the terminal, you will first go to the airline ticket counter. There, in exchange for your ticket, the airline agent will give you your boarding pass, which gives you permission to sit in a specific seat on the airplane.

The airline agent will attach a cardboard label to your baggage. The label has an identification number that matches one that is stapled to your boarding pass. The label also has a three-letter code, which identifies the airport at which you will land and helps the airline baggage handlers get your bags to the correct airplane. Your baggage will then travel on a conveyor belt into the underground ''belly'' of the airport. On international flights and some domestic flights, the baggage will be checked for weapons. A baggage handler will load all the baggage for your flight onto a cart, drive the cart to the airplane, and load the baggage onto the plane.

While you wait to board your plane, there may be time to visit some of the many shops located in the terminal. These include banks, newsstands and bookstores, restaurants and snack bars, and gift shops. Most international airports also have duty-free shops. If you are visiting a foreign country, you can buy goods at the duty-free shop and bring them home without having to pay duty, or import tax.

Some airports have an observation lounge, where large windows allow you to watch airplanes take off, land, and taxi (move slowly along the ground) to a gate. Gates are the points from which passengers leave the terminal and board the airplane.

Before heading to your gate, you will be screened by an electronic device that detects hidden weapons. Any bags that you are carrying on the plane will be passed through an X-ray machine to be sure they do not contain any weapons. These security checks are necessary to prevent the airplane from being hijacked.

The next stop is your gate, where your airplane is waiting. The distance between the main part of the terminal and the gate may be

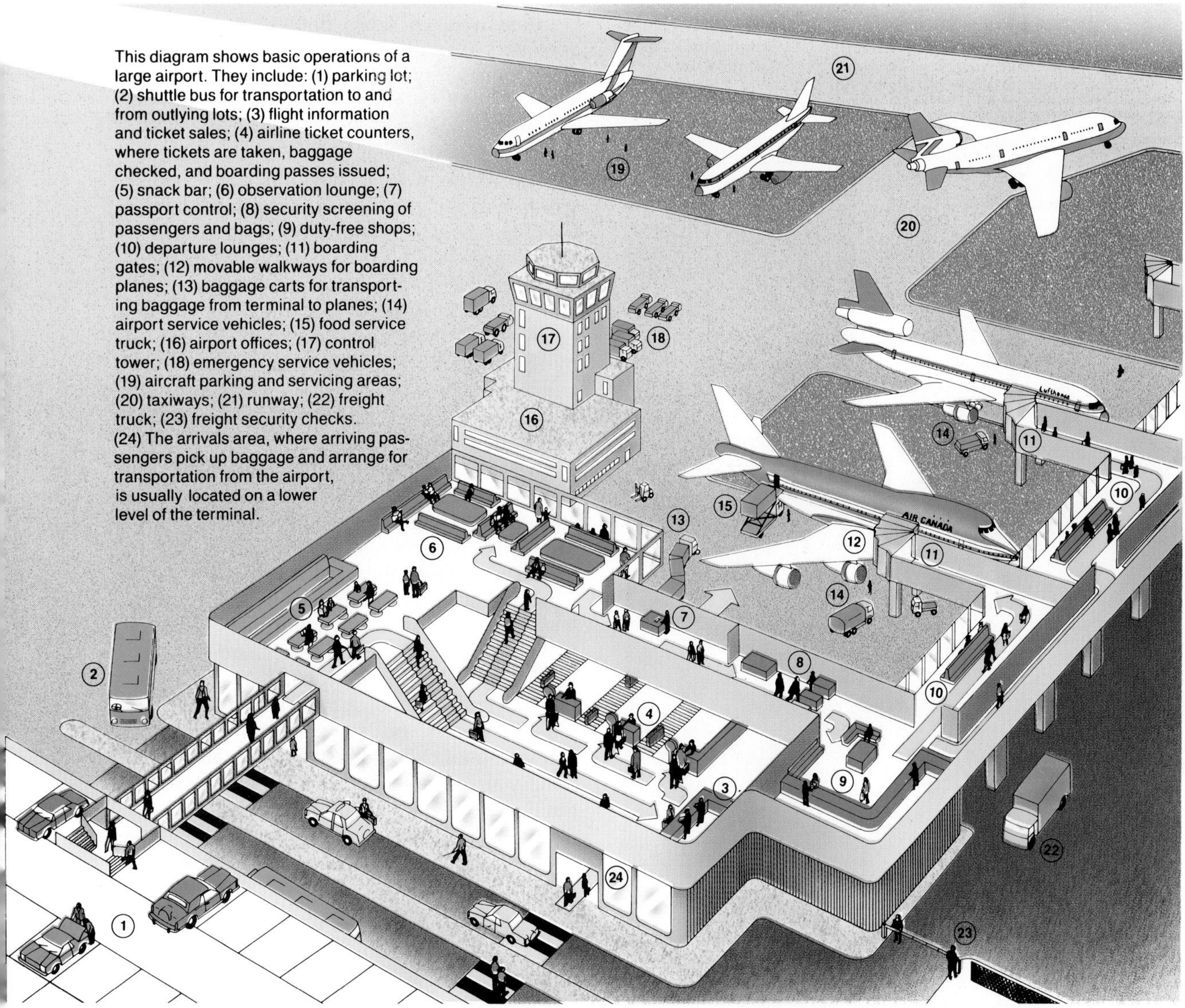

This diagram shows basic operations of a large airport. They include: (1) parking lot; (2) shuttle bus for transportation to and from outlying lots; (3) flight information and ticket sales; (4) airline ticket counters, where tickets are taken, baggage checked, and boarding passes issued; (5) snack bar; (6) observation lounge; (7) passport control; (8) security screening of passengers and bags; (9) duty-free shops; (10) departure lounges; (11) boarding gates; (12) movable walkways for boarding planes; (13) baggage carts for transporting baggage from terminal to planes; (14) airport service vehicles; (15) food service truck; (16) airport offices; (17) control tower; (18) emergency service vehicles; (19) aircraft parking and servicing areas; (20) taxiways; (21) runway; (22) freight truck; (23) freight security checks. (24) The arrivals area, where arriving passengers pick up baggage and arrange for transportation from the airport, is usually located on a lower level of the terminal.

Above: Airport firefighters perform a practice drill. Fire and other emergency teams are on call around the clock in case of accidents. *Below:* An airplane is serviced in an airport hangar. Planes are checked regularly; a major overhaul may take nearly two weeks.

too far to walk. In some airports, you will have to take a quick train ride. In others you will take a shuttle bus to a "mid-field" terminal, which is separate from the main terminal. In still other airports, passengers are transported to their gates on moving sidewalks. When you reach your gate, you will find yourself in a large, open waiting room. From here you will board your plane, most likely via a short, covered walkway.

The Runway. Airplanes take off and land on the runway. Jet planes require very long runways, sometimes as much as 2 miles (3 kilometers) in length. An air carrier airport typically has between two and four runways and may have as many as eight. A runway may look like an ordinary paved road. But, unlike roads built for cars, runways are made of special material able to withstand the impact of 830,000-pound (375,000-kilogram) airplanes. The runways will not crack under extreme cold or heat. Snowplows and salt spreaders keep them clear and ice free in winter. Drainage systems keep them from being flooded during rainy weather. Emergency fire and ambulance crews are always on duty.

The roads that run alongside the runways are called taxiways. They link the runways with the terminal and with other airport buildings, such as storage and service hangars. Lining the runway is a complex system of lights and signs with numbers and letters, which guide pilots in taking off, landing, and taxiing to and from the gates. Pilots are also guided by the ground crew, who steer airplanes into their gate parking positions. (Because airplanes cannot back up, they are often towed out of their gates by trucks.)

Air Traffic Control. Before the pilot can take off, or even start the plane's engines, permission must be given by the airport control tower. The control tower is the nerve center of the airport. From there, all approaches, landings, and takeoffs are directed by radio contact with the pilot. Air traffic controllers, the men and women in the control tower, are skilled at helping as many as 100 planes per hour take off and land without a collision. To do their job, they rely on sophisticated computers and communications systems. In the United States, air traffic controllers are employees of the Federal Aviation Administration (FAA).

Air traffic controllers in charge of ground control tell the pilot when to start the engines

When approaching an airport, the pilot of an airplane is guided by a system of lights that outline the runways and show where the plane should touch down.

and which taxiways and runway to use. After clearance (permission to take off) is given, the tower gives the pilot instructions to get clear of the airport area and proceed on course. Throughout the flight, the pilot must report at regular intervals to air traffic control centers located along the flight route. The pilot may be directed to change course or altitude to avoid bad weather or other air traffic. As the plane nears the end of its flight, the pilot contacts the control tower at the destination airport (where the plane will land). Air traffic controllers there direct the approach to the airport and the landing of the plane.

Other Facilities. Many operations are carried out at a major airport. Scores of buildings on airport grounds contain airline offices and food kitchens, fire and snow-removal equipment, and medical facilities. Large warehouses store cargo before and after it is shipped. Hangars house planes for servicing and maintenance.

All these operations employ staffs of workers. Additional airport workers include police and military personnel and, at international airports, customs and immigration officials. All together, up to 35,000 people may be employed at a large airport.

THE WORLD'S TEN BUSIEST AIRPORTS

Airport	Passengers (2000 Totals)
1. Hartsfield Atlanta International: Atlanta	80,171,036
2. O'Hare International: Chicago	72,135,887
3. International: Los Angeles	68,477,689
4. Heathrow Airport: London	64,607,185
5. International: Dallas/Ft. Worth	60,687,122
6. Tokyo International (Haneda): Japan	56,402,206
7. Frankfurt/Main: Germany	49,360,620
8. Paris (Charles de Gaulle): France	48,240,137
9. International: San Francisco	41,173,983
10. Amsterdam Schiphol Airport: Netherlands	39,604,589

Source: Airports Council International

OWNERSHIP AND CONTROL

All major civil airports in the United States are owned by the communities or states in which they are located. Airport policy is set by a board, commission, or department of public works. An aviation director is in charge of daily airport operations.

Even though most airports are publicly owned, they usually are not supported by taxpayers' dollars. Large airports are run mainly with money made from fees charged to airlines and other businesses operating in the airport.

More and more, airports are seeking to help their communities by controlling the noise produced by jet airplanes. Originally, most airports were built far from city centers. They have not moved, but the growth of cities has sometimes led to the building of homes near airports. Steps taken to reduce noise for nearby residents include forbidding the use of older, noisier aircraft and closing the airport during times when most people are sleeping.

At the same time, airports must expand to accommodate ever-growing numbers of passengers. One of the major challenges facing today's airport planners is to increase an airport's capacity while also making it acceptable to the community in which it is located.

ANDREW J. SOBEL
Former manager, Public Affairs
Airports Council International

AKRON. See OHIO (Cities).

ALABAMA

The name Alabama comes from an Indian word that scholars believe means "plant gatherers." It referred most likely to the agricultural practices of the Alabama, a tribe of Creek Indians who originally lived in the region.

Alabama's nickname, Heart of Dixie, comes from the state's location in the heart, or center, of the southeastern United States, a region popularly known as Dixie. There are several theories about the origin of the name "Dixie." One claims it came from the French word dix, *meaning "ten." This word was printed on $10 bills used in the state of Louisiana before the Civil War. The bills were called dixies, and eventually the name Dixie, or Dixieland, came to be used for all the cotton-growing states in the South.*

State flag

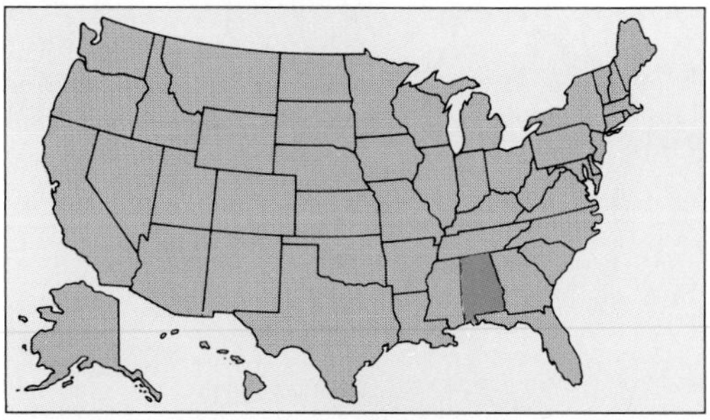

Alabama lies in the southeastern United States, in a region known as the Deep South. Part of its southern border includes the port of Mobile, which connects the state to the seaports of the world. Birmingham is Alabama's most populous city. Montgomery is its capital.

Like its neighbors, Alabama was once a predominantly agricultural state dominated by cotton farming. Although cotton is still grown, forest products and livestock are now more important to the economy. The development of the iron and steel industries in the 1880's, particularly around Birmingham, made Alabama the most industrialized state in the South. Local factories continue to make iron and steel products in addition to tires, textiles, and computer parts. Coal is also mined and processed. However, service-related jobs contribute the most to the state's economy.

Throughout its history, Alabama has experienced its share of conflict and rebellion. The Confederate States of America (CSA) was organized in Alabama in 1861, and Montgomery briefly served as its first capital. Alabama's history also is noteworthy for its long struggle with race relations. The modern civil rights movement began in Montgomery in 1955, when a black woman named Rosa Parks refused to yield her seat to a white person on a city bus. This bold action initiated a year-long boycott of the city bus system, which led to the passage of a federal law banning segregation on public transportation. Furthermore, mass demonstrations in Birmingham in 1963 forced the desegregation of public facilities. Then in 1965, more than 25,000 Americans, black and white, participated in a protest march, from Selma to Montgomery, to end discrimination at the polls and to secure voting rights for all African Americans.

LAND

From north to south, Alabama extends about 330 miles (531 kilometers) from its border with Tennessee to its shoreline on the warm Gulf of Mexico.

Land Regions

Five major land regions cover the state of Alabama. Although the northeastern corner of the state reaches into the Appalachian Mountain system, much of Alabama's interior is made up of flat or gently rolling plains.

The East Gulf Coastal Plain is by far the largest of Alabama's land regions. For many years this mostly flat plain formed the heart of the South's cotton fields.

The part of the plain that today lies within Alabama can be divided roughly into three areas: the **Central Pine Belt** in the northwest, so called because of its abundant pine forests; the **Mobile River Delta** in the southwest; and the **Wiregrass** area in the southeast, named for the coarse grass that used to grow there.

Clockwise from top left: **Oakleigh Mansion, near Mobile, is a graceful example of the antebellum (pre-Civil War) plantation homes of the Old South. Beaches along the Gulf of Mexico make excellent playgrounds. Birmingham is Alabama's largest and most industrialized city.**

State flower:
Camellia

State tree:
Southern pine

FACTS AND FIGURES

Location: Southeastern United States; bordered on the north by Tennessee, on the east by Georgia, on the south by Florida and the Gulf of Mexico, and on the west by Mississippi.

Area: 52,237 sq mi (135,293 km^2); rank, 30th.

Population: 4,447,100 (2000 census); rank, 23rd.

Elevation: *Highest*—2,407 ft (734 m), at Cheaha Mountain; *lowest*—sea level, along the Gulf of Mexico.

Capital: Montgomery.

Statehood: December 14, 1819; 22nd state.

State Motto: *Audemus jura nostra defendere (We dare defend our rights).*

State Song: "Alabama."

Nickname: Heart of Dixie.

Abbreviations: AL; Ala.

State bird:
Yellowhammer

The Black Belt is a long strip of nearly level land less than 50 miles (80 kilometers) wide. Named for its dark-colored soils, it is an especially fertile region and was once known for its large, productive plantations.

The Interior Low Plateau covers a small region of northern Alabama. It is dominated by the broad valley of the Tennessee River, which cuts through the knobby hills of the plateau and makes the soil suitable for farming.

The Appalachian Highlands reach their southernmost extension in northeastern Alabama, where they can be divided into two regions. The **Cumberland Plateau**, which is the southern portion of the Appalachian Plateau, has some good farmland, but it is mainly suited to lumbering and mining. The **Ridge and Valley Region** is made up of narrow valleys between steep mountain ridges. It is known for its mineral riches and picturesque forests of oak and pine.

The Piedmont is a wedge-shaped area to the south of the Ridge and Valley Region. It is made up of foothills, with some rolling land. The state's highest point, Cheaha Mountain, is located here. It rises 2,407 feet (734 meters) above sea level.

Rivers, Lakes, and Coastal Waters

Alabama's geography is marked by an abundance of rivers and lakes. Two main river systems cover the southern three-quarters of the state. The Alabama River and its main tributaries, the Coosa and Tallapoosa rivers, empty the eastern side of the state; the Tombigbee River and its tributary, the Black Warrior River, drain the western side. These two river systems join to form the Mobile River, which empties into Mobile Bay on the Gulf of Mexico. Their junction forms a delta area that covers several hundred square miles of marshes and cypress swamps.

The Tennessee River, flowing east to west, distinguishes the geography of northern Alabama. The Tennessee-Tombigbee Waterway, a canal completed in 1985, ties the Tennessee River system to the Tombigbee River, and thus to the port of Mobile. The Chattahoochee River in the southeast forms part of the border between Alabama and Georgia.

All of Alabama's larger rivers have been dammed, creating many beautiful lakes. The largest is Guntersville Lake, created in the 1930's by damming the Tennessee River.

Alabama's coastline on the Gulf of Mexico makes up a small part of the state's southern border. It stretches only 53 miles (85 kilometers), but because of many bays, inlets, and islands, there are actually 607 miles (977 kilometers) of shoreline. Of the offshore islands, Dauphin Island is the largest.

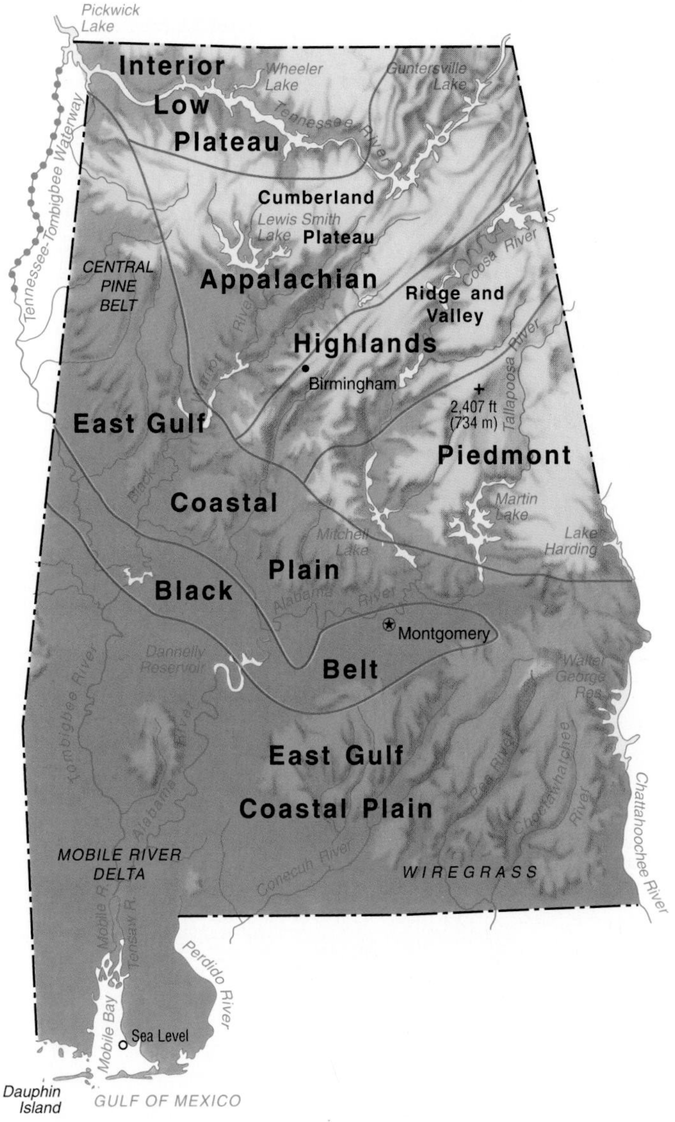

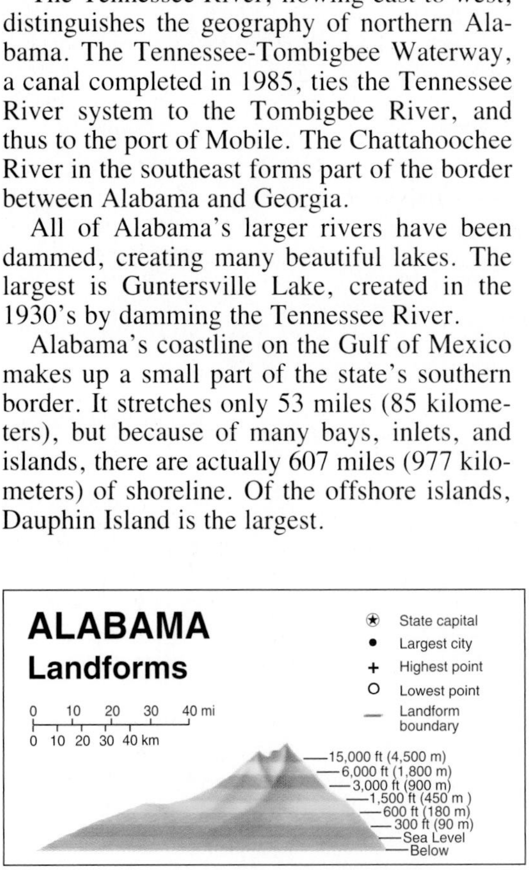

Loblolly pine trees surround the swamplands of Gulf Shores State Park, in one of Alabama's southernmost regions. The rare Cahaba lily (*inset*) grows only along some Alabama streams.

Climate

Alabama's climate is quite mild. Winter temperatures rarely drop below freezing and average about 52°F (11°C) in the south and 46°F (8°C) in the north. Summer temperatures tend to be about the same throughout the state, averaging about 80°F (27°C).

Snowfall is unusual, but rainfall is abundant, averaging 65 inches (1,651 millimeters) a year along the coast and about 53 inches (1,346 millimeters) in the northern regions. Hurricanes sometimes blow in from the Gulf of Mexico, occasionally causing damage to shoreline areas.

Plant and Animal Life

Alabama's many flowering trees and shrubs make spring and summer especially beautiful. Azaleas, mountain laurel, rhododendron, orchids, and wild roses dot the landscape. About two-thirds of Alabama is forestland. The pine is the most common tree, followed by oak, hickory, and cedar.

More than 300 species of birds live at least part of the year in the state. These include eagles, buzzards, hawks, ospreys, wild turkeys, ducks, and geese. Rabbits, squirrels, raccoons, foxes, and white-tailed deer are common. Black bears and alligators live in some areas.

Bass, crappie, bluegill, and catfish fill many of the state's freshwater lakes.The commercial products of Alabama's offshore waters include shrimp, snapper, oysters, and crabs.

Natural Resources

One of Alabama's most valuable resources is its waterways. Rivers were once the primary means of transport in the state before roadways were built. Still used for shipping, the rivers provide hydroelectric power from dams on the Coosa, Tallapoosa, Tennessee, Chattahoochee, and Black Warrior rivers.

The fertile soils of the East Gulf Coastal Plain were formed from sediment laid down in the oceans that once covered this region. Most of these soils are sandy loams or clay soils. Unfortunately erosion and many decades of farming have made Alabama's soils less fertile. Some farms are now planted with grasses to improve the soil and provide pasture for cattle, especially in the Piedmont and Black Belt regions.

The state's pine forests are a valuable source of wood pulp, used for making paper products. Tree farms have had the added benefit of controlling erosion and improving the worn-out soils.

Most of Alabama's minerals are found in the northern half of the state. Coal, limestone, marble, sand and gravel, and bauxite (an aluminum ore) are mined. Petroleum is found in the extreme southwestern counties. Iron ore, once an important local resource for steelmaking in the Birmingham area, is no longer heavily mined.

▶ PEOPLE

The majority of Alabamians are descendants of European settlers, mostly of English or Scotch-Irish ancestry. The influence of the Spanish and the French, Alabama's first European settlers, is still evident around Mobile.

About 26 percent of the population is African American. Those of Hispanic or Asian descent together make up about 2 percent of the population. One-half of 1 percent are of Native American heritage. Four major groups are native to the state—the Creek, Choctaw, Chickasaw, and Cherokee.

For many decades most of Alabama's population lived in rural areas. Starting in the 1940's, the number of people who worked on farms dropped steadily. By 1960, for the first time, more Alabamians lived in cities than in rural areas. Today 60 percent of Alabamians live in urban centers.

Education

Although public education in Alabama was established in 1854, the state's schools were poorly supported, and there were virtually no schools for black children. Since the early 1900's there have been efforts made to improve education, but Alabama's tax support for schools remains well below the national average. City schools are generally better funded than those in rural areas.

The University of Alabama is the state's oldest public university. Its football team, known as the Crimson Tide (*above*), is consistently ranked among the best in the nation. In the summertime, county fairs (*left*) are held throughout the state. These public festivals give people an opportunity to display and sell homemade foods and crafts.

PEOPLE

Population: 4,447,100 (2000 census).

Density: 85 persons per sq mi (33 per km²).

Distribution: 60% urban; 40% rural.

Largest Cities (2000 census):

Birmingham 242,820	Tuscaloosa 77,906
Montgomery 201,568	Hoover 62,742
Mobile 198,915	Dothan 57,737
Huntsville 158,216	Decatur 53,929

Source: U.S. Bureau of the Census

Persons per sq mi	Persons per km²
over 250	over 100
50-250	20-100
5-50	2-20
0-5	0-2

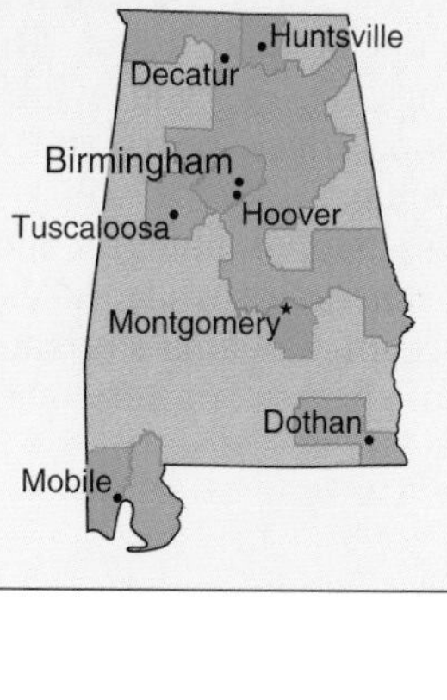

The state has many colleges and universities, including more than 40 community colleges built during the 1960's.

Athens State College, founded in 1822, is the oldest college in the state. The University of Alabama, founded in 1831, is the oldest state university, with campuses in Tuscaloosa, Birmingham, and Huntsville. Auburn University has the largest student body in the state. There are six other state universities and more than a dozen private colleges, including Tuskeegee University, established by Booker T. Washington in 1881.

Libraries, Museums, and the Arts

About 200 public libraries serve the people of Alabama. The largest are located in Birmingham, Montgomery, Huntsville, and Mobile. State history is explored in the Alabama Department of Archives and History in Montgomery and at the Civil Rights Institute, located in Birmingham.

Alabama has more than 50 museums. The Birmingham Museum of Art and the Montgomery Museum of Fine Arts have large collections of paintings and artifacts. The Anniston Museum of Natural History contains an unusual display of 900 specimens of birds. The George Washington Carver Museum at Tuskeegee Institute National Historic Site features agricultural exhibits. The U.S. Space and Rocket Center in Huntsville has more than 60 hands-on exhibits about spaceflight. It is Alabama's most popular tourist attraction.

The Alabama Shakespeare Festival, founded in Anniston in 1972, is located in Montgomery. This elaborate performing arts complex offers a variety of plays, from Shakespeare to Tennessee Williams, as well as concerts, lectures, and dance programs.

Alabama is an important center of traditional American music. Spirituals, gospel songs, and string-band music for banjos, fiddles, and guitars are popular.

Although Alabama has no professional sports teams, college football is a major pastime. The University of Alabama team, called the Crimson Tide, is consistently ranked among the best in the nation. The school's traditional rival, Auburn University, was the home of famed football coach John Heisman, in the 1890's. The prestigious Heisman Trophy, named for him, is awarded each year to the nation's best college football player.

Cotton thrives in Alabama's rich river valleys. It was once the state's single most important product, but today it is considerably less important to the economy.

ECONOMY

More than one hundred years ago, Alabama's economy was agricultural, based almost entirely on cotton. Manufacturing grew after the Civil War, with iron furnaces and steel mills providing many of the state's jobs. Today the service industries have surpassed agriculture and manufacturing to become the largest and fastest-growing part of Alabama's economy.

Services

More than 70 percent of Alabamians have jobs that provide services to their communities, such as health care, education, government services, police and fire protection, and banking, insurance, and real estate services. Services also include businesses that supply such necessities as food, clothing, transportation, and housing.

Manufacturing

About 23 percent of the state's workforce is employed in manufacturing jobs. Alabama's most important manufacturing industries are those that produce metals, wood products, and textiles. Many of these industries make use of

The manufacture of copper tubing and other fabricated metal products contributes significantly to Alabama's gross state product.

the state's own raw materials, such as coal and wood pulp.

About 90 percent of all the steelmaking in the South takes place in Alabama, mostly in and around Birmingham, Anniston, and Gadsden. Factories that make metal products are located throughout the state.

Alabama's forests supply lumber for furniture and other wood products as well as wood pulp for the paper industry. More than 500 paper mills are located in the state.

The textile industry produces yarn, thread, woven fabrics, clothing, and other goods. Chemicals, rubber, and plastics are additional important manufactured products.

Agriculture

For many years, cotton ranked first among Alabama's crops, but today cotton contributes only minimally to the state's total income from crops. Alabama produces substantial amounts of soybeans, peanuts, vegetables, corn, hay, and oats.

Livestock now brings more than twice as much income to Alabama than cash crops. Broilers (young chickens) are Alabama's single most important agricultural product. Cattle, hogs, dairy products, and seafood from the Gulf of Mexico also are important.

Mining and Construction

About 5 percent of the state's workforce is engaged in mining or construction activities, such as the ongoing building and repair of roads and bridges. Alabama is known for its production of coal and limestone. Other minerals produced in the state include oil, natural gas, clays and shale, marble, mica, sand and gravel, and bauxite.

The state's first producing oil well began operating in Choctaw County, in 1944. Today there are about 2,000 producing oil wells in the state, nearly all of them located in the southwest.

Transportation

Alabama has one of the nation's finest river transportation systems. Completed in 1985, the Tennessee-Tombigbee Waterway provides a water route from much of the eastern United States to the port city of Mobile. Alabama's first railway, between Decatur and Tuscumbia, was completed in 1835. Today the state's railroads are used mostly for freight. Alabama also has an excellent system of more than 140 local airfields. Major airports are located in Birmingham, Huntsville, Montgomery, and Mobile.

PRODUCTS AND INDUSTRIES

Manufacturing: Metals and metal products, paper and wood products, textiles, chemicals, rubber, plastics.

Agriculture: Broilers (young chickens), beef cattle, hogs, dairy products, greenhouse and nursery products, soybeans, cotton, peanuts, corn, hay, seafood.

Minerals: Coal, limestone, oil, natural gas, clays and shale, bauxite, sand and gravel, mica, marble.

Services: Wholesale and retail trade; finance, insurance, and real estate; business, social, and personal services; transportation, communication, and utilities; government.

Percentage of Gross State Product* by Industry

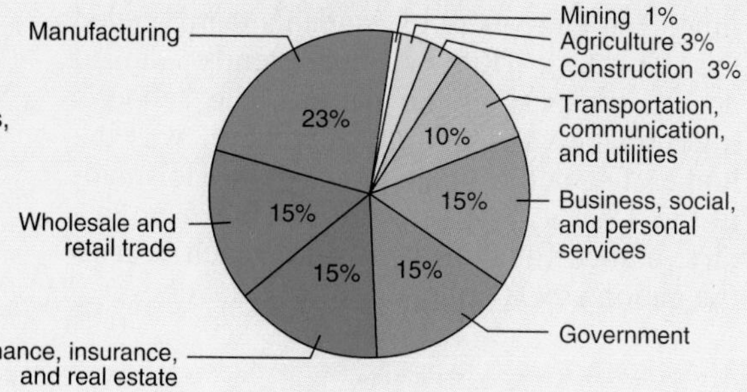

*Gross state product is the total value of goods and services produced in a year.

Source: U.S. Bureau of Economic Analysis

Communication

About 100 weekly newspapers are published in Alabama; another 24 are published daily. The *Birmingham News* has by far the largest circulation. The *Mobile Register*, founded in 1813, is the state's oldest newspaper still in existence.

Birmingham acquired the state's first licensed radio station, WBRC, in 1925 and its first television stations, WABT and WBRC-TV, both in 1949. Approximately 25 television stations and 240 radio stations operate within the state.

▶ CITIES

Alabama's cities are scattered throughout the state. Only four of them have populations exceeding 100,000.

Montgomery, Alabama's capital and second largest city, is often called the Cradle of the Confederacy because in 1861 it became the first capital of the Confederate States of America (CSA). Situated on the Alabama River, Montgomery is a center of agricultural trade. It is the leading cattle market in the southeastern United States, with large ranges and cattle herds in the surrounding area. Industries within the city include textile mills, meatpacking plants, and furniture factories.

Montgomery has several institutions of higher education, including Alabama State University. Auburn and Troy State universities each have a campus there. Faulkner University and Huntingdon College also are located in Montgomery.

Birmingham, Alabama's largest and most industrialized city, is located in central Alabama. It was founded as the small town of Elyton in 1871 and has been called the Magic City because of its rapid growth. Birmingham is the South's major producer of iron and steel. Other area industries manufacture cast-iron pipes, heavy machinery, chemicals, and textiles. Birmingham is also a cultural and educational center.

Mobile, the state's third largest city and only seaport, was founded by the French and named for the Mobile Indians. Known as Alabama's Gateway to the World, Mobile is a busy industrial and shipping center with chemical plants, shipyards, and seafood industries. It is also a gracious and beautiful resort city, known for its flowers and ancient oak trees draped with Spanish moss.

Huntsville, in the northern part of the state, was one of Alabama's first settlements. For many years it remained a small farming community, but it grew rapidly in the 1950's after the U.S. Army developed a missile research center at the Redstone Arsenal. Today Huntsville is known as Rocket City, U.S.A. The U.S. Space and Rocket Center, the U.S. Space Camp and Space Academy, and the George C. Marshall Space Flight Center, run by the National Aeronautics and Space Administration (NASA), are located there.

Mobile, Alabama's third largest city, is located on the Gulf of Mexico. It is the state's only seaport and a major center of shipping and transportation.

Places of Interest

Bellingrath Gardens and Home, in Theodore, is a beautifully landscaped estate once owned by Walter D. Bellingrath, a local industrialist. The formal gardens are world famous for their springtime displays of azaleas. The home itself is noted for its lovely art objects.

The Birmingham Civil Rights Institute, in Birmingham, is the centerpiece of the city's historic Civil Rights District. On permanent display is a chronological history of the city's role in the civil rights movement.

The Civil Rights Memorial, located outside the Southern Poverty Law Center in Montgomery, stands in tribute to forty people who lost their lives in the struggle for civil rights. It was designed by Maya Lin, the architect who designed the Vietnam War Memorial in Washington, D.C.

Dexter Avenue King Memorial Baptist Church, in Montgomery, was where Martin Luther King, Jr., preached from 1954 until 1960. Now designated a National Historic Landmark in memory of the slain civil rights leader, the church contains a mural depicting events in King's life.

Horseshoe Bend National Military Park, on the Tallapoosa River near Dadeville, marks the site of the last battle of the Creek War of 1813–14. It was there that General Andrew Jackson defeated the heavily outnumbered Creek Indians.

Ivy Green, in Tuscumbia, is the birthplace and childhood home of Helen Keller. Every June a theater company takes part in the Helen Keller Festival to reenact the period in Keller's life during which she learned to overcome her disabilities.

Azaleas in Bellingrath Gardens, in Theodore

First White House of the Confederacy, located in Montgomery, served as the residence of Jefferson Davis, the first president of the Confederacy, during the first months of the Civil War in 1861, when Montgomery was the Confederate capital. The house was originally built in 1835. Civil War items and many period furnishings are on display.

Mound State Monument, a state park and museum in Moundville, near Tuscaloosa, preserves prehistoric temple mounds. Visitors may also explore a reconstructed Indian village.

Russell Cave National Monument, near Bridgeport in northeast Alabama, is the site of Alabama's earliest known human inhabitants. The monument preserves evidence of almost continuous habitation in the cave from at least 7000 B.C. to about A.D. 1650.

Tuskeegee Institute National Historic Site, in Tuskeegee, includes Tuskeegee University, the George Washington Carver Museum, and Booker T. Washington's home, known as the Oaks. The museum includes displays of Carver's agricultural experiments with peanuts and sweet potatoes.

U.S. Space and Rocket Center, in Huntsville, is the world's largest space museum. Visitors can experience the sights and sensations of space travel through dozens of hands-on exhibits. Rockets, space shuttles, training facilities, and research laboratories are also on display.

The center also runs a number of enormously popular space camps, where children and adults can experience many aspects of spaceflight. For more information, see the article SPACE AGENCIES AND CENTERS in Volume S.

State Parks. Alabama has 4 national forests and more than 20 state parks. For more information, contact Alabama State Parks, 64 North Union Street, Montgomery, Alabama 36130.

U.S. Space and Rocket Center, in Huntsville

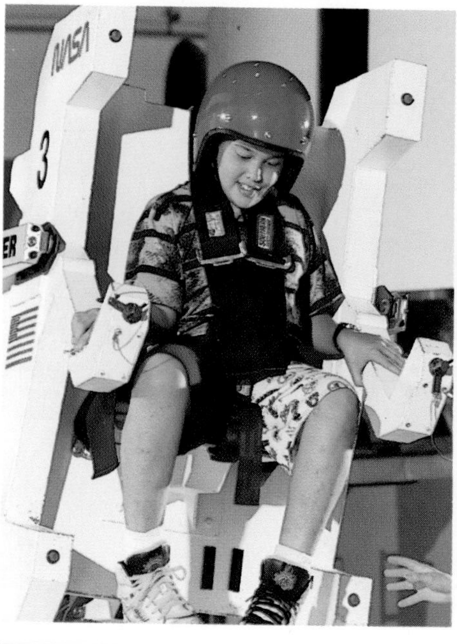

Sculpture near the Birmingham Civil Rights Institute

GOVERNMENT

Alabama's constitution, adopted in 1901, has been amended more than five hundred times. It contains provisions for three branches of government.

The head of the executive branch is the governor, who is elected by the people of the state. Other elected officials in the executive branch include the lieutenant governor, secretary of state, attorney general, treasurer, auditor, and commissioner of agriculture and industry.

The legislative department is made up of a senate and a house of representatives. The members of both of these bodies meet annually and serve 4-year terms.

The highest state court is the supreme court. It consists of a chief justice and eight associate justices elected statewide.

GOVERNMENT

State Government
Governor: 4-year term
State senators: 35; 4-year terms
State representatives: 105; 4-year terms
Number of counties: 67

Federal Government
U.S. senators: 2
U.S. representatives: 7
Number of electoral votes: 9

For the name of the current governor, see STATE GOVERNMENTS in Volume S. For the names of current U.S. senators and representatives, see UNITED STATES, CONGRESS OF THE in Volume U-V.

The state is divided into 67 counties. Each county is governed by a board of commissioners, known as the county commission.

HISTORY

Evidence shows that cave-dwelling Indians lived in Alabama as early as 9,000 years ago. By the time of first European contact in the early 1500's, Alabama was inhabited by the Mississippians, a sophisticated society of Indians frequently referred to as the Mound Builders.

European Exploration and Settlement

The Spanish explored Mobile Bay as early as 1519, but they did not venture into the interior until 1540, when Hernando de Soto led an expedition through northeastern Alabama. He took many Indians captive as he marched from one Mississippian village to the next, searching for gold and other treasure.

One of De Soto's prisoners, the chieftain Tuskalusa, secretly plotted a counterattack at the walled Mississippian town of Mabila, but armor and horses gave the Spanish a big advantage. By the time the Indians surrendered, about 3,000 of them had been killed.

In the late 1600's, English traders from the Carolinas and Georgia traded with the Indians in Alabama. In 1702 the French established Fort Louis on Mobile Bay, which was moved,

Alabama's state government finally settled in Montgomery in 1846. The following year, the capitol building (*above*) was erected in the Greek Revival style.

in 1711, to the present site of the city of Mobile. It became the first permanent white settlement in what is now Alabama.

After the French and Indian War, the Treaty of Paris (1763) ceded most of present-day Alabama to England, which in turn ceded it to the United States in 1783 following the American Revolutionary War. American settlers started moving into Alabama around 1800.

At that time, Alabama's four main tribes—the Creek, Cherokee, Choctaw, and Chickasaw—occupied much of Alabama's good farmland, and they resisted the settlers moving onto their lands. As a result, during the War of 1812 the Indians sided with the British against the Americans. In 1813, in retaliation against an American assault, the Indians at-

This engraving of a plantation in Clarke County in the 1800's shows slaves called field hands engaged in the backbreaking task of picking cotton by hand.

tacked Fort Mims, about 50 miles (80 kilometers) north of Mobile, killing approximately 250 settlers. The Tennessee militia, led by General Andrew Jackson, marched from one Indian village to another, burning and killing. The final conflict came on March 27, 1814, when Jackson defeated the Creek at the Battle of Horseshoe Bend. The Indians signed a treaty that gave most of their territory to the U.S. government. Almost immediately, thousands more settlers poured into Alabama.

Statehood and the Trail of Tears

Settlers organized the Alabama Territory in 1817. Two years later it became a state. Between 1819 and 1846, the state capital was moved three times due to transportation difficulties and Alabama's changing centers of population. State government finally settled in Montgomery in 1846.

In the early years of statehood, settlers pushed for the removal of all Indians from Alabama. In 1830, Andrew Jackson, who was by then the president of the United States, signed the Removal Act, using his power to force the migration of most of Alabama's Indians to Oklahoma. The route the Indians took, on which many thousands died throughout the 1830's, became known as the Trail of Tears.

Cotton, Slavery, and the Civil War

Between 1820 and 1860, due to a booming cotton market, Alabama became one of the wealthiest states in the Union. However, the state's large cotton plantations would not have been as profitable without the use of slave labor. Alabamians, therefore, fiercely resisted a growing movement in the North to abolish slavery, and they objected to the federal government interfering in the affairs of the South-

INDEX TO ALABAMA MAP

Abbeville •	(Henry)	D4
Alabaster	(Shelby)	C2
Albertville	(Marshall)	C1
Alexander City	(Tallapoosa)	D3
Andalusia •	(Covington)	C4
Anniston •	(Calhoun)	D2
Arab	(Marshall)	C1
Ashland •	(Clay)	D2
Ashville •	(St. Clair)	C2
Athens •	(Limestone)	C1
Atmore	(Escambia)	B4
Attalla	(Etowah)	C1
Auburn	(Lee)	D3
Bay Minette •	(Baldwin)	B5
Bessemer	(Jefferson)	C2
Birmingham •	(Jefferson)	C2
Boaz	(Marshall)	C1
Brewton •	(Escambia)	B4
Butler •	(Choctaw)	A3
Camden •	(Wilcox)	B4
Carrollton •	(Pickens)	A2
Centre •	(Cherokee)	D1
Centreville •	(Bibb)	B3
Chatom •	(Washington)	A4
Chickasaw	(Mobile)	A5
Clanton •	(Chilton)	C3
Clayton •	(Barbour)	D4
Columbiana •	(Shelby)	C2
Conecuh Nat'l Forest		C4
Cullman •	(Cullman)	C1
Dadeville •	(Tallapoosa)	D3
Daleville	(Dale)	D4
Daphne	(Baldwin)	B5
Decatur •	(Morgan)	C1
Demopolis	(Marengo)	B3
Dothan •	(Houston)	D4
Double Springs •	(Winston)	B1
Elba •	(Coffee)	C4
Enterprise	(Coffee)	D4
Eufaula	(Barbour)	D4
Eutaw •	(Greene)	B3
Evergreen •	(Conecuh)	C4
Fairfield	(Jefferson)	C4
Fairhope	(Baldwin)	B5
Fayette •	(Fayette)	B2
Florence •	(Lauderdale)	B1
Fort Payne •	(De Kalb)	D1
Fultondale	(Jefferson)	C2
Gadsden •	(Etowah)	C1
Gardendale	(Jefferson)	C2
Geneva •	(Geneva)	D4
Greensboro •	(Hale)	B3
Greenville •	(Butler)	C4
Grove Hill •	(Clarke)	B4
Guntersville •	(Marshall)	C1
Hamilton •	(Marion)	B1
Hartselle	(Morgan)	C1
Hayneville •	(Lowndes)	C3
Heflin •	(Cleburne)	D2
Homewood	(Jefferson)	C2
Hoover	(Jefferson)	C2
Hueytown	(Jefferson)	C2
Huntsville •	(Madison)	C1
Irondale	(Jefferson)	C2
Jackson	(Clarke)	B4
Jacksonville	(Calhoun)	D2
Jasper •	(Walker)	B2
Lafayette •	(Chambers)	D3
Lanett	(Chambers)	D3
Leeds	(Jefferson)	C2
Linden •	(Marengo)	B3
Livingston •	(Sumter)	A3
Luverne •	(Crenshaw)	C4
Madison	(Madison)	C1
Marion •	(Perry)	B3
Midfield	(Jefferson)	C2
Millbrook	(Elmore)	C3
Mobile •	(Mobile)	A5
Monroeville •	(Monroe)	B4
Montgomery★	(Montgomery)	C3
Moulton •	(Lawrence)	B1
Mountain Brook	(Jefferson)	C2
Muscle Shoals	(Colbert)	B1
Northport	(Tuscaloosa)	B2
Oneonta •	(Blount)	C2
Opelika •	(Lee)	D3
Oxford	(Calhoun)	D2
Ozark •	(Dale)	D4
Pelham	(Shelby)	C2
Pell City •	(St. Clair)	C2
Phenix City •	(Russell)	D3
Piedmont	(Calhoun)	D2
Pleasant Grove	(Jefferson)	C2
Prattville •	(Autauga)	C3
Prichard	(Mobile)	A5
Rainbow City	(Etowah)	C2
Roanoke	(Randolph)	D2
Rockford •	(Coosa)	C3
Russellville •	(Franklin)	B1
Saraland	(Mobile)	A5
Satsuma	(Mobile)	A5
Scottsboro •	(Jackson)	C1
Selma •	(Dallas)	B3
Sheffield	(Colbert)	B1
Southside	(Etowah)	C2
Sylacauga	(Talladega)	C2
Talladega •	(Talladega)	C2
Talladega Nat'l Forest		B3,D2
Tallassee	(Elmore)	D3
Tarrant	(Jefferson)	C2
Troy •	(Pike)	D4
Trussville	(Jefferson)	C2
Tuscaloosa •	(Tusculoosa)	B2
Tuscumbia •	(Colbert)	B1
Tuskegee •	(Macon)	D3
Tuskegee Nat'l Forest		D3
Union Springs •	(Bullock)	D3
Valley	(Lee)	D3
Vernon •	(Lamar)	A2
Vestavia Hills	(Jefferson)	C2
Wedowee •	(Randolf)	D2
Wetumpka •	(Elmore)	C3
Wheeler Nat'l Wildlife Refuge		C1
Wm. B. Bankhead Nat'l Forest		B1

• County Seat

Counties in parentheses

★ State Capital

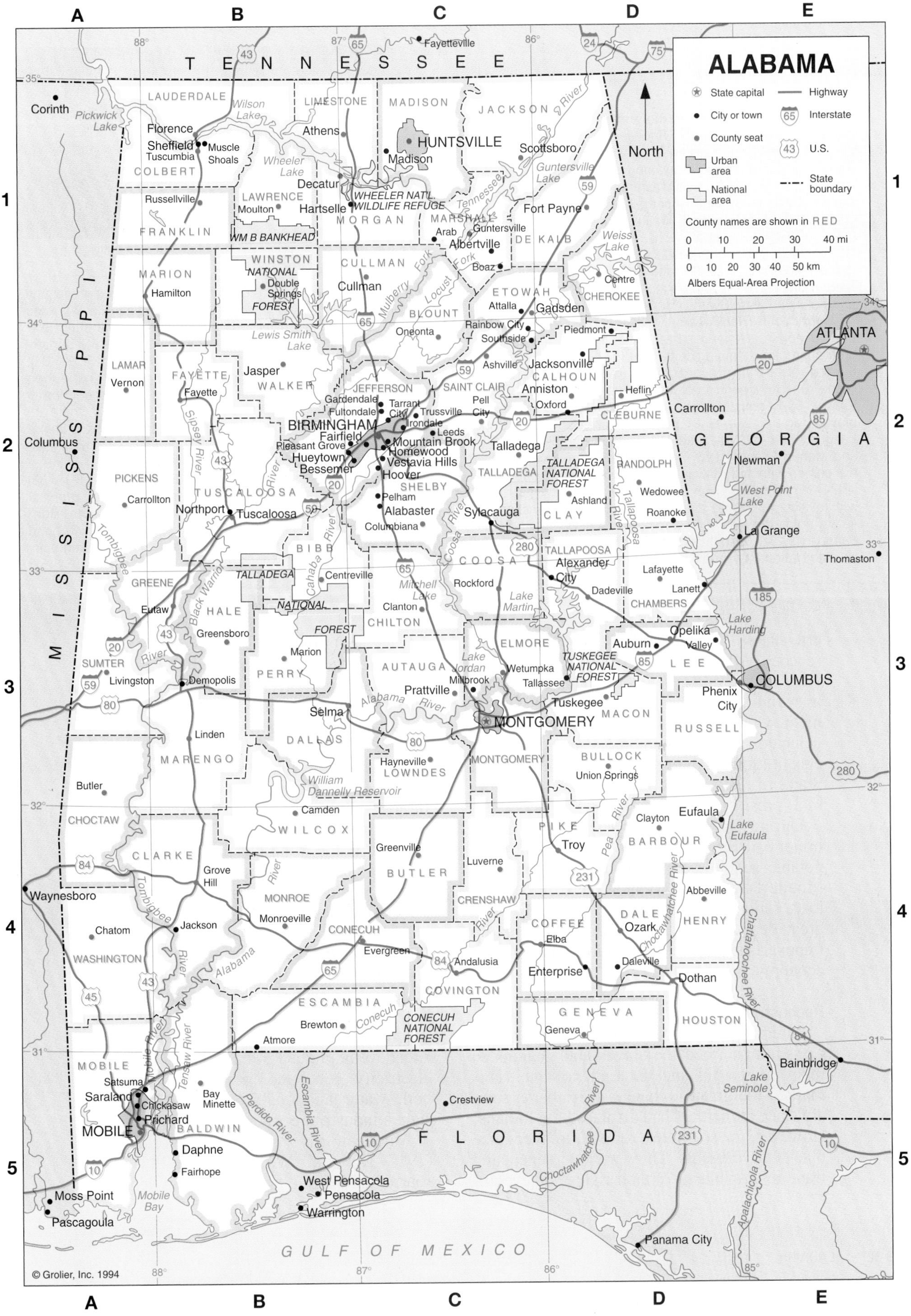
ALABAMA
State capital
City or town
County seat
Urban area
National area
Highway
Interstate
U.S.
State boundary
County names are shown in RED
0 10 20 30 40 mi
0 10 20 30 40 50 km
Albers Equal-Area Projection
North
A B C D E
1 2 3 4 5
TENNESSEE
GEORGIA
FLORIDA
MISSISSIPPI
GULF OF MEXICO
ATLANTA
COLUMBUS
Corinth
Pickwick Lake
Fayetteville
Columbus
Carrollton
Newman
West Point Lake
La Grange
Thomaston
Lake Harding
Phenix City
Lake Eufaula
Chattahoochee River
Bainbridge
Lake Seminole
Apalachicola River
Panama City
Crestview
Choctawhatchee
Perdido River
Escambia River
West Pensacola
Pensacola
Warrington
Moss Point
Pascagoula
Mobile Bay
Waynesboro
LAUDERDALE
Wilson Lake
Florence
Sheffield
Tuscumbia
Muscle Shoals
COLBERT
LIMESTONE
Athens
MADISON
HUNTSVILLE
Madison
JACKSON
Scottsboro
Guntersville Lake
Wheeler Lake
Decatur
WHEELER NATL. WILDLIFE REFUGE
Hartselle
LAWRENCE
Moulton
MORGAN
Russellville
FRANKLIN
WM B BANKHEAD
WINSTON
NATIONAL
Double Springs
FOREST
MARSHALL
Arab
Guntersville
Albertville
Boaz
Fort Payne
DE KALB
Weiss Lake
Centre
CHEROKEE
CULLMAN
Cullman
Mulberry Fork
Locust Fork
BLOUNT
Oneonta
ETOWAH
Attalla
Gadsden
Rainbow City
Southside
Piedmont
MARION
Hamilton
Lewis Smith Lake
LAMAR
Vernon
FAYETTE
Fayette
Jasper
WALKER
JEFFERSON
Gardendale
Fultondale
Tarrant City
Trussville
Irondale
BIRMINGHAM
Fairfield
Pleasant Grove
Hueytown
Bessemer
Mountain Brook
Homewood
Vestavia Hills
Hoover
Leeds
Pelham
Alabaster
Columbiana
SHELBY
ST. CLAIR
Ashville
Pell City
Jacksonville
CALHOUN
Anniston
Oxford
Heflin
CLEBURNE
Talladega
TALLADEGA
TALLADEGA NATIONAL FOREST
RANDOLPH
Wedowee
Roanoke
Ashland
CLAY
Tallapoosa River
Sylacauga
PICKENS
Carrollton
TUSCALOOSA
Northport
Tuscaloosa
Sipsey River
Black Warrior River
Tombigbee
BIBB
Cahaba River
Centreville
TALLADEGA NATIONAL FOREST
GREENE
Eutaw
HALE
Greensboro
COOSA
Rockford
Coosa River
Mitchell Lake
Clanton
CHILTON
Lake Martin
TALLAPOOSA
Alexander City
Dadeville
Lafayette
Lanett
CHAMBERS
Opelika
Auburn
Valley
LEE
SUMTER
Livingston
Demopolis
PERRY
Marion
AUTAUGA
Lake Jordan
Prattville
Millbrook
ELMORE
Wetumpka
Tallassee
TUSKEGEE NATIONAL FOREST
Tuskegee
MACON
RUSSELL
Selma
Alabama River
MONTGOMERY
DALLAS
Linden
MARENGO
Hayneville
LOWNDES
William Dannelly Reservoir
BULLOCK
Union Springs
Butler
CHOCTAW
Camden
WILCOX
PIKE
Troy
Pea River
Clayton
Eufaula
BARBOUR
CLARKE
Grove Hill
Greenville
BUTLER
Luverne
CRENSHAW
MONROE
Monroeville
Abbeville
HENRY
DALE
Ozark
Choctawhatchee River
Chatom
Jackson
WASHINGTON
CONECUH
Evergreen
COFFEE
Elba
Enterprise
Daleville
Dothan
Andalusia
COVINGTON
ESCAMBIA
Brewton
Conecuh
CONECUH NATIONAL FOREST
Atmore
GENEVA
Geneva
HOUSTON
MOBILE
Satsuma
Saraland
Chickasaw
Prichard
MOBILE
Mobile River
Tensaw River
Bay Minette
BALDWIN
Daphne
Fairhope
© Grolier, Inc. 1994

Famous People

Helen Keller

Booker T. Washington

Dr. Martin Luther King, Jr.

Consult the Index to find more information in *The New Book of Knowledge* about the following people who were born in or are otherwise associated with Alabama: educators George Washington Carver (1864–1943), Helen Adams Keller (1880–1968), and Booker T. Washington (1856–1915); blues great W. C. Handy (1873–1958); civil rights leaders Martin Luther King, Jr., (1929–68) and Coretta Scott King (1927–); and Olympic track-and-field star Jesse Owens (1913–80).

Henry Louis (Hank) Aaron (1934–), born in Mobile, is American baseball's all-time champion home-run hitter. In 1974 he broke Babe Ruth's record of 714 career home runs and went on to hit a career total of 755. For much of his career, Aaron played for the Braves of the National League, first in Milwaukee (1954–65) and then in Atlanta (1966–74). He ended his career with the Milwaukee Brewers (1974–76) of the American League. Along with a lifetime batting average of .305, Aaron holds the all-time record for runs batted in (2,297). In addition to being chosen the National League's most valuable player of 1957, Aaron won the Spingarn Medal in 1975 and was elected to the National Baseball Hall of Fame in 1982.

Ralph David Abernathy (1926–90), born in Linden, was a Baptist minister and civil rights leader. He and Dr. Martin Luther King, Jr., planned the 1955 Montgomery bus boycott to protest segregation, and together in 1957 they established the Southern Christian Leadership Conference (SCLC) to broaden the civil rights movement through nonviolent means. After King was assassinated in 1968, Abernathy led the Poor People's March on Washington, D.C. He served as SCLC president from 1968 to 1977. His autobiography, *And the Walls Came Tumbling Down,* was published in 1989.

Hugo La Fayette Black (1886–1971), born in Harlan, was an associate justice of the U.S. Supreme Court for 34 years (1937–71). A successful Birmingham lawyer, Black was elected to the U.S. Senate, where he served for ten years (1927–37). A Democrat, Black vigorously supported the New Deal policies of President Franklin Roosevelt, which led to his Court appointment in 1937. Black was a liberal judge who supported government protection of free speech and civil rights.

Paul William (Bear) Bryant (1913–83) is considered by many to be the greatest college football coach of all time. Born in Kingsland, Arkansas, Bryant was head coach at Maryland (1945), Kentucky (1946–53), and Texas A&M (1954–57)

ern states. On January 11, 1861, Alabama seceded (withdrew) from the Union and invited all the other Southern states to join her in withdrawal and in forming a new government. On February 4, 1861, a convention of delegates met in Montgomery and drew up a constitution for the newly formed Confederate States of America. Jefferson Davis was sworn in as president on February 18.

During the Civil War (1861–65), many minor battles took place in Alabama. The most notable action occurred at the naval battle of Mobile Bay in 1864, which the Confederates lost. Union raids late in the war destroyed a great deal of property and left Alabama so impoverished, it took generations to rebuild its economy.

Reconstruction

After the war, several amendments to the Constitution freed the slaves and guaranteed them citizenship and the right to vote. This marked the greatest change in Alabama society since the settlers had displaced the Indians. However, most whites refused to recognize blacks as citizens. They used violence and fraud to strip blacks of their rights and eventually created a system of legal segregation (separation of the races), which allowed whites to treat blacks unfairly. The final blow came in 1901, when Alabama revised its constitution and took away the blacks' right to vote.

Meanwhile, falling cotton prices made farming less profitable. At the instigation of Daniel Pratt, a cotton-gin and textile manufacturer, Alabama began to build railroads and encourage the development of industries. Pratt invested in the iron industry in the new city of Birmingham, which grew rapidly, and in the 1890's, many new cotton mills and sawmills were established.

Alabama in the 1900's

Economic growth accelerated in the 1900's with the expansion of the iron-and-steel, textile, and lumber industries. The development of chemical, rubber, and electronics plants added to the industrial base. An abundance of electricity, generated cheaply by the power of both water and coal, greatly advanced the state's industrial economy.

American involvement in World War I (1917–18) and World War II (1941–45) spurred industrial production and led to the before beginning his 24-year dynasty with the Crimson Tide of the University of Alabama (1958–82). Among his achievements were six national championships; three Coach of the Year awards; 15 victories in a record 29 bowl-game appearances; and a career record of 323-85-17. The Paul W. Bryant Museum in Tuscaloosa commemorates Bryant and University of Alabama football.

(Nelle) Harper Lee (1926–), born in Monroeville, achieved literary distinction with the publication of her only novel, *To Kill a Mockingbird* (1960). The story examines racial prejudice and social injustice in a small Alabama town, as seen through the eyes of an innocent and unbiased young girl. The book won the Pulitzer Prize for fiction in 1961 and was made into a popular film in 1962.

Joe Louis (Joseph Louis Barrow) (1914–81), born near Lafayette, was one of the all-time greatest professional boxers. He was the longest-reigning world heavyweight champion, defending his title 25 times between 1937 and 1949. He won his first heavyweight title in 1937 by knocking out James J. Braddock in 8 rounds. Nicknamed the "Brown Bomber," Louis won 68 victories and lost only 3 fights in his entire professional career.

Rosa Louise McCauley Parks (1913–), born in Tuskeegee, sparked the modern civil rights movement when she was arrested in 1955 for refusing to give her seat to a white passenger on a crowded Montgomery city bus, as required by city law. The incident led to a bus boycott, led by Dr. Martin Luther King, Jr., that increased national awareness about racial segregation and discrimination. Parks was awarded the Spingarn Medal in 1979 and the Congressional Gold Medal in 1999 for her contributions to the civil rights movement. Her memoir, *Rosa Parks,* was published in 1992.

Julia Strudwick Tutwiler (1841–1916), born in Tuscaloosa, was an educator and social reformer. She helped establish several schools for girls and successfully campaigned for the admission of women into the University of Alabama. Tutwiler also worked to reform the state prison system. She wrote *Alabama,* the state song.

George C. Wallace

George Corley Wallace (1919–98), born in Clio, served as governor of Alabama for four terms (1963–67; 1971–79; and 1983–87) and three times was an unsuccessful candidate for president of the United States (1968, 1972, and 1976). A staunch supporter of states' rights and segregation, Wallace came to national attention in 1963 when he defied federal law by attempting to block the enrollment of two black students at the University of Alabama. In later years, however, he softened on civil rights protections and formed a coalition of black and white supporters. While campaigning for the presidency in 1972, Wallace was paralyzed by a bullet in a failed assassination attempt in Laurel, Maryland.

establishment of several large military bases in the state. The Great Depression of the 1930's, which brought great suffering to Alabama's farmers, led to the establishment of the Tennessee Valley Authority (TVA) and other federal projects that helped build the state's economy. In the 1950's and 1960's, the nation's space program developed rockets at Huntsville Redstone Arsenal. Rockets built there were used to send up America's first satellite as well as the first astronauts to land on the moon.

Meanwhile, race relations remained strained. As early as the 1940's, African Americans in Alabama challenged racial discrimination in voting. However, their first victory was not achieved until 1956, following a year-long, nonviolent boycott of the Montgomery city bus system, organized by Dr. Martin Luther King, Jr., in response to the 1955 arrest of Rosa Parks. The protest led to the passage of a federal law in 1956 that made discrimination illegal on public transportation and marked the birth of the modern civil rights movement in the United States.

Demonstrations against the continued segregation of public facilities took place in Birmingham in 1963. Abuses by law enforcement officers, such as the use of high-powered water hoses against peaceful demonstrators and the deaths of four black girls, killed by a bomb while attending Sunday school, outraged the nation and prompted the passage of the Civil Rights Act of 1964. Then the following year, Dr. King led a peaceful march from Selma to Montgomery to protest discrimination against blacks at the polls, which directly led to the passage of the Voting Rights Act of 1965.

Meanwhile, many whites deeply resented integration and supported the pro-segregation position of Alabama's Governor George Wallace. By the 1970's, however, most Alabamians, including Governor Wallace, had adjusted to the new order and accepted the rights of all citizens. By 1991, Alabama led the nation in the number of African Americans elected to public office, clearly representing the state's progress toward achieving racial equality.

ROBERT J. NORRELL, PH.D.
Director, Center for Southern History and Culture, University of Alabama

ALAMO. See TEXAS.

ALASKA

State flag

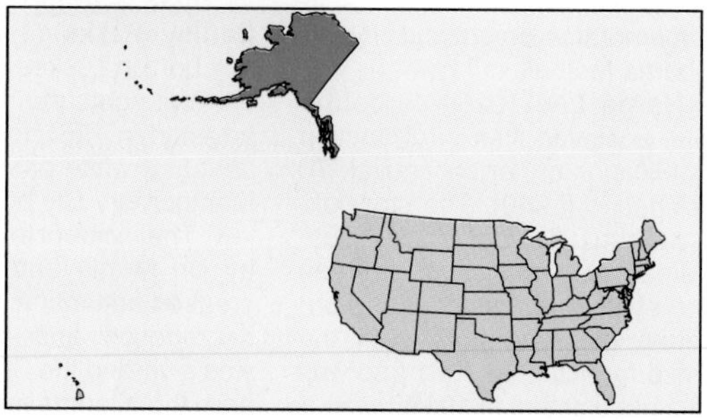

Alaska takes its names from the Aleuts—a people native to Alaska—who called their land alaxsxa. *Although there are several possible translations of the word, experts generally agree that it means "the main land."*

Alaska's nickname is the Last Frontier. For more than two hundred years, newcomers have sought their fortunes from its wealth of natural resources. Whether pursuing furs, gold, or oil, these hardy pioneers forged their way through an untouched wilderness. Even today, much of Alaska has never been settled or even explored.

Alaska gets more hours of sunlight in the summertime than any other state, giving the state another nickname, Land of the Midnight Sun. For nearly three straight months, from May through July, the sun never sets at Barrow, Alaska's northernmost point.

Alaska is a rugged peninsula located in the northwest corner of North America, approximately 500 miles (800 kilometers) from the "Lower 48" states. Covering an area more than twice the size of Texas, Alaska is by far the largest of the fifty states. Yet the U.S. 2000 Census reported that it had fewer residents than any other state except Wyoming and Vermont. More than one-quarter of northern Alaska lies within the Arctic Circle. It is covered by frozen, treeless tundra. Lush rain forests grow in the state's southeastern region.

Anchorage, Juneau (the capital), and Fairbanks are the three largest cities in Alaska. People there enjoy most of the same conveniences as other American cities. Yet beyond these urban areas, Alaska is rough, wild, and barely populated. Many places can only be reached readily by airplane.

Dog mushing, or sledding, is Alaska's official state sport. Once a major form of transportation in wintertime, the dog team and sled is still necessary in some rural areas. Since 1973, the Iditarod Trail Sled Dog Race has been Alaska's most famous sporting event. Dashing from Anchorage to Nome along a more than 1,000-mile (1,600-kilometer) route, mushers facing treacherous terrain take as long as three weeks to finish what has been called the Last Great Race on Earth.

The first people to inhabit Alaska came from Siberia, perhaps as long as 50,000 years ago. The descendants of these first settlers—the Yupik and Inupiat Eskimos, Aleuts, and various groups of Indians—still thrive in Alaska. Russian explorers discovered Alaska in the mid-1700's, and at once the territory was overrun with fur trappers and merchants. Within a hundred years, they had hunted sea otters and fur seals almost to extinction. When the United States offered to buy Alaska in 1867, many Americans believed Alaska was worthless, and they ridiculed its purchase until gold was discovered there in 1880. Soon tens of thousands of gold rushers swarmed into Alaska, hoping to strike it rich.

Alaska's modern history began when the territory achieved statehood on January 3, 1959, and even more important, when oil was discovered in Prudhoe Bay in 1968. Since then, oil has become the mainstay of Alaska's economy as well as the focus of many fierce battles between business people, who wish to develop the land, and environmentalists, who wish to preserve it in its natural state.

▸ LAND

Alaska is an enormous peninsula, surrounded on three sides by water. Its 6,640-mile (10,686-kilometer) coastline is longer than that of any of the other continental

Dall sheep and other wildlife thrive in Alaska's vast mountain ranges. Most Alaskans enjoy the challenge of living in such a rugged land and climate. A Russian Orthodox church graces Kodiak Island, where fur traders established their first permanent settlement in 1784.

State flower:
Forget-me-not

State tree:
Sitka spruce

FACTS AND FIGURES

Location: Northwestern North America; bordered on the north by the Arctic Ocean, on the south by the Pacific Ocean and the Gulf of Alaska, on the east by Canada (British Columbia and Yukon Territory), and on the west by the Bering Sea.

Area: 615,230 sq mi (1,593,444 km^2); rank, 1st.

Population: 626,932 (2000 census); rank, 48th.

Elevation: *Highest*—20,320 ft (6,194 m), at Mount McKinley; *lowest*—sea level.

Capital: Juneau.

Statehood: January 3, 1959; 49th state.

State Motto: *North to the Future.*

State Song: "Alaska's Flag."

Nicknames: Last Frontier; Great Land; Land of the Midnight Sun.

Abbreviation: AK

State bird:
Willow ptarmigan

states. The total shoreline, including offshore islands, bays, and inlets, is about 47,300 miles (76,150 kilometers) long.

Alaska encompasses more than 1,000 islands, mostly in the Alexander Archipelago and the Aleutian island chain. The Alexander Archipelago and the thin strip of mainland that borders British Columbia are known as the Panhandle.

Land Regions

Alaska's vast landscape contains four major land regions.

The Pacific Mountain System, in the south, contains the Coast Mountains in the southeast; the St. Elias, Wrangell, Chugach, and Kenai ranges around the Gulf of Alaska; the Aleutian Range, which sweeps southwestward through the Alaska Peninsula and the Aleutian Islands; and the Alaska Range farther inland. The Alaska Range is known for its high peaks and its many glaciers and rivers. Its crowning point is Mount McKinley. Rising 20,320 feet (6,194 meters), it is the highest peak in North America.

Mount McKinley is the highest mountain in all of North America. The Athabascan Indians call it *Denali*, meaning the Great One. Located in Denali National Park in the south central part of the state, it is the crowning point of the Alaska Range.

The Central Uplands and Lowlands, covering most of central Alaska, is made up of rolling hills, valleys, and low mountain ranges. Forests grow in its eastern and central valleys. Some areas are covered by permafrost, or permanently frozen subsoil. Others are covered with a dense growth of low vegetation.

The Rocky Mountain System reaches its northernmost extension at the Brooks Range. The highest mountains within this range are located in the northeastern part of the state and rise just above 9,000 feet (2,743 meters).

The Arctic Coastal Plain, also known as the Arctic Slope, lies entirely within the Arctic Circle. From the foot of the Brooks Range, this flat and treeless plain slopes northward to the Beaufort Sea and the Arctic Ocean. The soil is largely permafrost.

Rivers and Lakes

The Yukon is the great river of Alaska. It winds across central Alaska more than 1,400 miles (2,250 kilometers) and empties through a huge, swampy delta into Norton Sound. The largest of the Yukon's tributaries in Alaska are the Porcupine, the Koyukuk, and the Tanana rivers. Other major rivers are the Kuskokwim, Susitna, Copper, and Colville rivers.

Alaska has many natural lakes. Iliamna Lake, on the Alaska Peninsula, is the largest, covering about 1,000 square miles (2,600 square kilometers). Becharof Lake, south of Iliamna, is the second largest.

Climate

Alaska's climate varies widely from one region to another. The Panhandle and the coastal plain along the Gulf of Alaska have moderate temperatures and heavy precipitation. High mountains protect these areas from cold northerly winds, and ocean currents warm the shores. Winds off the Pacific Ocean lose their moisture as they collide with the mountains, drenching the area with rain. The average annual precipitation in this region is about 94 inches (2,388 millimeters), although some areas receive twice that amount. The average annual temperature is 41°F (5°C). The Copper River, Cook Inlet, and Bristol Bay areas have colder winters and less rainfall.

Summer and winter temperatures in the Interior are more extreme. Average annual precipitation there is about 15 inches (380 millimeters). The growing season in the Tanana Valley near Fairbanks averages only about 100 days, but long hours of summer sunlight help to make up for the short sea-

Lichens cover the ground in the tundra regions of Alaska. This type of vegetation is an important food source for caribou.

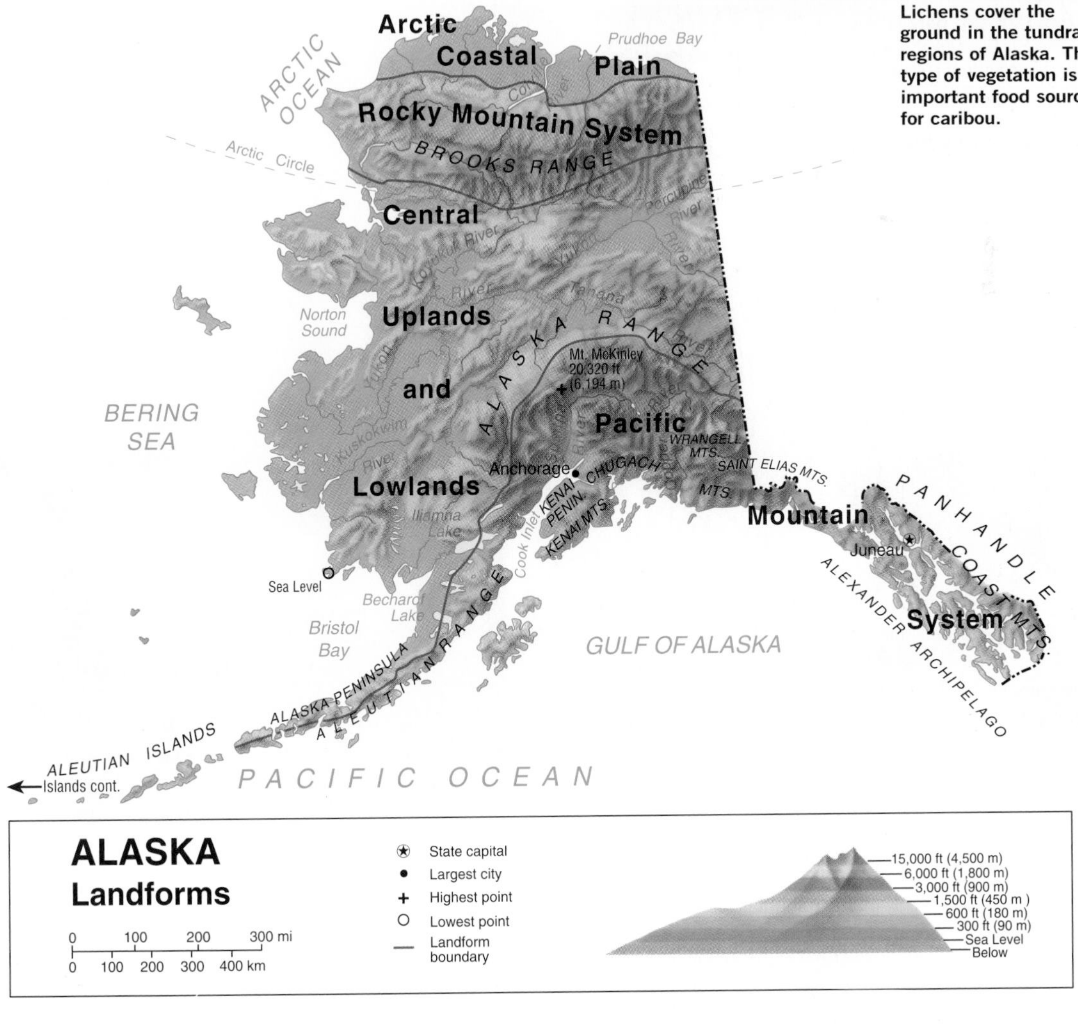

Places of Interest

In the vast expanse of Alaska, there are many places of scenic and historic interest, including remote arctic lands, sites of early Russian settlement, prospectors' trails, the seacoast, spectacular glaciers, and wilderness homes of Alaska's fascinating, varied, and abundant wildlife.

Denali National Park and Preserve, located midway between Anchorage and Fairbanks, contains Mount McKinley, the highest mountain in North America. Originally established in 1917 as Mount McKinley National Park, this popular park preserve contains deep lakes, glaciers, and approximately 300 peaks of the Alaska Range, as well as a wide variety of wildlife.

Gates of the Arctic National Park and Preserve lies completely north of the Arctic Circle. Located in the central Brooks Range, the area is a vast wilderness of mountains, valleys, glacial lakes, and rivers. It was designated a national park in 1980.

Glacier Bay National Park and Preserve, 100 miles (160 kilometers) west of Juneau, can be seen by boat or by air. The park contains more than forty great ice masses between two parallel mountain ranges—the St. Elias to the east and the Fairweather to the west. Whales and seals can be found in Glacier Bay.

Katmai National Park and Preserve, on the eastern shore of the Alaska Peninsula, is the site of the violent volcanic eruption in 1912 that turned green lands into the Valley of Ten Thousand Smokes. Also remarkable for its wildlife, it is the nation's largest grizzly bear sanctuary.

Totem Bight State Historical Park, near Ketchikan

Kenai Fjords National Park, south and west of Seward on the Kenai Peninsula, includes the Harding Icefield, one of the major ice caps in the United States.

Klondike Gold Rush National Historical Park, at Skagway, preserves historic buildings from the gold rush days, as well as the Chilkoot and White Pass trails, once trekked by prospectors.

Mendenhall Glacier, a popular attraction, is located in Tongass National Forest within a short distance of Juneau. The glacier is about 12 miles (19 kilometers) long and 1.5 miles (2.4 kilometers) wide.

Saint Michael's Russian Orthodox Cathedral, a landmark building in Sitka, houses a beautiful collection of icons, or religious paintings.

Sitka National Historical Park, at Sitka, preserves the site where the Tlingit Indians made their last stand against the Russian settlers in 1804. The park also includes a wildlife sanctuary and a collection of Tlingit totem poles.

Totem Bight State Historical Park, north of Ketchikan, features a collection of Haida and Tlingit totem poles from the 1800's.

Wrangell-St. Elias National Park and Preserve, east of Anchorage, is the largest unit of the National Park System. The Chugach, Wrangell, and St. Elias mountain ranges of the Pacific Mountain System converge here, forming North America's largest collection of peaks higher than 16,000 feet (4,877 meters).

State Parks. For information on state parks and other public lands, such as wildlife refuges, contact the Alaska Public Lands Information Center, 605 W. 4th Avenue, Anchorage, Alaska 99501.

Brown bear catching salmon. Katmai National Park and Preserve

Mendenhall Glacier, near Juneau

The Pribilof Islands in the Bering Sea serve as breeding grounds for some of the world's largest colonies of fur seals (*above*). Hunting of these animals is controlled by the federal government. Cook Inlet (*right*) is one of Alaska's three major oil-producing regions.

son. The waters of the Arctic Ocean keep Arctic Alaska warmer than the bitterly cold Interior. Precipitation there averages only about 7 inches (178 millimeters) a year.

Weather in the Aleutian Islands is influenced by the warm Pacific Ocean to the south and the cold Bering Sea to the north. The air is wet and foggy. Average annual temperatures are about the same as those along the Gulf of Alaska, but there is only half as much precipitation. Fierce, gusting winds called williwaws often lash the islands.

Plant and Animal Life

Forests cover about one-third of Alaska. The coastal forests—in the Panhandle and along the Gulf of Alaska—are dense, towering stands of western hemlock, Sitka spruce, and red and yellow cedar. The Interior forests contain mostly white spruce, birch, aspen, poplar, and willow. Muskeg bogs, common to much of Alaska, contain spongy masses of plant life—cranberries, crowberries, grasses, mosses, and lichens. The dead plants decay slowly because of the low temperatures.

Alaska is home to an astounding variety of wildlife. Black-tailed deer, mountain goats, moose, black bears and grizzly bears (including the Kodiak brown bears on Kodiak Island) are among the largest animals found in the south. Farther north, moose become more plentiful than deer, and wolves, lynx, and Dall sheep thrive. Caribou, or wild reindeer, increase in numbers toward the north, where they travel in herds of thousands. Polar bears live in the far north. Animals that are not native to Alaska but were brought there include reindeer, elk, musk oxen, and bison.

Nearly 400 species of birds make their home in Alaska, including geese, grouse, and ptarmigan and such predatory birds as bald eagles, falcons, hawks, and owls. Animals that are valued for their fur include marten, mink, and beaver. Major game fish include salmon, halibut, rainbow trout, and grayling. The most important commercial fish are salmon, cod, herring, halibut, crab, shrimp, clams, and scallops. Enormous numbers of marine mammals, such as walruses, whales, and seals, thrive in Alaska's bounteous waters.

Natural Resources

Traditionally, Alaska's most prized natural resources were fur, fish, and gold. Today they are petroleum and natural gas. Rich deposits have been found in Prudhoe Bay, the Kenai Peninsula, and Cook Inlet. Gold and silver are found in many areas. Alaska also has enormous reserves of coal, but much of it is of inferior quality and is difficult to reach.

Russians (*above*) were the first people to immigrate to Alaska in modern times. Eskimos (*right*) make up the largest segment of Alaska's native groups. They include the Inupiat of the northern regions and three Yupik groups—Siberian, Pacific Gulf, and Central Alaskan.

PEOPLE

Although Alaska is one of the least populous states in the nation, its population has grown tremendously in recent decades. Three out of every four Alaskans live in five major urban areas. The Anchorage borough is the most densely populated, followed by the Fairbanks North Star, Matanuska-Susitna, Kenai Peninsula, and Juneau boroughs.

Two out of every three Alaskans were born outside of the state. Many came from other U.S. states to work in Alaska's oil fields or for the government. There are pockets of African, Hispanic, and Asian Americans in urban areas.

The so-called Alaska Native groups make up approximately 17 percent of the state's population. The major groups are the Yupik and Inupiat Eskimos, the Aleut, and various Indian communities that include the Haida, Tsimshian, and Tlingit and twelve Athabascan groups. For more information, see the articles INUIT and INDIANS, AMERICAN (North American Indians Since 1500) in Volume I.

Education

The first schools in Alaska were established by the Russians with the settlement of Kodiak Island in 1784. After the United States purchased Alaska in 1867, missionaries carried out educational work among the native peoples. When settlement increased in the 1880's and 1890's, the federal government established public schools. Today each borough or rural district regulates its own public-school system, according to the policies of the State Board of Education. Homeschooling and correspondence courses are common in remote areas.

The state-supported University of Alaska was founded in 1917 in Fairbanks as the Alaska Agricultural College and School of Mines. Today main campuses also are located in An-

PEOPLE

Population: 626,932 (2000 census).

Density: 10 persons per sq mi (4 per km^2).

Distribution: 68% urban; 32% rural.

Largest Boroughs (2000 census):

Anchorage 260,283	Juneau 30,711
Fairbanks North Star 82,840	Ketchikan Gateway 14,070
Matanuska-Susitna 59,322	Kodiak Island 13,913
Kenai Peninsula 49,691	Sitka 8,835

Source: U.S. Bureau of the Census

Persons per sq mi	Persons per km^2
over 250	over 100
50-250	20-100
5-50	2-20
0-5	0-2

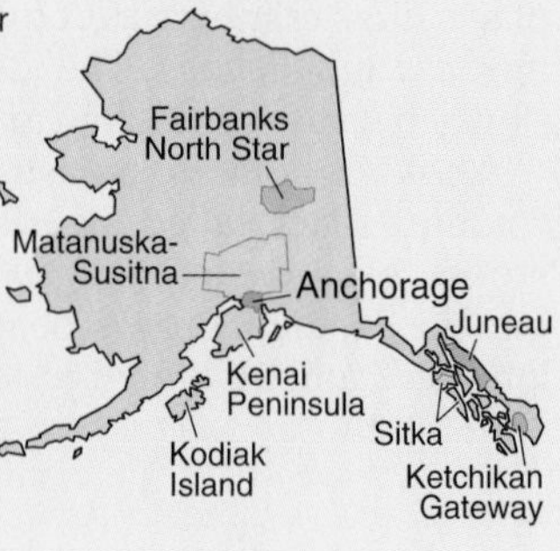

chorage and Juneau, with branch campuses in several communities. The state university system offers strong programs in arctic and petroleum engineering, marine sciences, geophysics, and international business and trade. There are three private colleges in the state: Alaska Pacific University, in Anchorage; Alaska Bible College, in Glennallen; and Sheldon Jackson College, the oldest college in the state, in Sitka.

Libraries, Museums, and the Arts

Anchorage's public library system circulates more than 1.5 million books a year. Statewide, there are about ninety public libraries and branches. The Alaska State Library in Juneau houses the largest collection of state-related books and documents.

The Alaska State Museum in Juneau is the state's leading natural history museum. Displays cover ancient and modern cultures, pioneer and mining history, and Alaskan wildlife. The Anchorage Museum of History and Art highlights centuries of Alaskan art and history. The University of Alaska Museum in Fairbanks features Alaskan history and natural sciences. The Sheldon Jackson Museum in Sitka houses an array of Alaskan artifacts. Other museums include the Living Museum of the Arctic, in Kotzebue; and the Trail of '98 Museum, in Skagway.

ECONOMY

Petroleum is Alaska's single most important product. Royalties and taxes on oil alone provide most of the state's revenues. Fish is Alaska's most valuable export.

Services

Service industries account for 70 percent of Alaska's annual gross state product (GSP)—the total value of goods and services produced in a year. Government is the largest segment, employing approximately 30 percent of the workforce, including national park workers. Other services, in descending order of importance, are transportation, communication, and utilities; business, social, and personal services, which include tourism; finance, insurance, and real estate services; and wholesale and retail trade.

Manufacturing

Alaska has relatively few manufacturing industries. Its most important manufactured goods are processed seafood products, such as canned salmon and smoked, salted, or frozen fish and shellfish. Wood is processed to produce round logs, lumber, wood pulp, wood chips, and paper.

Agriculture

Due to its harsh climate and rugged terrain, Alaska ranks last among the fifty states in the value of its farm production. Most of Alaska's farming is done in the Matanuska-Susitna Valley north of Anchorage and in the Tanana Valley near Fairbanks. Major farm products are milk, hay, potatoes, lettuce, greenhouse plants, and cattle.

Alaska leads the nation in the value of its seafood catch (*left*). Seaplanes (*below*) bring essential goods to people who live in Alaska's remote regions.

Alaska's fisheries, on the other hand, are extremely productive. They account for half the catch of the entire United States. Groundfish are the most valuable. These include pollack, cod, flatfish, rockfish, and sablefish. Pollack is Alaska's leading commercial fish, followed by salmon and shellfish. Crab—tanner, king, and Dungeness—are the major shellfish catches. Alaska also supplies much of the world's halibut.

Mining and Construction

Mining contributes more to Alaska's GSP than any other single enterprise. About 19 percent of all the petroleum produced in the United States comes from Alaska, making it one of the leading oil-producing states. More than 1 million barrels of crude oil are extracted from Alaska's oil fields every day. About 65 percent of all the state's oil comes from Prudhoe Bay and Kuparuk on the North Slope. They are the two largest known oil fields in North America. The state also produces about 1.3 billion cubic feet (36.4 million cubic meters) of natural gas daily.

After petroleum, zinc is Alaska's most valuable mineral product. The Red Dog Mine near Kotzebue is the largest zinc mine in the Northern Hemisphere. Large quantities of gold and silver are also found.

All three phases of mining—exploration, development, and production—require construction work, including the building of housing for workers. As new mineral reserves are continually being found, construction continues to be an important support industry in the state.

The Trans-Alaska Pipeline carries oil from Prudhoe Bay on the North Slope to the port of Valdez on Prince William Sound, a distance of 800 miles (1,287 kilometers).

Transportation

Most people do not realize that Alaska is as close to major European cities as it is to major Asian cities. Air and sea traffic take the polar route across the Arctic region between Europe and Alaska every day. Anchorage and Fairbanks have international airports that provide passenger and cargo service. Additional airports are located in Juneau, Ketchikan, Kodiak, Sitka, Wrangell, Petersburg, Nome, Barrow, Kotzebue, and Valdez. Bush pilots handle most of the travel into the rugged Interior.

Alaska has one road connection—the Alaska Highway—to Canada and the Lower 48 states. The Alaska Railroad is the only rail line. Both extend north as far as Fairbanks.

Perhaps Alaska's best-known transportation system is the 800-mile (1,287-kilometer) Trans-Alaska Pipeline, which was built in the 1970's to transport oil from Alaska's North Slope fields to the port of Valdez for shipping. Today, Valdez is the fourth busiest port in the country. Most of its traffic is domestic, and most of its cargo is oil.

PRODUCTS AND INDUSTRIES

Manufacturing: Processed foods, wood and paper products, electrical and nonelectrical machinery, sand and gravel materials, computer equipment, handcrafted goods.

Agriculture: Seafood, milk, hay, livestock feed, potatoes.

Minerals: Petroleum, natural gas, zinc.

Services: Wholesale and retail trade; finance, insurance, and real estate; business, social, and personal services; transportation, communication, and utilities; government.

Percentage of Gross State Product* by Industry

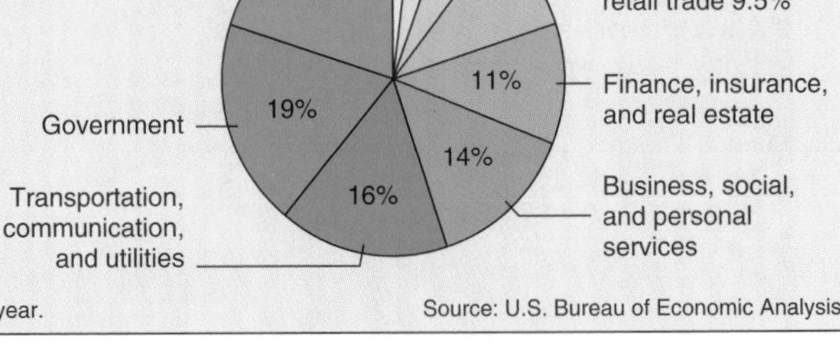

*Gross state product is the total value of goods and services produced in a year.

Source: U.S. Bureau of Economic Analysis

Communication

Alaska's major newspapers include the *Anchorage Daily News*, the Fairbanks *Daily News Miner*, *The Peninsula Clarion* in Kenai, and the *Juneau Empire*. More than sixty radio stations and a dozen television stations broadcast throughout the state.

▶ CITIES

Most of Alaska's large population centers, except for Fairbanks, are in the state's southern coastal region. Small towns and villages dot the Interior and the western coast.

Juneau, located in the Panhandle, is Alaska's capital. Founded by gold miners in 1880, it was named for Joe Juneau, one of the first prospectors to discover gold in the area.

Juneau, often called the Longest City in the World, occupies a long and narrow stretch of land that slopes from the foot of Mount Juneau down to a bustling waterfront on Gastineau Channel. Douglas Island, in the channel, also is part of the city. Mountains cut the city off from the mainland, so visitors must come in by boat or airplane. Attractions include the Alaska State Museum, St. Nicholas Russian Orthodox Church, and a fascinating historic district.

Anchorage, Alaska's most populous borough, is home to more than 41 percent of the state's residents. The metropolitan area, known as the Anchorage Bowl, lies between Cook Inlet to the east and the Chugach Mountains to the west.

The city was founded in 1915 when the Alaska Railroad was under construction. Today it is the state's commercial and financial center. Revenues from the booming oil industry financed the construction of the Alaska Center for the Performing Arts, Sullivan Sports Arena, and dozens of office towers and luxury hotels. Earthquake Park, commemorating the 1964 earthquake, offers a scenic view of the city and its surroundings.

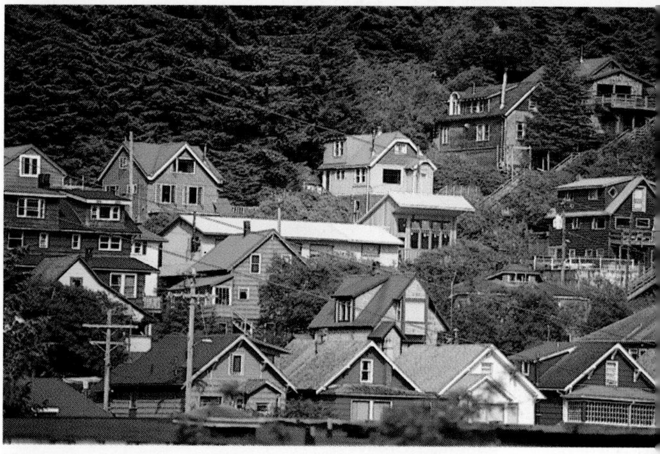

More than 41 percent of Alaska's population lives in the sprawling borough of Anchorage (*top*). Juneau (*above*), the state capital, has charming hillside neighborhoods.

Fairbanks is the heart of Fairbanks North Star, Alaska's second most populous borough. It is the only major population center in the Interior. Fairbanks is the northern endpoint of the Alaska Railroad and the state's major highways and thus is a transportation hub for the state's northern and western regions. Fairbanks' international airport provides service to and from Asia, Europe, Arctic Alaska, and the Lower 48 states.

Faribanks was founded in 1902 when gold was discovered nearby. Today it is a major trading center for the Yukon Valley. Attractions include the main campus of the University of Alaska and a theme park called Pioneer Park.

▶ GOVERNMENT

Alaska remained a territory for 47 years before it became a state. This was one of the

Four pillars of Alaskan marble and a statue of a Kodiak brown bear distinguish the entrance to the state capitol building in Juneau.

INDEX TO ALASKA MAP

Akutan C5
Alakanuk C3
Alaska Maritime Nat'l. Wildlife Refuge A5, B5, C5
Alaska Peninsula Nat'l. Wildlife Refuge D4, D5
Anchorage D4
Anderson D3
Angoon F4
Aniak C4
Aniakchak Nat'l. Monument and Preserve D4
Annette I. Indian Res. F4
Arctic Nat'l. Wildlife Refuge D2, E2
Barrow D2
Bering Land Bridge Nat'l. Preserve C3
Bethel C4
Cape Krusenstern Nat'l. Monument C2
Chevak C3
Chugach Nat'l. Forest D4, E4
Cordova E4
Craig F4
Delta Junction E3
Denali Nat'l. Park and Preserve D3
Dillingham D4
Dutch Harbor C5
Emmonak C3
Fairbanks D3
Fort Yukon E2
Galena D3
Gambell C3
Gates of the Arctic Nat'l. Park and Preserve D2
Glacier Bay Nat'l. Park and Preserve E4, F4
Haines F4
Homer D4
Hoonah F4
Hooper Bay C3
Houston D3
Izembek Nat'l. Wildlife Refuge C5
Juneau ★ F4
Kake F4
Kanuti Nat'l. Wildlife Refuge D2, D3
Katmai Nat'l Park and Preserve D4
Kenai D4
Kenai Nat'l. Wildlife Refuge D4
Kenai Fjords Nat'l. Park D4
Ketchikan F4
King Salmon D4
Klawock F4
Kobuk Valley Nat'l Park C2, D2
Kodiak D4
Kodiak Nat'l. Wildlife Refuge D4
Kotzebue C2
Kwethluk C4
Lake Clark Nat'l. Park and Preserve D4
McGrath D3
Metlakatla F4
Misty Fiords Nat'l Monument F4
Mountain Village C3
Ninilchik D4
Noatak Valley Nat'l. Park C2, D2
Nome C3
Noorvik C2
North Pole D3
Palmer D3
Petersburg F4
Point Hope C2
Quinhagak C4
St. Paul B4
Salamatof D4
Sand Point C5
Savoonga C3
Selawik C2
Selawik Nat'l. Wildlife Refuge D3
Seward D4
Sitka F4
Skagway F4
Soldotna D4
Thorne Bay F4
Togiak C4
Togiak Nat'l. Wildlife Refuge C4
Tok E3
Tongass Nat'l. Forest F4
Unalakleet C3
Unalaska C5
Valdez E4
Wasilla D3
White Mountains Nat'l Recreation Area D3
Willow D3
Wrangell F4
Wrangell-St. Elias Nat'l. Park and Preserve E3, E4
Yakutat E4
Yukon-Charley Rivers Nat'l. Preserve E3
Yukon Delta Nat'l. Wildlife Refuge C4
Yukon Flats Nat'l. Wildlife Refuge D2

★ State capital

longest territorial periods in the nation's history. Anxious for statehood, Alaskans adopted a constitution in 1956, three years before they joined the Union.

Like the United States government, Alaska's state government consists of three branches: executive, legislative, and judicial. The governor is the state's chief executive. Other executive branch officers include the lieutenant governor and the attorney general.

The state's legislative branch consists of a senate and a house of representatives. The legislature convenes every year in January. The normal 120-day lawmaking session can be extended ten days upon a two-thirds vote of the legislators.

The Alaska Supreme Court heads the judicial branch of government. There are also courts of appeals, superior courts, district courts, and local magistrates.

While most other states are divided into counties, Alaska is divided into 16 boroughs organized around population centers. Those parts of the state that do not belong to a particular borough are governed by the state legislature. Only one Alaskan community is

GOVERNMENT

State Government
Governor: 4-year term
State senators: 20; 4-year terms
State representatives: 40; 2-year terms
Number of organized boroughs: 16

Federal Government
U.S. Senators: 2
U.S. Representatives: 1
Number of electoral votes: 3

For the name of the current governor, see STATE GOVERNMENTS in Volume S. For the names of current U.S. senators and representatives, see UNITED STATES, CONGRESS OF THE in Volume U-V.

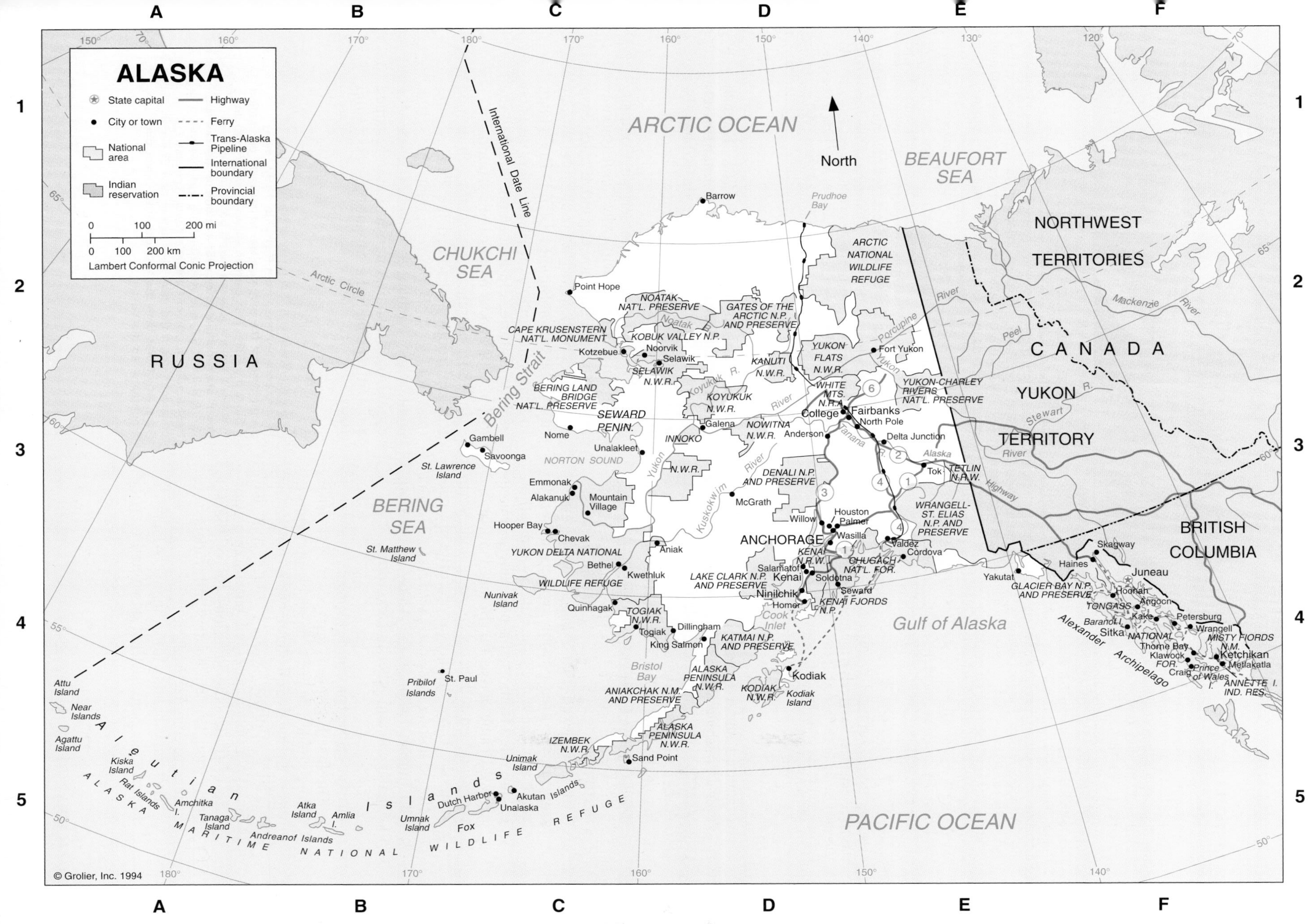
ALASKA
State capital
City or town
National area
Indian reservation
Highway
Ferry
Trans-Alaska Pipeline
International boundary
Provincial boundary
0 100 200 mi
0 100 200 km
Lambert Conformal Conic Projection
ARCTIC OCEAN
North
BEAUFORT SEA
CHUKCHI SEA
BERING SEA
Gulf of Alaska
PACIFIC OCEAN
RUSSIA
CANADA
NORTHWEST TERRITORIES
YUKON TERRITORY
BRITISH COLUMBIA
International Date Line
Arctic Circle
Bering Strait
NORTON SOUND
Bristol Bay
Cook Inlet
Prudhoe Bay
Barrow
Point Hope
Kotzebue
Noorvik
Selawik
Nome
Unalakleet
Gambell
Savoonga
St. Lawrence Island
St. Matthew Island
Emmonak
Alakanuk
Mountain Village
Hooper Bay
Chevak
Bethel
Kwethluk
Aniak
Nunivak Island
Quinhagak
Togiak
Dillingham
King Salmon
Galena
McGrath
Fort Yukon
Fairbanks
College
North Pole
Anderson
Delta Junction
Tok
Houston
Palmer
Willow
Wasilla
ANCHORAGE
Valdez
Cordova
Salamatof
Kenai
Soldotna
Seward
Ninilchik
Homer
Kodiak
Kodiak Island
Yakutat
Haines
Skagway
Juneau
Hoonah
Angoon
Kake
Petersburg
Wrangell
Sitka
Baranof I.
Thorne Bay
Klawock
Craig
Prince of Wales I.
Ketchikan
Metlakatla
Alexander Archipelago
St. Paul
Pribilof Islands
Sand Point
Unimak Island
Akutan
Unalaska
Dutch Harbor
Fox Islands
Umnak Island
Amlia I.
Atka Island
Andreanof Islands
Tanaga Island
Amchitka I.
Rat Islands
Kiska Island
Agattu Island
Near Islands
Attu Island
Aleutian Islands
ALASKA MARITIME NATIONAL WILDLIFE REFUGE
ARCTIC NATIONAL WILDLIFE REFUGE
NOATAK NAT'L. PRESERVE
GATES OF THE ARCTIC N.P. AND PRESERVE
CAPE KRUSENSTERN NAT'L. MONUMENT
KOBUK VALLEY N.P.
SELAWIK N.W.R.
KANUTI N.W.R.
YUKON FLATS N.W.R.
BERING LAND BRIDGE NAT'L. PRESERVE
SEWARD PENIN.
KOYUKUK N.W.R.
WHITE MTS. N.R.A.
YUKON-CHARLEY RIVERS NAT'L. PRESERVE
NOWITNA N.W.R.
INNOKO N.W.R.
DENALI N.P. AND PRESERVE
TETLIN N.R.W.
WRANGELL-ST. ELIAS N.P. AND PRESERVE
YUKON DELTA NATIONAL WILDLIFE REFUGE
KENAI N.R.W.
CHUGACH NAT'L. FOR.
LAKE CLARK N.P. AND PRESERVE
KENAI FJORDS N.P.
TOGIAK N.W.R.
KATMAI N.P. AND PRESERVE
ALASKA PENINSULA N.W.R.
KODIAK N.W.R.
ANIAKCHAK N.M. AND PRESERVE
IZEMBEK N.W.R.
GLACIER BAY N.P. AND PRESERVE
TONGASS NATIONAL FOR.
MISTY FJORDS N.M.
ANNETTE I. IND. RES.
Noatak
Koyukuk R.
Yukon
Porcupine
River
Tanana
Kuskokwim
Alaska Highway
Peel
Mackenzie River
Stewart River
Yukon R.
© Grolier, Inc. 1994

Famous People

Aleksandr Baranov

Vitus Bering

Joseph Juneau

Aleksandr Andreevich Baranov (1746–1819) became the first manager of the Russian-American Company, established in 1799, and served as the first governor (1799–1818) of Russian America. A successful fur trader, he extended Russian settlements in Alaska and sold furs to the United States, Canada, and China. Baranov's settlement at New Archangel (now Sitka) replaced Kodiak as the fur-trading capital. Baranof Island is named for him.

Vitus Bering (1680–1741), a Danish explorer employed by the Russian Navy, led the first European exploration of Alaska's coast. He also discovered the strait and the sea that now bear his name. A biography of Bering is included in Volume B.

Susan Butcher (1954–), a world-class sled dog racer, was born in Boston, Massachusetts. In 1979 she became the first person to drive a sled dog team to the top of Mount McKinley. In the annual 1,000-mile (1,600-kilometer) Anchorage-to-Nome Iditarod Trail Sled Dog Race, she took first place in 1986, 1987, 1988, and 1990, setting new course records in 1986, 1987, and 1990.

Sheldon Jackson (1834–1909), born in Minaville, New York, was a leading Presbyterian missionary. He went to Alaska in 1884 to minister to the native groups and became known as the Bishop of All Beyond. He helped save thousands from starvation by urging the U.S. government to import reindeer from Siberia. In 1885 he was appointed Alaska's first superintendent of public instruction. Jackson founded many free schools and traveled widely, collecting Alaskan artifacts on his way. He was a sponsor of Sitka Industrial School, which was later renamed Sheldon Jackson College.

Joseph Juneau (1836?–99), a French Canadian gold miner born near the city of Quebec, was prospecting with Richard Harris and three Tlingit Indians in 1880 when he discovered gold near present-day Juneau, touching off the Alaska gold rush. The town that sprang up on the site was named Juneau after him. It has been the capital of Alaska since 1900.

organized under federal law. This is the former Tsimshian Indian reservation of Metlakatla on Annette Island. Otherwise, Alaska's Indian affairs are conducted according to the 1971 Alaska Native Claims Settlement Act and its subsequent amendments.

▶ HISTORY

It is believed that Alaska's first settlers came to the area possibly as long as 50,000 years ago. These nomadic hunters and gatherers migrated from what is now Siberia, pursuing wild game across the Bering land bridge that once existed between Asia and North America. Three distinct groups of people developed among these early settlers: the Yupik and Inupiat Eskimos, the Aleut, and various Athabascan and other Indian groups.

Russian Exploration and Settlement

The first Europeans arrived in 1741, when Georg Steller, a crew member of explorer Vitus Bering's expedition, went ashore on Alaska's southern coast. Bering's crew had found not only a new land, but also a new article of trade—the luxurious fur of the sea otter. Soon, Russian hunters and traders were rushing to colonize Alaska.

The newcomers took many Aleuts as slaves, while some settled down and married native Alaskan women. In 1784, Russian traders established their first permanent settlement at Three Saints Bay on Kodiak Island. This new colony became known as Russian America.

By 1799 the Russian-American Company had been chartered, with Aleksandr Baranov as its manager. Baranov expanded trade eastward and built a fort near the present-day city of Sitka on Baranof Island. The Tlingit Indians, who could not tolerate this invasion of their centuries-old homeland, attacked the fort in 1802 and won back their ground.

In 1804, Baranov returned with armed Russian troops and forced the Tlingit to retreat for good. Baranov rebuilt the settlement, New Archangel, which became the capital of Russian America. Later renamed Sitka, it remained the capital of Alaska until 1900.

Near right: **When U.S. Secretary of State William H. Seward bought Alaska from Russia in 1867, many people thought the purchase was extravagant and called it Seward's Folly. This cartoon shows Seward (left) and President Andrew Johnson (right) preparing to "cool down" angry congressmen with a chunk of Alaskan ice.** ***Far right:*** **In 1897, one year after gold was discovered in the Klondike region of Canada's Yukon Territory, prospectors built the town of Skagway near Chilcoot Pass, which was then the shortest route—over the mountains—to the Yukon.**

Susan Butcher

William Louis Paul, Sr. (1885–1977), a politician and lawyer born in Port Simpson, British Columbia, was the first part-Indian ever to serve (1925–29) in the Alaska territorial legislature. He fought the Literacy Act in 1925 to protect Native Americans' voting rights. His advocacy of Tlingit and Haida rights in 1968 paved the way for the Alaska Native Claims Settlement Act of 1971.

William Henry Seward (1801–72), a statesman and outspoken opponent of slavery, was born in Florida, New York. Having served as a New York state senator (1831–34) , as governor of New York (1839–42), and as a U.S. senator (1849–61), he was appointed U.S. secretary of state by President Abraham Lincoln in 1861. During the Civil War (1861–65), he succeeded in preventing European nations from recognizing the Confederate States of America as a legitimate nation. In 1865, Seward was injured in the same assassination plot that killed Lincoln. After his recovery he continued in his post until 1869, under President Andrew Johnson. It was during this time that Seward, a territorial expansionist, purchased Alaska for the United States (1867).

Grigori Shelekhov (1747–95), a Russian fur trader, founded the first Russian colony in Alaska at Three Saints Bay on Kodiak Island in 1784. After his death, his business, the Shelekhov-Golikov Company, formed the basis of the Russian-American Company.

The Alaska Purchase

Russia's interest in Alaska soon declined. The colony was expensive to maintain, and the fur trade had ceased to be profitable. In 1867, U.S. Secretary of State William H. Seward arranged to purchase Alaska from Russia for $7.2 million. Many Americans believed it was a foolish idea. Newspaper articles and cartoons ridiculed Alaska, calling it Seward's Folly, Seward's Icebox, Icebergia, and Walrussia. But Seward believed Alaska was a land of great potential.

The Gold Rush

Seward's Folly soon turned to fortune. In 1880, near present-day Juneau, Tlingit guides led prospectors to rich deposits of gold. Year after year, new gold strikes brought additional waves of gold rushers. In 1896, fabulous deposits were found in the Klondike region of Canada's Yukon Territory, and tens of thousands of fortune hunters swarmed through Alaska's Panhandle to get there. After gold was discovered in Nome in 1899, a tent city sprang up overnight. Within a couple

PREPARING FOR THE HEATED TERM.

King Andy and his man Billy lay in a great stock of Russian ice in order to cool down the Congressional majority.

of years, more than 20,000 prospectors had arrived. To help keep order among the gold hunters, Alaska adopted a system of courts and laws in 1900. In 1912, Congress officially declared Alaska a U.S. territory.

The Long Road to Statehood

Alaskans first appealed to Congress for statehood in 1916, but the bill failed to pass. In 1941, when America declared war on Japan and entered World War II, Alaska's strategic importance became clear. More than 150,000 American troops and civilian workers were rushed to Alaska. In only nine months, a 1,488-mile (2,396-kilometer) road was built through Canada to Fairbanks as a military supply route. Now called the Alaska Highway, it is still the only road connecting Alaska with the Lower 48 states.

In 1942, Japan bombed the American naval base at Dutch Harbor in the Aleutian Islands and invaded the islands of Attu and Kiska. These were the only North American territories to be invaded during the entire course of the war. After more than 14 months of fierce resistance, and with heavy casualties on both sides, the Americans finally managed to free the islands.

After the war ended in 1945, the United States entered into the Cold War era with the Soviet Union, reinforcing Alaska's strategic importance. In 1958, Congress approved the Alaska Statehood Act, and on January 3, 1959, President Dwight D. Eisenhower proclaimed Alaska the 49th state.

Hardship and Prosperity

On March 27, 1964, a devastating earthquake, registering about 9.2 on the Richter scale, ravaged Anchorage and much of the Gulf coast and killed 131 people. This was the strongest earthquake ever recorded in North America. In 1967, flood waters rushed through Fairbanks, killing five people.

In 1968 the state's economy boomed when massive oil and natural gas reserves were discovered at Prudhoe Bay. Oil profits doubled the gross state product between 1973 and 1975. When construction of the Trans-Alaska Pipeline began in 1974, Alaska's population and labor force soared. After the pipeline was completed in 1977, revenues began flowing into the state treasury, allowing Alaskans to abolish the state income tax.

Alaska Native Claims Settlement Act

In 1971, President Richard Nixon signed the Alaska Native Claims Settlement Act. It awarded Alaska's native peoples approximately 44 million acres (18 million hectares) of land and more than $962 million in compensation for past infringements on their land and resources. Eventually 13 regional corporations were organized to manage the money and land development. But some communities resisted economic interests, choosing instead to preserve their territory.

Environmental Concerns

Many people worried that oil exploration might endanger caribou, polar bears, whales, and other animals that remained vital to the livelihoods of Alaska Native groups. In 1978, 56 million acres (23 million hectares) of Alaskan land were set aside as national parks, monuments, and wildlife refuges. While this protected Alaska's natural areas, it also closed off a vast amount of territory to mineral exploration. The state of Alaska sued to retain access to these lands, but lost. Two years later the Alaska National Interest Lands Conservation Act passed into law.

In 1989 came the worst environmental disaster in Alaska's history. The oil tanker *Exxon Valdez* ran aground in Prince William Sound, spilling millions of gallons of crude oil. Hundreds of miles of shoreline—as well as thousands of birds, fish, and other animals—were coated with thick, black oil. Federal, state, and local governments, oil companies, and environmentalists all joined forces to clean up the environment and sort out the damages. The disaster only heightened the debate between land developers and environmentalists.

In 2001, President George W. Bush reignited the environmental controversy when he announced his intentions to reopen the Arctic National Wildlife Refuge to oil and gas drilling in response to the rising costs of imports. Public concerns, however, forced his administration to abandon the plan. Meanwhile, scientists monitored the environment and worked with oil companies to find ways to prevent further problems.

Ann Heinrichs
Author, *Alaska*

Reviewed by Donna Freedman
Author, *City Smart Anchorage*

ALBANIA

Albanians call themselves Shqiptarë, which means "sons of the eagle." It is an appropriate name because many Albanians live in the high mountains just as eagles do. A fiercely independent people, the Albanians long suffered under foreign domination. For nearly 500 years Albania was a part of the Turkish Ottoman Empire, before winning its independence in 1912. In the early 1990's, Albanians freed themselves from a Communist system of government that had long ruled the country.

THE PEOPLE

Most of the people are Albanians. Greeks are the country's largest ethnic minority. The Albanians were formerly divided into two major groups—the Gegs, in the north, and the Tosks, in the south. The Shkumbi River was the dividing line between the two. The differences in speech and customs between the two groups were largely eliminated during the period of Communist rule. The population is concentrated mainly in and around the major cities of Tiranë (also spelled Tirana), Durrës, Vlorë, Elbasan, and Shkodër. Tiranë is the capital and largest city.

Many people of Albanian ancestry live outside their homeland. Most live in what was Yugoslavia. But there are also large Albanian communities in Greece, Italy, Western Europe, and the United States.

Way of life. In spite of many centuries of foreign occupation, the traditional Albanian way of life was preserved in the high mountain region. In the more isolated areas, the clan

Albania is a small, rugged country. Many of its people, like these schoolgirls, traditionally have lived in the high mountains that make up most of the land.

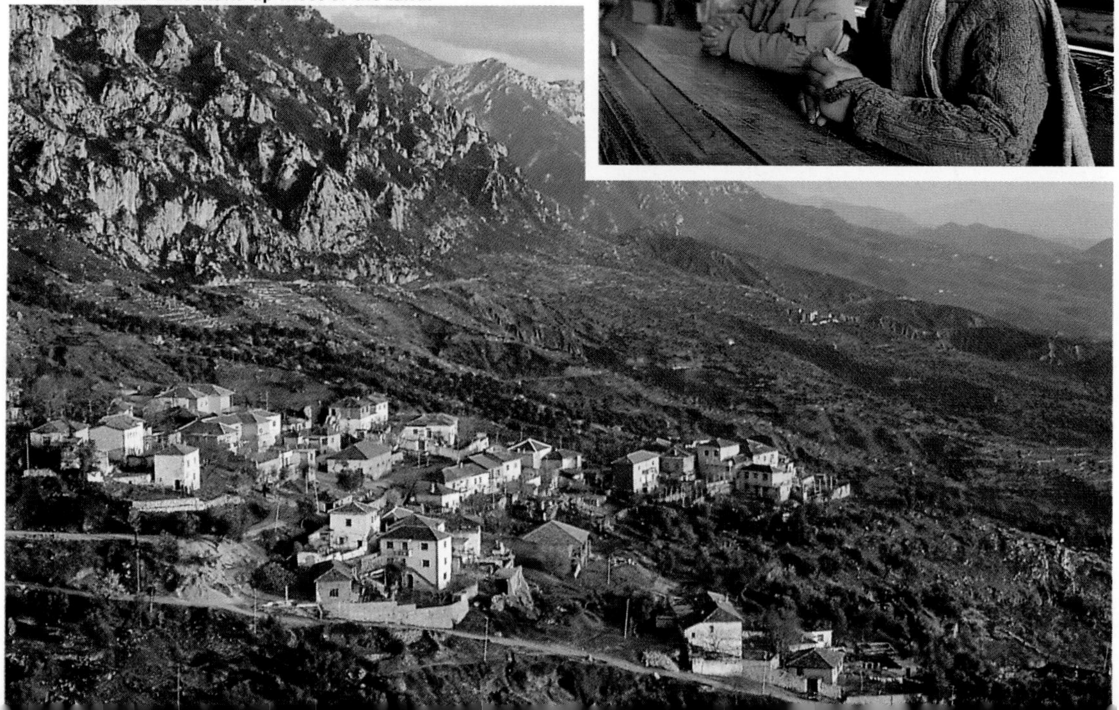

Albanian Muslims pray at a mosque near Tiranë, the capital. Albania is the only European country in which Muslims make up the majority of the population —a reminder of the centuries-long rule of the region by the Ottoman Turks. Other Albanians belong to the Eastern Orthodox and Roman Catholic churches.

system, based on family relationship, survived until the 1900's. After the Communists took over Albania, they broke up the clan system and seized the land owned by the landlords. The land was divided into small farms, which were then combined into collectives, run by a group of farmers in common, or large state farms, run by the government. This system is now being changed with the restoration of private ownership of farmland.

Striking contrasts between old and new are seen in all of Albania's cities. The huge new apartment houses, modern in appearance, are very different from the narrow, cobblestone streets and oriental-looking bazaars in older parts of the cities.

FACTS and figures

REPUBLIC OF ALBANIA is the official name of the country.

LOCATION: Southeastern Europe.

AREA: 11,100 sq mi (28,748 km²).

POPULATION: 3,400,000 (estimate).

CAPITAL AND LARGEST CITY: Tiranë.

MAJOR LANGUAGE: Albanian.

MAJOR RELIGIOUS GROUPS: Muslim, Eastern Orthodox, Roman Catholic.

GOVERNMENT: Republic. **Head of state**—president. **Head of government**—prime minister. **Legislature**—People's Assembly.

CHIEF PRODUCTS: Agricultural—wheat, corn, potatoes, cotton, tobacco, rice, sugar beets, fruits, nuts, livestock. **Manufactured**—refined petroleum products, processed foods, textiles, machinery, building materials, fertilizers. **Mineral**—chromite (chromium ore), petroleum, coal, copper, nickel, asphalt.

MONETARY UNIT: Lek (1 lek = 100 quindars).

Language and Religion. Albanian is one of the Indo-European group of languages, but it is unlike any other language spoken in Europe. The Albanian language is used throughout the country. Some Greek is also spoken in the southern part of Albania.

Although the government forbade religious observance, about 70 percent of the people are said to be Muslims; about 20 percent members of the Eastern Orthodox Church; and some 10 percent Roman Catholics. Albania is the only predominantly Muslim nation in Europe.

THE LAND

Albania lies on the west coast of the Balkan Peninsula, in southeastern Europe. Small in area, it extends about 200 miles (320 kilometers) from north to south and about 60 miles (100 kilometers) from east to west. To the west of Albania are the Adriatic Sea and the Strait of Otranto. Across the Strait of Otranto is the heel of Italy's boot. Serbia borders Albania on the north and east. Greece is on the south. Albania has three natural regions: the coastal lowland in the west, a central hilly belt, and the mountains in the east, north, and south.

The Coastal Lowland. Along the coast is a narrow, formerly marshy lowland. Fast-running streams flow from the mountains to this plain and often flood the land. Until recently mosquitoes thrived in the stagnant water, and few people lived here because of the dangers of malaria. The marshes have since been drained and the land reclaimed.

The Hilly Belt. A narrow strip of hilly land stretches across central Albania, where the mountains and the coastal lowlands meet. At this point the mountains are quite low, and their lower slopes are terraced and planted with tree crops. Here, too, the narrow mountain valleys widen into broad basins. The soils of these basins are fertile and are carefully cultivated. Tiranë, Shkodër, Elbasan, and Berat are important cities in this region.

The Mountains. Nearly three fourths of Albania is mountainous. The highest mountain is Mount Korab, which rises to 9,066 feet (2,763 meters) in northeastern Albania. In the north the mountains are deeply fissured. In the southern parts of the country, they are more rounded and often open up into broad, fertile basins.

Lakes, Rivers, Natural Resources. Albania has three large lakes. They are Scutari, in the north, and Ochrida and Prespa, in the southeast. The country's rivers are short and swift and are not navigable, or usable by ships, except for short stretches. These rivers are, however, an important source of hydroelectric power, which supplies much of Albania's electricity.

About one quarter of the land is wooded. Oak or scrub forests are found in the south, while pine, poplar, and chestnut trees grow along the rivers and at various elevations.

Albania has a number of valuable mineral resources. It is one of the world's leading producers of chromite (chromium ore). Other mineral deposits include petroleum, coal, copper, nickel, and asphalt.

Climate. The coastal lowland and the hilly belt have a Mediterranean climate, typically marked by mild winters and hot, sunny summers. A cold wind called the bora sometimes blows from the mountains to the lowlands. The mountains have a continental climate. Summers here are cool and winters cold and snowy. Although there is considerable rainfall, it is sometimes erratic.

THE ECONOMY

Historically, Albania has been one of Europe's least-developed countries. At one time most of its people were farmers, even though the largely mountainous terrain severely limits the amount of land suitable for agriculture. Under Communist rule, Albania had a centrally planned economy controlled by the state, which stressed industrial development.

Agriculture. About half the working population is still engaged in agriculture. The chief food crops include wheat, corn, and potatoes. The major commercial crops are cotton, tobacco, rice, sugar beets, and fruits and nuts. Sheep traditionally were the most important form of livestock. But chickens, goats, pigs, and cattle are also raised.

Industry and Trade. Manufacturing and mining currently employ about one third of the work force. The chief industrial products are minerals, refined petroleum products, processed foods, textiles, machinery, building materials, and fertilizers.

Albania's chief exports include chromite and other mineral ores, processed foods, and tobacco products. It imports chemicals, metals, and paper and rubber products. A lack of rainfall in the early 1990's forced the importation of grains and other foodstuffs.

Transportation and Communications. The country's most important railroad connects the port of Durrës with Tiranë and Elbasan. Airline service links Tiranë with capitals of neighboring countries. There are some asphalt roads, but many parts of the country have only dirt or gravel roads. In the rugged interior, people may still travel by horseback or in the traditional ox carts.

Radio, television, and other forms of communication were owned by the state.

HISTORY AND GOVERNMENT

Early History. The earliest known people of what is now Albania were the Illyrians. The Romans conquered the region in 167 B.C., but they were never able to subdue the mountain-

A nearly deserted factory reflects the economic failures that played an important part in the overthrow of Albania's Communist government.

Below: George Kastrioti, known as Skanderbeg, is Albania's national hero. He briefly united the country against the Ottoman Turks in the 1400's, before it again fell to the Turks after his death. *Right:* Modern Albanians in 1992 celebrated their victory over the Communist regime that had ruled the nation for more than 45 years and had made it the most isolated country in Europe.

ous areas completely. In the centuries that followed, the region fell to numerous rulers. The Ottoman Turks first invaded Albania in 1385. Opposition to the Turks was led by the national hero George Kastrioti, called Skanderbeg, who in 1443 united Albanians against them. After his death in 1468, however, Albania again fell under Turkish rule.

Independence to World War II. Albania declared its independence from a declining Ottoman Empire on November 28, 1912. The years between World War I and World War II were stormy ones for Albania. Ahmet Zogu was named president in 1925. Three years later he gave himself the title of King Zog I. Zog fled when Italy invaded Albania in 1939, just months before World War II began. In 1943, a German army occupied Albania. When the Germans evacuated Albania in 1944, the Communists took control of the country. Albania officially became a "people's republic" under a new constitution in 1946.

Communist Rule. Although Albania had an elected legislature, the People's Assembly, only the Albanian Labor Party, a Communist party, had been allowed to take part in elections. Real political power had always been in the hands of the party's top leadership.

Albania was led by Enver Hoxha from 1944 until his death in 1985. During these years, Albania followed its own rigid, solitary Communist road. It broke relations with the Soviet Union in 1961. For a time it had friendly relations with the People's Republic of China, but these also cooled. After Hoxha's death, Ramiz Alia assumed power.

Recent History. In 1991 the first elections were held in which non-Communist political parties were allowed to compete. The result, a Communist victory, led to national protests, forcing the government to resign. New elections were held in 1992, and Sali Berisha, the leader of the Democratic Party, was elected president. He was re-elected in 1996.

In 1997, charges of economic corruption led to demonstrations that were brutally suppressed by police. More than 10,000 Albanians fled across the Adriatic Sea to Italy, causing a state of emergency there. Elections were later held, and the People's Assembly, the legislative body, chose Rexhep Mejdani of the Socialist Party to succeed Berisha.

Albania's present government is based on a constitution adopted in 1998. The People's Assembly, the sole legislative body, is elected for four years. It elects the president, who appoints a prime minister to head the Council of Ministers.

George W. Hoffman
University of Texas at Austin
Reviewed by Nicholas C. Pano
Author, *The People's Republic of Albania*

ALBANY. See New York (Cities).

ALBEE, EDWARD. See Washington, D.C. (Famous People).

ALBERT

Albert was the name of one prince consort of Great Britain and two kings of Belgium.

Albert, Prince Consort of Great Britain (1819–61) was the husband of Victoria, queen of England, Scotland, and Ireland. Born Albert Francis Charles Augustus Emmanuel near Coburg, Germany, on August 26, 1819, he was the youngest son of Duke Ernest I of Saxe-Coburg-Gotha.

Albert married Queen Victoria, his first cousin, in London in 1840. He soon became her most trusted adviser. Victoria's ministers feared that Albert, a foreigner, would interfere in British politics, but he used his influence tactfully and wisely and in time became known as Albert the Good.

Prince Albert was known to be strict but kindhearted. He encouraged music and the arts and was extremely interested in science and education. He was instrumental in organizing the Great Exhibition of 1851 and in the founding of Imperial College, London. His other achievements ranged from the abolition of dueling to the introduction of the Christmas tree to England.

Prince Albert and Queen Victoria enjoyed an unusually happy marriage. Unfortunately, he died at 42 from typhoid fever at Windsor Castle on December 14, 1861. Victoria, who had idolized her husband, was so distraught by his early death that she withdrew completely from public life for the next 15 years.

Albert, Prince Consort of Great Britain, was husband and first cousin to Queen Victoria. A German prince by birth, Albert worked hard to prove his devotion to his adopted homeland. Although he was considered shy and cold, Albert was actually kindhearted, and it was largely due to his influence that slavery was abolished in the British colonies. Albert's high moral standards also shaped the rigid social conditions now associated with the Victorian era.

The popular King Albert I led the Belgian resistance against the Germans during World War I. He was one of the few European monarchs not to be overthrown in the political upheavals that followed the war.

Albert I, King of the Belgians (1875–1934) (r. 1909–34), born in Brussels, was the son of Philip, Count of Flanders, and the nephew of King Leopold II. The shy Albert was considered unsuited to his role as king when he succeeded his uncle in 1909. But his tolerant and progressive views, and the popularity of his German-born wife, Queen Elisabeth, won him the affection of his people.

In 1914, at the outbreak of World War I, Germany, disregarding Belgium's neutrality, invaded the country. Albert won the world's admiration for his courage in resisting the invasion. By ordering open the floodgates along the Yser River, flooding the Yser Valley, he prevented the Germans from achieving their critical goal of advancing to the English Channel coast. For the remaining four years of the war, Albert and his army resolutely held on to a few square miles of Belgian territory, becoming a symbol of Belgian resistance.

After the war, Albert continued to support social reform and to work toward improving relations between the opposing Flemish- and French-speaking sections of his population. An enthusiastic mountaineer, he was killed in a climbing accident in the Ardennes on February 17, 1934. He was succeeded by his eldest son, King Leopold III.

Albert II, King of the Belgians (1934–), born in Brussels, was the second son of Leopold III. He came to the throne in 1993, succeeding his brother, Baudouin I.

LANCE SALWAY
Author, *Queen Victoria's Grandchildren*

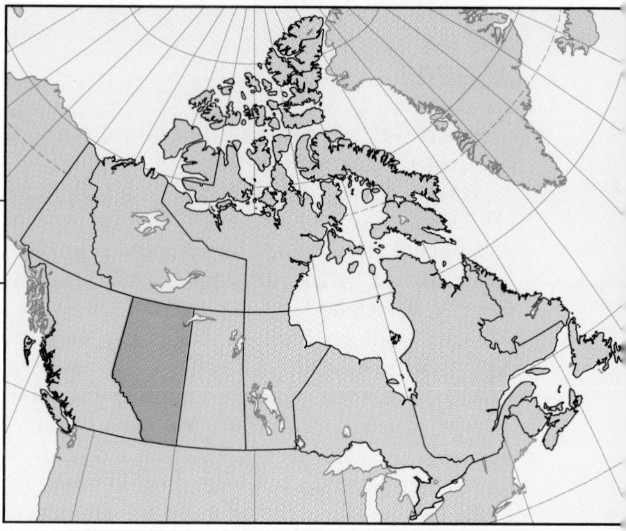

ALBERTA

Alberta's flag (above) and the coat of arms (opposite page) both feature a view of the province's wheatfields, plains, foothills, and mountains. The cross of St. George, patron saint of England, recalls Alberta's ties with Great Britain. The provincial bird is the great horned owl (right); the provincial flower is the rose (opposite page).

Alberta is one of Canada's three Prairie Provinces. It stretches from British Columbia and the towering, snow-clad Rocky Mountains in the west to the province of Saskatchewan in the east; and from the thinly settled Northwest Territories in the north to the state of Montana in the south. Within the boundaries of Alberta, fields of grain extend farther than the eye can see, and cattle ranches dot the foothills of the Rockies.

THE LAND

Alberta has a varied landscape that falls into three landform regions: the Canadian Shield, the Interior Plains, and the Mountains and Foothills.

The Canadian Shield. The northeast corner of Alberta lies in the Canadian Shield. This region occupies 3 percent of the land area of the province. Elevations in the Shield range from 650 to 1,300 feet (200 to 400 meters). Bare rock outcrops are found throughout the area. Only in a few places do patches of soil cover the rocks. The soils are thin and rocky and of little use for agriculture. Many marshes and lakes have formed in depressions created during the Great Ice Age.

The Interior Plains. The Interior Plains occupy almost 90 percent of the land. The plains lie between the Shield in the northeast and the Mountains and Foothills in the southwest. Elevations range from about 650 to 4,000 feet (200 to 1,200 meters).

Contrary to popular opinion about the flatness of the plains, they have a highly varied local relief. The land is flat only in places once covered by ancient glacial lakes. Elsewhere, the plains region is typically rolling. Deep river valleys and a number of hilly areas, especially in northern Alberta, contrast sharply with the surrounding plains. Some of the valleys are now dry (coulees), but at one time they carried away the meltwaters from the retreating ice sheets. The hills are flat-topped remnants of land that was eroded (worn away) by the rivers. The Cypress Hills in the southeast, the Swan Hills south of Lesser Slave Lake, and the Caribou Mountains in the north all rise at least 1,200 feet (370 meters) above the countryside. In a few areas the streams have cut deeply into softer rocks. Small sections of deeply eroded land called badlands have resulted, especially in the lower Red Deer Valley, where dinosaur fossils are often exposed by erosion.

The Mountains and Foothills. This region is located along the southwestern margin of the province. The mountains form the boundary between Alberta and British Columbia. They are also a continental drainage divide between waters flowing into the Pacific Ocean on the one hand, and the Arctic Ocean, Hudson Bay, and the Gulf of Mexico on the other.

Between the plains and the eastern wall of the Rockies lie the rolling foothills, which range in elevation from less than 4,000 to more than 6,000 feet (1,200 to 1,800 meters). West of the foothills tower the ranges of the Rocky Mountains. Here the landscape is composed of jagged, snow-clad peaks and broad, U-shaped valleys. Many small lakes and swift streams are found high in the rocky basins of

FACTS AND FIGURES

Location: Western Canada. **Latitude**—49° N to 60° N. **Longitude**—110° W to 120° W.

Joined Canadian Confederation: September 1, 1905 (with Saskatchewan, as the 8th and 9th provinces).

Population: 2,974,807 (2001 census). **Rank among provinces**—4th.

Capital: Edmonton, pop. 666,104 (2001 census).

Largest City: Calgary, pop. 878,866 (2001 census).

Physical Features: Area—255,540 sq mi (661,848 km²). **Rank among provinces**—4th. **Rivers**—Athabasca, Pembina, Smoky, Peace, Hay, North and South Saskatchewan, Oldman, Bow, Red Deer, Milk River. **Lakes**—Athabasca, Claire, Lesser Slave, la Biche, Cold, Utikuma, Beaverhill. **Highest point**—12,294 ft (3,747 m), Mt. Columbia.

Industries and Products: Mining; agriculture; food processing; oil refining; metals; machinery; chemical products; hydroelectric power; wood and wood products; fur; fishing.

Government: Self-governing province. **Titular head of government**—lieutenant governor, appointed by the governor-general in council. **Actual head of government**—premier, leader of the majority in the legislature. **Provincial representation in federal parliament**—6 appointed senators; 26 elected member(s) of the House of Commons. **Voting age for provincial elections**—18.

Provincial Bird: Great horned owl.

Provincial Flower: Wild rose.

Provincial Motto: *Fortis et liber* (Strong and free).

the mountains. Thirty of these peaks are at least 11,000 feet (3,300 meters) high. Many of them have glaciers similar to those that once covered the neighboring plains. The mountains offer the tourist some of the most spectacular scenery in the world.

Rivers and Lakes

All the important rivers of the province begin in the snow and ice fields of the Rocky Mountains. Many of the important rivers in central and southern Alberta flow eastward to Lake Winnipeg and then northward to form part of the Hudson Bay drainage system. The Milk River flows about 100 miles (160 kilometers) in Alberta near the southern border. It is a tributary of the Missouri and is part of the Gulf of Mexico drainage. The large rivers of northern Alberta flow northward and form part of the Arctic Ocean drainage.

There are thousands of lakes in Alberta. The largest is Lake Athabasca, although only one third lies in Alberta. The remaining two thirds is in Saskatchewan. Because of its beauty and the large number of tourists who visit it, Lake Louise in Banff National Park is perhaps the best-known lake in Alberta.

Climate

Alberta has a continental climate with long, cold winters and short, warm summers. In winter, the cold is sometimes broken by warm dry winds from the mountains. The Indians call these winds "chinooks," or "snow-eaters." The chinook can cause temperatures to rise sharply in less than an hour.

Except in the Rocky Mountains, annual precipitation ranges from about 16 inches (400 millimeters) in the plains to about 24 inches (600 millimeters) in hill areas. Westerly winds from the Pacific Ocean lose most of their moisture crossing the mountains. The Rockies thus have a higher annual precipitation—from 16 inches (400 millimeters) in the drier valleys to more than 55 inches (1,400 millimeters) in the higher areas. Precipitation there falls mostly as winter snow.

In the plains, most of the precipitation falls as rain in the summer, when it is needed for crops. Autumn is fairly dry, which is good for harvesting grain. The growing (frost-free) season varies from more than 120 days in the southern plains to less than 60 days in the far north and mountain valleys.

Natural Resources

Soils. Alberta's rich soil is one of its major resources. The black soils of the parkland are among the most fertile in the world. The brown soils of the prairies are also fertile, but they are located in the drier parts of the province. Ranching, dryland agriculture, and irrigation agriculture are important in this soil zone. The gray forest soils, which occupy the northern half of the province, have developed under the cover of trees and thus are less suited for agriculture.

Vegetation. The foothills, the eastern slopes of the Rocky Mountains, and large portions of northern Alberta are forested. The forestlands are one of the province's important natural resources.

Left: Erosion of soil and rock has produced the barren terrain of the badlands, in southeastern Alberta. *Above:* The more fertile soil of Alberta's prairies is well suited for growing wheat and other grain crops.

Right: Towering mountain peaks, majestic pine forests, and crystal-clear lakes are among the attractions of Banff National Park, in the Canadian Rockies.

Between the forest and the prairie lies the parkland. Parkland is a region of mixed trees and grassland. To the south and east of the parkland lie the prairies. Almost all the agriculture is located in the prairie and parkland regions.

Minerals. The most important of Alberta's widespread mineral deposits are the mineral fuels. The province contains vast deposits of both crude oil and natural gas. In addition, sulfur is an important nonfuel by-product of Alberta's natural-gas production.

The Athabasca tar sands (sands filled with thick, tarry oils), located along the Athabasca River, contain the richest reserves in the province. But recovery of the oil is costly. Two plants are now in production, and other pilot projects are under way.

Alberta has more than half of Canada's minable coal reserves. Most of the coal is bituminous (soft) coal. It underlies much of the plains area and also occurs in the foothills and along the eastern slopes of the Rockies.

Good-quality sand and gravel occur throughout most of the province; limestone is abundant in the Rockies, and clay and shale are found in the Medicine Hat area. Large deposits of low-grade iron are available in the Peace River district. Alberta also has deposits of gypsum, phosphate, salt, sodium sulfate, and silica sand.

THE PEOPLE

Alberta is one of the fastest-growing provinces in Canada. Its population, like those of the other Prairie Provinces, is made up of people from different backgrounds. The greatest number are British in origin. In addition there are large groups of German, Ukrainian, Scandinavian, French, Dutch, or Polish background. Smaller ethnic groups include Russians, Hungarians, Italians, Romanians, Yugoslavs, Finns, Chinese, and Japanese. About 89,000 native Indians, 67,000 métis (persons of mixed Indian and European heritage), and 1,300 Inuit make their homes in Alberta.

At the beginning of the 1900's more than 70 percent of the people lived on farms or in rural villages. Today more than 60 percent of the population lives in metropolitan Edmonton and Calgary, while 13 percent lives in smaller urban centers.

Agriculture was once the leading occupation in Alberta. Today less than 8 percent of the labor force is employed in agriculture. Increased use of farm machinery requires fewer people to operate the farms. Higher wages offered in other industries also account for the movement away from the farm.

More than half of the people now employed in Alberta work in service industries, including education, health, entertainment, recrea-

tion, transportation, communication, finance, and personal services. Many people are employed in wholesale and retail trades. Manufacturing, construction, mining, forestry, fishing, and trapping are other occupations.

EDUCATION

Schooling is free for all children in the province and is compulsory for those between the ages of 7 and 15.

Alberta has four universities—the University of Alberta in Edmonton, Athabasca University, the University of Calgary, and the University of Lethbridge. There are 13 community colleges and technical schools. The Banff Center in Banff offers many fine programs in music and the arts in a wilderness setting.

Alberta has about 250 public libraries. Museums include the Provincial Museum in Edmonton, Glenbow Museum in Calgary, and the Tyrrell Museum of Paleontology near Drumheller. Art galleries and other cultural institutions are widely distributed.

PLACES OF INTEREST

Banff National Park, in the Canadian Rockies, is noted for its majestic scenery and its wildlife preserve. An article on Banff National Park appears in Volume B.

Elk Island National Park, near Edmonton, is a preserve for buffalo and other plains animals.

Jasper National Park is also in the Rockies. An article on this park appears in Volume J.

Waterton Lakes National Park, bordering on Montana, is a recreational area. It shares the International Peace Park with Montana.

Wood Buffalo National Park, in northeast Alberta and the Northwest Territories, is famous for its herds of buffalo and other wild animals.

Alberta also has a number of provincial parks that offer a wide variety of recreational opportunities. Best known are **Peter Lougheed Park,** near the site of the 1988 Winter Olympic ski events; **Dinosaur Park,** which contains the fossil remains of prehistoric dinosaurs; and **Writing-on-Stone,** which features monumental stones with inscriptions made by prehistoric people.

INDUSTRIES AND PRODUCTS

Mining. Alberta ranks first among the provinces in mineral production. It produces some 85 percent of Canada's oil and natural gas, making the nation approximately self-sufficient in these mineral fuels.

The most important oil fields are at Pembina, Leduc-Woodbend, Redwater, Swan Hills, and Rainbow Lake. Development of the vast Athabasca tar-sands deposits began in 1964. The first oil was produced in 1967. A second and larger development started operating in 1978. Production from conventional oil wells has peaked and will now slowly decline. Deposits in the tar sands will be increasingly important. Reserves of natural gas are larger than those of conventional oil, and both production and proven reserves are still in the process of expanding.

Much of Alberta's other mineral production is made up of industrial minerals such as clay, sand, gravel, limestone, gypsum, salt, and phosphate. Sulfur, a by-product of natural gas production, is becoming more important. Alberta accounts for most of Canada's sulfur production. Alberta also has vast coal resources, which contain more energy than its oil and gas reserves combined. Much coal is exported each year to other countries. Diamonds have also been discovered in the province.

Manufacturing. The food and beverage industry, which includes slaughtering and meat-packing, flour milling, and various other types

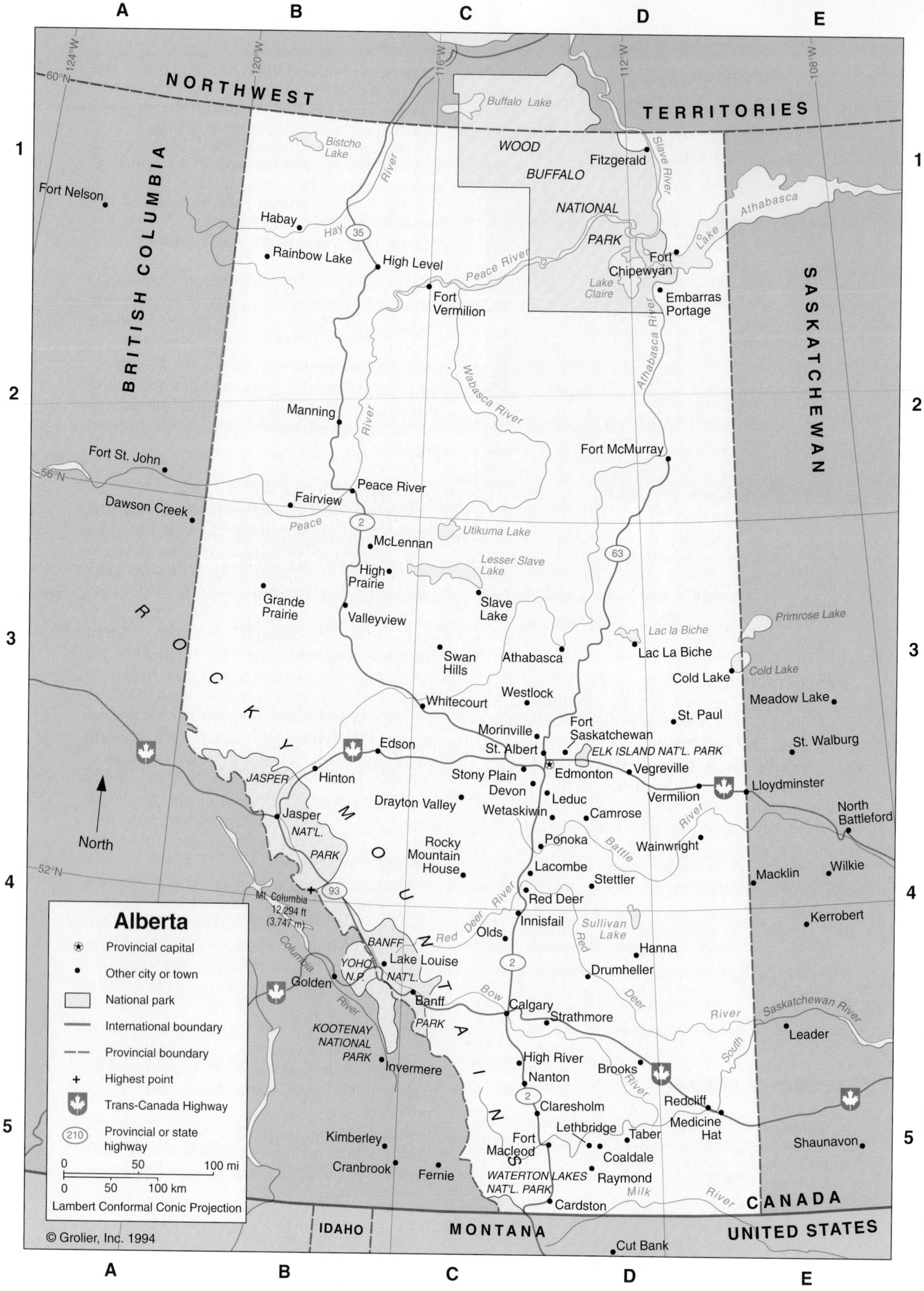
A
B
C
D
E
1
2
3
4
5
124°W
120°W
116°W
112°W
108°W
60°N
56°N
52°N
NORTHWEST
TERRITORIES
BRITISH COLUMBIA
SASKATCHEWAN
ROCKY MOUNTAINS
MONTANA
IDAHO
CANADA
UNITED STATES
Buffalo Lake
Bistcho Lake
WOOD BUFFALO NATIONAL PARK
Fitzgerald
Slave River
Fort Nelson
Habay
Hay
35
Rainbow Lake
High Level
River
Peace River
Fort Chipewyan
Lake Claire
Athabasca Lake
Embarras Portage
Fort Vermilion
Wabasca River
Athabasca River
Manning
River
Fort St. John
Fort McMurray
Peace River
Fairview
Dawson Creek
Peace
2
Utikuma Lake
McLennan
63
Lesser Slave Lake
High Prairie
Grande Prairie
Slave Lake
Valleyview
Primrose Lake
Lac la Biche
Lac La Biche
Swan Hills
Athabasca
Cold Lake
Cold Lake
Westlock
Meadow Lake
Whitecourt
St. Paul
Morinville
Fort Saskatchewan
St. Walburg
St. Albert
ELK ISLAND NAT'L. PARK
Edson
Edmonton
Vegreville
JASPER
Hinton
Stony Plain
Devon
Lloydminster
Leduc
Vermilion
Drayton Valley
Wetaskiwin
Camrose
North Battleford
Jasper
NAT'L. PARK
River
Battle
Ponoka
Wainwright
North
Rocky Mountain House
Lacombe
Wilkie
Macklin
Stettler
Mt. Columbia 12,294 ft (3,747 m)
93
Red Deer
River
Red Deer
Innisfail
Kerrobert
Sullivan Lake
Columbia
BANFF
Red
Olds
Red
Hanna
YOHO N.P.
Lake Louise
NAT'L.
2
Drumheller
Golden
Bow
Deer
River
Banff
Calgary
Saskatchewan River
PARK
River
Strathmore
Leader
KOOTENAY NATIONAL PARK
High River
South
Brooks
Invermere
Nanton
River
2
Claresholm
Redcliff
Medicine Hat
Lethbridge
Taber
Kimberley
Fort Macleod
Coaldale
Shaunavon
Cranbrook
Fernie
WATERTON LAKES NAT'L. PARK
Raymond
Milk
River
Cardston
Cut Bank
Alberta
Provincial capital
Other city or town
National park
International boundary
Provincial boundary
Highest point
Trans-Canada Highway
210
Provincial or state highway
0
50
100 mi
0
50
100 km
Lambert Conformal Conic Projection
© Grolier, Inc. 1994

INDEX TO ALBERTA MAP

Athabasca C3
Banff C4
Banff Nat'l. Park C4
Brooks D5
Calgary C5
Camrose D4
Cardston C5
Claresholm C5
Coaldale D5
Cold Lake D3
Devon C4
Drayton Valley C4
Drumheller D4
Edmonton C3
Edson B3
Elk Island Nat'l. Park D3
Embarras Portage D2
Fairview B2
Fitzgerald D1
Fort Chipewyan D1
Fort Macleod C5
Fort McMurray D2
Fort Saskatchewan D3
Fort Vermilion C2
Grande Prairie B3
Habay B1
Hanna D4
High Level B1
High Prairie B3
High River C5
Hinton B4
Innisfail C4
Jasper B4
Jasper Nat'l. Park B3,B4
Lac La Biche D3
Lacombe C4
Lake Louise C4
Leduc C4
Lethbridge D5
Lloydminster E4
Manning B2
McLennan B3
Medicine Hat D5
Morinville C3
Nanton C5
Olds C4
Peace River B2
Ponoka C4
Rainbow Lake B1
Raymond D5
Redcliff D5
Red Deer C4
Rocky Mountain House C4
St. Albert C3
St. Paul D3
Slave Lake C3
Stettler D4
Stony Plain C4
Strathmore C5
Swan Hills C3
Taber D5
Valleyview B3
Vergreville D4
Vermilion D4
Wainwright D4
Waterton Lakes Nat'l. Park C5
Westlock C3
Wetaskiwin C4
Whitecourt C3
Wood Buffalo Nat'l. Park C1,D1

of food processing, depends largely on farm production. It was the leading manufacturing industry in Alberta until the early 1980's, when the refined-petroleum and coal-products industries took the lead. The chemical and chemical-products industries have also expanded rapidly. Other products manufactured in Alberta include metals and fabricated metal products, machinery, cement and concrete, and wood products.

Agriculture. Grain is still the most important agricultural product, but there has been a steady trend toward mixed crop and livestock farming in recent years. Cattle ranching is important. Sugar beets, potatoes, and feed crops are grown in irrigated areas. Where there is enough rainfall, wheat is the most important grain crop. In the parkland region, barley, oats, rye, rapeseed, and flax are grown and livestock is raised.

Electric Power. Most of Alberta's electric power plants use coal and natural gas for fuel. Hydroelectric power plants are located along the Bow and North Saskatchewan rivers and their tributaries. These typically account for less than 5 percent of the electric power produced, because they are used mainly during peak-demand periods. Power generated from huge supplies of coal and gas, together with waterpower, makes Alberta one of the most energy-rich provinces.

An oil sands recovery plant at Fort McMurray. Production of synthetic crude oil from Alberta's vast tar-sands deposits is an important part of the oil industry.

Forestry. Forest products account for only a small part of the economy. But forests are so extensive that production could be greatly increased. Alberta's forest products include lumber, plywood, and pulp, as well as railway ties and Christmas trees. Pulp mills are located near Hinton and Grande Prairie.

Fishing and Trapping. Fishing and trapping are of minor importance today. Commercial fishing is confined largely to the northern lakes. Whitefish is the most valuable variety. There are several hundred fur farms in Alberta. Trapping is conducted primarily in the northern forest and, like fishing, is chiefly a part-time occupation.

▶CITIES

Most of Alberta's major cities are located in the southern and central part of the province. Many were first established near rivers that served as waterways. Today an extensive network of railways, highways, and airlines serves all the urban centers of the province.

Left: **Cowboys can test their riding skills at the Calgary Exhibition and Stampede, an annual agricultural fair and rodeo.** ***Right:*** **Edmonton, Alberta's capital, is a transportation hub of western Canada and a center of industry, culture, and provincial government.**

Edmonton, the capital, is located in central Alberta. It serves as a collecting and distributing center for industries connected with agriculture and petroleum and as a transportation hub for the mining regions in the Northwest Territories and the Yukon. Food processing, oil refining, metal production, and the production of petrochemicals are some of the city's important industries. Edmonton is the home of the Oilers, a National Hockey League team, and of the Eskimos, a Canadian Football League team. The city's metropolitan population is about 938,000. (An article on Edmonton appears in Volume E.)

Calgary, the administrative center of Alberta's oil industry, also has grown rapidly. Food and beverage processing, meat-packing, flour and feed milling, and the production of dairy products are important industries. The annual Calgary Exhibition and Stampede (rodeo) attracts thousands of visitors. The 1988 Winter Olympics were held in Calgary and in mountain areas to the west of the city. Calgary's metropolitan population is about 951,000.

Red Deer, a city of 68,000, is a rapidly growing service center midway between Edmonton and Calgary. The city is home to Red Deer College, and Sylvan Lake and Gaetz Park are popular tourist sites.

Lethbridge, with a population of about 67,000, is a major center for food processing. It lies in the center of the chinook belt and thus enjoys mild winters. Early settlers included Mormons, Hutterites, and Mennonites.

Medicine Hat, a city of almost 51,000, is noted for clay products and pottery. Its ample supply of natural gas provides fuel for factories and for heating Medicine Hat's thriving greenhouse industry.

Other important cities are **Fort McMurray**, **Grande Prairie**, **Camrose**, **Wetaskiwin**, **Lloydminster**, **Brooks**, and **Drumheller**.

TRANSPORTATION AND COMMUNICATION

Because most of the people live in the southern part of Alberta, transportation is more highly developed there. However, new roads are being built in remoter areas to aid in economic development and to attract tourists. Transportation by truck is important, and Alberta has a higher percentage of cars in proportion to population than other provinces.

Railways. Alberta is served by two transcontinental lines that provide year-round access to world markets for Alberta's products. Feeder lines serve most communities. One of the latest additions—the Great Slave Railway—will have far-reaching effects on the northern areas through which it passes.

Aviation. Aircraft are used to transport people, machinery, and supplies to the north, where there are few roads and railways. All of the major cities have regular passenger and air freight services, and various airlines link Alberta with the rest of Canada and the world.

Water Transport. Freighting by river was once the only means of shipping heavy goods in Alberta. It is of minor importance today. Water routes still in use today are the Athabasca River from Waterways to Lake Athabasca, and the Slave River between Athabasca and Great Slave Lake in the Northwest Territories. In summer, power barges haul heavy freight bound for northern settlements.

Pipelines. Pipelines are the most economical means of transporting the oil and gas produced in Alberta. Oil is transported by pipelines from Edmonton to Superior, Wisconsin; to Sarnia and Port Credit in Ontario; and to the Pacific coast.

Communication. Alberta has nine daily newspapers. Of these, the Edmonton *Journal* has the largest circulation. Numerous weeklies are also published. The province has 14 television stations and 35 AM and 23 FM radio stations. Cable television is available in most centers. In addition to the major Canadian networks, the major U.S. networks are picked up through Spokane, Washington.

GOVERNMENT

Alberta is a self-governing province. Like the other provinces, it is headed by a premier who represents the controlling party in the provincial assembly. A lieutenant governor, appointed by the Governor-General in Council, is the titular head of the province. He represents the Crown. Alberta is represented in the federal parliament by six senators appointed by the Governor-General and by 26 elected members of the House of Commons. The voting age for provincial elections is 18.

HISTORY

The first European to set foot in Alberta was probably Anthony Henday. In 1754 he set out from Hudson Bay to trade for furs with the Indians. Henday explored a large portion of southern Alberta.

After the surrender of New France to the English in 1763, fur traders from eastern Canada and the United States began to tap the rich fur resources of the Canadian west.

Peter Pond, an American from Connecticut, was the first of these men to reach Alberta. He established a trading post on the Athabasca River in 1778. In 1789, Alexander Mackenzie began his famous explorations to the Arctic Ocean; and, in 1793, to the Pacific Ocean.

The Hudson's Bay Company and the North West Company competed for the fur trade of the Canadian west. Soon much of the country between Hudson Bay and the Rocky Mountains was dotted with rival trading posts. Competition was so fierce that there was sometimes bloodshed. But the rivalry ended when the companies united in 1821 under the name of the Hudson's Bay Company.

In 1870 the Dominion of Canada acquired title to the company's lands, and five years later the area known today as the province of Alberta became part of the newly organized Northwest Territories.

Before the transfer of land to Canada, most of the settlers in Alberta were traders, Indians,

IMPORTANT DATES

1691	Henry Kelsey of the Hudson's Bay Company reached the eastern border of Alberta.
1754–55	Anthony Henday of the Hudson's Bay Company was the first European to enter Alberta.
1778	Peter Pond established the first trading post in Alberta.
1789	Alexander Mackenzie went down the Mackenzie River from Chipewyan to the Arctic Ocean.
1793	Alexander Mackenzie crossed Alberta via the Peace River.
1794	Fort Augustus founded on the site of Edmonton.
1861	St. Albert Mission founded by Father Lacombe.
1870	Canada acquired Alberta from the Hudson's Bay Company.
1874	North West Mounted Police posts established.
1882	The District of Alberta was created.
1883	The Canadian Pacific Railway main line was built across Alberta.
1905	Alberta admitted to Canadian Confederation.
1923	Alberta Wheat Pool organized.
1924	Turner Valley began producing oil.
1947	Oil discovered at Leduc.
1949	Mackenzie Highway to Hay River in the Northwest Territories completed.
1950–53	Interprovincial Pipeline built between Edmonton and Sarnia, Ontario.
1951	Completion of the St. Mary Dam near Spring Coulee provided irrigation for southeastern Alberta.
1964	Development of oil sands at Athabasca began.
1969	Alberta Resources Railway completed.
1976	The Alberta Heritage Fund established to invest oil and gas revenues and thus provide for Alberta's future welfare.
1979	Charles Joseph (Joe) Clark of Alberta became prime minister of Canada.
1988	Winter Olympic Games held in Calgary.
1992	Catherine Anne Fraser became the first woman to be appointed chief justice of Alberta.
1995	End of federally funded grain transport leads to closing of grain elevators and abandonment of railroad tracks throughout Alberta.

métis, and missionaries. The best-known mission was St. Albert Mission, founded by Father Lacombe in 1861. It was the province's first successful agricultural settlement.

In 1873 the Canadian Government organized the North West Mounted Police. Mounted Police posts were established in Alberta at Fort Macleod, Fort Saskatchewan, and Fort Calgary. The "Mounties" brought law and order to the region. One of their first acts was to stamp out an illegal whiskey trade.

The Canadian Pacific Railway reached Calgary in 1883. This was the turning point in the growth of settlement. The first settlers to take advantage of the rail line were ranchers who settled on the rich grazing land in the south.

Toward the end of the 1800's, Canada encouraged immigration by offering land to homesteaders. This, together with more railway construction in western Canada, attracted many settlers. They came from eastern Canada, the United States, and Britain and other European countries. The population of Alberta rose rapidly from about 73,000 in 1901 to more than 375,000 in 1911.

In 1905, Alberta became a separate province. Following World War I, the Depression and drought of the 1930's slowed economic growth. However, population doubled in the years between World War I and World War II. The discovery of oil at Leduc in 1947, followed by even larger oil discoveries elsewhere, touched off the greatest period of economic growth in Alberta's history. But by the early 1980's, economic growth had slowed, due in part to a decline in oil prices. Because of this economic recession, migration increased, leading to a decline in population. A partial recovery of oil and gas prices stimulated some economic activity, as did the 1988 Winter Olympics in Calgary and a free trade agreement with the United States that began in 1989.

D. Wayne Moodie
University of Manitoba
Reviewed by A. H. Laycock
University of Alberta

ALBRIGHT, MADELEINE. See Washington, D.C. (Famous People).
ALBUQUERQUE. See New Mexico (Cities).
ALCHEMY. See Chemistry, History of.

ALCOHOL

Alcoholic beverages have been known for many centuries, but it was not until the late Middle Ages that the substance alcohol was discovered. Someone—possibly an alchemist in southern Italy—collected a colorless, flammable liquid from heated wine. This liquid, first called *aqua ardens*, or "burning water," was named alcohol in the 1500's.

Today thousands of different alcohols are known. Some are clear, colorless fluids that evaporate readily and mix freely with water. Others are thick, oily liquids that hardly dissolve in water. Some are even solid at room temperature.

Alcohols are made up of atoms of carbon, hydrogen, and oxygen. The carbon atoms form a kind of framework around which the hydrogen and oxygen atoms are arranged. Each particular type of alcohol is typically determined by the number and arrangement of these three elements.

Most alcohols are very poisonous. Ethyl alcohol, or ethanol, is found in alcoholic beverages. It is poisonous when taken in large quantities. Methyl alcohol, also called wood alcohol, is so poisonous that a small amount may cause blindness or death. Denatured alcohol, an important industrial solvent, is ethanol to which poisonous chemicals or unpleasant-tasting substances have been added to make it unfit to drink.

Alcohols are used in enormous quantities in the manufacture of plastics, medicines, synthetic fibers, paints, and other common products. Because other substances mix easily with them, alcohols are used to extract, or remove, flavoring oils, perfumes, and drugs from plant and animal products.

In the home, ethanol is an ingredient in antiseptics, flavorings, perfumes, liquors, and many medicines. Because of its low freezing point (about –179°F, or –117°C), red-tinted ethanol is usually used in outdoor thermometers. Isopropyl alcohol, or rubbing alcohol, is commonly used in both homes and hospitals.

Reviewed by Louis I. Kuslan
Southern Connecticut State University

ALCOHOLISM

Alcoholism is a chronic illness of addiction to the sedative drug alcohol. Alcohol is one of the oldest and most widely used drugs, and many adults drink alcoholic beverages without becoming addicted. Addiction can be defined as the compulsive use of a substance, which the individual cannot control. Compulsive drinkers drink in spite of knowing that drinking is affecting their lives in a harmful way. Alcoholics sometimes stop drinking, but unless treated they almost always start drinking again.

Alcoholism is often diagnosed as either alcohol **abuse** or **dependence**. Alcohol abuse is a mild form of the illness. Alcohol dependence is a more severe form and is often, but not always, marked by tolerance to the effects of alcohol as well as by a withdrawal syndrome when the use of alcohol is stopped. About 13 percent of people in the United States will suffer from the illness of alcohol abuse or dependence during their lifetime.

Although alcoholism is known to be a hereditary illness, its causes are not clearly understood. There does not seem to be a particular type of personality likely to become an alcoholic. It has been noted that some alcoholics can at first drink large amounts of alcohol without feeling the effects of the alcohol and without having a hangover. This can make them think that they can drink alcohol without negative consequences. Also, the illness may show itself only after several years of drinking.

There has been a substantial increase in the use of alcohol among young people. More people under age 21 are killed by alcohol than by illicit drugs. Although it is illegal in all of the U.S. states for anyone under 21 to purchase or possess alcohol, the drinking of alcohol, especially **binge drinking**, has become an increasing problem among high-school and college students. Binge drinking is defined as consuming five or more drinks in a row for men and four or more in a row for women.

Effects of Alcohol. Alcoholics often show personality changes once they drink compulsively. They may become angry and argumentative, quiet, or depressed. Often a small amount of alcohol causes persons with alcoholism to feel even more anxious, sad, tense, and confused. They then seek relief by drinking more.

Many medical problems affect alcoholics. Serious damage to the liver, heart, stomach, and other organs, especially the brain, can result from the overuse of alcohol. Many alcoholics do not eat properly, and some of their ills are caused by poor nutrition as well as by the direct effects of alcohol on the body.

The problem of driving a car after consuming a defined amount of alcohol is known as drunk driving, described legally as Driving While Impaired (DWI) or Driving Under the Influence (DUI). Drunk driving has received increased attention in recent years. States have enacted tougher legislation to combat the offense. Mothers Against Drunk Driving (MADD), a nationwide organization, was founded in 1980 to help keep U.S. roads safe and to support victims of drunk driving.

Treatment for Alcoholism. Alcoholism can be treated through counseling, by attendance at mutual support groups, and, much less frequently, with medications such as antidepressant drugs.

Mutual help groups, such as Alcoholics Anonymous, give patients guidance, support, and hope. Attendance at mutual help groups also counteracts the tendency of alcoholics to want to be alone as their disease progresses to the more severe stage of dependence. Doctors, psychologists, and counselors familiar with alcoholism can help motivate the patient to enter into a plan for recovery. Private rehabilitation centers have been established to help alcoholics recover. Many large businesses have set up programs to help their employees who are alcoholics.

Several programs have been formed to help the families of alcoholics better understand the disease and its problems. Al-Anon is for the family and friends of alcoholics. Alateen, a division of Al-Anon, is for young people, primarily teenagers, who live in an alcoholic family situation. Adult Children of Alcoholics (ACA) helps adults who have problems because they grew up with an alcoholic parent. Research into methods of treatment and prevention will further help those affected by this major health problem.

Peter A. Mansky, M. D.
Department of Psychiatry
Albany Medical College of Union University

See also Drug Abuse.

Louisa May Alcott was one of the first authors to write novels for young people. Her best-loved work, *Little Women*, is based on her own girlhood experiences.

ALCOTT, LOUISA MAY (1832–1888)

Louisa May Alcott, best known as the author of *Little Women*, was among the first authors to write novels for young readers. She was born in Germantown, Pennsylvania, on November 29, 1832. Her father, Bronson Alcott, was a noted educator and lecturer. When Louisa was 2 years old, the family moved to Boston, Massachusetts, where her father opened a school. Six years later, the Alcotts moved to Concord.

There were five children in the Alcott family—Anna, Louisa, Elizabeth, May, and a boy who died in infancy. For the Alcott girls, childhood was not all play. Bronson Alcott's projects failed, one after another, and money became scarce. Louisa realized that she must find a way to help her family.

When she was 16, she began writing stories and sketches and sending them out for publication. She also worked as a teacher. In 1854, Louisa's first book, *Flower Fables*, was published. It was a collection of fairy stories she had made up to tell one of her pupils.

During the U.S. Civil War, Louisa May Alcott served as a nurse in a Union Army hospital in Washington, D.C. She wrote about her experiences in the book *Hospital Sketches*, published in 1863. Her first novel for adults, *Moods*, appeared the following year.

Louisa May Alcott wrote more than 200 books and stories, but her publisher had to urge her to write what became her most famous novel, *Little Women*. She wrote it while she was editor of *Merry's Museum*, a magazine for girls. She based the story on the Alcotts' family life in Concord. The book was published in two parts, in 1868 and 1869. It sold so well that at last she was able to take care of her family. She continued the story in *Little Men* (1871) and *Jo's Boys* (1886).

Many famous people of Concord were friends of the Alcotts. Henry David Thoreau, Ralph Waldo Emerson, and Oliver Wendell Holmes were among those from whom Louisa gathered ideas about the need for social reform. She worked for the abolition of slavery and later for women's right to vote.

Louisa May Alcott died in Boston on March 6, 1888, two days after her father's death.

LOUISE HALL THARP
Author, *The Peabody Sisters of Salem*

An excerpt from *Little Women* follows.

LITTLE WOMEN

"What in the world are you going to do now, Jo?" asked Meg, one snowy afternoon, as her sister came tramping through the hall, in rubber boots, old sack and hood, with a broom in one hand and a shovel in the other.

"Going out for exercise," answered Jo, with a mischievous twinkle in her eyes.

"I should think two long walks this morning would have been enough! It's cold and dull out; and I advise you to stay, warm and dry, by the fire, as I do," said Meg with a shiver.

"Never take advice! Can't keep still all day, and, not being a pussy-cat I don't like to doze by the fire. I like adventures, and I'm going to find some."

Meg went back to toast her feet and read "Ivanhoe"; and Jo began to dig paths with great energy. The snow was light, and with her broom she soon swept a path all around the garden, for Beth to walk in when the sun came out; and the invalid dolls needed air. Now, the garden separated the Marches' house from that of Mr. Laurence. Both stood in a suburb of the city, which was still country-like, with groves and lawns, large gardens, and quiet streets. A low hedge parted the two estates. On one side was an old, brown house, looking rather bare and shabby, robbed of the vines that in summer covered its walls, and the flowers which then surrounded it. On the other side was a stately stone mansion, plainly betokening every sort of comfort and luxury, from the big coach-house and well-kept grounds to the conservatory and the glimpses of lovely things one caught between the rich curtains. Yet it seemed a lonely, lifeless sort of house; for no children frolicked on the lawn, no motherly face ever smiled at the windows, and few people went in and out, except the old gentleman and his grandson.

To Jo's lively fancy, this fine house seemed a kind of enchanted palace, full of splendors and delights, which no one enjoyed. She had long wanted to behold these hidden glories, and to know the "Laurence boy," who looked as if he would like to be known, if he only knew how to begin. Since the party, she had been more eager than ever, and had planned many ways of making friends with him; but he had not been seen lately, and Jo began to think he had gone away, when she one day spied a brown face at the upper window, looking wistfully down into their garden, where Beth and Amy were snowballing one another.

"That boy is suffering for society and fun," she said to herself. "His grandpa does not know what's good for him, and keeps him shut up all alone. He needs a party of jolly boys to play with, or somebody young and lively. I've a great mind to go over and tell the old gentleman so!"

The idea amused Jo, who liked to do daring things, and was always scandalizing Meg by her queer performances. The plan of "going over" was not forgotten; and when the snowy afternoon came, Jo resolved to try what could be done. She saw Mr. Laurence drive off, and then sallied out to dig her way down to the hedge, where she paused, and took a survey. All quiet, —curtains down at the lower windows; servants out of sight and nothing human visible but a curly black head leaning on a thin hand at the upper window.

"There he is," thought Jo, "poor boy! all alone and sick this dismal day. It's a shame! I'll toss up a snowball and make him look out, and then say a kind word to him."

Up went a handful of soft snow, and the head turned at once, showing a face which lost its listless look in a minute, as the big eyes

Little Women tells of the daily lives of the four March girls—pictured here with their beloved mother—as they grow from schoolgirls to independent young women.

brightened and the mouth began to smile. Jo nodded and laughed, and flourished her broom as she called out, "How do you do? Are you sick?"

Laurie opened the window and croaked out as hoarsely as a raven,. "Better, thank you. I've had a bad cold, and been shut up a week."

"I'm sorry. What do you amuse yourself with?"

"Nothing; it's as dull as tombs up here."

"Don't you read?"

"Not much; they won't let me."

"Can't somebody read to you?"

"Grandpa does, sometimes; but my books don't interest him. . . ."

"Isn't there some nice girl who'd read and amuse you? Girls are quiet and like to play nurse."

"Don't know any."

"You know us," began Jo, then laughed, and stopped.

"So I do! Will you come, please?" cried Laurie.

Left: The Russian emperor Alexander I (reigned 1801–25) helped defeat Napoleon, but failed to fulfill his early promise as a reformer. *Above:* A terrorist's bomb ended the life and reign (1855–81) of Alexander II, who had freed the Russian serfs. *Right:* Alexander III, a son of the assassinated Alexander II, disapproved of reform. His reign (1881–94) was marked by repression and intolerance.

ALEXANDER

Alexander was the name of three emperors and czars of Russia. They set the course of Russian political history between 1801 and 1894 by resisting all efforts to limit their absolute power.

Alexander I (1777–1825) reigned as emperor from 1801 to 1825. As a boy he was raised at the court of his grandmother, the Empress Catherine II (the Great). He was taught, in the spirit of the Enlightenment of the 1700's, to seek justice and to right the social ills of his subjects. He came to the throne, at the age of 23, following a palace revolution that overthrew his father, the Emperor Paul I (ruled 1796–1801), who was murdered.

Alexander's greatest challenge came in 1812, when a French army under Napoleon invaded Russia and captured and burned Moscow. However, the French forces were virtually destroyed in their long retreat through Russia. With Napoleon's final defeat in 1814, Alexander emerged as the most powerful monarch in Europe. He was one of the dominant figures at the Congress of Vienna (1814–15), which restored the old balance of power in Europe after the fall of Napoleon. He was also a founder of the Holy Alliance (1815), which was largely a statement of religious faith and was adopted by most of the European rulers.

Under Alexander, Russia's boundaries were expanded to include central Poland, Finland, Bessarabia, and territories in Transcaucasia. The tragedy of his rule arose from his unwillingness to apply the liberal lessons of his youth to the problems of his country and his subjects. Russian government and institutions, including serfdom, remained much the same at the end of his reign as he had found them in 1801.

Toward the end of his life, Alexander grew moody and melancholy. A legend grew up that he did not die in 1825, but gave up his throne to become a wandering holy man, eventually dying in Siberia in 1864.

Alexander II (1818–81), the nephew of Alexander I, was emperor of Russia from 1855 to 1881. He earned the name of Czar Liberator for his freeing of the Russian serfs.

Alexander was conservative by instinct and sympathetic to the authoritarian style of rule of his father, Emperor Nicholas I (ruled 1825–55). When he succeeded to the throne, Russia was in the midst of the Crimean War (1854–56) against Britain, France, and the Turkish Ottoman Empire. Russia's poor performance in the war prompted Alexander to examine its many neglected problems.

Among these was the institution of serfdom, under which millions of Russian peasants were bound by law to the land of their lords. Beginning with the emancipation of the serfs in 1861, Alexander introduced further reforms in the system of local government, the law, finances, higher education, and the method by which soldiers were recruited.

Alexander expected universal approval of these reforms. Instead, he received demands for even greater reform, including a constitution to limit his absolute authority. After escaping an attempted assassination in 1866, he became disillusioned with his role as reformer and turned his attention to foreign affairs. He extended Russian influence and territory in Central Asia and led Russia into the Russo-Turkish War of 1877–78.

Alexander was killed by a bomb thrown by a member of a revolutionary terrorist group. The assassination occurred only hours after Alexander had signed an order granting some political concessions.

Alexander III (1848–94) was Russian emperor from 1881 to 1894. He succeeded his murdered father, Alexander II, on the throne. One of his first acts was to cancel the modest political concessions made by his father.

Alexander was a gruff, robust figure. Even before coming to the throne, he had been conservative and disapproving of reform. As emperor, he placed restrictions on education and imposed severe censorship of the press. He was intolerant of the many languages, cultures, and religions found among the numerous peoples of the Russian Empire. The Poles, Finns, and Jews became special targets of his repressive policy of "Russification." This was an attempt to force the Russian Orthodox religion and the Russian language on the subject peoples and thus reduce the religious and cultural differences within the empire.

In foreign affairs, Alexander avoided major military conflicts while pursuing a goal of expansion in the Ottoman territories in Europe and Asia. He also abandoned Russia's traditional alliance with Germany and replaced it with a French alliance.

PETER CZAP, JR.
Amherst College

See also CRIMEAN WAR.

ALEXANDER, LLOYD. See CHILDREN'S LITERATURE (Profiles).

ALEXANDER THE GREAT (356–323 B.C.)

Alexander III of Macedon, known as Alexander the Great, was one of the most extraordinary persons of all time. He was a military commander at the age of 18; king at 20; ruler of Greece, western Asia, and Egypt at 24; and conqueror of the Persian Empire at 28. He died at the age of 32, leaving a legend unmatched in history.

Alexander III of Macedon (Macedonia), known as Alexander the Great, was the foremost general of ancient times. During his brief lifetime of 32 years, he conquered most of the known world of the 4th century B.C. His conquests opened Egypt and western Asia to Greek culture and thought.

Early Years. Alexander was born in 356 B.C. in Pella, Macedon (or Macedonia), in what is now part of northern Greece but was then a separate kingdom. His father, Philip II, had made Macedon into a major power and had conquered the cities of Greece. King Philip hired the Greek philosopher Aristotle as a teacher for the young prince. Thus, Alexander acquired training in war and politics from his father and admiration for the culture of Greece from his teacher.

King of Macedon. When Philip was assassinated in 336 B.C., Alexander became king of Macedon and inherited his father's plans for an invasion of Asia. In 334 B.C. he led a well-trained army of Macedonians and Greek allies across the Hellespont (the Dardanelles)—a strait separating Europe from Asia—and declared war on the vast Persian Empire.

Conquest of an Empire. The young king proved himself to be one of the greatest generals in history. A natural leader of soldiers and a master of military planning, he defeated

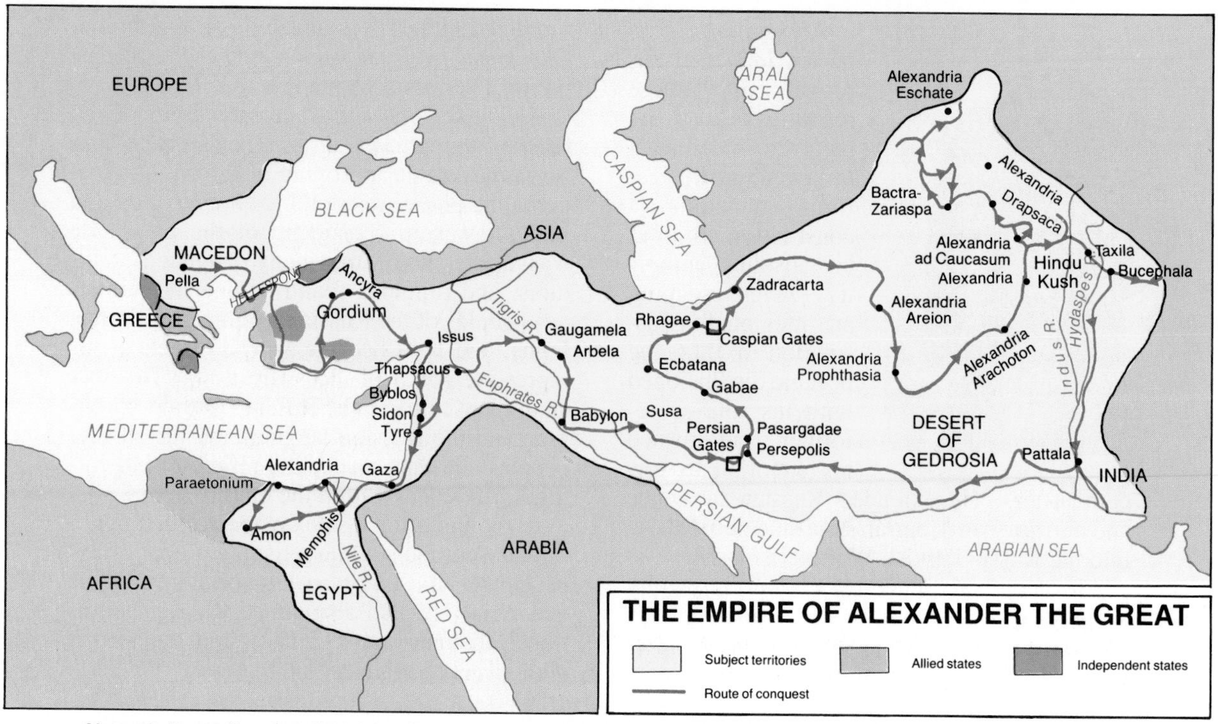

Alexander's empire stretched from Greece and Macedon to the borders of India and included Egypt and the Persian Empire. The arrows show his route of conquest.

a variety of armies, including the much larger forces of the Persian Empire. At the core of Alexander's army were the superb Macedonian infantry and cavalry, the best troops of the age.

Egypt, which had been a satrapy (province) of the Persian Empire, fell to Alexander in 331 B.C. Near the mouth of the Nile River he founded Alexandria, the most famous of the many cities he named after himself. In 331, at the Battle of Gaugamela (in present-day Iraq), he defeated the army of the Persian king, Darius III. When Darius was murdered by his own nobles after this defeat, Alexander succeeded him as the new Lord of Asia.

From 329 to 326 B.C., Alexander led his victorious army through the deserts and mountains of central Asia, to the borders of India. He might have crossed into India itself, except for a mutiny, or revolt, among his officers. What had begun as a military campaign to seize the riches and lands of the Persians had become an expedition of exploration. After years of war in lands strange to them, his weary soldiers wanted to return home.

Return Journey: The Death of Alexander. Yielding to his troops, Alexander led the army down the Indus River (in what is now Pakistan) to its mouth in the Arabian Sea. Splitting his forces, Alexander built a fleet to explore the coast between India and the Persian Gulf, while he and the army followed this route by land. The soldiers became lost in the hostile desert of Gedrosia and many of them died.

Eventually, Alexander and the army reached Babylon (in what is now Iraq), his capital in Asia, where he made plans for further explorations and military campaigns. But, after several weeks of illness, caused by malaria, exhaustion, and, perhaps, too many wounds suffered in battle, the 32-year-old Alexander died on June 10, 323 B.C.

His Achievement and Legend. Alexander opened western Asia to Greek thought and culture. His remarkable conquests (he never lost a battle) and his captivating personality established him as a legend. His brief, whirlwind career gave rise to the story that, at one point, he "wept because there were no more worlds to conquer."

EUGENE N. BORZA
The Pennsylvania State University
Author, *Philip II, Alexander the Great, and the Macedonian Heritage*

ALFRED THE GREAT (849–899)

Only one king in the history of the English people has been called "the Great." This was Alfred, who ruled the land of the West Saxons. The youngest son of King Aethelwulf of Wessex, Alfred was born in 849 in Wantage, a town in south central England.

Alfred's father was a very religious man and a friend of Pope Leo IV. Twice before his 10th birthday, Alfred traveled to Rome. Those visits made a lasting impression on the young boy. Alfred came to respect both religion and education, and in later years he learned to speak and read Latin. During Alfred's youth Danish sea rovers, whom we now call Vikings, raided England. The Danish invaders made settlements on the English coast and used these bases for raids farther inland.

Alfred Becomes King. Alfred's father died in 858. Soon afterward two of Alfred's older brothers were killed in battle. Aethelred, Alfred's last surviving brother, was king when a new invasion of Danes menaced the West Saxon kingdom in 870. The next year has been called "Alfred's year of battles" because he fought against the Danes in nine different places. The most important battle took place at Ashdown. The Saxons defeated the Danes, but Aethelred was wounded and died in the spring. Alfred then became ruler of the war-torn kingdom. He was 22 years old.

The only English king to be honored with the title "the Great," Alfred saved his country from foreign conquest and paved the way for the unification of England.

The next seven years saw times of peace and times of war. In the winter of 878, a Danish force attacked the castle where Alfred was celebrating Christmas. Alfred and a small band of loyal soldiers escaped and hid in the forest until Easter.

Many legends have grown up about Alfred's adventures during those trying times. The most famous is the story of Alfred and the cakes. According to that legend, Alfred, disguised as a farmer, took refuge in a hut in the forest. An old woman who lived there asked him to watch the cakes baking in her oven while she went about her work. Alfred was so busy worrying about his kingdom and planning new battles that he let the cakes burn. When the woman returned, she gave Alfred a severe scolding. But he did not embarrass her by telling her that he was the king.

In 876, Alfred defeated the Danes at Edington. All the nobles of England now turned to Alfred as their leader. Alfred and Guthrum, the pagan Danish chief, signed a peace treaty at Wedmore. Guthrum and many of his followers settled in England and were converted to Christianity. This was an important step toward uniting England. In 886 other Danish invaders attacked England, but Alfred defeated them, too.

Alfred's Reforms. Alfred turned his attention to strengthening England. English laws were rewritten and clarified. New forts and walls were built to protect towns. But Alfred's most important work was in restoring the learning and education that had existed in England before the Danish invaders swept through the country.

With the help of scholars, Alfred translated several books from Latin to English. These were among the first books ever written in the language of the country and were the foundation of English literature.

When Alfred died in 899, an unknown chronicler wrote, "There passed away Alfred the king . . . the famous, the warlike, the victorious, the careful provider for the widow, the helpless, the orphan and the poor; the most skilled of Saxon poets, most dear to his own nation, courteous to all, most liberal . . . most watchful and devout in the service of God."

Reviewed by KENNETH S. COOPER
George Peabody College
Vanderbilt University

ALGAE

Wherever there is moisture and light, algae are found. They are a diverse group of simple organisms that range in size from life-forms so small they can be seen only with a microscope to ones that are greater than 165 feet (50 meters) long! Water habitats such as oceans, rivers, lakes, and ponds are home to most algae. On land, they are present in all habitats where there is some water, including puddles, soil, plants, and even on the skin of tropical, tree-dwelling sloths!

Algae (plural of alga), classified in the Kingdom Protista, are ancient organisms. They are credited with being the life-forms that first released oxygen into the atmosphere, making it possible for life to develop on land. This varied group of organisms includes seaweeds, diatoms, and dinoflagellates.

▸ CHARACTERISTICS OF ALGAE

The simple forms and life processes of algae have not changed much in the millions of years since the first forms appeared.

Structure. Some algae consist of only one cell, while others consist of numerous cells that are joined to form a colony. Algae made up of rows of cells appear as long, threadlike forms called filaments. Some algae consist of a matted network of branching filaments rather than loose filaments. More complex in structure are some of the multicelled algae that form a thallus, or body, with leafy structures. Most seaweeds are examples of this.

Each cell of an alga, whether it is a single-celled or multicelled organism, is made up of the same components. An alga cell is enclosed by a thin, skinlike covering called the cell membrane. Within the cell are specialized structures, including a nucleus, chloroplasts, and a mitochondrion, that carry on the life processes of the cell. The nucleus directs all the cell's activities. Chloroplasts are the structures that contain chlorophyll and other pigments. It is through the action of chlorophyll, in the presence of sunlight, carbon dioxide, and water, that the food-making process of photosynthesis takes place. Once food is produced, the mitochondrion is responsible for transforming the food into energy that the cell can use.

Appearance. Although the insides of algae cells are the same, their outsides vary greatly. Some cells are naked cells. That is, they only have a cell membrane. Others have a cell wall

Some Common Kinds of Algae

Brown algae

Rich in minerals, these seaweeds are harvested for use as food and also for the chemicals in their cell walls, which are used to produce paints, cosmetics, and drugs. Kelp (*left*), a familiar brown algae, can be found anchored to rocks by a structure called a holdfast (*below*). Dense forests of kelp provide lush habitats for many marine animals.

Green algae

Hundreds of millions of years ago, green algae expanded their territory from habitats in the sea to those on the land, becoming the ancestor of all land plants. Today, green algae can be found clinging to rocks and trees, spreading across the surface of a pond (*above*), growing in colonies (*left*), and even covering the shells of turtles.

made up of a material called cellulose. Still others have microscopic scales that may contain hard minerals such as calcium or silica.

Despite the presence of chlorophyll, most algae do not appear green. Often other pigments block out the green, so algae can appear yellow-green, golden brown, or various shades of red depending on the combination of pigments present in the cells.

Reproduction. In some algae, specialized cells are produced during sexual reproduction. When two of these cells join, a new cell is formed that grows into the new alga. Other algae reproduce asexually by dividing into two or more parts. Each part then grows into a new alga. Vegetative reproduction occurs in algae that have seedlike cells called spores. Once set free, the spores grow into new algae wherever they settle.

THE IMPORTANCE OF ALGAE

Algae present a problem when their populations increase greatly. Some algae may grow to cover the surface of a body of water like a thick blanket. Called algal blooms, these growths can alter the natural cycle that keeps the water well oxygenated and smother the animal and plant life. Certain algae produce potent poisons, or toxins, that can harm or even kill both marine life and anyone who eats the infected animals. For example, toxins produced by a dinoflagellate called *Pfiesteria*, first found in the Chesapeake Bay area of the United States, can cause severe sores in fish and memory loss in people who come in contact with the organism.

These harmful effects, though serious, are outweighed by beneficial effects. Marine algae are the world's most important source of oxygen, which is produced as a by-product of photosynthesis. In aquatic environments, algae form the base of the food chain, providing food for fish and other animals that live in the water. In some cultures, algae are an important source of food for people; in others, they are added to livestock feed.

The most important commercial use of algae comes from the chemicals that are extracted from their cell walls. These chemicals are used as additives in paints, cosmetics, drugs, and many food products. Cell wall extracts also are important to research in microbiology and biotechnology.

Paul Gabrielson
William Jewell College

See also Cells; Microbiology.

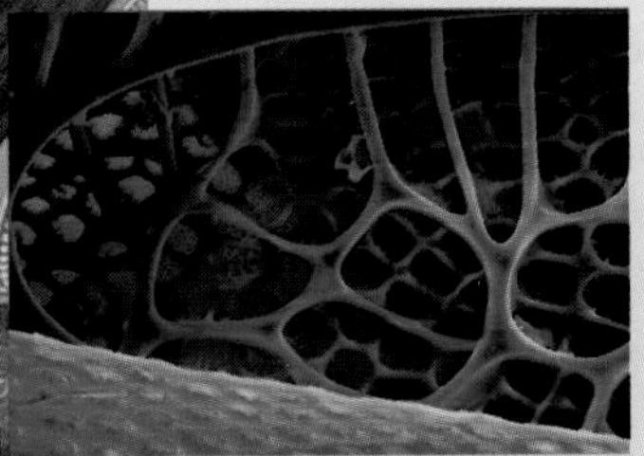

Diatoms

Members of this group (*left*) form one of the largest populations of living things. They are the most numerous organisms making up marine plankton and are the world's major oxygen producers. Their hard, glassy cell walls (*below*), which contain silica, give diatoms a jewel-like appearance.

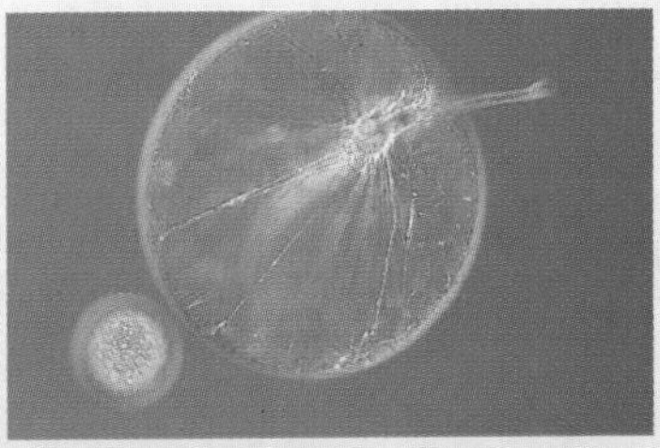

Dinoflagellates

These microscopic algae swim using tail-like flagella. Some species contain red pigment and produce a potent nerve poison. When they occur in great numbers, they cause the "red tides" that can kill millions of fish.

Red algae

Unlike other algae, these seaweeds can perform photosynthesis in the dim light hundreds of feet below the water's surface. Many species, including Irish moss (*above*), are important food sources.

ALGEBRA

Algebra is a branch of the science of mathematics that uses numbers, letters, and other symbols, and the basic operations of arithmetic (addition, subtraction, multiplication, and division) to solve problems involving unknown quantities.

Algebra is used constantly by engineers, scientists, and economists and by people who work with computers in banking and in many other industries. Algebra has many practical applications, too. For example, whenever we use a formula to figure out the amount of interest we will earn from a savings account, we are using algebra.

▶ USING VARIABLES FOR PROBLEM SOLVING

Arithmetic uses numbers to find answers to problems. You probably know addition problems such as $7 + 5 = 12$. Algebra uses numbers, too, but it also uses other symbols to represent unknown numbers or quantities. Most often these are letters written in italics, such as a, b, c, or x, y, z.

In algebra the letter x is most commonly used to represent an unknown quantity. However, x looks very similar to the multiplication sign $\times$. To avoid confusion, you can write $x \cdot y$ or xy or $(x) \cdot (y)$ to express x times y.

The mathematical statement $3 - 3 = 0$ is also a numerical equation. An equation is a mathematical statement in which the arrangement of numerals and letters and their operating signs on one side of an equals sign (=) is equal to an arrangement and its operating signs on the other side of the equals sign. (An arrangement of numerals, letters, and operating signs is often called an **expression**.) For example, this statement means that when 3 is subtracted from 3, the difference is 0. The statement $a - a = 0$ is an algebraic equation. It means that *any* number subtracted from itself has a difference of 0.

In algebra, a letter that can stand for any number is called a **variable**. If *any* number is substituted for a in the example above, the statement will be true. Therefore a is the variable. A number whose value never changes is called a **constant**. In the example above, 0, or zero, is a constant because no matter what a is, whenever it is subtracted from itself, the difference is always 0.

▶ ALGEBRAIC EQUATIONS

The use of variables in algebra makes it easier to solve complex problems. For example, consider this situation: A boy and a girl collected \$29 for the school fair. The girl collected \$3 more than the boy. How much money did each collect?

In algebra the problem would be expressed in this way: Let x represent the unknown number of dollars collected by the boy; then let $x + 3$ represent the unknown number of dollars collected by the girl. This results in the equation $x + (x + 3) = 29$.

When working with equations, it helps to **simplify**, or write a shorter form of, a problem. The first step in simplifying is combining like units, or units that have the same value. When simplifying, the equation must be kept in balance at all times—whatever you do to one side of the equals sign, you must do to the other. There are four ways to simplify:

1. Make both sides larger by adding the same number to both sides.
2. Make both sides smaller by subtracting the same number from both sides.
3. Multiply both sides by the same number, except for the number 0.
4. Divide both sides by the same number, except for the number 0.

These four rules can help us solve the equation $x + (x + 3) = 29$. First, combine the like units by changing $x + (x + 3)$ to $(x + x) + 3$, or $2x + 3 = 29$.

Then, make both sides smaller by subtracting 3 from each side and you will get $2x = 26$.

Now, divide both sides of the equation by the same number, the number 2, and you will get $x = 13$.

Since $x = 13$, we now know that the boy collected $13 and the girl collected $16. This same problem could have been solved using arithmetic, but it is more easily solved using the language of algebra.

Signed Numbers

Signed numbers are often used to solve equations. Signed numbers are **positive numbers** (numbers greater than zero) and **negative numbers** (numbers less than zero). They are sometimes written in parentheses, such as $(+4)$ or (-7), to separate them from the sign that tells you what operation to use.

Signed numbers are often pictured on a number line, with positive numbers to the right of zero and negative numbers to the left of zero.

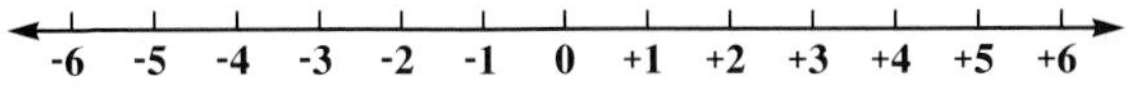

Adding Signed Numbers. Movement to the right (→) along a number line indicates addition. For example, let us say that at 6 A.M. the temperature was 5 degrees below zero $(-5°)$. By noon the temperature had risen 10 degrees $(+10°)$. What was the temperature at noon? In the equation $(-5) + (+10) = x$, the x represents the unknown rise in temperature. To solve the equation, start at (-5) on the number line and move 10 spaces to the right.

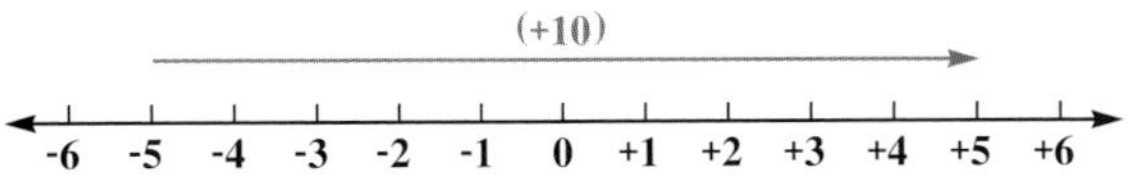

You can see that the temperature at noon was 5 degrees above zero $(+5°)$, so $x = (+5)$.

Other Operations with Signed Numbers. The number line can also be used to do subtraction with signed numbers. Movement to the left (←) on a number line indicates subtraction. All signed numbers can also be multiplied or divided.

Exponents

In algebra, just as in arithmetic, a short way of writing down particular numbers or expressions is frequently used. Using an **exponent** is a short way of writing a particular number or expression, and it is frequently used in algebraic equations.

In arithmetic, multiplication is a short way of adding equal groups. For example, $3 + 3 + 3 + 3 + 3 = 15$ can also be expressed as $5 \times 3 = 15$. Algebra uses a like procedure.

For example, $2 + 2 = 4$ can be expressed as 2^2, which is read as two squared, or 2 to the second power. Also, $2 \cdot 2 \cdot 2 = 8$ can be expressed as 2^3, which is read as two cubed, or 2 to the third power. The smaller-sized upper numeral in each expression is the **exponent**. The larger-sized lower numeral in each expression is the **base**. The exponent tells us that there is to be a multiplication, and it also tells how many times the base has to be repeated, or multiplied.

In the equation $2^2 \cdot 2^3 = 2^5$, the 2^2 means $(2) \cdot (2)$ and the 2^3 means $(2) \cdot (2) \cdot (2)$. So, $2^2 \cdot 2^3 = (2) \cdot (2) \cdot (2) \cdot (2) \cdot (2)$. The rule is, when multiplying two numbers with the same base, copy the base and add the two exponents. So $(2^2) \cdot (2^3) = 2^5$, or 32.

When you divide numbers containing exponents, you subtract the exponents. For example, $(2^5) \div (2^3) = 2^2$.

▶USING FORMULAS

Many algebraic equations are rules that apply to day-to-day situations. These equations are called **formulas**.

A common formula is used to find the area of a rectangle. It is expressed as $A = lw$, in which A stands for the area, l stands for the length of the rectangle, and w stands for the width of the rectangle. The formula tells us that to find the area of the rectangle, the length must be multiplied by the width. The answer will be expressed in square units.

Using this formula to find how much carpeting is needed for a room that measures 15 feet by 10 feet gives you 150 square feet.

▶COORDINATE GEOMETRY

Algebra is an even more powerful tool when it is combined with geometry to form a graph.

Any equation in algebra can be pictured as a graph. Problems involving more than one equation can be solved by finding where the graphs meet.

Many equations have more than one variable. Usually if one variable is x, the second variable is y, as in $2x + 3y = 12$. The graph of an equation such as $2x + 3y = 12$ is formed by plotting points on a plane, or flat surface, by using **coordinates**—pairs of numbers that give the location of a point. Each point is located by measuring how far it is from each of two lines. The horizontal line is called the x axis. The vertical line is called the y axis. For example, here is a point that is 3 units from the y axis and 2 units from the x axis.

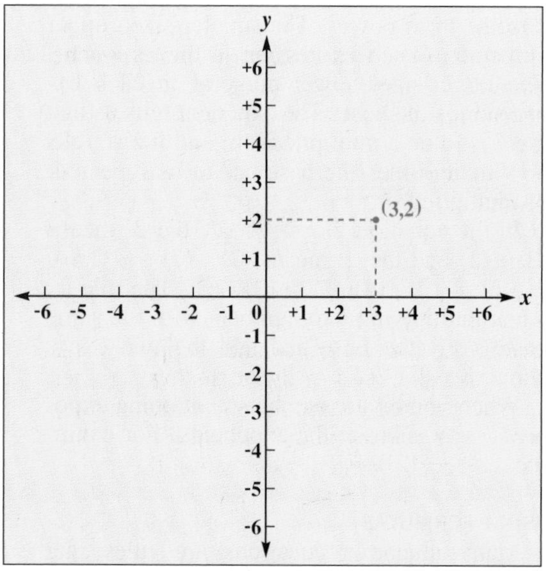

We think of this as 3 units in the $+x$ direction and 2 units in the $+y$ direction and write the location of the point as (3,2). When put into an equation, the point (3,2) is a point for which 3 can replace x and 2 can replace y. If the equation is true, when the variables are replaced by the location of the point on the graph in this way, the point is part of the graph. Because $2(3) + 3(2) = 12$ is true, $(6 + 6 = 12)$, the point (3,2) is on the graph of $2x + 3y = 12$.

Other points on the graph of $2x + 3y = 12$ are (0,4) on the y axis, and (6,0) on the x axis.

$$2(0) + 3(4) = 12$$
$$2(6) + 3(0) = 12$$

When all the points on the graph of $2x + 3y = 12$ are shown, the result is a graph that is a line. Making a graph of an equation often helps us understand the equation better and makes it easier to solve.

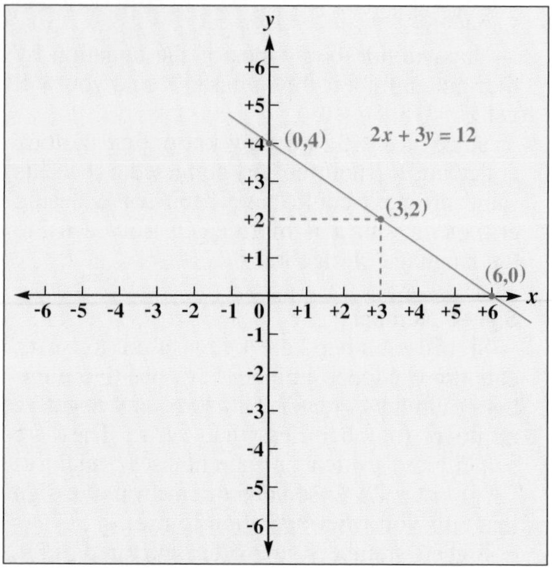

THE HISTORY OF ALGEBRA

The ability to solve algebraic equations goes back almost 4,000 years to the civilizations of Egypt and Babylonia. The algebra of these ancient peoples, however, used words instead of letters to solve equations. It was not until about A.D. 250 that Diophantus, a Greek, used some abbreviations and letter symbols to write out solutions to problems.

The word "algebra" comes from the Arabic word *al-jabr*, which was used about A.D. 825 in the title of a popular book written by the mathematician al-Khwarizmi, which set down the basic rules for solving equations.

Significant contributions to the field of algebra in modern times include the invention of coordinate geometry by René Descartes (1596–1650); the discovery of the *fundamental theorem of algebra* by Carl Friedrich Gauss (1777–1855); the creation of an algebra of logic by George Boole (1815–64); and important discoveries in modern abstract algebra by Emmy Noether (1882–1935).

BRYAN BUNCH
Pace University

See also ARITHMETIC; NUMBERS AND NUMBER SYSTEMS.

ALGER, HORATIO. See MASSACHUSETTS (Famous People).

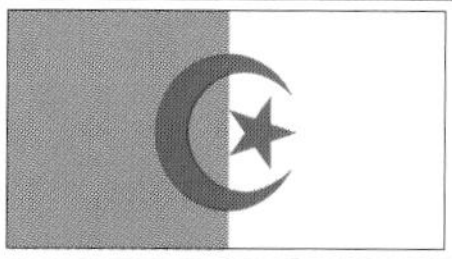

ALGERIA

Algeria, situated on the Mediterranean Sea, is the second largest nation in Africa, after Sudan. It is a country where old customs and traditions exist side by side with modern ways. The land itself is marked by contrast. Beyond a narrow, fertile area along the coast lies the Sahara, the world's largest desert.

Algeria was long occupied by a succession of foreign powers, including the Romans, the Ottoman Turks, and finally, the French, whose rule was characterized by brutal repression. But in 1962, after seven years of violent warfare, Algeria finally won its independence.

▶ PEOPLE

The first known inhabitants of Algeria were the Berbers, a nomadic people of unknown origin. Over the centuries, many conquering peoples invaded the land. The Arabs, who came in the A.D. 600's, introduced Arabic culture and the Muslim religion. Today's population is made up mostly of people of mixed Arab and Berber heritage.

Language and Religion. Almost all Algerians are Muslims belonging to the Sunni sect of Islam. Arabic and Berber are the official languages, and French is still widely spoken.

Education. Schooling, which begins at age 6, is mandatory for the first nine years. Most education is public and free for all. There are several universities in the country, the most prominent being the University of Algiers.

Way of Life. More than three-fourths of Algeria's people live in northern cities and towns. The rest live inland in small villages, or on patches of fertile ground in the desert (called oases). The country's few remaining nomads live in the desert. As the seasons change, they travel between the north and the south and settle temporarily in open fields with their herds of camels and goats.

▶ LAND

Algeria is part of the region known as the Maghrib (Arabic for "where the sun sets"), which includes Libya, Mauritania, Morocco, and Tunisia.

Land Regions. The long ranges of the Atlas Mountains divide Algeria into three physical regions—the Tell, the Sahara, and the High Plateaus.

The Tell (Arabic for "hill") is a narrow strip of coastal lowlands and hills along the Mediterranean. The fertile lowlands support farms and orchards. Forests grow on the lower slopes of the hills, and sheep and goats graze in the highlands. Most of Algeria's major cities are located in the Tell.

The Sahara (Arabic for "desert"), by far the largest of Algeria's regions,

The Berbers (*left*), a nomadic people of unknown origin, were Algeria's first-known inhabitants. Arabs (*below*) came to the Sahara desert region in the A.D. 600's and introduced Arabic culture and the Muslim religion.

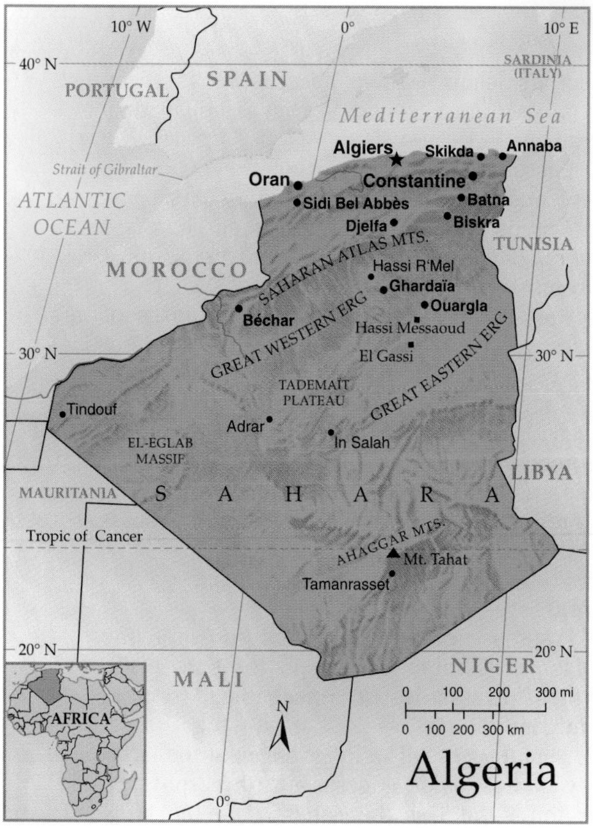

covers approximately 80 percent of the country. It is mainly a *hammada* (rocky plateau), flanked by *ergs* (areas of giant sand dunes). Mount Tahat, Algeria's highest peak, rises 9,852 feet (3,003 meters) in the Sahara's Ahaggar Mountains. Oases, watered by springs and wells, are scattered throughout the region.

Between the Tell and the Sahara lies a small region called the High Plateaus. The landscape there is covered with *chotts* (shallow salt lakes that are dry part of the year).

Rivers, Lakes, and Coastal Waters. Algeria's Mediterranean coastline is approximately 1,200 miles (1,930 meters) long. The country has many short rivers. The Chelif, the most important river, runs across the High Plateaus and through the Atlas Mountains.

Climate. The Tell has mild, rainy winters and dry, hot summers, although it is humid along the coast. The High Plateaus have hot and dry summers but colder winters, with little rainfall. Snow covers the high northern mountains in the winter. The Sahara is hot by day, but temperatures drop sharply at night. Rainfall is scarce. In the spring the sirocco (a hot, dry wind) from the south blows across the desert, causing fierce sandstorms.

Natural Resources. Algeria has extensive mineral resources, including oil and natural gas (mined in the Sahara), iron ore, phosphates, coal, lead, zinc, and uranium. Pine, cedar, cork oak, olive trees, and evergreens grow in the north. Animal life includes deer, otters, weasels, gazelles, jackals, and wild pigs. Monkeys, hyenas, and panthers live in the remote highlands.

▶ ECONOMY

Services. Nearly one-third of Algeria's economy is based on service industries, such as banking, real estate, wholesale and retail trade, tourism, and government. Government services alone employ 29 percent of the entire workforce.

Manufacturing. Algeria's manufacturing sector slowed during an economic crisis in the 1980's. Today's chief manufactured products include refined petroleum products, iron and steel, textiles, processed foods, fertilizers, assembled motor vehicles, electronic goods such as televisions and stereos, cement, bricks, cork, and paper.

Agriculture and Fishing. Only about 10 percent of Algeria's land is suitable for farming.

FACTS and figures

DEMOCRATIC AND POPULAR REPUBLIC OF ALGERIA is the official name of the country.

LOCATION: Northwestern coast of Africa.

AREA: 919,591 sq mi (2,381,740 km^2).

POPULATION: 32,000,000 (estimate).

CAPITAL AND LARGEST CITY: Algiers.

MAJOR LANGUAGES: Arabic and Berber (official), French.

MAJOR RELIGIOUS GROUP: Muslim.

GOVERNMENT: Republic. **Head of state**—president. **Head of government**—prime minister. **Legislature**—National Popular Assembly and the Council of the Nation.

CHIEF PRODUCTS: **Agricultural**— wheat, barley, oats, grapes, olives, citrus fruits, sheep, cattle. **Manufactured**—processed food, petroleum products, textiles, iron and steel, fertilizers, assembled motor vehicles, electronic consumer goods, bricks, cork, paper, cement. **Mineral**—petroleum, natural gas, iron ore, phosphates, coal, lead, zinc.

MONETARY UNIT: Algerian dinar (1 dinar = 100 centimes).

Algeria must import grain and other foods to meet its needs. Grains, wine grapes, olives, citrus fruits, and figs are grown on the Tell. On the High Plateaus, farmers grow wheat and barley and raise livestock. Nomads raise sheep, goats, and camels on the sparse grazing lands of the Sahara. Dates and other fruits, grains, and cotton are grown in Saharan oases. The waters of the Mediterranean yield sardines, shrimp, tuna, anchovies, and shellfish.

Mining. Petroleum and natural gas account for about 30 percent of Algeria's revenues and nearly all of its export income. The country's natural gas deposits are the fifth largest in the world. Natural gas is liquefied before it is exported by special tankers and by pipelines to Europe and elsewhere.

Algiers—the capital, largest city, and chief port of Algeria—rises beyond the half-moon-shaped Bay of Algiers, an inlet of the Mediterranean Sea.

▸ MAJOR CITIES

Most of Algeria's large cities are on the Mediterranean coast.

Algiers, with a population of more than 1.6 million, is Algeria's largest city. It is a major seaport and an important center of transportation, industry, and culture. The city's oldest section, the historic Casbah, will one day be made into a museum, after its inhabitants have been relocated.

Oran, with a population of more than 850,000, is Algeria's second largest city.

▸ CULTURAL HERITAGE

Algerian culture is the product of the blending of many cultures over many centuries: Berbers, eastern Arabs and Muslims, Spanish Moors, Ottoman Turks, and Saharan and West African Bedouins. These interactions have provided Algeria with a rich legacy of folk music, songs, and dances.

▸ GOVERNMENT

Algeria is a republic based on a 1976 constitution that has since been amended several times. A president, who is elected to a 5-year term, serves as head of state and appoints a prime minister to serve as head of government. The president may be re-elected only once.

A constitutional revision in 1996 reorganized Algeria's legislature into two branches. The lower house, the National Popular Assembly, has 389 members who are elected to 5-year terms. The upper house, the Council of the Nation, has 144 members elected to 6-year terms. Of these, 96 are elected indirectly and 48 are chosen by the president.

▸ HISTORY

The Berbers had long inhabited the region when the Phoenicians, a people of the eastern Mediterranean, began to establish colonies along the North African coast in the 1100's B.C. The Romans took over Algeria (then called Numidia) in 146 B.C. They were fol-

Natural gas is processed in the Sahara desert. Algeria's natural gas deposits are the fifth largest in the world.

lowed in the A.D. 400's by the Vandals, a Germanic people, but the region later fell to the Byzantine Empire. The Arabs began their conquest of the area during the 600's. From 1518 to 1830, Algeria was part of the Turkish Ottoman Empire.

In the 1700's, the city-states of Tripoli, Tunis, Algiers, and Tangier together became known as the Barbary States. Pirates from the region became legendary for their attacks against Spain, whose forces constantly raided the shores of North Africa.

Colonial Occupation. In 1830 the French invaded Algeria and later occupied it after forty years of armed resistance. Some historians believe the French invaded to avenge an insult suffered by the French ambassador.

During World War II (1939–45), Algeria was controlled briefly by Germany, but in 1942 it became the headquarters of the Allied forces in North Africa. After the war, France regained control over the colony.

Houari Boumédiene overthrew the government in 1965, then served as president until 1978.

The Algerian War (1954–62). The Algerians' struggle for independence began in earnest in 1954, when the Algerian National Liberation Front (FLN) launched a guerrilla campaign against the French. In 1962, after more than seven years of civil war, an agreement was reached between the FLN and the French government under President Charles de Gaulle, and Algeria officially became an independent country.

Algeria Since Independence. Ahmed Ben Bella, a leader in the struggle for independence, became president in 1963. He was overthrown in 1965 in a military coup led by Colonel Houari Boumédiene, who served as president until his death in 1978. He was succeeded in 1979 by Chadli Bendjedid, who was forced to resign in 1992.

Until 1989, the FLN was the only legal political party in Algeria. But in 1988 a weakening economy stimulated major youth riots. The government responded with violence, and hundreds of people were killed. However, it soon adopted more liberal policies, and in 1989 the constitution was amended to allow for additional political parties.

In local elections held in 1990, the Islamic Front for Salvation (FIS)—which sought to transform Algeria into an Islamic state—won control of 32 of the country's 48 provinces. However, in 1992 the military suspended further elections, and a High Council of State (HCS) was formed to run the country temporarily. The FIS was banned and its leaders were killed, leading to another violent rebellion.

Between 1992 and 2003, fighting between religious extremists and government security forces claimed more than 150,000 lives. The fighting also destroyed much of Algeria's social and economic infrastructure. Attacks against civilians in remote villages caused thousands of people to flee their homes.

Multiparty legislative elections were once again permitted in 1997 and 2002, but the FIS was still banned. Abdelaziz Bouteflika, who was supported by the military, won the 1999 presidential election by default when his six opponents withdrew from the race because of alleged electoral fraud. Voters then approved a peace plan (the National Concord).

As the Islamist rebellion subsided, the Berbers began to demand reforms, including the recognition of the Berber language as an official national language. The government agreed to the linguistic and other cultural demands, but a protest movement in the predominantly Berber region of Kabylie continued to press for major economic and political changes.

On May 21, 2003, a major earthquake struck the region of Algiers. Approximately 2,300 people were killed and 10,000 left homeless.

In 2004, Bouteflika was re-elected president in a landslide victory.

AZZEDINE LAYACHI
Associate Professor of Politics
St. John's University

ALGIERS. See ALGERIA (Major Cities).

ALGONKIAN INDIANS. See INDIANS, AMERICAN.

ALI, MUHAMMAD (1942–)

When the American boxer Muhammad Ali proclaimed himself "the greatest," he may have been right. Ali was one of the most charismatic and skilled athletes of all time.

Muhammad Ali was born Cassius Marcellus Clay, Jr., on January 17, 1942, in Louisville, Kentucky. Clay was introduced to boxing at the age of 12, and by the time he reached 18 he had won several amateur championships. His final amateur bout was at the 1960 Summer Olympic Games, where he won the light heavyweight gold medal.

Ali won his first professional heavyweight title in 1964 when he defeated Sonny Liston. That same year he joined the Nation of Islam (Black Muslims) and changed his name to Muhammad Ali. Ali was suspended from boxing and stripped of his title in 1967 for refusing to participate in the military draft. He returned to the ring three years later.

Ali regained the heavyweight crown in 1974 by defeating George Foreman. Ali also had famous matches with Joe Frazier. In a 1971 bout, Frazier defeated Ali in a unanimous decision. In a 1975 rematch, Ali took the title away from Frazier. Ali lost the heavyweight title in 1978 to Leon Spinks, but when he beat Spinks in a rematch eight months later, he became the first boxer to hold the title three different times. By his retirement in 1981, Ali had won 56 matches and lost only five. He was inducted into the International Boxing Hall of Fame in 1990.

In 1984, Ali was diagnosed with Parkinson's disease, which affected his muscles and speech. In 1996, he was given the honor of lighting the Olympic flame at the opening ceremony of the Summer Olympic Games in Atlanta, Georgia.

Reviewed by William E. Shapiro
Consultant, children's encyclopedias

ALIEN AND SEDITION ACTS. See Adams, John (President).

ALIENS

People who are not citizens of the country in which they live are called aliens. Aliens are required to obtain government permission in order to stay in a foreign country. United States Citizenship and Immigration Services (USCIS), a division of the U.S. Department of Homeland Security, handles alien affairs.

Temporary visitors must obtain visas (permits) from the State Department to enter the country. Visas allow them to travel, go to school, or conduct business for a limited time.

There are several million **permanent resident aliens** living in the United States. They enjoy most of the rights and privileges of American citizens, such as the right to hold a job or to own property. They also share many of the same duties, such as paying taxes. However, they cannot vote or hold most public offices. Resident aliens over the age of 18 must carry an identification card, more commonly known as a green card.

A third category is made up of **refugees**, who left their homelands because of war or persecution. Most refugees are admitted into the United States under a special procedure called parole. They may eventually achieve resident-alien status.

Any alien in the United States who does not follow U.S. government laws and regulations can be deported (required to leave the country), according to the Alien Act of 1798.

An **illegal alien** is a person who enters a country without the permission of that country's government or who stays beyond the term of his or her visa. Illegal aliens can cause complex problems because they place a burden on public services without paying the taxes that support them. The Immigration Reform and Control Act of 1986 set penalties for people who employ illegal aliens, but it also gave legal status to many illegal aliens living in the United States.

Christopher Bentley
Senior Public Affairs Officer
U.S. Citizenship and Immigration Services

See also Citizenship; Homeland Security, United States Department of; Immigration; Naturalization; Passports and Visas.

ALLEN, ETHAN (1738–1789)

Ethan Allen was a hero of the American Revolutionary War and a leader in the fight for Vermont's statehood. He was born in Litchfield County, Connecticut, probably on January 10, 1738. As a young man he fought in the French and Indian War (1754–63).

In 1769, Allen settled in Vermont, which was then known as the "New Hampshire grants." A heated dispute arose between the colonial governors of New York and New Hampshire because each claimed that land for his own colony. Allen felt that the original settlers from New Hampshire had the strongest claim. Unfortunately for them, Britain decided otherwise and granted the land to New York.

This action prompted Allen and his friend Seth Warner to organize a militia called the Green Mountain Boys. In 1770 the group took up arms against the intruding New Yorkers to prevent them from taking over their land. The governor of New York declared Allen an outlaw and offered a reward for his arrest.

In April 1775, the Revolutionary War began. On May 10, Allen, with his Green Mountain Boys and some Connecticut militia, succeeded in capturing the British fort at Ticonderoga, New York, on Lake Champlain. Four months later, Allen and his men failed in an attempt to capture Montreal, and Allen was taken prisoner.

After his release in a prisoner exchange in 1778, Allen returned to continue the fight for Vermont's independence. However, the Continental Congress refused to recognize Vermont's claim to statehood. Allen considered having Vermont annexed to Canada, but the plan fell through.

Ethan Allen died on February 12, 1789, in Burlington, Vermont. Two years later, Vermont became the 14th state of the Union.

Reviewed by Richard B. Morris
Editor, *Encyclopedia of American History*

ALLEN, RICHARD. See Pennsylvania (Famous People).
ALLEN, WOODY. See Motion Pictures (Profiles: Directors).
ALLENTOWN. See Pennsylvania (Cities).

ALLERGIES

An allergy is an abnormal response by the immune system to a foreign substance (called an allergen) that is normally harmless. Allergies often begin in childhood but can develop at any time. In the United States, an estimated 50 million people have them.

Symptoms of allergies vary and can range from mild to severe. The most common are sneezing, watery eyes, and nasal congestion (allergic rhinitis or hay fever); breathing difficulties (asthma); and skin rashes. Other allergy symptoms include itchy and swollen skin (hives), eye inflammation (conjunctivitis), digestive disturbances, and anaphylaxis. The latter, which is rare, is a severe reaction that causes swelling of body tissues, breathing difficulties, cramps, vomiting, and a rapid drop in blood pressure. If not treated immediately, anaphylaxis can be fatal.

Although some allergens, such as pollen, often cause a specific type of allergic response (hay fever), other allergens can produce different responses in different people. For example, an allergy to cat or dog dander may cause hives in one person and asthma in another.

How Allergies Develop. An allergy develops when the immune system—the body's defense mechanism against toxins, bacteria, and viruses—first mistakes a substance that is harmless for one that is harmful. This response stimulates the production of a special type of antibody, or protein, called immunoglobulin E (IgE). IgE antibodies then attach themselves to mast cells (found mainly in the respiratory and digestive system) or to white blood cells. When the person is exposed to the same substance again, the antibodies signal the mast cells or white blood cells to release chemicals that cause allergic symptoms. Chief among these is a powerful substance called histamine.

Causes. People can be allergic to many things. However, more are allergic to inhaled substances than anything else. Of these, the most troublesome are dust and pollen (fine powders from plants and trees), and molds, animal dander, feathers, and chemicals.

Many people are also allergic to foods such as peanuts, shellfish, and cow's milk, venom from insects (especially yellow jackets and other wasps and bees), and drugs such as penicillin.

The most common causes of allergic skin reactions are poison ivy and poison oak. But many other materials may cause reactions in sensitive individuals, including latex, soaps, various chemicals, and cosmetics.

A person with a family history of allergies is more likely to develop them than someone who comes from a nonallergic family. However, it is not the specific allergy that is inherited, but the tendency to be allergic.

Sneezing, watery eyes, and nasal congestion, called allergic rhinitis or hay fever, are among the most common allergy symptoms.

Diagnosis and Treatment. Doctors diagnose most allergies with a physical exam and skin or blood test (called a radioallergosorbent test, or RAST). In a skin test, a small dose of a purified allergen is injected just below the skin, or lightly scratched into the skin. After a short time, the skin is checked to see if an allergic reaction (usually redness and swelling) has occurred. For a RAST, a blood sample is taken to measure the amount of IgE antibodies to one or more possible allergens.

An allergy cannot be cured, but once it has been identified it can be controlled in several ways. Avoiding exposure to the allergen is the simplest. Unfortunately, this is not always possible. Although it may be easy to avoid certain foods or drugs, it is much more difficult to avoid things such as dust or pollen. In such situations, medications can be used to reduce or eliminate allergic symptoms. These include antihistamines (which prevent sneezing, watery eyes, and other effects of histamine), anti-inflammatory drugs (which reduce inflammation in the airways), and nasal decongestants. Other medications are breathed directly into the lungs with an inhaler. These relax the muscles around the airways to relieve coughing, wheezing, and shortness of breath.

When these methods are not effective, immunotherapy may be recommended. During immunotherapy, a doctor injects a small amount of the allergen into the patient's system. Gradually, the amount that is injected is increased. This causes the immune system to produce less of the antibodies that cause allergic symptoms. Allergy shots must be given for several years before they work. They are most effective for allergic rhinitis and allergies caused by insect stings.

Life-threatening allergic reactions are usually treated with injections of epinephrine (also known as the hormone adrenaline). This relaxes the muscles in the airways, making it easier to breathe, and tightens the blood vessels. Epinephrine can be administered by a medical practitioner or self injected with a prescription device called an Epi-pen if medical care is not available.

ADRIAN M. CASILLAS, M.D.
UCLA School of Medicine

Did you know that...

some schools are now banning peanut butter? This is because several studies have indicated that peanut allergies are on the rise, especially among children. And for some of these children, even minimal exposure to peanuts can result in a life-threatening reaction, or anaphylaxis.

No one is really sure why peanuts have become so risky, but doctors who treat allergies say there could be several reasons. One is that children are eating peanut butter at an earlier age, which increases their risk of developing an allergy. Another is that our exposure to peanuts and other nut products has increased; peanuts and peanut products are now added to many processed foods, as well as a number of lotions and creams.

ALLIGATORS. See CROCODILES AND ALLIGATORS.

ALLOYS

An alloy is a substance formed by combining a metal with other metals or non-metals. Brass is an alloy made with the metals copper and zinc. Steel is an alloy made with a metal—iron—and a non-metal—carbon. Alloys are usually made by melting the ingredients and mixing them together.

The special characteristics of a metal, such as its flexibility, hardness, strength, and resistance to corrosion, are called **properties.** Alloying makes it possible to create materials with just the right combination of properties for a particular use.

Almost every metallic substance used today is an alloy of some kind. But the idea of making alloys is not new. It was known by people in ancient times.

Thousands of years ago, people discovered that they could use copper instead of stone to make their tools. Copper was easier to work with than stone and was fairly easy to obtain. Perhaps the only trouble with copper was that it was not hard enough for some uses. About 3500 B.C. it was found that if tin, another fairly soft metal, was combined with copper, a very hard material was produced. This material was the alloy called bronze.

The discovery of how bronze is made was probably accidental, but it turned out to be an important event. Bronze was a better material for many purposes than either of the two metals that composed it. The alloy was so widely used that this period of history became known as the Bronze Age.

Bronze is only one example of an alloy that is used because it does a certain job better than many pure metals. Airplanes must be built of material that is both light and strong. Aluminum is light enough, but it is not strong enough for this purpose. Steel is strong enough, but it is too heavy. But combining aluminum with copper, magnesium, and other metals yields an alloy that is light, yet strong enough to stand up to the stresses of flight. Similarly, adding nickel, vanadium, chromium, and other metals to steel produces a stronger metal. This saves weight by making it possible to reduce the thickness of parts.

Steel is an extremely versatile and useful metallic material. In the United States alone, about 100,000,000 metric tons of steel are produced each year for use in everything from skyscrapers to saucepans.

Alloying steel with other metals produces materials called **alloy steels,** which are suitable for a wide variety of purposes. Manganese alloy steels are used to make machines such as rock crushers and power shovels, which must withstand extremely hard use. Stainless steel, which contains chromium and sometimes nickel and manganese, is a hard, strong substance that resists heat and corrosion. Stainless steels are used for such things as jet engines, automobile trim, knives, forks, and spoons, and kitchen equipment.

CLASSES OF ALLOYS

Alloys are divided into two main classes: ferrous and non-ferrous. The term **ferrous** (from the Latin word *ferrum,* meaning "iron") applies to alloys, such as steel, whose base metal is iron. Alloys that contain little or no iron, such as aluminum and copper alloys, are called **non-ferrous.**

There is an important difference between alloys and impure metals. Both are mixtures, but alloys are mixtures that have been deliberately combined in definite proportions. Impure metals are accidental mixtures that vary greatly in their make-up.

ALLOY STRUCTURES

Why does an alloy have different properties from the metals that compose it? To understand the answer to this question, something must be known about how atoms line up to form the inner structure of metals.

When a metal is melted, the atoms of the metal move about freely. When the metal cools and becomes solid, the atoms form clusters of a certain shape, called **crystals.** There are three main types of crystal structure. Two of these crystal structures are shaped like cubes, with the atoms at various places on the cubes. The third type is a more complicated structure that has a six-sided, or hexagonal, shape.

These clusters of atoms, or crystals, also form larger groups called **grains.** These grains can be seen with the aid of a microscope. In a pure metal, such as copper, all the grains look alike.

Certain metals can mix together so closely when they are melted that the grains all look

Clusters of metallic crystals form geometric shapes, called grains, in a sample of pure gold. The grain structure here is magnified 160 times.

When copper is added to gold to form an alloy, the atoms of each metal interact, and the grain structure changes. Magnification is the same as the photo at left.

alike when the alloy becomes solid, just as they do in a pure metal. When two metals are so completely mixed, they are said to be in **solid solution.** One such solid solution is the alloy of copper and nickel called cupronickel. In this alloy copper is the base metal; that is, more copper than nickel is used in making the alloy. Cupronickel is stronger and harder than copper but less able to conduct heat or electricity. The addition of nickel to the copper has created new properties that neither copper nor nickel alone has.

These new properties are created by the difference in the sizes of the atoms of copper and the atoms of nickel. When the nickel atoms enter the crystal structure of the copper, they replace some copper atoms. Because the nickel atoms are of a different size, the crystals of copper are distorted, or warped out of their normal shape. Although the grains of the alloy appear to have the same shape as the grains of the base metal (copper), the smaller units, the crystals, have been changed. This change in the shape of the copper crystals is the reason the alloy has different properties from the copper and nickel of which it is made. Every metal has atoms of different size from those of all other metals. Thus, whenever a solid-solution alloy is formed, a distortion of the crystal structure of the base metal will always take place, and new properties will be created.

Some metals do not mix completely with each other. These metals are said to be **partially soluble** in each other. They form two or more different kinds of grains when the alloy solidifies. The different kinds of grains are called **phases.** They are actually solid solutions containing different proportions of the two metals. Some kinds of brass, an alloy composed of copper and zinc, have this kind of structure.

There is a third type of constituent in some alloys. The metals combine to form an **intermetallic compound,** which has a crystal-and-grain structure quite different from either of the pure metals. In an aluminum-copper alloy, for instance, a small amount of copper goes into solid solution with the aluminum. The rest of the copper combines with aluminum atoms to form an intermetallic compound composed of two atoms of aluminum and one atom of copper. Thus, the aluminum-copper alloy is made up of three components: a large amount of aluminum, a small quantity of copper in solid solution, and tiny particles of the intermetallic compound.

Although intermetallic compounds are usually hard and brittle, their presence in an alloy in small amounts is very valuable. Such alloys combine the toughness of solid solutions with the hardness of intermetallic compounds.

We owe jet airplanes, television, and many other technical marvels to alloys. These metal mixtures made it possible to turn engineers' and scientists' ideas into reality.

John A. Ring
Union Carbide Corporation

See also Bronze and Brass; Iron and Steel; Metals and Metallurgy.

ALMANACS. See Reference Books.

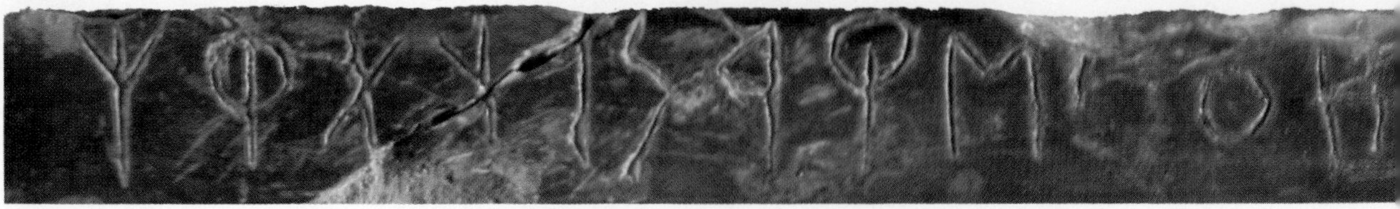

ALPHABET

An alphabet is a group of signs that is used to write a language. The signs—called letters—express all the individual sounds that people use when they speak.

We think of the letters of our alphabet as having a fixed order—beginning with A and ending with Z—but that is only because we learned it that way. The letters originally were made up as they were needed, rather than in any logical pattern. We could easily change the order of the letters in our alphabet and it would not affect the way we write or speak.

The ancestor of the alphabet we use for writing English was created more than 3,000 years ago. Our alphabet is called the Latin or Roman alphabet because it is taken directly from the alphabet used by the ancient Romans. The Romans adapted this alphabet from the one used by the Etruscans, another people who lived in Italy, who in turn had borrowed it from the Greeks. The Greeks had taken the alphabet from the Phoenicians, a Semitic people who lived along the eastern end of the Mediterranean Sea. Which Semitic people actually originated the concept of the alphabet remains a mystery. But by about 1000 B.C., several groups of peoples speaking related languages—including the Arameans, the Phoenicians, and the Hebrews—were all using this same basic system for writing their languages.

▶FORERUNNERS OF THE ALPHABET

An alphabet is a writing system that expresses the sounds of language. We call such a writing system phonetic ("by sounds"). An alphabet has signs for the smallest individual speech sounds. We call these individual sounds **phonemes** ("sound units"). Another type of phonetic writing system that is not considered an alphabet uses signs to stand for **syllables.** Syllables are speech units that are made up of phonemes. A syllable can be a complete word or part of a word, but it must contain a vowel sound.

A third type of writing system has signs that stand for complete words regardless of how many syllables the word has. Even though we have an alphabet, we sometimes use signs for complete words in order to save time and space. For example, all of our numerals are word signs. It is much easier to write 1945 than to use our alphabet to spell out "one thousand nine hundred forty-five." Other common word signs that we use include & for "and," + for "plus," and $ for "dollar."

Word Writing Systems. The earliest writing systems, which came into use about 3000 B.C., used almost all word signs. These were the hieroglyphic writing of ancient Egypt and the cuneiform writing of the ancient Sumerians. The main disadvantage to a writing system that uses only word signs is that it needs a large number of signs because there are many words in a language. Look at the size of the dictionary. Imagine having to learn a different sign for every word in the dictionary in order to be able to read and write.

Actually, in a word writing system the same sign often stands for several related words. The reader must decide which of the words the writer meant with the sign he used. But such a system still needs about 1,000 signs. Chinese is one of the only modern languages to use a word writing system.

Word-Syllabic Writing Systems. Because of the drawbacks of using only word signs, the Sumerians and Egyptians quickly developed signs for syllables, which they used in combination with word signs. This was a tremendous improvement over using word signs by themselves because the exact word the writer intended to use could be expressed more accurately.

The Sumerians indicated vowel sounds in their syllabic signs. This meant that they needed a sign for each consonant plus each vowel. (In English, for example, different signs would be needed to express the syllables ba, be, bi, bo, bu, da, de, di, do, du, and so on.) The Egyptian signs were simpler. They stood for the consonant plus any vowel. In this system the reader had to supply the correct

The Etruscan alphabet, which reads from right to left, is one of the ancestors of our alphabet. This carving, made about 700 B.C., was probably used for teaching.

vowel, which caused some confusion. It would be like writing "ht" in English and leaving it to the reader to decide whether the letters meant hot, hat, hit, or hut. The advantage of the system was that the number of syllabic signs needed was reduced to the number of consonants in the language.

Syllabic Writing Systems. The Semitic peoples of Syria and Palestine developed purely syllabic writing systems. Their systems were very simple because they eliminated word signs completely and, like the Egyptians, their signs expressed consonants plus any vowel. This simplification was an important step in the development of the alphabet.

Because vowels were not expressed by the writing, these syllabic systems—called **syllabaries**—were not true alphabets. Alphabets have a sign for each phoneme in the language. But the Semitic syllabaries developed into the alphabets used today. The most important of the Semitic syllabaries were the Phoenician, from which the Greeks developed their alphabet, and the Aramaic.

The Phoenician Writing System. The earliest example of Phoenician writing that we have is from the city of Byblos and dates from about 1000 B.C., but the writing system was surely in use before this. Byblos was a major center of commerce. It was so important in the trade in papyrus, a paperlike material used for writing, that its name gave the Greeks their word for "book" *(biblos)* and the English language its "Bible." Some scholars think that Byblos may have been the place where the Semitic writing system was first created, but there is no direct evidence for this.

The Phoenician writing system had 22 signs. Each sign had a name, the first sound of which was the sound that the sign represented. In many cases the signs can be recognized as pictures of the object that forms the name of the sign. The first sign was called *aleph,* which was the Phoenician word for "bull," and the sign looked like a bull's head.

The second sign, called *beth,* represented the sound "b." It was the Phoenician word for "house," and the letter looked something like the plan of a simple house. You can go all the way through the Phoenician script in this manner, finding meanings for almost all of the names of the signs and relating the signs to the names. The last sign was *taw,* which meant "sign" or "mark." It was in the shape of a simple cross.

This, then, was the writing system that the Greeks adapted to write their own language.

THE DEVELOPMENT OF THE ROMAN ALPHABET

Greeks. When the Greeks adapted the Phoenician writing system to their own language, some time before the 8th century B.C., they made a very significant change. They created signs for vowels and used them each time a vowel occurred. Simple as this sounds, it was the last important step in the development of writing systems that had been going on for more than 2,000 years. The Greek writing system was truly an alphabet, because each sound in the language now had its own sign. Every word could be written accurately with a system that used a very small number of signs.

The Greeks did not invent new signs for the vowels but simply converted some of the Phoenician signs that they did not need for their own language into vowel symbols. They also added some letters and later dropped others to create the 24-letter Greek alphabet. When the Greeks borrowed signs from the Phoenicians, they kept the names for the signs, although they had no meaning in Greek. Thus *aleph* became *alpha,* and *beth* became *beta*. It is from the names of these two letters that our word "alphabet" comes.

Etruscans. The next step in the alphabet's journey was to the Etruscans. They were a people of northern Italy who were influential during the 11th to 6th century B.C. The Etruscans wrote their language using an early Greek alphabet, with some modifications. The most important offshoot of the Etruscan alphabet was the Roman alphabet.

The Roman alphabet, which is used to write English and many other modern languages, developed over thousands of years. From left: The Phoenician syllabary was an important early writing system. From it the Greeks developed their alphabet, which spread to the Etruscans. The Romans adapted the Etruscan alphabet. By the 3rd century B.C., 21 of the capital letters that we use today had been perfected by the Romans.

Romans. The Romans adapted the Etruscan alphabet, probably beginning in the 6th century B.C. Of the 26 letters of the original Etruscan alphabet, the Romans accepted 20.

By the 3rd century B.C. the Roman alphabet consisted of 21 letters: A, B, C, D, E, F, G, H, I, K, L, M, N, O, P, Q, R, S, T, V, and X. Only J, U, W, Y, and Z remained to be added to the alphabet. When the Romans conquered Greece in the 1st century B.C., a large number of Greek words were taken into the Latin language. The Romans found it necessary to borrow some Greek letters in order to write these new words. The Greek letter *upsilon* had developed into a sound between *u* and *e*, and the Romans gave it the name *wye*. The letter *zeta* had been rejected five centuries earlier and its place in the order taken by G, but it was now

OTHER MAJOR ALPHABETS

The Roman alphabet is just one of the writing systems used by the world's people today. Other important alphabets are listed below.

Arabic	ا ب ت ث ج ح خ د ذ ر ز س ش ص ض ط ظ ع غ ف ق ك ل م ن لا و ي
Cyrillic	АБВГДЕЁЖЗИЙКЛМНОПРСТУФХЦЧШЩЪЫЬЭЮЯ
Gaelic	a b c d e f g h i l m n o p r s t u
Greek	ΑΒΓΔΕΖΗΘΙΚΛΜΝΞΟΠΡΣΤΥΦΧΨΩ
Hebrew	א בּ ב ג ד ה ו וּ ז ח ט י כּ כ ל מ נ ס ע פּ פ צ ק ר שׁ שׂ תּ ת
Hindi	अ आ इ ई उ ऊ ऋ ए ऐ ओ औ क ख ग घ ङ च छ ज झ ञ ट ठ ड ढ ण त थ द ध न प फ ब भ म य र ल व श ष स ह

accepted and along with Y placed at the end of the alphabet after X. This brought the total number of letters to 23. This was the alphabet used during the time of the Roman Empire. J, U, and W were added much later and were more a matter of developments in handwriting than of a real need for separate letters.

Capital and Small Letters. In ancient times, all writing was done in what we call capital (or uppercase) letters. Small (or lowercase) letters developed later.

The Roman letters were perfected by the 1st and 2nd centuries A.D.. The form known as square capitals was written with great precision, especially on stone, and the letters were very symmetrical and well proportioned. These forms are what we still use for our capital letters today.

The small letters of our modern alphabet developed more gradually. While square capitals were fine for stone inscriptions, everyday writing, done with a pen or brush on papyrus or parchment, required more flexibility and speed. The everyday script, which used much rounder forms of the letters (still capitals), was called cursive. Writing materials were expensive, so the scribes who copied books tried to fit as much lettering as possible on a page and in the process created a number of "book hands." These two factors—the need to write quickly and the need to save space—led to the development of our small letters.

TODAY'S ALPHABETS

Many different alphabets are used in the world today, but with the possible exception of the Korean alphabet all of them developed in one way or another from the Semitic writing system.

The Cyrillic Alphabet. We have already seen how the Greek alphabet developed from the Phoenician and how the Roman alphabet developed from the Greek. Two other alphabets also developed from the Greek but at a much later date. In the 9th century A.D., the Glagolitic and the Cyrillic alphabets were devised to write the Slavic languages. Both were based on the Greek alphabet then in use. Glagolitic was more popular at first but eventually was replaced by Cyrillic, which is not as complicated. Cyrillic in various forms is used today in Bulgaria, Russia, Ukraine, Belarus, and Serbia and Montenegro.

Other Alphabets. Except for those areas that use the Greek and Cyrillic alphabets, some form of the Roman alphabet is used throughout Europe. Almost all of the rest of the world's alphabets developed from the Semitic syllabary known as Aramaic. The alphabets derived from the Aramaic include those used to write the modern Semitic languages—Arabic, Hebrew, and Syriac. Alphabets used in India and Southeast Asia and the Mongol script are also derived from the Aramaic.

In the 3,000 years since its invention, the alphabet has proved to be a very durable and flexible tool for expressing language. It has been adapted successfully to many languages. Apparently it is here to stay.

ROBERT M. WHITING
The Oriental Institute
The University of Chicago

See also WRITING; articles on the individual letters of the alphabet.

The snowcapped Alps extend across much of south central Europe. The highest Alpine peak, Mont Blanc (to left of center), lies on the border between France and Italy.

ALPS

The Alps are a great mountain system of south central Europe, famed for the spectacular beauty of their snowcapped peaks.

Extent and Divisions. From the coast of the Mediterranean Sea, the Alps stretch for a distance of about 660 miles (1,060 kilometers). They form the boundary between France and Italy and extend across Switzerland, northern Italy, southern Germany, Austria, and the Balkan peninsula. They are usually divided into three main sections: Western, Central, and Eastern Alps. Some of the principal Alpine mountain ranges are the Maritime, Ligurian, Rhaetian, Pennine, and Bernese Alps in the Western and Central Alps; and the Noric and Carnic Alps, the Hohe Tauern and Dolomites, and the Julian and Dinaric Alps in the Eastern Alps.

Peaks, Glaciers, Rivers. Mont Blanc, on the border between France and Italy, is the highest peak in the Alps, rising 15,771 feet (4,807 meters). The Matterhorn, on the Swiss-Italian border, although lower in elevation, is noted for its steep, knifelike ridges, which have long challenged mountain climbers. There are more than 1,200 Alpine glaciers, or slow-moving bodies of ice. The largest, the Aletsch Glacier, covers an area of about 66 square miles (171 square kilometers). Several important rivers, including the Rhine, the Rhône, and tributaries of the Po, rise in the Alps.

Plant and Animal Life. A variety of plant and wild animal life thrives at elevations below the highest summits. Grapes are cultivated in the southern valleys. Oak, beech, and other trees grow on the lower slopes, while evergreens are found at higher elevations. Above the tree line are meadows, often used for grazing livestock. The edelweiss is the most famous of Alpine flowers. The chamois (a kind of antelope), ibex (a wild goat), and golden eagle all live above the tree line.

Passes and Tunnels. There are about 50 Alpine passes, or natural gaps in the mountains. Some of these were used in older historical times by invading armies crossing into Italy. The best-known passes include the Brenner, between Austria and Italy; the Great St. Bernard and the Simplon, between Switzerland and Italy; the Montgenèvre, the Little St. Bernard, and the Mont Cenis, between France and Italy; the St. Gotthard in Switzerland; and the Arlberg in Austria.

Numerous railroad and highway tunnels have made travel across the Alps much easier. The Simplon Tunnel, extending for 12½ miles (20 kilometers) between Switzerland and Italy, is one of the world's longest railroad tunnels. The St. Gotthard Road Tunnel in Switzerland, completed in 1980, is the world's longest highway tunnel, with a length of 10 miles (16.3 kilometers).

Reviewed by DANIEL JACOBSON
Michigan State University

ALTERNATIVE MEDICINE

Alternative medicine is any healing practice not commonly used in conventional, or traditional, Western medicine. The list of therapies classified as alternative changes constantly, as therapies proven to be safe and effective become part of conventional health care. When used together with conventional medicine, alternative therapies are called **complementary**.

While conventional medicine relies mainly on drugs and surgery to treat disease, practitioners of alternative medicine prefer to use less invasive therapies. People often seek alternative therapies for conditions, such as chronic pain, that have not responded to conventional treatment. Practitioners of holistic medicine—a health-care method that emphasizes treatment of the whole person—are likely to use alternative therapies. (See the article HOLISTIC MEDICINE in Volume H.)

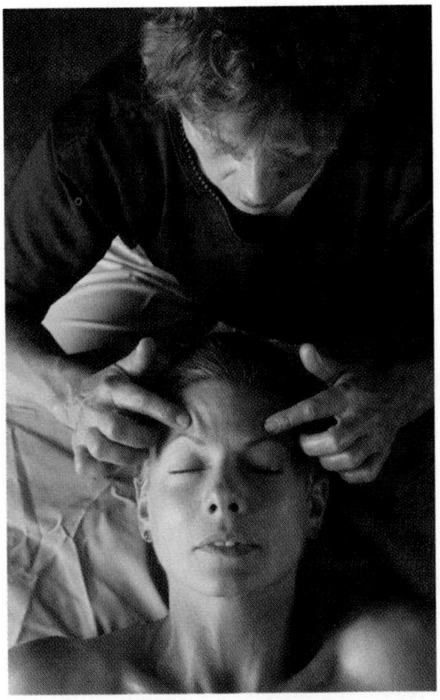

One popular alternative therapy is massage. It is used to treat injuries, relieve pain, and promote relaxation.

The use of alternative therapies in the United States has grown rapidly in recent years. In response to this trend, the National Institutes of Health established an Office of Alternative Medicine in 1992. Six years later, this expanded to become the National Center for Complementary and Alternative Medicine (NCCAM). It funds and coordinates research to evaluate the benefits and risks of alternative therapies.

The NCCAM classifies alternative therapies into five categories: mind-body interventions, biologically based therapies, alternative medical systems, manipulative and body-based methods, and energy therapies.

Mind-body interventions use techniques thought to enhance the mind's ability to affect bodily function and symptoms. One of the more common is meditation, which can help prevent or relieve stress-related illness by helping a person become more relaxed.

Biologically based therapies use substances found in nature, including certain foods, herbs, and nutritional supplements. These therapies—such as the use of vitamin C as a cold remedy—are considered alternative when their health benefits have not been proven by scientific study.

Alternative medical systems are based on complete systems of theory and practice. One example is traditional Chinese medicine, which has been practiced since ancient times and includes therapies such as acupuncture.

Manipulative and body-based methods involve moving or manipulating parts of the body to treat injuries or relieve pain. For example, chiropractors adjust the spine, joints, and muscles, and massage therapists manipulate muscle and connective tissue.

There are two main types of **energy therapies**. The first type, called biofield therapy, is thought to manipulate the energy that some believe surrounds or enters our bodies. One well-known biofield therapy is Reiki. It is based on the belief that when spiritual energy is channeled through a Reiki practitioner, one's spirit is healed. This, in turn, is said to heal the body.

Another type of energy therapy is believed to draw on the Earth's electromagnetic fields for healing. One example is magnet therapy, which consists of placing magnets on or near the body. Advocates claim that this has many benefits, including pain relief.

Although many kinds of treatments can be called alternative, not all are worthwhile. While some may be helpful, others may be harmful, especially when combined with other therapies or medications. Therefore, anyone considering an alternative therapy should discuss it with a physician.

Reviewed by CHRIS THOMSEN
National Center for Complementary and Alternative Medicine

ALUMINUM

In the 1800's, people already knew that aluminum was the most abundant metal in the Earth's crust. They had even been able to extract the bluish white metal from its ores. But the cost of refining it was still so high that Emperor Napoleon III of France still had his finest dinner spoons made of it in the 1860's. Metallurgists were in the position of having discovered a great treasure house of extremely useful metal without having found the key that would unlock it. When a way was found to refine the metal cheaply in 1886, aluminum became an important part of nearly every industry in the world.

Aluminum makes up between 7 and 8 percent of the Earth's crust. Although it is so abundant, its existence was not suspected for a long time. This is because it is never found in nature as a pure metal but is combined with other chemical elements in compounds that are very hard to break down.

Aluminum compounds are found in many minerals, and all clay contains aluminum. Many of the most beautiful precious stones are basically nothing but colored aluminum compounds. Rubies and sapphires, for example, are aluminum oxide with traces of other elements. Emeralds contain aluminum along with beryllium, chromium and silicon.

The most important ore of aluminum is bauxite, a type of clay. It generally contains from 40 to 60 percent aluminum oxide.

The existence of aluminum was predicted in 1808 by the English scientist Sir Humphry Davy. However, he was unable to solve the problem of extracting the metal from its ore. In 1825 the Danish scientist H. C. Oersted produced the first aluminum metal the world had ever seen—but in an amount too small even to conduct experiments. The German scientist Friedrich Wöhler succeeded in extracting aluminum in powder form in 1845 and made the first discoveries about aluminum's properties.

Aluminum's career as a luxury item ended in 1886 with the simultaneous discoveries of Charles M. Hall in the United States and Paul Héroult in France. The two men had independently hit upon the same solution to the problem of converting aluminum ore into the metal aluminum cheaply enough for everyday use.

The Hall-Héroult process is basically the same one used in today's two-step process of aluminum refining. Bauxite ore is refined to produce aluminum oxide, a white powder, which is also called alumina. Alumina in turn must be further processed to produce aluminum. It was this second step that held back aluminum production for so many years.

Hall and Héroult found that alumina could be dissolved in molten cryolite, an icy-looking mineral found primarily in Greenland, and then broken down by passing an electric current through the molten mixture. The current separates the alumina into aluminum and oxygen. The aluminum settles at the bottom of the cell and is drawn off. More alumina is added to keep the process going. About 2 pounds (0.9 kilogram) of alumina are needed to make 1 pound (0.45 kilogram) of aluminum metal.

Aluminum's many characteristics combine to make it suitable for many products. An important characteristic is its light weight. Aluminum weighs two thirds less than such common metals as iron, copper, nickel, or zinc. Its lightness makes aluminum useful in the manufacture of building materials, bus and truck bodies, and automotive and airplane parts. About 90 percent of the total weight of a typical four-engine aircraft is aluminum.

Aluminum also conducts electricity well. For this reason it has replaced copper for high-voltage electric transmission lines. Since it is lighter than copper, electric lines of aluminum need fewer supporting towers.

Because it is a good conductor of heat, aluminum makes good cooking utensils. If just one edge of an aluminum pan is heated, the heat will spread evenly through the pan. With

FACTS ABOUT ALUMINUM

CHEMICAL SYMBOL: Al

ATOMIC WEIGHT: 26.98

SPECIFIC GRAVITY: 2.7 (a little more than 2½ times as heavy as water).

COLOR: silvery white with a bluish tinge.

PROPERTIES: soft and easily shaped; resists corrosion; nonmagnetic; good conductor of heat and electricity; forms compounds that are hard to break down.

OCCURRENCE: third most abundant element in the Earth's crust (after oxygen and silicon); most abundant metal in the Earth's crust.

CHIEF ORE: bauxite.

CHIEF SOURCES: Australia, Guinea, Jamaica, Brazil, Russia.

In England and certain other countries, aluminum is called aluminium.

many other metals, "hot spots" that cause food to stick and burn may form.

Besides being a good conductor of heat, aluminum is also a good insulator. This is not as confusing as it seems. The metal's shiny surface reflects heat rays away.

Why doesn't aluminum rust? It would seem that aluminum's quickness to react with the oxygen in the air would make it subject to corrosion. But actually it is this very quickness to react with oxygen that protects aluminum against corrosion. When aluminum is exposed to the air, it immediately combines with some of the oxygen to form a thin, tough, colorless film that protects the metal against further chemical action and thus prevents rusting.

Aluminum also stands up well against most acids, but it is attacked by strong solutions of alkalies, such as lye and ammonia, and of salts, including common table salt. Salt solutions cause pitting and form a dull film on the metal. Aluminum boats that are used in salt water need a protective coating, usually of clear plastic. Aluminum cooking vessels do not usually show this pitting and dulling because in most homes they are shined with abrasive pads after use.

Although aluminum is naturally light and flexible, it is not especially strong for a metal. There are two ways to increase its strength. One is by cold-working (hammering or rolling the metal at room temperature). This compresses the metal and makes it harder. When very high strength is needed, the other method—alloying—must be used.

The metals most frequently alloyed with aluminum are copper, manganese, nickel, magnesium, zinc, iron, and silicon. Because of its higher strength, most of the aluminum used for machine parts and for structural parts in airplanes, automobiles, and buildings is in the form of alloys.

To help ensure a sufficient supply of aluminum in the future, the recycling, or reusing, of aluminum products such as soft-drink cans has become a major industry. In addition to conserving ore supplies, recycling uses much less energy than does refining.

ROBERT E. ABBOTT
Senior Associate Editor
Product Engineering magazine

ALVAREZ, LUIS WALTER (1911–1988)

Luis Walter Alvarez is known for his research on subatomic particles—the tiny particles of matter that make up the atom. Alvarez's research improved our understanding of the forces that hold together the **nucleus**, or center, of the atom. These forces are considered to be among the strongest in the universe.

Alvarez was born on June 13, 1911, in San Francisco, California. He studied physics at the University of Chicago, from which he received his Ph.D. in 1936. He then went on to become a professor of physics at the University of California at Berkeley.

In 1941, the United States entered World War II. Many scientists wanted to help the war effort, and Alvarez developed a type of radar system that was used to locate bombing targets, and a ground-controlled approach radar system that was used to land aircraft in bad weather. In 1943, Alvarez was asked to join the team of scientists at Los Alamos Scientific Laboratory in New Mexico that was developing the atomic bomb.

After the war, Alvarez returned to his study of the atom. With several associates at the University of California, he developed the liquid-hydrogen **bubble chamber**, which he used to identify many subatomic particles. In 1968, he won the Nobel Prize in physics for this research.

In 1980, he helped publicize the theory of his son, the geologist Walter Alvarez, that a large asteroid collision with the Earth may have led to the extinction of the dinosaurs. This theory is now widely accepted.

Alvarez died on September 1, 1988, in Berkeley, California.

RACHEL KRANZ
Editor, Biographies
The Young Adult Reader's Adviser

See also ATOMS.

ALZHEIMER'S DISEASE

Alzheimer's disease (AD) is a progressive brain disorder that causes disorientation, personality changes, and an increasingly severe decline in memory, thinking, and language skills. First described in 1906 by German physician Alois Alzheimer, it is the most common cause of dementia (the loss of mental abilities).

In the United States, an estimated 4.5 million people are thought to have AD. At least 95 percent of these people have a form called late-onset AD, which occurs mainly in those aged 65 and older. Although the risk of late-onset AD increases with age—nearly half of people 85 and older have it—it is not considered a normal consequence of aging.

Another, less common form of the disease is called early-onset AD. It typically affects people between the ages of 30 and 60 and accounts for less than 5 percent of all cases. It is usually inherited and has been linked to mutations in certain genes.

Early symptoms of Alzheimer's disease usually include forgetfulness, difficulty finding the right words for things, and subtle personality changes. Since these symptoms may be similar to normal signs of aging, they are often missed. As the disease progresses, however, memory declines even further. A person may routinely forget familiar names and faces and may become confused when driving a car or handling money. He or she may have trouble understanding what is being said and may appear to have no interest in others. Mood swings are also common, as is increasingly poor judgment. For example, a person with Alzheimer's disease may wear many layers of clothing on a hot day or not enough clothes on a cold day.

During the later stages of the disease, people become even more impaired—mentally and physically. They become bedridden and unable to care for themselves. This places them at greater risk for other life-threatening illnesses such as pneumonia. Death usually occurs when deterioration of the brain causes essential body functions to fail.

The course of the disease varies. The time from the appearance of symptoms to death ranges from three to twenty years. The average duration is eight years. Early-onset AD tends to progress more rapidly.

Causes. The brains of people with AD have been found to have two specific types of abnormal structures. Although these structures are the physical evidence of AD, it is still not known whether they are the primary cause of damage to the brain. Most experts agree that it is probably a complex set of genetic and nongenetic factors, rather than a single cause, that triggers the disease process. Except for the genetic mutations associated with early-onset AD, the only well-established risk factors are increasing age, a family history of the disease, and one gene that increases the risk of late-onset AD. Researchers have also found that the risk factors for heart disease, such as high blood pressure, may also increase the risk for AD. There is also evidence that remaining mentally active may be associated with a lower risk.

Diagnosis and Treatment. There is no single test to diagnose AD—it is not yet possible to detect the abnormal structures in the brain while the person is still alive. Doctors therefore make a diagnosis of "possible" or "probable" AD based on tests that assess memory and thinking skills. A physical exam is also performed to exclude other possible reasons for the person's symptoms.

Although scientists are working to develop drugs that prevent or slow the progression of AD, it still has no cure. However, some drugs may temporarily improve or stabilize memory or thinking skills, or slow their rate of decline. Doctors may also prescribe medications to treat symptoms, such as depression and insomnia, that often affect people with AD. Such drug therapies, as well as various care strategies, can make AD patients more comfortable and improve their quality of life.

Impact. A diagnosis of AD is usually very difficult for patients and their families. Often, people with AD are able to live at home and are cared for by a spouse or other family member. But as the disease progresses, the physical and emotional demands of home care may become too much for the family. In such cases, the patient must be placed in an extended-care facility. Support and information for AD patients and their families is available from organizations such as the Alzheimer's Association and from various community groups.

Alzheimer's Association

See also AGING; OLD AGE.

AMAZON RIVER

The Amazon is South America's most important river and the second longest river in the world. Only the Nile, in Africa, is longer. The Amazon carries more water than the Mississippi, the Yangtze (or Chang, the longest river in China), and the Nile together. In a single second the Amazon pours more than 55 million gallons (200,000 cubic meters) of water into the Atlantic Ocean. This tremendous flow is caused by heavy tropical rains and melting snow in the Andes mountains. The Amazon's huge drainage basin—the world's largest—covers more than one third of the South American continent.

The River's Course. The Amazon is about 3,900 miles (6,280 kilometers) long. It begins high in the snow-fed Andean lakes of Peru, tumbles rapidly down the mountains, and then flows eastward across the low plains of Brazil before emptying into the Atlantic Ocean. On its journey the Amazon gathers additional water from hundreds of tributaries, some are more than 1,240 miles (2,000 kilometers) in length. These include the Rio Negro and the Japurá, Juruá, Purus, Madeira, Tapajós, and Xingu rivers. In some places the river is so wide that one cannot see the opposite shore. During the rainy season the river frequently overflows its banks and floods the surrounding lowland areas.

The Amazon basin is only sparsely populated. Most of its inhabitants live along the course of the great river, which is their chief means of transportation.

Above: Timber is one of the Amazon basin's most valuable resources. The region also has deposits of gold, bauxite (aluminum ore), copper, tin, and other minerals. *Right:* Large oceangoing ships can travel up the Amazon for about 1,000 miles (1,610 kilometers), as far as the Brazilian river port of Manaus.

Exploration. In 1541 a Spaniard, Francisco de Orellana, became the first European to descend the Amazon. But while exploring the river, he and his group barely escaped an attack by female Indian warriors. Orellana named the river after the women, whom he believed were descended from the Amazons—a band of women warriors made famous in Greek mythology.

Resources and Development. Much of the sparsely populated Amazon basin is covered with some of the world's densest rain forests, a source of valuable timber. There are rich deposits of gold, bauxite (aluminum ore), copper, tin, manganese, and iron ore. Several highways have been built, but the river remains a major form of transportation. Oceangoing ships can travel upstream about 1,000 miles (1,609 kilometers) to Manaus, in Brazil. Smaller vessels travel as far as the port of Iquitos, in Peru.

The Amazon basin has been called one of the Earth's last frontiers. The eight countries of the Amazon basin—Bolivia, Brazil, Colombia, Ecuador, Guyana, Peru, Suriname, and Venezuela—signed the Treaty of Amazon Cooperation in 1978. They agreed to jointly develop and share the great wealth of the region. However, because the Amazon basin is home to unique varieties of plants and animals, many scientists have opposed large-scale development of the area.

In 2000, scientists finally confirmed the long-disputed source of the Amazon. It starts as the Nevado Mismi, a stream in southern Peru.

Reviewed by DANIEL JACOBSON
Michigan State University

AMERICAN COLONIES. See THIRTEEN AMERICAN COLONIES.

AMBULANCES

An ambulance is a specially equipped vehicle that rapidly transports sick or injured people to a hospital. Most often, it is a van or truck with flashing lights and sirens that allow it to move rapidly through traffic. But helicopters and airplanes are also used as ambulances, usually to transport patients from remote areas or over very long distances.

Ambulances have been used in the United States since the late 1800's. Early ambulances—first horse-drawn and later motorized—were minimally equipped, and their drivers were not trained to provide more than basic first aid. In 1966 federal standards were established for ambulances and emergency medical workers. Today ambulances are equipped and staffed to provide a range of emergency medical services.

All ambulances carry basic equipment such as stretchers, splints, bandages, and oxygen. Other supplies may include a defibrillator, which delivers an electrical shock to restart a patient's heart, and intravenous (IV) equipment, which delivers fluid and medicine through a vein in the arm or hand.

Ambulance workers, many of whom are volunteers, include emergency medical technicians (EMT's) and paramedics. EMT's are trained to provide basic life support: administering oxygen, performing cardiopulmonary resuscitation (CPR), bandaging wounds, and splinting broken bones. Paramedics are trained to provide advanced life support, such as using machines to monitor a patient's heartbeat and administering lifesaving medications. Ambulances may also be staffed by specially trained nurses. Others important to the Emergency Medical Services (EMS) system are dispatchers, who answer calls and send ambulances to the right locations, and the medical director, a doctor who oversees the EMS system.

In most parts of the United States, an ambulance can be called by dialing 911 or the local emergency number.

LAUREN SIMON OSTROW
CHARLOTTE OSTROW
EMS Best Practices, Inc.

AMERICAN CIVIL LIBERTIES UNION (ACLU)

The American Civil Liberties Union (ACLU) is an organization dedicated to protecting U.S. constitutional rights and freedoms. The ACLU works in courts, legislatures, and communities to protect freedom of speech and other freedoms guaranteed by the Bill of Rights. It works to preserve principles such as the right to equal protection under the law, the right to due process (fair treatment of persons accused of a crime), and the right to privacy.

The ACLU handles thousands of court cases each year, providing lawyers and legal advice in cases involving civil liberties. It seeks to ensure rights for groups that have been traditionally denied them, including minorities, women, and the poor.

The ACLU also lobbies Congress and testifies before Congressional committees. And it informs the public by conducting educational programs and by publishing pamphlets and other materials.

The ACLU was founded in 1920. Since then it has been involved in many important—and often controversial—cases. One of the most famous was the 1925 Scopes trial, popularly known as the monkey trial, in which the ACLU helped challenge a Tennessee law that banned the teaching of evolution. The ACLU has also supported the right of unions to organize, protested the internment of Japanese Americans during World War II, defended the right of American Nazis to demonstrate, challenged prayer in public schools, and defended women's reproductive rights.

The ACLU is nonprofit and nonpartisan (not affiliated with any political party). It has some 400,000 members, and chapters and affiliates in every state. Policy is set by a national board. The ACLU receives no government funding. Its work is financed by member dues and contributions and grants.

ANTHONY D. ROMERO
Executive Director
American Civil Liberties Union

AMERICAN COLONIES. See THIRTEEN AMERICAN COLONIES.

AMERICAN INDIAN MOVEMENT (AIM)

The American Indian Movement (AIM) is an activist group founded in 1968 in Minneapolis, Minnesota. Originally formed to help American Indians fight poverty and police discrimination in Minneapolis and St. Paul, it rapidly became a national civil rights organization. Today it is called the American Indian Movement Grand Governing Council.

AIM's objective has been to help Indians achieve economic independence through better education and health care, greater job opportunities, and improved legal representation. It has also advocated a return to traditional spiritual and cultural practices. It established "survival schools" for Indian children living in urban areas.

AIM has fought for the right of Indians to govern themselves within their reservations. It has called for reorganization of the U.S. Bureau of Indian Affairs (BIA) to eliminate what it considers excessive government control. It has also demanded international recognition of Native American treaty rights, which resulted in the 1977 International Indian Treaty Conference with the United Nations in Geneva, Switzerland.

Although many tribal peoples support AIM, some oppose the organization, which has been accused of provoking confrontations to achieve its objectives. These included a march on Washington protesting treaty violations in 1972 and a takeover of the South Dakota village of Wounded Knee in 1973. At Wounded Knee, the site of the last major clash between federal troops and American Indians, AIM demands included a review of broken treaties between the Native Americans and the federal government.

In 1978, AIM led the "Longest Walk" from San Francisco to Washington to focus attention on Native American concerns. More recently, it has protested the use of Indian caricatures as mascots for sports teams.

Reviewed by Clyde H. Bellecourt
National Executive Director
American Indian Movement
Grand Governing Council

AMERICAN LEGION

The American Legion is the largest and most politically powerful veterans' group in the world. The Legion has chapters in all 50 states as well as in Washington, D.C., Puerto Rico, France, Mexico, and the Philippines.

Membership in the American Legion is open to any man or woman who has served in any branch of the American armed forces during a period of armed conflict. Members of local posts elect delegates to state and national conventions, where policies are decided. The National Executive Committee, with headquarters in Indianapolis, Indiana, and offices in Washington, D.C., is the governing body.

The American Legion is a major advocate of programs to benefit veterans and their survivors. It conducts extensive lobbying and public education programs to promote national defense and security, including the maintenance of a strong and modernized military. It also works to promote patriotism, respect for the flag, and the preservation of traditional American values.

The American Legion sponsors a number of programs to benefit the welfare and development of children. In addition to educational programs in schools, it sponsors Boy Scout troops, the American Legion baseball program, an annual National Oratorical Contest, and the Boys' State and Girls' State programs, which teach boys and girls how local and state governments work. The Legion also sponsors various scholarship programs.

The American Legion was formed in Paris, France, in 1919 by American veterans of World War I to promote the memory of their wartime service, to ensure proper medical treatment and compensation for wounded comrades, and to promote American patriotism. It was formally incorporated by Congress on September 16, 1919. It played a key role in the establishment of the Veterans Administration in 1930 and the passage of the GI Bill in 1944. Today there are about 3 million members worldwide.

Charles R. Shrader
Independent Scholar

AMERICAN LITERATURE

From the beginning, the literature of America has been created by the many voices of its diverse people. Before the Europeans came to settle in the 1500's and 1600's, the many tribes of Native Americans created a rich oral heritage of songs, chants, and tales. With the arrival of white settlers, America's formal literature began: first in travel books, then in religious writing, finally in the poems, novels, and plays that would eventually record and reflect America's national development.

Over the past four centuries, as the country expanded politically and economically, literature has expressed the aspirations and achievements of all the races and creeds that make up the nation. What began as a small and elite literary culture on the eastern seaboard has grown to encompass a sprawling modern society. In spite of their differences, almost all Americans have shared a commitment to their country's democratic possibilities and a fascination with the meaning of American identity; these two themes have been recurrent topics in American literature.

THE COLONIAL EXPERIENCE

Because the Indians did not practice writing, their ancient traditional material has not survived in its original form. (See feature, Indian Art and Culture, on this page.) It was left to the white explorers and colonists, who brought books and writing with them from England, France, and Spain, to begin the written record that has become American literature.

Promotional Literature

European settlers came to the New World for many reasons. Some were seeking adventure or commercial profit, while others were fleeing religious persecution. All these men and women were urged on by a literature of exploration and promotion—the earliest American advertising—which pictured the New World as a fruitful garden, a land overflowing with abundance and opportunity. Captain John Smith's attractive account of Virginia (1608) was the first book written in English in America, and his *Description of New England* followed several years later. Other writers, such as Francis Higginson, also produced books, pamphlets, and poems celebrating the golden promise of America.

Throughout the first one hundred years of English settlement, beginning with Jamestown in 1607, most of the literary achievement of the colonies was the work of New England's Puritans. The Puritans were the best educated of the English colonists and the most firmly committed to literary activity. It was the Puritan settlers of Massachusetts who founded the colonies' first institute of higher learning. Harvard College (now Harvard University) was founded in 1636, just a few years after the colony itself was established. The first printing press was set up at Harvard in 1639, and the first book was published there the following year.

Indian Art and Culture

Indians lived on the American continent for hundreds of years before European settlers began to arrive in the 1500's and 1600's. They created a rich oral literature: songs, chants, fables, and stories. Because of language differences, it is hard for English-speaking readers to appreciate Indian literature. However, the two songs printed here in translation suggest the subtle power of the originals:

Love Song
A loon I thought it was
But it was
My love's
Splashing oar.
(Chippewa)

Song of Failure
A wolf
I considered myself,
But the owls are hooting
And the night
I fear.
(Teton Sioux)

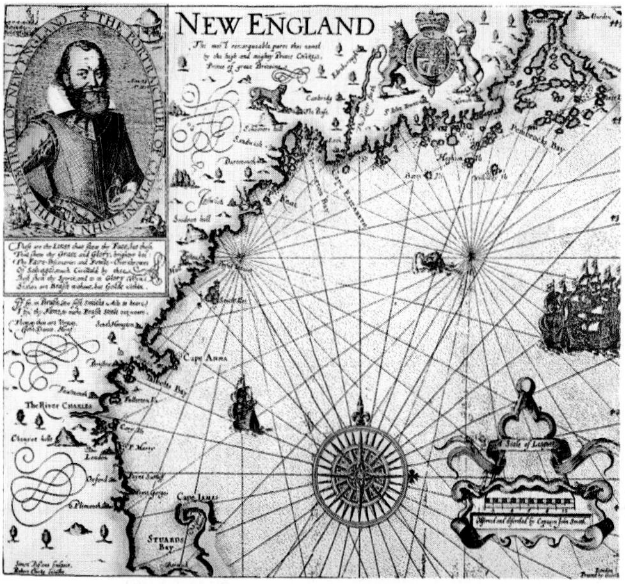

A portrait of English explorer John Smith and a map of the Massachusetts coastline appeared in his *Description of New England*, published in 1616.

Puritan Prose Writing

In their own opinion, the most valuable possession that Puritan men and women brought with them from England was their religion. Above all, they placed their faith in the Bible, which they believed contained the revealed word of God. At the center of their worship, they wanted to hear the Bible read and interpreted. The preacher was thus a leading figure in the community, and the sermons that were preached in Puritan meetinghouses became the first real literary texts produced in the English-speaking New World. The sermons followed a standard format, in which a phrase from the Bible was read and then explained at great length—some sermons went on for more than two hours. The most famous of all the Puritan preachers was Jonathan Edwards, who served as minister of Northampton, Massachusetts, for 24 years. He wrote important philosophical books, including *The Freedom of the Will* (1754), but he is best remembered for a sermon he preached in 1741, "Sinners in the Hands of an Angry God."

Religion was also the major theme of other Puritan writing, including the thousands of diaries produced by men and women alike. Their deep concern with sin and salvation led the Puritans into a habit of daily spiritual examination, which they recorded in their diaries. Part of the Puritan influence on later American literature was this preoccupation with the self. Thomas Shepard, Michael Wigglesworth, and many other Puritan diarists filled daily journals with the details of each day's religious striving. Over and over, they return to a few simple but profound themes: God's sovereign power and the complete dependence of each person on God's mysterious choices.

Puritan minister Jonathan Edwards wrote on religious and philosophical subjects. He is most famous for his sermon "Sinners in the Hands of an Angry God," which he preached to his congregation in 1741. It expressed the Puritan belief that eternal torment awaited sinners after death.

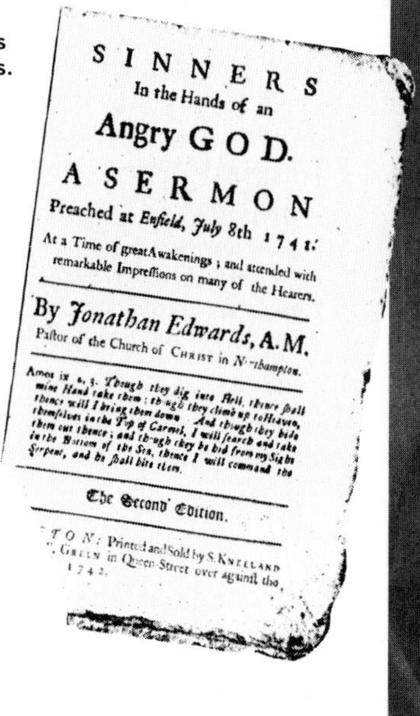
SINNERS
In the Hands of an
Angry GOD.
A SERMON
Preached at Enfield, July 8th 1741.
At a Time of great Awakenings; and attended with remarkable Impressions on many of the Hearers.
By Jonathan Edwards, A. M.
Pastor of the Church of CHRIST in Northampton.
The Second Edition.

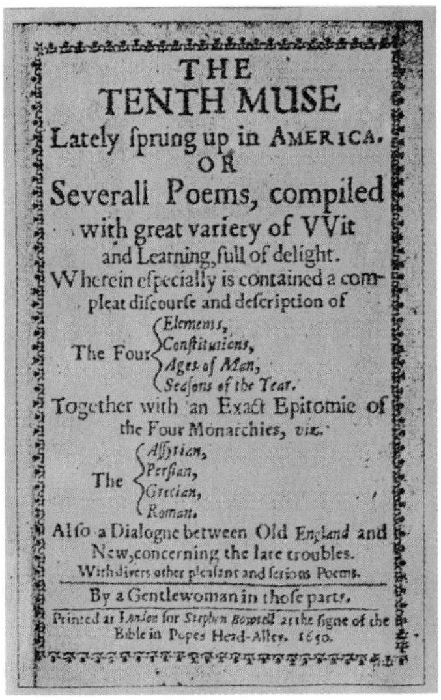
THE
TENTH MUSE
Lately ſpring up in AMERICA.
OR
Severall Poems, compiled
with great variety of VVit
and Learning, full of delight.
Wherein eſpecially is contained a com-
pleat diſcourſe and deſcription of
The Four *Elements*, *Conſtitutions*, *Ages of Man*, *Seaſons of the Year*.
Together with an Exact Epitomie of
the Four Monarchies, viz.
The *Aſſyrian*, *Perſian*, *Grecian*, *Roman*.
Alſo a Dialogue between Old England and
New, concerning the late troubles.
With divers other pleaſant and ſerious Poems.
By a Gentlewoman in thoſe parts.
Printed at London for Stephen Bowtell at the ſigne of the
Bible in Popes Head-Alley. 1650.

***The Tenth Muse*, a collection of poems by New England writer Anne Bradstreet, won praise in the American colonies and in England when it was published in 1650.**

Many of the Puritan diaries are grim and relentless, shrill warnings against any sort of human pleasure. At least one, however, written by Samuel Sewall, reveals a more modern point of view. While still respectful of Puritan values, the diary also introduces newer ideas of happiness and self-fulfillment. Sewall was a prosperous Massachusetts merchant whose long life spanned the end of the 1600's and the early decades of the 1700's. He presided over the Salem witchcraft trials (and later apologized for sentencing convicted "witches" to hang), and he wrote the first antislavery pamphlet in America, *The Selling of Joseph* (1700). Sewall's diary is one of the major works of early American literature. The daily entries provide a vivid self-portrait as well as a valuable record of daily life in colonial New England.

Along with their sermons and diaries, the Puritans also produced a large number of histories. These, too, are important literary texts. Like all the other writing of the Puritans, their histories were anchored in religious belief. *Of Plymouth Plantation* (1630–50), by William Bradford, *The Wonder-Working Providence of Sion's Savior in New England* (1653), by Edward Johnson, and *Magnalia Christi Americana* ("Christ's Great Deeds in America"; 1702), by Cotton Mather, all shared a God-centered view of history. The Puritan historians believed that human events acted out a divine plan—and they believed that they and their fellow Christians were at the heart of that plan.

Puritan Poetry

The men and women of colonial New England also wrote a great deal of poetry, though most of it was conventional and dull. Only a few Puritan poets rose above mediocrity, and only two, Anne Bradstreet and Edward Taylor, achieved real distinction.

Anne Bradstreet immigrated to New England with her husband in 1630 and lived the rest of her life in Massachusetts. She bore eight children and supervised a large, relatively prosperous household. Because she was a woman, she faced opposition as a writer, but her book, *The Tenth Muse, Lately Sprung Up in America* (1650), was the first volume of poems published by a resident of the New World. She wrote a number of long, formal epics. Her best poems, however, are briefer and more personal verses on her family and her daily domestic obligations. She wrote love poems to her husband, as well as other poems that celebrated the births and mourned the deaths of her children and grandchildren.

For 58 years, from 1671 until the end of his life, Edward Taylor served as minister of the frontier town of Westfield, Massachusetts. Nearly all his poems are closely connected to his preaching and devotions; more than two hundred, called *Meditations*, were written in response to the same biblical texts on which he was preaching. Taken as a group, they are among the most remarkable verse sequences in American literature. They draw on familiar religious traditions, combining the images of the Bible with the language of everyday colonial life. They tell of the encounter between God and the individual soul, often achieving great emotional power through the use of elaborate metaphors and dramatic action.

Southern Writing

Very little significant literature appeared in the South during the 1600's and 1700's. Ebenezer Cooke wrote a funny poem, "The Sot-Weed Factor" (1708), a savage attack on America's rude wilderness conditions. A more important text is the diary of William Byrd II, a wealthy Virginia planter who owned the largest library in the colonies and thought of himself as simply a transplanted Englishman. His diary, unlike those written by the Puritans, contains little reference to God or salvation. Rather, Byrd's diary records his everyday routine: what time he got up, what he ate and read, the journeys he took. Byrd's daily entries provide glimpses into middle-class life in Virginia, from farming practices to relations between masters and slaves.

Benjamin Franklin

By the late 1700's, America's several colonies had existed as dependencies of England for almost two hundred years. America was growing rapidly in population and economic importance, but its literary culture lagged behind. The first American whose work and writing received international recognition was Benjamin Franklin. A scientist, diplomat, businessman, and writer, he rose to success from humble beginnings and seemed to embody the American dream of opportunity.

Franklin's writing, from the humorous "Dogood Papers" (1722) he published as a teenager, through the hugely popular *Poor Richard's Almanac* (1733–38), is always marked by shrewd common sense and independent thought. His *Autobiography,* written between 1771 and 1788, is one of the landmarks of American literature. Franklin's self-portrait, written in a strong, straightforward style, captures the accents of real speech. That style is his chief legacy to the nation's literary tradition.

Political Writing

As America moved toward independence, literature reflected the changing political situation. Some of the most important writing of this period was produced in support of revo-

American Literature 1700–1900

This time line follows the progress of American literature from colonial days to the dawn of the modern era. The writing produced during those 200 years reflects the sweeping changes that took place as the United States transformed from a rural society of villages and small towns into a powerful industrialized nation. Biographies of the writers listed on the time line can be found in the appropriate volumes of this encyclopedia.

Benjamin Franklin

1733 First edition of *Poor Richard's Almanac* by Benjamin Franklin (1706–90)

1776 *Common Sense* by Thomas Paine (1737–1809)

1819–20 *The Sketch Book* by Washington Irving (1783–1859)

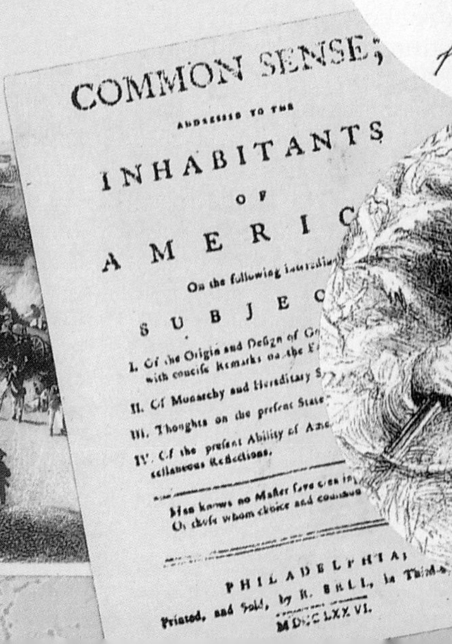

Rip Van Winkle

lution. Thomas Paine's *Common Sense,* published on the eve of the Revolutionary War in early 1776, sold more than 100,000 copies in two months and helped to lead the nation toward its demands for independence. The letters of men and women like John and Abigail Adams, Thomas Jefferson, and James Madison eloquently recorded a dangerous and pivotal period in history.

Out of the continuous discussion and debate emerged the Declaration of Independence and the Constitution, two documents of unequaled importance in political history, which have also earned a high place in American literature. The Declaration, which was officially submitted by a committee, was in fact mostly the work of one man, Thomas Jefferson. Although he was a southern aristocrat and slaveholder, Jefferson established himself as one of the nation's most articulate domestic voices. His library of about six thousand volumes served as the foundation of the Library of Congress, and his writings and building designs strongly influenced America's taste in architecture. His *Notes on the State of Virginia* (1784) made important contributions to American natural science.

Early Black Writing

The Constitution demonstrated the limits as well as the strengths of American democracy. Women were denied the vote, and black

1826 *The Last of the Mohicans* by James Fenimore Cooper (1789–1851)

1828 *American Dictionary of the English Language* by Noah Webster (1758–1843)

1832 *Poems* by William Cullen Bryant (1794–1878)

1836 *Nature* by Ralph Waldo Emerson (1803–82)

1840 *Tales of the Grotesque and Arabesque* by Edgar Allan Poe (1809–49)

1845 *Narrative of the Life of Frederick Douglass* by Frederick Douglass (1817–95)

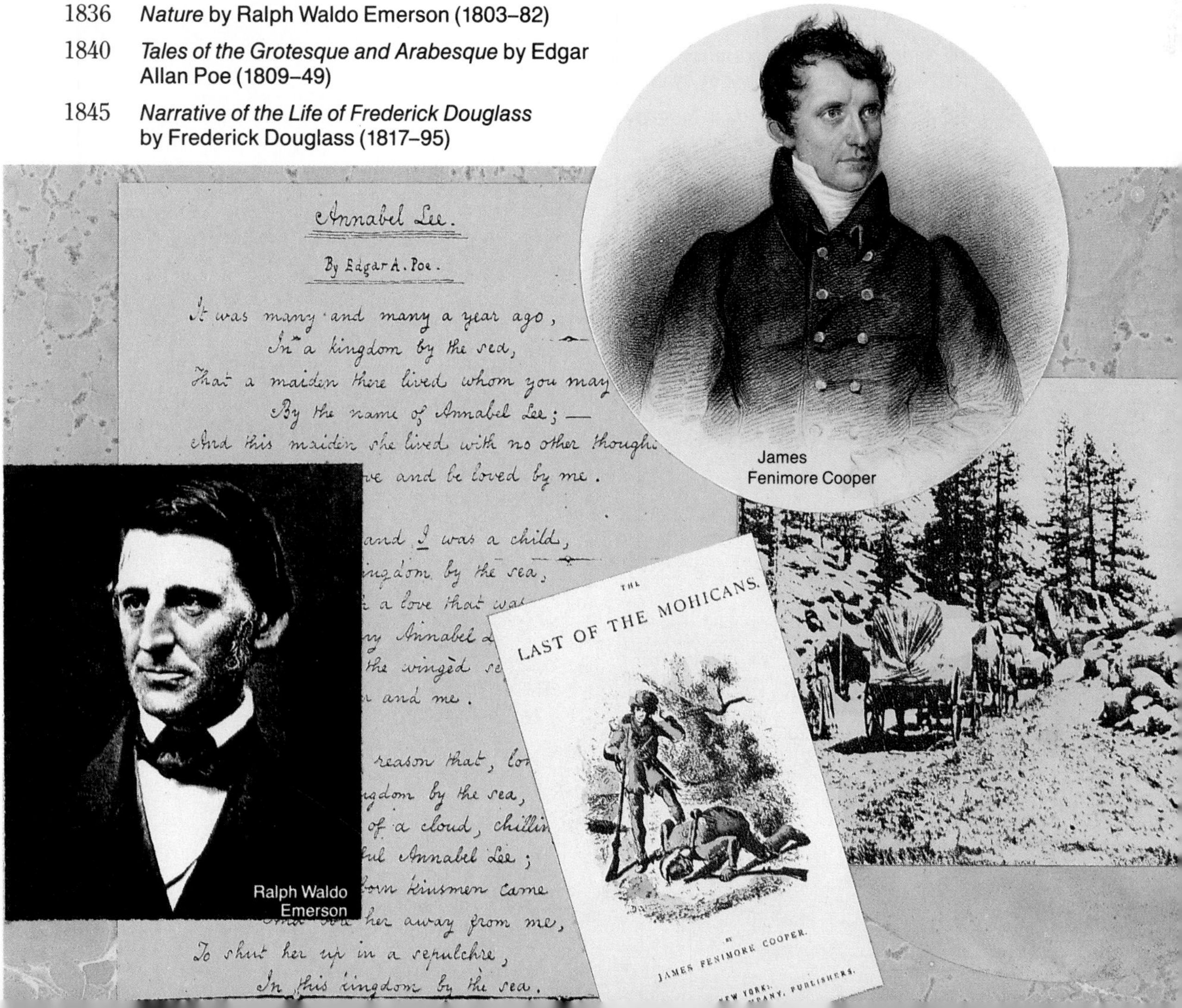

James Fenimore Cooper

Ralph Waldo Emerson

Americans were defined as property rather than human beings. Slavery had flourished from the earliest colonial settlements: the first slave ship arrived in Virginia in 1619, the year before the *Mayflower* brought the Pilgrims to Plymouth. Slavery was supported by the Constitution, but the debate over the place of black people would occupy an increasingly central role in the debate over the nation's identity throughout the 1800's and 1900's.

Much of African-American culture mingled the African tribal heritage with artistic forms adapted from white European traditions. Phillis Wheatley, the only black writer who gained national recognition in the colonial years, accepted a cooperative relationship to white society and religion. Her volume, *Poems on Various Occasions*, published in 1773, contains verse that is conventional in style and safely patriotic and Christian in sentiment.

An altogether different tone can be found in the work of Olaudah Equiano, known as Gustavus Vassa. Taken from Africa and enslaved as a child, Equiano eventually earned his freedom and became a leading figure in the abolition movement. His life story, *The Interesting Narrative of the Life of Olaudah Equiano, or Gustavus Vassa, the African* (1789), is an early and important black autobiography. The book contains unforgettable scenes that reveal the cruelty of slavery and the distance that still separated America's democratic ideals from

1850 *The Scarlet Letter* by Nathaniel Hawthorne (1804–64)

1851 *Moby-Dick* by Herman Melville (1819–91)

1852 *Uncle Tom's Cabin* by Harriet Beecher Stowe (1811–96)

1854 *Walden* by Henry David Thoreau (1817–62)

1855 *The Song of Hiawatha* by Henry Wadsworth Longfellow (1807–82); *Leaves of Grass* by Walt Whitman (1819–92)

1858 *The Autocrat of the Breakfast Table* by Oliver Wendell Holmes (1809–94)

reality. (See feature, Slave Narratives, on the following page.)

Literary Nationalists

In the years before and after the Revolution, writers and intellectuals tried to define America's cultural identity. In *Letters from an American Farmer* (1782), St. John de Crevecoeur asked, "What is an American?," and answered his own question by appealing to "a new race of men." One of the busiest groups of literary nationalists in the late 1700's was a band of New England poets and essayists known as the Connecticut (or Hartford) Wits. These men, including such figures as Timothy Dwight, Lemuel Hopkins, and painter John Trumbull, produced satires, epics, and hymns to the New World landscape.

Joel Barlow, one of the youngest members of this group, was more radical in politics and more talented as a writer. He believed that his most important work was *The Columbiad* (1807), a long and tedious narrative in couplets that celebrates American history from the time of Columbus. In fact, modern readers find the best of Barlow's many poems to be *The Hasty Pudding* (1793), a mock-epic in praise of the cornmeal mush eaten in farmhouses all across the nation. In a series of humorous scenes, Barlow contrasts America's plain but wholesome food with the tasteless delicacies favored in Europe.

1866 *Snow-Bound* by John Greenleaf Whittier (1807–92)

1868–69 *Little Women* by Louisa May Alcott (1832–88)

1884 *Adventures of Huckleberry Finn* by Mark Twain (1835–1910)

1890 *Poems* by Emily Dickinson (1830–86)

1895 *The Red Badge of Courage* by Stephen Crane (1871–1900)

1903 *The Ambassadors* by Henry James (1843–1916)

Huckleberry Finn

John Greenleaf Whittier

Emily Dickinson

Slave Narratives

Autobiographies written by ex-slaves made a major contribution both to the politics and the literature of the 1800's. No books told more about the reality of the slave system than the personal narratives of such men and women as Moses Roper and Harriet Jacobs. The most famous of these autobiographies was written by Frederick Douglass (pictured), who was also the leading figure in the black abolitionist movement before the Civil War. Douglass' *Narrative* (1845) is the eloquent story of his own successful quest for freedom. It inspired thousands of Americans, white as well as black, to join together to demand the end of slavery.

Such comparisons were common in the early years of the Republic. They form the entire theme of *The Contrast,* a play that Royall Tyler wrote and staged in 1784. It was the first significant play written in America and the first to be professionally produced.

Early Fiction

The Power of Sympathy (1789), by William Hill Brown, is usually identified as the first American novel. It was written in imitation of English sentimental fiction of the time. So, too, were the works of other writers in the early Republic. *Charlotte Temple* (1791), by Susanna Haswell Rowson, one of the first American best-sellers, and *The Coquette* (1797), by Hannah Foster, are both melodramatic tales involving seduction, desertion, and death. Charles Brockden Brown brought the mystery and violence of the European "gothic novel" to American settings in such novels as *Wieland* (1798) and *Arthur Huntley* (1801). *Modern Chivalry* (1815), by Hugh Henry Brackenridge, is a huge book that follows its characters across the American backwoods.

Among the most notable southern fiction was the work of William Gilmore Simms, whose *Yemassee* (1835) includes passages of realistic description and lively dialogue. A more sinister southern literary form was the "plantation novel," which defended slavery as a benevolent institution. John Pendleton Kennedy published the first such novel, *Swallow Barn,* in 1832.

Irving and Cooper

Two New Yorkers created some of the most memorable characters and stories in early American fiction. Washington Irving published his *Sketch Book* in 1820, which introduced the unforgettable Ichabod Crane and Rip Van Winkle, both of whom have become enduring parts of America's folklore. Irving's work was a triumph in Europe as well as the United States. The English novelist William Thackeray called him the first "ambassador" from "the New World of Letters to the Old."

The first novel by James Fenimore Cooper also appeared in 1820. Son of a wealthy landholder, Cooper was skeptical of democracy, but he invented several of the themes that would occupy the attention of later American novelists. *The Spy* (1821) is a melodrama about the Revolution, while *The Pilot* (1823) is a sea story based on the career of John Paul Jones. The most important of Cooper's novels are the five volumes in the Leatherstocking series, beginning with *The Pioneers* (1823) and including *The Last of the Mohicans* (1826) and *The Deerslayer* (1841). In these novels, Cooper dealt with the rapid westward march of white settlement and the destruction of the frontier. He also presented an idealized portrait of the woodsman. Natty Bumppo, badly dressed and poorly educated but brave and honest, is a figure of American myth.

Romanticism

Romanticism was a movement in art, music, and literature that began in the late

1700's and continued into the first half of the 1800's. It was a reaction against the Age of Reason of the 1700's, a period when reason was stressed as the best way to discover truth. In contrast, romanticism emphasized emotion and individual feelings over reason and logic. Followers of romanticism were drawn to the beauty of unspoiled nature. William Cullen Bryant was the first American poet to respond to the new movement. His poems "Thanatopsis" (1821) and "A Forest Hymn" (1825) spoke of nature with affection and reverence.

A more extreme kind of romanticism can be found in the work of Edgar Allan Poe. Poe earned very little success in his brief life, but he has had a great influence on European as well as American literature in the years since his death. His poetic theories were ahead of their time, insisting on beauty and the emotional nature of poetry. He pioneered in the mystery story, and the detective he invented, C. Auguste Dupin, looks forward to a later fictional detective, Sherlock Holmes. Poe's tales of the grotesque, such as "The Black Cat," "The Pit and the Pendulum," and "The Fall of the House of Usher," have fascinated generations of readers. No later writer has created images of fear and pain that are more vivid than Poe's.

▶THE EARLY 1800's

New England Poets

In the years before the Civil War, Boston, which traced its intellectual leadership back to the Puritans, remained the literary capital of the United States. In particular, the poets Henry Wadsworth Longfellow, Oliver Wendell Holmes, and John Greenleaf Whittier enjoyed national admiration.

Longfellow was professor of modern languages at Harvard for twenty years. His textbooks, as well as his volumes of poetry, were highly regarded in Europe as well as America. His long narrative *Song of Hiawatha* (1855), modeled on a Finnish epic, was once among the country's most popular poems. Longfellow's verse was always skillful, but his subjects tended to be familiar and his techniques were usually quite conventional.

Oliver Wendell Holmes, who was for many years professor of anatomy at Harvard, was a respected essayist and poet. He had a great talent for conversation, which he demonstrated in his most familiar book, *The Autocrat of the Breakfast Table* (1858).

John Greenleaf Whittier, the son of poor Massachusetts farmers, had no college education. He supported himself as a laborer and journalist and wrote a large number of popular poems celebrating the landscape and simple people of rural New England. For many years, he was also active in the cause of abolition, and he wrote many essays and poems demanding the end of slavery. In this cause, he was joined by other prominent New England writers, especially William Lloyd Garrison and James Russell Lowell.

Emerson, Fuller, and Thoreau

The 1830's and 1840's were the years of what was called "the American newness," and it was Ralph Waldo Emerson who gave that phrase its meaning. A graduate of Harvard and a minister, Emerson abandoned Christianity in his twenties and spent the rest of his long life proclaiming a new American philosophy. Above all, Emerson believed in the essential goodness of nature and the freedom of the individual. (See feature, Transcendentalism, on the following page.)

In 1836, Emerson published *Nature,* a small book but one of the most influential in American literature. In *Nature,* Emerson demanded that his fellow citizens reject the authority of the past and of Europe to create their own genuine culture. He repeated this argument the following year, in a lecture at Harvard on "The American Scholar." This speech has come to be regarded as America's declaration of literary independence. Emerson declared that every age must write its own books, and that each new generation must see the world for itself.

A remarkable group of men and women gathered around Emerson, including Margaret Fuller and Henry David Thoreau. Fuller was the first editor of the transcendentalist magazine *The Dial* and the author of a landmark book in the history of feminism, *Woman in the Nineteenth Century* (1845). She shared Emerson's anger at American materialism, but she went much further than Emerson in criticizing the inequalities of American society.

Thoreau also shared many of Emerson's ideas, including his belief in the spiritual power of nature and the need for individual self-reliance. On the Fourth of July, 1845, he

Transcendentalism

Transcendentalism is best known as a movement of New England writers and philosophers, led by Ralph Waldo Emerson and Henry David Thoreau (pictured), that occurred in the 1800's. Transcendentalism covered a wide range of ideas, but its central concepts remain influential: Transcendentalists' belief in the divinity of the human soul and the value of individual thought led to reforms in religion and education. Their philosophy of living in harmony with nature has become an accepted part of American thinking. Thoreau's concept of civil disobedience — the right to protest unjust laws by disobeying them — was adopted by such later reformers as Martin Luther King, Jr.

moved into a cabin he had built on the shores of Walden Pond in Massachusetts. He spent the next two years living alone—reading and writing, eating the vegetables he grew in his own garden and the fish he caught in the pond. Years later, he told the story of that experience in his most famous work, *Walden* (1854). The book is also a lesson in values, in which Thoreau argues for simple living and rejects the dependence of modern civilization on technology and machines. *Walden* continues to influence American attitudes toward nature and the environment.

Histories

In the 1800's, history was regarded as a form of literature. The country was still relatively young, but the search for a distinctive national identity included the rediscovery of the American past. Some historians wrote about the lives of individual heroes, such as Christopher Columbus, Thomas Jefferson, and especially George Washington. Other writers tried to include the whole nation; they wrote large narratives, often in several volumes, that treated American history as an epic tale. The most important of these books were *The History of the Conquest of Mexico* (1843), by William Hickling Prescott, *The Oregon Trail* (1849), by Francis Parkman, and the monumental *History of the United States* (1834–76), which George Bancroft worked on for half of his long life. These books express quite different attitudes toward the United States and its democratic politics, but all of them accept the assumption that America had a special destiny.

Nathaniel Hawthorne

The American past also provided Nathaniel Hawthorne with his main subject. His own ancestors had been among the Puritans who settled in early Massachusetts, and he was both fascinated and horrified by these grim, self-righteous religious crusaders. He had lived for a while in the utopian (model) community of Brook Farm, but that experiment was a failure and only convinced him that human nature was essentially flawed. He wrote one novel satirizing Brook Farm, called *The Blithedale Romance* (1852), but all his work is colored by his pessimism. He wrote only four novels, but one of them, *The Scarlet Letter* (1850), is among the major works in American literature. This sad account of human weakness and intolerance is set in Salem of the 1600's, a shadowy, mysterious landscape that is at the same time quite real.

Herman Melville

Herman Melville was one of Hawthorne's chief admirers, but his own work is much more concerned with the American present than its past. The years before the Civil War were a period of unprecedented expansion and exploration. The American frontier moved westward, and American ships sailed all the oceans of the world. That seafaring inspired a great many novels and travel books, including *Two Years Before the Mast* (1840) by Richard Henry Dana, Jr., a memoir of Dana's personal experiences as a common sailor.

Melville also worked as a seaman. He shipped on the whaler *Acushnet* in 1841 for an

18-month voyage to the South Pacific. This journey gave him the material for his first books, *Typee* (1846) and *Omoo* (1847), which were popular travel books. But Melville's voyaging also prepared him for his greatest novel, *Moby-Dick* (1851), in which the hunt for the white whale becomes a vast symbolic quest. The *Pequod*'s Captain Ahab, one of the most memorable characters in American literature, leads his men to their doom through the sheer strength of his will.

Moby-Dick was a commercial failure, as were the rest of Melville's writings. His novels, stories, and poems would only begin to receive recognition in the 1900's. He spent the last several decades of his life working as a customs inspector in the port of New York. During those years, he wrote little. However, one of his late works, *Billy Budd* (discovered and published after his death), which tells of an essentially decent man overtaken by tragedy, is among his masterpieces.

Whitman and Dickinson

America's two greatest poets were Walt Whitman and Emily Dickinson. Although they lived at the same time, their lives and their poetry were different in almost every respect.

Whitman lived most of his life in New York City, Long Island, and Camden, New Jersey. As a young man, he worked in dozens of different jobs, from carpenter to schoolteacher to journalist; in the Civil War, he served as a nurse for wounded soldiers. Out of his wide experience, he invented a radically new kind of poetry, using very little rhyme or conventional meter, which influenced all later generations of American writers. He said that the United States were themselves the greatest poem. Whitman wrote about himself as a way of writing about America and the nation's democratic beliefs. In the opening lines of his most famous poem, called "Song of Myself" (1855), he declared:

I celebrate myself and sing myself,
And what I assume you shall assume,
For every atom belonging to me as good belongs to you.

Emily Dickinson lived her entire life in Amherst, Massachusetts. Much of her poetry is based on the ordinary events that filled her daily life: housekeeping, gardening, reading, conversation. She had a sharp sense of humor, but she was also fascinated with death: nearly 600 of her 1,775 poems have to do with dying and death and funerals. Dickinson's poems are typically short, many of them only 8 to 16 lines. However, she compressed a great range of emotional experience into her verse.

Stowe, Lincoln, and the Civil War

In the 1840's and 1850's, the debate over slavery became the most serious crisis facing the United States. Politicians such as Senators Daniel Webster of Massachusetts and Henry Clay of Kentucky tried to find grounds for compromise, but the divisions between North and South grew increasingly bitter. Northern opposition to slavery was significantly hardened by the publication of *Uncle Tom's Cabin* (1852), which proved to be the most popular and the most influential novel published in America during the 1800's. The book's author, Harriet Beecher Stowe, was the daughter and wife of ministers. She had seen the evils of slavery firsthand, and she was committed to abolition. Abraham Lincoln said that *Uncle Tom's Cabin* started the Civil War; that was not literally true, but the novel did serve to crystallize the North's opposition to slavery.

The Civil War itself produced one great writer: President Abraham Lincoln. He had little formal schooling, but he read widely to educate himself. Like his personal style, his writing was plainspoken, earthy, and humorous. At the same time, he maintained a quiet dignity that helped the nation to endure the most serious crisis in its history. His speeches, including "The Gettysburg Address" and the Second Inaugural, are documents of supreme importance to American literature and politics.

▶THE LATER 1800's

The years following the Civil War were a period of unprecedented economic growth. The South had been devastated, but in the North, industry and prosperity increased greatly. Cities grew tremendously in size. For example, in the four decades from 1860 to 1900, New York City grew from 750,000 people to 3.5 million. The nation's population, including millions of immigrants, rapidly expanded westward. The new railroad system linked the most distant parts of the country in an efficient transportation network. New fortunes were created; men such as Cornelius

Vanderbilt, John D. Rockefeller, and J. P. Morgan became familiar figures in the daily press. Because of the country's fascination with wealth and material values, these years were sometimes called the "Gilded Age."

James and Twain

Many writers and artists found the culture of America to be unfriendly, anti-intellectual, and even uncivilized. As a result, several of them actually left the United States for longer or shorter periods to live and work in Europe. The most famous of these early expatriates was Henry James, one of the major novelists of the late 1800's and early 1900's. James used the contrast between Europe and America, which he called the "international theme," as a central subject in many of his stories and novels. He was especially interested in the psychology of his characters, and he employed a subtle prose style in order to reveal the inner life of his heroes and heroines. He also developed theories of fiction that would influence later generations of writers.

Unlike James, Mark Twain had begun as a poor boy and had worked in dozens of different jobs before finding his career as a writer. Although he believed in the promise of democracy, he was a stern critic of American society. His masterpiece, *The Adventures of Huckleberry Finn* (1884), is a brilliant comedy, but it also contains a strong attack on the slave system and the corruption of national ideals. Like all of Twain's best novels, including *The Adventures of Tom Sawyer* (1876), *Huckleberry Finn* employs a strong and believable colloquial (conversational) English. Twain said that "the soul of the people, the life of the people" was in their everyday speech, and his own greatest achievement was in his literary use of the ordinary language of America's people.

Henry James lived in England for many years. His novels often contrast the values of the young United States with the age-old traditions of Europe.

Frontier Humor

Twain's style grew out of the tall tales and frontier humor of the Old Southwest (a region stretching from Georgia to Missouri). The isolation and lawlessness of the frontier gave rise to an oral tradition of jokes and stories that eventually made its way into print. Some of the major humorists were Augustus Baldwin Longstreet, George Washington Harris, and Bret Harte. Harte's stories, such as "The Luck of Roaring Camp" (1868) and "The Outcasts of Poker Flat" (1869), were vivid portrayals of life in the mining camps of the California gold rush.

Realism

The emergence of the frontier humorists, who came from the West and South, demonstrated that American literature was becoming a more national achievement. Another important writer from the Midwest was William Dean Howells, who was born in Ohio and who eventually became one of the most influential novelists and editors of the late 1800's. In his fiction as well as his essays, Howells spoke as the champion of a new realism, which took ordinary, middle-class life as its subject. His many books include *The Rise of Silas Lapham* (1885) and *A Hazard of New Fortunes* (1890).

The years after the Civil War produced many important realist writers, including Rebecca Harding Davis, Edward Eggleston, and Hamlin Garland. Davis' "Life in the Iron Mills," which was published in the *Atlantic Monthly* magazine in 1861, was an angry work that revealed the oppression of workers. Eggleston's *Hoosier Schoolmaster* (1871) was set among the common people of Indiana, while Garland's *Main-Travelled Roads* (1891) exposed the hard and bitter lives of farmers and villagers in the Midwest.

New England Women Writers

New England continued to produce important writers in the later 1800's, including a group of remarkable women: Rose Terry Cooke, Mary E. Wilkins Freeman, and Sarah Orne Jewett. Each of these women, in different ways, explored the narrow, rural lives of men and women who had been left behind in the great changes that followed the Civil War.

Cooke's stories emphasized the loneliness and poverty of New England life. Freeman was especially interested in the sufferings of women. Her stories, collected in such volumes as *A Humble Romance* (1887) and *A New England Nun* (1891), portrayed the effects of isolation and outworn traditions on individual lives. Jewett emphasized the relationships among women that help them to cope and survive. In her masterpiece, *The Country of the Pointed Firs* (1896), men are mostly absent. The story centers on the daily lives of women, whose quiet activities—gardening, knitting, quilting, visiting, talking, praying—have replaced the more familiar adventures of male fictional heroes.

Southern Writing

Much of the literature produced by white writers in the South after the Civil War looked back affectionately at plantation life before the war. There were significant exceptions, including the work of George Washington Cable, Lafcadio Hearn, and Kate Chopin. Cable, who served in the Confederate army, later became a spokesman for black rights. His major novel, *The Grandissimes* (1880), was an attack on the racism and moral hypocrisy of the South.

Hearn was born in Greece and lived for a while in New Orleans before settling permanently in Japan. One of his early books, *Gombo Zhebes* (1885), was a collection of Creole proverbs. It was one of the earliest attempts to preserve American folk tales and treat them seriously.

Kate Chopin was born in St. Louis and also lived for a while in New Orleans. The mother of six children, she was widowed at the age of 30 and supported herself with her writing. Her most successful work, collected in *Bayou Folk* (1894) and *A Night in Acadia* (1897), was a series of sketches based on the Creole people and customs, which she had observed while she lived in New Orleans. Her tales provide vivid glimpses of the passion that lies beneath the surface of respectability. Her masterwork, *The Awakening* (1899), sympathetically explores the emotions and desires of its heroine.

Naturalism

The tremendous economic and political changes of the late 1800's were accompanied by a philosophy of competition and rugged individualism. Sometimes called "social Darwinism," this philosophy argued that human relations involved an endless struggle, in which only the "fittest" survived. Traditional concepts of justice and morality were threatened by a harsher view of human life in which individual choice mattered less than heredity and environment.

One literary outcome of this new point of view was the movement known as naturalism. Influenced by such European writers as Emile Zola and Gustave Flaubert, naturalism depicted men and women as controlled by instincts or passion, helpless in the face of economic and social circumstances.

Two of the major American naturalist writers were Stephen Crane and Frank Norris. Crane's poems and fiction continually assert the cruelty and indifference of the universe. *Maggie: A Girl of the Streets* (1893), which is set in the slums of New York's Lower East Side, tells the pitiable story of a young girl whose poverty drives her into prostitution, despair, and death. Crane's most famous novel, *The Red Badge of Courage* (1895), strips away the patriotic feeling surrounding the Civil War to reveal the horror of war's reality. The novel's young hero, Henry Fleming, experiences battle as confused, terrifying, and ultimately meaningless. Crane called the novel "a psychological portrait of fear." As such, it is a brilliant success.

Like Crane, Frank Norris believed that force ruled human lives. His major work was a projected three-volume "epic of wheat," which would take in the whole nation and its economic life. Only the first two volumes were completed before Norris' death, but the first of them, *The Octopus* (1901), is his chief work. Loosely based on California history, the novel is mainly a study in the power of destiny. In Norris' view, nature is a vast machine, and human beings are insignificant atoms in a large, mysterious design. It was a view widely shared as the 1800's ended.

THE EARLY 1900'S

Shortly after the turn of the century, Henry Adams said that, in the year 1900, "history broke in halves." He made the statement in his autobiography, which he called his *Education* (1907), a book that examines the sense of complete separation that divided the 1800's from the 1900's. What Adams had in mind was the transformation of the United States from a politically insignificant and agricultural society of villages and small towns into the world's leading industrial and military power. Technology, immigration, and the growth of large cities permanently changed the nature of American life. By 1900, the world of Henry Adams' childhood had disappeared.

Wharton and Dreiser

The city itself became a major subject of fiction and poetry. Novelists as different as Edith Wharton and Theodore Dreiser shared a deep interest in America's new urban life.

Wharton was the child of a socially prominent family in New York City, and many of her books reflect that background. Her finest book was *The House of Mirth* (1905). This novel, one of Wharton's earliest, traces the career of a poor but ambitious young woman whose failure in a money-driven society leads her to despair and death. Throughout the rest of her long career, Wharton wrote dozens of novels and stories in which her characters are defeated by the power of social convention.

Theodore Dreiser, who came from Indiana, grew up in poverty. His parents were German immigrants, and his books reveal his lifelong interest in the fate of poor and outcast people. His first novel, *Sister Carrie* (1900), was a landmark in American literature. Set in Chicago and New York, the novel provides the fullest and most realistic portrait of city life that any writer had yet created—from glamorous restaurants and theaters to sweat shops and tenements. The book's heroine is a poor girl who yearns for money and comfort. A creature of her desires, she is typical of all Dreiser's characters.

The Mass Media and the Muckrakers

At the turn of the century, new printing technologies made it possible to publish magazines and newspapers much faster and more cheaply than in the past. This was the period when the modern "mass media" developed, including hundreds of weekly and monthly magazines, and daily newspapers that sold as many as a million copies. Publishers competed ruthlessly with one another for readers by cutting prices and by introducing special features.

Some of the most important journalists were called "muckrakers." These were a group of men and women who investigated corruption and conspiracy in every aspect of American politics and business. They wrote articles on subjects ranging from oil companies and child labor to the life insurance industry and city government. Their exposés led to the passage of strong reform laws.

The most famous muckraking work was a novel, *The Jungle,* by Upton Sinclair. Published in 1906, this book shocked readers all over the country with its revelations about the Chicago meat-packing industry. The novel showed that the meat Americans were eating was unhealthy and that the workers in the packinghouses were severely exploited.

Willa Cather

Willa Cather began her career as an editor of *McClure's,* one of the principal muckraking magazines. Born in Virginia and raised in frontier Nebraska, Cather often used the Midwest and Southwest in her fiction. Her best novels, including *O Pioneers!* (1913) and *My Antonia* (1918), commemorate the efforts of prairie people, especially women, to maintain their dignity and find fulfillment despite the endless labor and harsh conditions of their lives. Much of her work looks back to an earlier America, in which values were supposedly simpler and more heroic.

Black Writing

For blacks, the early 1900's were a period of increased discrimination and oppression. In 1896, the Supreme Court had declared that segregation was legal. "Jim Crow" laws, which denied blacks equal access to education, employment, health care, and transportation, were passed throughout the South. The Ku Klux Klan, founded just after the Civil War, renewed its persecution of blacks; lynchings were a terrible feature of black life.

Black responses to this worsening racial situation were varied. Booker T. Washington, the most influential leader of his generation, argued for a gradual approach and for cooperation with whites. Washington's autobiogra-

Two writers of the early 1900's were Willa Cather and W. E. B. DuBois. Cather's novels chronicled the heroism of American pioneers, especially women. DuBois sought to combat racial prejudice and obtain equal opportunity for blacks through such writings as *The Souls of Black Folk* (1903).

phy, *Up From Slavery* (1901), tells the story of his progress from poverty and illiteracy to the presidency of Tuskegee University, a position that gave him international prestige.

W. E. B. DuBois felt that Washington was self-serving and compromised too often with white demands. DuBois, who was born in Massachusetts and earned his doctorate at Harvard, argued for a more militant position. He wrote many essays and books in the course of his long life, all of them devoted to combating white racism and demanding equal opportunity for blacks in all areas of American life. One of DuBois' most famous books was *The Souls of Black Folk* (1903). It was here that he gave his famous description of the "double consciousness" of American blacks: "an American, a Negro; two souls, two thoughts . . . two warring ideals in one dark body."

Some of the other important black writers of the early 1900's included poet Paul Laurence Dunbar and Charles Waddell Chesnutt, a novelist and short-story writer. Chesnutt offered realistic portraits of slavery and of the years that followed the Civil War. His novels *The House Behind the Cedars* (1901) and *The Marrow of Tradition* (1901) suggested that life for blacks in the United States was getting worse rather than better.

Modernism

In the early years of the 1900's, many different groups were demanding reform and renewal: black writers, labor organizers, supporters of women's rights, and muckraking journalists. The same spirit of protest also touched literature and the other arts. On both sides of the Atlantic, a dizzying variety of new artistic movements flourished. **Modernism**, as much of this new work and theory came to be called, was based on the belief that all the existing structures that governed life and art—social, religious, and political—had broken down. Order was replaced by fragments, and the typical modernist work often seems difficult to understand.

Three American writers who made major contributions to the modernist movement were Gertrude Stein, Ezra Pound, and T. S. Eliot.

Gertrude Stein studied philosophy and psychology with William James at Harvard. She went on to complete two years of medical school at the Johns Hopkins University before moving permanently to Paris early in the century. Her home became a famous meeting place for artists and writers. It was also a gallery for the dozens of paintings Stein collected —works by Picasso, Matisse, and many other modern masters. Her own writing, in such books as *Three Lives* (1909) and *Tender Buttons* (1914), was eccentric and often difficult to understand. However, her advice and her example made her a key figure in the new artistic developments.

Ezra Pound and T. S. Eliot joined forces briefly, in England before World War I (1914–18), to attempt to revitalize the art of poetry. They identified Victorian conventions and cliches as the enemy, and they insisted that all writers must work on new assumptions. Just before the war, Pound edited an anthology of "imagist" poetry that had an immense influence on later writers. Imagism, according to Pound, demanded that poetry be based on concrete images, and that it use the flexible rhythm of ordinary speech.

The first undeniable masterpiece of American modernism was Eliot's long poem "The Love Song of J. Alfred Prufrock" (1915). Opening with a passage from Dante's *Inferno,* "Prufrock" is the extended self-portrait of a timid middle-aged man.

Robinson and Frost

Despite modernism's influence, important work was done in the early 1900's of a more familiar sort. In particular, Edwin Arlington Robinson and Robert Frost used the scenes and voices of New England to create memorable poetry. Robinson's poems are often set in a fictional New England town called "Tillbury." His typical characters are joyless men and women who spend their days contemplating their own failure. "Eros Turannos" (1916), one of his finest poems, portrays a woman's desperate and self-destructive love for a man she knows will betray her.

Robert Frost was probably the best-known American poet of the 1900's. His first volumes, *A Boy's Will* (1913) and *North of Boston* (1914), gained him a popularity that he kept through half a century. Unlike the modernists, whose verse was difficult and obscure, Frost wrote poetry that was based on ordinary speech and was accessible to a large audience. He was born in California, but he lived most of his long life in New England. His poetry is filled with the landscapes, seasons, and people of that region.

The Chicago Renaissance

In the years before World War I, Chicago was the scene of important American experiments in poetry and fiction. The magazine *Poetry,* brilliantly edited by Harriet Monroe, published some of the most significant new verse, including the work of Carl Sandburg. Sandburg was the son of Swedish immigrants, and his poetry is always sympathetic to the concerns and experiences of ordinary men and women. He established his reputation with *Chicago Poems,* published in 1916.

The most important prose writer associated with the Chicago Renaissance was Sherwood Anderson. His third book, and his one masterpiece, was *Winesburg, Ohio* (1919), a collection of two dozen tales set in the small town of the volume's title.

The poet Carl Sandburg wrote about the life of ordinary people, most famously in *Chicago Poems*. He also collected folk songs and wrote tales for children.

BETWEEN WORLD WARS

The 1920's were known as the "Jazz Age": bootleg liquor was sold in spite of Prohibition, jazz bands played in illegal nightclubs, gangsters battled in city streets. The end of World War I brought a decade of prosperity to America, but it was also a period of moral disillusionment. Many people came to believe that the war had betrayed the ideals of freedom and democracy for which so many had fought and died. The most famous poem of the 1920's, T. S. Eliot's *The Waste Land* (1922), presented an image of the modern world as morally sterile. For Eliot and other writers, the postwar years were a time of anxiety and doubt. These themes were shared by many of the novelists, poets, and playwrights of the period.

Novelists

Sinclair Lewis wrote a series of important novels satirizing the materialism and prejudices of the American middle class. *Main Street* (1920) exposes the conformity and dullness of Gopher Prairie, a midwestern town based on Sauk Centre, Minnesota, where Lewis grew up. *Babbitt* (1922) was perhaps Lewis' most important book. The title character, a smooth-talking real estate salesman, embodies every vice that Lewis associated with America's culture of commerce: ambition, greed, and dishonesty.

Ernest Hemingway was one of several writers who had served in World War I. Born in the suburbs of Chicago, Hemingway found work as a reporter after graduating from high school. He went to Italy in the last months of the war as an ambulance driver and was seriously wounded. His novels, especially early ones such as *The Sun Also Rises* (1926) and *A Farewell to Arms* (1929), tell of the injuries that war inflicts on ordinary men and women. He developed a prose style of rigorous simplicity that influenced American writing throughout the rest of the 1900's.

F. Scott Fitzgerald gave the Jazz Age its name. He created memorable fictional portraits of the immoral but glamorous people who drank and danced through the decade. *The Great Gatsby* (1925) is his masterpiece, a book that T. S. Eliot called "the first step the American novel has taken since Henry James." Jay Gatsby is not merely a gangster and hustler. He is also a tragic figure, whose rise and fall comment sadly on the collapse of the American Dream in the 1900's.

Poets

The 1920's were a period of exceptional achievement in American poetry. The work of William Carlos Williams, Marianne Moore, and Wallace Stevens gave distinction to the decade; so too did the work of several important black poets. (See feature, The Harlem Renaissance, on this page.)

Williams was a physician who insisted that poetry must be faithful to everyday experience. He favored things over ideas, writing about daily life in a language of street-corner speech. Marianne Moore wrote in a more specialized vocabulary but also took the familiar scenes of the world as her subject. She wrote about everything, from animals in the zoo, to science, to baseball. Wallace Stevens was especially interested in the unique role of the creative imagination. He wrote in a richer, more elaborate style than Williams or Moore. Many of his poems explore the ways in which individuals might resist the growing power of the state.

The New Book of Knowledge contains biographies of many American writers of the 1900's. Consult the appropriate volumes to find entries on the following writers:

BALDWIN, James
BELLOW, Saul
BUCK, Pearl
DOS PASSOS, John
DREISER, Theodore
ELIOT, T. S.
FAULKNER, William
FITZGERALD, F. Scott
FROST, Robert
HEMINGWAY, Ernest
HUGHES, Langston
LEWIS, Sinclair
LONDON, Jack
LOWELL, Robert
O'NEILL, Eugene
SANDBURG, Carl
STEIN, Gertrude
STEINBECK, John
STEVENS, Wallace
WARREN, Robert Penn
WHARTON, Edith
WILLIAMS, Tennessee
WRIGHT, Richard

The Harlem Renaissance

The 1920's witnessed an outpouring of prose and poetry by black writers. The movement came to be called the Harlem Renaissance, because it was centered in Harlem, a community in New York City. Langston Hughes (pictured, bottom left, with other writers) was an important contributor to the movement. So, too, were Countee Cullen, Claude McKay, and Jean Toomer. The work of these writers had little in common, but all explored black American life from a black point of view. They often based their writings on black oral traditions and folklore; some of the poets used the rhythms of jazz in their verse. In 1925, Alain Locke published the landmark anthology *The New Negro*, which celebrated the diversity, skill, and self-confidence of the new black writers. The movement ended with the Great Depression of the 1930's, but its influence lived on in later black writers.

Eugene O'Neill

Beginning before World War I and continuing through the 1920's and 1930's, the work of Eugene O'Neill revolutionized American theater. O'Neill was an Irish Catholic and the son of a theatrical father, and his life is often revealed in his plays. He experimented constantly, using masks and other devices to dramatize the hidden psychological truths of his characters. His major plays include *The Emperor Jones* (1920), *The Great God Brown* (1926), *The Iceman Cometh* (1946), and *Long Day's Journey Into Night* (1954).

The Crash and the Great Depression

The Jazz Age ended when the stock market crash of October 1929 ushered in the longest and deepest economic depression in American history. Thousands of banks and factories closed, and millions of workers lost their jobs. The suffering was made worse by a sustained drought in the Midwest, the worst in a century. President Franklin D. Roosevelt used the programs of the "New Deal" to create jobs, but hardship continued throughout the 1930's.

Protest Literature

Some of the most popular writing of the 1930's—for example, Margaret Mitchell's *Gone With the Wind* (1936)—offered escape from the problems of the Depression. However, many writers were politically committed; most of them held left-wing (radical) beliefs. A group who sided with the workers in their struggles were known as "proletarian writers." Some of the most significant protest texts were left-wing plays, especially the work of Clifford Odets. Odets' *Waiting for Lefty* (1935) dramatizes a New York taxi strike and the efforts of oppressed workers to organize.

James T. Farrell wrote about the lower-middle-class Irish neighborhood in South Chicago where he had grown up. Although he published more than forty volumes of fiction, essays, and poetry, his most important books were his earliest, the three novels that make up the *Studs Lonigan* trilogy (1932–35). The three books follow Studs from his adolescence to his early death, a victim of his background and of his own greed and violence.

The two most influential protest writers of the 1930's were John Dos Passos and John Steinbeck. Dos Passos was a veteran of World War I; his work consistently took the side of the common man and woman against the forces of big government. His best books, the three volumes of the *U.S.A.* trilogy (1930–37), are a brilliant chronicle of American life in the early 1900's.

All of Steinbeck's work expresses his deep sympathy with the nation's poor and disadvantaged. *The Grapes of Wrath* (1939), which won the Pulitzer prize and was made into a motion picture, was one of the most controversial and important novels of the decade. The Joad family's journey to California in search of a new life is a true American epic.

Southern Writing

A significant group of southern writers appeared in the years between the two world wars. The earliest was Ellen Glasgow, who treated the southern past in a realistic and often ironic way. Many of her best novels, including *Virginia* (1913) and *Barren Ground* (1925), deal with the status of women in the changing South.

Two other important prose writers were Thomas Wolfe and Katherine Anne Porter. Wolfe's huge novels, especially *Look Homeward, Angel* (1929) and *Of Time and the River* (1935), are based on his own memories of his southern boyhood in North Carolina. Katherine Anne Porter's best works were her short stories and novellas, such as *Flowering Judas* (1935) and *Pale Horse, Pale Rider* (1939). Her work is distinguished for its superb craftsmanship and psychological subtlety.

A group of southern poets, known as "The Fugitives," gathered at Vanderbilt University in Tennessee. They were conservative in their opinions, supporters of earlier rural southern values against the pressure of northern industrialism. The group included John Crowe Ransom, Allen Tate, and Robert Penn Warren.

William Faulkner

The most highly regarded southern novelist of the 1900's was William Faulkner. Almost all of his books are set in the small Mississippi town in which he grew up. Turned into fiction as Yoknapatawpha County, this region became the scene of more than a dozen intricate and eloquent novels. Beginning with *The Sound and the Fury* (1929), and continuing through such books as *Absalom, Absalom!* (1936) and *Go Down, Moses* (1942), Faulkner created dozens of memorable characters and episodes. His principal theme was southern history. He was fascinated by the evil of slavery, and his novels often retell the collapse of the old southern slave empire in the catastrophe of the Civil War.

Black Writing

The range and diversity of black writing in the 1930's is demonstrated by the contrasting work of Zora Neale Hurston and Richard Wright. Hurston was trained as an anthropologist, and she was especially interested in the folk customs and tales of the South and the Caribbean. Her nonfiction writing, including the essays in *Mules and Men* (1935), made a distinguished contribution to African-American culture. Her finest novel, *Their Eyes Were Watching God* (1937), is set in the black communities of the South and also makes use of black oral traditions.

Richard Wright also insisted on the central importance of folklore to black life and literature. He grew up in poverty in rural Mississippi, moved to Chicago, and was active in radical politics in the Depression decade. His essays, stories, and novels all record his personal experience with American racism and oppression. His novel *Native Son* (1940) was a turning point in American literature. The violent story of a young black man named Bigger Thomas, this novel permanently expanded the range of black writing.

▸LITERATURE SINCE WORLD WAR II

World War II (1939–45) provided the subject for several important novels, in particular *The Naked and the Dead* (1948), by Norman Mailer, and *From Here to Eternity* (1951), by James Jones. The years since the war have been a period in which American dominance as an international power has been accompanied by doubts about America's proper global role. The international hostility of the Cold War defined relations between the United States and the other nations of the world for forty years.

In the shadow of that long conflict, America went through important transformations: the civil rights movement, along with the struggle of women and other groups toward equality; the upheavals of the 1960's, which called many traditional values into question; the Vietnam War, which deeply divided the nation for more than a decade. The poetry, drama, and fiction of these years have recorded the turmoil that has reshaped American society.

Postwar Poetry

Throughout the years since World War II, much excellent poetry has been written in traditional forms, using conventional subjects. The formal poets who did this work, including Elizabeth Bishop and Richard Wilbur, believed in the value of intelligence, contemplation, and civilization. Their verse tends to be restrained, ironic, and often complex.

Experimental Poets. The postwar years have also produced poetry of political protest and experimental verse of all sorts. (See feature,

The Beats

Beginning in the mid-1950's, a group of young writers known as the "beats" began publishing unconventional poems and novels that challenged middle-class American values. The members of the group celebrated freedom of the individual, and many of them were associated with the protest movements of the following decades. The most important beat works are probably *On the Road* (1957), an autobiographical novel by Jack Kerouac (pictured), and *Howl* (1956), a long poem by Allen Ginsberg. Other beat writers were the poets Lawrence Ferlinghetti and Gregory Corso and the novelist John Clellon Holmes.

The Beats, on preceding page.) A group of writers who became known as "confessional poets" published some of the most important recent verse. The confessional writers used their own lives, including their most intimate problems, as the subject matter of their poetry. The group included Robert Lowell, John Berryman, and Sylvia Plath.

Lowell's *Life Studies* (1959), which combined shocking personal revelations with superb craftsmanship, influenced a generation of writers. Berryman's *Dream Songs* (1964–68) was a kind of versified diary in which alcoholism, failure, and death are frequent topics. Plath, who committed suicide at age 30, wrote poems in which anger and despair merge in thoughts of dying; her best work was published, after her death, in *Ariel* (1965).

Black Poets. Gwendolyn Brooks won the first Pulitzer prize awarded to a black writer fór her second volume of poetry, *Annie Allen* (1949). Her poetry became increasingly militant after 1967, when she and other writers in the Black Arts Movement dedicated their work to the task of social change.

Robert Hayden made extensive use of black history and folklore in his poetry; his books include *Figures of Time* (1955) and *A Ballad of Remembrance* (1962). Hayden's "Runagate, Runagate" pays tribute to Harriet Tubman, who escaped from slavery and then helped hundreds of others to freedom.

Postwar Drama

In the years following the war, the leading playwrights were Arthur Miller, Tennessee Williams, and Edward Albee. Miller's *Death of a Salesman* (1949) has been perhaps the most important play of the postwar era; the tragedy of the central character, Willy Loman, went beyond personal failure to encompass the collapse of the American dream.

Tennessee Williams wrote more than two dozen full-length plays. Several of them, including *The Glass Menagerie* (1944), *A Streetcar Named Desire* (1947), and *Cat on a Hot Tin Roof* (1955), are among the classics of recent American theater. Edward Albee wrote more experimental plays than Miller or Williams, often short works influenced by the European "theater of the absurd." In a typical Albee play, a small group of characters engage in verbal and even physical abuse, sometimes for no apparent reason.

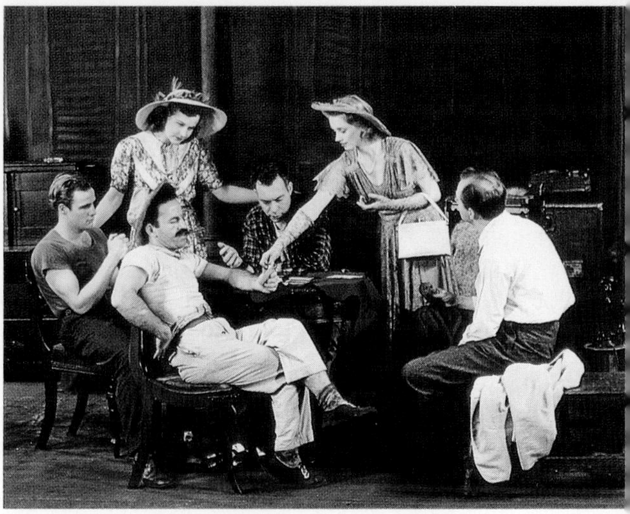

A scene from *A Streetcar Named Desire*, by Tennessee Williams. Williams wrote more than two dozen plays. Many have become classics of American theater.

More recent playwrights whose work has commanded attention include Sam Shepard and David Mamet. Many of the best contemporary dramatists have been women, including Wendy Wasserstein; Beth Henley, who won the Pulitzer prize for *Crimes of the Heart* (1981); and Marsha Norman, who won the Pulitzer for *'Night Mother* (1983).

Postwar Fiction

The early postwar mood of alienation and discontent was best captured in the 1951 novel *The Catcher in the Rye,* by J. D. Salinger, in which young Holden Caulfield dreams of protecting all the world's children from danger. Other writers of the period whose work focused on the anxieties of the middle class were John Cheever and John Updike.

Southern Fiction. Although the American economy had become increasingly national, the South remained a separate literary region after World War II. Some of the main writers of that region have included Robert Penn Warren, Eudora Welty, Flannery O'Connor, William Styron, and Walker Percy.

Warren won distinction both as a novelist and a poet. His best novels were his earliest ones, in particular the Pulitzer prize-winning *All the King's Men* (1949), a fictional account of the Louisiana politician Huey Long. Eudora Welty wrote some of the finest short stories of the century, memorably evoking the people and landscapes of the rural South. Her first collection, *A Curtain of Green and Other Stories* (1941), remains her masterpiece.

Flannery O'Connor's stories combine the grotesque and the supernatural; her work is filled with outcasts and marginal people. William Styron has chosen subjects that range from the Nazi death camps, in *Sophie's Choice* (1979), to an 1800's slave revolt, in *The Confessions of Nat Turner* (1967). Walker Percy, a physician and a Catholic, continually explored the decay of faith in the modern South. His novels include *The Moviegoer* (1961) and *The Last Gentleman* (1966).

Jewish Fiction. Among the most significant recent writers were several Jewish novelists who examined the debate over older values that followed World War II. This group included Saul Bellow, Bernard Malamud, and Philip Roth. Bellow, who won the Nobel prize in 1976, has created memorable characters and urban scenes. He writes in defense of the individual and of traditional culture; his finest novels are perhaps *Henderson the Rain King* (1959) and *Herzog* (1964).

Bernard Malamud's stories and novels often resemble folk tales and allegories. In much of his work, including his best book, *The Assistant* (1957), Malamud created characters who are defeated by circumstance but maintain their faith. Philip Roth has shown a lifelong interest in the problem of moral authority. His famous books include *Portnoy's Complaint* (1969) and the Pulitzer prize-winning *American Pastoral* (1997).

Black Writers. The past few decades have been a triumphant period for black writers. In 1952, Ralph Ellison published *Invisible Man*, one of the most important novels of the postwar era. The book combines realism, folklore, and fantasy to tell the story of its narrator's life and his discovery of American racism.

James Baldwin was the son of a storefront preacher, an eloquent and bitter man. Baldwin's first and best novel, *Go Tell It on the Mountain* (1953), is based on his own childhood experiences. In addition to fiction, he produced some of the most brilliant essays of his time. Collected in such volumes as *Notes of a Native Son* (1955) and *Nobody Knows My Name* (1961), these essays make up a passionate denunciation of racial injustice.

Postwar black writing has encompassed the remarkable accomplishment of gifted women, including Toni Morrison and Alice Walker. Morrison's fiction celebrates the language and the heritage of tales that define the American black experience. Her principal novels, such as *Song of Solomon* (1977) and *Beloved* (1987), for which she received the Pulitzer prize, combine a detailed knowledge of history with myth and fantasy. Alice Walker's major novel, *The Color Purple* (1982), is written as a series of letters that reveal the oppression and liberation of a woman named Celie.

Other talented black women writers have included Margaret Walker, Paule Marshall, Terry Macmillan, and Toni Cade Bambara.

Experimental Fiction. Over the past several decades, a number of writers have undertaken a wide range of technical experiments in fiction. Vladimir Nabokov, a Russian émigré, used parody, multilingual jokes, and intricate plots to focus attention on the nature of fiction itself. Donald Barthelme worked in fragments, word games, and fairy tales. His stories have been collected in such volumes as *Come Back, Dr. Caligari* (1964). John Barth has created narratives in which storytelling itself becomes the main subject.

Contemporary Diversity

The most evident hallmark of contemporary American literature is its great range and diversity. From the "minimalist" realism of Raymond Carver to the enormous and complex novels of Thomas Pynchon; from the brilliant reportage of Joan Didion to the finely crafted fables of Cynthia Ozick—recent American writing has represented the widest variety of styles and subjects.

The nation's ethnic minorities have produced distinguished work. Maxine Hong Kingston, in such books as *Woman Warrior* (1976), has dramatized the tensions between past and present in Asian-American culture. The main character of *Bless Me, Ultima* (1972), by Rudolfo Anaya, learns to base his life in the modern world on the foundation of tradition. The novels of the Native American writer Leslie Marmon Silko, including *Ceremony* (1978), combine realistic narrative with the songs and legends of the Indian past.

PETER CONN
University of Pennsylvania
Author, *Literature in America: An Illustrated History*

AMERICAN REVOLUTION. See REVOLUTIONARY WAR.

AMISH

The Amish are a conservative Protestant group that originated in Europe in 1693. They live in 28 U.S. states and the Canadian province of Ontario. About 65 percent live in Ohio, Pennsylvania, and Indiana. The total number of Amish is about 180,000, half of whom are under 18 years old. There are over a dozen subgroups with varied practices.

Beliefs and Practices. The Amish value humility and obedience and condemn pride. They place the welfare of the community above individual rights and choices and believe that salvation comes from obedient living in the community of faith. These values are expressed in guidelines for daily living called the Ordnung. The Ordnung is not written down and is modified as new issues arise.

The details of the Ordnung can vary by congregation. But all Amish are expected to wear special clothing: Women must wear plain long dresses, bonnets, and shawls, while men must wear full beards and broad-brimmed hats. The Ordnung also forbids certain forms of technology, attending high school and college, joining the military, and initiating divorce.

Most Amish speak a Pennsylvania German dialect, as well as English. They live apart from the rest of society in rural communities and travel by horse and buggy. Although many farm, about half own or operate small businesses.

The local congregation, which usually includes about 25 to 35 families, is the social and religious center of Amish life. Members meet for worship every other Sunday in one of their homes. Each congregation has several leaders who serve for life without formal training or pay.

Almost all Amish children attend one- or two-room private schools that go through eighth grade only.

The Amish must choose to be baptized. About nine out of ten request baptism, usually between the ages of 19 and 21. Between age 16 and baptism, some Amish youth do things that are forbidden by the church, such as going to movies, driving cars, and listening to popular music. At baptism, they renounce the devil and the world, confess their belief in Christ, and promise to submit to the church for the rest of their lives. The Amish usually marry by age 21 and often have seven or eight children. The extended family provides a strong sense of identity and social support in Amish society.

History. The Amish trace their history to the Anabaptist movement that began in Switzerland in 1525 during the Protestant Reformation. Anabaptists refused to baptize their babies. They argued that only adults who had voluntarily decided to follow Christ should be baptized. They were considered heretics and many were executed.

In 1693, the Amish emerged as a distinct group among the Anabaptists living in Switzerland and the Alsace region of France. Their leader, Jakob Ammann, called for shunning wayward members of the church to maintain its purity. Ammann's followers became known as Amish. The Amish migrated to the Americas in the mid-1700's and again in the 1800's.

Donald B. Kraybill
Cynthia L. Nolt
Elizabethtown College

WONDER QUESTION

What is shunning?

Among the Amish, shunning is the practice of avoiding church members who have refused to confess violations of major church teachings. Although personal communication does not necessarily stop, other members of the community may not receive rides or goods from offenders or sit with them during meals. Offenders may return to the community if they are willing to confess their sins.

AMISTAD REBELLION

Sengbe Pieh (Joseph Cinque) led the Amistad Rebellion, which occurred in 1839.

The Amistad Rebellion was one of the most famous cases of slave mutiny in U.S. history. It strengthened the U.S. abolition movement and sharpened the division between Americans over the issue of slavery.

The rebellion, led by Sengbe Pieh (later called Joseph Cinque), took place in 1839 aboard the Spanish ship *Amistad*. A group of 53 Africans, mostly Mende people from present-day Sierra Leone, had been captured by slave traders and brought to Havana, Cuba. There they were purchased by two Spanish planters, Pedro Montez and Joseph Ruiz. The captives were brought aboard the *Amistad* for what was meant to be a short sail to a port 300 miles up the Cuban coast.

Three days later, Cinque and the other slaves managed to free themselves and seize control of the ship, killing two crew members. They forced Montez and Ruiz to steer the ship toward the rising sun—back to Africa. Each night, however, the Spaniards secretly sailed the ship in the opposite direction. After two months of zigzagging, the ship was stopped in U.S. waters. The Africans were arrested on charges of piracy and murder and jailed in New Haven, Connecticut.

The Africans' plight attracted the attention of abolitionists and missionaries, who rallied to their defense. The case ultimately went to the Supreme Court, where former president John Quincy Adams argued for the Africans' release. In 1841, the court ruled that they had been kidnapped in violation of a treaty banning the international slave trade. It determined that they had a right to defend their freedom and that they should be released. Cinque and most of the other surviving Africans returned to Africa the following year.

RENEA HENRY
Amistad Research Center

AMMUNITION. See GUNS AND AMMUNITION.

AMNESTY

Amnesty usually refers to an act by a government or other sovereign power that allows a person or group of people to avoid punishment for a public offense. The term comes from a Greek word meaning "forgetfulness."

Governments throughout history have granted amnesty following wars or other political conflicts, in order to reunite their citizens. One of the earliest known amnesties was declared in 403 B.C., after the citizens of Athens, Greece, overthrew a group of repressive rulers known as the Thirty Tyrants. Their new leader, Thrasybulus, issued an amnesty for all citizens—except the former rulers—and asked them to forget the wrongs they had suffered under the previous government.

The U.S. Constitution gives the president power to grant amnesty, and several presidents have done so. In 1795, George Washington granted amnesty to Pennsylvanians who had participated in the Whiskey Rebellion. During the Civil War (1861–65), Abraham Lincoln offered it to all Confederates, except high-ranking army officers and officials, provided they take an oath of loyalty to the Union. After the war, President Andrew Johnson proclaimed a general amnesty.

After World War I (1914–18), amnesties and pardons were granted to people imprisoned for protesting the war. (Pardons are similar to amnesties except they are typically granted to individuals rather than groups, usually after a person has been convicted of a crime.) In 1974, President Gerald Ford offered amnesty to Vietnam War draft evaders and military deserters in exchange for public service work. President Jimmy Carter later pardoned most draft evaders.

The U.S. Congress can also grant amnesty. In 1986, Congress passed an act providing it to illegal aliens who had entered the United States before 1982. This allowed them to remain in the country permanently.

ELIZABETH MATTHEW
American University

AMOEBA. See MICROBIOLOGY.

AMPHIBIANS

They can be found under the damp logs on forest floors; propelling themselves through the waters of streams, lakes, and ponds; burrowing into the ground; bounding through woodlands with great leaps; or waddling across dry, sandy desert. These smooth-skinned **vertebrates** (animals with backbones) called amphibians inhabit all parts of the world except Greenland and Antarctica.

There are three main groups of amphibians: frogs and toads, salamanders and newts, and caecilians. As they go through their early growing stages, the three groups look similar; but as adults, they look very different. Frogs and toads have four legs and no tails. Their hind legs are long and strong. They use their well-developed back legs for jumping and swimming. Salamanders and newts have tails their entire lives. They also have four legs as frogs and toads do. However, their short, weak legs are suited to walking rather than jumping. Caecilians, which have no legs, are burrowing animals that look a lot like giant earthworms.

Scientists have identified more than 4,000 kinds, or **species**, of amphibians. More species are still being discovered, particularly in the rain forests of Africa, South America, and Southeast Asia.

▶CHARACTERISTICS OF AMPHIBIANS

Amphibians are ectothermic—that is, they depend on external heat sources, such as the sun, to raise their body temperature. Most amphibians spend the early part of their lives in water and the adult part on land. During the early, aquatic period, amphibians use gills for respiration. Later on land, most breathe through lungs. Amphibians can also absorb oxygen through their skin, which is generally smooth, moist, and scaleless. In some species of salamanders, the lungs do not function; all respiration is through the skin and the mucous membranes of the mouth.

Senses. Amphibian senses are well developed. Frogs and toads have excellent sight and depend on their eyes to find food. Salamanders have good eyes and also a keen sense of smell. When they hunt for food, they use both sight and smell. For the burrowing life of caecilians, good eyesight is not a necessity. They either have very small eyes or no eyes at all. Caecilians hunt mainly by smell. They have two tentacles, or feelers, near the mouth. As they move through the ground, the tentacles pick up food scents.

The American bullfrog (*left*) is the largest North American frog.

Eating Habits. In their aquatic larval stage, young amphibians vary in their diets. Some eat mainly plant material. Others eat only insects and other animals. Still others eat a mixture of plant and animal food. Adult amphibians, however, are almost entirely meat eaters and make insects the bulk of their diet.

A toad has a short, stout body with warty skin.

Producing Sounds. Most amphibians are able to produce some kind of sound. Frogs and toads use their voices to communicate warnings, defend themselves, and send mating calls. However, except for frogs and toads, amphibians do not have well-developed voices. Caecilians and most salamanders and newts are limited to sounds such as coughs and grunts. The sounds they produce are not used as a form of communication.

Defenses. Many different kinds of mammals, snakes, and birds hunt the amphibian. When threatened, amphibians that closely match the colors in their environment may hide from their enemies by simply staying very still. Some salamanders have tails that break off. The salamander quickly escapes as

its attacker chases the twitching tail. Many amphibians have poison-secreting skin glands. The poison irritates the mouth of the attacker, and it does not take much time before the attacker willingly lets go of its prey.

LIFE CYCLES

In most species of amphibians, the young animals, or **larvae**, that hatch from the eggs resemble fish in certain ways. They must live in water. They have tails that they use to propel themselves. They take in oxygen through gills. Gradually, the larvae undergo changes that turn them into land-dwelling adults. Such a change of form is called a **metamorphosis**.

As full-grown adults, most amphibians are small creatures. They usually are no longer than 6 inches (15 centimeters) and weigh less than 2 ounces (57 grams). The largest amphibian is the Japanese giant salamander, which grows to 5¼ feet (1.6 meters) in length. One species of caecilian also reaches lengths of more than 4 feet (1.2 meters).

Frogs and Toads. Frogs and toads are the most widespread of all the amphibians. They usually live in wet or moist places such as ponds, marshes, or rain forests, but there are some toads that are able to live in dry areas, including deserts. In frogs and toads, fertilization of the eggs is almost always external. The male fertilizes the eggs as they are being released into the water by the female.

The larva that hatches from an egg is called a **tadpole** or **polliwog**. It has a tail and gills. The larva grows and develops over a period of time that lasts from two weeks to two years; then, metamorphosis to the land stage begins. The gills are absorbed and the animal develops lungs. Legs develop and the tail disappears. Finally the animal has the characteristics of an adult frog. It climbs out of the water and onto land. It continues to grow until it reaches its full size. When it is mature, it returns to the water to mate and breed.

There are exceptions to this typical pattern. In one species, for example, the male frog carries strings of eggs wrapped around his hind legs until they hatch. In other species, there is no aquatic larval stage; the froglets that hatch from the eggs look like miniature adults.

Salamanders and Newts. Salamanders and newts generally live in lakes and streams and

An Amphibian Life Cycle

Most amphibians, such as this leopard frog, develop from eggs laid in water. When a frog egg hatches, a tadpole emerges. The young tadpole is very much like a fish—it has gills, lidless eyes, and a finlike tail. Slowly, the tadpole changes into an animal, with well-developed legs and lungs, that can live on land.

Arching its tail in warning is part of the defensive behavior of the salamander called ensatina (*opposite page*). In addition to the warning posture, the salamander secretes a poisonous slime that irritates and repels attackers.

During its land stage of development, which lasts two to three years, the red-spotted newt feeds on snails, small insects, and worms.

A salamander (*right*) can be identified by grooves that run down its sides.

under damp logs on forest floors. In most tailed amphibians, fertilization occurs internally within the female's body. After courtship, the male deposits a packet of sperm, called a **spermatophore**, on the bottom of the pond. In species that breed on land, the male places the spermatophore on moist ground. The female picks up the spermatophore and stores it in her **cloaca**, a chamber at the base of the tail that opens to the outside of the body. When the female lays her eggs, they pass through the cloaca, where the sperm fertilize them.

The larvae of salamanders and newts are similar in appearance to the adults. The main difference is that the young animal has feathery gills on the outside of its neck. After two to four months, the larva changes into an adult. It loses the gills and forms air-breathing lungs.

Caecilians. The caecilians are found only in the tropics and subtropics. Most live in underground burrows; however, there are caecilians that spend all their life in water.

Fertilization is internal in caecilians. Most species deposit their eggs in water. Some caecilians lay eggs on land. After depositing her eggs, the female caecilian may coil herself around them to keep the eggs safe from predators until they hatch. The caecilian larvae have tails and live in water. Like frogs and toads, they gradually lose their tails and turn into adults.

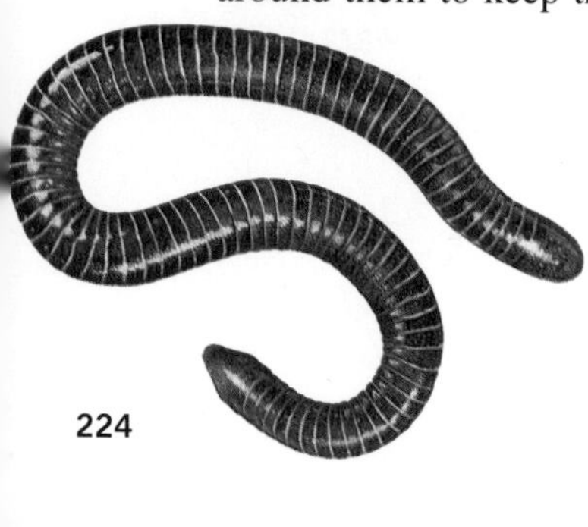

In its dark underground home, the caecilian picks up chemical cues with its tentacles that tell it when a food source is near.

AMPHIBIANS AND THEIR ENVIRONMENT

Amphibians have an important role in the environment. They help maintain the balance of nature in many areas: sometimes because they are food for other animals, including humans; other times because they eat large amounts of insect pests and larvae.

In many parts of the world, amphibians are disappearing from areas where they once were common. People's activities appear to be the main cause of this decline. Habitats are destroyed as marshes and other wetlands are drained; forests are cut down; and homes, roads, and other structures are built. Automobiles also kill thousands of amphibians each year. In many places, amphibians are run over as they cross the roads built between their homes and their spawning grounds. Chemical substances from acid rain and pesticides also harm amphibians when they are absorbed through their moist skin. Amphibians also absorb dangerous chemicals when they eat insects that contain pesticides.

As the important contributions of amphibians have become recognized, efforts have been made to protect them. Measures enacted by some countries that protect the environment from the harmful effects of acid rain and the misuse of pesticides also help protect amphibians. Countries, such as India, have banned the export of frog legs (considered a delicacy in some parts of the world) to protect their amphibian population. In many parts of Europe, toad tunnels have been built to help toads safely cross the roads that block their travel to spawning grounds.

JENNY TESAR
Author, *Introduction to Animals*
Reviewed by JOHN L. BEHLER
Curator, Department of Herpetology
The Bronx Zoo

See also FROGS AND TOADS.

AMSTERDAM

Amsterdam is the largest city of the Netherlands and the country's financial, commercial, and industrial center. Located in the province of North Holland, it is the official capital of the Netherlands, although the actual seat of government is at The Hague. A city of great charm, Amsterdam is distinguished by its many canals, streets of handsome old houses, museums and churches, and a vigorous cultural life. The population of the city proper is about 735,000, and more than 1 million people live in its metropolitan area.

Amsterdam is situated on the IJ, an inlet of the IJsselmeer, an enormous lake. Like much of the Netherlands, the city lies below sea level and is protected from the encroaching sea by dikes. Amsterdam takes its name from a dam that once restrained the Amstel River, which flows through the city.

The City. The best-known parts of the city are the tree-lined canals, where wealthy merchants in the 1600's and 1700's built their homes. The houses are now mainly used as offices or for other commercial purposes. The Old Church, built in the 1200's, is Amsterdam's oldest structure. On Dam Square, the central square, are the royal palace (formerly the town hall), dating from the 1600's, and the New Church, built in the 1400's. The Rijksmuseum (state museum) has a splendid collection of paintings by Rembrandt and other masters. Rembrandt's home is itself a museum. Other places of interest are the old Jewish quarter and the building in which Anne Frank and her family hid from the Nazis during World War II (1939–45) and where Anne wrote her famous diary. The hall of the Concertgebouw houses one of the world's great orchestras. The city has two universities, the University of Amsterdam and the Free University.

Economic Activity. Amsterdam is the country's second largest port, after Rotterdam. Its heavy industries include iron and steel, machinery, automobiles, and shipbuilding. Printing and publishing, oil refining, and clothing manufacture are also important. One of the city's oldest industries is the cutting and polishing of diamonds.

History. Amsterdam was founded in the 1200's. Originally a fishing port, it rapidly grew in commercial importance. By the 1600's it was the wealthiest city in Europe. It also became a refuge for those fleeing religious and political persecution elsewhere. Amsterdam declined as a port due to the gradual silting-up of its outlet to the sea, but the construction of the North Sea Canal in the late 1800's revitalized it. The city was occupied by the Germans from 1940 to 1945, during World War II, and its port was largely destroyed. The years following the war were marked by rebuilding and the expansion of the city to the surrounding suburbs.

Reviewed by JOHAN P. SNAPPER
University of California, Berkeley

Amsterdam, the official capital and largest city of the Netherlands, has one of the most extensive canal systems in all of Europe.

AMUNDSEN, ROALD (1872–1928)

Norwegian explorer Roald Amundsen was the first person to successfully lead an expedition to the South Pole. He was born on July 16, 1872, in Borge, Norway, to a family of sea captains.

He studied medicine for two years but left school to pursue his dream of being a polar explorer. In 1897 he sailed to the Antarctic with a Belgian expedition.

Between 1903 and 1906 Amundsen made the historic first crossing of the Northwest Passage, the route that connects the Atlantic and Pacific oceans by way of the Arctic waters of North America. During this trip, he determined the exact position of the north magnetic pole.

Amundsen planned to lead the first expedition to the North Pole but changed his plans when news arrived that an American, Robert Peary, had reached it. Amundsen decided instead that he would be the first to reach the South Pole. In June 1910 he secretly set sail. Although he knew a similar expedition had been launched by the British, under Robert Falcon Scott, Amundsen was determined to reach the pole before him. When he revealed his intentions several months later, the race for the pole attracted worldwide attention.

In October 1911, Amundsen and his men began the overland portion of their trip. Crucial to their success were survival techniques learned from the Eskimos, including the use of sled dogs. On December 14, 1911, Amundsen and his crew reached the South Pole—a month ahead of Scott. They raised the Norwegian flag and, three days later, began their journey home. Scott and his men were less fortunate; they died on their return trip.

In 1926, Amundsen flew over the North Pole in an airship piloted by Italian aviator Umberto Nobile. In June 1928, Amundsen set out to rescue Nobile, who had crashed an airship in the Arctic. Amundsen's plane disappeared and he was never seen again.

Reviewed by Byron J. Nordstrom
Gustavus Adolphus College

AMUSEMENT PARKS. See Parks and Playgrounds.

ANARCHISM

Anarchism is a political theory that regards government and other forms of central authority as harmful and unnecessary. Although anarchism is often linked with violence and chaos, advocates of "pure" anarchism claim it is just the opposite. They believe that power corrupts and that those in power eventually place their own interests before those of the people they are supposed to serve. According to anarchists, a free and just society is possible only when government is abolished and individuals freely cooperate as equals.

The first clear expression of anarchist beliefs can be traced to Taoists in China in the 500's B.C. Centuries later, in his book *An Enquiry Concerning Political Justice* (1793), British writer William Godwin formulated the concept of anarchism but did not give it that name. The first person to call himself an anarchist was French writer Jean-Pierre Proudhon. His work *What Is Property* (1840) predicted the eventual collapse of authority and the rise of a natural social order.

Mikhail Bakunin, a Russian noble, modified Proudhon's teachings. He advocated the violent overthrow of government and other existing institutions. He also believed that the means of production (basically land and goods) should be owned collectively (by all). This concept of collectivism was advanced by another Russian, Peter Kropotkin. In 1876 he introduced a theory of nonviolent social organization based on communes, or self-sufficient communities.

Anarchism gained hold in the United States in the late 1800's and early 1900's. One of the most prominent American anarchists was Emma Goldman, a Russian immigrant who first advocated and then rejected the use of violence. Later, in the 1960's and 1970's, anarchism briefly became popular among radical leftist groups.

Elizabeth Matthew
American University

ANASAZI

The Anasazi of the American Southwest built large, multistoried sandstone structures called great houses.

The Anasazi were a Native American people, the ancestors of the Pueblos, Zuni, and Hopi of present-day New Mexico and Arizona. Anasazi culture flourished from about A.D. 300 to 1500 in what is today called the Four Corners region of the Southwest—where the states of Utah, Colorado, Arizona, and New Mexico meet.

The name "Anasazi" is rarely used by their descendants. It is a Navajo word best translated as "ancestors of our enemies." It was first used in 1849, when American military surveyors visited mysterious ruins in New Mexico and asked their Navajo guides about the people who had lived there.

Society. Anasazi society began as scattered settlements of farmers living in small farmsteads called pueblos. At its peak in the 1050's, this society was centered on Chaco Canyon in New Mexico and included more than a hundred villages composed of huge, multistoried sandstone structures called great houses. More than a dozen great houses were clustered in Chaco Canyon itself. The Anasazi living in the canyon at this time are referred to today as Chacoans.

From studies of burial remains and grave offerings, archaeologists know that there were three classes of people in Chacoan society at its peak: The elite class lived in the great houses of Chaco Canyon and wielded the most power. The class below the elites lived in the outlying great houses. At the bottom of Anasazi society were the farmers, who typically produced more corn, beans, and squash than each family needed. Most of this surplus food was redistributed to other farms in need.

In 1050 the elite class had enough economic power to import pottery, turquoise, macaws, and shells for beads from people living hundreds of miles away. The Anasazi of the Chacoan era created magnificent buildings, fine black-on-white pottery, basketry, ornaments, and stone jewelry.

Decline. By the late A.D. 1000's, droughts and over-farming had greatly reduced crop production, and many farmers began to abandon their land. Conflicts arose, and Anasazi society began to break apart. Many people fled to the surrounding uplands for safety and to cultivate new land irrigated by the melting winter snows. Within a generation or two, these farmers had established large settlements at present-day Mesa Verde, Bandelier National Monument, and other locations. They flourished until severe droughts in the late 1200's drove them from the uplands to permanent creeks and rivers at lower elevations. There, they rebuilt their farming society based on independent, self-sufficient pueblos, twenty of which survive to this day.

DAVID E. STUART
Author, *Anasazi America*

ANASTASIA, ALBERT. See ORGANIZED CRIME (Profiles).

ANATOMY. See BODY, HUMAN.

ANCHORAGE. See ALASKA (Cities).

Egyptian hieroglyphics

Nimrud, Assyria (artist's rendering)

ANCIENT CIVILIZATIONS

The appearance of the world's first civilizations more than 5,000 years ago was a major development in human history. Before that time, people lived in small, scattered communities, moving from place to place in a constant search for food. Once they settled in areas suitable for growing crops, people learned to build permanent structures, express their creativity through art, and create large societies united by strong rulers and common beliefs.

When most people think of ancient civilizations, they think of famous ones such as those of the Egyptians or the Greeks. But the term "ancient civilization" covers many complex societies that existed between about 3500 B.C. and A.D. 1500 on almost every continent in the world. This article discusses only a small sampling from the vast and varied array of civilizations.

▸ CHARACTERISTICS OF ANCIENT CIVILIZATIONS

Ancient civilizations are also called **preindustrial civilizations** because they relied on human labor instead of "modern" machines for the harvesting of crops, the manufacturing of goods, the building of public works, and for other activities vital to their society. These civilizations developed from earlier village cultures and display great diversity, resulting from the different environments in which they flourished. But they all share a number of general features.

Ancient civilizations typically occupied large territories centered on cities. Because these societies were highly complex, they needed an effective form of government. This was provided by a ruler and a small class of nobles, officials, and priests who formed the center of the society. This centralized authority also controlled the economy, accumulating wealth by taxing a proportion of all crops and collecting payments, or tribute, from subject peoples. Such an economy allowed the rulers to support thousands of nonfarmers, such as officials, priests, soldiers, and artisans (metalsmiths, potters, and weavers).

Long-distance trade was the lifeblood of ancient civilizations, and merchants formed an important class in urban societies. They transported goods by land, river, and sea to and from distant lands. For example, southern Mesopotamia lacked metals, so it imported them from peoples in the nearby highlands. In return, Mesopotamian cities exported grain, dates, and fine clay vessels.

With long-distance trade came a need to keep accurate records of increasingly complex commercial transactions. Every early civilization developed a record-keeping system, usually a form of written script. The Mesopotamians impressed signs on clay tablets, the Egyptians wrote on rolls of papyrus reed, and the Inca knotted strings.

Every civilization erected elaborate public buildings such as royal palaces, temples, fortified citadels, and huge city walls. These public works provided a focus for the state, served as symbols of official religious beliefs, and proclaimed the power of the ruler. Other kinds of public works included the elaborate

Winnowing grain, Egypt

Mask of Agamemnon of Mycenae

Temple of Athena, Delphi, Greece

Civilizations emerged throughout the ancient world after people settled in areas suitable for farming. Most were complex societies centered on cities and united by powerful leaders. All developed writing systems, held distinctive religious beliefs, and built monumental structures such as palaces and temples.

Aztec god Quetzalcóatl

road systems built by the Inca, the enormous irrigation systems built in Mesopotamia, and the great pyramids built by the Egyptians. These projects required dozens, sometimes thousands, of laborers—often criminals, slaves, or prisoners of war.

Each of these civilizations also developed a set of distinctive religious beliefs. The ruler was typically perceived as a living god, the crucial link between the people and the other gods. These beliefs were commemorated by inscriptions on temple walls, in art, and in elaborate public ceremonies in which the ruler would appear before the people. For instance, the warrior-priests of the Moche (in present-day Peru) appeared before their subjects in glittering gold and silver dress that shone brilliantly in the rays of the sun. All rulers of early civilizations, whether Egyptian pharaoh, Minoan king, Chinese emperor, or Maya lord, were well aware that public performance was critical to ensuring obedience among their subjects.

Finally, each of these civilizations could not have been successful without exceptional individuals with strong leadership abilities. Although the names of most of these ancient leaders have been lost to time, some have endured through the ages or have been discovered through archaeological research. Among these great rulers were the pharaoh Menes, who unified Egypt about 3200 B.C., and Lord Pacal, who ruled the Maya city of Tikal between A.D. 615 and 683.

However, despite all their achievements, most pre-industrial states were remarkably unstable and short-lived. They rose to prominence rapidly, achieved a brief brilliance, then declined or utterly collapsed just as quickly, only to be succeeded by another state.

THE MIDDLE EAST

Some of the earliest civilizations developed in the Middle East. The world's first civilization arose in Mesopotamia, a fertile region centered on the Tigris and Euphrates rivers in modern-day Iraq. Other notable civilizations were those of the ancient Egyptians and the Hittites.

This shell plaque was carved in Sumer, where the world's first civilization arose.

Mesopotamia

Farmers began settling in southern Mesopotamia, in a smaller region called Sumer, by about 5500 B.C. Some of these early farming villages grew into small towns, each with their own religious shrine and patchwork of irrigation canals and fields. After 4000 B.C., farmers gathered into larger communities strategically located where large canals could feed extensive irrigation systems that sustained crops. These early settlements developed into the very first civilization. By 3500 B.C., some towns had become cities, each with their own leaders, officials, and priests who supervised irrigation and trade.

Sumerian cities such as Erech and Ur grew rapidly and developed into important religious and commercial centers. Each city had a large stepped temple called a **ziggurat**, atop which was a shrine to the city's god or goddess. The temple was both an administrative center and a place of worship; it included storerooms for trade goods and the grain that fed the hundreds of nonfarmers—traders, seamen, and artisans—living in the city. Trade brought metals, semiprecious stones, and many other goods from great distances. City officials created written records by inscribing clay tablets with wedge-shaped lines called **cuneiform**. The ruler of each city governed using his extensive political, religious, and military powers.

Sumerian civilization reached its peak after 2900 B.C. as a collection of small city-states

TIME LINE OF ANCIENT CIVILIZATIONS

3500 B.C. 3400 3300 3200 3100 3000 2900

SUMER (3500–2004 B.C.)

ANCIENT EGYPT (3200–30 B.C.)

HARAPPAN (3200–1700 B.C.)

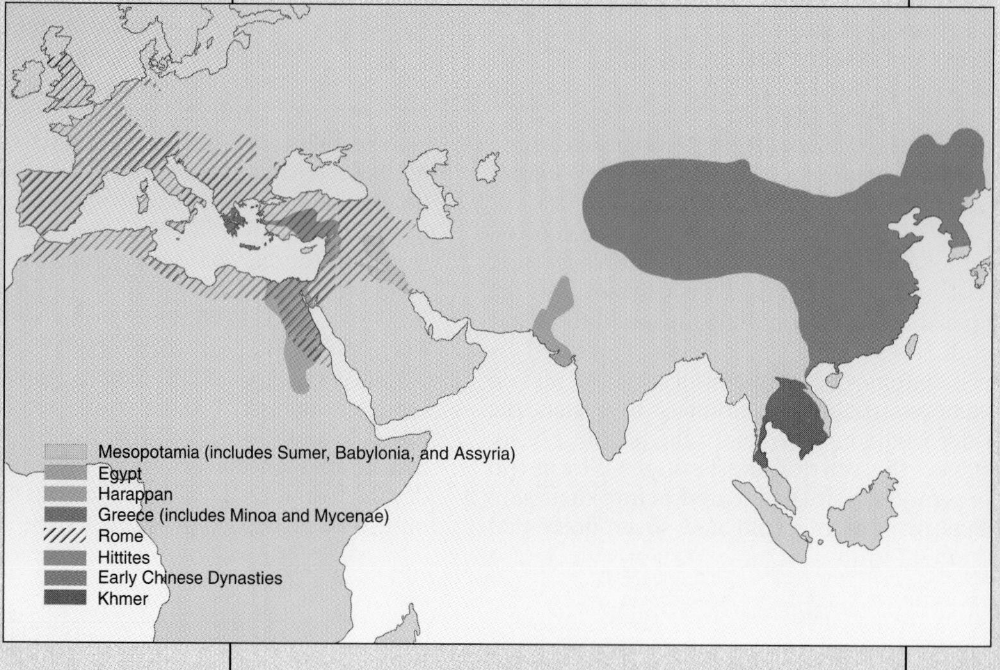

each with their own territory, irrigation canals, and patron gods. These city-states were in an almost constant struggle with each other for dominance in the region. The only unity in Sumerian civilization was a common technology, religion, and language. The Sumerians were brilliant inventors, who developed bronze and copper metallurgy and were among the first to use the wheeled vehicle and the sailing vessel.

By 2350 B.C., new kingdoms had developed upstream of Sumer around the cities of Akkad and Babylon. In northern Mesopotamia, important cities had developed along the Tigris River, in what was to become Assyria in later centuries. An able ruler named Sargon of Akkad conquered all of southern Mesopotamia about 2340 B.C. Akkadian rule endured for about one hundred years, before Gutians from what is now Iran overran its domains. About 2210 B.C., the Third Dynasty of Ur conquered its neighbors and established an empire that extended far into Assyria and eastward to the shores of the Mediterranean Sea. The empire was conquered by Elamite armies from the east in about 2004 B.C.

Babylonia and Assyria. The Akkadian and Ur empires began a Mesopotamian tradition of large, highly unstable empires that developed through military conquest, trade, ruthless administration, and the payment of tribute.

By 1990 B.C., Babylon controlled trade with the eastern Mediterranean and the Persian Gulf. The sixth king of Babylon was Hammurabi, who reigned from 1792 to 1750 B.C. He is best known for his written code of 285 laws, which was publicly displayed on stone columns at locations throughout the empire. Hammurabi was an

Above: **This sculpture may represent Sargon of Akkad, who established the first empire to control all of southern Mesopotamia.**

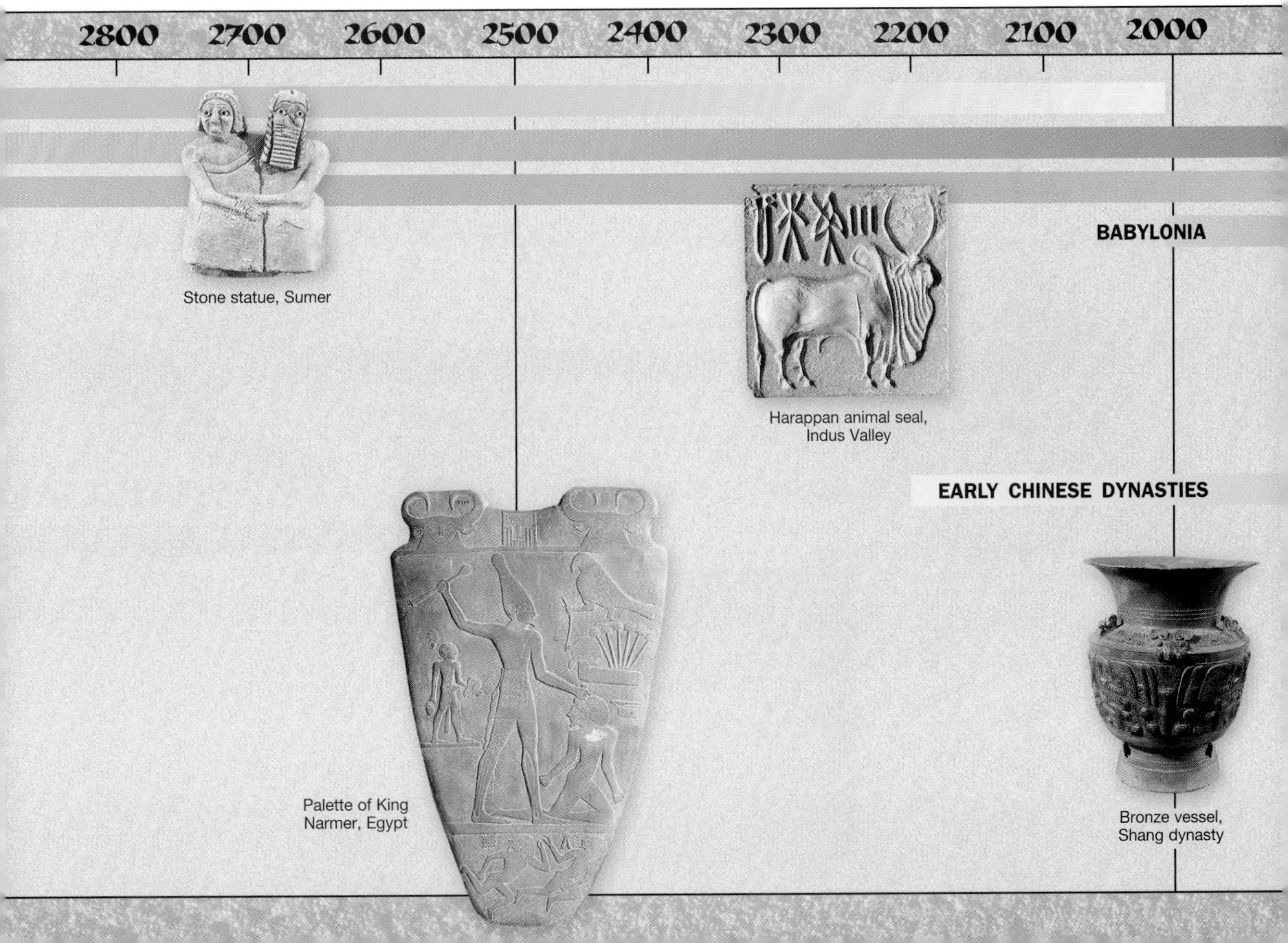

Stone statue, Sumer

Harappan animal seal, Indus Valley

Palette of King Narmer, Egypt

Bronze vessel, Shang dynasty

Ashurbanipal, shown in this relief hunting lions, was the last great king of northern Mesopotamia's Assyrian Empire.

able military man, but more important, he was an efficient administrator who spent much time improving irrigation and building public works.

The Babylonian empire declined after Hammurabi's death in 1750 B.C. The Assyrians, based in the city of Assur upstream on the Tigris River, rose to prominence as Babylon's empire weakened. For centuries, the merchants of Assur had traded far to the east and west. They also controlled all trade down the Tigris River to Babylon and beyond. Assur became very important during the reign of King Assur-uballit (1365–30 B.C.), who created a great empire through ruthless conquest and efficient administration. He maintained diplomatic contacts with the Egyptians, the Babylonians, and the Hittites.

Assur-uballit's empire also collapsed soon after his death, but it was revived in the 800's B.C. under a series of gifted kings. They expanded their domains through conquests and boasted of their victories in great friezes (long bands of continuous relief sculptures) carved on their palace walls. At the height of its power, Assyria's empire

1900 1800 1700 1600 1500 1400 1300 1200 1100

ANCIENT EGYPT (3200–30 B.C.)

HARAPPAN (3200–1700 B.C.)

BABYLONIA (2004–539 B.C.)

MINOANS (1900–1400's B.C.)

MYCENAEANS (1600–1200 B.C.)

HITTITES (1500–1200 B.C.)

EARLY CHINESE DYNASTIES (2200 B.C.–A.D. 906)

OLMECS (1500–500 B.C.)

Terra-cotta disc with Minoan written script

Bronze axe head, Hittite style

Glazed tile dragon from Ishtar Gate, Babylon

spread into Egypt, modern-day Israel, and the eastern Mediterranean coast. The last great Assyrian king was Ashurbanipal, who died in approximately 630 B.C. His empire fell apart rapidly when no strong ruler succeeded him.

Babylon soon became independent of Assyria, and an alliance of Persians and Babylonians overthrew the Assyrian capital at Nineveh in 612 B.C. For more than forty years, Mesopotamia was ruled by the king Nebuchadnezzar II of the Neo-Babylonian Empire, which extended as far as the eastern Mediterranean. Nebuchadnezzar's capital was protected by two walls and filled with mud-brick palaces, elaborate gardens, a processional way, and a huge ziggurat. When the armies of Cyrus the Great of Persia captured Babylon in 539 B.C., Mesopotamia became part of the Persian Empire.

For more information on the ancient civilizations of Mesopotamia, see the articles ASSYRIA in Volume A; Babylonia in Volume B; MESOPOTAMIA in Volume M; PERSIA, ANCIENT in Volume P; and SUMER in Volume S.

The Ishtar Gate was part of a fortified wall that surrounded the city of Babylon in the late 500's B.C. It was decorated with brightly colored glazed tiles.

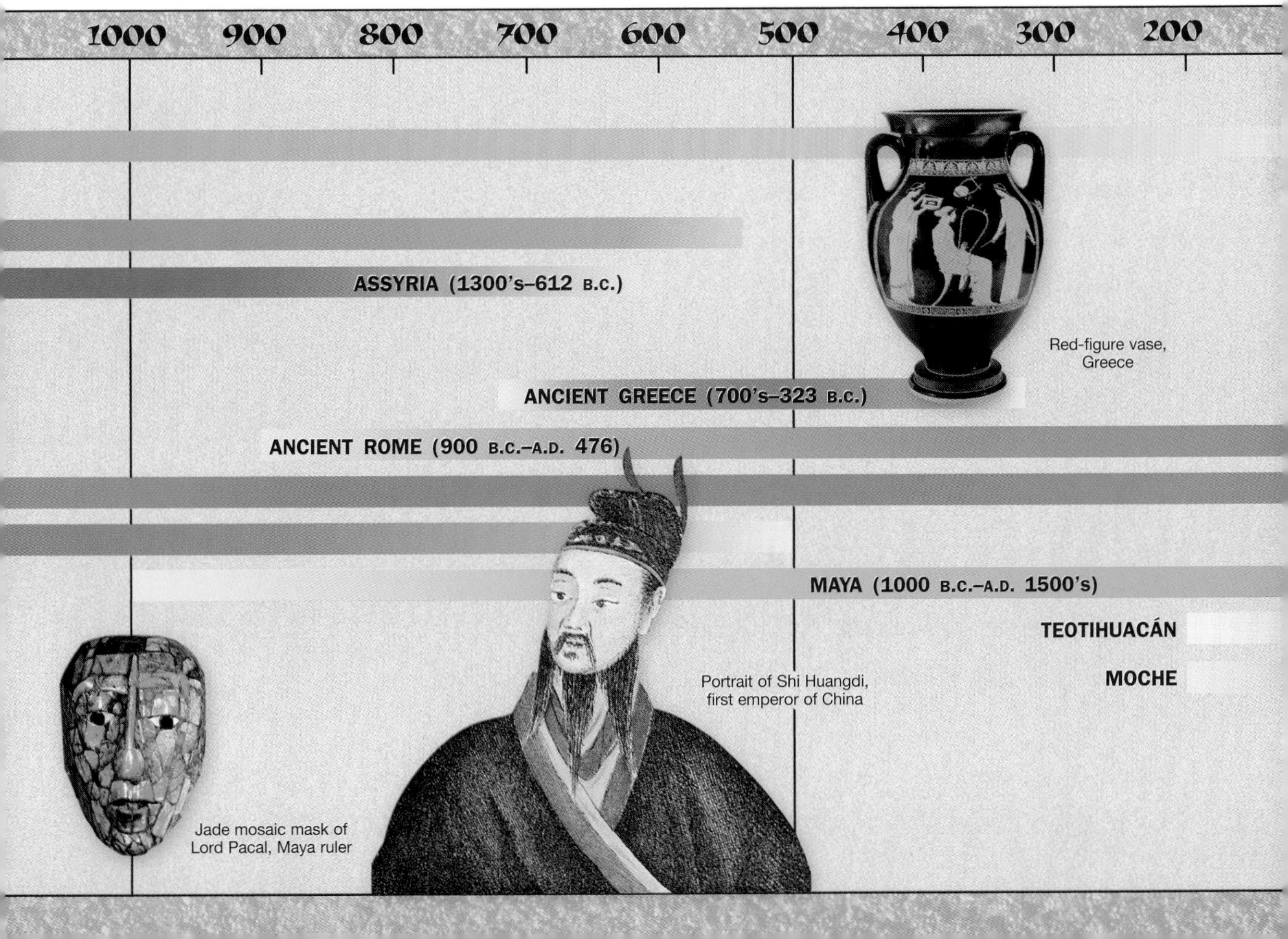

Red-figure vase, Greece

Portrait of Shi Huangdi, first emperor of China

Jade mosaic mask of Lord Pacal, Maya ruler

Ancient Egypt

The Nile River in northern Africa slices through the eastern Sahara desert like a green arrow, a fertile oasis flowing through some of the driest landscape on Earth. The valley is narrow except north of the modern city of Cairo, where it becomes a low-lying delta before flowing into the Mediterranean Sea. The annual flooding of the Nile fertilized the land along its banks, allowing local people to develop agriculture and establish small towns beginning about 4000 B.C. By the 3000's B.C., large kingdoms such as Nekhen in Upper Egypt (the southern half of the country) and Buto in Lower Egypt (the northern half) competed for political power. After generations of diplomacy and war, a ruler of Upper Egypt named Narmer united the two halves of the country into a single state in 3200 B.C. and established a civilization that would become one of the most successful in history.

Under pharaohs such as Ramses II, ancient Egypt reached the peak of its power and influence during the early 1000's B.C.

100 A.D. 1 100 200 300 400 500 600 700

ANCIENT EGYPT (3200–30 B.C.)

Machu Picchu, ancient Inca fortress city

Marble bust of Augustus, first emperor of Rome

ANCIENT ROME (900 B.C.–A.D. 476)

EARLY CHINESE DYNASTIES (2200 B.C.–A.D. 906)

MAYA (1000 B.C.–A.D. 1500's)

TEOTIHUACÁN (200 B.C.–A.D. 750)

MOCHE (200 B.C.–A.D. 700)

Carving, Khmer temple Angkor Wat

Ancient Egypt was ruled by a succession of kings, or pharaohs, who served as the representatives of the sun god, Re. The sun god was foremost among the many gods worshiped. The Egyptians also believed in life after death, so they carefully mummified their dead. This process preserved the body so it could be used by the deceased in the afterlife. For more information, see the article MUMMIES in Volume M.

The Egyptians built pyramids as burial chambers for early pharaohs. The construction of these colossal structures, particularly the three great pyramids in Giza, required the labor of thousands of people over decades. The Egyptians also built monumental temples to honor their kings and gods. For more information, see the article PYRAMIDS in Volume P.

The Egyptians were the first people to develop a system of hieroglyphic writing. This system consisted of pictures that represented ideas or whole words that were inscribed on stone monuments and written on papyrus. For more information, see HIEROGLYPHIC WRITING SYSTEMS in Volume H.

Ancient Egypt reached its peak after 1550 B.C. under pharaohs such as Amenhotep III, Seti I, and Ramses II. It colonized Nubia, a region south of Aswan in present-day Sudan, and turned the Nubian kingdom of Kush into an Egyptian province. It also extended its borders into eastern Mediterranean lands and assumed control of strategic trading ports along the coast. Egyptian civilization then declined as a series of conquerors, including the Assyrians, Nubians, and Persians, descended on the Nile beginning about 1075 B.C. Egypt came under Greek rule after 323 B.C., and in 30 B.C. it became part of the Roman Empire. For more information on ancient Egypt, see EGYPT, ANCIENT and EGYPTIAN ART AND ARCHITECTURE in Volume E.

Hittites

About 1500 B.C., a people called the Hittites formed a civilization in present-day Turkey and rose to power through conquest and clever political actions. While they adopted many customs from the people they conquered, they retained their own unique identity. At their peak, the Hittites competed

800 900 1000 1100 1200 1300 1400 1500

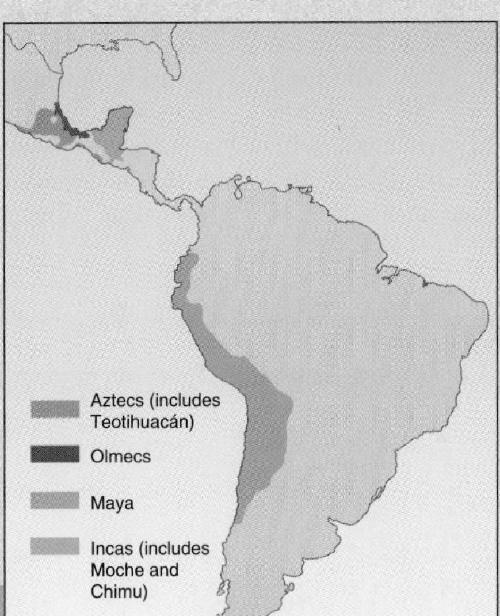

Francisco Pizarro, Spanish explorer

KHMER (A.D. 500–1431)

AZTECS (A.D. 1300's–1521)

CHIMU (A.D. 1373–1460)

INCAS (A.D. 1438–1533)

with Egypt for control of the vital trade routes that converged on the eastern Mediterranean coastlands. In the 1300's B.C., King Suppiluliumas expanded the empire as far as the borders of modern-day Lebanon.

The Hittite kings ruled from the capital city of Bogazköy, which was surrounded by several miles of walls, and obtained much of their grain from their fertile lands in today's Syria. After fighting the Egyptians at the Battle of Kadesh in the 1280's B.C., they formed an alliance with the pharaohs. Trade was too valuable to be upset by war.

The Hittites were the first people to smelt iron on a large scale, probably in the highlands south of the Black Sea. Because iron was ideal for making weapons and tools that needed tough, sharp edges, the Hittite rulers guarded the new technology. But by 1200 B.C., ironworking had spread through the Mediterranean world.

Political unrest and invasions from the north, as well as a widespread drought that hit the eastern Mediterranean, caused the Hittite civilization to collapse about 1200 B.C. into a collection of small city-states. These city-states became part of the Persian Empire centuries later. For more information, see the article HITTITES in Volume H.

THE MEDITERRANEAN

The Mediterranean region was home to several ancient civilizations: the Minoans, who lived on the island of Crete off the southeast coast of Greece; the Mycenaeans, who preceded the Greeks on the mainland; and the great civilizations of Greece and Rome.

The Minoans and Mycenaeans

The Minoan civilization developed about 1900 B.C. Unlike the Egyptians and Mesopotamians, the Minoans did not live in cities. Their civilization was centered on palaces that served as ceremonial centers, shrines, workshops, storehouses, and royal residences. The largest palace was Knossos in northern Crete, which was originally built about 1930 B.C. Knossos was a two-story structure, centered on a courtyard, with walls decorated with painted scenes of gods, goddesses, and acrobats leaping over bulls. Knossos was the hub of a civilization that thrived off trade with distant lands such as Egypt. The Minoans sailed as far as modern-day Syria and throughout the Aegean Sea.

The most dramatic event in Minoan history was the eruption in 1688 B.C. of a volcano on Santorini Island to the north, causing massive ash falls over Crete. Although this disaster must have greatly harmed agriculture, Minoan civilization survived. In the 1400's B.C., Knossos and other Minoan palaces were destroyed by fire. Mycenaean kings from the Greek mainland now dominated the Aegean world.

Mycenaean civilization, which arose by 1600 B.C., was also centered on palaces. The most important was a walled fortress in southern Greece called Mycenae, after which the civilization is named. Sections of the surrounding walls still stand, as does a famous gateway topped with two carved lions. Graves of Mycenaean lords, located just inside the walls, were excavated in the 1870's by the German archaeologist Heinrich

This frescoe of acrobats leaping over bulls decorated the walls of the Minoan palace Knossos, which was built about 1930 B.C.

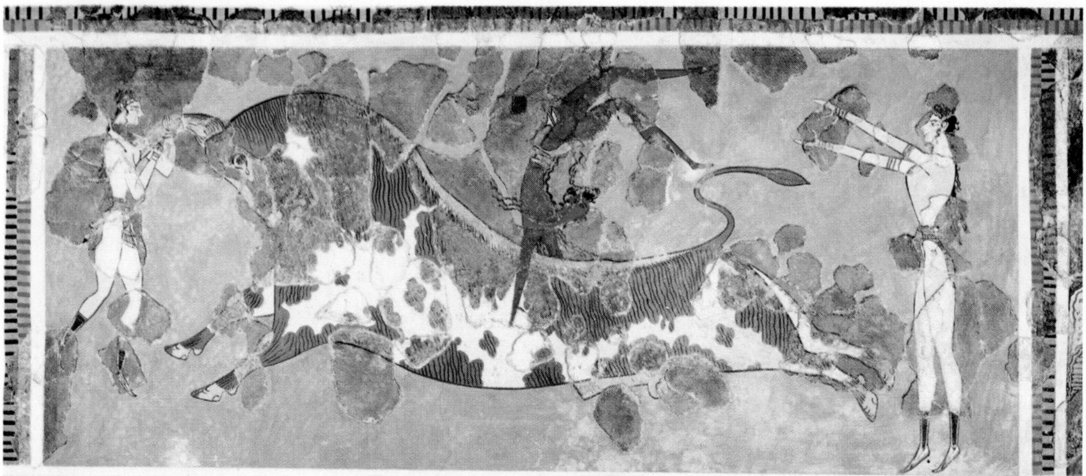

MUSIC IN THE ANCIENT WORLD

Music played an important role in most, if not all, of the world's ancient civilizations. It was performed for the same reasons as it is today: to entertain, to set the mood for performances or political events, as a form of artistic expression, and as a part of religious ceremonies.

Scholars have learned about the early history of music by studying the remains of instruments discovered at archaeological excavations; images of musicians, dancers, and singers painted on pottery or murals; and descriptions of musical performances in ancient texts. Although it is possible to approximate the sounds produced by certain instruments, there is no way to know exactly what ancient songs sounded like because few scores or notations exist for early music.

Many of the instruments played in ancient times are similar to those used today. The Sumerians of Mesopotamia played harps, lyres, flutes, oboes, and long-necked lutes. Musicians of ancient Egypt played harps, flutes, and double clarinets. The Egyptians also adopted Mesopotamian instruments such as double oboes and tambourines. Egyptian pharaohs even exchanged musicians, singers, and dancers with other rulers as gifts.

In ancient Greece, scholars studied music and developed various scales. The mathematician Euclid organized the scales into one system, with seven-note scales named for people and places, such as Dorian, Phrygian, and Lydian. The same names were used for scales in the Christian Church during the Middle Ages (A.D. 500–1450).

Music played an important role in ancient civilizations. This Sumerian mosaic of a musician playing a lyre dates from about 2800 B.C.

In Mesoamerica, the Maya had a rich musical tradition. The most common musical instrument found at Maya archaeological sites is the ocarina, a whistle or flute that was shaped like a person or animal. Other Maya instruments included long trumpets made from wood and gourds; drums made from wood or hollowed-out turtle shells that were struck with deer antlers; flutes; and rattles. The only known stringed instrument used by the Maya is the so-called friction drum, a gourd with a leather membrane stretched over the top and a single cord running up from the membrane. The cord was rubbed with a bow-like rasp or stick to make the membrane resonate and produce sounds.

JULIA L. J. SANCHEZ
Assistant Director
Cotsen Institute of Archaeology at UCLA

Schliemann. The lords had been buried with their weapons and were wearing golden masks depicting their features.

The Minoans and Mycenaeans used written scripts, known as Linear A and B, to record their trading activities and the administrative details of palace life. These scripts have been only partly deciphered, but they were a forerunner of Greek. Little is known of Minoan and Mycenaean religious beliefs, which may have involved a mother goddess responsible for the fertility of the soil.

Mycenae continued to dominate seaborne eastern Mediterranean trade routes until 1200 B.C. Thereafter, a combination of factors, including severe drought, foreign invasions, and political unrest, are thought to have caused the collapse of the civilization. For more information, see the article MYCENAEAN CULTURE in Volume M.

Greece

The collapse of the Mycenaean civilization in Greece about 1200 B.C. was followed by

Parts of the walled fortress Mycenae in southern Greece still stand, including this gateway topped with two carved lions.

many centuries of political change and uncertainty. Greece remained a land of small farming villages until the first city-states appeared during the 700's B.C. Greek settlements also flourished in Sicily, southern Italy, and on the shores of the Black Sea. Colonization carried Greek language and culture over large parts of the western Mediterranean and far inland.

Among the major city-states that were prospering by about 480 B.C. were Corinth, Sparta, and Athens. Corinth, famous for its fine perfumes, was a major manufacturing center governed by powerful tyrants. Sparta was an agricultural state in the Peloponnese peninsula of southern Greece. It relied on its powerful army to control much of the south. Athens was a commercial and manufacturing center that was blessed with fertile soils for agriculture. The Greek city-states frequently competed with one another in trade and war.

This Roman statue of Athena was copied from a Greek original carved in the 400's B.C.

During this period, the Greeks began developing their distinctive styles of architecture, sculpture, and painting. These styles constantly evolved during the history of ancient Greece, and they would exert a strong influence on many of the civilizations that followed.

Athens became a major cultural center during the 400's B.C. It was the birthplace of democracy, the rule of the people. (The term "democracy" comes from the Greek words *demos*, meaning "the people," and *kratos*, meaning "power.") Drama flourished in the hands of such well-known playwrights as Aristophanes, Aeschylus, and Euripides. The philosophers Plato and Socrates were justly famous, as was the historian Thucydides, who wrote a brilliant account of the Peloponnesian War (431–404 B.C.). Many examples of Athens' architecture were celebrated throughout the ancient world. These included the magnificent Parthenon, on the Acropolis (the highest point in the city); the Erechtheum, the holiest shrine in the city; and the two famous Long Walls that connected the city to the port of Piraeus, about 5 miles (8 kilometers) away.

In 480 B.C., Greece's various city-states united to defeat an invasion by the Persians. Greece then became an empire, under the rule of the most powerful city-state, Athens. This empire lasted until the Peloponnesian War. Athens was defeated by Sparta and other states, who maintained their autonomy until Philip II of Macedon (a kingdom in northern Greece) conquered the entire country in 338 B.C. and made them part of the Macedonian Empire.

Philip's son Alexander the Great reigned from 336–323 B.C., during which time he promoted Greek art and culture as he expanded his empire from Greece to India. He died unexpectedly and his generals divided the empire between them. This marked the end of Greece's classical age.

For more information, see the articles GREECE, ANCIENT; GREECE, ART AND ARCHITECTURE OF; and GREECE, LITERATURE OF in Volume G.

Rome

About 900 B.C., a people known as the Etruscans established a civilization in northern Italy. After 500 B.C., Etruscan civilization consisted of a network of self-governing city-states that had conquered territory to the north and south. Among the small settlements the Etruscans controlled was a town on the Tiber River called Rome. An Etruscan family named the Tarquins transformed Rome into a city, but they were expelled by the Romans in 510 B.C. The newly independent city-state became the basis of the great Roman republic.

Rome soon controlled all of Italy, and by 148 B.C. it had conquered Greece and parts of Asia. After a period of political turmoil, during which many individuals vied for control of the republic, the soldier and senator Octavian (later, Augustus) defeated Marc Antony and became Rome's first emperor in 31 B.C. The empire reached its greatest extent during the A.D. 100's, when its domain reached from Mesopotamia in the east to the Atlantic in the west, and from Britain in the North to Africa's Sahara desert in the south. A vast network of highways, roads, and tracks linked all parts of the empire.

Roman rule resulted in profound changes among conquered peoples, who nonetheless were permitted to retain their native cultures and languages. The Greek influence was great, especially in the east, where it was centuries old. Rome itself was a city of a half million people in Augustus' time, a glittering capital adorned with arches and columns commemorating imperial victories.

The Roman Empire never collapsed; it simply became something else. By A.D. 400, there were two empires, the eastern ruled from Constantinople (later Byzantium, now Istanbul), the western from Rome. The Eastern, or Byzantine, Empire survived for a thousand years. The Western Empire collapsed in the mid-400's and became a loose collection of independent kingdoms controlled by Germanic rulers.

But the legacy of Rome survives. The works of great writers such as Cicero, Vergil, and Ovid are still read today; and Latin, the language of the Romans, is the basis of modern-day French, Italian, Spanish, and Romanian. Roman law forms the basis of most Western legal systems. The Romans were also skilled builders; they perfected concrete and developed the stone arch, and their architectural styles can be seen in modern public buildings such as the White House and the Capitol in Washington, D.C. For more information, see the articles BYZANTINE EMPIRE in Volume B; LATIN LANGUAGE AND LITERATURE in Volume L; and ROME, ANCIENT and ROME, ART AND ARCHITECTURE OF in Volume QR.

The Romans were skilled builders. Among their contributions to architecture was the stone arch, as seen in the famous Colosseum.

▸ ASIA

Among the notable civilizations of Asia were the Harappan civilization, the early dynasties of China, and the Khmer of Southeast Asia.

Harappan Civilization

The fertile soils of the Indus and Saraswati River valleys in modern-day Pakistan were home to the Harappan civilization, which emerged after 3200 B.C. For 800 years, the Harappans lived in small villages and towns, trading for semiprecious stones and timber with people in the neighboring highlands to the north. After 2600 B.C., large cities developed along the two great rivers, although most Harappans still lived in smaller farming communities. At about the same time, the Harappans began to export cloth, wool, and cedar to Mesopotamia in exchange for gold, silver, and other items.

The writing on Harappan clay seals has never been deciphered.

Harappan civilization flourished over a vast area of about a half million miles, a region larger than modern Pakistan. Cities, towns, and smaller communities were linked by common religious beliefs, trade, and very loose political ties.

The civilization's two major cities, Harappa and Mohenjodaro, were home to perhaps 40,000 inhabitants each. They had high citadels protected by fortifications to keep out the summer floods. Nothing is known of their rulers because Harappan writing has not yet been deciphered. But it is believed that they rejected the lavish displays that marked Mesopotamian rulers and Egyptian pharaohs. The cities themselves were laid out in narrow streets lined by standardized houses made of baked brick and often arranged around courtyards. Many commoners lived in barrack-like dwellings at the edge of the city. Some areas of Harappa and Mohenjodaro served as markets, where beadmakers, potters, and other craftspeople labored in cramped workshops.

Little is known about Harappan religious beliefs. Some clay seals discovered by archaeologists depict gods, such as a three-headed figure wearing a horned headdress and surrounded by wild animals. Some Harappan experts believe this god was a forerunner of the Hindu god Shiva, Lord of the Beasts. In some respects, Harappan religion seems to resemble modern Hinduism.

Harappan civilization reached its peak in about 2000 B.C., when trade with Mesopotamia flourished. Three hundred years later, Harappa and Mohenjodaro were in decline and soon abandoned. This may be connected to drier climatic conditions, changes in trade patterns, or disastrous flooding along the Indus. At about this time, too, the Saraswati River dried up, causing a catastrophic disruption of farming along its banks.

Early Chinese Dynasties

Early Chinese civilization consisted of a succession of dynasties—ruling houses in which the leaders typically belonged to the same family. Occasionally, coexisting dynasties would compete with each other for power, as would rival rulers within individual dynasties. But throughout the rise and fall of these dynasties, Chinese culture remained relatively unchanged.

The early Chinese dynasties shared many common features. They were ruled by warlords who lived inside royal compounds with their families and attendants. This arrangement reflected the rigid social structure that separated the ruling class from the artisans, farmers, soldiers, and others who served them. Economies were based on agriculture, particularly the raising of cereal crops. Ancestor worship was central to their beliefs because a ruler's authority came from his ancestors.

The Xia and the Shang. Chinese legends tell of a famous leader named Huang Di who founded Chinese civilization in the Yellow River valley about 2698 B.C. In about 2200 B.C., a harsh ruler named Yu the Great founded China's first dynasty, the Xia.

The Xia lords were eventually succeeded by the Shang dynasty. The Shang dynasty was highly militarized and could muster an army of 10,000 men or more when needed. An

THE GREAT WALL OF CHINA

The Great Wall of China is an extensive fortification built by early Chinese dynasties to protect themselves from invaders to the north. It stretches across mountains and valleys in northern China for about 4,000 miles (6,400 kilometers)—greater than the distance between the east and west coasts of the United States. Like the pyramids of ancient Egypt and the Parthenon of ancient Greece, the Great Wall of China is an architectural and engineering marvel.

The Great Wall began as a series of smaller, separate walls built by various states between 685 and 221 B.C. for protection from attacks by their neighbors as well as by the Huns, a Mongolian people from central Asia. When Shi Huangdi of the Qin dynasty seized power and became China's first emperor in 221 B.C., he ordered that all the walls be connected to form one long fortification. Thousands of slaves, soldiers, and other laborers built the wall by stacking one layer of compacted dirt on top of another.

The wall was strengthened and lengthened during the Han dynasty (202 B.C.–A.D. 220), and towers were added at regular intervals to serve as guard posts. From these towers, sentries would light fires to alert forces along the wall that enemies were approaching.

Although later dynasties contributed to the wall's construction, the Ming dynasty (1368–1644) oversaw the final and most extensive work. Old sections were repaired, new sections and towers were added, and secondary walls were erected. The Ming reinforced their wall with an outer layer of brick and stone held together with a mortar of rice and lime. The guard towers were armed with iron canons.

Most of the wall that exists today dates from the Ming period. Its height ranges from 20 to 50 feet (6 to 15 meters) and its width from 13 to 40 feet (4 to 12 meters). A 13-foot-wide roadway runs along the top.

The Great Wall of China is an extensive fortification of dirt, brick, and stone. Most of the wall that exists today dates from the Ming dynasty (1368–1644).

Time, weather, and human activity have taken their toll on the Great Wall. Some sections have crumbled under centuries of wind and rain, while others have been covered by blowing sand. Other sections of the wall have been demolished to make room for new roads and other construction projects, while villagers living along its length have taken stones and bricks from the ancient structure to build homes.

elaborate kin organization that ran through society obligated people to serve the ruler when called upon. Like the Sumerian civilization, the Shang dynasty was a patchwork of small states. Its people were expert metalsmiths who produced fine bronze vessels.

One of the earliest Shang capitals was Ao, close to the Yellow River. Here the ruler lived in a compound surrounded by earthen walls, isolated from the surrounding farming villages. In 1400 B.C., the capital was moved to Anyang and a network of royal compounds, temples, and cemeteries were established that covered 120 square miles (310 square kilometers). Deceased Shang rulers were buried in deep pits along with their chariots, hundreds of superb bronze vessels and jade artifacts, and numerous sacrificial victims.

The Zhou and the First Emperor. The Shang was overthrown in 1027 B.C. by the Zhou dynasty, whose influence spread far into southern China. Although the Zhou consisted of several states or kingdoms that constantly fought with each other, the period of their rule was one of major innovations: After 700 B.C., walls of rammed (packed) earth were built around cities for protection; ironworking revolutionized warfare and improved agriculture; and commerce expanded with the development of the first Chinese coinage about 500 B.C. Another important development during the reign of the Zhou was the creation of the philosophical and religious doctrines of Taoism. Taoism provided the Chinese with a concept of order and harmony in the universe, and in later centuries it had a profound effect on China's artistic tradition and ideas of effective government.

This life-size terra-cotta soldier was one of thousands buried with Shi Huangdi, ancient China's first emperor.

The disputes among the Zhou came to an end in 221 B.C., when the ruthless leader of the Qin state conquered the others and unified China into a single empire. This leader took the name Shi Huangdi, or "first emperor." Under Shi Huangdi's rule, the Chinese built an extensive road system and began the construction of a vast wall of mud brick and rammed earth that stretched across the countryside to keep out nomadic invaders. Future dynasties strengthened and lengthened this wall, which eventually became the Great Wall of China.

The Han and the Decline of Ancient China. The Han founded a new dynasty and empire about 202 B.C. About 58 million people lived under Han rule, which extended from Mongolia to the margins of southeast Asia.

The Han expanded foreign trade along an extensive route called the Silk Road, which linked China with the West, and their ships sailed as far as India and the Indian Ocean. The Han emperors embraced Confucianism, which promoted the idea of a centralized monarchy and an educated bureaucracy to run the state. Among the important inventions developed by the Chinese during this period were paper, the crank handle, and the wheelbarrow.

The Han dynasty survived until A.D. 220, when weak imperial rule caused the centrally controlled empire to break apart. Three hundred and fifty years of chaos followed as the country cut itself off from the West. China was finally stabilized in A.D. 618 under the Tang dynasty, but foreign rulers later took over the country. The time of ancient Chinese civilization had passed. For more information, see the articles CHINA (History); CHINA, ART AND ARCHITECTURE OF; and CHINA, LITERATURE OF in Volume C.

The Khmer

Between 500 B.C. and the founding of China's first empire in 221 B.C., many small kingdoms developed in Southeast Asia. By the A.D. 100's, people in the Mekong Delta (in present-day Vietnam) traded extensively with China's Han dynasty. Beginning about 500, the greatest political power in the region was wielded by the Khmer. Like many ancient Southeast Asian peoples, the Khmer were influenced by Indian culture. They adopted India's belief in Hinduism and Buddhism, as well as Indian styles of art and architecture.

The Khmer formed an empire centered on the city of Angkor, located in a fertile region north of the Tonle Sap, a lake in present-day Cambodia. In 802 a dynamic Khmer monarch named Jayavarman II came to power. He developed a highly centralized form of government and promoted the idea that he was a god. Jayavarman ruled for 45 years and was succeeded by three dynasties of Khmer rulers between 900 and 1200.

Khmer monarchs called themselves *varman* ("protector"). They ruled over a state whose entire purpose was to serve the king and to build an elaborate holy temple for him. A series of rulers erected vast temple complexes in Angkor. One of the most magnificent was Angkor Wat, built in the 1100's. Nearby Angkor Thom was built in the 1200's as both a new capital and a shrine. These immense complexes—larger in scale than the Egyptian pyramids—are considered masterpieces of world architecture.

These huge building projects overstressed and weakened the empire, and in 1430–31 it fell to Thai armies. Descendants of the Khmer continue to live in present-day Cambodia, Thailand, and Vietnam.

▶ THE AMERICAS

Civilization in the Americas arose in two distinct regions. The first was in Mesoamerica, the name given by archaeologists to a region in Central America that stretches from central Mexico to northwest Costa Rica. The second was in South America, in the shadows of the Andes mountains in what is today Peru. The civilizations of this region are referred to as Andean.

Mesoamerica

The roots of civilization in Mesoamerica go back at least 3,500 years. At a time when ancient Egypt was at the peak of its power and prosperity, the first complex societies in the Americas appeared in the tropical lowlands by the Gulf of Mexico.

The Olmecs. The Olmecs formed a series of kingdoms in the Veracruz region of Mexico, along the shores of the Gulf of Mexico, beginning about 1500 B.C. Their homeland was low-lying and tropical, and it was rich in fish and other animals that were prominently featured in a sophisticated style of art that eventually spread throughout much of Mesoamerica. The Olmec rulers considered themselves links between the living world and the supernatural realm, as did later Mesoamerican rulers. The lords built great mounds and pyramids surrounding plazas to impress their followers with their overwhelming power. At places like San Lorenzo and La Venta, huge carved heads depict these rulers, whose names are unknown. The Olmecs' simple form of writing, which remains largely undeciphered, was probably the first developed in the Americas. In some ways it resembled the writing used by the Maya. The Olmec civilization disappeared about 500 B.C. for reasons still unknown.

The Olmecs of Mesoamerica carved enormous heads depicting their rulers, who considered themselves links to the supernatural realm.

The Maya. Olmec cultural traditions formed part of Maya civilization, which developed in the Yucatán Peninsula before 1000 B.C. Classic Maya civilization emerged about A.D. 300. Maya society consisted of an ever-changing pattern of city-states that competed ferociously with one another, although they shared a common language and religious beliefs. Great cities such as Calakmul, Copán, Palenque, and Tikal were ruled by powerful royal families. Maya rulers were divine lords who built their cities as symbolic representations of the Maya world: Cut-stone pyramids represented the mountains, plazas represented the plains, and carved obelisks represented forests. The religious powers of the lords and their expertise in battle led to constant warfare between the city-states.

Maya civilization was based on sophisticated swamp agriculture that focused on the cultivation of maize and beans. Extensive trading networks linked each city and the lowlands with the highlands to the south. Traders imported volcanic glass for mirrors and toolmaking, while the feathers of tropical birds and other products were exported. The Maya were also expert astronomers and mathematicians.

The Maya were so successful at water control that their population exploded during centuries of good rainfall. At the same time, the number of nobles increased and the pressure on the food supply grew to the point that there was political unrest. During the 800's, a series of severe droughts devastated crops in the region. The ancient Maya civilization collapsed in the south but survived in the north until it was conquered by the Spanish in the 1500's. Descendents of the ancient Maya still live in Latin America today. For more information, see the article MAYA in Volume M.

Above: **This section of a Maya limestone lintel (horizontal beam) depicts a blood-letting ceremony.** ***Right:*** **The Mesoamerican city of Teotihuacán was dominated by a vast complex of pyramids and plazas and a broad avenue known today as the Street of the Dead.**

Teotihuacán. Maya cities such as Tikal were strongly influenced by Teotihuacán, a powerful highland state on the edge of the Basin of Mexico. Between 200 B.C. and A.D. 750, Teotihuacán grew from a series of villages into a city covering 8 square miles (20 square kilometers) that was home to more than 150,000 people. Early rulers drew up an ambitious master plan for the city, which was unchanged over many centuries. A vast ceremonial complex of pyramids and plazas dominated the north end of the city. A broad avenue, known today as the Street of the Dead, intersected with another avenue that ran from east to west. At the intersection sat a temple and a huge market. Teotihuacán collapsed about 750, either as a result of conquest or severe drought.

The Aztecs. Teotihuacán's collapse created a political vacuum in the Basin of Mexico. This void was filled briefly by the Toltec civilization, centered on the city of Tula. Toltec civilization disintegrated in 1200 and was replaced by Aztec rule in the 1300's.

Originally a small tribe, the Aztecs rose to prominence through military skill. By the 1420's, they were the dominant power in Mesoamerica, expanding their domain until they ruled from the Pacific coast to the Gulf of Mexico and as far south as Guatemala. Their empire was a patchwork of alliances, held together by tribute. Thousands of war prisoners were sacrificed to the sun god, Huitzilopochtli. The Aztecs also worshiped the feathered serpent god Quetzalcóatl.

However, by the time Spanish adventurer Hernando Cortés landed in the lowlands in 1519, the Aztecs were already in decline. Their often brutal rule and the excessive tribute they demanded from the people they conquered had led to rebellions on the outer fringes of the empire. Cortés created alliances with rebellious rulers and marched on the Aztec capital, which fell in 1521. The entire civilization soon followed. For more information, see the article AZTECS in Volume A.

Andean Civilizations

By 2500 B.C., large villages flourished along the coast of present-day Peru. After 1800 B.C., these villages had grown into small kingdoms located in valleys, where mountain floodwater could be used to irrigate crops of maize, beans, and cotton. Elaborate ceremonial centers built around adobe pyramids housed the leaders, who supervised increasingly complex irrigation works.

A second culture developed in the highlands around Lake Titicaca, on the border between Peru and Bolivia, where small ceremonial centers grew rapidly. Their prosperity depended on trading textiles, wool, and fish meal with the coastal kingdoms.

Between 900 and 200 B.C., new religious ideas spread from a shrine in the Andes

foothills of central Peru, where priests communicated with the supernatural realm. They created an elaborate, highly distinctive art style that spread with the new religious ideas throughout the lowlands and highlands. This style of art and these religious ideas gave Andean civilization a basic unity, although it consisted of many separate political states. Despite their differences, the highlands and lowlands depended on one another for such essentials as fish meal from the Pacific and potatoes from the Andes.

About 200 B.C., the Moche state developed along the north coast of Peru. For 900 years, a small number of royal families, headed by warrior priests, ruled over thousands of irrigation farmers in the desert valleys. They ruled by military force and with a strict belief system that included human sacrifice and the worship of the sun and the moon. Much of what is known about these rulers comes from archaeological excavations of royal burials in the modern village of Sipán. (For more information, see ARCHAEOLOGY (Great Discoveries in Archaeology: The Lords of Sipán) in Volume A.) The major royal capital was a complex of huge pyramids, which was largely destroyed by catastrophic rains and major droughts in the 500's. The Moche civilization collapsed about A.D. 700.

After 1373, an expanding Chimu state conquered neighboring coastal valleys and organized a kingdom based on the city of Chan Chan in Peru. There, each Chimu ruler built his own compound where he lived in seclusion. He was mummified after his death, and his mummy remained in the compound. Chimu rulers were expert generals and diplomats, but they were unable to prevent the Inca from conquering them in 1460.

The Incas. About 1438, a brilliant warrior of the Inca tribe near the modern city of Cuzco conquered his neighbors and set about transforming his kingdom into a major state. Over the next sixty years, a series of able Inca rulers expanded their domains as far north as Ecuador, into the Lake Titicaca region, to the coast, and to the edges of the Amazon Basin on the eastern slopes of the Andes. The empire was named *Tawantinsuyu* ("the land of the four quarters") and was centered on the capital city of Cuzco. The Incas were brilliant conquerors and administrators, who linked their domains with extensive road systems throughout all kinds of terrain. At its height, the empire consisted of 6 million people.

By the early 1500's, the Inca civilization was in decline. Thousands of people had died from smallpox and other diseases introduced by the Spanish in the North; disputes arose over royal succession; and there was no suitable land left for each new ruler to conquer. The empire was in a state of civil war when Spanish adventurer Francisco Pizarro and a small band of soldiers landed in Peru in 1532. The Spanish conquered the capital city a year later, and soon the world's last pre-industrial civilization collapsed. For more information, see the articles INCAS in Volume I and PIZARRO, FRANCISCO in Volume P.

BRIAN FAGAN
Emeritus Professor of Anthropology
University of California, Santa Barbara
Coauthor, *Ancient Civilizations*

See also ARCHAEOLOGY; CUNEIFORM; GREEK MYTHOLOGY; INDIANS, AMERICAN; MYTHOLOGY; PERSIA, ANCIENT; POMPEII; WONDERS OF THE WORLD.

ANDERSEN, HANS CHRISTIAN (1805–1875)

No collection of fairy tales would be complete without the works of the Danish author Hans Christian Andersen. In fact, Andersen's life was like a fairy tale in many ways. Out of the poverty, hardship, and loneliness of his youth, he came to be one of the most honored men of his time. Many of the more than 160 fairy tales he wrote, including "The Ugly Duckling," "The Princess and the Pea," and "The Little Mermaid," have become literary classics enjoyed by children and adults alike.

Andersen was born on April 2, 1805, in Odense, Denmark. His parents were poor; his father worked as a shoemaker and his mother was a washerwoman. His father, who died when Andersen was 11, entertained him with old Danish legends and stories from *The Arabian Nights*.

The people of Odense never knew what to make of the tall, awkward boy. When he recited long passages from plays or did a clumsy dance or insisted on singing, they could hardly help laughing. Everyone advised him to learn a trade, but this he would not do. He was forever saying that he was going to be famous.

In 1819, Andersen moved to the capital city of Copenhagen, where he hoped to become an actor in the Royal Theater. Many people of the theater and wealthy families of the city tried to help him, without much success. His dancing master gave up, and so did his singing teacher. Directors of the Royal Theater sympathized with his efforts to write plays but finally concluded that Andersen needed an education. One of the directors raised money to send him away to school. The next few years were the unhappiest of his life. Andersen was much older than the other students, and the schoolmaster found endless ways to make fun of him. Finally when word of Andersen's plight reached his benefactors in Copenhagen, he was removed from the school and put into the hands of a private tutor. He later attended and graduated from Copenhagen University.

After his schooling, Andersen spent many years traveling and writing poems, books, and plays, which met with some success. It was not until he was 30 that he wrote any fairy tales. His first small book of fairy tales became popular almost immediately, and from then on his fame grew rapidly, spreading from country to country.

Andersen put many pieces of his own life into his fairy tales. He never forgot that his mother as a young girl had been forced to go begging. This led him to write "The Little Match Girl," a story full of compassion for the unfortunate ones of this Earth. And his own personal experiences are reflected in "The Ugly Duckling," which points out that sometimes the qualities that make you feel lonely, different, and out of place are the very qualities that, when properly used, can make you shine.

In 1867 he returned to Odense to be honored by his country. Standing on the balcony of the hall where the ceremony was held, he saw below him the city square, full of people who cheered him, and bright with thousands of candles burning in the windows of all the buildings. Andersen published his last fairy tales in 1872, and after a long illness, he died in Copenhagen on August 4, 1875.

DANNY KAYE

Danny Kaye (1913–87), the author of this article, was a popular actor and comedian who starred in the 1952 motion picture *Hans Christian Andersen.*

Kaye was born David Daniel Kominsky in Brooklyn, New York. He developed a talent for mime, improvisation, and reciting tongue-twisting lyrics and lines, which he displayed in motion pictures, television programs, and Broadway plays. Kaye also entertained children around the world on behalf of the United Nations Children's Fund (UNICEF).

On the following pages is one of Hans Christian Andersen's best-loved fairy tales.

THE EMPEROR'S NEW CLOTHES

Many years ago there lived an Emperor who was so exceedingly fond of fine new clothes that he spent all his money on being elaborately dressed. He took no interest in his soldiers, no interest in the theater, nor did he care to drive about in his state coach, unless it were to show off his new clothes. He had different robes for every hour of the day, and just as one says of a King that he is in his Council Chamber, people always said of him, "The Emperor is in his wardrobe!"

The great city in which he lived was full of gaiety. Strangers were always coming and going. One day two swindlers arrived; they made themselves out to be weavers, and said they knew how to weave the most magnificent fabric that one could imagine. Not only were the colors and patterns unusually beautiful, but the clothes that were made of this material had the extraordinary quality of becoming invisible to everyone who was either unfit for his post, or inexcusably stupid.

"What useful clothes to have!" thought the Emperor. "If I had some like that, I might find out which of the people in my Empire are unfit for their posts. I should also be able to distinguish the wise from the fools. Yes, that material must be woven for me immediately!" Then he gave the swindlers large sums of money so that they could start work at once.

Quickly they set up two looms and pretended to weave, but there was not a trace of anything on the frames. They made no bones about demanding the finest silk and the purest gold thread. They stuffed everything into their bags, and continued to work at the empty looms until late into the night.

"I'm rather anxious to know how much of the material is finished," thought the Emperor, but to tell the truth, he felt a bit uneasy, remembering that anyone who was either a fool or unfit for his post would never be able to see it. He rather imagined that he need not have any fear for himself, yet he thought it wise to send someone else first to see how things were going. Everyone in the town knew about the exceptional powers of the material, and all were eager to know how incompetent or how stupid the neighbors might be.

"I will send my honest old Chamberlain to the weavers," thought the Emperor. "He will be able to judge the fabric better than anyone else, for he has brains, and nobody fills his post better than he does."

So the nice old Chamberlain went into the hall where the two swindlers were sitting working at the empty looms.

"And so the Emperor set off in the procession under the beautiful canopy, and everybody . . . said 'Oh! how superb the Emperor's new clothes are!' "

"Upon my life!" he thought, opening his eyes very wide, "I can't see anything at all!" But he didn't say so.

Both the swindlers begged him to be good enough to come nearer, and asked how he liked the unusual design and the splendid colors. They pointed to the empty looms, and the poor old Chamberlain opened his eyes wider and wider, but he could see nothing, for there was nothing. "Heavens above!" he thought, "could it possibly be that I am stupid? I have never thought that of myself, and not a soul must know it. Could it be that I am not fit for my post? It will never do for me to admit that I can't see the material!"

"Well, you don't say what you think of it," said one of the weavers.

"Oh, it's delightful—most exquisite!" said the old Chamberlain, looking through his spectacles. "What a wonderful design and what beautiful colors! I shall certainly tell the Emperor that I am enchanted with it."

"We're very pleased to hear that," said the two weavers, and they started describing the colors and the curious pattern. The old Chamberlain listened carefully in order to repeat, when he came home to the Emperor, exactly what he had heard, and he did so.

The swindlers now demanded more money, as well as more silk and gold thread, saying that they needed it for weaving. They put everything into their pockets and not a thread appeared upon the looms, but they kept on working at the empty frames as before.

Soon after this, the Emperor sent another nice official to see how the weaving was getting on, and to enquire whether the stuff would soon be ready. Exactly the same thing happened to him as to the Chamberlain. He looked and looked, but as there was nothing to be seen except the empty looms, he could see nothing.

"Isn't it a beautiful piece of material?" said the swindlers, showing and describing the pattern that did not exist at all.

"Stupid I certainly am not," thought the official; "then I must be unfit for my excellent post, I suppose. That seems rather funny—but I'll take great care that nobody gets wind of it." Then he praised the material he could not see, and assured them of his enthusiasm for the gorgeous colors and the beautiful pattern. "It's simply enchanting!" he said to the Emperor.

The whole town was talking about the splendid material.

And now the Emperor was curious to see it for himself while it was still upon the looms.

Accompanied by a great number of selected people, among whom were the two nice old officials who had already been there, the Emperor went forth to visit the two wily swindlers. They were now weaving madly, yet without a single thread upon the looms.

"Isn't it magnificent?" said the two nice officials. "Will Your Imperial Majesty deign to look at this splendid pattern and these glorious colors?" Then they pointed to the empty looms, for each thought that the others could probably see the material.

"What on earth can this mean?" thought the Emperor. "I don't see anything! This is terrible. Am I stupid? Am I unfit to be Emperor? That would be the most disastrous thing that could possibly befall me.—Oh, it's perfectly wonderful!" he said. "It quite meets with my Imperial approval." And he nodded appreciatively and stared at the empty looms—he would not admit that he saw nothing. His whole suite looked and looked, but with as little result as the others; nevertheless, they all said, like the Emperor, "It's perfectly wonderful!" They advised him to have some new clothes made from this splendid stuff and to wear them for the first time in the next great procession.

"Magnificent!" "Excellent!" "Prodigious!" went from mouth to mouth, and everyone was exceedingly pleased. The Emperor gave each of the swindlers a decoration to wear in his buttonhole, and the title of "Knight of the Loom."

Before the procession they worked all night, burning more than sixteen candles. People could see how busy they were finishing the Emperor's new clothes. They pretended to take the material from the looms, they slashed the air with great scissors, they sewed with needles without any thread, and finally they said, "The Emperor's clothes are ready!"

Then the Emperor himself arrived with his most distinguished courtiers, and each swindler raised an arm as if he were holding something, and said, "These are Your Imperial Majesty's knee-breeches. This is Your Imperial Majesty's robe. This is Your Imperial Majesty's mantle," and so forth. "It is all as light as a spider's web, one might fancy one had nothing on, but that is just the beauty of it!"

"Yes, indeed," said all the courtiers, but they could see nothing, for there was nothing to be seen.

"If Your Imperial Majesty would graciously consent to take off your clothes," said the swindlers, "we could fit on the new ones in front of the long glass."

So the Emperor laid aside his clothes, and the swindlers pretended to hand him, piece by piece, the new ones they were supposed to have made, and they fitted him round the waist, and acted as if they were fastening something on—it was the train; and the Emperor turned round and round in front of the long glass.

"How well the new robes suit Your Imperial Majesty! How well they fit!" they all said. "What a splendid design! What gorgeous colors! It's all magnificently regal!"

"The canopy which is to be held over Your Imperial Majesty in the procession is waiting outside," announced the Lord High Chamberlain.

"Well, I suppose I'm ready," said the Emperor. "Don't you think they are a nice fit?" And he looked at himself again in the glass, first on one side and then the other, as if he really were carefully examining his handsome attire.

The courtiers who were to carry the train groped about on the floor with fumbling fingers, and pretended to lift it; they walked on, holding their hands up in the air; nothing would have induced them to admit that they could not see anything.

And so the Emperor set off in the procession under the beautiful canopy, and everybody in the streets and at the windows said, "Oh! how superb the Emperor's new clothes are! What a gorgeous train! What a perfect fit!" No one would acknowledge that he didn't see anything, so proving that he was not fit for his post, or that he was very stupid.

None of the Emperor's clothes had ever met with such a success.

"But he hasn't got any clothes on!" gasped out a little child.

"Good heavens! Hark at the little innocent!" said the father, and people whispered to one another what the child had said. "But he hasn't got any clothes on! There's a little child saying he hasn't got any clothes on!"

"But he hasn't got any clothes on!" shouted the whole town at last. The Emperor had a creepy feeling down his spine, because it began to dawn upon him that the people were right. "All the same," he thought to himself, "I've got to go through with it as long as the procession lasts."

So he drew himself up and held his head higher than before, and the courtiers held on to the train that wasn't there at all.

ANDERSON, MARIAN (1897–1993)

Visitors to a small church in Philadelphia, Pennsylvania, were amazed by the beautiful voice of a 6-year-old girl singing in the choir. She was Marian Anderson, born in Philadelphia on February 27, 1897. She loved to sing all kinds of songs, but her favorites were church hymns. This little girl eventually became one of the greatest singers of her time.

It was not easy for Marian Anderson to acquire a musical education. She was black in a racially prejudiced society, and her family was poor. But when she was in her twenties, she won a scholarship. It enabled her to travel and study in Europe. She made her European concert debut in Berlin, and her fame spread quickly. Her singing delighted huge audiences in every major European city. The great composer Jean Sibelius dedicated a song to her when she visited him in Finland.

News of her success in Europe reached America. At her homecoming concert in New York City in 1935, she received thunderous applause. But in 1939 she was prevented from giving a concert at Constitution Hall in Washington, D.C. Many people felt that her race was the reason. Undaunted, on Easter Sunday of the same year, she gave a free concert for an audience of 75,000 from the steps of the Lincoln Memorial.

As her fame increased, Marian Anderson toured all parts of the world. In 1955 she became the first black singer to appear with the Metropolitan Opera. The U.S. State Department sent her on a goodwill tour of Asia in 1957, and the following year, she served as a U.S. delegate to the United Nations. She was awarded the Presidential Medal of Freedom in 1963. The Marian Anderson Award, which she established in 1942, helped young students pay for their musical education.

Marian Anderson, a contralto with a rich, mellow voice, overcame racial prejudice to become one of the greatest singers of modern times.

On April 18, 1965, Marian Anderson gave a farewell concert at Carnegie Hall, in New York City. She died in Portland, Oregon, on April 8, 1993. Her autobiography is *My Lord, What a Morning* (1956).

Reviewed by Florence Jackson
Author, Blacks in America series

ANDERSON, MAXWELL. See North Dakota (Famous People).

ANDERSON, SHERWOOD. See Ohio (Famous People).

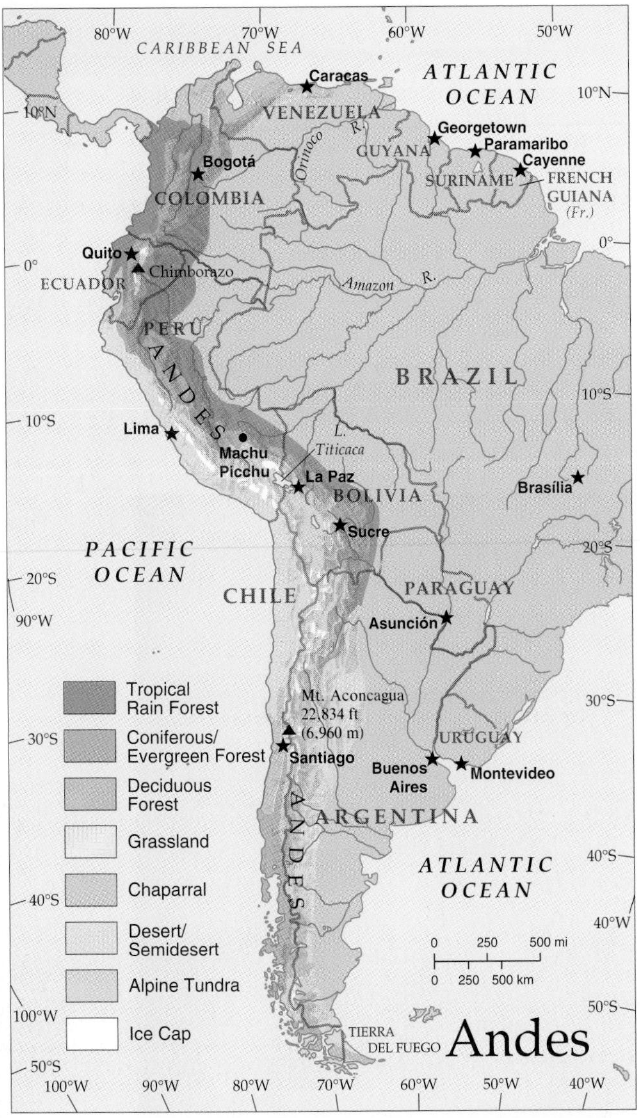

Cotopaxi, located in the Andes south of Quito, Ecuador, is the world's highest active volcano.

ANDES

The Andes form the longest and one of the highest mountain systems in the world. Only the Himalayas in south central Asia are taller and more rugged. The ranges of the Andes stretch about 7,200 kilometers (4,500 miles) along the west coast of South America, from the Caribbean Sea in the north to Tierra del Fuego, an island group at the southern tip of the continent.

Within the Andes there are many different kinds of lands and ways of life. There are great modern cities and small Indian villages where people live much as their ancestors did centuries ago. There are dense forests and barren plains, fertile farmlands, and stony soil where little grows. The capitals of four South American countries lie high in the Andes—Caracas, Venezuela; Bogotá, Colombia; Quito, Ecuador; and La Paz, Bolivia.

Many peaks in the Andes are over 6,100 meters (20,000 feet) high—taller than any peaks in North America. Aconcagua, in Argentina, is the highest mountain in the Western Hemisphere. It rises to 6,960 meters (22,834 feet). Many Andean peaks are volcanic. Some are inactive, but others still erupt at times. Cotopaxi, in Ecuador, is the highest active volcano in the world. It rises to 5,897 meters (19,347 feet).

There are few passes through the Andes, and the mountains form a great barrier to transportation and communication in South America. The northern Andes lie in Colombia, Venezuela, and Ecuador. The central Andes are in Bolivia, Peru, northern Chile, and northern Argentina. The mountains in some parts of the central Andes are extremely high and wide. The southern Andes, at the tip of the continent in Argentina and Chile, are the lowest part of the system.

Two of South America's major river systems—the Amazon and the Orinoco—begin in the Andes. High in the mountains between Bolivia and Peru is Lake Titicaca. It is the highest lake in South America and the highest navigable lake in the world.

The climate in the Andes changes with the elevation above sea level. At the lowest elevation, below 900 meters (about 3,000 feet), the climate is tropical. This is called the *tierra caliente* ("hot land"). It is a region of dense green jungles and rivers filled with crocodiles. Crops such as fruits and vegetables, cotton, and tobacco grow well at these elevations.

At slightly higher elevations, the climate is cooler. In the northern Andes, this region is the source of much of South America's fine coffee. At 2,100 meters (7,000 feet) the *tierra fría* (''cold land'') begins. Evergreen trees and wheat grow well here.

Between 3,000 and 4,000 meters (10,000 and 13,000 feet) is the treeless, windswept region known as the puna. Only a few hardy crops like potatoes and barley can be grown on these high mountainsides. High above, between the puna and the snowfields, is the *páramo* (''wasteland''), where nothing but mosses and lichens can survive.

The Andes provide the world with many important minerals such as copper, tin, and petroleum. There are smaller quantities of gold and silver. Coal deposits are limited.

Many interesting animals live in the Andes. There are llamas, guanacos, alpacas, and vicuñas—all members of the camel family. Chinchillas are highly prized for their valuable fur. There are cougars, or mountain lions, and small deer called guemal. Tiny hummingbirds, brilliantly colored, dart about in the Andean forests. Soaring above the towering, snowcapped Andes are the huge condors, the largest of the vultures and one of the world's largest flying birds.

About a third of all the people in South America live in the Andes, most of them in crowded cities and towns. In the Andes of Bolivia, Peru, and Ecuador, there are many descendants of the ancient Incas and other Indians who lived in the area before the Spanish conquest in the 1500's. Many of these peoples still speak only Indian tongues. The southern Andes are sparsely populated.

Deep gorges, steep slopes, and towering heights make it difficult and costly to build roads and railroads through the Andes. The Central Railroad of Peru, for example, is one of the world's highest railroads. It climbs to an elevation of 4,836 meters (15,865 feet). But in recent times the airplane and some modern highways have opened up areas that were once almost completely cut off from the outside world.

Reviewed by DANIEL JACOBSON
Michigan State University

A girl of the Peruvian Andes sits by the roadside above terraced fields. Below: Llamas parade before Sacsahuamán, a fortress built by the Incas outside Cuzco.

ANDORRA

Andorra is a tiny country located high in the Pyrenees mountains of southwestern Europe, between France and Spain. Although few people know much about it, Andorra is an ancient land, whose people have lived in the region since Roman times and whose form of government dated from the Middle Ages.

▶THE PEOPLE AND THEIR LAND

In addition to the native Andorrans, the population includes many Spaniards and a small French minority. The official language is Catalan, which is spoken in the Spanish province of Catalonia. Spanish and French are also widely used. The people are Roman Catholics.

Andorra is a rugged land. Surrounded by the high peaks of the Pyrenees, the country is broken by deep gorges and narrow valleys. It is drained by the Valira River and its tributaries. Andorra's beautiful mountain scenery and cool, dry summer climate make it popular with tourists. In winter there are heavy snowfalls, which have led to the development of several fine ski resorts. Andorra has neither railroads nor a major airport and can be reached only by automobile or bus.

▶THE ECONOMY

Because of its location and isolated mountainous terrain, Andorra served for centuries as a corridor through which goods were smuggled between France and Spain. So profitable was the smuggling business that it was often called Andorra's national industry. Today, however, tourism dominates the economy, accounting for most of Andorra's income.

Since little of Andorra's land is suitable for farming, agriculture is not a main source of wealth, and Andorra must import much of its food. The leading crops are oats, barley, and fruit. Tobacco is grown for export. Many mountain pastures are dotted with flocks of sheep. Mining, stone quarrying, and lumbering are carried out on a limited basis. Andorra also has a number of hydroelectric plants that supply electric power to Spain. Until 1983, Andorra had no income tax. Until recently, it had no customs duties (taxes), and many items are imported into the country for sale to tourists at bargain prices. Andorra also receives income from the sale of its beautiful postage stamps to collectors around the world.

▶HISTORY AND GOVERNMENT

According to tradition, Andorra was established late in the 700's when the emperor Charlemagne granted the people a charter of independence for their help in fighting the Muslim Moors, who had invaded the region from Spain. Nevertheless, for many years, Andorra was fought over by the French counts of Foix and the Spanish bishops of Urgel. Finally, in 1278, a treaty was signed at Les Escaldes, a small town near Andorra la Vella, the capital. By the terms of this treaty, the count of Foix and the bishop of Urgel were made co-princes of Andorra. Later the rights of the count of Foix were inherited by the kings of France, and when France became a republic, by the president of France.

Following a centuries-old custom, Andorra sent each of its two co-rulers a token tribute each year. The French president received the sum of 960 francs, while the bishop of Urgel received 460 pesetas, together with a supply

FACTS and figures

PRINCIPALITY OF ANDORRA (Principat d'Andorra) is the official name of the country.

LOCATION: Southwestern Europe.

AREA: 175 sq mi (453 km²).

POPULATION: 58,000 (estimate).

CAPITAL AND LARGEST CITY: Andorra la Vella.

MAJOR LANGUAGES: Catalan (official), Spanish, French.

MAJOR RELIGION: Roman Catholic.

GOVERNMENT: Co-principality. **Heads of state**—president of France, bishop of Urgel (co-princes). **Head of government**—chief executive (president) of the Executive Council.

CHIEF PRODUCTS: Agricultural—tobacco, oats, barley, fruit, livestock. **Manufactured**—tobacco products, lumber. **Mineral**—iron ore, building stone.

MONETARY UNIT: French franc (1 franc = 100 centimes), Spanish peseta (1 peseta = 100 céntimos).

of chickens, cheeses, and hams from each of the districts of Andorra. Each of the "princes," as the co-rulers are still referred to, sent a representative to Andorra. These representatives served as joint chiefs of the small Andorran police force and as judges in the criminal courts.

Because of the dual relationship with France and Spain, there are two school systems, one supported by France, the other by Spain. There is both a French- and a Spanish-owned radio station, each broadcasting in its own language. Andorra uses both French francs and Spanish pesetas as its legal money.

The Andorran legislative body is the General Council of the Valleys, which is made up of 28 elected members, four from each of the seven districts. The council chooses the chief executive, or president, who selects and heads the Executive Council, or cabinet of ministers.

A break with Andorra's past came in 1993, when Andorrans, in a referendum, approved the country's first constitution, which provides for a parliamentary form of government. It retains the Spanish and French co-princes as heads of state, but with much reduced powers.

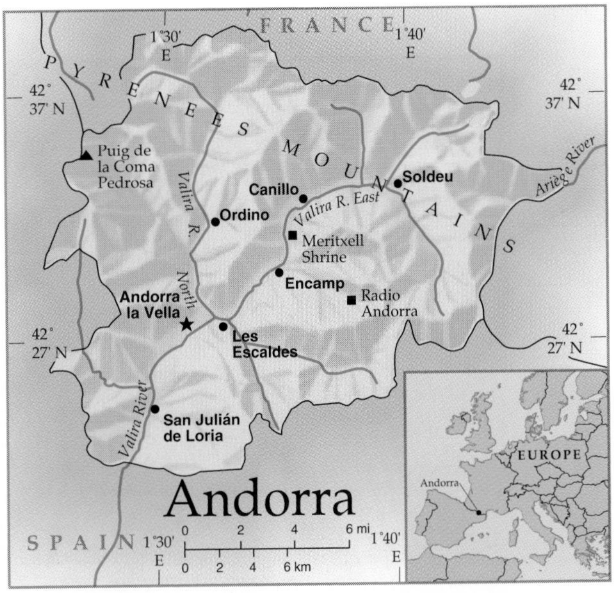

Andorra's traditional diplomatic isolation is also likely to undergo some changes with its admission to the United Nations, also in 1993.

PAUL C. HELMREICH
Wheaton College (Massachusetts)

ANDRÉ, MAJOR JOHN. See ARNOLD, BENEDICT; SPIES (Profiles).

ANEMIA. See DISEASES.

Andorra's rugged mountains (*left*) long kept the country isolated. Signs on buildings in Andorra la Vella, the capital (*right*), are in Catalan, Andorra's official language.

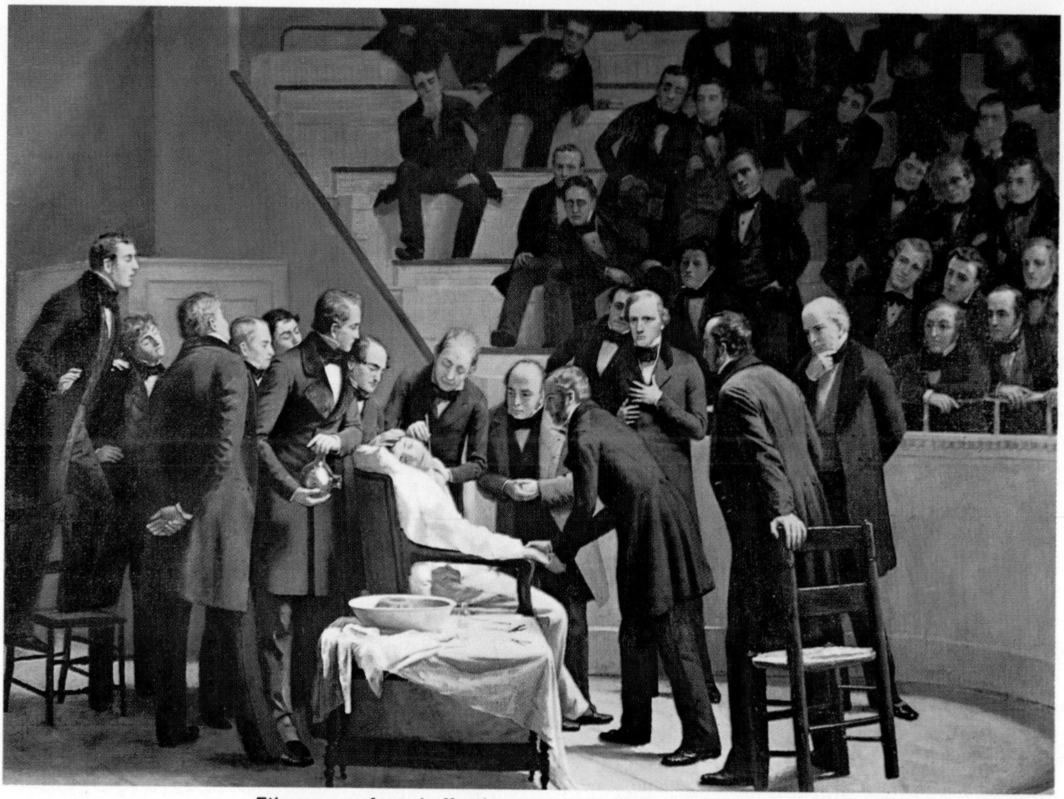

Ether as a safe and effective anesthetic during surgery was first demonstrated in public in 1846 by William T. G. Morton (the man holding the flask in the painting above).

ANESTHESIA

When you have to have an operation, you are given an **anesthetic.** This is a substance that keeps you from feeling pain. Some anesthetics prevent the nerves from sending messages of pain to the brain; others affect the brain itself. In either case you feel nothing when you are operated on. This condition is called anesthesia.

▶PAIN RELIEVERS OF OLD

From the earliest times people have looked for ways to relieve pain. They discovered that drugs made from certain plants could be used to kill pain. Doctors then tried using the same drugs during operations. Among these drugs were opium, mandrake, and hashish. But none of them was really very good. Small amounts had little effect. Large amounts often killed the patient.

Alcoholic drinks were tried as a means of inducing anesthesia (making the patient unconscious). But the patient often regained consciousness as soon as the first cut was made.

Even as late as the 1840's there seemed to be no safe and satisfactory way of putting a patient out of pain during an operation. So in most cases the patient was simply held or tied down, and the doctor worked as quickly as possible. Operations were limited to those that could be done in a few minutes. Even so, many patients did not survive the pain and shock.

▶THE START OF MODERN ANESTHETICS

The story of modern anesthetics begins with scientific studies of gases and ways they could be used. As early as 1799 the English chemist Humphry Davy had described nitrous oxide as a gas that was "capable of destroying physical pain." But many years passed before anyone used it as an anesthetic.

In the meantime people had discovered that breathing small amounts of nitrous oxide produced a pleasant sensation. In fact, nitrous oxide was known as laughing gas. By the 1840's people had also discovered the pleasures of breathing in ether. (Ether is a liquid that quickly turns into a gas when exposed to air.) They held parties called "ether frolics." Such parties were silly, but one good came from them. Many medical students and doctors were introduced to these gases at the parties.

One doctor who learned about ether at a frolic was Crawford W. Long of Jefferson, Georgia. In 1842 he painlessly removed tumors from the neck of a patient who had breathed in ether. This was probably the first truly effective anesthetic ever used in an operation on a human being. But Dr. Long did not publish his discoveries, and other doctors did not learn of his success.

By this time many doctors were experimenting with anesthetic gases. Horace Wells, a dentist in Hartford, Connecticut, was working with nitrous oxide. Unfortunately, when he tried to demonstrate it in public, something went wrong. The patient screamed with pain as his tooth was pulled. Dr. Wells fled to the sound of boos.

Success came to Wells's former partner, William T. G. Morton. At the Harvard Medical School, Dr. Morton met Charles T. Jackson, who suggested trying ether. Morton did. First he tried it on animals, including his own dog. Then he tried it on himself. It proved to be a safe and effective anesthetic.

By 1846, Morton was ready to demonstrate how ether could be used in surgery. He persuaded John C. Warren of the Massachusetts General Hospital to try operating on a patient who had been given ether. The day set was October 16. A group of doctors and students had been invited to observe. Many of them were sure that the ether would not work and had come only to laugh at Morton.

The patient was strapped to a chair in the usual way. Morton placed a tube in his mouth. The tube was connected to a glass globe filled with ether. Breathing the fumes into his lungs, the patient fell asleep.

Dr. Warren began to operate. Expecting the usual outcry, he made the first cut. There was silence. The doctor finished the operation. When the patient became conscious, he announced that he had felt no pain.

News of this success spread quickly. The way to modern, painless surgery was open. Oliver Wendell Holmes, an American doctor and poet, applied the term "anesthesia" to the condition produced by ether. The word is from the Greek and means "loss of feeling."

The search for more and better anesthetics was stepped up. James Simpson, an English doctor, was dissatisfied with ether because it irritated the lungs. Seeking a substitute, he found that chloroform had an anesthetic effect. In 1847 he gave it to a woman during childbirth, and she suffered no pain. Chloroform became very popular after 1853, when Queen Victoria took it during delivery of her seventh child.

Since then many anesthetics have been developed, each with its own special properties. Today, doctors can choose from many anesthetics the one best suited to the patient and the operation.

▶GENERAL AND LOCAL ANESTHETICS

There are two main types of anesthetics: general and local.

A general anesthetic makes the patient lose consciousness. A local anesthetic affects only part of the body. For example, if you have your tonsils out, you are given a general anesthetic so that you sleep through the operation. But if you need only a few stitches in your arm, you are given a local anesthetic that kills pain only in that area.

General Anesthetics

A general anesthetic works by first entering the bloodstream. The blood carries the drug to the central nervous system. Once there, the anesthetic acts on the nerve cells of the brain. These cells lose their ability to send and receive messages. No sensations are felt, and the patient loses consciousness.

General anesthetics are usually given either as a gas to be breathed in or as a liquid to be injected into a vein. The anesthetic may be given by an **anesthesiologist,** a physician who specializes in this work. Sometimes it is given by an **anesthetist,** a specially trained nurse or technician. Monitoring, or watching, the patient's vital signs is a very important part of giving an anesthetic. This means that the anesthetist must closely observe the pulse, blood pressure, color of the skin, and appearance of the eyes to check the depth of anesthesia.

The Local Anesthetic

A local anesthetic blocks the nerves at the area of the operation. The chemical may be applied to the surface of the body, to act on the nerve endings in the skin. Or it may be injected with a needle, to block nerve impulses to the brain and thus prevent the feeling of pain. Tooth extractions are often done in this way, with the anesthetic injected into the gum.

A method called spinal or regional anesthesia may be used for some abdominal operations or for the delivery of a baby. Nerves to the lower part of the body branch from the spinal cord. A single injection into the fluid surrounding the spinal cord blocks large numbers of nerves. The patient remains conscious and relaxed and feels no pain.

SOME WELL-KNOWN ANESTHETICS

These are all chemical anesthetics, identified by names in common usage. All are made in a laboratory.

GENERAL ANESTHETICS

CHLOROFORM: Clear liquid with a sweet odor. Quickly changes into gas. Stronger than ether, but not as safe in large amounts. Unlikely to burn or explode. Can damage liver. An early anesthetic, now rarely used.

CYCLOPROPANE: Colorless, sweet-smelling gas. Produces quick and deep anesthesia. Useful especially in diseases of the heart and respiratory system, when a high level of oxygen must be provided to the tissues. But its use is limited because it can explode.

ETHER: The chemical ethyl ether or diethyl ether. A colorless liquid that quickly changes into gas. Produces deep but safe anesthesia for long operations. Strong odor. Irritates breathing passages and lungs. Leaves patient feeling sick after operation. Burns and explodes easily. An early anesthetic, now replaced by newer ones.

FLUOTHANE: Trade name for the chemical halothane. A liquid that quickly changes into gas. Stronger than ether. May cause liver damage in a few patients. No unpleasant aftereffects. Unlikely to burn or explode. Now the most widely used anesthetic.

NITROUS OXIDE: Colorless, sweet-smelling gas. Produces unconsciousness quickly. No unpleasant aftereffects. Unlikely to burn or explode. Produces light anesthesia and must be used with stronger drugs. Used often in dental work or short operations. One of the first anesthetics. Also known as laughing gas.

PENTOTHAL: Trade name for thiopental sodium. A chemical solid that is dissolved in liquid before being injected into veins. Puts patients to sleep and makes them forget operation. Not a true anesthetic, so must be used in combination with other anesthetics for long operations. Few unpleasant aftereffects, but not safe for people with heart or lung trouble.

LOCAL ANESTHETIC

NOVOCAIN: Trade name for the drug procaine hydrochloride. Injected into area of pain. Commonly used in dental work and minor operations. Related anesthetics include those known by trade names Carbocaine, Metycaine, Nupercaine, Pontocaine, and Xylocaine.

WHY A RANGE OF ANESTHETICS IS NEEDED

Every anesthetic has both advantages and disadvantages. There is no single all-purpose anesthetic. Doctors choose what seems best for the patient and the kind of operation. They may choose one particular anesthetic. Or they may use several together.

Any good anesthetic must free the patient from pain, be safe and dependable, and prevent struggling movements. In most cases the muscles must be relaxed in order for an operation to be performed successfully.

Ideally, an anesthetic should also be pleasant to take, put the patient to sleep rapidly, have the smallest possible effect on the heart and lungs, and wear off quickly, leaving no unpleasant aftereffects.

A preanesthetic (before the anesthetic) drug is given to help prepare the patient for the anesthetic. It makes sure that the anesthetic will work smoothly and reduces anxiety, especially in children. The drugs most frequently used as preanesthetics are Demerol or Seconal, which make the patient drowsy, and Valium, which relaxes the patient. These drugs also help to reduce the aftereffects of anesthesia, such as nausea.

OTHER KINDS OF ANESTHESIA

Anesthetics are drugs that act chemically on the nerves of the body. But there are other ways to produce anesthesia.

One way is to lower the temperature of a part of the body—an arm, for example—by packing it in crushed ice. As the temperature goes down, sensation in that part is dulled. The same effect can be produced by spraying the area with a fast-evaporating chemical, such as ethyl chloride. The chemical evaporates quickly, causing the skin to cool sharply so that all sensation is lost. A quick operation can then be performed.

For operations on internal organs, the body is cooled by a technique called **hypothermia.** The body is cooled well below its normal temperature of 37°C (98.6°F), and a general anesthetic is given. With this technique the body's need for oxygen is lowered, and the heartbeat is reduced or even stopped. This allows surgeons to perform difficult brain and heart operations, because the body part under surgery is nearly bloodless.

Hypnosis is a very old way of producing a state of anesthesia. Before the development of chemical anesthetics, it was often the most effective way to control pain. The hypnotist-doctor suggests to the patient that no pain will be felt. The sensation of pain is then absent until the patient is awakened. But not everyone can be successfully hypnotized. And hypnosis cannot be used in major operations.

Acupuncture is a method of anesthesia that was developed in China, where it is routinely used in place of, or in addition to, conventional anesthesia. In acupuncture, fine needles are inserted at certain points under the skin and twirled rapidly. In acupuncture anesthesia, the patient remains conscious and relaxed and does not suffer the nausea or other unpleasant aftereffects of chemical anesthesia.

Today anesthesia makes it possible to perform long and difficult lifesaving operations. However, the search for better anesthetics continues. So do efforts to learn more about how anesthesia works.

SARAH R. RIEDMAN
Author, science books for children

See also DRUGS; MEDICINE (Medical Milestone: Conquest of Pain).

ANGELICO, FRA (1400?–1455)

One of the most beloved artists in history was the Italian painter Fra Angelico. He was considered so saintly that legends grew up around him. One story relates that when he fell asleep while working on a painting, angels came down from heaven to finish it for him.

Fra Angelico was born about 1400 near Florence. His real name was Guido di Pietro. He took the name Fra Giovanni da Fiesole at about the age of 20, when he entered a monastery in Fiesole. There he became famous for his paintings and illuminated manuscripts (handwritten books decorated with painted pictures or designs).

In 1436, Fra Angelico was transferred to the San Marco monastery in Florence. It is said that when the pope saw San Marco after Fra Angelico redecorated it, he offered to make the artist archbishop of Florence. But Fra Angelico refused, explaining that he could better serve the church by painting. About 1445 the pope called him to Rome to paint frescoes (wall paintings done on wet plaster) at the Vatican. Fra Angelico's frescoes use soft, yet clear colors and graceful lines to tell stories from the Bible.

Fra Angelico died in Rome on February 18, 1455. The names Fra Angelico ("angelic brother") and Il Beato ("the blessed one") were given to him after his death because he was devout—in his life and in his art.

Reviewed by S. J. FREEDBERG
National Gallery of Art (Washington, D.C.)

A detail from Fra Angelico's 1437 altarpiece at Perugia, Italy. The scene is from the life of St. Nicholas.

ANGELOU, MAYA (1928–)

In her collection of highly acclaimed autobiographies and poems, the American author Maya Angelou provides a candid and moving view of the African American experience. Her works stress courage and strength in the face of adversity.

Angelou was born Marguerite Johnson on April 4, 1928, in St. Louis, Missouri. She studied acting and dance in high school and performed in various musicals and plays throughout her young adulthood. Her brother gave her the nickname Maya, and she later took the last name Angelou from her first husband.

Angelou began her writing career as a journalist working overseas for African publications in the 1960's. The first of her autobiographical works, *I Know Why the Caged Bird Sings*, was published in 1970 and chronicles her life up to age 16. It was nominated for a National Book Award and remains her most famous work. Her first volume of poetry, *Just Give Me a Cool Drink of Water 'fore I Diiie*, was published in 1971 and was nominated for a Pulitzer Prize. She continued the story of her life in works such as *Gather Together in My Name* (1974), *The Heart of a Woman* (1981), *All God's Children Need Traveling Shoes* (1986), and *A Song Flung Up to Heaven* (2002). Angelou has also written children's books, including *Kofi and His Magic* (1996). In 1993, she was given the honor of reciting her poem "On the Pulse of Morning" at the inauguration of President Bill Clinton.

Angelou has continued to act throughout her career, appearing in—and sometimes writing and producing—films, plays, and television programs. She has also been a prominent civil rights activist and feminist.

PRISCILLA R. RAMSEY
Associate Professor of Afro-American Studies
Howard University

ANGELS

According to many religious traditions, spiritual beings called angels exist to serve God as attendants and messengers. The word "angel" comes from a Greek word meaning "messenger." Judaism, Christianity, and Islam all accept the existence of angels. The teachings of many other religions, including Hinduism, Buddhism, and Zoroastrianism, refer to similar beings, although they are given different names and functions.

Although they are not physical beings, angels are thought to take visible form in order to deliver messages from God. A number of sacred texts, including the Bible and the Koran, describe angels appearing to people in human or animal form. Often angels are said to have one, two, or even three pairs of wings.

Some faiths include a belief in guardian angels that watch over and protect humans. Muslims (followers of Islam) believe that two "writing" angels accompany each person throughout life, noting all good and bad deeds.

One of the most important angel messengers is the archangel Gabriel, who figures in Jewish, Christian, and Muslim traditions. Christians believe it was he who announced to the Virgin Mary that she was to be the mother of Jesus. Muslims believe that Gabriel appeared to the prophet Mohammed bearing messages from God. These messages, or revelations, eventually became the foundation of Islam.

Like humans, angels are believed to possess intelligence and free will. In fact, some angels are said to have rebelled against God. The most famous of these "fallen angels" is Satan, who according to some traditions is said to have led the rebellion and established his own kingdom—hell—after God expelled him from heaven.

MARY FROHLICH
Catholic Theological Union

ANGLO-SAXONS. See ENGLAND, HISTORY OF; ENGLISH LANGUAGE.

ANGOLA

The nation of Angola is located on the southwestern coast of Africa bordering the Atlantic Ocean. One of the largest countries on the African continent, it is greater in area than France, Germany, and the United Kingdom combined, although its population is relatively small for its size. Angola was for centuries a colony of Portugal. It finally gained its independence in 1975, but in the years that followed, the country was torn by a bitter and destructive civil war.

People. The people of Angola are related to the Bantu of central and southern Africa. Of the many Bantu groups, the largest in Angola are the Ovimbundu, the Kimbundu, and the Bakongo, who together make up about 75 percent of the population. The Ovimbundu, the largest group, live in the central highlands and are known for their skill as traders and ironworkers. The Kimbundu live near the cities of Luanda, the capital, and Malange, and have been most influenced by European ways. The Bakongo live in the northwest.

Angolans of mixed European and African ancestry are called mestiços. Although they form a small percentage of the population, they play an important part in the country's economic and political life. About 400,000 Portuguese once lived in Angola, but most left after its independence. Portuguese remains the official language, but various Bantu languages are widely spoken. Some Angolans are Christians, while others follow traditional African religions.

Land. Most of Angola consists of a vast plateau, which rises to its greatest height at Bié in the central region. A narrow strip of lowland runs along the Atlantic coastline, and the northern region is covered with tropical rain forests. In the south, Angola borders the northern edge of the great Kalahari Desert. Angola's land also includes a small area in the far north called Cabinda, which is separated from the rest of the country by the territory of the neighboring Democratic Republic of Congo. Most of the major rivers rise in the central plateau and empty into the Atlantic.

Angola's climate varies with location and elevation. The coastal area and south are generally hot and dry. The plateau region is cooler and receives more rainfall.

Economy. Agriculture and mining are the basis of the country's economy. Most Angolans are subsistence farmers, who grow food for their own use. Their chief food crops are corn, cassava (a starchy root), sweet potatoes, and bananas. The most important commercial crops are coffee and sugarcane, followed by cotton and sisal (used in making

Luanda is Angola's capital and largest city, a major port, and the country's economic center. Founded by the Portuguese in 1575 and situated on Angola's long Atlantic Ocean coastline, it is considered one of Africa's most attractive cities.

FACTS and figures

REPUBLIC OF ANGOLA is the official name of the country.

LOCATION: Southwestern coast of Africa.

AREA: 481,351 sq mi (1,246,700 km²).

POPULATION: 12,300,000 (estimate).

CAPITAL AND LARGEST CITY: Luanda.

MAJOR LANGUAGES: Portuguese (official), various Bantu languages.

MAJOR RELIGIOUS GROUPS: Christian, traditional African religions.

GOVERNMENT: Republic. **Head of state and government**—president. **Legislature**—National Assembly.

CHIEF PRODUCTS: **Agricultural**—coffee, sugarcane, cotton, sisal, corn, cassava, sweet potatoes, bananas. **Manufactured**—processed food, fish meal, textiles, beverages. **Mineral**—petroleum, diamonds, iron ore.

MONETARY UNIT: Kwanza (1 kwanza = 100 lwei).

cord and twine). Angola is rich in minerals, especially petroleum, which provides the bulk of its export income. It also has large deposits of diamonds, iron ore, and other minerals.

Many skilled European workers left Angola after independence. During the civil war that followed, farmers were driven from their fields, and government funds were spent on the war rather than on reconstruction.

History and Government. Bantu peoples first moved into Angola from central Africa in the 1300's. The country was named for Ngola, the ruler of an ancient Kimbundu kingdom.

European penetration of the region began with the Portuguese explorer Diogo Cão, who reached the mouth of the Congo River in 1482. The Portuguese founded the capital city, Luanda, in 1575. However, disease, the tropical climate, and resistance by the Africans prevented them from gaining complete control of the territory until 1918.

Armed revolts against Portuguese rule broke out in 1961. They were followed by years of guerrilla warfare, until a new government in Portugal granted independence to Angola in 1975.

The Popular Movement for the Liberation of Angola (MPLA) set up a Communist-style government, headed by Agostinho Neto as president. He was succeeded by José Eduardo dos Santos in 1979. The MPLA government was opposed by the National Union for the Total Independence of Angola (UNITA), led by Jonas Savimbi. The Soviet Union and Cuba sent troops to help the MPLA, while the United States and South Africa backed UNITA. Government support for the independence movement in neighboring Namibia involved Angola in clashes with South Africa, which then administered Namibia. An agreement to withdraw Cuban forces from Angola, signed in 1988, was one of several conditions for Namibian independence (achieved in 1990). In 1991, after the dos Santos government agreed to hold democratic elections, a peace accord was signed.

In the 1992 presidential election, neither dos Santos nor Savimbi won a majority. Dos Santos remained in power, but the civil war resumed. In 1997, a new legislature was installed with representatives from both parties. Yet the peace accord collapsed in 1999.

In 2002, Savimbi was killed by government troops. Shortly thereafter, dos Santos declared a cease-fire, ending 27 years of civil war, in which nearly 1 million Angolans had been killed. Angola then faced the challenge of rebuilding its society and economy.

HUGH C. BROOKS
Director, Center for African Studies
St. John's University (New York)

ANIMAL RIGHTS

In recent years, a growing number of people have come to believe that it is wrong to use animals for food, clothing, entertainment, or research. These people believe that animals are entitled to certain moral and legal rights that protect them from being killed, abused, or exploited for any reason. This concept is called animal rights.

Supporters of animal rights (sometimes called animal rightists) cite studies demonstrating animals' ability to reason and their capacity for feeling pain and experiencing emotional distress. They condemn the unhealthy conditions found in many modern "factory farms," in which large numbers of animals are crowded into small, confined spaces to make production more efficient. Animal rightists oppose experimenting on animals for medical research and using them to test cosmetics and other consumer products. They object to any activity—such as hunting, bullfighting, and dog racing—in which animals are killed, injured, or mistreated for sport. Animal rightists also oppose circuses, rodeos, and zoos, arguing that animals should not be kept in cages or made to perform tricks for human enjoyment.

Most people agree that animals should not be abused. This concept, called animal welfare, has been promoted since the 1800's by such organizations as the American Society for the Prevention of Cruelty to Animals (ASPCA) and the Humane Society of the United States. However, supporters of animal welfare usually believe it is acceptable to use animals for food, entertainment, and certain research purposes so long as they are treated as humanely as possible. They maintain that the benefits to humans—for example, lifesaving medical breakthroughs—outweigh the costs to the animals. They focus on improving conditions for animals used in agriculture, research, and entertainment.

Animal rightists, in contrast, seek to eliminate such activities rather than to reform them. Instead of animal experimentation, for example, they urge the use of alternative methods that they claim are just as effective. And they point out that most people do not need to eat meat in order to have a healthy diet. Numerous activist groups have been formed to promote animal rights. One of the best known is People for the Ethical Treatment of Animals (PETA).

Animal rights supporters participate in an anti-fur march.

The more extreme views of some activists have not been generally accepted. But public awareness of the issues surrounding animal use has grown. Many consumers now seek out products that have not been tested on animals. Some choose clothing made from synthetics instead of leather or fur. Others avoid eating meat or purchase only "free-range" products, from animals that have not been forced to live out their lives in overcrowded conditions. Other developments reflect this changing perception of the way animals should be treated. Many zoos have done away with small, barred cages in favor of spacious environments that resemble the animals' natural habitats. Some circuses have stopped using animal acts. Computer simulations and clay models have replaced animal dissection in many schools.

Laws have also been passed to protect animals. In many countries, and in every state in the United States, laws have been enacted that make animal abuse a crime. A few nations have gone even further. In 2002, Germany voted to extend constitutional rights to animals. The United Kingdom has laws banning the use of the great apes in research that causes pain.

Animal rights will likely remain a major ethical issue for some time to come. Scientific and technological advances, such as the cloning and genetic engineering of animals, continue to raise important questions regarding humans' treatment of other species.

MARC BEKOFF
Editor, *Encyclopedia of Animal Rights and Animal Welfare*

ANIMALS

A herd of elephants, great ears fanning to and fro, marches across the African plains toward a water hole. Sponges brighten the underwater landscape of a coral reef in a tropical sea. Ants spill out of their nest to repair the damage done by feet tramping across the ground. Elephants, sponges, and ants may seem very different. However, they share something in common with about a million other kinds of living things, including human beings—all of these are animals.

Most of us spend our lives surrounded by animals of one kind or another, although sometimes we are not aware of them.

Insects abound, sometimes in places where they are not particularly welcome. Small fish, frogs, and salamanders live in streams, ponds, and lakes and even in the middle of big cities. Some animals, such as raccoons, are out and about only after dark.

Animals live almost everywhere on Earth. They inhabit the deepest, darkest parts of the sea, where plants cannot survive. They are found on the highest mountain peaks and can survive in the coldest parts of Antarctica, where temperatures plunge to –72°F (–22°C). Even hot springs, with water heated to more than 100°F (38°C), are home to some kinds of insects.

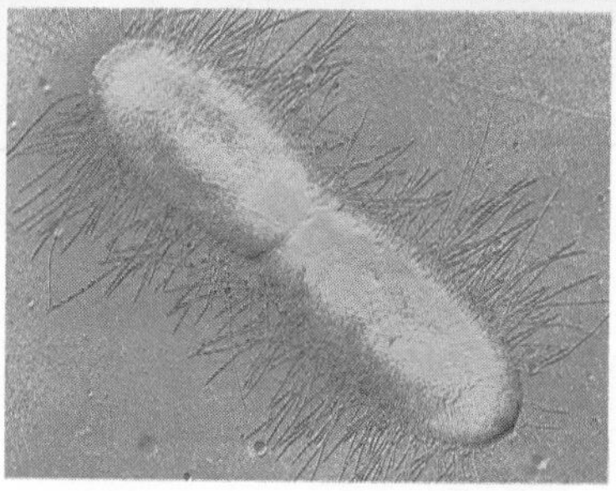

The classification of living things started when early humans grouped organisms according to whether they were considered helpful or harmful. Today living things, such as plants (*above left*), fungi (*above*), and bacteria (*left*), are separated into groups based on shared traits.

THE WORLD OF LIVING THINGS

Scientists classify all living things by assigning them to related groups according to similar characteristics, or traits. This orderly arrangement of all living things is called **scientific classification**. The largest groups of living things are called kingdoms.

For a long time, all living things were divided into just two kingdoms: animals and plants. If a living thing had body parts, such as a head, eyes, and limbs, and could move about, it was considered an animal. If a living thing was green, had leaves, and was stationary, it was considered a plant. However, even using such characteristics, scientists found it difficult to place some living things in either kingdom. A few kinds of plants, such as the Venus's-flytrap, move as they open and close their leaves to catch insects and feed on them. Some animals do not have heads or limbs; others, such as sponges, are anchored in place for most of their life and cannot move around.

Another characteristic, the method of getting food, was also used to group living things into kingdoms. Animals cannot make their own food; they must take food from their surroundings. In order to get the nourishment they need, they must eat either plants or animals that feed on plants. Plants, on the other hand, are able to make the food they need to survive by taking carbon dioxide from the air and water and nitrates from the soil, along with energy from sunlight. But even when they used the method of nourishment as a characteristic, scientists found organisms that were difficult to classify as either a plant or an animal. Some did not seem to belong to either group.

Over time, it became clear that all living things could not be assigned to just two groups. As a result, most scientists now divide all living things into five kingdoms. Animals make up one kingdom. Plants make up another. Certain one-celled organisms, some of which have characteristics of both plants and animals, belong to yet another kingdom, called Protista. Bacteria and fungi each have their own kingdoms, too. The living things in the same kingdom share more of the same characteristics than the living things in different kingdoms.

Within a kingdom, organisms are separated into subgroups depending on the characteristics they share. Major groups, called phyla, include animals that share one or more characteristics. Animals within each phylum are also separated into groups called classes according to certain differences between the animals. The classes are further divided into orders; the orders into families; the families into genera; and the genera into species.

With each subdivision, the relationship between the living things becomes stronger and the members of the group share more of the same characteristics of body structure and behavior. With the final separation into species, the members of a species share so many of the same basic characteristics that they look alike. Within a species, the members can mate with others in their group and produce offspring. The young develop in the same manner as the parents and grow to look very much like the parents. Human beings are a species. So are raccoons, American robins, and bullfrogs.

For more detailed information on how scientists classify living things, see the article LIFE in Volume L.

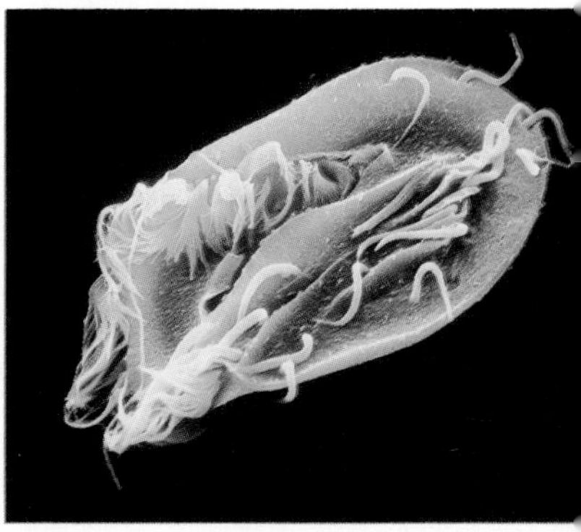

With tiny microscopic creatures, such as this protozoan, it is sometimes impossible to tell which are plants and which are animals. Many scientists prefer to group these forms into a separate kingdom called Protista.

THE ANIMAL KINGDOM

The animal kingdom can be divided into two general main groups: **vertebrates**, made up of animals that have a backbone, and **invertebrates**, made up of animals that do not have a backbone. Throughout the animal kingdom, there are about 40,000 different species of vertebrates and more than 1 million known species of invertebrates.

Vertebrates, which include human beings, have a bony structure, or skeleton, inside the body. The skeleton, which grows as the animal does, is the framework that gives an animal its body shape. The skeleton also supports and protects the soft insides of an animal's body.

Many invertebrates, such as insects, crabs, and lobsters, wear their skeleton outside their body. The tough outer coat, which is like a shell enclosing the body, is called an **exoskeleton**. The hard but lightweight structure is made up of sections, like the armor of a medieval knight. When invertebrates outgrow their exoskeleton, the shell splits and a new one is formed. Some invertebrates have no skeletons. Instead, they have soft bodies held together by strong, flexible fibers.

There is an endless variety of shapes, sizes, and traits within the animal kingdom, yet groups of animals are similar in certain ways. Some, such as humans (*right*), have two pairs of limbs; others, such as crabs (*below right*), have tough outer coats covering their bodies; still others, such as elephants (*below*), eat only plants.

Although they are very different looking, the flamingos (*above left*), the tree frog (*above*), the cheetah (*far left*), and the tree python (*left*) share certain characteristics as members of the animal group called vertebrates. All vertebrates have a backbone formed from cartilage or bony tissue, or both. In addition, the body of a vertebrate is usually divided into a head and a trunk and has two-sided symmetry —that is, the left and right sides are alike.

Animal Groups

Vertebrates and invertebrates can be further divided into subgroups. Each subgroup has its own unique combination of traits.

Vertebrates. Human beings are **mammals**, as are elephants, dogs, and whales. It may be hard to imagine that such different-looking animals have some of the same characteristics, but they do. Mammals are the only vertebrates that have hair and feed on milk from their mothers when they are babies. Mammals also are the only vertebrates whose young grow within the mother and receive nourishment from her before birth, although a few primitive kinds, such as the platypus, hatch from an egg.

Whether they live in the water like a whale or on land like a person, mammals breathe air through their lungs. They are also **warm-blooded** animals, which means they are able to maintain a constant body temperature no matter what the temperature of their surroundings is.

Similar to mammals, **birds** are warm-blooded and breathe air through lungs. However, birds are feathered instead of hairy. They hatch from eggs and bring food to their young. Unlike most vertebrates, birds do not have teeth. Instead, they have a hard beak, or bill, that is used to get food.

Reptiles are covered with scales instead of hair or feathers. They are **cold-blooded**—that is, their body temperature depends on the temperature of their surroundings. If a reptile, such as snake or crocodile, is too hot, it must move to the shade. If it needs warmth, it must get into the sun. Like birds and mammals, however, reptiles breathe air. Reptiles hatch from eggs, either inside or outside the mother.

Frogs, salamanders, and caecilians are **amphibians**. These cold-blooded animals are free of hair, scales, and feathers. Most live part of their life in water and part on land. Young amphibians use gills to breathe oxygen from the water. As they grow into adults, their body changes and they can live on land, using lungs to breathe air.

Fish, another vertebrate class, mainly use gills to breathe. Like reptiles and amphibians, fish are cold-blooded and cannot regulate their body temperature internally. Fish, which appeared about 500 million years ago, were the first animals to have a backbone.

Invertebrates. As a group, **arthropods** contain the largest number of species in the animal kingdom. The great variety in this group includes insects, spiders, crabs, lobsters, centipedes, and millipedes. All arthropods have jointed legs and an exoskeleton that contains a stiff, horny material called chitin.

Sponges are a group of animals that live at the bottom of oceans and other bodies of water. They spend their adult lives attached to rocks and other underwater objects. Although sponges vary widely in shape, color, and size, they all have a skeleton made up of either minerals or a protein called spongin.

There are about 100,000 known kinds of **mollusks**, which include snails, scallops, slugs, clams, oysters, and octopuses. The soft, boneless body of the mollusk is usually protected by a hard shell. Wherever mollusks live—in water or on land—they must keep their bodies moist to stay alive.

Did you know that ...

these tiny invertebrates, called leaf-cutter ants, are industrious weight lifters who can carry cut up leaves and flowers more than twice their own size and ten times their own weight? The ants lug their cargo back to their underground colony where the plant fragments are used as a garden bed for fungus to grow on. The ants then feed on the fungus.

The **coelenterates** include jellyfish, sea anemones, corals, and sea fans. Coelenterates are soft-bodied animals with a body wall formed by at least two layers of cells. Most of the 9,000 species live in the sea.

The invertebrates commonly referred to as "worms" actually consist of four major groups—**flatworms**, **roundworms**, **ribbon worms**, and **segmented worms**. All have soft, slender bodies, but no limbs. Earthworms, tapeworms, and leeches are among the several thousand kinds of worms.

The sea is home to many invertebrates. Under the water's surface, coral animals (*below*) display a riot of colors, while the red crab (*below right*) scrambles along the seashore.

▶THE VARIETY OF ANIMAL LIFE

Groups of animals may share some traits, yet every kind of animal has its own life-style and way of surviving. Sometimes the traits that make the living patterns different are very small; the great blue heron and the little blue heron are an example. They both are long-legged birds that wade into water to stalk small creatures, such as fish and frogs. They both live in marshes or other wetlands. However, the great blue heron is about twice the size of the little blue heron. The difference in size means that they feed in the same place, in a similar manner, but at different depths.

Each kind of animal is suited to living in a particular kind of environment, or **habitat**. An animal fits into a **niche** within its habitat—that is, it has a specific role within its community. Wetlands, such as marshes, are the habitat of herons, while their niche is that of a bird that wades to catch small water animals.

The heron's behavior and body structures enable it to survive within its particular habitat and niche. While wading, a heron will freeze its movements; motionless, it looks for a fish or a frog. When the heron sees its prey, it quickly extends its long neck and with its bill seizes the startled prey.

The climbing perch, an Asian fish, has another type of life-style. It lives in small ponds that sometimes dry up during times of drought. When this happens, the perch behaves in an unusual way for a fish: It creeps over the ground to another pond that still holds water. The climbing perch can do this because it has strong, flexible fins that act almost like legs. It also has a lunglike organ that allows it to breathe air as it travels out of water and over land.

The difference in their sizes allows the great blue heron (*top*) and the little blue heron (*bottom*) to have separate niches within the same shared habitat.

The traveling behavior, fins, and air-breathing organ of the climbing perch are like the heron's long legs and hunting behavior. They are all changes, or **adaptations**, of a living thing geared to a particular way of life. Every animal has its own special adaptations that improve its chances of survival.

Animals do not adapt on purpose; they adapt by chance. The adaptation of the giraffe's ancestors is an example. It may appear that the ancestors of the giraffe grew a long

Did you know that . . .

the bird called an oxpecker spends almost its entire life clinging to the back of a hoofed animal such as this impala? The oxpecker performs a valuable pest-removal service by removing bloodsucking ticks and blood-flies from the impala's body. In return, the impala allows the oxpecker to rest and sleep and even court and mate on its back.

There are many patterns of living within the same forest community. Some animals are most active during the day, others are most active during the night.

Animals of the Day

Clockwise from top right: woodpecker, cardinal, chipmunk, rabbit, coyote, lynx, and squirrel.

Animals of the Night

Clockwise from top right: flying squirrel, red fox, badger, woodcock, raccoon, mule deer, barn owl, and bat.

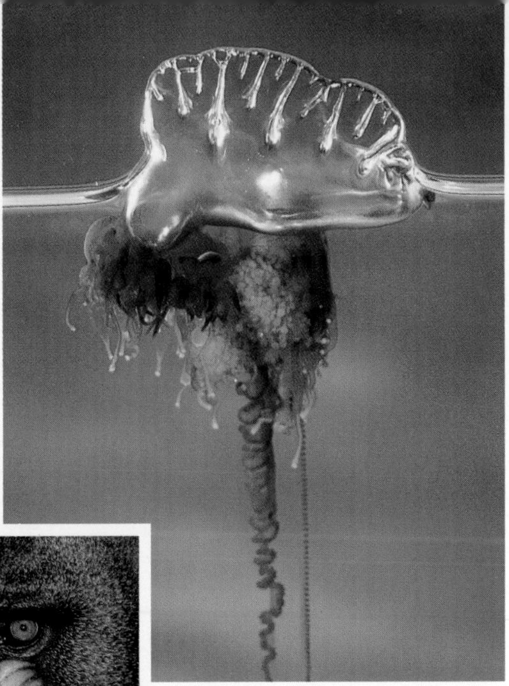

The Temminck's snapper (*above*) lures fish with an inviting wiggle of its pink-tipped tongue. The long tentacles of the Portuguese man-of-war (*above right*) have a paralyzing sting used to capture prey. The colorful face of the mandrill (*right*) becomes brighter with excitement.

neck so they could feed on leaves in trees; however, that is not the way it happened. Millions of years ago, a giraffe ancestor was born with a neck that was longer than the neck of the other animals in its group. It was not much longer than the neck of the others, but long enough so the animal could reach higher for food than the rest of the group. All the offspring of the long-necked ancestor had the same trait. Because more food was available to them, the long-necked animals had a better chance of surviving. As time passed, they survived in greater numbers than their short-necked relatives. Slowly the long-necked animal developed into the giraffe of today.

Amazing Animals

Adaptations create the astounding variety within the animal kingdom. Some animals are brilliantly colored; others are drab. Some animals are huge; others are so tiny that they cannot be seen without a microscope. Some are slightly unusual; others are utterly fantastic. Some animals share the traits of many animals; others seem to have traits that are quite unique.

The Colorful. The mandrill, a large baboon from Africa, is one of the most colorful mammals. Its face is bright red and blue. Many birds are also brilliantly colored, especially the males. The bird of paradise is one of the most colorful, and beautiful, birds. It lives in the jungles of the South Pacific islands. Its feath-

Did you know that . . .

the bee hummingbird, which weighs about 1/20 ounce (1.6 grams) and grows to about 2 inches (5 centimeters) in length, is the smallest living bird? Tiny and quick, this flying machine moves its wings at the fantastic rate of 70 times a second, propelling it along at speeds of up to 60 miles (97 kilometers) per hour.

The fierce-looking Komodo dragon is the biggest lizard in the world. It can reach 12 feet (3.6 meters) in length and more than 250 pounds (113 kilograms) in weight.

ers of scarlet, yellow, green, and blue form long trailing plumes or feathery capes. The shimmering colors gleam like metal in bright sunlight. In South America lives a group of frogs, known as poison dart frogs, that are as colorful as any birds. The small animals are bathed in vivid greens, reds, yellows, and black.

The Curious. The tapir is a jungle animal with an unusual appearance. Big as a pony, the tapir looks like a combination of several animals. It has a body shaped like that of a rhinoceros; a large, tapering head similar to that of a pig; and a nose, or snout, that looks like a shortened version of an elephant's trunk.

The Portuguese man-of-war is an interesting-looking water animal. Its body contains a balloonlike float that acts like a sail. Long tentacles dozens of feet long hang from its body and trail through the water as winds blow the man-of-war across the ocean.

Coral animals, which build reefs by secreting (giving off) limestone, have tubelike bodies with colorful tentacles, resembling petals, around the top.

The Big, the Small. When it comes to large size among animals, most people think of the extinct prehistoric reptiles called dinosaurs. Although not all dinosaurs were large animals (some were no bigger than a house cat), there were some plant-eating dinosaurs more than 85 feet (25 meters) long and weighing 80 tons.

As immense as some of the dinosaurs were, no dinosaur was as large as one animal that lives today. The great blue whale is the largest animal ever known. It grows up to 100 feet (30.4 meters) in length and may weigh more than 130 tons—that is more than the combined weight of thirty elephants. The huge bulk of the whale is supported by water. A land animal of the same size would need such a heavy skeleton and large muscles to support all its weight that it probably would not be able to lift its legs.

Some land animals do reach enormous size. The biggest land animal is the African elephant, which can be more than 13 feet (3.9 meters) high at the shoulder and weigh about 9 tons (10 metric tons). The African white rhinoceros is another heavyweight. It weighs up to 6,000 pounds (2,721 kilograms). Even certain birds can be considered giants. The ostrich, the largest living bird, can tower 8 feet (2.4 meters) high and weigh almost 300 pounds (136 kilograms).

At the other end of the size scale, the smallest animals with a backbone include the goby fish of the Philippines and the Cuban pygmy tree frog, neither of which grows to more than half an inch (0.5 centimeter) in length. The insect-eating shrew, which is the smallest mammal on land, weighs about as much as a dime.

Did you know that ...

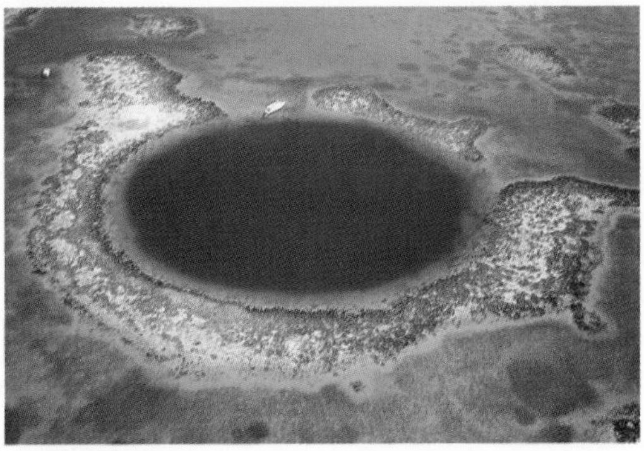

the largest structures ever built by living creatures are coral reefs? Some reefs are more than 1,000 miles (1,609 kilometers) in length. The reefs, such as this one surrounding a blue lagoon off the coast of Belize in the Caribbean Sea, consist of living coral polyps and their skeletal remains piled on top of one another. The strange and beautiful formations take millions of years to build.

The polar bear fears only killer whales and walruses as it makes its way along the Arctic shores. A thick coat of fur and a layer of fat keep the polar bear warm on the cold and barren tundra.

▶ANIMALS AND THEIR HABITATS

A polar bear, its black nose twitching, makes its way across the treeless landscape along the shores of the Arctic Ocean, hunting for small mammals, such as ground squirrels, and eating berries. This cold, icy, dry region is called a **tundra**. During the summer, the sea fringing the tundra is free of ice. When one area of the tundra is picked clean of food, the polar bear will swim miles through the sea to reach a new destination.

In winter when the ocean freezes over, the bears wander hundreds of miles across the ice hunting for seals. Finding an opening in the ice, the bear crouches near the hole, waiting patiently to ambush a seal when it comes up from the water below for a breath of air.

Winter lasts six months in the Arctic, and during most of that time the sun never rises. Temperatures drop far below 0°F (–18°C). Polar bears are adapted in many ways to life in the northernmost part of the world. Under its skin lies a thick layer of fat, called blubber, that serves as insulation to protect the bear against the cold. Over the skin is a thick, woolly undercoat of hair, which also helps the bear keep warm. An outer coat of stiff hairs, which sheds water like a raincoat, helps the bear stay dry. In addition to its layer of fat, keeping dry helps the bear stay warm. Such adaptations enable the bear to live in its cold, harsh environment.

The polar bear would not survive on the hot, open **grasslands** of East Africa. The climate is too warm and dry for the bear. Although the short-legged polar bear is not slow, it is not adapted for rapid pursuit, which is something it would need in order to catch the fast-running antelopes that live in large herds on the African grasslands.

The cheetah, a medium-sized spotted cat, is suited to hunting antelopes. Long-legged and swift as an arrow, the cheetah can catch fast-running antelopes, such as gazelles. The cheetah lacks blubber, and its fur is not as thick as the bear's. Just as a bear would not last long on the grasslands of the African plains, a cheetah would perish in the Arctic.

Because animals are adapted to different environments, the distribution of animal life throughout the world changes from place to place. The animals in one area can be very different from the animals living in another area. Climate and plant life are the main factors that determine the community of animals that live in a particular region. The African plains, for example, do not receive enough rain for forests to grow. But there is enough rain for grasses to thrive on the plains. Large herds of antelopes and zebras feed on the grasses. In turn, cheetahs, lions, and other predators (animals that kill others for food) stalk the herds.

Parts of Africa that are rainy enough for trees have vast forests, often called **rain forests**, or **jungles**. Grass eaters cannot find enough food in the forests. If the grass-eating antelopes and zebras are not in the forest, neither are the lions or cheetahs. But the jungle teems with other types of animals—monkeys, birds, snakes, and frogs are just a few of the kinds of animals that fill the jungle from the damp, shaded floor to the tops of the tall trees that shoot hundreds of feet into the air.

Some African animals, such as the elephant and buffalo, inhabit both grasslands and forest. However, forest elephants and buffalo generally are smaller than their grassland relatives. Smaller size makes it easier for an ani-

The boldly colored poison dart frog (*right*), which is usually less than 2 inches (5 centimeters) long, carries in its skin glands the most powerful animal poison known.

Animals abound amid the thick tangle of plants in the rain forest (*below*). Many of the animals spend their entire lives in the trees and never descend to the ground.

mal to get around among the trunks of the giant jungle trees.

Other types of animals live in **deciduous forests**, which are found in areas with moderate temperatures and rainfall and cold winters. The leaves of many of the trees in a deciduous forest turn from green to vibrant shades of red, yellow, and orange. The colorful display occurs once a year before the trees shed their leaves. Along with the white-tailed deer, which feeds largely on buds, new shoots, and leaves, nut-eating gray squirrels, bobcats, and many types of birds can be found in the deciduous forests of the northeastern United States.

Farther north are cold **coniferous forests**, with cone-bearing evergreens such as pines and spruces. Moose, which are the largest member of the deer family, feed on water plants in the many wet areas that dot the forests. The large hooves of the moose spread out to keep it from sinking into the waterlogged soil as it wanders through the forest. The many seeds of pine and spruce cones are food for the birds, red squirrels, and other small mammals that make their home in the coniferous forest.

The animals that live in **deserts** are very different from the animals that are found in the tundra and forests. Desert animals must be able to stand scorching heat and go without water for a long time. To escape the sun's heat, many desert animals, such as certain lizards, spend the warmest part of the day in underground burrows. Some animals, such as kangaroo rats, have developed so that they do not need to drink water. They get all the moisture they need from the juices of the plants they feed on.

The marten (*left*), a tree-climbing member of the weasel family, leaps gracefully from branch to branch as it hunts squirrels and other prey in the coniferous forest.

Animals of the northern coniferous forest (*below*) are well adapted to the cold winters. Some animals hibernate, while others travel to warmer climates to seek food and shelter.

Desert wildlife (*above*) must adapt to scorching daytime heat, cool night temperatures, and a scarce supply of water. The land iguana (*below*) nibbles on desert plants, such as cactus, for nourishment and water.

Like the polar bear and cheetah, all species are adapted to particular environments. Polar bears and cheetahs are each bound to just one environment. Even so, they move through many different habitats within their environment. The polar bear roams through the tundra from an ice field to the rocky seashore. Cheetahs hunt on grasslands so dry that they are almost desert, as well as on those that are dotted with thorny shrubs.

Some species manage to live in more than one environment and habitat. The wolf travels from the coniferous forest, where it hunts moose, farther north to the tundra, where it hunts musk oxen. Coyotes, which eat plant and animal products, roam deciduous and coniferous forests, grasslands, deserts, mountains, and lowlands. They can live in climate that is hot or cold, moist or dry.

In contrast to the coyote and wolf, there are species that live in only a tiny habitat within an environment. The Devil's Hole pupfish is one. All Devil's Hole pupfish inhabit a single freshwater pool near Death Valley in western Nevada. Within the pool, the pupfish stay over a ledge about the size of a basketball court. No other species of vertebrate lives within such a confined area.

Wherever it lives, each species of animal has its own way of life unlike that of any other. There are as many different life-styles among animals as there are species.

Broad, winglike fins propel the stingray through water (*above*). Victims have a difficult time escaping the fatal clasp of the bald eagle's talons (*right*).

THE BODY OF AN ANIMAL

By looking at the different body structures of an animal, it is possible to get information about how an animal lives. A shape, foot, bill, jaw, and tooth can all be clues to an animal's life-style. For example, it is reasonable to assume—by looking at its long neck—that the plant-eating giraffe eats leaves high in trees.

Shape. Whales and fish are totally different types of creatures. However, the body of a typical fish has the same streamlined and torpedo-shaped body as that of a whale. Their similar shapes are both adaptations to living in the water. With a streamlined shape, an animal can move through water with less effort. The pointed head of a water animal, such as a fish, wedges water aside. The long, slender body glides behind, almost as if it is following through a "hole" in the water made by the head.

Other fish, such as the stingray, have flattened bodies that resemble a pancake. Even though their bodies are not torpedo-shaped, they are streamlined in another way. A stingray's body can grow to about 5 feet (1.5 meters) wide. However, from the top surface of its body to the bottom, it is only a few inches deep.

Another fish, the moray eel, has a long, slender, snakelike body. Its shape allows it to slither into crevices and holes in reefs after the octopuses and crabs that are its prey. Water animals are not the only animals that need flexible, streamlined bodies. The weasel, a land animal, also has a snakelike body. Its slender, flexible body enables it to snake through underground burrows to catch the rabbits and rodents it feeds on.

Feet and Legs. The feet of some birds have powerful toes tipped with sharp, hooked claws, or **talons**. Talons are characteristic of birds that hunt, such as eagles and hawks. With the talons, the hunter bird seizes its prey. Once it has the victim within its grasp, the talons automatically tighten to hold the victim fast.

The favored diet of birds of prey varies greatly. The red-tailed hawk catches rodents, ground birds (such as pheasants), lizards, and snakes with its strong talons. The bald eagle feeds largely on fish that are caught near the surface of the water.

The curved, sharp claws of cats are used in much the same manner to grab and hold prey. However, the cat has an additional feature important to a land animal: It can withdraw, or retract, its claws into sheathes within the toes. This protects the claws when they are not needed to grasp prey. Withdrawing its claws also allows the cat to step softly when stalking its prey. Cats—from lions to house cats—creep up as close as they can to their prey before they pounce on it with a final rush.

The sidewinder uses a series of flat S-shaped loops to move its long, limbless body over the desert sand.

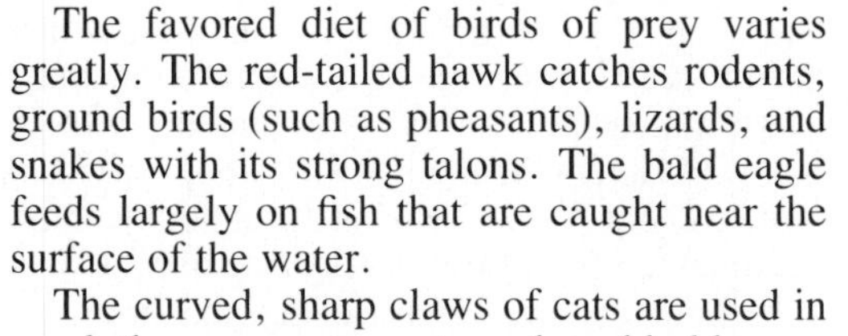

One cat is an exception—the cheetah. It has blunt claws, similar to a dog's, that it cannot withdraw. It also hunts more like such members of the dog family as wolves and African wild dogs than a cat. The cheetah does not quietly stalk its prey before pouncing and grabbing with its claws; rather, the cheetah runs down its prey, knocking it to the ground, and with its strong jaws grabs the throat of its victim and suffocates it.

The lynx, a cat that lives in the cold coniferous forest, has large, broad feet. As the lynx travels over the snow in search of prey, its feet act like snowshoes, keeping the cat from sinking into the snow. The spider monkey and the gibbon have unusually long fingers and toes, which they hook over branches as they swing through the trees.

Jaws and Teeth. Because animals have different ways of feeding, the body structures used for eating are different—even within the same family of animals. All birds use their beaks, or bills, to obtain food; however, among birds, there are many different kinds of bills. The woodpecker uses its chisel-like bill to chip away the bark and wood from trees and get to the insects hiding underneath. The pine grosbeak uses its short, heavy bill to crush seeds. The heron uses its long, spearlike bill to grab fish and frogs.

The spotted hyena hunts other animals, but it also feeds off the remains of animals killed by other predators, such as lions. With its large, powerful jaw muscles, the hyena is able to carry off and eat the bones and other remains that most animal jaws cannot crack.

A fish with strong jaws and heavy, wide teeth is the parrot fish. Similar to the hyena, the parrot fish uses its jaws for crushing. Found in the warm waters surrounding coral reefs, the parrot fish crushes the rock-hard coral to feed on the small, soft animals that secrete it.

The teeth and jaws of animals that eat plants are different from those of animals that eat other animals. Plant-eating animals, such as horses, generally have broad, flat-edged teeth for chewing leaves and grass; meat-eating animals, such as dogs, have long, sharp teeth for tearing and chewing flesh.

The spider monkey (*far left*) uses its long slender limbs to swing from branch to branch as it quickly makes its way through the tropical rain forest habitat. The anhinga (*left*) is a long-necked diving bird that uses its pointed bill to spear fish. Once it has captured its prey, it tosses it into the air and gulps it down. The distinctive body of the platypus (*below*) is well equipped for swimming. It has webbed feet and a broad flat tail that the water-loving platypus uses to steer itself.

▶HOW ANIMALS MOVE FROM PLACE TO PLACE

Animals move from place to place in different ways. Some animals travel through air or water; others travel across land. Animal movement requires work. The body must be lifted or moved forward or both. A variety of body structures help animals move. Microscopic animals that live in fluid are able to travel by moving hairlike body extensions called **cilia**. Other animals depend on fins, legs, or wings to help them move.

Animal Movement in Water

Some water animals use a form of jet propulsion to move. The squid fills its body with water and then forces it out the end of its body in a violent rush. The backward force of the water pushes the squid ahead.

A streamlined shape and fins enable fish to move through water. Fish propel themselves by pushing the tail fin back and forth against the water. Muscles along the fish's body contract and relax, first on one side, then on the other, causing the tail to sweep forcefully from side to side. The tail fin does the majority of the work while the other fins are used by the fish to keep its balance in the water.

Other water animals, such as whales and dolphins, also have streamlined bodies and tail fins that do the bulk of the swimming work. However, rather than a side-to-side motion, they are propelled through the water by powerful up-and-down movements of their tails.

Animal Movement on Land

Most land animals move around on legs that extend from the sides or undersides of their body. The legs of an animal must be strong enough to support and lift it. The best support is provided when the legs are extended directly under the body, as in most mammals. Animals such as amphibians and reptiles often have legs that extend outward from the sides of the body and use them to leap or crawl along rather than stand and walk.

An animal with two legs must keep one in contact with the ground to stay upright. An animal with four legs needs to have three of them on the ground, at least when walking. Three legs hold up the body while the fourth moves forward into a new position. When a four-legged animal runs, it has only two legs planted at the same time—each foot is lifted just before setting down the one ahead of it. However, the motion is so quick the animal does not fall down. Some large, fast animals, such as elks, lift all four feet in the middle of a galloping stride.

The Speed of Animals

How fast animals can move from place to place varies greatly among animals. The fastest speed (which is presented here) and the slowest speed of an individual animal also can be quite different.

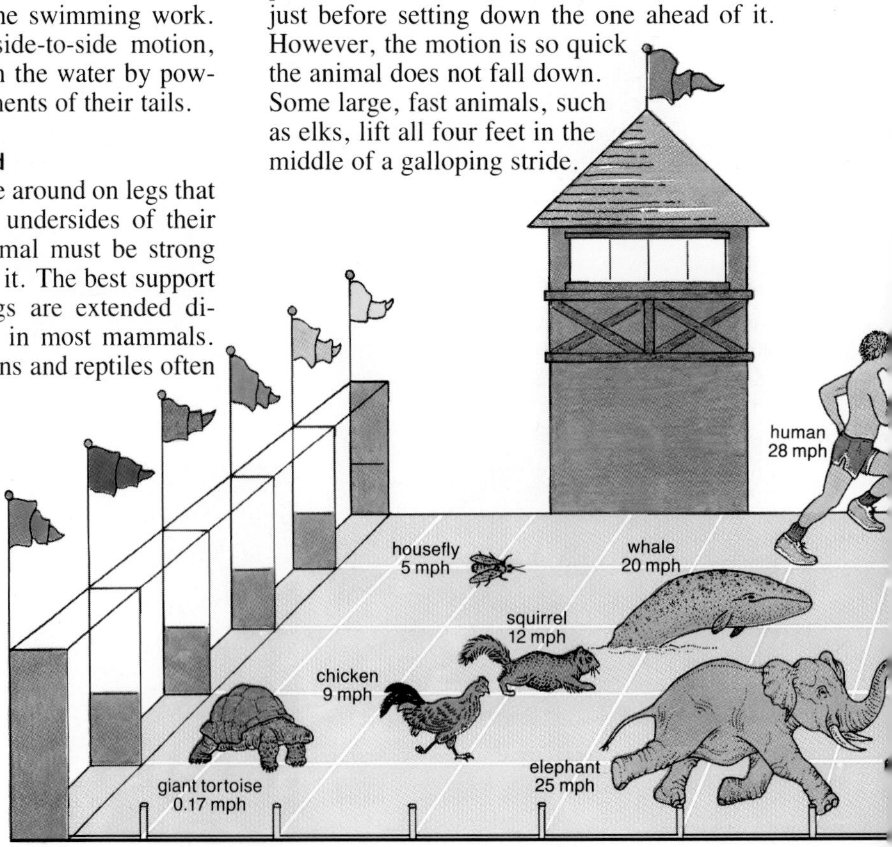

They may look clumsy, but manatees (*left*) are expert swimmers. Clocked at speeds of more than 200 miles per hour, the peregrine falcon (*above*) is the fastest animal in the world. Other cats wait and then pounce, but the cheetah (*right*) races after its prey.

Animal Movement in the Air

Animals travel through the air by gliding and by powered flight. Gliding animals, such as the flying squirrel, have thin flaps of skin extending from the sides of their body. The skin flaps act as parachutes to support them as they leap from a tree into the air. Along with the gliding squirrel, there are gliding frogs, lizards, and fish.

Powered flight requires wings that lift an animal by pushing down against the air. (See the article BIRDS for a detailed description of bird flight.) Most birds and many insects fly. The only mammal that flies is the bat.

▶HOW ANIMALS FEED

Animals spend much of their time seeking the food they need to survive. Animals that feed on meat, such as tigers and wolves, are called **carnivores**. Some meat-eating animals do not hunt for themselves; instead, they clean up the remains of animals killed by other predators. Such animals are called **scavengers** and include hyenas and vultures. Animals that only feed on plants are called **herbivores**. Some animals feed on both meat and plant matter. They are called **omnivores**.

Each species of animal has evolved its own special way of finding the food it needs. Some animals hunt for food in groups, while others hunt alone. Some animals have highly developed senses that help them find food, and others have special body structures that help attract food to them. Some animals gather food, but others lie in wait to trap food.

Animals That Eat Meat. The hunting styles of carnivores are related to the type of prey on which they feed. Wolves and cheetahs hunt

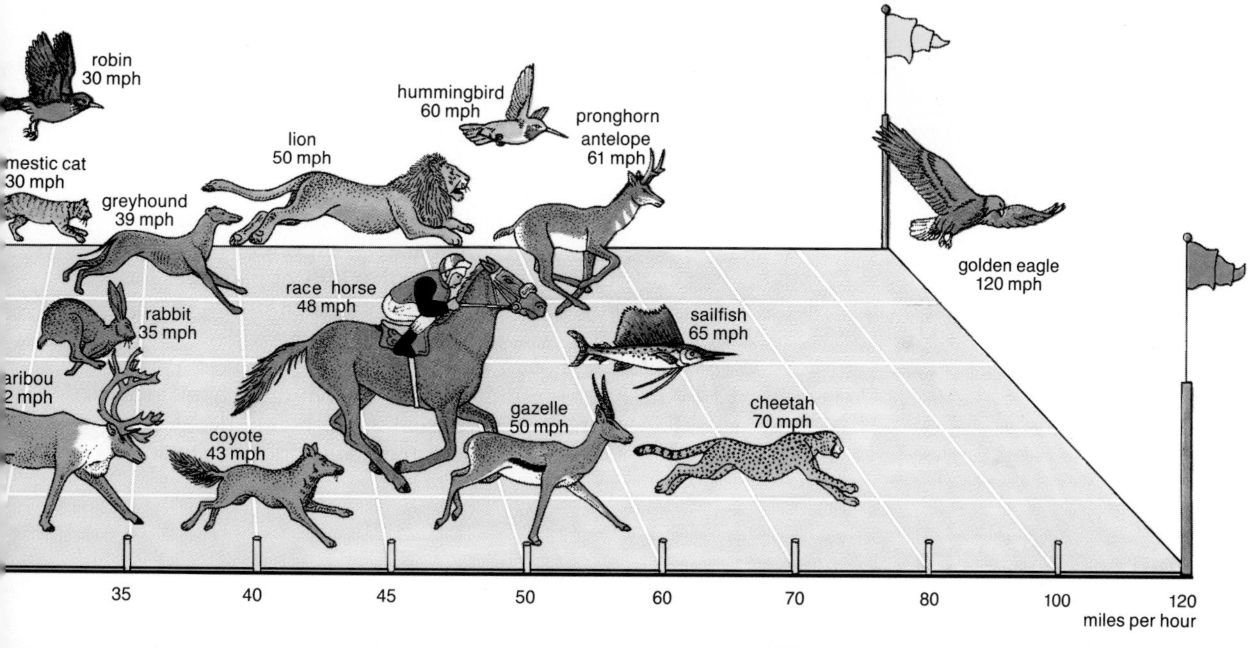

A pack of wild African dogs (*above*) tears at the flesh of a trapped wildebeest. The deadly emerald tree boa (*right*) wraps around its prey and tightens its coil until its victim suffocates.

fast-running, four-legged herbivores. Both kinds of animals pursue the same prey, but in different ways. The cheetah's pursuit, reaching speeds of over 50 miles per hour (80 kilometers per hour), is rapid but brief. If it does not catch its prey within about 600 feet (183 meters), it gives up and searches for another victim.

Wolves, which are very intelligent, hunt in groups, or packs. The members of a wolf pack take turns chasing their victim. They are able to stay fresh during a chase that sometimes lasts for miles. The prey is left exhausted—an easy target for the hungry pack. Wolves also set up ambushes. It is common for a wolf pack to surround its prey, circling in closer and closer until the victim is trapped. There is little chance that the frantic victim will escape the group attack.

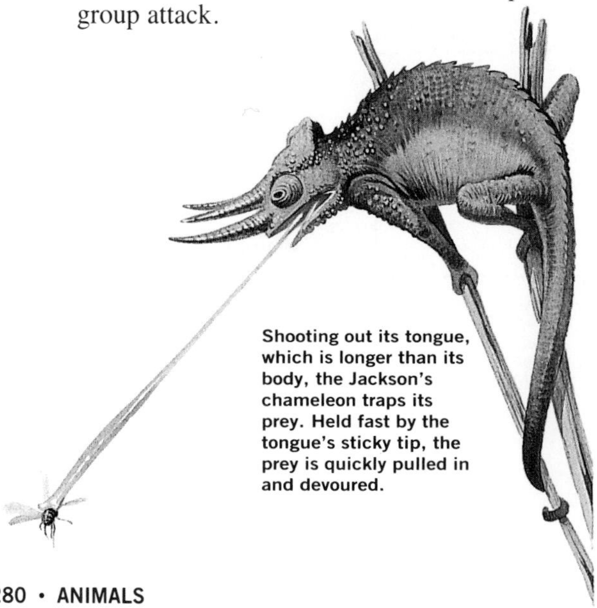

Shooting out its tongue, which is longer than its body, the Jackson's chameleon traps its prey. Held fast by the tongue's sticky tip, the prey is quickly pulled in and devoured.

There are spiders that hunt insects and other small invertebrates in the same manner as some large animals hunt their prey. In fact, some of these spiders are called "wolf" spiders. They are able to pursue their prey with astonishing speed. Most spiders, however, wait for food to come to them. They build webs to trap insects that fly and holes in the ground, with trap doors, to catch insects that crawl.

Rattlesnakes usually hunt at night for small mammals. Special organs in the rattlesnake's head sense the heat given off by the mammal's body. Once it finds its prey, the rattlesnake attacks. Two long fangs inject a poisonous material called venom into the victim. A rattlesnake's venom kills most victims in seconds. Immediately, the injected venom begins to digest the prey—before the snake has even swallowed it.

The jellyfish, a water animal, also uses special organs and venom to catch its prey. The long tentacles of the jellyfish, which can reach up to 50 feet (15 meters) in some species, trail underneath its body as it floats in the water. The tentacles are armed with cells that have stingers. When the cells touch something, the stingers are immediately triggered and shoot out to deliver venom that kills or paralyzes the prey. The helpless prey is then drawn in and eaten.

Although many animals do not have a separate sense organ just to help them hunt, one or more of their senses are highly developed and serve to help them find food. Predatory birds, such as hawks and owls, hunt by sight. Not only are they able to see their small animal prey from great distances, they also have a wide field of vision. Sight, along with a keen sense of smell, helps many animals, such as dogs and wolves, locate their prey.

A water animal that uses a lure to capture its prey is the angler fish. Projecting from its head is a long stalk with a colorful tab of fleshy tissue at the end. When prey swim near, the angler fish wiggles the brightly colored lure. As the victim comes close to examine the wormlike flesh, the angler fish's jaws open wide and the prey is sucked in.

Some animals, such as barnacles, are stationary and must gather food from the surrounding environment. Barnacles spend their adult life attached to rocks or floating objects. Inside its shell, the barnacle is a small, shrimplike animal with long, feathery limbs. As the tide washes over the barnacle, the top of its shell opens and out pop the feathery limbs. The barnacle sweeps its limbs through the water, catching tiny water animals and then kicking the trapped food into its mouth.

Some animals catch food while performing a service for another animal. Cleaner shrimp creep over the bodies of fish, removing pests and parasites as they go along. In the exchange, the shrimp gain a meal and the fish is rid of harmful pests.

Animals That Eat Plants. Plant eaters range from very tiny insects, such as aphids, to huge land animals, such as elephants. In much the same way as meat-eating animals have developed special feeding patterns, each species of plant eaters has evolved its own way of finding and eating food. Some plant eaters feed on grasses; others feed on leaves, seeds, or flowers; still others feed only on plant products, such as nectar. One thing that is common to all animals that only eat plants is that most of their time is spent searching for food and eating it.

Most plant eaters need to take in large amounts of food to get the nourishment they need. The colobus monkey of Africa spends most of its time in trees gathering and eating leaves. Most other monkeys, which have a varied diet, cannot digest leaves. The colobus has a special stomach that allows it to digest the approximately 6 pounds (2.7 kilograms) of leaves that it gathers daily to meet its energy requirements. Even with that amount of food, the colobus dozes as often as possible to conserve energy.

Water plants are an important source of food for animals such as canvasback ducks, brants (a kind of small goose), manatees, and marine iguanas. The marine iguana, a seagoing lizard that lives on the remote Galápagos Islands, feeds mainly on a type of seaweed called sea lettuce. The spiny invertebrates called sea urchins graze on algae in the water. With its rough, sandpaperlike teeth, the sea urchin scrapes off the algae growing on rocks and other surfaces.

The praying mantis (*right*) grasps its insect prey with the sharp hooks on the ends of its long, strong forelegs. Its usual diet consists of insects; however, the praying mantis may seize and eat small tree frogs.

At a height that can reach up to 18 feet (5.5 meters), giraffes (*below*) are the tallest animals in the world. They are able to browse among the branches of trees and tall shrubs, plucking the succulent vegetation with their long tongues.

When under attack, musk oxen (*right*) form a defensive circle with their horns pointing outward. The young are safe on the inside of the circle. Because the armadillo (*below right*) is protected by a powerful wall of body armor, it does not have to be quick to flee from an enemy.

Hummingbirds are among the animals that feed on plant products. The hummingbird uses its long bill to reach deep into flowers and extract the sweet nectar. Some species of bats also feed on nectar, lapping it up with long, thin tongues.

Animals That Eat Everything. Raccoons and people have something in common. They are both omnivores—that is, they eat all sorts of plant and animal products. Omnivores are among the most successful of all animals because they are not restricted to one food, or even a few foods. If one kind of food runs out, they turn to another. Adaptability to many foods enables an animal to exist in many different habitats. Raccoons are able to live in forests, grasslands, wetlands, and even in big cities. Rodents, sheep, deer, gourds, and insects can all be meals for the coyote.

Some human activities create a greater variety of food for omnivores. Raccoons and other animals, such as bears, relish the food garbage produced by people. Another food source created by people is the remains of animals killed by vehicles on the highway.

HOW ANIMALS DEFEND THEMSELVES

A species cannot survive unless it can defend itself against its enemies. The threat of attack from other animals, including human beings, is ever present. The risk of battle is the same for each animal: There is a winner and a loser. Yet even the winner may be wounded, sometimes seriously, making it more likely that it will be the loser in the next battle.

Animals have general and specialized methods of defense. In most situations, animals prefer to escape danger without fighting. Animals use two general defenses to avoid fighting—freezing and fleeing. When danger appears, an animal will remain motionless in an attempt to make itself undetectable to its predator, sometimes even playing dead. If the danger continues and the predator gets too close, the animal will flee. How close different predators can come before they pose a threat and the animal flees is known as **flight distance**. For example, a herd of Thompson's gazelles will graze without concern even though lions are within sight, as long as they are far enough away. If a lion comes too close, within about 200 yards (183 meters), the gazelles will take flight.

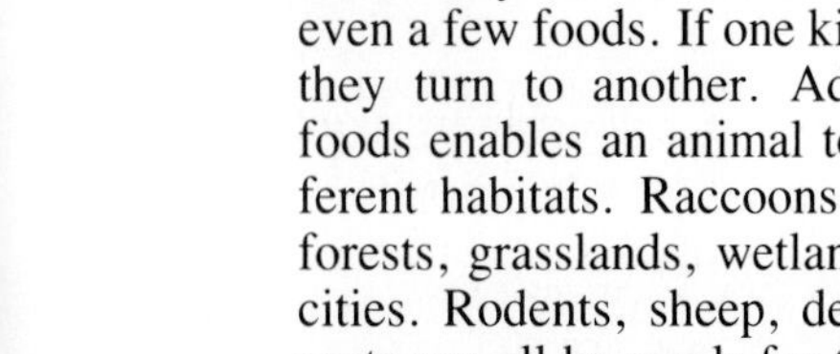

Although it has a preference for small water creatures, the raccoon has a large and varied diet that includes birds' eggs, corn, fruit, nuts, seeds, and small land animals.

Camouflage. Natural camouflage is a way of hiding in the open. When an animal blends into or resembles its surroundings, it can often remain undetected if it stays still. This not only helps an animal avoid enemies, it also helps an animal get close to its prey.

Color and shape can conceal an animal. Insects known as walking sticks have bodies that resemble brown twigs in shape and color. A walking stick will spend long periods of time without moving. Frozen in place on a branch of a tree or shrub, the insect seems to be part of the plant. Many tree-dwelling jungle animals, such as the tree python of Asia, are green like the year-round color of their environment. It is difficult—for an enemy and prey—to detect the python when it is coiled in the branches.

Warning Signals. The bright colors and patterns of some animals are a warning signal to enemies that they should stay away. Some boldly colored animals are venomous; others have glands that emit (give off) a harmful or irritating substance; still others sting or taste bad. At times the signal is hidden until danger appears. When threatened, the foul-tasting Oriental fire-bellied toad turns over to reveal its brightly colored belly.

The striking pattern of the black-and-white fur of the skunk, the vivid colors of the poison dart frogs, and the bright bands of the poisonous coral snake all say "stay away!" However, if a predator ignores the signal, one encounter is generally enough for any predator, if it can survive, to learn to avoid such animals.

Bright colors can also be useful to animals without a built-in defense—when the colors or patterns are the same as those of animals that are harmful. An example is the harmless hoverfly that is safe from many attacks because it looks like a stinging wasp.

Chemical Warfare. Some creatures defend themselves with chemical weapons. The chemicals are delivered in a variety of ways, such as the foul-smelling spray of the skunk, the venomous bite of a snake, the fierce stings of a jellyfish, and the stab of a stingray.

Not all chemicals are injected or sprayed. Some animals have skin glands that produce poisonous substances. The chemical oozes out onto the animal's skin. When a predator grabs hold with its jaws, it is poisoned. Other animals, such as the stonefish, have body parts containing poison that is released on contact.

Camouflaged by long grasses, the tiger can quietly stalk its prey and avoid its enemies. Without its striped markings, the shape of the tiger would stand out from the background of plants and earth in its habitat.

Armor. Scales, shells, and spines provide many animals with protective armor. The pangolin (or scaly anteater) is an ant-eating mammal covered on its back and sides with tough triangular scales that have razor-sharp edges. If threatened, the pangolin can raise its scales to slash its enemy or roll up into a tight ball, protecting its unarmored belly.

The soft flesh of turtles, tortoises, clams, crabs, and many other marine animals is protected by a hard shell. When danger threatens, they simply pull their body back into their snug enclosure and wait for the danger to pass.

The hedgehog, echidna (or spiny anteater), and porcupine are protected by a covering of strong, thick spines. Under attack, the spiny animals will protect exposed underparts and offer the enemy a sea of sharp, powerful spikes.

HOW ANIMALS COMMUNICATE

Animals use many signals, including some that are silent, to communicate with one another. Each species shares a language of sound and behaviors that is recognized by all its members.

Animal Calls. Each animal sound has a meaning. Calls are used for many reasons, including to warn or defend, to claim territory, to help find a mate, and to announce that food has been found. If frightened, a young alligator utters a shrill distress call. The call alerts other young alligators to the danger. The call also draws adult females to the young alligators. The nearness of the adult females provides protection for all the young, so the call serves as a warning and a defense.

A distress call can also confuse an enemy. When a frog is frightened, it lets out a loud squeak. The sudden loud sound can startle the enemy just long enough for the frog to jump away.

Animals that live in large groups such as bird flocks often use food calls that let the group know where a source of food can be found. A tern (a type of small gull) that sights a school of small fish swimming through the water utters a screamlike call.

Not all animal sounds are made with the voice. The ruffed grouse is known for its drumming sound. A male ruffed grouse trying to establish its territory or attract a mate will stand on a log and beat the air with its wings, creating a thumping sound. Although the beating is slow at first, it ends with a rapid whirring noise.

Coyotes, which live throughout the United States, Canada, and Mexico, communicate by howling. The eerie howl of the coyote is usually heard during the evening, night, or early morning.

Silent Signals. Body characteristics and behaviors provide the silent signals that many animals use to communicate. The shape of a body part, the color of fur, or a pattern of movement can send a message from one animal to another.

Some signals are used so that members of a particular species can identify one another. The horns of each species of antelope have a unique shape—some are straight spikes, others are spiraled, and still others are long and curved. Antelopes are able to recognize one another by the shape of the horns.

Scent is an important communication tool that some animals use to establish ownership. A male wolf urinates on shrubs and bushes to let other males know he is around and in charge of his territory. Scent is also used by members of the same species to identify one another and in mating.

Another silent mating signal is the flashing light that the firefly emits. Fireflies use their flashing signal to attract members of the other sex. Each species of firefly has its own pattern of flashes.

Using postures and facial expressions, animals can transmit a great number of messages that are either friendly or hostile. When a young animal whose mother is disciplining it turns over on its back exposing its soft stomach, it means the offspring knows the mother is in charge. In a meeting of two adult animals, the animal that assumes the same posture is saying "I give up."

HOW ANIMALS REPRODUCE

For a species to exist, its members must reproduce their kind. There are two main types of reproduction in the animal kingdom: asexual reproduction, in which a new offspring is produced by one parent, and sexual reproduction, in which a new offspring is produced by two parents.

Asexual Reproduction. Asexual reproduction is carried on by simple animals, such as sponges, jellyfish, flatworms, and those that make coral. When a coral animal reproduces, small projections, called buds, form on its body. The buds grow on the parent and develop their own feeding organs. Soon they split off the parent as a new, separate offspring.

During sexual reproduction, the sponge (*above*) releases sex cells into the surrounding water. The courting frigate bird (*above right*) inflates its huge red pouch to attract females. Orangutans and their young (*right*) enjoy a close relationship.

Another form of asexual reproduction is called **fragmentation**. During fragmentation, an animal, such as a flatworm, divides into two halves. After dividing, each fragment of the flatworm forms the body parts it is missing and becomes a complete new individual.

Sexual Reproduction. During sexual reproduction, two sex cells, an egg cell from a female and a sperm cell from a male, join to create a new offspring. The sperm of some animals, such as mammals, unites with the egg inside the female's body in a process called fertilization. The fertilized egg grows inside the female until the offspring is fully developed and ready for birth.

The fertilization process does not always take place inside the female during sexual reproduction. Some animals produce young without ever coming together to mate. Many fish and aquatic animals, such as frogs, release eggs and sperm into the water when individuals of both sexes are near one another. Fertilization is then a matter of luck. The chances of it occurring are increased in animals that send out signals to attract the opposite sex to them during the release of the cells. Male frogs, for example, emit mating calls that draw the females to them.

Care of the Young. Typically, animals that release sex cells but do not stay around to care for the offspring produce vast numbers of eggs. The female ocean sunfish, which can weigh 1,000 pounds (454 kilograms), can produce 28 million eggs in a single season. The unprotected eggs of the sunfish are threatened by wind, waves, and predators. But because so many eggs are produced, some have a chance of surviving and continuing the species.

Animals that have small numbers of young usually provide some sort of care for them. The female Pacific salmon builds a nest of pebbles and gravel for her 800 eggs. Birds and mammals, which may have only a few, or even a single, offspring, protect and feed their young. Some mammals, such as human beings, care for their young over many years.

▶CYCLES AND PATTERNS OF ANIMAL LIFE

The lives of animals involve regular cycles and patterns that are related to changes in their surroundings. There are many cycles of varying length that occur in an animal's life. Cycles may correspond with an animal's need to find food, a mate, or a new, less-crowded home.

Migration

Many animals, such as the wildebeest, monarch butterfly, gray whale, and Pacific salmon, are great travelers. The regular movement of animals over a set route is called a **migration**. Although all sorts of animals—mammals, fish, insects, and amphibians—migrate, birds are the best-known animal migrants. In the autumn, many birds travel south to spend the winter in a warmer climate. In the spring, they return north to nest and breed.

The champion travelers are the Arctic terns. Each year, Arctic terns travel between the Arctic and Antarctic, logging up to 25,000 miles (40,225 kilometers) of travel. Other birds migrate very short distances. Ptarmigans, which are ground birds common to the cold regions of the Northern Hemisphere, simply move down the mountainside a few hundred yards to escape severe winter weather.

Hibernation

Some cycles help animals survive sharp seasonal changes in temperature. **Hibernation** is a sleeplike state that protects animals against the cold and decreases their need for food. Many different kinds of animals hibernate, including some species of birds, mammals, insects, reptiles, and amphibians. When cold weather approaches, animals that hibernate burrow into the ground, curl up under leaves, or tuck away in dens. Their heartbeat, breathing, and other bodily functions slow down. They do not move. Because they are inactive, they do not need food. Most hibernating animals eat large quantities of food during the autumn. The food is stored in their body as fat and supplies the energy as they need it during hibernation.

Population Cycles

Some species go through cycles in their population. The ruffed grouse, a chickenlike bird of North America, has a population cycle of six or seven years. At the height of the cycle, the numbers of grouse explode. Then they decrease, year by year. At the lowest point of the cycle, the numbers gradually begin to increase.

Such cycles are partly tied to food supply. When food is abundant, more animals survive and have young. Eventually, however, the number of animals exceeds the food supply. Animals die and the population drops. With fewer animals around, food becomes increasingly more available. As it does, the population of the animals once again begins to increase.

Dense clouds of monarch butterflies (*below*) travel from Canada and the northern United States as far south as Mexico to escape the winter's cold. Huge herds of wildebeests (*right*) migrate over the grassy plains of Africa in search of food and water.

ANIMALS AND PEOPLE

Animals provide people with food, transportation, and protection. Animals also spread disease, such as rabies and Lyme disease, and compete with humans for food. In the long run, however, the fate of the animal kingdom is in human hands. People and their activities have so changed the balance of nature that many species will only survive if they have help from humanity.

People have long hunted wild animals as a source of food and clothing. Scientists believe that the need to band together and hunt helped human society become more complex. Actually, we still depend on hunting for an important food source—fish. Harvesting fish from the sea really is just another form of hunting wild animals.

Domestic Animals. Our domestic animals, such as cows, horses, and dogs, were bred from their wild ancestors by people. Dogs were domesticated about 14,000 years ago. Their ancestors probably were wolves that fed on garbage near human camps and then became tame. Dogs help people hunt, serve as guards, and, most of all, bring them happiness as pets.

Cattle and horses were domesticated from wild ancestors more than 5,000 years ago. Ever since, they have served as a means of transportation and, more important, have provided food. People have controlled the breeding of domestic animals to produce types with beneficial characteristics. Wild cattle, for instance, can be fierce. Early cattle breeders eliminated the fierceness by allowing only certain cattle to mate—those that seemed more docile (easy to control) than others. They passed this docile tendency on to their descendants.

Animal Symbols. Animals have always served as symbols for people. This is still true today. Evidence of animals used as symbols can be found throughout the world—in the names given to sports teams, in the art that is produced, and in the religions that consider some animals to be sacred.

Diseases from Animals. Some animals pass diseases to people. Many animals, such as raccoons, can spread rabies. If a rabid animal bites someone, that person will die unless treated. At one time, a person with rabies was doomed, but modern medical treatment has ended this threat.

Giraffes, elands, and rhinoceroses roam an animal preserve in Woburn, England. Preserves are part of an effort to protect and breed endangered animal species.

In recent years, another disease spread by animals has been on the increase. It is called Lyme disease, after the town in Connecticut in which it was first discovered. It is carried by a tick that can live on deer and other animals. Fortunately, not all ticks carry Lyme disease, and, with antibiotics, it is treatable.

WILDLIFE CONSERVATION

Humans present far more danger to animals than they to us. All over the world, species of animals are threatened with extinction because of people. Human populations are exploding. People need land, food, and natural resources. This means that habitats on which animals depend are taken up for human wants. Human activities cause pollution that destroys habitats and the animals that rely on them. The same pollution threatens human life.

Animals help keep the balance of nature. Moreover, they should be appreciated for themselves, as well as for what they do for us. While people are a threat to animals, people can also help them. Across the world, conservationists are working to keep animal species healthy, to save them from extinction, and to make our world better for animals—and for people.

EDWARD R. RICCIUTI
Coauthor, *The Audubon Society Book of Wild Animals*

See also AMPHIBIANS; BIOLOGICAL CLOCK; BIRDS; ENDANGERED SPECIES; FISH; HOMING AND MIGRATION; INSECTS; LIFE; MAMMALS; MOLLUSKS; REPTILES; SPONGES; WORMS.

The Road Runner always gets the better of Wile E. Coyote, his hapless pursuer, in a popular series of animated cartoons. Through the technique of animation, imaginary creatures appear to live and move.

ANIMATION

The word "animate" comes from the Latin word *anima*, or soul, and literally means "to give life to." In filmmaking, animation is a technique that makes inanimate (lifeless) drawings or objects appear to live and move. Animation is most often used to make cartoon movies and television shows. It can also be used in television commercials or in educational films. Animation is sometimes used in combination with live action in movies.

Unlike live-action films, which record the movements of living actors, animated films create an illusion of motion. Bugs Bunny never really dove down his rabbit hole, Mickey Mouse never really kissed Minnie, and Gumby never really waved good-bye. The movements of these imaginary creatures occurred only on film.

Because animation is not limited to recording things that really happened, it can show viewers many things that live action cannot, from the movements of a single atom to a view of an entire galaxy. An animated character can fly without wings, fall off a cliff without getting hurt, or be squashed flat as a pancake and pop back into shape. The only limits to what animation can show are the limits of the artist's imagination.

ANIMATION TECHNIQUES

There are two basic types of animation. In one technique, two-dimensional (flat) drawings are animated. The other technique involves the animation of three-dimensional objects such as puppets or clay figures. (A third type of animation, done with computers, is discussed in the box "Computer Animation" on page 290.)

To make an animated film, a series of drawings—or an object placed in a series of positions—is photographed, one picture at a time, by a motion picture camera. In each picture, or **frame**, the subject's position is changed slightly. When the completed film is run, the subject appears to move.

Artists and writers first prepare a **storyboard**, which is an illustrated script. The storyboard looks like a giant comic strip, with sketches showing the action of the story and dialogue (the characters' spoken lines) written under each sketch. Next, the music and the dialogue are recorded. Then the work of animation begins.

Two-Dimensional Animation. The animation of drawings is the technique most often used to create animated films and television shows.

The animators follow a chart listing the length of time and number of frames needed for each word, sound, and action in the entire script. To look smooth and natural, a single action that takes one second of screen time may require as many as 24 drawings. For example, if a script calls for a character to raise his hand, the first picture the animators draw shows the character with his hand at his side. In the next drawing, his hand is raised slightly, and a third drawing shows his hand still higher. Drawing after drawing is made in this way until, in the 24th drawing, the action is completed. More than a million drawings may be used in an animated feature film. Most television cartoons use fewer drawings per second. As a result, the characters' movements may not look as lifelike.

The animators draw every movement of every character that will appear in the film. When the drawings are completed, they are traced onto sheets of clear plastic called **cels**. Colors are then painted on the reverse sides of the cels. Other artists paint the backgrounds in the film. The finished cels are laid over the backgrounds and photographed with a special camera that shoots one frame of film at a time. The camera operator follows a chart that tells the proper sequence of the cels and which background is needed for each frame. The operator takes a picture, removes the cel and replaces it with the next one, then takes another picture. The soundtrack, containing the music, dialogue, and sound effects, is added after the photography is completed.

Some animated films are made without using cels. Instead, the drawings themselves are photographed. Pencil, charcoal, and colored pencil can produce subtle, shaded effects that are very different from the bright colors of the painted cels.

Three-Dimensional Animation. Three-dimensional figures and objects can be animated using a process called **stop-motion photography**. Animators often work with special puppets, which are made of flexible plastic molded around a jointed metal "skeleton." In recent years, figures and objects made of clay have become popular subjects of stop-motion animation.

Using a special motion picture camera, animators film the figure or object. After each frame is photographed, the camera is stopped,

Below: Three favorite animated characters are Elmer Fudd, Bugs Bunny, and Daffy Duck. _Below right:_ In the film _Who Framed Roger Rabbit?_, humans appeared to interact with cartoon characters. _Right:_ Animated clay figures enliven a television ad for California raisins.

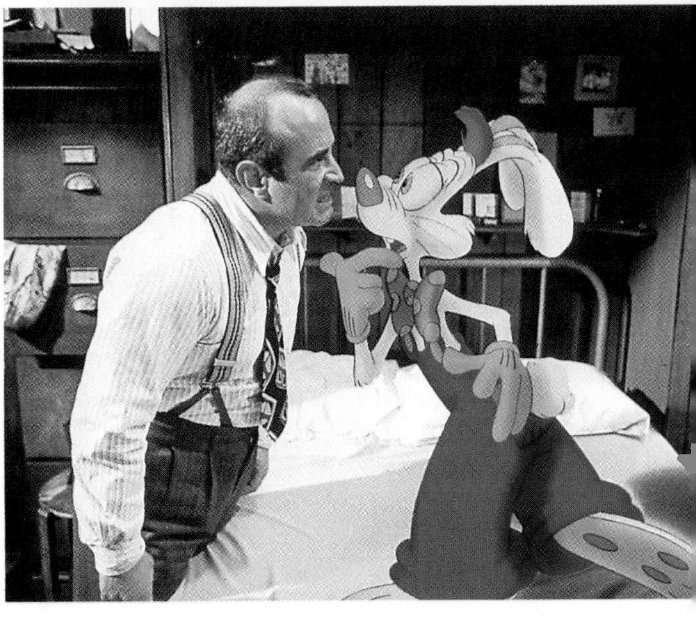

and the animators adjust the figure's position slightly. When the film is developed and projected, the figure appears to move.

Stop-motion photography is used to make short animated films and television commercials. It is also used to animate the imaginary creatures that appear in live-action fantasy and science-fiction movies. The giant ape King Kong, as well as some of the creatures in the *Star Wars* series, were animated using stop-motion techniques.

The title character from the computer-animated film *Tin Toy*, which won an Academy Award in 1989.

Computer Animation

Some of the most exciting developments in animation are taking place in the field of computer graphics, in which artists use computers to produce images and animate them. Computer animation is used to create video games and films, as well as graphics and special effects for television and movies.

Computer graphics techniques vary, depending on the kind of equipment and the software (instructions that tell the machine what to do) that are used. But most computer graphics systems have certain features in common.

The inside surface of a computer screen is coated with thousands of tiny dots of light-sensitive chemicals called phosphors. Each dot is called a picture element, or **pixel**. The pixels are arranged in clusters of three, with each pixel responsible for producing one of the three primary colors of light: red, blue, and green. These colors can be combined to produce all the colors an artist might need. Using a computer graphics program, the artist tells the computer which pixels to light up. The glowing pixels create the image on the screen.

The amount of detail in the image depends on the number of pixels on the screen. Most home computer screens have comparatively few pixels, and pictures drawn on them often show little detail. But a powerful computer used by an animator may have millions of pixels on the screen. With these machines it is possible to produce highly detailed images.

Once the artist has produced an image and stored it in the computer, the machine can be instructed to calculate all the slight adjustments in position that are needed to give the appearance of motion. It can also make all the necessary changes in light, shading, and perspective. Each succeeding computer-generated image is photographed and used to make a single frame of film. When the film is run, the effect is one of movement.

Computer animation can be used to create effects that would be difficult or impossible to achieve using drawings. For example, surfaces such as metal, glass, and plastic can be given extremely lifelike textures. For this reason, computer animation is often used to create realistic settings and backgrounds. However, some filmmakers continue to use traditional animation techniques to bring characters to life.

CHARLES SOLOMON

HISTORY OF ANIMATION

The first animated film, *Humorous Phases of Funny Faces*, was made in 1906 by J. Stuart Blackton, an American newspaper illustrator. Blackton filmed a series of faces that had been drawn on a blackboard and also used a variety of other techniques. Another early animated film, *Gertie the Dinosaur*, was created by the American cartoonist Winsor McCay in 1914. In this film, for the first time, a character drawn of lines seemed to live and breathe on the screen.

Audiences liked these animated cartoons. Soon many American film studios were producing animated films, which were shown in movie theaters before the feature films. The Pat Sullivan studio produced one of the most famous characters of the silent-film era, Felix the Cat. The Fleischer studio produced cartoons featuring the character Ko-Ko the Clown and later created Betty Boop, Popeye, and Superman cartoons.

The first successful animated cartoon with sound was *Steamboat Willie* (1928), which introduced the character Mickey Mouse. This film was produced by Walt Disney, who was to become the most famous American producer of animated films. Disney's series of Mickey Mouse cartoons and another series called *Silly Symphonies* were very popular with audiences.

The success of his early cartoons enabled Disney to launch an ambitious training program for his artists. They studied anatomy, drawing, acting, and motion to improve their animation. The results of this training can be seen in Disney's *Snow White and the Seven Dwarfs* (1937), which was the first feature-length animated film made in the United States. Other important Disney films followed, including *Pinocchio* (1940), *Fantasia* (1940), *Dumbo* (1941), and *Bambi* (1942).

Right: Snow White and the Seven Dwarfs, released by the Walt Disney studio in 1937, was the first feature-length animated film made in the United States.

Below: The beloved Disney character Mickey Mouse made his first appearance in 1928 in *Steamboat Willie*, the first successful animated cartoon with sound.

By the end of World War II (1939–45), leadership in the field of animation had passed to two major film studios, Metro-Goldwyn-Mayer (MGM) and Warner Brothers. At MGM, William Hanna and Joseph Barbera made cartoons featuring Tom and Jerry, a cat and a mouse. Warner Brothers cartoons, directed by Tex Avery, Chuck Jones, and Friz Freleng, starred Bugs Bunny, Daffy Duck, and many other characters. During the 1950's, United Productions of America (UPA) introduced a flat, modernistic drawing style in cartoons featuring Gerald McBoing-Boing and Mr. Magoo.

During the 1960's, television networks began broadcasting children's cartoons on Saturday mornings. Some cartoons were shown in the evenings. The most successful television animation studio was Hanna-Barbera, which introduced the Flintstones, the Jetsons, Yogi Bear, and hundreds of other characters.

In the 1980's and 1990's, animation became popular once again in films. The Disney studio produced such modern classics as *The Little Mermaid* (1989), *Aladdin* (1993), and *The Lion King* (1994). Computer animation (see box) has expanded the artistic possibilities of this field, creating the remarkably realistic dinosaurs of *Jurassic Park* (1993) and making barnyard animals appear to speak in *Babe* (1995). Full-length feature films, such as *A Bug's Life* and *Antz* (both 1998), have been made entirely by this technique. And with shows such as *The Simpsons* and *King of the Hill*, animation on television has become as popular with adults as it is with children.

CHARLES SOLOMON
Author, *Enchanted Drawings: The History of Animation*

See also DISNEY, WALT.

ANNAN, KOFI. See UNITED NATIONS (Profiles).
ANNAPOLIS. See MARYLAND (Cities).
ANNE, SAINT. See SAINTS (Profiles).
ANOREXIA NERVOSA. See DISEASES (Descriptions of Some Diseases).

A vast ice sheet (*far right*) covers Antarctica, making the continent inhospitable to life. The only human inhabitants are scientists from many nations, who have established bases (*right*), where they spend part of the year studying the frozen continent. Penguins (*below*) and other animals thrive in the waters off Antarctica.

ANTARCTICA

Antarctica is the coldest, windiest, most desolate continent on earth. Almost all of its area is covered with a vast ice sheet, which reaches a thickness of about 5 kilometers (3 miles) near the South Pole. This ice sheet holds 70 percent of the world's fresh water. Even so, much of Antarctica is considered a desert because many places receive so little precipitation—less than 76 millimeters (3 inches) a year, in the form of snow.

No people are native to Antarctica, but about 40 scientific stations are scattered around the continent. Each summer some 2,000 scientists come to Antarctica to study its environment. About 250 people spend the harsh winters there.

▶THE LAND

Larger than the United States and Mexico combined, Antarctica covers an area of about 14,000,000 square kilometers (5,405,000 square miles). Much of the continent is mountainous, and high peaks protrude through the ice sheet. A great mountain range, the Transantarctic Mountains, divides the continent and ice sheet into East Antarctica and West Antarctica.

At the edges of Antarctica lie enormous ice shelves—some as large as the state of Texas. Mountain glaciers (slow-moving masses of ice) flowing from the continent's center feed into the ice shelves. Regularly, pieces of ice break off to become icebergs, some of which may be 60 to 100 kilometers (37 to 62 miles) wide.

The ocean around Antarctica is formed by the southern parts of the Pacific, Atlantic, and Indian oceans. Much of this southern ocean is frozen all year long. In winter a thick belt of ice 480 to 1,600 kilometers (300 to 1,000 miles) wide surrounds Antarctica. Although much of the ice melts during the summer, the sea ice still extends between 160 and 800 kilometers (100 and 500 miles) from the continent.

▶THE CLIMATE

Surprisingly, Antarctica receives more sunlight than the equator, but the snow-covered ice sheet and the sea ice surrounding the continent reflect the heat back into space. Although the weather along the coast is considerably milder, inland the average winter temperature is about −70°C (−94°F). In July, 1983 (in the middle of the Antarctic winter), Soviet scientists at their Vostok Station recorded the world's lowest temperature: −89.2°C (−128.6°F).

Fierce winds, called katabatic winds, control Antarctica's weather and make the climate inhospitable to people. Gravity draws cold air

from the interior down the slopes of the ice sheet to the coast. As the air becomes colder, the wind speed increases—up to 322 kilometers (200 miles) an hour along the coast.

ANIMAL LIFE

Although plants and animals may have once thrived in Antarctica, today the continent itself is almost empty of life. Only a few hardy insects, primitive plants such as mosses, and one type of grass survive along the warmer coast of the Antarctic Peninsula near South America. Farther inland, in areas free of ice, lichens and simple organisms called algae have adapted to the cold, dry environment by living in the cracks of rocks. In 1996, British and Russian scientists found evidence of a large body of liquid water, the size of Lake Ontario, beneath the Antarctic ice sheet near Vostok. Some experts believe this "Lake Vostok"—hidden from the sun's light under the ice—may contain previously unknown aquatic organisms.

The sparseness of life on land contrasts greatly with the variety of life in the southern ocean. About 27 types of seabirds breed in the Antarctic region. Among these are the penguins—the most familiar of which are the small Adélie penguins and the larger emperor penguins. Six types of seals frequent the southern ocean. Of these, Weddell, Ross, crabeater, and leopard seals breed in or near Antarctica. Blue, fin, sei, humpback, and sperm whales also are common. Tiny sea creatures called krill are especially important to Antarctica's marine (sea) ecosystem—the community of living organisms and their environment. Shrimplike animals, krill serve as food for whales, seals, birds, and fishes. In turn, krill feed on plants and smaller animals.

ANTARCTICA'S PAST

More than 200 million years ago, Antarctica, South America, Africa, Australia, and India formed one enormous continent that scientists call Gondwana. Gradually, large pieces of the earth's crust separated, and Antarctica was isolated from the other continents. (For more information on how the continents were formed, see the articles EARTH and EARTH, HISTORY OF.)

Although the ice hides much of Antarctica's past, scientists have uncovered the fact that millions of years ago the continent had a tropical climate. Coal, petrified (mineralized) tree trunks, and fossils (the remains or imprints) of leaves and sea creatures have been discovered in Antarctica. In 1969, American geologists discovered the fossil jawbone of a small, four-legged reptile in the Transantarctic Mountains. This reptile had lived in Antarctica more than 200 million years ago.

For many years scientists searched for fossils of mammals. In 1982, American geologists discovered fossils of a small, rodentlike

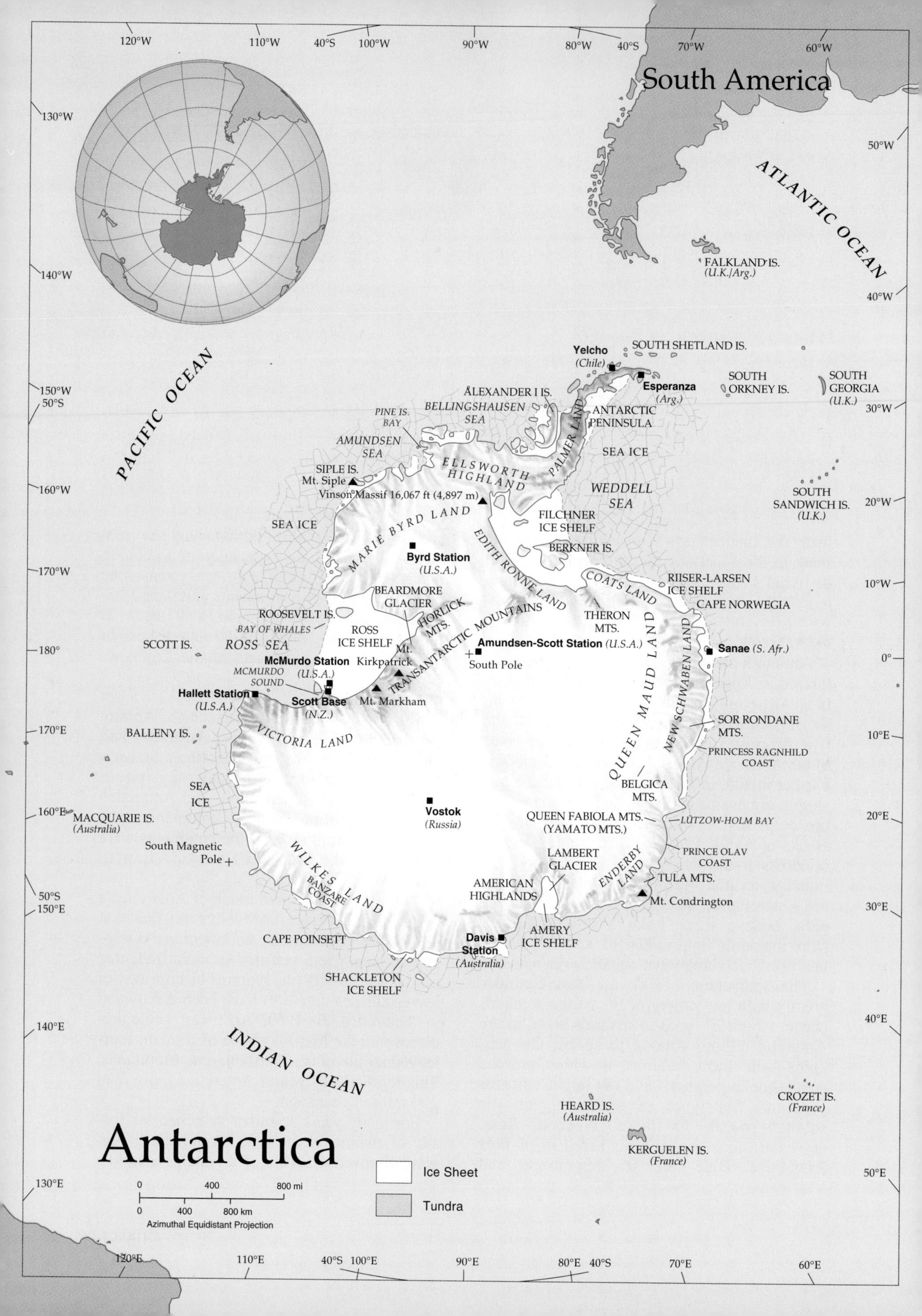
Antarctica
South America
ATLANTIC OCEAN
PACIFIC OCEAN
INDIAN OCEAN
FALKLAND IS. (U.K./Arg.)
SOUTH SHETLAND IS.
Yelcho (Chile)
Esperanza (Arg.)
SOUTH ORKNEY IS.
SOUTH GEORGIA (U.K.)
ALEXANDER I IS.
BELLINGSHAUSEN SEA
PINE IS. BAY
AMUNDSEN SEA
ANTARCTIC PENINSULA
PALMER LAND
SEA ICE
SIPLE IS.
Mt. Siple
ELLSWORTH HIGHLAND
WEDDELL SEA
Vinson Massif 16,067 ft (4,897 m)
SOUTH SANDWICH IS. (U.K.)
FILCHNER ICE SHELF
MARIE BYRD LAND
EDITH RONNE LAND
BERKNER IS.
Byrd Station (U.S.A.)
COATS LAND
RIISER-LARSEN ICE SHELF
CAPE NORWEGIA
BEARDMORE GLACIER
HORLICK MTS.
THERON MTS.
ROOSEVELT IS.
BAY OF WHALES
ROSS ICE SHELF
TRANSANTARCTIC MOUNTAINS
SCOTT IS.
ROSS SEA
Amundsen-Scott Station (U.S.A.)
South Pole
Mt. Kirkpatrick
QUEEN MAUD LAND
NEW SCHWABEN LAND
Sanae (S. Afr.)
McMurdo Station (U.S.A.)
MCMURDO SOUND
Hallett Station (U.S.A.)
Scott Base (N.Z.)
Mt. Markham
BALLENY IS.
VICTORIA LAND
SOR RONDANE MTS.
PRINCESS RAGNHILD COAST
SEA ICE
BELGICA MTS.
Vostok (Russia)
MACQUARIE IS. (Australia)
QUEEN FABIOLA MTS. (YAMATO MTS.)
LUTZOW-HOLM BAY
South Magnetic Pole
LAMBERT GLACIER
PRINCE OLAV COAST
WILKES LAND
BANZARE COAST
ENDERBY LAND
TULA MTS.
AMERICAN HIGHLANDS
Mt. Condrington
CAPE POINSETT
Davis Station (Australia)
AMERY ICE SHELF
SHACKLETON ICE SHELF
HEARD IS. (Australia)
CROZET IS. (France)
KERGUELEN IS. (France)
Ice Sheet
Tundra
0 400 800 mi
0 400 800 km
Azimuthal Equidistant Projection
120°W 110°W 40°S 100°W 90°W 80°W 40°S 70°W 60°W
130°W 140°W 150°W 50°S 160°W 170°W 180° 170°E 160°E 50°S 150°E 140°E 130°E
50°W 40°W 30°W 20°W 10°W 0° 10°E 20°E 30°E 40°E 50°E
120°E 110°E 40°S 100°E 90°E 80°E 40°S 70°E 60°E

marsupial (a pouched mammal like an opossum) that lived in Antarctica between 55 million and 40 million years ago. Because this marsupial was similar to mammals found in South America and Australia today, the discovery supported the theory that Antarctica was once joined to these two continents. The largest fossil yet found in Antarctica, that of a 9-meter (30-foot)-long whale said to be 40 million years old, was discovered in 1987.

EXPLORATION AND DISCOVERY

For centuries it was believed that an Antarctic continent existed, but its existence remained unproved. Between 1772 and 1775 the British navigator Captain James Cook sailed around Antarctica but did not sight it. In 1820 an American sealing ship under Captain Nathaniel Palmer reached the Antarctic Peninsula. Palmer, a British naval officer named Edward Bransfield, and a Russian admiral named Fabian von Bellingshausen are all generally credited with having "discovered" Antarctica at about the same time.

Between the 1820's and 1900, expeditions from the United States, France, and Britain explored the oceans and coast of Antarctica. In the early 1900's, explorers turned their attention landward. The race to be the first to reach the South Pole, at approximately the center of the continent, was the climax of the heroic age of Antarctic exploration. Although many men tried, the first to reach the South Pole was Roald Amundsen of Norway on December 14, 1911. Close behind him was Robert F. Scott, a British naval officer, who reached the pole on January 17, 1912, but died along with his men on the return trip.

In the years that followed, explorers and scientists from many countries traveled to Antarctica. Among them was Admiral Richard E. Byrd of the United States. Byrd led three expeditions to Antarctica between 1928 and 1941. In 1929 he became the first to pilot an airplane over the South Pole. Byrd and others changed Antarctic exploration by introducing tractors, airplanes, icebreaking ships, and radios and prepared the way for modern scientific investigation of the continent.

The modern age of Antarctic research began with the International Geophysical Year (IGY) of 1957–58. During the IGY, twelve nations established 55 scientific stations in Antarctica.

THE ANTARCTIC TREATY

In December, 1959, in Washington, D.C., Argentina, Australia, Belgium, Chile, France, Japan, New Zealand, Norway, South Africa, the Soviet Union, the United Kingdom, and the United States (all participants in the IGY) signed the Antarctic Treaty. The treaty became official in 1961. Since then, four additional nations have signed it, and 16 others have agreed to observe its provisions.

The Antarctic Treaty provides that Antarctica shall be used only for peaceful purposes. Ordinary military activities, nuclear tests, and the disposal of nuclear wastes are forbidden. The treaty also guarantees the free exchange of scientific ideas and information among the nations. It does not recognize the many territorial claims by countries to Antarctica. In addition, there are several special international agreements designed to preserve Antarctica's environment.

ANTARCTICA: PRESENT AND FUTURE

Scientists study Antarctica not only to learn its secrets but also to solve problems that affect the whole world. Antarctica's climate, the ice sheet, and the southern ocean have an effect on weather and oceans worldwide. The question of the ice sheet's stability is vital to scientists studying how carbon dioxide affects our climate. What will happen to the ice sheet if increased carbon dioxide in the atmosphere makes our climate warmer? Scientists are also concerned about the atmosphere's thinning ozone layer, a problem severe over Antarctica.

Antarctica's future may not be limited to providing scientists with information. Some countries now catch krill to feed people and animals. Antarctica is believed to have valuable mineral resources, including petroleum, coal, and precious metals. However, Antarctica's harsh climate makes finding and developing these resources difficult. In addition, people and governments want to ensure that Antarctica's unique environment will continue to be protected. In 1991, after more than two years of negotiations between members of the Antarctic Treaty, 24 countries signed an agreement that prohibited mining and oil drilling for 50 years.

WINIFRED REUNING
Division of Polar Programs
National Science Foundation

See also ARCTIC.

Roaming through the tall grass with her offspring clinging tightly to her back, the female giant anteater searches for her favorite prey—ants and termites.

ANTEATERS

The solitary creature journeys slowly through the dry grass, sniffing the ground with its long tubelike snout. Finding a hidden ant or termite nest, it uses its strong front claws to slash it open. Its wormlike tongue, which can reach 2 feet (0.6 meter) in length, darts in and out of the nest, greedily licking up the ants. Each day, this hungry mammal—the giant anteater—eats thousands of insects.

The three species, or kinds, of anteaters can be found roaming rain forests and grassy plains from southern Mexico to northern Argentina. Anteaters belong to a group of mammals, called Edentata (meaning "without teeth"), that also includes sloths and armadillos. Other animals are sometimes called anteaters, such as aardvarks and spiny anteaters; however, they are not part of the same family.

There is a wide range in size among the species of anteaters. The giant anteater measures about 6 feet (1.8 meters) from its head to its bushy tail and can weigh up to 110 pounds (50 kilograms). The tamandua, or collared anteater, measures about 42 inches (106 centimeters) from head to tail and weighs about 9 pounds (4 kilograms). The silky, or pygmy, anteater, which is about the size of a squirrel, measures about 13 inches (34 centimeters) from head to tail and weighs about a pound (0.45 kilogram).

Anteaters and Their Young. Anteaters live solitary existences, each one within its own territory. Males and females only come together to mate. About 180 days after mating, the female anteater gives birth to one baby.

Immediately after birth, the baby anteater climbs up onto its mother's back. It leaves its secure spot only to nurse or when the mother feeds. When it is about 3 months old, the young anteater ventures from its mother to find food for itself. The baby anteater stays with its mother until the mother becomes pregnant again.

The Life of an Anteater. The giant anteater lives on the ground—usually in open forests and savannas. Unlike its smaller night-feeding relatives that spend most of their lives in the trees, the giant anteater stays on the ground and seeks its food chiefly by day. When resting, the giant anteater often takes over the empty burrow of another animal or sinks into a shady ditch, covering itself with its broad tail.

Walking about on the knuckles of its front feet to protect its long sharp claws, the giant anteater spends most of the day searching for food. It uses its keen sense of smell to find nests of ants and termites. The giant anteater is a careful diner, quickly taking a small portion of the insect population before it can be bitten by the ants. The food is swallowed whole and broken down in its muscular stomach. The quantities of earth, sand, tiny twigs, and small stones that the giant anteater regularly takes in also help in the digestion of its food.

The Anteater and Its Environment. The enemies of the giant anteater include jaguars and pumas. When defending itself, the giant anteater will stand up and slash out with its strong front limbs and long claws.

Humans are also a threat to anteaters. In the process of clearing land for crops, grazing, and construction, they destroy the anteater's environment. Even though the anteater helps control the populations of insect pests, many people consider the anteater too dangerous to protect.

Reviewed by JAMES G. DOHERTY
Curator of Mammals
The Bronx Zoo

See also MAMMALS.

Bounding gracefully across the plains of Africa, impalas (*above*) can jump as high as 8 feet (2.4 meters) in a single leap. Safe within the protective camouflage of tall grasses, a baby Grant's gazelle (*left*) is nuzzled by its mother.

ANTELOPES

Antelopes are usually slender, graceful mammals that have two-hoofed toes on each foot and hollow horns. Although they are sometimes thought to be part of the deer family, antelopes are actually more closely related to cattle. Antelopes, cattle, and other animals such as bison, buffaloes, goats, and sheep all belong to the same family, called Bovidae.

Most antelopes live in Africa. There are also several species, or kinds, of antelopes found in Asia. While there are no true antelopes in North America, a close relative of the antelopes, the mountain goat, makes its home in the Rocky Mountains of North America.

▶CHARACTERISTICS OF ANTELOPES

There is great variety in the size of antelopes. The smallest, the royal antelope of Africa's western coast, is about the size of a rabbit. It measures about 10 inches (25 centimeters) high at the shoulder and weighs about 8 pounds (3.8 kilograms). The largest antelope, the giant eland of West Africa, is about the size of a large cow. It measures 6 feet (1.8 meters) high at the shoulder and can weigh more than 1,200 pounds (544 kilograms).

The appearance of the various species of antelopes seems to vary as much as the size does. Their smooth coat of hair is generally brightly colored with variations of white, gray, or brown. Several species have more distinctive coloring, such as the bongo, which is red with vertical white stripes, and the male sable antelope, which is nearly all black with white markings on its face, belly, and rump.

In some kinds of antelopes, both males and females have horns; in others only males have horns. Antelopes keep the horns all their life, unlike the antlers of deer, which are shed each year. The horns can be many different shapes and sizes—long and curved, short and ringed, spiral, or lyre-shaped.

The strong slender legs of the antelope enable it to leap high and run fast. The impala can jump 8 feet (2.4 meters) high, and the black buck of India can reach speeds of about 60 miles (97 kilometers) per hour.

Plants, such as leaves and grasses, make up the diet of the antelope. The antelope must tear its food from the plant by pressing the front teeth in the lower jaw against a hard pad in the upper jaw. The food is only slightly chewed before it is swallowed. After the food

Although actual fights between antelopes are rare, these greater kudu males have locked horns in a pushing match to resolve a territorial conflict. One of the males will eventually give in and withdraw from the match with head lowered and tail tucked between his legs.

passes to the stomach, it is called cud. At a later time, the cud is forced back into the mouth to be chewed thoroughly with the back molars before it is swallowed again. Antelopes and other animals, such as deer, cattle, sheep, and goats, that eat in this manner are called cud-chewers, or **ruminants**.

ANTELOPES AND THEIR YOUNG

Some male and female antelopes mate throughout the year, while others mate at a certain time of the year. The time between mating and the birth of the offspring varies from about five and a half months to about nine months, depending on the kind of antelope. Usually, only one baby is born at a time.

Most females living in herds leave the herd and find a secluded area in which to give birth. After giving birth, the mother licks the baby antelope, or calf, to rouse it. Within minutes, the calf is able to stand on its own.

In the first few months of life, the mother antelope may hide the calf in tall grass or bush when she feeds. Because calves, as well as sick and old antelopes, are easy catches for predators, many do not reach adulthood.

THE LIFE OF THE ANTELOPE

Antelopes, which live in herds, alone, or in pairs, can be found in a variety of habitats, or environments: grassy plains, dense tropical forests, hot deserts, high mountains, and even swamplands. The antelope spends much of the day, except for the hot afternoon, feeding, drinking, and ruminating (chewing its cud). During the afternoon when the sun is at its hottest, the antelope rests.

Many kinds of antelopes are territorial. This means that males mark an area as their own and guard it against other males. Although males spend much of their time defending their territory from other males, females are allowed to enter the territory so that mating can take place.

Hyenas, wild dogs, and large cats (such as lions and leopards) prey on antelopes. The smaller antelopes are also threatened by eagles, small cats, and pythons. These shy creatures often protect themselves by running away from predators. Some antelopes that live in herds use signals to warn others of danger; the springbok is one antelope that alerts others by leaping high into the air when it senses an enemy is near.

ANTELOPES AND THEIR ENVIRONMENT

For at least 2 million years, humans have hunted antelopes for food. The beauty of some antelopes has made them a target for hunters who desire their skins or horns. Others have hunted them solely for sport.

The long years of hunting have left some antelopes, such as the bontebok and the giant sable, scarce; others, such as the bluebuck, have been completely wiped out. Recent efforts have been made to protect some antelopes in parks and in private reserves. Additional efforts have focused on preserving the wild antelopes by establishing game ranches where antelopes would be raised, much like cattle, for meat. With commercial antelope meat available, it would be less likely that the wild antelopes would be hunted as a food source.

LYNN MARCINKOWSKI WOOLF
Science Writer

Reviewed by JAMES G. DOHERTY
Curator of Mammals
The Bronx Zoo

See also HOOFED MAMMALS.

ANTHONY, SUSAN B. (1820–1906)

For more than fifty years, Susan B. Anthony was a leading force in the women's rights movement and a tireless campaigner for woman suffrage. The 19th Amendment, which finally granted women the right to vote, was not ratified until 1920, 14 years after her death. However, in recognition of her lifelong struggle to gain equality for women, it is often called the Susan B. Anthony Amendment.

Born in Adams, Massachusetts, on February 15, 1820, Susan Brownell Anthony was the second of eight children. Although she grew up at a time when society discouraged women from voicing their political viewpoints, Anthony was raised by her Quaker parents to believe that women are equal to men and deserve equal opportunities.

Due to her parents' influence, Anthony eventually became involved in two important reform movements of the day—antislavery and temperance (to stop people from drinking alcoholic beverages). While working for temperance, Anthony developed extraordinary leadership skills.

In 1850, Anthony met Elizabeth Cady Stanton, an eloquent leader in the developing women's rights movement, and the two women developed a lifelong friendship and working partnership.

Anthony and Cady Stanton realized that no matter how capably led, women would never have the power to bring about changes in society unless they first won control over their own money and won the right to vote. They therefore petitioned the New York state legislature to pass a law giving women the right to keep any money they earned. (At that time, the law stated that a married woman's earnings belonged to her husband.) It took them six years, but in 1860 the state finally voted in favor of women's property rights.

Anthony also became active in the antislavery movement, and during the Civil War she promoted passage of the 13th Amendment. When slavery was finally abolished in 1865, Anthony believed that the antislavery and women's rights reformers should continue working together to win voting rights, both for the newly freed slaves and for women. To her dismay, many of the antislavery reformers chose to focus on black suffrage, and they turned away from the women's cause.

Susan B. Anthony's efforts on behalf of women's rights led to woman suffrage in 1920.

In 1870, the 15th Amendment was ratified, giving the vote to black men, but not to women. To test the law, Anthony went to the polls in Rochester, New York, in 1872 to vote in the presidential election. Her bold attempt got her arrested, and she was tried and fined $100 (which she refused to pay). Although she lost her case, Anthony's trial won additional support for her cause.

In the late 1800's, many new states were being admitted to the Union, and Anthony traveled through each one, urging people to make woman suffrage part of their state's constitution. After covering thousands of miles by train, wagon, and on horseback, she realized she would have to change her tactics. Instead of fighting the same battle state by state, Anthony began to push for an amendment to the United States Constitution. In 1878 a woman suffrage amendment was put before Congress for the first time, but it was defeated.

In 1890 the National Woman Suffrage Association, formed by Anthony and Cady Stanton in 1869, merged with another women's group and became the National American Woman Suffrage Association. Anthony continued to be a guiding force and took over the presidency of the newly merged organization in 1892. When she retired in 1900, the organization's annual convention was crowded with members from all over the country.

Susan B. Anthony died in Rochester, New York, on March 13, 1906, confident that the new generation of reformers would achieve her goal and obtain the vote for women.

In 1979 and 1980 the Susan B. Anthony dollar coin was minted in her honor. She was the first woman ever to be pictured on a U.S. coin in general circulation.

SUSAN MALONEY CLINTON
Author, *The Story of Susan B. Anthony*

See also STANTON, ELIZABETH CADY.

ANTHRAX. See DISEASES (Descriptions of Some Diseases).

ANTHROPOLOGY

Anthropology is the study of human beings and their ways of life. (The Greek word *anthropos* means "human being.") The people who work in this field are called anthropologists.

Anthropology emerged as a science in the mid-1800's as Western scholars became interested in the peoples encountered by explorers and missionaries. At that time most anthropologists studied isolated, non-Western cultures. Today anthropologists study people all over the world, in many different settings.

Many other fields—economics, sociology, psychology—study human beings, but only certain aspects. Anthropology is different. Its goal is to develop a broad and comprehensive understanding of what it means to be human. To gain this understanding, anthropologists use a holistic approach, which means they study all aspects of human beings—biological and social. It also means they focus on human societies as whole systems composed of interacting parts. An economist might be interested in how societies produce and exchange goods; a sociologist in how humans interact with others in their society; a psychologist in how humans think and feel. Anthropologists study all these aspects of social life and their interrelationship.

To discover what it means to be human, anthropologists look for what makes all humans similar as well as what makes them unique. To do so, they use a comparative approach, studying all societies, past and present. Some anthropologists compare humans to their close animal relatives to reveal what is uniquely human. One significant difference between humans and other animals is that humans develop complex systems of meaning known as culture. Culture is the entire way of life that a group of people learns—everything it has, makes, thinks, believes, and passes on to children. Culture includes knowledge, beliefs, art, morals, law, custom, and all other habits and abilities that members of the group acquire.

Anthropologists also compare human groups to determine what makes them different, both biologically and culturally. Understanding why humans differ is essential for developing an appreciation of human diversity. It helps overcome prejudices that many people may have about those who look and behave differently than they do.

Anthropologists study the similarities and differences between peoples and groups, including methods of obtaining food. *Top:* An Indonesian farmer cultivates rice. *Center:* Inuit hunters capture a ring seal. *Right:* An American woman buys produce in a supermarket.

Because anthropology seeks to understand humans fully, it is divided into four main subfields: biological anthropology, cultural anthropology, archaeology, and linguistic anthropology. Most anthropologists have broad training in each of these areas but specialize in one.

Many anthropologists, regardless of subfield, use their knowledge to develop practical solutions to social problems. They are called applied anthropologists. They often work for governments or private agencies, helping officials understand the impact of proposed programs or development projects on a culture. They may also analyze how to best introduce a program into a particular cultural setting. For instance, applied anthropologists have advised physicians on the most effective ways to introduce new AIDS medications in Africa. Others have helped governments identify their country's prehistoric sites so they can be preserved before development projects begin.

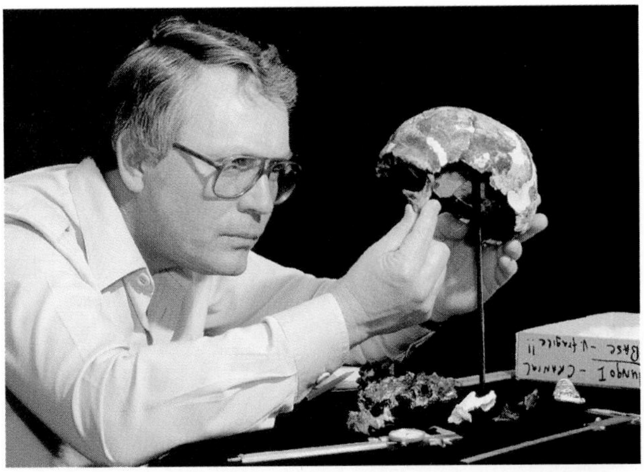

A biological anthropologist reconstructs an ancient human skull. Biological anthropology focuses on humans as physical creatures.

BIOLOGICAL ANTHROPOLOGY

Biological, or physical, anthropologists focus on humans as physical creatures. They study human biological evolution and variation, past and present.

Paleoanthropologists are one type of biological anthropologist. They study the fossil remains of ancient peoples to learn about human beginnings. They study the bones, teeth, and sometimes the DNA of human ancestors as old as several millions of years. They also reconstruct the environments of early humans to understand why humans evolved and why they look the way they do.

Because humans are closely related to animals known as primates, a group including monkeys and apes, some biological anthropologists study them for clues about the origins and evolution of early humans. These anthropologists are called primatologists.

Most biological anthropologists investigate how and why populations of living people differ in their biological makeup. They carry out human variation studies, measuring and comparing physical characteristics such as skin color, blood type, and genetic composition to understand how human populations have adapted to a range of environments. They study how the forces of evolution act on human populations to change them over time. Today, studies of human biological differences help answer questions such as why certain diseases afflict some populations more than others or how urban noise levels can impair children's development.

CULTURAL ANTHROPOLOGY

Cultural anthropologists study how people live throughout the world, focusing on their culture. This area of anthropology has two main goals: (1) to describe all cultures and (2) to explain their similarities and differences.

Cultural anthropologists learn about a culture by immersing themselves in it. This is called doing fieldwork. They learn the language of the people they study. They observe, and participate in, all aspects of a group's cultural life to get firsthand knowledge of it. They return from their fieldwork to write an **ethnography**, a description and explanation of a culture.

Traditionally, cultural anthropologists traveled alone to distant places to study a group's way of life. Today many anthropologists work in teams, studying people living in urban centers and in complex societies.

Because cultural anthropologists are interested in broad and holistic knowledge about humans, they concentrate on many different aspects of people's lives, including how they make a living and spend their earnings, how they educate their children, how they choose marriage partners and organize themselves

A cultural anthropologist takes notes as she watches a tribal woman weaving cloth. Cultural anthropologists study the different cultures of people throughout the world.

into families, how they protect themselves and make decisions about leadership, what they think about their environment, what they believe about God and other supernatural beings, and what kind of music and art they produce.

Since it is very difficult to know everything about a culture, especially the complex ones anthropologists tend to study today, cultural anthropologists often specialize in particular areas of interest. A medical anthropologist might focus on how different ideas about the body affect people's responses to illness. An urban anthropologist might study why some people are drawn to cities and how this movement affects their religious beliefs or the size of their families.

ARCHAEOLOGY

Archaeologists are anthropologists who focus on ancient human societies. By digging up and examining the remains of extinct societies, they help shed light on the human cultural past. Like cultural anthropologists, archaeologists add to our understanding of what it means to be human and of cultural similarities and differences.

Archaeologists use tools as simple as dental picks and shovels to carefully uncover the skeletal remains of ancient people, the objects they made, and the remains of their environment. They also use sophisticated technology to do their work: for example, they might rely on radar to locate ancient sites and spectrometers to analyze the age of an artifact. (A spectrometer is a device that measures radiation wavelength emissions from an object.) Archaeologists want to understand how early humans adapted to their environments and how they organized their societies to survive.

Archaeologists also help us understand how cultures have changed over centuries. By studying the past, they discover long-range trends. For example, they have traced the development of Mexico's political systems from those based on small family groups to powerful states. They have discovered how writing systems developed in the Middle East from earlier uses of pictures to communicate ideas.

LINGUISTIC ANTHROPOLOGY

Linguistics is the study of language. Linguistic anthropology focuses on the relationship of language to culture. Although it was once believed that humans were the only ani-

Archaeologists examine the remains of ancient societies. By shedding light on the human cultural past, they add to our understanding of what it means to be human.

mals with language, this idea has recently been challenged. Some studies show that chimpanzees and gorillas can learn words and can be taught to communicate with them, even if they do not actually speak these words but convey them with symbols. Regardless of whether humans are unique in their capacity for language, there is no doubt that language has been important to the development of human societies. Language is the primary means by which culture is transmitted.

Linguistic anthropology developed in the 1800's because the languages of the people many anthropologists studied were dying out. Anthropologists developed an international system of symbols (International Phonetic Alphabet) to represent the sounds of these languages, thereby preserving them.

Linguistic anthropologists study the characteristics and structure—or grammar—of existing languages. They compare the sounds, words, sentence structures, and meanings of languages to understand how different people think and view the world. For example, some languages have no past, present, or future tenses, which reflects and affects a people's understanding of time. One important finding of linguistic anthropology is that all languages are complex and allow for complicated meanings to be conveyed.

Historical linguists study the relationships among different languages to determine how languages have changed over time. By comparing different languages, they can trace how today's languages branched off from earlier languages. This splitting occurred at different times as groups of people moved away from one another and developed other habits. By looking at the similarities and differences among languages like these, historical linguists can uncover relationships that may have once existed between various groups.

HISTORY OF ANTHROPOLOGY

Anthropology took shape in the late 1800's in Europe and the United States. Until then, few individuals had made a serious study of different peoples. European explorers had long brought back stories about the people of Africa, Asia, and the Pacific islands, who differed in many ways from people in the Western world. Many Westerners considered these people primitive and inferior and thought they should become more like Westerners. By the late 1800's, some people began to hold different ideas. They thought it was important to understand other ways of life, not to condemn them. From such ideas grew the field of anthropology.

Renowned anthropologist Margaret Mead did much of her fieldwork in the early 1900's. Her ethnographies of Pacific Islanders are still read today.

Early anthropologists wanted to compare all known societies to understand their differences; they were particularly interested in learning why some societies were relatively simple and others complex. They thought that perhaps societies adapt and evolve to survive just as animals do. Their way of thinking came to be known as **social evolutionism**.

These anthropologists also thought they could learn about different cultures from the reports brought back by missionaries and colonizers. Soon, however, it became clear that such reports were biased. The social evolutionists were criticized for using faulty information. One flaw in their thinking was the belief that the culture and the race of a people were linked. They thought that darker skinned people developed simple cultures because they were incapable of developing complex ones. When it became apparent that this was not the case, the ideas of social evolutionists were widely viewed as invalid.

Franz Boas was one of the most important critics of social evolutionism. He was a German-born scholar who traveled to the United States in the early 1900's to study Native Americans. Boas established almost all of anthropology's goals and approaches. He showed the importance of gaining firsthand knowledge of a culture through extensive fieldwork. He was also the first to define the four subfields of anthropology.

Boas was among the leading anthropologists to show that culture and race are not linked. Native Americans, he argued, did not develop inferior cultures. They were only thought inferior by many Europeans because of ethnocentrism (judging others according to one's own cultural ideas and values). Boas emphasized the importance of understanding another culture on its own terms, rather than simply judging it as inferior because it is different. This approach came to be known as **cultural relativism**.

Boas was concerned that Native American cultures were quickly vanishing. He urged other anthropologists to collect information about them so that their customs and languages could become part of the record of human diversity. Out of this desire to preserve the fast-disappearing languages of Native Americans emerged the subfield of linguistic anthropology.

Boas trained many students in his methods of anthropology. One, Margaret Mead, became one of the best-known anthropologists in history. Although Mead did much of her fieldwork in the early 1900's, her ethnographies of Pacific Islanders are still widely read today.

Some anthropologists living in Europe during the early 1900's also questioned social evolutionary views. One of these, Bronislaw Malinowski, believed as Boas did in the need to conduct long-term fieldwork to understand a culture. The Polish-born Malinowski spent years studying the people of the Trobriand Islands in the South Pacific. He was interested in how the various parts of Trobriand society—its economic, political, and social systems—functioned together to help these people survive. This approach is called **functionalism**. Malinowski inspired many other anthropologists to use this approach to study how cultures work.

Since anthropology's beginnings, many new approaches to understanding human diversity have developed. Some anthropologists have focused on how societies are structured, while others have focused on how humans use symbols to create meaning. Still others are interested in how humans adapt to their physical surroundings. Regardless of the particular emphasis, anthropologists continue to seek ways to understand the full range of human societies. Today they propose new concepts and approaches to keep pace with an ever-changing world.

ANTHROPOLOGY TODAY

The world is a very different place today than it was when anthropology first developed more than 100 years ago. Today's world is an interdependent one—few human groups remain isolated. Decisions about oil production in the Middle East, for example, can have a major impact on people living in Australia, Asia, or the United States. We live in a truly global community—people everywhere are connected through travel and vast communications networks.

Some scholars think such connections will make humans more and more alike in their ideas and behavior. But anthropologists have

As communities become more culturally diverse, the work of anthropologists to help us understand and appreciate cultural differences has become ever more important.

Kurdish refugees carry their belongings across the Iran-Iraq border. The study of such population movements is a growing area of interest for anthropologists.

shown that people make very different uses of the products and information that circulate globally, interpreting them within the beliefs and values of their own traditions.

The work of anthropologists has become especially important in today's changing world. Understanding and appreciating human diversity is essential for developing ideas and policies that can help human groups coexist peacefully.

One important change that has occurred due to globalization is that cultural ideas and practices may no longer be tied to specific places or shared by all people in those places. This weakening of the tie between culture and place is called **deterritorialization**. It has required many anthropologists to rethink traditional approaches, including where and how they do their research. Until recently, most anthropologists traveled to one place to study a people's culture, but now it might be necessary for them to do fieldwork in several locations. For example, an anthropologist studying the Hmong would have once just traveled to Laos in Southeast Asia. Today, to understand Hmong culture fully, an anthropologist would also have to travel to California and Minnesota, where more than 100,000 contemporary Hmong live.

The separation of ideas and people from traditional locations has led many anthropologists to study **hybridity**, new forms of culture that develop on borders between groups (for example, the boundary between ethnic neighborhoods in urban centers).

The movement of populations is another growing area of interest. Many recent studies focus on immigrants, exiles, and refugees as they travel across traditional boundaries and come to live in new places.

A number of new issues are raised by today's population movements. People and groups are less likely than those in the past to settle in the first place to which they move. This can make it difficult to develop the shared group identity associated with culture. But this situation also produces opportunities for the creation of new cultural ideas and practices, providing anthropologists with many new places to undertake their study of what it means to be human.

CAREERS IN ANTHROPOLOGY

Although most anthropologists work at colleges and universities, where they teach and conduct research, anthropologists today may also be employed in almost any area where knowledge of human behavior can help institutions accomplish their goals. Archaeologists and cultural anthropologists work for museums and government agencies. Biological and cultural anthropologists have found employment in medical settings and mental health facilities, and with population councils and urban planning groups. Some anthropologists work as researchers for marketing firms and other companies doing business worldwide.

FRANCES E. MASCIA-LEES
Sarah Lawrence College

See also ANCIENT CIVILIZATIONS; ARCHAEOLOGY; LANGUAGES; PREHISTORIC PEOPLE; RACES, HUMAN.

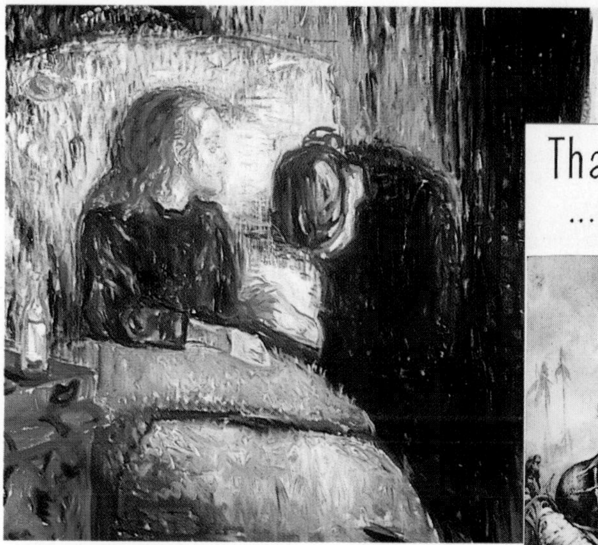

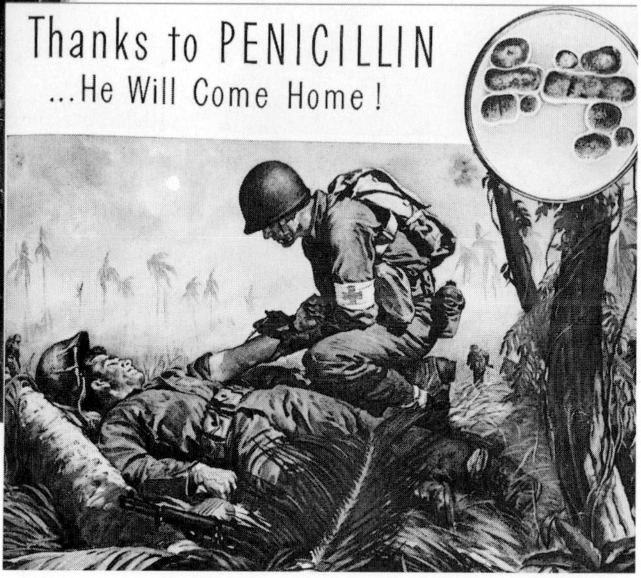

The Sick Child (*left*), a painting by Edvard Munch, is a reminder of the once-untreatable effects of tuberculosis, while the World War II poster (*below*) testifies to the dramatic impact antibiotics have had on our lives.

ANTIBIOTICS

Some battles rage silently, invisible to the naked eye. An infection is one such battle. During an infection, the fight that rages is between the body's defenses and disease-producing microbes. Sometimes microbes, or micro-organisms, can get the advantage in this battle. They multiply in large numbers and cause damage to tissues that results in disease. Antibiotics are substances produced by microbes that can kill or stop the growth of bacteria, fungi, and other microbes that cause disease and so restore an individual's health.

Antibiotics have had a major impact on our lives. These drugs, most of which have been developed only since the mid-1940's, have had such dramatic effects that they have often been called wonder drugs. Because of antibiotics, diseases that once meant almost certain death can now be controlled, adding years to the average life span.

KINDS OF ANTIBIOTICS

It was not until 1928 with the discovery of penicillin, an antibiotic produced by a mold, that scientists realized the potential for using substances produced by microbes. Penicillin cured many, but not all, diseases. Scientists scoured the world for microbes that could produce other types of antibiotics. Soil, which contains millions of molds and bacteria, was a common place to search.

While it was relatively easy to find new antibiotics, only a limited number were safe for human use. Scientists increased their efforts to design antibiotics in the laboratory. During the late 1950's and early 1960's, enormous strides were made in producing laboratory-designed antibiotics based on the by-products of molds and bacteria found in nature. Because these drugs were not true antibiotics but did fight disease-causing microbes, they were called **antimicrobials**. Today, the terms antibiotic and antimicrobial are often used interchangeably to mean any drug that fights infectious microbes.

As more antimicrobials were discovered, designed, and studied, scientists found that they had different properties. Some of these properties, including how they were made, how they affect microbes, and their range of activity, were used to classify antibiotics. Because the majority of antibiotics are used to treat bacterial infections, this section and the following text are based on how antibiotics and bacteria interact.

Natural, Semisynthetic, and Synthetic Antibiotics

One of the broadest ways of classifying antibiotics is based on whether they are found in nature or made in a laboratory. Those that are produced from living sources, such as penicillin, are called **natural** antibiotics.

Chemists learned that they could change the structure of natural antibiotics to make new and better drugs. These chemically modified drugs are called **semisynthetic** antibiotics because they are made partly by nature and partly in a laboratory. One such drug is produced when chemists change the form of penicillin, a natural antibiotic, to make a slightly different drug called ampicillin that can be used to treat different types of infections than penicillin is used to treat. Scientists can now develop a whole family of drugs by creating various forms of a single natural drug. Each drug in the family has slightly different properties. Sometimes a drug is changed so that it can be taken as a pill rather than by being injected. Other chemical changes can make the drug work longer in the body. The family of penicillin drugs can do many more things than the first penicillin molecule.

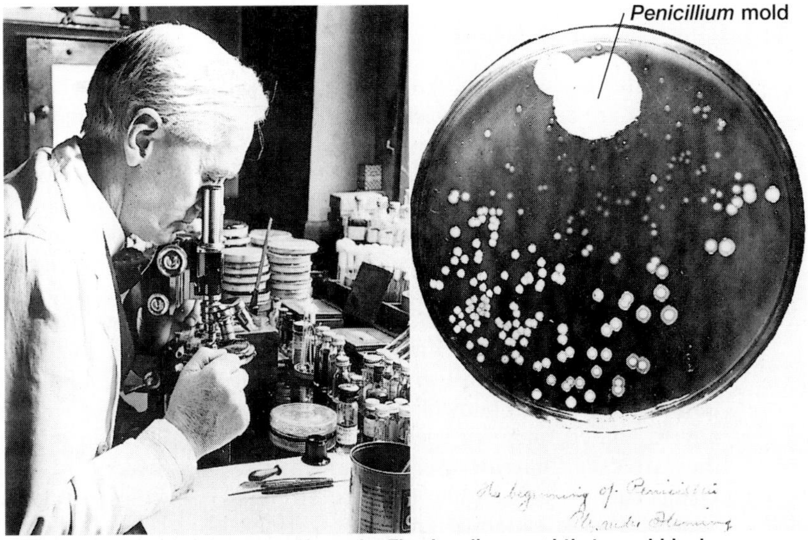

While working in his laboratory, Alexander Fleming discovered that a mold had contaminated a bacterial culture (original culture plate is shown) and stopped the bacteria's growth. He named the mold's antibacterial substance penicillin.

Studying the chemical structures of antibiotics, scientists determined that some had very simple structures. Chemists discovered that it was easier to make these antibiotics than to isolate them from microbes. These drugs, such as chloramphenicol, that are produced by using only laboratory chemicals are called **synthetic** drugs.

Bacteriostatic and Bactericidal Antibiotics

Another way of classifying drugs is based on how they affect bacteria. Antibiotics that stop the multiplication of bacteria are called **bacteriostatic**. Bacteriostatic drugs control microbes until the immune system of the individual can build up its defenses and

See For Yourself

How to Grow a *Penicillium* Mold

You will never see them, but spores of *Penicillium* mold are floating in the air all around you. You can prove that they are there by growing your own *Penicillium* mold on bread. Do not eat or taste the bread or mold that develops. Step 1: Microbes need moisture to grow, so sprinkle a piece of bread with a few drops of water. Leave the moistened piece of bread uncovered, exposed to the air for several hours. Step 2: Place the bread in a clear glass jar and cover it. Step 3: In a few days, check the jar. Although most bread contains chemicals to slow the growth of molds, it will not be long before several different molds are growing. If one of these colonies is bluish green, it is probably *Penicillium* mold.

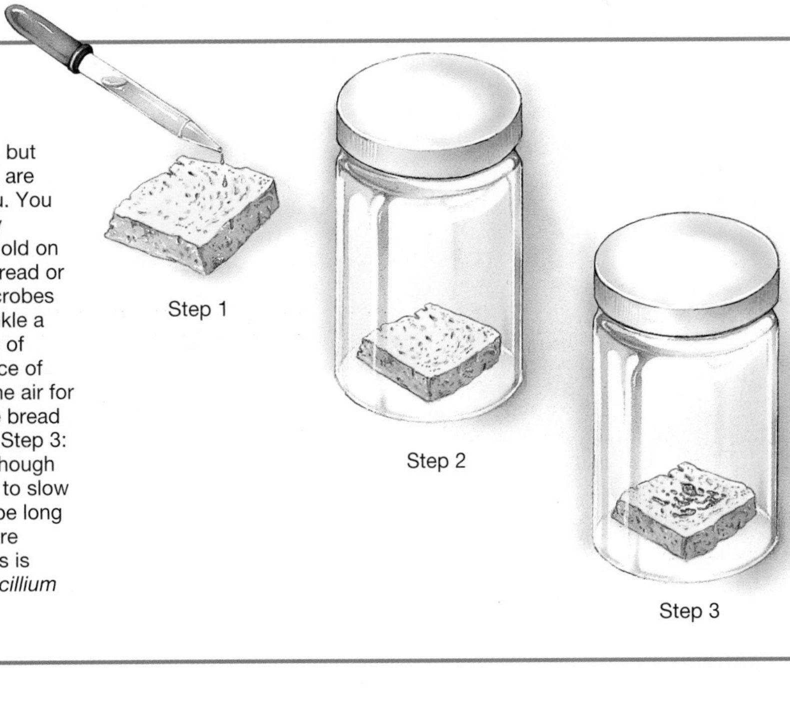

eliminate the infection. Antibiotics that kill bacteria are called **bactericidal**.

Narrow- and Broad-Spectrum Antibiotics

Antibiotics can also be classified according to the type of bacteria, identified as either gram-negative or gram-positive, they are most effective against. Some antibiotics, such as penicillin, are most effective in fighting gram-positive bacteria. Others, such as gentamicin, are used against gram-negative bacteria. Because both penicillin and gentamicin have a limited range, or spectrum, of activity, they are called **narrow-spectrum** antibiotics. Drugs such as tetracycline that are effective against a wide range of gram-negative and gram-positive bacteria are called **broad-spectrum** antibiotics.

HOW ANTIBIOTICS WORK

Antibiotics stop microbes in several ways. Most often they block the building of the microbial cell or interfere with activities that are needed for cell life. Each drug tries to hit a perfect target—some molecule or process that is present in the bacteria but not in humans—so that the drug affects the microbe while doing little damage to human cells. Different antibiotics do this in different ways.

Prevention of Cell Wall Formation

Some drugs stop the construction of the thick covering of the bacterial cell. This outer layer, called the cell wall, protects the bacteria against the harsh environments in which they live. The cell wall is a perfect target for antibiotics because it is made up of chemicals unique to bacteria. Human cells do not make cell walls nor do they have the types of molecules that make up cell walls. Penicillin, its family of drugs, and other antibiotics prevent the proper joining of the cell wall chemicals. The cell wall is greatly weakened, and the cell falls apart and dies.

Changes to the Cell Membrane

The cell membrane is a part of all living cells. In bacteria, it is a thin skin located just below the cell wall. It encloses all the molecules and fluid needed for life. The cell membrane is the gatekeeper of the cell; that is, it decides what gets in and what gets out of the cell. Certain antibiotics make the membrane leaky so that the cell loses important molecules. The microbes can no longer carry out their daily work because they have lost essential parts of their cell.

Changes to Chemical Processes

Antibiotics can also attack the machinery needed to manufacture proteins. Proteins are molecules that help cells digest food, recycle nutrients, produce energy, and make new cell parts. They are manufactured in structures called ribosomes. Although both human cells and bacterial cells have ribosomes, the two types are chemically different. Some antibiotics can target the unique molecules in the bacterial ribosomes while not attacking the human ribosomes. Antibiotics such as tetracycline bind to the bacterial ribosome and prevent it from making proteins. Without the proteins, the bacterial cells stop growing and eventually die.

Antibiotics can stop the production of the information molecules of the cell, called nucleic acids. Nucleic acid molecules are organized into a unique pattern to make genes, which are the hereditary units that ensure that our characteristics are passed on to the

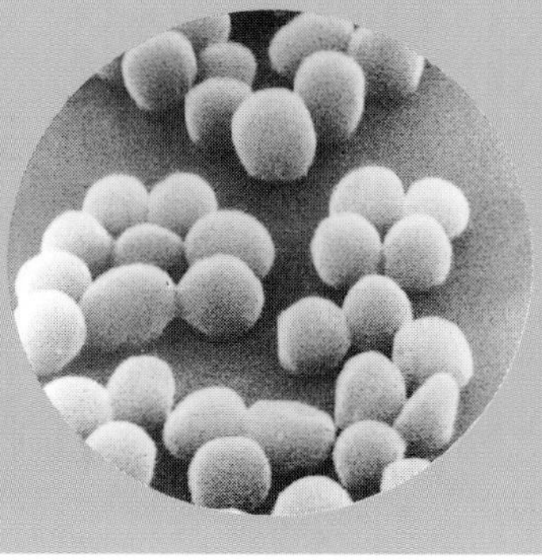

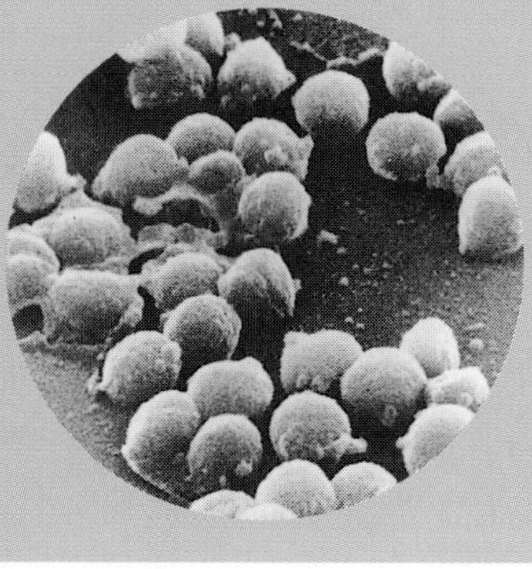

Before exposure to the antibiotic ampicillin, the cell walls of the bacteria *Staphylococcus aureus* (*far left*) are intact. After exposure, with walls weakened (*left*), the bacterial cells collapse and die.

Scientists use a variety of techniques, including the well method, to test the microbe-fighting abilities of antibiotics. Each well in this culture plate of live bacteria is filled with a different antibiotic. The clearer the zone around a well, the more effective the antibiotic is in controlling bacterial growth.

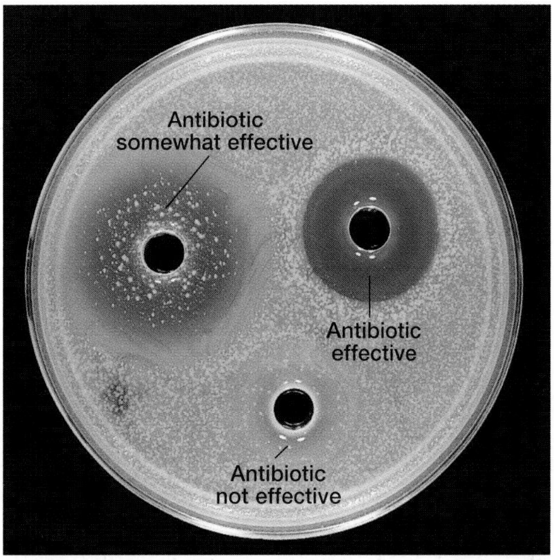

next generation. Specialized protein molecules are needed to correctly retrieve the information from the genes. Quinolones, a new family of antibiotics, bind to these specialized proteins and stop the retrieval of information, so that new bacteria cannot be made and the infection is controlled.

Some antibiotics mimic the natural building blocks used by bacterial cells to manufacture substances such as folic acid that are necessary for basic processes in the cell. Because sulfa drugs imitate the natural molecules that are used to make folic acid, bacterial cells are fooled into choosing the antibiotic, and by not using the natural molecules, the folic acid cannot be made. The normal work of the bacteria does not occur without this essential substance, and the bacteria soon die.

ADVERSE EFFECTS AND LIMITATIONS OF ANTIBIOTICS

Antibiotics have saved many lives, but they are not without problems. Ideally, antibiotics should not affect human beings in any way. But unfortunately, they can sometimes cause unwanted changes or damage to human cells. These harmful side effects can range from a

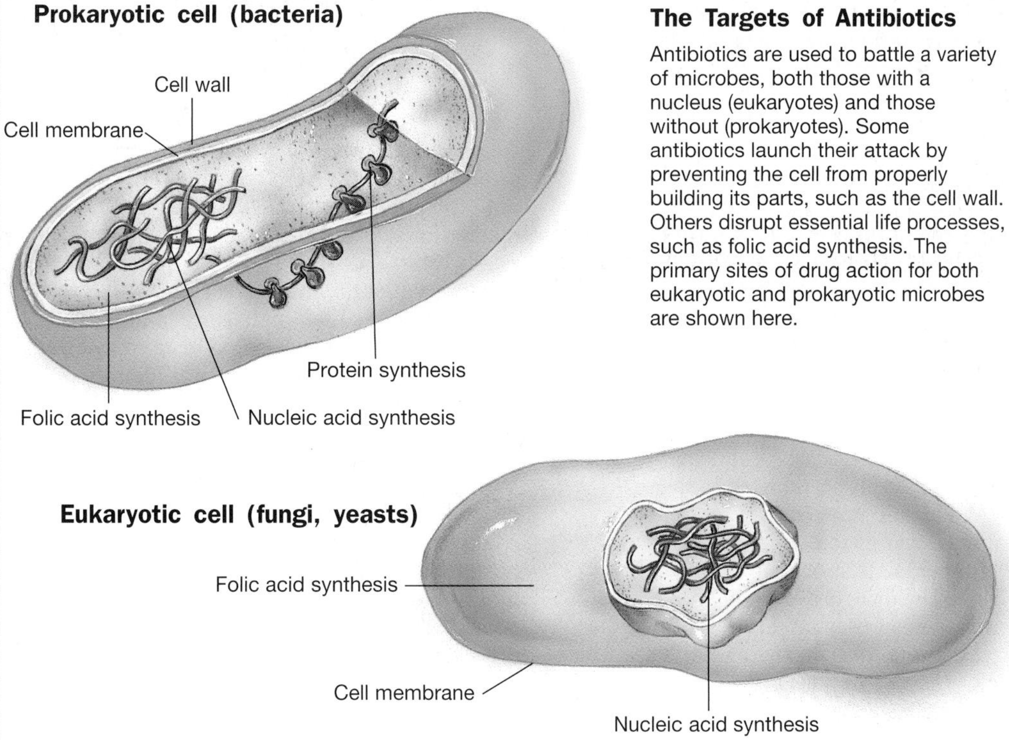

The Targets of Antibiotics

Antibiotics are used to battle a variety of microbes, both those with a nucleus (eukaryotes) and those without (prokaryotes). Some antibiotics launch their attack by preventing the cell from properly building its parts, such as the cell wall. Others disrupt essential life processes, such as folic acid synthesis. The primary sites of drug action for both eukaryotic and prokaryotic microbes are shown here.

very mild, unusual taste in the mouth to severe allergic reactions that can result in death. The benefits of the drugs must always be weighed against the dangers of the harmful effects. Antibiotics that are very toxic, or poisonous, would be used only for serious infections and when there are few other usable drugs available.

Allergic Reactions

Although all antibiotics can cause allergic reactions, few actually do. You may know of someone who is allergic or sensitive to antibiotics. A mild reaction such as a rash might occur after they take the antibiotic. Unfortunately, a more severe reaction can occur in some people. When they take the antibiotic, a chain of events takes place that causes the immune system to react inappropriately. It can produce a harmful, sometimes life-threatening, allergic reaction. People allergic to certain drugs should avoid using them.

Damage to Tissues and Organs

Some antibiotics can cause damage to tissues and organs. Drugs taken in pill form can cause common side effects such as an upset stomach or diarrhea. This problem usually occurs after the drug has been taken for a few days.

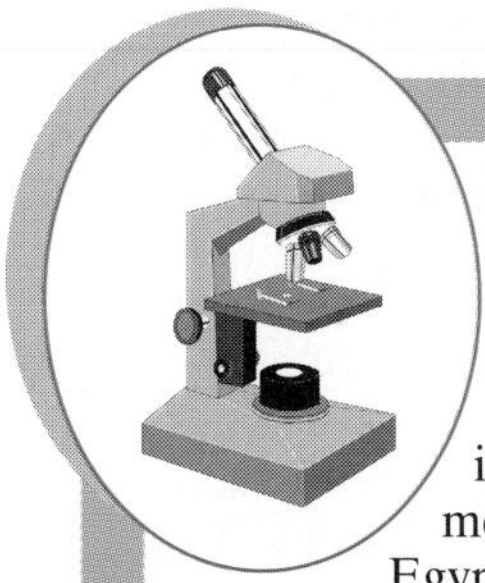

The Discovery of Antibiotics

Descriptions of the treatment of wound infections appear in early medical records from China and Egypt dating back to 1500 B.C. Wounds were dressed with the moldy or fermented products of substances such as dung. These were effective in treating superficial infections, but it was not known why. Even before the scientific study of antibiotics could begin, there had to be an understanding of how infectious diseases occurred. That understanding did not begin until the late 1800's when the French chemist Louis Pasteur discovered that bacteria could cause infectious diseases.

Once the infectious disease process was understood, scientists searched for drugs to treat serious infectious diseases. They tried many chemicals from their laboratory shelves. Many of these chemicals killed the microbes, but they also damaged human tissues. In the early 1900's, German scientist Paul Ehrlich realized the need for a "magic bullet." Such a chemical would find and destroy disease-producing microbes without harming an individual; that is, it would be selectively toxic. He combined and tested hundreds of chemicals and found one that could treat the disease syphilis. The drug proved to be too toxic for widespread use, but it did stimulate the interest of other scientists to search for a magic bullet. Other drugs were discovered using this chemical approach.

Many disease-fighting drugs that we use today are not chemically produced but are naturally occurring substances that are obtained from living creatures. The first such drug was discovered by accident. British bacteriologist Alexander Fleming was studying the disease-causing bacteria *Staphylococcus aureus.* He was trying to understand how it caused certain diseases and skin boils. He grew the bacteria in culture plates filled with a gelatinlike food, or medium. One day, Fleming noticed the presence of a green mold that had accidentally settled onto the surface of the same medium as the bacteria. He observed something curious—there was a clear area around the mold where the bacteria were not growing. Many other scientists had made similar observations, but Fleming pursued his discovery. He explored the possibility that the mold was making chemicals that could kill bacteria and that these natural chemicals could be used to cure disease. The green mold was identified as *Penicillium.* And the liquid he collected from it, which he called penicillin, could kill many types of bacteria.

Intensive research followed Fleming's discovery. Scientists showed that penicillin could cure infections without harming the host. Efforts were made to find *Penicillium* molds that would produce large amounts of penicillin. When a high-yielding mold was discovered, penicillin production increased greatly. It became the magic treatment for many diseases.

In the body, the kidneys and liver process and filter various molecules from the blood, including drugs. As the drugs pass through these organs, they can damage them. Usually the effects are mild and the tissue cells are repaired. In rare instances, though, the damage can be serious.

Superinfections

Antibiotics cannot tell the difference between normal, harmless microbes and disease-producing microbes. We live in a world filled with microbes, and many of them are found on and inside our bodies, such as on the skin or in the throat or intestine. These normal bacteria are a benefit to us because they compete with and control the growth of disease-causing microbes. Broad-spectrum antibiotics can destroy many of these beneficial bacteria along with disease-causing microbes. The microbes that survive can then multiply in large numbers, causing a superinfection. These microbes may be drug-resistant forms of the original bacteria causing the infection. Or they may be microbes that are normally present but only in small numbers. Often the microbes producing the superinfection prove to be harder to control than those of the original bacterial infection.

Resistance to Antibiotics

Another major problem that has resulted from the increased use of antibiotics is the appearance and spread of altered microbes that are resistant to various drugs. When antibiotics were first used in the early 1940's, they could easily kill many disease-producing bacteria. The dramatic cure of diseases that once had no treatment led to an increased use of antibiotics, and this popularity led to their use for infections they could not cure. For example, they were used to treat such viral infections as the common cold or sore throat that are not affected by antibiotics. This type of overuse produces microbes that are not easily killed by antibiotics, and many develop their own defenses to counteract or resist antibiotics. The resistance to antibiotics often means that more of the drug has to be used or, worse, that the original drug may no longer work and new drugs have to be found. A few microbes that can cause serious infections are now resistant to most of the known antibiotics.

The more exposure different bacteria get to an antibiotic, the more likely they are to produce new defenses against it. More than forty years ago, an accidental discovery showed that adding small amounts of antibiotics to animal feed helped make the animals grow faster and allowed farmers to send them to market sooner. Today, almost half the antibiotics made in the United States are fed to animals raised for food, such as cattle, hogs, chickens, and fish. Unfortunately, this overuse of antibiotics has produced more drug-resistant microbes that can potentially be transferred to humans or other animals. A balance must be found between the benefits of antibiotics to the farmer and the risks of resistant organisms to human health.

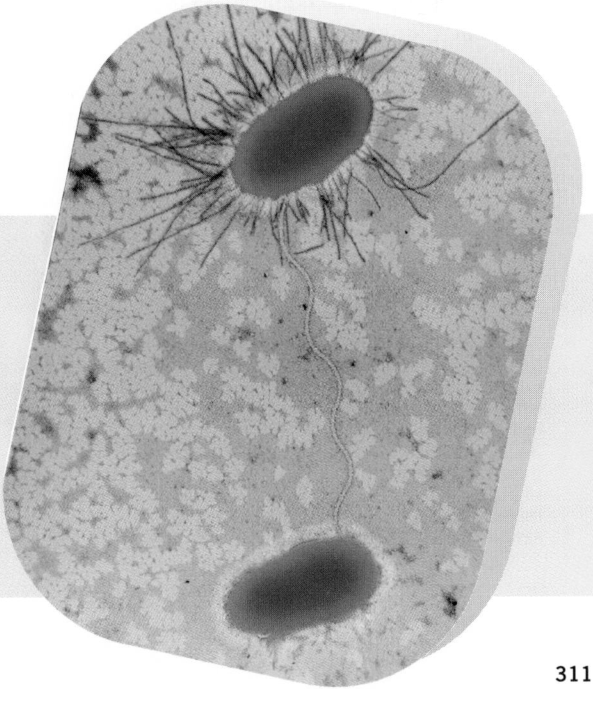

Bacteria have proven to be hardy organisms that are able to develop new defenses to resist the attacks of antibiotics. Here, an *Escherichia coli* bacterium transfers a copy of its resistance genes to a second bacterium. Each bacterium can repeat this process until most of the bacteria in a group are resistant to an antibiotic.

In the commercial production of antibiotics, large vats called fermentors are used to grow billions of antibiotic-producing microbes.

The continued use of antibiotics has allowed microbes to change, adapt, and become harder to destroy. By chance, a bacteria can change its genes and become better able to survive a drug's effect. These resistant bacteria can also share this new resistance trait with their neighboring bacteria. Bacteria can also pass on a copy of the genes when they divide into new bacteria. Soon large numbers of bacteria are resistant to the antibiotic. Some bacteria can even transfer genes that make them resistant to several antibiotics at once, creating so-called supergerms that are difficult to stop.

Some bacteria can pump out the antibiotic as soon as it gets into the cell. Other bacteria can change the chemicals in their cell walls so that the antibiotics cannot get in. Still other bacteria make special molecules that counteract the antibiotic before it kills them. They can also switch the molecules the antibiotic normally attacks so that the antibiotic can no longer recognize its target.

One approach to controlling drug-resistant microbes focuses on preventing the unnecessary use of antibiotics. Methods include monitoring milk and food supplies for antibiotics and educating health providers on the dangers of overprescribing drugs for mild infections. Providing information to the public on how to use antibiotics is another method. If antibiotic treatment is stopped before the prescribed date, the most resistant bacteria might survive and spread.

An additional approach seeks to eliminate existing forms of resistant strains. Public health officials are carefully tracking supergerms when they appear and informing health providers of their existence. Health providers can then act quickly to control the new microbes. New therapies, such as using a combination of drugs, have been found to be effective. It is harder for bacteria to escape the killing action of two drugs at once, and because less of each drug can be used, the likelihood of side effects is reduced. There is also a reduced chance of producing a resistant form of the bacteria.

Did you know that...

our current antibiotics are focused on stopping only bacteria? Finding drugs to kill other microbes, including fungi, protozoa, and parasitic worms, is a more difficult task. The cells of these creatures have molecules that are very similar to molecules found in humans, so it is hard to find a target that is unique to the microbe. Viruses are even harder to attack with drugs because they take over human cells and direct cell processes. Any drug used against them must control the virus but not affect human cells.

ANTIBIOTIC RESEARCH

Scientists are actively working to find new antibiotics and to understand how bacteria fight off these drugs. Using computers, scientists can work with models to see whether a drug is likely to work on a microbe. New natural products are being found in plants and animals. Sharks and frogs contain small protein molecules, called defensins, that scientists hope to develop into antibiotics.

Some scientists are testing new molecules that stop the spread of bacteria rather than kill them. These molecules keep the bacteria from attaching to cells and starting an infection. But whether antibiotics stop the spread of bacteria or kill them, the goal of antibiotic research is to eliminate microbial disease. The lives of many people depend on it.

CYNTHIA V. SOMMER
University of Wisconsin at Milwaukee

See also BACTERIA; DISEASES; FLEMING, SIR ALEXANDER; FUNGI; MICROBIOLOGY.

ANTIBODIES AND ANTIGENS

The human body is quick to recognize foreign organisms that enter it. "Foes" must be attacked or otherwise got rid of. The most common of these foes are viruses, bacteria, and other microscopic organisms. The body recognizes these foes by the chemicals within them called **antigens**. To counteract these foreign invaders, the body produces its own chemicals, protein molecules called **antibodies**. Each kind of antigen causes the production of a specific kind of antibody. Antibodies appear in the body fluids such as blood and lymph and in the body's cells.

Doctors learned to make use of the antibody system for defense against invaders long before they had any idea that antibodies existed. As early as 1796, Edward Jenner, an English country doctor, discovered that if he gave people a case of the mild disease cowpox, he prevented them from getting the serious disease smallpox. What Jenner did not know is that the diseases are caused by closely related viruses. They are so closely related that the cowpox antibody will counteract the smallpox antigen.

Injecting an antigen to start the production of antibodies is now called **vaccination**. (It is one kind of immunization—making a person immune.) The antigen injected is a **vaccine**. These terms are based on *vacca*, the Latin word for "cow," because Jenner's vaccine was made from the cowpox virus.

Today doctors know of several ways that people become immune to diseases. Some people inherit a natural resistance to certain diseases. Over the years they build up an immunity that keeps them from ever getting certain diseases. But most antibodies are acquired only after the body has been exposed to a known antigen. The antigen may be carried by some organism that enters the body on its own, or the antigen may be artificially injected with a needle.

When a specially prepared antigen is injected into a person, it is called **active immunization**. The person actively produces the antibodies that fight off the foreign matter. The antibody defense system then remains on the alert, ready to deal with any later invasion. This procedure can be used to protect people against a number of diseases, including measles, mumps, tetanus, poliomyelitis, diphtheria, chicken pox, whooping cough, hepatitis A, and hepatitis B.

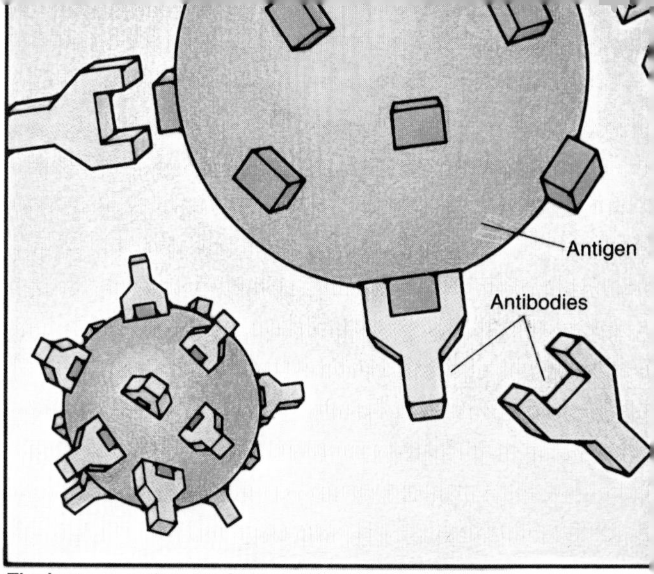

The immune system produces antibodies that match the patterns of specific antigens, much like a lock and key match each other. When antibodies (shown in blue) and an antigen (shown in red) meet, the antigen is put out of action when the antibodies lock onto it.

Antibodies may also be produced in animals by injecting them with antigens. The antibodies are then transferred directly to a person. These antibodies are immediately ready for action. This is called **passive immunization** because the person plays no part in the production of antibodies. Passive immunization disappears within a few weeks. Active immunization gives much more lasting protection.

The substance taken from the immunized animal or person for passive immunization is called **antiserum**. If used early enough, it can prevent such diseases as measles and tetanus. Sometimes an antiserum can be used after the antigen has entered a person's body, as in measles, tetanus, and diphtheria. Antiserums against bee and snake venom have also been developed.

Both antigens and antibodies are large molecules. Scientists believe that the antibody molecule combines with a particular antigen molecule, the two fitting like a key and a lock. In the chemical reaction that takes place, the antigen loses its power to cause the disease.

L. D. HAMILTON
Brookhaven National Laboratory

See also IMMUNE SYSTEM; VACCINATION AND IMMUNIZATION.

ANTIDOTES. See POISONS (Poison Centers).

ANTIGUA AND BARBUDA

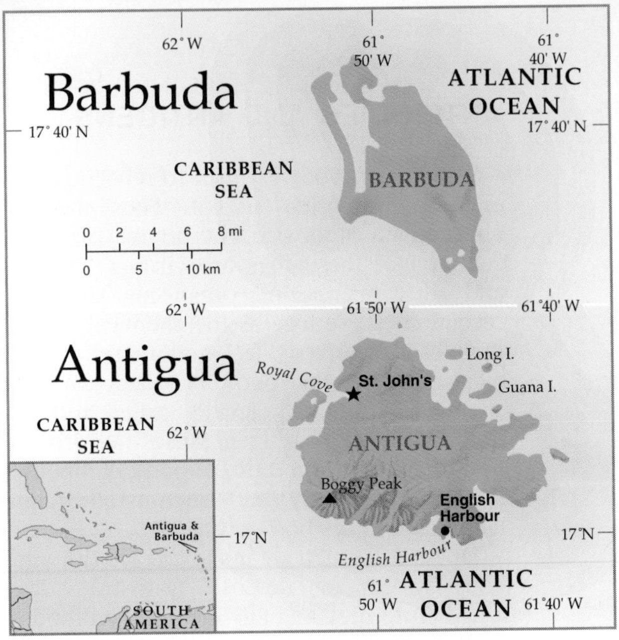

The nation of Antigua and Barbuda forms part of the Leeward Islands chain in the eastern Caribbean Sea. The country is made up of three islands—Antigua, Barbuda, and the tiny, uninhabited island of Redonda. A former British dependency, Antigua and Barbuda gained full independence in 1981.

THE PEOPLE AND THE ECONOMY

Over 90 percent of the people are of black African descent. The rest are of British, other European, Asian, or mixed ancestry. English is the official language. Most of the people live on Antigua, the largest island. St. John's, the capital, located on Antigua, has almost one-third of the total population.

Sugar and cotton were once the most important products of the islands. Tourism is now the main source of the country's income, employing about one-quarter of the labor force. Industries include the manufacture of rum, clothing, and household appliances and the assemblage of automobiles. An oil refinery on the island of Antigua processes imported crude oil for export.

FACTS and figures

ANTIGUA AND BARBUDA is the official name of the country.

LOCATION: Caribbean Sea.

AREA: 171 sq mi (442 km²).

POPULATION: 66,000 (estimate).

CAPITAL AND LARGEST CITY: St. John's.

MAJOR LANGUAGE(S): English (official).

MAJOR RELIGIOUS GROUP(S): Christian.

GOVERNMENT: Constitutional monarchy. **Head of state**—British monarch, represented by a governor-general. **Head of government**—prime minister. **Legislature**—Parliament (consisting of a House of Representatives and a Senate).

CHIEF PRODUCTS: Sugar, cotton, vegetables, rum, clothing, household appliances, assembled automobiles.

MONETARY UNIT: East Caribbean Dollar (1 EC dollar = 100 cents).

THE LAND

The island of Antigua is largely flat but has some rolling hills that are covered with lush vegetation. Barbuda is a wooded island and is noted for its fine beaches of pink and white sand. The climate is generally sunny and warm, with temperatures ranging from 71 to 86°F (22 to 30°C). Rainfall is light. The islands are subject to hurricanes. One of the most destructive, Hurricane Hugo, struck in 1989.

HISTORY AND GOVERNMENT

Christopher Columbus visited Antigua in 1493. The first Spanish and French colonists were succeeded by the British. Antigua officially became a British colony in 1667. Barbuda became part of the colony in 1860.

Tobacco was the first commercial crop. It soon gave way to sugarcane, which was harvested by slaves brought from Africa. The slaves were freed in the 1830's, when slavery was abolished in the British colonies.

After a period of internal self-government, the islands became independent as Antigua and Barbuda on November 1, 1981.

The British monarch, represented by a governor-general, is recognized as the nation's head of state. The head of government is the prime minister. The legislature, or Parliament, consists of an elected House of Representatives and an appointed Senate.

HOWARD A. FERGUS
University of the West Indies (Montserrat)

ANTILLES. See CARIBBEAN SEA AND ISLANDS.

ANTIQUES AND ANTIQUE COLLECTING

Antiques are objects once in everyday use that are prized today for their artistic, decorative, or historical value. Opinions vary on how old an object must be to be considered an antique, but most collectors agree on an age of at least one hundred years.

The most valuable antiques are masterpieces of furniture, glass, pottery, and metal made by skilled artisans in past centuries. Because these items are rare and highly sought after, they are often too expensive for the casual collector. But another category of antiques is available to almost everyone at reasonable prices: Everyday glassware and furniture, old bottles and tools, cracker boxes and tobacco tins are all popular for decorating homes. They have special appeal as reminders of life in the past.

FURNITURE

One of the most important fields of antique collecting is furniture. Most in demand is furniture made before 1830, when mechanized factory production became widespread. Furniture of the 1700's is especially desirable because of its fine design.

In England, beautifully crafted furniture was made during the reign of Queen Anne (1702–14). Queen Anne chairs, tables, highboys, and other pieces are distinguished by a gracefully curving leg, called a **cabriole** leg. The Queen Anne style remained popular for many years. After about 1740, English furniture design was strongly influenced by three outstanding cabinetmakers and furniture designers: Thomas Chippendale, George Hepplewhite, and Thomas Sheraton. Their names were given to the styles they designed.

A distinctly French style of furniture design was established during the reign of Louis XIV (1643–1715) and lasted until the French Revolution (1789–99). Many collectors believe that furniture made during the reign of Louis XV (1715–74) is among the finest ever made. Louis XV furniture is characterized by serpentine (curving) shapes and luxurious carving and inlays.

In colonial America, cabinetmakers copied English designs to produce beautiful furniture in native American woods. Some of the finest American formal furniture of the period was made in New York, Philadelphia, and Boston. Other furniture was produced in smaller towns, such as Newport, Rhode Island, and in rural communities, such as those of the Pennsylvania Dutch and the Shakers, a religious community. Shaker furniture, in particular, is admired for its sturdy construction and the simple beauty of its design.

Left: A highboy made in Massachusetts about 1750 has the curving cabriole leg characteristic of Queen Anne furniture. _Below left:_ A French desk from the reign of Louis XV has a graceful form and decorative inlaid patterns. _Below right:_ Shaker furniture, made by members of an American religious community, is admired today for its simple beauty.

The condition of antique furniture is an important consideration for collectors. Much antique furniture has remained in good condition because of its sound hand-crafted construction. A piece of furniture in good original condition, retaining the beautiful glow (patina) that age has given to its surface, is highly desirable. However, careful restoration can enhance the value of a damaged piece.

▶GLASS

Antique glass is one of the most popular collectibles. A wide range of glass objects—tumblers and goblets, vases and pitchers, plates and candlesticks—was produced in many countries, and collectors delight in the variety of patterns and colors. One of the earliest kinds of glass was blown glass, which is formed by blowing air through a pipe into a lump of hot, melted glass. Later varieties include pressed glass, in which the hot glass is shaped and given a surface pattern by being pressed into a mold; and cut glass, in which glass is decorated with patterns cut into the surface. (More information about these glass-making processes can be found in GLASS, in Volume G.)

One of the most famous American glass companies was founded in Sandwich, Massachusetts, in 1825. Sandwich pressed glass, which was made in many shapes and colors, is prized by modern collectors.

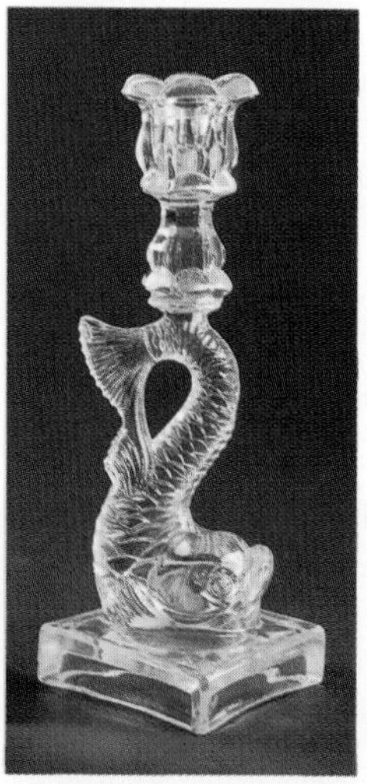

A pressed-glass candlestick in the shape of a dolphin was made by the Sandwich Glass Company about 1850. Pressed glass is shaped by pressing the hot glass into a mold.

Glass made in the late 1800's by master glassmakers has also become collectible. Some of the most famous makers of this "art glass," which included vases, bowls, and lampshades, were Emile Gallé of France, Thomas Webb of England, and Louis Comfort Tiffany of the United States.

It is difficult to tell old glass from new. Experts look for an irregular shape, signs of wear on the base, or imperfections such as bubbles in the glass itself. One way to identify handmade blown glass—early or modern—is to check the base for a **pontil mark**. A pontil is an iron rod used to handle the hot glass while it is being shaped. When the glass is broken off the pontil, a mark is left on the base. The pontil mark may be either rough or, if polished, smooth.

A lamp with a glass shade in the "dragonfly" design is one of many works created in the late 1800's and early 1900's by American glassmaker Louis Comfort Tiffany.

▶POTTERY

Clay can be shaped and baked into plates, cups, and other useful articles; this is called pottery. Many types of pottery, such as earthenware, are very porous, that is, they are easily penetrated by liquids. Therefore, pottery was often given a thin, glassy coating called a glaze. Glazes could be

A salt-glazed stoneware jug decorated with a bird design in cobalt blue was made in the United States in the first half of the 1800's. Sturdy stoneware vessels were often used to store food.

This teapot is an example of jasperware, a kind of unglazed stoneware made by the potter Josiah Wedgwood in Staffordshire, England. Jasperware usually features white figures silhouetted against a pastel background—often the delicate shade that has come to be called "Wedgwood blue."

decorative as well as protective.

One type of earthenware is called redware because of its red color. Redware was sometimes decorated with a cream-thick slip (fine clay mixed with water and coloring). The slip was placed in a funnel and applied to the piece before its final baking, much the way a baker decorates the top of a cake.

A very strong kind of pottery called stoneware does not require a protective glaze to resist water. This quality made it very useful for food storage. Many sturdy and practical stoneware crocks, jugs, churns, and milk pans were made in colonial times. The pieces most in demand today are those decorated with cobalt blue designs and covered with a transparent salt glaze.

The finest kind of pottery is porcelain (also called china because it was first made in China). It is hard and translucent, that is, light will show through it.

Some of the most collectible pottery was made in Staffordshire, England, during the 1700's and 1800's. A famous Staffordshire potter, Josiah Wedgwood, created jasperware, a kind of unglazed stoneware decorated with classical scenes. Staffordshire ware includes many other types of pottery, including fine china made by Josiah Spode and Thomas Minton and pottery molded in the shapes of dogs and other figures.

Potters have marked their wares with many different signs. The marks scratched, indented, or painted on pottery may tell who made the piece and from what country it came. A well-known mark is the crossed swords that appear on Germany's Meissen china (also called Dresden). However, many old pieces of china are unmarked. For this reason, a collector also judges the value and age of a piece by inspecting its condition, checking for wear on the base, and examining its glaze for small age cracks (called crazing). The shape of a piece and its decoration are also considered.

METALWORK

Because metalworking techniques changed greatly after 1830, age is an especially important factor to collectors of metal objects. Silver made in London during the 1700's is of great interest to serious collectors. American and French antique silver is also popular.

Some of the earliest silver items were cups and tankards (drinking mugs). Later silversmiths made tea sets, knives and forks, and other tableware. English silver was stamped

Right: This painted-tin coffeepot was made in the northeastern United States about 1825–50. Tin objects decorated with colorful painted designs are called toleware.

Below: This silver porringer is an example of the work of Paul Revere, a leading American silversmith who became famous as a Revolutionary War patriot.

Biscuit boxes, washstands, copper pots, and old railroad signal lights are just a few of the many collectible items that can be found at an outdoor flea market. Though not always beautiful or rare, objects such as these are valued as reminders of life in the past. They are generally available at reasonable prices, making them especially appealing to beginning collectors.

with marks identifying the maker, the year, and the town in which the piece was made. The thousands of marks are explained in books, which help collectors identify silver pieces.

Pewter, a metal made by combining tin and copper, was also used to make tableware. Like silver, pewter was often marked with symbols, such as an eagle or a rose and crown, that can help identify a piece's origin.

Brass, an alloy of copper and zinc, is an attractive metal that was used to make fireplace andirons, candlesticks, and other useful objects. Many have become highly sought-after antiques. Copper, like brass, is a soft metal that is easy to form and has good color. It is also an efficient conductor of heat, so it was often used to fashion cooking pots. The insides of the pots were coated with tin so that food would not come into contact with the copper. Copper was also made into weathervanes, which today are often used indoors as folk-art decorations. The green color acquired by weathered copper is also admired.

Tin-coated steel was shaped into candlesticks, lanterns, and all kinds of boxes and trays. Tin objects sometimes were decorated with painted designs; these objects are called **toleware**.

Antique iron is also collected. Cooking forks, pot trivets, and other wrought-iron objects, hand-forged by blacksmiths, were used in American colonial times. Cast-iron objects, which are shaped by casting hot metal in a mold, include everything from old cooking pots to decorative urns.

Samplers were hand-stitched by girls to show their needlework skills. The name and dates on this sampler tell us that it was made by a 10-year-old girl in 1773.

OTHER KINDS OF ANTIQUES

Antique clocks are very popular objects to collect. Clocks were mass-produced in Connecticut during the 1800's, and examples are fairly easy to find today. More highly valued are clocks made during the 1600's and 1700's, which show outstanding craftsmanship. Antique guns and powderflasks, swords, lamps, and books each have a following.

In recent years, collectors have shown increased interest in textiles, mainly handmade quilts and **samplers**—examples of handstitching created by girls to show their embroidery skills. Many other items are considered "collectibles," including early toys, dolls and dollhouse furniture, penny banks, buttons, old signs and posters, and even vintage postcards. These objects are not always beautiful or rare. But they provide a fascinating glimpse of the people and customs of earlier times. Follow your interests and let them lead you into the adventures of collecting.

Reviewed by WAYNE MATTOX
President, Woodbury (Connecticut) Antiques Dealers Association

See also FOLK ART; FURNITURE.

ANTISEPTICS. See DISINFECTANTS AND ANTISEPTICS.

ANTITOXINS. See DISEASES (Prevention of Disease); VACCINATION AND IMMUNIZATION.

ANTONY, MARK (83?–30 B.C.)

Mark Antony (Marcus Antonius) was a Roman general and statesman and one of the rulers of Rome after the death of Julius Caesar. His love for the Egyptian queen Cleopatra was the subject of William Shakespeare's tragedy *Antony and Cleopatra*. He is also a major figure in Shakespeare's *Julius Caesar*.

Mark Antony was one of the rulers of ancient Rome after the assassination of Julius Caesar. His struggle for supreme power with a co-ruler, Octavian, led to his defeat and death. Antony's love for Cleopatra, queen of Egypt, was the subject of William Shakespeare's tragedy *Antony and Cleopatra*.

Antony was born in 83 or 82 B.C. into an aristocratic Roman family. Through his mother, Julia, he was a cousin of Julius Caesar. Antony served with distinction under him during the conquest of Gaul (most of present-day France) in 54–50 B.C. He also backed Caesar in his struggle with the Roman general Pompey. In 48 B.C. he brought precious reinforcements to Caesar and commanded his left wing at the Battle of Pharsalus, in Greece, where Pompey was defeated.

In 44 B.C., Antony shared the consulship, Rome's highest office, with Caesar. When Caesar was assassinated that same year, Antony seized power for himself. He negotiated between opposing groups—republicans, who had conspired in the assassination, and Caesar's followers—to prevent civil war.

Antony's greatest rival for power in Rome was to be the young Octavian, Caesar's adopted son and heir. Octavian first sided with Cicero, an orator and a leader of the republicans, to weaken Antony. But he then joined Antony and Lepidus, Caesar's former lieutenant, in a triple alliance, the Triumvirate. Cicero and other republicans were executed.

In 42 B.C., Antony defeated the republican forces led by Brutus and Cassius, Caesar's assassins, at the Battle of Philippi in Greece and won control of Rome's eastern provinces. He later attempted and failed to conquer the Parthian Empire and tried to strengthen himself by an alliance with Cleopatra. Relations with Octavian remained strained, in spite of Antony's marriage to his sister, Octavia, in 40 B.C. Their struggle ended when Antony was defeated in the naval Battle of Actium in 31 B.C. He and Cleopatra fled back to Egypt, where they both committed suicide. The triumphant Octavian went on to become (as Augustus) the first emperor of Rome.

ALLEN M. WARD
University of Connecticut
Coauthor, *A History of the Roman People*

See also CAESAR, GAIUS JULIUS; CICERO, MARCUS TULLIUS; CLEOPATRA.

ANTONY, SAINT. See SAINTS (Profiles).

ANTONYMS. See SYNONYMS AND ANTONYMS.

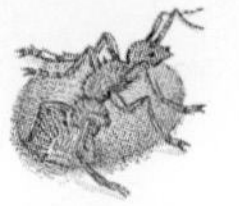

ANTS

Ants emerged on the earth more than 100 million years ago. Since that time, these tiny insects have developed amazingly varied kinds of existences. But no matter how different their lives are, none live alone. Ants are social insects, that is, they live together in organized communities, or **colonies**. The population of an ant colony varies depending on the species of ant. Some ants live in colonies that contain only a few members. Others are part of colonies that contain hundreds, thousands, or even millions of members.

Ants, which along with bees and wasps make up the insect order Hymenoptera, can be found on every continent except Antarctica. **Myrmecologists**, biologists who study ants, have discovered and given scientific names to almost 9,000 species, or kinds, of ants. Each year many new kinds are discovered, and scientists estimate that there may be as many as 20,000 different species in the world.

▸THE CHARACTERISTICS OF ANTS

Ants are small, usually drably colored creatures that range in size from 1/25 inch (0.1 centimeter) to more than 1 inch (2.5 centimeters) in length. The many different species of ants all share similar body structures.

The Body of an Ant

Like all insects, the ant is an invertebrate (animal without a backbone) with a body divided into three main sections: head, thorax, and abdomen. Within these sections are organs that allow ants to sense the world around them, breathe, process food, communicate with others, move, and reproduce. The delicate internal organs are protected by an **exoskeleton**, which is the hard outer covering of the body. Along with protecting the ant's internal organs, the strong exoskeleton gives the ant its body shape and provides places of attachment for the muscles.

Head. The head of an ant has several important structures: antennae, scent glands, eyes, and mouth.

The antennae of an ant are the most noticeable structures of the head. The antennae serve as organs of smell and touch, performing tasks much like those of the human nose and fingertips. The antennae are also used in communication. Ants may tap other ants with their antennae to beg for or offer food or to recruit other ants to go to a food source located outside the nest.

The scent glands are used in another form of communication. Messages are sent through chemicals, called **pheromones**, given off by the scent glands. The smell of these chemicals warns other ants in the nest of danger.

The mouth of an ant is a small hole at the front end of the head. On either side of the mouth is a pair of strong, bladelike jaws called **mandibles**. The shape of the mandibles may be quite different in different kinds of ants and may also vary within a species. Ants use their mandibles for a variety of purposes. They use them to carry their tiny, delicate eggs, cut up food, attack prey, and fight enemies. Mandibles are even used for communication. Some ants bang their mandibles on the floor of their

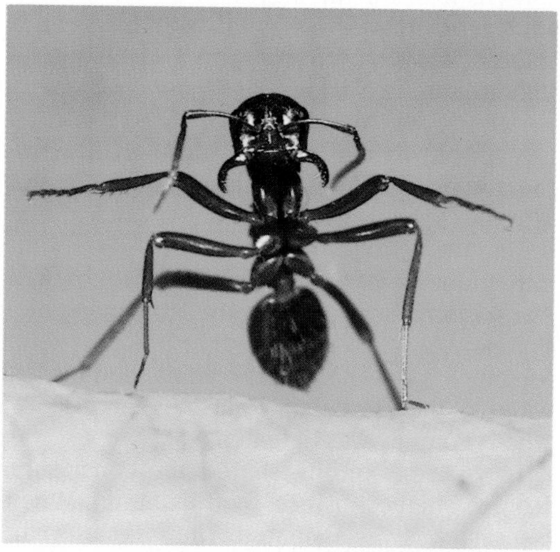

Each ant species has characteristics that are suited to its own way of life. An army ant (*above*) displays the menacing mandibles that it uses to overwhelm prey. The long, muscular hind legs of a jumping ant (*below*) help it to jump several times its body length!

nests or snap them together to produce a danger signal that can be heard by other ants.

While some kinds of ants have very small eyes or no eyes at all, most ants have two different kinds of eyes—compound eyes and simple eyes. The large compound eyes, one on each side of the head, are made up of many lenses placed close together that work to produce a single visual image. The three simple eyes, or **ocelli**, are near the center of the head. The ocelli sense the brightness and the direction of light. Using the ocelli, ants can sense polarized light, a form of light humans cannot see. Using polarized light, ants can find the position of the sun in the sky. Ants use the position of the sun as a compass point to find their way to and from their nest.

Thorax. The thorax is the middle part of an ant's body. There are three pairs of legs attached to it. The front legs, which are used to dig through soil, are thicker and stronger than the middle and hind legs. In most ants the middle and hind legs are very similar in size. But in the jumping ants of South America, the hind legs are longer and more muscular than the middle legs.

In ants that have wings, the two pairs are attached to the upper sides of the thorax. In most species of ants, the males and young queens have wings; workers do not. Winged ants use their wings only during the mating flight. Once they have mated, the males die and the young queens break off their wings because they no longer need them.

Abdomen. An ant's abdomen has three major parts. The first part, which lies close to the thorax, is called the **propodeum**. On its surface, the propodeum often has spines, ridges, or bumps that are unique to each species of ant. The middle part, or **pedicel**, is made up of one or, sometimes, two moveable segments. The pedicel has a slender, waistlike form. Like the propodeum, the pedicel also has surface features unique to each ant species. These surface features are useful in recognizing different species.

The large rounded part of the abdomen is known as the **gaster**. Some species of ants have a sting at the end of the gaster. Because the sting developed from an egg-laying device, only the female can have a sting. The sting is used mainly to capture prey and for defense. **Venom**, or poison, produced in

The Body Structures of an Ant

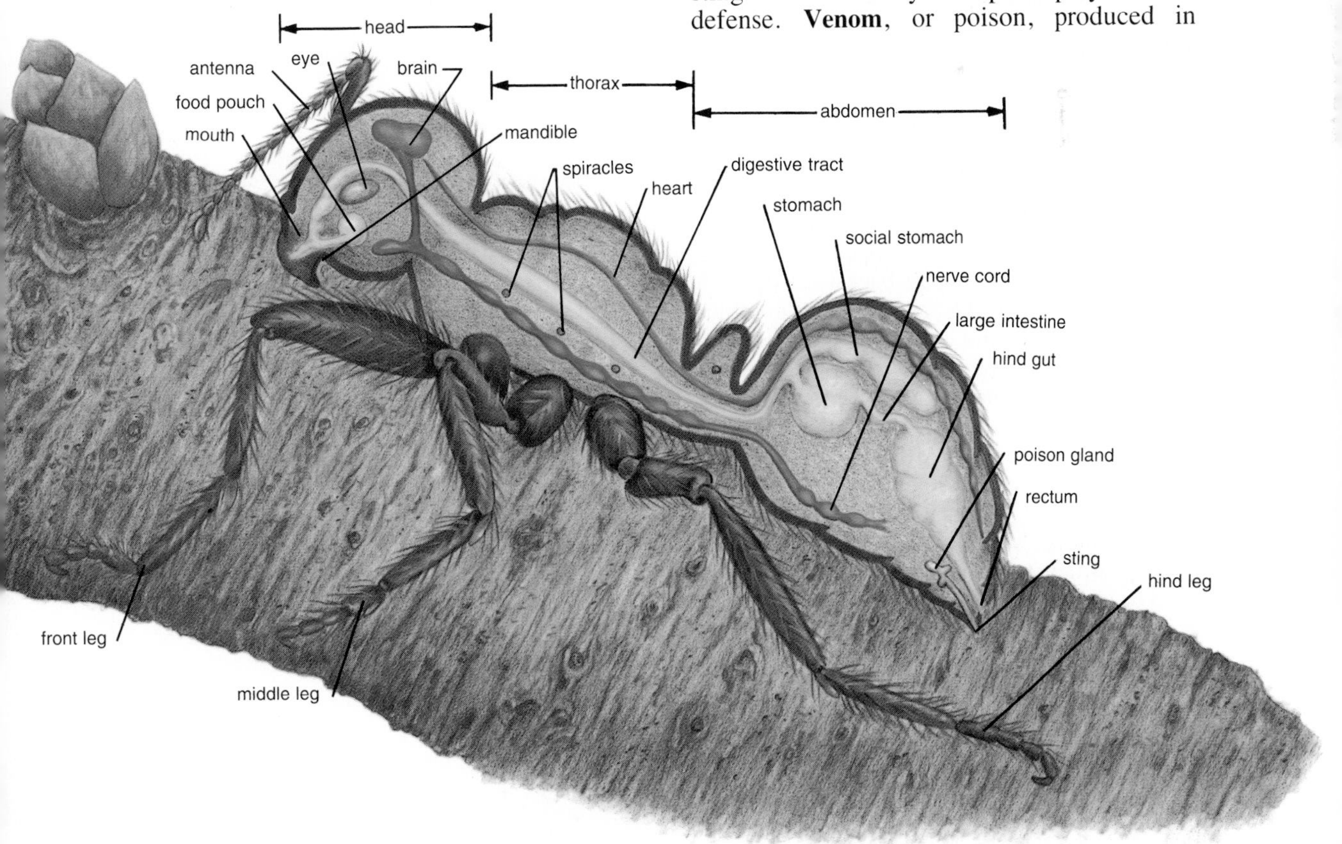

glands at the tip of the gaster is injected into the victim through the sting. But not all ants have useful stings. Some have stings so small or shaped so that they cannot be inserted into prey. Some of these ants produce formic acid or other kinds of venom that are sprayed or dabbed onto prey.

Inside the Body. The nervous system of an ant consists of the brain, nerve cord, and nerves. The brain is very tiny, but compared to the ant's body size, it is one of the largest brains in the insect world. The brain serves as the control center for all the body functions and processes. From the brain, a nerve cord extends along the lower side of the ant's body to the tip of the gaster. Nerves branch out along the nerve cord, carrying messages from the brain to other parts of the body and from other body parts to the brain.

Like other animals, ants take in oxygen during the process of respiration. The oxygen enters the body through small holes called **spiracles** on the sides of the thorax and abdomen. A network of tubes carries the oxygen throughout the ant's body. Carbon dioxide, a waste product formed during energy production, leaves through the spiracles.

The blood system of the ant is responsible for bringing digested food to the organs, muscles, and nervous system. It also takes away waste material. The ant's heart is part of a long tube that runs along the top of the ant's body from the head to the gaster. Blood is sucked up into the heart through tiny openings along the tube. As the heart contracts, blood is forced toward the head of the ant. There, blood pours out through an opening, bathing the brain and then flowing backward through the rest of the body. The cycle repeats continuously, nourishing and cleansing the body.

An ant's digestive system is a long tube that extends from the mouth to the end of the gaster. Within the abdomen, the tube widens to form pouchlike organs. An important organ of the digestive system is the **crop**, or "social" stomach. Liquid food, gathered during feeding expeditions, is stored in the crop. Ants returning to their nest regurgitate (bring up) the food to share with colony members. Food that is not stored in the crop passes to the stomach, where it is digested, then to the hind gut, where most of the food is absorbed into the blood. Material that is not absorbed travels through the hind gut to the rectum. Waste absorbed from the blood also is deposited in the rectum. After most of the water is reabsorbed from the waste material, it passes out of the body through an opening called the **cloaca**.

THE LIFE OF ANTS

Although there is great variety in how ants live, there is one trait they all share—all ants live in colonies. Within the different colonies, ants perform similar tasks: making nests, producing young, and feeding.

Members of the Colony

Ant colonies contain male and female members. However, most of the time the colony is populated only by females. Each ant colony has at least one queen, who is more of an egg-producing factory than a ruler. Some ant species have several queens in a colony, while a few kinds have hundreds. Male ants have short life spans, appearing in great numbers during the mating season. Once their job—flying out and mating with the winged queens from another colony—is accomplished, they die. Most of the colony is composed of workers, small wingless females that do not breed. Some colonies also have larger, big-headed workers called major workers.

Members of an Ant Colony

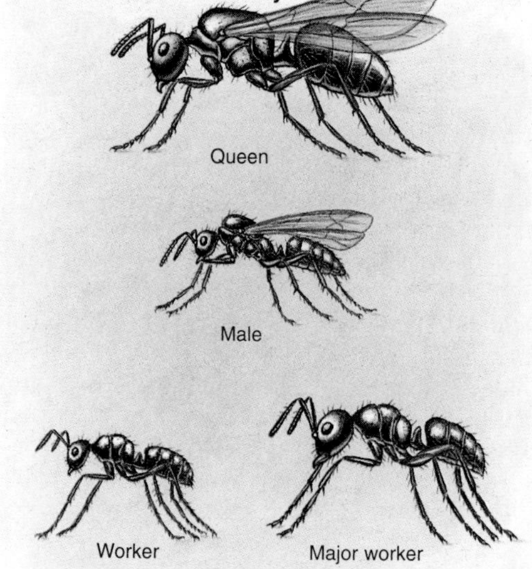

The Life Cycle of an Ant

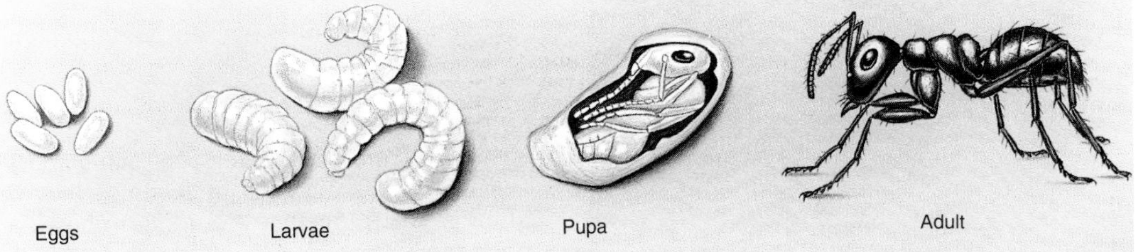

From the eggs the queen ant lays, wormlike larvae hatch. The larvae spend their time eating and growing. They enter the pupal stage when their growth as larvae is complete. During the pupal stage, an ant slowly takes on the adult form.

There may be more than one species of ant in a colony. For example, slave-making ants kidnap other ants and bring them back to work in the colony. Young queens of other kinds of ants leave their own colony to take over another species' colony. After killing the colony's queen, the invader queen forces the workers to raise its young. Eventually all the host ants are replaced by the invading ants.

Other kinds of animals, usually other invertebrates, may be "guests" of the colony. The guests are usually scavengers, eating leftover food or waste in the nest. Sometimes these invertebrates feed on the young or adult ants. The invaders may also use special chemicals to repel attacking ants or to fool ants into accepting them into the colony. In tropical rain forests, social wasps, bees, or even birds may live in part of an ant nest, or they may build separate nests nearby.

The Ant's Life Cycle

There are four stages in the development of an ant: egg, larva, pupa, and adult. The mating flights of males and young queens mark the beginning of the cycle. During the flight, a male deposits sperm (male sex cells) inside a queen's body. The queen stores the sperm until she is ready to lay eggs.

With mating accomplished, the male has fulfilled his only function for the colony, and he dies. The queen busily searches for a favorable location to start a new nest. When she finds a suitable place, she settles in, breaking off the wings she will never need again. After the queen prepares a nest, she lays a few eggs each day. As the eggs pass out of her body, they are fertilized by the stored sperm.

Within a few days of being laid, the eggs hatch. From the eggs, the wormlike forms called larvae (plural of larva) emerge. The larvae are fed by the queen. Depending on what they are fed, the larvae will develop into either queens or workers. The larvae, which spend most of their time eating, grow in size over the next few weeks. When their growth is complete, they enter the pupa stage. Some pupae (plural of pupa) spin a protective cocoon of silk; others are covered only by their skin. During the pupal stage, the ant slowly takes on the form of an adult. After about two or three weeks, its development is complete and the adult ant emerges.

The Ant's Home

Most ants make their homes in soil or rotting wood. Nests in soil or wood consist of chambers and narrow tunnels. Ants travel the tunnels to reach the chambers and the outside. In the tropics, many species nest in plants.

Some soil-nesting ants build a mound full of chambers and tunnels. The mounds are built of soil, small pebbles, twigs, grass blades, and leaf fragments. Some kinds of ants build nests without soil. They make nests with a paperlike

Did you know that . . .

ants were used as the first method of biological pest control? More than 2,000 years ago in southern China, farmers gathered the silk nests of the green tree ant. They took the nests from nearby forests and moved them to the orange groves on their farms. Because the ants are aggressive predators, eating any and all insects that cross their path, the ants helped keep the groves free of pests.

Ant mounds can hold interesting collections of objects. The chambers and tunnels of some have yielded fossils, minerals, even tiny nuggets of gold.

material, called **carton**, made of plant fibers stuck together with saliva. The carton nest may be simple sheets of material covering the spaces in bark or rocks in which the ants live. Or the nest may have a ball-like structure.

In addition to soil and carton, parts of plants also are used to make nests. Certain species of tropical tree ants weave a nest of leaves and silk. Groups of workers pull leaves together while others move silk-producing larvae (newly hatched ants) back and forth from the edge of one leaf to the other until the two leaves are firmly attached.

How Ants Obtain Food

Ants feed on a wide range of foods. Some ants eat only plant matter, such as seeds. Others feed on the fungus they carefully grow. But most kinds of ants are predators and scavengers—with a taste for sweets. They catch and eat small invertebrates, especially other insects, and they also eat already dead prey. They even steal prey from other small predators. Ants satisfy their taste for sweets by consuming plant sap, nectar, and fruit. The resourceful ants also get their sugary treats by raiding the hives of honeybees and the homes of human beings.

KINDS OF ANTS

Because ants have developed such elaborate and distinctive methods of feeding, they are often grouped together according to how they obtain food.

Harvester Ants

Seeds are part of the diet of many kinds of ants. However, they make up almost the entire diet of harvester ants, who gather seeds directly from plants or from the ground. These ambitious ants gather many more seeds than can be eaten at one time. The uneaten seeds are stored in special chambers in their nests, so there is always a ready supply of food.

Before the seeds can be eaten by the adults, they must be processed by the larvae. Workers break up the seeds into small pieces and feed them to the larvae. The larvae are able to digest the starchy seeds because they have a starch-digesting enzyme, which is missing in the adults. In the stomach of a larva, the seeds become a soft, pulpy mass. The larvae regurgitate some of this partially digested food for the adult ants. The different digestive abilities of the adults and larvae help ant colonies make use of food resources neither could use without the other.

Fungus-Grower Ants

Fungus-grower ants, found in the warmer portions of North and South America, have a very specialized diet. They have nests with large chambers deep in the soil. In these chambers, fungus growers cultivate special molds. The molds produce swellings that are eaten by the ants.

The fungus must be grown on beds of compost (decayed organic matter). Most fungus-grower ants farm their fungus crop on compost made from the droppings of plant-eating insects, such as caterpillars. Leaf-cutter ants are fungus-grower ants that make compost from pieces of fresh leaves, flowers, and fruits. The ants drink some of the plant juice from these materials but use most of it to raise the fungus that they and their larvae dine on.

Slave-Maker Ants

Slave-maker ants raid the nearby nest of a closely related species and steal its brood. The

slavers carry the stolen brood to their home nest, where the slave ants already present eat most of the brood that is brought in. The brood that is not eaten matures and adds to the slave force of the colony.

To establish a new colony, mated slave-maker queens find a young or weak colony of a related species and invade it. The invaders kill the colony's queen and get the orphaned workers to raise their babies. The population of the colony increases as the slave-maker offspring mature and begin raiding other colonies. The colony remains a mixture of slave-maker ants and kidnapped ants.

Gatherer Ants

Several ant species have certain workers called **repletes** that, like other ants, store liquid food in their crops. Most replete-former ants are known as honey ants. They live in the deserts of North America and Australia. The liquid, usually honeydew or nectar, is gathered during the rainy season when plant growth is rapid and sap-feeding insects are abundant. Storing the liquid food allows these ants to have energy and water available during long dry spells.

Another replete-former lives in the oak woodlands of North America. This unusual ant is active in autumn, on warm winter days, and in early spring. Its main food is the rotting flesh of dead insects and earthworms. The ants collect the liquid from this softened meat during the time of year when many dead invertebrates are available. During summer, these "winter ants" stay underground and raise the year's brood with the liquefied invertebrate flesh stored in the crops of the repletes.

When its abdomen becomes so swollen with liquid food that it can barely walk (*left*), the gatherer ant called a replete must remain in the nest.

Slave-maker ants must depend on their slaves to perform such tasks as grooming the queen (*below left*), raising their brood, and building their nest.

Like miniature gardeners, leaf-cutter ants gather leaves (*below*) and other vegetation to prepare a bed on which to grow their fungus crop.

A herder ant "milks" aphids to get honeydew by stroking the insects with its antennae. It may also eat some of the aphids for meat.

Herder Ants

Herder ants live with sap-feeding insects in a special relationship that resembles the way human beings tend and herd cattle and other livestock. Some herder ants live underground with small insects called root aphids. The aphids feed on the sugary sap of the roots growing through the ant nests. To get rid of the excess sugar and water in their sap diet, the aphids discharge a sweet secretion called honeydew. Ants love to eat this sweet waste product. At times the ants also eat some of the aphids for meat. Ants that live this way often get all of their nutrition from aphids.

The herder ants of the Asian rain forest live with relatives of aphids called scale insects. These ants live in the warm, humid rain forest. The queen ant and her brood hide in the middle of swarms of workers on the soft new growth of forest shrubs. The scale insects suck sap from the plant twigs, and the ants harvest honeydew and scale insect meat for food. When the nest twig grows old and woody, the ants move, transporting their scale insects to a new "pasture"—that is, a new young twig.

Army Ants

When it comes to feeding, many ants are specialists, seeking out and preying on only one kind of food. Army ants are one such example. Many army ants only attack the nests of other ants, stealing and eating their broods. However, they have been accused of eating just about everything—from invertebrates to dogs, even humans!

Army ants have no permanent home. Each night the workers come together, creating a shelter out of their joined bodies. With the morning sun, bands of ants stream out from their temporary quarters, searching for food. When they find their prey, these ferocious ants swarm around it, attacking the victim with their long mandibles.

▸ANTS AND THEIR ENVIRONMENT

Ants serve several valuable functions. They help maintain the balance of nature by consuming large numbers of other insects and serving as a food source for other animals. They enrich the soil as they dig their burrows, loosening and mixing the dirt. Ants benefit human beings when they feed on insect pests, such as those that attack cotton plants and orange trees. But some of the same habits that make them helpful make them harmful. Ants can be household pests, infesting food and sometimes delivering painful stings. Some ants damage homes and other buildings by burrowing into the wood. They are agricultural pests when they feed on crops.

Over the years, myrmecologists have watched the same changes in the health of ant populations as in other species. Ants characteristic of endangered ecosystems—including the eastern tall grass prairie of North America, the rain forests of Asia, the savannas of northern Africa, and the hay meadows of Europe—are headed for extinction along with the other life-forms found in those habitats. In every way, the future of ants is linked to that of other life on our planet. Some species will increase; many others have already decreased and will continue to do so. Some may become victims of extinction.

JAMES C. TRAGER
Editor, *Advances in Myrmecology*

See also ANTEATERS; INSECTS.

APACHE INDIANS. See INDIANS, AMERICAN.

Size is the major characteristic that distinguishes the two groups of apes. The hulking gorilla (*above*) belongs to the group known as great apes, while the dainty gibbon (mother and daughter, *right*) belongs to the group known as lesser apes.

APES

Apes are hairy, long-armed animals without tails. They are intelligent creatures with large and complex brains, belonging to a group of mammals called **primates**. Human beings, monkeys (which are sometimes mistaken for apes), and a number of more primitive animals, such as lemurs, also are primates.

Of all existing animals, apes resemble human beings the most. The similarities between apes and human beings have led most scientists to believe that millions of years ago, apes and human beings shared a common ancestor. Some of the shared characteristics include highly developed nervous systems, excellent eyesight, broad flat chests, and flexible fingers and toes with nails instead of claws.

Although apes and human beings share many characteristics, there are significant differences. People, who are capable of more complicated tasks, have larger, more complex brains. Human beings also take longer to develop, have less body hair, and longer life spans. But probably the most important differences are that people have the ability to communicate with spoken language and to stand upright and walk on two legs.

CHARACTERISTICS OF APES

All apes are divided into two families, or groups, based chiefly on size. There are great apes and lesser apes. The great apes, which belong to the family Pongidae, include four species, or kinds, of apes: the gorilla, orangutan, chimpanzee, and bonobo, or pygmy chimpanzee. The largest of the great apes, and the largest primate, is the gorilla. A male can weigh about 600 pounds (272 kilograms) and stand more than 5 feet (1.5 meters) tall. The lesser apes, which belong to the family Hylobatidae, include nine species of gibbons. Gibbons are the smallest apes. They usually weigh 10 to 20 pounds (4.5 to 9 kilograms) and stand about 2 feet (0.6 meter) tall.

The various species of apes share many of the same characteristics. Their lively faces are more or less naked with flat noses and jaws that are thrust forward. Because they have mobile facial muscles, apes are able to display a wide range of facial expressions. Their eyes, which are directed forward, are capable of full-color vision. Hairless external ears are positioned on the sides of their heads. The trunk is well muscled with arms longer than legs. The siamang gibbon is the ape with the longest arms. Its arms, which may be more than twice as long as its body, span a distance of about 5 feet (1.5 meters). Apes have long-fingered hands with flat nails and opposable thumbs, that is, thumbs that can be placed against other fingers. Hair, varying in color from black to shades of reddish brown, covers their bodies.

Apes live in a variety of habitats. Gorillas are forest animals, found in tropical Africa. One population, the western lowland gorilla, lives in west central Africa. The eastern lowland gorilla lives about 600 miles (965 kilometers) away, in central Africa. Still another population, the mountain gorilla, inhabits mountains in east central Africa. Orangutans are also forest animals. However, their habitats on the Indonesian islands of Borneo and Sumatra distinguish them from other great apes—they are the only existing great apes of Asia. Chimpanzees are adaptable apes that make their home in Africa. They live in forests and in grasslands near wooded areas. Tropical forests in central Africa are home to the bonobos. Gibbons inhabit the airy heights of forests of Southeast Asia.

The devoted mother orangutan will spend years alone with her young offspring, roaming through the forest.

Apes are both land- and tree-dwellers. On land, apes typically move about on all fours with the knuckles of their front hands on the ground. Exceptions are the orangutan, which closes its hands into fists, and the gibbon, which walks with its long arms held high. Although all apes can climb trees, some are much more comfortable moving about high above the ground—the orangutan and gibbon seldom come down from their lofty habitats, while gorillas rarely climb trees.

Most apes are very social animals. In fact, they need to be around each other. When apes do not have contact with each other, they become depressed and dejected. Their sociability extends to their mode of parenting. Apes are dedicated parents that spend a lot of their time raising their offspring. Rather than have many offspring, apes produce a few young that are cared for by both male and female parents. Their care extends over several years until the young are able to take care of themselves.

THE LIFE OF APES

Except for the solitary orangutan, apes live in groups. Some groups, like those of the gibbons, are small and consist of an adult pair and their young. A gorilla group, which may reach two dozen members, includes a few adult males, some younger males, and females and their offspring. Chimpanzees live in groups of between 15 and 80 individuals. The largest groups, or communities, are formed by the bonobos. A single community can have close to 150 members.

The gibbon is well adapted to a tree-dwelling existence. When it must navigate an open space between trees, the gibbon projects itself through the air for distances up to 32 feet (10 meters).

To get sufficient nourishment, a gorilla (*above*) consumes huge quantities of plant matter. A chimpanzee (*left*) uses a stick tool to search a rotted log for tasty insect morsels.

Although the various groups may be large and noisy, apes are generally peaceful creatures. Apes engage in threatening displays or aggressive behavior when guarding their territories against intruders or when males compete with each other for status, or rank, within a group. Males with the highest status usually mate with the most females. Gibbons are an exception. The male mates with only one female, and it stays with that female for life.

Apes are active during the day hunting and foraging for food. Gorillas are strict vegetarians. Other apes have a varied diet but feed mostly on plant matter. The fruit, roots, and leaves of plants and the bark of trees are consumed. Gibbons often eat birds' eggs, insects, and spiders as well as plants. Chimpanzees and bonobos add small mammals to their plant diet. In their quest for food, apes—especially chimpanzees—will develop and use tools. The episodes of eating are broken up by naps and playtimes with offspring.

When apes are sexually mature, at about 7 years of age, they are able to mate. Although twins are sometimes born, generally only a single offspring is produced by the female. The offspring stays with its mother for three to six years. The young apes are sheltered by their family group as their elders prepare them for the tasks of their adult lives.

At night, apes retire to sleeping nests. Some, like the tree-dwelling orangutan, build their nests high above the ground by bending twigs and branches to form a springy platform in the trees. Other apes, such as the gorilla, gather leaves, grasses, and other plant material to make their ground nests comfortable.

APES AND THEIR ENVIRONMENT

Few animals threaten the lives of apes. Large cats, such as tigers and leopards, do hunt apes for food. But it is people who have seriously reduced the ape population. People have hunted apes for food and captured and traded them to stock zoos and for use in scientific research.

By far the greatest threat to apes is the loss of their habitats. Tropical forests and woodlands throughout the world, including those inhabited by apes, are being eliminated by human activity. Some are cut for lumber. Others are cleared to make room for agriculture or industries such as mining. As people have cleared land for development, apes have been pushed from their homes into lands that are poor habitats. The inferior lands cannot supply the apes with what they require to survive. Consequently, their numbers have dwindled.

Various methods are being used to protect the world's ape population. In many countries, laws have been enacted that make hunting or trading apes illegal. No longer are apes taken from the wild to supply zoos and research centers. Instead, apes are bred in captive-breeding programs, which also ensures that the various species of apes will not become extinct. In addition, many conservation groups are working hard to establish forest sanctuaries where apes can be protected and their habitat preserved.

Edward R. Ricciuti
Coauthor, *The Audubon Society Book of Wild Animals*

See also Mammals.

APHRODITE. See Greek Mythology (Profiles).
APOLLO. See Greek Mythology (Profiles).

This famous painting, *The Last Supper*, was painted by Leonardo da Vinci on a wall of Santa Maria delle Grazie, a church in Milan, Italy.

APOSTLES, THE

The Apostles were 12 men especially appointed by Jesus Christ "that they should be with him, and that he might send them forth to preach, and to have power to heal sicknesses, and to cast out devils." Later Jesus sent them forth two by two. He "gave them power over unclean spirits; and commanded them that they should take nothing for their journey, save a staff only; no scrip, no bread, no money in their purse."

The word "apostle" comes from a Greek word meaning "to send away." Today it is sometimes used for religious missionaries.

Christ's 12 Apostles came from different backgrounds. Four were fishermen. Matthew, a tax collector, was the only wealthy man.

Like people everywhere, the Apostles had different personalities. Peter was a dependable leader with an independent nature. James the Younger was strict and severe, but respected for his justice. Philip liked to ask questions. Christ nicknamed James the Elder and his brother John "Sons of Thunder" because they had quick tempers. Thomas is known as "Doubting Thomas" because at first he would not believe that Christ had risen from the dead. Some of the Apostles were quiet men, content to listen and to learn. Others were impatient. Because Peter, James the Elder, and John had a deeper understanding of Jesus' teachings, they were chosen to be with Jesus at the most important times.

Following Jesus' lifetime the Apostles traveled near and far. It is believed that Thomas went to India and Andrew reached what is now Russia. The teachings of Christ were spread throughout Asia Minor and most of the Roman Empire. The experiences of some of the Apostles are recorded in the New Testament.

According to a custom of the time, some of the Apostles were given new names when they took up their new responsibilities. The 12 Apostles are usually named in this order:

Simon, renamed Peter; a fisherman. Christ said, "Thou art Peter, and upon this rock I shall build my church."

Andrew, a fisherman; brother of Simon Peter. Saint Andrew's cross is so named because of the traditional belief that Andrew died on a cross made in the form of an X. He is the patron saint of Scotland, Greece, and Russia.

James the Elder (also called James the Greater), a fisherman; son of Zebedee. James was the first to die as a martyr in Jerusalem.

John, a fisherman; brother of James the Elder; author of the Fourth Gospel. He was known as "the disciple whom Jesus loved."

Philip of Bethsaida, who, when he became an Apostle, led his friend Nathanael (renamed Bartholomew) to Christ.

Bartholomew, Philip's friend. He was the son of Talmai (Bar Talmai in Hebrew). It is thought that his new name, Bartholomew, came from Bar Talmai.

Matthew, a tax collector. He preached in Judea, and is the traditional author of the First Gospel. Tradition also says that he brought Christianity to the East.

Thomas (also called Didymus, which means "twin"). He showed great faith by offering to accompany Jesus to Jerusalem, where some sought to stone him.

James the Younger (also called James the Less, or James the Little), son of Alphaeus. Some scholars say that this is the James who welcomed Saint Paul to Jerusalem when many were suspicious of Saint Paul's conversion to Christianity.

Jude, or Judas (also called Thaddaeus), brother of James the Younger (though some scholars think he was the son of James).

Simon the Cananaean, martyred in Persia. "Cananaean" means one who is zealous or eager. Simon was so named for his devotion to Judaism before becoming a Christian.

Judas Iscariot. He betrayed Jesus for 30 silver coins. When Jesus was condemned to death, Judas repented and hanged himself.

Matthias was chosen by the 11 Apostles to replace Judas Iscariot. Tradition says he brought Christianity to ancient Ethiopia and Macedonia.

Paul of Tarsus (originally named Saul) was not one of the chosen 12, but is called an Apostle and is as respected as the others.

Reviewed by JAMES I. MCCORD
President, Princeton Theological Seminary

APPALACHIAN MOUNTAINS. See NORTH AMERICA.

APPENDICITIS. See DISEASES (Descriptions of Some Diseases).

APPLE

The apple is the most important tree fruit of the temperate regions of the world. Apples have been grown and used as food since the dawn of history. Charred remains found in Stone Age lake dwellings in central Europe show that prehistoric peoples ate apples. There are carvings of apples on ancient tombs and monuments in the Middle East.

The apple appears often in the myths and folklore of ancient civilizations. In Greek mythology, Hercules (Heracles) traveled to the end of the world to bring back the golden apples of the Hesperides. A golden apple—the apple of discord—caused a quarrel that led to the Trojan War. A Norse myth tells of magic apples that kept people young forever. The Halloween game of bobbing for apples had its beginning among the ancient Celts as a way of foretelling the future.

Apples were brought to America by the earliest European settlers. At first apples were used mainly for cider, which was a popular beverage in England and northern France, where most of the early colonists came from. Cider is another name for apple juice. Hard cider is apple juice that has fermented. It contains a small percentage of alcohol—about as much as beer.

As the frontier moved westward across the continent, apple trees followed. One of the first things a settler did after clearing the land and building a cabin was to plant a few apple trees in the yard.

▶ USES OF APPLES

Apples have many uses. They are eaten fresh, cooked, dried, and canned. Their juice is used for drinking and for making vinegar. Apples furnish valuable minerals and vitamins and add bulk to the diet.

The United States produces about 5½ million tons of apples every year, and more than half the crop is sold to be eaten fresh. Lower-quality apples are made into juice or applesauce. Some are also canned as fillings for pastries and pies. Apples can be processed to make sweet cider, hard cider, liqueurs, and apple cider vinegar. The processing remains can even be distilled to make perfumes used in shampoos and cosmetics.

▶ ORIGIN OF THE APPLE

Although there are numerous kinds of wild, or crab, apples native to different parts of the world, the kind from which the familiar cultivated apple developed came from the mountains of southwestern and central Asia, between the regions of the Black and Caspian seas and eastward from there. This ancestor of the modern apple, which still grows wild, is smaller and more sour than our present varieties, but the tree on which it grows resembles our cultivated trees.

People selected the best fruit from the wild trees for eating and used seeds from the better fruit for planting. In this way the quality of apples was gradually improved.

▶ VARIETIES

A number of distinct varieties of apples were raised in the lands north of the Mediterranean Sea several centuries before the time of Jesus. Since then thousands of varieties have been named and grown in different parts of the world. Most of these have now disappeared from commercial production, although many different varieties are still grown in various parts of the world.

In the United States and Canada, about 25 varieties are grown extensively, although there are small plantings of many other kinds. Apple varieties must meet certain requirements before growers are willing to invest time, money, and labor in them. First of all, the trees must be productive. Second, the fruit must be attractive-looking and of good size. Its flavor and texture must appeal to most people. Finally, the fruit must keep well in storage. This is why so few varieties are grown on a large scale.

Nearly all our present important varieties originated as chance seedlings. Since about 1900, scientific breeding work has resulted in the development of some fine new varieties. Most of these, however, are not yet widely grown.

The leading variety of apple in the United States is the Red Delicious, which originated from a seedling tree found on a farm in Peru, Iowa, about 1881. Most Red Delicious apples are now raised in the Northwest Pacific states and British Columbia, Canada, though some are grown in most apple-growing regions.

The McIntosh is the leading variety in Canada, New York, and the New England states. McIntosh trees are all descended from one chance seedling found on a pioneer farm in Ontario, Canada, in 1796. The original tree survived, bearing apples, until 1908, although it was badly damaged by a fire.

Other leading varieties include the Golden Delicious, Rome Beauty, Gala, Jonathan, and York Imperial.

Apples from Far Away

Among America's most popular apples are two that came from far away. The Granny Smith apple originated in Australia in the late 1860's. Mrs. Anne Smith found a young tree bearing large, hardy green apples that were good for cooking and eating. In the 1930's, the locally popular Granny Smith apples were exported from Australia. By the 1960's, successful strains were introduced to Wash-

Of the many apple varieties commonly grown in the United States and Canada, these are some of the most popular for eating and cooking (*clockwise from far left*): Red Delicious, Rome Beauty, Granny Smith, Fuji, Yellow Delicious, and McIntosh.

Carefully maintained orchards—those that are properly fertilized, sprayed, and pruned—often produce a showy display of pink apple blossoms in the spring, followed by a bountiful crop of valuable fruit in the fall.

ington State. Now Granny Smith is one of Washington's leading apples. But the Granny Smith faces increased competition from another foreign apple, the Fuji, from Japan. This apple was first grown in 1939. It has gained popularity in the United States and, like the Granny Smith, is becoming one of Washington State's leading varieties.

Older Varieties

For more than 200 years, one of the most popular commercial apples was the Rhode Island Greening. Renowned even in the 1700's, this apple originated in Newport, Rhode Island. Up until the 1960's, the Rhode Island Greening was quite popular in the eastern United States. It is very difficult to find today. The Northern Spy was another American apple popular for more than a century. It arose from a seedling in a New York orchard around 1840. A major commercial apple until the 1960's, the Northern Spy is still grown on a small scale today. Its roots are resistant to some diseases, so the rootstock is commonly used for apple breeding. The Rome Beauty is an older variety that is still very common today. This apple, which dates to the 1840's, became famous for its bright red color and for its storage ability.

THE TREE

In good soils, unpruned apple trees will reach 30 to 40 feet (9 to 12 meters) in height. But when apples are grown for market, the trees are pruned to prevent them from becoming this tall. The trees in most commercial orchards are kept to a height of less than 20 feet (6 meters).

The apple tree is "rounded"—that is, it is about as broad as it is high. The branches are twisted and spreading. The fruit of most commercial varieties is red, but there are also varieties that bear yellow, green, russet (reddish brown), and striped fruit. Apple wood is dense, hard, and heavy. Because the tree has a short trunk and many branches, it is not used for lumber. Apple wood is sometimes used for carved ornaments and in furniture.

Apple trees generally do not begin to blossom and bear fruit until they are 5 to 8 years old. They reach maximum production at about 20 years, and commercial orchards are generally replaced when the trees are 35 to 40 years old. Although the trees would live much longer, the fruit produced on old trees is generally smaller and poorer in appearance.

Apple pickers climb tall ladders to harvest ripe fruit from the treetops. Small batches of apples gathered from the trees are transferred to large containers on the ground.

▶ MANAGING THE APPLE ORCHARD

A great deal of intensive work must be performed in the commercial orchard. Each year the trees should be pruned, usually in late winter. This prevents them from becoming too tall or too thick and bushy and results in larger, better-colored fruit. The trees must be fertilized to make them grow and bear properly. Nearly all apple orchards need nitrogen fertilizers. Other elements such as potassium and magnesium may also be needed.

Frost, insect pests, and fungus diseases are among the most serious problems the apple grower faces. Apple trees must be tended carefully throughout the growing season. Apple trees bloom in the early spring, bearing delicate, fragrant blossoms that range in color from white to dark pink. Because open apple blossoms die when the temperature drops a few degrees below freezing, crops are often lost when late frosts occur. Commercial orchards generally are planted on slopes or high ground to reduce this danger, since cold air tends to sink. Commercial growers may use heaters or spray the blossoms with water on cold nights. Water cools much more slowly than air, so a soaking with water can help keep blossoms from freezing even when the air temperature falls below 32°F (0°C). While the tree is in bloom, many growers bring in beehives so that there are plenty of bees to pollinate the flowers. The apple, which develops from the ovary of the flower, is the end product of the pollination.

Many insects attack the apple tree. One of the worst is the codling moth, which lays its eggs on or near the fruit. When the eggs hatch, the larvae bore into the fruit and a "wormy" apple results. Other insect pests include scales, aphids, and mites. Diseases caused by fungi and bacteria, such as apple scab and fire blight, can also infect the flowers, fruit, and leaves of the apple tree.

Repeated spraying is often necessary to keep the fruit free of insects and diseases. Be-

See For Yourself

How to Sprout Apple Seeds

1. The first step in sprouting apple seeds is to collect some seeds from an apple. Once you have gathered the seeds, soak them in warm water overnight.

2. There are a number of different kinds of containers you can plant your seeds in—flowerpots, milk cartons, or coffee cans. The container should have one or more drain holes in the bottom and be able to hold about 1 quart (0.9 liter) of moist soil. To prepare the container, place small stones or pebbles in the bottom and fill it to the top with soil. Water the soil and press it down farther into the pot. Make sure there is a dish underneath to catch the water that drains out of the soil. To plant the seeds, place a few seeds on top of the soil about 1 inch (2.5 centimeters) apart. Then push them about 1/2 inch (1 centimeter) under the surface with your finger. Gently pat the soil down and water it again.

3. The pot should be kept in a warm, sunny place. Be sure to check the soil every day and keep it moist. It may take several weeks for you to see tiny green stalks and leaves pop through the soil. Once the seedlings have grown about 2 inches (5 centimeters), each one can be put in its own container to grow. As they grow, the seedlings will continue to need sunshine and water. You also can fertilize them with houseplant fertilizer. Eventually the apple plants will need to be replanted in larger containers. Check with your local garden center to find out at what intervals they will need to be transplanted.

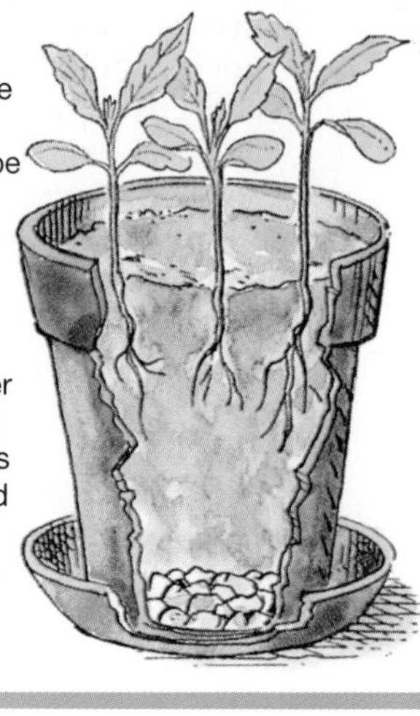

cause pests appear at different times of the growing season, some areas may need 12 to 14 sprays per year. New varieties of apples are now being bred that are resistant to certain kinds of insects and fungi. This reduces the need to spray so often.

▶ PROPAGATION

Apple trees do not "breed true." That is, new trees grown from seeds do not produce fruit that is exactly like the parent tree's. Trees for orchards are therefore produced by budding or grafting. A bud or a short piece of a twig taken from a parent tree is inserted into a young seedling tree so that it grows and forms the top of the new tree. The new tree will then produce fruit exactly like that of the tree from which the bud was taken.

By budding or grafting onto certain kinds of roots, it is possible to produce trees that never become very large. Such trees are called dwarfs. Dwarf trees, besides being easier to spray, prune, and collect harvests from, usually bear fruit earlier. They are popular for home planting and are used commercially on a large scale. Since dwarf trees can be planted close together, the yield of fruit is generally increased.

▶ HARVESTING AND STORAGE

Some varieties of apples mature in midsummer and others ripen in late fall. However, most kinds are ready for picking in September and October. The fruit must be picked by hand and carefully handled, for it will spoil if it is bruised.

The fruit is firm when picked but softens quite rapidly after picking unless it is put into cold storage. Apples will soften as much in one day at room temperature as they will in ten days in cold storage. Therefore, if the fruit is to be held for winter or early spring markets, it must be put into cold storage immediately and cooled rapidly to about 32°F (0°C). It is held there until time for marketing.

Apples will keep even better in controlled atmosphere storage: The fruit is put into airtight rooms, where the oxygen level is reduced from the 20 percent present in normal air to about 3 percent. At the same time the carbon dioxide content, normally present only in trace amounts, is increased to 2 to 5 percent. (The exact figures vary for different kinds of apples.) This slows down the life processes of the fruit cells and helps keep the fruit from softening. The controlled atmosphere, together with low temperatures, can keep some kinds of apples in good eating condition for up to a year. But very few apples are stored longer than nine months.

WONDER QUESTION

Who was Johnny Appleseed?

The legend of Johnny Appleseed is based on the life of a real person—John Chapman. Born in Massachusetts in 1774, Chapman became a wandering pioneer who made it his mission to spread the apple tree across the country. Throughout the early 1800's, he provided seeds and seedlings for settlers heading westward. He traveled thousands of miles, planting single trees and starting orchards in West Virginia, Ohio, and Indiana. Many apple orchards throughout the Midwest owe their start directly or indirectly to Chapman. Chapman's kindness to animals, love of nature, skill with herbal remedies, and love of the Bible inspired the stories behind the legend of the eccentric but much-loved character, Johnny Appleseed.

▶ LEADING APPLE AREAS

Apples can be grown in nearly all the temperate areas of the world. Most kinds can endure winter temperatures down to –20°F (–29°C), and some kinds can withstand temperatures as low as –40°F (–40°C).

In the United States, the leading producers of apples are Washington, New York, Michigan, Pennsylvania, and California. In Canada, British Columbia, Ontario, and Nova Scotia lead. Other major apple-producing countries around the world include China, Italy, France, Poland, Turkey, Argentina, Chile, Spain, Russia, Germany, and Japan. Apples do not thrive in the tropics, for the trees require a period of cold and dormancy to grow and bear fruit properly.

Reviewed by ELIZABETH KAPLAN
Author, *Biology Bulletin Monthly*

See also FRUITGROWING.

APPLIQUÉ. See NEEDLECRAFT.

April

No one really knows how April got its name. Some people think the month was named for Aphrodite, the Greek goddess of love. Others think that it came from the Latin word *aperire,* meaning "to open," referring to the opening of spring buds and flowers.

Place in year: 4th month.
Number of days: 30.
Flowers: Sweet pea and daisy.
Birthstone: Diamond.
Zodiac signs: Aries, the Ram (March 21–April 19), and Taurus, the Bull (April 20–May 20).

1
- **William Harvey** born 1578
- **Otto von Bismarck** born 1815
- *April Fools' Day*

2
- **Charlemagne** born 742
- **Hans Christian Andersen** born 1805
- **Émile Zola** born 1840
- U.S. mint established, 1792
- First American motion picture theater opened, Los Angeles, California, 1902

3
- **Washington Irving** born 1783
- Pony Express began in U.S., 1860

4
- Redesigned American flag adopted, 1818
- North Atlantic Treaty signed, 1949
- Martin Luther King, Jr., assassinated, 1968
- Liberation Day in Hungary
- National holiday in Senegal

5
- **Jean Honoré Fragonard** born 1732
- **Joseph Lister** born 1827
- **Booker T. Washington** born 1856

6
- **Raphael** born 1483
- Church of Jesus Christ of Latter-Day Saints (Mormon) founded, 1830
- Robert Peary and Matthew Henson reached the North Pole, 1909
- U.S. declared war on Germany, entering World War I, 1917

7
- **William Wordsworth** born 1770

8
- Ponce de León claimed Florida for Spain, 1513

9
- **Charles Steinmetz** born 1865
- First tax-supported public library in America founded by people of Peterborough, New Hampshire, 1833
- General Robert E. Lee surrendered the army of Northern Virginia to General Ulysses S. Grant, ending U.S. Civil War, 1865

10 • **Matthew C. Perry** born 1794
• **Joseph Pulitzer** born 1847
• London and Plymouth companies chartered by King James I of England, 1606

11 • **Charles Evans Hughes** born 1862
• Napoleon I abdicated, 1814

12 • **Henry Clay** born 1777
• U.S. Civil War began at Fort Sumter, 1861
• Salk polio vaccine declared effective, 1955
• Soviet Major Yuri Gagarin orbited the earth, 1961
• U.S. space shuttle Columbia launched, 1981

13 • **Thomas Jefferson** born 1743
• Edict of Nantes freed the French Huguenots, 1598
• Metropolitan Museum of Art founded in New York City, 1870

14 • First edition of Noah Webster's dictionary published, 1828
• Abraham Lincoln assassinated, 1865
• *Pan American Day*

15 • **Leonardo da Vinci** born 1452
• **Henry James** born 1843
• The ocean liner *Titanic* sank, 1912

16 • **Wilbur Wright** born 1867
• **Charlie Chaplin** born 1889
• Queen's birthday in Denmark

17 • **Nikita Khrushchev** born 1894
• National holiday in Kampuchea
• Evacuation Day in Syria

18 • **Clarence Darrow** born 1857
• Paul Revere's ride, 1775
• Great earthquake and fire, San Francisco, 1906
• Independence Day in Zimbabwe

19 • The American Revolutionary War began in Lexington, Massachusetts, 1775
• Republic Day in Sierra Leone

20 • **Adolf Hitler** born 1889
• U.S. abandoned the gold standard, 1933

21 • **Charlotte Brontë** born 1816
• **Elizabeth II** born 1926
• Legendary founding of Rome, 753 B.C.
• Spanish-American War began, 1898
• *San Jacinto Day* in Texas

22 • **Immanuel Kant** born 1724
• **Vladimir Lenin** born 1870
• Oklahoma Territory opened to settlers, 1889
• *Arbor Day* in Nebraska

23 • **William Shakespeare** born 1564
• **Joseph M. W. Turner** born 1775
• **James Buchanan** born 1791
• **Stephen A. Douglas** born 1813
• **Sergei Prokofiev** born 1891
• **Lester Pearson** born 1897

24 • U.S. Library of Congress established, 1800

25 • **Oliver Cromwell** born 1599
• **Guglielmo Marconi** born 1874

26 • **John James Audubon** born 1785
• **Eugène Delacroix** born 1798
• An explosion and resulting meltdown at the Chernobyl nuclear plant near Kiev, Ukraine, led to the worst crisis in the history of commercial atomic power, 1986
• Union Day in Tanzania

27 • **Samuel F. B. Morse** born 1791
• **Ulysses S. Grant** born 1822
• National holiday in Afghanistan; Togo

28 • **James Monroe** born 1758
• Maryland became the 7th state, 1788
• Mutiny on the British ship *Bounty,* 1789

29 • Emperor's birthday in Japan

30 • George Washington inaugurated as first president of the U.S., 1789
• Louisiana Purchase, 1803
• Louisiana became the 18th state, 1812
• War in Vietnam ended, 1975
• Queen's Day in the Netherlands
• King's birthday in Sweden

Second or Third Sunday in April: *National Library Week* begins. **First Sunday in April:** Daylight Savings Time begins for much of the U.S. **Third Monday in April:** *Patriots' Day* in Maine and Massachusetts. **Third Friday in April:** *Arbor Day* in many states. **Holidays or holy days that may occur in either April or March:** *Palm Sunday; Holy Week and Easter; Passover.* **In April or May:** Independence Day in Israel.

The calendar listing identifies people who were born on the indicated day in boldface type, **like this.** You will find a biography of each of these birthday people in *The New Book of Knowledge.* In addition to citing some historical events and historical firsts, the calendar also lists the holidays and some of the festivals celebrated in the United States. These holidays are printed in italic type, *like this.* See the article HOLIDAYS for more information.

Many holidays and festivals of nations around the world are included in the calendar as well. When the term "national holiday" is used, it means that the nation celebrates an important patriotic event on that day—in most cases the winning of independence. Consult *The New Book of Knowledge* article on the individual nation for further information on its national holiday.

AQUACULTURE

Aquaculture is the raising of fish and other animals and plants in controlled water environments. Most often these organisms are raised for food, but they also can be raised for scientific or industrial purposes or for recreational use, such as sport fishing.

Many kinds of animals and plants are raised successfully through aquaculture. Fish, especially carp, trout, salmon, and catfish, are the most important crops. About 10 percent of the world's supply of fish is produced through aquaculture. Shellfish, such as clams, mussels, oysters, and shrimp, are an important part of the industry. Octopuses, squid, pearl oysters, and seaweed, which is used for food in many Asian cultures, also are raised through aquaculture.

Aquaculture can take place in tanks on land or in artificial or natural bodies of water. Depending on the species, or kind, of organism being raised, salt water, fresh water, or brackish (somewhat salty) water is used. Sometimes flooded lands, such as rice paddies or coastal wetlands, serve as aquaculture pens. Aquaculture is even possible in open water, such as rivers or ocean coastlines, if the plants or animals can be confined with nets or cages.

There are many advantages to raising animals and plants in this manner. Each harvest is predictable, which is an improvement over traditional fishing methods. The quality of the animals and plants can be controlled through diet, breeding programs, and the use of medicines. In addition, crop productivity can be improved because the organisms are more easily protected from predators and contamination by pollutants.

Aquaculture is a rapidly expanding industry. China, which has a long history of aquaculture, is the leading producer of aquatic products. However, many countries contribute to the world's commercial harvests, including the United States, Norway, Japan, Thailand, and Ecuador. As the supplies of fish and shellfish from the world's oceans decrease, the aquaculture industry is destined to gain in importance as a way of supplying the world's growing population with food.

BARBARA WIESE
Science Writer

See also FISH FARMING; FISHING INDUSTRY.

AQUARIUMS

If you like watching all different kinds of fish and want an opportunity to see a variety of water-dwelling animals and plants, you will enjoy visiting an aquarium. Aquariums are zoos for fish and other aquatic animals. Like other zoos, aquariums re-create as natural an environment as they can for their animals, some of which they collect from the wild. Aquariums educate the public about the animals and the environments they come from. They also run breeding programs for endangered species of fish and marine mammals and help people understand why it is important to reduce pollution in our oceans and keep our waterways clean.

Aquariums, such as this swim-through aquarium, offer visitors a unique opportunity—a close-up view of the hidden life that exists under the water's surface.

Some aquariums contain only small tanks of fish, with just one or a few species in each tank. Other aquariums include huge tanks that re-create entire environments. **Oceanariums** are large, often outdoor, pools where marine mammals and fish are kept. Such pools may hold more than a million gallons of water. Some aquariums that are built along the edge of the ocean have turned the seashore into an exhibit.

Many people work together at an aquarium. **Aquarists**, people who maintain the aquarium, collect fish and other aquatic creatures for the aquariums and help feed and

Vancouver Public Aquarium

AQUARIUMS OF THE WORLD

Aquarium of the Americas (New Orleans, Louisiana). It features fish and other animals from North and South America and re-creates an Amazonian rain forest, a Caribbean coral reef, a Gulf coast community (including a barnacle-encrusted oil rig platform), and the Mississippi River bottom.

Genoa Aquarium (Genoa, Italy). Built on a pier that juts out into the Mediterranean Sea, the Genoa Aquarium helps educate visitors about the rich natural world of this now polluted body of water and inspires people to help restore it.

John G. Shedd Aquarium (Chicago, Illinois). Opened in 1930, the Shedd Aquarium is the largest indoor aquarium in North America.

Monterey Bay Aquarium (Monterey, California). Focusing on the marine life of Monterey Bay, the aquarium highlights the richness of one of the world's most diverse habitats, or environments.

National Aquarium in Baltimore (Baltimore, Maryland). This aquarium features not just fish and marine mammals but a live rain forest with birds, amphibians, and reptiles.

Nausicaa (Boulogne sur Mer, France). Visitors can experience what it would be like to be caught in a fishing net with hundreds of fish and learn about aquaculture—how people farm the seas.

New England Aquarium (Boston, Massachusetts). Built in 1969, the New England Aquarium was the first aquarium to try to give visitors the sense that they are underwater with the fish.

New York Aquarium (Brooklyn, New York). Penguins, walruses, seals, sea lions, and sea otters frolic together in the rocky coast habitat of the oldest aquarium in America.

Osaka Ring of Fire Aquarium (Osaka, Japan). Visitors descend through seven stories of exhibits as they explore nine different habitats of the Pacific Ocean.

Port of Nagoya Public Aquarium (Nagoya, Japan). Fish from around the world are displayed in exhibits that make visitors feel as if they are descending the depths in a submarine, exploring the Antarctic coast, or snorkeling through a coral reef.

Sydney Aquarium at Darling Harbor (Sydney, Australia). The aquatic habitats in and around Australia are features at this aquarium. Part of the aquarium floats on barges in Sydney's harbor, making up the largest floating aquarium in the world.

Vancouver Public Aquarium (British Columbia, Canada). A long-time leader in innovative exhibits and educational programs, this aquarium was the first to show salmon spawning.

Monterey Bay Aquarium

care for the animals in the collection. Biologists study the animals, help design and maintain healthy environments for them, and, in some cases, coordinate breeding programs with other aquariums and zoos. Veterinarians treat any animals that have contracted diseases. Electricians and plumbers help maintain the aquarium's pumps and water filters. Exhibit designers create appealing displays, and educators help people identify and understand the different types of animals in the aquarium. With the help of the aquarium staff, we get a glimpse of a variety of fascinating underwater worlds that otherwise would remain largely invisible to us.

ELIZABETH KAPLAN
Series Coauthor, *Ask Isaac Asimov*

See also FISH; FISH AS PETS.

AQUINAS, SAINT THOMAS (1225?–1274)

Saint Thomas Aquinas was one of the great religious thinkers of the Middle Ages and had a powerful influence on his time. Yet as a student, his silence in the classroom and his heavy build earned him the nickname of "dumb ox." His fellow students and professors soon discovered, however, that he was not stupid, but rather a deeply intelligent, although humble, man.

Thomas was born in the castle of Rocca Secca near Aquino, Italy. His father was Landulf, Count of Aquino, and his mother was Theodora, Countess of Teano. When he was 5, he was taken to the abbey of Monte Cassino for his schooling. He stayed there until he was about 13 and later studied at the University of Naples for five years.

When Thomas was about 19, he joined the Dominican order, despite the objections of his family. He was eventually allowed to complete his studies in Paris and Cologne under Albertus Magnus, the most renowned professor in the Dominican order.

Thomas himself became famous as a teacher, winning admiration for the clarity and power of his thought. He developed a philosophy that combined Christian beliefs with the teachings of the Greek philosopher Aristotle.

About 1266, Thomas began writing his most famous work, the *Summa theologica*, a scientifically arranged study of theological teaching and Christian philosophy. He never finished it. On December 6, 1273, he experienced such a spiritual revelation at Mass that he could write no more. The revelation made all his writings appear as nothing to him.

Thomas died on March 7, 1274. He was made a saint in 1323 and a doctor of the Church in 1567. His writings fill 20 thick volumes and include much on Aristotle.

HARRY J. CARGAS
Editor, *The Queen's Work*

AQUINO, CORAZON C. (1933–)

Corazon Aquino served as president of the Philippines from 1986 to 1992. The widow of Benigno Aquino, Jr., a Filipino political leader assassinated by his opponents, she led a "People Power" revolution, in 1986, to overthrow President Ferdinand Marcos, who had held office since 1965. She campaigned to replace his government with one based on "justice, morality, decency, freedom, and democracy."

Corazon Cojuangco Aquino was born in Manila on January 25, 1933, the fourth of the six children of Jose Cojuangco and Demetria Sumulong. As a young woman she attended the College of Mount St. Vincent in the United States. In 1953 she married Aquino, a journalist and politician. They had five children.

Benigno Aquino rose quickly in politics. When in 1973 it appeared that he could win the Philippine presidential election, Marcos declared martial law and put his popular rival in jail. In 1980, Aquino was permitted to go to the United States for medical treatment, and Corazon accompanied him.

In 1983, Benigno Aquino was shot and killed when he returned to the Philippines. Many people held Marcos responsible for his death. Corazon, a housewife with no political experience, returned to the Philippines to lead the opposition movement against Marcos in her husband's place. In 1985, more than 1 million Filipinos petitioned her to run for president.

Marcos appeared to be the victor in the election of February 7, 1986, but many charged that he had tried to fix the election. With the support of the military, Aquino led the people in a campaign of nonviolent resistance and forced Marcos to resign.

When Aquino took office, she established a newly elected Congress, called for a new constitution, freed Marcos' political prisoners, and restored the people's civil liberties.

Aquino's new administration faced many serious challenges: Rivals tried to overthrow her government, and Communist rebels threatened the new democracy. Aquino was also faced with reviving the economy, which had suffered after years of corruption under Marcos. In 1992, Aquino was succeeded as president by her former defense minister, Fidel V. Ramos.

ISABELO T. CRISOSTOMO
Author, *Cory: Profile of a President*

ARABIA. See MIDDLE EAST; SAUDI ARABIA.

ARABIAN NIGHTS

Hundreds of years ago professional storytellers in India and the Middle East made up the stories now known as *The Arabian Nights*. Later on, groups of these stories were put together. One group was translated from Arabic to French by Antoine Galland in the early 1700's. His *Mille et une nuits,* or *A Thousand and One Nights,* introduced these Oriental tales to the Western world.

All the collections have one thing in common. A heroine, Scheherazade, tells the different stories. She recites the tales for a very good reason: She must save her life.

Scheherazade was married to Sultan Shahriyar, who had killed his first wife when she was unfaithful to him and then all his later wives in revenge against women. Scheherazade did not want to suffer the same fate. On her wedding night she began to tell her husband a story and stopped just before she reached the end. The Sultan allowed her to live another day in order to hear the end of her tale. The next night she finished the story and began another one even more fascinating than the first. Again she stopped before the ending, gaining another day of life.

And so it went, for a thousand and one nights. Finally the Sultan realized that Scheherazade was a good and faithful wife, and the couple lived happily ever after.

The stories supposedly told by Scheherazade are understandably popular. Nowhere does one find treasures more magnificent, beasts more fabulous, or magicians more cunning. Excerpts from two of the best-known stories follow.

In **Aladdin and the Wonderful Lamp** a magician poses as a long-lost uncle to the unsuspecting Aladdin. The two leave the city and arrive at a secret place, where the magician kindles a fire, throws powder on it, and says some magic words. The earth trembles and opens, revealing a flat stone with a brass ring to raise it by. With the help of more magic words, the stone is moved and steps appear.

"Go down," said the magician. "At the foot of those steps you will find an open door leading into three large halls. Tuck up your gown and go through them without touching anything, or you will die instantly. These halls lead into a garden of fine fruit trees. Walk on till you come to a niche in a terrace where stands a lighted lamp. Pour out the oil it contains and bring it to me." He drew a ring from his finger and gave it to Aladdin, bidding him prosper.

Aladdin found everything as the magician had said, gathered some fruit off the trees and, having got the lamp, arrived at the mouth of the cave.

The magician cried out in a great hurry, "Make haste and give me the lamp." This Aladdin refused to do until he was out of the cave. The magician flew into a terrible passion, and throwing some more powder on the fire, he said something, and the stone rolled back into its place.

The magician left Persia forever, which plainly showed that he was no uncle of Aladdin's, but a cunning sorcerer who had read in his magic books of a wonderful lamp which would make him the most powerful man in the world. Though he alone knew where to find it, he could only receive it from the hand of another. He had picked out the foolish Aladdin for this purpose, intending to get the lamp and kill him afterward.

For two days Aladdin remained in the dark, crying and lamenting. At last he clasped his hands in prayer, and in so doing rubbed the ring, which the magician had forgotten to take from him.

Immediately an enormous and frightful genie rose out of the earth, saying, "What wouldst thou with me? I am the slave of the ring and will obey thee in all things."

Aladdin fearlessly replied, "Deliver me from this place," whereupon the earth opened, and he found himself outside. As soon as his eyes could bear the light he went home, but fainted on the threshold. When he came to himself he told his mother what had passed, and showed her the lamp and the fruits he had gathered in the garden, which were in reality precious stones. He then asked for some food.

"Alas, child," she said, "I have nothing in the house, but I have spun a little cotton and will go and sell it."

Aladdin bade her keep her cotton, for he would sell the lamp instead. As it was very dirty she began to rub it, that it might fetch a higher price. Instantly a hideous genie appeared and asked what she would have.

She fainted away, but Aladdin, snatching the lamp, said boldly, "Fetch me something to eat!"

The genie returned with a silver bowl, twelve silver plates containing rich meats, two silver cups, and a bottle of wine.

Another *Arabian Nights* favorite is **The Forty Thieves**. The hero, Ali Baba, is a poor woodcutter. Here is how he finds out what the forty thieves are up to.

One day, when Ali Baba was in the forest, he saw a troop of men on horseback, coming toward him in a cloud of dust. He was afraid they were robbers and climbed into a tree for safety. When they came up to him and dismounted, he counted forty of them. They unbridled their horses and tied them to trees.

The finest man among them, whom Ali Baba took to be their captain, went a little way among some bushes and said, "Open, Sesame!" so plainly that Ali Baba heard him. A door opened in the rocks and, having made the troop go in, he followed them and the door shut again of itself.

They stayed some time inside and Ali Baba, fearing they might come out and catch him, was forced to sit patiently in the tree. At last the door opened again and the forty thieves came out. As the captain went in last he came out first, and made them all pass by him; he then closed the door, saying, "Shut, Sesame!" Every man bridled his horse and mounted, the captain put himself at their head, and they returned as they came.

Then Ali Baba climbed down and went to the door concealed among the bushes and said, "Open, Sesame!" and it flew open. Ali Baba, who expected a dull, dismal place, was greatly surprised to find it large and well lighted, and hollowed by the hand of man in the form of a vault, which received the light from an opening in the ceiling. He saw rich bales of merchandise—silk stuffs, brocades, all piled together, gold and silver in heaps, and money in leather purses. He went in and the door shut behind him. He did not look at the silver but brought out as many bags of gold as he thought his asses, which were browsing outside, could carry, loaded them with the bags, and hid it all with fagots. Using the words, "Shut, Sesame!" he closed the door and went home.

Reviewed by CAROLYN W. FIELD
The Free Library of Philadelphia

ARABIC LITERATURE

“Arabic literature” means literature written in the Arabic language. Today, Arabic is the primary language of the Arab countries of North Africa and the Middle East. (See the following article, ARABS, for a list of these countries). All people whose native language is Arabic are considered Arabs, regardless of their religion.

In early times, Arabic was the language of Muslims, followers of the Islamic faith, who lived in a much broader geographical area than today's Arab world. (See the article ISLAM in Volume I.) The Koran (Quran), the sacred text of Islam, is written in Arabic and is regarded as the highest model of beautiful Arabic style.

With the spread of Islam in the 600's, Arabic became a major world language. During this period, people of many different ethnic origins used Arabic as their literary language, even if they spoke Persian, Turkish, or another language as their native tongue. Classical Arabic literature was composed in courts and kingdoms from northern India in the east to Spain in the west.

The content of the Koran has also influenced Arabic literature, just as the Bible has influenced the literature of the Western world. For example, the stories of Joseph, Solomon the Wise, and other biblical figures who also appear in the Koran came to be used as symbols in classical and modern Arabic literature.

Arabic literature has influenced other literatures and has been influenced by them in turn. One example of this cultural exchange is *Kalila and Dimna*, a collection of fables featuring animal characters. Originally written in Sanskrit, the story was later translated into Old Persian (Pahlavi). In the 700's it was translated into Arabic and became one of the first works of Arabic prose literature. Five hundred years later, *Kalila and Dimna* was translated into Spanish and became one of the earliest works of Spanish literature.

Arabs are very proud of the beauty of their language and regard literature, and poetry in particular, as one of the highest achievements of Arab culture.

EARLY POETRY

The earliest form of Arabic literature is a kind of long oral poem called *qasida*, which developed in the 400's and 500's. During this period, poets were highly respected members of their tribes. They would compose, memorize, and recite long poems that chronicled the victories of their tribes, described desert life, and recounted sad love stories.

Poetry was first written down during the Umayyad dynasty (661–750). Poems were still performed aloud, however, and often set to music and sung. During the Abbasid dynasty (750–1258), considered the high point of medieval Arabic and Islamic culture, outstanding poetry was written. This classical poetry dealt with such themes as the glory of the king, hunting, mysticism, victories in battle, and wine. People still read these early *qasidas* today.

ADAB

Today the Arabic word *adab* means “literature,” but during the Abbasid dynasty it meant “refinement.” It referred to prose writing that educated and refined readers by pro-

Top left: **A portrait of a scribe from an Arabic manuscript written in 1287.** ***Below:*** **An illustrated page from the** ***Book of Animals*****, a famous example of** ***adab*****.**

An elaborately decorated page from a Moroccan Koran of the 1800's. The Koran is regarded as a model of Arabic literary style.

viding information about the world around them. *Adab* included essays and book-length works on such topics as language and style, the history of various peoples and nations, scientific subjects, intellectual and philosophical questions, and human nature.

FICTION

Throughout early and medieval times, educated Arab people did not take a great interest in fiction. Most fiction took the form of epic poems and stories, which were passed down orally from generation to generation by professional storytellers, who performed them on special occasions. Because the tradition of oral performance is dying out, these stories survive today mainly in written form.

The most famous work of Arabic fiction around the world is the *Thousand and One Nights*, also known in English as the *Arabian Nights*. This work features fantastic tales about all kinds of people and creatures, including the magic spirits called genies (a name that comes from the Arabic word *jinn*). *Thousand and One Nights* originated with a small collection of stories written in Persian and translated into Arabic in the 800's. Over the centuries many storytellers contributed to its development and expansion into the large work it is today. After it was translated into English and French in the 1700's, it became well-known among Western readers and has inspired such popular works as the animated Disney film *Aladdin* (1993). Excerpts from two of the best-known tales are given in the preceding article, ARABIAN NIGHTS.

MODERN LITERATURE

The 1800's saw a revival of classical Arabic literature, which helped bring about a modern Arabic literature. Arabs in present-day Syria and Lebanon, many of whom were Christian, took a renewed interest in the tradition of Arabic literature and created a neoclassical school of poetry. In Egypt, writers revived forms of medieval prose, which contributed to the later development of the novel and short story. Khalil Gibran, a Lebanese Christian who immigrated to the United States, belonged to a school of writers called the emigré writers. These writers left Lebanon and Syria to live abroad in the United States and South America, but they maintained their Arab ties and contributed to both American and Arabic literature.

Poetry remains an important form of literature in contemporary Arab society. The forms of poetry have changed over the centuries, and much modern poetry is composed in free (unrhymed) verse. Its main subjects are love and social and political topics. Although modern poetry looks and sounds quite different from its ancient counterpart, modern poets still consider classical poetry an important part of their tradition.

In addition to poetry, modern Arabic literature includes three forms of fiction used in Western literature: the short story, the novel, and drama. Of these, the novel and the short story are the most popular. The Egyptian writer Naguib Mahfouz, who won the Nobel Prize for literature in 1988, is considered by many to be the father of the modern Arabic novel. Other popular writers include short story writers Yousef Idris, an Egyptian, and Ghassan Kanafani, a Palestinian; novelists Abd al-Rahman Munif from Saudi Arabia and Tayeb Saleh from Sudan; Syrian poets Adonis and Nizar Qabbani; and Egyptian playwright Tawfiq al-Hakim. Works by these and many other authors have been translated into English.

For many years, France controlled the countries of Morocco, Algeria, and Tunisia, building schools that taught French rather than Arabic. Today some Arab authors from these countries write in French rather than Arabic. The Moroccan writer Taher Ben Jelloun is among the North African Arab writers who have won distinguished literary prizes in France.

KRISTEN E. BRUSTAD
Emory University

Originally nomads of the desert, most Arabs today live in cities such as Cairo (*left*). The capital of Egypt and the most populous city in the Arab world, Cairo was founded in the A.D. 900's by Arab conquerors. Only a relatively few Arabs, such as these Bedouins in Qatar (*below*), still follow the nomadic way of life, traveling over age-old routes, seeking pasture and water for their livestock.

ARABS

The name "Arab" refers to the peoples who speak Arabic as their native language. The Arabs originated in the deserts of what is now Saudi Arabia, which occupies most of the vast Arabian Peninsula. However, the impression that Arabs are still people of the desert—that is, Bedouins or nomads—is inaccurate. Most Arabs today are city dwellers. Nomads make up less than 5 percent of the Arab population, which numbers nearly 220 million.

▶ THE ARAB WORLD

Geographically, the Arab world stretches across North Africa and includes most of the countries of the Middle East, except for Iran, Turkey, Israel, and Cyprus. The nations of the Arab world are Algeria, Bahrain, Comoros, Djibouti, Egypt, Iraq, Jordan, Kuwait, Lebanon, Libya, Mauritania, Morocco, Oman, Qatar, Saudi Arabia, Somalia, Sudan, Syria, Tunisia, the United Arab Emirates, and Yemen.

In addition, about 2.7 million Palestinian Arabs live on the West Bank of the Jordan River and in the Gaza Strip, territories occupied by Israel since the 1967 Arab-Israeli War. Nearly 1 million Arabs live in Israel itself. Arabs have also emigrated to many parts of the world. It has been estimated that in the United States there are about 3 million Americans of Arab origin.

The Arabs are a diverse people, but there are basic elements that link most of them. The most important of these are the Islamic religion and the Arabic language, and the culture and history associated with them.

Religion. Most Arabs are Muslims, or followers of Islam. There are also many Christian Arabs, particularly in Egypt, Lebanon, and Syria and among the Palestinians. In Lebanon, Christians of various denominations make up approximately 30 percent of the population.

Islam originated in the Arabian Peninsula more than 1,300 years ago. It spread rapidly through much of Asia and Africa, so that today some of the largest Muslim countries and communities are outside the Arab world.

Islam, whether Arab or non-Arab, has two major branches—Sunni and Shi'ite. Sunni is the larger branch and most Arabs are Sunnites. However, Shi'ites are a majority in Iraq and make up the single largest religious community in Lebanon. Bahrain's population is

An Arab girl and her brother (*left*) study the Koran (Qur'an), the sacred book of Islam, the religion of Muslims. Islam originated in the Arabian Peninsula in the 600's and spread to much of Asia and Africa. A miniature painting of the 1200's (*right*) depicts a caravan of Arab pilgrims on the way to Mecca, the holiest city of Islam. If they are able to do so, Muslims are expected to make at least one pilgrimage (*hajj*) to Mecca (in Saudi Arabia) in a lifetime.

about 70 percent Shi'ite, while some other small Persian Gulf states have important Shi'ite minorities.

For more information, see the article ISLAM in Volume I.

The Arabic Language. Arabic belongs to the Semitic group of languages, which also includes Hebrew. The languages of Arabs and Jews are thus closely related. More broadly, Arabic is a part of the Hamito-Semitic family, which can be traced back to ancient Egyptian and includes some languages of Ethiopia.

Arabic developed among the Bedouins. Its growth was greatly encouraged by a tradition of poetry that was highly elaborate in its spoken form before being written down. With the emergence of Islam in the A.D. 600's, the Koran (Qur'an), the sacred book of Islam, became the model for the future use of the language. It was the one text that all Arab (and later all non-Arab) Muslims learned. Educated Muslims memorized the Koran completely, and it became the standard for classical Arabic.

As the Koran accompanied the Arab conquests, its message and style spread across the Islamic world. Although variations in the spoken language developed, all Arabs share a common written language. Arabs also can communicate orally by speaking the same Arabic used for writing.

See ARABIC LITERATURE preceding this article, and the article KORAN in Volume JK.

ARAB HISTORY AND CIVILIZATION

References to Arabs as nomads and camel herders of northern Arabia appear in writings dating back to the 800's B.C. The name was later applied to all inhabitants of the Arabian Peninsula.

Arabs were then a tribal society. They were grouped together according to family heritage, tracing their origins back to a common ancestor. But tribal society in the Arabian Peninsula was always fragmented because of the harsh desert conditions. Tribes broke up into smaller clans, which roamed the desert, stopping at oases (fertile areas) and wells for food and water. No great Arab state appeared until the coming of Islam.

Islam originated in the city of Mecca, in what is now western Saudi Arabia. Mecca was the birthplace of Mohammed (or Muhammad), one of history's most important figures. Born about A.D. 570, he is considered the prophet of Islam. Mohammed preached a monotheistic religion (belief in one God) like that of Jews and Christians. When opposed by the people of Mecca, he fled to Medina, to the north. This journey occurred in A.D. 622, which became known as the year of **Hegira**, or "migration." Later, it was made the first year of the Islamic calendar. Today, Mecca and Medina are Islam's two holiest cities.

See the article MOHAMMED in Volume M.

The Spread of Islam. At the time of Mohammed's death in 632, Mecca and most of the tribes of the Arabian Peninsula had accepted Islam. A century later an Islamic empire, under Arab leadership, ranged from Spain across North Africa and most of the present-day Middle East to Central Asia and northern India. Spain, conquered by Arabs from North Africa in 711, was the center of a great Arab-Islamic civilization, with major contributions by Jews, until the end of the 1400's.

Islam was the motivating force behind this conquest, but non-Muslims were not forcibly converted to Islam. Different religions were tolerated. Christians and Jews were permitted to practice their faiths as long as special taxes were paid to Muslim rulers.

The Caliphates. The Muslim rulers who came after Mohammed were known as caliphs. There were two great caliphates or dynasties of Arab origin—the Umayyad and the Abbasid. Umayyad rule lasted from 661 to 750 and was centered in Damascus (the present capital of Syria). The Abbasids ruled between 750 and 1258 from their capital of Baghdad (the modern-day capital of Iraq).

Arab Achievements. Islamic civilization, including both Arab and Persian (Iranian) influences, flourished under the Abbasids. Its accomplishments included advances in literature, philosophy, agriculture, and medicine. Greek philosophy, including the works of Plato and Aristotle, was translated into Arabic as well. The translations passed, by way of Muslim Spain and Sicily, to European Christian scholars, thus preserving one of the great heritages of Western civilization. Islamic medical texts were used in Europe until the 1600's.

Arab scholars also made important contributions in mathematics. What we call Arabic numerals (the symbols we use for our numbers) actually originated in India and were modified by the Arabs. But Muslim mathematicians invented algebra, which comes from the Arabic *al-jabr*.

The Arabs also developed a distinctive style of art and architecture. See the article ISLAMIC ART AND ARCHITECTURE in Volume I for information on this subject.

Arab Decline. At the height of its power, the Abbasid Caliphate was immensely wealthy, dominating trade between Europe and Asia. But the collapse of the dynasty in 1258 meant the end of Arab leadership of the Islamic world. Its later rulers were the Ottoman Turks, whose empire, centered in Constantinople (present-day Istanbul), included most of the Arab lands.

As the Ottoman Empire itself declined in the 1800's, many of the Arab lands were taken over as colonies by European powers. By the start of World War I in 1914, all of

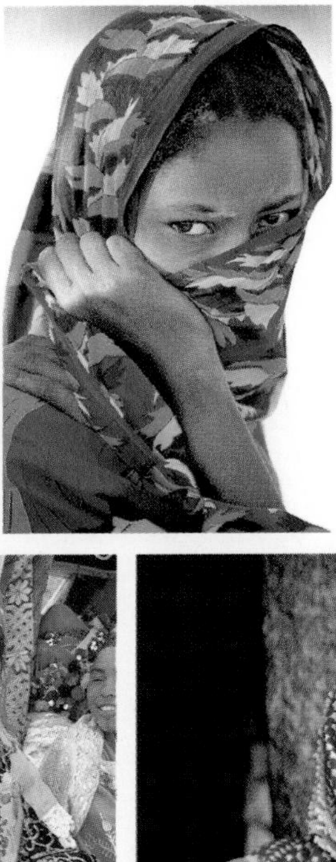

The Arabs are a diverse people, but there are basic elements that link most of them. These include the religion of Islam (although some Arabs are Christians), the Arabic language, and the culture and history associated with both. The many faces of the Arab world include a Somalian woman (*left*), a group of Egyptian men (*far left*), a group of Moroccan women (*below left*), and a Jordanian man (*below*). Although some Arabs wear western-style clothing, others wear traditional garments and head coverings.

North Africa was under European control. Algeria, Tunisia, and Morocco were ruled by France; Libya was an Italian colony; and Egypt was dominated by Britain. Even though most of the Arab territories were under some form of Turkish or European domination, people in these lands were inspired by a feeling of nationalism and began to identify themselves as Arabs. By 1918, when the war ended, what was left of the Ottoman Empire had fallen apart.

At the 1919 peace conference, Britain and France were awarded the remaining Arab lands, with the understanding that they would foster the development of the peoples of these regions toward self-government. Syria and Lebanon went to France, and Iraq and Palestine went to Britain.

Palestine represented a special case. During World War I, British officials had suggested to Arab leaders that Palestine would be included in areas to be granted Arab self-determination. The British then promised Palestine to leaders of the Zionist movement, which called for a Jewish state in Palestine. The origin of the Arab-Israeli conflict lies in

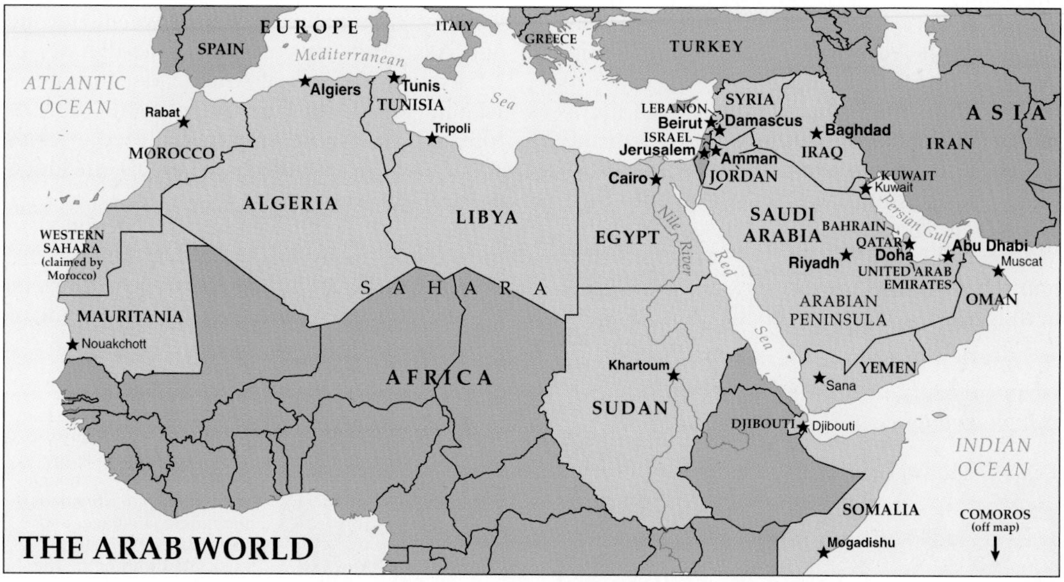

The landscape of the Arab world is as varied as its people. An Iraqi farmer (*below*) plows a fertile area in the upper valley of the Tigris and Euphrates rivers. By contrast, most of the Arabian Peninsula (*right*) is made up of desert.

the history of these conflicting promises as well as Palestinian Arab opposition to Jewish claims in the region.

See the article PALESTINE in Volume P and the one on Zionism in Volume WXYZ.

Recent History. Most of the Arab lands won their independence in stages after World War II ended in 1945. Some did so peacefully, others after a struggle. The creation of the Jewish state of Israel in part of Palestine in 1948 set off hostilities that led to five Arab-Israeli wars—in 1948, 1956, 1967, 1973, and 1982. The conflict continues today inside Israel, particularly over the claims of the Palestinian Arabs to their own state in the West Bank and Gaza, under the Palestine Liberation Organization (PLO). The PLO, which most Palestinian Arabs look to for leadership, is an organization of various Palestinian groups that is dedicated to freeing Palestine from what they claim is an illegal Israeli state.

In addition to Arab-Israeli hostility, there have been clashes between Arab regimes or within the countries themselves because of territorial ambitions or ideological differences. The civil war that wracked Lebanon from the mid-1970's to late 1990 reflected the struggle for political power between different religious communities.

Iraq's invasion of Kuwait in 1990 was caused by its desire to gain more shoreline on the Persian Gulf as well as control of Kuwait's vast oil reserves. The quick defeat of Iraq in a short war in 1991, by a coalition led by the United States, ended this threat, but the long-term results of the war still remain to be seen.

Workers drill for offshore oil in the Red Sea. Oil is the most valuable resource in the Arab world, with the largest deposits found in Saudi Arabia.

In 2001, a group of extremists from the Arab world launched suicide attacks that destroyed the World Trade Center in New York City and damaged the Pentagon in Washington, D.C. Most of the nations in the Arab world denounced these crimes and promised their cooperation in helping the United States bring the criminals to justice. Along with their fellow citizens, most Arab-Americans were shocked and saddened by these events.

ARAB COUNTRIES TODAY

Arab countries today vary greatly in economic development. Agricultural productivity is high in Arab lands, but good farmland is often scarce because of a limited water supply. Population growth, which is considered too high in countries such as Egypt, is another important factor in the future of the Arab world. Except for oil, most have little in the way of natural resources. Saudi Arabia and the small Persian Gulf states, once home only to small numbers of nomadic peoples, now have incredible wealth due to oil. At the same time, countries with rich historical pasts—Egypt, for example—are poor today. This disparity has led educated people from the poorer Arab nations to seek work in the wealthy Persian Gulf states. It has also bred resentment among some of the poorer countries.

In spite of these and other differences, the Arabs are united by many things. In addition to a common written language and values rooted largely in Islam, Arabs also have a shared history. This includes both greatness under past Muslim dynasties and, more recently, forced submission to foreign rulers.

Traditional Arab cultural values have always strongly stressed family ties and unity, which can be important in forming political factions. Such relationships have become less common in the large cities, where the growth of modern professions has created new political and economic alliances.

CHARLES D. SMITH
San Diego State University
Author, *Islam and the Search for Social Order in Modern Egypt*

Reviewed by JOHN E. WOODS
Center for Middle Eastern Studies
University of Chicago

See also ISRAEL; MIDDLE EAST; and articles on the individual Arab countries.

Each kind of arachnid has special traits. The scorpion (*far left*) gives birth to live young, the spider (*left*) produces silk, and the tick (*above*, before and after feeding) lives on other animals.

ARACHNIDS

Arachnids are very small, typically land-dwelling animals that belong to the class Arachnida. Arachnids are members of a larger group of animals called arthropods, which include insects, crabs, and other invertebrates with segmented bodies.

Among the approximately 74,000 species of arachnids, the best known are spiders, scorpions, mites, ticks, and daddy longlegs. Arachnids range in size from mites that are only 1/250 inch (0.1 millimeter) long to scorpions that can reach 7 inches (18 centimeters) in length. Most, however, are less than 1 inch (2.5 centimeters) long.

In their basic appearance, arachnids resemble insects. Both arachnids and insects have segmented bodies, jointed legs, and a tough, hard outer covering, or **exoskeleton**. Under close examination, however, the two groups are seen to be quite different. While insects have three main body parts, wings, six legs, compound eyes, and antennae, arachnids have two main body regions, eight legs, simple eyes, and two pairs of limbs that are modified for grasping, biting, and touching. Unlike insects, they do not have wings or antennae.

Each kind of arachnid has distinguishing characteristics that set it apart from the others. **Spiders** possess venom glands and inject venom into their prey through fangs on their jaws. They also have abdominal glands that produce silk, which is used for special tasks such as capturing prey, courting a mate, and forming a sac for their eggs. Because spiders consume large amounts of insects, they are important biological-control agents.

Scorpions are easily recognized by their tapered bodies and their large size. Clawlike appendages alongside the jaw are used to seize prey. With the prey in its grasp, the scorpion whips its tail, which is tipped with a venomous stinger, forward and over the back to deliver an injection of toxic venom. Among the larger arachnids, scorpions are unusual because rather than laying eggs, they give birth to living young.

Mites and **ticks** are the smallest arachnids. Their bodies are saclike and appear to have only a single region. The feeding habits of mites and ticks vary. Ticks are parasitic; that is, they live on other creatures and are harmful to them in the process. Mites can be parasites as well as plant eaters, predators, and scavengers. Both ticks and mites can be harmful to people. Ticks can carry serious diseases, such as Rocky Mountain spotted fever and Lyme disease. Plant-eating mites are major agricultural pests, while other mites are human and animal pests. The common dust mite is thought to be a trigger of asthma. Some mites also carry disease.

Daddy longlegs, or **harvestmen**, are named for their extremely long, slender legs. When attacked by a predator, a daddy longlegs can shed a leg to avoid capture. A new leg will regrow at the next molt, when the daddy longlegs sheds its skin. Many species have an additional defense—they have glands that produce secretions disagreeable enough to discourage predators. Most species of daddy longlegs are scavengers, feeding on dead insects and fallen fruit.

MAY R. BERENBAUM
Department of Entomology
University of Illinois

See also SCORPIONS; SPIDERS; TICKS.

ARAFAT, YASIR (1929–)

Yasir Arafat has been the head of the Palestinian National Authority (PNA), the governing authority over Arabs in Palestine, since 1996. His goal has been to establish an independent Arab state in the West Bank and the Gaza Strip, two areas of Palestine that are effectively under the control of Israel.

Arafat was born on August 24, 1929, either in Jerusalem or in Cairo, Egypt. After graduating with a degree in civil engineering from Cairo University, Arafat became involved in politics. In 1956 he helped found Al-Fatah, an anti-Israeli guerrilla group that made its first attacks on Israel in 1965.

In 1969, Arafat was elected chairman of the Palestine Liberation Organization (PLO), a loose union of guerrilla groups fighting for the establishment of a Palestinian state.

Arafat's goal seemed within reach in 1993. On September 13, Israel and the PLO signed an interim peace accord. For this accomplishment, Arafat and Israeli leaders Yitzhak Rabin and Shimon Peres shared the 1994 Nobel Peace Prize. But peace was still far away.

In 2000 a failed attempt by Arafat, Israeli prime minister Ehud Barak, and U.S. president Bill Clinton to reach a final peace agreement led to an uprising by Palestinian militants and suicide bombings aimed at Israeli civilians. This prompted a tough crackdown by Israel. Chances for a Palestinian state seemed further reduced when Ariel Sharon, who considered Arafat a terrorist, was elected Israeli prime minister in 2001.

After Sharon broke off all ties with Arafat in late 2001, Arafat appealed to the Palestinians for calm. But militant attacks continued, leading the Israelis to surround Arafat's headquarters in the West Bank city of Ramallah, keeping Arafat a virtual prisoner. Arafat was released in May 2002, but his authority was weakened. In 2003, the Palestinian legislature created a position for a prime minister, making it possible to renew peace negotiations.

Reviewed by DANIEL GOURÉ
Vice President, The Lexington Institute

ARBITRATION

When people, companies, or even nations have disputes with one another, they have choices about what to do. Parties who disagree usually work things out by bargaining with each other (**negotiation**). If that does not work they may go to court (**litigation**). But sometimes there is no court that can take the case, or court proceedings would take too long. In that event the parties may decide to pick a third person (or small group of people) to decide what the outcome should be. This is **arbitration**. The person picked to settle the argument is called an arbitrator.

Sometimes parties ask an arbitrator to decide their case just by looking at arguments and evidence they submit on paper. More likely, they will want to question witnesses in front of the arbitrator, in a **hearing**, which is like a trial, although usually much less formal. Once the hearing is over and the parties have had a chance to explain their arguments, the arbitrator will issue a decision, called an **award**. If necessary, courts will enforce awards. More than 130 nations have signed the United Nations Convention on the Recognition and Enforcement of Foreign Arbitral Awards.

In major league baseball and hockey, some players each year are eligible for **salary arbitration**. When a team and player cannot agree on what that player's salary should be for the next season, each tells the arbitrator what their last offer was, and why. In baseball, the arbitrator has to pick one figure or the other. In hockey, the teams and players have agreed to let the arbitrator pick any figure between what the club offered and what the player asked for.

ROBERT N. COVINGTON
Professor of Law
Vanderbilt University Law School

ARBOR DAY. See HOLIDAYS.

ARBUS, DIANE. See PHOTOGRAPHY (Great Photographers).

ARCHAEOLOGY

Imagine trying to learn about the lives of your ancestors from a fork, a piece of an alarm clock, a bone from a pot roast, or an automobile hubcap. It would be impossible to create a complete picture from so few pieces, but this is what archaeologists try to do. Archaeologists learn as much as they can about people who lived long ago by studying **artifacts**—tools, weapons, and other objects those people left behind.

Archaeology is the study of ancient human behavior. The word "archaeology" comes from the Greek words *archaios*, which means "ancient," and *logos*, which means "word." Archaeology is a branch of anthropology, the study of people and their cultures. Archaeology includes human paleontology (or paleoanthropology), the study of ancient human fossils.

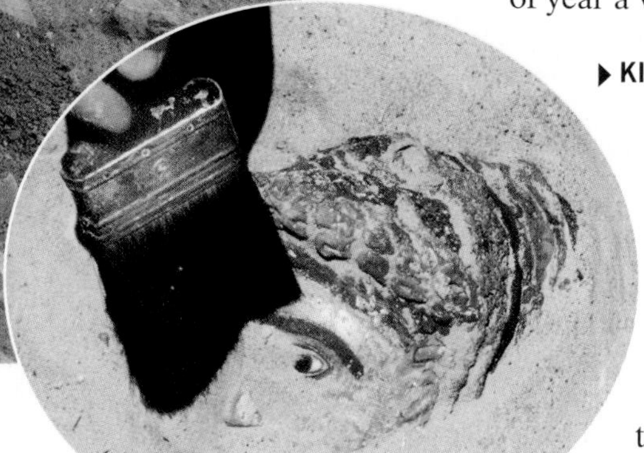

Archaeologists conduct careful and systematic excavations to uncover ancient artifacts and bones. From their discoveries, they piece together fragments of the past to learn how people lived long ago.

To determine how ancient people lived, archaeologists try to establish what events happened in the past, as well as when, where, and why they happened. They look to answer specific questions, such as, Why did humans begin making stone tools? When did humans develop agriculture and domesticate animals? Did a particular group of people survive by hunting, gathering plants, or by farming? Another very important part of archaeology is the preservation of archaeological sites for future generations, an activity known as **cultural resource management** (CRM) in North America and as **heritage management** elsewhere.

Archaeology is a complex science that relies on careful research, planning, excavation, and documentation, as well as sophisticated technology. A modern archaeologist can determine the direction of the wind on the day of an ancient hunt, the precise location a stone spear point came from, or what time of year a village was occupied.

▸ KINDS OF ARCHAEOLOGISTS

Archaeology is such a vast and complicated field that it would be very difficult for an archaeologist to be an expert in every area of study. Most archaeologists specialize in studying a specific region of the world or a specific time period.

Archaeologists who focus on a particular region include **Egyptologists**, who specialize in ancient Egyptian civilization; **Mayanists**, who study the ancient Maya civilization in Central America; **biblical archaeologists**, who study the societies of the eastern Mediterranean lands mentioned in the Old and New Testaments of the Bible; and **classical archaeologists**, who study the ancient Greek and Roman civilizations. Archaeologists who focus on a particular period of history include **prehistorians**, who study prehistoric times—from the first appearance of human beings more than 3 million years ago to the development of writing (and thus written records) about 5,000 years ago; and **industrial archaeologists**, who investigate sites dating from the Industrial Age—from the Industrial Revolution in the late 1700's through today.

Other kinds of archaeologists include **zooarchaeologists**, who are experts on the bones of ancient animals; **historical archaeologists**, who use written records as well as archaeological research to reconstruct the past; and **underwater archaeologists**, who examine shipwrecks, sunken ports, and other archaeological sites on the bottoms of lakes, rivers, and oceans. There are also specialists in ancient plant remains, prehistoric fishing, the manufacture of pottery and stone tools, the environments of the past, and many other aspects of the ancient world.

INVESTIGATING THE PAST

Properly studying evidence of people who lived long ago is a painstaking process involving many steps. A site must be chosen and accurately surveyed; if excavation is necessary, it must be carried out carefully and systematically. Artifacts and other items recovered during the excavation must be properly labeled and cataloged and then must be analyzed in a laboratory to discover exactly what they are and what information they can provide about the site and the people who once lived there.

Choosing and Surveying a Site

Archaeological sites are everywhere. Some are very prominent and have been known for a long time, such as Stonehenge in England; the Temple of Athena on the Parthenon in Athens, Greece; and the great city of Teotihuacán in Mexico. Other sites are not so obvious, sometimes consisting of little more than a handful of discarded stone tools or broken clay pot fragments.

Some archaeological sites are discovered by accident, such as during highway construction, quarrying, and other activities. For instance, excavation for a subway in Mexico City revealed many traces of the Aztec civilization. Nature also uncovers archaeological sites, such as when an earthquake formed Olduvai Gorge in East Africa 100,000 years ago. The gorge cuts through the bed of an ancient lake, around which early

GREAT DISCOVERIES IN ARCHAEOLOGY

The Rosetta Stone

The Rosetta Stone was discovered in 1799 by a French army officer building fortifications at the city of Rosetta in northern Egypt. The stone dated from 196 B.C. and contained text praising the Egyptian king Ptolemy V Epiphanes. The Rosetta Stone was unique and of great historic value because it provided the same text written in three different scripts—Egyptian hieroglyphs, demotic (a later, cursive form of Egyptian writing), and Greek. At the time, the meaning of Egyptian hieroglyphic writing was unknown. By comparing the hieroglyphs to the Greek text, French scholar Jean François Champollion deciphered the mysterious symbols in 1822. This allowed modern scientists to read the ancient Egyptian texts for the first time.

Because it contains the same text written in three different scripts, the Rosetta Stone was the key to deciphering Egyptian hieroglyphic writing.

GREAT DISCOVERIES IN ARCHAEOLOGY

The Tomb of Tutankhamen

Tutankhamen was a minor ruler of ancient Egypt. He was born about 1357 B.C., assumed the throne when he was about 9 years old, and had an unremarkable reign until his death in 1339 B.C. When his tomb was discovered in 1922 in Egypt's Valley of the Kings by British archaeologist Howard Carter, it became the most famous archaeological discovery ever made. What made the tomb so significant was that it had survived thousands of years relatively intact.

Every pharaoh's tomb found before had been looted by robbers long ago. Tutankhamen's tomb had also been robbed twice in ancient times, but very little was taken. When discovered, the tomb held a vast collection of artifacts, including disassembled chariots, animal-shaped couches, numerous chests, jewelry of many shapes and sizes, containers of preserved food, jars of wine and oils, games, and many religious items. The tomb also contained the mummy of Tutankhamen, which was enclosed in a solid gold coffin and adorned with jewelry and a magnificent gold mask inlaid with colored glass, stone, and ceramic.

The tomb of Tutankhamen was discovered virtually intact in 1922. In addition to a dazzling collection of artifacts, it contained the mummy of the pharaoh.

humans lived about 2 million years ago. However, archaeologists find most sites with a deliberate search, or survey.

Aerial and satellite photography are important tools in discovering sites that may not be recognizable from the ground, such as ancient travel routes or the widely scattered remains of a settlement. For instance, airborne radar was used to detect the remains of swamp gardens built by the Maya, gardens once so fertile they produced two harvests or more a year.

Once a site has been identified, fieldworkers can pinpoint its location using the Global Positioning System, or GPS—a network of orbiting satellites that continually transmit signals to all points on Earth. Using a GPS receiver, fieldworkers can determine the exact longitude, latitude, and altitude of the site. This information, along with data about the site's soil composition, terrain, and rainfall, can then be fed into a geographic information system (GIS). This computer system allows archaeologists to

Aerial photography is helpful in locating archaeological sites that may not be recognizable on the ground, such as this serpent-shaped mound in Ohio.

Ground-penetrating radar allows archaeologists to study the size, shape, and location of buried objects before they excavate a site.

compare a particular site with others nearby, as well as to analyze how the local environment may have affected where ancient people decided to establish their settlements.

Excavation

Excavation is a destructive process. Even when using the most careful methods and the most delicate tools, the act of excavation often destroys a site's historical importance. Sometimes the only evidence of a site after it is excavated are the artifacts found, the notes taken, and any report published by the archaeologists afterward. Because of this, archaeologists avoid digging unless it is absolutely necessary. They use devices such as ground-penetrating radar, which bounces sound waves off buried objects to create accurate images of their shape and location, to study what lies below the surface of a site before it is disturbed by excavation.

Once the decision to excavate has been made, the archaeologist develops a plan for the dig (such as where to begin and what tools to use). This plan establishes the best ways to discover the age of the site, how many different societies occupied it and for how long, and how the lives of the site's inhabitants changed over the centuries. The archaeologist often works with a team, which includes experts from other sciences. Geologists study a site's layers of soil and rocks to determine how it formed, zooarchaeologists examine animal bones to reconstruct ancient hunting and herding practices, and botanists study minute fossils of plant pollen to determine the kind of vegetation that existed at the site long ago.

Many archaeologists make a distinction between vertical and horizontal excavation. **Vertical excavation** involves digging small trenches straight down from the surface to sample any remains left by a site's inhabitants. **Horizontal excavation** (also called area excavation) is used to uncover much larger areas, such as entire villages, the foundations of a palace, or a network of streets.

GREAT DISCOVERIES IN ARCHAEOLOGY

The Royal Burials of Ur

In 1922, British archaeologist Leonard Woolley began excavations at the ancient Sumerian city of Ur in present-day southern Iraq. There he discovered the remains of a tiny village, which appeared to be the original settlement around which the city—and the entire Sumerian civilization—arose. In the remains of the village, Woolley found spectacular royal burials, particularly one belonging to a prince who died about 2100 B.C. The prince was buried, wearing an elaborate headdress, necklaces, rings, and other fine jewelry, in a stone chamber at the bottom of a huge pit. His body was surrounded by those of his attendants, who had been sacrificed for the burial. Also in the pit was a pair of oxen, which had been buried pulling a wooden wagon. Woolley's excavations provided the most detailed and complete portrait of the Sumerians, who established the earliest known civilization.

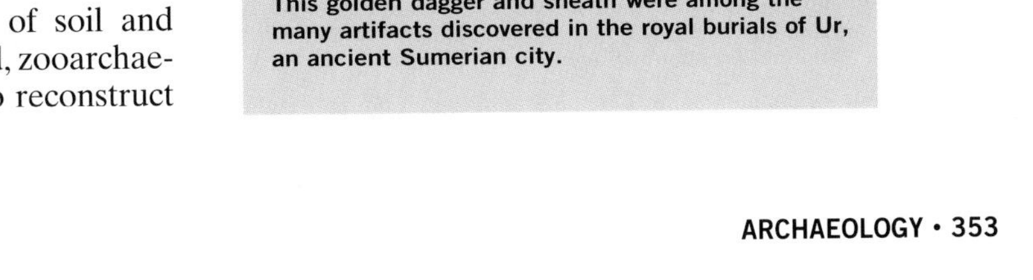

This golden dagger and sheath were among the many artifacts discovered in the royal burials of Ur, an ancient Sumerian city.

GREAT DISCOVERIES IN ARCHAEOLOGY

The Lords of Sipán

In the late 1980's, Peruvian archaeologist Walter Alva faced down desperate and potentially dangerous looters to excavate a burial site inside a pyramid at Sipán, Peru. The burial consisted of mud brick chambers that contained the bodies of two lords and a warrior-priest of the Moche civilization. Their bodies were placed inside wooden coffins and adorned with golden masks, crescent-shaped golden headdresses, ornate breastplates made of shells and copper beads, and tunics covered with small gold plaques. Included in the burials were the bodies of sacrificial victims, both men and women, and hundreds of clay pots. Before this time, very little was known about the Moche, who flourished along Peru's north coast from about 200 B.C. until A.D. 700. Alva's excavation was remarkable not only for its detailed reconstruction of the tombs' contents but also for its preservation of a site on the verge of complete destruction at the hands of looters.

A burial site within a pyramid at Sipán, Peru, containing three richly adorned bodies, narrowly escaped looting. Its excavation revealed important information about an ancient civilization.

A vital part of excavation is the recording of a site's layers of occupation and the items that are found in each. This layering occurs when people live at the same location over many centuries, building new settlements on top of the ruins of previous ones. The lowest layer of occupation is the earliest one, and each layer above that is slightly later. The study of this sequence of successive layers, or strata, at a site is called **stratigraphy**.

Artifacts and other remains can vary considerably from one layer to the next, and their differences reflect changes in the societies that left them. A gradual change indicates a culture's regular, natural development over time, while a sudden change in the style or material used to make artifacts could indicate the presence of an entirely new culture in the area. The clusters of artifacts and other remains in relation to one another can reveal much about ancient activities. For example, a concentration of charcoal lying near a pile of partially burned animal bones may be evidence of cooking, or a bundle of copper wire, tongs, and hammers may represent the remains of a workshop for making wire bracelets.

The actual digging of a site is done either by student volunteers or paid laborers. Mechanical excavators are used to remove large areas of soil, but most excavation is done with picks and shovels, or often just small trowels and brushes.

The excavation team passes all soil through fine screens to recover small objects such as beads or tiny bones. Sometimes the soil is passed through a machine that rinses it with water before catching any artifacts in thin meshed screens.

As the dig progresses, every detail of the site is documented with photographs and drawings, including detailed plans of any structures and their contents. Where possible, electronic surveying devices are used to pinpoint the location of objects found within the site. Such thorough records are very important because they represent the permanent record of a site now destroyed. Detailed site notebooks provide a complete record of the excavation as it unfolds.

Other team members process any artifacts that are found. They clean, sort, and label each piece, then pack them in special bags or containers. The site's laboratory workers also keep detailed records of each artifact, and describe, draw, or photograph exceptionally important finds.

Once the excavation is complete, the excavators carefully refill their trenches and return the site to as close to its original state as possible. Conserving artifacts and sites is just as important as the knowledge obtained from them.

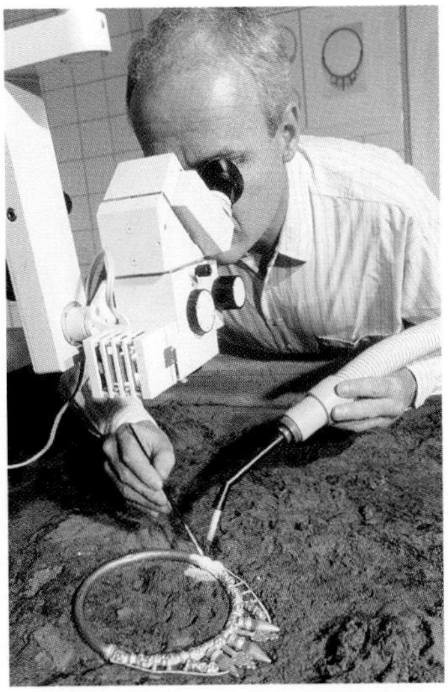

Using a brush, a suction device, and a high-powered microscope, an archaeologist brings an ancient gold necklace back to its original state.

Laboratory Work

Archaeologists spend more time in the laboratory than in the field. In the laboratory, each object found at a site is analyzed to reveal as much information as possible about the past.

The first step in analyzing archaeological objects is to classify them according to similar characteristics. In **typology** classification, objects are organized according to their appearance, the material they are made from, or their function. In **seriation** classification, objects of one type are organized in a series to show how their characteristics changed over time. For instance, pottery found at various levels of a site may be grouped according to the type of clay used to make them. The pieces of one type are then arranged from the oldest, simplest examples with no decoration to the later, delicate pieces with sophisticated decoration.

The objects are then examined by experts, using many different kinds of tools, and compared with objects found at other sites. By studying the distribution of similar artifacts over a wide area, archaeologists can sometimes trace ancient trade routes where stone was exchanged over long distances. Spectrographs, devices that measure the wavelengths of light given off by a mineral when it is heated, can reveal the chemical elements in a stone tool, which may indicate where the stone came from. High-powered microscopes can reveal if the subtle wear patterns on the working edge of the same stone tool were caused by scraping skins, working leather, or butchering animals. In recent years, scientists have made remarkable advances in the microscopic study of the powdery residues found in ancient wine jars from Egypt and the eastern Mediterranean, leading to new insights into ancient wine trade.

Botanists examine remains of plant life, such as charred seeds from abandoned hearths or impressions of grain left in pottery fragments. Such remains help build a picture of an area's vegetation in the past. They can also shed light on how human activity affected the landscape. For instance, plant remains at the early farming village of Abu Hureyra on the Euphrates River in Syria led botanist Gordon Hillman to discover that droughts had killed nut-bearing trees in the region after 10,500 B.C. This forced the villagers to turn to wild grasses for food and then eventually to plant and harvest their own crops.

Ancient bones and bone fragments are extremely delicate. They must be cleaned, sorted, and labeled with great care.

Zooarchaeologists piece together bone fragments like a jigsaw puzzle, identifying the animals hunted and eaten by the inhabitants of a site and learning about the butchering methods used to process the carcasses. Zooarchaeologists also study the remains of domesticated animals to determine the ages at which animals were slaughtered and how herds were managed. Specialist zooarchaeologists may be called in to offer their expertise on the remains of birds or fish.

Once all the items retrieved are analyzed, the archaeologist writes a complete report on the site. The report covers everything from

Animal bones can shed light on the behavior of ancient peoples. Marks on this elephant leg bone may have been made by primitive stone tools used to butcher the animal.

GREAT DISCOVERIES IN ARCHAEOLOGY

The Terra-Cotta Army of Shi Huangdi

In 1974, farmers in the Chinese town of Xi'an were digging a new well when they came upon the remains of a large pottery figure. Archaeological excavation at the site led to the discovery of an army of more than 7,000 life-size terra-cotta soldiers and horses guarding the tomb of Shi Huangdi, China's first emperor, who died in 210 B.C.

The soldiers and horses were buried in three long pits lined with timber and were arranged in ranks as if marching into battle. The soldiers included cavalrymen, infantrymen, and archers carrying weapons such as axes, crossbows, spears, and swords. The figures were depicted wearing armor or tunics, and many had been given unique hairstyles. They had originally been painted in bright colors, but most of the colors had faded over time.

Although the terra-cotta army is one of the most unique and important archaeological finds of all time, the area around the site promises to reveal more treasures in the future. The actual tomb of Shi Huangdi lies nearby beneath a great burial mound which, according to legend, contains a miniature of the emperor's world: models of palaces, rivers represented by a network of flowing mercury, and a jewel-encrusted ceiling representing the stars of the night sky.

A vast army of life-size terra-cotta soldiers and horses guards the tomb of China's first emperor, Shi Huangdi.

the excavation methods used and layers of the site to its dating and the lives of the people who lived there. It is a portrait of ancient life, pieced together from hundreds of small fragments of evidence. Using the same evidence, the archaeologist also compares the site with others nearby and farther away to see if there are any similarities. Every settlement, however small, is part of a larger picture of the past.

Dating the Past. Written records chronicle the past only as far back as about 3200 B.C., and then only in Egypt and Mesopotamia (an ancient region in the Middle East). To date artifacts and events older than that, archaeologists rely on a variety of methods.

One of the simplest methods of dating sites and events is called **dendrochronology**, which uses the annual growth rings of trees. Tree rings grow wide or narrow, depending on each year's weather. Based on the comparison of bands of many trees, a master chart is made that shows the weather for each year in a particular region. When a piece of wood from an ancient site in the region is found, its pattern of bands can be matched against the master chart. In this way an archaeologist can tell when the wood was cut and first used. Ancient dwellings in the American Southwest have been dated with rings from their door and roof beams. Tree rings from European oaks provide an accurate timescale for dating wood from prehistoric sites as far back as 8000 B.C.

In 1949, the American chemist Willard Libby developed a method of dating the remains of organisms—people, animals, and plants—called **radiocarbon dating**. All living things absorb carbon-14 atoms, or radiocarbons, either from the atmosphere or in their food. When an organism dies, radiocarbon is no longer absorbed and the amount already absorbed begins to decay, or break down, at a regular rate. Knowing this rate of decay, archaeologists can measure the amount of radiocarbon in an old bone and determine how old it is. This method can date objects up to 50,000 years old.

Another method, **potassium argon dating**, is used to establish the age of volcanic rocks (formed from cooling lava) that are more than 100,000 years old. Potassium, found in most minerals, contains small amounts of radioactive atoms called potassium-40. Over time, some of the potassium-40 atoms decay into the gas argon-40, and this decay can be measured to establish the age of a volcanic rock and thus any artifacts in or around it. For more information on radiocarbon and potassium

GREAT DISCOVERIES IN ARCHAEOLOGY

The Iceman

In 1991, German mountain climbers high in the Italian Alps discovered the frozen corpse of a man who had lived more than 5,000 years ago. The body was so well preserved, or mummified, by ice and cold that it proved to be one of the greatest sources of information ever discovered about the Europeans who lived during the Neolithic, or late Stone, Age.

The discovery of the mummified "Iceman" in the Italian Alps provided a wealth of information about the Europeans of the late Stone Age.

Medical examinations of the Iceman, as he came to be called, determined he was about 40 years old at the time of his death and stood about 5 feet 2 inches (160 centimeters) tall. His right shoulder had been wounded by an arrow, and his right hand bore dagger wounds. His stomach was empty, indicating he died hungry, and his lungs were black from breathing the smoke of campfires. For clothing, the Iceman wore an outer coat of animal skins, a grass cape, and a hat and boots made from bear and deer skins. He had carried with him a leather backpack on a wooden frame, a flint dagger, a longbow of yew wood, and 14 arrows.

argon dating, see the article RADIOACTIVE DATING in Volume QR.

CAREERS IN ARCHAEOLOGY

Movies and television often portray archaeology as exciting and adventurous. In fact, it is a demanding science that requires years of study in school and long days of searching and excavating in the field.

An advanced academic degree is required for a career in archaeology. A master of arts (M.A.) degree is required to teach at a college or to become involved in cultural resource management. A doctorate (Ph.D.) is required for a research-based career. Courses are taken in subjects such as anthropology, geology, history, and biology. Many archaeologists also receive instruction in conservation methods as well as in the legal requirements for protecting and managing archaeological sites.

Further education is typically needed to become a specialist. A classical archaeologist studies art history, classical literature, and the Greek and Latin languages. An Egyptologist needs to be able to read Egyptian hieroglyphic writing.

Until recently, most archaeologists were employed by universities or museums and spent much of their time conducting excavations and field surveys or working in the laboratory. Today governments and large private companies employ large numbers of archaeologists to conserve, protect, and manage archaeological sites. But there are only a few thousand employment opportunities for archaeologists in the world, so it is quite hard to make a living at it. Many people follow archaeology as a hobby.

HISTORY OF ARCHAEOLOGY

Archaeology began during the Renaissance (1300–1600), with a renewed interest in the art and architecture of ancient Greece and Rome. In the 1700's, upper-class gentlemen in Great Britain and Europe began searching for artifacts, drawing famous monuments, and eventually conducting excava-

WOMEN IN ARCHAEOLOGY

Before 1900, archaeology was practiced mostly by men. Excavation was not considered a suitable activity for women, although some were permitted to work in laboratories. Despite the limitations put on them by society, several women made significant contributions in the early years of archaeology.

Gertrude Bell (1868–1926) of Great Britain was one of the first women to break through archaeology's all-male barrier. Self-taught and an experienced traveler in the Middle East, Bell conducted pioneering archaeological surveys at a variety of sites in Syria and Mesopotamia. After World War I (1914–18), she was named director of antiquities for the newly formed country of Iraq and drafted laws to prevent the export and destruction of the country's ancient relics.

Harriet Hawes (1871–1945) of the United States traveled to Greece in 1896 on a classical archaeology scholarship, but she was not permitted to work in the field. Arthur Evans, who had discovered the remains of the Minoan civilization on the island of Crete off Greece's southern shore, offered Hawes his support and encouraged her to work on the island. She was the first woman to lead an archaeological expedition in the region, directing the excavation of the ancient Minoan town of Gournia.

Gertrude Bell

Gertrude Caton-Thompson (1889–1985) of Great Britain was one of the most respected archaeologists to study the Stone Age (2,500,000–3000 B.C.). While still a student, Caton-Thompson began the first archaeological exploration of northern El Faiyûm, a region in Egypt rich in artifacts. In 1929, she excavated the great ruins of the Zimbabwe culture in southeastern Africa, and she later served as president of the British Prehistoric Society.

tions. These excavations, mainly of ancient burial mounds, were sloppy by today's standards. Records were not kept, artifacts from one layer were mixed with artifacts from other layers, and only objects such as those made of gold or ivory were considered valuable. Little thought was given to what could be learned from what was found.

When Napoleon Bonaparte's French army invaded Egypt in 1798, they brought scientists with them who studied many wonders of ancient Egyptian civilization, including the Great Sphinx and the pyramids of Giza. Their research was published and read around the world, sparking widespread interest in ancient Egypt and archaeology. By the 1800's, Egyptology had turned from tomb robbing to a science.

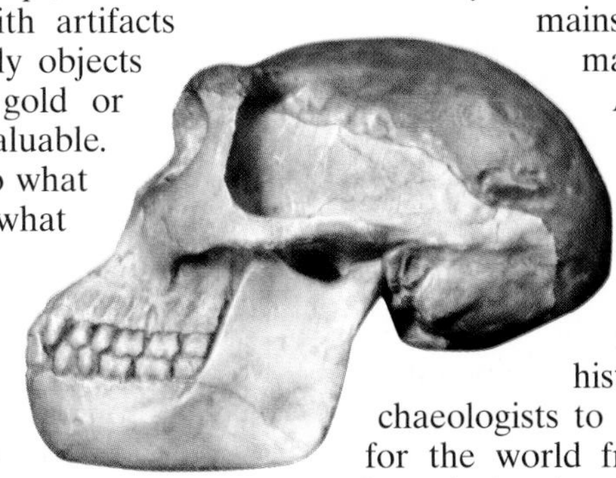

In the 1800's, discoveries of the fossilized bones of primitive humans, such as this *Homo erectus* skull, provided new clues about the age of humanity.

The 1800's

During the 1800's, archaeology continued to be practiced primarily by amateurs and adventurers who used crude methods of excavation and cared little for preserving sites.

Archaeological artifacts were first organized into unique categories in 1816 by the Danish museum curator Christian Jürgensen Thomsen. Thomsen arranged the archaeological collection of the National Museum in Copenhagen according to the Three Age System. In this system, artifacts were assigned to the Stone Age, the Bronze Age, or the Iron Age, according to their characteristics. Thomsen's Three Age System was widely accepted and proved valid by later excavations.

It was also during the 1800's that scientists began wondering about the age of humanity. Until this time, the biblical date for the origin of humankind—about 4000 B.C.—was widely accepted. However, excavations began revealing ancient stone tools and the bones of animals long extinct, suggesting that people and all other life on Earth were far older than previously thought. When Charles Darwin published his *Origin of Species* in 1859, his theories of evolution and natural selection provided a framework for the study of human origins.

By the end of the 1800's, skeletal remains of ancient, primitive humans had been found in Africa; evidence of the world's earliest writing and agriculture had been discovered in the Middle East; and the vast ruins of Maya cities were revealed in Central America. These historic discoveries allowed archaeologists to establish a rough time line for the world from the dawn of humans, through the rise of civilization, and to the fall of the last ancient cultures.

The 1900's

Archaeology became a true science during the 1900's, with strong ties to the study of history and the natural sciences. Systematic methods of excavation and accurate record-keeping were established. After the end of World War I (1918), aerial photography became a common tool for locating sites.

Until the 1960's, archaeologists were generally content to just describe artifacts and ancient societies. Since then, they have focused on explaining what they found. After the 1970's, concern grew about the destruction of archaeological sites due to war, looting, and simple neglect.

Archaeology Today

Modern-day archaeologists seek to manage and preserve sites for future generations with a minimum of excavation, while using increasingly sophisticated methods to explain and reconstruct the past.

In the future, archaeology will continue to focus on preserving the past by protecting sites and artifacts. Research will intensify in parts of the world where much of human history remains unknown, such as in China and Central and Southeast Asia. Every new discovery provides a clearer and more complete picture of ancient people and the world in which they lived.

BRIAN FAGAN
University of California, Santa Barbara

See also ANCIENT CIVILIZATIONS; ANTHROPOLOGY; AZTECS; MAYA; MUMMIES; PREHISTORIC PEOPLE; RADIOACTIVE DATING; UNDERWATER ARCHAEOLOGY.

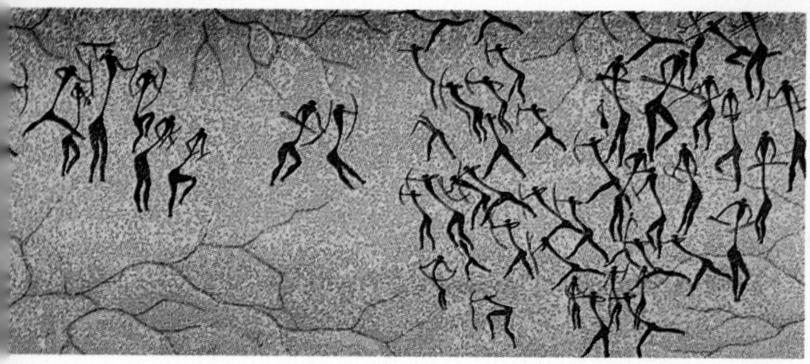

A photograph of the wall of a cave located in the central Sahara region of Africa shows a painting of what are thought to be people of the Stone Age hunting with bows and arrows.

ARCHERY

Ancient arrowheads found in North Africa suggest that bows and arrows were in use more than 50,000 years ago. Even though archaeologists (scientists who study how people lived in the past) have not been able to determine exactly how and when these arrowheads were first used, the early existence of archery and archery's importance to the survival of human beings have been documented in cave paintings that show people hunting with bows. For many centuries, bows and arrows were also used as weapons of war. They were such effective weapons that nations rose and fell because of them.

Today, archery—the activity of shooting with bows and arrows—is enjoyed primarily as a sport.

▸ EARLY BOWS AND ARROWS

The earliest known bows were made from whatever materials were available in a particular area. The wood from yew trees was often favored, but ash, willow, elm, aspen, pine, and other woods were also used. When wood was unavailable, bows were made from a combination of the horn, bone, tendon, or gut of animals.

An early bow called the longbow (far right) is still used by some archery enthusiasts.

Early archers may have shot only sharpened sticks from their bows. The first arrows were crafted from wood and other materials. Straight, well-seasoned wood that was free of knots was used to make the shafts. Arrowheads were carved from stone, flint, hardwood, and the horn, bone, or teeth of animals. They were made in different shapes, but the tip was always a sharp point.

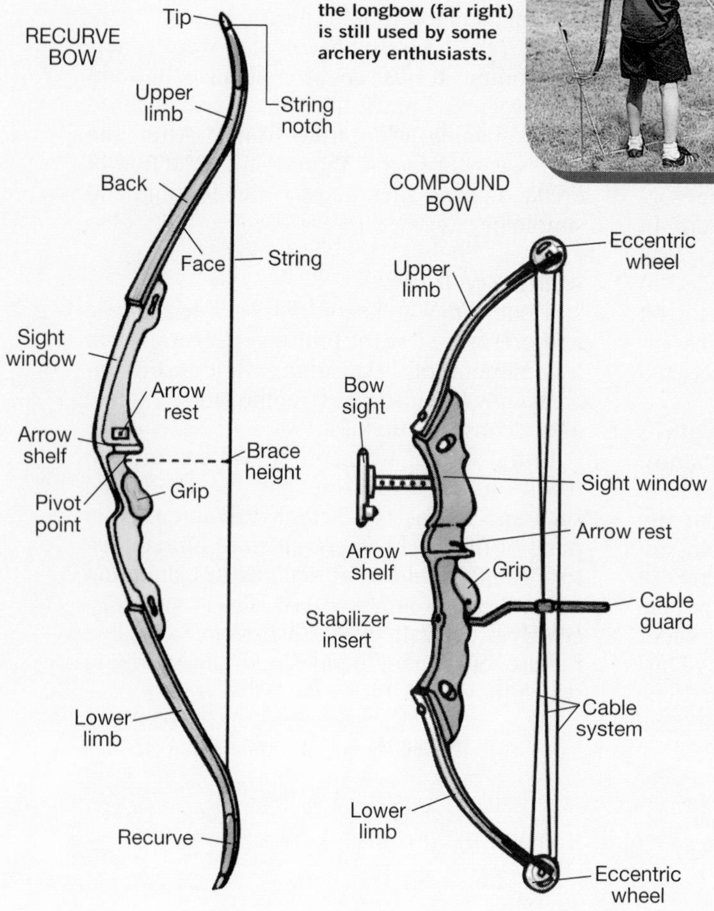

▸ MODERN ARCHERY EQUIPMENT

Today, most archers use either **recurve bows**, which have backward-bending limbs and are drawn (pulled back) with the fingers, or **compound bows**, which are drawn with a mechanical release. H. W. Allen filed for a patent on an early version of the compound bow on June 23, 1966. It uses a series of cables and pulleys that enables the archer to exert less energy while pulling the bow string back to aim. This innovation was welcomed by those who were fascinated with archery but lacked the strength to participate in the sport. The compound bow is viewed as a major factor in the growth of modern archery.

In recent years, new materials have enhanced the accuracy and durability of bows and arrows. The handle, or **riser**, of the bow is now made from a lightweight aluminum. The **limbs**, the parts of the bow that project beyond the handle, are made of laminated wood, fiberglass, or a combination of fiberglass and carbon.

Various accessories have helped to improve the performance and accuracy of bows. A mechanical release aid has become more popular than the shooting glove and **finger tab**, a piece of leather worn on the fingers to protect against string pressure. This mechanical aid is clamped onto the bow string and pulled back. The arrow is then released by squeezing a trigger similar to that of a gun. Accessories to increase accuracy include adjustable rests that aid in obtaining good arrow flight and sights that allow the archer to aim with precision.

Prior to the 1940's, arrows had been made primarily from wood. Arrow technology took a giant step forward in the early 1940's with the invention of the aluminum arrow, which is much lighter than an arrow made of wood or fiberglass. It is also more consistently straight. In the late 1980's, the use of carbon material made arrows even lighter and stronger.

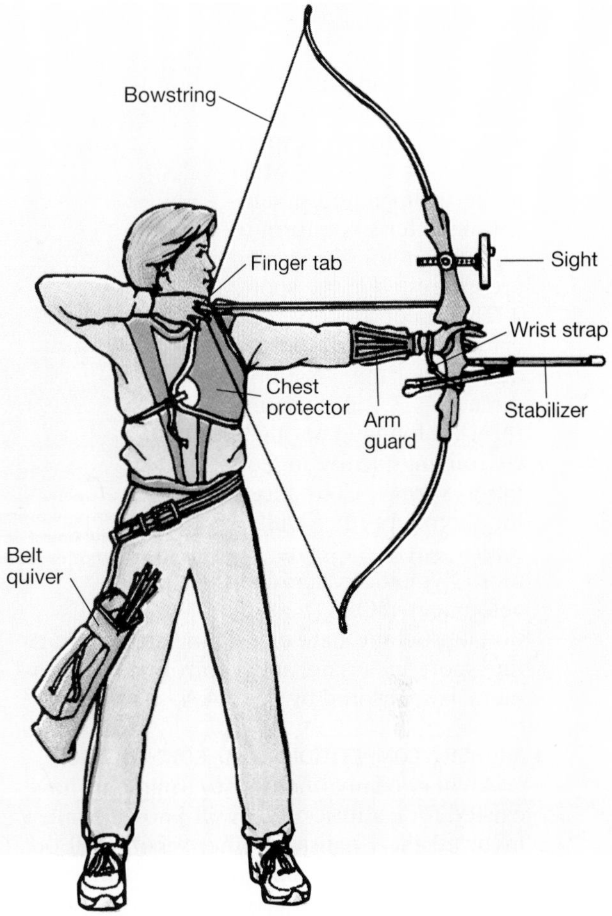

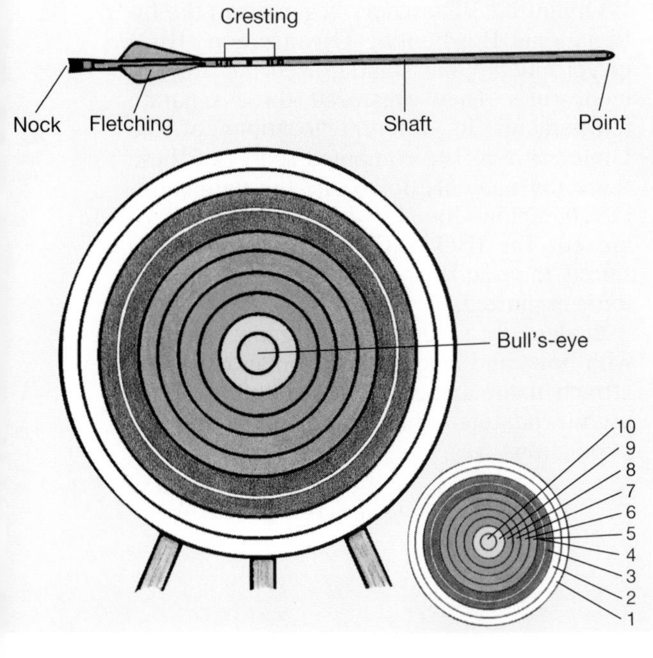

There are several arrow accessories. Special inserts are made to fit snugly inside an arrow shaft, which allows replaceable arrowheads to be threaded in and out of the shaft. The feathers on an arrow—called **fletching**—are made of turkey feathers or plastic. Fletching is glued to the back of the arrow shaft to help stabilize the arrow in flight. **Nocks** are U-shaped plastic notches that fit on the tail of the arrow and help hold it in place on the string of a bow. The place where the notch of the arrow fits on the bowstring is called the **nocking point**.

Such new equipment has captured the interest of many people. Yet traditional equipment still has a place in archery for those who wish to experience its earlier forms.

▶ LEARNING ARCHERY

Modern bows are powerful, and arrows can be very dangerous. It is important, therefore, for young archers to be supervised by an adult. In addition, all beginners should seek instruction from experienced archers. Most archery shops and organizations offer some form of instruction for those who are interested in the sport.

The major archery association in the United States is the National Archery Association (NAA), founded in 1879. Its training facility in Colorado Springs, Colorado, is the home of the United States Archery Team. Junior Olympic Archery Development (JOAD), a national program that helps young archers learn the sport in a safe and controlled environment, is sponsored by the NAA.

Target archery is a popular and very competitive sport. Competing archers practice long hours perfecting every aspect of their form, from setting up and aiming to shot execution.

ARCHERY COMPETITIONS AND BOWHUNTING

Archery competitions or tournaments have existed for centuries. One well-known contest involved the English folk hero Robin Hood. He beat England's champion archer by splitting his competitor's arrow with his own on the final shot of their contest. The term "Robin Hood" is still used on the tournament range today when an archer splits an arrow.

There are three forms of tournament archery today: Target, Field, and 3-D. Each has its own set of shooting rules and equipment guidelines. Men, women, and children of all ages can participate.

Target Archery. Target archery is the most familiar form of tournament archery. It takes place both indoors and outdoors. Indoors, the shooting distance is 20 yards (18 meters). Outdoors, the distance can vary from 33 to 99 yards (30 to 90 meters). The archery field is always flat and open. The bull's-eye targets, which have ten scoring rings, are set up at varying distances. The sizes of the target's scoring rings change depending upon the distance. Archers use either recurve bows or compound bows, and all archers compete against their peers.

Field Archery. Field archery can take place on varied terrain. Archers take four shots at each of 28 different bull's-eye targets. These targets are set at varying distances ranging from 20 feet (6 meters) to 80 yards (73 meters). Any type of archery equipment can be used. The archers in the competition are matched with one another according to age and equipment.

3-D Archery. 3-D archery closely simulates hunting with bows and arrows, and it takes place over a wide variety of terrain. Each competitor shoots one arrow per target over a 40-target course. The targets, set at distances that are unknown to the competitors, resemble game animals, and each one has scoring rings that represent vital parts of an animal's body. Bowhunters often enter these tournaments to improve their skill in estimating distances, shooting accurately, and performing under pressure.

Organized 3-D archery began when the International Bowhunting Organization (IBO) in Vermilion, Ohio, standardized 3-D tournament rules. They organized three separate tournaments in different locations of the United States. The combined scores of these three tournaments determine the national 3-D champion for 13 different classes of archers. The IBO National Triple Crown inspired thousands of other 3-D tournaments to be organized.

Bowhunting. Hunting for game animals with bows and arrows is a popular sport that attracts many archers. Some wildlife agencies use bowhunters to help them regulate animal populations.

JOHN SIELICKI
Professional Archer and Writer

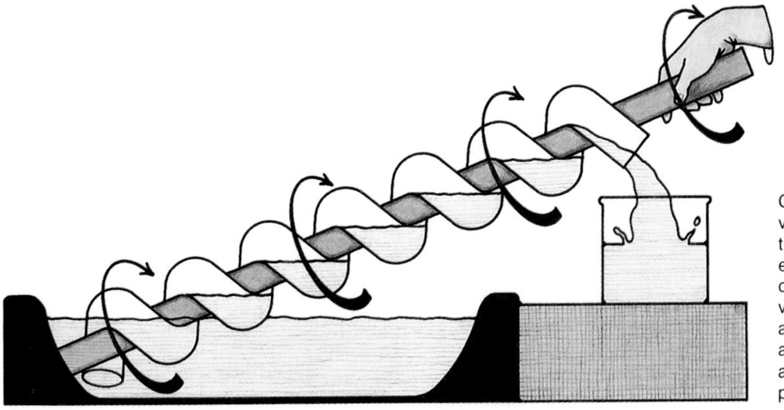

One of Archimedes' many clever inventions is the water screw. As it turns, water is scooped into the lower end and moves upward through the coils. You can make this simple device with a few feet of flexible tubing, a sturdy rod such as a broomstick, and some cloth tape to hold the top and bottom ends of the tubing in place.

ARCHIMEDES (287?–212 B.C.)

"Give me a place to stand, and I can move the world." The man who is supposed to have spoken those words was Archimedes, a Greek mathematician and inventor who lived some 2,200 years ago. It was not an idle boast. Archimedes was one of the first people to develop the science of mechanics. He understood that a person with a mechanical device such as a lever could move many times his or her own weight. Challenged by the king to prove his point, Archimedes did so. He arranged a device that allowed the king to move a large ship all by himself.

Archimedes was born about 287 B.C., in Syracuse, a Greek settlement on the island of Sicily. Little is known about his personal life except that his father was an astronomer and may have been related to the king of Syracuse. Also, at some time in his life, Archimedes studied in Alexandria, Egypt, a center of Greek culture.

Archimedes is best known for his many inventions. Among other things, he invented a compound pulley; a sphere that imitated the motions of the heavenly bodies; and a water screw to raise water. He himself most valued his work in mathematics and scientific theory. But his fame rests on inventions and the legends that grew up around him.

One legend tells how Archimedes made his most important discovery. The king, it seems, had ordered a new crown. It was supposed to be made of solid gold, but the king suspected the jeweler of cheating. He asked Archimedes to tell him if the crown was solid gold.

At first Archimedes could not think how to do this. Then one day the answer came to him as he was getting into his bath. Legend has it that he rushed naked into the streets shouting, "Eureka [I have found it]!"

What had happened was very simple. The bath was full, and it overflowed as Archimedes climbed into it. This started him thinking about the way objects displace water. And he suddenly saw how to solve his problem.

First he took a quantity of gold and a quantity of silver, each equal in weight to the crown. The weights of gold and silver were equal, but their volumes were not. The silver, being less dense, was bulkier than the gold.

Next Archimedes took two vessels filled to the brim with water. He placed the gold in one and the silver in the other. The silver, being bulkier, caused more water to overflow. Archimedes concluded that when a solid sinks in water, it displaces its own volume of water.

Finally he tested the crown against the equal weight of gold. When placed in water, the crown caused more overflow. Therefore, the crown had to contain metal other than gold. This metal made it bulkier and caused the greater overflow.

Further experiments resulted in what is now known as Archimedes' principle: An object in a fluid is buoyed up by a force equal to the weight of the displaced fluid.

When Archimedes was an old man, the Romans attacked Syracuse. He turned his creative mind to defense and invented several weapons that held off the enemy. It is claimed that he built a huge system of mirrors that burned Roman ships by concentrating the sun's rays on them. Syracuse, however, was defeated in 212 B.C., and Archimedes was killed. The story goes that he was drawing mathematical figures in the sand when a Roman soldier struck him down. But Archimedes was so highly respected that the Roman commander buried him with full honors.

JOHN S. BOWMAN
Author, *Prehistory and Early Civilization*

ARCHITECTURE

Architecture is the art and technology of building. But it is much more than that. Buildings reflect the beliefs, aspirations, and culture of the people who construct them. Over the centuries, most of the world's best-known buildings have been made for those with wealth and power—pharaohs, kings, popes, and, more recently, governments and corporations. Today, however, architectural historians also recognize the value of **vernacular architecture**—structures built by and for ordinary people.

Architects—those who design buildings—must be both artists and technicians. Buildings must be pleasing in appearance, but they also must meet practical requirements. They must be of sound construction, and they must be well suited to their function.

We know the history of architecture mainly through the structures themselves. Many buildings continue to stand today, including some that are thousands of years old. Other important structures have fallen or been torn down. They must be studied through written records or archaeological excavations. Architectural historians also study the lives and activities of the people who built the structures so that they can understand architecture in its context.

ARCHITECTURE OF THE ANCIENT WORLD

The first human settlements that consisted of structures more complex than caves or primitive wooden huts emerged about 6000 B.C. in the ancient Middle East. There, people settled in well-watered, fertile areas and began to farm. With permanent settlements came the need for permanent shelters. Archaeological excavations of ancient towns in present-day Jordan and Turkey provide some of the best evidence of these early agricultural settlements. Houses were made of mud bricks and timber frames. They were clustered together for stability and protection from invaders. Among the houses were shrines with colorfully painted walls decorated with bulls' heads and horns.

About 3000 B.C., the Sumerians, a people living in

The Parthenon, a Doric temple built during the 400's B.C., is one of the best examples of Greek temple architecture.

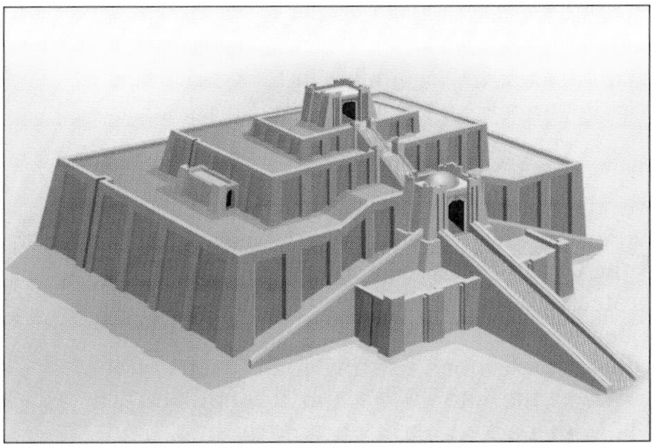

The stepped ziggurats of ancient Mesopotamia were built of sun-dried mud bricks and were topped with a temple or shrine used for religious rituals.

an ancient Middle Eastern region known as Mesopotamia, began building large cities. At the center of these cities were large temple compounds dominated by stepped structures called **ziggurats**, which were constructed out of sun-dried mud bricks. This style of architecture and city design was adopted by later Mesopotamian people, including the Akkadians and the Babylonians.

The Babylonians adorned their palaces with brightly colored glazed tiles. The Ishtar Gate, part of a fortified wall that surrounded the city of Babylon during the late 500's B.C., was covered with colorful tiles forming lively patterns and sculptures of animals that projected slightly from the flat background (a technique known as **low relief** or **bas relief**).

Egypt

The best-known examples of ancient architecture are the monumental pyramids and temples built by the ancient Egyptians, several of which have survived to the present day.

Pyramids. Until about 3100 B.C., the Egyptians buried their royalty under rectangular, mud brick structures with slanted sides and flat tops. These tombs, called **mastabas**, were often clustered together and housed the burials of entire royal families.

A new kind of tomb was developed during the 2600's B.C. by Imhotep, the first architect known to history. Built for King Zoser at the city of Saqqara, the tomb was essentially a series of mastabas stacked one on top of the other and decreasing in size from bottom to top. This was the earliest known pyramid and the first structure ever built with massive blocks of cut stone. Because each side of this pyramid resembled a series of steps, it came to be known as the Step Pyramid.

The Step Pyramid, in Egypt, is the earliest known pyramid. Its construction was overseen by Imhotep, the first architect known to history.

The three famous pyramids of Giza, built between 2660 and 2560 B.C., were constructed out of massive limestone blocks. The largest of the three pyramids measures 756 feet (230 meters) on each side and originally reached a height of 481 feet (147 meters). Its base covers 13 acres (5.2 hectares).

Later Egyptian pyramids were built of mud brick and only encased in stone. After about 1640 B.C., the Egyptians stopped building pyramids and turned to carving tombs in hillsides or valley floors. For more information, see the article PYRAMIDS in Volume P.

Temples. The ancient Egyptians also built many temples. Queen Hatshepsut's funerary temple at Deir el-Bahri, across the Nile River from Luxor, is one of the most magnificent temples still in existence. Carved into the side of a towering limestone cliff about 1470 B.C., it features a series of terraces supported by rows of columns, or **colonnades**, and connected by ramps.

Freestanding temples built at Luxor and Karnak were meant to honor important people during their lifetimes. At the center of these temples were large halls surrounded by colonnades. The central section of the hall,

This article provides a broad overview of architecture's development throughout history. The architecture of individual countries is surveyed in numerous articles, such as ITALY, ART AND ARCHITECTURE OF and UNITED STATES, ART AND ARCHITECTURE OF. Biographies of architects Philip Johnson, Le Corbusier, Ludwig Mies van der Rohe, I. M. Pei, Louis Sullivan, Christopher Wren, and Frank Lloyd Wright can also be found in the appropriate volumes of this encyclopedia.

called the **hypostyle hall**, was taller than the side sections, and its raised ceiling had side openings to allow in light. This was the earliest known example of a **clerestory**. The clerestory and other formal characteristics of ancient Egyptian temples influenced the development of classical achitecture in Greece and, later, Rome. For more information, see EGYPTIAN ART AND ARCHITECTURE in Volume E.

ASIAN ARCHITECTURE

China

China's history is marked by a long series of dynasties and emperors. However, throughout this long history, Chinese architecture changed very little in style or materials used.

The earliest Chinese structures, including tombs and city walls, were built of packed earth and timber frames. During the early 200's B.C., methods of framing with timber became more advanced, and structures with two levels, or stories, became common. These structures typically had peaked, tiled roofs with wide eaves to provide shelter from rain. The wooden beams and supporting brackets were decoratively carved.

With the introduction of Buddhism in the 500's, **pagodas** (shrines for Buddhist relics) became a staple of Chinese architecture. They were made of timber or brick and consisted of several stories with gently sloping roofs.

Chinese architecture reached its peak with the Forbidden City. This vast complex of about 9,000 buildings in the center of Beijing was built over a span of 500 years, beginning in 1368, as a home for the emperors. The timber and brick structures were lavishly decorated with ceramic tiles, red and gold lacquer, enamel, carved wood, and stone and jade inlays.

Perhaps the most famous Chinese structure is the Great Wall of China, begun in 214 B.C. to protect China from invasion. The wall was extended and rebuilt many times over the years; the sections existing today were built between the late 1300's and the mid-1600's. Made of packed earth encased in brick and stone, the wall winds across mountains and through valleys for some 4,000 miles (6,400 kilometers). Towers, erected at regular intervals along the wall, were used as guard posts and platforms from which smoke signals were sent to warn of approaching enemy forces.

Japan

Japanese architecture was influenced by the traditions of China, Buddhism, and Shinto, the native religion of Japan. Shinto shrines were finely crafted wood structures with thatched roofs. Since ancient times, they have been torn down and rebuilt on the same plan every twenty years.

Japanese domestic architecture, from teahouses to the Katsura Villa in Kyoto (1615–63), was simple and undecorated but finely crafted. Houses had wood frames and pitched roofs with wide eaves. Inside, rooms often had built-in bookshelves and were separated by screens of fabric or paper. The dimensions of all parts of the Japanese house were based on the proportions of the traditional Japanese straw mat called a tatami, which was 3 feet (1 meter) wide by 6 feet (2 meters) long.

India

Indian architecture reflects many religious and cultural traditions. Buddhists cut temples into rock cliffs and built mud brick mounds, called **stupas**, from the 200's

Chinese buildings, such as this temple in Beijing, were often lavishly decorated with colorful lacquer, enamel, and ceramic tiles.

One of the most notable examples of pre-Columbian architecture is Machu Picchu, a complex of terraced structures built by the Incas high in the Peruvian Andes.

B.C. to about A.D. 800. Beginning about 600, Hindus built freestanding, rock-cut temples as residences for their gods. India is also home to an Islamic tradition, which can be seen in the famous Taj Mahal. Completed at Agra in 1648, the Taj Mahal is a tomb of gleaming white marble built by a Mogul ruler for his deceased wife. Its great central dome is surrounded by four smaller ones, and a slender tower, or **minaret**, rises from each corner of the marble terrace. The tomb's inner walls are inscribed with verses from the Koran. (A separate article on the TAJ MAHAL can be found in Volume T.)

LATIN AMERICAN ARCHITECTURE

The architecture of ancient Latin America is called pre-Columbian, which refers to the time before the arrival of Columbus and other European explorers. Between about A.D. 100 and 800, the Zapotec and Maya people founded rich cultures in the areas of present-day Mexico and Central America. Their towns of stone and wood buildings were laid out in alignment with the patterns of the stars in the night sky. Farther south, in parts of present-day Peru, the Incas built a highly advanced society. They were masters of engineering. About 1450, they built Machu Picchu, a vast complex of terraced structures high in the Andes that served as a country estate for Inca royalty.

The arrival of Europeans beginning in the late 1400's marked a distinct change in the region, as European cultural traditions gradually replaced those of the native people. In the 1600's and 1700's, Spanish colonizers brought Europe's baroque style to Latin America. This style, characterized by a sense of movement and drama, would define Latin American architecture into the modern era.

AFRICAN ARCHITECTURE

The architecture of northern Africa includes the pyramids and temples of ancient Egypt as well as the mosques built by Islamic peoples. The architecture of sub-Saharan Africa has only recently been well studied. It includes temporary beehive-shaped structures made of branches, leaves, and other natural materials built by nomadic peoples. More permanent structures, including large mosques and palaces, were built of mud brick over bamboo frames.

Perhaps the most notable ancient African structure south of the Sahara is the fortified city of Great Zimbabwe (from which the country Zimbabwe took its name). The site today consists of several immense walls built of granite blocks and a tall conical tower resembling a grain silo.

GREEK ARCHITECTURE

More than any civilization before them, the ancient Greeks worked to perfect architectural form. They carefully calculated geometry and proportion to create buildings whose various elements blended together to form a unified whole.

The earliest Greek temples were probably built of wood. The Greeks then took the elements of those early wood structures and used them to create temples of stone masonry, many of which still stand today. Greek temples were built with a simple construction system called **post-and-lintel**, in which vertical

The ancient Romans developed the arch and other structural forms, as seen in this aqueduct, a system for transporting water.

columns (posts) support horizontal beams (lintels).

One of the most lasting developments of Greek architecture is the system of styles, or orders, used to build Greek temples. The orders, called Doric, Ionic, and Corinthian, are best identified by the tops, or **capitals**, of the columns. The **Doric** order had simple capitals and was the least decorated. **Ionic** capitals were more delicate and ornate, resembling scrolls. **Corinthian** capitals were the most decorative, featuring ornately carved acanthus leaves. Although Greek temples were built on these regular orders, there was great variety in the temples, from the earliest to the latest, reflecting a spirit of experimentation within the system.

The Parthenon, a Doric temple, is one of the best examples of Greek temple construction. Built between 447 and 432 B.C., it contained an enormous statue of the god Athena. Carved sculptures were located in the Parthenon's **pediments** (the triangular spaces at each end of the building, just beneath the roof) and **friezes** (decorative horizontal bands of continuous relief sculptures directly above the columns).

Every Greek city had an **agora**, the center of economic, political, social, and religious activity. Long covered walkways called **stoas** ran along two or more sides, housing small shops and stores. For more information, see the article GREECE, ART AND ARCHITECTURE OF in Volume G.

ROMAN ARCHITECTURE

The architecture of the ancient Romans blended local traditions with influences from other cultures, especially Greece. Until fairly recently, the Romans were thought to have merely copied Greek architecture. Today, however, ancient Rome's many contributions to architecture are considered as significant as those of any other culture.

The Romans were particularly skilled at building with bricks and stones. With these materials, they developed new roof forms using arches, vaults, and domes. To create an **arch**, wedge-shaped stones or bricks, called **voussoirs**, were placed with the narrow ends on the inside of the arch and the wide ends on the outside. The top or center voussoir, called the keystone, held all the other voussoirs in place. The Romans typically used round or pointed arches to span openings in walls or to support heavy roofs.

Other forms of the arch developed by the Romans include the **barrel vault**, which is like a series of arches built next to one another to form a tunnel, and the **groin vault**, which consists of two arches or barrel vaults that inter-

The arch was developed to span wall openings or support heavy roofs. It became the basis for other structural forms. A barrel vault is a series of arches placed one behind the other to form a tunnel-like roof. A groin vault is formed by the intersection of two barrel vaults. A dome can be thought of as a series of arches arranged in a circle.

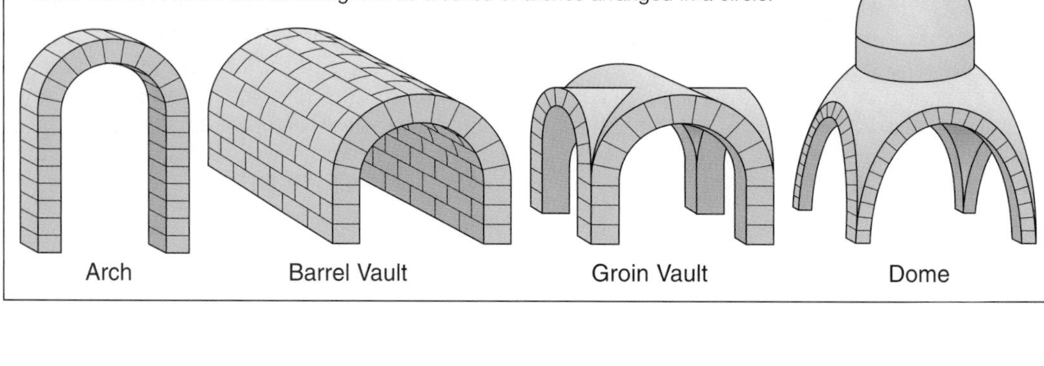

The domed cathedral Hagia Sophia, built in the A.D. 500's, is one of the greatest examples of the Byzantine style of architecture.

sect at the top. A **dome** can be thought of as a series of arches built in a full circle around a center point.

Another important architectural development of the ancient Romans was the perfection of concrete. Roman concrete was a mixture of crushed or small stones, lime, water, and volcanic ash. It was as strong as stone but cheaper to make and easier to work with. Concrete could be molded into forms such as vaults and domes. A famous example is the dome of the Pantheon, one of the largest Roman temples, built about A.D. 120. The dome has a diameter of 142 feet (43 meters). The Romans always covered concrete with small tiles of marble, brick, or other masonry materials.

The center of a Roman city was the **forum**, or public square. The typical forum had a small temple at one end and a courtyard flanked by colonnades. Also in a forum was a **basilica**, a rectangular structure with semi-circular spaces called **apses** at each end. The central space had shorter side aisles and was lit by clerestory windows. Basilicas were used to hold crowds gathered for legal, social, or commercial activities.

The Romans were also talented engineers. The long, arched aqueducts that carried water into Roman cities from as far away as 50 miles (80 kilometers) still stand today. For more information, see the article ROME, ART AND ARCHITECTURE OF in Volume QR.

CHRISTIAN ARCHITECTURE

The spread of Christianity throughout the Roman Empire beginning in the early 300's led to a need for new churches. Christian worship demanded a style of architecture very different from the religious architecture of Greece and Rome. The earlier temples had served as a house for the god, a storehouse for treasures, and as a background for outdoor ceremonies. Christians worshiped together inside their churches. So the plan of early Christian churches was based on Roman basilicas, which had plenty of open space and windows to let in light.

One of the earliest examples of Christian architecture was the old St. Peter's church in Rome, completed in 333. Colonnades divided the interior into three parts: a central **nave** (where the congregation gathered) and two aisles on either side. The altar stood in an apse at the far end of the nave, underneath which was the tomb of Saint Peter. With the addition of a cross-aisle (called a **transept**), the plan of the old St. Peter's looked like a crucifix—the symbol of the Christian church. This basic plan, with variations, can be seen in many Christian basilicas and cathedrals to this day.

Byzantine Architecture

Early Christian art and architecture influenced by Eastern traditions is called Byzantine, after the city of Byzantium (modern-day Istanbul). Byzantium became the capital of the Eastern Roman Empire in A.D. 330, when it was renamed Constantinople by the emperor Constantine I.

Byzantine churches were round or in the form of a cross with arms of equal length (a shape known as a Greek cross). Such plans are described as centralized because they focus attention on the center of the space rather than the end.

One of the greatest examples of the Byzantine style is Hagia Sophia (Greek for "holy wisdom"), built in Constantinople between 532 and 537. The center of the church is a vast open space lined on each side by two-story colonnades. Towering 180 feet (55 meters) above the nave is a great dome about 100 feet (30 meters) in diameter and covered in gold mosaics. The dome was supported by **pendentives**, triangular braces with curved sides that rose from massive columns at each corner of the walls beneath. Half-domes flanked the great dome on two sides.

The Byzantine style of architecture spread to Greece, Russia, and finally through Venice to western Europe. For more information, see the article BYZANTINE ART AND ARCHITECTURE in Volume B.

Rib vaulting, a structural system developed by Romanesque architects, made possible the lighter and taller vaults often found in Gothic cathedrals.

ISLAMIC ARCHITECTURE

Islamic architecture, which developed about 650, is best represented by mosques (where Muslims go to worship). Mosques are typically entered through a long court that opens into a large prayer hall. On one wall is an arched niche that indicates the direction of Mecca, the holy city of Islam. The faithful are called to prayer from the minarets standing outside the mosque. Most mosques have one or more domes.

Like Christian basilicas, mosque designs varied according to local traditions. The mosque at Cordoba, Spain (late 700's), mixed Spanish and Islamic architectural customs. In the Middle East, mosques such as Masjid-i-Jami (early 1000's) in Iran were often decorated with colored, glazed tiles. The tiles were typically covered with scripture from the Koran and abstract geometric or floral designs (a style called **Arabesque**). For more information, see the article ISLAMIC ART AND ARCHITECTURE in Volume I.

ROMANESQUE ARCHITECTURE

After the fall of Rome in A.D. 476, many construction techniques and architectural styles were lost. But by about the year 1000, there was a significant revival of architecture. The buildings built during the 1100's and 1200's have elements of the architectural forms of ancient Rome, so this style came to be called **Romanesque**. Romanesque buildings, however, appear more massive and stocky than the buildings of ancient Rome. They have thick walls, small windows, dark interiors, round arches, and short columns. And Romanesque buildings were made of stone instead of concrete.

The Romanesque cathedral was built on the typical basilica plan but was more complex than its Roman and early Christian ancestors. More altars were added along the side aisles and the apse, decoratively carved arches were placed over doors, and towers often rose above each side of the entrance.

Flying buttresses, shown here on Notre Dame cathedral, supported the walls of Gothic buildings from the outside.

Romanesque architects experimented with vaults, developing a new structural system called **rib vaulting**. It was first used in cathedrals in Caen, France (1068), and Durham, England (1100). Over square or rectangular sections of the nave, supporting ribs sprang from four corner columns and crossed like a groin vault at the ceiling's peak. This structural system made possible the lighter and taller vaults that would characterize Gothic cathedrals. For more information, see the article ROMANESQUE ART AND ARCHITECTURE in Volume QR.

▶ GOTHIC ARCHITECTURE

Buildings designed in the Gothic style, particularly cathedrals, appear to reach toward heaven. This effect is achieved by the combination of three building techniques: rib vaults, pointed arches, and flying buttresses.

Rib vaults helped create very steep, slanting roofs. Pointed arches over doors and windows stressed the vertical line of the building's design. **Flying buttresses** were arched braces that supported the walls of a building from the outside. The weight of the ceiling was transferred from the walls to the flying buttresses, so the walls could be made thinner. The vertical emphasis of a Gothic cathedral was further enhanced by tall, slender spires and extensive use of stained glass windows that filled the interiors with light.

Although its roots are in Romanesque architecture, Gothic architecture is generally considered to have originated with the work of a French abbot named Suger. In his design for a new choir in the apse of St. Denis (1144), Suger used rib vaults to open the space to the light coming through the stained glass windows. Flying buttresses were first used extensively on the nave of Notre Dame's cathedral (1163 to about 1250) in Paris. For more information, see GOTHIC ART AND ARCHITECTURE in Volume G.

▶ RENAISSANCE ARCHITECTURE

The Renaissance (meaning "rebirth"), which began about 1400, marked a deliberate break with the art and literature of the immediate past. The Italians, in particular, wanted to revive what they viewed as the greatness of ancient Rome and Greece. A new interest arose in the architectural styles of those cultures, which are commonly known as classical architecture.

The center of the early Renaissance was Florence. There, Filippo Brunelleschi designed what is commonly considered the first Renaissance building: the Ospedale degli Innocenti (Foundling Hospital) for orphans (1421). The front, or **facade**, of the building was composed of a row of wide arches, called an **arcade**, that rose above slender Corinthian columns. Brunelleschi's design for the Old Sacristy at the Church of San Lorenzo in Florence (1421–28) demonstrates the balance and proportion that Renaissance architects favored. The building, organized on geometric principles, was a perfect cube topped with a half-circle dome. Brunelleschi used pendentives between the base and the dome.

In 1506, construction began on a new church to replace the old St. Peter's in Rome.

Baroque architecture, as seen in St. Peter's Basilica, Rome, gives the impression of movement through ornate, lively designs and curved shapes.

The new St. Peter's Basilica became one of the greatest achievements of the Renaissance and one of the world's most famous buildings. Donato Bramante created the original plan for the building. He was followed by a series of talented Renaissance architects, each of whom modified the preceding designs. Michelangelo took over the project in 1546, and the church was completed on his design. His greatest contribution to the church was its magnificent dome.

The Renaissance arrived in France, Spain, and England in the late 1500's, but those nations never fully adopted the pure form of classicism achieved in Italy. In France, Renaissance forms borrowed from Italy were blended with the French Gothic tradition. In addition to churches and other religious structures, the Renaissance also shaped the design of palaces, including Louis XIV's famous palace at Versailles, completed in 1685. For more information, see the article RENAISSANCE ART AND ARCHITECTURE in Volume QR.

BAROQUE ARCHITECTURE

Baroque architecture developed between the late 1500's and the early 1700's in Italy, France, Austria, and other nations. Where Renaissance architecture expressed stability, baroque architecture gave the impression of movement through ornate and lively designs, contrasts of light and shadow, and curved shapes. Circles were replaced by ovals, columns were doubled or twisted, pediments were broken, and **cornices** (horizontal moldings that project over the edges of roofs) were curved. Giovanni Lorenzo Bernini best represented the baroque style in Rome with his designs for St. Peter's in 1656, particularly the two curving colonnades of the piazza, or square. For more information, see BAROQUE ART AND ARCHITECTURE in Volume B.

NEOCLASSICISM AND THE EARLY ARCHITECTURE OF THE UNITED STATES

Beginning in the 1700's, there was another revival of interest in classical architecture. This movement, called **neoclassicism** ("new classicism"), developed out of two broad trends. The first trend was **Palladianism**, a revival of classical architecture through the study of the works of the Italian Renaissance architect Andrea Palladio. In 1715, Palladio's writings on architecture were first published in English. These books spurred architects in England to look to buildings such as Palladio's Villa Rotunda (1550–67) for inspiration. In 1725, Richard Boyle (Lord Burlington) designed a villa called Chiswick House, in Middlesex, England, that followed the Renaissance classicism of the Villa Rotunda.

The second trend that defined neoclassicism was the development of the field of archaeology. Beginning in the 1700's, scholars from England and France grew increasingly interested in studying the architecture of ancient Greece and Rome firsthand. The English architect Robert Adam developed a popular neoclassical style, based on his examinations of the archaeological ruins of ancient Rome. The interior of Adam's Syon House (1762–69), built in Middlesex, was inspired by the design of ancient Roman baths. The design of columns, friezes, and other elements in this house were influenced by Adam's careful study and measurement of ancient Roman decoration.

Because neoclassicism coincided with the reign of the English kings George I–IV (1714–1830), in England this style of architecture was referred to as Georgian. The popularity of Georgian, neoclassical architecture also coincided with the birth of the United States and defined the first significant architecture built in the new nation. Thomas Jefferson's design for his house, called Monticello, was influenced by Palladian neoclassicism. His design for the Virginia State Capitol (1785–96), with its simple rectangular form and front colonnade topped by a pediment, was directly inspired by an ancient Roman temple called the Maison Carrée (about 16 B.C.).

In most cases, neoclassicism did not result in pure revivals of classical styles. The United States Capitol building (completed 1863), for example, reveals the architectural influence of ancient Greece and Rome, as well as the Renaissance.

MODERN ARCHITECTURE

Modern architecture arose out of two important developments that occurred in the rapidly changing world of the 1800's. For the first time in centuries, new building materials—including cast and wrought iron, steel, and reinforced concrete—were available. And new kinds of buildings—such as factories, railroad stations, and tall office buildings—were needed to accommodate new ways of living and working.

The 1800's

Toward the end of the 1800's, architects began to experiment with new materials. Structures such as St. Pancras train station in London (1865) and the Eiffel Tower in Paris (1889), which were built using wrought iron, were feats of engineering that showed the strength and potential of industrial materials. In 1892, French builder and engineer François Hennebique patented a system of embedding steel rods inside concrete columns and beams. Concrete that is reinforced in this manner is a relatively light yet very strong material that can be used in a variety of ways.

With so many new methods, materials, and building types to choose from, architects debated which style was appropriate for the times. Some, such as those involved in a revival of the Gothic style, looked to the past. Others, including those associated with the movement called **art nouveau** ("new art"), tried to create new styles, looking to nature and other sources for inspiration.

The American architect Louis Sullivan was among the first to analyze the relationship between the design of a modern building and its use. His design for the Wainwright Building (1891) in St. Louis, Missouri, reflected his theory that tall office buildings should be designed in three parts. The base, or ground floor, of the building had large openings of glass to provide light for shopping and other commercial activities. The middle section consisted of numerous floors of offices, all exactly the same. The top level provided space for equipment to operate the building. This concept continues to influence skyscraper design today.

Typical of neoclassical architecture, Thomas Jefferson's design for Virginia's state capitol building recalls an ancient Roman temple.

The Early 1900's

Most of the advances in engineering that occurred in the late 1800's and early 1900's

The American architect Frank Lloyd Wright designed houses, such as Fallingwater, that were in harmony with their natural surroundings.

took place in the United States. Many European architects praised American engineering but criticized the continued use of decoration on buildings. In 1908 an Austrian architect, Adolf Loos, wrote an influential essay in which he argued that architectural ornamentation of any kind was no longer needed in a modern, advanced society.

One American who captured the admiration of European architects was Frank Lloyd Wright. Working mainly in the Chicago area, Wright completely transformed the American house. The interiors of Wright's houses, which he called prairie houses, were open and spacious. Low-pitched roofs and deep overhanging eaves created long, low silhouettes that were in harmony with the flat midwestern landscape. Wright's revolutionary designs were admired by young German architects such as Walter Gropius, who later founded Bauhaus, a famous school of modern design.

Another important German architect, Ludwig Mies van der Rohe, designed the German pavilion at the 1929 International Exhibition, held in Barcelona, Spain. The one-story building, which was about the size of a house, showed how new materials could be used to create entirely new types of spaces. The pavilion had a light, steel structure that supported a flat roof. The interior spaces were defined not by traditional walls but by free-standing slabs of thin marble.

One of the most famous and influential of all modern architects was Charles Édouard Jeanneret, known as Le Corbusier. In 1929, Le Corbusier designed a house called the Villa Savoye, built outside Paris. The house was raised up on thin columns, called **pilotis**, so that it seems to hover over the ground. Inside, rooms were connected by a series of ramps that led to an outdoor terrace on the flat roof. Long, horizontal openings in the walls, called ribbon windows, lit the interior.

The International Style

In 1931, the architectural designs of Walter Gropius, Mies van der Rohe, Le Corbusier,

Lever House, a skyscraper in New York City, features the simple geometric lines and large areas of glass that characterize the international style.

After the 1950's, architects began using concrete in bold new ways. Le Corbusier's chapel Notre Dame du Haut in France (*right*) features smooth, curving shapes. Frank Lloyd Wright's Guggenheim Museum in New York City (*below right*) consists of ramps that spiral around a central atrium.

and others were showcased at an exhibition at the Museum of Modern Art in New York. The exhibition organizers noted that the new architecture was light rather than massive, expressed its function clearly, and did not rely on styles of the past. It was characterized by simple, geometric lines and the use of concrete, steel, and large areas of glass. They called this new architecture the **international style**.

After World War II (1939–45), the international style dominated modern architectural design around the world, especially for office buildings. A typical example is Lever House (1950–52), a skyscraper built in New York by the architectural firm of Skidmore, Owings, and Merrill. Lever House had a horizontal base elevated on pilotis. From that base rose a rectangular tower covered in a thin sheath of aluminum and glass. Soon, similar towers defined the skylines of cities across the United States, Europe, and elsewhere. German architects such as Gropius and Mies van der Rohe, who had emigrated to the United States, became educators and trained an entire generation of young architects in the style. However, the influence of the international style was short-lived.

New Trends and Postmodernism

After the 1950's, architects began to explore new means of expression. Several architects expanded the use of reinforced concrete. Le Corbusier led the way with his design for the chapel Notre Dame du Haut (1955), in Ronchamp, France. It has a boldly curved roof made of a thin shell of reinforced concrete held together by concrete struts. A narrow strip of windows just below the roof makes it appear to float. Numerous other windows pierce the thick walls, filling the inside of the chapel with an otherworldly light.

American architect Louis Kahn also used concrete in his design for the Salk Institute in La Jolla, California. The design and materials lent themselves to the creation of both large open spaces for group research and quiet, private areas for individual study. The buildings were carefully designed to reflect the character of the site, with its dramatic ocean views.

Other architects used concrete to create bold, expressive forms. Frank Lloyd Wright designed the galleries of New York City's Guggenheim Museum (1959) as a series of ramps spiraling around a central atrium, or court. The TWA Terminal (1956–62) at Kennedy International Airport in New York, designed by Finnish architect Eero Saarinen, features curved concrete shells that resemble a bird about to take flight.

An often overlooked but important influence on architecture after World War II was the growing movement to the suburbs. U.S. cities saw a tremendous loss in population as families moved to new housing developments in outlying areas. One of the first of these developments was Levittown, built on Long Island, New York, in 1948. Its designers adapted methods of mass production used in industry, enabling houses to be built quickly and cheaply. In 1956, Southdale, the first fully enclosed, environmentally controlled shopping center, opened in a suburb of Minneapolis. Its architect, Victor Gruen, intended the center to be the new "town square" of the suburbs, with places for people to socialize as well as shop. That same year, General Motors opened a complex of offices and research facilities in suburban Detroit, designed by Eero Saarinen. Soon other businesses were relocating to the suburbs.

THE NEW WORLD TRADE CENTER

In 2003, a design by the American architect Daniel Libeskind was chosen for the rebuilding of the World Trade Center in New York City. The new World Trade Center site will consist of several office buildings, a new transportation terminal, and a 1,776-foot (541-meter) tower, which will be the tallest in the world. The site will also include a memorial plaza dedicated to the victims of the terrorist attack that destroyed the original World Trade Center on September 11, 2001.

During the 1960's, a group of architects emerged who were dissatisfied with what they viewed as the plain simplicity of the international style. The followers of this movement, which later became known as **postmodernism**, decorated their buildings with elements that recalled historical styles. The American architect Robert Venturi, an early leader of the movement, thought architecture should reflect life by being complex and filled with contradictions. Michael Graves' design for the Portland (Oregon) Public Service Building (1983) featured historical elements such as columns that were simulated (not structural) with colors and bas relief, Philip Johnson topped his design for AT&T's headquarters in New York City (1984) with a classical pediment, and I. M. Pei's design for the new entrance to the Louvre in Paris (1989) featured a pyramid constructed of steel and glass.

Venturi and fellow architects Denise Scott Brown and Steven Izenour wrote a book called *Learning from Las Vegas* (1972), in which they suggested that architects should also look to commercial shopping centers and other common neighborhood features for inspiration. The book accompanied a growing interest in vernacular architecture.

Throughout the 1970's, many architects focused their attention on historic preservation and the architecture of the city. Projects such as the 1976 renovation of Quincy Market in Boston drew shoppers back into the city from the suburbs and reminded people of the rich history and character of cities.

Most architects strive to make balanced structures that are in harmony with their surroundings. Other architects purposely seek to make their structures clash jarringly with their surroundings. This movement is called **deconstructivism** because the architects seem to deconstruct, or take apart, a conventional building and reassemble its various elements in an apparently random or jumbled fashion. In his design for the Wexner Center (1989) on the campus of Ohio State University, the American architect Peter Eisenman combined forms from buildings that had previously existed at the site with forms from the existing campus. This resulted in walls and other parts of the building intersecting one another at unexpected angles.

Buildings designed by the American architect Frank Gehry resemble deconstructivist architecture, but Gehry had a different method and purpose. He used computer modeling programs to calculate structural systems and create buildings in shapes that would have been impossible to achieve even 20 years earlier. Gehry's Guggenheim Museum (1997) in Bilbao, Spain, looks like an explosion of curving forms clad in a shiny skin of titanium.

Computer modeling programs have also made possible the structural feats of designers such as Richard Rogers, Norman Foster, and Santiago Calatrava. They designed bridges, train stations, airports, and exhibition halls with sweeping roofs supported by columns, trusses, or cables. Calatrava's addition to the Milwaukee Art Museum (2001) has a roof that looks like two great wings spreading out from the building. In fact, these wings actually move. Such buildings recall the great engineering feats of early modernism. And they point to a future of increasingly dynamic buildings, based on a new era of materials and structural techniques.

The sweeping lines and wing-like roof of the Milwaukee Art Museum's newest addition point to a future of dynamic architectural designs.

Computer modeling programs help architects design buildings in revolutionary shapes, such as the Guggenheim Museum in Bilbao, Spain.

CAREERS IN ARCHITECTURE

Although architects design buildings, they are not the only people involved in constructing them. They usually work with many related professionals, such as engineers, interior designers, landscape architects, and urban designers. Architects themselves must have broad knowledge of all these fields. Architects typically must earn a four-year undergraduate degree, followed by a two- or three-year program of graduate study, leading to the Master of Architecture (M.Arch) degree. Once the architecture student graduates, he or she works as an intern to gain experience in all the different aspects of design and construction. After this period, the intern takes a registration exam. Only after passing this exam may the intern take the title and full responsibilities of an architect.

NANCY A. MILLER
University of Minnesota

See also ANCIENT WORLD, ART OF THE; BUILDING CONSTRUCTION; CATHEDRALS.

ARCTIC

Surrounding the geographic North Pole is a deep, ice-covered ocean, the Arctic Ocean, which is bordered by the northern parts of the continents of North America, Europe, and Asia. This is the Arctic region. Here, periods of continuous daylight alternate with periods of continuous darkness for days to months at a time. Cold pervades the region. But unlike the southern polar region of Antarctica, which has no native human inhabitants, people have lived in the Arctic for thousands of years. Because of its location, its geography and climate, and its wealth of natural resources, the Arctic region is politically, scientifically, and economically important.

The boundaries of the Arctic region are measured in different ways. The Arctic is sometimes defined as the area north of the Arctic Circle, an imaginary line around the globe at 66° 30′ (66 degrees, 30 minutes) north latitude. Other ways of determining the region's limits include the tree line, the most northerly point at which trees will grow, and the extent of polar sea ice and of permafrost, or land that is permanently frozen.

▶GEOGRAPHY OF THE ARCTIC

The Arctic is dominated by the Arctic Ocean and a vast treeless plain called the tundra. Unlike Antarctica, which is an ice-covered continent, much of the Arctic consists of ice-covered seas.

The Arctic Ocean. The Arctic Ocean, which covers approximately 5 million square miles (13 million square kilometers), makes up about two thirds of the Arctic region. East of the island of Greenland, the Arctic Ocean connects with the Atlantic Ocean. West of Greenland the Arctic flows through Baffin Bay, Davis Strait, and shallow outlets between the northern islands of Canada. The Arctic Ocean joins the Pacific Ocean through the Bering Strait, which separates Alaska from what is now northeastern Russia (formerly part of the Soviet Union). Although its extent varies from summer to winter, ice covers the Arctic Ocean year-round, making navigation frequently difficult and dangerous. From October to June the ocean is completely ice-locked, and only submarines can cross it completely by passing under the ice. At times, icebergs, which break off the ends of glaciers, float south into the shipping lanes of the Atlantic Ocean and create hazards to navigation.

The Tundra. The tundra begins on the land area of the Arctic about where the tree line ends. When the summer sun melts the ice and snow cover, the Arctic tundra becomes a rich green living carpet of plants. But beneath a thin layer of soil lies ground that is always frozen. This permafrost forms whenever the temperature of the ground stays continuously

The frozen Arctic Ocean (*far left*) dominates the Arctic region. The people of the Arctic have survived in their harsh environment by developing simple but useful equipment, such as the dog sled (*center*). When the summer sun melts its covering of ice, the tundra (*left*) blooms with plants and flowers.

below the freezing point, 32°F (0°C), for two or more years. Most of Greenland, much of Alaska, half of Canada, and parts of Scandinavia, Russia, Mongolia, and Northeast China are affected by permafrost. Its greatest recorded thickness—4,900 feet (1,500 meters)—is in Siberia.

Not all of the land in the Arctic region is covered by the tundra. Rocky, mountainous islands quite different from the flat tundra are scattered around the Arctic Ocean. Greenland is almost completely covered by a large ice sheet, with mountains ringing its coast.

See the article TUNDRA in Volume T.

CLIMATE

Although low temperatures are the major characteristic of its climate, the Arctic is not always bitterly cold. During the summer, temperatures over the Arctic Ocean are near 32°F (0° C). Winter temperatures, however, average between –22° and –31° F (–30° to –35°C). It is colder over land areas, especially over the Greenland ice sheet, where a winter temperature of –87° F (–66° C) has been recorded. In the subarctic, a region just south of the Arctic, winters are colder but summers are warmer. The lowest temperature ever recorded here was –90° F (about –68° C) in Siberia.

Like Antarctica, the Arctic receives little precipitation (rain or snow). The generally low temperatures limit the amount of moisture that can be held in the air and consequently the amount of snow that will fall. In March and April, when the greatest amount of snow covers the ground, the average depth in the Arctic is 8 to 20 inches (20 to 50 centimeters). The snow remains for 10 months of the year.

The Arctic year is divided into a long, cold winter and a short, cool summer. Because of its geographical position, the Arctic is marked by long periods of darkness and daylight. At the North Pole the sun remains above the horizon for six months at a time and below the horizon for another six months, giving in effect six months of daylight, followed by six months of darkness.

PLANT AND ANIMAL LIFE

Plants and animals are plentiful in the Arctic. More than 90 types of plants grow not far from the North Pole. Closer to the Arctic Circle scientists have identified 450 varieties of plant life. In summer the tundra is covered with flowers and various plants, including lichens, mosses, grasses, and small shrubs. More than a hundred types of birds live in the Arctic. Musk oxen, caribou, reindeer, foxes, wolves, bears (including polar bears), valuable fur-bearing animals such as ermine and sable, snowshoe hares, and lemmings (small, mouse-like animals) thrive in the region. The Arctic waters are rich in fish, including salmon, cod, and rockfish, and many kinds of seals, whales, and porpoises.

ARCTIC PEOPLES

The Arctic has been populated by small groups of people for thousands of years. They probably followed herds of reindeer, caribou, and musk oxen from Central Asia northward and eventually adapted to the environment. One of the most widespread peoples in the region are the Inuit, formerly called Eskimos. They are found in Alaska and Canada, as well as Greenland and Siberia. Indians also live in some areas of the North American Arctic region, especially in Alaska and Canada. For more information on the Inuit, see the article INUIT in Volume I.

Perhaps the best-known people of the European Arctic region are the Sami (formerly called Lapps), who live in the northern areas of Finland, Norway, and Sweden and in parts of Russia. Many Sami still follow their traditional ways of life as hunters and reindeer herders. But as the Arctic is increasingly exploited for its natural resources, they are being trained for more settled occupations, such as farming and mining. For more information on the Sami, see the article LAPLAND in Volume L.

In Siberia, in the Asian Arctic region of Russia, the native peoples include the Chukchi, Koyaki, and Yakuts, as well as some Inuit and Sami. Most continue to follow their traditional occupations—herding reindeer, hunting, fishing, and fur trapping. See the article on Siberia in Volume S.

All of the native Arctic people have developed a unique ability to survive in their harsh environment by skillfully using the few materials available to them. From snow, ice, and animal skins and bones they have fashioned a simple technology that enables them to build shelters, weapons, and such forms of transportation as sleds and kayaks (small, skin-covered boats). Land and sea animals and fish provide their main source of food.

NATURAL RESOURCES

The natural resources of the Arctic can be divided into four main groups—furs, whale products, fish, and minerals. In the early days of Arctic exploration, seals attracted fur traders. Because of the region's large whale population, a booming industry soon developed in whale oil, whalebone, and other products from these great creatures. Today, because many marine animals are in danger of being wiped out, their hunting is limited by international agreements.

The Arctic seas provide some of the oldest and most productive fishing areas in the world. The amount that can be caught by any country, however, is controlled by national territorial limits and by other internationally recognized agreements.

The Arctic's mineral resources include coal, copper, diamonds, gold, iron, lead, zinc, nickel, and tin. Large petroleum and natural gas deposits exist in the northern areas of Alaska, Canada, and Russia. Petroleum from Alaska and Canada is transported south by pipelines.

EXPLORATION AND DISCOVERY

The first recorded explorers of the Arctic were the Norsemen who sailed from Norway to Iceland, Greenland, and North America. By the mid-1500's, British and Dutch merchants and sailors began exploring the Arctic in search of a northeast passage to China and India. Although these explorers did not find the passage, they did learn more about the Arctic. These searches also opened up sea trade with Russia and led to the development of the whaling and sealing industries.

About the same time, other British explorers were searching for a northwest passage to Asia around the North American continent. In 1576, Martin Frobisher sailed for the first time to Canada's Baffin Island. Within the next 40 years, Davis Strait, Baffin Bay, and Hudson Bay had been explored. For more information, see the article HUDSON, HENRY in Volume H. Between the early 1600's and 1800's the attention of merchants and explorers focused on developing land routes to support the fur trade. As a result of these explorations, two British explorers, Samuel Hearne and Alexander Mackenzie, followed Canadian rivers northwest to the Arctic Ocean. For more information, see the article MACKENZIE, ALEXANDER in Volume M.

During the 1700's and 1800's explorers continued to search the Arctic for the elusive Northwest Passage. This route was not found until the early 1900's, when Norway's Roald Amundsen became the first person to sail northwest from the Atlantic Ocean through the Arctic to the Pacific Ocean. His voyage lasted from 1903 to 1906. (Amundsen later commanded the first expedition to reach the South Pole of Antarctica.)

Once the Northwest Passage was discovered, explorers turned their attention to the North Pole. During these expeditions much scientific information also was obtained, including data on sea ice and the Arctic Ocean collected by the Norwegian explorer Fridtjof Nansen. In 1909 an American expedition led by Robert E. Peary successfully reached the North Pole for the first time. See the article on Peary in Volume P.

Since the beginning of the 1900's, advances in technology have expanded Arctic exploration. The American explorer Richard E. Byrd claimed to have made the first flight over the North Pole in 1926. (An article on

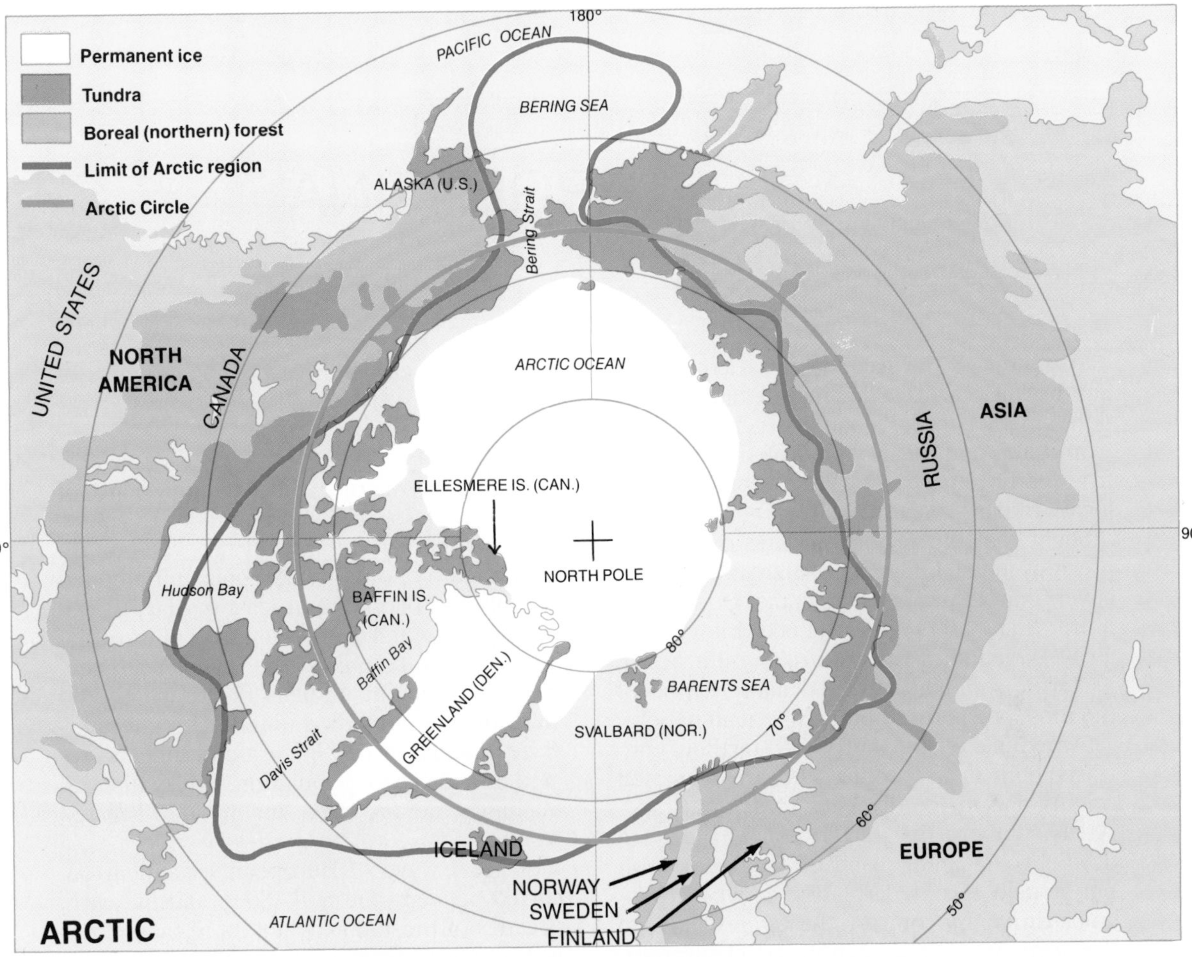

The strategic importance of the Arctic region lies in its central location between the continents of North America, Europe, and Asia.

Byrd appears in Volume B.) In 1958 the U.S. nuclear-powered submarine *Nautilus* became the first ship to reach the North Pole, by traveling under the Arctic ice. In 1977 the nuclear-powered Soviet icebreaker *Arktika* was used to explore the frozen Arctic Ocean. Scientists completed a 7-year exploration project on the ecology of the Bering Sea in 1983.

THE ARCTIC TODAY

Political and Strategic Importance. National territorial rights are recognized for all Arctic land areas. But the extent to which nations can control Arctic coastal waters is still unresolved. With the growth of the offshore oil industry in the Arctic, control of its waters will become more important. The Arctic's strategic importance lies in its central position between North America, Europe, and Asia. In 1993, Russia, Norway, Sweden, Finland, Iceland, and Denmark formed the Council of the Euro-Arctic Region, to promote trade and to clean up areas contaminated by pollution.

Research and Environmental Protection. Most scientific research in the Arctic concentrates on its climate and its unusual geographical and physical characteristics. In addition, environmental research and protection have become increasingly important as new technology enables us to tap the mineral resources of the region. This is vital because the ecology of the Arctic can be easily disrupted or damaged and recovers very slowly and sometimes not at all. As a result, many nations have established strict measures to protect this unique, fascinating, and invaluable region of the world.

WINIFRED REUNING
Division of Polar Programs
National Science Foundation

See also ANTARCTICA.

ARES. See GREEK MYTHOLOGY (Profiles).

ARGENTINA

Argentina is the second largest country of South America, exceeded in area and population only by Brazil. Its name, which is derived from Latin and means "land of silver," came from early European explorers, who saw the local Indians wearing silver jewelry and thought that the region must be rich in the precious metal. Only much later did they discover that the silver had come from Peru, more than 1,000 miles (1,600 kilometers) away. Argentina's real natural wealth lies in its fertile soil, which helped make it one of the most prosperous South American nations.

Argentina is a country of startling contrasts, both in its people, who are of varied origins, and in the diversity of its landscape. At its southern tip are the islands of Tierra del Fuego, meaning "land of fire" in Spanish but actually a cold, desolate area where penguins thrive. By contrast, the Gran Chaco, in the north, is a hot, densely forested subtropical region. The towering mountains of the Andes make up most of its western region, while in the east lie the vast, open plains of the Pampas.

▸ PEOPLE

The great majority of Argentines are of European descent. The remainder are chiefly mestizos (persons of mixed European and Indian ancestry) along with some full-blooded Indians and people of at least partial African descent. The first European settlers were the Spanish, who colonized the region beginning in the 1500's. The Indians they encountered were mostly nomadic hunters. The intermarriage of some of the Spanish and Indians created the mestizo population. Today the remaining Indians live mainly in isolated reservations.

A great wave of European settlement occurred between the mid-1800's and the early decades of the 1900's, when more than 6 million immigrants arrived in the country. Argentines of Spanish and Italian ancestry are now the most numerous. But there are also

The spectacular Iguazú Falls lie on Argentina's border with Brazil. The numerous falls, separated by islands, average 200 feet (61 meters) high.

descendants of French, Swiss, Austrian, German, and British settlers, as well as some of Eastern European and Asian origin. More recent immigration has been from neighboring South American countries.

Language. Spanish is the official language, although Argentine Spanish has been strongly influenced by other languages, Italian in particular. This is especially so in Buenos Aires, the capital. Some Argentines speak more than one language, and in Buenos Aires, newspapers are published in a dozen or more languages. Several Indian languages are also spoken.

Religion. More than 90 percent of Argentines are Roman Catholics, and the constitution still requires that the president be a Roman Catholic. There are also significant Protestant and Jewish minorities and a small Muslim community. Religious freedom is guaranteed to all.

Education. Some 95 percent of the population is able to read and write, giving Argentina one of the continent's highest literacy rates. Schooling is required by law for all children between the ages of 6 and 14. At 14, students can take examinations to enter one of the various kinds of secondary school. Some prepare them to enter a university, while others train them for a career in business, industry, or trade. Argentina has several national universities. The largest is the University of Buenos Aires, with more than 100,000 students. Education is free through the university level.

Urban Life. Argentina is one of the most highly urbanized countries in the Western Hemisphere, with more than 85 percent of its people living in cities and towns. About one-third of the population lives in Greater Buenos Aires. Wealthy and middle-class Argentines in the largest cities generally live in comfortable houses or apartments. Most of the better-off workers also have decent homes, built by their unions, the government, or through their own efforts. Large numbers of poorer people from the rural areas and from neighboring countries have also moved into the cities, particularly Buenos Aires. Many of these newer migrants live in slums and squatter colonies and often find it hard to obtain full-time employment.

Argentines usually eat their evening meals quite late. Although the children may eat

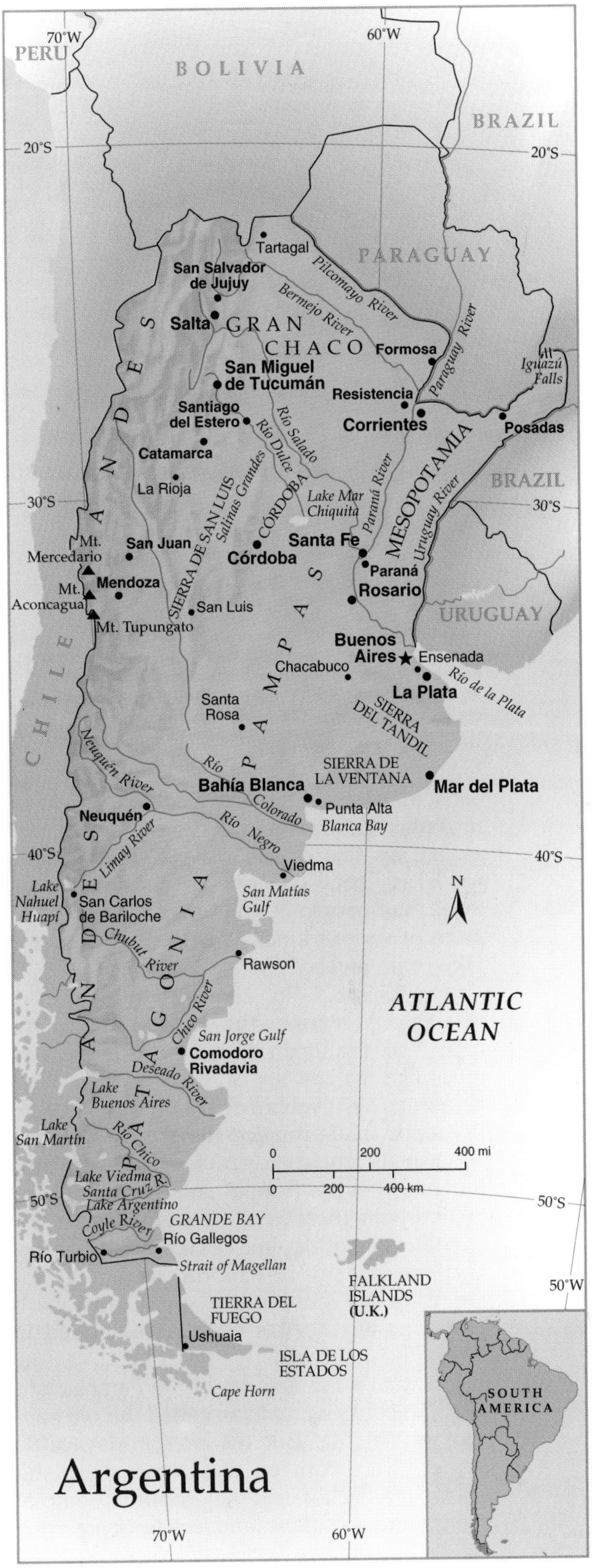

Argentina is one of the most highly urbanized countries in the Western Hemisphere, with about 85 percent of its people living in cities and towns. These Argentines are in Buenos Aires, the capital and largest city.

early in the evening, adults seldom sit down to dinner until eight o'clock, and sometimes as late as nine or ten o'clock. The favorite foods are beef—Argentines consume more meat than people of any other country—and pasta of various kinds. Wine is almost always taken with meals.

The Gaucho. In contrast to the city-dwelling Argentine, the gaucho made his home on the open Pampas. A horseman, much like the cowboy of the American West, he earned his livelihood from the wild cattle that once freely roamed the great plains. He was usually a mestizo, who fought the Indians for control of the Pampas and was instrumental in driving them from the region.

The gaucho became a legendary figure. Distinguished by his colorful dress and admired for his independent spirit and superb horsemanship, he was often romanticized in Argentine literature.

Eventually, the division of the Pampas into large ranches, or *estancias*, ended the old gaucho way of life. But the present-day cattle herders who work on the *estancias* are still known as gauchos, and they continue some of the traditions of their predecessors.

Sports. Argentines are avid sports fans. Soccer is by far the most widely followed sport, drawing many thousands of spectators to arenas. The heritage of the gaucho has also given Argentines a passionate interest in all sports related to horsemanship, including horse racing and polo, the latter introduced by the British. *Pato*, a game resembling polo, was first played by the gauchos. Basketball, boating, skiing, and automobile racing are also quite popular.

LAND

About one-third the size of the United States, Argentina occupies most of the narrow, southern part of South America.

Land Regions. The country can be divided into five natural regions: the Andean region, the Gran Chaco, Mesopotamia, the Pampas, and Patagonia. The Gran Chaco and Mesopotamia are sometimes grouped in a single Northern or Northeastern region.

The Andes mountains form most of Argentina's western border with Chile, and they occupy about one-third of Argentina's total land area. Snowcapped Aconcagua, at 22,834 feet (6,960 meters) the mightiest of the An-

FACTS and figures

ARGENTINE REPUBLIC (República Argentina) is the official name of the country.

LOCATION: Southern part of South America.

AREA: 1,068,297 sq mi (2,766,889 km^2).

POPULATION: 37,000,000 (estimate).

CAPITAL AND LARGEST CITY: Buenos Aires.

MAJOR LANGUAGE: Spanish (official).

MAJOR RELIGIOUS GROUP: Roman Catholic.

GOVERNMENT: Republic. **Head of state and government**—president. **Legislature**—National Congress (consisting of the Senate and Chamber of Deputies).

CHIEF PRODUCTS: **Agricultural**—wheat, corn, cotton, sugarcane, soybeans, fruits, livestock (especially cattle and sheep). **Manufactured**—processed livestock products (especially beef, wool, leather goods), other processed foods, petroleum products, wine, iron and steel, chemicals, paper, machine tools, automobiles. **Mineral**—petroleum, natural gas, coal, iron ore.

MONETARY UNIT: New peso (1 peso = 100 centavos).

Patagonia (*above*) is a vast but thinly populated region of Argentina, consisting mainly of dry, windswept plateaus. The snowcapped Andes (*right*) form most of Argentina's border with Chile.

dean peaks, is Argentina's highest mountain as well as the highest in the Western Hemisphere. In the north the Andes rise from a high plateau called the Puna. The mountains of the southern Andes are lower, reminding visitors of the Swiss Alps. They are, in fact, often referred to as the Alps of Argentina and are among the country's most popular tourist areas, particularly for skiers and other winter-sports enthusiasts.

The Gran Chaco, situated in the far north, is an enormous lowland covered by areas of thick rain forest and swamp. Four broad rivers—the Pilcomayo, Bermejo, Salado, and Dulce—cross this region. These rivers often overflow their shallow banks in the wet season and flood large parts of the region. At other times the region may suffer from drought.

Mesopotamia, like the ancient region of Mesopotamia in the Middle East, takes its name from a Greek word referring to a land "between rivers." Lying to the east of the Gran Chaco, Mesopotamia consists of a rolling plain lying between the Paraná and Uruguay rivers. In the northeast the Paraná joins the Iguazú (or Iguaçú) River, forming a series of waterfalls that make up the spectacular Iguazú Falls. The region is suitable for grazing livestock and growing several kinds of crops.

The Pampas is the heartland of Argentina. It is the center of the country's agriculture and cattle raising and the site of its major cities and manufacturing industries. Although it makes up only about one-fifth of Argentina's land, it is the home of nearly four-fifths of its people. Extending from the Gran Chaco and Mesopotamia in the north to the Río Colorado in the south, the Pampas forms a huge semicircle of fertile plains, centering on Buenos Aires. The only elevated areas are in the south, where hills rise to more than 4,000 feet (1,200 meters).

Patagonia, which stretches from the Río Colorado to the southern tip of Argentina, is a large, sparsely populated region of cold, dry, windswept plateaus. Its thin soil makes sheep raising the chief economic activity. The region includes Tierra del Fuego, which Argentina shares with Chile.

Climate. Most of Argentina has a temperate climate, but there is great regional variation. The northern Gran Chaco is the hottest region, with summer temperatures of 113°F (45°C) not uncommon. The lowest temperature, 3°F (–16°C), was recorded at the southern tip of Patagonia. Average temperatures, however, are much more moderate. Rainfall is heaviest in Mesopotamia, which receives 60 inches (1,500 millimeters) a year. It diminishes toward the west and south. Since Argentina lies in the Southern Hemisphere, the seasons are reversed. January is the warmest month and June and July the coldest months.

Natural Resources. Argentina's most valuable natural resource is the fertile soil of the Pampas, which has produced much of its wealth. Forests cover about one-fifth of the land, providing timber and other wood products, including tannin, made from the bark of the red quebracho tree and used in tanning leather. Petroleum and natural gas are the most important mineral resources. There are also deposits of coal, iron ore, tin, and other minerals. Argentina's rivers are a source of hydroelectric power, which supplies close to half of its energy needs.

The Pampas is Argentina's most fertile region. The country's economy traditionally has been based on the production of beef cattle and wheat and other grains.

▶ ECONOMY

Argentina's economy traditionally has been based on agriculture, chiefly cattle raising and the production of wheat and other grains, with meat and grains making up most of its exports. Certain technological advances made it possible to exploit the potential wealth of the Pampas, beginning in the second half of the 1800's. With the invention of the steel plow, extensive cultivation of the soil became feasible. The advent of barbed wire made it easier to fence in the land and permitted the large-scale breeding of cattle, while the development of refrigerated ships made it practicable to export large quantities of meat to distant markets.

The high point of this economy, dependent on the export of agricultural products, came in the early 1900's. Thereafter, the economic direction of the country changed substantially, due in large part to two world wars and the Great Depression of the 1930's. These made it difficult to obtain manufactured goods from abroad, forcing Argentina to begin developing its own industries, chiefly to meet the needs of the domestic market. At the end of World War II in 1945, the government began to actively encourage industrialization. Since then, manufacturing and service industries have become dominant.

Manufacturing. Manufacturing is concentrated in the east, particularly around the cities of Buenos Aires, Córdoba, and Rosario. Major industries are based on meat packing, other food processing, and the manufacture of leather goods and wool textiles. The production of iron and steel, machine tools, chemicals, and refined petroleum is also important. A variety of consumer goods are manufactured as well, including paper, tobacco products, beverages, automobiles, and clothing.

Agriculture. In spite of the growth of manufacturing and other industries, however, agriculture is still vital to the economy, and Argentina remains one of the world's major food-producing countries. Corn and soybeans are major crops, in addition to wheat. Cotton is produced in the Gran Chaco and sugarcane in some of the northern provinces. Wine grapes and a variety of other fruits are grown in the foothills of the Andes. Sheep are raised in numbers second only to cattle, particularly in the southern Pampas and Patagonia, and wool is an important export.

Trade. Along with Brazil, Paraguay, and Uruguay, Argentina belongs to the Southern Common Market, or Mercosur. This trade organization officially came into being in 1995, forming the world's second largest customs union.

Transportation. Argentina has the most extensive transportation system in South America. Railroads link Buenos Aires with almost every part of Argentina and with neighboring countries. Buses and trucks have also become increasingly important as a source of passenger and freight traffic. Aerolínas Argentinas is the national airline. The country's main navigable waterway is the Río de la Plata system (the combined Paraná and Uruguay rivers).

MAJOR CITIES

Buenos Aires, the capital and largest city, lies on the Río de la Plata. It is Argentina's chief port and a center of its commerce and industry. See the article on Buenos Aires in Volume B.

Rosario, on the Paraná River, is Argentina's second largest city. An important port and railroad hub, it is a natural link between the Gran Chaco, Mesopotamia, and the Pampas. Its major industries include meatpacking and sugar refining.

Córdoba, the third largest city, is famed for its university, founded in 1613, one of the oldest in the Western Hemisphere. Economically, it is a center of automobile production.

CULTURAL HERITAGE

Symphony concerts, opera, the theater, ballet, and other cultural activities are popular among Argentines. Argentina is one of the leading movie-producing countries in Latin America and its films are widely shown in other Spanish-speaking nations. It is a major Spanish-language publishing center and has a long literary tradition of its own. Perhaps the most famous modern Argentine author, Jorge Luis Borges (1899–1986), was known for his short stories, essays, and poetry. He was often considered for, but never granted, the Nobel Prize for literature.

Argentine popular music includes a variety of dances. In addition to the well-known tango are the *chacarera*, *zamba*, and *milonga*. Argentine folk tunes combine Spanish and Indian music, frequently accompanied by the guitar. Argentina has also produced a number of important classical composers. One of the most acclaimed of contemporary composers was Alberto Ginastera (1916–83), who is best known for his opera *Bomarzo*.

For more information on Argentine literature and music, see the articles LATIN AMERICA, LITERATURE OF and LATIN AMERICA, MUSIC OF in Volume L.

GOVERNMENT

Argentina has a federal type of government based on a constitution adopted in 1853, as amended in 1994. Executive power rests with the president, who is elected, to-

Lights illuminate the Plaza de la República in the heart of Buenos Aires. The obelisk in the center commemorates the founding of the city more than 400 years ago.

gether with a vice president, directly by the people for four years. The president may seek re-election to a second consecutive 4-year term. (Previously, presidents were elected by an electoral college to a 6-year term and were not eligible for immediate re-election.) The office of prime minister was also created under the amended constitution.

The legislative body is the National Congress, composed of the Chamber of Deputies and the Senate. Deputies are elected by popular vote for four years; senators are chosen by provincial legislatures for terms of nine years. The third branch of government, the judiciary, consists of the federal court system, headed by a supreme court.

Argentina includes 22 provinces, the Federal District of Buenos Aires, and the National Territory of Tierra del Fuego. Each province has an elected governor and legislature. Argentina also claims the Falkland Islands (which it calls Islas Malvinas), other islands in the South Atlantic, and territory in Antarctica. Argentine claims to the Falklands, a British possession since 1833, led to a brief war between the two countries in 1982.

HISTORY

Various Indian tribes lived in Argentina before European explorers arrived. The first European to visit Argentina was Juan Díaz de Solís, a Spanish navigator, who sailed into the Río de la Plata in 1516. An early attempt at colonization failed and the first permanent Spanish settlement was eventually established at Santiago del Estoro in 1553. During the first two centuries of Spanish colonial rule, Argentina was a part of the Viceroyalty of Peru. By law, all Argentine trade was required to pass westward, through Peru and Bolivia, which hampered the development of Buenos Aires but encouraged the growth of towns in the interior.

In 1776, Spain established the separate Viceroyalty of the Río de la Plata, with its capital at Buenos Aires. This stimulated the city's growth as a port and political center. It also began a long conflict between the people of Buenos Aires, known as *porteños*, and those of the interior over conflicting economic interests.

Independence. In 1806 the *porteños* repulsed an effort by the British to seize Buenos Aires, an event that heightened Argentine feelings of self-reliance. Four years later, after Napoleon invaded Spain and placed his brother on the Spanish throne, the *porteños* revolted in support of the deposed king, Ferdinand VII. When a restored Ferdinand ignored their demands for greater self-government, however, a struggle began for Argentine independence, which was formally proclaimed in Tucumán on July 9, 1816. Argentine forces, led by José de San Martín, subsequently crossed the Andes, helping to liberate Chile and Peru from Spanish rule as well. See the article on José de San Martín in Volume S.

Age of the Caudillos. The early decades of independence were turbulent. Caudillos, or military chieftains, ruled the various provinces. The most powerful was Juan Manuel de Rosas, who became governor of the province of Buenos Aires and dominated most of the others from 1835 to his overthrow in 1852. In 1853 a new constitution was adopted, patterned on that of the United States. Buenos Aires Province did not join the federation, however, until 1862.

Growth of the Nation. The second half of the 1800's and the early 1900's were a time of tremendous growth. The country was ruled by governments representing the rural aristocracy and their allies, who pushed for the economic development of the Pampas. They

After liberating Argentina from Spanish rule, José de San Martín (on left) led an army across the Andes in 1817 to help liberate Chile and Peru as well

expanded farming and livestock grazing on their great estates, fostered the development of the railroad system, and encouraged massive immigration from Europe. Under Domingo Sarmiento, president from 1868 to 1874, the school system was reorganized and education made compulsory. Sarmiento had earlier won fame as the author of *Facundo*, an attack on the early caudillos.

Reform and Reaction. Control of the government, however, remained in the hands of the great landowners, who maintained their hold on power by rigging most elections. Although there was considerable freedom of press and assembly, movements thought dangerous were ruthlessly suppressed.

Opposition groups fought for and won passage, in 1912, of a new election law expanding the right to vote and providing for a secret ballot. In 1916, Hipólito Irigoyen, leader of the Radical Party, became the first Argentine president to be elected by popular vote. He won re-election in 1928, but in 1930, he was overthrown in a military coup backed by conservatives, restoring effective control of the government to the large landowners.

The Perón Era. A military coup, in 1943, during World War II, ended this period of Argentine history and soon began a new era. One of the coup leaders, Colonel Juan Perón, seeking a popular base of support for his own ambitions, turned toward the organized labor movement, which had either been largely ignored or actively opposed by previous governments. As secretary of labor in the new government, he supported unions in negotiations with employers, enacted extensive labor legislation, and persecuted those unionists who refused to support him politically. Within two years, he had won the support of most of the labor movement and become the country's most important political leader. In 1946 he was elected president.

In addition to his role as the supposed defender of the workers, Perón stressed Argentine nationalism. This was reflected in his strong support of industrialization and his takeover of important foreign-owned businesses. Although he and his second wife, María Eva Duarte (known as Evita), had wide popular support, his regime became an increasingly harsh dictatorship. In 1955, Perón was himself overthrown by the country's military leaders.

Juan Perón, shown with his wife, Eva, ruled Argentina from 1946 to 1955, when he was overthrown. He returned to power in 1973 but died the following year.

Period of Chaos. Return of Perón. The ouster of Perón began a chaotic 18-year period of rapidly alternating governments. Of the eight succeeding presidents, none completed a full term of office. Perón remained in exile, and his supporters, the Peronistas, were long forbidden from running candidates in elections. In 1973, however, Héctor Cámpora, a Peronista, won the presidency. Two months after taking office, Cámpora resigned, paving the way for a new election, won by Perón, whose new wife, Isabel, became vice president. Perón's return to power was to be brief, however. Mortally ill, he died only nine months after taking office.

As vice president, Isabel Perón succeeded her husband as president, but she proved incapable of handling the many problems facing the country. She was finally overthrown in still another military coup, in 1976.

Recent History. The seven years of military rule that followed constituted the most cruel and oppressive regime in 20th-century Argentine history. In the name of putting down left-wing terrorism, which it accomplished, the government jailed, tortured, and killed many thousands of its opponents. At the same time, its economic policies caused unemployment without curbing the inflation they were intended to remedy. The government collapsed in 1982 after Argentina was defeated by Britain in a war over the Falkland Islands.

Raúl Alfonsín, the Radical Party candidate, won the 1983 presidential election. He restored political democracy but was unable to halt runaway inflation. He was succeeded as president in 1989 by Carlos Saúl Menem, the candidate of the Peronistas, who adopted free-market reforms and dramatically reduced inflation. After a constitutional amendment made it possible for him to run for re-election, Menem won a second term as president in 1995. But in 1999 he was defeated by the Radical Party candidate, Fernando de la Rúa. Menem later faced corruption charges.

Carlos Saúl Menem was president of Argentina from 1989 to 1999.

Continuing economic crises plagued the new administration. To avoid the collapse of the banking system, de la Rúa placed limits on money withdrawals. But this extreme measure caused widespread riots, and he was forced to resign. Congress appointed Eduardo Alberto Duhalde president until new elections could be held. Meanwhile, Argentina's unemployment rate soared to more than 20 percent.

Elections finally took place in 2003. Peronist candidate Néstor Kirchner succeeded as president when his opponent, former president Menem, withdrew from the race.

Robert L. Carmin
Ball State University
Reviewed by Robert J. Alexander
Author, *Juan Domingo Perón: A History*

ARIKARA. See Indians, American (On the Prairies and Plains).

ARISTOTLE (384–322 B.C.)

Aristotle was one of the most important citizens of ancient Greece. He never won a battle or held a political office, but he was a famous teacher and one of the greatest philosophers who ever lived.

Only a few facts are known about Aristotle's childhood. We know he was born in Stagira, a town in northeastern Greece, in 384 B.C. His father was court physician to Amyntas II, king of Macedonia, who was the grandfather of Alexander the Great. It seems likely that Aristotle learned something about science from his father.

ARISTOTLE THE STUDENT

When Aristotle was about 17 years old, he went to study in Athens, an important Greek city-state. He became a pupil of the finest teacher of his day, the philosopher Plato.

The young men at Plato's Academy spent several years studying mathematics, astronomy, and government. When they had mastered these studies, they were asked to think about some of the problems at the heart of Greek philosophy: What is happiness? What is the good life? Plato's method of teaching stressed learning how to think clearly.

Aristotle studied under Plato for about twenty years. He was an excellent student. Plato called him "the mind of the school." When Plato died in 347 B.C., Aristotle left the academy and began to develop his own method of teaching.

There was nothing, it seemed, that did not capture Aristotle's interest. How does the mind work? How can we learn what is true and what is false? What is the best form of government? These were only a few of the problems with which Aristotle wrestled.

Aristotle tried to find the answers by observing the world around him. He believed that every event had a logical explanation and that conclusions could be formed from investigation and observation.

ARISTOTLE THE TEACHER

Aristotle's fame was great by the time he left Plato's school. When King Philip II of

Macedonia was looking for a teacher for his son Alexander, he chose Aristotle. It is hard to know how much Aristotle influenced Alexander the Great, but we do know that teacher and pupil became lifelong friends.

After Alexander became king of Macedonia, Aristotle returned to Athens. In 335 B.C., with money contributed by Alexander, Aristotle opened a school called the Lyceum. It is from Aristotle's school that the high schools of France and Italy take their names: *lycée* and *liceo*.

Many subjects were taught at the Lyceum, and there were various aids for learning. Aristotle collected the first large library of ancient times. There was a museum of natural science, a garden, and a zoo.

After the morning classes Aristotle lectured to anyone who wanted to listen while he paced up and down the covered walk (called the *peripatos*) outside of his school. For this reason those who accepted his philosophy were called **Peripatetics**.

Aristotle lived and taught in a world that was very different from the one that Plato knew. In Plato's time every citizen understood the part he was to play in the life of Athens and his responsibility to the government of the city-state.

While Aristotle taught at the Lyceum, Athens lost its independence and became only a small part of Alexander's empire. As citizens of an empire, the Athenians had to adjust to a new form of government.

Aristotle urged each man to seek his own place in the world by learning how to live a good and useful life. A happy life could be found by living according to the "golden mean." By the "golden mean" Aristotle meant the middle way between two extremes. For example, he said the middle way "between cowardice and rashness is courage."

Twelve years after Aristotle opened his school, word reached Athens that Alexander the Great had died. At that time the people of Athens were divided into two groups—those who had learned to live under Alexander's rule and those who still hated it. When news of his death came, Alexander's enemies turned on his friends. Aristotle was prosecuted, like Socrates, for offending against religion. Rather than stand trial, he left Athens. He died soon afterward, in 322 B.C.

Copied from a Greek original, this Roman statue of Aristotle is in the Spada Gallery, Rome.

ARISTOTLE'S BOOKS

Of the 400 books that Aristotle is said to have written, only a small number have come down to us. But they are remarkable books. Aristotle's works seem to have been an encyclopedia of Greek learning of the 4th century B.C. There are books on astronomy, physics, poetry, zoology, oratory, biology, logic, politics, government, and ethics.

Aristotle's books were studied after his death. They were used as textbooks in the great centers of learning: Alexandria, Rome, and the universities of medieval Europe. No other man influenced the thinking of so many people for so long.

Even today Aristotle's books are an important influence because we still use his method of investigation and observation. He classified and related all the knowledge of his time about the world. Modern scientists have found that many of the observations he made more than 2,000 years ago are correct. He showed us that every statement should be supported by evidence. Aristotle's key to knowledge was logic and his basis for knowledge was fact.

Reviewed by GILBERT HIGHET
Author, *The Classical Tradition*

ARITHMETIC

When you keep score in a game, when you count your change, when you compare baseball batting averages or try to balance your checkbook, you are doing arithmetic. Arithmetic is a way of working with numbers. It is a branch of the science of mathematics.

▶NUMBERS AND NUMERALS

People begin using arithmetic when they are very young. Their earliest experiences, however, have to do with quantity, not with counting. Just by looking at them, a child too young to count knows that four toy blocks are more than two.

We think that early human beings had the same kind of **number sense**. They could not count, but they could tell by looking that they had as much of something as they needed or wanted.

As time passed, people needed more than just a sense of quantity. They needed to keep an actual count of things, such as how many sheep were in a herd or how many days it took to travel to a good hunting spot. People probably first used pebbles or their fingers to count. Then, at some unknown time thousands of years ago, numbers were discovered and number names were invented. These numbers are called **counting numbers**, which we also call **natural numbers**. Much later, zero was added to the counting numbers. Zero and the counting numbers together make up **whole numbers**.

People in ancient civilizations also developed different numeral systems, or ways of writing numbers. The Babylonians, Egyptians, Greeks, and Romans all had their own systems. These early systems were complicated and difficult to use. Then around 750 A.D., a new numeral system came into use. It was developed by the Hindus in India and was spread to other parts of the world by Arab traders. The Hindu-Arabic system includes only ten symbols. These symbols are 1, 2, 3, 4, 5, 6, 7, 8, 9, 0. The ten symbols of the Hindu-Arabic system can be used to write any number, no matter how great or how small, and they are still used today.

▶OPERATIONS WITH WHOLE NUMBERS

Once people had numbers and written numerals, they were able to work with them in different ways to solve everyday problems. They discovered that numbers can be used to perform four basic processes, or operations. These operations are addition, subtraction, multiplication, and division. Each operation is represented by a sign: + for addition, − for subtraction, × for multiplication, and ÷ for division. Another way to show division is with this sign: $\overline{)}$

It is important to know when to use the different operations and how they relate to one another.

Addition

Addition is a way of operating with numbers. It is the process of putting groups of like things together to find their total number or quantity. Counting forward is another way of finding a total number or quantity. Addition is faster than counting forward except when you are counting forward only a few numbers.

In order to add, you must know the basic addition facts. An addition fact is made up of two parts: two numbers from 0 to 9 that are to be added, called the **addends**, and their **sum**, or the answer to the addition.

$$\mathbf{4 + 6 = 10} \qquad \mathbf{9 + 8 = 17}$$

In the first example, 4 and 6 are the addends and 10 is the sum. In the second example, 9 and 8 are the addends and 17 is the sum.

ADDITION TABLE
This table can be used to find the basic addition facts, the sums of any two numbers from 0 to 9. To find the sum of 3+ 4, for example, find the 3 in the far left-hand column. Go along that row until you get to the column with 4 at the top. You will be on the 7, and 3 + 4 = 7.

+	0	1	2	3	4	5	6	7	8	9
0	0	1	2	3	4	5	6	7	8	9
1	1	2	3	4	5	6	7	8	9	10
2	2	3	4	5	6	7	8	9	10	11
3	3	4	5	6	7	8	9	10	11	12
4	4	5	6	7	8	9	10	11	12	13
5	5	6	7	8	9	10	11	12	13	14
6	6	7	8	9	10	11	12	13	14	15
7	7	8	9	10	11	12	13	14	15	16
8	8	9	10	11	12	13	14	15	16	17
9	9	10	11	12	13	14	15	16	17	18

This next problem lets us compare addition and counting forward. Suppose you cycled 8 miles on Monday and 5 miles on Tuesday. You could find out how many miles you cycled in all by counting forward or by adding.

Counting forward	**or**	**Addition**	
8 9, 10, 11,		**8**	**addend**
12, 13		**+ 5**	**addend**
		13	**sum**

When you are adding large numbers, it can be helpful to look at the numbers as if they were written in columns. Each column has a value and each one can be added in a sequence from right to left. The column names are **ones**, **tens**, **hundreds**, and **thousands**. If you were adding 1,268 and 2,159 this way, you would begin in the ones column to the far right and move left to the tens column, then to the hundreds column, and then to the thousands column.

Thousands	**Hundreds**	**Tens**	**Ones**
1	**2**	**6**	**8**
2	**1**	**5**	**9**
3	**4**	**2**	**7**

The greatest number you may write in any column is 9. What do you do when the sum in a column is more than 9?

In this example, the sum in the ones column is 17. You may think of 17 as 1 ten and 7 ones. Write 7 in the ones column and add the 1 ten to the other numbers in the tens column.

Add in the tens column: 1 + 6 + 5 = 12. Think of the 12 tens as 1 one hundred and 2 tens. Write 2 in the tens column. Add 1 to the hundreds column.

Adding in the hundreds column, you get 1 + 2 + 1 = 4. Write 4 in the hundreds column.

Adding in the thousands column, you get 1 + 2 = 3. Write 3 in the thousands column. The sum is 3,427.

Subtraction

Subtraction is the opposite of addition. One kind of subtraction involves finding the number of objects remaining in a group after some of the objects have been removed. Counting back is another way of finding the number remaining. Subtraction is usually quicker than counting back. To use the subtraction method you must know the basic subtraction facts. For every addition fact there is a related subtraction fact. They can each be written down in two ways, which are shown below.

Addition Fact	**Related Subtraction Fact**
6 + 5 = 11	**11 − 5 = 6**
6	**11**
+ 5	**− 5**
11	**6**

When you use subtraction, you subtract from a number called the **minuend**. The number you subtract is the **subtrahend**, and the answer you get is the **difference**.

Suppose you had 15 postage stamps and you used 7 of them to mail letters. You could find out how many stamps you had left by counting back or by subtracting.

Counting back	**or**	**Subtracting**	
15 14, 13, 12,		**15**	**minuend**
11, 10, 9, 8		**− 7**	**subtrahend**
		8	**difference**

When you are subtracting large numbers from one another, the idea of place value can be useful. For example, if you are subtracting 35 from 92, you could think of the numbers in this way:

92 = 9 tens and 2 ones
−35 = 3 tens and 5 ones

The 9 tens and 2 ones can also be written as 8 tens and 12 ones. All you do is change 1 ten into ten ones. This gives the following:

92 = 8 tens and 12 ones		**minuend**
−35 = 3 tens and 5 ones		**subtrahend**
57 or 5 tens and 7 ones		**difference**

You can check your results by adding the difference to the subtrahend. You should get the minuend.

Subtraction is also used to compare numbers. Suppose you compare the temperatures of a 19-degree day and a 35-degree day to find out how much warmer the 35-degree day is. You may think, What number added to 19 will make 35? You can do it this way:

19° to 20°	=	**1 degree**
20° to 30°	=	**10 degrees**
30° to 35°	=	**5 degrees**
		16 degrees

On paper, the operation of subtraction will provide a quick answer:

35 degrees
−19 degrees
16 degrees

x	1	2	3	4	5	6	7	8	9
1	1	2	3	4	5	6	7	8	9
2	2	4	6	8	10	12	14	16	18
3	3	6	9	12	15	18	21	24	27
4	4	8	12	16	20	24	28	32	36
5	5	10	15	20	25	30	35	40	45
6	6	12	18	(24)	30	36	42	48	54
7	7	14	21	28	35	42	49	56	63
8	8	16	24	32	40	48	56	64	72
9	9	18	27	36	45	54	63	72	81

MULTIPLICATION TABLE
This table can be used to find the basic multiplication facts, the products of any two numbers from 1 to 9. To find the product of 6 x 4, for example, find the 6 in the far left-hand column. Go along that row until you get to the column with 4 at the top. You will be on the 24, and 6 x 4 = 24.

Multiplication

Multiplication is a quick way of adding equal, or same-size, groups.

To do multiplication, you must know the basic multiplication facts. For example, you know that $3 \times 8 = 24$ is a basic multiplication fact. Read it as "3 eights equal 24." In a multiplication fact, the number being multiplied by another number is the **multiplicand**; the number used to multiply by is the **multiplier**; and the answer is called the **product**.

Suppose a pack of bubble gum contains 5 pieces; how many pieces are there in 3 packs? You can get the answer by adding equal groups or by multiplying.

Adding equal groups or **Multiplying**

$$\begin{array}{r} 5 \\ 5 \\ +\ 5 \\ \hline 15 \end{array} \qquad \begin{array}{rl} 5 & \textbf{multiplicand} \\ \times\ 3 & \textbf{multiplier} \\ \hline 15 & \textbf{product} \end{array}$$

Division

Division is the process of splitting a group into equal parts or groups. It is the opposite of multiplication.

To divide you must know some basic division facts. For example, $6 \div 3 = 2$ is a division fact. In a division fact, the number to be divided by another number is called the **dividend**; the number it is to be divided by is called the **divisor**; and the answer is called the **quotient**.

Suppose you have 24 soccer cards. If you can put 8 cards on each page in a photo album, how many pages will you fill? To find the number of pages, you can subtract equal groups or you can divide.

Subtracting equal groups of 8 or **Dividing by 8**

$$\begin{array}{r} 24 \\ -\ 8 \\ \hline 16 \\ -\ 8 \\ \hline 8 \\ -\ 8 \\ \hline \end{array} \qquad \textbf{divisor}\ 8\overline{)24}\ \textbf{dividend} \quad (\text{quotient } 3)$$

You can check your division results easily by using multiplication. Multiplying the quotient and the divisor should give you the dividend: $3 \times 8 = 24$.

In division you cannot divide by zero. For example, you may know that 24 cannot be divided into groups of 0.

Operations with Fractions and Decimals

You have been reading about addition, subtraction, multiplication, and division. All of the numbers in the examples you have seen are whole numbers. There are other kinds of numbers as well.

Fractions are numbers that represent parts of a whole, for example, one-half ($\frac{1}{2}$) of an apple, two-thirds ($\frac{2}{3}$) of a mile, or one-fourth ($\frac{1}{4}$) of a dozen.

Another way to express fractions is with decimals. For example, the fraction $\frac{1}{4}$ is 0.25 when written as a decimal.

Working with fractions and decimals is more complicated than working with whole numbers. However, the basic operations of arithmetic—addition, subtraction, multiplication, and division—can be applied to fractions and decimals.

▶USING CALCULATORS AND COMPUTERS

The operations of arithmetic can be performed by different methods. Calculations that may not have to be exact can often be done in your head. Sometimes using a pencil and paper helps you get an accurate answer quickly. When you need to do many operations or work with large numbers, calculators and computers are the most efficient way to work.

USING ESTIMATION STRATEGIES

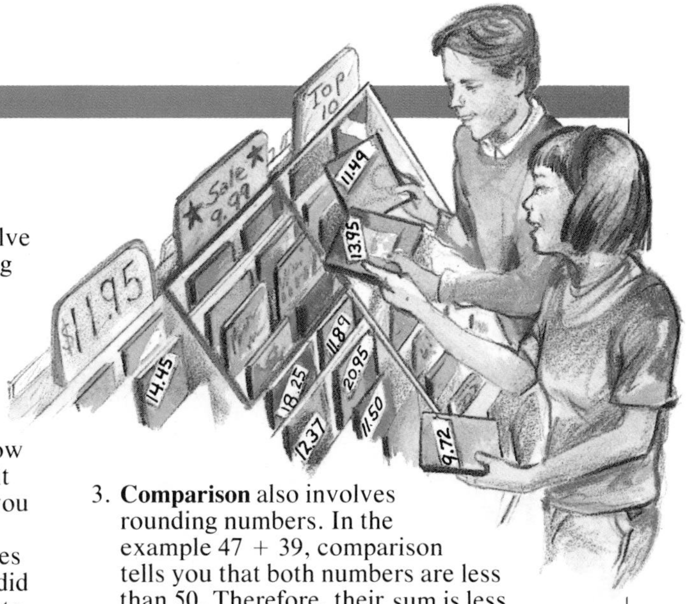

Estimation is an important step in the process of using arithmetic operations to solve number problems. Estimation involves using clues to make a sensible guess, or estimate. For example, an estimate tells *about* how many of something there may be, or *about* how large or small something may be. You have probably used estimation many times. For example, you may have estimated how long it might take you to get to school, or how much money you might need to buy an outfit for a special occasion, or how much wood you might need to make a bench. Until you actually made the trip or priced the purchases or made specific measurements, you really did not have an accurate amount. But an estimate gave you a good enough picture to begin with. All estimation strategies involve using numbers that are easy to work with mentally.

Here are several strategies:

1. One way to estimate is to **round** each number to the nearest ten, hundred, thousand, and so on, before you add, subtract, multiply, or divide. For example, to estimate the sum of 48 + 11 + 42 + 29, round each number to the nearest ten, then add.

$$\begin{array}{rcr} \mathbf{48} & \longrightarrow & \mathbf{50} \\ \mathbf{11} & \longrightarrow & \mathbf{10} \\ \mathbf{42} & \longrightarrow & \mathbf{40} \\ \underline{\mathbf{+\,29}} & \longrightarrow & \underline{\mathbf{+\,30}} \end{array}$$

2. **Clustering** is used when several numbers cluster near a single number. In the example 43 + 59 + 61 + 38, two of the numbers cluster near, or are close to, 40 and two are close to 60. The sum can thus be estimated as 2 × 40 plus 2 × 60, or 200.
3. **Comparison** also involves rounding numbers. In the example 47 + 39, comparison tells you that both numbers are less than 50. Therefore, their sum is less than 100.
4. Estimation can also be done by using front digits. This is called **front-end** estimation. To estimate 7,556 − 1,321, subtract the thousands: 7,000 − 1,000 = 6,000. Then adjust the answer: 556 is more than 321, so the answer must be *more than* 6,000.
5. A way to estimate quotients is to use **compatible numbers**, or numbers that are close to each other. For example, to divide 355 by 12, think of a number close to 355 that can be divided by 12 evenly: 360 ÷ 12 = 30.
6. In situations that require an exact answer, estimation is also helpful. Whether you compute with pencil and paper or with a calculator, it is a good idea to use estimation to check yourself and determine whether a particular answer to a problem is reasonable. If it is not, you should do the computation again.

Using estimation when you work with numbers will help you avoid careless errors.

Imagine, for example, that a recycling center collected 5,937 glass bottles, 7,365 plastic bottles, 3,779 metal cans, and 6,985 paper bags. What method would you use to calculate the total number of containers collected? It might be difficult to get an exact answer by performing this addition mentally. An accurate answer could be found in a reasonable amount of time using a pencil and paper. But a calculator would probably be the best choice to provide the correct answer quickly. Although computers can be used to perform lightning-fast calculations, they are best used for complex tasks, including organizing and displaying mathematical data, setting up graphs, and exploring mathematical patterns.

LYNN FLETCHER
Educational Writer

Reviewed by WILLIAM M. FITZGERALD
Professor of Mathematics
Michigan State University

See also DECIMAL SYSTEM; FRACTIONS AND DECIMALS; MATHEMATICS; NUMBERS AND NUMBER SYSTEMS; NUMERALS AND NUMERATION SYSTEMS.

ARIZONA

State flag

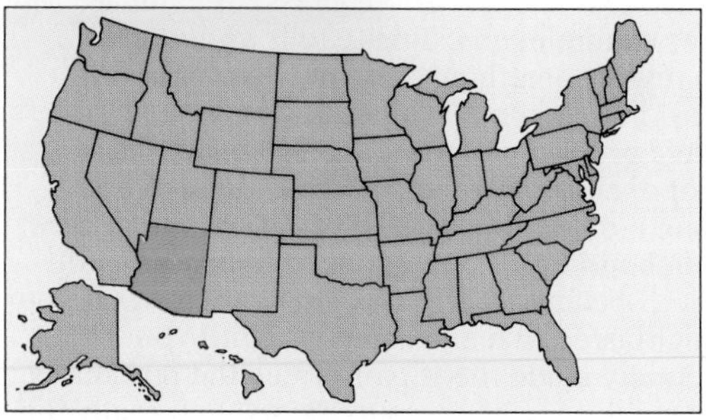

In 1736, a Yaqui Indian prospector discovered chunks of silver lying on the ground near a Spanish mining camp known as Arizonac. Pima Indians, who call themselves the O'odham ("the People"), lived in the region where the silver was found. Some scholars believe that the name Arizonac came from two Pima Indian words, ali *and* shonak, *which mean "small springs." Because many of the first European miners and settlers were Basques from northern Spain, other scholars think that the word derived from the Basque term* arritza onac *("valuable rocky places"). Whatever its origin, the name Arizonac eventually became Arizona.*

Because of its dry climate and sparse vegetation, Arizona is a state where the geological bones of the earth—its mountains, canyons, mesas, and valleys—dominate the landscape. In the north, the Grand Canyon of the Colorado River cuts a mile deep through rock formations that are nearly 2 billion years old. In the south, the Sonoran Desert stretches in a series of broad valleys and rugged mountain ranges deep into Mexico.

Arizona has one of the most varied natural environments in North America. North of Tucson, the Mount Lemmon Highway climbs 6,000 feet (1,830 meters) up the Santa Catalina Mountains, passing in the course of a one-hour drive through desert, oak woodland, pinyon pine and juniper woodland, pine forest, and spruce-fir forest.

Arizona's cultural environment is just as varied. Arizona is part of the American Southwest, a region where many different groups encountered one another and fought for control of water and land. The descendants of those peoples continue to live there today. Arizona is a state in which many different ways of life coexist.

It is also a place where the past exists side by side with the present. People have inhabited Arizona for at least 11,000 years; today it is one of the fastest growing states in the nation. Despite its well-deserved reputation for wide-open spaces, Arizona is one of the most urban states as well, with most of its population residing in metropolitan areas.

Most Arizonans work in those cities at manufacturing jobs or in service industries. Tourism is particularly important to the economy. Arizona's spectacular national forests, parks, and monuments draw millions of visitors to the state each year.

These national treasures underscore the importance of the federal government in Arizona. The U.S. government controls some 70 percent of Arizona's land. It also funded the giant water projects that provide much of the state with water for drinking, irrigation, and hydroelectric power.

LAND

Arizona is the sixth largest state in area. The Colorado River forms the western boundary with California. The northeastern corner touches the borders of Utah, New Mexico, and Colorado to form the Four Corners—the only point in the United States where four states meet. Although Arizona is landlocked, its southwestern border with the Mexican state of Sonora is less than 50 miles (80 kilometers) from the Pacific Ocean's Gulf of California.

Land Regions

Three major land regions—the Colorado Plateau, the Central Mountain Zone, and the Basin and Range—cross the state, giving Arizona great biological diversity as well as stunning natural beauty.

***Clockwise from left:* A desert vista includes ancient rock inscriptions left by Arizona's first inhabitants. Sightseers descend into the Grand Canyon—the state's best-known landmark—on mules. Native American culture is a vital part of modern Arizona life.**

State flower:
Saguaro cactus blossom

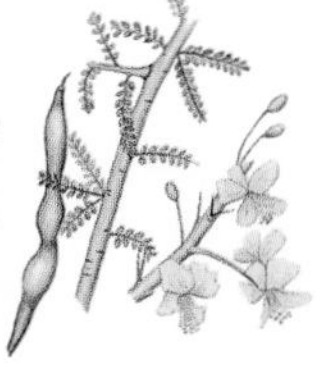

State tree:
Paloverde

FACTS AND FIGURES

Location: Southwestern United States; bordered on the north by Utah, on the east by New Mexico, on the south by Mexico, and on the west by Nevada and California.

Area: 114,006 sq mi (295,276 km^2); rank, 6th.

Population: 5,130,632 (2000 census); rank, 20th.

Elevation: *Highest*—12,633 ft (3,853 m) at Humphreys Peak; *lowest*—70 ft (21 m) along the Colorado River in Yuma County.

Capital: Phoenix.

Statehood: February 14, 1912; 48th state.

State Motto: *Ditat Deus* ("God enriches").

State Song: "Arizona."

Nickname: Grand Canyon State.

Abbreviations: AZ; Ariz.

State bird:
Cactus wren

The Colorado Plateau is Arizona's largest land region. Stretching into Utah, Colorado, and New Mexico, it extends across Arizona from the northwest to the southeast. The Colorado River and its tributaries have carved steep gorges into the layers of sedimentary rock that form the region. The deepest and best known of these gorges is the Grand Canyon. In between are high **mesas** (flat-topped hills), broken by volcanic craters and peaks.

The southern edge of the Colorado Plateau is the Mogollon Rim, which rises north of Prescott and runs south and east into New Mexico. With elevations of more than 7,000 feet (2,130 meters), it supports the largest stand of ponderosa pines in the world. The rest of the Colorado Plateau is lower and drier, with sparser vegetation. It includes the Painted Desert, famous for its barren rock landscapes, and Monument Valley, where spires of eroded rock tower over the high desert floor.

The Central Mountain Zone, below the Mogollon Rim, is an arc of mountain ranges that separates the Colorado Plateau from the Basin and Range. It is one of the wildest, most rugged regions of Arizona. Ranges such as the Bradshaws, Mazatzals, and Sierra Anchas cross northwestern and central Arizona. To the east are the White Mountains and the Blue Range. Much of Arizona's mineral wealth is concentrated in this region.

The Basin and Range, Arizona's third land region, extends across the western United States and Mexico. Most of Arizona's Basin and Range belongs to the Sonoran Desert, two-thirds of which lies in Mexico.

The Basin and Range is composed of isolated mountain ranges separated by broad, fertile valleys. As the region approaches Tucson, the valleys narrow and the mountains loom higher, reaching elevations of 8,000 to 12,000 feet (2,440 to 3,660 meters). Biologists call these high ranges **mountain islands**. By that they mean that the mountains contain plants and animals not found on the valley floors—the desert "oceans"—that surround them. Mountain islands occur throughout the state, but they are most distinctive in southeastern Arizona.

Above: The Mogollon Rim forms the southern edge of the Colorado Plateau. *Below:* The San Francisco Peaks, north of Flagstaff, are the state's highest mountains.

Rivers and Lakes

Although much of Arizona is desert country, rivers have shaped its landscape and its history. The Colorado River, the greatest river in the West, flows through or along Arizona's borders for nearly half its length. All other major rivers and streams in Arizona empty their waters into the Colorado.

The major tributary of the Colorado in northern Arizona is the Little Colorado River, which arises in the White Mountains. The Gila River and its major tributary, the Salt River, drain central and southern Arizona. They also provide most of the water that irrigates Arizona farms. The Verde River in central Arizona and the Santa Cruz and San Pedro rivers in southern Arizona also flow into the Gila system.

All of Arizona's major rivers have been dammed to provide water for irrigation and hydroelectric power. Those dams have created artificial lakes where Arizonans fish, boat, and water-ski. Major dams along the Colorado River include Hoover Dam, which formed Lake Mead, and Glen Canyon Dam, which flooded magnificent Glen Canyon to create Lake Powell. Roosevelt Lake, Apache Lake, Canyon Lake, and Saguaro Lake are strung like beads along the Salt River.

Hoover Dam, on the Colorado River between Arizona and Nevada, generates hydroelectric power and supplies water for agricultural and human use.

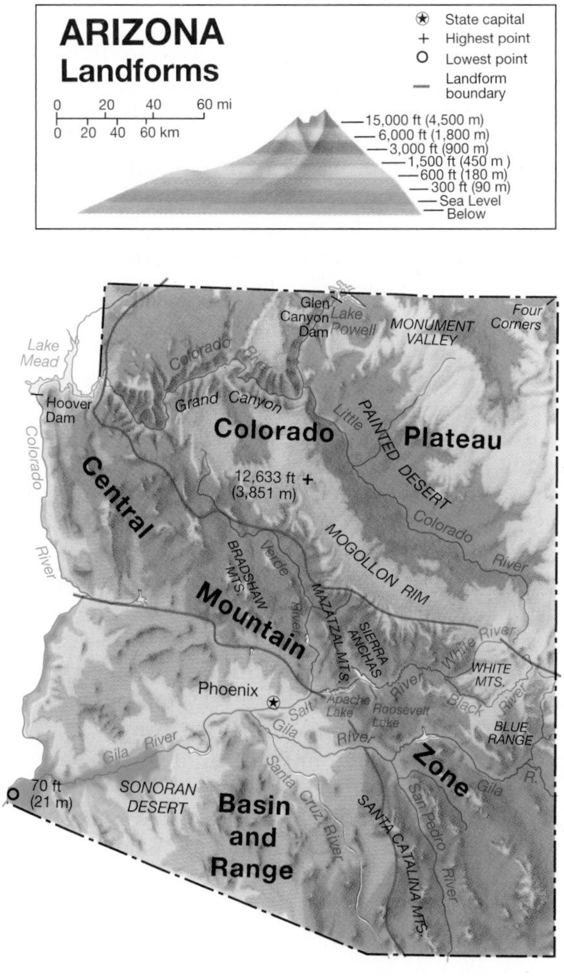

Climate

Most of Arizona has a very dry climate. Precipitation (rain and snow) varies throughout the state according to the elevation of the land. Lowland areas like Yuma in the southwest average less than 5 inches (127 millimeters) of rain a year. Rain or snow on the tallest mountain peaks may exceed 30 inches (762 millimeters).

Arizona's moisture arrives during two distinct rainy seasons. During July and August, summer thundershowers provide about two-thirds of the annual rain. Winter storms bring about one-third.

Much of Arizona is as hot as it is dry. Average temperatures for January range from 50°F (10°C) in the lowlands to 30°F (− 1°C) in the highlands. July temperatures average 90°F (32°C) in the lowlands and 65–75°F (18–24°C) in the mountains. Temperatures in the

Far left: Plants, such as the saguaro cactus, that have adapted to the desert climate are a distinctive part of the Arizona landscape. *Near left:* The heritage of the Old West lives on in Arizonans such as this foreman of a ranch near Wilcox.

deserts occasionally reach 120°F (49°C) in summer. Many portions of the desert endure more than 100 days of 100°F (38°C) heat a year.

Because Arizona is so hot and dry, farming is impossible without irrigation. The average number of days without a killing frost ranges from 240 around Yuma to 100 days at higher elevations in northern Arizona.

Plant and Animal Life

Arizona's varied environments support many different species of plants and animals. Black bears and elk inhabit the Mogollon Rim and the high mountain country. Herds of pronghorn antelope dart across the grasslands while bighorn sheep clamber over the summits of desert mountain ranges. Coyotes, mountain lions, bobcats, and mule deer range from the deserts to the mountains.

Perhaps the most distinctive plants and animals are those that have adapted to the hot, dry climate of the desert. Cacti such as the giant saguaro and the thorny cholla have broad, shallow root systems that quickly suck up scarce moisture, which is stored in their spongy stems. The tiny kangaroo rat has specialized kidneys that enable it to extract moisture from seeds, so it does not need to drink.

Natural Resources

Arizona is rich in minerals, particularly silver, gold, and copper. Black Mesa in northern Arizona contains enormous deposits of coal. Forests of ponderosa pine and Douglas fir stretch across the Mogollon Rim, while broad valleys in central and southern Arizona have soils suitable for farming. The only limitation on agriculture is water.

Because there are no major rivers south of the Gila, southern Arizona obtains most of its water from aquifers (underground deposits of water). Until 1993, Tucson was the largest city in the United States that pumped all its water from below ground. Now the canals and pipelines of the Central Arizona Project bring water from the Colorado River 335 miles (540 kilometers) across the desert to Phoenix, Tucson, and the farmers of south central Arizona.

▶ PEOPLE

After 1940, Arizona transformed itself from a rural to an overwhelmingly urban state. On the eve of World War II, 499,261 people lived in Arizona. By the year 2000, Arizona's population had soared to more than 5 million. More than 85 percent of those people live in cities and towns.

Most Arizonans come from other places, particularly California and the Midwest. Arizona society is mobile: For every ten people who settle in Arizona, seven move away.

Native Americans, in contrast, have inhabited Arizona for thousands of years and today make up about 5 percent of Arizona's population. Most belong to the 14 major Native American groups that occupy Arizona—

the Navajos or Diné (the largest group), Hopis, Western Apaches, Yavapais, Hualapais, Havasupais, Quechans, Mojaves, Maricopas, Cocopahs, Akimel O'odham, Tohono O'odham (formerly called Papago), Yaquis, and Southern Paiutes. Some 70 percent of Native Americans live on the state's 22 reservations.

Hispanic Americans make up about 25 percent of the state's population. Most are recent immigrants from Mexico, particularly Sonora. Others come from families that have lived in Arizona for nine or ten generations.

Americans of European descent make up about 64 percent of Arizona's population. African Americans compose 3 percent, and about 2 percent of the state's residents are Asian Americans. All these relatively new arrivals join with American Indians and Mexican Americans to make Arizona one of the most multicultural states in the nation.

Education

The Arizona territorial legislature established the first public school system in 1871. There are three state universities. The University of Arizona in Tucson and the Arizona Territorial Normal School (now Arizona State University) in Tempe were founded in 1885. Northern Arizona University in Flagstaff was created in 1899.

Arizona also has numerous public community colleges, including Navajo Community College, which is run by the Navajo Nation. Private institutions include the University of Phoenix, in Phoenix; Prescott College, in Prescott; and the American Graduate School of International Management, in Glendale.

Libraries, Museums, and the Arts

Arizona has an active public library system, with bookmobiles and computers connecting rural communities with libraries in larger towns. The Arizona Historical Society,

Authentic dances of old Mexico are performed at a festival in Sedona. Arizona shares many cultural traditions with Mexico, its neighbor to the south.

founded in 1884, operates its main museum in Tucson. Museums that focus on Arizona's Native American heritage include the Arizona State Museum of the University of Arizona in Tucson; the Museum of Northern Arizona in Flagstaff; and the Heard Museum in Phoenix.

Museums and botanical gardens devoted to the biological diversity of Arizona and the Sonoran Desert include the Arizona-Sonora Desert Museum west of Tucson, the Boyce Thompson Southwestern Arboretum near Superior, and the Desert Botanical Garden in Phoenix. The Phoenix and Tucson art museums contain important collections of Western, Mexican, and Native American art.

The Arizona Theater Company and other professional theater companies present plays in Tucson and Phoenix. Both Phoenix and Tucson have professional symphonies.

Arizona is internationally renowned for research in astronomy, anthropology, biology, and geology. One of the most important research institutions is the Desert Laboratory on

PEOPLE

Population: 5,130,632 (2000 census).

Density: 45 persons per sq mi (17 per km²).

Distribution: 87% urban; 13% rural.

Largest Cities (2000 census):

Phoenix 1,321,045	Scottsdale 202,705
Tucson 486,699	Chandler 176,581
Mesa 396,375	Tempe 158,625
Glendale 218,812	Gilbert 109,697

Persons per sq mi	Persons per km²
over 250	over 100
50-250	20-100
5-50	2-20
0-5	0-2

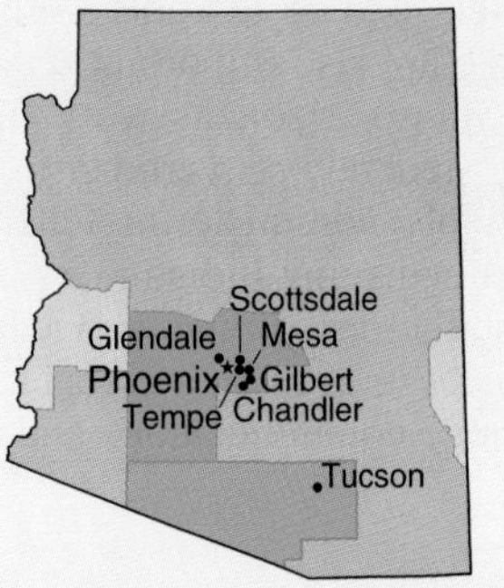

Source: U.S. Bureau of the Census

Above: Kitt Peak National Observatory, west of Tucson, is a world-renowned center of astronomical research. *Right:* Technicians inspect computer chips. Many Arizonans are employed in the electronics industry.

Tumamoc Hill in Tucson, where scientists have been studying the ecology of the Sonoran Desert for nearly a century. Another is the Kitt Peak National Observatory, west of Tucson.

ECONOMY

Before World War II, Arizona's economy was dominated by the so-called Three C's: copper, cattle, and cotton. Those industries remain important, but today most Arizonans work in the manufacturing or service sectors of the economy. More job growth was anticipated with the passage in 1994 of the North American Free Trade Agreement (NAFTA), which established a free-trade zone among Mexico, Canada, and the United States.

Services

More than 75 percent of Arizona's workers are engaged in service occupations. Many of these industries arose to serve the large numbers of tourists who visit the state each year. Businesses located along the Arizona-Sonora border rely heavily on customers from Mexico. Among the most important service industries are business, social, and personal services, such as banking, health care, and hotels and restaurants. Wholesale and retail trade are also important service activities.

Many Arizonans work for the local, state, or federal government, running public schools, administering federal and state lands, and managing Indian reservations and military installations. Other service industries are finance, insurance, and real estate and transportation, communicaton, and utilities.

Manufacturing

Manufacturing employs about 15 percent of Arizona's workforce. Leading products are machinery, transportation equipment, and electrical and electronic equipment.

Many manufacturing jobs are in the electronics and aerospace industries and rank high in terms of average annual salary. However,

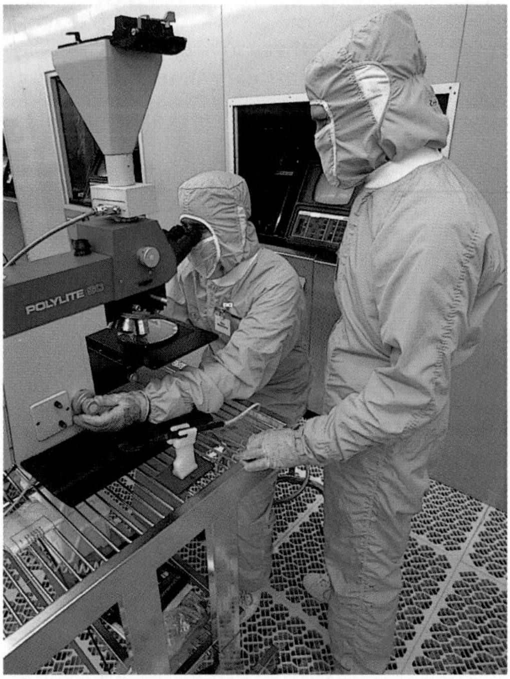

because many of these companies depend on government defense contracts, employment in manufacturing can be uneven. For example, the collapse of the Soviet Union and the end of the U.S.-Soviet arms race in the early 1990's led to layoffs in some Arizona electronics and aerospace companies. Nonetheless, the general trend in manufacturing seems to be expansion.

Mining and Construction

Mining, especially copper mining, was formerly the most important industry in Arizona. Today mining employs less than 1 percent of Arizona's workforce. The copper industry slumped in the 1980's, and although production rose again in the early 1990's, fewer miners were needed because of changes in technology.

A cattle drive on the Fort Apache Indian Reservation. Ranching, once a mainstay of the Arizona economy, remains an important industry in rural areas of the state.

Coal mining is restricted to Black Mesa in northern Arizona. On thousands of acres leased from the Navajo Nation and the Hopi tribe, coal is stripped from the ground with enormous draglines. Some of the coal fuels the Navajo Generating Station at Page. Mixed with water, the rest slides down a 274-mile (441-kilometer)-long pipeline to a power plant on the Colorado River in southern Utah.

Arizona's rapid growth has created employment opportunities in the construction industry. Federal projects such as the digging of irrigation canals also employ construction workers.

Agriculture and Forestry

Agriculture, ranching, and forestry remain important industries in rural Arizona. Arizona is a leading producer of cotton. Thousands of acres of alfalfa, wheat, vegetables, and citrus fruit are also cultivated. Although agriculture uses 80 to 85 percent of Arizona's water, it employs less than 3 percent of the state's workforce.

Ranching is a statewide industry, with most ranchers grazing their cattle and sheep on Arizona's public lands. About 40 percent of Arizona's total dollar value for agricultural production comes from livestock sales. The logging industry employs almost as many Arizonans as copper mining. Nearly all the timber is cut in northern Arizona, where most of the sawmills are located as well.

Transportation and Communication

Arizona is linked to the rest of North America by five interstate highways and two transcontinental railroads, the Santa Fe and Southern Pacific.

Two major international airports in Phoenix and Tucson connect Arizona to the nation and the world. More than 20 million people pass through Sky Harbor Airport in Phoenix each year. Because of its sunny skies, Arizona also has several major air bases, including Luke Air Force Base outside Phoenix and Davis-Monthan in Tucson.

All major Arizona cities have daily newspapers, and many rural communities have weekly newspapers. Radio and television stations, most originating from Phoenix and Tucson, broadcast throughout the state.

PRODUCTS AND INDUSTRIES

Manufacturing: Electrical and electronic equipment, transportation equipment, aerospace equipment, machinery.

Agriculture: Cattle, cotton, dairy products, lettuce, wheat, citrus fruit, sheep.

Minerals: Copper, silver, gold.

Services: Wholesale and retail trade; finance, insurance, and real estate; business, social, and personal services; transportation, communication, and utilities; government.

Percentage of Gross State Product* by Industry

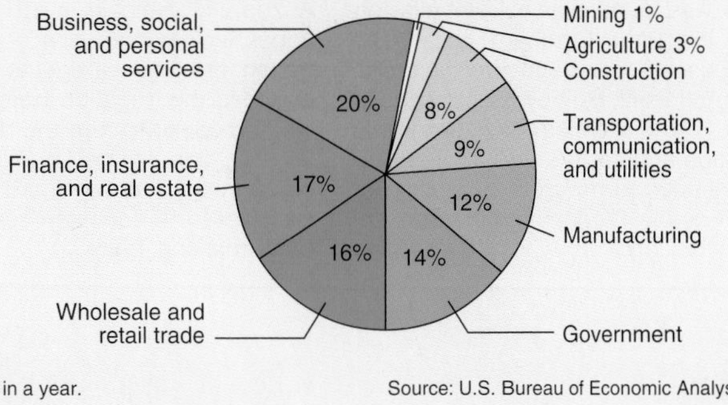

*Gross state product is the total value of goods and services produced in a year.

Source: U.S. Bureau of Economic Analysis

Places of Interest

Grand Canyon National Park

Mission San Xavier del Bac

Petrified Forest National Park

Betatakin Cliff Dwelling, Navajo National Monument

Many of Arizona's spectacular natural attractions are preserved as national forests, parks, and monuments. Some of the most outstanding are included in the descriptions below.

Canyon de Chelly National Monument, on the Navajo Nation in northeastern Arizona, is a sandstone canyon shaped like the talon of a hawk. At Spider Rock, a great sandstone spire, the cliffs rise nearly 1,000 feet (305 meters) above the canyon floor. Canyon de Chelly contains Anasazi Indian ruins built at the base of cliffs and in caves. The two most spectacular ruins are White House and Antelope House. Navajo (Diné) Indians farm small plots and graze their herds of sheep and cattle within the canyon.

Grand Canyon National Park is perhaps the most famous national park in the world. Set aside as a forest reserve in 1893 and a national park in 1919, the Grand Canyon attracts millions of tourists each year. An article on the Grand Canyon can be found in Volume G.

Kitt Peak National Observatory, on the Tohono O'odham Reservation, is a world-renowned center of astronomical observation and research.

London Bridge, in Lake Havasu City, is a historic stone bridge originally built in London, England, that was taken down and reassembled in Arizona. It spans an inlet of the Colorado River.

Mission San Xavier del Bac, south of Tucson, was founded as a Jesuit mission among the Pima O'odham Indians by Padre Eusebio Francisco Kino in 1700. The church itself, built by Franciscans in the late 1700's, is a magnificent example of baroque architecture and art. San Xavier continues to be used as a place of worship by the O'odham of the San Xavier Reservation.

Navajo National Monument, in northern Arizona, contains some of the most spectacular Anasazi cliff dwellings in the Southwest. Cliff dwellings such as Keet Seel and Betatakin appear to be timeless extensions of the sandstone cliffs to which they cling; in fact, anthropologists believe they were built, occupied, and abandoned between A.D.1267 and 1300.

Petrified Forest National Park, east of Holbrook, preserves prehistoric trees that turned to rock millions of years ago. The fallen trees and logs are scattered over thousands of acres. The park includes a portion of the **Painted Desert**, a barren area whose rock formations are tinted in shades of red, blue, and purple.

Roosevelt Dam, on the Salt River east of Phoenix, is the foundation of modern Arizona. Completed in 1911 by the National Reclamation Service, the dam controlled flooding along the Salt. It also provided the irrigation water and hydroelectric power to turn the Salt River Valley into one of the largest agricultural oases in the Southwest and Phoenix into the largest metropolitan center between California and Texas.

Saguaro National Park consists of two units east and west of Tucson. Both protect dense stands of giant saguaro cactus in the Tucson Mountains and the foothills of the Rincon Mountains. Tohono O'odham (Papago Indians) are still allowed to harvest saguaro fruit in the park in the early summer.

San Pedro Riparian Conservation District, along the San Pedro River in southeastern Arizona, was set aside by the federal Bureau of Land Management to preserve one of the last stretches of natural river habitat in Arizona. It protects great forests of cottonwoods and many species of birds and animals.

Tombstone, in Cochise County, became a mining boomtown after silver was found in the area in the 1870's. It is the site of the O.K. Corral, where Wyatt Earp, Doc Holliday, and other gunfighters took part in a famous shootout.

State Areas. Arizona maintains numerous state parks that preserve its natural beauty and its historical heritage. For more information, contact the Arizona State Parks Office, 800 W. Washington, Suite 415, Phoenix, Arizona 85007.

CITIES

Arizona has two major metropolitan areas. The largest is Phoenix and its satellites of Mesa, Glendale, Tempe, and Scottsdale. The other is the Tucson metropolitan area.

Phoenix is Arizona's capital and largest city. It became the territorial capital in 1889 and the state capital in 1912. Today it is a center of commerce and industry. Sun City, one of the first planned retirement communities in the United States, is part of the Phoenix metropolitan area. An article on Phoenix appears in Volume P.

Tucson, Arizona's second largest city, is located on the Santa Cruz River in the south central part of the state. Its name comes from a Pima Indian phrase meaning "the spring at the foot of the black mountain." Tucson was founded by the Spanish in 1775. It was the territorial capital from 1867 to 1877. An article on Tucson appears in Volume T.

Mesa, Arizona's third largest city, was founded by Mormon settlers in 1878. Originally an agricultural center, Mesa now anchors the rapidly urbanizing eastern portion of the Salt River Valley known as the East Valley.

Glendale began as an agricultural community promoted by canal-company developers in the late 1800's. Today it is the key city in the northwestern portion of the Phoenix metropolitan area. The American Graduate School of International Management is located there.

Tempe was known as Hayden's Ferry when it was founded in 1872 at a crossing on the Salt River. Like other cities in the Salt River Valley, its agricultural origins have largely given way to urban and industrial growth. Arizona State University is located there.

Above: **The state capitol in Phoenix. *Below left:* The capital since 1912, Phoenix is also Arizona's largest city and a center of commerce and industry.**

Scottsdale, located east of Phoenix, was founded in 1896 by Winfield Scott, a former army chaplain. Today the city, which calls itself "The West's Most Western Town," has many popular resorts and is a center of Western and Native American art markets.

Yuma, on the Colorado River in the southwestern portion of the state, is the center of a thriving agricultural area that includes the Wellton-Mohawk Valley along the lower Gila River. Thousands of tourists winter in the Yuma area each year.

GOVERNMENT

The state constitution was drafted in 1910 and approved by the people in 1911.

The governor heads the executive branch of the state government. The legislative branch is composed of a senate and a house of representatives. The judicial branch includes a supreme court of five justices.

Elected boards of supervisors administer Arizona's 15 counties. Most cities have city managers and city councils as well as mayors.

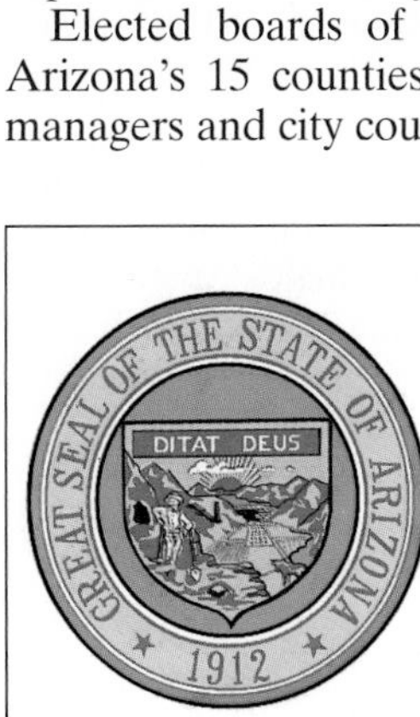

GOVERNMENT

State Government
- Governor: 4-year term
- State senators: 30; 2-year terms
- State representatives: 60; 2-year terms
- Number of counties: 15

Federal Government
- U.S. senators: 2
- U.S. representatives: 8
- Number of electoral votes: 10

For the name of the current governor, see State Governments in Volume S. For the names of current U.S. senators and representatives, see United States, Congress of the in Volume U-V.

▶ HISTORY

People have occupied Arizona for at least 11,000 years. Early peoples survived by gathering wild plant foods and hunting game. Farming began about 1000 B.C. in well-watered areas such as the Tucson Basin.

Beginning about A.D. 200, Arizona's three major pre-European cultures developed. The Anasazi inhabited the Colorado Plateau, where they built cliff dwellings and large pueblos. The Mogollon occupied the highlands of eastern Arizona and western New Mexico. The Hohokam lived in central and southern Arizona. Along the Salt and Gila rivers, the Hohokam created the largest pre-European system of irrigation canals in North America.

Spanish Exploration and Settlement

The first European to enter Arizona was Fray Marcos de Niza, a Franciscan missionary. In 1539, the Spanish government sent him to search for the legendary Seven Cities of Cībola, which were supposedly made of gold. A year later, a much larger expedition led by Francisco Vásquez de Coronado investigated de Niza's claims that he found the Seven Cities among the Zuni Indians of northwestern New Mexico. Those claims proved false, and Spain lost interest in Arizona until the late 1600's. Between 1687 and his death in 1711, Jesuit missionary Eusebio Francisco Kino established missions in northern Sonora and southern Arizona.

The arrival of the Europeans changed Indian life in Arizona in both good ways and bad. Old World diseases, such as smallpox and measles, killed thousands of Native Americans. But the Europeans also introduced horses, cattle, and sheep as well as crops, such as wheat, that could be grown in the winter.

Some Indians, such as the Pimas, became reluctant allies of the Spaniards. But others, particularly the Apaches, resisted the Spaniards and raided their settlements for horses and cattle. Because of Indian resistance, Spanish Arizona was confined to the valley of the Santa Cruz river. The first major Spanish settlement was Tubac, founded as a **presidio** (military garrison) in 1752. In 1775, the Spaniards transferred the presidio to Tucson.

Mexican Arizona

When Mexico won its independence from Spain in 1821, Arizona became part of the new republic of Mexico. The Mexican government awarded nine large land grants to Mexican ranchers in southern Arizona. However, by the 1840's the ranchers had been driven from the land by the Apaches.

In 1846, war broke out between Mexico and the United States. The Treaty of Guadalupe Hidalgo in 1848 ended the war and gave to the United States the territory of New Mexico, which included present-day Arizona north of the Gila River. Six years later, in 1854, Mexico sold southern Arizona to the United States under the Gadsden Purchase.

INDEX TO ARIZONA MAP

Place	County	Grid
Akchin Indian Reservation		C4
Apache Junction	(Pinal)	D4
Apache Nat'l. Forest		F4
Avondale	(Maricopa)	C4
Benson	(Cochise)	E6
Bisbee	(Cochise)	F6
Buckeye	(Maricopa)	C4
Bullhead City	(Mohave)	A2
Cabeza Prieta Nat'l. Wildlife Refuge		F1
Camp Verde	(Yavapai)	D3
Canyon De Chelly Nat'l. Monument		F1
Carefree	(Maricopa)	D4
Casa Grande	(Pinal)	D5
Cave Creek	(Maricopa)	C4
Chandler	(Maricopa)	D4
Chino Valley	(Yavapai)	C3
Cibola Nat'l. Wildlife Refuge		A4
Clarkdale	(Yavapai)	C3
Clifton •	(Greenlee)	F4
Coconino Nat'l. Forest		D3
Colorado	(Mohave)	B1
Colorado River Indian Reservation		A3
Coolidge	(Pinal)	D5
Coronado Nat'l. Forest		E5,E6,F6
Cottonwood	(Yavapai)	D5
Douglas	(Cochise)	F6
Eagar	(Apache)	F3
El Mirage	(Maricopa)	C4
Eloy	(Pinal)	D5
Flagstaff •	(Coconino)	D2
Florence •	(Pinal)	D4
Fort Apache Indian Reservation		E4
Fort Mojave Indian Reservation		A3
Fredonia	(Coconino)	C1
Gila Bend	(Maricopa)	C5
Gila Bend Indian Reservation		B4
Gila River Indian Reservation		D4
Gilbert	(Maricopa)	D4
Glendale	(Maricopa)	C4
Globe •	(Gila)	E4
Grand Canyon Nat'l. Park		B1
Guadalupe	(Maricopa)	C4
Havasu Nat'l. Wildlife Refuge		A3
Havasupai Indian Reservation		C1
Holbrook	(Navajo)	E3
Hopi Indian Reservation		E2
Holbrook •	(Cleburne)	E3
Huachuca	(Cochise)	E6
Hualapai Indian Reservation		B2
Imperial Nat'l. Wildlife Refuge		A5
Kaibab Indian Reservation		C1
Kaibab Nat'l. Forest		C1
Kearny	(Pinal)	D4
Kingman •	(Mohave)	B2
Kofa Nat'l. Wildlife Refuge		B4
Lake Havasu City •	(Mohave)	A3
Lake Mead Nat'l. Rec. Area		A1
Mammoth	(Pinal)	E5
Marana	(Pima)	D5
Mesa	(Maricopa)	D4
Miami	(Gila)	E4
Navajo (Dine') Indian Reservation		D1
Navajo Nat'l. Mon.		E1
Nogales •	(Santa Cruz)	E6
Organ Pipe Cactus Nat'l. Mon.		C5
Oro Valley	(Pima)	E5
Page	(Coconino)	D1
Papago (Tohono O 'odham) Indian Reservation		C5
Paradise Valley	(Maricopa)	D4
Parker •	(La Paz)	A3
Payson	(Gila)	D3
Peoria	(Maricopa)	C4
Petrified Forest Nat'l. Park		F3
Phoenix ★	(Maricopa)	C4
Pima	(Graham)	F5
Pinetop- Lakeside	(Navajo)	E3
Prescott	(Yavapai)	C3
Prescott Nat'l. Forest		C3
Prescott Valley	(Yavapai)	C3
Safford •	(Graham)	F5
Saguaro Nat'l. Park		D5
St. Johns •	(Apache)	F3
Salt River Indian Reservation		D4
San Carlos Indian Reservation		E4
San Luis	(Yuma)	A5
San Xavier Indian Reservation		D6
Scottsdale	(Maricopa)	D4
Sedona	(Coconino)	D3
Show Low	(Navajo)	F3
Sierra Vista	(Cochise)	E6
Sitgreaves Nat'l. Forest		E3
Snowflake	(Navajo)	E3
Somerton	(Yuma)	A5
South Tucson	(Pima)	D5
Springerville	(Apache)	F3
Superior	(Pinal)	D4
Surprise	(Maricopa)	C4
Taylor	(Navajo)	E3
Tempe	(Maricopa)	C4
Thatcher	(Graham)	F5
Tombstone	(Cochise)	F6
Tonto Nat'l. Forest		D3
Tucson •	(Pima)	E5
Wellton	(Yma)	A5
Wickenburg	(Maricopa)	C4
Willcox	(Cochise)	F5
Williams	(Coconino)	C2
Winslow	(Navajo)	E2
Wupatki Nat'l. Monument		D2
Yuma	(Yuma)	A5

• County Seat   Counties in parentheses   ★ State Capital

ARIZONA
State capital
Highway
City or town
Interstate
County seat
U.S.
Urban area
State boundary
National area
Indian reservation
County names are shown in RED
0 20 40 60 mi
0 20 40 60 km
Albers Equal-Area Projection
A B C D E F
1 2 3 4 5 6 7
UTAH
NEVADA
CALIFORNIA
NEW MEXICO
COLO.
SONORA
MEXICO
North
Las Vegas
Lake Mead
GLEN CANYON NAT'L. REC. AREA
Lake Powell
San Juan River
Colorado City
Fredonia
Page
KAIBAB IND. RES.
KAIBAB NAT'L. FOREST
NAVAJO
(DINÉ)
INDIAN
RESERVATION
NAVAJO NAT'L. MON.
GRAND CANYON NATIONAL PARK
HAVASUPAI IND. RES.
Colorado River
Little
KAIBAB NAT'L. FOREST
HOPI INDIAN RESERVATION
CANYON DE CHELLY NATIONAL MONUMENT
Chinle Creek
LAKE MEAD NAT'L. REC. AREA
HUALAPAI IND. RES.
Lake Mohave
MOHAVE
COCONINO
WUPATKI NAT'L. MON.
APACHE
NAVAJO
Puerco River
Kingman
Williams
Flagstaff
Bullhead City
FORT MOJAVE IND. RES.
KAIBAB NAT'L. FOR.
COCONINO NATIONAL
Winslow
Holbrook
PETRIFIED FOREST NATIONAL PARK
HAVASU NWR
PRESCOTT
YAVAPAI
Sedona
Clarkdale
Cottonwood
Chino Valley
NAT'L.
Prescott Valley
Camp Verde
FOREST
Lake Havasu City
Prescott
SITGREAVES NATIONAL FOREST
Snowflake
Taylor
St. Johns
Bill Williams River
Santa Maria River
Verde River
Parker
Payson
TONTO NATIONAL FOREST
Show Low
Pinetop-Lakeside
Springerville
Eagar
COLORADO RIVER IND. RES.
LA PAZ
Wickenburg
Hassayampa River
Cave Creek
Carefree
Theodore Roosevelt Lake
FORT APACHE INDIAN RESERVATION
APACHE NATIONAL FOREST
Surprise
El Mirage
Peoria
Glendale
PHOENIX
Paradise Valley
Scottsdale
SALT RIVER IND. RES.
Salt River
Black River
GILA
CIBOLA NAT'L. WILDLIFE REF.
Avondale
Buckeye
Tempe
MESA
Apache Junction
Guadalupe
Gilbert
Chandler
Miami
Globe
SAN CARLOS INDIAN RESERVATION
GREENLEE
KOFA NATIONAL WILDLIFE REFUGE
MARICOPA
Superior
San Carlos Lake
GILA RIVER IND. RES.
GRAHAM
Clifton
IMPERIAL NAT'L. WILDLIFE REF.
GILA BEND IND. RES.
AK-CHIN IND. RES.
Gila River
Gila Bend
Kearny
Florence
Coolidge
Casa Grande
PINAL
San Pedro
CORONADO
Thatcher
Pima
Safford
Yuma
Wellton
Eloy
Mammoth
Somerton
YUMA
NATIONAL FOREST
San Luis
San Luis Río Colorado
Santa Cruz
Marana
Oro Valley
PAPAGO
(TOHONO O'ODHAM)
INDIAN RESERVATION
CABEZA PRIETA NAT'L. WILDLIFE REFUGE
SAGUARO NAT'L. PARK
TUCSON
CORONADO NATIONAL FOR.
Willcox
ORGAN PIPE CACTUS NAT'L. MON.
South Tucson
SAGUARO NAT'L. PARK
COCHISE
SAN XAVIER IND. RES.
Benson
CORONADO NAT'L. FOR.
Tombstone
CORONADO NAT'L. FOR.
PIMA
CORONADO
SANTA CRUZ
NAT'L. FOR.
Huachuca City
Sierra Vista
Bisbee
Nogales
Douglas
Agua Prieta
Cananea
Magdalena
Caborca

Famous People

Bruce Babbitt (1938–), who grew up in Flagstaff, was elected attorney general of Arizona in 1974. From this position he unexpectedly succeeded to the governorship of the state on the death of the incumbent governor in 1978. Elected to two terms in his own right, Babbitt crusaded against land fraud and forged the Groundwater Management Act, which strictly regulated the pumping of Arizona's groundwater. President Bill Clinton appointed Babbitt U.S. secretary of the interior in 1993.

Cochise (1810?–74) was chief of the Chokonen band of the Chiricahua Apaches. He was one of the greatest Apache war leaders and diplomats of the 1800's. From his homeland in southeastern Arizona, Cochise and his fellow Chiricahuas fought both the U.S. and Mexican governments. He finally made peace with the United States in 1871. Cochise spent the last years of his life trying to negotiate a lasting peace between the Chiricahuas and the United States government.

Barry Goldwater (1909–98), born in Phoenix, was one of the architects of the modern conservative movement in the United States. He served as U.S. senator from Arizona from 1953 to 1987. In 1964, he won the Republican nomination for president but lost the national election to Lyndon Johnson. Goldwater served as chairman of the Senate's Armed Services Committee and its Intelligence Committee.

Barry Goldwater

Carl T. Hayden (1877–1972) was born in Tempe. He grew up watching the farmers of the Salt River Valley battle floods and droughts, especially during the disastrous years of the 1890's, and developed a lifelong interest in water control. He pursued this interest when, upon Arizona's admission to the Union in 1912, he became the state's first representative in Congress. Hayden remained in Congress until 1927 and then entered the U.S. Senate, serving from 1927 to 1969. In 1968 he secured approval for the Central Arizona Project, fulfilling his lifelong dream.

George W. P. Hunt (1859–1934), a rancher in the Salt River Valley, was president of Arizona's constitutional convention (1910) and was elected the state's first governor (1912). He went on to win re-election six more times. Hunt was a champion of the Arizona labor movement and an enemy at times of the big copper companies. He also was the president of a bank in Globe.

Helen Hull Jacobs (1908–97), born in Globe, was a tennis champion in the 1930's. She was the first person to win the U.S. Open women's singles title four years in a row. She also took the singles title at Wimbledon, England,

Territorial Arizona

During the Civil War (1861–65), most Arizonans favored the South. Confederate troops occupied Tucson in 1862 but were soon driven out by Union forces. Arizona was separated from the territory of New Mexico in 1863. Prescott, the center of a mining district, became the first capital of the Arizona Territory.

After the Civil War, more prospectors, ranchers, and farmers moved to Arizona. The newcomers invaded the traditional lands of several Indian groups, who defended their homelands and tried to drive the miners and ranchers out. By the 1870's, most of these groups had been defeated and settled on reservations. But the Chiricahua Apaches, under such leaders as Cochise and Geronimo, waged brilliant campaigns of guerrilla warfare against both the U.S. and Mexican governments. With the surrender of Geronimo in 1886, Apache armed resistance ended.

Development and Statehood

The arrival of railroads in the early 1880's transformed Arizona's economy, enabling Arizona's major products—cattle, copper, and cotton—to be transported throughout the country.

The number of cattle in the territory increased from about 5,000 in 1870 to 1.5 million in the early 1890's. Arizona ranchers shipped most of their cattle by railroad to California or the Midwest to be slaughtered.

Copper mining did not become feasible until technological changes in the late 1800's enabled mining companies to extract low-grade ores. Huge underground and open-pit copper mines in Bisbee, Superior, Ajo, and other boomtowns made Arizona the largest producer of copper in the United States.

Large-scale agriculture could not take place in Arizona until rivers had been dammed to control floods and provide irrigation water. The Salt River Project, a federally funded irrigation project, constructed the Theodore Roosevelt Dam on the Salt River near Phoenix. The dam, which was completed in 1911, allowed farmers in the Salt River Valley to cultivate several hundred thousand acres of land.

A movement to make Arizona a state arose in the 1890's, but not until 1910 did Congress allow Arizona to draft a constitution and apply for statehood. Arizona became the 48th state on February 14, 1912. Phoenix, which had been made the territorial capital in 1889, became the state capital.

where she was a six-time finalist. Jacobs was elected to the Tennis Hall of Fame in 1962.

Estevan Ochoa (1831–88), with his partner Pinckney Randolph Tully, operated one of the largest long-distance freighting companies in the Arizona Ter-

Helen Hull Jacobs

Estevan Ochoa

ritory. Ochoa also was a territorial legislator and a founder of the Arizona public school system. During the 1870's, he was a leading citizen of Tucson, serving as the first Mexican mayor of the city in 1875.

Sandra Day O'Connor (1930–) grew up on her family's ranch in Duncan. She served in the Arizona state senate and as a judge in the Arizona court system before becoming, in 1981, the first woman appointed to the U.S. Supreme Court. O'Connor is profiled in SUPREME COURT OF THE UNITED STATES in Volume S.

Linda Ronstadt (1946–), born in Tucson, is a well-known pop singer. Having first gained fame in the world of rock and country-rock, she later returned to her Southwest roots, recording albums of Mexican folk songs. Ronstadt springs from a musically prominent Tucson family. Her paternal grandfather, a native of Mexico who moved to Tucson as a young man, founded one of the city's first orchestras. Her aunt, **Luisa (Ronstadt) Espinel** (1892–1963), was a well-known performer of Spanish and Latin-American folk music during the 1920's and 1930's.

Stewart Udall (1920–), born in St. Johns, won fame as both a politician and an environmentalist. He practiced law in Tucson and served in the U.S. House of Representatives from 1955 until 1961, when President John F. Kennedy appointed him U.S. secretary of the interior. He held that post until 1969. His brother, **Morris Udall** (1922–98), succeeded him in Congress, serving from 1961 until 1991.

Later Developments

Beginning with World War II (1939–45), Arizona transformed itself from a rural to an urban state. Because of Arizona's good flying weather, the War Department built air bases throughout the state, training thousands of pilots there. The government also opened defense plants in Arizona. In addition, the war increased the demand for Arizona copper and other products.

Growth continued after the war ended. Wartime military and defense activities triggered a boom in electronics and aerospace manufacturing. The state's population grew as soldiers who had been stationed in Arizona returned there to live. Arizona's sunny, dry climate, now tempered by the use of air conditioning, attracted many new residents.

Arizona's Native Americans, who had been denied the right to vote in state elections until 1948, also profited from the economic boom. In the 1960's several tribes opened businesses on their reservations. In 1974 a long-standing land dispute between Hopi and Navajo tribes was settled by Congress. Land in northeastern Arizona that had been used jointly by the two tribes was divided between them. But the new boundary lines forced the relocation of many Indian families, and the settlement became a source of bitter controversy between Hopis and Navajos.

As the shift from rural to urban land uses continued, Arizona cities competed with farmers for water. The Salt River Project, which had turned the Phoenix area into an agricultural oasis in the early 1900's, now provided the water and power for Phoenix's phenomenal urban growth.

Arizona also tapped the water of the Colorado River. Under the terms of the Colorado River Compact, which Arizona signed in 1945, the state was entitled to 2.8 million acre-feet (3.5 billion cubic feet) of water from the Colorado each year. (An acre-foot equals enough water to cover an acre with a foot of water.) Congress finally approved the Central Arizona Project (CAP) in 1968. The CAP water was originally destined for agricultural use. By the time it finally reached Tucson in 1993, however, people were consuming much of it. As Arizona continues to grow, the struggle for water among various groups will undoubtedly intensify.

THOMAS E. SHERIDAN
Curator of Ethnohistory
Arizona State Museum

ARKANSAS

Early French explorers are credited with naming Arkansas after the Arkansa (or Arkansea) Indians. These Indians called themselves the Quapaw, meaning "downstream people," because they had settled in Arkansas after migrating down the Mississippi River. It was the tribes native to the region who named the newcomers the Arkansa, which in their own language meant "south wind people."

When the United States acquired Arkansas as part of the Louisiana Purchase of 1803, the spelling was changed to Arkansaw *to match its pronunciation, but it was soon changed back again. Ongoing confusion over the spelling and pronunciation finally prompted the state legislature to pass a law in 1881: The name of the state would be spelled* Arkansas, *but it would be pronounced* Arkansaw.

State flag

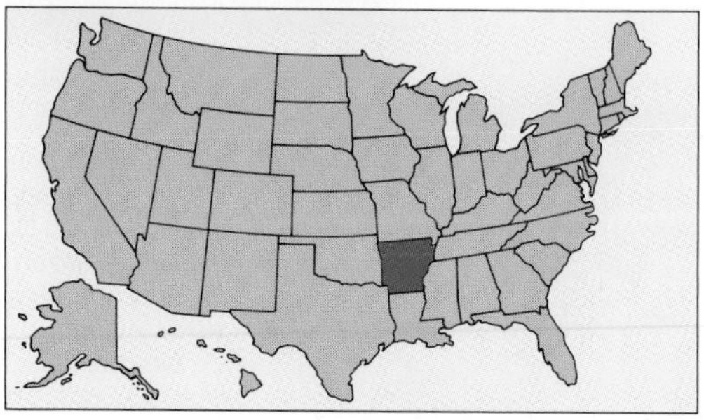

Arkansas is a southern state, located along the western bank of the Mississippi River. Its eastern and southern regions are covered by open plains that support large plantations on which cotton, soybeans, rice, and other cash crops are grown. To the north and west lie rugged highlands, featuring the beautiful Ozark Plateau and the Ouachita Mountains.

Much of Arkansas's history is linked to its agricultural past. Until 1865, state politics were dominated by slave-holding plantation owners, who supported withdrawal from the Union during the Civil War; in the 1880's dissatisfied small-scale farmers founded a new political party to protect their interests; and during the Great Depression of the 1930's, black and white tenant farmers and sharecroppers joined together to form the nation's first biracial farmers' union.

Despite the steady growth of manufacturing and the service industries in more recent years, the state continues to be associated with its agricultural production. Today Arkansas is the nation's leading producer of rice and poultry.

The largest segment of Arkansas's population lives in the farming regions in the south and east. However, the entire state is becoming increasingly urbanized and large numbers now live in central Arkansas, in or near Little Rock, the state's capital and largest city. The population in the northwest is also expanding due to the growth of tourism, the poultry industry, and retirement communities.

The state's official nickname, the Land of Opportunity, was adopted in 1953 to advertise the state's many assets and to attract new industries. The nickname the Natural State, which appears on Arkansas's state license plates, is the state slogan.

LAND

From east to west, Arkansas rises from the plains of the Mississippi Delta to the Ozarks and the Ouachita Mountains.

Land Regions

The land is divided into two main geographic regions—the lowlands in the southeast and the highlands in the northwest.

The Lowlands include the Mississippi Alluvial Plain, often called the Delta, and the West Gulf Coastal Plain. The Delta, which lies in the east along the Mississippi River, covers nearly one third of the state. The West Gulf Coastal Plain lies in the south-central part of the state and extends into neighboring Louisiana and Texas. The entire lowland area is relatively flat. It was once swampland, but most of it has been drained and put to agricultural use.

Natives of the Ozarks dedicate themselves to preserving regional customs and the unspoiled rural beauty of the Highlands. Ozark heritage celebrations, such as the annual Arkansas Folk Festival in Mountain View, feature traditional folk music, arts, and crafts.

State flower: Apple blossom

State tree: Shortleaf pine

FACTS AND FIGURES

Location: South central United States; bordered on the north by Missouri, on the east by Tennessee and Mississippi, on the south by Louisiana, and on the west by Oklahoma and Texas.

Area: 53,182 square miles (137,742 km²); rank, 28th.

Population: 2,673,400 (2000 census); rank, 33rd.

Elevation: *Highest*—2,753 feet (839 m) at Magazine Mountain; *lowest*—55 feet (17 m) along the Ouachita River.

Capital: Little Rock.

Statehood: June 15, 1836; 25th state.

State Motto: *Regnat populus* ("The people rule").

State Song: "Arkansas."

Nickname: Land of Opportunity (official); Natural State; Diamond State.

Abbreviations: AR; Ark.

State bird: Mockingbird

The Highlands are dominated by the Ozark Plateau and the Ouachita Mountains, with the Arkansas Valley between them. The Ozarks are sometimes referred to as mountains, but they are actually three eroded plateaus of increasing height: the Salem Upland, the Springfield Upland, and the Boston Mountains. The Ouachita Mountains, located in west-central Arkansas, rise more than 2,000 feet (610 meters). They are heavily wooded and known for their natural hot springs. The Arkansas Valley is lower-lying than the two regions it separates, and yet it has several high peaks of its own, including Magazine Mountain, the highest point in the state.

Rivers, Lakes, and Springs

Four great rivers flow through Arkansas: the Mississippi, the Arkansas, the Red, and the White. The Mississippi forms most of the state's eastern border. The Arkansas flows southeastward through the center of the state and empties into the Mississippi. Both rivers play important roles in transportation. Along with the White River and the Red River, they also serve as homes for wildlife and as places for recreation.

Dams have been constructed in a few of the smaller rivers, creating large artificial lakes. These lakes are chiefly in the Highlands and provide flood control, hydroelectric power, and recreation. Lake Chicot in the southeast is the state's largest natural lake.

Thermal springs attract tourists and other people who believe that bathing in them is good for their health. The water temperature at Hot Springs, a well-known resort, reaches about 140°F (60°C) at the surface. Mammoth Spring near the Missouri border is another well-known hot spring.

Climate

Arkansas enjoys a humid subtropical climate. Because of its inland location, Arkansas receives cold air masses from the heart of the North American continent in winter and hot air masses in summer. Far enough south, it also receives warm, moisture-laden winds from the Gulf of Mexico. The result is a relatively mild climate and an eight-month growing season that permits the cultivation of a wide range of crops.

July temperatures average about 80°F (27°C). The Highlands enjoy cooler summer nights than do the Lowlands. Similarly, the Highlands have somewhat colder winters. Average January temperatures in the state range between 36°F (2°C) and 48°F (9°C).

Most of the precipitation falls as rain, with the southern half of the state receiving more than the north. Snow sometimes falls in the northern mountains, but it is rare in the south. Arkansas ranks seventh among all 50 states in the amount of rainfall received. It averages about 49 inches (1,245 millimeters) per year.

Far left: The sandstone cliffs of Petit Jean Mountain overlook the beautiful Arkansas Valley. *Left:* Agriculture thrives in Arkansas's fertile Mississippi Delta region. *Right:* The soothing effects of the natural hot mineral springs in the Ouachita Mountains attract tourists from all over the world.

Plant and Animal Life

One hundred years ago, Arkansas was nearly covered by great forests of deciduous and evergreen trees, but today the majority of wooded land in the Mississippi and Arkansas river valleys has been cleared for farmland. Arkansas also has grasslands on its eastern prairies and in two counties in the northwest.

Many kinds of wildlife abound in Arkansas. Deer, fish, wild turkeys, and migrating ducks and geese, which feed in the rice fields, are abundant. Trout, largemouth bass, and smallmouth bass are among the many popular game fish. Squirrels, opossums, rabbits, weasels, and many other small mammals are found throughout the state. Black bears, which had nearly disappeared from the state, have been brought back and now thrive in the Boston Mountains.

Natural Resources

Arkansas's soils, forests, and minerals provide the raw materials that are so important to the economic life of the state.

The state's most fertile soils are its limestone and alluvial soils, which produce many different crops when properly fertilized and cultivated. The soils in the rice-growing areas have a subsoil that will not let water drain easily, which helps irrigate the rice.

Despite clearing by early settlers, forests still cover approximately one half of the state and are important economically. Softwood forests of shortleaf pine and loblolly pine are found in the south; hardwood forests of oak and hickory are found in the north, in the Mississippi Valley, and along southern streams.

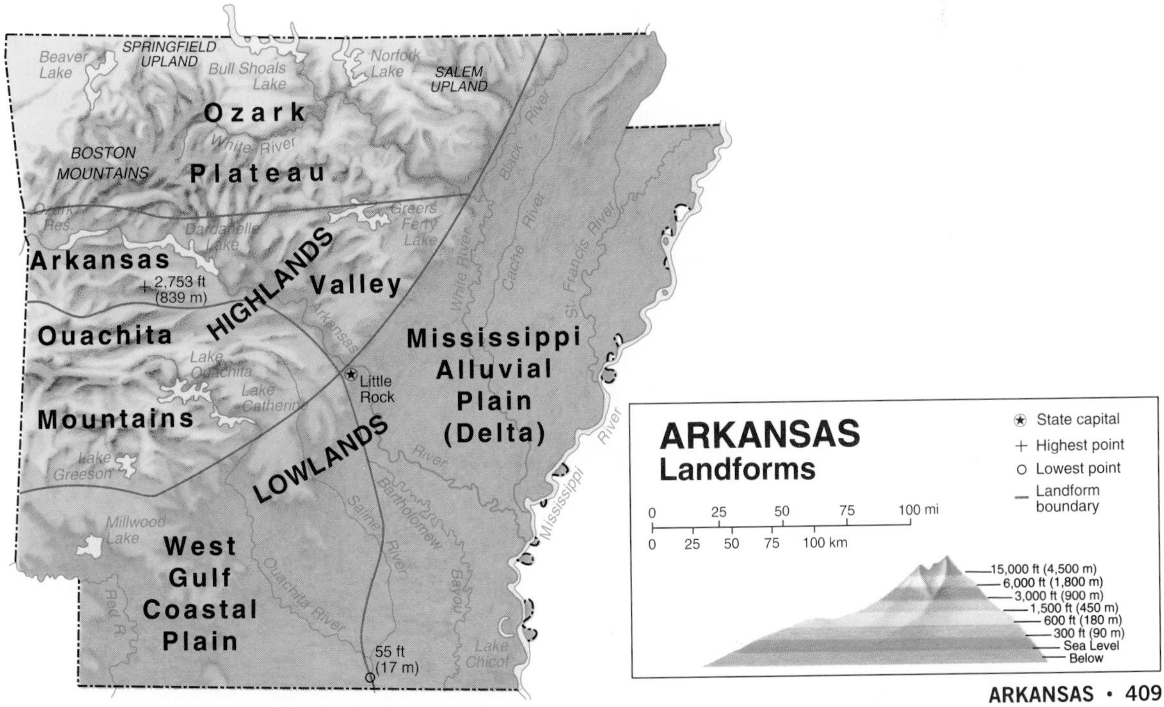

Left: **Arkansans who live in rural areas enjoy the benefits of country living. But increasing numbers are moving to urban areas in search of economic opportunities.** ***Above:*** **University of Arkansas football fans huddle for warmth at Razorback Stadium in Fayetteville.**

Most of the state's minerals are located in the West Gulf Coastal Plain and the Arkansas Valley. They include petroleum, natural gas, natural-gas liquids, clays, coal, and bauxite, from which aluminum is obtained. Stone is quarried in the highlands. Diamonds also are found in abundance, although they are no longer mined commercially.

▶ PEOPLE

The people of Arkansas are known as Arkansans or Arkansawyers. Approximately 54 percent live in urban areas; the other half live in rural areas—places with fewer than 2,500 residents. The Lowlands are more populous than the Highlands due to the Lowlands' productive agriculture, mineral wealth, and transportation facilities. The Highlands attract retired people because of the beautiful scenery, moderate cost of living, and pleasant climate.

The Caddo, Osage, and Quapaw Indians originally inhabited Arkansas, but few remain there today. In the 1800's, most were forced onto reservations in Oklahoma as a result of the westward expansion of Anglo-Americans.

Most of the Anglo settlers that first came to Arkansas were descendants of colonial southerners, most of whom had originally come from northwestern Europe. They brought with them to Arkansas the traditions and practices of the Old South, notably cotton production and slavery. Later settlers included Germans, Italians, Chinese, and Lebanese, who came to work on Arkansas's farms and railroads and in the lumber mills and mines.

Since the 1970's, Arkansas has shown a consistent gain in overall population. The African American population, however, has declined and today stands at about 16 percent.

PEOPLE

Population: 2,673,400 (2000 census).

Density: 50 persons per sq mi (19 per km²).

Distribution: 54% urban; 46% rural.

Largest Cities (2000 census):

Little Rock 183,133	Jonesboro 55,515
Fort Smith 80,268	Pine Bluff 55,085
North Little Rock 60,433	Springdale 45,798
Fayetteville 58,047	Conway 43,167

Source: U.S. Bureau of the Census

Persons per sq mi	Persons per km²
over 250	over 100
50-250	20-100
5-50	2-20
0-5	0-2

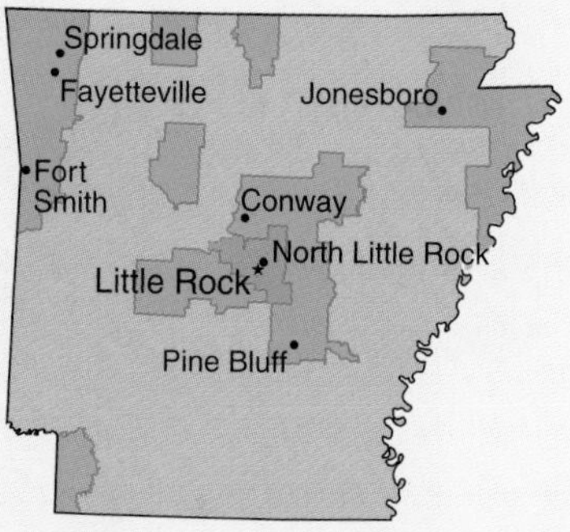

Education

When Congress created the Arkansas Territory in 1819, it set aside a section of land in each county for public schools. In 1843, the state legislature established a system for public education, but until the Civil War, most of the schools in operation were private. Today's public school system is largely based on a plan established by the state constitution in 1868.

Arkansas has 17 accredited four-year colleges and universites. The largest is the University of Arkansas, which has its main campus at Fayetteville; other campuses at Little Rock, Monticello, and Pine Bluff; and a medical sciences campus at Little Rock.

Other state-supported four-year institutions are at Jonesboro, Conway, Russellville, Magnolia, and Arkadelphia. Private four-year colleges include the University of the Ozarks in Clarksville, Hendrix College in Conway, and Harding University in Searcy.

Libraries, Museums, and the Arts

Arkansas's first library system was established in the mid-1800's. However, the growth of public libraries was slow, partly because the people lived in widely scattered rural areas. The Arkansas Library Commission was established in 1935 to address this problem. It maintains a book collection at Little Rock from which volumes are sent by mail to individuals, schools, and organizations. Bookmobiles operate throughout the state, and most of the cities support free public libraries.

The fine arts are represented in Arkansas by various activities. Little Rock has a choral society, an opera company, a repertory theater, and a symphony orchestra. Fort Smith and Pine Bluff also have symphony orchestras. Poets and writers have settled in Eureka Springs in northwest Arkansas where they have developed a lively and productive literary and artistic community.

The Arkansas Arts Center, in Little Rock, contains the state's most important collection of paintings and other fine arts. Also of note in Little Rock is the Museum of Science and History. The University of Arkansas Museum in Fayetteville contains Arkansas Indian artifacts and many science and natural history exhibits.

Arkansas is rich in folklore and legends. The Ozark Folk Center in Mountain View celebrates Arkansas folk culture. It provides live demonstrations of traditional arts and crafts during the summer. The library at the University in Fayetteville has a large and unusual Arkansas folklore collection that includes tape-recorded histories and stories told by Arkansas residents.

ECONOMY

In the past, Arkansas depended almost entirely on its farm products for its income. Products such as cotton, livestock, and poultry remain important income producers. However, in recent years services and manufacturing have become the state's primary economic activities.

Services

Arkansas's various service industries employ 70 percent of the state's entire work force. Wholesale and retail trade (the buying and selling of industrial and personal goods) are the most profitable within the services category. They are followed by financial services (banking, insurance, and real estate); professional and personal services (such as medical, tourist, and other social services); and government (which includes the maintenance of state-supported schools, hospitals, and the like). Remaining service industries are in transportation and communication.

Most people in Arkansas make a living in the service industries. Personal services include such everyday activities as barbering and hairdressing.

Arkansas is the nation's leading producer of rice (*above*) and broiler chickens (*right*). The state's economy once depended on agriculture, but today it is based more on the service industries and on manufacturing, particularly food processing.

Manufacturing

Manufacturing employs about 25 percent of Arkansas's work force. The most important manufacturing industry is food processing, including the canning of fruits and vegetables and the processing of poultry and livestock.

Industries that make electrical equipment also are profitable. Among Arkansas's many products are electric motors, refrigerators and ranges, air conditioners, television sets, and lightbulbs. Arkansas factories also produce clothing, plastic and metal products, and chemicals.

Agriculture

Arkansas's Lowlands belong to a wider region of the South known as the Cotton Belt, and farmers there once grew only this crop. Cotton production has since declined in importance, but it still brings much income to the state. Today Arkansas ranks sixth in the nation in cotton production.

Today rice and soybeans are Arkansas's most profitable cash crops. In fact, Arkansas rice farmers supply an international market, including Japan. Arkansas is also the nation's leading producer of broiler chickens.

Arkansas's forests provide the raw material for many of its manufacturing industries. Pine is used for wood pulp, which is used to make paper; oak and hickory are used to make furniture, barrels, and railroad ties.

PRODUCTS AND INDUSTRIES

Manufacturing: Food processing, electrical machinery and equipment, lumber and wood products, paper products, fabricated metal products, chemicals, nonelectrical machinery, rubber and plastic products.

Agriculture: Broiler chickens, soybeans, rice, wheat, cotton, eggs, milk, beef cattle, turkeys, sorghum grain, cottonseed, hogs, oats, hay, corn, grasses, grapes, snap beans, tomatoes.

Minerals: Petroleum, natural gas and natural gas liquids, bauxite, barite, coal, granite, gypsum, sand and gravel, limestone, marble.

Services: Wholesale and retail trade; finance, insurance, and real estate; business, social, and personal services; transportation, communication, and utilities; government.

*Gross state product is the total value of goods and services produced in a year.

Percentage of Gross State Product* by Industry

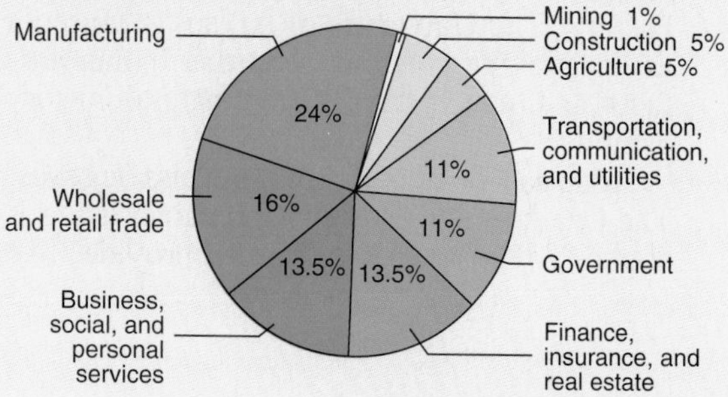

Source: U.S. Bureau of Economic Analysis

Mining and Construction

Petroleum and natural gas are important mineral products as are quartz crystals and crushed stone. Arkansas is the nation's leading producer of bauxite, the principal source of aluminum. It is also a leading producer of barite, a mineral used in the manufacture of paper, rubber, and other products. Mining and construction activities employ approximately 4 percent of the work force.

Transportation

The Mississippi River, the greatest river transportation system in the United States, has always been an important trade route to Arkansas. The Arkansas River also is used for limited amounts of freight traffic.

Four major and 24 short-line railways, covering 2,500 miles (4,000 kilometers) of tracks, operate within the state. Three of its rail systems are among the nation's largest: Burlington Northern, Inc.; the Union Pacific Railroad Company; and the Southern Pacific Transportation Company. Bus passenger service and bus and truck freight services also are important to the state's transportation systems. Arkansas has approximately 270 airports and airfields, and about one dozen commercial airlines serve the state. The principal airports are located in Little Rock and Hot Springs.

Communication

Until recently, Little Rock published two major daily newspapers, the *Arkansas Democrat* and the *Arkansas Gazette*. The *Gazette*, first published in 1819, had been the oldest newspaper in continuous publication west of the Mississippi River. The two newspapers combined to form the *Arkansas Democrat-Gazette*. More than 200 radio stations and 17 television stations broadcast throughout the state.

▶ CITIES

Six cities in Arkansas have populations exceeding 50,000. Only one, Little Rock, has more than 100,000 people.

Little Rock, the state capital and largest city, was founded in 1820. Its name comes from a rocky outcropping on the Arkansas River that marked the early settlement. Located near the center of the state, Little Rock is a major market for cotton, soybeans, and other agricultural products. It is also the leading transportation and trade center and the home of a large number of industries. Many historic buildings, such as the old Capitol, are located here.

Fort Smith, a historical border city between Arkansas and what was once called Indian Territory, grew up around a fort built in 1817. It is now an important market center on the Arkansas River, serving western Arkansas and eastern Oklahoma. It is also a leading industrial center, producing refrigerators, heating equipment, paper cups, light metal products, and furniture.

North Little Rock is an industrial city across the river from Little Rock. Among its products are clothing, cosmetics, wood products, ma-

Little Rock is Arkansas's capital and largest city. It was named after a small formation of rocks on the Arkansas River, where the city was founded in 1820.

Places of Interest

Crater of Diamonds State Park, near Murfreesboro

Ozark Folk Center, in Mountain View

Blanchard Spring Caverns, near Mountain View

Buffalo National River, in the Ozarks

Arkansas Post National Memorial, near Gillett at the mouth of the Arkansas River, marks the first permanent European settlement (1686) in the Lower Mississippi River Valley. Founded by Henri de Tonti, it served as Arkansas's first territorial capital (1819–21).

Buffalo National River was the first in the United States to be designated a national river (1972). Canoeists and rafters enjoy its exciting rapids and waterfalls and its scenic canyons, cliffs, and forests. It winds for 132 miles (212 kilometers) through the Ozarks.

Blanchard Spring Caverns, located near Mountain View in the Ozark National Forest, is one of the largest caverns in the United States. It contains many dramatic stalactite and stalagmite formations. The surrounding forest, one of three national forests in the state, is known for its rugged beauty.

Crater of Diamonds State Park, near Murfreesboro, is the only active diamond mine in North America. Discovered by farmer John M. Huddleston in 1906, it is no longer mined commercially. Visitors, however, may hunt for diamonds and keep whatever they find. More than 60,000 gems have been collected, some with a value of more than $100,000.

Eureka Springs, a resort town in the Ozarks, is known for its picturesque Victorian homes and tourist entertainments.

Hot Springs National Park, in Hot Springs, features a health spa and resort. Its naturally hot mineral waters reach a temperature of about 140°F (60°C). One million gallons flow from the spring each day. Visitors come to bathe in the mineral waters, which are said to be beneficial to one's health. The site was established as a national park in 1921. Thoroughbred racing is featured at nearby Oaklawn Park from February through April.

MacArthur Park, in downtown Little Rock, is home of the Arkansas Arts Center and the Museum of Science and History. The museum occupies the Old Arsenal Building, built in 1838, which was the birthplace of General Douglas MacArthur. The park is named for him.

Ozark Folk Center, in Mountain View, preserves Ozark folk arts. Craftspeople demonstrate traditional skills, such as blacksmithing, candle making, quilting, and weaving. Musicians also give live folk-music performances.

Pea Ridge National Military Park, located near Rogers, commemorates the largest Civil War battle fought west of the Mississippi River. More than 26,000 troops took part in the battle, which took place March 7–8, 1862. At the battle's end, Union forces had defeated the Confederate troops.

Toltec Mounds, in Scott, is an ancient ceremonial complex made of earthen mounds. The mounds once had buildings on them, probably used for religious purposes. They were built between A.D. 700 and 950 by people of the Plum Bayou Culture. Mistakenly named for Indians from Mexico, they are among the largest and most complex ancient sites in the Lower Mississippi River valley.

State Parks. Arkansas has 44 state parks and 3 state museums. For information, contact Arkansas State Parks, Department of Parks and Tourism, One Capitol Mall, Little Rock, Arkansas 72201.

chinery, and food products. Together with Little Rock it forms a large metropolitan area with a population of more than 580,000.

Pine Bluff, founded in 1819, is a commercial center in a rich agricultural region. It produces paper and other wood products, clothing, and light metal products. It is a major transportation hub for the southeastern part of the state.

▶ GOVERNMENT

Arkansas's government is organized under the constitution adopted in 1874 (the state's fifth) and its various amendments. The first was adopted in 1836 when Arkansas became a state. The second was adopted when Arkansas withdrew from the Union in 1861. Others were adopted as a result of the Civil War and its aftermath.

All of the constitutions have provided for three branches of government, with largely separate powers. The legislative branch, called the General Assembly, consists of two bodies: the Senate and the House of Representatives. Senators are elected to 4-year terms, representatives to 2-year terms.

The executive branch consists of a governor and six other state officers—the lieutenant governor, secretary of state, attorney general, treasurer, auditor, and land commissioner. Each is elected by the people to a 4-year term. Other members of the executive branch are appointed by the governor, with approval by the state senate often required.

The judicial branch interprets and applies the law. Four kinds of state courts make up this branch. They are the minor courts, the circuit courts, the chancery courts, and the Supreme Court. The Supreme Court consists of a chief justice and six associate justices, all elected to 8-year terms.

County and city governments have authority in various local matters, including taxation. Important county officers are the county judge, county and circuit clerks, sheriff, assessor, collector, and treasurer.

Arkansas's state capitol in Little Rock was modeled after the United States Capitol in Washington, D.C. The granite and marble structure was completed in 1915.

▶ HISTORY

Three Indian groups lived in the Arkansas region at the time of first contact with European explorers: the Quapaw in the east, the Caddo in the Ouachita and Red river valleys of the southwest, and the Osage in the west.

European Exploration

The first Europeans to visit Arkansas were Spanish explorers, who arrived in 1541 looking for gold. They were led by Hernando de Soto, who died in Arkansas the following year.

The next wave of visitors came 130 years later, when French explorers Father Jacques Marquette and Louis Jolliet traveled by canoe down the Mississippi River and reached the Arkansas River in 1673.

In 1682, a French explorer and fur trader named Robert Cavelier, Sieur de La Salle, also traveled down the Mississippi to claim the river and its wide valley for the king

GOVERNMENT

State Government
Governor: 4-year term
State senators: 35; 4-year terms
State representatives: 100; 2-year terms
Number of counties: 75

Federal Government
U.S. senators: 2
U.S. representatives: 4
Number of electoral votes: 6

For the name of the current governor, see STATE GOVERNMENTS in Volume S. For the names of current U.S. senators and representatives, see UNITED STATES, CONGRESS OF THE in Volume U-V.

French explorers Father Jacques Marquette and Louis Jolliet first encountered the Quapaw Indians in 1673 when their expedition reached the Arkansas River.

of France. His faithful lieutenant, Henri de Tonti, returned to Arkansas in 1686, and at the mouth of the Arkansas River he founded a settlement the French called *Aux Arcs* (pronounced Ozarks), Arkansas's first permanent European settlement. Later it was renamed Arkansas Post.

The Louisiana Purchase and Statehood

Arkansas, which was claimed at various times by both France and Spain, was part of an enormous region that was called Louisiana. In 1803, the French emperor Napoleon I sold the territory to the United States. After the Louisiana Purchase, Arkansas was part of the Missouri Territory. Then in 1819 it became its own territory, with its own territorial governor. On June 15, 1836, Arkansas became the 25th state.

Withdrawal from the Union

In the early 1860's, with the threat of civil war surrounding the question of slavery, Arkansas voted against seceding (withdrawing) from the Union, unlike many other Southern states that seceded and formed the Confederate States of America. But after the Civil War began at Fort Sumter, South Carolina, on April 12, 1861, Arkansas joined the Southern states and seceded from the Union on May 6.

INDEX TO ARKANSAS MAP

Arkadelphia •	(Clark)	**B3**
Arkansas City •	(Desha)	**D4**
Ashdown •	(Little River)	**A4**
Ash Flat •	(Sharp)	**D1**
Augusta •	(Woodruff)	**D2**
Barling	(Sebastian)	**A2**
Batesville •	(Independence)	**D2**
Beebe	(White)	**D2**
Benton •	(Saline)	**C3**
Bentonville •	(Benton)	**A1**
Berryville •	(Carroll)	**B1**
Big Lake Nat'l Wildlife Refuge		**E2**
Blytheville •	(Mississippi)	**F2**
Booneville •	(Logan)	**B2**
Brinkley	(Monroe)	**D3**
Bryant	(Saline)	**C3**
Cabot	(Lonoke)	**C3**
Camden •	(Ouachita)	**C4**
Charleston •	(Franklin)	**A2**
Clarendon •	(Monroe)	**D3**
Clarksville •	(Johnson)	**B2**
Clinton •	(Van Buren)	**C2**
Conway •	(Faulkner)	**C2**
Corning •	(Clay)	**E1**
Crossett	(Ashley)	**D4**
Danville •	(Yell)	**B2**
Dardanelle •	(Yell)	**B2**
De Queen •	(Sevier)	**A3**
Dermott	(Chicot)	**D4**
Des Arc •	(Prairie)	**D3**
De Valls Bluff •	(Prairie)	**D3**
De Witt •	(Arkansas)	**D3**
Dumas	(Desha)	**D4**
Earle	(Crittenden)	**E2**
El Dorado •	(Union)	**C4**
England	(Lonoke)	**D3**
Eudora	(Chicot)	**D4**
Eureka Springs •	(Carroll)	**B1**
Fayetteville •	(Washington)	**A1**
Fordyce •	(Dallas)	**C4**
Forrest City •	(St. Francis)	**E2**
Fort Smith •	(Sebastian)	**A2**
Gosnell	(Mississippi)	**E2**
Greenwood •	(Sebastian)	**A2**
Hamburg •	(Ashley)	**D4**
Hampton •	(Calhoun)	**C4**
Harrisburg •	(Poinsett)	**E2**
Harrison •	(Boone)	**B1**
Heber Springs •	(Cleburne).	**C2**
Helena •	(Phillips)	**E3**
Hope •	(Hempstead)	**B4**
Hot Springs •	(Garland)	**B3**
Huntsville •	(Madison)	**B1**
Jacksonville	(Pulaski)	**C3**
Jasper •	(Newton)	**B2**
Jonesboro •	(Craighead)	**E2**
Lake City •	(Craighead)	**E2**
Lake Village •	(Chicot)	**D4**
Lewisville •	(Lafayette)	**B4**
Little Rock ★	(Pulaski)	**C3**
Lonoke •	(Lonoke)	**D3**
McGehee	(Desha).	**D4**
Magnolia •	(Columbia)	**B4**
Malvern •	(Hot Spring)	**C3**
Marianna •	(Lee)	**E3**
Marion •	(Crittenden)	**E2**
Marked Tree	(Poinsett)	**E2**
Marshall •	(Searcy)	**C2**
Maumelle	(Pulaski)	**C3**
Melbourne •	(Izard)	**D1**
Mena •	(Polk)	**A3**
Monticello •	(Drew)	**D4**
Morrilton •	(Conway)	**C2**
Mountain Home •	(Baxter)	**C1**
Mountain View •	(Stone)	**C2**
Mount Ida •	(Montgomery)	**B3**
Murfreesboro •	(Pike)	**B3**
Nashville •	(Howard)	**B4**
Newport •	(Jackson)	**D2**
North Little Rock	(Pulaski)	**C3**
Osceola •	(Mississippi)	**E2**
Ouachita Nat'l Forest		**A3, B3**
Ozark •	(Franklin)	**B2**
Ozark Nat'l Forest		**B2, C1**
Paragould •	(Greene)	**E1**
Paris •	(Logan)	**B2**
Perryville •	(Perry)	**C2**
Piggott •	(Clay)	**E1**
Pine Bluff •	(Jefferson).	**C3**
Pocahontas •	(Randolph)	**D1**
Prescott •	(Nevada)	**B4**
Rison •	(Cleveland)	**C4**
Rogers	(Benton)	**A1**
Russellville •	(Pope)	**B2**
St. Francis Nat'l Forest		**E3**
Salem •	(Fulton)	**D1**
Searcy •	(White)	**D2**
Sheridan •	(Grant)	**C3**
Sherwood	(Pulaski)	**C3**
Siloam Springs	(Benton)	**A1**
Springdale	(Washington)	**A1**
Star City •	(Lincoln)	**D4**
Stuttgart •	(Arkansas)	**D3**
Texarkana •	(Miller)	**B4**
Trumann	(Poinsett)	**E2**
Van Buren •	(Crawford)	**A2**
Waldron •	(Scott)	**A3**
Walnut Ridge •	(Lawrence)	**D1**
Warren •	(Bradley)	**C4**
West Helena	(Phillips)	**E3**
West Memphis	(Crittenden)	**E2**
White Hall	(Jefferson)	**C3**
White River Nat'l Wildlife Refuge		**D3**
Wynne •	(Cross)	**E2**
Yellville •	(Marion)	**C1**

• County Seat Counties in parentheses ★ State Capital

The Civil War and Reconstruction

The Civil War brought devastation and bitterness to Arkansas. About 60,000 Arkansans fought for the Confederacy; however, as many as 15,000 joined the Union forces. The largest battle that was fought west of the Mississippi River took place in Arkansas, at Pea Ridge on

ARKANSAS
State capital
City or town
County seat
Urban area
National forest
Highway
Interstate
U.S.
State boundary
County names are shown in RED
0 10 20 30 40 mi
0 10 20 30 40 km
Albers Equal-Area Projection
North
A
B
C
D
E
F
1
2
3
4
MISSOURI
KENTUCKY
TENNESSEE
MISSISSIPPI
OKLAHOMA
TEXAS
LOUISIANA
BENTON
CARROLL
BOONE
MARION
BAXTER
FULTON
RANDOLPH
CLAY
GREENE
LAWRENCE
SHARP
IZARD
MADISON
WASHINGTON
NEWTON
SEARCY
STONE
INDEPENDENCE
CRAIGHEAD
MISSISSIPPI
CRAWFORD
FRANKLIN
JOHNSON
POPE
VAN BUREN
CLEBURNE
JACKSON
POINSETT
CROSS
CRITTENDEN
SEBASTIAN
LOGAN
CONWAY
FAULKNER
WHITE
WOODRUFF
ST. FRANCIS
YELL
PERRY
SCOTT
PRAIRIE
LEE
MONROE
PULASKI
LONOKE
SALINE
GARLAND
MONTGOMERY
POLK
PHILLIPS
ARKANSAS
JEFFERSON
GRANT
HOT SPRING
HOWARD
PIKE
CLARK
DALLAS
CLEVELAND
LINCOLN
DESHA
SEVIER
LITTLE RIVER
HEMPSTEAD
NEVADA
OUACHITA
CALHOUN
DREW
BRADLEY
MILLER
LAYFAYETTE
COLUMBIA
UNION
ASHLEY
CHICOT
OZARK NATIONAL FOREST
OZARK NAT'L. FOREST
OUACHITA NATIONAL FOREST
ST. FRANCIS NAT'L FOREST
BIG LAKE NAT'L WILDLIFE REFUGE
WHITE RIVER NAT'L. WILDLIFE REFUGE
Bentonville
Rogers
Siloam Springs
Springdale
Fayetteville
Eureka Springs
Berryville
Huntsville
Harrison
Jasper
Yellville
Mountain Home
Salem
Pocahontas
Corning
Piggott
Ash Flat
Melbourne
Walnut Ridge
Paragould
Jonesboro
Kennett
Gosnell
Blytheville
Dyersburg
Marshall
Mountain View
Batesville
Osceola
Jackson
Brownsville
Trumann
Harrisburg
Marked Tree
Tahlequah
Sallisaw
Van Buren
Ozark
Clarksville
Clinton
Heber Springs
Newport
Fort Smith
Barling
Charleston
Paris
Greenwood
Booneville
Dardanelle
Russellville
Morrilton
Conway
Searcy
Augusta
Wynne
Earle
Marion
Millington
West Memphis
MEMPHIS
Poteau
Danville
Beebe
Forrest City
Waldron
Perryville
Cabot
Des Arc
Jacksonville
Sherwood
Brinkley
Maumelle
LITTLE ROCK
North Little Rock
Lonoke
De Valls Bluff
Clarendon
Marianna
Mena
Mount Ida
Hot Springs
Bryant
Benton
England
Stuttgart
West Helena
Helena
Malvern
Sheridan
White Hall
Pine Bluff
De Witt
Clarksdale
De Queen
Murfreesboro
Arkadelphia
Nashville
Idabel
Rison
Star City
Dumas
Prescott
Fordyce
Ashdown
Hope
Camden
Hampton
Warren
Monticello
McGehee
Arkansas City
Dermott
Cleveland
Greenwood
Greenville
Texarkana
Lewisville
Magnolia
El Dorado
Hamburg
Lake Village
Crossett
Eudora
Mount Pleasant
Table Rock Lake
Beaver Lake
Bull Shoals Lake
Norfolk Lake
Greers Ferry Lake
Lake Dardanelle
Ouachita Lake
DeGray Lake
Millwood Lake
Lake Texarkana
White River
Buffalo River
Black River
St. Francis River
Little Red River
Arkansas River
Caddo River
Saline River
Ouachita River
Little River
Red River
Sulphur River
Mississippi River
62
55
63
67
40
65
30
79
95°
94°
93°
92°
91°
90°
89°
36°
35°
34°
33°

Famous People

Maya Angelou

Bill Clinton

Maya Angelou (1928–), born Marguerite Johnson in St. Louis, Missouri, was raised in Stamps. Her autobiography, about growing up during the civil rights movement, is entitled *I Know Why the Caged Bird Sings* (1970). Other works include *All God's Children Need Traveling Shoes* (1986) and *I Shall not be Moved* (1990). In 1993 she read a poem at the presidential inauguration of Bill Clinton that she wrote especially for the occasion.

Hattie Wyatt Caraway (1876–1950) was born near Bakersville, Tennessee, but later settled in Arkansas. A Democrat, she was the first woman elected to the U.S. Senate. In 1931 she completed her deceased husband's Senate term and was elected in her own right in 1932 and 1938. She sponsored an early version of the Equal Rights Amendment.

Johnny Cash (1932–2003), born in Kingsland, was a popular country music singer, guitarist, and composer. His hit songs included "I Walk the Line" (1956), "Folsom Prison Blues" (1956), and "A Boy Named Sue" (1969). In 2003 he won his 11th Grammy Award for the song "Give My Love to Rose," and an MTV Video Music Award for his video "Hurt." He also appeared in films and on television.

William Jefferson (Bill) Clinton (1946–), born and raised in Hope, was 42nd president of the United States (1993–2001). A biography of Bill Clinton appears in Volume C.

Jay Hanna (Dizzy) Dean (1911–1974), born in Lucas, was one of baseball's greatest pitchers. As a member of the St. Louis Cardinals, he led the National League in strikeouts for four years (1932–36) and in 1934 he won thirty games and the NL Most Valuable Player Award. He was traded to the Chicago Cubs in 1938 and later became a sports announcer. He was elected to the National Baseball Hall of Fame in 1953.

March 7–8, 1862. Union forces won the battle and secured much of Arkansas and Missouri for the United States. After Union forces captured Little Rock in September 1863, the war was effectively over for Arkansas, although the civilians continued to suffer greatly. Arkansas was readmitted to the Union in 1868 but was occupied by federal troops until 1874.

Politics and Segregation

In the 1880's, many of Arkansas's tenant farmers and sharecroppers suffered due to low farm prices. In part, they blamed the Democrats who ruled the state legislature, and in 1886 they formed their own protest organization, the Agricultural Wheel, and ran "Wheeler" candidates for political office. The Democrats, in order to control dissent and drive a wedge between white "Wheelers" and black "Wheelers," passed laws that made it difficult for blacks to vote. Also, lynchings and other violence toward blacks increased.

Improvements and Reforms

In the early 1900's, during a period known as the Progressive Era, Arkansas's educational system was improved; a board of health was created; and a commission was formed to oversee the state's business interests. But in spite of this era of optimism, Arkansas soon faced many setbacks.

In the 1920's a major depression in agriculture ruined many farmers. Then a tragic flood in 1927 killed many people and destroyed much of that year's crops. Four years later, as the Great Depression of the 1930's was getting underway, a great drought again ruined crops. The government's New Deal programs brought relief to farm owners but to few farmworkers. As a result, black and white tenant farmers and sharecroppers banded together to form the Southern Tenant Farmer's Union, the first biracial union in the nation's history. The group succeeded in bringing attention to the plight of farm laborers.

In the early 1940's, World War II helped Arkansas's economy, but at the same time, thousands of people left the state, either to serve in the armed forces or to work in defense-related industries. With the work force depleted, farmers began to rely more on machinery to harvest the crops, and eventually agriculture became fully mechanized.

Integration

In 1954, the U.S. Supreme Court declared that segregating black and white students in separate schools was unconstitutional. Arkan-

James William Fulbright (1905–95) was born in Sumner, Missouri, but grew up in Fayetteville. A Rhodes scholar and lawyer, he served two terms as a U.S. representative (1942–45) and served five terms as a U.S. senator (1945–74) from Arkansas. In 1946 he sponsored the Fulbright Act, which provides scholarship funds to students studying abroad. As chairman of the Senate Foreign Relations Committee (1959–74), he was one of the chief congressional opponents of American involvement in the Vietnam War. The College of Arts and Sciences and the Institute of International Relations, both at the University of Arkansas, have been named for him.

John Harold Johnson (1918–   ), born in Arkansas City, founded (1942) the Johnson Publishing Company, which publishes *Ebony* and *Jet* magazines. Johnson has also been highly successful in the fields of book publishing, radio broadcasting, and cosmetics. He was awarded the Spingarn Medal in 1966.

Scott Joplin (1868–1917) was probably born in the border town of Texarkana. The son of former slaves, this musical genius became known as the King of Ragtime. Joplin's lively compositions include the still-popular "Maple Leaf Rag" and "The Entertainer." However, he was not recognized as a serious composer until long after his death; he was awarded a Pulitzer Prize in 1976.

Douglas MacArthur (1880–1964), born in Little Rock, was one of the United States' most brilliant generals. As commander of the U.S. Army in the Pacific during World War II (1941–45), his bold stategies helped defeat the Japanese. MacArthur also commanded (1950–51) the United Nations forces during the Korean War. A biography of Douglas MacArthur appears in Volume M.

Douglas MacArthur

Edward Durell Stone (1902–78), born in Fayetteville, was a noted architect. Often his buildings were designed around a courtyard, with bands of filtered light coming through the roofs and ceilings. Among his best-known designs are the Museum of Modern Art (1937) in New York City; the U.S. Embassy (1954-58) in New Dehli, India; and the Kennedy Center for the Performing Arts (1964-69) in Washington, D.C.

In 1957 federal troops were sent to Arkansas to protect the first black students to enroll at the all-white Little Rock Central High School.

sas resisted the courts and continued to segregate the students until 1957, when nine black students attempted to attend the all-white Little Rock Central High School. Governor Orval E. Faubus called out the Arkansas National Guard to prevent them from entering the school.

In response to this, President Dwight D. Eisenhower ordered federal troops to Arkansas to enforce the integration. After a period of crisis and adjustment, the schools integrated without further incident.

Recent Trends

Today the farm economy of Arkansas is struggling, and some of its counties are among the poorest in the nation, especially those in the Delta region. However, the state's economy is growing overall, and population continues to rise. New businesses are coming to the state, and some industries are growing rapidly, especially tourism. Arkansas is working harder than ever to live up to its nickname as a land of opportunity for all.

JEANNIE M. WHAYNE
Arkansas Historical Association

ARLINGTON NATIONAL CEMETERY. See NATIONAL CEMETERIES.

ARMADA, SPANISH. See SPANISH ARMADA.

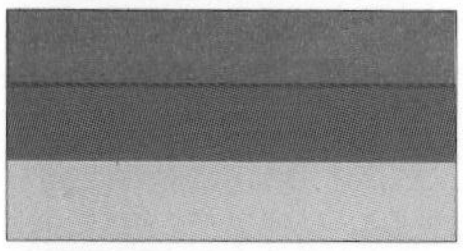

ARMENIA

The ancient homeland of the Armenians was a large, mountainous plateau in western Asia, which included part of what is now eastern Turkey. Armenians had inhabited the plateau continuously from the 500's B.C. Their kingdoms could be found in the region from earliest times to 1375. From this date until 1918, however, no Armenian state existed.

For most of this period its people were ruled as part of the Ottoman Turkish, Persian, and Russian empires. Between 1918 and 1920 a free Armenian republic struggled to survive, before becoming a part of the Soviet Union. Armenia remained a Soviet union republic until 1991, when it declared its independence. The present-day Republic of Armenia occupies a small area in the northeastern corner of its historic homeland.

▸THE PEOPLE

A Dispersed People. Armenians have been dispersed, or scattered, to many corners of the world. About half now live outside Armenia. Armenian communities have grown up in the Middle East, Russia, Western Europe, and the United States, among other places.

More than 90 percent of the Armenian republic's people are Armenian. Ethnic minorities include Azerbaijanis and Russians. The capital and largest city is Yerevan (sometimes spelled Erevan), with a population of more than 1 million.

Language and Religion. Armenian is a distinctive language with its own alphabet. Although it belongs to the large Indo-European language family, it is not related to any other living language.

Armenians have been Christians since the early A.D. 300's and claim to be the first to have adopted Christianity as their official state religion. Outside of Armenia, the church is often the center of Armenian social and community life. The head of the Armenian Apostolic Church is the Catholicos, who resides in the holy city of Echmiadzin, near Yerevan.

Custom and Tradition. Although Christmas and Easter are the most important holidays, two others are widely observed by Armenians. Vartanantz celebrates an event in A.D. 451, when Armenians under Vartan Mamikonian fought to the death against the Persians to preserve their religion. And on April 24th, Armenians commemorate the destruction, in 1915, of the Armenian community in Turkey. (See History section.)

Armenian foods are similar to that of other Middle Eastern peoples. A typical Armenian

FACTS and figures

REPUBLIC OF ARMENIA is the official name of the country.

LOCATION: Western Asia.

AREA: 11,500 sq mi (29,800 km²).

POPULATION: 3,300,000 (estimate).

CAPITAL AND LARGEST CITY: Yerevan (Erevan).

MAJOR LANGUAGE(S): Armenian.

MAJOR RELIGIOUS GROUP(S): Christian.

GOVERNMENT: Republic. **Head of state**—president. **Head of government**—prime minister. **Legislature**—parliament.

CHIEF PRODUCTS: Chemicals, electronic equipment, synthetic rubber, textiles, wheat, barley, cotton, fruits and nuts, copper.

meal might include lamb, rice pilaf, eggplant, yogurt, and a sweet dessert like baklava. Armenians pride themselves on their close family ties and the importance of hospitality. Children are taught respect for Armenian culture and traditions.

Notable Armenians. Armenians have gained renown in many fields. Among those prominent in Soviet life were the composer Aram Khachaturian, the astrophysicist Victor Ambartsumian, former world chess champion Tigran Petrosyan, and the onetime president of the Soviet Union, Anastas Mikoyan. Notable Americans of Armenian ancestry include the playwright William Saroyan, composer Alan Hovhaness, former California governor George Deukmejian, Jr., singer and actress Cher (who is also part Cherokee Indian), and businessmen Alex Manoogian and Kirk Kerkorian.

THE LAND

The Armenian plateau is a rugged highland averaging about 5,000 feet (1,500 meters) in elevation. It is crossed by numerous valleys and by swift-flowing rivers, broken by rapids and falls. Historic Armenia had its chief population centers in the valley of the Araks River (also called Aras or Araxes) and the region around Lake Van. Lake Van now lies within Turkey. Two other great lakes can be found on the plateau—Sevan in Armenia, and Urmia, now part of Iran.

The highest point on the plateau, Mount Ararat (Masis to Armenians), now lies in Turkey. Mount Aragats, the highest peak in the Armenian republic, rises 13,435 feet (4,095 meters) above sea level. The history of the land has been marked by destructive earthquakes. In 1988 two Armenian cities were devastated by a massive earthquake that killed more than 25,000 people.

Armenia has a generally dry climate, often with extremes of temperature. Winters are long and cold; summers are usually short and hot. Despite the harshness of the climate in winter, Armenia was one of the earliest agricultural areas cultivated by humans. The soil can be quite fertile, especially when irrigated. Copper is the chief mineral resource.

THE ECONOMY

Until the mid-1900's, most Armenians were peasant farmers. But with the great drive toward industrialization in the Soviet Union during the 1930's, Soviet Armenians began to

Most of Armenia consists of a high, rugged plateau ringed by mountains and crossed by numerous valleys and swift-flowing streams. The woman at right wears traditional Armenian dress.

move to the towns to work in factories. Today the majority of Armenians live in urban areas (cities and towns) and industry is the most important element of the economy. Major manufactured products include chemicals, electronic equipment, synthetic rubber, and various textiles, including fabrics.

The chief crops include wheat, barley, cotton, and fruits and nuts—particularly apricots, peaches, walnuts, and grapes for Armenian cognac, or fine brandy. Livestock include cattle, sheep, and goats.

▶ HISTORY AND GOVERNMENT

Urartu to Tigranes I. The first important state in what became Armenia was the kingdom of Urartu, with its center around Lake Van. In the 600's B.C., new tribes migrated to the region, probably from the west. They mingled with the earlier inhabitants to form a distinct people, first mentioned as "Armenians" in the mid-500's B.C. Ruled for many centuries by the Persians, Armenia became a buffer state between contending Greeks and Romans to the west and Persians and Arabs to the south.

Armenia reached the height of its power under King Tigranes I (the Great), who ruled from 95 to 55 B.C. Tigranes founded an empire of many different peoples, but it was eventually conquered by the Romans.

Christianity and Conflict. In A.D. 314, the Armenian king Tiridates III was converted to Christianity. In the early 400's, Saint Mesrob (also known as Mashtots) created an Armenian alphabet, and religious and historical works in that language began to appear. And yet, despite their common language and religion, Armenians frequently fought amongst each other and with their kings.

The invasion of the Seljuk Turks in the 1000's led to the collapse of the independent Armenian kingdoms, and a new state, Lesser Armenia, was formed along the Mediterranean Sea. It was overrun by Mamelukes from Egypt in 1375.

In the 1500's most of historic Armenia was conquered by the Ottoman Turks, who ruled it until the early 1900's. Eastern Armenia was ruled by Persia until it was absorbed into the Russian Empire in 1828.

Ottoman Rule. For centuries, the Ottomans maintained relatively peaceful relations with the Armenians in Turkey. But by the late 1800's, the Armenians had begun to suffer relentless persecution. Between 1894 and 1896, hundreds of thousands of Armenians were massacred on the orders of Sultan Abdul-Hamid II.

After the so-called Young Turk revolution of 1908, the Armenians hoped a period of peace and cooperation would follow. But in 1914, World War I broke out and Turkey went to war against Russia. In 1915 the Armenians, whose sympathies lay with the Russians, were banished by the Turks into the Syrian desert. In the process, between 600,000 and 1.5 million died of hunger and thirst or were killed outright. This barbarous act has been called the first genocide of the 20th century.

Soviet Republic. Some survivors fled abroad. Others went to Russian Armenia, where in 1918, after the Russian Revolution, an independent Armenian republic was established. It survived only briefly. Threatened by a nationalist movement in Turkey, the government turned the new state over to the Soviet Communists in 1920.

Armenia became the smallest of the 15 republics making up the Soviet Union. It remained under Communist control until the Soviet Union broke apart in 1991. Armenia then became an independent nation.

Independence. In 1991, voters elected Levon Ter-Petrosyan president of the new republic. A constitution, adopted in 1995, greatly strengthened the president's powers. Ter-Petrosyan was re-elected in 1996.

In the late 1980's, a bitter conflict flared between Armenia and its neighbor Azerbaijan over Nagorno-Karabakh, a territory that lies in Azerbaijan but whose people are mostly Armenian. A cease-fire was declared in 1994, but the political struggle continued, damaging the economies of both countries and causing great hardship among the people. The conflict remains unresolved.

In 1998, Ter-Petrosyan's political opponents forced him to resign, and he was succeeded by the prime minister, Robert Kocharian. Then in 1999, Premier Vazgen Sarkisian was assassinated, plunging Armenia into deeper political crisis. Kocharian was re-elected president in 2003, but activists took to the streets to protest voting irregularities.

RONALD GRIGOR SUNY
University of Michigan
Author, *Armenia in the 20th Century*

The use of armor peaked between the 1300's and the mid-1500's. The soldier's suit was worn in France about 1550. The horse displays Venetian armor dating from 1575.

ARMOR

When primitive people began to use weapons, they were faced with new problems. Their bodies needed more protection. They learned to use shields of wood or tough animal hide to protect themselves from the enemy's clubs or stone axes. This was the earliest armor.

Later the ancient Egyptian and Assyrian soldiers wore heavy cloth jackets or shirts to add to their protection. These were made of many layers of quilted linen.

METAL ARMOR

The first metal armor was made of bronze. It was probably used by the Greeks about 2000–1800 B.C. They hammered bronze into helmets to protect their heads. They also covered their wooden shields with thin metal sheets.

The Romans were the first to make wide use of iron for armor. Roman soldiers protected their bodies with leather vests covered with thin strips of bronze or iron. Sometimes they covered their legs with metal shin guards. Helmets shielded the head. Roman helmets had broad, curving metal sidepieces to protect the cheeks. Brims came down to cover the forehead and the back of the neck.

Steel was not used in armor much before the Middle Ages. Armor made of steel was even stronger and more flexible than that made of iron. Whole suits of steel protected the medieval knight from head to toe. Sleeves, shin guards, and even gloves with jointed fingers were carefully shaped from thin metal plates. Hinges, joints, and rivets fastened the suits to make them flexible. Helmets had movable visors, or lids that dropped over the face when fighting began.

Some knights wore flexible armor of chain mail. Such armor was made of hundreds of tiny steel rings linked together to form a kind of steel cloth. Shirts of chain mail slipped over the head and reached to the knees.

Plate armor had to be carefully fitted to the body. The armorer heated the metal and

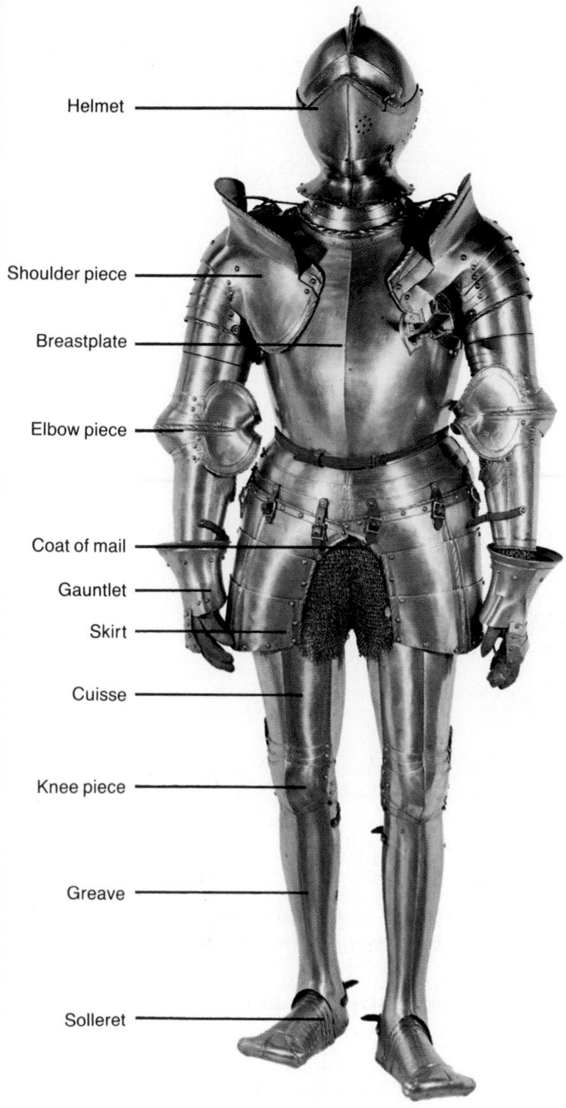

The fully covered "knight in shining armor" as shown at far left was a gradual development. Knights once wore shirts of chain mail, a fabric made from interlinked iron rings. Later, leather or metal plates were attached to the mail. In the 15th-century Italian suit at left, the steel plates have been made flexible by leather straps and rivets. Helmets, too, evolved. The bronze Corinthian battle helmet above dates from the 5th century B.C. The lion's head parade helmet at top is from Italy, 1460.

shaped it with tools. Working like a tailor, the armorer measured, tried on, and shaped again. Sometimes beautiful designs were etched into the steel. The shield was usually decorated with inlaid metal in several colors.

Full armor had many disadvantages. Because it was so expensive to make, only the well-to-do noble or knight could afford a suit of armor. Even worse was its great weight. A special servant or knight-in-training called a squire had to help the knight put on his armor and mount his horse. Drawings from the Middle Ages show knights being hoisted onto their horses by derricks or cranes. If the knight was thrown to the ground by his enemy, he was usually unable to struggle to his feet. His opponent could then easily kill him with his sword or spear.

▶THE DECLINE OF ARMOR

Gunpowder (invented centuries before by the Chinese) reached Europe about the end of the Middle Ages. A foot soldier with a gun could now pierce the heaviest armor that a man was able to carry on his body. Armor began to lose its usefulness. However, early explorers of the American continent continued to use armor against Indian arrows. But by the time of the American Revolution, armor appeared only in fancy-dress uniform.

Far left: A suit of Japanese armor dating from the 16th century is made of steel, silk braid, gilt bronze, deerskin, bear pelt, and gilt wood. Center: A suit of English armor dating from the 16th century is made of brass, leather, and velvet. It was fashioned at the Royal Workshop at Greenwich, the finest armor maker in England. Above: A parade helmet, made of silver and bronze, and shield, made of brass, silver, and gold, were crafted for King Louis XIV of France about 1700.

▶ARMOR IN MODERN FORM

In the two world wars, metal helmets were used to protect the head and neck from pieces of flying metal. Fliers in World War II and in Korea wore thick coveralls padded with fiberglass. These gave protection from cold as well as from shell fragments. Some police officers wear armor in the form of bulletproof vests. Still another type of modern armor is the protective helmet such as those worn by construction workers or motorcyclists.

Today a new type of armor has been designed to help astronauts explore outer space. Space suits are thickly padded and fit snugly from neck to toe. A helmet, covering the entire head, is fitted with earphones, microphones, and a supply of oxygen. With such protection astronauts can face the great strains of rocket launching and space travel. As long as people must protect their bodies against enemy weapons and the forces of nature, they will try to design better armor.

James Hoerger
John F. Kennedy School
(Great Neck, New York)

ARMORED VEHICLES. See Tanks.

ARMS CONTROL. See Disarmament.

ARMSTRONG, LOUIS. See Louisiana (Famous People).

ARMSTRONG, NEIL A. (1930–)

On July 20, 1969, American astronaut Neil Armstrong became the first man ever to walk on the moon.

Neil Alden Armstrong was born in Wapakoneta, Ohio, on August 5, 1930. After receiving his degree from Purdue University in 1955, Armstrong became a civilian research pilot for the National Advisory Committee for Aeronautics (NACA), later renamed the National Aeronautics and Space Administration (NASA). He worked seven years as a test pilot before being accepted in the astronaut program in 1962. Among his early major assignments was the command of the *Gemini 8* mission, which accomplished the first manual space-docking maneuver (March 16, 1966).

In January 1969, Armstrong was chosen to command the *Apollo 11* space mission. He was accompanied by fellow astronauts Edwin E. "Buzz" Aldrin and Michael Collins. On July 16, 1969, a *Saturn 5* booster rocket launched *Apollo 11* and its crew into space. Four days later, on July 20, the lunar module, the *Eagle*, landed on the moon, in a smooth region called the Sea of Tranquility. Armstrong thrilled the world when he radioed NASA with the declaration, "The *Eagle* has landed." Then, at 10:56 P.M. eastern standard time (EST), Armstrong became the first human being to set foot on the moon. The event was immortalized in his statement, "That's one small step for a man, one giant leap for mankind." For nearly 22 hours, Armstrong and Aldrin explored and collected samples of the moon's surface.

On July 24, the *Apollo 11* crew re-entered the Earth's atmosphere, splashing down in the Pacific Ocean at 12:50 P.M. EST. Hailed as heroes, the astronauts were each awarded the Presidential Medal of Freedom. Armstrong resigned from NASA in 1971.

Reviewed by AMOS J. LOVEDAY, JR.
Ohio Historical Society

ARMY. See CANADA, ARMED FORCES OF; UNITED STATES, ARMED FORCES OF THE.

ARNOLD, BENEDICT (1741–1801)

Benedict Arnold was a brave soldier, a patriot—and the most notorious traitor in American history.

Born in Norwich, Connecticut, on January 14, 1741, Arnold fought in the French and Indian War at the age of 14 and later became a captain in the Connecticut militia. When the Revolutionary War began in 1775, he helped Ethan Allen capture Fort Ticonderoga and then proposed a daring plan to capture Quebec, the key to British Canada. The attack failed, but Arnold proved himself a heroic soldier. In 1777 he played a key role in bringing about the British defeat at Saratoga, a major victory for the Americans.

In June 1778, Arnold was placed in command of Philadelphia, where he married Peggy Shippen, the daughter of a British sympathizer. In 1779 he was charged with using his position for personal profit and employing soldiers in his command as servants. A court martial cleared him of most of the charges, but General George Washington was required to reprimand him. Arnold, resentful of such treatment, plotted revenge.

In 1780, Arnold was given command of the strategic fort at West Point, New York, which he immediately plotted to surrender to the British. For this he was promised money and a promotion. But Arnold's British contact, Major John André, was intercepted by American soldiers and executed as a spy. Arnold fled to a British ship.

The British paid Arnold and gave him command of a small force, with which he fought against Americans in Virginia and Connecticut. After the war, he moved with his family to England. He died in London on June 14, 1801, scorned by Americans and British alike. Had he not betrayed his country, Arnold would be remembered today as one of the nation's greatest heroes.

Reviewed by RICHARD B. MORRIS
Editor, *Encyclopedia of American History*

ARNOLD, HENRY ("HAP"). See WORLD WAR II (Profiles: Allied Powers).

ART

Art is one of humanity's oldest inventions. It existed long before a single farm was planted, before the first villages were built. Art was already thousands of years old when writing appeared; in fact, the letters of the first alphabets were pictures. People were probably shaping objects and scratching out images even as they turned their grunts and cries into the first systematic spoken languages.

People are still making art; they have never stopped. Just about every society, from the oldest to the youngest and from the most primitive to the most advanced, has created works of art. No wonder that the sum of all this creation is called "the world of art." Art is a world in itself, a world as round and full and changeable as the world we live in and, like the earth, a whole of many distinct parts. Removing a wedge from the whole and studying it is like touring a country or visiting an era in the past. One wedge describes the ideals of the ancient Greeks. Another defines the interests of the French in the Middle Ages. Still another demonstrates the ideas that shaped the Renaissance in Italy. Another reflects the traditions that had meaning in Japan in the 1700's, or China in the 900's, or India in the 1600's. But seen as

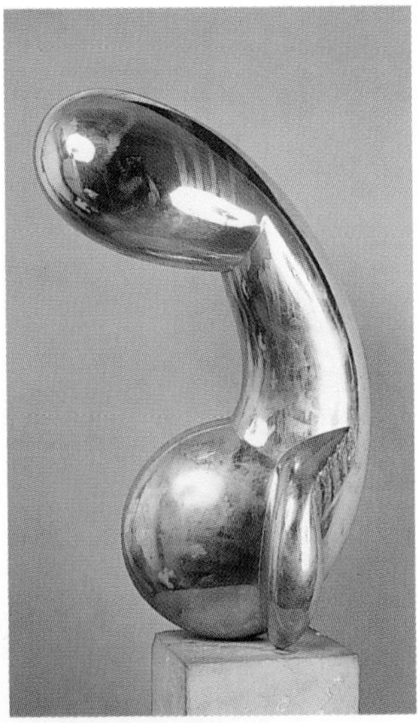

The Metropolitan Museum of Art, Gift of Renate Hofmann, 1975.

Every society, in every time and place, has created art. *Clockwise from top:* Artists use a variety of styles and techniques to depict the world around them, from the detailed realism of Albrecht Dürer's *Hare*, to the utter simplicity of *Princesse X*, by Constantin Brancusi. Hans Hofmann's *Rhapsody*, on the other hand, is completely abstract —it does not represent any recognizable object. The Inuit artist who carved a polar bear from whale bone chose a familiar subject and a readily available material.

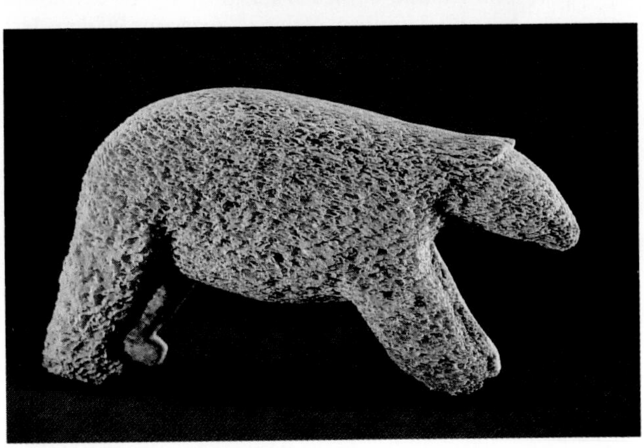

This article discusses theories about the origins and meanings of art. It also suggests ways in which we can learn about a people or culture by studying the art they created. *The New Book of Knowledge* contains many articles that provide specific information on the arts of various cultures. For example, the arts of the peoples of Africa are discussed in AFRICA, ART AND ARCHITECTURE OF. The arts of individual countries are surveyed in numerous articles, including CHINESE ART; FRANCE, ART AND ARCHITECTURE OF; INDIA, ART AND ARCHITECTURE OF; JAPANESE ART AND ARCHITECTURE; LATIN AMERICA, ART AND ARCHITECTURE OF; and UNITED STATES, ART AND ARCHITECTURE OF THE.

Look up the names of periods and styles of art to find such articles as GOTHIC ART AND ARCHITECTURE, IMPRESSIONISM, ISLAMIC ART AND ARCHITECTURE, and MODERN ART.

The basic components of art are discussed in COLOR and DESIGN. There are also articles on art forms, such as COLLAGE, DRAWING, PAINTING, SCULPTURE, and WATERCOLOR. Other articles cover the history and collections of famous art galleries, including HERMITAGE MUSEUM, LOUVRE, METROPOLITAN MUSEUM OF ART, and NATIONAL GALLERY OF CANADA. Consult the Index to find the many biographies of artists contained in this encyclopedia.

Below: Prehistoric people may have created likenesses of animals, such as this bison carving, as a form of hunting magic. Left: Kachina figures made by Pueblo Indians are representations of ancestral spirits.

a whole, the world of art reveals a broad picture of all of humanity; it summarizes the ideals, interests, and ideas of all people in all eras. It tells us what has been on people's minds in generation after generation, from the dawn of humanity to the present day.

Art, then, is a product of the human mind and a mirror of that mind—a record of human progress. And like the mind, and like the societies that progress has created, art is rich, complicated, and sometimes quite mysterious.

THE MEANINGS OF ART

Actually, most people do know what art is. The trouble comes when they try to define it. No one definition satisfies everyone's idea. No one definition seems broad enough to cover every object in an art museum. And some definitions are too broad—they may apply to everything in the museum, but they also apply to many things that clearly are not art.

Despite the difficulty of defining art, we can make certain observations that help us to understand what art is. Art is a product made by people that expresses the uniqueness of the maker, of the society to which the maker belongs, of all humanity, or of all of these. The product appeals to the intellect and to the senses, especially to the sense of beauty. The product can assume a variety of forms—a musical composition, a ballet, a play, or a novel or poem. This article, however, deals only with the "fine" arts: drawing, painting, sculpture, and architecture.

It is our intellect that makes humans unique. People have created religion, science, and technology to make their struggle for survival easier. They have created art to measure the worth of these and all human enterprises against the quality of life. European medieval art dealt almost exclusively with religion. Italian Renaissance art reflected the growing interest in the sciences. Much Oriental art conveys the idea of a harmonious, well-ordered universe. Art of the modern era is very much a product of the age of technology.

Art—or at least great art—almost always gets at the truth. Great artists are expert observers and their work reflects life as they see it.

ART AS A RECORD

The earliest art that we know about was painted on the walls of caves during the Old Stone Age—roughly 20,000 years ago. Most of the pictures depict animals—bison, reindeer, ibex—the animals that early people hunted and depended on for survival. We cannot be completely sure why these images were painted, but we can guess that hunters created likenesses of their prey in order to capture its spirit. Having taken the spirit, the hunters found it easier to take the body. And since early people were very good hunters, whose mastery of weapons gave them an advantage over much stronger creatures, they must have believed that the magic worked.

About 5,000 years ago, the first great civilization began emerging from humanity's intelligent struggle for survival. And with them came monumental art—art created to proclaim the greatness of a civilization and to last forever. In Egypt and Mesopotamia gigantic pyramids were erected, the tombs within decorated with carvings and paintings showing the great deeds of the rulers buried there. Clearly, these ancient peoples had no intention of ever disappearing. Even their utensils and vessels were meant to last eternally.

Mesopotamian and especially Egyptian art dwelt on the achievements of rulers. This was so mainly because the rulers were thought to be gods, or at least to have intimate contact with gods. And it was fitting, too, because the ruler was regarded as the living embodiment of the nation: Pharaoh and Egypt were one and the same. The individuality of the human being was seldom even recognized, much less celebrated.

Then came the Minoans and Mycenaeans and the Greeks, and people had their day. The early statuary of the Aegean peoples was said to represent gods and goddesses, but the forms were becoming ever more recognizably human. This in itself seems to indicate that people were beginning to appreciate their own importance. Like the ancient Hebrews, they proclaimed themselves made in their gods' image—not perfect, perhaps, but nonetheless godlike. By the Classical Age (400's B.C.) in Greece, even that pretense was dropped. Greek sculptors began portraying spear bearers and charioteers with bodies as perfect as those of the gods Apollo and Dionysus.

Greek art idealized the human form. We do not believe that there were no Greeks with pot bellies or bowlegs; but we can conclude that the Greeks thought enough of themselves to find great satisfaction in showing themselves as ideal beings. And so we admire the Greeks not so much for what they were, but for the ideals they set up for themselves.

The Greeks' high regard for the individual is also reflected in their architecture. Greek architects took great pains to proportion their structures so that people could use them comfortably: The ceilings are never so high, the rooms never so massive that a person feels small or lost within. This is another example of how we use art, which expresses ideals, to learn about a people of the past.

Roman art, like Roman civilization, was based to a large extent on the Greek model. But the Romans carried their concern with the individual a step further. One Roman statue is a representation of an old, big-nosed citizen with a stern expression on his face. No one would call it an idealized portrait. Yet, as one studies it, the face gradually appears handsomer; it seems to reflect great character, wisdom, integrity. With such works the Romans are saying that the individual need not meet prescribed standards to be beautiful.

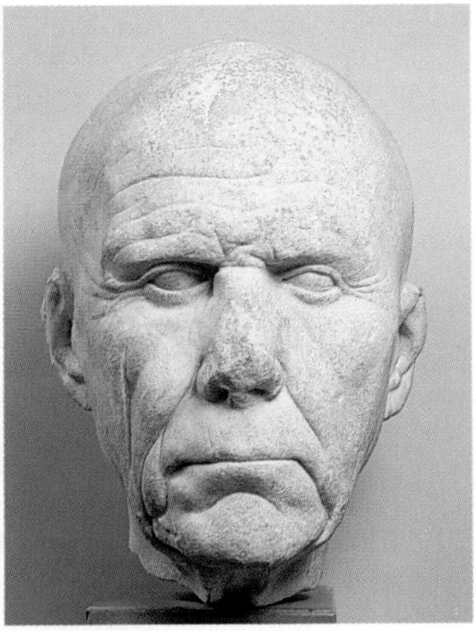

Portrait sculptures by Roman artists show their interest in portraying subjects realistically. The deeply lined face and stern expression of this sculpture of an old man reflect his individuality and character.

When invasions by Germanic tribes into western and southern Europe became too troublesome for the Romans to deal with, the emperor Constantine (280?–337) moved his capital eastward to the site of the old city of Byzantium. The new capital was called Constantinople, in his honor. Constantine also was the first Christian emperor, and thus his eastern empire, called the Byzantine Empire, became the first Christian civilization. There the traditions of ancient Greek and Roman art were remolded to fit the needs of Christianity. Under the emperor Justinian (483–565), Constantinople was built up as the first great Christian city.

The soaring heights and rich decoration of Gothic cathedrals, such as Reims Cathedral in France, were meant to inspire churchgoers with the glory of God.

The Roman Empire in western Europe came to an end in the A.D. 400's. The following period, from about 500 to 1500, is called the Middle Ages. The Germanic peoples who established kingdoms in the former empire were greatly influenced by Roman civilization. They learned the Roman tongue and adopted Christianity. They turned their artistic skills to making Christian art, using the intricately carved and decorated style that characterized their art.

The early Middle Ages were years of confusion and disorder in western Europe. Yet during this period the great Frankish king Charlemagne established a large empire that included much of western and central Europe. Elsewhere—in the Byzantine Empire, northern and western Africa, and the Far East—great civilizations flourished.

During the later Middle Ages, a new and monumental style of architecture called Gothic (the name was given to it much later) developed in the West. All over France, Germany, and England, grand cathedrals rose, one after another, each more lavish than the others. Nearly all the art of this period, which lasted into the 1500's in some parts of Europe, was devoted to decoration of the cathedrals. Columns were surrounded with statues; doorways were richly carved; beautiful stained-glass windows colored the sunlight pouring in; carefully cut and polished wood formed the altars; huge, heavy tapestries hung between chapels; mosaic tiles formed mazelike patterns on the floors. It was as if all artistic creativity was focused on the glorification of God and the church.

Gothic architecture tells us a great deal about how society regarded people. The Gothic cathedral is high, heaven-reaching, enormously empty. Inside, one cannot help feeling small and humble. And all the statues—the saints on the columns, the demons over the doors—are watching and warning.

Early in the 1400's, the God-centered outlook of the Middle Ages slowly began to change. First in Italy and then throughout Europe, the individual human being became a main concern of art. This attitude, known as humanism, is what distinguished the Renaissance from earlier periods. It is what made the Renaissance go down in history as a great age for humanity. And again, it was in art that the spirit of humanism was expressed most clearly.

Humanism affected not only the content of art but the very way in which art was created. For if art said that people were individuals, worthy of recognition for their beliefs, were not the people who made art very special individuals, deserving credit for their accomplishments? So, with the Renaissance, the artist took on a new importance. And the recognition that the artist received added a new facet to art.

In Eastern lands, as in the West, art from its earliest days was an ever-growing record of what was most important to people. Art in Japan often reflects an appreciation for the beauty of nature. Early Japanese painting tended to be delicate, airy, and romantic, reflecting the graceful life of the Japanese court. Later, when Japan was ruled by militaristic

The Metropolitan Museum of Art, Bequest of Mrs. H. O. Havemeyer, 1929.

***Left: The Great Wave off Kanagawa*, a woodcut by the Japanese artist Katsushika Hokusai. The development of woodcut techniques in Japan allowed prints to be reproduced inexpensively and helped bring Japanese art to a wider audience.**

***Below:* Artists in the Eastern world developed original and expressive styles of manuscript illustration. This page is from a Persian manuscript of the 1400's.**

emperors, art became harsher and more realistic. The 1700's and 1800's saw the development of the Japanese woodcut. Woodcuts, which are inexpensive to reproduce, were meant to reach a wider audience—to bring beauty within reach of the hardworking common people.

The arts in India have almost always had a religious content. However, this was often combined with an interest in earthly life. Sculpture, in particular, often portrayed gods and goddesses as vital and lifelike beings. Indian painters developed original and expressive styles of manuscript illustration.

China's artistic tradition is one of the oldest in the world, dating back to 5000 B.C. A respect for tradition and reverence for nature is reflected in Chinese art and architecture. Calligraphy, the art of beautiful writing, was considered one of the most important visual arts.

▶ART OF THE ARTIST

Art since the Renaissance has remained a record of humanity and a reflection of the ideas that concern people. But since the Renaissance this record has come down to us in a series of very personal statements.

The great Italian artist Michelangelo believed that the truth of any matter existed in nature. The artist's job was to seek that truth and capture it in his art. He once described sculpture as the act of "liberating the figure from the marble that imprisons it." In other words, the forms that he depicted so dramatically in his work already existed; his job was to find them and free them.

A later Italian painter, Caravaggio, sought the truth in everyday occurrences, such as the pleasures of making music. Even in his paintings of religious events, he clothed the participants in the apparel of his own time, and placed them in commonplace settings, such as taverns. Saints were often pictured as poor people with plain garments and bare feet. Caravaggio seemed to be saying that all people, even the most humble, have value.

The paintings of the Dutch artist Rembrandt may represent the peak of humanism. In a very special way, Rembrandt's subject matter was the soul of man. He painted religious subjects, portraits of prosperous Dutch citizens, and he painted simple portraits of poor people and of himself. But whatever he painted, his figures always appear lit from within, as if they were filled with all the suffering—and the beauty—of humanity. Rembrandt is telling us that with all the pain, corruption, and helplessness that characterize human life, the human spirit is still filled with all the glory and good of God's light.

The 1600's and 1700's were the "age of kings" in Europe. The courts of the European nations dominated much artistic activity. Many artists were dependent on the kings and aristocrats who

Above: **In his painting *The Jewish Bride*, Dutch artist Rembrandt van Rijn portrays the tender affection of a newly married couple. Rembrandt's work, in its expression of the dignity of the human spirit, may represent the peak of humanism in art. *Right:* In *The Third of May, 1808*, Spanish artist Francisco Goya protests the invasion of his country by Napoleon's armies—and attacks the nature of war itself.**

Collection, The Museum of Modern Art, New York. Gift of Mrs. Simon Guggenheim.

The Metropolitan Museum of Art, Purchase, 1983.

Near left: **A sculpture made by the Kota people of Gabon represents the spirit of the dead. It is constructed of wood covered with sheets of copper and other metals. The shapes and patterns of African art influenced many modern European and American artists, including Pablo Picasso.** ***Far left:*** **Picasso, like other modern artists, experimented with new ways of looking at things.** ***Girl Before a Mirror*** **uses bright colors and flattened shapes in its portrait of a young woman.**

ruled the continent. And yet great artists can never be slaves—except to the search for truth. As the abuses of the monarchs stirred the common people to greater and greater resentment, the artists often joined in the protests. For example, when Napoleon's armies invaded Spain in 1808, the Spanish artist Francisco Goya turned his talents to an assault on the French. His paintings and engravings include works that are savage attacks on the French invaders, and even more savage—and lasting—attacks on war itself.

Another Spaniard, Pablo Picasso, made a similar statement 130 years later. His well-known painting *Guernica* tells the story of the Spanish Civil War as directly as any text. And it is not only about a destroyed Spanish city; it is about war.

The 1800's and 1900's saw a remarkable increase in the speed at which civilization changes. We have come through an Industrial Revolution into an age of technology into a space age. Artists have kept pace with all these changes.

The ways in which artists approach art have been in a state of constant re-evaluation since the mid-1800's. The impressionists began a process that led to a breakdown in the importance of subject matter. With these French artists came an interest in the technique used to apply paint to canvas. Concern with forms for their own sake led to cubism and then to abstractionism, in sculpture as well as painting. By the mid-1900's painting and sculpture seemingly came together in a search for new forms.

The 1900's also saw a growing appreciation of the arts of non-Western cultures. Once dismissed as "primitive," the arts of African and Native American peoples were now admired for their vitality and directness of expression. African sculpture, in particular, influenced a number of modern artists, including Picasso. As modern communications have allowed ideas about art to become ever more widely spread, the influence of cultures on one another has continued.

What is the truth of our own age, as expressed in art? As we study the art of our age, each of us can draw our own conclusions.

David Jacobs
Author, *Master Painters of the Renaissance*

ART DECO. See Decorative Arts (The Industrial Age).

ARTEMIS. See Greek Mythology (Profiles).

ARTERIOSCLEROSIS. See Diseases (Descriptions of Some Diseases).

ARTHRITIS. See Diseases (Descriptions of Some Diseases).

CHESTER ALAN ARTHUR (1829-1886)
21st President of the United States

FACTS ABOUT ARTHUR
Birthplace: Fairfield, Vermont
Religion: Episcopalian
College Attended: Union College, Schenectady, New York
Occupation: Lawyer
Married: Ellen Lewis Herndon
Children: William, Chester, Ellen
Political Party: Republican
Age on Becoming President: 50
Office Held Before Becoming President: Vice President
President Who Preceded Him: James A. Garfield
Nickname: "The Gentleman Boss"
Years in the Presidency: 1881–1885
Vice President: None
President Who Succeeded Him: Grover Cleveland
Age at Death: 56
Burial Place: Albany, New York

DURING ARTHUR'S PRESIDENCY
Below, left: The U.S. Senate ratified (1882) the Geneva (or Red Cross) Convention of 1864. Congress passed the Pendleton Civil Service Act, which established the U.S. Civil Service Commission (1883). *Below:* The Brooklyn Bridge was completed (1883); at the time it was the world's longest bridge. Construction of the first building known as a skyscraper, the 10-story Home Insurance Building, was begun in Chicago (1883). The Linotype, the first practical typesetting machine, was patented (1884) by Ottmar Mergenthaler. *Above:* The Washington Monument in Washington, D.C., was dedicated (1885).

ARTHUR, CHESTER ALAN. On July 2, 1881, President James A. Garfield was shot in the back by an insane man. For two months the President lay between life and death. On September 19, Garfield died, and early the next morning Vice-President Chester Alan Arthur became the new president of the United States.

Arthur was a handsome man. Tall and broad-shouldered, he impressed people with his dignified bearing and elegant manners. He was courteous and friendly.

But many people considered the handsome vice-president unfit to be president. Arthur had long been associated with the spoils system. Under this system government jobs were awarded for service to a political party, whether the candidates were honest and able or not. In fact, the man who killed President Garfield explained that he did so because he had been refused a government job. People were alarmed that Arthur, a product of the spoils system, had become president.

Arthur's administration, however, proved to be quite different than his country expected. It was marked by honesty and by the replacement of the spoils system with the present Civil Service system based on merit.

EARLY YEARS

Chester Alan Arthur was born October 5, 1829, in Fairfield, Vermont. He was the oldest son in a family of seven children. His father, William Arthur, was a Baptist minister.

The Arthur family moved about a great deal. The Reverend William Arthur was a man of strong beliefs and did not hesitate to speak his mind to his congregations. As a result, he did not stay in one place very long. At the age of 15, Chester entered Union College, in Schenectady, New York. He helped pay for his college expenses by teaching school during vacations. He studied hard and, in 1848, graduated with honors. Arthur then studied law. But he continued to teach to support himself until 1853, when he went to New York City to begin his career as a lawyer.

The future president first gained prominence when he became involved in the slavery question that was soon to lead to civil war. William Arthur had been opposed to slavery, and Chester shared his father's feelings. He sympathized with the plight of blacks and took part in two important cases in their defense. In one his law firm gained freedom for eight blacks accused of being runaway slaves.

The other case dealt with the problem of segregation. It arose when Lizzie Jennings was not allowed to ride on a streetcar in New York City because she was black. Arthur won $500 for her in damages. And the court decision stated that blacks had the same right to ride on New York streetcars as anyone else.

ARTHUR ENTERS POLITICS

Like most lawyers of the time, Arthur also took part in politics. In 1860 he helped organize the New York State Republican Party, and he supported its candidate for governor. As a reward the governor made Arthur engineer in chief and then quartermaster general of New York State. During the Civil War Arthur's position was very important, for all Union Army volunteers were equipped by the state before they were sent on to the Army. Arthur proved skillful and honest in providing thousands of New York soldiers with food, shelter, guns, tents, and other equipment.

COLLECTOR OF NEW YORK

Arthur's work for the Republican Party brought him to the attention of Senator Roscoe Conkling, the political boss of New York State. Arthur became Conkling's lieutenant and worked with him to win the election of Ulysses S. Grant in 1868. For his help President Grant in 1871 appointed Arthur collector of customs for the port of New York.

The collector was in charge of the New York Custom House, which received most of the customs duties of the United States. He also had the power to distribute more than 1,000 jobs. Under the spoils system these jobs went to faithful Republicans. They were expected to work for the party as well as for the Custom House. In the years that Arthur held the position, he simply followed the old system, although he himself remained an honest and able administrator.

In this newspaper cartoon of the 1880's (*above*), President Arthur turns his back on his old crony, Boss Roscoe Conkling. The woman represents the Republican Party. After President James A. Garfield was assassinated in 1881, Chester Arthur was inaugurated as 21st president at his home in New York City (*below*).

But many people were becoming angry about the inefficiency of the spoils system. They wanted a merit system, under which officeholders would be chosen on the basis of ability. In 1877 Rutherford B. Hayes, a believer in the merit system, became president. Hayes ordered an investigation of the New York Custom House, and in 1878 Arthur was dismissed from his post. The conflict caused a deep split in the Republican Party. The supporters of the old system became known as Stalwarts. The reformers were called Half-Breeds.

VICE-PRESIDENT

In 1880 the Republicans who met to pick a new candidate for president were still bitterly divided. The delegates voted 36 times before they agreed on a candidate whom no one had expected—James A. Garfield, a Half-Breed. However, Senator Conkling was Garfield's political enemy. And to gain the support of the Stalwarts, the Garfield men nominated Arthur for the vice-presidency. The Republicans won in a close election. Ten months later Garfield was dead, and Arthur became the 21st president of the United States.

Ellen Lewis Herndon (*below*) married Chester Alan Arthur in 1859. She died in 1880, before he became president. Their young daughter, Ellen, was raised in the White House by President Arthur's sister.

PRESIDENT ARTHUR SURPRISES MANY PEOPLE

As president, Arthur surprised both his friends and enemies. Arthur wished to make a good record for himself and was eager to be renominated and re-elected. He knew that he would never gain the support of reform and independent voters if he acted simply as a tool of Boss Conkling.

Arthur therefore determined not to let his administration be disgraced by the spoils system. He also tried earnestly to deal with some of the serious political problems the nation faced. But he was not so successful as he wished because he never had the full support of Congress.

For many years the Senate and the House of Representatives had gained power at the expense of weak presidents. Even such a strong personality as Abraham Lincoln had trouble with Congress. And his successors—Johnson, Grant, and Hayes—had let themselves be dominated by powerful Congressional leaders. Arthur was especially defenseless. He had become president by accident, and he did not command the support of any strong group in Congress.

Furthermore, Congress was itself divided. Both the Democratic and Republican parties were split into warring groups like the Stalwarts and the Half-Breeds. Some questions, such as the tariff (the tax on goods imported into the country), also divided the legislators. Other issues, such as the currency, set farmers, laborers, and manufacturers fighting one another.

Most important of all, the country was expanding and growing rich. Many people thought only of what they could get for themselves. Their representatives did not vote according to what was best for the nation as a whole. Instead they voted for laws that would gain the most for their supporters. Under such conditions it was difficult even for an able president to work out a good national policy. Arthur tried his best. But his achievements were limited.

The Pendleton Act and the Merit System

Before Arthur took office, it became known that some postal officials had collected money illegally in arranging mail routes. They were brought to trial in the famous Star Route cases. They were never convicted, but the

IMPORTANT DATES IN THE LIFE OF CHESTER ALAN ARTHUR

1829	Born at Fairfield, Vermont, October 5.
1848	Graduated from Union College.
1854	Became a lawyer in New York City.
1859	Married Ellen Lewis Herndon.
1860	Appointed engineer in chief of New York.
1862–1863	Quartermaster general of New York.
1871–1878	Collector of customs for the port of New York.
1880	Elected vice-president of the United States.
1881	Garfield assassinated; Arthur inaugurated president of the United States, September 20.
1881–1885	21st president of the United States.
1886	Died in New York City, November 18.

trial made many more Americans aware of the evils of the spoils system.

With President Arthur's support, Congress now tried to introduce the merit system. In 1883, Arthur signed a law that helped take thousands of government jobs out of politics. This was the Pendleton Civil Service Act. It required candidates for many government jobs to pass tests before they could be accepted. Men who qualified were protected against being dismissed for political reasons. The Pendleton Act was the beginning of the present United States Civil Service.

Too Much Money and Chinese Exclusion

During the 1880's the United States had an unusual problem: there was too much money in the treasury. In one year the government collected $80,000,000 more than it spent. This kept money out of circulation, hurt business, and caused prices to fall. Arthur wanted to solve the problem by lowering the tariff. Congress, however, refused to do so. It preferred to spend the money on a "pork-barrel" bill. This was a law that authorized federal funds to be spent on river and harbor improvements. Such a law won votes for the congressmen and senators of the favored states. Arthur rejected the bill even though he knew that this would make him unpopular. But Congress passed it over his veto, and the tariff problem was not solved during Arthur's term in office.

Congress also passed the Chinese Exclusion Act of 1882 against the president's wishes. Its aim was to prevent Chinese from immigrating to the United States. Arthur opposed the bill because it violated a treaty between China and the United States. His opposition forced Congress to rewrite the law so that it had fewer harsh restrictions against the Chinese.

NOT ALL WAS POLITICS

In 1859 Arthur had married Ellen Lewis Herndon, the daughter of a Virginia naval officer. Mrs. Arthur died in 1880, before her husband became president. Each day President Arthur honored her by placing fresh flowers in front of her picture.

The President's favorite sport was fishing. He was considered one of the best salmon fishermen in the country. Arthur was also fond of good food and companionship. He enjoyed the dinners to which he was invited and hated to leave. Since none of the guests could politely leave before the President, the dinners sometimes lasted until midnight.

Arthur liked elegant surroundings, and he had the White House completely redecorated. He installed new plumbing, a new bathroom, and the first elevator in the White House. His sister, who acted as hostess, helped him make it Washington's social center.

ARTHUR IS REJECTED BY THE REPUBLICANS

In 1884 the Republicans did not renominate Arthur for president. The Half-Breed reformers were still not satisfied with him, and his old Stalwart friends, of course, were now against him. James G. Blaine was nominated and later lost the election to Democrat Grover Cleveland.

Arthur returned to his old law practice. But his health was failing. On November 18, 1886, at the age of 56, he died at his home in New York.

Chester Arthur was an honest and courageous president. But the political situation of his times did not permit him to deal successfully with the country's great problems. The greatest achievement of his administration was the Pendleton Civil Service Act. However, he will be best remembered as the spoils system politician who became president by accident, and who proved himself a better man than anyone expected.

OSCAR HANDLIN
Harvard University

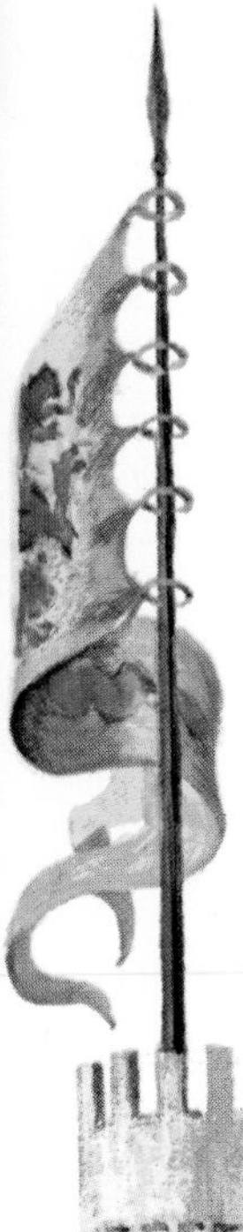

ARTHUR, KING

In romance and legend, in music and art, King Arthur and his Knights of the Round Table are among the world's best-known heroes. For centuries they have been favorites of storytellers in many different countries.

The tales, as they are most often told today, are set in Arthur's court at Camelot, in a castle with noble towers and a great hall. In the great hall stood the Round Table, where only the best and most valiant knights could sit. Because the table had no head and no foot, all the knights seated around it were of equal rank. Each knight has his own seat with his name carved on it. The knights were bound by oath to help one another in time of danger and never to fight among themselves.

The tales tell of the wise and courteous Sir Gawaine; the brave Sir Percival; Sir Lancelot, who loved King Arthur's wife, Guinevere; the traitor Sir Modred, who seized the throne and tried to wed Queen Guinevere; the noble Sir Bedivere, who received Arthur's last commands before he died; and Sir Tristram, the knight of many skills. One seat at the Round Table had no name on it. It was reserved for the knight who found the Holy Grail, the cup supposedly used by Christ at the Last Supper. The seat was finally won by Sir Galahad, the purest and noblest of all the knights.

Religion and magic run through all the stories about Arthur and his knights. On the side of good was the mighty magician Merlin, who was Arthur's adviser. On the side of evil was the wicked sorceress Morgan le Fay.

THE STORY OF ARTHUR

The story of King Arthur and his knights, as told in *Le Morte Darthur* ("The Death of Arthur") by Sir Thomas Malory, begins with the death of Arthur's father, King Uther Pendragon. Following the king's death, there was strife and civil war among England's nobles. The nobles finally gathered in a church to ask God to show them who their rightful king should be. As they came out of the church they saw a sword in an anvil mounted on a great stone. On the sword it was written that whoever could pull the sword out of the stone would be the next king of England. None of the nobles could withdraw the sword.

Although he was the king's son, Arthur was not with his father when he died. Arthur had been given to the magician Merlin for safekeeping shortly after his birth. Merlin had known that King Uther's death would cause a struggle for power among the nobles and that Arthur's life would be in danger, so Merlin gave the baby to Sir Ector and his wife to raise as their own, not telling them that the baby was King Uther's son.

Some months after the sword appeared in the stone, a great tournament was held and Sir Ector, his son Sir Kay, and the young Arthur all attended. When Sir Kay discovered that he had left his sword at the inn where they were staying, he sent Arthur after it. The inn, however, was closed because everyone had gone to the tournament. But Arthur remembered seeing a sword stuck in a stone in the churchyard nearby. Without knowing what it meant, he removed the sword easily, and, after further proofs, Arthur became king.

His reign was full of victories. Many of these he owed to another sword, an enchanted one called Excalibur. Here is Malory's tale, adapted by Mary MacLeod, of how he got it.

Leaving Sir Pellinore, King Arthur and Merlin went to a hermit, who was a good man, and skilled in the art of healing. He attended so carefully to the King's wounds, that in three days they were quite well, and Arthur was able to go on his way with Merlin. Then as they rode, Arthur said, "I have no sword."

"No matter," said Merlin, "near by is a sword that shall be yours if I can get it."

So they rode till they came to a lake, which was a fair water and broad; and in the midst of the lake, Arthur saw an arm, clothed in white samite, that held in its hand a beautiful sword.

"Lo," said Merlin, "yonder is the sword I spoke of."

With that they saw a damsel rowing across the lake.

"What damsel is that?" said Arthur.

"That is the Lady of the Lake," said Merlin, "and within that lake is a rock, and therein is as fair a place as any on earth, and richly adorned. This damsel will soon come to you; then speak you fair to her, so that she will give you that sword."

Presently the damsel came to Arthur, and saluted him, and he her again.

"Damsel," said Arthur, "what sword is that which yonder the arm holdeth above the water? I would it were mine, for I have no sword."

"Sir Arthur, King," said the damsel, "that sword is mine; the name of it is Excalibur, that is as much as to say *Cut-Steel.* If you will give me a gift when I ask you, ye shall have it."

"By my faith," said Arthur, "I will give you what gift ye shall ask."

"Well," said the damsel, "go you into yonder barge, and row yourself to the sword, and take it and the scabbard with you, and I will ask my gift when I see my time."

So King Arthur and Merlin alighted, and tied their horses to two trees, and went into the barge, and when they came to the sword that the hand held, Arthur lifted it by the handle, and took it with him. And the arm and the hand went under the water; and so they came to the land, and rode away.

Some years later, Arthur married Guinevere, the daughter of a king he had helped in battle. After their marriage, Arthur set up his court at Camelot. There he gathered the most chivalrous princes to be his Knights of the Round Table. The stories of their feats and adventures—tournaments, battles, and quests for the Holy Grail—are all part of the Arthurian legends.

At the end of Arthur's reign, while he was away from Camelot, Sir Modred tried to take over the kingdom and marry the queen. But Arthur returned and defeated Modred in battle, killing him with his own hands. As Modred fell, he lifted up his sword and mortally wounded Arthur. Arthur's body was mysteriously carried away to the island of Avalon. According to legend, King Arthur would return one day.

▶SOURCES OF THE ARTHURIAN LEGENDS

The book that is the chief source today for all the legends about Arthur and his knights was written by an Englishman, Sir Thomas Malory. It was printed in 1485 and was one of the first books to come from the press of the first English printer, William Caxton. Although the tales were written in English, the title of the book, *Le Morte Darthur* ("The Death of Arthur"), is French and most of the tales were adapted from various French versions of the legends.

Tales about Arthur were particularly popular in France during the 1100's and 1200's. Originally, however, the Arthurian tales came from Celtic sources—from myths belonging to the Irish and British races and from early accounts of the history of Britain.

The first of these histories to mention Arthur was written in Latin by Nennius, a Welsh priest who lived in the 800's. He tells of a Celtic military commander named Arthur who in the 500's won twelve battles against the Saxon invaders of Britain. This is the original Arthur and it is all we know of him. Legends grew up around him, however, and he became a popular Welsh hero. When some of the Celtic people migrated from Britain to France, they carried the tales about Arthur to their new neighbors, the French and the Normans. Wandering minstrels spread the tales even farther as they visited the courts of Europe and Followed European armies into lands of the eastern Mediterranean.

About this same time, in the 1100's, another Welsh priest, Geoffrey of Monmouth, wrote down some of these tales in a book called *Historia Regum Britanniae* (History of the Kings of Britain). Although he pretended that the book was a translation into Latin of "a very old book in the British language," it was his own creation. He made Arthur into a king and surrounded him with nobles and barons from western Europe. In 1155, a Norman monk named Wace translated Geoffrey's *Historia* into French, adding material from other sources and leaving out parts. His *Roman de Brut* contains the first mention of the Round Table. Wace's poem was used by a priest named Layamon, who was the first to write about Arthur in English.

Between 1170 and 1181, a Frenchman, Chrétien de Troyes, wrote poems based on the Arthurian legends that were highly regarded for their style. His material was probably taken from Celtic origins. He is an important source for the story of the Holy Grail.

The Arthurian legends have attracted many writers in English since Layamon. Stories about Arthur were written in the 1400's by Sir Thomas Malory; in the 1800's by Lord Tennyson, Algernon Swinburne, Matthew Arnold, and William Morris; and in the 1900's by T. H. White.

The Arthurian legends have also been expressed in music and art. In music, the most famous composer to make use of these legends was Richard Wagner. In art, several of John Singer Sargent's mural paintings depict the quest for the Holy Grail.

Reviewed by CAROLYN W. FIELD
The Free Library of Philadelphia

ARTICLES OF CONFEDERATION. See UNITED STATES, GOVERNMENT OF THE; UNITED STATES, HISTORY OF THE.
ARTIFICIAL INTELLIGENCE. See COMPUTERS.
ARTIFICIAL RESPIRATION. See FIRST AID (Rescue Breathing).
ARTILLERY. See GUNS AND AMMUNITION.
ART NOUVEAU. See DECORATIVE ARTS (The Industrial Age).

ASBESTOS

Asbestos is the common name for a group of fire-resistant minerals that are made up of soft and flexible fibers. The threadlike fibers can be woven into cloth or mixed with a binding material and molded into any shape.

Asbestos comes in two main forms. Ninety-five percent is chrysotile, from the mineral serpentine. The other form, amphibole, includes five minerals—crocidolite, amosite, anthophyllite, tremolite, and actinolite.

Both forms of asbestos developed when cracks in the earth's rocks filled with water containing many minerals. Over millions of years, heat and pressure evaporated the water but left the fibers of asbestos.

The biggest deposits of asbestos are found in Canada, the Russian Federation, and South Africa. Smaller deposits are located in the United States. Asbestos is mined like coal—from open pits or through tunnels.

Asbestos is a most valuable substance. It will not burn or melt. It resists acids as well as other strong chemicals, and it is a good insulator against heat or the flow of electricity.

The ancient Greeks and Romans were among the early users of asbestos. They wove the fibers into burial cloths, tablecloths, and long-lasting lamp wicks.

By the 1900's, asbestos was used in a wide variety of products, such as automobile brake linings, roofing shingles, furnace linings, floor tiles, and firefighter suits.

In the 1960's, scientists discovered that inhaling asbestos fibers can cause cancer or serious lung disease. In 1989, the U.S. government decided to phase out the manufacture, use, and export of most asbestos products while safer substitutes could be found. Asbestos was also removed from many schools and other buildings.

Some studies have shown that asbestos is not always harmful. Its danger depends on the type of asbestos and the amount and size of the fibers in the air. Still, experts urge people to avoid exposure to asbestos.

GILDA BERGER
Science Writer

ASCORBIC ACID. See VITAMINS AND MINERALS (Vitamin C).
ASHE, ARTHUR. See TENNIS (Great Players).
ASHLEY, WILLIAM HENRY. See FUR TRADE IN NORTH AMERICA (Profiles).

ASIA

Asia is the largest and most heavily populated of the world's continents. It occupies nearly one-third of the earth's total land surface and is home to about 60 percent of its people. Asia is bounded on three sides by oceans (and their various seas): the Arctic Ocean on the north, the Pacific Ocean on the east, and the Indian Ocean on the south. On the west its traditional boundaries are the mountains and bodies of water separating it from Europe. The Suez Canal divides Asia from Africa on the southwest; and the narrow Bering Strait, which links the Arctic and Pacific oceans, separates it from North America.

Asia is a continent of enormous extremes. It has the world's highest peak—Mount Everest, on the border between Tibet, a region of China, and Nepal. It also has the lowest point on the earth's surface—the shoreline of the Dead Sea, on the Israel-Jordan border. Asia has some of the most densely populated regions in the world, including the two most populous countries, China and India. At the same time, large areas of Asia are too dry, too cold, or too mountainous to support any but limited numbers of people.

Asia was the birthplace of the world's earliest civilizations and its major religions. It was the site of once-vast empires of great wealth and cultural and scientific achievement. These great empires declined with the rise to power

Some of the many aspects of Asia: *Opposite page:* the Royal Mosque in Isfahan, Iran, one of the glories of Islamic architecture; Bengal tigers, native to the Indian subcontinent; the skyline of Tokyo, capital of Japan; the Great Buddha at Kamakura, Japan. *Above:* fertile rice fields of Indonesia; the Great Wall of China; and a pensive boatman on the Jumna River at Agra, India, with the fabled Taj Mahal in the distance.

of European nations, several of which ruled large regions of Asia as colonies until the mid-1900's. The end of colonial rule marked the emergence of the nation-states of present-day Asia.

▶THE LAND

Physically, Asia forms the much larger, eastern portion of an enormous landmass known as Eurasia (Europe and Asia), which stretches from the Atlantic to the Pacific oceans. But although physically linked, Europe and Asia have had such distinct histories that they are usually considered separate continents. The generally accepted dividing line between them runs along the Ural Mountains, the Caspian Sea, the Caucasus Mountains, the Black Sea, and the Bosporus and Dardanelles straits that connect the Black Sea with the Mediterranean.

Numerous islands, including those making up the nations of Japan, Indonesia, and the Philippines, ring the continent and form part of it. The interior is marked by some of the world's most imposing physical features. In the heart of the continent, standing like an enormous wall, is the great chain of the Himalayas, of which Everest is a part. The Himalayas are themselves part of an even larger mountain system that runs from Turkey in the west to China in the east. Asia has some of the most forbidding deserts on earth, including the Gobi of Mongolia and China, the Syrian, and the Rub' al Khali (Empty Quarter) of

Saudi Arabia. Vast treeless plains, or steppes, cover much of Central Asia. Farther north is the broad belt of forest known as taiga.

Regions of Asia

Asia can be divided into a number of distinct regions, although geographers do not always agree on which countries belong in which regions.

East Asia is one of the centers of Asian civilization. It consists of China, Korea, Japan, and Taiwan. Historically and geographically, East Asia is dominated by China, which includes more than 75 percent of the region's territory.

Three important rivers flow through parts of China: the Huang He (Yellow River) of North China, the Chang Jiang (Yangtze) of Central China, and the Xijiang (Si Kiang) of South China.

Korea is a long, mountainous peninsula, situated between China and Japan. Japan itself consists of four large islands and a number of smaller ones lying off the eastern coast of Asia. The island of Taiwan lies off the southeastern coast of the Chinese mainland. Historically a province of China, it is the seat of the Republic of China, which opposes the Communist government of the People's Republic of China on the mainland.

Central, or Inner, Asia is a rather imprecisely defined region. Included within it are Tibet and the Xinjiang-Uygur Autonomous Region of western China. Kazakhstan, Kyrgyzstan, Tajikistan, Turkmenistan, and Uzbekistan, which gained independence with the breakup of the Soviet Union in late 1991, are usually considered part of Central Asia, although they are sometimes included in North Asia. Mongolia is often considered a part of the region, too.

Covering a vast area, Central Asia consists mainly of high plateaus, mountains, deserts, and steppe land. Tibet, for example, forms one great plateau rising some 15,000 feet (4,500 meters). Because of its mountainous terrain, limited rainfall, and generally poor soil, however, the region has a relatively small population for its size.

South Asia includes India, Pakistan, Bangladesh, Afghanistan, Sri Lanka, Maldives, and the small Himalayan countries of Nepal and Bhutan. This region is mainly one of great population density, with a variety of climates. It extends from the high Himalayas in the north to the Indian Ocean in the south, forming a huge triangle, dominated by India. The Arabian Sea is situated on one side of this triangle and the Bay of Bengal is on the other.

Much of Southwest Asia consists of desert, such as the Rub' al-Khali of Saudi Arabia (*left*). Southeast Asia, by contrast, has large areas of tropical rain forest (*right*).

Southeast Asia includes areas on both the Asian mainland and neighboring islands. Myanmar (Burma), Thailand, Laos, Cambodia, and Vietnam are situated on the mainland. East Timor, Indonesia, Singapore, and the Philippines are island countries. Malaysia lies on both the mainland and islands.

Mount Everest, the world's highest peak, rises in the great mountain chain of the Himalayas, which stands like an enormous wall in the heart of Asia.

Tiny, oil-rich Brunei, the smallest of the Southeast Asian nations, is located on the large island of Borneo, the rest of which belongs to Malaysia and Indonesia. Indonesia is the largest and most populous country.

The climate is tropical, with numerous areas of dense population. Four great rivers flow through mainland Southeast Asia—the Mekong, the Chao Phraya, the Salween, and the Irrawaddy.

FACTS and figures

LOCATION AND SIZE: Mainland Asia extends from: **Latitude**—1° 16´ N to 77° 41´ N. **Longitude**—26° 04´ E to 169° 40´ W. **Area**—approximately 17,297,000 sq mi (44,780,000 km²). **Highest Point**—Mt. Everest, 29,035 ft (8,850 m). **Lowest Point**—Dead Sea, about 1,300 ft (400 m) below sea level.

POPULATION: 3,737,000,000 (estimate).

PRINCIPAL LAKES: Aral, Baikal, Balkhash, Tungting, Urmia, Koko Nor.

PRINCIPAL RIVERS: Yangtze (Chang), Huang He (Yellow River), Amur, Lena, Mekong, Yenisei, Ob, Indus, Irtysh, Brahmaputra, Salween, Euphrates, Amu Darya, Ganges, Olenek, Kolyma, Syr Darya, Irrawaddy, Tarim, Xijiang (Si Kiang), Tigris, Chao Phraya (Menam).

PRINCIPAL MOUNTAIN RANGES: **Himalayas**—Mt. Everest, Kanchenjunga, Lhotse I, Makalu, Lhotse II, Cho Oyu, Dhaulagiri, Nanga Parbat, Annapurna; **Karakoram**—K2 (Mt. Godwin Austen), Gasherbrum I, Broad Peak; **Kunlun**—Ulugh Muztagh; **Hindu Kush**—Tirich Mir; **Tien Shan**—Pobeda Peak, Khan Tengri; **Elburz**—Mt. Demavend; **Altai**—Tabun Bogdo, Belukha; **Barisan**—Mt. Kerinchi; **Taurus**—Ala Dag; **Sulaiman**—Takht-i-Sulaiman, twin peaks; **Ural Mountains**—Naroda.

PRINCIPAL DESERTS: Gobi, Rub` al Khali, Syrian, Nafud, Taklamakan, Kara Kum, Thar, Kyzyl Kum.

Southwest Asia. Southwest Asia makes up most of the region called the Middle East. It includes the countries of Turkey, Iran, Syria, Lebanon, Israel, Jordan, Iraq, Kuwait, Saudi Arabia, Yemen, Oman, the United Arab Emirates, and the island nation of Cyprus. The Sinai Peninsula, a territory of Egypt lying east of the Suez Canal, is also considered a part of Asia geographically.

Southwest Asia has a generally hot and dry climate, with little rainfall. But an area of rich soil in the shape of a semicircle, called the Fertile Crescent, stretches between the Mediterranean Sea and the Persian Gulf. Here,

Bactrian camels graze on the high steppe that makes up much of Central Asia. Although one of Asia's largest regions, it has a relatively small population.

INDEX TO ASIA PHYSICAL MAP

Aden, Gulf of .A5
Altai Mts. .D3
Altyn Tagh .E3
Amu Darya .C3
Amur River .F2
Anadyr Range .F1
Andaman Islands .D5
Andaman Sea .E5
Arabian Sea .B4
Arafura Sea .H6
Aral Sea .C3
Ararat, Mt. .B2
Baikal, Lake .E2
Balkhash, Lake .D3
Baltic Sea .B1
Banda Sea .H6
Barents Sea .C1
Bengal, Bay of .D5
Bering Sea .G1
Black Sea .B2
Brahmaputra River .D4
Borneo (Kalimantan) .F6
Bosporus, Straits of .A2
Caspian Depression .B2
Caspian Sea .B3
Caucasus Mts. .B2
Celebes (Sulawesi) .G6
Celebes Sea .G6
Central Siberian Plain .E2
Ceram .H6
Chang River (Yangtze) .F4
Chao Phraya (Menam) River .E5
Cherski Range .F1
Chukchi Sea .F1
Dead Sea .A3
Deccan Plateau .C5
Demavend, Mt. .B3
Don River .B2
Dongting Lake .F4
East China Sea .G4
East Siberian Sea .F1
Eastern Ghats .D5
Elbrus, Mt. .B2
Elburz Mts. .B3
Euphrates River .A3
Everest, Mt. .D4
Flores .G6
Formosa Strait .F4
Ganges River .D4
Gobi Desert .E3
Godwin Austen, Mt. (K2) .C4
Greater Khingant Mts. .F2
Hainan .F5
Halmahera .G6
Helmand River .C4
Himalayas .D4
Hindu Kush .C4
Hokkaido .G2
Hong (Red) River .E5
Honshu .G3
Hwang Ho (Yellow) River .F4
Indian Ocean .C6
Indigirka River .F1
Indus River .C4
Iran, Plateau of .B4
Irrawaddy River .E5
Irtysh River .D2
Japan, Sea of .G3
Java .F6
Java Sea .F6
K2 (Mt. Godwin Austen) .C4
Kamchatka Peninsula .G1
Kara Sea .D1
Kara Kum .C3
Karakorum Range .D4
Khyber Pass .C4
Kolyma Range .F1
Kolyma River .F1
Koryak Range .F1
Kunlun Mts. .D4
Kuril Islands .G2
Kuznetsk Basin .D2
Kyrgyzstan Tien Shan .D3
Kyushu .G3
Kyzyl Kum .C3
Laccadive Islands .C5
Laptev Sea .E1
Lena River .E1
Luzon .G5
Macassar Strait .G6
Malacca, Strait of .E6
Malay Peninsula .E6
Maldives .C6
Manchurian Plain .F2
Mediterranean Sea .A2
Mekong River .E5
Mindanao .G5
Mindoro .G5
Minya Konka .E4
Mongolia, Plateau of .E3
Mount Sinai .A3
Nafud (Red Desert) .A4
Nan Shan .E4
Negros .G5
New Guinea .H6
New Siberian Islands .E1
Nicobar Islands .D6
Ob River .D2
Okhotsk, Sea of .G1
Okinawa .G4
Oman, Gulf of .B4
Palawan .G5
Panay .G5
Persian Gulf .B4
Philippine Sea .G4
Qinghai Lake .E4
Red Basin .E4
Red Desert (Nafud) .A4
Red (Hong) River .E5
Red Sea .A3
Rub' Al Khali .B4
Ryukyu Islands .G4
Sakhalin .G2
Salween River .E5
Samar .G5
Sayan Mts. .E2

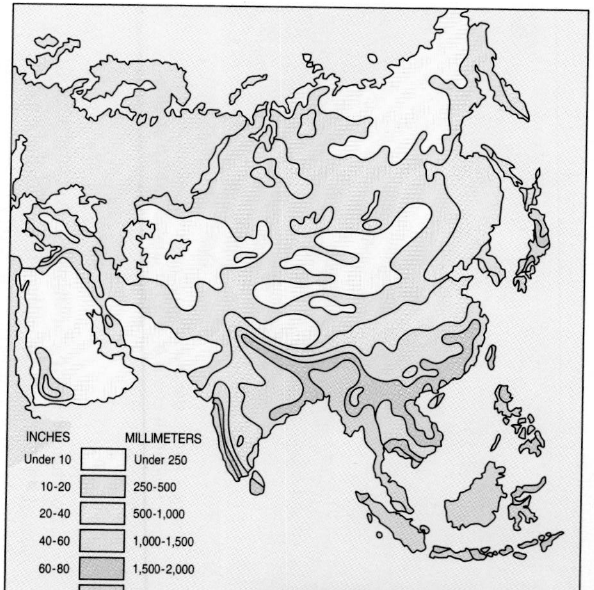

AVERAGE ANNUAL PRECIPITATION

Severnaya Zemlya .E1
Shandong Peninsula .F3
Shikoku .G3
Si Kiang (West River) .F4
Siberia .E2
Sinai Peninsula .A3
Socotra .B5
South China Sea .F5
Sri Lanka .D6
Stanovoi Range .F2
Suez Canal .A3
Sulu Sea .G5
Sumatra .E6
Sumba .G6
Sumbawa .G6
Syr Darya .C3
Syrian Desert .A3
Taimyr Peninsula .E1
Taiwan .G4
Taklamakan Desert .D4
Tarim River .D3
Tarim Pendi Basin .D3
Taurus Mts. .A3
Thailand, Gulf of .E6
Thar Desert .C4
Tien Shan .D3
Tigris River .B3
Timor .G6
Timor Sea .H6
Tonkin, Gulf of .F5
Tsinling Mts. .E4
Turfan Depression .D3
Ural Mts. .C2
Ural River .C2
Urmia, Lake .B3
Ust-urt Plateau .B3
Verkhoyansk Range .E1
West River (Si Kiang) .F4
Western Ghats .C5
Western Siberian Plain .D2
Wrangel Island .F1
Xizang Plateau .D4
Yaiu River .F3
Yangtze (Chang) River .F4
Yellow (Hwang Ho) River .F4
Yellow Sea .F3
Yenisei River .D2
Zagros Mts. .B3

Asia
Two-Point Equidistant Projection
0 500 1000 1500 mi
0 500 1000 1500 2000 km
Tropical Rain Forest
Coniferous/ Evergreen Forest
Deciduous Forest
Chaparral
Grassland
Desert and Semidesert
Tundra
Alpine Tundra
Ice Sheet
ARCTIC OCEAN
PACIFIC OCEAN
INDIAN OCEAN
Europe
Africa
RUSSIA
SIBERIA
WESTERN SIBERIAN PLAIN
CENTRAL SIBERIAN PLAIN
KARA SEA
LAPTEV SEA
SEVERNAYA ZEMLYA
TAIMYR PENINSULA
CHUKCHI SEA
WRANGEL I.
EAST SIBERIAN SEA
NEW SIBERIAN ISLANDS
ANADYR RANGE
KORYAK RANGE
BERING SEA
Kolyma R.
Indigirka R.
CHERSKI RANGE
VERKHOYANSK RANGE
Lena River
Yenisei River
Ob River
Irtysh
URAL MTS.
Ural River
KAMCHATKA PEN.
SEA OF OKHOTSK
SAKHALIN
KURIL ISLANDS (Russia-Claimed by Japan)
HOKKAIDO
HONSHU
JAPAN
SHIKOKU
KYUSHU
SEA OF JAPAN
N. KOREA
S. KOREA
STANOVOI RANGE
GREATER KHINGANT MTS.
MANCHURIAN PLAIN
Lake Baikal
SAYAN MTS.
KUZNETSK BASIN
ALTAI MTS.
PLATEAU OF MONGOLIA
MONGOLIA
GOBI DESERT
KAZAKHSTAN
Lake Balkhash
ARAL SEA
Syr Darya
Amu Darya
KYZYL KUM
UZBEKISTAN
UST-URT PLATEAU
CASPIAN DEPRESSION
CASPIAN SEA
TURKMENISTAN
KARA KUM
KYRGYZSTAN
TAJIKISTAN
AFGHANISTAN
TIEN SHAN
TURFAN DEPRESSION
ALTYN TAGH
Tarim R.
TARIM PENDI BASIN
TAKLAMAKAN DESERT
KUNLUN MTS.
NAN SHAN
Qinghai L.
HINDU KUSH
K2 (Mt. Godwin Austen)
KARAKORUM RANGE
XIZANG PLATEAU (PLATEAU OF TIBET)
CHINA
TSINLING MTS.
Huang Ho (Yellow) River
Minya Konka
RED BASIN
Chang (Yangtze) River
Dongting L.
West (Si) River
Red (Hong) R.
HONG KONG
SHANDONG PENINSULA
YELLOW SEA
EAST CHINA SEA
OKINAWA (Japan)
RYUKYU ISLANDS
Formosa Strait
TAIWAN
PHILIPPINE SEA
HIMALAYAS
Brahmaputra R.
NEPAL
Mt. Everest 29,028 ft (8,848 m)
BHUTAN
BANGLADESH
INDIA
THAR DESERT
PAKISTAN
Khyber Pass
Helmand R.
Indus River
DECCAN PLATEAU
WESTERN GHATS
EASTERN GHATS
SRI LANKA
LAKSHADWEEP ISLANDS (India)
MALDIVES
ANDAMAN ISLANDS (India)
NICOBAR ISLANDS (India)
BAY OF BENGAL
ANDAMAN SEA
MYANMAR (BURMA)
Salween R.
Chao Phraya R.
THAILAND
LAOS
Mekong River
VIETNAM
CAMBODIA
GULF OF TOLKIN
HAINAN
GULF OF THAILAND
SOUTH CHINA SEA
MALAY PENINSULA
MALAYSIA
SINGAPORE
BRUNEI
BORNEO
SUMATRA
JAVA
JAVA SEA
SUMBAWA
FLORES
SUMBA
TIMOR
EAST TIMOR
TIMOR SEA
ARAFURA SEA
BANDA SEA
CERAM
CELEBES
CELEBES SEA
Macassar Strait
INDONESIA
HALMAHERA
NEW GUINEA
LUZON
PHILIPPINES
SAMAR
MINDORO
PANAY
NEGROS
PALAWAN
SULU SEA
MINDANAO
TURKEY
Straits of Bosporus
BLACK SEA
CAUCASUS MTS.
Mt. Elbrus
GEORGIA
ARMENIA
Mt. Ararat
AZERBAIJAN
L. Urmia
TAURUS MTS.
CYPRUS
LEBANON
ISRAEL
SYRIA
JORDAN
SINAI
Mt. Sinai
Suez Canal
Dead Sea
Euphrates River
Tigris River
IRAQ
SYRIAN DESERT
ELBURZ MTS.
Mt. Demavend
ZAGROS MTS.
IRAN
PLATEAU OF IRAN
SAUDI ARABIA
NAFUD
KUWAIT
BAHRAIN
QATAR
PERSIAN GULF
UNITED ARAB EMIRATES
RUB' AL KHALI
OMAN
GULF OF OMAN
YEMEN
GULF OF ADEN
SOCOTRA (Yemen)
ARABIAN SEA
RED SEA
MEDITERRANEAN SEA
A B C D E F G H
1 2 3 4 5 6
40°N 50°N 60°N 70°N 80°N
40°E 50°E 60°E 70°E 80°E 90°E 100°E 110°E 120°E 130°E 140°E
10°W 0° 10°E 20°E 30°E
30°N 20°N 10°N 0° 10°S
180° 170°W 170°E 160°E 150°E
20°E 40°E 60°E 80°E 100°E 120°E 140°E 160°E 180°

North Asia is a vast but thinly populated region. It is often frozen in winter, when reindeer sleds (*right*) become a convenient form of transportation. The Chang Jiang (or Yangtze River) (*below*) is East Asia's major river and China's longest. Nearly half of China's people live in the river's great basin.

where the Tigris and Euphrates rivers provide sufficient water for irrigation, some of Asia's and the world's oldest civilizations arose thousands of years ago.

To the region's traditional nations three countries can be added—Armenia, Azerbaijan, and Georgia, which also gained independence from the former Soviet Union in 1991. They are sometimes called Transcaucasia or the Transcaucasian republics because of their location on or near the Caucasus mountain range between Europe and Asia.

COUNTRIES OF ASIA*

COUNTRY	CAPITAL
Afghanistan	Kabul
Armenia	Yerevan
Azerbaijan	Baku
Bahrain	Manama
Bangladesh	Dhaka
Bhutan	Thimphu
Brunei	Bandar Seri Begawan
Cambodia	Phnom Penh
China, People's Republic of	Beijing
Cyprus	Nicosia
Georgia	Tbilisi
India	New Delhi
Indonesia	Jakarta
Iran	Tehran
Iraq	Baghdad
Israel	Jerusalem
Japan	Tokyo
Jordan	Amman
Kazakhstan	Astana
Korea, North	P'yŏngyang
Korea, South	Seoul
Kuwait	Kuwait
Kyrgyzstan	Bishkek
Laos	Vientiane
Lebanon	Beirut
Malaysia	Kuala Lumpur
Maldives	Male
Mongolia	Ulaanbaatar
Myanmar (Burma)	Yangon
Nepal	Kathmandu
Oman	Muscat
Pakistan	Islamabad
Philippines	Manila
Qatar	Doha
Saudi Arabia	Riyadh
Singapore	Singapore
Sri Lanka	Colombo
Syria	Damascus
Tajikistan	Dushanbe
Thailand	Bangkok
Timor, East	Dili
Turkey	Ankara
Turkmenistan	Ashkhabad
United Arab Emirates	Abu Dhabi
Uzbekistan	Tashkent
Vietnam	Hanoi
Yemen	Sanaa

*Russia includes territory in both Asia and Europe, but the majority of its people live in Europe. Azerbaijan, Georgia, Kazakhstan, and Turkey also have areas of territory in Europe.

North Asia. This is another vast but thinly populated region, which extends across the northern part of the continent from the Ural Mountains to the Pacific Ocean. Most of North Asia consists of the region known as Siberia and lies within present-day Russia. Bordering the Arctic Ocean on the north, with the coldest winter temperatures on the continent, it is often inhospitable to human settlement, although it is rich in mineral resources.

See the separate articles on the Himalayas, the Middle East, Mount Everest, Palestine, Siberia, and Southeast Asia in the appropriate volumes.

Natural Resources

Minerals. Asia is rich in mineral resources, although a good part of its mineral wealth is still untapped. Deposits of coal, iron ore, and copper are found in East Asia, while South Asia is rich in manganese. Southeast Asia is

WONDER QUESTION

What and where is Asia Minor?

Asia Minor, also known as Anatolia, is a peninsula that forms the westernmost part of Asia and includes most of the land area of Turkey. It is bordered on the north by the Black Sea, on the south by the Mediterranean Sea, and on the west by the Aegean Sea, an arm of the Mediterranean. The land consists mainly of a high, rugged central plateau, ringed by mountains in the north and south.

Historically, Asia Minor was one of the earliest areas of human settlement. It was the site of numerous ancient kingdoms, most notably that of the Hittites, who flourished in the region from about 1900 to 1200 B.C. Some of the first Greek colonies were established on the peninsula's western coast. The legendary city of Troy (actually several cities), scene of Homer's *Iliad*, was located on the northwestern coast of Asia Minor.

The Greeks first used the name "Asia" to refer to the western part of the peninsula. Later, the name Asia Minor, meaning smaller or lesser Asia, was given to the entire region, to distinguish it from the rest of the vast Asian continent.

As a natural gateway between Europe and Asia, Asia Minor was a prize fought over by many conquerors through the centuries. Between 500 B.C. and A.D. 1500, it fell, in succession, to the Persians, the armies of Alexander the Great, the Roman and Byzantine empires, Arabs, Seljuk Turks, Mongols, and Ottoman Turks. With the collapse of the Ottoman Empire and the establishment of a republic in 1923, the region became the heartland of present-day Turkey.

Fishing begins at sunrise on the Mekong River, the chief waterway of Southeast Asia. The plains and delta of the river form a fertile rice-growing area, traditionally cultivated with the aid of water buffalo, probably the most useful domesticated animal of the region.

one of the world's chief sources of tin, with Malaysia being the world's largest producer. North Asia's extensive mineral resources include bauxite (aluminum ore), iron, gold, lead, zinc, and silver.

Southwest Asia, particularly the Persian Gulf area, is the world's single largest source of petroleum, with an estimated one-half of the total supply. Other important sources of petroleum are in Azerbaijan, China, and Indonesia. China also has the world's largest deposits of anthracite (hard coal) and tungsten. Turkey has large chromium deposits, and India has enormous deposits of mica.

Soils and Vegetation. Much of Asia has poor soils, particularly in the interior, which is too high, dry, or cold for good soil to have developed. Nor are the soils of the subtropical and tropical regions necessarily very productive. The most fertile places, where crops can most readily be grown, are located along the river valleys and some coastal areas, and it is here that the densest populations are found. In a few cases, such as the island of Java in Indonesia, the soils are fertile because of their volcanic origin.

Vegetation ranges from the mosses and other simple plant life of the frozen tundra along the North Asia coast to the lush tropical rain forests of Southeast Asia. Between the two lie the belt of northern forest (taiga), the grasslands of the semi-arid steppes, and deserts with little or no vegetation at all.

Its forests are among the continent's major natural resources. The taiga belt is the world's largest area of woodlands, and Southeast Asia's tropical rain forests include such valuable hardwoods as teak and mahogany. Logging, however, has suffered from a lack of transportation in some areas, and in others from overcutting.

Animal Life. Asia is home to a variety of wild and domestic animal life. Most wild animals inhabit the less-populated areas.

Polar and brown bears, Arctic foxes and hares, mouse-like lemmings, the rare Siberian tiger, reindeer, elk, and such valuable fur-bearing animals as ermine and sable are found in North Asia. The Bactrian (two-humped) camel is a vital beast of burden in the arid lands of Central Asia, while the Arabian (one-humped) camel performs the same function in the deserts of Southwest Asia. The hardy yak, a shaggy-haired ox, thrives in the high, windswept Tibetan plateau, where it is the most important form of livestock.

Animals unique to Asia include the Komodo dragon, largest of the lizards; the shy orangutan; and the Indian (or Asian) elephant, which has smaller ears than its African cousin.

Birds are found throughout the continent. The most gorgeously plumaged inhabit the tropical areas of South and Southeast Asia, which are also home to monkeys and apes. The orangutan lives only in the dense tropical forests on the islands of Sumatra and Borneo. India has a number of large mammals, including the Bengal tiger, the Indian rhinoceros, and the Indian (or Asian) elephant. The water buffalo is probably the most important domesticated animal of the region, invaluable in plowing its rice fields.

Large reptiles include crocodiles and a wide variety of snakes, among them the deadly Indian cobra and the enormous python. The Komodo dragon, the world's largest lizard, can be found on a few of the Indonesian islands. East Asia's most distinctive mammal is the giant panda, which is native only to the bamboo forests of interior China.

Climate

Asia has almost all the varieties of climates known. In general, it has what is called a continental climate—that is, one marked by wide seasonal and temperature ranges and limited rainfall. Much of the continent is cold and dry in the winter and warm and dry in the summer. Because of its great size, many areas are far from the sea. As a result, the interior of Asia is never touched by the winds that bring moisture from the oceans. Most of Central Asia is alternately cold and warm, but always dry.

Temperature. The high mountain ranges that cross Asia act as a huge wall. They keep the cold winds of the Arctic from blowing to the south and the hot winds of the south from blowing north. Therefore, average temperatures in the areas north of the mountains are lower than they would normally be at the same latitude elsewhere in the world. Siberian winters, for example, are among the coldest on earth. The average January temperature is about −60°F (−51°C). In the town of Verkhoyansk, in northeastern Siberia, the winter temperature has dropped to −90°F (−68°C).

The hottest parts of Asia are in the southwestern region. The area around the Persian Gulf is one of the hottest in the world, with land temperatures often reaching 120°F (49°C).

Rainfall. Rainfall in Asia is also affected by the size of the continent and its mountain ranges. Some regions receive a great deal of rain, while others receive little. Winds carrying moisture from the ocean bring rain to the near side of the mountains, leaving the far side of the high mountains generally dry.

Examples of this uneven rainfall can be seen throughout Asia. Parts of Southwest Asia receive as little as 4 inches (100 millimeters) of rain a year, while northeastern India is one of the wettest regions on earth. Southeast Asia is often hit by heavy rains, which may cause widespread flooding. Parts of southern China also receive much rainfall. Most of the rest of the continent tends to be dry.

Winds. Many parts of Asia are subjected to very strong winds. One such wind, called the Seistan, blows through Iran, in Southwest Asia, for about six months of the year at extremely high speeds. Many desert areas in Central Asia have similar winds. Winds from the plateau of Tibet have blown thousands of tons of soil (loess) hundreds of miles eastward to China. The heating and cooling of the land in interior Asia causes great masses of air to rush in and out of this area. Because of the height and location of the mountains, the winds usually move in an east–west direction.

The monsoons of the Indian Ocean are seasonal winds. For about six months each year they blow from northeastern India across the peninsula, carrying warm air out to the Indian Ocean. From June to September they reverse their direction and blow from the southwest. They then carry rain to the land, creating the wet monsoon season. If these returning winds do not carry enough rain, then crops fail and famine may result. The farmers of South and Southeast Asia are thus dependent upon the wet monsoon for their livelihood.

THE PEOPLE

Asia's population, already very large, is growing rapidly. This is due partly to the high birthrate in some of the Asian nations and partly to the declining death rate. Modern medicines, better public health care, improved nutrition, and other advancements in living standards have helped increase the average life span of most Asian people.

Population Density

Asia's population is not spread out evenly over the continent. Most of the people live in three regions—South, Southeast, and East Asia. Therefore, even though more than one-half of Asia's land lies in North and Central Asia, less than one-tenth of Asians live there.

Population densities vary widely. Southwest Asia has fewer than 60 people per square mile (25 per square kilometer). But in South, Southeast, and East Asia, the highest population densities in the world are found. Often the population is even denser than the figures would indicate, since the bulk of the people are concentrated in the most fertile areas, usually along riverbanks or in coastal regions. In China, for example, the great majority of the people live in the eastern part of the country, along the coast and in the fertile basins drained by the great rivers. The average population density in these areas can be as high as four to six times the overall density of the country.

Racial and Ethnic Groups

Asians are as varied as their landscape. Attempts to classify them differ, but they can be divided into a number of broad categories.

Mongoloid peoples, including Chinese, most Japanese, Koreans, Mongols, and Tibetans, make up by far the largest group. The Han Chinese, who constitute most of China's population but are concentrated in the east, are the largest single ethnic group.

Turkic peoples occupy a vast area stretching from northwestern China across Central Asia to Turkey and Azerbaijan. North Asia is also home to some Turkic ethnic groups, as well as to considerable numbers of European Russians.

Malay peoples inhabit Indonesia and the Philippines, while most mainland Southeast

Asians are a Malay-Mongoloid mixture. South Asia includes two main ethnic groups: Indo-Aryans in northern India, Pakistan, Bangladesh, and most of Afghanistan and Sri Lanka; and Dravidians in southern India and part of Sri Lanka. Aside from Turkey, the Transcaucasian countries, and Iran (whose people are mainly Indo-Aryan), the great majority of Southwest Asians are Semites, chiefly Arabs but also including Jews, most of whom live in Israel. The people of Cyprus are of Greek (the majority) and Turkish ancestry.

Other distinctive Asian racial groups include the few remaining Ainu of northern Japan and the Negritos and hill people of South and Southeast Asia. These are believed to be the original inhabitants of the regions.

Languages

The peoples of Asia can also be defined by their languages. The language names are similar to, but not always the same as, the ethnic classifications.

South Asia has two major language divisions—the Indo-Iranian (or Indo-Aryan), part of the large Indo-European family; and the Dravidian. The Indo-Iranian branch is divided into dozens of languages, including Hindi, Urdu, Bengali, Punjabi, and Sinhala. The many languages of the Dravidian family of southern India include Tamil, Telugu, Kanarese, and Malayalam. Persian, spoken in Iran, and the Pashto and related languages of Afghanistan are also Indo-Iranian.

Chinese, Tibetan, and most of the languages of mainland Southeast Asia belong to the Sino-Tibetan family. Mandarin Chinese is the world's most widely spoken language. Japanese and Korean are separate languages, sometimes classified in the Altaic family. The Malayo-Polynesian family includes languages of Malaysia, Indonesia, the Philippines, and most of the Pacific islands.

The major language of Southwest Asia, Arabic, belongs to the Semitic family (as does Hebrew, spoken in Israel). The Osmanli Turkish of Turkey, the Azeri Turkish of Azerbaijan, and their related languages of Central and North Asia are Altaic. Armenian and the Greek spoken on Cyprus are Indo-European, while Georgian belongs to the small Caucasian language family.

Opposite page, clockwise from top left: **A wealthy Saudi Arabian with a gold-plated cellular telephone; elderly Tajiks from Central Asia; a Russian mother and daughter from Siberia, in North Asia; a Sri Lankan woman gathering tea leaves; and an Israeli woman.** ***This page, clockwise from right:*** **A girl from the Philippines; a boy from India; schoolchildren in Japan; a man from China.**

INDEX TO ASIA POLITICAL MAP

Abu Dhabi........B4
Aden........A5
Ahmadabad........C5
Al Basrah........B3
Almaty........D3
Amman........A3
Amritsar........C4
Anadyr........F1
Ankara........A2
Ashkhabad........B3
Astana........C2
Baghdad........B3
Baku........B3
Bandar Seri Begawan........F6
Bandung........F6
Bangalore........C5
Bangkok........E5
Banjarmasin........F6
Beijing........F3
Beirut........A3
Bishkek........C3
Blagoveshchensk........F2
Bombay (Mumbai)........C5
Bratsk........E2
Calcutta........D5
Changchun........F3
Chelyabinsk........C2
Chengdu........E4
Chita........E2
Chongqing........E4
Cochin........C5
Colombo........D6
Da Nang........F5
Dalian........F3
Damascus........A3
Davao........G5
Delhi........D4
Dhaka........D5
Dili........G6
Doha........B4
Dushanbe........C3
Esfahan........B3
Fuzhou........F4
Gorkiy
(Nizhnly Novgorod)........B2
Guangzhou........F4
Hanoi........E5
Harbin........F3
Hiroshima........G3
Ho Chi Minh City........F5
Hohhot........F3
Hong Kong........F4
Hyderabad (India)........C5
Hyderabad (Pakistan)........C4
Inchon........F3
Irkutsk........E3
Islamabad........C4
Izmir........A2
Jahrum........B4
Jaipur........C4
Jakarta........F6
Jayapura........H5
Jerusalem........A3
Jiddah........A4
Jinan........F3
Kabul........C4
Kandahar........C4
Kanpur........D4
Karachi........C4
Karaganda........D3
Kashi........D3
Katmandu........D4
Kerman........B4
Khabarovsk........F2
Kobe........G3
Komsomolsk........F2
Kota Kinabalu........F6
Krasnoyarsk........D2
Kuala Lumpur........E6
Kunming........E4
Kuwait........B4
Kyoto........G3
Lahore........C4
Lanzhou........E4
Lhasa........D4
Lucknow........D4
Macao........F4
Madras (Chennai)........D5
Madurai........C5
Magadan........F1
Magnitogorsk........C2
Male........C6
Manado........G6
Manama........B4
Mandalay........E5
Manila........G5
Mashhad........C3
Mecca........A4
Muscat........B4
Nagasaki........G3
Nagpur........G3
Nanjing........F4
Nanning........F4
New Delhi........C4
Nicosia........A3
Norilsk........D1
Novokuznetsk........D2
Novosibirsk........D2
Omsk........D2
Osaka........G3
Padang........E6
Palembang........F6
Pavlodar........D3
Phnom Penh........E5
Pyongyang........F3
Qingdao........F3
Quezon City........G5
Riyadh........A4
Sana........A4
Sapporo........G2
Semipalatinsk........D3
Sendal........G3
Seoul........F3
Shanghai........F4
Shenyang........F3
Singapore........E6
Srinagar........C4
Sukkur........C4
Surabaya........F6
Tabriz........B3
Taegu........F3
Taipei........F4
Taiyuan........F3
Tashkent........C3
Tbilisi........B3
Tehran........B3
Thimphu........D4
Tianjin........F3
Tokyo........G3
Tomsk........D2
Ujung Pandang........G6
Ulaanbaatar........E3
Ulan-Ude........E3
Urumqi........D3
Victoria........F4
Vientiane........E5
Vladivostok........G3
Wenzhou........F4
Wuhan........F4
Xiamen........F4
Xian........E4
Yakutsk........F2
Yangon (Rangoon)........E5
Yekaterinburg........C2
Yerevan........B3
Yokohama........G3
Zhengzhou........F4

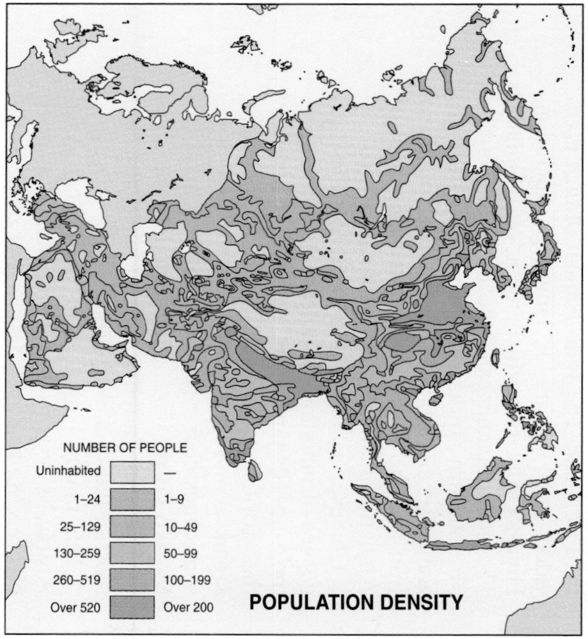

POPULATION DENSITY

Chief Cities in Asia (by population)

Over 7,000,000

Beijing† (Peking), China
Bombay (Mumbai),* India
Calcutta (Kolkata),* India
Delhi, India
Istanbul,* Turkey
Jakarta, Indonesia
Seoul, South Korea
Shanghai,† China
Tianjin (Tientsin),* China
Tokyo, Japan

3,000,000 to 7,000,000

Baghdad, Iraq
Bangkok, Thailand
Dhaka, Bangladesh
Guangzhou (Canton), China
Ho Chi Minh City (Saigon),* Vietnam
Karachi, Pakistan
Madras (Chennai), India
Pusan, South Korea
Shenyang, China
Singapore, Singapore
Tehran, Iran
Wuhan, China
Yokohama, Japan

2,000,000 to 3,000,000

Ankara, Turkey
Bandung, Indonesia
Bangalore, India
Chengdu (Chengtu), China
Chittagong, Bangladesh
Chongqing (Chungking), China
Hanoi, Vietnam
Harbin, China
Hyderabad, India
Inchon, South Korea
Lahore, Pakistan
Nagoya, Japan
Nanjing (Nanking), China
Osaka, Japan
Pyongyang, North Korea
Surabaya, Indonesia
Taegu, South Korea
Taipei, Taiwan (Republic of China)
Yangon (Rangoon), Myanmar

*Metropolitan area
†Municipality, including surrounding counties

Asia
0 500 1000 1500 mi
0 500 1000 1500 2000 km
Two-Point Equidistant Projection
A B C D E F G H
1 2 3 4 5 6
ARCTIC OCEAN
PACIFIC OCEAN
INDIAN OCEAN
Europe
Africa
RUSSIA
KAZAKHSTAN
MONGOLIA
CHINA
INDIA
JAPAN
N. KOREA
S. KOREA
TAIWAN
PHILIPPINES
INDONESIA
MALAYSIA
BRUNEI
SINGAPORE
VIETNAM
CAMBODIA
THAILAND
LAOS
MYANMAR (BURMA)
BANGLADESH
BHUTAN
NEPAL
SRI LANKA
MALDIVES
PAKISTAN
AFGHANISTAN
TAJIKISTAN
KYRGYZSTAN
UZBEKISTAN
TURKMENISTAN
IRAN
IRAQ
SYRIA
LEBANON
ISRAEL
JORDAN
CYPRUS
TURKEY
GEORGIA
ARMENIA
AZERBAIJAN
SAUDI ARABIA
KUWAIT
BAHRAIN
QATAR
UNITED ARAB EMIRATES
OMAN
YEMEN
EAST TIMOR
SINAI
XINJIANG-UYGUR AUTONOMOUS REGION
XIZANG AUTONOMOUS REGION (TIBET)
KURIL ISLANDS (Russia)
OKINAWA (Japan)
SOCOTRA (Yemen)
LAKSHADWEEP (India)
ANDAMAN ISLANDS (India)
NICOBAR ISLANDS (India)
Suez Canal
MEDITERRANEAN SEA
BLACK SEA
CASPIAN SEA
ARAL SEA
RED SEA
PERSIAN GULF
GULF OF OMAN
GULF OF ADEN
ARABIAN SEA
BAY OF BENGAL
ANDAMAN SEA
GULF OF THAILAND
GULF OF TONKIN
SOUTH CHINA SEA
EAST CHINA SEA
YELLOW SEA
SEA OF JAPAN
SEA OF OKHOTSK
BERING SEA
PHILIPPINE SEA
SULU SEA
CELEBES SEA
BANDA SEA
ARAFURA SEA
TIMOR SEA
JAVA SEA
BARENTS SEA
KARA SEA
LAPTEV SEA
EAST SIBERIAN SEA
CHUKCHI SEA
Izmir
Ankara
Nicosia
Beirut
Jerusalem
Amman
Damascus
Tbilisi
Yerevan
Baku
Tabriz
Baghdad
Al Basrah
Kuwait
Tehran
Esfahan
Mashhad
Ashkhabad
Kerman
Jahrum
Riyadh
Manama
Doha
Abu Dhabi
Muscat
Jiddah
Mecca
Sana
Aden
Karachi
Hyderabad
Ahmadabad
Sukkur
Kandahar
Kabul
Islamabad
Srinagar
Lahore
Amritsar
Delhi
New Delhi
Jaipur
Kanpur
Lucknow
Katmandu
Thimphu
Dhaka
Calcutta (Kolkata)
Chittagong
Nagpur
Bombay (Mumbai)
Hyderabad
Bangalore
Madras (Chennai)
Cochin
Madurai
Colombo
Male
Dushanbe
Tashkent
Bishkek
Almaty
Kashi
Urumqi
Lhasa
Magnitogorsk
Chelyabinsk
Yekaterinburg
Astana
Omsk
Karaganda
Novosibirsk
Pavlodar
Semipalatinsk
Tomsk
Krasnoyarsk
Novokuznetsk
Norilsk
Bratsk
Irkutsk
Ulan-Ude
Chita
Ulaanbaatar
Yakutsk
Magadan
Anadyr
Komsomolsk
Blagoveshchensk
Khabarovsk
Vladivostok
Harbin
Changchun
Shenyang
Dalian
Beijing
Tianjin
Hohhot
Taiyuan
Jinan
Qingdao
Zhengzhou
Xian
Lanzhou
Nanjing
Shanghai
Wuhan
Wenzhou
Chengdu
Chongqing
Changsha
Fuzhou
Taipei
Xiamen
Guangzhou
Hong Kong
Macao
Kunming
Nanning
Hanoi
Pyongyang
Seoul
Inchon
Taegu
Sapporo
Sendai
Tokyo
Yokohama
Kobe
Kyoto
Osaka
Hiroshima
Nagasaki
Mandalay
Yangon (Rangoon)
Vientiane
Da Nang
Bangkok
Phnom Penh
Ho Chi Minh City
Quezon City
Manila
Davao
Kota Kinabalu
Kuala Lumpur
Medan
Kuching
Banjarmasin
Manado
Ujung Pandang
Padang
Palembang
Jakarta
Bandung
Surabaya
Dili
Jayapura
40°N 50°N 60°N 70°N 80°N
30°N 20°N 10°N 0° 10°S
10°W 0° 10°E 20°E 30°E 40°E 60°E 80°E 100°E 120°E 140°E 160°E 170°E 180° 170°W 150°E
40°E 50°E 60°E 70°E 80°E 90°E 100°E 110°E 120°E 130°E 140°E

Religions

Three of the world's great religions, Judaism, Christianity, and Islam, originated in Southwest Asia. Islam, the religion of the Muslims, eventually became the dominant faith of the region and spread to Central Asia and parts of South Asia (chiefly what are now Pakistan, Bangladesh, and Afghanistan) and Southeast Asia (mainly present-day Indonesia and Malaysia). Together with Hinduism and Buddhism, Islam remains one of the major religions of Asia.

Christianity was re-introduced to Asia by missionaries, and Judaism was re-established as the religion of Israel in recent times. Today, Christians predominate in Cyprus, Armenia, Georgia, and the Philippines, and make up about 40 percent of the population of Lebanon. Most of the Russians of North Asia are Christian, and there are significant communities in other parts of Asia.

Hinduism originated in India and is the chief religion of that populous country, which also has an important Muslim minority. India's religious heritage also includes Sikhs, Jains, and Parsees, or Zoroastrians. The origins of Zoroastrianism were in ancient Persia (Iran), where it was eventually supplanted by Islam. Buddhism also developed in India, based on the teachings of Siddhartha Gautama, called the Buddha. But it has relatively few followers in India today. Most Buddhists are now found in China, Japan, Korea, and mainland Southeast Asia.

Taoism is a native religion of China, which developed from the philosophy of Lao-tzu, while Shinto is the original faith of Japan. China has also been strongly influenced by Confucianism. Named for its founder, Confucianism is not a religion but a system of ethical teachings. Through China, it has influenced the thinking of other countries of East Asia as well as areas of Southeast Asia, partic-

Asia was the birthplace of the world's major religions: an orthodox Jew at the Western Wall in Jerusalem (*top*); Muslims kneeling in prayer (*right*); a Buddhist monk with statues of the Buddha (*below*); Christian dignitaries (*below right*); a Hindu holy man (*opposite page, top*).

ularly Vietnam. In addition, such early religious beliefs as animism and shamanism still survive in some parts of Asia.

Articles on the major religions of Asia can be found in the appropriate volumes. An article on Confucius appears in Volume C. Also consult RELIGIONS OF THE WORLD in Volume QR.

The Arts

Many Asian countries have a long tradition of cultural achievement in art, architecture, and literature. For detailed information on this aspect of Asia, see the following articles in the appropriate volumes of this encyclopedia: ANCIENT WORLD, ART OF THE; CHINA, ART AND ARCHITECTURE OF; CHINA, LITERATURE OF; INDIA, ART AND ARCHITECTURE OF; INDIA, LITERATURE OF; ISLAMIC ART AND ARCHITECTURE; JAPANESE ART AND ARCHITECTURE; JAPANESE LITERATURE.

Education

The scholar has always been a respected member of the community in Asia. In China, the most revered figure, Confucius, was a scholar and teacher. Asia's tradition of learning is also very old, the first Chinese university having been founded in 124 B.C. But until modern times education was a privilege enjoyed only by the well-to-do, and the great mass of Asians could neither read nor write. Not until the latter half of the 1800's did most Asian countries begin to adopt the goal of universal education for all of their people.

The majority of Asian countries today have compulsory school attendance laws, and almost all of them have policies designed to keep children in school longer. Fees that prevented many children from attending school have been gradually abolished or lowered. The literacy rate (the percentage of people able to read or write) has risen dramatically, although it still varies widely from country to country. In higher education, there is at least one college in every major city, and many cities have several colleges and universities. The academic standards of many of them compare favorably with those of the best universities in the world.

▸ CITIES

Although the majority of its people live in rural areas, Asia has some of the largest cities to be found anywhere in the world. Population trends are also marked by increasing urbanization, or the movement of people from rural areas to the cities.

The largest urban centers are located in East, South, and Southeast Asia. They include Tokyo, the capital of Japan; China's great municipalities of Shanghai; Beijing, the capital; and Tientsin (Tianjin); South Korea's rapidly growing capital of Seoul; the Indian cities of Bombay, Calcutta, and Delhi; and Jakarta, Indonesia's capital.

Many cities originated close to natural transportation routes. Istanbul, Turkey's largest city, one of the most favorably located, lies on the waters separating Europe and Asia. Formerly called Constantinople, it is the only city situated on two conti-

Jakarta is the capital of Indonesia and the largest city of Southeast Asia. Like other rapidly growing Asian cities, it has new sections built in the most modern style.

Istanbul (*left*), Turkey's largest city, is strategically located on the waters separating Europe and Asia. Formerly called Constantinople, it was once the capital of the Roman Empire. Jerusalem (*above*) is an ancient city holy to three religions—Judaism, Christianity, and Islam.

nents. Other Southwest Asian cities, such as Iraq's capital of Baghdad, while smaller, are also of great historical and cultural interest. The importance of Jerusalem, a city holy to three religious faiths, far outweighs its relatively small size.

Articles on the cities mentioned can be found in the appropriate volumes.

THE ECONOMY

About two-thirds of Asia's people earn their livelihood from the land. The most fertile areas are in South and Southeast Asia and in the eastern part of East Asia. Here, where the continent's population is most densely concentrated, every bit of usable land is intensely cultivated. In recent decades, to keep up with population growth, Asian countries have used modern technology to increase farm output.

Industrialization has been the major goal of nearly every economic development program carried out in Asia since the end of World War II in 1945. Japan is the greatest example of an Asian nation that has succeeded dramatically in industrializing itself. Rich mineral deposits, particularly oil and natural gas, have also fueled regional growth. In addition, many international companies have moved their manufacturing activities to Asia to take advantage of its skilled workforce and relatively low wages. By the late 1990's, however, economic growth in much of East and Southeast Asia had slowed.

Agriculture

Rice, which needs a warm and wet climate to grow, is the major crop in the southern regions of Asia. Southeast Asia, eastern India, southern China, Korea, and Japan are the important rice-growing areas. Farther north, in the drier regions, cereal grains such as wheat, barley, and millet are grown. China, northern India and Pakistan, and Central Asia are major wheat- and corn-growing areas.

Rubber is an important commercial crop in Thailand, the world's leading producer of natural rubber, and other countries of Southeast Asia. Most of the world's tea comes from India, China, and Sri Lanka. Sugarcane is grown mainly in India, China, and Thailand. Cotton is a major product in China, India, and countries of Central Asia. Asia's soybeans and the world's silk come largely from China. Jute, used to make burlap and twine, is Bangladesh's chief export. Coconuts come from Indonesia and the Philippines, while peanuts are grown in China and India. Dates and oranges are specialties of Southwest Asia.

Nomadic herders in Southwest and Central Asia, where the land is often suitable only for grazing, depend largely on their livestock. Many small farmers throughout Asia raise poultry for food. India and North Asia produce much cheese and butter, and North Asia and China lead in beef, pork, mutton, and lamb. Wool is a major product in Central Asia.

Manufacturing

Japan is not only the most highly industrialized nation in Asia; it ranks among the top two or three world industrial powers. It is the world's chief shipbuilding country and, along with the United States, the largest producer of automobiles and other motor vehicles. It is either first or among world leaders in the manufacture of steel, aluminum, chemicals, television sets and videocassette recorders, and computers and other high-technology products. Japan has achieved this with few mineral resources of its own. It must import the raw materials with which to manufacture these goods for export.

India and China are a distant second to Japan in industrial output. India is an important producer of textiles, cotton clothing, steel, electrical machinery, and electronic equipment. China's industrial heartland has traditionally been in its northeastern region (sometimes called Manchuria), the site of large iron and coal deposits. A main goal of the country's leaders is to make China one of the world's major industrial powers by the early 2000's.

South Korea, Taiwan, Singapore, and Israel have developed modern industrial economies in recent decades, and Turkey has long had a significant industrial capacity. Until the late 1990's, when much of Southeast and East Asia experienced a serious economic downturn, countries such as Thailand, Indonesia, and Malaysia were also industrializing rapidly.

Mining and Fishing

Asia has virtually all the minerals needed for industrial growth, although some deposits remain to be developed, particularly in the lightly populated North Asia region. For detailed information on these minerals and where they are found, see the section Natural Resources (Minerals).

Fishing is an especially important industry in Asia. Japan's fishing industry is one of the most modern in the world, equipped with floating canneries that process the fish right after they are caught. China also has a major fishing industry, and Thailand has become the world's largest exporter of seafood (mostly farm-raised shrimp). The Persian Gulf waters

About two-thirds of Asians earn their livelihood from the land. Rice, here being planted in China's Sichuan province, is one of the continent's major crops. Automobiles are assembled at a plant in South Korea, which is rapidly becoming one of Asia's leading industrial areas.

Oil refineries such as this one in Saudi Arabia process much of the world's fuel supply. Southwest Asia has about half of the world's known oil reserves.

are famed for their natural pearls, while Japan produces much of the world's supply of cultured pearls.

Lumbering

Russia is the world's leading producer of sawed wood, and a large part of its lumbering is done in Asia. Japan is also an important world producer of sawed wood. In spite of its rich forest resources, Asia as a whole has a shortage of lumber. Many Asian countries are now carrying out reforestation programs—that is, the planting of trees for future use. These projects, which replace lost timber areas, also help prevent floods and soil erosion.

Transportation

Geography has hindered the development of both transportation and trade in Asia. Transportation has been easiest on or near the coasts and along the great rivers, which have been the main avenues of transportation in much of the continent for centuries. In the North, however, the Arctic climate keeps the coastal areas icebound for the better part of the year. In parts of Asia transportation is still a matter of using old caravan trails. Merchants still cross the deserts of Southwest and Central Asia on camels, although the camels are gradually being replaced by vehicles designed for desert travel.

The first Asian railroads were built after the arrival of the Europeans, mainly during the late 1800's and early 1900's. Some new lines were built after World War II, and others are now under construction. The Trans-Siberian Railroad is the only rail line crossing the whole vast expanse of Asia. It is also the world's longest continuous railroad, linking the Russian capital of Moscow in Europe with the Pacific Ocean port of Vladivostok. The line was expanded in recent years, but the harsh climate and rugged terrain make further work difficult. Today, Japan, India, and China have the most extensive rail systems.

The roads and highways of Asia, with some exceptions, are generally poor. Increasingly, air transport is being used to reach formerly inaccessible areas.

Modern methods of transportation in Asia can be seen in Japan's system of turbo trains. Popularly known as "bullet trains" because of their shape and high speed, they can travel at 160 miles (260 kilometers) an hour. Here the bullet train passes Mount Fuji on the main Japanese island of Honshu.

The sculpture at left was discovered at Mohenjo-Daro, part of the Indus Valley civilization. One of three main sites of early Asian civilization, it flourished 5,000 years ago in what is now Pakistan. Later Greek and Roman influence is reflected in the ruins at Palmyra, in modern-day Syria, a city-state that briefly held power during the A.D. 200's.

HISTORY

The history of Asia began in three great river valleys—the Tigris-Euphrates in Southwest Asia, the Indus in South Asia, and the Huang He (Yellow River) in East Asia. In these three areas, civilizations developed that give Asia its special place in the world today.

Early Civilizations

The Tigris-Euphrates Valley was the site of several early civilizations. From 3500 B.C. to 600 B.C., a succession of great states arose in the region. The Sumerians, Babylonians, and Assyrians developed writing, law, and commerce. The code of Hammurabi (about 1800 B.C.) was one of the first written law codes in the world. Around 600 B.C., the Persians, under Cyrus the Great, established an empire that stretched from the shores of the Mediterranean Sea to northern India. The empire was expanded by later Persian kings, among them Darius the Great.

The ruins of Harappa and Mohenjo-Daro are signs of early civilization in the Indus Valley of South Asia. In about 1500 B.C., Indo-Aryan invaders came through the mountains of northwestern India to establish the Hindu civilization. Traces of this early beginning remain to this day, and the tradition of Hinduism is still one of the most important influences in modern India.

For additional information on these periods of Asian history, see the articles ANCIENT CIVILIZATIONS (sections on Sumerian, Babylonian, and Indus Valley civilizations); and PERSIA, ANCIENT.

The earliest civilization in China developed along the northern reaches of the Huang He during the 1500's B.C. China's history was marked by successive dynasties, or ruling families. Some ruled for centuries; others for only a short period. The last dynasty, the Qing (or Manchu), was overthrown and a republic established in 1912.

Period of Development and Expansion

After 500 B.C., several great religions and empires grew up in Asia. In 334 B.C., Alexander the Great began his conquest of western Asia. His invasion brought Asia into direct contact with Greek civilization. Meanwhile the first great Indian empire, the Maurya, was established in the 320's B.C., creating unity in India. Under its greatest ruler, Asoka, Buddhism briefly flourished and the great monumental art of India began.

Farther east, in China, the Han dynasty (202 B.C.–A.D. 220) established an empire and extended its influence into Central and Southeast Asia. Under its great emperor Wu Ti, the Han adopted Confucianism. During this period other great religions took form. Chris-

Confucius, China's great sage and teacher, lived from about 551 to 479 B.C. His system of ethics has influenced Chinese thinking from ancient times to the present.

IMPORTANT DATES

About 3200 B.C.	Beginnings of civilization: Sumerians develop cuneiform writing; early urban culture in the Indus Valley; China emerges from the Stone Age.
About 1750 B.C.	Hammurabi, king of Babylonia, introduces world's first uniform code of laws.
About 1500 B.C.	Shang dynasty flourishes.
About 1300's B.C.	Phoenicians develop the first alphabet.
1200's B.C.	Moses leads the Exodus, receives the Ten Commandments.
1028–25	Chou dynasty: beginning of China's Iron Age.
600–300 B.C.	Upanishads written; crystallization of the caste system in India.
500's B.C.	Cyrus the Great founds the Persian Empire.
274–232 B.C.	Asoka unites two-thirds of India; rules according to Buddhist laws; sends out missionaries.
202 B.C.–A.D. 220	Han dynasty: height of ancient Chinese civilization; paper and porcelain invented.
A.D. 330	Constantine I moves the capital of the Roman Empire to Byzantium, renamed Constantinople (now Istanbul).
618–906	Tang dynasty in China: printing invented.
622	Mohammed (570–632) flees from Mecca to Medina and organizes the Commonwealth of Islam.
632–1100	Growth of Arabic civilization under the influence of Islam.
960–1279	Sung dynasty in China: beginning of modernity; use of compass; gunpowder developed.
998–1030	Muslims invade Punjab: mixing of Hindu and Muslim cultures.
1096–1290	Era of Crusades: increased contact between East and West.
1206–27	Genghis Khan (1167?–1227) establishes the Mongol Empire, conquers large parts of Asia and Europe.
1260	Kublai Khan becomes emperor of China.
1271–95	Travels of Marco Polo bring first detailed knowledge of Asia to Europe.
1368–1644	Ming dynasty drives out Mongols, reunifies China.
1369–1405	Tamerlane conquers much of Southwest Asia, invades India.
1453	Constantinople captured by the Ottoman Turks: end of the Eastern Roman (Byzantine) Empire; beginning of the Ottoman Empire.
1498	Vasco da Gama sails to India, opens water route to the East.
1514	Portuguese make first landing in China.
1521	Ferdinand Magellan claims Philippines for Spain.
1526	Mogul Empire in India founded by Babur.
1549–51	St. Francis Xavier introduces Christianity in Japan.
1600–1868	Tokugawa period in Japan: ban on all foreigners begins a long era of isolation.
1644–1912	Qing (Manchu) dynasty rules China.
1756–63	Britain becomes dominant power in India after the Seven Years' War.
1839–42	Opium War between Britain and China.
1853–54	U.S. Commodore Matthew Perry lands in Japan: end of Japanese isolation.

1857–58	Sepoy Rebellion (Indian Mutiny) in India.
1868	Meiji Restoration begins in Japan.
1869	Suez Canal opens.
1894–95	Sino-Japanese War.
1898	Spanish-American War: United States acquires the Philippines.
1900	Boxer Rebellion in China.
1904–05	Russo-Japanese War: Japan emerges as world power.
1911–12	Revolution in China led by Sun Yat-sen: China becomes a republic.
1923	Turkey becomes a republic.
1931	Japan invades Manchuria.
1941	Japan attacks Pearl Harbor, bringing United States into World War II.
1945	Atomic bombs dropped on Hiroshima and Nagasaki; Japan surrenders; World War II ends.
1946	Jordan and the Philippines gain independence.
1947	India and Pakistan gain independence.
1948	Israel created; Burma (now Myanmar) and Ceylon (now Sri Lanka) become independent; North and South Korea established.
1949	Communists win control of mainland China: Nationalist government retreats to Taiwan; Indonesia gains independence.
1950–53	Korean War.
1950	Chinese troops enter Tibet.
1954	North and South Vietnam, Laos, and Cambodia established.
1957	Malaya gains independence.
1960	Cyprus gains independence.
1961	Kuwait gains independence.
1963	Malaysia formed.
1965	Maldives and Singapore gain independence.
1967	Yemen (Aden) gains independence.
1971	Bangladesh gains independence.
1975	Vietnam War ends; civil war in Lebanon.
1976	North and South Vietnam united.
1979	Egypt and Israel sign peace treaty; Shah overthrown in Iran; Soviet forces invade Afghanistan.
1980–88	War between Iran and Iraq.
1984	Brunei gains independence.
1988–89	Soviet Union withdraws from Afghanistan.
1990	Yemen (Sana) and Yemen (Aden) are united; Iraq invades and occupies Kuwait.
1991	Gulf War ends with defeat of Iraq; breakup of the Soviet Union creates eight new Asian nations.
1993	First of a series of accords on Palestinian self-rule is signed by Israel and the Palestine Liberation Organization (PLO).
1997	Hong Kong is returned to China.
1998	India and then Pakistan conduct nuclear tests.
2000	North and South Korea hold their first summit meeting in 50 years.
2001	China is admitted to the World Trade Organization.
2002	East Timor gains independence from Indonesia.
2003	American-led forces invade Iraq, ending the regime of its dictator, Saddam Hussein.

tianity appeared in Southwest Asia, and Buddhism began to spread to East Asia.

The A.D. 600's saw the rapid rise of Islam. Its followers conquered most of North Africa, Southwest Asia, and northern India. In East Asia, China flourished under the Tang and Sung dynasties from about A.D. 600 to 1200. In the 1200's, Genghis Khan, the Mongol conqueror, gained control of much of Asia, from China to Russia.

Period of Colonialism

With the arrival in India of the Portuguese navigator Vasco da Gama in 1498, Europeans actively entered the life of Asia. Aware of Asia's many riches, the Europeans began to carve out colonial empires. In the 1500's, Portugal established colonies in India, and Spain acquired the Philippines. The English, French, and Dutch joined the rush for colonies in the 1600's. By the end of the 1800's, Britain governed most of what is now India, Pakistan, Bangladesh, Sri Lanka, Malaysia, Singapore, and Cyprus. France ruled modern Vietnam, Laos, and Cambodia; and the Netherlands controlled Indonesia. Among the few remaining independent Asian states were China, Japan, Korea, Siam (now Thailand), Persia (now Iran), and the Ottoman Turkish Empire. The United States won the Philippines from Spain, and Korea was later colonized by Japan, in 1910. Russia and the Soviet Union also ruled a great Asian empire.

Nationalism and Independence

The desire for self-rule and unity—called nationalism—was the most powerful force in Asia during the 1900's. Asian nationalism grew rapidly. It reached its height in the years after World War II, when the following nations were born: Mongolia in 1945; Jordan and the Philippines in 1946; India and Pakistan in 1947; Burma, Ceylon (now Sri Lanka), Israel, and North and South Korea in 1948; and Indonesia in 1949.

Amid great pomp, Suleiman I (*top*) ascends the Ottoman Turkish throne in 1520. The Ottoman Empire lasted nearly 400 years more, but gradually diminished in power. A British warship (*right*) fires on flimsy Chinese craft in the first Opium War (1839–42), which arose over Chinese efforts to bar imports of the drug. China's defeat forced it to cede Hong Kong to Britain and to open ports to foreign trade.

Indian leader Mohandas K. Gandhi achieved independence for his country by leading a campaign of nonviolent resistance to British rule.

Cambodia, Laos, and North and South Vietnam became independent in 1954. The Federation of Malaya followed in 1957; Cyprus in 1960; and Kuwait in 1961. Malaysia (made up of Malaya, Singapore, Sarawak, and Sabah) was established in 1963. Maldives won independence in 1965, as did Singapore, which seceded from Malaysia. South Yemen won its independence in 1967, and Bangladesh (formerly East Pakistan) did so in 1971.

In 1976, following the end of the long Vietnam War, North and South Vietnam were united. Brunei gained independence in 1984; and in 1990, South Yemen (Aden) and North Yemen (Sana) were united into a single republic. And the Soviet republics of Armenia, Azerbaijan, Georgia, Kazakhstan, Kirghizia, Tajikistan, Turkmenistan, and Uzbekistan all won independence in 1991.

Perhaps the most far-reaching effect of Western tradition on Asia was in the introduction of its political ideas and institutions. Some of the newly independent Asian nations adopted Communist forms of government. Others developed parliamentary systems. Most Asian countries, however, assumed a nonaligned, or neutral, position in their dealings with the great powers. This policy had first been announced officially at the Bandung Conference in Indonesia in 1955.

Recent History

The nations of Asia are playing an ever-increasing role in world affairs. Japan's economic strength makes it respected, and sometimes feared, by other nations. China, with more than one-fifth of the world's people, is a major power, especially since the breakup of the Soviet Union. India's size and great population make it dominant in South Asia, and the oil-producing countries of Southwest Asia are vital to the world economy.

The ideal of peace envisioned at the Bandung Conference, however, has been difficult to achieve. In the years since, war has erupted in many parts of Asia.

In South Asia, India and Pakistan went to war several times, chiefly over the region of Kashmir. Afghanistan experienced years of military upheaval. Sri Lanka was torn by violent ethnic hatreds. Civil conflict also raged in Cambodia, until a fragile peace was agreed to in 1991. And riots in Indonesia forced the resignation of its long-term president in 1998. In Southwest Asia, Israel fought numerous wars with its Arab neighbors. Lebanon was devastated by years of conflict. Iran and Iraq fought between 1980 and 1988. And Iraq's invasion of Kuwait in 1990 led to war in the Persian Gulf. (For more information, see the article PERSIAN GULF WAR in Volume P.)

Elsewhere in the Middle East, a series of accords signed by Israel and the Palestinian Arabs beginning in 1993 eventually

A mushroom cloud marked the atomic bombing of the Japanese city of Hiroshima by the United States in 1945, which hastened the end of World War II.

brought the Gaza Strip and nearly half of the West Bank under the control of an elected Palestinian government. Israel and Jordan also signed a peace treaty in 1994. The United States and Vietnam restored diplomatic ties in 1995. In 2000, North and South Korea held their first summit meeting since the Korean War (1950–53).

However, conflict continued on the continent. After the September 11, 2001, attacks on the United States, a U.S.-led war on terrorism ousted the Taliban regime from Afghanistan. But efforts failed to prevent additional terrorist episodes, notably in Yemen, Indonesia (on the island of Bali), and Saudi Arabia. Furthermore, the unstable situation in the Middle East was inflamed by a new wave of Israeli-Palestinian violence. India and Pakistan came to the brink of another war over Kashmir. In 2002, the international community welcomed East Timor to the world of nations after it gained independence from Indonesia. However, civil war later erupted in Indonesia's Aceh province.

The United States led a successful military campaign in 2003 to remove the Iraqi dictator, Saddam Hussein, from power and thus eliminate Iraq's ability to produce nuclear, biological, and chemical weapons. The removal of Hussein was welcomed throughout the Muslim world, although many protested the American presence in the region. International attention then shifted to other nations possessing banned weapons of mass destruction, notably Iran and North Korea.

EDWARD W. JOHNSON
Montclair State College

HYMAN KUBLIN
Author, *The Rim of Asia*

See also articles on individual Asian countries.

ASIAN AMERICANS

Asian Americans are U.S. citizens who were born in Asia or whose ancestors emigrated from Asia. They are one of the country's fastest-growing minority groups. According to the U.S. Census, some 12 million Americans—approximately 4 percent of the total population—claim Asian ancestry. This percentage was expected to grow to 10 percent by 2050.

The majority of Asian Americans—more than 20 percent—are of Chinese origin. Americans of Filipino ancestry form the next largest group, followed by Asian Indian, Vietnamese, Korean, and Japanese Americans. Increasingly, the term **Asian Pacific Americans** is used, to encompass people from the Pacific Islands (including native Hawaiians).

About half of all Asian Americans live in three states: California, New York, and Hawaii. Influential cities with large Asian populations include New York City, Los Angeles, San Francisco, and Honolulu.

A Vietnamese American family gathers for a group portrait. Most Asian American families are close knit, and several generations may live within one household.

WAY OF LIFE

The traditional Asian American way of life emphasizes family values, a reverence for education, a strong work ethic, religious observance, and participation in community events.

Family Life. Most Asian American families are close knit, with several generations sometimes living within one household. Respect for elders and the importance of study and hard work are among the values passed along to younger family members. Traditional values sometimes conflict with the American ideal of individual freedom. For example, Asian American women have sought to gain greater equality in the home and workplace while remaining respectful of traditional roles.

Religion. Asian Americans practice a number of different religions, depending on their ethnic origins. Buddhism, Confucianism, Hinduism, Islam, and Taoism are among the

Right: **Asian Indian women in traditional dress take a lunch break in Pasadena, California. Many women of Asian descent have blended successfully into American society while maintaining their cultural identity.** ***Below:*** **Business associates review design plans. Asian American business professionals work in many different fields.**

leading faiths. Christianity is also widely practiced—many U.S. Christian denominations have been reinvigorated by the presence of active Korean and Chinese churches.

Holidays and Cultural Celebrations. For Chinese and Vietnamese Americans, the lunar New Year holiday is an occasion for celebration and renewal. The Korean Harvest Festival and the Chinese Moon Festival, both celebrated in September, are times to give thanks for the gifts and abundance of the year.

Several Asian American groups celebrate Children's Day on May 5 to honor future generations. In summer, Japanese Americans celebrate Nisei Week, a cultural festival first held in 1934. Many Asian Indian Americans celebrate two national holidays of India: Independence Day, on August 15, and Republic Day, on January 26. In May of each year, Asian American Heritage Month commemorates the Asian American experience with festivals, conferences, and readings.

INFLUENCES ON AMERICAN CULTURE

Asian influences can be found in many areas of American culture. For example, the English language has been enriched by words with Asian origins, including tycoon (a powerful businessperson), guru (a spiritual guide or teacher), and yen (a strong desire or craving).

Left: **Young girls adorned with flowers march in a parade to celebrate the Laotian New Year.** ***Right:*** **Men perform a traditional Dragon Dance for the Chinese New Year.**

Most Americans are familiar with Chinese foods such as dim sum (assorted appetizers) and Japanese sushi (raw fish with rice). Indian curries and tandoori dishes (meats and breads cooked in a clay oven) are increasingly popular. Other well-known Asian dishes include kimchi (spicy pickled cabbage) from Korea; pad thai, a noodle dish from Thailand; and pho bo, Vietnamese noodle soup. Many chefs have adapted Asian seasonings and cooking techniques to create a cuisine known as Asian fusion.

Most of the best-known martial arts originated in Asia—judo, karate, and aikido in Japan; kung fu in China; and tae kwon do in Korea. Yoga, an ancient Indian discipline, is widely practiced today as a form of exercise and relaxation. Many Americans practice tai chi chuan, an ancient Chinese system of exercises.

Chinese Americans introduced holistic healing—an approach to health care that considers the whole person—to American medicine, as well as alternative therapies such as acupuncture. Western design has been influenced by the Chinese concept of feng shui, which aims to achieve balance and harmony in one's environment. And many Americans have embraced Zen Buddhism, a form of the Buddhist faith that stresses the practice of meditation as a means of enlightenment.

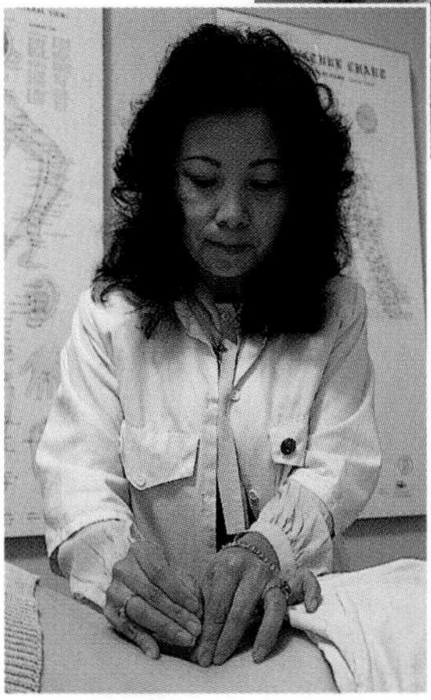

Above: **A Korean grocer welcomes a customer to his market in Los Angeles. The city has one of the country's largest populations of Asian Americans. *Left:* An acupuncturist works with a patient. Acupuncture, a traditional form of Chinese medicine, is one of many Asian influences on American culture.**

▶ NOTABLE ASIAN AMERICANS

Asian Americans have made important contributions to nearly every aspect of American life. In politics, Dalip Singh Saund became the first Asian American to serve in the U.S. Congress, in 1956. In 2000, Norman Yoshio Mineta became the first Asian American member of a U.S. presidential cabinet. In science, Tsung Dao Lee and Chen Ning Yang were the first Asian Americans to receive the Nobel Prize, for their work in physics in 1957. Entrepreneurs Charles Wang and Jerry Yang are leaders in technology.

Many Asian Americans have had distinguished careers in the arts, including orchestra conductors Seiji Ozawa (the first Asian American to direct a major American symphony orchestra) and Zubin Mehta, cellist Yo-Yo Ma, and violinists Sarah Chang and Midori. The elegant and functional designs of I. M. Pei are landmarks of modern architecture. Authors Maxine Hong Kingston, Amy Tan, Jhumpa Lahiri, and Bharati Mukherjee have told of the Asian immigrant experience in their work, as have filmmakers Ang Lee and Wayne Wang.

Asian American athletes have excelled in a variety of sports. Divers Sammy Lee and Vicki Manalo Draves won gold medals at the 1948 Olympic Games. Kristi Yamaguchi, the first Asian American to win an Olympic gold medal in figure skating (1992), and Michelle Kwan are leading figure skaters. Other important Asian American athletes include tennis player Michael Chang and golfer Tiger Woods (who is of both African American and Asian American heritage).

▶ HISTORY

Early Asian Immigration. The first Chinese immigrants went to the United States in 1849, attracted by the discovery of gold in California. Thousands more immigrated to the state in 1865 to help build the transcontinental railroad. The Chinese were paid very low wages for this backbreaking work. Many other workers regarded cheap Chinese labor as a threat. This led to outbreaks of violence and, in 1882, the Chinese Exclusion Act, which barred all Chinese laborers from immigrating to the United States.

Meanwhile, Japanese immigrants arrived in Hawaii to work on the sugar plantations and in California to work on farms. After the United States acquired the Philippines from Spain in 1898, many Filipinos went to work in agriculture and in the cannery industries along the Pacific Coast. In 1903, the Pensionado Act gave Filipino students the opportunity to study in the United States. (The students were called pensionados because they were supported by government stipends.)

Asian Exclusion. Although Asian immigrants were establishing themselves in the United States, they were excluded from full participation in American society. For example, California and other western states passed alien land laws that prohibited Asians from owning land. At various times, the U.S. government restricted or prohibited immigration from certain Asian countries. See the article ORIENTAL EXCLUSION ACTS in Volume O.

Despite the obstacles they faced, Asian Americans created vibrant communities. In the 1880's, Chinese residents of San Francisco established laundries that became bustling places of business, and the area soon evolved into the city's famous Chinatown. Other Chinatowns flourished, as did Koreatowns, Little Tokyos, and Manilatowns.

Japanese Americans line up at a relocation center in Manzanar, California, in 1942. During World War II, thousands of persons of Japanese ancestry were forced into detention camps.

World War II. Japan's surprise attack on the U.S. naval base at Pearl Harbor in 1941 caused the United States to enter World War II (1939–45). In 1942 a combination of hysteria and mistrust of the Japanese led to the forced imprisonment of more than 110,000 Japanese Americans in relocation camps in desolate regions of the country. Even U.S.-born citizens of Japanese ancestry were forced to abandon homes, schools, and businesses. To show their patriotism, many Japanese Americans from the camps volunteered to serve in the U.S. Army. The all-Japanese American unit, the 442nd, was the most highly decorated of the war.

However, conditions for other Asian groups improved during wartime. Chinese and Filipinos were employed in the booming war industry or joined the army to fight. Their contributions were recognized, and the U.S. government changed a number of laws that had prevented Asians from exercising their rights. The Chinese Exclusion Act was repealed in 1943, allowing Chinese to become citizens. With the passage of the Luce-Cellar Act in 1946, citizenship rights were granted to Filipinos and Asian Indians.

After World War II, Congress passed the War Brides Act, which allowed women—including Asian women—to immigrate to America as brides of U.S. servicemen. Other legislative changes resulted in the granting of citizenship rights to Japanese and Koreans and the repeal of the alien land laws in 1956.

A New Wave of Immigration. In 1965, amendments to the Immigration and Nationality Act removed the national origins quota system—in effect since 1924 and amended in the 1950's—that had limited Asian immigration to the United States to anywhere from zero to several hundred immigrants per year. As a result, the Asian American population grew dramatically. Asians immigrated to the United States not only from China, Japan, and the Philippines but from elsewhere in Asia—India, Thailand, Taiwan, Malaysia, and Burma. They came for both economic and educational opportunities.

The aftermath of the Vietnam War (1957–75) brought more immigrants from Southeast Asia, including Vietnamese, Lao, and Cambodians. They have added diversity to a number of cities. Vietnamese, for example, have established an important center in Orange County, California, known as Little Saigon.

Modern-Day Issues. As the Asian American population has grown, new challenges have arisen. The perception of the Asian American as a high-achieving "model minority" has sometimes caused those in need of social services to be overlooked.

In the late 1960's an Asian American movement arose. Inspired by the African American civil rights movement, it sought equality, social justice, and political empowerment for Asian Americans. Departments of Asian American studies were established at major universities. Japanese Americans, after years of silence about the detention camps of World War II, fought to redress the wrongs that had been done. Under the 1988 federal Civil Liberties Act, the government apologized and paid reparations to survivors.

Asian Americans continue to work toward a better America through numerous organizations. Advocacy groups such as Asian Immigrant Women Advocates and the Asian Law Caucus work for immigrant rights and other reforms. The Committee Against Anti-Asian Violence fights racial hatred.

Ethnic Origins of Asian Americans

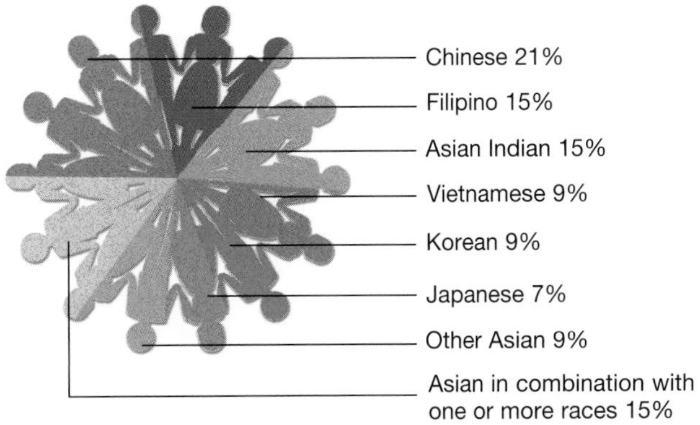

Source: U.S. Bureau of the Census (2000 census).

Institutions such as the Wing Luke Asian Museum in Seattle, Washington, and the Asia Society in New York City promote awareness of Asian culture. Newspapers such as *The Rafu Shimpo* and *AsianWeek* help educate and inform Asian Americans as well as the wider community.

JUDY SOO HOO
UCLA Asian American Studies Center

ASIMOV, ISAAC. See SCIENCE FICTION (Profiles).

ASQUITH, HERBERT HENRY (1852–1928)

British statesman Herbert Henry Asquith, 1st Earl of Oxford and Asquith, served as prime minister from 1908 until 1916. He was the last leader of the Liberal Party to serve as prime minister.

Asquith was born on September 12, 1852, in Morely, Yorkshire. He was a brilliant student at Oxford University and later became a successful lawyer in London. In 1886, Asquith won his first election to Parliament. He quickly became a leader within the Liberal Party, serving as home secretary (1892–95) and as chancellor of the exchequer (1905–08). He succeeded as premier following the death of Henry Campbell-Bannerman in April 1908.

Legislation passed during Asquith's first years in office included massive social reforms, including the provision of old-age pensions, unemployment insurance, national health insurance, minimum wage standards for miners, and protection of trade unions. However, Asquith was at his best when dealing with constitutional issues, such as limiting the power of the House of Lords, accomplished by the Parliament Act of 1911, and negotiating home rule for Ireland.

In 1914, Britain entered World War I. Unfortunately, Asquith did not prove himself an effective war leader, and in the third year of the war he was pushed out of office in favor of the more dynamic David Lloyd George. Although he continued to lead the Liberal Party until 1926, Asquith never again held office. In 1925 he was created Earl of Oxford and Asquith, and he entered the House of Lords. He died on February 15, 1928.

ROY JENKINS (LORD JENKINS OF HILLHEAD)
Author, *Asquith*

ASSINIBOIN. See INDIANS, AMERICAN (On the Prairies and Plains).

ASSYRIA

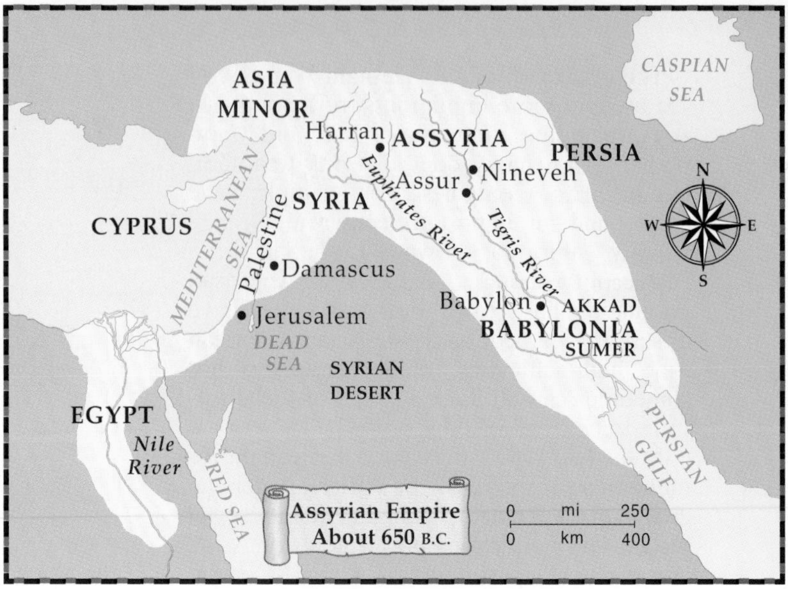

Assyria was an ancient kingdom located in what is now northern Iraq. It was part of a larger region in the Middle East called Mesopotamia. At its peak, Assyria was one of the most powerful of the world's earliest civilizations.

The Assyrian language was a form of Akkadian, a Semitic language spoken throughout Mesopotamia. The Assyrians developed their own version of cuneiform, a writing system whose characters were formed by wedge-shaped lines usually impressed onto wet clay. Works of literature, scholarship, and science were mainly imported from Babylonia, Assyria's neighbor to the south. Royal inscriptions and other literary works were composed in a Babylonian dialect, while the Assyrian language was used mostly for legal and administrative documents. Despite Babylonia's influence on Assyrian culture, the royal court at Assyria's capital city of Nineveh attracted scholars from throughout the region and became the world's first great intellectual center.

Ashur was the primary god worshiped by the Assyrians. The king served as the high priest, acting as a mediator between the gods and his people. He was often portrayed in stone relief carvings, Assyria's chief art form. Many such carvings have been found in the remains of ancient palaces.

History. Assyria began as a city-state centered on the town of Assur on the Tigris River. It was ruled by foreign empires until it achieved full independence during the mid-1300's B.C. The Assyrian kings began to expand their territory, colonizing surrounding lands. The most powerful kings of this time were Tukulti-Ninurta I (about 1244–1208 B.C.), who conquered Babylonia and briefly united all of Mesopotamia under his rule, and Tiglath-Pileser I (about 1114–1076 B.C.). Foreign invasions then forced Assyria into a decline until about 900 B.C.

Stone relief carvings were the chief art form of the Assyrians. These carvings often portrayed the Assyrian king, who also served as the high priest.

Assyria rose to power again during the 800's B.C. under the reigns of Ashurnasirpal II (883–859 B.C.) and Shalmaneser III (858–824 B.C.). The military destroyed conquered towns, massacred prisoners, and removed entire populations from their homelands. Conquered territories were turned into provinces whose administrators were directly responsible to the king. This was the first such political structure in world history.

Under the Sargonid dynasty (721–610 B.C.), Assyria's domain spread in all directions and even reached as far as Egypt. The Assyrian civilization was at its most powerful during the reign of Ashurbanipal (668–630 B.C.). However, his successors were unable to withstand attacks by the Babylonians and the Medians (an Iranian people). Nineveh was captured and sacked in 612 B.C., followed by Harran two years later, and a Babylonian empire became the dominant power in the region.

PAUL-ALAIN BEAULIEU
Harvard University

See also BABYLONIA.

ASTAIRE, FRED. See MOTION PICTURES (Profiles: Movie Stars).

ASTEROIDS. See COMETS, METEORITES, AND ASTEROIDS.

ASTHMA

Asthma is a long-term disease affecting the airways to the lungs. It causes breathing difficulties that may be mild, moderate, or severe. Asthma often begins in childhood, but a person can develop it at any time of life. In the United States, more than 10 million adults and nearly 5 million children have asthma.

In many people with asthma, the airways to the lungs become inflamed and more likely to be irritated when exposed to certain physical and environmental triggers. This can start breathing difficulties that result in an asthma attack. An attack can come on suddenly or slowly and can last from a few minutes to several days.

Asthma is a long-term disease that causes breathing difficulties. It is often treated with medication that is inhaled into the lungs.

During an asthma attack, bands of muscles surrounding the airways tighten, the lining of the airways swells, and glands inside the airways produce excess mucus. These three things reduce the opening of the airways and make it difficult to breathe. Symptoms of an attack include coughing, shortness of breath, tightness in the chest, and wheezing.

Most mild or moderate asthma attacks can be controlled with medicine. Sometimes, however, an attack can be severe and even life threatening. Symptoms such as extreme difficulty breathing or talking and blue lips or fingertips indicate an emergency, and 911 or the local emergency number should be called immediately.

Causes. Asthma has no single cause. Instead, attacks are brought on by a variety of triggers, acting alone or in combination. In many people, attacks are brought on by allergic reactions to pollen, dust, grass, mold, animal dander, foods, and other allergens. Other triggers include tobacco smoke, air pollution, viral infections such as colds, and strenuous physical exercise. Emotions can also play a role. Although they do not cause asthma, they can trigger symptoms in some people with the disease. Asthma is known to run in families.

Between 1980 and 1994, the number of reported cases of asthma in the United States rose by 75 percent. Possible causes for this increase include greater exposure to air pollutants and to indoor triggers such as dust mites and cigarette smoke. Researchers are studying the possible causes of asthma to find additional ways of preventing and treating it.

Treatment. Although there is no cure for asthma, it can be controlled with medication. It is important to have a doctor diagnose and treat asthma. Once a diagnosis is made, a doctor can prepare a personalized asthma action plan. This tells the patient how to use asthma medicines and what to do if symptoms appear. Fast-acting medicines can stop an attack by relaxing the muscles around the airways. Long-term treatment includes the use of steroids to control inflammation and swelling, thus preventing attacks. Most asthma medication is breathed directly into the lungs with an inhaler. All asthma medicines are safe and cause few or no side effects when used according to a doctor's instructions.

Asthma can also be controlled by avoiding the triggers that cause airway irritation. (People with asthma should not avoid exercise, however; instead, they should use medicine to control the reaction.) If the trigger is an allergen, special skin or blood tests can identify the substance so that it can be avoided or the allergy treated.

Part of an asthma action plan may include self monitoring with a small handheld device called a peak flow meter. By blowing forcefully into the meter, patients can measure how well their lungs are working and thus better manage their asthma.

Adrian M. Casillas, M.D.
UCLA School of Medicine

ASTOR FAMILY

John Jacob Astor, a German immigrant, founded the American Fur Company and became America's first millionaire.

The Astors were an important and influential family in the United States in the 1800's and 1900's. With a fortune originally made in fur trading and real estate, they became one of New York City's most prominent families, building hotels, developing real estate, and investing in publishing. They also used their fortune to buy newspapers in Great Britain, establishing a publishing dynasty closely tied to British politics.

The family dynasty was founded by **John Jacob Astor** (1763–1848), a fur trader, real estate developer, and financier. He was born in Waldorf, Germany, and immigrated to the United States at age 21, landing in Baltimore in 1784. On a voyage to New York, the ship carrying him was frozen in Chesapeake Bay for part of the winter. While waiting for a thaw, he met a trader on board who told him stories of fur trading in the Pacific Northwest. Intrigued, he decided to enter the business although he had no experience in hunting or trapping.

By 1790, Astor was already fully involved in the fur trade. With the profits from these ventures, he began to buy land. His business of trading furs and land would continue into the future and earn him a large fortune. In 1808 the American Fur Company was chartered in New York, and by the end of 1811 he had established Astoria, a trading post on the Columbia River in Oregon. He was also trading furs overseas with Europe and China. His land purchases in New York City made him one of the city's largest landowners. Parts of the city were eventually named after him, notably Astoria, in the borough of Queens.

Although the American Fur Company would continue to operate for decades, the death of his grandson in 1819 reduced Astor's involvement in business. Leaving most of his affairs to his son, he sailed to Europe, where he remained for the rest of his life.

John Jacob Astor was known as the wealthiest American of his day and was the first American millionaire. When he died in 1848, Astor had a net worth of $20 million. In his will, he bequeathed $400,000 for the establishment of a reference library in New York City that later became part of the New York Public Library.

The family legacy was continued by his son **William Backhouse Astor** (1792–1875), known as the landlord of New York. William inherited most of his father's estate and invested it successfully, doubling its value. **John Jacob Astor IV** (1864–1912), a grandson of William Backhouse, helped manage the family real estate holdings, wrote science fiction, and was an inventor. He died in the sinking of the *Titanic* ocean liner in 1912. **William Waldorf Astor** (1848–1919), another grandson of William Backhouse, graduated from Columbia University law school and was a state assemblyman and senator in New York before serving as a diplomat to Italy (1882–85). He then moved to Britain, becoming a British citizen in 1889. He bought a British newspaper, the *Pall Mall Gazette*, and became closely tied to the Liberal Party. In 1917, he was awarded a peerage and became known as Viscount Astor of Hever. His son, **Waldorf Astor** (1879–1952), served as private secretary to Prime Minister David Lloyd George and was publisher of a newspaper, *The Observer*. Waldorf's wife, **Nancy, Lady Astor** (1879–1964) (born Nancy Langhorne in Virginia) became the first woman to serve in Parliament, succeeding him after he entered the House of Lords as the second viscount Astor. Waldorf's brother, **John Jacob Astor** (1886–1971) bought the London *Times* newspaper in 1922. **Vincent Astor** (1891–1959), son of John Jacob IV, attended Harvard, served in the U.S. navy during both world wars, and later became one of the publishers of *Newsweek* magazine in the United States. Vincent's wife, socialite **Brooke Astor** (1902–), managed the Vincent Astor Foundation, which has donated more than $150 million to charitable and cultural causes.

CHARLES GEISST
Author, *Deals of the Century*

See also FUR TRADE IN NORTH AMERICA.

ASTROLOGY

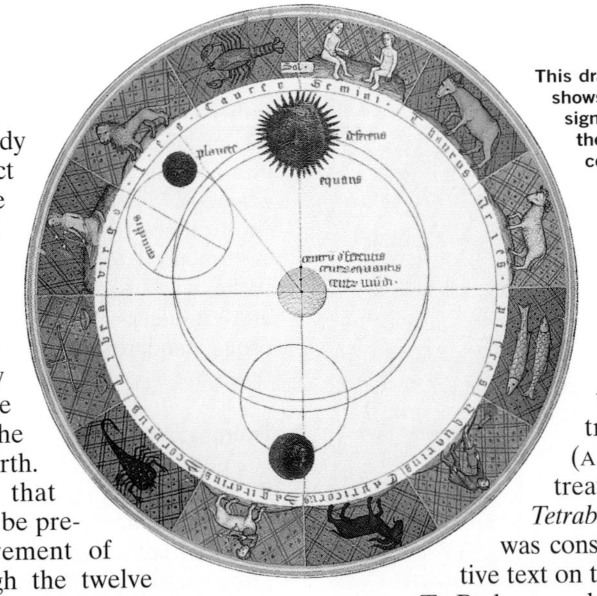

This drawing from the 1500's shows the twelve astrological signs encircling the Earth, then believed to be the center of the universe.

Astrology is the study of the supposed effect of the stars and the planets on Earth and its inhabitants. People who practice astrology believe that a person's character is influenced by the positions of the heavenly bodies at the time of his or her birth. They also believe that events on Earth can be predicted by the movement of these bodies through the twelve signs of the zodiac: Aries, Taurus, Gemini, Cancer, Leo, Virgo, Libra, Scorpio, Sagittarius, Capricorn, Aquarius, and Pisces.

Unlike astronomy—the study of the physical properties of objects in the universe—astrology is not today considered a science. But it is widely practiced. Newspapers all over the world publish daily astrological forecasts, called horoscopes, and astrologers prepare more detailed predictions for thousands of believers.

Newspaper horoscopes are generally based on one's sun sign. This is the sign of the zodiac in which the sun appears to lie when a person is born. This simplified form of astrology implies that everyone born under a particular sign shares the traits associated with that sign. It also suggests that all people with the same sign are affected by the movement of celestial bodies in the same way.

A more personalized interpretation is possible by determining the exact positions of the sun, moon, and planets in the heavens at the time of birth. This information is obtained by casting a chart (also called a horoscope). A visual representation of a chart consists of a circle divided into twelve sections called houses. Each house is related to certain aspects of life. Planetary movement through each house is believed to affect the areas it represents.

History of Astrology. Astrology goes back to ancient times. It can be found in almost every culture, from the Americas to China. In the West, astrology originated with the ancient Babylonians, who used it to make predictions for the ruler. The ancient Greeks and Romans expanded astrology to include individual horoscopes and predictions of natural and political events.

In the A.D. 100's, the great Greek astronomer Ptolemy (A.D. 90?–168?) wrote a treatise on astrology, the *Tetrabiblos*. For centuries it was considered the authoritative text on this topic.

To Ptolemy and his followers, astrology and astronomy were the sister sciences of the stars. Astronomy was concerned with predicting and mapping the movements of the sun and moon and the known planets, while astrology dealt with their influences on the Earth.

For centuries thereafter, astrology was an important part of the scientific worldview in the West. It was taught along with the sciences in most European universities from the 1300's through the 1600's.

Astrology's status changed during the scientific revolution of the 1600's and 1700's. By the end of this period it was no longer viewed as a true science. Some historians attribute this to the influence of Nicolaus Copernicus, who is considered the founder of modern astronomy. Copernicus challenged the system of astronomy that existed at the time, which placed the Earth at the center of the universe. Acceptance of his view—that the planets instead revolved around the sun—raised doubts about whether the heavens were created to direct changes on Earth.

However, Johannes Kepler and Galileo Galilei, two important astronomers who promoted Copernicus' views, were both practicing astrologers. This has led some historians to observe that other factors may also have helped remove astrology from the realm of legitimate science.

Darrel Rutkin
Dibner Institute for the History of Science and Technology
Massachusetts Institute of Technology

See also Zodiac.

Sally Ride, aboard the *Challenger*, learned how to eat in the weightlessness of space. Notice the special food tray designed for the astronauts.

ASTRONAUTS

Throughout history, a few people have dared to dream that one day human beings might leave the surface of the Earth and explore the heavens. During the last thirty years that dream has come true, and a select group of men and women from several nations have journeyed into space.

The men and women who travel in space for the United States are called **astronauts** (from a Greek word meaning "sailors of the stars"). Those sent into space by the former Soviet Union are called **cosmonauts** (from a Greek word meaning "sailors of the universe"). Astronauts and cosmonauts may be sent into space for different reasons. Their mission may be to gather information about the Earth, the moon, or the rest of our solar system; to perform experiments; to launch, repair, or retrieve space satellites or telescopes; to study how being in space affects people and other living organisms; and to learn what effect space has on nonliving substances.

Selecting Astronauts

The people who become American astronauts are selected by NASA, the National Aeronautics and Space Administration. Today, some astronauts are test pilots, others are scientists or engineers. All astronauts must have graduated from college and have at least a bachelor's degree. They must also have either extensive experience as jet pilots or an advanced degree or professional experience in engineering or in the biological or physical sciences. There is no age limit. The height limit ranges from 64 to 76 inches (163 to 193 centimeters) for pilots, and from 58½ to 76 inches (149 to 193 centimeters) for scientists and engineers. All astronauts must meet rigorous standards of physical health and mental fitness.

Training Astronauts

Today's American astronauts are trained to fly in the space shuttle. They must learn how to control the spacecraft, monitor its many systems, launch satellites, and conduct scientific experiments. Astronauts must also be prepared to handle any emergencies that might happen and to endure the physical and emotional stresses that occur during spaceflight.

Astronauts are trained at NASA's Johnson Space Center near Houston, Texas. They learn the space shuttle's propulsion, navigation, environmental, and computer systems. They learn how to use the shuttle's long robot arm to release satellites into orbit and how to use the tools and equipment carried on board the shuttle. Astronauts also learn how to put on, and work in, the space suits that must be worn if they venture outside the shuttle. In addition, they take classes in subjects such as astronomy, navigation, geology, oceanography, and meteorology.

Astronauts also fly a certain number of hours each month in training jets—the pilots practice flying, the scientists and engineers develop navigation and communication skills and practice working as part of a crew.

Once an astronaut is assigned to a spaceflight, she or he begins training with the other members of the crew. A typical crew is composed of two astronauts with test pilot backgrounds and three or more astronauts with either science or engineering backgrounds. The crew trains together to learn to work as a team and to learn about the experiments or space satellites on their particular flight. An important part of the training takes place in the spaceflight simulator—a device that reproduces many of the shuttle's maneuvers and responses during flight. In the flight simulators, astronauts practice all phases of spaceflight, including launch, orbit, re-entry, and landing. They also learn how to respond when a system malfunctions and how to communicate with mission control.

Living and Working in Space

Being in space is quite different from being on Earth. This is because astronauts and all the objects around them are weightless. Astronauts move around in the shuttle by pushing off from a wall and floating from one place to another. They can perform somersaults and can easily lift satellites that would weigh thousands of pounds on Earth.

Weightlessness also makes eating and sleeping different from what astronauts are used to on Earth. Most of the food is similar to what is eaten on Earth, but some of it is specially prepared. Foods that are sticky, like beef stew or pudding, are the easiest to eat because they stick to utensils instead of floating away before they can be eaten. A drink cannot be poured in space because the liquid would simply float out of the pitcher or glass. To solve this problem, liquids are served in closed containers, and astronauts drink through straws.

When they sleep, some astronauts strap themselves into sleeping bags, which can be attached to the walls with a fabric like Velcro so that they do not float around; others float freely in the middle of the room as they sleep. They can sleep right side up, upside down, or sideways—all positions feel exactly the same in weightlessness.

Compared with earlier spacecraft, today's shuttle is relatively roomy. The air inside is the same as in any living room and the temperature is controlled. Astronauts wear regular clothes during spaceflight. But if they have to go outside, either to conduct experiments or to repair something, they must put on pressurized space suits that provide breathable air and that protect them against the vacuum of space.

During spaceflight, astronauts are very busy conducting experiments, operating equipment, and monitoring different systems. There is some time, though, for just looking at the Earth through the small windows of the shuttle.

Milestones

Yuri Gagarin of the former Soviet Union became the first person in space on April 12, 1961. In February 1962, John Glenn became the first American to orbit the Earth. The first woman in space was Valentina Tereshkova of the former Soviet Union, who orbited the Earth in June 1963. In March 1965, Soviet cosmonaut Alexei Leonov became the first person to leave a spacecraft on a "spacewalk." On July 20, 1969, the American astronauts Neil Armstrong and Edwin Aldrin became the first human beings to set foot on the moon. John Young and Robert Crippen were the first astronauts to fly in the space shuttle, in April 1981. Sally Ride, who orbited the Earth in the shuttle in June 1983, was the first American woman in space.

The achievements of these and many other brave men and women have made the human dream of space travel come true. These individuals are truly sailors of the skies.

SALLY K. RIDE
Professor of Physics
University of California, San Diego

See also ARMSTRONG, NEIL A.; GLENN, JOHN H., JR.; SPACE EXPLORATION AND TRAVEL; SPACE SHUTTLES.

WONDER QUESTION

Why are astronauts weightless?

During spaceflight, the space shuttle is held in orbit around the Earth by gravity. This means that astronauts are not "away from gravity," as many people think. Astronauts are weightless because they and the space shuttle are continually falling toward Earth under the force of gravity—just as you would be if you jumped out of an airplane. Imagine jumping out of an airplane carrying a scale to weigh yourself. If you could stand on the scale while you and it were falling, the scale would read zero—you would be weightless. This is exactly the same situation that astronauts find themselves in when they are in orbit. The shuttle and everything inside it, including astronauts, are weightless because they are not resisting gravity—they are all falling together under the force of gravity.

If the space shuttle is falling, why does it not crash into the Earth? The reason is that although the shuttle is falling toward Earth, it is also traveling very fast horizontally. The speed given to the space shuttle by its rockets when it is launched allows it to reach and travel at a certain altitude in space. It is the force of gravity at that altitude that forces the shuttle to fall just enough to stay in a circular orbit that is always at the same distance from the Earth.

ASTRONOMY

Astronomy is the study of everything in the universe. It is also one of the oldest sciences. For thousands of years, people have gazed at the sky to try to learn about the stars, the planets, and all of the other objects in the universe. Paintings of astronomical events thought to be about 10,000 years old have been found in caves in Europe; and marks that may represent the phases of the moon have been found on artifacts more than 30,000 years old. Aside from such examples, however, the earliest astronomers left no written records of their studies.

THE ORIGINS OF ASTRONOMY

Long before the invention of the telescope people noticed many things in the sky. They noticed, for example, that the stars move across the sky from east to west during the course of an evening. They noticed that certain other points of light, which we now know are planets, move through the sky at different speeds. They also observed that the moon goes through phases, or seems to change shape night after night.

Starting about 10,000 years ago, people used their knowledge of the changing positions of the sun and stars to determine when to plant and harvest crops. Between 4,000 and 5,000 years ago, people in England constructed a grouping of large stones to act as a kind of astronomical observatory. Known as Stonehenge, we believe this grouping of stones was used to measure the changing position of the sun as it rises. These positions could in turn be used to determine the changing of the seasons.

Stonehenge may have been an early observatory used to study the movement of the sun across the sky.

The movements of the sun, moon, and planets also became the basis for the study of **astrology**, which held that such movements had an effect on people's lives. Although astrology was unscientific, it led to careful studies of the heavens and to the development of the science of astronomy. The first records of astrologers date back to ancient Babylon about 3,000 years ago. But people also studied the skies in ancient Egypt, China, Mexico, and other parts of the world.

ASTRONOMERS OF ANCIENT GREECE

Since the earliest astronomers lived before recorded history, we can only guess at what they knew. Our first real knowledge of ancient astronomy dates from about 2,500 years ago, when ancient Greek astronomers carefully recorded what they had learned.

Among the earliest Greek astronomers was Thales (640–546 B.C.), who was supposed to have predicted an eclipse of the sun around the year 580 B.C. An eclipse of the sun occurs when the moon moves in front of the sun and blocks its light. Supposedly, the sudden darkness caused by this eclipse was so startling that soldiers laid down their arms in the middle of a battle and called a truce. Whether this story is true or not, it is probably true that Thales had the ability to predict eclipses. This tells us that Greek astronomy had reached a fairly advanced stage by Thales' time.

Our knowledge of other Greek scientists is more accurate. The mathematician Pythagoras (582?–500? B.C.) suggested that the Earth was round, which we now know is true. The astronomer Eratosthenes (275?–195? B.C.) calculated, quite accurately, the diameter of the Earth. He did this by comparing the length of shadows cast at noon in two different cities. He knew that the Earth must be round because the shadows were of two different lengths, which told him that the sun was shining at different angles on these two cities. By comparing the length of the shadows, he could calculate the Earth's diameter. In fact, he came very close to the correct diameter. The philosopher Aristarchus (310?–230? B.C.) suggested that the Earth and other planets revolved around the sun, but this idea did not catch on for more than 2,000 years.

Early astronomers, like those in this tapestry, helped change ideas about the order of the universe. By the 1500's, astronomy had become an important science, and careful measurements were being made of the changing positions of the sun, moon, stars, and planets.

The most famous and influential Greek astronomer was Aristotle (384–322 B.C.), a philosopher whose reputation extended into many areas of study. Aristotle's greatest contributions in astronomy dealt with **cosmology**, the study of the nature of the universe. Aristotle believed that the Earth was at the center of the universe and that the stars and other planets were inside crystal spheres surrounding it. According to Aristotle, these spheres rotated around the Earth at different speeds, which was why the stars and planets moved through the sky at different speeds.

The Greek thinker Ptolemy (A.D. 90?–168?) also believed that the Earth was at the center of the universe. His book on astronomy, which became known as the *Almagest* (Arabic for "the greatest"), was one of the most influential books in the history of astronomy. The idea of an Earth-centered universe, known as the Ptolemaic System, was the accepted view for more than 1,000 years.

A number of articles cover topics relating to astronomy and space. For more information about them, see Astronauts; Black Holes; Comets, Meteorites, and Asteroids; Constellations; Cosmic Rays; Eclipses; Gravity and Gravitation; Milky Way; Moon; Nebulas; Observatories; Planetariums and Space Museums; Planets; Pulsars; Quasars; Radiation Belts; Radio Astronomy; Rockets; Satellites; Satellites, Artificial; Solar System; Space Agencies and Centers; Space Exploration and Travel; Space Probes; Space Research and Technology; Space Shuttles; Space Stations; Space Telescopes; Stars; Sun; Telescopes; Universe; and articles on the individual planets Mercury, Venus, Earth, Mars, Jupiter, Saturn, Uranus, Neptune, and Pluto.

A REBIRTH OF ASTRONOMY

During the Middle Ages in Europe, little scientific knowledge was accumulated, and the science of astronomy was nearly forgotten. However, the knowledge of the ancient Greeks was preserved by the Arabs, who translated Greek works into Arabic. If not for the Arabs, most Greek knowledge, including astronomy, would have been lost forever.

By the 1200's, Europeans had begun to reexamine Greek knowledge. But it was not until the 1500's that new ideas in astronomy had begun to form. One of the first people to suggest that Aristotle and Ptolemy were wrong was the Polish astronomer Nicolaus Copernicus (1473–1543). Copernicus believed that the sun, not the Earth, was at the center of the universe. He also revived Aristarchus' idea that the Earth revolved around the sun. In fact, Copernicus believed that all the planets revolved around the sun in circular orbits and that the moon revolved around the Earth. As it turned out, parts of his theory were wrong, but Copernicus was closer to the truth than Aristotle or Ptolemy.

One of the most significant points of Copernicus' theory was its explanation for the phenomenon of **retrograde motion**, in which some of the planets sometimes appear to slow down and move backward in the sky. Copernicus explained that the planets revolve in their own orbits around the sun. As

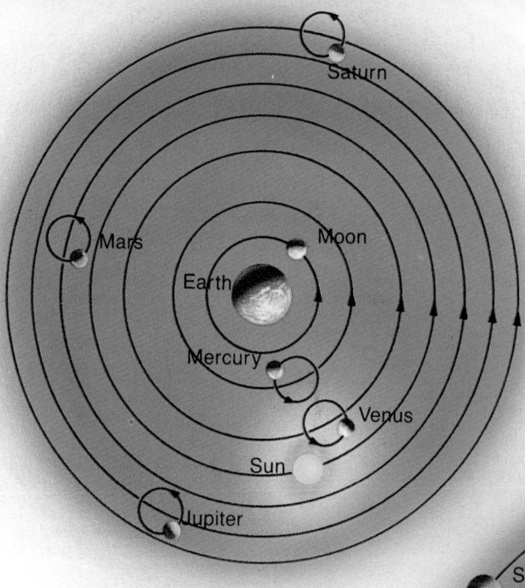

Ptolemy thought that the Earth was the center of the universe and that the sun and planets circled the Earth. Planets also moved in smaller circles, called epicycles.

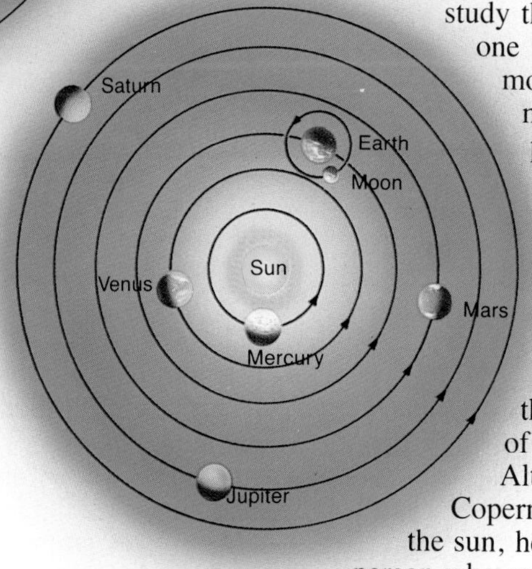

Copernicus was the first to realize that the Earth, moon, and planets orbit the sun. However, he was wrong in believing that the orbits were perfect circles.

the Earth overtakes another planet and passes it, it appears from Earth that the other planet is slowing down and then moving backward. In fact, the planet's direction is not changing at all. What the observer is experiencing is an effect that is similar to the feeling people have that objects in their field of vision are moving backward as they pass them. For example, a car moving next to your car will seem to go backward as you are going by it.

Copernicus' theories were published in 1543 in a book entitled *De revolutionibus orbium coelestium* ("On the Revolutions of the Heavenly Spheres"). This important book influenced the work of many generations of astronomers.

Later in the 1500's, Danish astronomer Tycho Brahe (1546–1601) built an observatory to study the heavens. Although telescopes had not yet been invented, Brahe designed sophisticated instruments to measure the movements of the stars and planets. Like Copernicus, Brahe believed that the sun was at the center of the universe. Brahe's young assistant, Johannes Kepler (1571–1630), also believed in the theories of Copernicus. When Brahe died, he left his records to Kepler, who used them to make a remarkable discovery about the planets. He discovered that the planets were moving around the sun in ellipses (ovals), rather than in circles as Copernicus had assumed.

At about this same time, the Italian scientist Galileo Galilei (1564–1642) was making even more remarkable discoveries. Galileo was the first astronomer to use a telescope to study the sky, and he saw things no one else had ever seen. He saw mountains and valleys on the moon, four moons around the planet Jupiter, and strange dark spots on the sun. He even saw something that he called "handles" sticking out of the side of the planet Saturn. They later turned out to be its famous rings. Galileo supported Copernicus' theories and attacked the ideas of the ancient Greeks.

Although Galileo believed, like Copernicus, that the planets orbited the sun, he could not explain why. The person who answered that question was the English scientist Isaac Newton (1642–1727). Newton discovered that all objects produce a force called gravity that attracts other objects. A large object like the sun produces enough gravity to hold the planets in orbit around it. Moons orbit planets for the same reason. Because of Newton's discoveries, scientists came to accept Copernicus' idea that the Earth and other planets revolve around the sun.

▶DISCOVERIES ABOUT THE UNIVERSE

The discoveries of Isaac Newton marked the beginning of modern astronomy. But there was still much to be learned about the solar system and the universe. Since Newton's time, astronomers have learned a great deal.

The Planets and Their Moons

Until the 1700's, astronomers believed that there were only six planets: Mercury, Venus, Earth, Mars, Jupiter, and Saturn. Then, in 1781, the astronomer William Herschel (1738–1822) and his sister Caroline Herschel (1750–1848) discovered a seventh planet. The discovery of this planet, called Uranus, caused

great excitement because it was the first new planet to be discovered since ancient times. Prompted by this discovery, astronomers began looking for other new planets. In 1846, the German astronomer Johann Galle (1812–1910) spotted the planet Neptune, although its presence had been predicted earlier by the English astronomer John Couch Adams (1819–92) and the French astronomer Jean Joseph Leverrier (1811–77). Finally, in 1930, the American astronomer Clyde Tombaugh (1906–97) located the planet Pluto, which had been predicted by the American astronomer Percival Lowell (1855–1916).

The existence of the Earth's moon has always been known. But the existence of other moons, or satellites, in the solar system was not known until Galileo discovered moons orbiting Jupiter in 1610. Gradually, other moons were discovered as well. The only planets that have no moons are Mercury and Venus.

Comets and Asteroids

For thousands of years, people had seen strange streaks of light pass through the night sky every few years. The English astronomer Edmund Halley (1656–1742) realized that these streaks of light were actually small objects orbiting the sun. These objects, known as comets, begin their long elliptical orbits far beyond the outermost planets. Attracted by the sun's gravity, they fall inward toward the sun and are then propelled back out to the outer reaches of the solar system.

Comets are made mostly of ice and dust. As a comet nears the sun, evaporation causes gases in its head, or **coma**, to glow. The solar wind (electrically charged particles from the sun) blows back some of these gases to form a brilliant, glowing tail that may be more than 60 million miles (100 million kilometers) long. Scientists think that comets come from a cloud of ice and dust orbiting the sun at a distance of more than 10 trillion miles (16 trillion kilometers). This cloud, called the Oort Cloud after Dutch astronomer Jan Oort (1900–92) who first predicted its existence, is left over from the earliest days of the solar system.

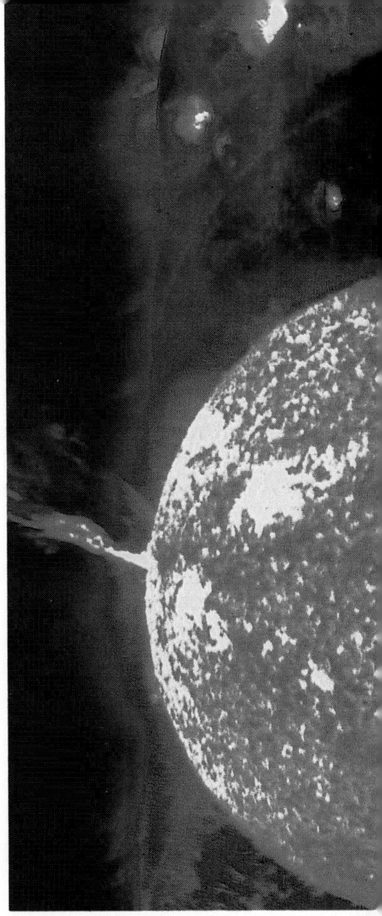

We have learned a great deal about objects in space. Comets like Halley's (*above*) are made of ice and dust. The sun (*right*) is a star made of hot gases that often shoot miles above its surface.

Another group of objects in the solar system are asteroids, a number of small bodies located between the orbits of Mars and Jupiter. Asteroids may be the remains of a planet that never quite formed. The first asteroid was discovered in 1801 and was named Ceres. Since then, thousands more have been discovered.

The Sun and the Stars

After Galileo observed dark spots on the sun, it was many years before other discoveries about it were made. Beginning in 1826, the German astronomer Heinrich Schwabe (1789–1875) began counting sunspots. Over time, he discovered that these sunspots appear in cycles during which their number varies. In 1851, the Scottish astronomer Johann von Lamont (1805–79) noted that disturbances in the Earth's magnetic field happened during the periods of greatest sunspot activity. These early discoveries opened the way for other discoveries about the sun's effects on the Earth, the sun's temperature, and the process that causes the sun's heat and light.

In time, astronomers realized that the universe is much larger than our solar system and that the sun is actually a star just like others in the night sky. These stars are globes of extremely hot gas heated by nuclear reactions in their interiors. One of the first to try to measure the distance to a star was the Dutch astronomer Christiaan Huygens (1629–95). Huygens was unsuccessful, but in 1838, the German astronomer Friedrich Wilhelm Bessel (1784–1846) measured the distance to a star named 61 Cygni (the star numbered 61 in the constellation Cygnus) and found that it was 66 trillion miles (106 trillion kilometers) away.

Stars beyond our solar system are so far away that astronomers invented a new unit to measure their distance. That unit, known as the **light-year**, represents the distance a beam of light travels in a year. Although light seems to travel instantly from place to place it does not. It actually moves at an extremely fast speed, about 186,000 miles (300,000 kilometers) per second. A light-year is about 6 trillion miles (9.6 trillion kilometers). The star 61 Cygni is therefore 11 light-years from Earth.

Soon after Bessel measured the distance to 61 Cygni, the Scottish astronomer Thomas Henderson (1798–1844) measured the distance to Alpha Centauri at 4.33 light-years. A star's distance in light-years indicates how long ago the light we see now left that star. With Alpha Centauri, for example, the light we see today left the star 4.33 years ago. This means that we actually see Alpha Centauri as it was 4.33 years in the past. Most stars are millions of light-years away, and the light we see left them millions of years ago.

Binary and Variable Stars. Once astronomers began to study the stars beyond our solar system, they made a number of surprising discoveries. Most stars have other stars orbiting with them, making them part of multiple star systems. Some of these systems consist of only two stars, called **binary stars**. ("Binary" means "made up of two things.") Other systems consist of more than a dozen stars moving around one another in complex orbits.

Astronomers also discovered that stars do not always shine with a consistent brightness. Some grow brighter and dimmer over a period of time. These stars are called **variable stars**.

Classification of Stars. Some of the most important discoveries about stars have been based on their spectra, the plural form of **spectrum**. A spectrum is the range of colors observed in an object that produces light, such as a star. A rainbow is an example of a spectrum. Scientists can study the spectrum of a star by letting the light from the star pass through special instruments. Sometimes certain colors are found to be missing. Because these missing colors appear as dark or bright lines in the spectrum, they are called spectral lines. These lines tell astronomers about the chemical elements that the star is made of.

The first astronomer to photograph the spectrum of a star was Henry Draper (1837–82) in 1872. In the 1880's, American astronomers Edward Pickering (1846–1919) and Annie Jump Cannon (1863–1941) divided stars into classes based on the lines in their spectra and the bright background, or **continuum**, on which the lines are observed. The star classes they created, named O, B, A, F, G, K, and M, are arranged according to temperatures, with the hottest stars in class O and the coolest in class M.

THE TWENTY NEAREST STARS

STAR	DISTANCE IN LIGHT-YEARS	STAR	DISTANCE IN LIGHT-YEARS
Sun	about 8.3 light-mins.	Yale 343.1*	9.0
		Ross 154	9.6
Proxima Centauri*	4.3	Yale 5736	10.3
Alpha Centauri A*	4.3	Epsilon Eridani	10.8
Alpha Centauri B*	4.3	Yale 5475	10.9
Barnard's Star*	6.0	Yale 2730	10.9
Wolf 359	7.7	61 Cygni A*	11.1
+36° 2147	8.3	61 Cygni B*	11.1
Sirius A*	8.7	Epsilon Indi	11.4
Sirius B*	8.7	Procyon A*	11.5

*member of binary or multiple star system

Omega Centauri, the brightest star cluster in the sky, is 22,000 light-years from Earth. Halley's comet, above it, is about 4 light-minutes from Earth in this picture.

Most stars fall in the area of the H-R diagram known as the main sequence because they obey the rule that hotter stars are brighter and cooler stars are dimmer. However, a few stars are cool and bright or hot and dim and they fall outside the main sequence.

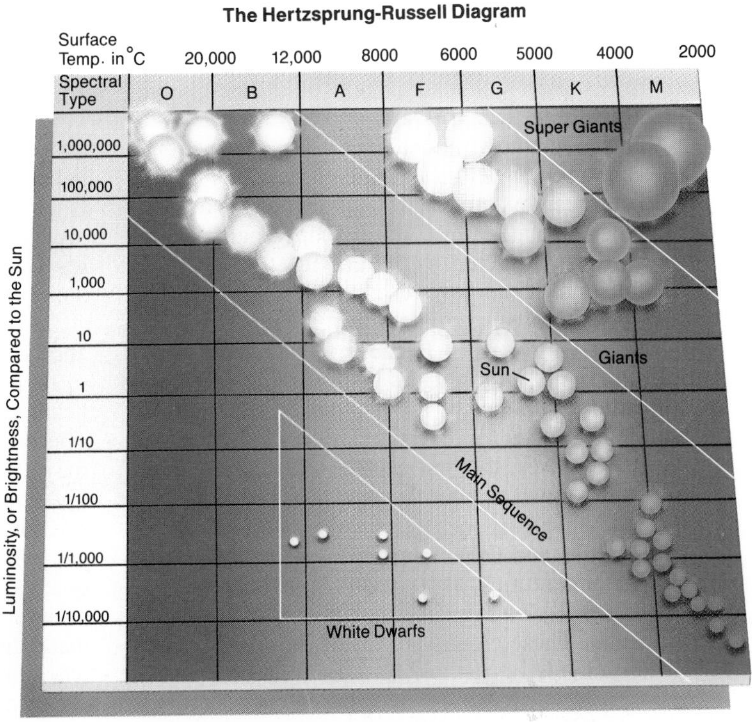

In the early 1900's, the Danish astronomer Ejnar Hertzsprung (1873–1967) and the American astronomer Henry Norris Russell (1877–1957) studied both the spectral classes of stars and their **luminosity**, or brightness. They discovered that temperature and brightness are closely related, with the hotter stars being brighter and the cooler stars being dimmer. These two scientists created a diagram, known as the Hertzsprung-Russell (or H-R) diagram, showing these relationships. This diagram has helped scientists learn how stars are born and how they die.

Detailed analysis of star spectra led British-American astronomer Cecilia Payne (1900–79) to conclude that most stars are made of the same chemical elements. This information also contributed to our understanding of the lifetimes of stars and why stars shine.

The Birth and Death of Stars. A star begins its life as a cloud of mostly hydrogen gas and dust floating in space. If something disturbs this cloud, such as a passing star, it can begin to collapse, and the gravity that is produced attracts other particles of gas and dust. As the cloud shrinks, the speed at which these particles fall toward the center of the cloud causes it to heat up and glow, forming what astronomers call a **protostar**. When the protostar reaches a certain temperature, a process known as hydrogen fusion begins, fueled by the hydrogen gas present. Hydrogen fusion creates such tremendous heat that the protostar tries to explode outward, but the powerful gravity of the gas and dust particles prevents this from happening. Instead, the protostar remains perfectly balanced between exploding and collapsing, and it becomes a star.

Stars have life expectancies ranging from a hundred or so million years to trillions of years, depending on their size. A very massive star uses up, or burns, its nuclear fuel very rapidly and has a relatively short life span. A star with a very low mass burns its fuel much more slowly and lasts much longer. Medium-sized stars, like our sun, use up their hydrogen in about 10 billion years.

Eventually, a star begins to run out of hydrogen gas and hydrogen fusion ceases. At that point, it begins to collapse again, generating even more heat. The star becomes so hot that other gases, such as helium, begin new processes of fusion. These new fusions generate such tremendous heat that the star expands greatly, becoming what is known as a **red giant**. While the outer layers of red giants are relatively cool, these stars are very bright because of their tremendous size.

As a red giant runs out of fuel, it collapses once more. If the original star was relatively small, the red giant will collapse into a small, dense form called a **white dwarf**. A white dwarf appears very dim because of its small size, but it is very hot. If the original star was massive, the collapsing red giant will generate so much heat that the star explodes. The resulting explosion is called a **supernova** and is millions of times brighter than an ordinary star. The part of the star left behind by the explosion becomes a **neutron star**, a rapidly spinning star that is even smaller and denser than a white dwarf. If the original star was extremely massive before it exploded, the neutron star would also collapse and would never stop collapsing. It would become a **black hole**, which is so dense and has such an enormous gravitational pull that even light cannot escape from it. A black hole has never been seen but would probably appear as a dark hole surrounded by a spiral-shaped halo of hot particles attracted by its gravity. Matter that falls into it can never escape.

Neutron stars often emit bursts of radio waves into space. Because the neutron stars spin rapidly, these radio waves are detected by radio telescopes as a pulsating signal, with a single pulse for every rotation. Because of these pulses, the first neutron stars discovered were known as pulsating stars, or **pulsars**.

Galaxies and Other Objects

For centuries, astronomers have been aware of small glowing clouds of matter in the universe. These clouds are called **nebulas**. Some are clouds of gas and dust left behind by supernova explosions like the Crab Nebula, which formed more than 900 years ago, or by other interstellar events. Others are protostars starting to form.

In the early 1900's, scientists discovered that some nebulas are actually very distant **galaxies**, or great clouds of stars. Our sun is part of the Milky Way galaxy. As astronomers studied these distant galaxies with telescopes that became more and more powerful over time, they saw that there are billions of galaxies in the universe. Most are clustered together in groups. The Milky Way galaxy is part of a small cluster known as the Local Group. When astronomers look at galaxies they see bright stars and glowing gases. But they have also learned that much of the matter in galaxies is invisible. This dark matter makes up about 90 percent of all the mass of the universe.

Certain galaxies, called Seyfert galaxies, appear to have violent explosions taking place in their centers, which may result from heat generated by giant black holes at their centers. There is some evidence that such a black hole may exist inside the Milky Way galaxy.

At the very edge of the visible universe, scientists have detected extremely bright objects known as **quasars** (short for "quasistellar objects"). Some of these quasars are billions of light-years away. Because the light from these distant objects takes billions of years to reach us, quasars may be galaxies at early stages of their existence.

The Development of the Universe

By the 1920's, astronomers had noticed that galaxies outside the Local Group were moving away from our galaxy. The American astronomer Edwin Hubble (1889–1953) also noticed that the farther away a galaxy was, the faster it was moving. In fact, clusters of galaxies were moving away from one another, suggesting that the universe was expanding.

Profiles

Friedrich Wilhelm Bessel (1784–1846) is considered to be one of the most skillful and diligent astronomical observers of his time. A self-educated astronomer, Bessel's calculations on the orbit of Halley's comet in 1804 brought him fame and a position at Lilienthal Observatory in Germany. His contributions included the determination of the positions of more than 75,000 stars and the first accurate calculation of the distance of a star from the earth, which was perhaps his greatest achievement.

Annie Jump Cannon (1863–1941) is recognized as one of the foremost woman astronomers. After studying astronomy at Radcliffe College, Cannon was appointed to the staff of Harvard College Observatory in 1896, where she worked for the rest of her life. She was one of the first women to receive a Harvard faculty appointment. One of her greatest achievements was her preparation of *The Henry Draper Catalogue*, a system still used to classify stars. Cannon proved that stars could be grouped into a few basic types arranged according to their color, which indicated a star's surface temperature. During her lifetime, Cannon classified well over 350,000 stars. She received numerous honors, including an honorary doctorate from Oxford University, the first awarded to a woman.

Annie Jump Cannon

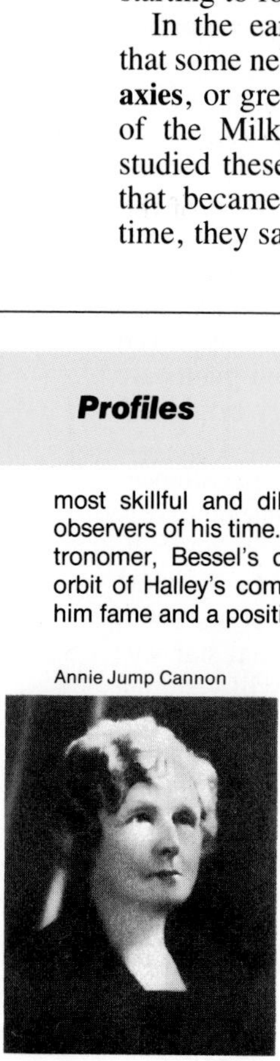

Sir Arthur Stanley Eddington

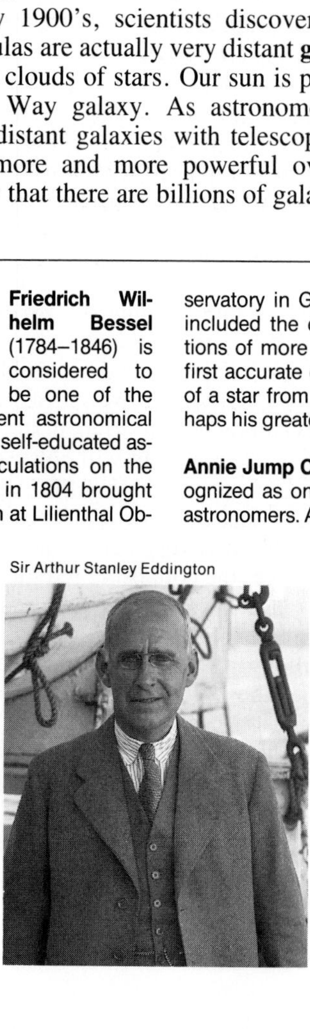

Sir Arthur Stanley Eddington (1882–1944) is noted for his work on the internal dynamics of stars. After graduating from Trinity College at Cambridge, England, Eddington served first as chief assistant at the Royal Observatory at Greenwich and then as director of the Cambridge Observatory. His pioneering work on stars proved that a star's energy is transported by radiation from its interior to its surface. He also determined the relationship between a star's mass and its brightness. Eddington became an important supporter of Einstein's theory of relativity. His observation that starlight is deflected (bent) around the sun during solar eclipses provided evidence to confirm Einstein's theory that gravitation causes light to bend. Eddington won many honors for his work.

Astronomers realized that if the universe is expanding, there must have been a time when all the galaxies were closer together. In fact, at some time in the distant past, all the galaxies may have been crushed into an area in space made up of a dense soup of particles smaller than atoms. By studying the speed at which galaxies are moving apart, astronomers theorized that about 10 to 15 billion years ago a tremendous explosion, which they call the Big Bang, may have started the expansion of the universe. At that time, these particles, which make up most of the matter in space, formed into hydrogen and helium atoms, and began to expand and move outward. Over millions of years, stars and galaxies began to form, but scientists are not sure how these particles formed galaxies in the shapes and patterns that exist in the universe today.

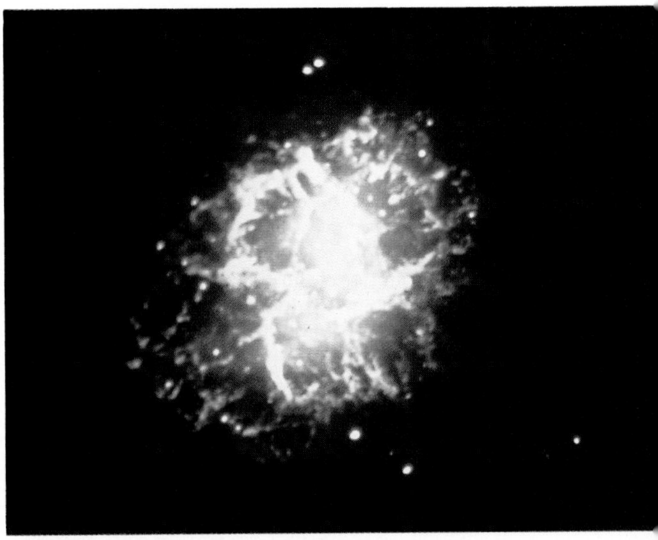

Telescopes help astronomers study the Crab Nebula, the remains of a supernova with a neutron star at its center, about 5,000 light-years from Earth.

THE TOOLS OF ASTRONOMY

Most objects studied in astronomy are so far away that astronomers must gather information about them from a distance by using special instruments. The first astronomical instrument, of course, was the human eye, and many early astronomers devised instruments to measure the motion of the stars and planets.

One of the most important instruments ever developed by astronomers is the optical telescope. ("Optical" means "making use of light.") The lenses and mirrors of optical telescopes focus the light entering them in such a way that distant objects appear larger and brighter. Optical telescopes also allow astronomers to see many more objects than are visible to the naked eye. The earliest type of optical telescope, developed in the 1600's, was the **refracting telescope**, which is basically a tube with a lens at each end. Another type of optical telescope is the **reflecting telescope**. In a reflecting telescope, one of the lenses is replaced with a mirror. Most of the larger telescopes are reflecting telescopes.

George Ellery Hale (1868–1938) was one of America's foremost astronomers. Hale studied physics at Massachusetts Institute of Technology but devoted much of his spare time to astronomy. One of his first achievements was the invention of the spectroheliograph, an instrument for photographing the sun. His greatest achievements, however, involved telescopes. His first triumph was in overseeing the construction of the 40-inch refracting telescope at Yerkes Observatory in Wisconsin—the largest of its kind in the world. Hale was also involved in the construction of a 100-inch reflecting telescope at the Mount Wilson Observatory in California and the 200-inch reflecting telescope at Mount Palomar Observatory in California.

The **Herschel Family** were distinguished English scientists of German origin who were noted for their work in astronomy. **William Herschel** (1738–1822) was a pioneer in almost every branch of modern astronomy. An avid builder of telescopes, he established his reputation in 1781 with the discovery of the planet Uranus. William is also noted for his classifications of star clusters and nebulas, his discovery of binary (double) star systems, and his theories on the structure of the universe. He was the first to establish the motion of the solar system and to try to determine the direction of its movement. He was also the first to suggest the existence of infrared radiation. **Caroline Lucretia Herschel** (1750–1848), William's sister, began her work in astronomy as her brother's assistant. However, she is also noted for her own research. In 1786 she observed her first comet, and by 1797 she had discovered seven more. She also discovered many new nebulas. **John Frederick William Herschel** (1792–1871), the son of William Herschel, began a career in mathematics and law but devoted himself to astronomy after his father's death in 1822. John Herschel discovered more than 1,000 binary stars and almost 2,000 nebulas and star clusters in the skies of the Southern Hemisphere. He also pioneered the use of photographic techniques in astronomy. A founding member of the Royal Astronomical Society, he received a knighthood for his achievements.

George Ellery Hale

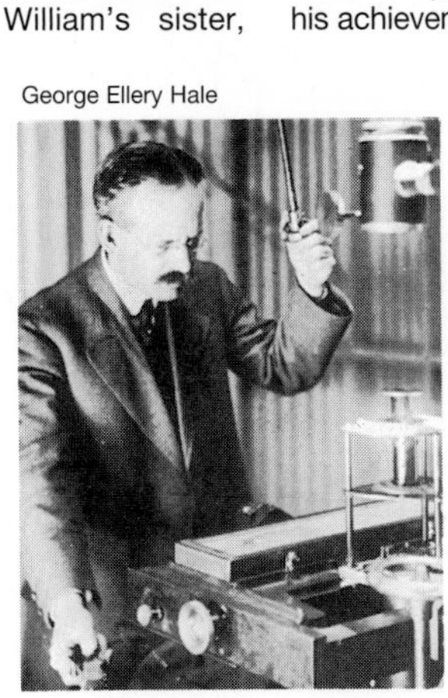

William Herschel

WONDER QUESTION

How do astronomers measure distances in space?

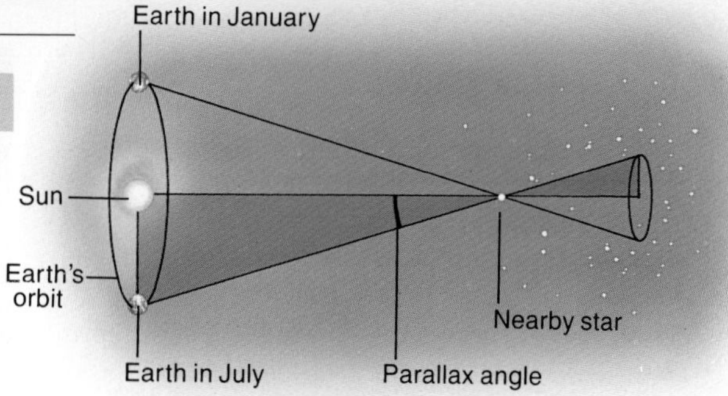

Astronomers have different methods of measuring the distance of objects in space. One way is through something called the **parallax**. When viewed from two different points, a star appears to shift position slightly in the sky. The angle of the parallax is the amount of this shift. Astronomers determine a star's parallax by observing the star at intervals of several months, during which time the Earth has moved between different points of its orbit. Astronomers can calculate the star's parallax from these observations and then use mathematical formulas to determine the star's distance from the Earth.

The parallax method works well for nearby stars but not for measuring the distance of stars and galaxies that are very far away. To do this, astronomers compare the luminosity, or actual brightness, of an object with its brightness as observed through a telescope. This method is based on the fact that the fainter an object appears when viewed from Earth, the greater its distance.

Astronomers often use this method to measure distances to variable stars. The luminosity method can also be used to measure the distance of galaxies.

To measure the most distant objects in space, astronomers use a method involving the objects' spectral lines of light, as measured by special instruments. Astronomers have discovered that if the spectral lines of an object shift toward the red end of the spectrum, it means the object is moving away. The greater the shift, the faster the object is moving. Astronomers also discovered that the farther away an object is, the faster it is receding. Using these facts, astronomers are able to calculate the distance of even the most remote galaxies and quasars.

In the late 1800's and early 1900's, telescopes were combined with cameras to take photographs of objects in the universe. Photographic plates can gather light from objects better than the human eye can, and because of this, very dim objects not visible to the eye can be seen in a photograph. Other instruments, such as **spectrometers** and **photometers**, can also be attached to telescopes to measure the spectrum of an object or the brightness of its light. A telescope receives information carried by visible light. Because it

Profiles

Marquis Pierre Simon de Laplace (1749–1827) was a noted French mathematician and astronomer. Laplace's greatest achievements were in the area of celestial mechanics. He explained the properties and motions of the sun, the planets, and the moon, and the gravitational interactions among them. His work was especially significant in that it proved that the solar system was basically a stable system. Laplace is also noted for his nebular hypothesis, which theorized that the solar system evolved from a rotating mass of gas that condensed to form the sun, the planets, and their various satellites.

Henrietta Swan Leavitt

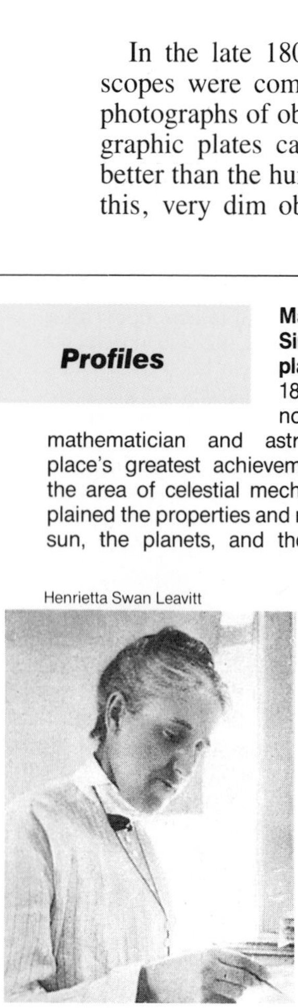

Percival Lowell

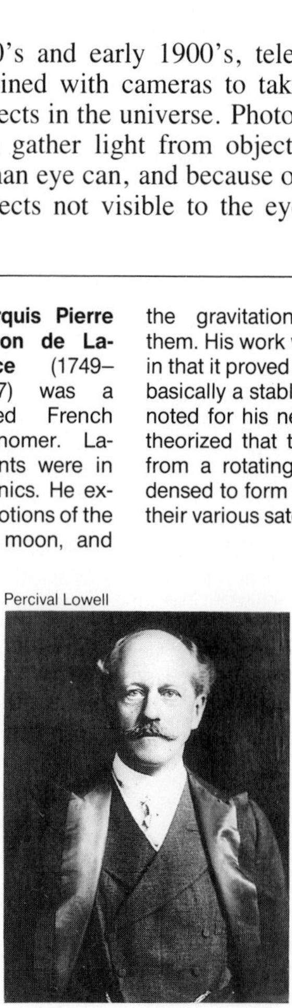

Henrietta Swan Leavitt (1868–1921) became interested in astronomy at Radcliffe College. In 1902 she was appointed to a permanent position at Harvard College Observatory and soon became head of its department of photographic photometry. Leavitt's job was to determine the photographic magnitudes, or brightness, of the light from distant stars. Her work was the basis for statistical investigations of the Milky Way galaxy until the 1940's. Leavitt is also noted for her study of variable stars—stars whose brightness varies. During her career she discovered roughly 2,400 variable stars—about half of all those known at the time. Of particular importance was her observation that the brighter the star, the longer its period of brightness. This discovery enabled other astronomers to determine the size of the Milky Way galaxy and its distance from other galaxies.

Percival Lowell (1855–1916) studied Mars from his own private observatory near Flagstaff, Arizona. He claimed to see clear signs of vegetation on the planet's surface, a view finally disproved by unmanned probes in the 1960's and 1970's. Lowell predicted a planet lying beyond Neptune, but it was not until after his death that the planet Pluto was discovered. He was the first to realize that the best observations require superior atmospheric conditions. His observatory was one of the first to be built far away from the lights and smog of civilization.

radiates outward from a light-producing object such as a star, visible light is said to be a form of radiation. The visible light that radiates from stars is one of several types of radiation known as **electromagnetic radiation**. Other types of electromagnetic radiation are listed above. Many stars and other astronomical objects produce these other types of radiation, but they are invisible to the human eye. Astronomers have built special telescopes that operate from space satellites. These are used to study forms of radiation that cannot be detected easily on the Earth's surface because our atmosphere blocks them.

The Earth's atmosphere tends to distort visible light from the stars as well. This distortion is what makes stars seem to twinkle, and it interferes with astronomers' studies. In the late 1980's, the United States launched a reflecting telescope, the Hubble Space Telescope, into orbit around the Earth where it could photograph stars and gather information about distant galaxies without many of the distortions caused by the Earth's atmosphere. The Hubble has taken many striking photographs for astronomers to study.

Some of the newest telescopes use a technique known as adaptive optics to compensate for atmospheric distortion. The lenses of these telescopes are computer controlled and can actually change shape to help eliminate distortion. Astronomers often watch what these telescopes are viewing on video screens and use computers to analyze and create images of the new information.

One of the most important advances of modern astronomy has been the development of space probes. Launched by rockets or by space shuttle crews, space probes examine the planets and moons of the solar system at a closer distance and send the information they gather back to Earth. In our solar system, many of the larger moons and all of the planets except Pluto have been studied by space probes. This has led to a new science called comparative planetology, which compares other planets with the Earth and expands our understanding of the geology of the Earth.

EXTRATERRESTRIAL INTELLIGENCE

People have long wondered whether the Earth is the only place in the universe with intelligent life. So far, there have been no conclusive signs of extraterrestrial life (life "outside the Earth"). In the late 1990's, scientists discovered tiny structures that resembled bacteria-like fossils in several meteorites that had crashed on the Earth. The meteorites are believed to be from Mars. But whether the structures found in them are really the remains of Martian life has yet to be proved.

It is possible that life exists elsewhere in the universe. After all, it is a vast place, with billions of galaxies and trillions of stars.

Charles Messier (1730–1817), a French astronomer, was noted for his discoveries of comets and his catalog of nebulas. While working as clerk for the astronomer Joseph Nicolas Delisle, Messier observed many comets and began compiling lists of nebulas. His list of nebulas, published in a catalog in 1784, remains his most enduring contribution to astronomy. This list includes the Crab Nebula and the Andromeda galaxy. Messier gave each a number prefixed by the first letter of his last name (such as M31 for the Andromeda galaxy), many of which are still used today. Messier also observed eclipses, sunspots, and the new planet Uranus. A skilled observer, he left mathematical calculations to others.

Harlow Shapley

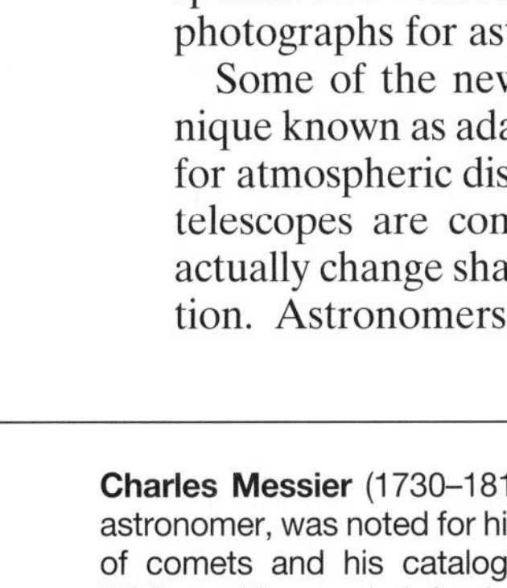

Maria Mitchell

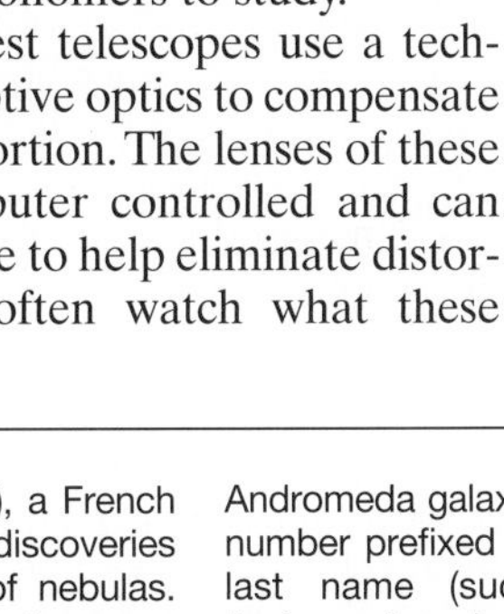

Maria Mitchell (1818–89) was the first woman astronomer in the United States. Mitchell was introduced to astronomy by her father, a noted amateur astronomer. While working as a librarian at the Nantucket Atheneum, Mitchell discovered a faint comet and was awarded a medal from the king of Denmark for her achievement. From 1849 to 1868, Mitchell worked at the U.S. Nautical Almanac Office, where she computed the positions of Venus at regular intervals. When Vassar College opened in 1865, Mitchell was appointed professor of astronomy and director of the college observatory. Mitchell was also an activist in women's causes. In 1848 she became the first woman elected to the American Academy of Arts and Sciences.

Harlow Shapley (1885–1972) began a career as a crime reporter and took up astronomy largely by accident while studying in college. From 1914 to 1921, Shapley worked at the Mount Wilson Observatory in California. While there, he began to study a group of variable stars called Cepheids. His research, coupled with observations by Henrietta Swan Leavitt on star magnitudes, helped him determine the size of the Milky Way galaxy and the location of the solar system within it. From 1921 to 1952, Shapley served as director of the Harvard College Observatory. One of his major discoveries was the identification of two dwarf galaxies. Shapley was also instrumental in developing the Harvard observatory into a major research institution.

Astronomers have detected signs of planets, called **extra-solar planets**, orbiting stars not far from our own sun. However, while there is strong evidence now for Jupiter-size extra-solar planets, no Earth-like ones have yet been found. But if such planets do exist, some may have the right conditions for life. Perhaps there may even be intelligent life elsewhere in the universe. This study of life in outer space is called **exobiology**.

In recent decades, a group of scientists have supported a research effort they call SETI, the *s*earch for *e*xtra*t*errestrial *i*ntelligence. These scientists use large radio telescopes to listen for special signals with patterns different from ordinary radio waves that might signal other civilizations. So far, no such signals have been detected.

▶CAREERS IN ASTRONOMY

Astronomers do far more than study the sky. Some astronomers are theoretical astronomers, who devise theories that attempt to explain what others observe. Other astronomers are in charge of space probes and the data they send back from the planets and other objects in the solar system and beyond. Still other astronomers, called archaeoastronomers, study the history of astronomy in the distant past. Others teach at schools and universities. A few very lucky astronomers fly in space shuttles, where they can perform experiments in space itself.

Astronomy is one of the most exciting areas of modern science, and over the last few centuries, astronomers have completely changed our view of the universe. Should you choose to become an astronomer, you could have the very same opportunity.

CHRISTOPHER LAMPTON
Author, *Astronomy: From Copernicus to the Space Telescope*
Reviewed by KATHERINE HARAMUNDANIS
Coauthor, *An Introduction to Astronomy*

ATATÜRK, KEMAL. See WORLD WAR I (Profiles: Central Powers).

ATHEISM

Atheism most commonly refers to the belief that there is no God. It is the opposite of theism, or belief in God. Atheism is different from agnosticism, which is the belief that it is not possible to know whether or not God exists.

Many atheists believe that there is no scientific explanation for the existence of a supreme being and that such a being would be an exception to the laws of nature. Some regard the existence of evil and human suffering as proof that there cannot be a loving and all-powerful God.

Most atheists think that the universe came into existence by chance and that people have the ability to love and care for each other without divine assistance. They often embrace a philosophy called secular humanism, which emphasizes the worth of each individual, a code of ethical and moral behavior, and humanity's responsibility for itself.

Atheism conflicts with the teachings of many faiths, including Judaism, Christianity, and Islam. But it is compatible with certain religions, such as Taoism and some types of Buddhism, that are not based on belief in a supreme being.

Like many other philosophies and belief systems, atheism has been accepted by some groups and cultures over time and rejected by others. Where it has been rejected or condemned, atheists have sometimes been severely persecuted.

Over the past several centuries, acceptance of atheism in the West has been influenced by various movements (the Enlightenment, for example) and by prominent individuals. Famous atheists have included Sigmund Freud, Albert Einstein, Charles Darwin, and Karl Marx (who influenced some former Communist societies to adopt atheism as their official doctrine).

No one knows how many people consider themselves atheists, but some surveys claim there are as many as 240 million worldwide. Although most atheists do not belong to organized groups, some participate in organizations such as American Atheists or the Atheist Alliance. Such groups work to support the separation of church and state and eliminate persecution of atheists.

FRANK KIRKPATRICK
Trinity College

ATHENA. See GREEK MYTHOLOGY (Profiles).

ATHENS

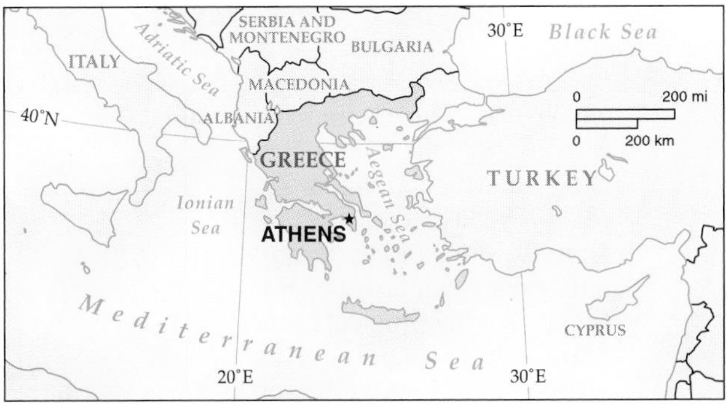

Athens (*Athínai* in Greek) is the capital and largest city of Greece. Its population is estimated at about 750,000, and more than 3 million live in the Greater Athens metropolitan area. Renowned as the cradle of Western civilization, Athens has long been one of the world's most famous cities. It was named for Pallas Athena, the ancient Greek goddess of wisdom.

The city of Athens is situated on the Attic plain in southeastern Greece, about 6 miles (10 kilometers) from the major port of Piraeus. Piraeus, part of Greater Athens, lies on the Saronic Gulf, an inlet of the Aegean Sea, itself part of the Eastern Mediterranean.

Most of Athens lies between the rivers Cephisus (to the northwest) and Ilissus (to the southeast). Both rivers are wholly or partly dry in summer, and neither is navigable. The city receives only about 15 inches (380 millimeters) of rainfall annually. Winters are cool, but the weather is very hot and dry in summer. The city's water supply comes from the Marathon reservoir.

Except on its southwest side, which reaches toward the sea, Athens is surrounded by hills: Mount Aegaleos lies to the west, Parnes to the north, Pendelikón to the northeast, and Hymettus to the east. Some ridges lie within the city itself. The highest of these, northeast of the city center, is Mount Lycabettus. But the most famous of all is the Acropolis.

The City. The Acropolis, the original nucleus of the city, is a flat-topped hill that is about ¼ mile (0.4 kilometer) wide. It was a natural site for a fortress, as it rises abruptly from the plain and has only one approach, through the Propylaea (ceremonial gate). The Parthenon, a famous temple atop the Acropolis, was built following the Persian Wars in the 400's B.C. in honor of the goddess Athena. It is among the greatest surviving examples of classical Greek architecture.

Other ancient structures on the Acropolis are the temples of Erechtheum and Athena Nike. Historic sites near the Acropolis include the Areopagus (where the ancient council of elders met) and two ancient theaters, the Odeon and the Theater of Dionysus. There are many Roman remains in the eastern city district (called New Athens),

Athens is the capital and largest city of Greece. Its most famous landmark, the ancient temple known as the Parthenon (rear right), sits atop a hill called the Acropolis.

which was built during the reign of the emperor Hadrian. Much archaeological work has been done at all these sites, and dozens of museums, such as the National Archaeological Museum, house many of the artifacts that have been found.

Athens has several universities, including the University of Athens and National Technical University. The National and Capodistrian University of Athens, founded in 1837, is the seat of the presiding archbishop of the Orthodox Church.

Artistic achievements in the ancient city-state of Athens made it the cultural center of the classical world.

Economic Activity. Athens is the hub of Greece's economic life. The country's industry is largely concentrated there, particularly along the route toward Piraeus. Shipbuilding and the production of textiles, machine tools, carpets, and chemicals are all important industries.

As the capital of Greece, Athens is served by a large transportation network, including highways, railways, and a subway system. Athens Eleftherios Venizelos International Airport is located just northeast of the city. Much passenger and cargo ship traffic enters by the port of Piraeus, including ferry service to Crete and other islands in the Aegean.

History. The earliest settlement in Athens was built on the Acropolis before 3000 B.C. As the community grew, it spread northward and developed around the agora, or marketplace. The ancient city was connected to the port at Piraeus by two parallel lines of fortifications called the Long Walls. These enabled Athens to receive supplies from abroad, delivered by the ships of the powerful Athenian navy.

The 400's B.C. became known as the Golden Age of Greek civilization, and the city-state of Athens was the cultural center of the classical world. During this period, great advancements were made in the fields of government, art and architecture, literature, and philosophy. But as Athens grew, other Greek city-states, particularly Sparta, began to resent its influence and power. The rivalry eventually led to the Peloponnesian War (431 to 404 B.C.), which ended when the Spartans defeated the Athenian navy. (For more information, see the article PELOPONNESIAN WAR in Volume P.) Athens then began to decline, and eventually it came under Roman rule. It became part of the Byzantine Empire when the Roman Empire split in A.D. 395.

After the Fourth Crusade to the Holy Land (1202–04), Athens came under the rule of French, and later Italian, dukes. But in 1458 it fell to the Ottoman Turks, and it remained in their hands until 1833, when it became capital of the newly independent Kingdom of Greece.

The building of modern Athens was begun in the 1800's after Greece achieved independence. It was designed as a city of broad boulevards, all leading to Syntagma (Constitution) Square, where the old royal palace (now the Parliament Building) is located. In 1896, Athens hosted the first modern Olympic Games.

The city's population swelled after 1922 with the arrival of Greek refugees from the newly established Republic of Turkey. During World War II, the Germans occupied Athens from April 1941 to October 1944. It escaped destruction, but Piraeus was bombed and had to be rebuilt. A great unplanned expansion in the 1950's brought urban traffic problems, and air pollution increasingly damaged the ancient structures. An earthquake in 1999 killed 95 people and left 70,000 more homeless.

In the 1990's Athens was transformed after the city was chosen to host the 2004 Summer Olympic Games. Traffic and air pollution were brought under control. Other improvements in public transport included a new subway system, a new airport, and a new highway around the city.

ARTHUR CAMPBELL TURNER
Coauthor, *Power and Ideology in the Middle East*

ATHLETICS. SEE OLYMPIC GAMES; PHYSICAL EDUCATION; articles on individual sports.

ATLANTA

Atlanta, the capital of Georgia, is the largest center of trade, transportation, and industry in the southeastern United States. Today more than 4.1 million people live in Atlanta's greater metropolitan area. Approximately 416,000 live within the city limits.

Transportation has played an important part in Atlanta's history. The city was founded in 1837 at the terminus, or end, of the Western and Atlantic Railroad. At first the city was called Terminus. Its name was changed to Atlanta in 1845.

During the Civil War (1861–65), Union general William T. Sherman recognized Atlanta's importance as a Confederate supply center. His troops took the city in 1864 and burned most of its buildings. But Atlanta was rapidly rebuilt after the war, and it became the state capital in 1868. By 1900, the city was prosperous and growing. Today Atlanta is a major city.

Banking, retailing, and tourism are important to Atlanta's economy. The city is also the headquarters of several world-famous companies, including Coca-Cola, Delta Airlines, United Parcel Service (UPS), and the Cable News Network (CNN), located in the CNN Center. Manufacturing industries produce transportation equipment, textiles, electronics equipment, and processed foods.

Atlanta, founded as a railroad depot in 1837, became the capital of Georgia in 1868. Today it is the largest center of transportation, trade, and industry in the southeastern United States.

At the heart of Atlanta is an intersection called Five Points. Office buildings, hotels, banks, shops, and restaurants spread out from this point. Nearby is an underground mall called Underground Atlanta, with storefronts that show what Atlanta looked like before the Civil War. To the north of Five Points runs Peachtree Street, Atlanta's best-known avenue. To the south stands the gold-domed state capitol. To the east, on Auburn Avenue, is the Martin Luther King, Jr., National Historic Site, which includes the birthplace and tomb of the slain civil rights leader.

Atlanta is a center of education and culture in the Southeast. Georgia State University, Emory University, Morehouse College, Spelman College, Atlanta College of Art, and Georgia Institute of Technology are among its institutions of higher learning. The arts are well represented. The Atlanta Ballet performs at the Fox Theatre. The Atlanta Symphony Orchestra, the Alliance Theatre Company, the Atlanta College of Art, and the High Museum of Art are housed in the Robert W. Woodruff Arts Center. Notable museums include the Jimmy Carter Presidential Library-Museum, the Atlanta History Center, and the Fernbank Natural History Museum. Grant Park, one of the city's largest parks, is home to Zoo Atlanta.

Atlanta has several sports stadiums. The Atlanta Falcons of the National Football League play in the Georgia Dome. The Atlanta Hawks of the National Basketball Association and the Atlanta Thrashers of the National Hockey League play in the Philips Arena. The Atlanta Braves, a National League baseball team, play at Turner Field. Various other sports facilities were built for the Summer Olympic Games, which Atlanta hosted in 1996.

JOHN RAYMOND
The Atlanta Constitution

ATLANTIC OCEAN

The Atlantic Ocean is the world's second largest body of water. Covering about one fifth of the earth's surface, it is exceeded in size only by the vast Pacific Ocean. As a link between four continents—Europe, Africa, North America, and South America—the Atlantic Ocean has played an important role in modern world history.

The word "Atlantic" is derived from Greek mythology, referring to the Titan Atlas, who gave his name to the Atlas mountain range of North Africa. To the later Romans, the Atlantic was the region beyond the Atlas Mountains. The Atlantic Ocean was also thought to be the site of the legendary land of Atlantis, which was said to have been swallowed up by the sea many centuries ago.

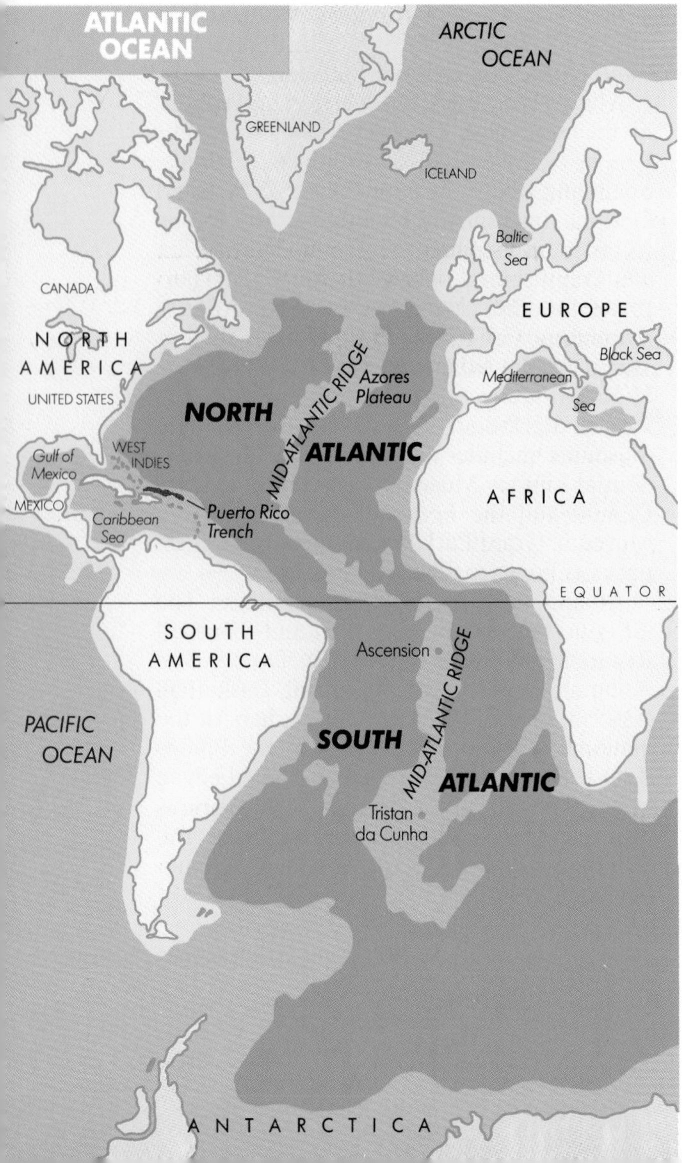

Area and Location. Counting all its adjacent seas, the Atlantic Ocean has an area of more than 41,000,000 square miles (106,000,000 square kilometers). Without them, the ocean still covers an area of some 31,830,000 square miles (82,440,000 square kilometers). The Atlantic Ocean extends from the Arctic region in the north to Antarctica in the south. Some geographers consider the Arctic Ocean to be a separate body of water, while others consider it a part of the Atlantic. The Atlantic is bounded on the east by Europe and Africa, and on the west by North and South America.

At its narrowest, between the bulge of Brazil (in South America) and the city of Dakar in Senegal (in Africa), the Atlantic is about 1,850 miles (2,980 kilometers) across. At its broadest, between Florida and the Strait of Gibraltar, it is more than 4,000 miles (6,400 kilometers) wide. The Atlantic Ocean is divided by the equator into two major parts, the North Atlantic and the South Atlantic.

The Ocean Floor. The Atlantic Ocean has an average depth of about 12,800 feet (3,900 meters). The deepest spot is in the Puerto Rico Trench, in the North Atlantic, which reaches a depth of 27,510 feet (8,385 meters).

The ocean floor is divided into two valleys by the Mid-Atlantic Ridge. This S-shaped ridge runs from north to south and rises about 6,000 feet (1,830 meters). Where it rises above the surface, the ridge forms a number of small islands, including the Azores, Ascension, St. Helena, and Tristan da Cunha.

Shorelines and Coastal Waters. Compared to the fairly straight coast of the South Atlantic, the North Atlantic has a very irregular shoreline. The greatest indentations are on the eastern side of the Atlantic. They are formed by the Baltic, North, Mediterranean, and Black seas. The coastal waters on the western side include Hudson Bay, the Gulf of Saint Lawrence, the Gulf of Mexico, and the Caribbean Sea. Water from most of the great river systems of the world flows into the Atlantic. These rivers give the Atlantic the largest drainage area of any ocean. Such drainage, from about half of the world's land area, includes many dissolved minerals and makes the Atlantic the saltiest of the oceans.

Currents: Warm and Cold. The North and South Atlantic have several strong currents that affect the climate of nearby land areas. The direction of these water currents is similar to that of the wind currents. In the North Atlantic they flow in a clockwise direction; in the South Atlantic, counterclockwise.

The Gulf Stream of the North Atlantic carries warm water northward from the tropics along the eastern coast of the United States and then turns northeast toward Europe. The Gulf Stream makes western Europe warmer than areas of the same latitude in eastern North America. The cold Labrador Current flows from the Arctic Ocean along the eastern coasts of Greenland and Canada until it meets the Gulf Stream. It is the Labrador Current that gives northern New England and eastern Canada their cold climates. It also carries icebergs and fog southward, where they often endanger shipping. In the South Atlantic the warm Brazil Current travels south from the equator along the eastern coast of Brazil.

The Sargasso Sea, a part of the Atlantic lying between the West Indies and the Azores, is a region of relatively still water and little wind. In the days of sailing ships, vessels were often becalmed there.

History. To the ancient Greeks and Romans, the Atlantic Ocean marked the boundary of the known world. Few early peoples, except for the seafaring Phoenicians, ventured beyond the Mediterranean Sea. Vikings later colonized Iceland and Greenland, and in about A.D. 1000 founded a short-lived settlement in Canada. It was not until Christopher Columbus' epic voyage of 1492, however, that large-scale exploration of the Atlantic began. Trade routes were established, followed by European settlement in the Americas. The Atlantic, which had once been a barrier to human expansion, became a vital highway between the Old World of Europe and the New World of America. The importance of this link has since continued.

DANIEL JACOBSON
Michigan State University

ATLANTIC PROVINCES. See NEW BRUNSWICK; NEWFOUNDLAND AND LABRADOR; NOVA SCOTIA; PRINCE EDWARD ISLAND.

ATLASES. See MAPS AND GLOBES.

ATMOSPHERE

The Earth is surrounded by layers of gases we call air, or our atmosphere. Our atmosphere serves us in many ways. It keeps a portion of the sun's radiation from reaching the Earth's surface, which prevents our planet from becoming boiling hot during the day. At night, it keeps the heat that is generated by the sun's rays during the day from escaping too quickly. This protects the Earth's surface from temperatures of extreme cold. Because the atmosphere moderates temperatures and screens out dangerous radiation from the sun, the Earth is able to support life.

The atmosphere also helps make the Earth a more pleasant place to live. Air carries sound waves, which let us hear voices and music. The molecules, particles, and water droplets in the air can scatter sunlight, giving rise to blue skies, red sunsets, and rainbows.

WHAT OUR ATMOSPHERE IS MADE OF

Air—our atmosphere—is a mixture of colorless gases, water vapor, and dust particles. Nitrogen is the most abundant gas in the atmosphere. Almost four fifths of air is made up of nitrogen. The next most abundant gas is oxygen. Nearly one fifth of air is oxygen, which is an essential element for almost all life. People need oxygen to breathe and to turn food into energy. Another gas in the atmosphere is carbon dioxide. Although it is present in very small amounts, it is vital to life on Earth. Green plants use carbon dioxide in the process of making their food.

Our air contains traces of still other gases. Helium and hydrogen are found in very small amounts, as are argon, krypton, neon, and xenon. Some gases, such as methane and nitrous oxide, are emitted into the atmosphere from the Earth's surface largely as a result of biological processes in plants and animals. Others, such as carbon monoxide and a class of molecules called *chlorofluorocarbons* (CFC's), enter the atmosphere as a result of human activities, especially industry. Molecules such as ozone are formed in the atmosphere usually as a result of chemical reactions caused by sunlight acting on the other molecules there.

Water vapor in the atmosphere is water in a gaseous form. It is found mostly in the lowest few miles of the atmosphere, but it can be found higher up as well. It enters the atmosphere from bodies of water such as oceans, lakes, and rivers, and by evaporation from the Earth's surface. When conditions are right, clouds and fog can form from this vapor. The water in clouds can evaporate back into the atmosphere or fall to Earth as precipitation, such as rain, sleet, or snow.

The lower atmosphere is filled with countless specks of dust—tiny particles of matter from soil, fires, plants, salt spray, volcanoes, or meteors, most too small to be seen.

AIR HAS MASS AND EXERTS PRESSURE

Although it may feel as though air does not have mass, it does. A cubic centimeter of dry air has a mass of about 0.00118 grams when it is at sea level and at a temperature of 77°F (25°C). If we could measure the mass of all of the molecules in the atmosphere, the total would be staggering, about 5,700,000,000,000,000 (quadrillion) tons.

The air presses down on us and against us from all sides. Something like a ton of air is pressing against you at this moment. You are not aware of this because pressure within your body balances the pressure of the air outside of it.

Air pressure is 14.7 pounds per square inch (1.036 kilograms per square centimeter) at sea level. It is greatest there because that is the bottom of the atmosphere. The higher you go, the thinner the air becomes. For example, at 10 miles (16 kilometers) above sea level, the density of the air is only about one tenth of the density at the Earth's surface.

LAYERS OF ATMOSPHERE

Our atmosphere is made up of the troposphere, the stratosphere, the mesosphere, the thermosphere, and the exosphere.

The Troposphere

This lowest layer of the atmosphere is where we live, and it is also the layer that we know the most about. Like the other atmospheric layers it varies in size. The troposphere extends from sea level to an altitude of almost 12 miles (19 kilometers) above the equator, but only about 5 miles (8 kilometers) above the North and South poles.

Most of the Earth's population lives within the area about 1 mile (1.6 kilometers) above sea level. But scientists have learned that peo-

OZONE DEPLETION

Scientists have been monitoring concentrations of ozone in the upper stratosphere since evidence for ozone depletion was found over Antarctica in the mid-1970's. Ozone acts as a shield that protects us from much harmful ultraviolet radiation from the sun. Ozone depletion occurs when chlorofluorocarbons exposed to the strong ultraviolet radiation in the stratosphere release chlorine atoms. The chlorine atoms help break down ozone into ordinary oxygen, reducing the amount and effectiveness of ozone in our atmosphere. Chlorofluorocarbons are industrially produced molecules used for air conditioning and refrigeration, as propellants for aerosol sprays, and as blowing agents for foams.

The total amount of ozone over a station in Antarctica where people were living and working was shown to have decreased by about one third between the mid-1970's and the mid-1980's. Measurements from a satellite showed this depletion occurred over all of the continent. By the early 1990's the amounts of ozone over Antarctica were about half those of the 1970's. The TOMS (Total Ozone Mapping Spectrometer) program continues to map daily levels of ozone over Antarctica from satellites in space. In this photograph, the wide bands of lavender and dark purple indicate areas of ozone depletion on this date.

A unique spectrometer maps levels of ozone in the Earth's atmosphere in Dobson units, a measure of the thickness of ozone over a broad area.

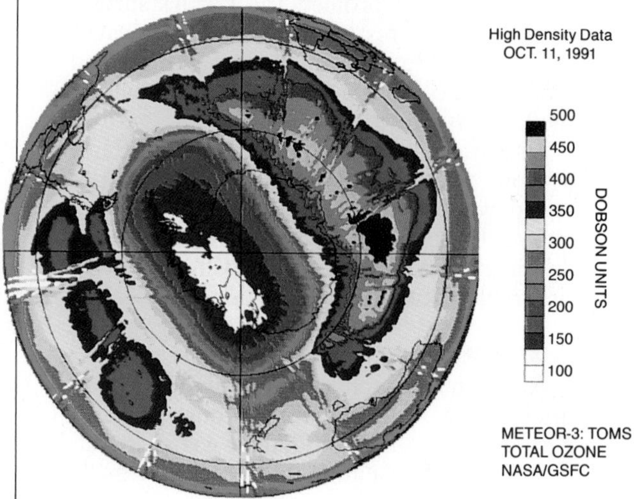

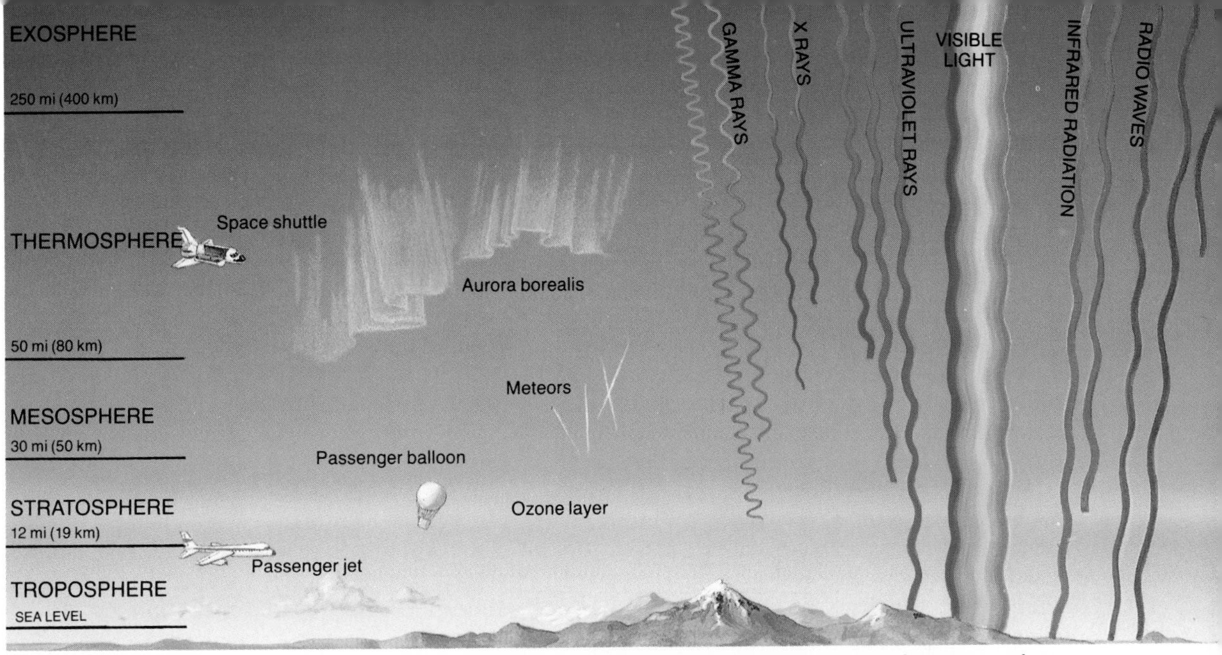

The many layers of the Earth's atmosphere—the troposphere, stratosphere, mesosphere, thermosphere, and exosphere—protect us from much harmful radiation from space.

ple can go about 3½ miles (5.6 kilometers) above the Earth's surface before they must use pressure suits and oxygen masks.

Most of our weather takes shape in the troposphere. Winds pick up water vapor from which clouds and rain form. Air currents move up and down, while winds blow north, south, east, and west, carrying warm or cold air.

Instruments carried aloft in balloons and on satellites have proven that the temperature in the troposphere drops steadily as one goes higher. There is a drop of about 3.5 to 5.5°F for each 1,000 feet (2 to 3°C for each 300 meters). At the top of the troposphere the temperature usually approaches −70°F (−56°C). Under certain conditions, temperatures as low as −117°F (−82°C) can be reached. This process slows near the top of the troposphere.

The area in which the temperature stops changing as you go higher in altitude is called the tropopause. This marks the boundary between the troposphere and the stratosphere. Winds reach their greatest force at the level of the tropopause. Most of the fast-moving winds called jet streams are found here. They move along at speeds of up to 200 miles (320 kilometers) an hour.

The Stratosphere

The second layer of air is the stratosphere. Temperatures in the stratosphere increase with altitude from the lower boundary (the tropopause) to the upper boundary (the stratopause). The stratopause is about 30 miles (50 kilometers) above sea level and the temperature there is typically about 32°F (0°C). The increase in temperature is caused by a layer of ozone. This gas absorbs most of the ultraviolet radiation that comes from the sun and changes it to heat energy, which is transmitted to other gas molecules in the stratosphere.

Ordinarily only between one and ten of every million molecules in the stratosphere are ozone molecules, but these molecules are very important to life on Earth. Ozone absorbs much of the sun's ultraviolet radiation, which can cause skin cancers and cataracts in people, so that only small amounts reach Earth.

The stratosphere is very stable, with little or no upward or downward movement of air. The air in the stratosphere is very dry, with only two to six molecules of water for every million molecules of air.

The Mesosphere

Above the stratosphere, the air becomes even thinner, and the temperature again falls. Beginning at a height of about 30 miles (50 kilometers) and extending up to about 50 miles (80 kilometers) is the mesosphere. At the top of the mesosphere, temperatures may be lower than −103°F (−75°C).

The Thermosphere and the Exosphere

The thermosphere reaches a height of perhaps 250 miles (400 kilometers) above sea level. It is remarkable for its electrical activity and range of temperatures. At the bottom of this layer, temperatures are below freezing. At the top, they exceed 2200°F (1200°C), caused by direct exposure to solar radiation.

Atoms and molecules of gas in the very thin air of the thermosphere are bombarded by radiation from the sun. They are broken into smaller, electrically charged particles called **ions** in a region referred to as the **ionosphere**. Here electric currents can flow, as they do in a neon tube or fluorescent light.

The ionosphere reflects some radio waves back to Earth. This allows radio communication between widely separated places on Earth. For example, radio waves beamed from North America bounce off the ionosphere and can be received in Africa. Without the bounce, the waves would simply continue out into space.

WONDER QUESTION

Is the Earth's atmosphere warming?

Many scientists think that small changes in its composition will cause the atmosphere at the Earth's surface to become warmer. They are alarmed because the amounts of gases such as carbon dioxide, methane, and nitrous oxide in our atmosphere are increasing. These gases tend to trap the radiation that reaches the Earth from the sun. Because the amount of radiation we receive tends to be constant, if less radiation escapes from our atmosphere, the atmosphere could become warmer.

The problem is complex because many factors need to be considered. For example, if the surface atmosphere of the Earth warms, glacial ice may melt, causing sea levels to rise. Also, more water may evaporate from the Earth's surface. This would affect the formation of clouds and the amounts and patterns of wind and rainfall. Both of these changes could affect temperatures around the world, but precisely how (and for how long) is not fully understood.

Records going back many years show a temperature increase, but the increase has been interrupted by cooling periods. The evidence continues to suggest, however, that "global warming" is occurring. Because the effects of global warming could be so serious, research is continuing on a global scale.

The exosphere, the outermost layer of the atmosphere, continues out into space until it eventually merges with the atmosphere of the sun. The atmosphere here is extremely thin. Atoms and molecules travel so rapidly, particularly at the upper levels, that they regularly escape the Earth's gravitation and become part of the gases in space.

CHANGES IN THE ATMOSPHERE

The atmosphere has remained fairly stable for many millions of years, but its temperature and composition change with time. Natural occurrences can cause changes in the composition of the atmosphere, for example, when ashes and hot gases are thrown into the atmosphere during volcanic eruptions.

People also cause changes in the atmospheric composition. The burning of fossil fuels such as coal and gasoline release carbon dioxide into the atmosphere. Agricultural activities such as cattle raising, rice production, and the burning of tropical rain forests and grasslands release methane, carbon monoxide, and nitrogen oxides. Many industrial processes release oxides of sulfur and nitrogen and traces of metals into the atmosphere. Some processes send chlorofluorocarbons into the stratosphere. Since the start of the Industrial Revolution during the late 1700's, the amount of carbon dioxide in the atmosphere has increased by 30 percent and the amount of methane has doubled.

Increased carbon dioxide in the atmosphere may cause temperatures on Earth to rise. Chlorofluorocarbons in the stratosphere cause the loss of ozone, which can allow unsafe levels of ultraviolet radiation to reach the Earth. Because of their impact, human activities that can cause changes in the Earth's atmosphere need to be better understood and controlled. Today there are many tools used to study atmospheric changes, including the research balloons, space shuttles, and space satellites that make observations and collect data and sophisticated computers that help scientists interpret it.

DR. JACK A. KAYE
Office of Space Science and Applications
Earth Science and Applications Division, NASA

See also AIR POLLUTION; CLIMATE; EARTH; WEATHER; WINDS.

ATOMIC BOMB. See NUCLEAR ENERGY.

ATOMIC ENERGY. See NUCLEAR ENERGY.

ATOMS

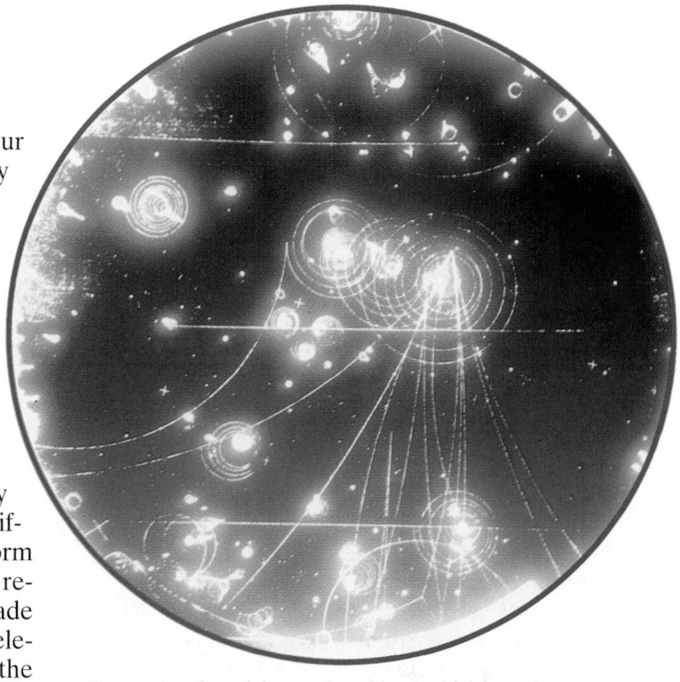

The tracks of particles produced by the high-speed collision between a photon and the nucleus of an atom of hydrogen can be seen in a bubble chamber, a particle detector used to expose such collisions for scientists to study.

Atoms are the basic building blocks of our world. These tiny particles make up every type of matter in the universe—solid, liquid, or gas. Matter is anything that takes up space and has weight.

An atom is the smallest bit of uncombined matter that retains the properties or characteristics of larger portions of the same matter. A group of atoms bound together tightly is called a **molecule**. When atoms of the same type combine with one another, they form the molecules of a **chemical element**, usually referred to simply as an **element**. When different types of atoms combine, they form molecules of a **chemical compound**, often referred to as a **compound**—a substance made up of two or more elements in which the elements are always combined in exactly the same proportion. Water, for example, is a chemical compound made up of hydrogen and oxygen. A single molecule of water contains one atom of oxygen and two atoms of hydrogen. Most of the objects we encounter in everyday life are made up of such combinations of atoms.

▶ PROVING THE EXISTENCE OF ATOMS

The idea of atoms is not new. More than 2,500 years ago, Greek scholars originated the idea of such tiny particles after reasoning that matter could be divided again and again but only so far before reaching a limit. They also imagined that the diverse and colorful world around them was built up from a relatively few different kinds of atoms. The word "atom" itself comes from the Greek word *átomos*, meaning something that cannot be cut or divided into smaller parts.

Even though the Greeks were able to imagine the idea of atoms, they could not prove that they existed. It was not until more modern times that scientists proved the existence of atoms. This scientific proof comes from both chemical and physical evidence.

Chemical Evidence

The laws of chemistry provide powerful indirect evidence for the existence of atoms. Every chemical compound has a precise recipe—it contains specific amounts of certain elements. This is known as the **law of definite proportions**. For example, when the elements hydrogen and oxygen combine to form water, the required amounts of each element, by weight, are eight parts of oxygen for every one part of hydrogen. It is not possible to combine hydrogen and oxygen in any other proportion and end up with water.

Furthermore, if a given set of elements can be used to create more than one compound, then the weights of the various compounds have simple relationships among them. This is known as the **law of multiple proportions**. For example, hydrogen and oxygen can also be combined to produce hydrogen peroxide instead of water. This compound contains 16 parts of oxygen for each part of hydrogen. Notice that this ratio—16:1—is twice the 8:1 ratio needed to produce water.

Scientists have concluded from these chemical laws that each molecule of water must contain two hydrogen atoms and one oxygen atom and that each molecule of hydrogen peroxide contains two hydrogen atoms and two oxygen atoms.

Physical Evidence

In 1827, the Scottish scientist Robert Brown observed a slight but continual and

Robert Brown

random motion of small visible particles in a liquid under a microscope. As a result of observations and analyses since that time, scientists know that this constant jostling of particles, called **Brownian motion**, is due to the randomly moving atoms or molecules of the liquid. It is possible to estimate the weight of atoms using measurements of Brownian motion because the abruptness of the jostling motion depends on the weight of the atom compared to the weight of the particle being jostled.

Two inventions of the late 1900's, the scanning tunneling microscope (STM) and the atomic force microscope (AFM), allow scientists to capture images of solid surfaces that clearly show arrangements of atoms on the surface. Although these images are not photographs in the ordinary sense, they provide additional physical evidence for the existence of atoms.

BASIC FACTS ABOUT ATOMS

Atoms are so small that they cannot be seen under the most powerful microscopes. But scientists have developed methods to determine the size of atoms and their **mass**, which is the quantity of matter in them regardless of their volume. Scientists also know how to identify and distinguish one type of atom from another.

The Size and Mass of Atoms

An atom is unimaginably tiny. The period at the end of this sentence has a diameter of about 0.02 inch (about 0.5 millimeter). If the period were made up of pure carbon, its diameter would contain about 2 million carbon atoms placed side by side. Another way to imagine the size of atoms is to think of magnifying the period so that each of the 2 million carbon atoms along its diameter is about as large as the period itself. The magnified period would be about 1.2 miles (2 kilometers) across. The diameters of the atoms that make up the other elements are not very different from those of carbon. The largest atoms have only about twice the diameter of the smallest atoms.

The mass of a single atom is also extremely small. Imagine fine grains of pollen, which have diameters of about 0.000004 inch (0.001

Figure 1. The Structure of an Atom

Scientists think that the inner structure of an atom looks like a tiny solar system. At its center is a nucleus made up of subatomic particles called protons and neutrons, which in turn are made up of particles known as quarks. Orbiting the nucleus are particles called electrons. Electrons are thought to be elementary particles, those that cannot be divided into smaller parts. The number of electrons in an atom is equal to the number of protons.

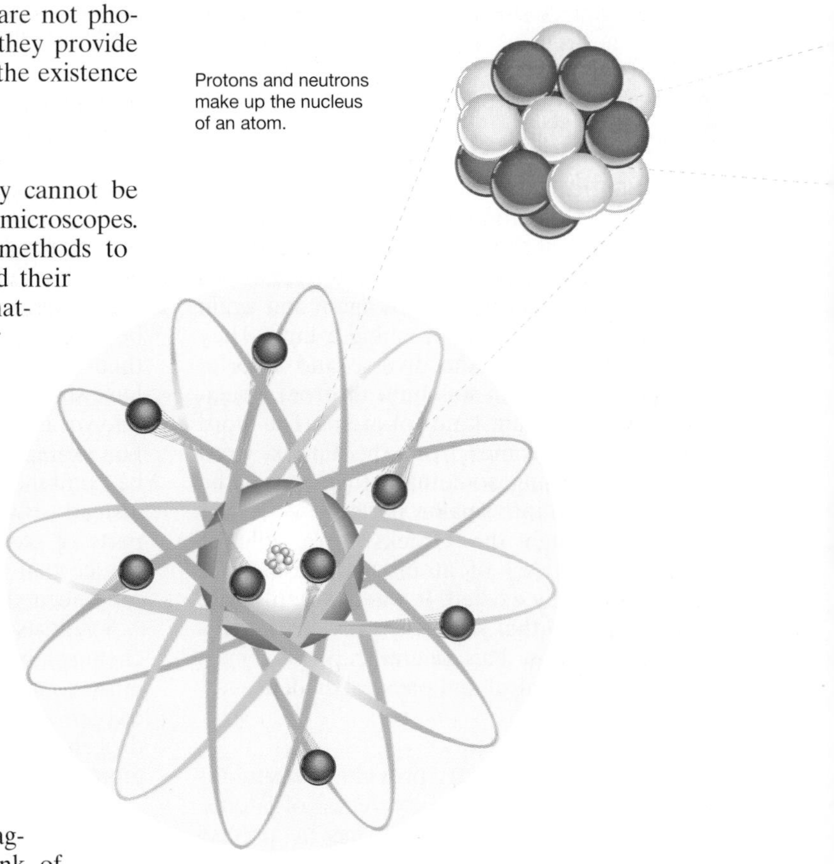

millimeter). It would take about 2 trillion grains of pollen to make up 0.035 ounce (1 gram) of mass, which is about the mass of a paper clip. Yet each one of those tiny pollen particles would contain about 20 billion atoms.

The differences in the mass of atoms are more extreme than the differences in atomic size. Hydrogen, the lightest atom, has about one-twelfth the mass of a carbon atom. The heaviest known atom, unnilennium, has about 22 times the mass of carbon and more than 260 times the mass of hydrogen.

Types of Atoms

Although there are millions of different chemical compounds, their molecular structures are made from a limited collection of different types of atoms. A good way to understand this is to consider the following comparisons: The millions of different words in the English language have been constructed from an alphabet of only 26 different letters, and the thousands of musical tunes that exist have been created from twelve basic musical tones.

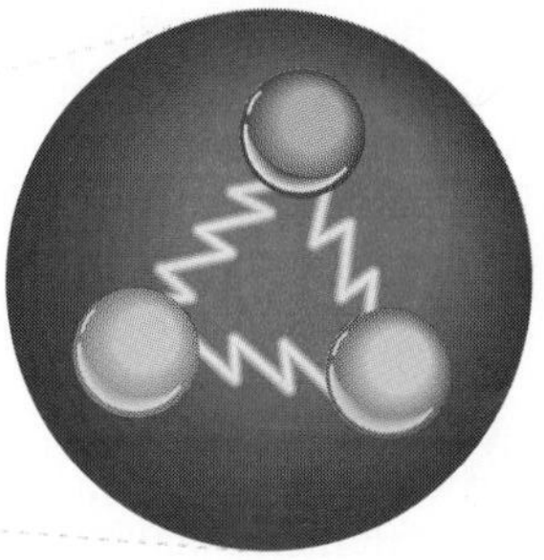

Each proton and neutron is composed of other particles called quarks.

Scientists have identified 92 elements that occur naturally on Earth, and each one represents a particular type of atom. Of these naturally occurring elements, the most common ones are oxygen, silicon, aluminum, iron, magnesium, calcium, potassium, and sodium. They make up more than 95 percent of all the atoms on Earth. Iridium, polonium, promethium, protactinium, and xenon, which make up fewer than one-billionth of the atoms on Earth, are the five rarest of the naturally occurring elements.

Another 20 elements, often called artificial elements, have been produced in limited quantities in nuclear reactors or scientific laboratories. All of the artificial elements are very unstable, which means they quickly decay or break down into other elements. This helps explain why they are not found in nature. Even if they had been present on Earth in the distant past, they would have decayed completely by now.

THE STRUCTURE OF ATOMS

Since the early 1900's, scientists have known that atoms contain even tinier particles of matter called **subatomic particles** and that these particles make an atom look like a miniature solar system (see Figure 1). At the center of the atom is a **nucleus** (the plural is **nuclei**). This nucleus contains two kinds of subatomic particles—protons and neutrons. A **proton** is a particle that carries a positive charge of electricity. A **neutron** is a particle that carries no electrical charge and has a mass about equal to that of a proton. Because protons and neutrons are found together in the nucleus, they are sometimes called **nucleons**.

Traveling around the nucleus are particles called **electrons**, which carry a negative electrical charge. In an atom of hydrogen, which is the simplest element, a single electron orbits a single proton. The force that binds these two particles together is an electrical attraction between the negatively charged electron and the positively charged proton. The two particles pull equally hard on one another. However, because the mass of a proton is more than 1,800 times greater than the mass of an electron, the proton barely moves in response to the electron's attraction. It is the electron that does most of the moving.

In its normal form, an atom has an equal number of electrons and protons, which means that it is electrically neutral. Some atoms, however, have fewer or more electrons than normal. An atom with fewer electrons than protons is called a **positive ion**. An atom with more electrons than protons is called a **negative ion**.

Atomic Number

Atoms differ from one another in the number of particles they contain. Oxygen, for example, has 8 electrons, 8 protons, and 8

Figure 2. The Carbon-12 Atom

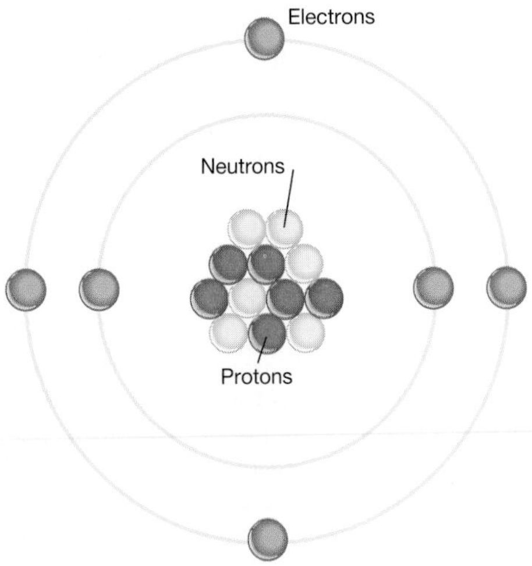

The mass number of an atom is based on the total number of protons and neutrons in its nucleus. The nucleus of a carbon-12 atom has six protons and six neutrons; therefore its mass number is 12. It also has six electrons.

neutrons; aluminum has 13 electrons, 13 protons, and 14 neutrons. The chemical identity of any given element depends on its **atomic number**, which is the number of protons in its nucleus. For example, the atomic number is 1 for hydrogen, which has 1 proton, 6 for carbon, which has 6 protons, and 13 for aluminum, which has 13 protons. Among the naturally occurring elements, the atomic numbers range from 1 for hydrogen to 92 for uranium. (A list of the elements and their atomic numbers is in the Periodic Table in ELEMENTS, CHEMICAL in Volume E.)

Mass Number and Isotopes

While the atomic number is the same for all atoms of a given element, the masses of these atoms may differ. The **mass number** of an atom is the total number of protons and neutrons in the nucleus. Most atoms of hydrogen, for example, have a mass number of 1—the nucleus contains only one proton. However, a tiny percentage of hydrogen atoms contain a proton and a neutron. Such atoms of hydrogen are called deuterium, or heavy hydrogen, and they have a mass number of 2.

Atoms that have the same atomic number but differing mass numbers are called **isotopes**. There are actually three isotopes of hydrogen: ordinary hydrogen, with a mass number of 1; deuterium, with a mass number of 2; and tritium, with a mass number of 3.

Many isotopes do not occur naturally and are produced only under special conditions created by scientists. Such artificial isotopes generally are unstable and exist for only brief periods of time before they begin to lose extra particles and decay. After an isotope decays, it turns into a stable atom.

Atomic Weight

The **atomic weight** of an element is the average weight of the element's atoms. This weight is concentrated in the protons and neutrons in the nucleus of the atoms.

Scientists have adopted a scale based on a unit of measurement called the **dalton** to express atomic weight. The dalton is named for British scientist John Dalton, who proved in 1808 that atoms exist. A dalton is defined as one-twelfth the mass of an atom of carbon-12, a carbon isotope with six protons and six neutrons (see Figure 2). An atom of this isotope, therefore, has an atomic weight of 12 daltons. Carbon-12 was adopted for the standard because carbon can be chemically combined with almost any other element, making it easier to do experiments that allow scientists to compare atomic masses.

Did you know that...

Ernest Rutherford

it was not until the late 1890's that scientists began to understand the internal structure of the atom. In 1897, the British physicist J. J. Thomson discovered that atoms contained negatively charged particles, which later became known as electrons. This discovery suggested that atoms must also contain a positive electric charge in order to balance the negative charge of the electrons. About 1909, another British physicist, Ernest Rutherford, probed atoms with particles he had produced in experiments with radioactivity. He found a positive charge concentrated in a very small nucleus of an atom. Rutherford's work led to the theory on which the structure of the atom is based, that the atom consists of a small, heavy nucleus surrounded by one or more electrons.

An atom that weighs twice as much as carbon-12 would have an atomic weight of 24 daltons. However, because atomic weight is an average, it is rarely a whole number. The chlorine atom, for example, has an atomic weight of 35.5 daltons.

The Size of the Nucleus

The size of an atom is defined by the diameter of the orbits of its outermost electrons. The nucleus of the atom is much smaller than the atom itself. Imagine, for example, that a carbon atom were enlarged until its diameter was about the same as a domed sports stadium. At this scale, the carbon nucleus would be about the size of a peppercorn. Moreover, the nucleus of an atom contains more than 99.9 percent of the atom's total mass, yet the volume of the atom is about one thousand million million times greater than the volume of the nucleus.

HOW ATOMS COMBINE

The atoms of most elements do not exist singly in nature. Exceptions to this rule are the atoms of the noble gases—helium, neon, argon, krypton, xenon, and radon. The atoms of these six elements almost never combine with themselves, with one another, or with any other elements. For this reason, these noble gases are said to be **inert**. All other elements are chemically **active**—that is, they combine with one another to form chemical compounds.

Arrangements of Chemical Bonds

When atoms of different kinds combine to form molecules of a chemical compound—such as water (H_2O) or methane (CH_4)—the atoms are arranged in a specific pattern within each molecule (see Figure 3). In a molecule of water, for example, the single oxygen atom occupies a central location, with the two hydrogen atoms connected to it forming an angle of about 105°. In a molecule of methane, the single carbon atom is at the center, and the four hydrogen atoms are connected to it in the form of a tetrahedron, or pyramid shape.

The Force Holding Molecules Together. The force that holds the atoms of a molecule together is the electrical attraction between the electrons and the nuclei of the atoms. The outermost electrons, also called **valence electrons**, are actually what constitute the "glue" with the nuclei. A common type of bond between atoms is a **covalent bond**, or electron-pair bond. This consists of a pair of electrons shared between two atoms. In some cases, adjacent atoms may be joined by two, or even three, pairs of electrons; these are known as double or triple bonds.

Differing Bonds. Atoms of different elements are able to form differing numbers of bonds. Hydrogen atoms can form only a single bond, in which each atom has, in effect, two electrons: its own and one from an adjacent hydrogen atom. Most other elements, however, form bonds according to the **octet rule**, or rule of eight, which states that each atom undergoes bond formation until a total of eight electrons surround it.

Figure 3. Molecules

Carbon Dioxide (CO_2)

A carbon dioxide molecule consists of two oxygen atoms and one carbon atom. Each of the two oxygen atoms forms a double bond with the one carbon atom.

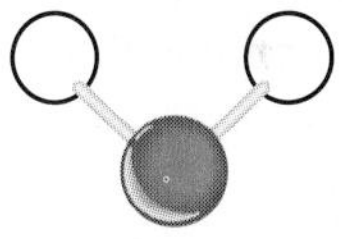

Water (H_2O)

A water molecule consists of two hydrogen atoms and one oxygen atom. Hydrogen atoms can form only a single bond.

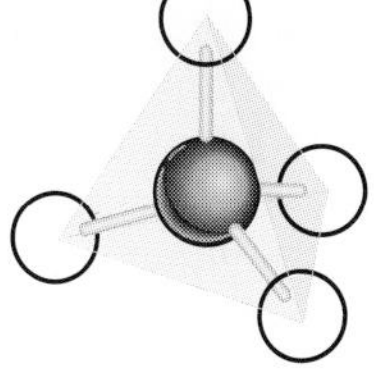

Methane (CH_4)

A methane molecule consists of four hydrogen atoms and one carbon atom. The hydrogen atoms are connected to the carbon atom with a single bond. If you connected the hydrogen atoms, as shown here, you would form a figure called a tetrahedron.

Figure 4. Covalent Bonding

In covalent bonding, pairs of the outer, or valence, electrons from each atom form bonds with one another. In a carbon dioxide molecule, each oxygen atom shares a pair of valence electrons with the one carbon atom. This gives each oxygen molecule eight valence electrons circling its nucleus—six of its own and two shared with the carbon atom. The carbon atom also has eight valence electrons circling its nucleus—four of its own and four shared, two with each oxygen molecule.

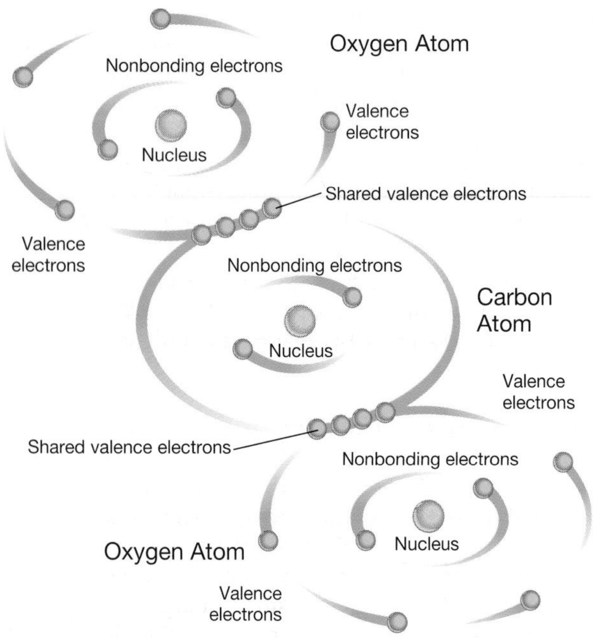

Molecule of Carbon Dioxide (CO_2)

Although there are exceptions to the octet rule, it is a very good rule of thumb. For example, consider carbon dioxide (CO_2) as shown in Figure 4. In a carbon dioxide molecule, each of the two oxygen atoms forms a double bond with the one carbon atom. Each oxygen nucleus, therefore, has eight valence electrons around it: the six it started with plus two from the carbon. Furthermore, the carbon atom also has eight valence electrons—the four it started with plus two more from each oxygen atom.

The Stability of Atomic Particles

The electron is generally believed to be a stable particle—one that will not decay into some smaller particle. This is because there is no known lighter particle into which it could decay. Scientists have tried unsuccessfully to find evidence that protons decay. Their experiments have established that if the proton is unstable, it must have a lifetime of at least 100,000,000,000,000,000,000,000,000,000,000 (10^{32}) years. Free neutrons—ones that are not bound within a nucleus—are known to be unstable and short-lived. A free neutron decays into a proton, an electron, and a neutral particle called an electron antineutrino. However, when a neutron is part of a nucleus, it becomes stable.

▸ OTHER SUBATOMIC PARTICLES

At one time, scientists thought electrons, protons, and neutrons were **elementary particles**—that is, particles that could not be divided into any smaller parts. Scientific knowledge now suggests that the electron is an elementary particle but that protons and neutrons are composed of even more fundamental particles, known as quarks.

Quarks

Some scientists think that **quarks** are the fundamental building blocks of matter. But others think that researchers will discover that quarks themselves are composed of even smaller and more fundamental particles.

According to scientific evidence, there are six different kinds of quarks, each with a rather whimsical name: **up**, **down**, **charmed**, **strange**, **top**, and **bottom**. (Some scientists prefer the names **truth** and **beauty** for the last two types.) Because there are six types, scientists often say that quarks come in six flavors.

One of the most extraordinary properties of quarks is that they have fractional electrical charges. In the past, scientists considered the amount of charge carried by an electron to be the basic unit of electrical charge. Until the discovery of quarks, they did not think anything had less charge than an electron. They now know, however, that the up quark

The Six Flavors of Quarks

Name	Symbol	Charge*
Up	u	$+\frac{2}{3}$ e
Down	d	$-\frac{1}{3}$ e
Charmed	c	$+\frac{1}{3}$ e
Strange	s	$-\frac{1}{3}$ e
Top	t	$+\frac{2}{3}$ e
Bottom	b	$-\frac{1}{3}$ e

*Charge as a fraction of the charge of an electron.

has a positive charge equal to two-thirds the charge of an electron. The down quark is negatively charged, with one-third the charge of an electron.

A proton is made up of three quarks in two flavors—two ups and one down. Thus its total electrical charge is +1. A neutron is also made up of three quarks—two downs and one up. Its electrical charge is thus 0. The various flavors of quarks can be combined in similar ways to produce other types of known particles.

Leptons

Electrons belong to a different family of subatomic particles, the **leptons**. The word "lepton" comes from the Greek word *leptós*, meaning small or slight. The lepton family consists of six particles. The most familiar is the electron itself. The other particles are the muon, the tau particle, and three types of neutrino associated with each, the electron neutrino, the muon neutrino, and the tau neutrino. These six particles generally are regarded as being three pairs. The first pair consists of an electron and an electron neutrino. The second pair consists of a muon and a muon neutrino. The third pair is made up of a tau particle and a tau neutrino. Leptons are now considered to be one of the basic constituents of matter.

Bosons

The **bosons** are fundamental particles that transmit forces between other particles. Scientists have identified four forces that bind the particles of an atom together. In the **electromagnetic force**, the electrons of an atom are tied to the nucleus by the attraction of opposite electrical charges. This electromagnetic force is transmitted by a type of boson called a **photon**.

There are three other forces that bind together the elementary particles that make up atoms. Each of these forces has one or more different bosons. The **strong force** binds quarks together and also holds the nucleus together. The boson that transmits this force is called a **gluon**. The familiar **force of gravity**, the force that keeps the Earth in orbit around the sun, is associated with a boson called the **graviton**. The fourth force, called the **weak force**, is responsible for beta radioactivity, the process by which some unstable atoms break down. The weak force is transmitted by three bosons called the **W+ particle**, the **W– particle**, and the **Z particle**.

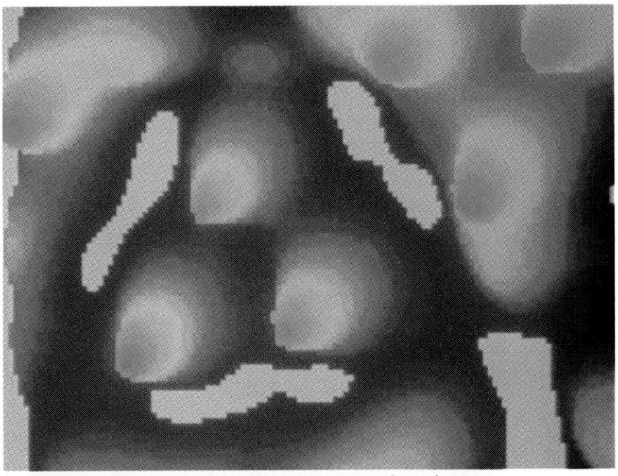

A scanning tunneling microscope can produce images of the arrangement of atoms on solid surfaces, here on a layer of silicon. Added color clarifies each element.

Antimatter Particles

Scientists have discovered that antiparticles also exist. An antiparticle has the same mass as its corresponding particle but the opposite electrical charge. The first antiparticle was discovered in 1931. This particle—the antielectron, or positron—has the same mass as an electron, but it has a positive charge instead of a negative one. Antiprotons and antineutrons were discovered in the 1950's. Scientists think that all subatomic particles have their corresponding antiparticles.

Antiparticles are sometimes referred to as **antimatter**. When antimatter particles encounter one another, they annihilate, or wipe out, each other. This reaction produces a burst of energy. For example, when an electron and a positron encounter each other, they produce energy in the form of gamma rays.

Scientists have long suspected that if an antielectron and an antiproton encountered one another, an atom of "antihydrogen" could be formed. In the late 1900's, this hypothesis was confirmed by European scientists, who were able to produce eleven atoms of antihydrogen in their experiments.

WILLIAM H. INGHAM
Professor of Physics, James Madison University

See also CHEMISTRY; ELEMENTS, CHEMICAL; FISSION; MATTER; NEON AND OTHER NOBLE GASES; NUCLEAR ENERGY; RADIOACTIVE ELEMENTS.

ATTILA (406?–453)

Attila, the legendary king of the Huns, devastated the western half of the Roman Empire between A.D. 451 and 452. He was so feared by Christians, he became known as the Scourge of God, meaning the instrument of God's wrath.

The Huns were originally a nomadic tribe of Mongols, who came out of central Asia in the late 300's and invaded Europe. They were good horsemen, arming themselves with short, powerful bows, which they shot from horseback with devastating effect. About A.D. 400 they settled in the region later known as Hungary.

In 434, Attila succeeded his uncle as leader of the Huns. He won such respect as a warrior that Hunnish communities from the western borders of China to the Danube River accepted his kingship. In 445 Attila launched a campaign against the Roman Empire. In 447 his horsemen overran the Balkan lands, raiding the whole of Greece and threatening Constantinople, the seat of the Roman Empire in the East.

In 451 Attila turned westward and, in his most famous campaign, crossed the Rhine River, penetrating deeply into Gaul (France). Although he successfully besieged the city of Orléans, Attila was defeated later that year in the decisive battle of Châlons by the Roman general Flavius Aetius, who had formed an alliance with Theodoric I, King of the Visigoths.

The defeat did not prevent Attila from embarking on another campaign in 452. That summer his horsemen crossed the Alps to ravage Italy, and Pope Leo I allegedly paid Attila protection money to save Rome from attack.

Attila died suddenly in 453. Although he probably died from heart failure, legend says he was murdered by his bride, a Burgundian princess. His scattered empire disintegrated with his death, but so terrible was his impact on Christian Europe that Attila appears in the epic poems of several countries, most notably as Etzel in the German *Nibelungenlied.*

ALAN PALMER
Author, *Quotations in History*

ATTLEE, CLEMENT (1883–1967)

Clement Richard Attlee, leader of Great Britain's Labour Party from 1935 to 1955, served as prime minister (1945–51) following World War II. As the first prime minister to have a Labour majority in Parliament, Attlee introduced a series of social welfare programs, most notably the National Health Service.

Born in 1883 in a London suburb, Attlee studied at Oxford University, practiced law for four years, then became a social worker. His sympathy for the poor in London's East End slums led him to join the Labour Party.

Elected member of Parliament (MP) in 1922, he held junior cabinet posts in the short-lived Labour governments of 1924 and 1929–31 and became the Labour Party leader in 1935. During World War II, Attlee served as deputy prime minister (1942–45) in Winston Churchill's wartime coalition (multiparty) government. Then, with a landslide victory in 1945, he became prime minister.

At home, Attlee introduced national health care and brought the utilities and railroads into public ownership. In foreign affairs, he backed the creation of the North Atlantic Treaty Organization (NATO) and supported the United Nations' stand against Communist aggression in Korea. Attlee himself regarded the transition of the British Empire to a Commonwealth, marked especially by the government's granting of independence to India and Pakistan (1947), as his greatest achievement.

Although Attlee narrowly won the 1950 election, economic difficulties led to his defeat the following year. After his retirement in 1955 he was given a title of nobility as 1st Earl Attlee. He died on October 8, 1967.

ALAN PALMER
Author, *The Penguin Dictionary of Modern History*

ATTUCKS, CRISPUS. See REVOLUTIONARY WAR (Profiles).

AUDIO SYSTEMS. See HIGH-FIDELITY SYSTEMS; SOUND RECORDING.

AUDUBON, JOHN JAMES (1785–1851)

In the early 1800's John James Audubon was living on the American frontier. He dressed in buckskin and wore his hair long, but he was a different kind of pioneer. His work was the lifelike painting of birds in their natural surroundings.

Audubon was born on his father's plantation in Les Cayes, Santo Domingo (now Haiti), on April 26, 1785. The father, a trader and sea captain, returned to France in 1789, taking his son with him. In the town of Nantes, young Jean Jacques—the French for John James—went to school, but his real interests were the outdoors and painting.

In 1803 John was sent to live at Mill Grove, an estate his father owned near Valley Forge, Pennsylvania. After a short time he went back to France, returning to Pennsylvania in 1806. Audubon later moved to Louisville, Kentucky, where he set up a general store. In 1808 he married Lucy Bakewell, a neighbor from Mill Grove, and took her to Louisville. But the store soon failed, as did all the other business ventures that Audubon tried. Instead of attending to business, he was usually exploring the wilderness.

At first Audubon hunted for food and sport, but he became more and more interested in studying birds. He sketched them in the wild. Then, to get more detail, he began to bring specimens home. He made his paintings in watercolor and chalk. Audubon also made the first known banding experiments on American wild birds. He tied thread around the legs of baby birds and later observed that some had returned to their place of birth to nest.

By 1819, Audubon was bankrupt. He now had only one aim: to complete his collection of bird paintings for publication. In 1821 he traveled down the Ohio and Mississippi rivers, searching for birds and earning a little money by painting portraits. When he arrived in New Orleans, he sent for his wife and two sons. Lucy became a governess and was the main support of the family for the next twelve years.

Audubon began a search for someone to publish his work. Reproduction of his paintings required great skill and expense. In 1826, having failed to find a publisher in America, Audubon went to England and Scotland, where he was well received. He was elected to the Royal Society of Edinburgh in 1827.

A painting of meadowlarks nesting in a field by John James Audubon, who roamed the wilderness identifying, observing, and drawing the birds of North America.

In London that same year, Audubon finally found financial support, as well as an engraver who could reproduce his bird paintings. During the next eleven years, *Birds of America* appeared in four large volumes, one of the rarest and most ambitious works ever published. Between 1831 and 1839, with the help of the Scottish naturalist William Macgillivray, Audubon also wrote five volumes of text to accompany the engravings. This work contained life histories of nearly 500 bird species.

The books brought him money and fame. In 1841, Audubon was able to buy a Hudson River estate. He worked on a book and paintings of the animals of North America, which his sons completed after his death on January 27, 1851.

Audubon's interest in all wildlife is honored by today's National Audubon Society, which is dedicated to the protection of wild creatures and their habitats.

JOHN S. BOWMAN
Author and Science Writer

August

August was the sixth month of the early Roman calendar. It was called *Sextilis,* which means "sixth." The Roman emperor Augustus renamed the month August in honor of himself.

Place in year: 8th month.
Number of days: 31.
Flower: Poppy.
Birthstone: Sardonyx or peridot.
Zodiac signs: Leo, the Lion (July 23–August 22), and Virgo, the Virgin (August 23–September 22).

1
- **Herman Melville** born 1819
- Colorado became the 38th state, 1876
- Confederation Day in Switzerland

2
- First federal census in the U.S. began, 1790

3
- Christopher Columbus began his famous voyage from Spain and eventually reached the New World, 1492

4
- **Percy Bysshe Shelley** born 1792
- John Peter Zenger acquitted of libel, 1735
- U.S. agreed to buy Danish West Indies (now Virgin Islands) from Denmark, 1916

5
- Cyrus Field completed first transatlantic cable, 1858
- First U.S. corporation tax adopted by Congress, 1909
- U.S. atomic submarine *Nautilus* became first vessel to cross the North Pole underwater, 1958

6
- **Daniel O'Connell** born 1775
- **Alfred, Lord Tennyson** born 1809
- **Sir Alexander Fleming** born 1881
- Gertrude Ederle became first woman to swim across the English Channel, 1926
- Hiroshima bombed by the U.S. in first military use of an atomic bomb, 1945
- Independence Day in Bolivia

7
- **Ralph Bunche** born 1904
- Dedication of the International Peace Bridge between the U.S. and Canada, 1927

8
- The Spanish Armada defeated by Britain, 1588

9 • **John Dryden** born 1631
• Richard M. Nixon resigned as president, 1974
• National holiday in Singapore

10 • **Herbert Hoover** born 1874
• Missouri became the 24th state, 1821
• Smithsonian Institution founded, 1846
• Independence Day in Ecuador

11 • Independence Day in Chad

12 • Thomas Edison invented the phonograph, 1877
• The U.S. annexed Hawaii, 1898

13 • **Annie Oakley** born 1860
• **Fidel Castro** born 1926

14 • U.S. Social Security Act approved, 1935
• End of fighting, World War II, 1945
• Strike began at Lenin Shipyard in Gdansk, Poland, leading to gain of workers' rights never achieved before in a Communist regime, 1980

15 • **Napoleon I** born 1769
• **Sir Walter Scott** born 1771
• Panama Canal officially opened, 1914
• National holiday in Congo; South Korea

16 • The American colonists won the Battle of Bennington (Vt.), 1777

17 • **Davy Crockett** born 1786
• Robert Fulton's *Clermont* sailed up Hudson River to become first commercially successful steamboat, 1807
• National holiday in Gabon
• Independence Day in Indonesia

18 • Virginia Dare became first English child born in America, 1587

19 • **Orville Wright** born 1871
• **Manuel Luis Quezon** born 1878
• American ship *Constitution* won naval battle with the British *Guerrière,* 1812

20 • **Bernardo O'Higgins** born 1778
• **Oliver Hazard Perry** born 1785
• **Benjamin Harrison** born 1833

21 • Lincoln-Douglas debates began, 1858
• Hawaii became the 50th state, 1959

22 • **Claude Debussy** born 1862
• The *Savannah,* first American steamship to cross the Atlantic Ocean, launched, 1818

23 • Liberation Day in Romania

24 • Mount Vesuvius erupted in Italy, destroying Pompeii, A.D. 79
• Massacre of St. Bartholomew. Under orders from Charles IX, numerous Huguenots, or Protestants, massacred, 1572

25 • **Althea Gibson** born 1927
• Independence Day in Uruguay

26 • **Antoine Lavoisier** born 1743
• **Geraldine Ferraro** born 1935
• The 19th Amendment to U.S. Constitution gave women the right to vote, 1920

27 • **Lyndon Baines Johnson** born 1908

28 • **Johann Wolfgang von Goethe** born 1749
• **Leo Tolstoi** born 1828
• Martin Luther King, Jr., delivered "I have a dream . . ." speech to 250,000 citizens at the "March on Washington" to demand passage of new civil rights laws, 1963

29 • **John Locke** born 1632
• **Oliver Wendell Holmes** born 1809
• **Charles Franklin Kettering** born 1876

30 • **Lord Ernest Rutherford** born 1871

31 • National holiday in Malaysia; Trinidad and Tobago

The calendar listing identifies people who were born on the indicated day in boldface type, **like this**. You will find a biography of each of these birthday people in *The New Book of Knowledge.* In addition to citing some historical events and historical firsts, the calendar also lists the holidays and some of the festivals celebrated in the United States. These holidays are printed in italic type, *like this.* See the article HOLIDAYS for more information.

Many holidays and festivals of nations around the world are included in the calendar as well. When the term "national holiday" is used, it means that the nation celebrates an important patriotic event on that day—in most cases the winning of independence. Consult *The New Book of Knowledge* article on the individual nation for further information on its national holiday.

AUGUSTA. See MAINE (Cities).

AUGUSTINE, SAINT (354–430)

Saint Augustine, one of the most respected Christian thinkers, was born on November 13, 354, in Tagaste, a small town in North Africa, which was then part of the Roman Empire. (It is now in Algeria.) His mother, later known as Saint Monica, was a devout Christian. His father, a Roman government official, was converted to Christianity only shortly before his death.

As a young man, Augustine was often in trouble. His parents sent him away to school to keep him busy. He studied Greek, Latin, and philosophy. In 370 he went to Carthage, the center of learning in Africa, where he later opened a school. During his years there, Augustine searched for a way to worship God and to live his life, but no one religion fully satisfied him.

In 383 he traveled in Italy. There he came under the influence of Saint Ambrose, then bishop of Milan. Ambrose instructed him in the Christian faith, and in 387 Augustine was baptized a Christian. In 388, Augustine returned to Tagaste, where he lived a quiet life of prayer and studied to become a priest. He was ordained in 391 and was made bishop of the nearby city of Hippo in 395. Augustine continued to write and to preach there until his death on August 28, 430.

Today, Saint Augustine is best remembered for his writings. In addition to his sermons and letters, he wrote more than 200 books, the most famous of which are *The City of God* and the *Confessions of Saint Augustine.* In *The City of God*, he defends Christianity and the Catholic Church. In the *Confessions*, Augustine retraces his life and his search for faith. He was the first to use "confessions" as a form of autobiography. His frankness, keen mind, and self-knowledge make this life story one of the most interesting and inspiring ever written. Saint Augustine's feast day—the day on which the Catholic Church honors him—is August 28.

Reviewed by MSGR. JOHN PAUL HAVERTY
Archdiocese of New York

AUGUSTUS (63 B.C.–A.D. 14)

Augustus was the first emperor of Rome. He achieved power ruthlessly but proved himself to be a great statesman, who brought peace, prosperity, and order to the Roman Empire, which before him had been torn by civil war. Born Gaius Octavius, he was given the name Augustus (meaning "revered") by the Roman Senate.

Early Years and Character. Octavian, as he is usually referred to before becoming emperor, was born on September 23, 63 B.C., into a wealthy and prominent family. His mother, Atia, was the niece of Julius Caesar, who prepared the young man for a public career. His father had died while Octavian was still a child, and at the age of 18, he was adopted by Caesar, who had no son of his own. When Caesar was assassinated by his enemies in 44 B.C., Octavian set out both to avenge his murder and to surpass his achievements.

Throughout his life, Octavian frequently suffered from illness, especially in times of stress, and he preferred to live and eat simply. Somewhat vain, he wore high-soled shoes to look taller than his 5 feet 7 inches, and his official portraits always emphasized his best features. He could be friendly, humorous, and tactful, but he was also calculating and cruel at times.

Struggle for Power. In his struggle for power, the young Octavian was opposed by Caesar's friend Mark Antony. Octavian at first cooperated with Caesar's assassins to defeat

Antony. This forced Antony and his ally Marcus Lepidus to join with Octavian. In 43 B.C. the three men, known as the Second Triumvirate, were given power by the Roman Senate to reconstruct the government. They proceeded to destroy their opponents, who included the great orator Cicero.

In 42 B.C., Octavian's and Antony's troops defeated the forces of Brutus and Cassius, Caesar's chief assassins, at the battle of Philippi in Greece. While Antony sought to consolidate his power in Rome's eastern provinces, Octavian returned home, where over the next ten years he strengthened his own position by alliances and marriages. Eventually only Antony, supported by the Egyptian queen Cleopatra, remained as a rival. Their defeat at the great naval battle of Actium in 31 B.C. and their subsequent deaths left Octavian the sole ruler of the Roman world.

Ruler of Rome. Although Octavian became the first Roman emperor, most of the various offices and powers he held were traditionally those of the old Roman Republic. In 27 B.C. the Senate, which was filled with his followers, conferred on him the name Augustus, which would be assumed as a title by succeeding emperors.

The long reign of Augustus was marked by considerable accomplishment. He expanded the empire, stabilized its frontiers, reorganized the army, and created a permanent navy. The provinces prospered under a fairer and more efficient administration and the promotion of trade and agriculture. It was an era of profound peace and the golden age of Latin literature.

Augustus married three times. His only child was a daughter, Julia, by his second wife, Scribonia. Because he had no son, he eventually chose his stepson, Tiberius, son of his third wife, Livia, to be his heir. After Augustus' death in A.D. 14, at the age of 76, Tiberius peacefully succeeded him.

ALLEN M. WARD
University of Connecticut
Coauthor, *A History of the Roman People*

See also ANTONY, MARK; CAESAR, GAIUS JULIUS; CICERO, MARCUS TULLIUS; CLEOPATRA.

AUSTEN, JANE (1775–1817)

Jane Austen wrote novels about life in the small villages and country houses of her native England. Today her works are considered classics of English literature.

Austen was born on December 16, 1775, in Steventon, Hampshire, where her father was a parson. As a child she wrote stories making fun of the fashionable novels of the day, in which ladies were very delicate. In *Love and Friendship*, which she wrote when she was 14, her two heroines "fainted alternately on the sofa."

The first of Austen's novels to be published was *Sense and Sensibility*, in 1811. Two years later came *Pride and Prejudice*. The Prince Regent (later King George IV) read *Mansfield Park*, which was published in 1814. He admired it so much that he asked the author to dedicate her next novel to him. *Emma*, with the royal dedication, was published in 1816. But Austen still did not sign her name to her novels. Some of her friends would talk to her about them without knowing she was the author.

In her novels she wrote about the kind of life she knew best—"three or four families in a country village"—instead of inventing colorful people and adventures. Yet within the limits of this subject area she examined universal human traits with great wit and insight. Sir Walter Scott, the famous historical novelist of Austen's time, wrote of her "exquisite touch which renders ordinary commonplace things and characters interesting."

Although each of her heroines acquires a husband, Austen herself never married. She led a busy life, however, fitting in her writing among her many social and household activities. Often, she said, "Composition seems to me impossible with a head full of joints of mutton and doses of rhubarb." She was often ill during the writing of her last novel, *Persuasion*, and she died in Winchester on July 18, 1817. *Persuasion* and *Northanger Abbey* were published the next year.

JULIET MCMASTER
University of Alberta (Canada)

AUSTIN. See TEXAS (Cities).

AUSTRALIA

Australia is both a country and a continent. It is, at the same time, the world's smallest continent and its sixth largest country in area. Australia's name is derived from the Latin word for "southern" and refers to its location in the Southern Hemisphere. Its location, between the Pacific and Indian oceans and surrounded by extensive seas, served to isolate Australia, historically, from other landmasses. One result of this was the development of forms of animal and plant life that are found nowhere else on earth.

The Commonwealth of Australia, the country's official name, is made up of six states. Five are on the mainland—New South Wales, Victoria, Queensland, South Australia, and Western Australia. The sixth is the island state of Tasmania. There are also two federal territories on the mainland—the large Northern Territory and the small Australian Capital Territory, which includes Canberra, the national capital.

Australia also administers a number of small islands in the Pacific and Indian oceans, as well as the Australian Antarctic Territory.

▸ THE PEOPLE

Origins. Australia's earliest inhabitants were the ancestors of the present-day Aborigines, who migrated from the Southeast Asian region in prehistoric times. The first European settlers arrived from Britain in 1788. Later British groups founded the colonies that eventually became the Australian nation. Although Australians of British ancestry still make up the majority of the population, in recent decades there has been in-

The varied look of Australia and the Australians: The boldly modern Sydney Opera House, resembling a ship's billowing sails (*left*); a backyard chef offering spiny lobster and an artist displaying her work (*top and above*); and (*opposite page*) the desolate Outback; an Aborigine, descendant of the country's earliest inhabitants; a rancher; and an elderly Australian of Chinese ancestry.

creased immigration from other European countries and Asia.

Language and Religion. English is the language of Australia, but it is spoken with a distinctive accent by many Australians. The Australians also have enlivened the language with a rich variety of their own expressions—so much so, in fact, that their conversation is sometimes hard for an English-speaking foreigner to follow. An added complication is that Australian English (locally known as "Strine,") is gradually being supplanted by American English, so some confusion has developed about what a typical Australian sounds like.

About 75 percent of Australians acknowledge belonging to one or another Christian denomination. According to the most recent census, in percentages of people responding, Roman Catholics (28 percent) and Anglicans, or members of the Church of England (24 percent), are the main religious groups. The Uniting, Presbyterian, and Orthodox churches are the next largest. There are also small but significant Muslim, Buddhist, and Jewish communities.

Education. Education is compulsory for all Australian children between the ages of 6 and 15 (age 16 in Tasmania). Most children, however, start in infants' classes at the age of 5. Government-run schools providing free education exist in all populated parts of the country. There are, in addition, many fee-charging schools affiliated with the various religious denominations. In recent years, the number of students attending these fee-charging schools has increased dramatically, particularly among Roman Catholics. The state governments have overriding responsibility for education, although funds are also provided by the federal government at all levels. Australia has about twenty universities and a number of colleges that offer courses leading to both undergraduate and advanced degrees.

The Aborigines. The Aborigines are Australia's distinctive native people. Their origins date back 40,000 years or more, when the first groups reached the northern coast of Australia from the island chain that extends from the Malay Peninsula to New Guinea. Most traveled by canoe or raft. The migration was aided by the lower sea levels of the time, before the rising

About 15 percent of Australia's people live in rural areas. Much of rural life revolves around sheep and cattle raising.

ocean formed a major water barrier between these islands and Australia.

As the early arrivals moved inland, they established religious sites in various areas. Patterns were chipped into rocks, and the rock faces were adorned with the tracks of kangaroos, emus, and other native animals—in some cases, huge creatures now extinct. Newcomers continued to arrive, although in steadily decreasing numbers, as the surrounding seas rose, isolating the Australian continent. Food was obtained by hunting and fishing and by gathering edible plants, the seeds of trees, and berries. Since the people were nomads, traveling from place to place, they usually built only simple, temporary shelters.

From the ancient rock carvings, the Aborigines developed legends centered around the Dreamtime, the period when mythical creatures were shaping the world. Believing in a link between the individual and the environment, they came to terms with their often harsh land. Their lifestyle was adapted to the conditions of the natural world around them, and they reinforced their ancient beliefs with sacred ceremonies. As nomads, they developed no feeling of permanent property but, instead, held to the concept of tribal ownership. Thus, while land was not considered to belong to any individual, the right to hunt in any given area belonged to those with a traditional claim to it.

In addition to the Aborigines, Australia has a smaller group of native people, the Torres Strait Islanders, whose original home was in the islands of the Torres Strait, between New Guinea and the northernmost tip of Australia, Cape York.

In a recent census, a little over 265,000 people identified themselves as of aboriginal or Torres Strait Islander ancestry. The largest number live in the states of Queensland and New South Wales. See the separate article on the Aborigines in this volume.

The New Australians. Since the late 1940's, Australia has become home to some 4 million immigrants. About 40 percent of these new arrivals were from the United Kingdom and the remaining 60 percent from various countries of Europe and Asia. Until the 1970's, European immigration was emphasized, but since then, the sources of immigration have increasingly been countries of Asia. By the mid-1990's, some 4 percent of the total population was of Asian ancestry.

Cattle ranches, called stations, are found mainly in the northern areas. The cattle are handled by stockmen, many of whom are Aborigines.

The newcomers of non-British ancestry arrived from countries where dozens of different languages were spoken, and about 10 percent of today's Australians speak English with difficulty. The earlier policy of assimilating, or absorbing, the newcomers into the prevailing British culture was changed to one of support for a multicultural society. Funds have been allocated to establish ethnic television stations and ethnic schools. At the same time, ethnic community councils have been formed in every state and their efforts coordinated through a National Ethnic Communities Council.

WAY OF LIFE

Characteristics. Australians in general enjoy one of the world's highest standards of living. Most of the people live along the coast, more than 75 percent of them in the fertile southeastern crescent-shaped region. (See Population Density map.) The majority of Australians own their own homes and a large proportion have automobiles. Nearly all households are equipped with a variety of electrical appliances, such as refrigerators, vacuum cleaners, and television sets, while video recorders, personal computers, and mobile telephones are increasingly in use. Pay-TV services opened in the major cities in 1995.

In spite of the faster pace of modern life, Australians have not lost their easygoing, informal manner, or their tolerance. These habits date back to pioneer days when hardiness and practical ability, as well as cooperation and helpfulness to neighbors, were needed in the struggle to create a new nation.

City Life. About 85 percent of Australians now live in cities and other urban areas. The main centers of population are the state capitals—Sydney, Melbourne, Brisbane, Adelaide, Perth, and Hobart—and Canberra and Darwin in the federal territories. These cities typically have tall office buildings, large and elaborate shopping areas and supermarkets as well as busy smaller shops, attractive parks and gardens, and extensive residential suburbs, where most of the people have their homes.

Everyday life in Australian cities is much like life in any modern city. Men and women leave for work in the morning, while the children go off to school neatly dressed in their school uniforms. Child care facilities are available for children under 6, so that young mothers can take jobs in order to increase family income.

Rural Life. About 15 percent of the population lives in rural areas. Although country life retains its distinctive features, television and radio keep the people closely in touch with daily events, and the automobile provides mobility. As a result, there is little sense of isolation, except in the more remote areas.

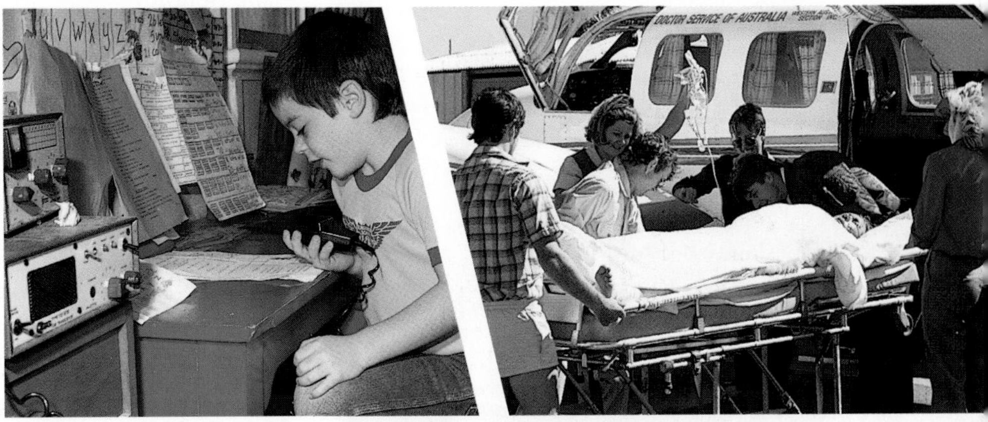

Children in the remote Outback, far from any schools, receive instruction by radio from the School of the Air (*left*). The Royal Flying Doctor Service (*right*) provides medical services to the isolated regions.

Much of rural life revolves around sheep raising, which has long been a major economic activity.

Large sheep stations (Americans would call them ranches) dot the dry inland plains of the east and southwest, while smaller ones are found in other parts of the country. In the late winter and early spring, shearing crews come to clip the sheep. A good shearer can clip 150 to 200 sheep a day. The wool is then baled and transported to the city for sale at auction. It has become traditional to hold picnics, dances, horse races, and other celebrations when shearing is over.

Where sheep do not thrive, particularly in the tropical areas of the north, cattle are raised. The cattle stations, some of which are enormous in size, employ teams of cowboys (known as stockmen) to handle the animals. In some cases a small helicopter is called in to assist the stockmen. The big cattle stations and some of the larger sheep stations form small communities in themselves. In areas where there is adequate rainfall or irrigation, usually not far from the coast, a variety of crops are grown.

The Outback. The sparsely settled interior of Australia is known as the Outback. Those who live here must be hardy individuals and self-reliant enough to deal with the isolation. Radio has reduced some of the loneliness, allowing people to keep in touch with neighbors who are often too far away to visit easily. Television, available by satellite, also helps ease the loneliness.

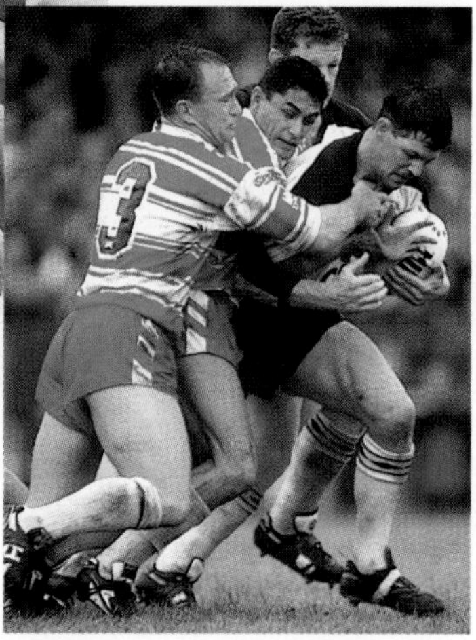

Australians are sports enthusiasts. Surfboat teams (*above*) prepare for a race in the coastal waters. Rugby (*right*) is an especially rugged sport, a cross between soccer and American football.

Children in the Outback are far from any schools. Although some attend boarding schools in the cities, most receive instruction at home from a program called School of the Air. Assignments are given out over the radio, and the children mail in their homework to be graded. Radio is also used to summon help when people become ill. The Royal Flying Doctor Service (RFDS) makes doctors, nurses, and dentists available throughout the Outback. Some of the doctors fly vast distances every year in caring for their scattered patients.

Many of the large sheep and cattle stations in the Outback have their own airstrips for light airplanes. To deliver supplies to the stations and transport cattle to market, "road trains" have been specially devised, consisting of a powerful engine unit with three trucks towed behind it. These have replaced the older method of driving cattle on long overland journeys. And for some tasks, ranch workers on horses have given way to crews in trailer trucks.

Sports. Australians are enthusiastic about sports, both as spectators and participants. Australian Rules football, soccer, and rugby are the most popular spectator sports. Cricket (like rugby, a British invention) is a favorite summer pastime. Tennis, lawn bowling, golf, and horse racing all have keen followings, while the closeness of most Australians to the coast makes it easy for them to enjoy swimming, sailing, and other water sports. The country has produced numerous world-class athletes, particularly in tennis, swimming, and track.

▸THE ARTS

Literature. Australia's early poets and novelists were new arrivals who found both the land and the society unfamiliar. It was some time before Australia's literature truly reflected the Australian scene and developed national characteristics. The work of the "bush balladists" of the late 1800's is still remembered. These were the poets who saw their country through the eyes of the pioneers who were building it. Foremost among them were Andrew Barton ("Banjo") Paterson and Henry Lawson. Paterson wrote the ballad "Waltzing Matilda," now widely regarded as the national song of Australia.

In a development paralleling the American experience (particularly with such American writers as Mark Twain and Bret Harte), the short story became a vital force in Australian

In his stark *Sunday Evening*, the contemporary painter Russell Drysdale depicted the harsher aspects and loneliness of the Australian landscape.

literary expression. Lawson, Paterson, and many lesser writers found a regular outlet for their stories in the *Bulletin*, a weekly journal that, from 1880, encouraged writers and artists to record rural life and give literary tone to the campfire yarn.

The novel in Australia has developed its own character since the publication, in 1917, of *The Fortunes of Richard Mahony* by Henry Handel Richardson (the pen name of Ethel Richardson). Among later novelists whose works received worldwide distribution are Xavier Herbert, Patrick White (who won the Nobel Prize for literature in 1973), Morris West, Colleen McCullough, Peter Carey, David Ireland, and Thomas Keneally. Keneally's novel *Schindler's List*, published in 1982, was made into an award-winning film.

Painting. As with literature, painting in Australia began as a reflection of European values of form and light. Most of the early paintings were by artists with fond memories of their homelands. A distinctive style emerged in the 1880's as artists began to define the landscape with authenticity and insight. A group of Melbourne-based landscapists—Arthur Streeton, Tom Roberts, Fred McCubbin, and others—found the technique of the French Impressionists an ideal starting point for the naturalistic painting of Australian scenes; they were the originators of the Heidelberg school (named for a town in Victoria). After them came Hans Heysen and others whose work had a more formal approach.

Beginning in the 1950's, styles became either starker or more complicated, with international influences playing a greater role as art horizons widened. Practitioners of the bolder approach included Sidney Nolan, Arthur Boyd, Albert Tucker, Russell Drysdale, and William Dobell. Dobell was an exuberant romantic with a firm sense of color whose work displayed superb technique. Roger Kemp was a leader of a vigorous abstractionist movement. A distinctive Aboriginal art style has also gained attention. Based on ritual ground paintings, it captures the art and lifestyle of the desert Aboriginal groups.

Music, Theater, and Film. Australians have won renown in

Australians renowned in the arts include composer Percy Grainger (*right*); novelist Patrick White (*center*), winner of the 1973 Nobel Prize for literature; opera singer Joan Sutherland (*top*); and popular singer Olivia Newton-John.

Australia

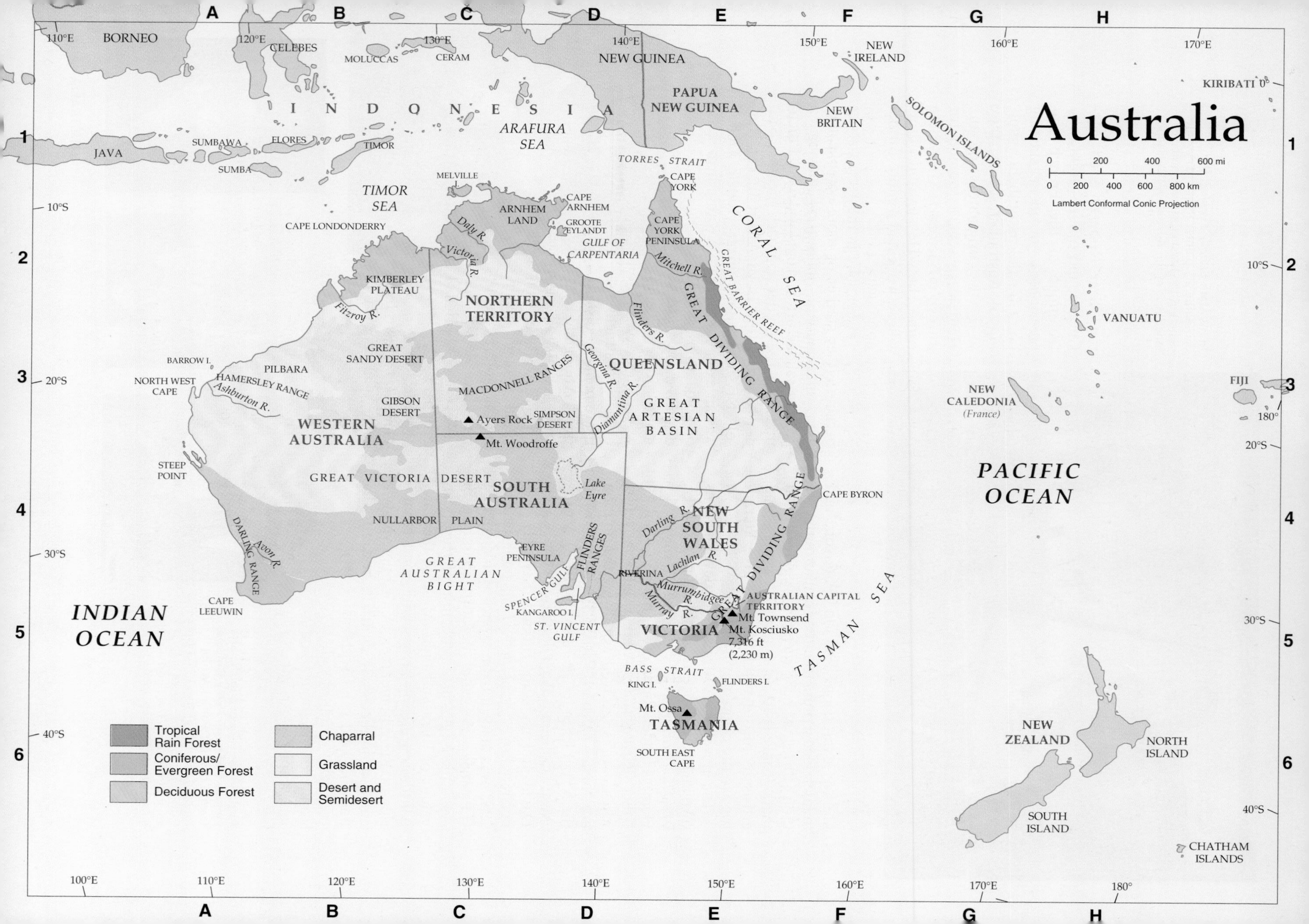

Australia
0 200 400 600 mi
0 200 400 600 800 km
Lambert Conformal Conic Projection
BORNEO
CELEBES
MOLUCCAS
CERAM
NEW GUINEA
PAPUA NEW GUINEA
NEW IRELAND
NEW BRITAIN
SOLOMON ISLANDS
KIRIBATI
I N D O N E S I A
ARAFURA SEA
JAVA
SUMBAWA
FLORES
TIMOR
SUMBA
TIMOR SEA
TORRES STRAIT
CAPE YORK
MELVILLE I.
ARNHEM LAND
CAPE ARNHEM
GROOTE EYLANDT
GULF OF CARPENTARIA
CAPE LONDONDERRY
CAPE YORK PENINSULA
CORAL SEA
Daly R.
Victoria R.
Mitchell R.
GREAT BARRIER REEF
KIMBERLEY PLATEAU
NORTHERN TERRITORY
Fitzroy R.
Flinders R.
GREAT DIVIDING RANGE
VANUATU
GREAT SANDY DESERT
BARROW I.
PILBARA
QUEENSLAND
Georgina R.
MACDONNELL RANGES
NORTH WEST CAPE
HAMERSLEY RANGE
Ashburton R.
GIBSON DESERT
GREAT ARTESIAN BASIN
Diamantina R.
NEW CALEDONIA (France)
FIJI
Ayers Rock
SIMPSON DESERT
WESTERN AUSTRALIA
Mt. Woodroffe
STEEP POINT
PACIFIC OCEAN
GREAT VICTORIA DESERT
SOUTH AUSTRALIA
Lake Eyre
CAPE BYRON
NULLARBOR PLAIN
Darling R.
NEW SOUTH WALES
DARLING RANGE
Avon R.
EYRE PENINSULA
FLINDERS RANGES
GREAT AUSTRALIAN BIGHT
Lachlan R.
RIVERINA
SPENCER GULF
Murrumbidgee R.
AUSTRALIAN CAPITAL TERRITORY
Murray R.
Mt. Townsend
TASMAN SEA
INDIAN OCEAN
CAPE LEEUWIN
KANGAROO I.
ST. VINCENT GULF
VICTORIA
Mt. Kosciusko 7,316 ft (2,230 m)
BASS STRAIT
KING I.
FLINDERS I.
Mt. Ossa
TASMANIA
SOUTH EAST CAPE
NEW ZEALAND
NORTH ISLAND
SOUTH ISLAND
CHATHAM ISLANDS
Tropical Rain Forest
Coniferous/ Evergreen Forest
Deciduous Forest
Chaparral
Grassland
Desert and Semidesert
100°E
110°E
120°E
130°E
140°E
150°E
160°E
170°E
180°
0°
10°S
20°S
30°S
40°S
A B C D E F G H
1 2 3 4 5 6

INDEX TO AUSTRALIA PHYSICAL MAP

Place	Grid	Place	Grid
Arafura Sea	C1	Kangaroo Island	D5
Arnhem, Cape	D2	Kimberley Plateau	B2
Arnhem Land	D2	King Island	E5
Ashburton River	A3	Kosciusko, Mt.	E5
Ayers Rock	C3	Lachlan River	E4
Barrow Island	A3	Leeuwin, Cape	A5
Bass Strait	E5	Londonderry, Cape	B2
Byron, Cape	F4	MacDonnel Ranges	C3
Cape York Peninsula	E2	Melville Island	C1
Carpentaria, Gulf of	D2	Mitchell River	E2
Coral Sea	E2	Murrumbidgee River	E5
Daly River	C2	Murray River	E5
Darling River	E4	North West Cape	A3
Darling Range	A4	Nullarbor Plain	C4
Diamantina River	D3	Ossa, Mt.	E6
Eyre, Lake	D4	Pilbara	B3
Eyre Peninsula	D4	Riverina	E5
Fitzroy River	B2	Simpson Desert	D3
Flinders Island	E5	South East Cape	E6
Flinders Ranges	D4	Spencer Gulf	D5
Flinders River	D3	St. Vincent Gulf	D5
Georgina River	D3	Steep Point	A4
Gibson Desert	C3	Swan River	A4
Great Artesian Basin	E3	Tasman Sea	F5
Great Australian Bight	C4	Timor Sea	B1
Great Barrier Reef	E2	Torres Strait	D1
Great Dividing Range	E3	Townsend, Mt.	E5
Great Sandy Desert	B3	Victoria River	C2
Great Victoria Desert	C4	Woodroffe, Mt.	C3
Groote Eylandt	D2	York, Cape	E1
Hamersley Range	A3		

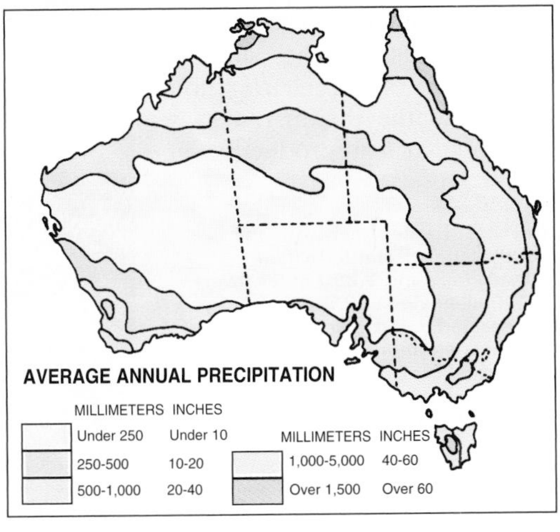

music, theater, and film as well. The voices of opera singers Nellie Melba, Peter Dawson, Marjorie Lawrence, and Joan Sutherland have delighted music lovers the world over. Composers such as Percy Grainger and Peter Sculthorpe have also won international fame. Well-known figures in the popular field include jazz musicians Ray Price, Don Burrows, and the Little River Band, and singers such as the Bee Gees, Peter Allen, Olivia Newton-John, and Helen Reddy.

An expanded interest in the performing arts led to the creation of new centers of cultural expression, of which Melbourne's arts center is among the most opulent. The most striking, however, is the Sydney Opera House, with its multiple-roof design in the shape of gigantic ships' sails. Meanwhile, in the theater, after years in which imported stage spectaculars were the accepted formula for success, Australian plays began to win greater attention through the success of playwright David Williamson.

Filmmaking developed early in Australia; one of the first feature-length films was made

FACTS and figures

COMMONWEALTH OF AUSTRALIA is the official name of the country.

LOCATION: Southern Hemisphere, between the Pacific and Indian oceans.

AREA: 2,967,895 sq mi (7,686,848 km^2).

POPULATION: 31,000,000 (estimate).

CAPITAL: Canberra.

LARGEST CITY: Sydney.

MAJOR LANGUAGE: English.

MAJOR RELIGIOUS GROUP: Christian.

GOVERNMENT: Federation of states. **Head of state**—British monarch, represented by a governor-general. **Head of government**—prime minister. **Legislature**—Federal Parliament (made up of the Senate and the House of Representatives).

CHIEF PRODUCTS: **Agricultural**—wheat, barley, wool, beef, mutton, dairy products, sugarcane, fruits. **Manufactured**—automobiles, construction materials, chemicals, processed foods, electronic equipment, agricultural and earth-moving equipment, plastics, optical fibers, fertilizers, pharmaceutical products. **Mineral**—bauxite (aluminum ore), iron ore, copper, coal, petroleum, natural gas, lead, uranium, industrial diamonds, gold, silver.

MONETARY UNIT: Australian dollar (1 dollar = 100 cents).

there in 1906. Beginning in the 1970's, the industry gained international attention though the work of filmmakers Bruce Beresford, Peter Weir, Gillian Armstrong, and Fred Schepisi. Many of these directors went on to further fame in Hollywood.

THE LAND

Overview. Australia occupies an area roughly equal to that of the United States, excluding Alaska and Hawaii. It extends from Cape York in the north to South East Cape in the south—a distance of about 2,300 miles (3,700 kilometers)—and from Steep Point in the west to Cape Byron in the east—a distance of about 2,600 miles (4,000 kilometers). Off the northeastern coast lies the Great Barrier Reef, the world's longest coral formation.

Australia's major landforms are low mountains in the east and level plains and broad plateaus elsewhere. Three natural regions extend as broad bands from north to south across the continent. These are the Eastern Highlands, the Central Lowland, and the Western Plateau.

Eastern Highlands. The Eastern Highlands consist of a series of hills and plateau sections extending along the great curve of the Pacific coast. They form a series of watersheds dividing the flow of the rivers in the region. Elevation varies from between 1,000 and 2,000 feet (300 to 600 meters) over the northern half of the region to more than 3,000 feet (900 meters) in the more southerly part. Near the southeastern corner of the region are the Australian Alps, which are snow-covered in winter. Their highest peak, Mount Kosciusko, rises to 7,316 feet (2,230 meters).

The eastern slopes of the highlands are still largely forested and support logging in some areas. Rainfall is abundant, and rivers flowing to the coast are short and swift and subject to sudden flooding. Rivers on the western slopes flow into the Central Lowland. Here, however, rainfall is intermittent, and during the long dry spells, the same rivers become no more than a string of waterholes.

Central Lowland. This is an extensive, generally flat region with the lowest elevation in Australia. It has three shallow drainage basins. In the north are the rivers flowing into the Gulf of Carpentaria; in the center is the Lake Eyre Basin; and in the south is the Murray-Darling river system, which gathers together the main rivers flowing from the western slopes of the Eastern Highlands. The Murray River and its branches support a number of large irrigation areas, and the region ranks as Australia's most productive in

The Great Barrier Reef (*top*), the world's largest coral formation, extends for some 1,250 miles (over 2,000 kilometers) off Australia's northeastern coast. Farmland and vineyards are found in the relatively few fertile areas of South Australia (*right*). Queensland's varied landscape includes tropical rain forests (*opposite page*).

Ayers Rock rises 1,100 feet (335 meters) above the desert of northern Australia. It is called Uluru by the Aborigines, who consider it sacred.

terms of livestock raising and general output of farm products.

Lake Eyre, the lowest point on the continent, lies in the western part of the region. Its surface averages about 39 feet (12 meters) below sea level. For most of the time it consists of a vast expanse of dried, salty mud. Only two or three times in 100 years does it receive enough water to turn it into a true lake.

Underlying most of the Central Lowland is the Great Artesian Basin, a vast underground reservoir. When deep bores are drilled into the basin, warm water flows to the surface, making livestock raising possible when no other water is available.

Western Plateau. The largest of the three regions, the Western Plateau covers almost half of Australia. It has an average elevation of about 1,000 feet (305 meters), with a higher section in the northwest called the Kimberley Plateau. The arid interior includes three deserts—the Great Sandy Desert, the Gibson Desert, and the Great Victoria Desert. To the south is the Nullarbor (meaning "treeless") Plain. The most important agricultural area is in the southwest, where enough rain is received in winter for wheat and sheep farming. The Eyre Peninsula in the south is another significant farming area. Although often desolate, the region has much of Australia's mineral wealth.

Climate. Because Australia lies in the Southern Hemisphere, the seasons are reversed. Winter comes in June and summer in December. The northern third of the country has a tropical climate, marked in summer by warm, moist air and monsoon rains. Two or three times each year, the heavy rainfall along the coast results in serious flooding. The south has a temperate climate. Summers are generally hot and often rainless. But in

winter and spring the westerly winds bring rain to parts of Western and South Australia, most of Victoria and southern New South Wales, and Tasmania, thus sustaining the country's most fertile agricultural regions.

January and February are the hottest months and July is the coolest. Temperatures are highest in the tropical north and the arid interior. Darwin, on the northern coast, averages about 86°F (30°C) in January and about 77°F (25°C) in July, while Melbourne, on the southern coast, averages about 68°F (20°C) in January and 48°F (9°C) in July. In the desert interior and other arid regions, summer temperatures often exceed 100°F (38°C).

Rainfall can vary widely. The northern, eastern, and southwestern coasts receive more than 40 inches (1,000 millimeters) a year, while large areas of the interior receive less than 10 inches (250 millimeters). The areas of heaviest rainfall are along the Pacific coast, particularly in Queensland, which can receive as much as 160 inches (4,000 millimeters) annually.

Mineral Resources. Australia ranks among the wealthiest nations in terms of mineral resources. It is a leading producer of bauxite (aluminum ore), iron ore, copper, lead, uranium, industrial diamonds, gold, and silver. Huge coalfields have been opened up, while oil and natural gas fields (the largest are offshore) yield abundant energy. In addition, nearly 100 other minerals, including nickel and manganese, are mined in significant amounts.

A road sign alerts motorists to an approaching kangaroo crossing. Kangaroos are the country's best-known animals.

▶ WILDLIFE

Australia's extraordinary varieties of animal wildlife are a result of its long isolation from other lands. When Australia split off from other continental landmasses, it included early forms of furred, warm-blooded animals as well as reptiles and birds. The earliest of the furred creatures had characteristics of both reptiles and warm-blooded animals. They were the ancestors of the present-day platypus and echidna (also known as the spiny anteater), which are unique in that they lay eggs and also produce a milk-like substance to feed their young. The platypus also has a duck-like bill and webbed feet.

Australia is home to most of the world's marsupials, or pouched mammals, of which kangaroos are perhaps the best known. There are a number of species, including the red kangaroo and the gray kangaroo, that grow to be as tall and heavy as human adults, and the wallaby, which is about the size of a small child. See the article on marsupials in Volume M. An article on kangaroos appears in Volume J-K.

Another distinctive animal is the tree-dwelling koala, which eats only the leaves of eucalyptus trees. The dingo, a wild dog, was brought to Australia by Aboriginal groups, who used it in hunting.

The emu is a large, flightless bird that, along with the kangaroo, appears on the Australian coat-of-arms. Its smaller relative is the cassowary. Another bird, the kookaburra, is known as the laughing jackass because its song sounds like rowdy laughter. Most numerous among the birds, however, are the parrots, which include many species in beautiful multicolored plumage.

Several animals introduced by Europeans have run wild in Australia. Among these are water buffalo, rabbits, goats, camels, and foxes. Rabbits, first brought in during the 1850's, multiplied so rapidly that they became major pests, and Australians have been trying to reduce their numbers ever since. Wild horses, known as brumbies, roam free in some mountain districts and in wilderness areas in the interior.

▶ THE ECONOMY

A Diversified Economy. Australia has a diversified economy, combining agriculture, mining, and manufacturing. Although it has only limited fertile land, Australia is a major producer and exporter of agricultural products. Its wealth of mineral resources has made mining vital to the economy. Manufacturing is now central to the national prosperity, but the country's fastest-growing economic activity involves the provision of services. Australia's trade, which was once mainly with Britain and Europe, has increasingly been directed toward Asia and the Pacific.

Nearly as familiar as the kangaroo is the koala, which feeds only on leaves of the eucalyptus tree. Much of Australia's wildlife is found nowhere else on earth.

Manufacturing and Services. Australia's manufacturing industries grew in the 1950's and 1960's, eventually employing one-quarter of the workforce. But stagnation set in during the 1970's and a restructuring began, with the steel and metalworking industries leading the revival. New industries emerged in the 1990's, and manufacturing has rebounded to engage nearly one-fifth of the labor force.

The industries that have prospered the most are those associated with technological changes and rising standards of living. Factories are turning out, and often exporting, a wide range of goods. These include automobiles, construction materials, chemicals, and electronic equipment. In addition, Australian industry produces agricultural and earthmoving equipment, plastics, optical fibers, fertilizers, and pharmaceuticals.

Among service industries, finance, business and community services, and communications have risen the most in recent decades. Wholesale and retail trade have fallen slightly.

Agriculture and Livestock Raising. Australia has long been the leading sheep-raising coun-

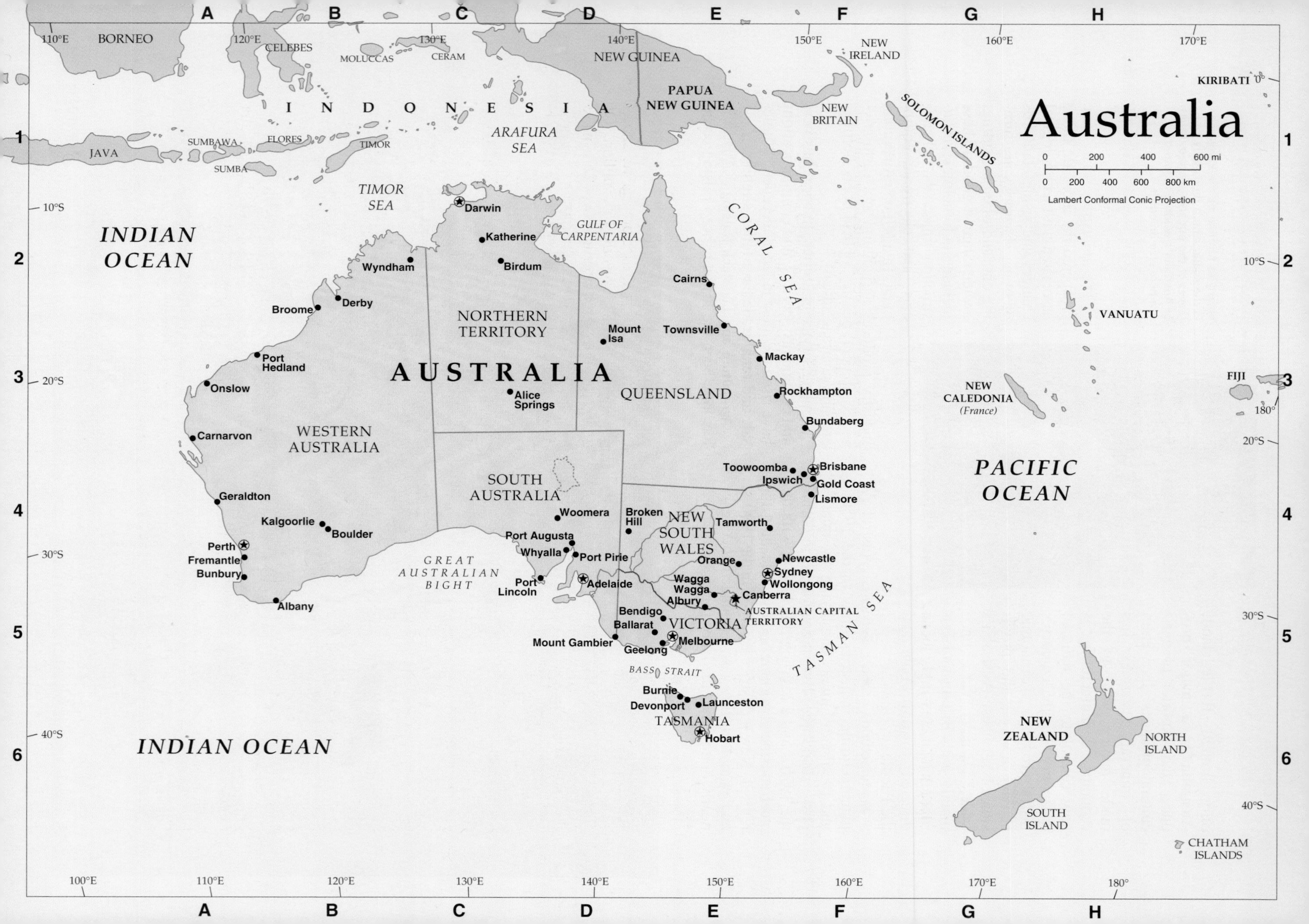
Australia
0 200 400 600 mi
0 200 400 600 800 km
Lambert Conformal Conic Projection
BORNEO
CELEBES
MOLUCCAS
CERAM
NEW GUINEA
PAPUA NEW GUINEA
NEW IRELAND
NEW BRITAIN
KIRIBATI
SOLOMON ISLANDS
I N D O N E S I A
JAVA
SUMBAWA
FLORES
TIMOR
SUMBA
ARAFURA SEA
TIMOR SEA
GULF OF CARPENTARIA
CORAL SEA
INDIAN OCEAN
VANUATU
FIJI
NEW CALEDONIA (France)
PACIFIC OCEAN
AUSTRALIA
NORTHERN TERRITORY
WESTERN AUSTRALIA
SOUTH AUSTRALIA
QUEENSLAND
NEW SOUTH WALES
VICTORIA
AUSTRALIAN CAPITAL TERRITORY
TASMANIA
Darwin
Katherine
Birdum
Wyndham
Derby
Broome
Port Hedland
Onslow
Carnarvon
Geraldton
Kalgoorlie
Boulder
Perth
Fremantle
Bunbury
Albany
Alice Springs
Mount Isa
Cairns
Townsville
Mackay
Rockhampton
Bundaberg
Toowoomba
Ipswich
Brisbane
Gold Coast
Lismore
Woomera
Port Augusta
Whyalla
Port Pirie
Port Lincoln
Adelaide
Broken Hill
Tamworth
Newcastle
Orange
Sydney
Wollongong
Wagga Wagga
Albury
Canberra
Bendigo
Ballarat
Melbourne
Geelong
Mount Gambier
GREAT AUSTRALIAN BIGHT
BASS STRAIT
TASMAN SEA
Burnie
Devonport
Launceston
Hobart
NEW ZEALAND
NORTH ISLAND
SOUTH ISLAND
CHATHAM ISLANDS
INDIAN OCEAN
110°E
120°E
130°E
140°E
150°E
160°E
170°E
100°E
180°
0°
10°S
20°S
30°S
40°S
A
B
C
D
E
F
G
H
1
2
3
4
5
6

INDEX TO AUSTRALIA POLITICAL MAP

Adelaide	**D5**	Kalgoorlie	**B4**
Albany	**B5**	Katherine	**C2**
Albury	**E5**	Launceston	**E6**
Alice Springs	**C3**	Lismore	**F4**
Ballarat	**E5**	Mackay	**E3**
Bendigo	**E5**	Melbourne	**E5**
Birdum	**C2**	Mount Gambier	**D5**
Boulder	**B4**	Mount Isa	**D3**
Brisbane	**F4**	Newcastle	**E4**
Broken Hill	**D4**	Onslow	**A3**
Broome	**B2**	Orange	**E4**
Bunbury	**A5**	Perth	**A4**
Bundaberg	**F3**	Port Augusta	**D4**
Burnie	**E6**	Port Hedland	**A3**
Cairns	**E2**	Port Lincoln	**D5**
Canberra	**E5**	Port Pirie	**D4**
Carnarvon	**A3**	Rockhampton	**E3**
Darwin	**C2**	Sydney	**E5**
Derby	**B2**	Tamworth	**E4**
Devonport	**E6**	Toowoomba	**F4**
Fremantle	**A4**	Townsville	**E3**
Geelong	**E5**	Wagga Wagga	**E5**
Geraldton	**A4**	Whyalla	**D4**
Gold Coast	**F4**	Wollongong	**E5**
Hobart	**E6**	Woomera	**D4**
Ipswich	**I4**	Wyndham	**C2**

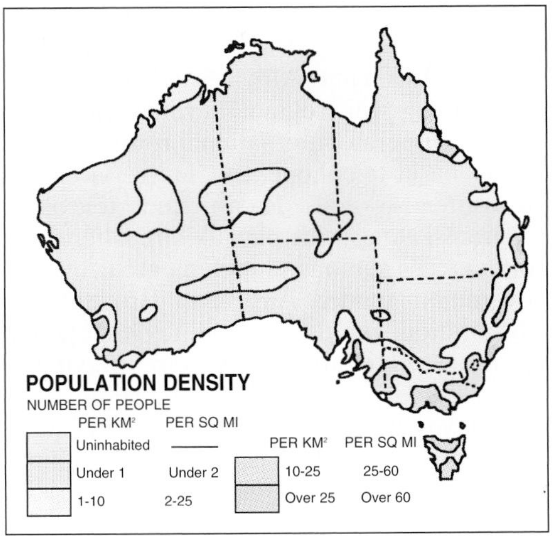

SOME AUSTRALIAN WORDS AND PHRASES

beano—a feast
billabong—a waterhole
billy—can for boiling water
bludger—idler
bonza—good, great
bush—forest country
dinkum—honest, true, genuine
ear basher—a talkative bore
galah—a silly, talkative person
give him the drum—tell the true facts
go crook—get angry
grizzle—to complain
larrikin—a hoodlum
never-never—back country
nong—useless person
no-hoper—a stupid person
ratbag—someone not to be taken seriously
ropeable—extremely angry
spine bashing—reclining
squatter—owner of a large sheep station
wake-up—someone sharp; no fool
whinge—complain
yacker—hard work

try, producing more than half of the world's fine-quality wool used in clothing. Its sheep population usually exceeds 150 million. Of these, two-thirds are merinos, which provide the finest wool. New South Wales has the largest number of sheep, with about 40 percent of the total.

Dairy farming is important near the main cities along the eastern and southern coasts and in irrigated areas in Victoria. Wheat and other grains are widely grown in eastern and southwestern Australia, usually on large, mechanized farms. Much of the wheat is exported. Most grain farmers also keep sheep as an additional source of income.

Australia produces a variety of fruits. Pineapples and other tropical fruits are grown on the north Queensland coast. Peaches, plums, and citrus fruits flourish in irrigated areas, and apples are produced in Tasmania. The Brossa Valley in South Australia is a wine-making center. Australia is one of the world's leading exporters of sugarcane, which is grown along the northeastern coast.

Mining and Energy. The discovery of large gold deposits in the 1850's made Australia

Agriculture and mining are an important part of the country's diversified economy. The vast flocks of sheep raised in New South Wales and other states (*below*) have made Australia the world's leading sheep-producing country, providing more than half of its supply of fine wool. Wheat farming (*left*) is highly mechanized. Gold is mined chiefly in Western Australia (*opposite page*).

the world's largest producer of the precious metal, and new goldfields continued to be found, although on a lesser scale, for decades. Kalgoorlie, in Western Australia, is the main gold-producing site. Iron ore, mined chiefly in the Pilbara region of Western Australia, is one of the country's most valuable exports. Australia leads the world in bauxite output, with 38 percent of the total production. The bauxite is mined in Queensland, in the Darling Range of Western Australia, and in the Northern Territory.

The discovery of oil and natural gas fields, beginning in the 1960's, transformed Australia's energy potential. Oil fields in Bass Strait, off the coast of Victoria; in southern Queensland; and in Western Australia supply most of the country's oil and natural gas needs. Increasing quantities of liquefied natural gas are now being exported from wells in the Timor Sea, particularly to Japan. Coal is mined in large quantities in central Queensland, both for export and for domestic use. Lignite (brown coal) is produced in Victoria.

Transportation and Communications. Transportation is generally well developed. Australia is one of the most highly motorized countries in the world, with an average of one motor vehicle for every two people, and there is an extensive network of roads along the coast. In the Outback, however, many of the roads are unpaved. Trains are fast and modern, and excellent internal air service is provided by Qantas Airways and Ansett Australia, along with regional airlines. Both airlines also operate international routes.

The basic telephone and fax services are government-owned. Radio and television programs, along with pay-TV, are offered by commercial stations, supplemented by the government-funded Australian Broadcasting Corporation. The use of satellites has opened up the remote areas that were previously served only by local stations. The larger cities each have several daily newspapers, including *The Australian*, which is published nationwide. A wide range of magazines and books are also published.

THE STATES AND TERRITORIES

New South Wales. Nearly one–third of Australia's people live in New South Wales, the most populous state. Most are concentrated along the eastern coast, and more than half live in Sydney, the capital and largest city. Sydney is also the heart of the state's manufacturing, commerce, finance, and transportation. Newcastle, the second largest city, is a center of steel production.

The narrow coastal lowlands of New South Wales have a succession of short river valleys well suited to farming. The country's highest point, Mount Kosciusko, is in the south, and the surrounding region is popular with skiers and other winter-sports enthusiasts. The western slopes of the Eastern Highlands include large areas of good crop and grazing land.

Nearly two-thirds of the state's area lies beyond the highlands. These western plains are crossed by the Darling and other rivers, which provide irrigation for growing citrus fruits, rice, and other crops. Wheat is also grown on the plains, and large numbers of sheep, particularly merinos, and some beef cattle are raised here as well.

Victoria. Victoria is the second smallest state in area and the second largest in population. Most of its inhabitants live in the south. Melbourne is the capital and largest city. Other important towns include Geelong and Ballarat.

Victoria occupies a wedge of territory in Australia's southeastern corner, in the heart

of what is known as the fertile crescent. With the state's mild, moist winter climate, Victoria's agriculture is highly productive, particularly its truck and dairy farms, which supply the main cities with fresh fruits, vegetables, and milk. The state's main energy source is its deposits of lignite, which have aided its industrial development. It also has offshore deposits of natural gas and oil. Victoria is the center of Australia's automobile production and manufactures a wide range of other goods as well.

Queensland. Queensland, Australia's second largest state in area, occupies the northeastern part of the country. Most of its people live along the narrow coastal strip, where

STATE	CAPITAL
New South Wales	Sydney
Queensland	Brisbane
South Australia	Adelaide
Tasmania	Hobart
Victoria	Melbourne
Western Australia	Perth
TERRITORY	**CAPITAL**
Australian Capital Territory	Canberra*
Northern Territory	Darwin

*National capital

Australia's major cities are located in the coastal areas. Brisbane (*top*), the capital of Queensland and the country's third largest city in population, is also an important port and manufacturing center. The newer Queensland city of Gold Coast (*left*) is a popular tourist resort.

Brisbane, the capital, and Gold Coast, the second largest city, are located. The interior is only sparsely populated.

Queensland's pleasant climate, beautiful beaches, offshore islands, and tropical rain forests have made tourism an important industry. Increasing numbers of retired people have also settled here. Mining is a major economic activity and includes the production of coal, copper, aluminum, and other minerals. The bulk of Australia's sugarcane is grown and processed in the tropical north, while the interior of the state is given over to sheep raising. Large numbers of cattle are grazed in the north and west, making Queensland the chief beef-producing state.

South Australia. Most of South Australia's people, farms, and industries are situated in the southeastern part of the state. Adelaide, the capital, is home to about three-quarters of the state's population.

Only a very limited area of the state is suitable for farming. Wheat and some barley is grown in the Eyre Peninsula and east of Spencer Gulf. Sheep also thrive in these regions. Along the lower reaches of the Murray River, irrigated land produces a variety of fruits, including grapes used in wine making. Dry, unproductive land makes up most of the remainder of the state, except for deposits of iron ore, uranium, and opals (a semi-precious stone). The Aboriginal groups have been granted title to vast areas of the virtually uninhabited interior.

Western Australia. Nearly 400 years ago, Europeans first reached the coast of what is now Western Australia. They described it as a rugged, dry, and inhospitable land, and their description still fits all but its southwestern corner. The largest of Australia's states, it consists largely of barren desert, only occasionally broken by an isolated mining town or cattle station.

Nearly all of Western Australia's people and most of the wheat farms, sheep stations, and fruit orchards are in the southwestern part of the state. Perth, the capital, is the major urban center. Australia's only transcontinental rail line cuts across the empty Nullarbor Plain to the east.

Gold was first discovered in Western Australia in 1885, and mining towns sprang up overnight. The richest finds were at Coolgardie and nearby Kalgoorlie, towns lying on the fringe of the desert and dependent on a pipeline from Perth for their water. Kalgoorlie continues to be a world leader in gold production. The state is also rich in iron ore, mainly from the Pilbara region in the Hamersley Range. Oil is extracted at Barrow Island, and natural gas is piped in from the Timor Sea.

Tasmania. Tasmania, the island state, is the smallest in area of Australia's states. Sometimes called the Apple Isle because it produces most of Australia's apples, it is also famous for its rugged scenery. Hobart, the capital and largest city, lies at the foot of Mount Wellington. Other important towns are Launceston and Devonport. A ferryboat connects Devonport with Melbourne on the mainland across Bass Strait.

The western half of the island is mountainous, with heavy rainfall and dense forests. To the east, the climate is more suited to sheep raising and the cultivation of hops, various fruits, and potatoes. The abundance of water has encouraged hydroelectric development, and this has attracted industry to the island. Tin is also mined.

Northern Territory. The Northern Territory, which became self-governing in 1978, is the least populated and least developed part of Australia. Crocodiles and wild buffalo still live in some of the marshy coastal swamps. Darwin, the capital, is the only large settlement in the northern part of the territory. Almost entirely destroyed by a tropical cyclone in 1974, the city has since been rebuilt. Katherine (a former mining town) has grown with the establishment of an air force station and the development of tourism and cattle raising. Alice Springs, generally called Alice, is the largest town in the south and is linked by rail with Adelaide.

Australian Capital Territory. The Australian Capital Territory is an enclave within New South Wales surrounding the national capital, Canberra. The federal territory also includes the area of Jervis Bay, transferred from New South Wales in 1915 for use by the Royal Australian Navy.

Melbourne (*below*), the second largest city, is the capital of Victoria and a major port and financial center. Sydney (*right*), capital of New South Wales, is Australia's largest city and the country's chief port. The monorail is a distinctive feature of the city's transportation system.

▸ MAJOR CITIES

Sydney, Australia's largest city, industrial center, and the capital of New South Wales, was founded in 1788. It was the first European settlement in the country. See the separate article on Sydney in Volume S.

Melbourne, the second largest city and the capital of Victoria, is a major port and a financial center of the nation. An article on Melbourne appears in Volume M.

The national coat of arms incorporates the kangaroo and the emu, a large, flightless bird. Both animals are distinctive to Australia.

Brisbane, the capital of Queensland and third largest in population, is the only large Australian city with a subtropical climate. Numerous parks and gardens have made it one of Australia's most beautiful cities. It is Queensland's business and cultural center, and it handles much of the state's tourist trade. A monument in the city commemorates the cooperation between Australia and the United States during World War II.

Perth, the capital of Western Australia, has grown to become Australia's fourth largest city. Said to be Australia's most beautiful city, it reminds many Americans of cities in southern California. Its port is Fremantle, at the mouth of the Swan (Avon) River. The mining boom brought dramatic changes to Perth. At one time the highest building was 15 stories. Today several skyscrapers are many stories taller. Among the notable recent additions to the city are an entertainment center, a new art gallery, and extensive freeways. The Perth industrial complex extends to Fremantle, about 10 miles (16 kilometers) away, site of the world's largest wheat terminal.

Hobart, the capital of Tasmania, was founded in the early 1800's and is Australia's second oldest city. Mountains provide a beautiful background for the city, which is surrounded by a flourishing agricultural area. Ores, wood and metal products, and food and beverages are exported through the port of Hobart.

Canberra is an important seat of learning and scientific achievement as well as being Australia's national capital. See the article on Canberra in Volume C.

▸ GOVERNMENT

Australia is an independent member of the Commonwealth of Nations. The federal government in Canberra conducts national affairs. Each state has its own parliament and

IMPORTANT DATES

1642	Abel Tasman sighted and named Van Diemen's Land (Tasmania).
1770	New South Wales was claimed for Britain.
1788	First British settlement was founded at Port Jackson (Sydney Harbour).
1803	Matthew Flinders circumnavigated (sailed around) the Australian coast.
1825	Van Diemen's Land separated from New South Wales.
1829	Swan River colony (Western Australia) was begun.
1836	Colony of South Australia was first settled.
1851	Victoria separated from New South Wales.
1853	Van Diemen's Land was renamed Tasmania.
1859	Queensland separated from New South Wales.
1862	John McDouall Stuart crossed Australia.
1892–93	Gold was discovered in Western Australia.
1901	Commonwealth of Australia was formed.
1914–18	Australia fought alongside Britain in World War I.
1927	Parliament moved from Melbourne to Canberra.
1939–45	Australia fought on the side of the Allies in World War II.
1945	Australia became one of the original members of the United Nations.
1950	Australia contributed forces to the United Nations in the Korean War.
1951	ANZUS Security Treaty between Australia, New Zealand, and the United States was signed.
1956	Melbourne hosted the Summer Olympic Games.
1978	The Northern Territory was granted internal self-government.
1988	Australia Day marked the bicentennial (200th anniversary) of British settlement in Australia.
1994	Legislation was enacted to give Aboriginal groups and Torres Strait Islanders authority to claim land under "native title."
2000	Sydney hosted the Summer Olympic Games.
2003	The last link in Australia's long-awaited north-south transcontinental railway was completed.

governor. Australia was the first country to use the secret ballot, and every Australian citizen over 18 years of age is required to vote.

Legislative authority rests with the Federal Parliament, made up of the Senate and the House of Representatives. Each state has ten senators, and each territory has two. The House of Representatives is elected on the basis of population. Its membership is required to be, as nearly as possible, twice that of the Senate. A governor-general represents the British monarch, who is the ceremonial head of state. Political power rests with the prime minister, who heads the government. The prime minister is the leader of the governing party or parties in the parliament and is assisted by a cabinet of ministers.

The High Court of Australia is the supreme legal authority, with the power to override all other courts in the land. It interprets the constitution and settles disputes between the states.

HISTORY

Discovery and Exploration. As early as the Middle Ages (and possibly earlier), stories were told about the existence of a large continent in the Southern Hemisphere. But Europeans had never seen it, and they referred to it as *terra australis incognita*, Latin for "the unknown southern land."

The Dutch were the first Europeans to see Australia, sighting it while making journeys between the Netherlands and their colonies in what is now Indonesia. But although they had seen the western coast of the continent, they did not know how far to the east it extended. In 1642 the Dutch navigator Abel Tasman was sent out to discover what lay in the east. Tasman sailed too far south to see the mainland, but he did visit the island that is now called Tasmania in his honor but which he named Van Diemen's Land. Tasman then continued eastward to New Zealand and later explored Australia's northern coast.

No careful explorations of the continent were made until 1770, when James Cook, a British naval officer and explorer, sailed along its eastern coast and named it New South Wales. He visited Botany Bay, near what is now modern Sydney, and reported that the bay and much of New South Wales looked suitable for settlement. See the article on James Cook in Volume C.

First Settlements. The first settlement came about after Britain had lost its colonies in what is now the United States. Looking for an alternate place that it could use to relieve its overcrowded prisons, the government decided to establish a penal colony at Botany Bay. The first shipload of convicts and a few British soldiers commanded by Captain Arthur Phillip landed on January 22, 1788. Four days later, Phillip moved the settlement a little farther north to a better location at Port Jackson, which he named Sydney. More convicts followed, and new colonies were established in Tasmania and other parts of the continent.

Further Exploration. Most of the coastline was only vaguely known at this time and further explorations were carried out. In 1798, George Bass, a naval surgeon and explorer, sailed along the southern coast and showed that Tasmania was an island. Bass Strait, which separates the island from the mainland, was named after him. In 1801, Matthew Flinders, a captain in the Royal Navy, discovered and charted Kangaroo Island and Spencer and St. Vincent gulfs along the south coast. (Flinders Ranges and Flinders Island were named for him.) The Blue Mountains, which lay behind Sydney, were first crossed in 1813.

The first British settlement in Australia was established at Port Jackson (Sydney Harbour) in 1788 by Captain Arthur Phillip, after their initial landing at Botany Bay.

The Early Colonies. Life was very difficult during the early years in Sydney. Attempts at farming failed in the poor soil, and it was not until better land was found along Nepean Bay, to the west, that successful farms were established and food supplies improved. The successful breeding of Merino sheep, which proved well suited to the climate, led to the development of a flourishing wool industry. At the same time, whaling in the South Pacific brought trading ships to Sydney.

Free English settlers began arriving in the 1820's, and the first free colony was established at Swan River, in what is now Western Australia, in 1829. South Australia was settled in 1836, and settlers from Tasmania crossed Bass Strait and occupied the Port Phillip district from 1835 to 1837. This later became the colony of Victoria.

Expansion Inland. In the 1820's, settlers had begun taking their flocks of sheep across the Blue Mountains. Hoping to find more good land, explorers went farther inland. Captain Charles Sturt first explored the Darling River; then in 1829–30, he followed the Murrumbidgee River to the Murray. Continuing on to sea, he reported on the excellence of the grassy plains. In 1836, Major Thomas Mitchell found fertile land south of the Murray River. Close behind the explorers came the sheep herders, settling where they found good pasture.

In spite of optimistic hopes, later explorers found dry and mainly unrewarding land. One was Edward John Eyre, who in 1841 discovered the great salt lake that bears his name. Another was Wilhelm Ludwig Leichhardt, who in 1844–45, traveled overland from Brisbane to the northern coast. In 1862, John McDouall Stuart crossed Australia from Adelaide in the south to the site of Darwin in the north.

The six colonies grew rapidly and all became self-governing during the latter half of the 1800's.

Nationhood. Realizing the merit of acting together on matters of common interest, the colonies decided to seek a basis for federation. A first constitution was drawn up in

Exploration of Australia's rugged interior (*above*) was essential to its development. Nationhood was finally achieved in 1901, after which the first federal parliament was convened (*below*) in Melbourne, the early national capital.

Australians celebrated the 200th anniversary of British settlement in 1988. The event was highlighted by a fireworks display in Sydney Harbour.

1891, and a second in 1898. After it won approval from Australian voters, the British Parliament passed a constitution act, and the six colonies became states in the new Commonwealth of Australia on January 1, 1901.

With the outbreak of World War I in 1914, Australia joined forces with Britain and its allies. During World War II (1939–45), Australia again fought on the side of Britain, and after the entry of the United States into the war, it became a support base for U.S. forces. Its forces took part in campaigns first in the Middle East and then in the Pacific. In 1942 the city of Darwin was bombed by Japanese planes.

Australia became increasingly active in world affairs after World War II. It was an original member of the United Nations, and in 1950, when the Korean War erupted, Australian troops were sent to Korea as part of the United Nations command. In 1951, Australia signed the ANZUS defense pact with New Zealand and the United States. A significant proportion of Australia's national income each year is allocated to assisting the developing countries.

Economic Growth and Immigration. Growing demand and scarcity of imports during World War II provided a major stimulus to Australian industry. To strengthen development after the war, the government encouraged immigration from Britain and other parts of Europe, and over time, millions of new Australians were resettled successfully.

During the 1980's, however, the large-scale immigration from Britain and Europe fell off sharply. Many of the new arrivals were from countries in Asia—especially refugees from Vietnam, China, and Cambodia and business and professional people from Hong Kong.

Recent History. In 1988, Australians marked the 200th anniversary of British settlement. The occasion became one of review and redirection. This was especially so in relations with the Aboriginal people, who had suffered dispossession from their lands during the settlement of the country. Among the government's measures to bring about reconciliation for past injustices were increased welfare spending and other social programs. In 1994 legislation was enacted to give Aborigines and Torres Strait Islanders authority to claim land under "native title."

Financial deregulation in the mid-1980's led to an economic boom, which collapsed in 1990 and was followed by a sharp recession. Many industries declined, causing high levels of unemployment. The government advocated the removal of barriers to international trade. It also directed its efforts to gaining access to the fast-growing markets in the Asia and Pacific area.

Proposals to replace the constitutional monarchy with a republican form of government gained ground in the mid-1990's. But in 1999, Australians voted to keep Great Britain's monarch as their head of state.

In 2000, Sydney hosted the Summer Olympic Games, just as Melbourne had 44 years earlier. And in January 2001, Australia celebrated the centennial, or 100th, anniversary of its federation. In 2003, Australia was one of the few countries to send troops in support of the American-led war in Iraq.

CHARLES M. DAVIS
University of Michigan

R. M. YOUNGER
Author, *Australia and the Australians*

AUSTRIA

Austria is a landlocked nation in central Europe, bordered by eight different countries. The people of Austria call their country Österreich, meaning "eastern realm." The origin of the name dates back to the A.D. 800's, when the emperor Charlemagne made Austria an eastern border region of the Holy Roman Empire. From this beginning, Austria itself grew into a great empire. It reached its height in the 1500's, when the Habsburgs, its ruling family, controlled lands that stretched from Austria to Spain and included vast Spanish colonial possessions in the Americas.

Although the empire declined from this high point, it survived for another 400 years, until its collapse in 1918, at the end of World War I. From its ruins, modern Austria emerged, along with other present-day nations of central and eastern Europe.

The snow-covered Grossglockner (meaning "great bell") is the highest peak in the Austrian Alps.

PEOPLE

The Austrians are of various ethnic backgrounds, but most share a common language, religion, and culture.

Language. German, the official language of Austria, is spoken by almost all its people. Austrians also take pride in their regional dialects of German, such as the *Wienerisch* spoken in Vienna, the capital. The chief non-German-speaking residents—the Czechs, Slovenes, Croats, and Hungarians—speak German as their second language.

Religion. The great majority of Austrians are Roman Catholics. Many saints' days and church holidays are widely celebrated. Only a small number of people belong to various Protestant churches. Austria has a sizable Muslim population. It once had a large Jewish population, but few Jews remained in Austria after their persecution during World War II (1939–45).

Education. School is compulsory for Austrian children between the ages of 6 and 14. All children must attend elementary school, or *Volksschule*, for four years. Students may then go on to several different kinds of secondary schools. A student wishing to prepare for college attends a *Gymnasium*. Trade and technical schools train students for non-academic careers. The University of Vienna, founded in 1365, is the oldest and best known of Austria's universities.

Dress. Austrians in the large cities wear modern clothing. But for holidays and special occasions, people sometimes

Life in Vienna, Austria's capital and largest city, is both colorful and elegant. ***Top left:*** Folk musicians provide outdoor entertainment. ***Above:*** Coffeehouses have been popular meeting places since coffee was first introduced in the 1600's. ***Left:*** The members of the famed Vienna Boys' Choir perform wearing their traditional sailor suits.

put on traditional local costumes. The women wear a dirndl, which is a colorful dress, with aprons and elaborately embroidered headdresses. Men and boys wear short leather pants, called lederhosen, and simple shirts and jackets made of homespun linen or a coarse woolen cloth called loden.

Holidays. Holidays are joyful occasions in Austria. A favorite holiday throughout the country is December 6, or Nikolo Day. This is the day when Nikolo, or Saint Nicholas (Santa Claus), visits Austrian children. The night before, children leave their shoes where Nikolo will find them. In the morning, children who have been good find presents in their shoes. But those who have been naughty find only potatoes and lumps of coal.

In January and February, just before the Roman Catholic period of Lent, Austrians enjoy the carnival season, known as *Fasching*. Elaborate costume balls are often part of the festivities, especially in the cities.

Sports and Recreation. Mountain climbing, swimming, waterskiing, and sailing are favorite summer sports. The cold, snowy winters are perfect for skiing and ice-skating. Skiing is so much a part of the Austrian way of life that schoolchildren take ski courses between February and April as part of their schoolwork.

Soccer is Austria's most popular spectator sport. Large cities have huge stadiums and regularly scheduled soccer games. Soccer players are great heroes to Austrian children. Even the smallest Austrian village has its own amateur soccer team.

Another favorite pastime of Austrians is a visit to a coffeehouse. There one can meet friends, chat, read the newspapers, and enjoy delicious coffee and pastries.

▶ LAND

Austria is wedged between eight other countries. Switzerland and tiny Liechtenstein lie to the west and Germany to the northwest. The Czech Republic and Slovakia are situated on the north, Hungary on the east, and Italy and Slovenia on the south.

Land Regions. Austria has five natural regions—the eastern Alps, the Alpine Foreland, the Granite Uplands, the Vienna Basin, and the Styrian Basin.

The Alps, which cover about two-thirds of the country, have three main divisions—the Northern Limestone Alps, the Central Alps, and the Southern Limestone Alps. The highest mountains are in the Central Alps. Many of these are covered by large glaciers. Austria's highest peak, the Grossglockner ("great bell"), is located there. Deep valleys lie between the main ranges.

The Alpine Foreland lies between the Alps and the Danube River in the provinces of Salzburg, Upper Austria, and Lower Austria. It is a region of fertile hills and valleys where cattle graze and vegetable crops are grown. The cities of Salzburg and Linz are both in this region.

Just north of the Danube River are the rolling, forest-covered hills of the Granite Uplands. They occupy the parts of the provinces of Lower Austria and Upper Austria that lie north of the Danube River.

The Vienna Basin, in eastern Austria, is the country's heartland. It contains all of Austria's best farmland and is also the center of Austrian industry. Vienna lies in the middle of the Vienna Basin.

FACTS and figures

REPUBLIC OF AUSTRIA (REPUBLIK ÖSTERREICH) is the official name of the country.

LOCATION: Central Europe.

AREA: 32,378 sq mi (83,858 km^2).

POPULATION: 8,200,000 (estimate).

CAPITAL AND LARGEST CITY: Vienna.

MAJOR LANGUAGE: German (official).

MAJOR RELIGIOUS GROUP: Christian (mainly Roman Catholic).

GOVERNMENT: Republic. **Head of state**—president. **Head of government**—chancellor. **Legislature**—Federal Assembly (composed of a National Council and a Federal Council).

CHIEF PRODUCTS: **Agricultural**—wheat, barley, and other grains; potatoes; sugar beets; livestock; dairy products. **Manufactured**—heavy machinery, transportation vehicles, processed foods, and chemicals. **Mineral**—magnesite, iron ore, graphite, lignite (brown coal), zinc, lead, petroleum, natural gas, bauxite, copper.

MONETARY UNIT: Euro (1 euro = 100 cents).

The Styrian Basin, in the province of Styria, is situated to the south of the Vienna Basin. It is quite fertile, with grain crops and fruit grown in its broad valleys.

Rivers. The Danube is Austria's most important river and one of Europe's major commercial waterways. Other important rivers are the Inn, Salzach, and Enns. All are tributaries (branches) of the Danube. Fed by melting glaciers in the Alps, they flow too swiftly for river traffic. But they are an important source of hydroelectric power, which provides much of Austria's energy. Hydroelectric power is also exported to neighboring countries.

Climate. Three of Europe's major climatic regions meet in Austria. Northern Austria has an Atlantic type of climate with mild, rainy winters and cool, moist summers. Southern Austria has a Mediterranean climate with hot, dry summers and mild, rainy winters. Eastern Austria has the hot summers and cold winters typical of the continental climate.

The mountains have their own characteristic climate, marked by heavy snowfall in winter. An unusual feature of the mountain climate is the foehn, a warm, dry wind that blows from the high mountains. The foehn "eats up" the snow from the ground. Farmers are delighted to see the snow disappear, for it means that they can soon drive their livestock up to the mountain pastures for the summer. But they also fear the destructive avalanches that sometimes hurtle down the mountainside when the melting snow becomes dislodged.

Natural Resources. Austria has a number of valuable mineral resources. It is the world's leading producer of magnesite, a component of heat-resistant materials, and an important producer of graphite. Most of Austria's iron ore comes from the Erzberg ("Ore Mountain") in Styria. Bauxite (aluminum ore), lignite (low-grade brown coal), copper, lead, and zinc are also mined. Austria has some petroleum and natural gas, but it still must import fuel.

ECONOMY

The Austrian economy is based chiefly on industry. Agriculture, although still important, plays a much smaller role economically than in the past.

Services. Austria's largest economic sector is made up of services. These include banking, insurance, wholesale and retail trade, government activities, and businesses related to tourism. Austria's spectacular ski resorts, scenic attractions, historic sites, and cultural events draw millions of visitors every year.

Manufacturing. Industry employs nearly 30 percent of the workforce. It provides a similar percentage of the country's gross national product (the total value of goods and services produced in a year). The leading manufactured goods include heavy machinery, transportation vehicles and parts, processed foods, chemicals, lumber, and paper products.

Agriculture and Forestry. Because Austria is so mountainous, only about 20 percent of its land can be cultivated. Nevertheless, Austrian farmers supply most of the country's food. Most of the suitable farming land is in the Alpine valleys. Wheat, barley, and other grains; potatoes; and sugar beets are the leading crops. Various fruits and vegetables are grown and some wine is produced. Cattle and sheep provide large quantities of meat, milk, butter, and cheese.

Austria's forests provide valuable lumber and the raw materials for a variety of wood products, including paper.

Trade. Austria has been a member of the European Union (EU) since 1995. Its primary trading partner is Germany, followed by Italy, the United States, and France. Its major exports include machinery and equipment, motor vehicles and parts, paper and paperboard, metal goods, chemicals, iron and steel, and textiles. Its major imports are oil and food.

MAJOR CITIES

The majority of Austrians are city-dwellers. About one-third of the people live in the five largest cities—Vienna, Graz, Linz, Salzburg, and Innsbruck.

Vienna is Austria's capital and largest city. Its location on the Danube River at the edge of the East European plain has made it an important city throughout history. See the separate article on Vienna in Volume UV.

Graz is Austria's second largest city and the capital of the province of Styria. A manufacturing center, it is also noted for its many parks and gardens. **Linz** is the capital and cultural heart of Upper Austria.

Salzburg, situated on the Salzach River, is considered one of the world's most beautiful cities. Its annual music festival attracts many visitors. **Innsbruck**, the capital of Tirol (or Tyrol), is probably best known for its ski resorts. It was the site of the 1964 and 1976 Winter Olympic Games.

CULTURAL HERITAGE

Austria and lands that were once part of the Austrian empire have produced many important figures in the world of music, literature, and art. Only a relatively few names can be cited here.

Music. Much of the world's great music was written by Austrians or by composers who made Austria their home.

The greatest period of Austrian music, from about 1730 to 1830, produced Joseph Haydn, Wolfgang Amadeus Mozart, Ludwig van Beethoven (who lived in Vienna most of his life), and Franz Schubert.

The two giants of music in the 1800's were Anton Bruckner and the German-born Johannes Brahms (who spent the last twenty years of his life in Vienna). The Strauss family, especially Johann, Jr., and Johann, Sr., made the Viennese waltz world famous. Gustav Mahler continued the great Viennese tradition into the early 1900's. Arnold

Austria's cultural heritage includes many great figures in music, literature, and art. Among the most notable are (*top row, from left*) composers Joseph Haydn, Wolfgang Amadeus Mozart (as a boy), and Franz Schubert; (*bottom row, from left*) authors Arthur Schnitzler and Franz Kafka; and the artist Oskar Kokoschka (in a self-portrait).

Schoenberg and Alban Berg were two of the leading modern composers.

Austria is also the birthplace of one of the most famous Christmas carols—"Silent Night" (*Stille Nacht*), written on Christmas Eve, 1818, by Franz Gruber and Joseph Mohr.

Three music festivals that are held in Austria each year attract thousands of music lovers from all over the world. The Vienna drama and music festival is held in June. The Salzburg festival, held in August, features the works of Mozart (who was born in Salzburg) and other composers. The Bregenz festival, also held in August, specializes in light opera.

For more information on music associated with Austria and Germany, see the article GERMANY, MUSIC OF in Volume G.

Art. The beginnings of the modern period of Austrian art are reflected in the paintings of Gustav Klimt. Klimt, who died in 1918, was a leader in the movement that led to expressionism. His work influenced two other important Austrian artists of the 1900's, Oskar Kokoschka and Egon Schiele.

Literature. In literature, Austrians have made important contributions to drama, poetry, the short story, and the novel. In the 1800's, the dramatist Franz Grillparzer combined the German classical tradition with Austrian and modern elements. Hugo von Hofmannsthal wrote plays and poems, as well as librettos for operas by the German composer Richard Strauss, in the late 1800's and early 1900's. At about the same time, Arthur Schnitzler was writing plays and stories on psychological themes.

The poet Rainer Maria Rilke and the short-story writer and novelist Franz Kafka are two of the greatest literary figures from this same period. Kafka (whose short life was spent in Prague, the capital of today's Czech Republic) wrote symbolic stories about the anxiety of modern life. Other important authors from the first half of the 1900's include novelists Robert Musil, Stefan Zweig, and Franz Werfel.

GOVERNMENT

Austria is a federal republic made up of nine provinces: Burgenland, Carinthia, Lower Austria, Upper Austria, Salzburg, Styria, Tirol, Vienna, and Vorarlberg. Each of the provinces has its own legislature and governor, with control over its local affairs.

The national legislature is the Federal Assembly, composed of the National Council and the Federal Council. Members of the

National Council are elected by the people to 4-year terms. The Federal Council, which has only limited powers, is elected by the provincial legislatures.

The president of Austria, who is elected for six years, is the head of state. The president appoints the chancellor (prime minister) to head the government. The chancellor and ministers of the government are usually members of the political party with the largest number of seats in the National Council, and they are responsible to that body.

HISTORY

The discovery of ancient burial grounds shows that Austria was inhabited in prehistoric times. The region was conquered by the Romans about 15 B.C. One of their settlements, Vindobona, eventually became the city of Vienna. With the collapse of the Roman Empire in the West in the A.D. 400's, the region fell to eastern invaders. Not until the time of Charlemagne's empire in the 700's was a stable government re-established.

In 976 the Holy Roman emperor Otto II gave part of Austria to Leopold of Babenberg. The Babenbergs ruled for 300 years. When the line died out, Austria passed to the kingdom of Bohemia (now part of the Czech Republic).

The Habsburg Dynasty Begins. In 1278, Rudolf of Habsburg (or Hapsburg), who was then Holy Roman emperor, defeated the Bohemian king Ottokar II at the Battle of Marchfeld. Rudolf acquired the Austrian lands, which he and his descendants were to govern continuously until 1918. During that time, Austria became the center of a vast Habsburg empire that often dominated the rest of Europe. The German princes elected a Habsburg to rule the Holy Roman Empire for all but five years between 1438 and 1806, when the empire came to an end.

The Habsburgs frequently sealed military alliances by offering their sons and daughters in marriage to the children of other rulers. The greatest matchmaker of all was Emperor Maximilian I. His marriage to Mary of Burgundy in 1477 eventually gave him control of the prosperous Low Countries (present-day Belgium, the Netherlands, and Luxembourg) and parts of northern France. Maximilian then arranged for his son Philip to marry Juana (Joanna the Mad), heiress to the Spanish thrones of Castile and Aragon.

In 1516, Philip's son, Charles of Ghent, inherited the throne of Spain as King Charles I. When Charles's grandfather Maximilian died in 1519, he became emperor, as Charles V, as well. Charles ruled over more territory than any previous European monarch.

Rulers of Two Empires. Charles's empire was so vast that he gave Austria to his younger brother Ferdinand in 1522. Through his marriage to Anne of Hungary and Bohemia, Ferdinand was chosen ruler of both these kingdoms in 1526. The House of Austria now governed two empires. Through Charles V, the Spanish branch ruled Spain, the Low Countries, much of Italy, and Spain's American colonies. At the same time, the Austrian branch headed by Ferdinand ruled in Austria, Hungary, Germany, Bohemia, Moravia, Silesia, Croatia, Slovenia, half of Romania, and parts of northern Italy.

The Habsburgs' empire soon came under attack from two directions. From the east the Ottoman Turks conquered most of Hungary, which they held until the end of the 1600's. To the west other European rulers attacked Austria and Spain because they feared that the Habsburgs had grown too powerful. Most notable of the conflicts was the Thirty Years' War, which began in 1618 and involved most of Europe before ending in 1648. Although

The Habsburg family ruled Austria for some 600 years. This painting from the early 1500's shows the Holy Roman emperor Maximilian I (left) with his wife, Mary of Burgundy (right), their son Philip (next to Mary), and their grandson, the future Charles V (center).

The Pragmatic Sanction, which allowed a woman, Maria Theresa, to inherit the throne, led to the War of the Austrian Succession (1740–48).

defeated in the Thirty Years' War, Austria was able to win back Hungary from the Turks. See the article on the Thirty Years' War in Volume T.

In 1701 the Habsburgs were at war again. The last Spanish Habsburg, Charles II, had died the previous year, and Louis XIV of France claimed the vacant throne for his grandson Philip of Anjou. England and the Netherlands joined Austria and the Holy Roman Empire against France in the so-called War of the Spanish Succession. The war ended in compromise in 1714. Louis' grandson Philip got Spain and its American colonies. Austria received what was left of the Spanish Netherlands (today's Belgium and Luxembourg) as well as most of Spain's possessions in Italy.

The War of the Austrian Succession. Yet another war of succession broke out in 1740, when Emperor Charles VI died without male heirs. Normally, women could not inherit the throne. But before he died, Charles VI had issued a will, called the Pragmatic Sanction, that left his entire empire to his eldest daughter, Maria Theresa. Immediately after Charles's death, several foreign rulers tried to seize Maria Theresa's inheritance, in what became known as the War of the Austrian Succession. After eight years of war she lost the wealthy province of Silesia to Prussia but held on to the rest of her empire.

Maria Theresa strengthened the power of Austria's ruler against the country's powerful nobles and church leaders. She also continued the Habsburg policy of making political marriages. She ended nearly three centuries of hostility between France and Austria by marrying her daughter Marie Antoinette to the future king of France, Louis XVI. Unpopular in France, Marie Antoinette was later executed during the French Revolution. See the biography of Marie Antoinette in Volume M.

Maria Theresa's son, Joseph II, helped his mother rule. After her death in 1780, he became sole ruler. Among his many reforms, Joseph freed the serfs, who had been bound by law to the land they tilled, and drastically reduced the power of the nobles and the church. His Edict of Tolerance granted religious freedom to Protestants and Jews in the Austrian lands.

Metternich and the Congress of Vienna. The outbreak of the French Revolution in 1789 renewed Austria's age-old rivalry with France. The victories by the French general Napoleon brought about many changes, including the destruction, in 1806, of the Holy Roman Empire that Austria had controlled for so long. To save Austria itself, the new emperor, Francis II (who had come to the throne in 1792), gave his daughter, Archduchess Marie-Louise, to Napoleon in marriage in 1810.

The clever policies of Austria's chief minister, Prince Klemens von Metternich, contributed to the final defeat of Napoleon and France in 1814. In that year, Metternich invited the other European rulers to meet in Vienna. At this Congress of Vienna, many of the borders Napoleon had redrawn and monarchs he had overthrown were restored.

For more than thirty years, Metternich used repressive measures in an effort to protect Europe's rulers from the growing forces of liberalism and nationalism. But it was impossible to ignore the increasing feelings of nationalism among the Austrian empire's many different peoples.

The Revolution of 1848 and the Dual Monarchy. In 1848 a revolution erupted, which was put down only after much bloodshed. Metternich was dismissed, and Emperor Ferdinand, who had come to the throne in 1835, abdicated in favor of his 18-year-old nephew, Francis Joseph.

Francis Joseph was forced to agree to several constitutional reforms. The most lasting was the Great Compromise of 1867, which gave Hungary equal status with Austria in the new Dual Monarchy of Austria-Hungary.

Tensions remained, however, between the various ethnic groups, especially the Czechs and Germans of Bohemia. In addition, neigh-

The empire of Austria-Hungary reached its peak in 1914, just before the outbreak of World War I. The empire collapsed in 1918, with Austria-Hungary's defeat.

boring countries desired those parts of the empire that contained peoples who spoke their language.

In 1914 a Serb nationalist assassinated the heir to the imperial throne, Archduke Francis Ferdinand. The event led to the outbreak of World War I (1914–18), in which Austria-Hungary and its allies were defeated.

The aged Francis Joseph died in 1916, after a reign of 68 years. His successor, Charles I, the last emperor, was compelled to accept the breakup of the empire in October 1918. Peace terms divided Austria and Hungary into two much smaller republics. Most of their former territory went into the creation of two new nations (Czechoslovakia and Yugoslavia) and part of a re-established Poland. Italy received much of the Austrian Tirol, while Romania acquired Transylvania from Hungary.

The Republic of Austria. With the loss of its empire, the young Austrian republic faced severe economic difficulties. Economic problems led to political strife. Most Austrians favored *Anschluss*, or union, with Germany, although this had been forbidden by the peace treaties. In 1938, Nazi Germany's dictator Adolf Hitler sent in troops to take over Austria, which then became the German state of Ostmark. Thus Austria was part of Germany during World War II.

When the war ended in 1945, the Republic of Austria was restored. But the country and its capital were divided into American, British, French, and Soviet zones of occupation. The occupation forces left Austria in 1955, after it signed a treaty agreeing to a policy of permanent neutrality.

In 1986, Kurt Waldheim, a former secretary-general of the United Nations, was elected president. Thomas Klestil succeeded him in 1992 and was re-elected in 1998.

Recent Events. For many years, Austrian government officials pressed for membership in the European Union (EU). However, many Austrians were reluctant to abandon the country's neutral position or to sacrifice their separate identity, distinct from their German neighbors. But on January 1, 1995, Austria joined the EU, along with Finland and Sweden. In 2002, Austria was one of eleven EU members that formally adopted a common currency known as the euro.

In February 2000, the EU imposed sanctions against Austria for accepting the Freedom Party, a right-wing group known for its Nazi sympathies, into its coalition government. Sanctions were lifted that September, and Austria was fully reinstated into the EU.

President Klestil died on July 6, 2004, two days before his term ended. He was succeeded by Heinz Fischer, who had won the presidential election in April.

GEORGE W. HOFFMAN
Author, *Austria*

CHARLES W. INGRAO
Author, *The Habsburg Monarchy, 1618–1815*

See also HABSBURGS; HOLY ROMAN EMPIRE.

AUTISM

The word "autism" comes from the Greek word for "self." The syndrome of autism was first described in 1943 by Dr. Leo Kanner. He studied eleven children who had unusual behaviors and interests and seemed unable to relate to people and situations in the ordinary way.

One of the children Dr. Kanner wrote about was a 6-year-old named Frederick. Frederick's mother said he was not good at playing with other children and did not play with the usual childhood toys. He was terrified of machines such as elevators and vacuum cleaners, and he did not like change or to try new things.

Most of the time, Frederick ignored the people around him—even his grandparents. He spoke a few words before the age of 2 but after that would seldom speak. When he did speak, he would often mix up his personal pronouns. For example, when receiving a gift he would say, "You say thank you."

Diagnosis of Autism and Related Conditions. Autism is now recognized as a group of conditions with similar behavioral characteristics. These conditions may be referred to as **autism spectrum conditions** or **pervasive developmental disorders**. There are five conditions that are formally grouped as pervasive developmental disorders: Autism, Asperger's Disorder, Childhood Disintegrative Disorder, Rett Syndrome, and Pervasive Developmental Disorder-Not Otherwise Specified.

As was the case with Frederick, children with autism have symptoms that can be grouped into three categories: problems with language and communication, problems with social interaction, and unusual interests and behaviors. Examples of difficulty with language include delays speaking in sentences and confusion of pronouns such as "me" and "I." Children with autism may make up their own words for things, repeat the same words over and over again, and say words at unusual times. Nonverbal communication, such as shaking the head to mean "no" or pointing out objects to others, is frequently absent.

Even though they might want to have friends and play with others, children with autism have a difficult time doing so. They may avoid physical contact and appear to ignore those around them. Some scientists think that people with autism cannot put themselves in another person's position. The unusual interests and behaviors of people with autism might include a fascination with simple items such as string, traffic lights, or license plates. Or they may enjoy the way it feels when they twirl around and so repeat this action again and again.

Asperger's disorder takes its name from Dr. Hans Asperger, who, like Dr. Kanner, wrote about children whose behaviors were unusual. Like people with autism, children with Asperger's disorder have unusual preoccupations and interests and have trouble understanding how their behavior is viewed by others. However, children with Asperger's disorder do not have early language problems and may learn to talk and read very early.

Childhood Disintegrative Disorder is characterized by the same symptoms as autism. However, with this disorder children seem to develop normally until about 2 years of age. Then they begin to lose many of the skills that had developed up to that time and typically stop talking and playing normally as autistic behaviors appear.

Rett syndrome usually occurs in girls. The disorder was named for Dr. Andreas Rett, who described a group of girls who developed normally in early childhood but then lost all of their acquired skills, including the use of their hands. The cause of Rett syndrome is now known to be an abnormal gene on the X chromosome.

In addition to the disorders described above, there are many children who have some symptoms in common with autism but who do not have all of the symptoms necessary to diagnose it. In these cases, the diagnosis of **Pervasive Developmental Disorder-Not Otherwise Specified** is often made. This means that the person has an autism spectrum disorder but the condition is different in some way from the other disorders described above.

How Common Is Autism? Autism is probably more common than was once believed. Early studies suggested that five children out of 10,000 had the disorder. More recently, perhaps because of a better recognition of milder cases, it is thought that as many as two out of every 1,000 children have a pervasive developmental disorder. Boys are four to five times more likely than girls to have a pervasive developmental disorder. Rett syndrome is the exception, occurring in about one in 10,000 to one in 15,000 female children.

Causes and Treatment. Scientists believe that genes may be partially responsible for autism because the disorder can run in families. In the case of identical twins, if one has autism, the other is likely to have it 50 percent of the time. Because the likelihood is not 100 percent, it indicates environmental factors may also play a role. Autism is also commonly associated with other neurological conditions, such as mental retardation and epilepsy.

There are no specific cures for autism. Early and intensive behavioral therapy seems to be helpful, and different strategies are used. At school it is not uncommon for children with autism to have special aides to help them with tasks that are especially challenging. Therapists who help with speech and language, behavior, and physical skills may all be involved in a child's treatment team. In some situations, medication can also be helpful. There is hope that as scientists learn more about the causes of autism, they will continue to find better treatments.

People with Autism Have Strengths. Although people with autism have problems with language and social skills in common, it is important to remember that every person with autism is unique. It makes no more sense to say that all tall people are alike than it does to suggest the same for people with autism. Some children with autism are talented artists, some are amazing mathematicians, and some have exceptional memory. Like everyone, people with autism are sons, daughters, brothers, sisters, neighbors, and friends.

BRYAN H. KING M.D.
Dartmouth Medical School

AUTOBIOGRAPHY. See BIOGRAPHY, AUTOBIOGRAPHY, AND BIOGRAPHICAL NOVEL.

AUTOGRAPHS

Asking your friends to write in an autograph album may start you on a hobby that will last the rest of your life. Though popularly thought of as a signature, an autograph is any handwritten document. The word comes from the Greek word *autographos*, meaning "self-written."

People have been collecting autographs since ancient times. The ancient Romans prized the letters of Vergil and Caesar. In medieval and Renaissance Europe, students collected messages from friends and prominent persons in pocket-sized albums called *alba amicorum*. Today, fans collect the signatures of their favorite sports stars, performers, and authors, while serious collectors spend enormous sums to add letters and historical documents to their collections.

The most popular collection in the United States is a set of the presidents' autographs. These can be either simple signatures cut from documents or letters handwritten and dated while the president was in office. In other countries there is a similar interest in autographs of heads of state. It is not always easy to obtain an authentic presidential signature. Many presidents have used "proxy signers"—persons who have learned to imitate the signatures of other persons. And today mechanical devices make it possible to sign thousands of letters automatically, reducing the number of original signatures.

Another desirable collection is a set of autographs of the signers of the U.S. Declaration of Independence. But this set is difficult to complete: Because of their early deaths, the signatures of two signers, Button Gwinnett of Georgia and Thomas Lynch, Jr., of South Carolina, are extremely rare.

Authors' original manuscripts are also prized. Today many writers donate their col-

Did you know that...

one of the rarest autographs is that of William Shakespeare? Only six authentic ones are known to exist. If another authentic signature were to turn up, it would sell for at least $5 million!

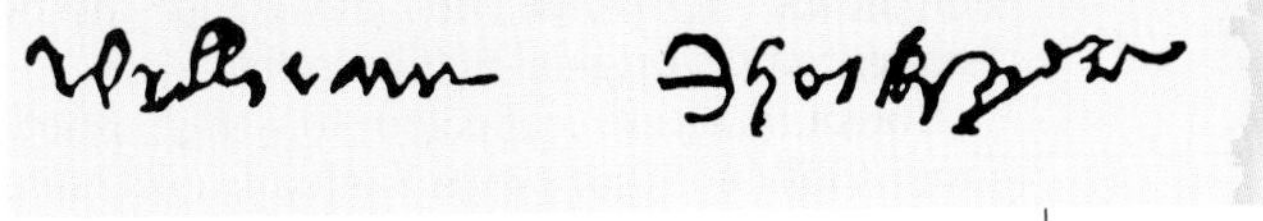

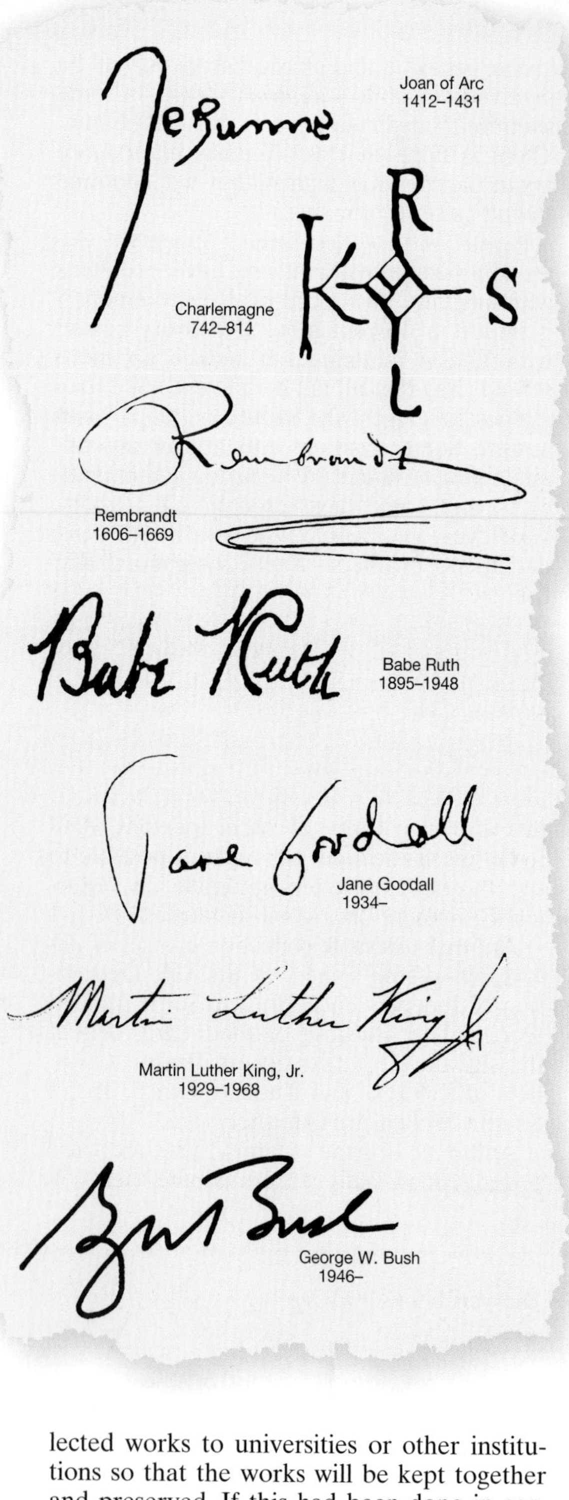

lected works to universities or other institutions so that the works will be kept together and preserved. If this had been done in earlier times, we would not have lost all of Shakespeare's original manuscripts.

Books that are collected for their autographs fall into four types. Signed books have only the author's signature in them. Inscribed books contain an inscription from the book's author to its owner. A presentation book is one the author presents to someone, writing in it to show it is a gift. The fourth type is quite different. It is valued for its association with something or someone that interests the collector. Usually it is a book that has belonged to a famous woman or man and has a signature or inscription inside to prove it.

Letters fall into two categories. A typewritten letter signed by its author is collectible. But letters both written and signed by their authors in longhand are more valuable. Of course, the contents of a letter also have a great deal to do with its value. Even the correspondence and diaries of ordinary people can be valuable if they shed light on a historic event or period. For example, a soldier's letter describing his experiences during the Civil War may add much to our knowledge of that conflict.

Rather than purchase historical documents, many collectors prefer to solicit signatures and letters from living celebrities in person or by mail. If you write to famous persons for their signatures, be sure to enclose stamped, self-addressed envelopes for the replies. Signatures are collectible, but letters are more interesting and usually more valuable. It is often a good idea to ask your correspondent a thought-provoking question.

Condition is a major factor in determining the value of an autograph. In caring for your collection, it is wise to follow a few simple rules: Never attempt to make repairs yourself. Do not fold your documents, and remove any paper clips and staples. Avoid exposing your autographs to direct light; do not frame valuable items. Store your collection in a cool, dry place in special acid-free folders and boxes.

Whatever type of collection you have, you will find many other enthusiastic collectors who will trade with you. Dealers will help you buy and sell autographs and check whether an autograph is authentic. Dealer and hobbyists' Websites provide useful information on available autographs, current prices, and sources for archival storage materials. Many museums and libraries have excellent autograph collections on display.

Reviewed by Charles Hamilton
Author, *Collecting Autographs and Manuscripts*

AUTOMATION

Without automation our world would be a very different place. Each part of every product we use would have to be made by hand; therefore, we would have fewer products and they would cost more. Our selection at the supermarket would be limited because food items would need to be planted, harvested, and packaged by hand. Our daily tasks would take more time. For example, every dirty shirt, sock, and towel would have to be washed by hand. And we would have to talk to an operator every time we placed a telephone call.

WHAT IS AUTOMATION?

The term "automation" refers to machinery or equipment that operates with little or no human control. Automation is possible whenever a process can be broken down into simple, repetitive procedures. Generally, automation is used to perform tasks that would be dangerous, boring, or unpleasant for humans to do. Any job that requires human effort or time, but little conscious thought, is a good candidate for automation.

Automation is different from other mechanized processes because it can operate without human intervention. The equipment must be designed, set up, and programmed by humans, but it is then able to run independently to accomplish the desired task. In order to do this it must be designed to have certain capabilities, such as the ability to adjust to feedback, coordinate movements, sequence actions, and make decisions.

Adjustment to Feedback

An important characteristic of automated equipment is the ability to self-adjust in response to **feedback**. A good example of a self-adjusting automated system is a home heating system controlled by a thermostat. A person sets the desired temperature on the thermostat. If the temperature in the house falls below the set temperature, the thermostat senses this and automatically turns on the furnace. When the temperature in the house reaches the set temperature, the furnace is automatically turned off. Through the process of feedback, a nearly constant temperature is maintained inside the house.

More complicated examples of feedback in automation can be found in paper mills or chemical processing plants. In these factories, computers monitor different variables, such as the temperature of ovens or the speed of conveyor belts. When necessary, the computers signal the processing equipment to make adjustments so that these variables are maintained within a desired range.

A home heating system is a simple example of self-adjusting automation. It keeps the temperature in a room at the same level as the setting on a thermostat in the room. The breaker arm of the thermostat reacts to changes in the room's temperature. As the temperature gets cooler or warmer than the setting, the breaker arm closes or opens a switch that turns the furnace on or off—to make the room warmer or to let it cool down.

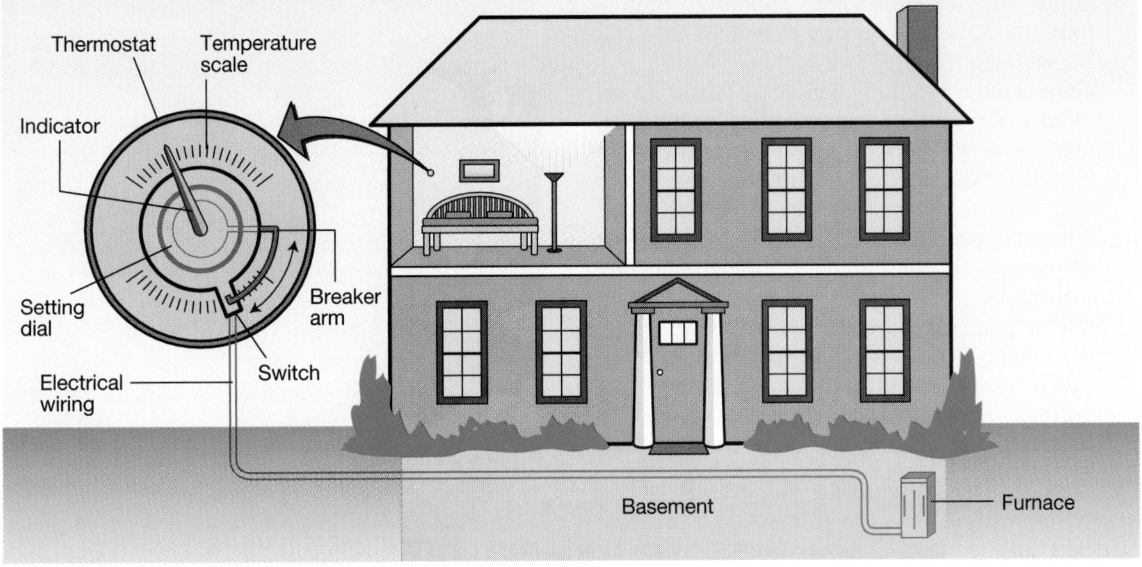

In some factories, such as this cannery, products move from start to finish along an assembly line, and no human assistance is necessary.

Coordination of Movements

Another important property of automated equipment is self-coordination. A machine that is self-coordinated can perform several different actions at the same time. Some delicatessen meat slicers are self-coordinated. The deli worker places a large piece of meat into the carriage of the slicer, selects the slice thickness by adjusting the distance from the carriage to the slicing blade, and turns the slicer on. The slicer then coordinates three motions. The blade that will cut the meat is spun, the meat is pushed into the blade by the carriage, and the carriage automatically moves back and forth across the blade. Each pass across the blade yields a uniform slice of meat without any effort from the worker.

Sequencing of Actions

Automated equipment that is self-sequencing can execute several different actions one after another in a correct order. Some of the electronic animated figures found at amusement park attractions are run by self-sequencing automation. An **audio-animatronic** figure of a man that moves its mouth, face, hands, and body in a synchronized way with a sound track appears to be singing and dancing along with the music each time the sound track is played. The animatronic man is able to act out a scene for an amusement attraction many times each day without becoming tired or hoarse, as a human might.

In some factories, self-sequencing automation is used to ensure the correct assembly of products. Automated conveyor belts or trolley cars transport products from one work site to the next. At each work site, another step toward finishing the product is carried out. For the product to be assembled correctly, the work sites must be visited in the proper order. Some semiconductor processing factories operate in this manner to produce integrated circuits for electronics products.

Decision-Based Automation

Automation that is decision-based can choose its next action based upon the outcome of a decision. The decision that the equipment makes may be conditional, requiring only if-then decisions. Or it may be more complex and involve artificial learning or artificial intelligence. (Artificial intelligence is software that tries to simulate certain aspects of human intelligence. For more information see the article COMPUTERS in Volume C.) Coin sorters found in banks use if-then decision making. The bank teller places unsorted coins into a bin and turns on the machine. The conditional logic the machine uses is simple: If the coin is the size of a dime, then it is dropped into the dime container; if it is the size of a penny, it is dropped into the penny container, and so forth.

ROBOT SYSTEMS

Robots are a sophisticated and versatile type of automation. While most automated equipment is designed for one specific task, robots can be set up and programmed to perform several different jobs and to change

Audio-animatronic figures, such as this life-size Furby, sometimes attract large audiences who are fascinated by their lifelike movements.

Robot arms, each programmed to perform a precise sequence of tasks, work tirelessly on an automobile assembly line.

their own operation in response to the working environment. Some of today's automated factories use robots that have all the characteristics of automation listed above.

Consider a robot that removes parts from a conveyor belt and assembles them into a product. The robot has mechanical devices, called **actuators**, that control its movements. Each actuator self-adjusts to reach a programmed position. The robot has a control computer that coordinates the movements of each actuator. The motions of the robot are also self-sequenced so that each part is picked up from the conveyor belt in the proper order and placed in the correct location to assemble the product.

Robots use decision-based action to handle unexpected conditions. For example, if the robot reaches for a part but does not obtain one, it automatically makes a decision about how to continue based upon its program. It may be programmed to try to grasp the part again, to reach in an alternative location for the part, or to stop and notify the operator that something has gone wrong.

Further, the robot may be programmed with the ability to assemble several different types of products. If so, it would have an internal computer listing the components needed for each different type. The robot would consult its computer before assembling each product to determine the proper parts to use and their locations. For more information about how robots work, see the article ROBOTS in Volume R.

AUTOMATION TODAY

Automation has been developed for almost every aspect of our daily lives. Factory automation frees laborers from dangerous or repetitive work. Automation within the home saves hours of undesirable chores. Automation within our communications systems allows fast and limitless connections to people around the world. Automation in the farming industry enables a few workers to grow enough food to feed thousands of people. And automation within our transportation system permits the organized and safe transport of millions of passengers each day.

Industrial Automation

There are many examples of automation used in industry. Some factories use automation for a single process. In others, production lines are fully automated from start to finish. The automobile industry was one of the first to use automation on a large scale. A robot with a welding tool can be set up to automatically weld a set of joints in an automobile assembly line. Another robot carrying a spray painting gun can be set up to smoothly proceed through a set of motions so that a car body is evenly painted.

Other manufacturers use automation as well. Automated steel-working plants start with a large block of hot metal and squeeze it through rollers to make sheets of specified thicknesses. In automated glass-making plants, molten glass moves from huge vats to machines that mold it into everything from candy dishes to ornamental vases. Some factories for other industries, such as oil refining, chemical production, and prescription drug manufacture, are also automated.

Business Automation

Nearly every aspect of business today is affected by the use of computer-based automation for the storage, arrangement, and retrieval of information. Banking is one area that has changed dramatically in recent years. Account information at banks is automated using computers and special-purpose software applications. Because of automation, people no longer have to go to the bank teller to receive money. Instead, automatic teller machines (ATM's) allow people to make financial transactions, including deposits and withdrawals, at any time. The information is sent to a computer, which automatically updates the banking records.

Retail stores use automation to maintain their inventories. Each store item is labeled with a bar code. Automated checkout devices equipped with laser scanners read the bar codes to determine the identity and price of each item. A computer keeps track of how many units of an item are sold and subtracts them from the number last ordered. The store manager is then able to determine which items need to be reordered.

Libraries use similar bar codes to keep track of books. With the touch of a keyboard, a librarian can determine if a book is checked out, by whom, and when it is due.

Home Automation

There are many devices in our own homes that save time by automating everyday tasks. For example, dishwashers automatically wash and dry large numbers of dishes, and clothes washers automatically run through the appropriate wash cycles to get clothes clean. Answering machines automatically answer the telephone, play greetings, and record messages so that we can receive calls even when we are not at home. Coffee makers can be programmed to have hot coffee waiting when we wake up in the morning. Even a loaf of bread can be kneaded and baked automatically using an automated bread maker. While these machines are doing their jobs, we can spend our time doing something else.

Other Automation

Many other examples of automation can be found that do not fit within the categories listed above. We encounter automation when we travel. For example, traffic lights keep vehicles flowing smoothly on the roadways. Some toll roads have automated tollbooths that allow a driver to simply pull up and deposit coins. When the proper amount of toll has been paid, the machine will raise a gate and permit the car to pass. The speed of certain cars can be automatically maintained using cruise control.

People traveling longer distances may encounter other types of automation. There are automated systems for transporting and routing luggage throughout an airport. Airplanes have autopilots that can control the plane during periods of uneventful flying. Even in space travel, automation is heavily relied upon due to the danger and expense of having astronauts perform certain tasks.

The handling of mail by the United States Postal Service is also highly automated at cer-

Laser scanning devices linked to computers read bar codes on products and automatically record the price and update the store inventory.

Many household tasks are now automated. Dishwashers automatically move through cycles to wash, rinse, and dry many dishes at the same time.

tain locations. Optical scanning devices read ZIP codes and print a bar code on each envelope. Then mechanical shuttling tracks read the bar codes and route letters so that those going to the same destination are grouped.

Today engineers and architects benefit from the use of automated drawing software called computer-aided design (CAD). There are even printer-like machines, which will produce a functional three-dimensional prototype of a designed part from a CAD file.

EARLY AUTOMATION

Early forms of automation were technologies developed by inventors to solve specific problems. The automated loom was invented in 1801 by a French weaver named Joseph-Marie Jacquard. His loom could automatically make cloth with complicated woven patterns. It was controlled by cards with holes punched in them. As each card moved through the machine, it adjusted the loom to weave part of the pattern. Another advance came when the sewing machine was developed in the mid-1800's to avoid the time-consuming task of sewing cloth by hand.

Near the end of the 1800's, an automated tally machine helped total the results of the United States census. The director of the Bureau of the Census devised a system for handling this huge and complicated task using an automated machine and punched cards. The holes on each card were arranged in a pattern that stored the information gathered by the census takers. For instance, a man's age, the city where he lived, and the number and ages of his children might all be recorded by holes punched in particular positions on the card. These cards were then fed into the automated machine that tallied the data and gave the Census Bureau correct totals.

Computers can be seen as a method of automated computation. The first computer was developed by scientists during World War II. The machine, called the Electronic Numerical Integrator and Calculator (ENIAC), filled an entire room. It was designed to solve problems related to the effective use of weapons. Today we can buy an inexpensive calculator that fits in a pocket and is more powerful than the ENIAC.

HOW AUTOMATION AFFECTS OUR LIVES

Automation is progressing rapidly. Perhaps the most noticeable effect that automation has on our lives is through its impact on manufacturing. Automated factories can manufacture products faster, and with higher quality than is otherwise possible. Because machines operate quickly and do not get tired or bored, we can mass-produce products in high volumes. And because the costs of parts and materials are lower when higher volumes are purchased, the products themselves can be made and sold at lower prices than would be possible if only small volumes were made.

In this scenario, everyone can benefit. The owners of the factories can benefit from the profits they are able to make. The consumer also benefits from the availability of quality products at low cost. In the short term, automating a particular task may mean that some workers become unemployed. However, in the longer term, the lives of those workers can benefit by their transfer to jobs that may be less tedious, strenuous, or hazardous and more enjoyable and rewarding.

PATRICK F. MUIR
Carnegie Mellon University

See also COMPUTERS; MANUFACTURING; ROBOTS; TECHNOLOGY; UNEMPLOYMENT AND UNEMPLOYMENT INSURANCE.

AUTOMOBILE MODELS

How would you like to own a large fleet of motor vehicles—everything from luxury cars and racing cars to trucks and vans, from station wagons and buses to four-wheel drive jeeps? You might even have vehicles representing different periods in automotive history. Owning such a fleet is possible—in miniature—for those who build and collect automobile models.

▶HOBBY WITH A HISTORY

People began collecting toy cars shortly after the first cast-metal models were made in the early 1900's. The first model-car building kits did not appear until the 1930's, and they were only blocks of wood with wheels. Plastic model kits appeared after World War II. During the 1950's and 1960's, automobile dealers offered assembled plastic models of new full-size cars. These models are rare, and they have become valuable collector's items.

The first model automobiles with internal-combustion engines were available in the 1930's. These models burned fuel to produce power. They were guided by rollers along elevated rails on a wood or concrete track. Some were guided by control lines like those used on model airplanes.

Model cars with electric motors did not become widely available until the 1950's. At first these cars were guided by rails. But by 1960 most were guided by a system using a slot, or narrow opening, in the track. A slotless system, in which cars are guided by a curb or wall, appeared in the early 1970's. Radio control was being used in model cars with fuel-burning engines by 1965. By about 1975 a combination of rechargeable batteries and an electric motor controlled by radio signal was perfected.

▶TYPES OF MODELS

Automobile models are the most popular type of hobby miniature. There are models of every imaginable type of vehicle. Most models are available ready-made in metal or in plastic or as plastic kits to be put together. There are also powered racing models that duplicate both the action and the appearance of full-size automobiles.

The size of a model as compared to the size of the real vehicle is called its **scale**. The scale is expressed as a proportion (such as 1:43) or as a fraction (such as $\frac{1}{43}$). The larger the proportion or fraction, the larger the model. A $\frac{1}{43}$ scale model automobile is about the size of a credit card; a $\frac{1}{8}$ scale model is about the size of a briefcase. The smallest size, $\frac{1}{87}$ scale, is known as HO scale.

Collector's Cars

Unpowered, ready-made model cars are by far the most popular. These vehicles can range from tiny plastic cars costing a couple of dollars to all-metal desk-size models costing hundreds or thousands of dollars. The most popular collector's cars are metal models with some plastic details, in $\frac{1}{43}$ scale.

Most plastic model kits must be glued together and painted. But kits with simple snap-together construction are also available. Both types of kits include full interior, engine, and chassis details, such as windshield wipers, chrome trim, and hoods and doors that open and close. The most common scale for American model kits is $\frac{1}{25}$, but there are hundreds of kits available in sizes ranging from $\frac{1}{87}$ to $\frac{1}{8}$ scale.

Racing Cars

The two main types of model racing cars are tabletop racers, which run on special tracks, and radio-controlled models, which are usually raced outdoors.

Tabletop Racers. Racing slot and slotless model cars requires almost as much "driving" skill as racing full-size automobiles. Slot cars must stay in a narrow slot to get the electric power needed to move them. The cars must be carefully guided through turns so they do not spin out of their slots.

This $\frac{1}{16}$ scale 1957 Chevrolet has working doors.

Left: A 1/12 scale electric-powered radio-controlled racing car. **Right:** If carefully guided, electric slot racers can zoom around a curved track at terrific speeds.

Slot cars are run by an electric-powered motor, which turns gears that drive the rear axle. Metal strips on each side of the slot carry the electric power. When these strips make contact with the metal pickup strips on the bottom of the car, which are called shoes, electricity is transferred from the track to the car motor. A hand-held control is used to change the car's speed.

Slotless cars are also powered by electricity but it is supplied by batteries carried inside the cars. These cars can be run on the floor or on the ground in straight-line races. When they are used on an oval or wiggly track, however, walls are used to guide the cars. Such tracks are really troughs that force the cars to steer when they push against the walls. Usually, each car has its own trough or lane and the race continues until the batteries run down or the cars are picked up by hand and turned off. There is no remote control with these simple electric racing cars.

Radio-Controlled Racers. In radio-controlled cars, a hand-held transmitter sends radio signals to a receiver in the car. These signals control the car's speed and direction. Most radio-controlled cars are powered by battery-operated electric motors. But some are powered by internal-combustion engines fueled by gasoline.

The most popular size for radio-controlled model cars is 1/12 scale. Some of these models can exceed speeds of about 30 miles (50 kilometers) an hour. The radio-controlled cars respond quickly to any movement of the transmitter levers. With practice, the "driver" can duplicate all the maneuvers of a real racing car.

More expensive radio-controlled cars have powerful transmitters and receivers that use different radio frequencies. This allows several cars to be raced at one time. In the United States, people using these larger transmitters must obtain special permits from the Federal Communications Commission.

Both electric- and gasoline-powered radio-controlled cars can be raced outdoors. Paved parking lots and school yards are ideal places. Some cities even have special tracks. Electric-powered cars can be raced indoors, but they need a very large area. Radio-controlled dune buggies an other off-road vehicles are raced outside in the dirt.

ROBERT SCHLEICHER
Author, *Model Car Racing: Tabletop & Radio-Control*

Left: **The start of the Indianapolis 500. Cars begin the race in eleven rows of three. The starting positions are determined in time trials that take place during the days just before the race.**

Below: **Formula One cars roar through the curving streets of Monaco during a Grand Prix race.**

AUTOMOBILE RACING

When automobile racing began in the 1890's, the speeds were like those of a fast horse and buggy. The first major race, held in 1895, was from Paris to Bordeaux, France, and back. The winner averaged only 15 miles (24 kilometers) an hour. But the speeds of racing automobiles increased every year. By the 1960's, the racing automobile was nearly as fast as some kinds of airplanes.

Automobile racing includes events and classes for almost every kind of four-wheeled vehicle. The racing rules and formulas are established so that the vehicles in each class perform as much like the others as possible.

Racing takes place on many kinds of tracks. There are oval tracks, drag strips, and twisting tracks built around oval tracks. There are also cross-country races on public roads or on dirt and sand. If a car is designed for one type of track, it can sometimes be raced on other tracks if minor changes are made to the car.

The emphasis in automobile racing has shifted away from pure speed. Race car designers now concentrate on improving the cornering speeds, braking, and fuel economy of their machines. Top speeds on a straight course have not increased much since the 1960's. But racing cars are getting around the tracks faster. This is because of improvements in tires, design, brakes, and aerodynamics (the study of the way in which air affects moving objects). It can be said, then, that winners of races are determined by the abilities of the drivers, the car designers, and the mechanics.

Modern racing cars have been made safer with stout metal frame bars, nonexploding fuel tanks, and built-in fire extinguishers. Race courses are now usually lined with safety barriers to help stop cars that go out of control. Safety helmets and fireproof driving suits provide more protection for the driver. But racing is still a dangerous sport, and the driver must be highly skilled.

GRAND PRIX RACING

Grand Prix racing and sports-car racing are the only forms of automobile racing that are popular worldwide. The Grand Prix cars are meant to be the best road-racing machines. The top Grand Prix class is Formula One. It has this name because the cars must be built according to a set formula. The overall winner of Grand Prix Formula One races is really the "world champion" because many countries compete only in this type of racing.

The Grand Prix cars look and perform much like the cars that race in the famous Indianapolis 500. But they have smaller engines, better brakes, and more cornering speed. They have only one seat, are low to the ground, and have no fenders. In the past, Grand Prix races were held on public roads. Today many places, including Monaco; Long Beach, California; and Miami, Florida, use downtown streets for open-wheel race car events. All other races are held on tracks. Whether on public-road courses or on racetracks, Grand Prix races are about 150 to 250 miles (240 to 400 kilometers) long.

SPORTS-CAR RACING

No other mass-produced vehicle is as fast as a sports car over winding and twisting roads. Racecourses that imitate such conditions are called road racetracks. These tracks are used for both production and prototype classes of sports-car racing. The production cars are regular sports cars. They are rebuilt for more reliability. But the parts are all regular parts. Only a roll bar and an open exhaust system are allowed as modifications of the cars that the public can buy. The prototype sports cars are built almost exactly like Grand Prix cars. They have a special body and engine not found in sports cars for sale to the public.

There are several sports-car classes, which are based on engine size. Sports-car races range from 30-minute regional races to international endurance events like the 12-hour racing at Sebring, Florida, and the 24-hour race at Daytona, Florida.

SPEEDWAY RACING

The most common type of speedway track is oval and measures about 1 mile (1.6 kilometers) around. Many classes of cars—such as Midgets, Sprint cars, Quarter Midgets, and Indianapolis-500-style "Championship" cars—race on these tracks. All but the "Championship" cars often compete in regional or local racing series that use both paved and dirt tracks.

The "Championship" cars have a single-seat cockpit, a powerful engine in the rear, and no fenders. Throughout the year, "Championship" cars compete in races, some as short as 100 miles (160 kilometers) and some as long as 500 miles (800 kilometers). "Championship" racing climaxes at the Indianapolis (Indiana) Motor Speedway each Memorial Day weekend at the end of May. The famous Indianapolis 500 race (so named from its length of 500 miles) is held at that time on the speedway's $2\frac{1}{2}$-mile (4-kilometer) oval track.

STOCK-CAR RACING

There is something especially exciting about watching a race when the automobiles

Left: During a "pit stop" at the Indianapolis 500, mechanics make repairs and fill the fuel tank in a matter of seconds. _Right:_ Tightly bunched cars in a stock-car race vie for the lead position.

Smoke pours out from the engine as this specially built "dragster" accelerates quickly to begin its run.

look like the family car. In racing, such automobiles are called stock cars. There are many different stock-car classes. A stock car can be a car manufacturer's latest model, or it can be an old model called a jalopy. Some stock cars can reach 180 miles (290 kilometers) an hour on the banked turns of the large paved oval tracks. Jalopies are often the stars of the races held on dirt-track ovals at county fairs. In some countries, stock cars are raced on road racetracks.

The rules for most classes of stock-car racing specify that only the outward appearance of the car and some of the major parts must be truly "stock," or standard. All the other parts —including the wheels, brakes, and moving engine parts—are special racing parts. A tubular steel frame is welded inside the "stock" body to protect the driver and to provide the extra strength needed for faster cornering speeds.

▶DRAG RACING

Short races in which automobiles accelerate to top speed on straight courses have become very popular. These races are called drag races in the United States and sprint races in many other countries. The fastest drag racers can accelerate from a standing start to more than 300 miles (480 kilometers) an hour on a 1/4-mile (0.4-kilometer) track in less than five seconds. There are drag-racing classes for just about every type of automobile from compact sedans (enclosed cars) to hot-rod roadsters (open cars) and from stock to "hopped up" cars. Some specially built "dragsters" are about twice as long as normal passenger cars. Often they have no fenders.

▶THE LAND SPEED RECORD

Racing enthusiasts used to have areas closed off on weekends for speed contests. Today only a few of these areas are left. The most famous is Bonneville Salt Flats near Wendover, Utah. Most of the world's land speed records have been set there. Malcolm Campbell went 301.1 miles (484.5 kilometers) an hour in 1935. Craig Breedlove reached 600.6 miles (966.4 kilometers) an hour in 1965, and Gary Gabelich drove 622.4 miles (1,001.4 kilometers) an hour in 1970. In 1979, Stan Barrett went 739.7 miles (1,190.2 kilometers) an hour. Andy Green drove 763.0 miles (1,228.4 kilometers) an hour in 1997, setting the first supersonic land speed record.

▶OFF-ROAD RACING

Vehicles with four-wheel drive—such as Jeeps, dune buggies, and special rear-engine racing machines—compete in a variety of automobile races on dirt, off regular roads. The best-known off-road vehicle races are those on the dirt roads and trails of Baja, Mexico. Similar natural courses are sometimes laid out around the outside of paved race courses. Off-road vehicles also compete on many of the dirt-track ovals. Or they use the same types of twisting dirt or sand tracks with jumps that motorcycles race on. There are even some "sand drag" acceleration races for off-road vehicles, where sand dunes or beaches are the race courses.

ROBERT SCHLEICHER
Author, *The Model Car, Truck & Motorcycle Handbook*

See also KARTING.

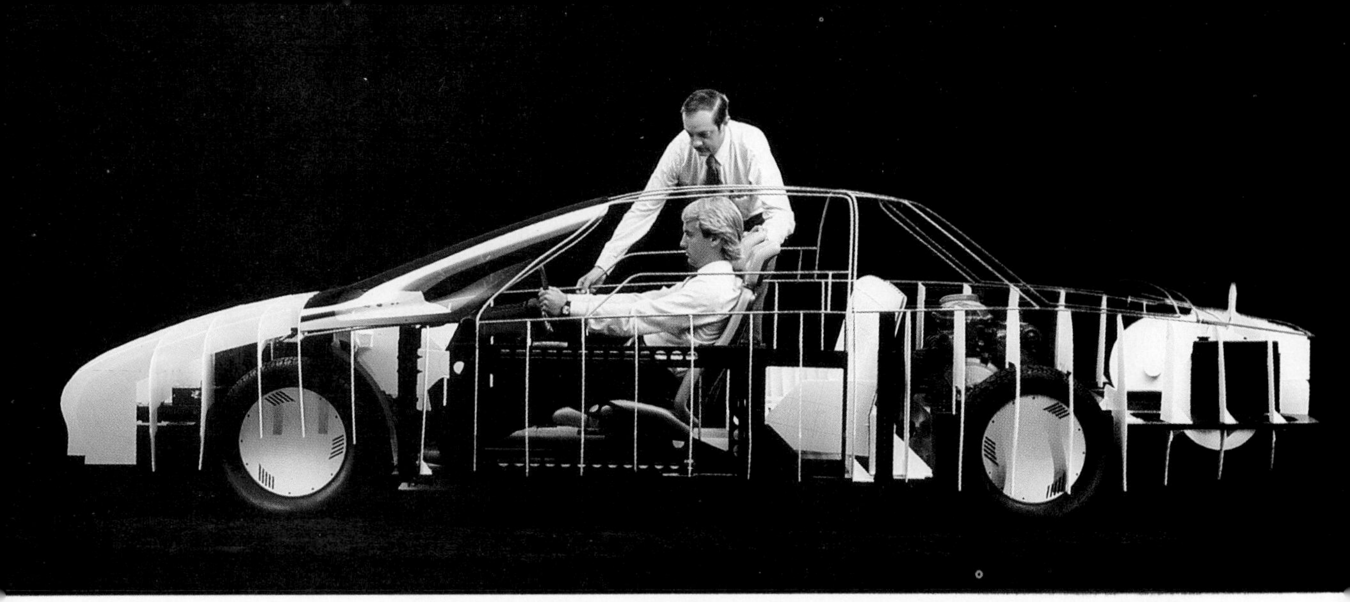

The comfort of the driver is studied in an open model of the design for a new automobile.

AUTOMOBILES

Frightened English farmers rushed to their windows on Christmas Eve, 1801, when they heard loud clanking and hissing on their quiet country road. What they saw was a smoke-belching, steam-powered horseless carriage. It was driven by their neighbor, Richard Trevithick, who had built the odd carriage.

None of them knew it at the time, but it was the first practical use of mechanical power to move a vehicle. Other strange machines had been invented before, and some of them had even moved on their wheels. But Trevithick's was the first to actually do what it was supposed to do—making it the world's first true "automobile."

An automobile is a self-propelled land vehicle that can carry passengers or freight. Unlike a train, an automobile can travel on land without rails. Trucks and buses are automobiles designed for special uses. Race cars are automobiles that run on a race course, and offroad vehicles are automobiles that run on rough ground or sand.

Trevithick's self-propelled carriage could carry passengers over land at a speed of nearly 10 miles (16 kilometers) per hour. Neither his neighbors nor even Trevithick himself appreciated the importance of his achievement. He considered his noisy carriage—with its huge wood and metal wheels and horizontal boiler that puffed out clouds of wood smoke—little more than a toy. He finally took it apart so that he could sell the engine to a mill owner.

The First Experiments

No one person invented the automobile. Many inventors living and working in different countries and at different times contributed to its development. Many of the inventions that went into the creation of the automobile were small in themselves, but together they were important.

The first recorded use of a self-powered vehicle was in 1769. Nicolas Cugnot, a French military engineer, designed and built an awkward but workable three-wheeled vehicle powered by a steam engine. The vehicle was intended as a tractor for hauling heavy cannons. It had a short career. It went out of control during a trial run and crashed.

Only a few years after Trevithick's steam engine, American inventor Oliver Evans built a steam-powered dredge (a machine used to clear sediment from waterways). The machine was equipped with wheels so that it could move on land. To demonstrate to the public that steam could move land vehicles as well as boats, Evans drove his machine around Philadelphia's Center Square for several days. Then he put it to work dredging the waters around the docks in the Schuylkill River. Evans hoped the demonstration would persuade wealthy people to back him in manufacturing steam vehicles. But most people of those days did not think his invention was practical.

Because of the work of Trevithick and Evans, steam-powered vehicles rapidly gained popularity in England. A number of compa-

Built by Nicolas Cugnot in 1769, the earliest self-propelled vehicle was powered by a steam engine. It was almost impossible to steer and crashed on a trial run.

nies were formed to operate steam-powered passenger coaches. But these early steam coaches soon ran into opposition. Stagecoach and railroad operators resented and feared their competition. Farmers disliked the noisy, smelly coaches, and turnpike owners charged them extra high fees. They did this to make up for the damage the steam vehicles supposedly did to the roads. Beginning in 1831 the British Parliament passed a series of very strict laws regulating the use of self-propelled vehicles. The strictest was the Red Flag Act of 1865. It was so named because one of the provisions of the law required a person to walk ahead of all "road locomotives" to warn of their approach. The various laws imposed such high taxes and so many limitations that steam coaches could not operate without losing money. This hurt automobile development in England until the Red Flag Act was repealed in 1896.

Forerunners of the Modern Automobile

Meanwhile, experiments in Europe and in the United States were pushing ahead. Building on the work of earlier scientists and engineers, French engineer Jean Joseph Étienne Lenoir completed a workable internal-combustion engine in 1860. This one-cylinder engine ran on coal gas ignited by an electric spark. The Lenoir engine was designed as a stationary power plant for factories. But a small model was used experimentally in 1863 to power a road vehicle.

About 1865 an Austrian inventor, Siegfried Marcus, built and road tested a simple four-wheeled vehicle with an internal combustion engine that used liquid fuel. Ten years later he produced a second liquid-fueled vehicle. It also ran successfully and is now preserved in a museum in Vienna.

Nikolaus A. Otto, a German inventor, built the most direct ancestor of today's automobile engine in 1876. Otto's engine used the four-stroke principle of operation—intake, compression, power, and exhaust. Automobile engines of today operate on this principle. Otto's original engine, like Lenoir's, operated on coal gas, but it was soon adapted for use with other fuels. Otto's invention provided a relatively light and powerful engine that was important to later developments.

Gottlieb Daimler and another German, Karl Benz, are usually credited with being the earliest builders of successful automobiles with internal-combustion engines. Each produced a motor car in 1886. Daimler's greatest contribution was his light, reliable, medium-speed gas engine. The design formed the basis for the modern automobile engine. Daimler's first machine was intended mainly for testing an all-purpose engine that could be used in boats, trains, and airplanes. But Benz concentrated on the idea of a vehicle fitted with a gasoline motor. He worked hard on a design combining the motor, body, chassis (frame and wheels), and other parts into an efficient unit.

In the early 1890's, a French engineer, Emile Levassor, produced a chassis to fit Daimler's engine. The resulting vehicle, called a Panhard-Levassor, is regarded by many automobile historians as the first real forerunner of the modern automobile. It was the first motor vehicle in which the frame was made separately from the body and suspended from the axles by springs. It also was the first to have the engine in front and the now-standard clutch-and-gear transmission.

Between 1880 and 1900, the concept of the automobile emerged. It was still a rarity that only a wealthy person could own. But people were beginning to take it seriously as a method of transportation. Most of these early automobiles were powered by steam or electricity. But the internal-combustion engine was soon to take its place as the standard automobile engine.

The electric car was superior to the steamer or the gasoline car in several ways. It ran quietly and smoothly, without the vibration and

DEVELOPMENT OF THE AUTOMOBILE
In the panel at the right and in panels on the pages that follow, the history of the automobile is shown through photographs. Each car is a notable example of the engineering or design of its time.

smelly fumes of its rivals. It was easy to control. It did not require a complicated set of gears or clutches to transmit the power to the wheels or to run in reverse. There were few moving parts to wear out. But it had a serious defect. It could not carry with it an adequate power source. The batteries ran down, usually after a distance of about 20 to 40 miles (30 to 65 kilometers), and had to be recharged. It was obviously more convenient to add a few gallons of gasoline to a fuel tank than to recharge or replace a heavy battery. Besides, batteries large enough to power an automobile were very costly. Another disadvantage of the electric automobile was its generally low speed—12 miles (19 kilometers) per hour was a good speed for most electric cars in 1900.

Steam-driven cars were even more popular than electrics in the late 1890's and early 1900's. More than 100 different makes of American steamers were placed on the market in those years. Steamers offered more power than electrics, quiet operation, and smooth

Electric cars were briefly popular. They were quiet and easy to operate but slow. Most could travel only about 40 miles before their batteries needed recharging.

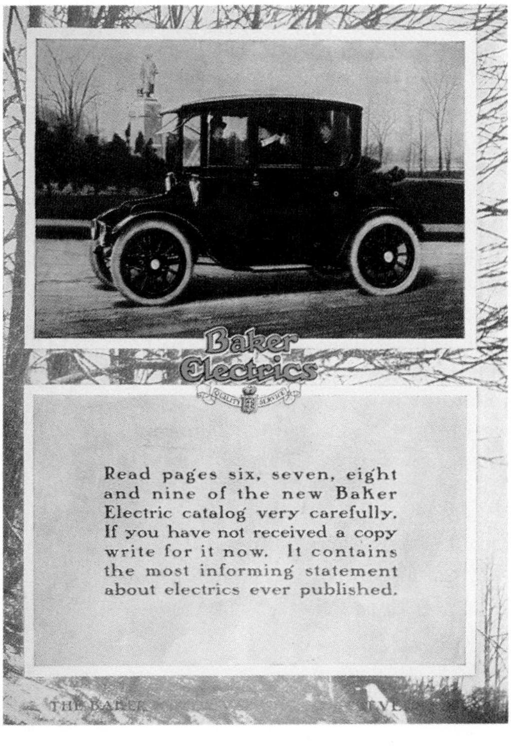

1896 Benz

1906 Stanley Steamer

1907 Rolls Royce Silver Ghost

1909 Model T Ford

1928 Model A Ford

1931 Bugatti Type 41 Royale

1934 Chrysler Airflow

1935 Dusenberg SSJ

1937 Cord

1941 Lincoln Continental

performance. But their drawbacks were serious. It took a long time to build up steam, and doing so was a complicated procedure. Owners feared, sometimes with good reason, that a boiler explosion or accident might result from the fire under the boiler.

Today, the best remembered of the steam cars are the Stanley Steamers. They were made in Newton, Massachusetts from the late 1890's well into the 1920's by Francis and Freelan Stanley, who were identical twins. In 1906 a Stanley Steamer set a new world's land speed record at Ormond Beach, Florida. It hurtled across the sand at 127.6 miles (205.9 kilometers) per hour. By the time the last steamers were made in the mid-1930's, some very efficient and dependable machines were being produced.

The internal-combustion engine is much more complicated than either the steam engine or the electric motor. It has many more moving parts that can wear out. In its early days, it was tricky and temperamental. It frequently broke down or simply refused to start. But there are good reasons why it eventually became the standard power plant for automobiles. With all its failings, it produced more power in relation to its weight than the other engines. When it broke down, it was relatively easy to repair. Its cruising range was limited by the amount of fuel in its tank and not by the availability of water or the endurance of batteries.

The Early Years

Two brothers, Charles E. and James F. Duryea, were the first Americans to manufacture and market a successful gasoline-powered automobile. James Duryea completed the first Duryea automobile in 1893, in Springfield, Massachusetts, working with his brother's design. Their second car was the winner of the first American automobile race, on Thanksgiving Day, 1895. The course was about 55 miles (88 kilometers) long, from Chicago to Evanston, Illinois, and back. In 1895 the Duryeas established the first American automobile manufacturing company.

Ransom E. Olds opened his first factory in 1899 in Detroit, Michigan. When the factory burned down in 1901, Olds came up with an idea that enabled him to continue production and that was a major breakthrough in automobile manufacturing. Instead of making all the

Henry Ford created the first assembly line to manufacture automobiles. At the stage shown, Model T chassis move along the line while the car bodies are lowered onto them. At the next step, the body will be fastened in place.

parts in his factory, he developed careful specifications and had the parts made with great precision by a number of small manufacturers. The parts were then brought to the factory for assembly into cars.

The idea of standardized parts was further developed by Henry M. Leland who founded the Cadillac Company. His cars were made of completely interchangeable parts. In a test in 1908, three Cadillac cars were completely taken apart by the Royal Automobile Club of Britain, and three cars were reassembled using a mixture of parts from the original cars. The three reassembled cars ran perfectly.

Although Olds and Cadillac developed the idea of standardized and interchangeable parts, it was Henry Ford who developed mass production. In 1908 the Ford Motor Company produced the famous Model T Ford. His idea was to produce a motor car that the average person could afford, operate, and maintain. The first Model T Ford sold for $850.00, but Ford knew that he could bring the price down if he could develop an efficient way of manufacturing the cars. Ford developed the first assembly line in 1914.

The basic idea of the assembly line was to move the car on a moving conveyor belt while workers on each side added parts as the car moved along. Often the parts were brought to the workers on another conveyor belt. Each worker had a specific relatively simple task to perform as compared with assembling an entire engine. The use of standardized interchangeable parts also produced a better product that could be easily repaired at lower cost. Before the assembly line, it had taken more than twelve hours to assemble a Model T. New Model T's now came off the assembly line at the rate of one car every 24 seconds. By 1915 the price of a Model T had dropped to $440.00, and by 1925 a Model T could be bought for $290.00

A major advance in 1912 was the invention of the electric starter, an electric motor that starts the gasoline engine. Before the development of the electric starter, the gasoline engine had to be started by cranking it by hand. This took considerable strength and was also dangerous. If the car were not cranked properly, the crank could kick back and cause a fractured thumb or arm.

World War I proved the value of the gasoline automobile. Trucks and ambulances were used in great numbers during the war, and the war proved to be a testing ground for automotive design. In addition, members of the armed services became familiar with automobiles and what they could do.

In the period 1900 through 1920, a great many changes took place in the automobile. During this time, closed cars that protected the drivers and passengers from sun and rain became more common. However, it was not until 1923 that closed sedans became more common than open cars.

Many technical advances improved the function of the automobile. The braking system of the cars improved as cars became more powerful and traffic increased. Early cars had brakes only on the rear wheels, requiring a great deal of force from the driver to stop the car. In the 1920's, cars first had mechanical brakes on all four wheels. By the 1930's most cars had hydraulic brakes. Low-pressure balloon tires took the place of hard-riding high-pressure tires. Safety glass that did not shatter when broken was introduced in the 1920's and helped prevent serious injury. During the 1930's most cars were also equipped with heaters and radios. Cars also began to take on a smoother shape to offer less wind resistance.

During World War II, vast numbers of automobiles and trucks were manufactured for use by the military. Again the war provided a testing ground for new ideas. By the late 1940's, many cars had automatic transmissions, power brakes, and power steering.

During the 1950's, cars became lower, longer, and wider. Many cars were styled with rear fins and great amounts of chrome.

In the 1960's the United States became increasingly concerned with air pollution caused by automobiles. Devices added to engines decreased the amount of harmful chemicals released into the air. In 1970, the Federal Clean Air Act set standards to control the amount of harmful gases emitted by automobiles.

In the 1970's a gasoline shortage and an increase in gasoline prices created a great interest in smaller cars that used less fuel. The federal government passed laws requiring that new automobiles average 27.5 miles per gallon by 1985. Laws were also passed requiring automobiles to better withstand crashes.

In the 1970's and 1980's the trend shifted to smaller cars that were fuel efficient. Other conveniences such as air conditioning and power windows, seats, seat belts, and door locks became common.

In the 1990's, fuel conservation became less important as gasoline prices fell. Larger vehicles were popular once again. Air bags became a standard safety feature on many new automobiles. And battery-powered electric cars were introduced to control the continuing problem of air pollution.

By today's standards the early automobiles were uncomfortable and difficult to operate. But the many inconveniences did not discourage potential buyers. The fact that a person could have independent transportation by mechanical means was considered a miracle of technology. It has certainly proved to be so.

1942 Jeep

1947 Volkswagen Beetle

1951 Studebaker

1957 Ford Thunderbird

1959 Cadillac

1964½ Ford Mustang

1988 Acura Legend

1965 Toyota Corona

1998 Chevrolet Blazer

1973 Mercedes Benz 280 SEL

1998 Ford F-250

1973 Honda Civic

1998 Dodge Caravan

1978 Volvo

1998 Saturn EV1

▶ HOW AN AUTOMOBILE WORKS

Modern automobiles are complex machines made up of thousands of metal, plastic, glass, and rubber parts. They are reliable, comfortable, and safe. Although the sleek, modern automobile has changed greatly from the noisy and smelly cars of the 1890's, it has the same basic systems.

Most cars are powered by an internal-combustion engine. An **electrical system** provides the power to start the engine and, in gasoline engines, provides the sparks that ignite the fuel. Electricity is also required for electric devices such as lights, horns, radios, and heater fans.

Engines have **lubrication systems** to reduce the friction of their moving parts. They have **cooling systems** to carry away the great heat created by combustion. They have a **fuel system** to store and carry fuel to the engine. An **exhaust system** carries away the waste products of combustion.

The engine and all the parts that carry power to the wheels make up the **drive train.** In addition to the engine, the parts of the drive train include the **transmission,** the **drive shaft,** the **differential,** the axles, and the wheels that move the car, called the **drive wheels.** Some cars have the drive wheels in the front, some have drive wheels in the rear, and in other cars, all four wheels are drive wheels.

All cars have a **steering system** to connect the steering wheel to the front wheels. A **brake system** slows and stops the car. A **suspension system** protects the car and passengers from the bumps and dips in the road.

The basic structure to which all these parts are attached is the **chassis.** The **body** of the car consists of the external parts such as the fenders, hood, roof, doors, and trunk lid and the internal fittings of the passenger compartment. These fittings include the seats and the dashboard, which displays instruments that monitor such things as engine temperature, oil pressure, speed, and distance driven.

The Engine

The engine is the first part of the drive train. Most cars today are powered by internal-combustion engines. These engines burn a gaseous mixture of air and either gasoline or diesel fuel inside hollow cylinders. Most modern automobile engines have four, six, or eight cylinders. The cylinders in four-cylinder engines are generally arranged in a line. The cylinders in six-cylinder engines are arranged either in a

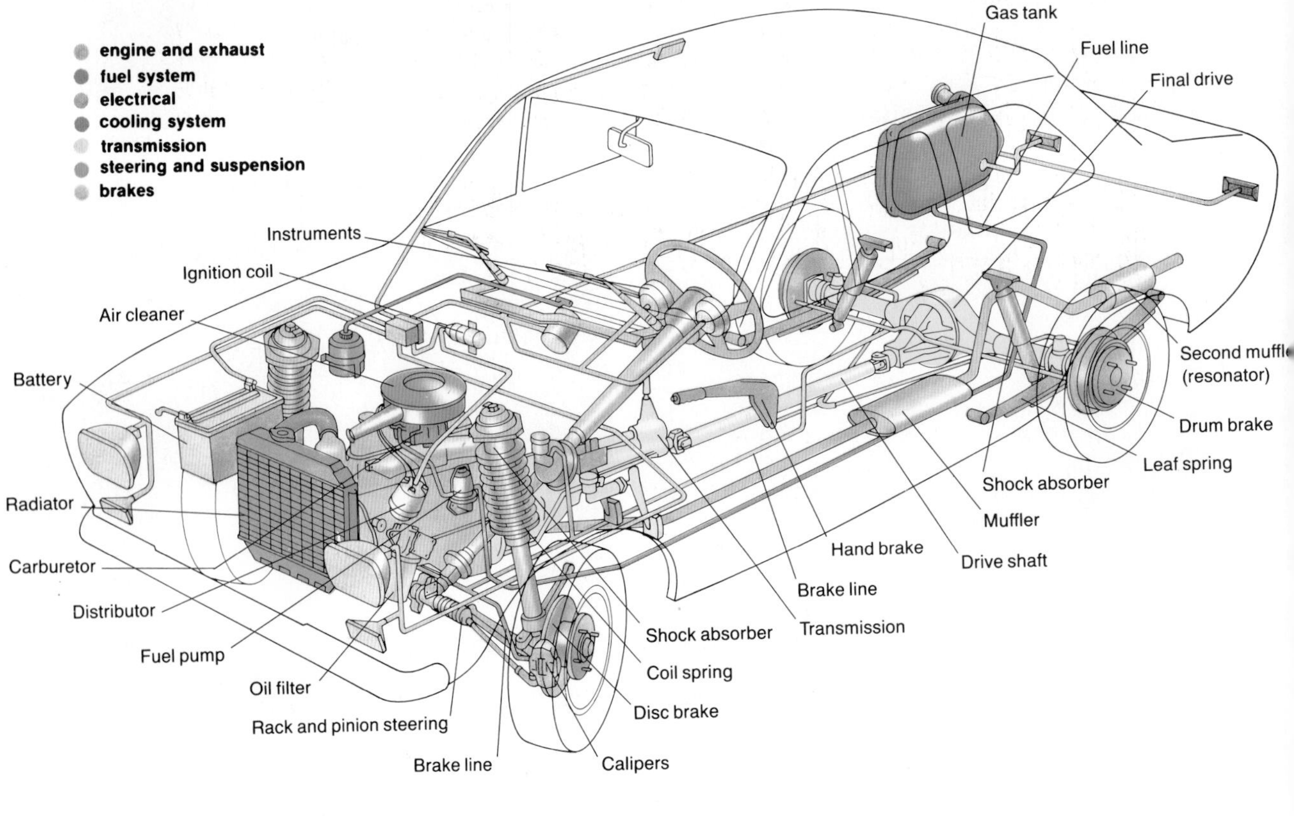

line or in a V-shape with three cylinders in each arm of the V. These engines are called V-6's. The cylinders in an eight-cylinder engine are nearly always arranged in a V, and such engines are called V-8's. Generally, the more cylinders that an engine has, the more powerful that it is.

When an internal-combustion engine is running, the burning gas expands, pushing a piston inside the cylinder. This happens very rapidly, one piston after the other, in each of the engine's cylinders. A connecting rod connects each piston to a shaft, called the **crankshaft**. As each piston is pushed by the gas, it forces the crankshaft to turn. This turning motion is passed through the drive train to the drive wheels. For more information on how these engines work, consult the articles INTERNAL-COMBUSTION ENGINES and DIESEL ENGINES in this encyclopedia.

The Fuel System

Fuel stored in the automobile's fuel tank is drawn to the engine by a **fuel pump.** A **carburetor** then mixes the fuel with air and sends the gaseous mixture to the **intake manifold** and on into the cylinders of the engine. Instead of a carburetor, some cars have a **fuel-injection system** that sprays controlled amounts of gasoline into intake ports close to the cylinders. The fuel-air mixture goes into the cylinder when an **intake valve** opens.

Filters in the fuel line clean the fuel, but they can block the flow of fuel when they get clogged with dirt. They need to be changed regularly or the engine will not run properly.

Some modern, high-performance cars have **turbochargers** that suck in extra air and force it into the cylinders of the engine. This creates more pressure as the fuel is burned and enables the engine to produce greater power.

The Exhaust System

When the fuel burns inside an engine, gases are formed. These gases must be removed from the engine so that new fuel may be burned. This is a fast-moving, continual process. The operation of the piston in each cylinder forces the gases out an **exhaust valve** and then into an **exhaust manifold** that collects exhaust gases from all the cylinders. The gases then pass through **mufflers**, into **tail pipes**, and out the rear of the automobile. They must be forced away from the car because they are poisonous and can cause death when breathed by the driver or passengers.

Most automobiles have one or more mufflers in the exhaust system to muffle the loud noise of the burning fuel. Modern cars also have **emission-control devices** to reduce the amount of carbon monoxide, hydrocarbons, and nitrogen oxide, the harmful chemicals in the exhaust gases. Some cars pump some of the exhaust back through the engine to use every last bit of the fuel. Others have devices such as a **catalytic converter** to convert (change) the harmful gases to a less harmful form. Most states have laws to regulate the maximum amounts of harmful chemicals that may be present in automobile exhaust gases.

The Electrical System

Electrical energy is stored in a rechargeable battery that, on most modern cars, provides 12 volts of electricity. Whenever the engine is running, the battery is kept charged by an electrical generator called an **alternator.** The alternator is driven by a **belt,** a flexible loop attached to an engine-driven wheel. You will find more information on generators and alternators in the article ELECTRIC GENERATORS in Volume E. An article explaining how BATTERIES work is in Volume B.

When a driver turns the ignition key to the "start" position, power from the battery operates the electric starter motor. This motor turns the crankshaft, which pushes the pistons up and down, thus causing the gasoline engine to start. One part of the electrical system, called the **ignition system,** provides power to

The Ignition System

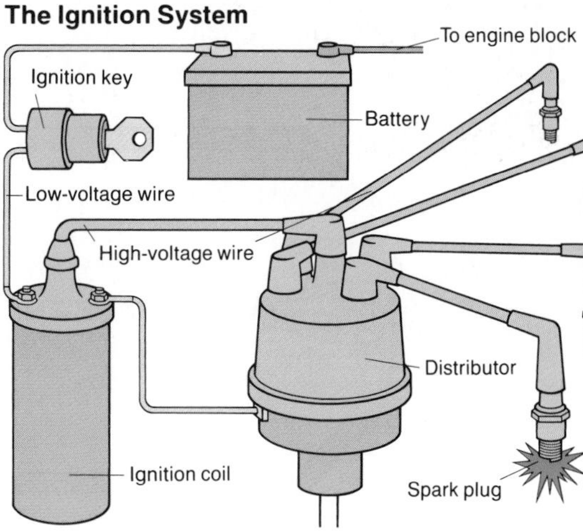

the spark plugs, which ignite the gas in the cylinders.

A spark strong enough to ignite the fuel requires far more than 12 volts of electricity. Thus the electricity from the battery is sent through an **ignition coil** that increases the voltage to about 20,000 volts. The current then passes through a **distributor** that sends it to the spark plug in each cylinder at the right time to ignite the gas in that cylinder.

The car's battery also provides electricity to operate the car's radio, horn, clock, instruments, lights, tape player, and other electric devices.

An automobile with a diesel engine has an electrical system to provide electrical energy for the starter motor, lights, and accessories. A diesel engine does not have spark plugs. Fuel is ignited when its temperature is raised to the burning point by very high compression of the fuel-air mixture in the cylinders.

The Lubrication System

Oil is essential to an internal-combustion engine. Oil coats the moving parts so that metal is not rubbing against metal inside the engine. Without lubrication, friction would cause the metal to become so hot that the engine would be destroyed. An **oil pump** in the engine forces the oil to every moving part.

Several quarts of oil are stored in the **crankcase** (the oil pan at the bottom of the engine). The oil pump draws oil from the crankcase and forces it around the engine. Eventually the oil drips back into the crankcase where it can be drawn up again. An oil filter in the system removes any dirt or tiny particles from the oil so they will not harm delicate engine parts. The oil and oil filter must be changed regularly to keep the engine running well.

The Cooling System

Modern internal-combustion automobile engines become very hot inside. They must be kept at an operating temperature that is cool enough to prevent damage from overheating yet warm enough for the most efficient operation. Some engines are **air-cooled.** As the car moves, air flows through the engine compartment to carry away excess heat. Other engines have **liquid cooling systems.** In these engines the cylinders have double walls. An engine-driven **water pump** forces **coolant** to flow between these walls. The coolant is usually a mixture of one-half water and one-half ethylene glycol, which acts as an antifreeze to keep the water from freezing. Usually anti-rust and anti-corrosion chemicals are added to the ethylene glycol. The coolant picks up heat from the cylinders and is then pumped through a **radiator** where airflow carries away the heat. A thermostat controls the flow of the coolant to keep the engine operating at the correct temperature.

Transmission and Final Drive

The engine is located at the beginning of the drive train of an automobile. The transmission receives the power from the engine and passes it on (transmits it) to the drive shaft, which in turn passes the power on to the drive wheels.

The transmission contains a series of gears that can be connected in different ways to produce different **gear ratios.** These permit the speed of the drive shaft to change in relation to the speed of the engine. The lowest gear ratio is called first gear and provides the greatest amount of torque, or twisting force, from the engine to the drive wheels. This gear is used for starting the car from a standstill. All cars have at least three gear ratios, and some

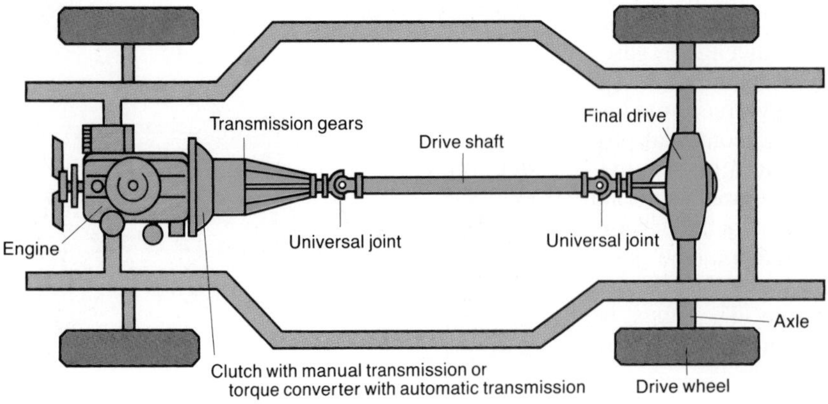

The Drive Train

The series of parts that carry power from the engine to the drive wheels is called the drive train. In the diagram the drive train is shown for a car with an engine located at the front of the car and with the drive wheels at the rear of the car. Front-wheel drive cars have the transmission and final drive located at the front. These cars do not have a drive shaft.

Manual Transmission

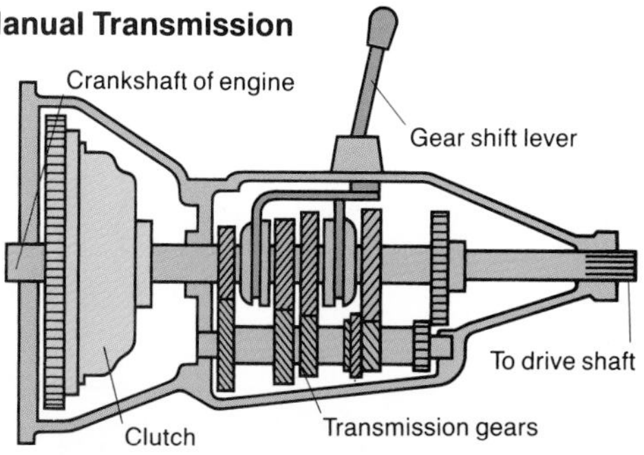

In a car equipped with a manual transmission, the driver selects the correct set of gears to match the engine speed to the road speed. In addition to a reverse gear, a manual transmission will have a neutral position and three, four, or five gears for forward movement.

Automatic Transmission

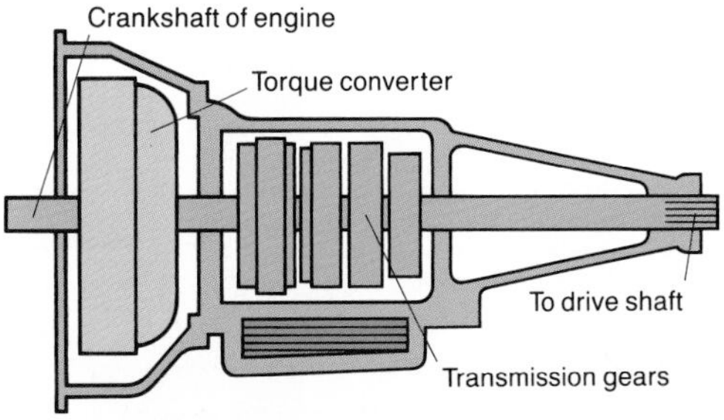

In a car equipped with an automatic transmission, the gears are shifted automatically from low to high as the car moves from a standing position to cruising speed. The transmission may shift into lower gears for climbing hills or for passing when more power is needed from the engine.

have four or even five. At the higher gear ratios, less torque is supplied to the drive wheels, but greater speed results at the drive shaft and at the drive wheels. The high gear ratios are used for highway travel. Transmissions also have a reverse gear that changes the direction in which the drive wheels turn, so that the car can back up. All transmissions also have a neutral position in which the engine is not connected to the drive shaft at all. This position permits the engine to run at any speed without the drive shaft or drive wheels turning.

Manual Transmissions. Some cars have a manual transmission that permits the driver to select the gear ratio best suited for the driving conditions. When changing from one gear to another, it is necessary to disconnect the transmission from the engine. This is accomplished by the **clutch,** which is located in the drive train between the engine and the transmission. When the clutch pedal is pushed down, the engine is disconnected from the transmission and the gears can be shifted. When the clutch pedal is allowed to come back up, the engine is again connected to the transmission and power flows to the drive wheels.

Automatic Transmission. An automatic transmission shifts the gears for the driver. All the driver must do is press down on the **accelerator** pedal (the "gas" pedal); the automatic transmission selects its lowest gear. Then, as speed increases, the transmission shifts itself into higher gears. No clutch is needed for a modern automatic transmission because it has a **fluid** (transmission oil) **coupling** between the gears and the engine.

If the car is going up a steep hill, the automatic transmission shifts itself down to a lower gear so that the engine can turn faster and provide more power. At the top of the hill, when the extra power is no longer needed, the transmission shifts back to a higher gear.

Many drivers prefer the direct control of a manual transmission. Others prefer the ease of an automatic.

For more detailed information on how a modern transmission works, consult the article TRANSMISSIONS in Volume T.

Drive Shaft. In a front-engine car with rear-wheel drive, power from the transmission is carried to the final drive at the rear of the car by a drive shaft. The drive shaft is coupled to the transmission by means of a **universal joint.** This is a flexible joint that permits the rear axle of the car to move up and down without bend-

The Final Drive

The final drive carries power from the drive shaft to the drive wheels. It contains the differential gears that permit each of the drive wheels to turn at a different speed.

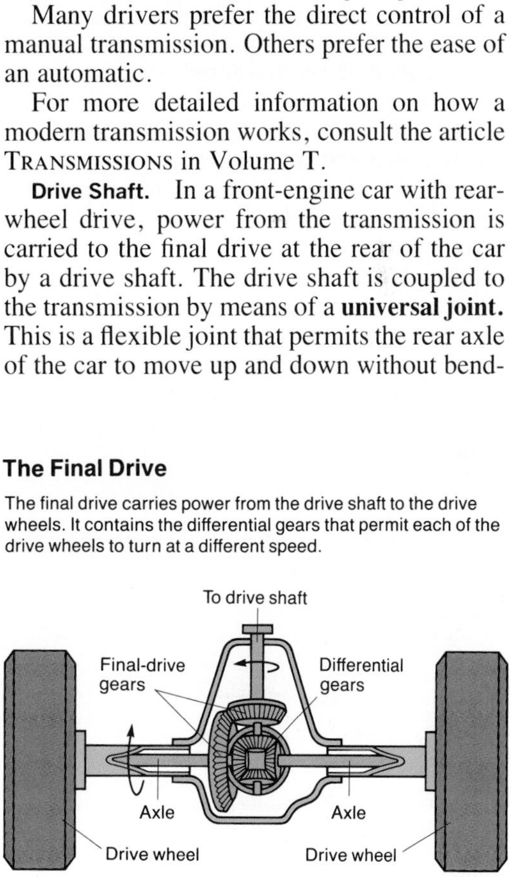

Rack and Pinion Steering

The steering system enables the driver to turn the front wheels and to control the direction of the car's movement. Some cars have power-assisted steering that uses power from the engine to make steering easier for the driver.

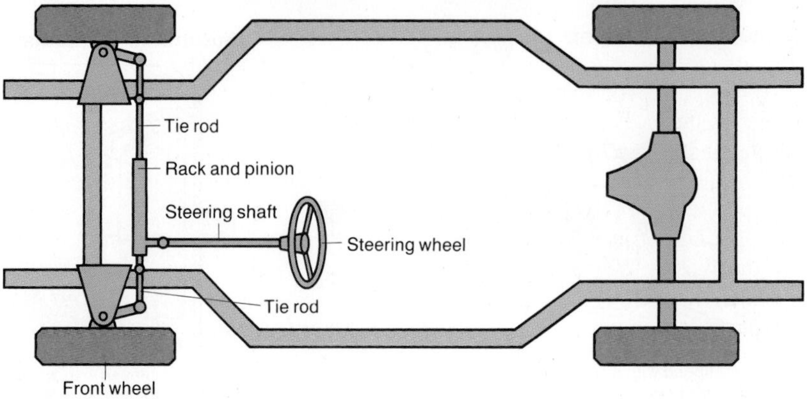

ing the drive shaft as the car goes over bumps. In a front-engine car with front-wheel drive, the transmission is connected directly to the final drive. A four-wheel drive car usually has two drive shafts and two final drives, one for each pair of drive wheels.

The final drive consists of a series of gears that carries the power from the drive shaft to the axles that turn the drive wheels. One set of gears causes the axle to turn at a slower speed than the drive shaft, and thus more torque is delivered to the drive wheels. A second set of gears, called the **differential,** permits each drive wheel to turn at a different speed when the car turns a corner. Because the inner wheel travels a smaller distance than the outer wheel, the inner wheel must turn at a slower speed to avoid skidding.

The Steering System

When the driver turns the steering wheel, gears are turned inside a **steering box** and this moves shafts attached to the front wheels. Some cars have a **rack-and-pinion** type of steering mechanism, in which gears act against a row of teeth.

If the car has power steering, a pump powered by the engine operates a hydraulic system that makes it easier for the driver to turn the wheels. The power assist works only when the engine is running.

Some automobiles have **four-wheel steering.** When the steering wheel is turned, both front and rear wheels turn. With four-wheel steering, a car can make U-turns in much less space. It is also easier to make the tight turns required to park in a small space.

The Brake System

The brake system enables the driver to slow down and to stop the car. The brake systems of modern cars operate on all four wheels and are either **drum brakes** or **disc brakes.** The basic principle of both types of brakes is the same: A friction pad is pressed against a rotating steel part that turns with the wheel, slowing or stopping the car. In drum brakes the metal part is cylinder-shaped, and the friction material is mounted on curved pieces called **brake shoes** that fit inside the drum. In disc brakes a steel disc turns with the wheel, and the friction material is in the form of **pads** that

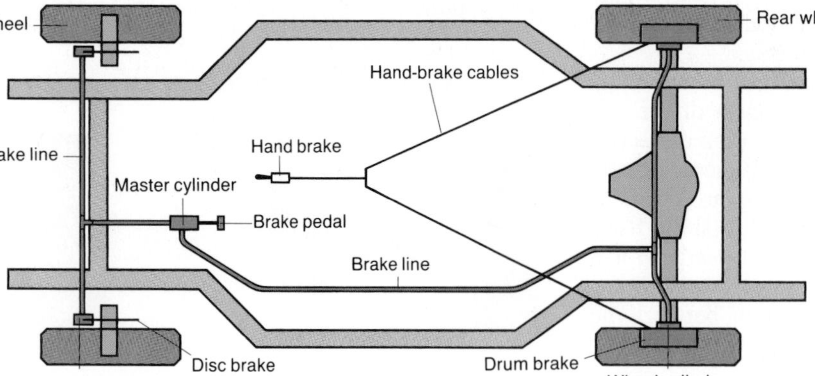

Brake System

All modern cars have hydraulic brakes that operate on all four wheels. Separate brake lines operate the front and rear brakes so that at least two wheels will have operating brakes if part of the system is damaged. The car shown has disc brakes in front and drum brakes in the rear.

are squeezed against both sides of the disc by a device called calipers.

Both types of brakes are operated by a hydraulic system. The main parts of the system are a **master cylinder** connected by steel tubes, called **brake lines,** to **wheel cylinders** at each wheel. When the driver steps on the brake pedal, a force is applied to a piston inside the master cylinder. The force is passed by the hydraulic fluid to a cylinder at each wheel where it moves another piston that pushes the friction material against the metal drum or disc. At the same time, an electric switch connected to the brake pedal turns on a red light at the rear of the car.

Many cars now have **power-assisted brakes** in which a vacuum system or a hydraulic pump operates on the master cylinder to increase the pressure applied by the driver. The power assist works only while the engine is running. All cars also have an emergency or hand brake that works independently of the hydraulic brake system.

A diagram of a hydraulic brake system appears in Volume H in the article HYDRAULIC AND PNEUMATIC SYSTEMS.

The Chassis and Body

The chassis includes the steel frame, the engine, drive train, and steering, brake, and suspension systems to which the body is fastened. The body includes the passenger compartments, the hood and trunk, and the fenders that cover the wheels. In earlier years the frame was manufactured first, and the body was then bolted to it. This method is still followed in the manufacture of cars that have fiberglass bodies and of trucks. Most modern automobiles are manufactured using **unitized body construction** in which the frame and body are made of a number of stamped steel panels that are welded together to make a one-piece combined chassis and body.

The Suspension. The suspension system supports the chassis and body and attaches them to the wheels. It absorbs the shock of hitting bumps in the road and improves safety by keeping good contact between the wheels and the road. The main parts of the suspension system are **springs** and **shock absorbers** located between the axles and the chassis at each wheel. The springs and shock absorbers resist pressure against the wheel caused by bumps in the road, smoothing out the movement of the chassis. Usually **coil springs** are used at the front wheels and **leaf springs** are used at the rear wheels. Some cars use coil springs at all four wheels or use **torsion bars** instead of springs. A torsion bar is a steel bar mounted so that a twisting force acts on it when the wheel moves up and down. The bar is elastic and resists the twisting force, acting much like a spring. Most cars have **independent suspension** at the front wheels that enables each wheel to move up and down separately. Shock absorbers are hydraulic devices that resist rapid changes of movement and smooth out the up and down movements of the wheels as they pass over bumps. There is usually one shock absorber at each wheel.

Wheels and Tires. Automobile wheels are made of pressed steel or an aluminum alloy. They are bolted to **hubs,** which are connected to the axles. The bolts are often covered by **hub caps** but must be easy to reach so that they can be removed when it is necessary to

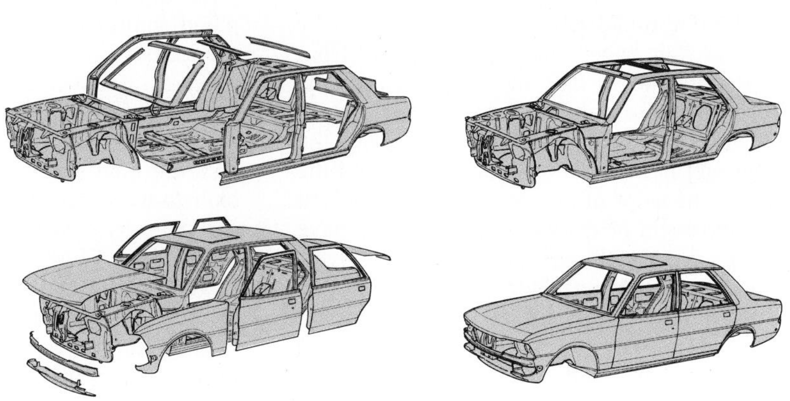

In unitized body construction, different parts of the body are stamped from sheet steel and welded together. The welding is often done by robots controlled by computers. The hood, trunk lid, front fenders, and doors are then added to complete the body.

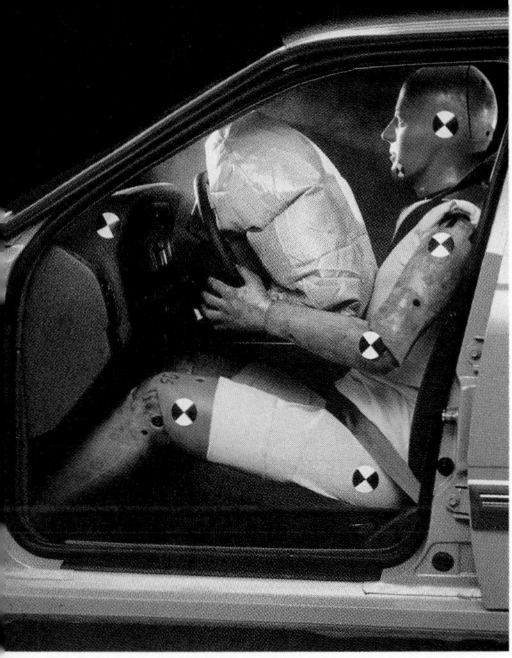

Left: In a test crash, an air bag inflates in a fraction of a second. The air bag prevents the dummy from smashing into the steering wheel or the windshield when the car stops abruptly. *Above:* Cars for sale in the United States are built so that the front end of the car will crumple and absorb some of the force that stops the car in a front-end accident.

remove a wheel, as in case of a flat tire. Modern tires are called **pneumatic tires** because they are filled with air that helps to cushion the ride. There are three kinds of tires used on automobiles: bias-ply, belted-bias, and radial. For more information about each type, see the article TIRES in Volume T.

Safety Features

All cars today have seat belts or some other restraint system to protect drivers and passengers in case of an accident. Many states now require people to fasten their belts every time they get into the car. In 1978 the state of Tennessee passed a law requiring that infants and children be placed in special restraints, and since then many states have passed similar laws. Seat belts have been proven to help prevent injury and save lives.

Since the mid-1990's, most new cars have also had "air bags" that rapidly inflate from the steering wheel hub, the dashboard, or the doors if the car suddenly stops, such as in a collision. The resulting "balloons" keep the driver and passengers from slamming into the front or the sides of the car, or from flying out the windshield or the windows. Air bags have been credited with saving thousands of lives. However, some early air bags inflated too forcefully, posing a threat to children and small adults. Engineers are refining air bag systems to make them safer for everyone.

Other safety laws exist. Automobile bodies must be strong and often reinforced with steel bars in critical areas such as doors to protect the driver and passengers in case of accidents. Doors must have special locks that are crash resistant. Bumpers are now built to absorb some of the force of an impact. Brakes must meet certain performance standards, and fuel systems must be able to withstand crashes without spilling their flammable contents. Interiors of cars must be well padded, and outside mirrors must be available. Even the steering column on a modern car must be built to collapse, or otherwise absorb the impact of a crash. Tires, transmissions, and windshields must all be built with safety rules in mind.

How a New Model Is Created

A new model is made as a blend of what the public wants and needs and what the manufacturer thinks the public will buy. When the manufacturer decides to build a new model, the ideas of many people are considered. Engineers, stylists, designers, and economists decide how the car should look and perform and how much it should cost. Detailed drawings are then sent to hundreds of skilled specialists who plan the actual production of the car. Step-by-step they build the car from the ground up. They design and make working models of the various parts that will go into the car. Engineers may design and build a new engine for the new model. Other engineers may experiment with various types of axles, gears, brakes, and other components to see which will perform best for the new model.

Styling engineers select paint finishes, interior fabrics, and trim and also design the instrument panel and other accessories.

Finally a prototype, or sample version, of the car is built. It has probably taken months, even years, of careful research, design, and engineering to produce the final model. But questions still remain. Will the car perform correctly? Is it really the car the public wants?

Testing A New Model. The sample car is put through test after test to see if anything is wrong with it. It is placed in special "torture chambers" where it is frozen and thawed, drenched with water, heated and allowed to cool, and shaken and twisted until any flaws have been spotted and corrected. When the laboratory tests have been completed, the sample car is driven over a test track at the company proving ground. There it is subjected to far more severe punishment than the average automobile will have to face. Sample cars are also road tested to see how they perform on steep twisting mountain roads, on long flat straight roads, and in crowded city traffic. All this testing often leads to changes in design and then to more testing.

Mass Production of Automobiles

While the prototype model is going through its tests, engineers are planning how to manufacture the car in quantity. They design machines that will turn out the various parts of the car. Some of these machines, such as those that stamp out the roofs or fenders or doors, are the size of a small building. Other machines are designed so that parts, such as engine blocks, automatically move from one machine to another as different drilling, grinding, and other operations are performed.

Today's mass production of automobiles takes precise timing of every operation. Before mass production starts, engineers must determine the most efficient way to assemble the cars. Their plan must make sure that each machine manufacturing a part works in coordination with all the other machines so that the right parts meet at the right time and place on the final assembly line.

When everything is organized, full-scale production begins. Modern automobile production is like a great river. The main river is fed by side rivers, which are fed by streams. The "main river" of an automobile factory is

Right: Computers play a major part in the development of a new model. The shape of the car and the way people will fit in the car can be tried on a computer before even a model is made. _Below:_ For some models, a new engine may be designed and tested to achieve the desired performance. _Below right:_ A model of the new car is scanned by a device that records the car's shape. The data will be used in determining the final design.

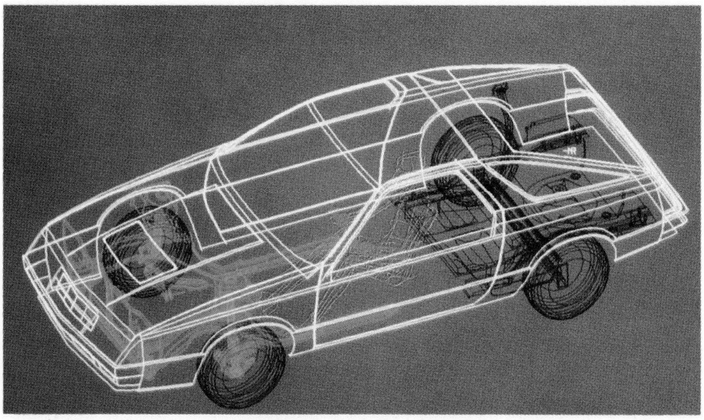

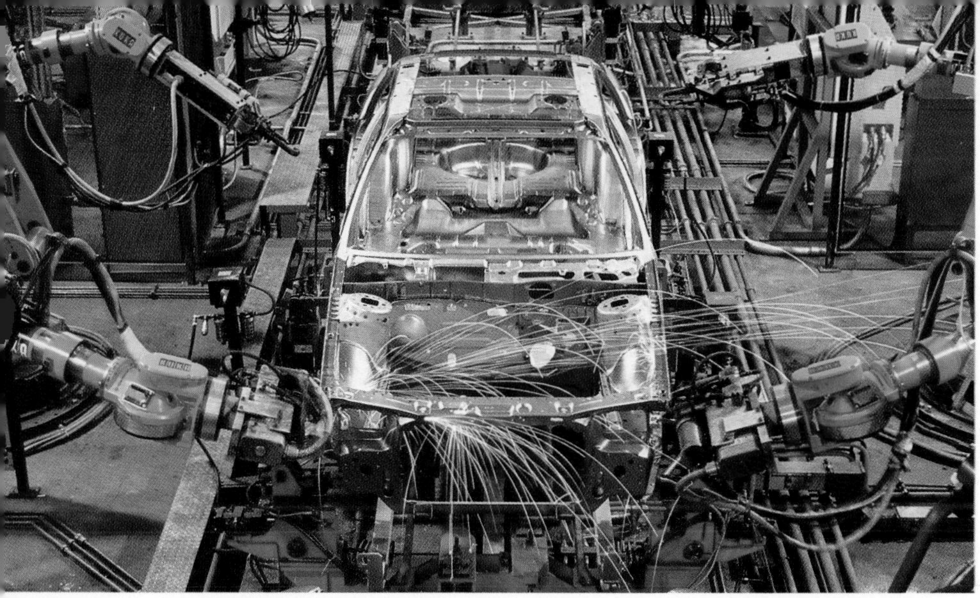

Left: Computer-controlled robots do much of the tedious and dangerous work in assembling cars. Robots weld the several pieces of stamped sheet steel together to create the automobile body. *Right:* Final assembly and checking of an engine still require a skilled human. *Far right:* As the car nears completion, body and engine come together.

the final assembly line, an endless moving belt or chain that carries main components such as engine blocks.

The many sub-assembly lines are like the side rivers and streams, bringing parts and assembled sub-units—such as carburetors, fuel pumps, or alternators—into the main assembly line where they are attached by automatically controlled machines or by workers. A modern automobile has almost 20,000 separate parts, ranging in size from the roof and engine hood to tiny screws used inside the speedometer. Almost every part has been transported on an assembly line before it becomes a part of a finished automobile.

Once the engine and other sub-assemblies have been completed on their assembly lines, they are ready to be attached to the three major parts of the car—the chassis, the engine, and the body. With some models, the first two sub-assembly lines—carrying the chassis and the engine—meet and are fitted together. Then the chassis-engine assembly is joined to the body to produce a nearly completed car.

Other car models use an integrated, or single-unit, type of construction. Here, the body and chassis are welded together to make one instead of two major sub-assemblies.

Many additional operations are performed as the car moves down the assembly line. Parts are added at each station. Seats and floor carpets are installed, and the electrical systems are hooked up. Water hoses are attached, and various pieces of trim are added. Finally, at the very end of the line, gasoline is pumped into the tank and coolant into the radiator. Oil has already been added to the engine on the engine's assembly line. A worker slides behind the wheel, starts the engine, and drives the car off the line.

But it is still not ready for its first owner. Quality-control inspectors examine the car for flaws. They adjust headlights and check details such as door, hood, and window fit.

Finally, the car is ready for the road.

The Automobile Industry

The automobile industry is one of the world's biggest producers and merchandisers of a product. It is also one of the biggest buyers. The industry consumes huge quantities of raw materials such as iron, copper, and rubber. In the United States it uses up one fourth of the country's steel production.

Excluding agricultural work, one out of every nine jobs in the United States is directly related to the manufacture, sale, and use of motor vehicles. These jobs support approximately 14 million Americans. The center of automobile manufacturing in the United States is the Detroit area in Michigan, although major manufacturing plants are located in several other states.

Beginning in the early years of the industry, manufacturers of automobiles have merged to form large corporations. In the United States, the three major manufacturers have traditionally been General Motors, Ford, and Chrysler, each of which has produced cars that still bear the names of the original independent companies. General Motors cars include Chevrolet, Pontiac, Oldsmo-

bile, and Cadillac. Cars manufactured by the Ford Motor Company include Ford, Mercury, and Lincoln. Chrysler Corporation cars include Chrysler, Plymouth, and Dodge. In Great Britain the major manufacturer of automobiles is the Rover Group, which produces the Land Rover and the Range Rover. Rolls-Royce Motor Cars in England produces the famous Rolls-Royce and Bentley cars. In Germany the leading manufacturing companies are Volkswagen, Daimler-Benz (Mercedes), and BMW (Bayernische Motoren Werke). In France the leading manufacturing companies are Peugeot-Citroen and Renault. In Italy, the largest manufacturer of passenger cars is Fiat. In Japan, the leading producers are Toyota, Nissan, and Honda.

In the 1990's, automobile companies continued to merge. BMW took over the Rover Group. The makers of Mercedes and Chrysler joined to form DaimlerChrysler. And Volkswagen bought Rolls-Royce.

In the mid-1990's more than 50 million motor vehicles were manufactured worldwide each year. Of these, more than 37 million were passenger cars and the remainder were trucks and buses. The five leading producers of passenger cars are Japan, United States, Germany, France, and South Korea, in that order. Other countries that have a sizable automobile industry include Spain, Canada, the United Kingdom, Brazil, and Italy. All of these countries export a large percentage of their output.

Throughout the world there are more than 646 million cars on the road. If every person around the world climbed into an automobile at the same moment, there would be an average of twelve people in each car. But the number of people per automobile varies widely throughout the world. In the United States there are about two people per car, in Europe there are about five people per car, in Russia there are about 24 people per car, but in China there are more than 1,300 people per car.

In the mid-1990's, there were more than 135 million passenger cars on the road in the United States. More than two thirds of all the households in the United States have more than one motor vehicle. American motorists traveled just about 2 trillion miles in one year.

People in the United States own more than 30 percent of the world's cars, trucks, and buses. Japan is in second place in the number owned. Other countries where ownership is high are Germany, France, Italy, the United Kingdom, and Canada.

When the automobile rolls off the assembly line, a number of businesses become involved. Trucking firms haul new cars from the factory to the dealers. The dealers employ staffs of salespeople and mechanics. Their advertisements bring business to newspapers and radio and television stations. Service stations supply gasoline and oil to keep the cars running. Service stations in turn purchase their supplies from oil companies. Cars need regular servicing, and this keeps many thousands of mechanics busy. In the United States, the automobile industry accounted for nearly $300 billion in sales of motor vehicles in 1997 alone.

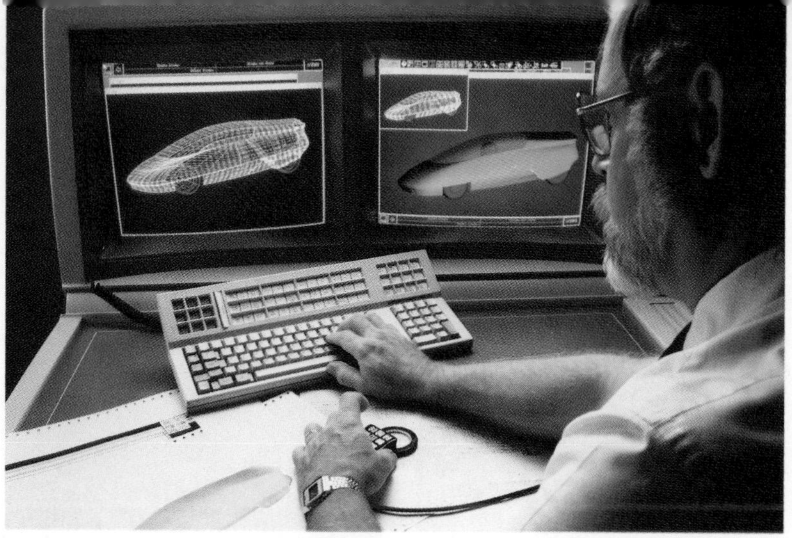

The car of the future may look like some cars of today, but it will be very different in the way that it operates. As new ideas and developments take place, they will be tried on a computer long before they are tested on the road.

Careers in the Automobile Industry

Manufacturing, selling, and servicing cars offer a wide range of career opportunities. Manufacturers employ many college graduates. Marketing experts determine what features the customers may want. Engineers, scientists, and artists design the cars. Production experts decide how to build them.

Manufacturing employees, such as machinists and tool and die workers, may have learned their skills in trade schools. They may serve several years as apprentices learning particular manufacturing skills. Others may be trained on the job to assemble cars.

Car dealers employ salespeople who are skillful in persuading customers to buy cars. Salespeople must be able to explain the cars' features and tell why these are desirable. This requires some mechanical knowledge.

Servicing cars offers a wide range of jobs—from pumping gas to making complicated repairs. Mechanics may be specialized in repairing certain areas such as transmissions, electrical systems, or car body repairs. Some of these skills may be learned in trade schools. Others may be taught by manufacturers' representatives or learned on the job. Large repair facilities have service managers and supervisors who make sure the work is done properly and efficiently.

The Car of the Future

The modern automobile is a marvelous machine. It is fast, sleek, comfortable, and beautiful to look at. But most automobile engineers know that the modern car will look like yesterday's noisy, smelly car when compared with the automobile of the future.

Experts predict that cars of the future will be made of plastics and carbon fibers that will be much stronger than steel and much lighter in weight. Even engines will be made of these materials.

Cars of the future will be smaller and lighter, but their design will probably be similar to the sleekest of the modern sports cars. There will probably not be any extreme design changes for a long time.

The real frontier for cars of the future lies not in body design but with computer activation. Cars may someday actually drive themselves. Highways would be wired so that cars could be programmed to travel a certain route and could make the trip with or without a driver. Everyone in the car would be able to relax, even take a nap, as the car speeds along at 200 miles (322 kilometers) per hour. The car would be radar- and computer-controlled to never touch other driverless cars or trucks and buses on the road. Changes of destination along the way could be made from the car, and a central computer could notify a computer at home.

Eventually the car would ease over to the right and pull off the high-speed roadway, navigate the city streets, and finally stop at the programmed destination.

Most automobile engineers believe that these cars are certain to be built, maybe even in the early 21st century—which would make it in your lifetime.

Ross R. Olney
Author, *Car of the Future*

See also Buses and Bus Travel; Diesel Engines; Internal-Combustion Engines; Transmissions; Trucks and Trucking.

AVALANCHES AND LANDSLIDES

On a sunny winter day, snow on a steep slope fractures and tumbles down a mountainside. The avalanche, a violent movement of snow that can also contain ice, soil, and rock, buries everything in its path.

On a rainy spring day, a huge water-soaked mass of land suddenly breaks away and falls down a steep hill, taking entire houses and roads along with it. Such a large movement of rock and soil is called a landslide.

Avalanches and landslides start for different reasons. However, they can both have a devastating impact on nearby settlements and recreation areas.

The violent movement of snow can be seen in this photo of an avalanche on Mt. McKinley, Alaska. Avalanches can occur wherever snow accumulates on steep slopes.

AVALANCHES AND THEIR CAUSES

In order for avalanches to occur, there must first be an accumulation, or buildup, of snow on a steep mountainside over time. During the winter, storms continually deposit fresh layers of snow on existing snow, creating a snowpack. Because each layer is built up under different weather conditions, the tiny ice crystals making up the snow may form strong bonds between some layers but weak bonds between others. If the bonds between layers are too weak, the top layers of snow can barely resist the downward pull of gravity.

At this stage, all that is needed for an avalanche to start is a so-called trigger event. This could be anything from the weight of new snow or a passing skier or animal to the impact of small chunks of snow and ice falling from above. Even a loud noise can set off an avalanche.

There are two main types of avalanches. A loose snow avalanche occurs when snow on or near the surface does not bond with the snow beneath it and begins to slide down a slope, gathering more and more snow as it continues down. The more common and deadly slab avalanche occurs when a weak layer of snow buried under a strong layer makes an entire snowpack unstable. A trigger event can then cause a single large plate, or slab, of snow to break off and fracture as it falls down the slope.

Snow builds up on a mountainside in layers. If a weak layer is buried under a strong one, the weight of a skier could trigger an avalanche.

Avalanches are a danger wherever snow accumulates on steep slopes. The deadliest avalanche ever occurred in 1970, when an earthquake off the coast of Peru triggered an ice avalanche near the summit of Mount Huascarán. The descending mass of ice and rocks accelerated to a speed of more than 170 miles (280 kilometers) an hour, destroying villages below. More than 18,000 people were killed.

▸ LANDSLIDES AND THEIR CAUSES

A landslide occurs when part of a hillside becomes too weak to support its own weight. This weakening can be caused by earthquakes or when the ground becomes soaked with rain or melting snow. Some types of landslides move seasonally, during rainy periods of the year. Others may lie dormant (inactive) for long periods of time, moving only once every number of years.

A landslide on this California hillside caused these houses to collapse. Soaking rains of the season had weakened the ground.

Landslides are more frequent in areas where there is a lot of erosion—the gradual wearing down and carrying away of land. Erosion is especially noticeable along some streams, rivers, and seacoasts. But landslides also occur far from areas of active erosion.

Human activities can also contribute to landslides. For example, the construction of buildings on hillsides may involve excavating material from the bottom of a slope and adding material higher up to create a more level lot. As a result, the slope can become overloaded, meaning that it cannot safely support the weight of the added material.

There are three main types of landslides: slides, falls, and flows. Slides are large bodies of land that move together along a sloping surface. Slides that rotate backward along a curved surface are called slumps. Translational slides are slides along a straight sloping surface. Slumps and translational slides can move up to 100 feet (30 meters) a day, although some move much more slowly. Debris slides and rockslides can move slowly or rapidly.

Falls of rock and soil occur on cliffs and steep slopes. Large rockfalls can be catastrophic events. Even small falls can be hazardous. Every year, small amounts of falling rock kill motorists, hikers, and campers in mountainous areas.

Flows are landslides in which materials move more like a fluid. Debris flows are rapid movements of wet mud and debris, while earthflows are movements of wet, clay-rich material. Debris flows triggered by storms have caused many deaths and much property damage in the United States. There are also dry flows, in which dry materials flow rapidly over long distances. In 1920, an earthquake in China's Gansu Province triggered a large, rapid flow of dry loess (silt deposited by wind) that killed some 100,000 people.

▸ PREVENTION AND DAMAGE CONTROL

In ski areas and along highways and railways, explosives are used to intentionally trigger small avalanches rather than allowing the slabs to build up to large and destructive avalanches. Heavy-duty fencing can hold snow in place, and specially designed deflecting walls can turn snow away from an area to be protected. Avoiding avalanche-prone slopes when skiing or hiking is the best way to prevent triggering an avalanche or being caught in one.

A number of methods are used to prevent landslides as well. One way is to capture and drain excess water before it reaches a potential landslide area. Walls and buttresses are used to prevent deep-seated landslide movements. Special fences and nets can keep falling rocks from reaching highways. And maps of landslide-prone areas help builders and planners avoid dangerous areas.

Reviewed by Dale Atkins
Colorado Avalanche Information Center
Rex L. Baum
U.S. Geological Survey

See also Earthquakes; Floods.

The ancient dream of flying has come true. These air show pilots are giving a thrilling demonstration of aerobatic flying, trailing white smoke to mark their paths in the sky.

AVIATION

People have always wanted to fly. The dream of flight appears in legends and myths of many cultures. It has been painted on cave walls, carved in stone, and inscribed on clay tablets. Through the centuries, stories have been told of magic flying carpets, winged horses, and chariots pulled by flying dragons.

The materials for simple aircraft have always been available. It would have been possible for ancient Chinese, Egyptians, or Incas to have made a hot-air balloon or a simple glider. Perhaps in a tiny village or on a remote mountainside someone did make a successful flight that was never recorded.

In the early 20th century, the dream finally became a reality. Millions of people have since flown in aircraft as varied as hot-air balloons, gliders, helicopters, huge airliners, and supersonic military fighters.

EARLY ATTEMPTS TO FLY

One of the earliest concepts of flight came from watching the effortless soaring of birds. Many individuals tried to fly by strapping wood and fabric wings to their arms and jumping from a tower or a cliff—only to plunge straight to the ground.

A successful introduction to flight appeared in China several centuries before the birth of Christ. In a war a soldier could be sent up on a large kite to spy on the enemy army. But it was not the answer to the dream of flying, because the kite had to be attached to the ground by a long rope.

In the 16th century the great Italian artist, scientist, and inventor Leonardo da Vinci had many ideas for ways in which humans could fly. He drew designs for parachutes, helicopters, and human-powered ornithopters (aircraft with flapping wings) and may have experimented with kites and balloons. Da Vinci's sketches did not get people off the ground, but his work did prepare the way for the scientists of the 18th and 19th centuries who in turn set the stage for the explosion of flight that would take place after 1903.

This article is an overview of the subject of aviation. It covers major events in the history of flight. The development of commercial, military, and private aviation is discussed. Other subjects covered here are government regulations and safety standards, aircraft manufacture, and careers in aviation.

Descriptions of specific kinds of aircraft appear in the articles AIRPLANES; BALLOONS AND BALLOONING; GLIDERS; and HELICOPTERS. The physical laws of flight are found in AERODYNAMICS; the subject of flying faster that the speed of sound is covered under SUPERSONIC FLIGHT. The kinds of engines used on aircraft are described in detail in JET PROPULSION; INTERNAL-COMBUSTION ENGINES; and ROCKETS.

Other articles containing information related to aviation are AIRPORTS; NAVIGATION; PARACHUTES; RADAR AND SONAR; and UNITED STATES, ARMED FORCES OF.

Balloons

Over the centuries, people have observed that the smoke and sparks from a fire are carried upward in the currents of hot air. But no one thought to catch the hot air in a bag until the 18th century when the French brothers Joseph Michel and Jacques Étienne Montgolfier began experiments with balloons. They made a huge balloon, 100 feet (30.5 meters) around, which was a linen bag lined with paper. Lifted by hot air from a straw-fed fire, the balloon rose into the air on June 5, 1783. It was the first successful step on the road to flight.

About the same time, another French scientist, J. A. C. Charles, found that the newly discovered element hydrogen, which is lighter than air, could also lift a balloon. On August 27, 1783, he demonstrated his hydrogen balloon in Paris to a group that included an American inventor, Benjamin Franklin.

These two methods of balloon flight—gas-filled and hot-air balloons—are still in use today. Because hydrogen is flammable, helium now fills weather balloons, blimps, and even toy balloons. Hot-air ballooning has become a popular sport. Several people ride in a "basket" carried aloft by a large, brightly colored balloon that travels with the wind.

But balloons were not the solution for practical air transportation. Although they could lift heavy loads into the air, there was no way of controlling the direction of their flight.

Airships

In the late 18th century, efforts were being made to develop a balloon with power and a means to steer it. But it was not until 1852 that the first powered airship was flown. A French engineer, Henri Giffard, flew over Paris in a hydrogen-filled **dirigible**. Dirigible is the French word for "steerable" and is sometimes used as a name for powered, steerable lighter-than-air craft. Giffard's dirigible had a steam-powered propeller. Later dirigibles were powered by electric batteries or internal-combustion engines. Giffard's dirigibles were **nonrigid airships**, which means their shape was maintained by the pressure of the gas with which they were filled. They were shaped like huge, fat cigars. The British called them **blimps**, a term that is still used today.

In 1900 the first **rigid airship** flew. It was built by a German company owned by Ferdinand von Zeppelin. The shape of these **zeppelins**, as rigid airships are often called, was maintained by an internal metal framework which contained hydrogen-filled bags. Zeppelins had internal-combustion engines to power their propellers. More than 100 of these rigid airships were built, but they were not the ideal aircraft. The future of aviation was with the more slowly developing heavier-than-air craft.

Gliders

In the early 1800's, Sir George Cayley, an English inventor, believed it would be possible to build a heavier-than-air craft. Based on his observation of the flight of birds such as seagulls, which soar for long distances without flapping their wings, he built model gliders with wings curved like a bird's wing. He added a combination rudder-elevator to make the glider turn and to climb or descend. These inventions are so important to all later

◀ Leonardo da Vinci drew plans for a glider (*far left*) in the 16th century. Otto Lilienthal (*left*) flew his first successful glider in 1891.

▶ The Wright brothers had studied Lilienthal's designs. In 1903 they made the first powered flight at Kitty Hawk, North Carolina.

aircraft designs that Cayley is often called the "father of aeronautics."

Power-driven model airplanes were being flown by the middle of the 19th century. The first was a steam-powered model designed and built by John Stringfellow, an English engineer. Steam remained the most popular source of power until the end of the 19th century. While tiny steam engines worked well enough in small model airplanes, steam engines large enough to power a full-size plane were too heavy to be practical. The development of the internal-combustion engine, light yet powerful, would one day be the solution. However, before powered flight was achieved, experiments with gliders large enough to carry a pilot solved the many problems of aircraft design and control.

Otto Lilienthal, a German, was one of the most successful designers of gliders. His first glider, built in 1891, was made of wood and cloth. The pilot hung from a frame in the center of the wing. Lilienthal took off in his glider by running down a hill with it until he was moving fast enough for the wind to lift the craft. He controlled the direction of flight by moving his body to one side or the other. Lilienthal made more than 2,000 flights. He was killed in 1896 while testing one of his new gliders.

▶ POWERED FLIGHT

Lilienthal was the first engineer-pilot, designing, building, and flying his own aircraft. His work was an inspiration to two brothers from Ohio who made their living building bicycles. They were Wilbur and Orville Wright.

The Wright Brothers

In the amazingly short time of four years, the Wright brothers identified and solved the basic problems of flying a heavier-than-air craft. These were:

(1) Wings with enough surface area and the proper curve to provide lift.

(2) A means to control the direction of the aircraft's movement.

(3) Proper placement of weight to keep the aircraft balanced.

(4) A lightweight source of power.

(5) Efficient propellers.

(6) Piloting skills needed to fly the aircraft.

While the Wright brothers were solving these problems, others were also racing to be the first to fly in a powered aircraft. The Wrights' closest competitor may have been Samuel Pierpont Langley of the Smithsonian Institution.

After years of patient experiments and trials with models, Langley completed a full-size airplane called the *Aerodrome* in 1903. Langley's gasoline-powered machine was to be launched from the top of a houseboat in the Potomac River. On the first flight the *Aerodrome* crashed into the river. It was fished out and repaired and then launched again, only to crash a second time. Discouraged by the failures and by heavy criticism in the newspapers, Langley gave up his experiments.

The Wrights meanwhile had been creating a series of gliders. They had also built a wind tunnel, in which a fan forced air through a large tube. In this they could observe the effects of airflow on models of their aircraft designs. By 1903 they also had designed and built a lightweight internal-combustion engine and propellers to be connected to the engine by bicycle chains.

The First Flight

On December 17, 1903, a windy day at Kitty Hawk, North Carolina, Wilbur and Orville Wright made the first successful powered flight in a heavier-than-air craft. The first flight, made by Orville, was short—120 feet (36.6 meters) in 12 seconds—but it was followed by three more flights with the brothers taking turns. The last flight that day was made by Wilbur. It lasted for 59 seconds and covered 852 feet (260 meters). That distance would have been longer if there had not been a strong headwind.

Early Designers and Pilots

After the Wright brothers had solved the basic problems of powered flight, more people became excited about aviation and began to build and fly their own planes, often learning by trial and error. In Canada, Alexander Graham Bell, the inventor of the telephone, established the Aerial Experiment Association in 1907. One of the association's members was Glenn Hammond Curtiss, a designer of lightweight engines and a record-setting motorcycle racer. The association built several aircraft including the *June Bug,* in which Curtiss won a prize offered for flying more than 1 kilometer (.62 miles).

In France, interest in aviation was very high. Alberto Santos-Dumont, a Brazilian who lived there, made the first European flight in a powered biplane in 1906.

In 1909, Louis Bleriot, of France, became the first person to fly a plane across the English Channel. He made the flight in a monoplane that he had designed himself. Bleriot had added several new features to his airplane. The pilot sat in the cockpit of a covered fuselage (the body of the craft). He controlled the flight with a control stick and pedals, just as airplanes are flown today. The rudder and the elevators were at the rear of the plane. Bleriot's design became the standard for later airplane builders.

Soon the new designs created in Europe surpassed those in the United States. One reason for these rapid advances was that the military forces of the various European governments supported aviation development.

▶WORLD WAR I, 1914–1918

Although aircraft were only a small part of the total military effort in World War I, aviation was important right from the beginning of the conflict.

Airships were used by both sides for gathering information behind enemy lines. The British used blimps for spotting enemy submarines that could then be attacked by airplanes or ships. The Germans continued their pre-war development of zeppelins and used them in 53 bombing raids against England. Such raids were more notable for the fright they caused than for actual damage. By the end of the war, the disadvantage of airships was apparent. Zeppelins moved very slowly, making them easy targets. Gunfire from hostile airplanes or ground artillery could cause the hydrogen gas to burst into flames.

During the early years of the war, airplanes were also used for flying over enemy lines to gather information. But soon there were also squadrons of fighters and bombers with specialized airframes, engines, and weapons.

In 1914 a typical British aircraft was the B.E. 2a, a fragile biplane with a 35-foot (10.6-meter) wingspan and weighing only 1,274 pounds (573 kilograms). With its 70-horsepower Renault engine, it had a top speed of 70 miles (113 kilometers) per hour. It carried a pilot and an observer. Its weapons were pistols and hand-held bombs.

At the war's end, in November, 1918, the British Royal Air Force was flying the Handley-Page V/1500. The V/1500 had a wingspan of 126 feet (38.4 meters), weighed 24,000 pounds (10,800 kilograms), and was powered by four 375-horsepower Rolls-Royce engines. Its top speed was 97 miles (156 kilometers) per hour. The fighters were capable of speeds in excess of 140 miles (225 kilometers) per hour and strong enough to make the high speed turns, dives, and other maneuvers of air combat. There were aircraft carrying five machine guns and bombs weighing hundreds of pounds.

▶PEACETIME AVIATION, 1919–1938

After the war, former military pilots and many others used aircraft for peaceful purposes. They crossed the oceans, flew to unexplored areas of the world, and always tried to fly higher and faster.

Record Flights

In the ten years after World War I, the speed record went from 171 miles (275.2 kilometers) per hour to 370 miles (595 kilometers) per hour. The altitude record increased from 33,113 feet (10,093 meters) in 1920 to 43,166 feet (13,157 meters) in 1930.

The first aircraft to cross the Atlantic Ocean was the U.S. Navy's Curtiss NC-4. This four-engine **flying boat** (an aircraft that takes off and lands on the water) completed the trip in 19 days in May, 1919. The first nonstop flight across the Atlantic was made in the next month. British Lieutenants John Alcock and Arthur Whitten Brown flew a two-engine Vickers Vimy from Newfoundland to Ireland, a distance of 1,890 miles (3,043 kilometers), in 16 hours and 28 minutes.

In May, 1923, the first nonstop flight across the United States was made in a U.S. Army Air Service Fokker T-2, that was flown coast to coast in 26 hours and 50 minutes. In September, 1924, two U.S. Army Douglas World Cruisers completed a round-the-world flight that had taken 175 days.

The record-making flight that most excited the public was Charles A. Lindbergh's solo flight from New York to Paris. On the morning of May 20, 1927, he took off from Roosevelt Field on Long Island in a silver Ryan monoplane named the *Spirit of St. Louis.* Thirty-three hours and 30 minutes later, he landed in Paris where he was given a hero's welcome. His later flights and many public appearances created enthusiasm for aviation that speeded its progress for the next decade.

Early Commercial Aviation

For several years after World War I, the practical use of airplanes was limited because they were not large enough, reliable enough, or able to fly in bad weather. This meant that businesses could not make a profit by carrying passengers, nor could they compete economically with the railroads as freight carriers.

One thing airplanes could carry was the mail. In 1918 the United States Government established its own airmail service, with airfields and beacon lights across the country. In 1925, private companies were given the job of carrying the mail. They also began to carry other cargo and some passengers.

Aircraft design and construction improved, and the number of passengers began to grow. In 1926, Congress passed the Air Commerce Act, which set a system of licensing for airlines and pilots and established a federal airways system with light and radio beacons to mark the routes. Safety was improved with the addition of de-icers—devices on the wings that reduce the accumulation of ice in bad weather. Ice is dangerous because it destroys smooth airflow thus reducing lift. It also adds weight. Fire-extinguishing systems were installed, and new instruments and radio aids were developed to improve navigation and to allow safer flying. In 1927 more than 18,000 passengers traveled on commercial airlines.

Charles A. Lindbergh (*left*) stands beside the plane in which he made the first solo flight across the Atlantic Ocean (1927). Amelia Earhart (*right*) was the first woman to fly alone across the Atlantic (1932) and from Hawaii to California (1935).

In 1909, Louis Bleriot made the first flight across the English Channel, a distance of 23½ miles (37.8 kilometers).

The Spad XIII biplane was one of the best World War I fighters. It was built by the French and flown by many Allied pilots, including the American ace Eddie Rickenbacker.

The Curtiss JN4, or "Jenny," was used to train military pilots in 1916. After the war, Jennys carried airmail and flew in air shows.

The all-metal Ford Trimotor, a ten-passenger plane, was one of the first successful airliners.

Zeppelins. As airplanes began their first commercial flights, they had growing competition from rigid airships. The Germans built giant zeppelins. The first, in 1900, had been 419 feet (128 meters) long. By 1938 they had built a zeppelin that was 803 feet (245 meters) long, had four diesel engines, and could carry 30 tons of cargo across the ocean.

But the possibility of damage by storms or from the use of highly flammable hydrogen gas made airship travel hazardous. When the zeppelin *Hindenburg* burst into flames while docking in Lakehurst, New Jersey, in May, 1937, the public rejected them as a passenger aircraft. By that time, airplanes had become safer and more convenient. In 2001 a German company began offering commercial airship flights again. The new zeppelins are filled with nonflammable helium.

Successful Airliners. One of the first successful passenger planes was also used for explorations such as the pioneering flights made by American Rear Admiral Richard E. Byrd in Antarctica. The plane was the Ford Trimotor, one of the first all-metal aircraft. This ten-passenger plane was introduced in 1926, and many were still flying in the late 1930's.

In 1933, Boeing Aircraft Company introduced the 247, an all-metal plane with many new design features. Its cantilever wings were routed through the fuselage. The two engines had streamlined **cowling** (covers) into which the landing gear retracted. The new features were successful, but this plane also carried only ten passengers—too few for the growing airline businesses. However it paved the way for the first passenger plane capable of earning a profit. This was the legendary Douglas DC-3, introduced in 1936.

Douglas Aircraft Company engineers incorporated into the DC-3 all of the current technical developments of the time—all-metal structure, engine cowling, and retractable landing gear. It had **radial engines** (cylinders in a circle around the crankshaft) that were cooled by the air flowing over them, so they did not need heavy, complicated liquid cooling systems. The controllable pitch propellers could be changed to the most efficient angle for taking off or cruising. The landing flaps allowed the plane to land at lower speeds. In addition, the DC-3 carried 21 passengers. This plane made the United States a world leader in airline travel.

In the 1930's, intercontinental air travel increased. Giant zeppelins (*left*) carried passengers between Europe and North and South America. Flying boats, such as the Boeing 314 (*above*), were able to land on harbors and rivers next to many of the world's major cities.

The DC-3 was copied by many manufacturers in other countries and was the basis for airline growth all over the world. In World War II it was called the C-47 for use as a military transport. More than 13,000 civilian and military versions were built, many of which were still flying in the late 1980's.

Flying Boats. Another important passenger aircraft used in the 1930's was the flying boat. It was particularly useful for traveling long distances over oceans. It could land at many of the world's major cities that had no airports but were located on oceans, lakes, or rivers. Small flying boats were used for short trips in Europe, but only those built in the United States were capable of traveling long distances such as the 2,400 miles (3,900 kilometers) across the Pacific Ocean from California to Hawaii. Special piers were built for the flying boats to unload passengers and cargo. Sikorsky Aircraft Company's S.40 and S.42, the Martin M-130, and the Boeing 314 flew to the Far East, South America, and Europe. Flying boats were popular from the late 1930's until the end of World War II. By then, large airfields had been built all over the world, and there were land aircraft capable of carrying more passengers than the flying boats.

WORLD WAR II, 1939–1945

The technical advances used in the design of the DC-3 were also applied to the fighters and bombers of all the air forces that fought in World War II. The German Luftwaffe (air force) had already tested modern military aircraft such as the Messerschmitt Bf 109 fighter and Heinkel He 111 bomber in the Spanish Civil War. Civilians had learned the terrors of air warfare when German planes bombed and destroyed the Spanish city of Guernica. In 1939 and 1940 the Luftwaffe used tactics it had developed in Spain to support the German army in the conquest of Europe.

The English had matched the German aircraft development with its own fighters, the Spitfire and Hurricane. These were used to fight the Battle of Britain in August and September of 1940. By maintaining control of its own skies, the British Royal Air Force was able to prevent the Germans from invading or forcing a British surrender by heavy bombing. Although London and many British industrial cities were bombed, production of aircraft continued and the people's morale remained high.

The British had developed four-engine heavy bombers—the Short Stirling, Handley-

The British Spitfire was a World War II fighter. It could fly at more than 350 miles (560 kilometers) per hour.

The B-17 Flying Fortress, a World War II bomber, could carry 3 tons of bombs to targets 600 miles (966 kilometers) away.

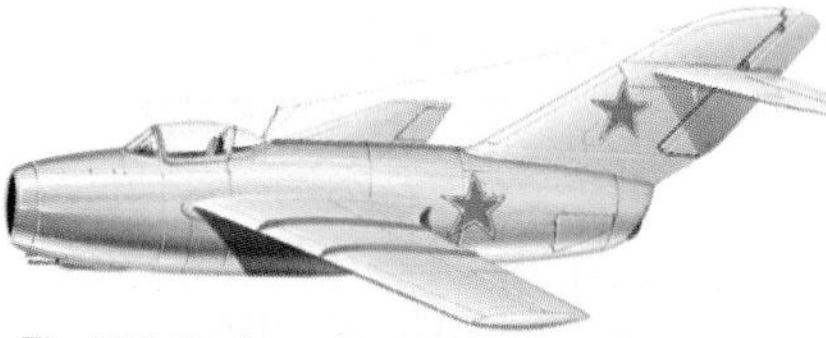

The MiG 15, shown here with North Korean markings, was a Russian-built fighter used in the Korean War. Its top speed was 668 miles (1,075 kilometers) per hour.

The B-52 Strato Fortress was in service from the late 1950's through the 1980's. It can carry bombs to targets 12,500 miles (20,000 kilometers) away.

The F-15 Eagle is a U.S. jet fighter used in the 1980's. It can climb to 98,000 feet (30,000 meters) in 2.5 minutes.

Page Halifax, and Avro Lancaster. These, with the American Boeing B-17s and Consolidated B-24s, eventually carried large bomb loads deep into German territory, sometimes maintaining round-the-clock bombing of military, industrial, and railroad targets, as well as of major cities.

The Japanese and Allied forces used aircraft in combination with ships throughout the war in the Pacific. On December 7, 1941, the Japanese used carrier-based aircraft to attack Pearl Harbor, the U.S. Naval base in Hawaii. The first important aerial blow struck by the United States was a bombing raid in April, 1942. B-25s, normally land-based, were launched from aircraft carriers to attack Tokyo and other Japanese cities. Allied strength in the air grew, with carrier-based and land-based planes playing important parts in the war in the Pacific. The last blow of the war was struck in August, 1945, by two B-29s, each carrying a single atomic bomb.

The B-29 was one of two aircraft that demonstrate the effect the war had on aircraft design and technology. It could fly at 400 miles (644 kilometers) per hour, had a range of 5,333 miles (8,583 kilometers), and could carry up to 10,000 pounds (4,545 kilograms) of bombs. This was later increased to 20,000 pounds (9,000 kilograms).

The second plane was Germany's 550-mile (885-kilometer)-per-hour Messerschmitt Me 262 fighter, whose jet engines and swept wings clearly showed the way for future aircraft design.

Other important aviation developments came out of the war. One was the use of radar for aircraft identification, control, navigation, and bombardment. Another was the helicopter, which was used as a rescue aircraft.

Other developments included a worldwide network of landing fields, navigational aides, meteorological (weather forecasting) facilities, and repair sites. These helped the huge expansion of air travel in the next decade.

1945 TO THE PRESENT

Before World War II, new designs of aircraft had been limited by the power available from current engines. The jet engine changed this situation. It was so powerful that stronger, more streamlined airframes were required.

New Designs. One of the most visible design changes was the swept wing that had been used on the Me 262. These wings were used on the new fighters and bombers and, in 1954, on the prototype (original model) of the Boeing 707, which became the world's first successful jet airliner. New metals and new manufacturing techniques were also developed to meet the special needs of high speed and high altitude flight.

The jet engine was not the only new form of propulsion. In October, 1947, the Bell XS-1 research rocket plane flew faster than the speed of sound (about 760 miles, or 1,225 kilometers, per hour). Rockets were usually used in research aircraft and as auxiliary power to help heavily loaded military planes take off.

The North American F-100, the first supersonic fighter, was put into service in 1953. Three years later the first supersonic bomber, the delta-winged Convair B-58, followed. In 1969, co-operative effort by Britain and France made possible the flight of the Concorde, the first successful supersonic airliner.

New Records. The new technology meant that speed and altitude records would continue to be challenged and broken. An intense international rivalry developed. The first official postwar speed record of 603 miles (971 kilometers) per hour was set in 1945 by a British Gloster Meteor F4.

In 1956 a British Fairey Delta 2 exceeded the 1,000-miles-per-hour mark at a speed of 1,132 miles (1,823 kilometers) per hour. A Russian Mikoyan Type E166 raised this to 1,666 miles (2,682 kilometers) per hour in 1962. By 1976 a U.S. Lockheed SR-71A—nicknamed the "Blackbird"—flew at 2,193 miles (3,531 kilometers) per hour. After the war, speeds were referred to in **"Mach" numbers**—multiples of the speed of sound, which is called Mach 1.

Although the records are not official, the highest and fastest aircraft ever flown is the North American X-15 research plane. In 1963 the X-15 reached an altitude of 354,200 feet—over 67 miles (108 kilometers). Because this is considered to be a space flight, the pilots were awarded astronaut wings. In 1967 the X-15A-2 achieved a speed of Mach 6.72, or 4,534 miles (7,300 kilometers) per hour.

While speed and altitude records were made and broken, one major goal of flight in the atmosphere had not been achieved. This was a nonstop, nonrefueled flight around the world. In December, 1986, this goal was reached in *Voyager,* a fragile-appearing airplane built by Burt Rutan, an American aircraft designer. It had a wingspan of 111 feet (33.8 meters)—longer than a Boeing 727—weighed 2,680 pounds (1,206 kilograms), and carried almost 1,200 gallons (4,560 liters) of fuel, which weighed four times as much as the plane itself.

The flight of 26,718 miles (43,016 kilometers) was made in 9 days by pilots Dick Rutan and Jeana Yeager. It was a triumph of high-technology materials, computer-aided design, and the personal skill and bravery of its pilots.

Left: **The DC-3, introduced in 1936, is one of the oldest airplanes in use today. This one is dropping fire fighters near a forest fire.**

Right: Voyager **is one of the latest airplane designs. In 1986 it made the first nonstop, nonrefueled flight around the world.**

The Boeing 747 (*above*) has its cockpit above the passenger area. The Concorde (*right*) had an adjustable nose section, shown here in the lowered position, which allowed the pilot to see the runway better.

COMMERCIAL AVIATION TODAY

Air travel has changed our lives in many ways. Where once only the wealthy traveled from country to country, now the average citizen can do it, too. Two things that make this possible are larger airplanes and more fuel efficient engines. An airplane like the Boeing 747 can carry 400 people at a cost 25 percent lower per person than the 100-passenger 707.

Another factor in lowering the cost of flying is deregulation of the airlines. In 1984 the United States government dissolved the Civil Aeronautics Board (CAB), the agency that had controlled the routes, fares, and some other airline activities. Now airlines compete for passengers by offering lower fares, better schedules, or different routes—things that once were set for them by the CAB.

Growth and Problems. After deregulation there was tremendous growth in the U.S. airline industry. But this growth has created problems, one of which is crowded airports. One of the busiest, O'Hare Field in Chicago, serves about 70 million passengers a year. In such busy conditions, baggage sometimes gets lost, or more tickets are sold for a flight than there are seats on the airplane. Delays caused by weather or maintenance problems may result in lines of airplanes waiting for takeoff or circling overhead waiting for their turn to land. Air traffic controllers must direct growing numbers of flights of arriving and departing aircraft as well as those en route. Airport administrations, airline companies, and the federal government are all trying to solve these problems.

The growth in passenger flying has created a need for new large and small airliners. The United States is the world leader in the manufacture of large planes such as the Boeing 767 and McDonnell Douglas MD11. But U.S. airlines also buy from foreign manufacturers. Regional airlines use smaller planes such as the German Fokker 100 and the British de Havilland DHC-7.

Although many technical improvements have been made in passenger airplane construction, speeds have increased very little. The original Boeing 707s had a maximum cruising speed of about 600 miles (966 kilometers) per hour. A modern 747 can attain about 625 miles (1,006 kilometers) per hour. Most airliners fly at about 550 miles (885 kilometers) per hour. The supersonic Concorde was the fastest airliner until it was withdrawn from service in 2003.

FLIGHT SAFETY

The airlines have had a very good safety record, and statistics show it is safer to travel by airplane than by car. But many people remain concerned about the dangers of flying. The government agency setting and maintaining aviation safety standards is the Federal Aviation Administration (FAA). The FAA regulates air traffic, investigates accidents, and makes rules for aircraft construction and maintenance and pilot licensing and training.

Because accident investigations often focus on pilot error, the FAA pays close attention to the training requirements of pilots. It gives pilot candidates written and flying tests for different levels of skill. A pilot is not allowed to fly for purposes beyond the level of the license earned. Airlines also test their pilots periodically.

Following the September 11, 2001, terrorist attacks, new security measures were established to ensure flight safety. The responsibility for airport security was assumed by the federal government. Also, all cockpit doors were strengthened and locked, and flight crews received additional training for handling emergency situations. (Also see HIJACKING in Volume H.)

GENERAL AVIATION

Aviation other than military or airline is called general aviation. The United States has long led the world in the number of private planes registered and in the total number of pilots licensed. In the mid-1990's, there were over 180,000 active general aviation aircraft, flown by some 640,000 active pilots.

Flying corporate executives in swift jets and fighting forest fires in water bombers are general aviation activities. Others include delivering organs for transplants, controlling traffic and other police work, and sport flying.

The number and variety of airplanes using large airports have created problems: Each type of plane flies at a different airspeed when approaching to land, yet it is necessary to maintain a safe distance between them. The pilots may be students in training or experienced flyers.

In the late 1980's, pilots, owners and manufacturers of small planes, and the FAA were seeking ways to protect flyers without overly restricting the use of the public airports. Controlled airspace around large airports is restricted to planes with two-way radios. In many such areas an aircraft must also have a **transponder**—a device that sends a signal identifying its position on the controller's radar screen.

AIRCRAFT MANUFACTURING

The cost of the new electronic equipment is high, as are the costs of buying, insuring, and maintaining aircraft. Flying lessons and renting airplanes are also expensive. This reduced by about 85 percent the number of new general aviation aircraft sold between the late 1970's and the late 1980's.

Total shipments of U.S. aircraft were about 2,400 in 1995 (not including off-the-shelf military aircraft). During World War II, U.S. manufacturers produced 100,000 aircraft per year. But modern planes are far more com-

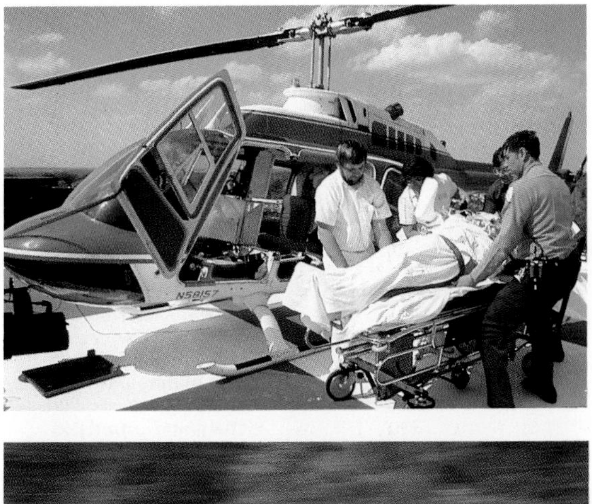

Aircraft serve many important purposes. Helicopters can be used to carry the ill or injured to hospitals (*top left*). Seaplanes carry people and supplies into remote areas where there are no airports (*bottom left*). Airplanes drop chemicals or water on forest fires (*below*).

plex. It may take seven years from the initial design to production of a warplane, and four years for a commercial airliner.

Every aspect of the design must be considered in order to achieve the combination of large size, high speed, and requirements for safety, reliability, and fuel economy. Engineers use many computer-aided design techniques. Before the first parts are built, there are computer tests of the design for strengths and weaknesses. New metals and composite materials such as plastic resins and graphite fibers are used because they combine strength and light weight. Sophisticated electronic equipment is also designed with the aid of computers.

The new materials and equipment and the time spent designing and building new planes are very costly. But planes are far more durable today than in the past. Whereas the early jet engines had to be overhauled every 25 hours of flying time, modern jet engines serve for tens of thousands of hours with much less maintenance. They last so long that weather-induced corrosion is more of a problem than are parts worn out by use. With careful maintenance and replacement of some parts with ones of newer design, an airliner can last 20 or 30 years, flying thousands of hours. This repays the owner's investment many times over.

▶CAREERS IN AVIATION

As airline services grow, so does the need for highly trained pilots and other aviation professionals. Because there are often a large number of qualified pilots seeking positions with the airlines, the standards for hiring can be very high. However, many new pilots are required every year as older pilots retire. For this reason, airlines are looking for ways to have enough pilots with the necessary training and experience. Some are providing their own training programs in which the entire training of a pilot is done by the airline's methods, right from the start. These may be combined with college degree programs.

Another source of qualified pilots is former military flyers. Military flying training standards are very high, and the equipment used is up to date. However, pilots earning their wings in the military service have to serve a number of years before returning to civilian life. In addition, the military pay is now more competitive with that of civilian pilots.

There are also a number of independent civilian flight training schools. It may cost a student as much as $25,000 to earn ratings to qualify as a professional pilot. Such a course would include 260 hours of flying time. Graduates of these schools might work for small commuter airlines, air taxi services, businesses owning airplanes, or in other jobs in which they are paid to fly with passengers. For all of these positions, candidates must be 18 years old and have a commercial license, which requires at least 250 hours of flying time. They must also take a written test and pass a physical examination.

Airline pilots must meet stricter requirements. To obtain an Airline Transport Pilot license, extensive training and experience with airline equipment is required. As well, written, physical, and flight examinations must be passed. Many airline pilots start out as flight engineers, for which they usually

In 1988, world records were set for distance and time aloft in a human-powered plane. Greek cycling champion Kanellos Kanellopoulos pedaled the American-built *Daedalus* for 3 hours and 54 minutes to complete the 74-mile (119-kilometer) flight between the Greek islands of Crete and Santorini.

The Beech Starship, a business plane, is built of light, strong composite materials. It has small forward wings, called canards, and winglets—sharply angled wingtips.

need both a commercial pilot's license and a flight engineer's license earned by passing written and practical tests.

Two licenses can be earned to become an airplane mechanic—either an airframe or engine mechanic's license; some positions require both. Aircraft mechanics maintain the complicated modern airliner. They often receive further training by the airline and by the manufacturer of the planes they maintain.

Each airline sets its own requirements and training for flight attendants. Their most important job is to see that the passengers are safe in normal operations and in emergencies. They also try to make the flight comfortable and enjoyable for the passengers.

Manufacturers employ engineers in many fields to design aircraft. Mechanics, electricians, and other expert workers are involved in the construction of the aircraft, and pilots are employed to test-fly them.

The FAA employs and trains air traffic controllers to work in airport control towers and other control centers. FAA pilots check the performance of commercial pilots, give flight exams to people seeking a pilot's license, and perform many safety-related tasks. Agency investigators try to discover the causes of all aviation accidents in order to prevent future ones.

THE FUTURE IN AVIATION

Since the first brief powered flight in 1903, aviation has undergone huge changes and has brought equally great changes to the world. Millions of people fly for business and pleasure. Two world wars and many other conflicts have shown the devastation of aerial conflict. And world leaders fly from one capital to another to attempt settlements of small wars before they become large ones.

The field of aviation will continue to change. New ideas in aircraft design will result in higher speeds and greater fuel economy. In the early 21st century, it may be possible to fly from New York City to Tokyo in less than two hours in a plane that flies at the edge of space.

Short flights from city center to city center will become more frequent with the further development of vertical-takeoff aircraft. The helicopter is a familiar version. Others will be similar to the tilt-rotor Bell XV-22, on which the angle of the engines can be changed for vertical or horizontal flight.

Cargo planes will be larger and able to carry heavier loads. The total weight of an aircraft, its fuel, and cargo might be as much as 1,000,000 pounds (450,000 kilograms). Cargo aircraft may be built in different shapes to carry certain large items. There are already specially modified planes that carry a single huge rocket engine. A modified 747 is used to carry the space shuttle on its back. More such uses will be devised.

Military aircraft will also have new shapes and be built of new materials. Some already have wings swept forward, and others have wings that can be moved from straight to swept positions. On-board computers assist in

MILESTONES OF AVIATION

1783 Jacques Étienne and Joseph Montgolfier of France launched first balloon (June).

1785 Jean Pierre Blanchard, French balloonist, made first successful voyage across English Channel.

1804 First winged glider made by Sir George Cayley, English aviation pioneer.

1848 John Stringfellow (English) constructed first successful power-driven model airplane.

1852 Henri Giffard flew steam-driven airship over Paris.

1891 Otto Lilienthal of Germany began his glider experiments.

1903 Wright brothers made first sustained, controlled flights in powered heavier-than-air craft at Kitty Hawk, North Carolina.

1909 Louis Blériot (French) made first crossing of English Channel in an airplane.

1911 Galbraith P. Rogers flew across United States, New York to California; flying time, 49 days.

1912 Harriet Quimby flew across English Channel, first woman to perform this feat.

1918 First airmail route established in United States.

1919 First crossing of Atlantic by air, accomplished by U.S. Navy seaplane; flying time, 54 hours.

First nonstop air crossing of Atlantic made by two English airmen, Captain John Alcock and Lieutenant Arthur Whitten Brown.

1923 Two U.S. Army pilots made first nonstop transcontinental flight, New York to San Diego, California, in 26 hours, 50 minutes.

1924 U.S. Army pilots made first round-the-world flight, which was also first transpacific flight; flying time, 175 days.

1926 Lieutenant Commander Richard E. Byrd, U.S. Navy, and Floyd Bennett flew across the North Pole, May 9.

1927 Charles A. Lindbergh made first solo nonstop transatlantic flight, New York to Paris; flying time, 33 hours, 30 minutes.

1929 Lieutenant James H. Doolittle, U.S. Army, made first flight using instruments only.

Commander Richard E. Byrd and crew made first flight across South Pole, November 29.

Fritz Opel of Germany flew first rocket plane.

1932 Amelia Earhart became first woman to fly Atlantic solo.

1939 First flight by jet aircraft made, in Germany.

1947 Captain Charles Yeager, USAF, made first supersonic flight.

1949 A USAF B-50, *Lucky Lady II*, completed first nonstop round-the-world flight.

1963 The X-15 flew to an altitude of 67 mi (108 km).

1965 Commander J. R. Williford, U.S. Navy, made longest direct helicopter flight—2,105 mi (3,388 km).

1967 First nonstop crossing of North Atlantic made by two USAF helicopters.

The X-15A-2 achieved the speed of Mach 6.72 (4,534 mi, or 7,300 km, per hour).

1969 First flights of Supersonic Transports (SST's)—Soviet TU-144 and Anglo-French Concorde.

1970 Boeing 747's made first commercial flights.

1976 Concorde began first passenger-carrying supersonic service.

1979 A human-powered aircraft, the *Gossamer Albatross*, was flown across the English Channel.

1981 Space shuttle orbiter *Columbia*, the first reusable spacecraft, made an airplane-like landing after completing its first space mission.

Stephen Ptacek flew *Solar Challenger*, powered by solar cells, across the English Channel.

1986 Richard Rutan and Jeana Yeager flew *Voyager* on the first nonstop, nonrefueled flight around the world.

1988 Record for distance (74 mi, or 119 km) and time aloft (3 hours, 54 minutes) set in a human-powered plane, the *Daedalus*.

1997 Steve Fossett flew a record distance (9,672 mi, or 15,572 km) in his balloon, *Solo Spirit*.

2004 The first manned commercial space flight was made by the rocket plane *SpaceShipOne*, piloted by Michael Melvill.

the controlling of the aircraft and its weapons. New materials for the surface of the aircraft will make it less visible on radar.

New fuels such as hydrogen, methane, or nuclear fuels will be used. Solar energy has already been used to power a very lightweight experimental aircraft. Other experiments are being conducted in which ground antennas beam microwaves to an aircraft where they are converted to electric power.

New materials and designs will also be used in general aviation aircraft. Some of these ideas will come from those modern aviation pioneers, the designer-pilots. These pilots follow the path of the Wright brothers, sometimes setting world records and leading the way for aircraft manufacturers. Many of the pilots and companies exchange information and encouragement through such organizations as the Experimental Aircraft Association of Oshkosh, Wisconsin.

Sport planes may soar with the birds, fighters may roar 10 feet above the terrain, and airliners may whisk 1,000 passengers from New York City to Honolulu. All of these aircraft will be products of the human spirit that produced the original dream of flight. They are a tribute to the men and women who devote their lives to aviation.

WALTER J. BOYNE
Former Director
National Air and Space Museum
Smithsonian Institution

See also AERODYNAMICS; AIRPLANES; AIRPORTS; BALLOONS AND BALLOONING; GLIDERS; HELICOPTERS; INTERNAL-COMBUSTION ENGINES; JET PROPULSION; NAVIGATION; RADAR AND SONAR; ROCKETS; SUPERSONIC FLIGHT; TRANSPORTATION; UNITED STATES, ARMED FORCES OF THE.

AZERBAIJAN

Azerbaijan is a country situated in the eastern part of Transcaucasia—the region lying along the great Caucasus Mountain range, which traditionally forms part of the dividing line between Europe and Asia. The present-day borders of Azerbaijan date from the early 1800's, when it was divided between Russia and Persia (now Iran). Russian, or northern, Azerbaijan was briefly independent, from 1918 to 1920, before it was absorbed by the Soviet Union, which succeeded the Russian Empire. When the Soviet Union itself fell apart in late 1991, northern Azerbaijan declared its independence.

The People. The Azeri, or Azerbaijanis, are descended from Turkic-speaking peoples who migrated to the region from Central Asia in ancient times. Today, Azeri Turks make up about 85 percent of the country's population. The two largest ethnic minorities are Russians and Armenians. Azeri Turkish is the official language, although Russian continues in common usage. (In Iranian Azerbaijan, Persian is widely used.) The Azerbaijanis are Muslims, the Russians and Armenians Christians. There are also a small number of Jews, some of whom have preserved their faith since the days of the Khazar Kaganate, a once-powerful Turkic state in the region.

About half the people live in urban areas. The capital and largest city, Baku, is Azerbaijan's chief port on the Caspian Sea. With some 2 million people in its metropolitan area, Baku has more than one-quarter of the country's total population.

Azerbaijan's territory includes the Nagorno-Karabakh and Nakhichevan regions. Nagorno-Karabakh has been the scene of much bloody fighting between ethnic Armenians and Azeris. The Armenians, who make up a majority of its population, seek unification with Armenia.

The Land. Azerbaijan has a ruggedly beautiful landscape. Nearly half the land is covered by mountains. The Greater Caucasus forms Azerbaijan's natural boundary on the north; the Lesser Caucasus separates it from Armenia on the west; and the Talysh Mountains border

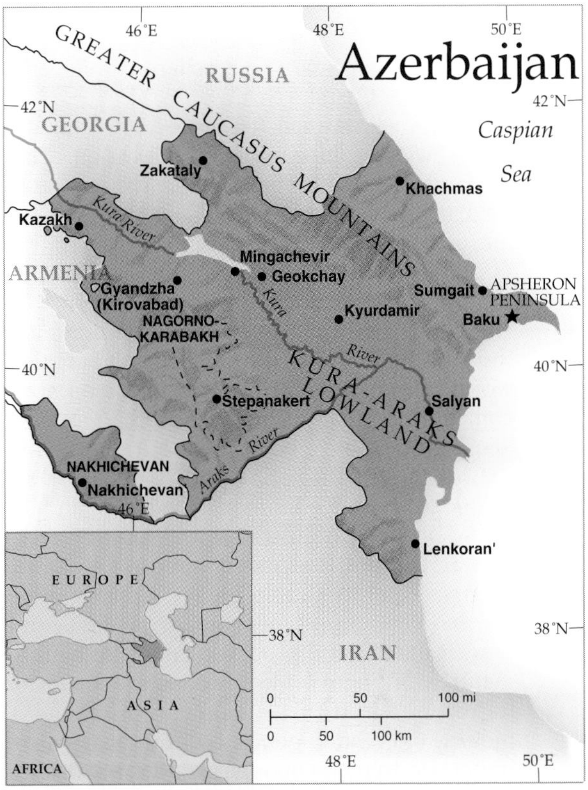

Looking as rugged as the mountains of her homeland, a woman of Azerbaijan contemplates her country's future. Azerbaijan was a constituent republic of the Soviet Union, before winning its independence as a result of the Soviet Union's collapse in 1991.

Iran to the south. Eastern Azerbaijan lies open to the Caspian Sea, which, despite its name, is the world's largest lake. Beyond the Caspian Sea are the deserts of Central Asia.

The Kura-Araks Lowland, which makes up the remaining land, takes its name from the country's two major rivers, the Kura and the Araks. The Araks marks the boundary with Iran. Fertile lowland plains, watered by the rivers and streams, stretch from the mountains to the Caspian Sea. The Apsheron Peninsula juts into the Caspian Sea.

Climate and Natural Resources. The climate varies widely, depending on elevation. The lowlands generally have mild winters and long, hot, and dry summers. Lowland temperatures in summer average 80°F (26°C). In the upper valleys and highlands, snow covers the ground in winter, while summers are cool.

Azerbaijan is rich in mineral resources. In the early 1900's it produced half of the world's petroleum. Most of the crude oil now comes from offshore oil fields in the Caspian Sea. Pipelines have been built to transport oil to ports on the Black Sea.

The Economy. Economically, Azerbaijan has well-developed industry as well as a diversified agriculture that meets almost all of the food needs of its people. Heavy industry is by far the most important segment of the economy. It includes oil processing and the manufacture of petroleum products, chemical fertilizers, electrical equipment, machinery, metals, and related goods. Light industry, also important to the economy, includes processed agricultural products, textiles, footwear, and electrical household appliances and other consumer goods.

The varied climate enables farmers to grow a variety of crops. These include wheat and other grains, cotton, tea, tobacco, and almost all kinds of vegetables and fruits. Sheep graze on mountain pastures in summer and in the lowlands in winter. The Caspian Sea teems with fish, including sturgeon, whose roe (eggs) are the source of the finest caviar.

History. As the only convenient land route through the Caucasus between Europe and Asia, Azerbaijan has been crossed by invading armies and migrating peoples since earliest times. The formation of Azerbaijan nationality dates from the A.D. 1000's, with the arrival of the last Turkic tribes, whose common language became Azeri Turkish. Only one time in its history was all of Azerbaijan united under a single national ruler: In the 1500's, a native Azeri dynasty of the Safavids (or Safawids) created a great empire that eventually reached from Central Asia to the Persian Gulf. But in the 1600's the dynasty fell under Persian rule.

The 1700's were marked by the struggle between Persia, Ottoman Turkey, and Russia for control of Azerbaijan and the rest of Transcaucasia. Under treaties signed in 1813 and 1828, Russia acquired the half of Azerbaijan north of the Araks River.

In 1918, a year after the Russian Revolution, Azeri leaders proclaimed an independent republic. It lasted only until 1920, when Azerbaijan was invaded by forces of the Soviet Union. It became a constituent republic of the Soviet Union in 1922.

With the collapse of the Soviet Union in December 1991, Azerbaijan regained its independence. A 1995 cease-fire halted the fighting in Nagorno-Karabakh, but tensions between Azerbaijan and Armenia over control of the region continued.

Government. The country's legislative body is the National Assembly (Milli Mejlis). Executive authority is held by the president, who appoints a council of ministers (headed by a prime minister) to handle the day-to-day operations of the government. Heydar A. Aliyev was elected president in 1993, the same year Azerbaijan joined the Commonwealth of Independent States (CIS). Aliyev was re-elected in 1998, although the opposition claimed he did not win the two-thirds majority of votes required. The election of his son Ilham Aliyev in 2003 brought further charges of vote tampering.

ALEC RASIZADE
The W. Averell Harriman Institute
Columbia University

FACTS and figures

AZERBAIJANI REPUBLIC is the official name of the country.

LOCATION: Southwest Asia.

AREA: 33,436 sq mi (86,600 km²).

POPULATION: 7,800,000 (estimate).

CAPITAL AND LARGEST CITY: Baku.

MAJOR LANGUAGE: Azeri Turkish (official).

MAJOR RELIGIOUS GROUP: Muslim.

GOVERNMENT: Republic. **Head of state**—president. **Head of government**—prime minister. **Legislature**—National Assembly (Milli Mejlis).

CHIEF PRODUCTS: **Agricultural**—wheat and other grains, cotton, tea, tobacco, vegetables and fruits, livestock. **Manufactured**—petroleum products, chemical fertilizers, electrical machinery, metals, processed agricultural products, textiles, consumer goods. **Mineral**—petroleum and natural gas, aluminum, iron, copper, and zinc ores.

MONETARY UNIT: Manat (1 manat = 100 qepik).

AZTECS

The Aztecs were an American Indian people of central Mexico, best known as the builders of an empire that swiftly fell under Spanish control during the years 1519 to 1521.

The defeat of the Aztecs was no ordinary conquest. The capital of their empire was a city larger than Rome. In its beauty it resembled Venice, set in the middle of a lake with canals for streets.

Although the city was demolished in the final battle of 1521, its fame has endured. Aztec civilization is remembered today for its elaborate religious life, complex social organization, elegant literature, and monumental works of sculpture.

SOCIAL ORDER

What made Aztec society run smoothly? How was it organized?

Such questions cannot be answered fully. Yet there is a wealth of information in the writings of conquerors and missionaries. Aztecs themselves learned to use alphabetic script, and some of them wrote descriptions of life as it had been before the Spanish Conquest. These early accounts are our sources.

Family and Community

When a man tied the end of his cloak to the corner of a woman's blouse, she became his wife and he could marry no other. Though he might take one or more secondary "wives," only the children of his actual wife could inherit his property.

A man's duties included farming, soldiering, and the various trades, such as carpentry and metalwork. A woman took care of the home, wove cloth, or practiced medicine.

Children had responsibilities of their own. Girls helped with the weaving. Boys fetched firewood or went to the marketplace to pick up scraps of maize (corn) and beans left by the merchants.

Settlements. Families lived in villages, towns, or cities. Every town had neighborhoods, each with its chief. A city with many neighborhoods might be divided into four quarters, each quarter with its chief. These divisions made it easy to recruit people for military service or large work projects.

In the Valley of Mexico, the center of the Aztec world, there were dozens of cities. The largest was the capital, called Tenochtitlán, which may have had a population of 200,000. Tenochtitlán and its twin city, Tlatelolco, were located on islands in the middle of a shallow lake. The islands were connected to the mainland by earthen causeways.

Today the capital of the republic of Mexico is Mexico City. It is on the same site, but the lake, over the years, has been mostly drained.

Social Classes. Like cities today, the Aztec capital was a place of bustling activity, filled with people of all kinds. Everybody, however, fit into one of three categories: nobles, commoners, and *tlatlacotin*. The *tlatlacotin* were poor people who had sold themselves as permanent workers. Their children, however, were born free.

This drawing by Ignacio Marquina shows the Aztec capital Tenochtitlán as it appeared in 1519. It is based on the descriptions of Spanish conquerors and the remains of Aztec monuments.

High officials were usually chosen from the noble class. Commoners were also selected, if of proven ability.

Government

Each city was ruled by a king, who gave orders to neighborhood chiefs and to kings of cities under his control. There was no single chain of command but several, each ending with one of the important kings. These kings made alliances among themselves. Since Tenochtitlán was the strongest of the cities, its ruler can be called emperor or king of the empire.

Tribute. The reason for controlling other cities was to make them pay taxes, or tribute. Tribute goods included cloaks, hides, timber, stone, precious feathers, jewels, gold, and various foods.

Warfare. People did not like giving tribute to a king in a distant city. They were loyal to their own town. But if they refused to pay, they were threatened with armed attack.

Aztec armies were well equipped with bows and arrows, spears, and a kind of wooden sword, called *macana*, which was edged with sharp bits of stone.

If the governors or emperor heard of a faraway city rich in goods, they sent warriors to conquer it. Afterward they divided up the tribute and made sure that it kept coming regularly. This is how the empire grew.

▶WAY OF LIFE

Traditional Aztec wisdom preached caution. The saying "The world is slick and slippery" meant it is easy to make mistakes in life. Aztecs also said, "Not twice on earth," meaning you only live once, so enjoy life while you can.

From Birth to Death

When a girl was born, she was presented with a tiny sewing basket. A boy was given a miniature shield and four little arrows. Before the age of 4, children had their ears pierced. At 5 or 6, children could go out to play, if they had finished their chores.

Education. At 10, children were legally responsible for their actions and could be sentenced to punishment. At this age all boys and girls were sent to neighborhood boarding schools. Some students learned trades. Others studied history, music, the art of speaking, and the interpretation of dreams.

At 15 a young woman was ready for marriage. The typical young man became a warrior and would marry later.

Dress. Men wore loincloths and simple cloaks knotted over one shoulder. Women wore sleeveless blouses and wrap-around skirts of cotton cloth.

Shelter and Food. Houses were of one story and might have several rooms, each facing a central courtyard. The kitchen with its fireplace was in the rear. A young family often lived in a single room in the house of the husband's father.

Maize, beans, squash, and turkey were important foods. Crops were grown on island gardens called *chinampas*, made of fertile soil scooped from the lake bottom.

Commerce. More unusual foods, such as cacao, pineapples, and vanilla, were brought by merchants from the lowlands. Cacao beans, the source of chocolate, were often used as money in the great marketplaces, where goods from all over the Aztec world were traded.

Goods came to market on the backs of porters. There were no beasts of burden and no wheeled vehicles. Water transport was by dugout canoe.

Old Age. Alcohol was restricted by law. But the elderly could drink as much as they wanted. This, along with retirement from work, was a privilege of old age.

Fragment of an Aztec Song

We merely come to stand sleeping,
we merely come to dream. It
is not true, not true that
we come to live on earth.
We come to do as herbs in spring:
and though our hearts come
sprouting, come green, those
few flowers of our flesh
that open wither away.

— translated by John Bierhorst from *Cantares Mexicanos*, a manuscript written in the 1500's.

Aztec statues are noted for their massive size and mysterious details. *Left:* The great statue of the earth goddess Snake Skirt wearing a carved necklace of human hands and hearts. *Above:* The famous "calendar stone." In the center is the face of an Aztec earth god.

Funerals. Long prayers were said for a dead person. The corpse was either buried or cremated, together with a sewing basket and weaver's tools (for a woman) or weapons (for a man).

It was believed that most people went to the dead land beneath the earth. Those who had drowned went to the paradise of the rain god. The most honored dead were men killed in battle and women who had died in childbirth. They went to the sky to live with the sun.

Religion

Aztecs worshipped many gods in addition to the rain god and the sun. There was the fire god, called Old God. There was an earth goddess, called Snake Skirt, and a goddess of love, named Flower Plume.

Merchants and hunters had special gods who received their prayers. The city of Tenochtitlán had a tribal god, Huitzilopochtli (wee-tseel-oh-POACH-tlee), who protected the city's warriors.

Feasts and the Calendar. The year was divided into 18 "months," each with 20 days. In each of these months there was a feast in honor of one or more gods. The rain god and the maize god were remembered in the spring. One of the fall months was devoted to Cloud Snake, god of hunting. Religious feasts were marked by parades and music. At the end of the year were five unlucky days, when people stayed indoors.

At the close of every 52 years a special ceremony was held. All fires were put out. Then a priest kindled a new fire using a drilling stick. Runners with torches carried the new fire to each of the settlements in the Valley of Mexico.

The Payment. Aztecs believed that the gods demanded payment, perhaps an offering of food or a sacrifice of quail. For the new fire ceremony and other important feasts it was necessary to make the "human payment"—the sacrifice of a human being.

Arts

Architects, painters, and musicians were skilled professionals who enjoyed prestige in Aztec society.

The most impressive works of architecture were the pyramids, built in tiers like a wedding cake. At the top of a pyramid were one or more temples, housing statues of gods.

Gods were also depicted in books, made from long sheets of bark paper, rolled or folded. There were no words, only numbers and pictures that were outlined with black and filled in with brilliant colors. The books were used to record history, to explain the functions of gods, and to list the tribute each city had to pay.

Aztec literature as we know it today was not preserved in these old-style books. It was written after the Spanish Conquest, using the alphabetic script learned from missionaries.

It includes poetic speeches, myths, histories, and the texts of songs.

Songs, both before and after the Conquest, were accompanied by two kinds of drums: a skin drum, played with the hands, and a two-toned log drum, played with mallets. Songs, as well as speeches, often touch upon historical incidents that are explained more fully in other longer works of literature.

HISTORY

Traditional Aztec histories begin with myths of world creation. They continue with legends about the Aztecs' predecessors, the Toltecs, who archaeologists have determined flourished between A.D. 900 and 1200. Their capital, Tula, now in ruins, is located 45 miles (72 kilometers) north of Mexico City. These legends are followed by historical accounts of the kings who built the Aztec empire.

Origin of the Aztecs

Aztecs claimed to have come from a region far to the north, migrating south toward Tula and into the Valley of Mexico. At about this time—according to legend—Tula's last ruler, the priest-king Quetzalcóatl (keh-tsahl-KOH-ahtl) broke his priestly vows and fled in disgrace to the eastern seashore. He disappeared over the water, promising one day to return. After he had gone, an Aztec tribe called Mexica founded Tenochtitlán, in 1325.

The Rise and Fall of the Aztec Empire

After years of warring with its neighbors, Tenochtitlán formed an alliance with two other cities, Texcoco and Tlacopán. This occurred about 1430. The new alliance, or empire, grew rapidly. By the time of the emperor Montezuma II, Aztecs controlled a territory stretching from the Pacific Ocean to the Gulf of Mexico and south to the present border of Guatemala.

A close-up view of the tiers of a Teotihuacán pyramid located outside Mexico City. Teotihuacán means "Palace of the Gods."

Spanish Conquest. It was Montezuma II who greeted the conqueror Hernando Cortés in 1519 (or the year 1 Reed by the Aztec calendar). According to legend, Montezuma believed Cortés was the legendary Quetzalcóatl, who was to return in the year 1 Reed, and was hesitant to give offense.

Montezuma was taken prisoner by the Spanish and mysteriously killed. Unable to restrain the populace by peaceful means, Cortés resorted to force. Firearms, horses, and steel armor gave the Spanish an edge. But they could not have won without the help of other Aztec cities, eager to see Tenochtitlán humbled. The capital was reduced to rubble during the fierce battle of the summer of 1521. A new Spanish city began to rise in its place.

Aftermath. Smallpox and other diseases brought from Europe greatly diminished the Aztec population. The succession of kings continued through the 1500's. Now known as *gobernadores* (governors), they served under Spanish authority. Although the *gobernadores* eventually lost what remained of their powers, people continued to read and write the Aztec language through the 1700's and to keep up many of the ancient customs.

Legacy of the Aztecs

The modern Aztec language, known as Nahuatl or *mexicano*, is still spoken by more than a million Nahua, who continue to plant maize, weave cotton cloth, and play instruments like the log drum. The Nahua live mostly in small towns and villages in central Mexico.

Nationally, Aztec art is recognized as an essential feature of Mexico's heritage. Aztec painting and sculpture have influenced Mexican artists such as Diego Rivera and Miguel Covarrubias. Modern poets such as Octavio Paz have been inspired by Aztec literature.

Perhaps the most widely known legacy of Aztec culture is in the realm of foods and recipes. *Avocado, chili, chocolate,* and *tomato* are all Aztec words. If you have been to a Mexican restaurant or have prepared Mexican food at home, you may have had *enchiladas, guacamole, tacos,* and *tamales*. These are dishes made with ingredients that go back to Aztec times.

JOHN BIERHORST
Author, *The Mythology of Mexico and Central America*

See also CORTÉS, HERNANDO; INDIANS, AMERICAN; MONTEZUMA II.

HOW TO USE THE INDEX

When travelers visit a large city, they use maps or guides to find their way about. When you want to find information in an encyclopedia, you need a guide, too. The Index is your guide to all the information in THE NEW BOOK OF KNOWLEDGE.

Each volume of THE NEW BOOK OF KNOWLEDGE contains the corresponding alphabetical division of the Index.

USING THE INDEX

When you look something up in this encyclopedia, you should always refer to the Index first. It will tell you where you can find what you want to know. Sometimes, if you need just one key fact, it will tell you all you want to know.

The Index brings together all the references to information about a particular subject. It tells you where that subject—and every subject related to it—is discussed. In most cases when you use the Index to look up a topic, you will find along with it a short definition or identifying phrase. This brief definition explains a term that may be unfamiliar to you and helps you make sure you have found the topic you are looking for.

HOW THE INDEX IS ARRANGED

The model entry and text in the next column and the diagram below explain what you will see if you look up a subject in the Index.

Anthropology (study of human beings and human culture) **A:300–305** *see also* Human beings; Sociology
archaeology related to **A**:349, 362
Boas, Franz **B**:261
Leakey family **L**:96–97
Mead, Margaret **M**:195
prehistoric people **P**:438–42
races, human **R**:28–31

The subject you are looking up, **Anthropology**, is called the **heading** and is in boldface type. Next to the heading are a few words that identify the topic —"study of human beings and human culture." These words are called the **identification**. A volume letter and page numbers follow the identification—**A:300–305**. The volume letter is always in boldface type and tells you in which volume to look for the information about the subject. The page numbers tell you on which pages of the volume to look. If they are also in boldface type, they are directing you to an entire article about the subject; if they are in lightface type, the information is in another article. The heading, its identification, and its volume and page numbers together make up the **entry**.

Following the page number of the entry, you will find the words "*see also*," followed by two index headings. The "*see also*" listings are called **cross-**

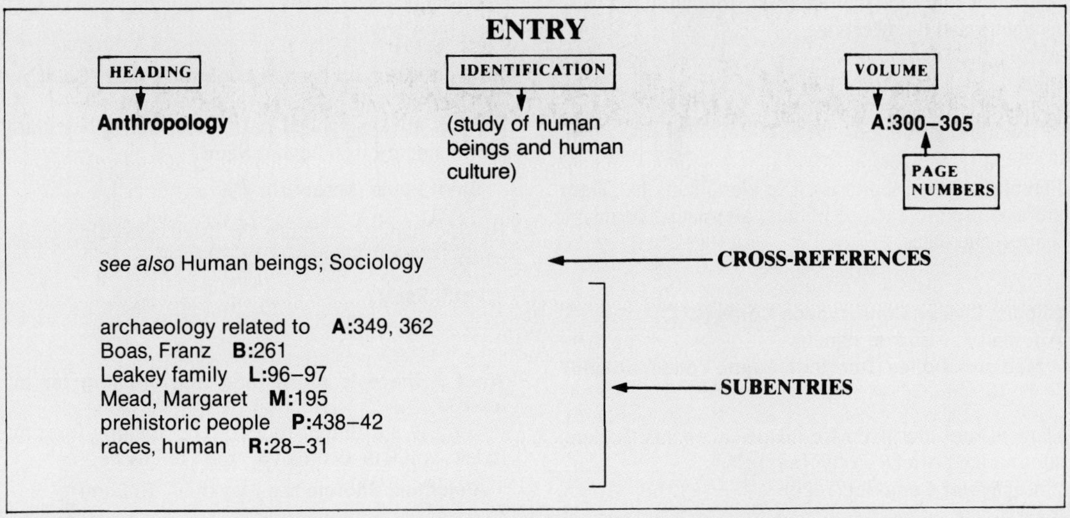

references. They tell you where to look to find more information related to your subject. Cross-references are guides to Index entries, not to article titles.

Beneath the entry there is a list of additional references to your subject. These references are called **subentries**. They are indented and arranged in alphabetical order. The subentries refer to all the important information about your subject throughout the set. Unless you look in the Index, you may not think of all the points about your subject that have been covered in the encyclopedia. (Subentries, in turn, may appear as main entries in other parts of the Index under their own initial letters.)

In the case of **Anthropology** there are only a few subentries. But if you look up a broad topic, such as **Vocations**, you may find dozens of subentries. Subentries are helpful if you want to review the whole of a particular field.

Illustrations are indicated by the words *"diagram(s)"* or *"picture(s)"* following the subject entry and its subentries.

Circles (in geometry) *diagram(s)* **G:**122
Bridges B:395–401
picture(s)
swinging bridge **J:**157

Country, state, and province articles each include at least one map, often with its own index. These maps are not listed in the Index, but other types of maps are indicated by the word *map(s)*, following the subject entry and its subentries.

Pigs
map(s)
world distribution **W:**265

Parentheses are used to enclose identifications. They are also used to enclose initials, alternative forms of names, and dates.

Initials: **Civilian Conservation Corps (CCC)**
Alternative forms of names:
Madison, Dolley (Dorothea Payne Todd Madison)

Dates: Dates are given for historical events that are summarized briefly in the Index.
Mayflower Compact (1620)

What should I look for?
Think of the specific word about which you need information and look for that. Go directly to the name you usually use for the thing you want. If you want to find out about baseball, turn directly to **Baseball** in the Index. You do not have to hunt first under **Sports**, although you would find baseball listed there, too.

How do I look up a person's name?
Look for the last name, just as you do when you use the telephone book.

Blake, William (English poet and artist) **B:250b**

How do I look up names that begin with "Mac" or "Mc"?
Names beginning with "Mac" and "Mc" are placed in alphabetical order, just as they are spelled.

MacArthur, Douglas
Macbeth
Mac Cool
Machine language
Maze
M' Bochi
McAuliffe, Christa
McKinley, William

What if the person is known by more than one name?
Some persons are known by more than one name. Such entries are listed by their best-known names—**Buffalo Bill**; **Twain, Mark**; **Napoleon**. However, if you should look under the person's official name, a cross-reference will tell you the right place to look.

Bonaparte, Napoleon *see* Napoleon I
Clemens, Samuel Langhorne *see* Twain, Mark
Cody, William Frederick *see* Buffalo Bill

How do I look up names beginning with "Saint" or "St."?
Saint is always spelled out. Place names beginning with Saint are listed under **Saint**.

Saint Louis (Missouri)

But the names of saints are listed according to the name. "Saint" is placed after the name.

Paul, Saint

What if there is more than one spelling for my topic?
If you use a different (but correct) spelling from the Index, you will also find a *"see"* reference.

Aleichem, Sholem *see* Aleykhem, Sholem

How are the headings in the Index arranged?
Because this is a Dictionary Index, it is arranged like a dictionary, letter by letter.

Mink
Minneapolis
Minnesingers
Minnesota

What if a heading is made up of more than one word?
Even when headings are made up of more than one word, they are still arranged alphabetically, letter by letter.

New Amsterdam
Newark
Newbery, John
New Castle

When there is a comma in the heading, the letter-by-letter arrangement goes through to the comma only—so that all the same names will be brought together.

Black (color)
Black, Hugo La Fayette
Black, Joseph
Blackball
Black Hills
Black market

What about words in parentheses, titles, and Roman numerals?
The alphabetical arrangement of headings is not affected by words in parentheses, titles, or Roman numerals. Just look up the heading as if it did not contain these added words or symbols.

John I, II, and III (books of the New Testament)
John (king of England)
John II (king of France)
John XXIII (pope)
John, Saint (apostle of Jesus Christ)

How do I look up a heading that begins with a number?
If a number is the first word in a heading, the number is spelled out and put in its alphabetical place.

Seven Cities of Cíbola
Seven Sisters
Seventeenth Amendment (to the United States Constitution)
Seven wonders of the ancient world

When numbers appear in any other place in a heading, they come before letters.

Carbon
Carbon-14
Carbon black

Do I look up "A," "An," and "The"?
"A," "an," and "the" are not used in alphabetizing. If any one of these words is part of the title of the book or play, the word is put at the end of the title.

Cat in the Hat, The
Midsummer Night's Dream, A

How are initials indexed?
You will find initials in their proper alphabetical order. A *"see"* reference along with them will lead you to the heading for which the initials stand.

CIA *see* Central Intelligence Agency

How do I look up the abbreviation "Mt."?
Mount is always spelled out and is placed after the name.

Everest, Mount

The word "lake," too, as a geographical term, is placed after the name.

Michigan, Lake

But you can look up the names of forts, towns, and rivers just as you would say them.

Fort Dearborn
Lake Placid
Mississippi River
Mount Vernon

How do I look up a poem?
Poems are listed individually by name and also by their authors.

"Jabberwocky" (poem by Carroll) **N:**273

Carroll, Lewis
"Jabberwocky" **N:** 273

How do I look up a story?
If the story you are looking for has been included in its complete form, you will find it listed under the heading **Stories** (told in full). If the story you want is part of a longer work, you will find it listed individually by its name.

Oliver Twist (book by Charles Dickens)
excerpt from **D:**151–52

Other listings similar to **Stories** are **Experiments and other science activities; Hobbies; How to.**

Index

A (first letter of the English alphabet) **A:1** *see also* Alphabet
AA (organization) *see* Alcoholics Anonymous
Aa (type of lava) **V:**382
AAA *see* Agricultural Adjustment Administration
Aachen (Germany) **F:**421–22; **W:**313
Aachen, Treaties of *see* Aix-la-Chapelle, Treaties of
Aalto, Alvar Henrik (Finnish architect and designer) **F:**138
  furniture **F:**517
  picture(s)
    molded plywood chair **F:**515
AAM (air-to-air missiles) **M:**345, 349; **U:**110
Aamodt, Kjetil Andre (Norwegian athlete) **O:**117–18
Aardvark, African (animal) **H:**216
  picture(s) **M:**72
Aardwolf (animal) **H:319**
  picture(s) **H:**319
Aarhus (Denmark) *see* Århus
Aaron (in the Old Testament) **B:**159
Aaron, Henry Louis (Hank) (American baseball player) **A:**142 *profile;* **B:**88 *profile,* 93
  picture(s) **B:**88
AAU *see* Amateur Athletic Union of the United States
Abaca (plant fiber) **F:**109; **R:**333, 334
Abacha, Sani (Nigerian political leader) **N:**258
Abacus (counting device) **A:2–3; N:**404–5
  computers, history of **C:**489
  early office machine **O:**59–60
  Japanese soroban **J:**30
Abbai (name for the Blue Nile in Ethiopia) **E:**331
Abbas, Mahmoud (Palestinian prime minister) **A:**349; **P:**43
Abbasid (Muslim dynasty) **A:**341, 345; **I:**315, 351
Abbas the Great (Persian shah) **I:**308
Abbate, Niccolo dell' (Italian painter) **F:**424; **R:**171
Abbe, Ernst (German physicist) **E:**163; **M:**286
Abbey Theatre (Dublin, Ireland) **I:**326–27; **T:**161; **Y:**354
Abbot, Margaret (American golfer) **O:**112
Abbott, Sir John Joseph Caldwell (Canadian prime minister) **C:**76 *profile*
Abbreviations **A:4–5** *see also* individual letters of the alphabet
  amateur radio **R:**63
  library filing **L:**186
  Postal Service abbreviations **P:**401–2
  states *see* individual state articles
  used as slang **S:**191
Abdication (of a monarch) **G:**276
Abdomen (part of the body)
  bees **B:**116
  beetles **B:**124
  insects **I:**230, 231
  shrimps **S:**167
  picture(s)
    CAT scan **X:**351
Abdul-Jabbar, Kareem (Lew Alcindor) (American basketball player) **B:**95i *profile*
  picture(s) **B:**95i
Abdullah II (king of Jordan) **H:**307; **J:**132
Abdullah Ahmad Badawi (prime minister of Malaysia) **M:**59
Abdullah ibn Hussein (king of Jordan) **J:**132
Abdul Rahman, Tunku *see* Rahman, Tunku Abdul
Abdul-Rauf, Mahmond (American basketball player)
  picture(s) **B:**95d
à Becket, Saint Thomas *see* Becket, Saint Thomas à
Abegweit (Micmac name for Prince Edward Island) **P:**460
Abel (in the Old Testament) *see* Cain and Abel
Abelard, Peter (French philosopher) **M:**294 *profile*
Aberdeen (Scotland) **S:**87; **U:**56
Aberdeen (South Dakota) **S:**318, 324
Abernathy, Ralph David (American minister and civil rights leader) **A:**142 *profile;* **S:**115
Aberrations (of lenses) **L:**148–49
Abhorrers (early English political party) **P:**369
Abidjan (working capital of the Ivory Coast) **I:**420–21
  picture(s) **I:**417
Abilene (Kansas) **K:**184; **O:**282
  picture(s) **K:**177, 184
Ability
  individual differences in learning abilities **L:**106
  measurement by tests **P:**501; **T:**118
AbioCor artificial heart **M:**208g; **O:**227
  picture(s) **M:**208g; **O:**227
Abizaid, John P. (American general) **I:**316b
Abkhazia (autonomous region in the Republic of Georgia) **G:**148
Able-bodied seamen (in the Merchant Marine) **U:**126
ABM systems *see* Antiballistic missile systems
Abnaki Confederacy (of Native Americans) **I:**177; **S:**25; **V:**310, 316
Åbo (Finland) *see* Turku
Abolition movement (United States history) **A:6–6b,** 79f–79g; **U:**183
  Adams, John Quincy **A:**19
  Anthony, Susan B. **A:**299
  Brown, John **B:**411
  Civil War issue **C:**333, 334, 335, 340
  Douglass, Frederick **D:**289
  Dred Scott case **D:**321
  Grimké, Sarah and Angelina **G:**381
  New York, history of **N:**224
  Ohio **O:**76
  Pennsylvania **P:**139
  political parties, history of **P:**371
  Schurz, Carl **W:**207
  Tubman, Harriet **T:**328
  Underground Railroad **U:**15–17
  What were the Gag Rules? **A:**6b
  Whittier, John Greenleaf **W:**169
  women's rights movement **W:**212–12a
Abomasum (section of the stomach of a ruminant) **H:**218
Abomey (capital of the kingdom of Dahomey) **B:**144
Abominable Snowman **H:**137–38
Aborigines, Australian (native people of Australia) **A:7,** 496, 497–98, 512, 517
  desert nomads **D:**127–28
  funeral customs **F:**495
  painting **A:**501
  picture(s) **A:**7, 497
Abortion (early ending of pregnancy) **A:8**
  Bush, George W., administration **B:**469
  ethics and society **E:**329
  Supreme Court of the United States **S:**509; **W:**213
Abraham (father of the Jews) **A:8–9**
  Dome of the Rock mosque in Jerusalem **J:**82
  Isaac was the son of **I:**345
  Islam **I:**346, 349; **K:**293
  Jews, history of the **J:**101
  Judaism, beliefs of **J:**144
  Muslim traditions **M:**199
  Old Testament **B:**159
  religions of the world **R:**147
  picture(s) **A:**8; **B:**162; **I:**347
Abraham, Plains of (site of the Battle of Quebec) **F:**465; **Q:**16, 17
Abraham's Sacrifice (etching by Rembrandt)
  picture(s) **D:**364
Abramowitz, Shalom Jacob *see* Mendele Mocher Sefarim
Abrams, Elliot (American public official) **I:**310
Abrasives (materials used for grinding and polishing) **G:**391–92
  ceramics **C:**178
  grinding machines **T:**232
  optical glass grinding **O:**185
  woodworking tools **W:**231
Abruzzo, Ben (American balloonist) **B:**36

Absalom (in the Old Testament) **B**:159
Absalom and Achitophel (play by Dryden) **D**:342
Absalon (Danish bishop) **C**:552
Absaroka Range (mountains, Wyoming) **W**:336
picture(s) **M**:430
Abscisic acid (plant hormone) **P**:312
Abscission (shedding of leaves by trees) **L**:115
Absentee ballots (for voting in elections) **V**:392
Absolute magnitude (of stars) **S**:428
Absolute monarchy (government by ruler without checks on power) **F**:414; **G**:273
Absolute zero **H**:87, 89
Absorbent papers **P**:56
Absorption (process by which one substance takes in another substance or energy) **C**:424; **H**:94; **L**:216
Absorption refrigerating system **R**:133–34
Absorption spectrum (in which colors are separated by dark spaces) **L**:225–26; **S**:489
Abstinence (from sexual intercourse) **B**:251
Abstinence syndrome *see* Withdrawal
Abstract algebra **M**:169
Abstract art (art movement) **M**:396b
American art **U**:132
Cézanne's influence **I**:106
collage **C**:402
concern with form **A**:433
cubism **C**:612
Dutch painting **D**:368
France **F**:432
Germany's Blue Rider group **G**:172
Guggenheim Museum (New York City) **M**:526
Kandinsky, Wassily **K**:173
Latin America **L**:65
Léger, Fernand **L**:136
Mondrian, Piet **M**:410
Russia, art of **R**:379
Abstract expressionism (art movement) **E**:424; **M**:396b; **P**:31, 32; **U**:134
Pollock, Jackson **P**:378
Spain, art of **S**:385
Still, Clyfford **N**:335
surrealism's influence on **S**:518
Abstract thought **C**:226
Abstract words **P**:92; **S**:116
Absurdist drama **D**:303
Abubakar, Abdulsalam (Nigerian president) **N**:258
Abu Bakr (Islamic caliph) **I**:350
Abu Dhabi (United Arab Emirates) **U**:45
Abu-Gurab (site of ancient Egyptian temple) **E**:111–12
Abuja (capital of Nigeria) **N**:256
Abuse of alcohol *see* Alcoholism
Abuse of children *see* Child abuse
Abu Simbel (site of ancient Egyptian temples) **D**:21; **E**:108, 114, 115
Abyssal plain (of the ocean floor) **O**:21
Abyssal zone (of the ocean habitat) **O**:23
Abyssinia *see* Ethiopia
Abyssinian cats **C**:138
A.C. *see* Alternating current
Acacia trees **P**:317
Academic dress **U**:223
Academic skills disorders **L**:107
Academy (school in Athens started by Plato) **P**:330
Academy (school in early America started by Benjamin Franklin) **E**:83, 84
Academy of Arts (Russia) **R**:377
Academy of Model Aeronautics (Washington, D.C.) **A**:107
Academy of Natural Sciences (Philadelphia) **P**:131
Academy of Painting and Sculpture (France) **F**:425, 430
Academy of Sciences (Russia) **R**:369
Acadia (French name for the area that is now Nova Scotia and New Brunswick) **C**:81; **N**:138g, 350, 357
Acadiana (region of Louisiana) **L**:322
Acadia National Park (Maine) **M**:44
picture(s) **M**:38, 44; **U**:77
Acadians (original French settlers of New France) **C**:51; **N**:138g, 356, 357 *see also* Cajuns
Acadian Village (New Brunswick) **N**:138e
Louisiana **L**:327
Maine settlers **M**:41
A cappella (musical term) **C**:283; **M**:536
Acapulco (Mexico) **M**:247
picture(s) **M**:243
hurricane damage **W**:81
Acasta gneisses (rocks) **R**:268
Accelerando (musical term) **M**:536
Accelerated erosion (caused by misuse of land) **E**:319
Accelerated motion (in physics) **M**:474
Acceleration (change in speed of an object)
falling bodies, laws of **F**:34
forces **F**:365
gravity and gravitation **G**:320, 322
human body, effects on **S**:340L–341
measurement **W**:116–17
motion **M**:475–76
rockets and Newton's laws of motion **R**:258
Accelerators, particle *see* Particle accelerators
Accelerometer (instrument to show changes in speed) **S**:340k
Accents (in music) **M**:536, 538
Accents (marks of stress in pronunciation) **P**:486
Accessories (interior design) **I**:261
Accidentals (in music) **M**:535, 536
Accident insurance *see* Insurance, accident
Accidents
avoiding health hazards **H**:76
blindness, causes of **B**:256
disabled people **D**:176–77
driver education courses **D**:324–27
first-aid treatment for **F**:156–62
occupational health and safety **O**:13
poisoning **P**:355–56
police investigate traffic accidents **P**:364
retardation, mental, can be caused by **R**:191
safety **S**:3–5
space exploration and travel **S**:352
workers' compensation **W**:253
Accipiters (woodland hawks) **H**:64
Accommodation, power of (of the eye) **E**:430; **L**:149–50
Accordion (musical instrument) **K**:240; **W**:185
picture(s) **F**:321; **K**:239
Accounting **B:311, 312–14**
Account manager (Executive) (at advertising agencies) **A**:33
Accra (capital of Ghana) **G**:196, 197
Accreditation (of hospitals) **H**:252
Accreditation (of universities and colleges) **U**:224
Accretion (buildup of new material on mollusks' shells) **S**:149
Accretion hypothesis (of origin of solar system) *see* Solar system—theories of formation
Accumulation (process in water cycle) **R**:93
A.C.E. (abbreviation used with dates) **C**:16
Ace (in tennis) **T**:90
Acesulfame-K (artificial sweetener) **S**:484
Acetate fibers **F**:110; **N**:436, 440
Acetic acid (in vinegar) **F**:344
Acetone (chemical) **F**:91
Acetylcholine (neurotransmitter) **B**:363; **N**:118
Acetylene torches **O**:289; **W**:118
picture(s) **O**:289
Achaeans (a people of ancient Greece) **T**:316
Achaemenid dynasty (ancient Persia) **I**:308; **P**:154–55
Achard, Franz Carl (German chemist) **S**:484
Achebe, Chinua (Nigerian writer) **A**:76d; **N**:257
Acheson, Edward (American inventor) **G**:391
Achievement tests **P**:501; **T**:118, 119–20
Achilles (in Greek mythology) **G**:355, 369; **I**:61; **T**:316
Achilles' heel **G**:369
Achromatic lenses **M**:286; **T**:58
Acid dyes **D**:377

Acid rain (precipitation that contains chemical pollutants) **A:9–10,** 124, 125; **W:**54, 69
coal burning causes **C:**391
conservation movement, history of the **C:**526
endangered species **E:**209
environmental problems **E:**304
European environmental issues **E:**351
fire and the environment **F:**144
forest, enemies of the **F:**376
sulfurous acid **S:**486
picture(s)
effects of **A:**10
Acids **C:**204 *see also* the names of acids
acid rain **A:**9–10
experiments and other science activities **E:**390
fatty acids **O:**79–80, 81
Acid soils **S:**238
Ackia Battleground Monument (Mississippi) **M:**358
ACLU *see* American Civil Liberties Union
Acne **A:**24; **C:**281; **D:**187; **G:**228
picture(s) **D:**187
Acoma (Indians of North America) **I:**172, 183
Aconcagua (highest peak in Andes) **A:**250, 384–85; **M:**504; **S:**274, 276
table(s)
first ascent **M:**500
Acorns (fruit of oak trees) **I:**187
Acoustic-electric guitars **G:**412
Acoustic guitars **G:**411–12
Acoustics (science of the behavior of sound) **P:**229; **S:**260–61
How do musical instruments make sounds? **M:**546–47
Acquired immune deficiency syndrome *see* AIDS
Acre (measure of area) **A:**98; **W:**113
Acrisius (in Greek mythology) **G:**365
Acrobatics *see* Gymnastics
Acronyms (words formed from the initial letters in a phrase or title) **A:**4
Acropolis (highest area of a Greek city) **A:**476c; **G:**341
Acrostics (word games) **W:**236
Acrylic fibers **F:**111; **N:**437
Acrylic (Plastic) paint **P:**30
Acta Diurna ("Acts of the Day") (public announcements in ancient Rome) **N:**204
Actin (protein in muscle cells) **M:**521
Acting **T:**157–58
charades **C:**186–87
how to put on a play **P:**335–38
Acting president (duty of the vice president) **V:**324
Actinide series (of elements) **E:**170
Actinium (element) **E:**170
Actinolite (mineral) **A:**438c
Action (mechanism of a piano) **P:**240
ACTION (United States government agency for volunteer help) **P:**104
Action and reaction (Newton's third law of motion) **M:**476; **R:**258
Action films (type of motion picture) **M:**497
Action painting (work of some abstract expressionists) **M:**396b; **P:**31
Action potential (nerve impulse) **B:**363
Actium, Battle of (31 B.C.) **A:**495
Active galaxies **U:**215
Active immunity **A:**313; **I:**95
Active learning **L:**105
Active solar heating systems **H:**97
Active volcanoes **V:**381
Activity games **G:**18–19
Act of God (legal term for a natural event of overwhelming force) **L:**88
Act of Settlement (England, 1701) **E:**248
Act of Union *see* Acts of Union
Actors and actresses **P:**336, 337, 338
Barrymore family **B:**74
Chaplin, Charlie **C:**185–86
clowns **C:**386–87
motion pictures **M:**481, 489
Shakespeare, William **S:**132–34
theater **T:**157–58
ACTP *see* American College Testing Program
Acts of the Apostles, The (book of the New Testament) **B:**165–66
Acts of Union
England and Ireland (1801) **E:**252; **I:**323; **P:**265
England and Scotland (1707) **E:**248; **S:**88
England and Wales (1536) **W:**4
Upper and Lower Canada united (1840) **C:**83; **Q:**16
Actuaries (mathematics experts in insurance companies) **I:**252
Actuators (mechanical devices controlling a robot's movements) **A:**531
Acuff, Roy (American singer) **C:**571
Acupuncture (medical treatment) **A:**257; **D:**239; **M:**207, 513
picture(s) **A:**459; **D:**239
Acura Legend (automobile)
picture(s) **A:**545
Acute angles (in geometry) **G:**121; **T:**312
diagram(s) **G:**121
Acute diseases **D:**181
Acyclovir (drug) **D:**194
A.D. (abbreviation used with dates) **C:**16
Adab (Arabic literature) **A:**341–42
Adagio (musical tempo) **M:**536
Adam, James and Robert (British architects and furniture designers) **A:**372–73; **E:**260; **F:**512
picture(s)
chair **D:**69
Adam and Eve (in the Old Testament) **B:**159
earliest palindrome **W:**236
picture(s) **B:**160
Adam and Eve (painting by Holbein) **H:**159d
Adam Bede (novel by Eliot) **E:**190
Adam de la Halle (French poet-musician) **F:**444
Adamkus, Valdas (Lithuanian president) **L:**263
Adams, Abigail Smith (wife of John Adams) **A:**12, 16; **F:**165; **W:**165
picture(s) **A:**13; **F:**164
Adams, Ansel (American photographer) **P:**210 *profile*
picture(s)
Snake River, photograph of **P:**210
Adams, Charles Francis (American historian and diplomat) **A:11**
Adams, Henry (American historian and writer) **A:11,** 214
picture(s) **A:**11
Adams, John (2nd president of the United States) **A:12–15**
Adams, John Quincy **A:**16
casting vote of vice presidents **V:**325
favored Independence Day celebrations **I:**112
helped to write the Declaration of Independence **D:**60
quoted on George Washington **W:**40
picture(s) **D:**58; **P:**445
Adams, John Couch (English astronomer) **A:**471; **N:**111
Adams, John Quincy (6th president of the United States) **A:**6b, **16–19,** 221; **E:**132
picture(s) **P:**445; **U:**142
Adams, Louisa Johnson (wife of John Quincy Adams) **A:**17; **F:**167
picture(s) **A:**18; **F:**167
Adams, Mount (New Hampshire)
picture(s) **N:**152
Adams, Samuel (American Revolutionary patriot and statesman) **A:20; F:**392; **R:**196, 197
Adam's apple (bulge in the throat) **S:**395
Adams family (in American history) **M:**144
Adamson Act (United States, 1916) **W:**181
Adams-Onís Treaty *see* Transcontinental Treaty

Adaptation (in biology) **A:**268, 270; **B:**197; **L:**197–98 *see also* Ecology; Estivation; Hibernation; Plant defenses; Protective coloration
animals adapted to different environments **A:**272–75
animals living in caves **C:**158
cactus **C:**4–5
camels **C:**39
camouflage of fish **F:**200
deep-sea life **O:**26–27
dinosaurs, the end of the **D:**174–75
evolution theory **E:**377–78
extinction **E:**425
fish **F:**186, 192–94
lizards **L:**276–77
mammals **M:**71–72
seals **S:**107
Adaptive optics **A:**476a
Addams, Jane (American social worker) **A:21; P:**106
Addends (in arithmetic) **A:**388
Adders (snakes) **S:**216
picture(s) **S:**210
Addiction, drug *see* Alcoholism; Drug addiction
Adding machines **C:**489–90; **O:**59–60
Addis Ababa (capital of Ethiopia) **E:**332–33
Addison, Joseph (English essayist) **E:**278, 321; **M:**19
Addition (in mathematics) **A:**388–89
abacus **A:**2
algebra **A:**182, 183
decimal fractions **F:**401
fractions **F:**398–99
Gauss' way to find sum of first 100 counting numbers **N:**387
number systems **N:**398–99
vector quantities **F:**366
picture(s)
abacus **A:**3
Additive inverse property (of numbers) **N:**399–400
Additives (chemicals)
food preservation **F:**342–43
food regulations and laws **F:**346
gasoline **G:**62
health foods **H:**79
lubricants **L:**335
plastics **P:**323, 324
Additive systems (type of numeration systems) **N:**403–4
Additivity (of colors of light) **C:**425
Address, forms of (in speaking and writing) **A:21–22**
Adelaide (capital of South Australia) **A:**512
Adelie penguins **P:**120b–122
Aden (Yemen) **Y:**358
Adena people (of the Ohio region) **I:**168; **O:**70, 74
Adenauer, Konrad (German statesman) **G:**165
Adenine (one of the bases that make up genes) **B:**298; **G:**77–78
Adenoids (lymph tissue in nasal passages) **D:**203; **L:**350
Adenosine deaminase (ADA) **B:**190; **G:**89
Adenosine triphosphate *see* ATP
Adenoviruses
picture(s) **V:**368
Adeodatus I, Saint (pope) **R:**292
Adeodatus II (pope) **R:**292
***Adeste Fideles* ("O Come, All Ye Faithful")** (carol) **C:**118
ADHD (Attention-Deficit Hyperactivity Disorder) **A:23; D:**332; **L:**108; **M:**224
Adhémar, Joseph A. (French mathematician) **I:**15–16
Adhesion (in physics) **L:**254
picture(s) **L:**254
Adhesives **G:242–43; S:**173
Ad hoc committees (of organizations) **P:**82
Adiabatic cooling (of air) **C:**382
Adi Granth (sacred book of Sikhism) **R:**151
Adipose tissue **G:**228
Adirondack Mountains **N:**212, 213, 215
picture(s) **N:**213
Adjaria (autonomous region in the Republic of Georgia) **G:**147, 148
Adjectives (words that modify nouns) **P:**93
Adjustable cameras **P:**202, 213
Adjutant General's Corps (of the United States Army) **U:**102
Adler, Dankmar (American architect and engineer) **S:**486
Adler Planetarium and Astronomy Museum (Chicago, Illinois) **M:**524
Administration, Office of (United States) **P:**451
Administrative sanctions (imposed by federal agencies for rule violations) **L:**87
Administrator (feminine: **administratrix**) (of a will) **W:**177
Admiralty Islands (Papua New Guinea) **I:**361; **P:**8; **W:**309
Admissions policies (of universities) **U:**225
Adobe (sun-dried bricks) **B:**391; **H:**186
Adolescence (period of transition from childhood to adulthood) **A:24–26**
acne **D:**187
alcohol use **A:**173
child abuse **C:**222
child development **C:**225, 226
drug abuse **D:**329, 330
foster care **F:**390
grief **G:**380
juvenile crime **J:**167–70
menstruation **M:**219–20
mental illness **M:**223, 224
motion pictures **M:**495
nutritional needs of adolescents **N:**426
orthodontics **O:**232–33
Red Cross youth memberships **R:**127
rock music **R:**262a–262b, 262c, 264
sleep needs of adolescents **L:**104
smoking **S:**207
suicide **S:**485
volunteerism **V:**390
young adult library services **L:**177
picture(s)
Bulgarian teenagers **B:**442
drug-abuse counseling **D:**332
Adonis (Syrian poet) **A:**342
Adoption (of children) **A:27–28; F:**390; **S:**229
Adoption and Safe Families Act (United States, 1997) **F:**390
Adoration, prayer of **P:**430
Adoration of the Kings, The (painting by Leonardo da Vinci) **L:**153
Adoration of the Magi (painting by Gentile da Fabriano)
picture(s) **U:**3
Adoration of the Magi, The (painting by Botticelli) **R:**161
picture(s) **N:**37
Adoration of the Magi, The (painting by Rubens) **B:**66
picture(s) **B:**67; **D:**362
Adoration of the Shepherds, The (painting by El Greco)
picture(s) **G:**330; **S:**383
Adoula, Cyrille (prime minister of the Congo) **C:**503
Ad points (in tennis) **T:**89
Adrastea (moon of Jupiter) **J:**162
Adrenal glands **B:**292; **E:**203; **G:**228
Adrenaline (hormone) *see* Epinephrine
Adrian I (pope) **L:**151; **R:**292
Adrian II (pope) **R:**292
Adrian III, Saint (pope) **R:**292
Adrian IV (pope) **H:**178; **R:**292
Adrian V (pope) **R:**293
Adrian VI (pope) **R:**293
Adrianople, Battle of (378) **B:**103e
Adult Children of Alcoholics (counseling program) **A:**173
Adult education **D:**109; **E:**76
picture(s) **E:**76
Adult Space Academy **S:**340a
Ad valorem tariff **T:**23
Advance (paid when a contract is signed) **B:**324
Advanced Medium Range Air-to-Air Missile **U:**115
Advanced Photo System (APS) film **P:**202

Advanced Weather Interactive Processing Systems (AWIPS) **W**:92
Advanced X-Ray Astrophysics Facility *see* Chandra X-Ray Observatory
Advection fog **F**:290
picture(s) **F**:291
Advent (religious season) **C**:299; **R**:155
picture(s)
candle lighting **R**:153
Adventitious roots (of plants) **P**:303
Adventure clubs (of Camp Fire Boys and Girls) **C**:43
Adventure fiction **F**:114; **M**:563
Adventures of Augie March, The (book by Bellow) **B**:141
Adverbs (words that modify verbs, adjectives, or other adverbs) **P**:93–94
Advertising **A:29–35**
book publishing **B**:333
commercial art **C**:456
consumer protection **C**:535
department stores **D**:118
Federal Trade Commission monitors food advertising **F**:346
folklore, American **F**:314
folk sculpture **F**:294
food ads aimed at children **F**:338
how radio broadcasting is financed **R**:57
how to be an entrepreneur **B**:472
magazines **M**:19, 20
mail order **M**:34–35
mass marketing **M**:88
modeling, fashion **M**:384–85
motion picture distribution **M**:486
newspapers **N**:197, 203
opinion polls **O**:169
photography **P**:203
political campaigns **P**:373
posters **P**:402
prescription drugs **D**:334
radio programs **R**:59, 60, 61
sales and marketing **S**:20, 21
saving money by watching supermarket advertisements **F**:347
silk-screen printing **S**:176
smoking ads banned on radio and television **S**:207
statistics can be misleading **S**:442
television **T**:68
trade and commerce **T**:265
trademarks **T**:266
What is the difference between public relations and advertising? **P**:517
Advertising agency **A**:33–34, 35
Advocates *see* Lawyers
Adze (tool) **T**:227–28
AEC *see* Atomic Energy Commission
A.E.F. *see* American Expeditionary Force
Aegean civilization **A**:429; **P**:15–16; **S**:94–95
Aegean Sea **G**:334
picture(s) **M**:211
Aegis Combat System (of the United States Navy) **U**:118
Aeneas (hero of Vergil's *Aeneid*) **A**:36; **G**:369
Aeneid (epic poem by Vergil) **A:36; G**:361; **P**:353; **T**:316; **V**:304–5
Latin literature **L**:75
Aerial acrobatics (Aerials) (in free-style skiing) **S**:184d
Aerial acts (in a circus) **C**:307
picture(s) **C**:308, 309
Aerial Experiment Association **A**:562
Aerial perspective (in drawing) **D**:311–12
Aerial photography **P**:208
archaeological sites, search for **A**:352, 359
ore, search for **M**:319
petroleum, search for **P**:168–69
photogrammetry **O**:183–84
Aeries (eagles' nests) **E**:2
Aerobatic flying
picture(s) **A**:559
Aerobic exercise **J**:111
Aerobic fitness *see* Cardiovascular fitness
Aerobraking (to slow a spacecraft) **S**:340d
Aerodrome (Samuel Langley's airplane) **A**:561
Aerodynamics (science of air in motion) **A:37–41**
airplane design **A**:109, 567
birds, flight of **B**:218–19
experiments and other science activities **E**:394
glider flight **A**:560–61; **G**:239
heavier-than-air craft **A**:561–62
How does a helicopter fly? **H**:104–5
hydrofoil boats **H**:315
supersonic flight **S**:499–502
picture(s)
automobile design **A**:539
Aeroflot-Russian International Airlines **R**:364
Aeronautics *see* Aviation
Aerosol containers **G**:61
Aerospace engineers **E**:225
Aerospace industry **A**:569–70 *see also* Space exploration and travel
Aeschylus (Greek dramatist) **D**:297; **F**:114; **G**:356
Aesir (race of Norse gods) **N**:279, 280
Aesop (Greek author of fables) **F**:2–3, 114; **H**:292; **S**:196
profile
"The Ant and the Grasshopper" **F**:5
"The Four Oxen and the Lion" **F**:5
"The Lion and the Mouse" **F**:4
picture(s)
"The Fox and the Crane" **C**:233
Aesthetics (branch of philosophy) **P**:192
Aether (Aristotle's fifth element) **C**:207
Aetna, Mount *see* Etna, Mount
Afar (language) **E**:316
Afars (a people of northeastern Africa) **D**:232, 233
Afars and the Issas, French Territory of the *see* Djibouti
AFDC *see* Aid to Families with Dependent Children
Afewerki, Isaias (president of Eritrea) **E**:317
Affect (facial expression that communicates an emotion) **E**:203
Affiliated areas (of the United States National Park System) **N**:56
Affiliate stations (in television industry) **T**:68
Affinity (in the dyeing process) **D**:376
Affirmative action (to overcome discrimination) **L**:8
Afghanistan **A:42–45**
Communism **C**:474
guerrilla warfare **G**:400
NATO peacekeeping troops in **N**:305
poetry **P**:354
refugees **R**:136
terrorism, war on **A**:457; **B**:468; **P**:40a; **T**:116–17
USSR's invasion **U**:43–44
map(s) **A**:42
picture(s)
farmers plowing with oxen **A**:43
flag **F**:226
Mazār-e Sharīf mosque **A**:42
Muslim woman **A**:45
Pashtun man **A**:42
Aflatoxin (toxin made by molds) **F**:500; **L**:270
AFL-CIO *see* American Federation of Labor–Congress of Industrial Organizations
Afonso I (king of Portugal) **P**:394
Africa **A:46–69** *see also* the names of countries
African American history **A**:79d
African Union **A**:81
agriculture **A**:92–93
art and architecture *see* Africa, art and architecture of
Congo River **C**:507
continents **C**:537, 538
dance **D**:32

doll making **D:**272
drought **D:**328–29
education **E:**75; **T:**43
exploration and discovery **E:**412–13
folk dance **F:**300, 301–2
folk music **F:**320–21, 325
food **F:**332
France's former territories **F:**412, 420
immigration **I:**94
lakes of the world **L:**33–34
literature *see* Africa, literature of
malaria is a public health problem **V:**284, 285
modern age **W:**274–75
mountains **M:**505–6
music *see* Africa, music of
mythology **M:**573
national parks **N:**56
Nile River **N:**260–61
Organization of African Unity **O:**221
plant and animal community **A:**272–74
population growth **P:**386, 388
poverty **P:**418, 420
proverbs **P:**498
refugees **R:**136
Sahara **S:**6–7
slavery, history of **A:**79d–79e
Stanley and Livingstone explored **S:**424
theater **T:**162
universities **U:**226
What and where are the Mountains of the Moon? **A:**61
World War I **W:**285
World War II **W:**299, 300–301, 307, 308
yellow fever is a public health problem **V:**284
map(s)
colonial partition to 1914 **A:**68
physical map **A:**51
political map **A:**59
population **A:**58
precipitation **A:**50
prehistoric people's remains **P:**439
World War II in North Africa **W:**297
picture(s)
rain forest **A:**49
savanna **A:**52
traditional hairstyle **H:**6
table(s)
waterfalls **W:**63
Africa, art and architecture of A:70–76
architecture **A:**367
art of the artist **A:**433
Nigeria **N:**257
pottery **P:**411
use by Modigliani **M:**400
picture(s)
terra-cotta sculpture **P:**411
Africa, literature of A:76a–76d; N:363
Africa, music of A:77–79; M:542–43
picture(s) **M:**545
Africa Corps (German army in World War II) **R:**320
Africa Hall (Addis Ababa, Ethiopia) **E:**333
African American literature A:205–6, 208, 214–14a, 215, 217, 218, 219
Angelou, Maya **A:**258
Baldwin, James **B:**21
children's literature **C:**238
Dove, Rita Frances **O:**77
Du Bois, W. E. B. **D:**342
Dunbar, Paul Laurence **D:**351
folklore **F:**313–14, 316
folklore: "Wiley and the Hairy Man" **F:**317–19
Hansberry, Lorraine Vivian **C:**221
Harlem Renaissance **A:**79k
Hughes, Langston **H:**275
Johnson, James Weldon **J:**118
Morrison, Toni **M:**462
novels **F:**116; **N:**363
trickster stories carried from Africa **A:**76b
Washington, Booker T. **W:**28
Wright, Richard **W:**327
African American music
folk music **F:**324
hymns and spirituals **F:**324; **H:**324–25
jazz **J:**56–64; **U:**208
jazz-style big bands **R:**262a
rhythm and blues music **R:**262a, 262b
rock music **R:**262c
African Americans A:79a–80; U:157 *see also* the names of African Americans
abolition movement **A:**6–6b
Alabama, history of **A:**142, 143
Amistad Rebellion **A:**221
Arkansas's population **A:**410
baseball **B:**92
Bluford, Guion, first African American in space **S:**348
Boston's Black Heritage Trail **B:**342
Buffalo Soldiers **B:**431
civil rights **C:**326, 327
civil rights movement **C:**328–30
Civil War, United States **C:**332–36, 347
Confederate States **C:**496
Delaware, history of **D:**93
Dred Scott decision **D:**321
Emancipation Proclamation **E:**200–201
English language **E:**267
food-service workers **F:**333
heart disease, risk factors for **H:**84
Henson, Matthew, among first Americans to reach North Pole **H:**115
human rights **H:**285
Jemison, Mae, first African American woman in space **S:**348
Jim Crow laws **J:**109
Kwanzaa **H:**162
Langston, John Mercer, first popularly elected black official in the U.S. **V:**359
Liberia settled by freed American slaves **L:**165, 168
literature *see* African American literature
Los Angeles **L:**304
Maryland's population **M:**124
motion pictures, history of **M:**489–90
music *see* African American music
National Association for the Advancement of Colored People (NAACP) **N:**25–26
newspapers: Baltimore's *Afro-American* **M:**127
New York's population **N:**216
Olympic Games, first African American women in **O:**112
percentage of United States population **U:**74
racism **R:**34c
Reconstruction Period **R:**117–20
segregation **S:**113–15
slavery **S:**194–97
Spingarn Medal **S:**409–10
Stokes, Carl, first African American mayor of major city **O:**77
Tennessee **T:**78
thirteen American colonies **T:**166, 178
Uncle Tom's Cabin by Harriet Beecher Stowe **S:**465
Underground Railroad **U:**15–17
universities and colleges **U:**220
urban poverty rates **P:**419
voting rights **V:**393
Washington, D.C., history of **W:**30, 36
What is Kwanzaa? **A:**80
Wilder, Lawrence Douglas, first elected African American governor in U.S. **V:**359
picture(s)
Congress, first African American members of **U:**143
girl awaiting baptism **M:**354

African Americans
picture(s) (cont.)
Little Rock school integration (1957) **A:**419
schoolteacher **N:**295
thirteen American colonies **T:**168
Tuskegee Airmen **W:**292
United States, population of the **U:**72
African American studies
Gates, Henry Louis, Jr. **W:**138
Woodson, Carter Goodwin **V:**359
African buffalo **B:**430
African elephants **A:**271; **E:**179–81
picture(s) **M:**69
African gray parrot **B:**250
African hunting dog
picture(s) **D:**240
African kingdoms, early **A:**65–66, 79d
Dahomey **B:**144
Kimbundu in Angola **A:**260
Mali **M:**62
Nigeria, history of **N:**257
picture(s)
Zimbabwe, ruins of **Z:**383
African Methodist Episcopal Church **P:**140
African National Congress (ANC) **M:**78; **S:**273
African sleeping sickness (disease) *see* Sleeping sickness, African
African Union **A:**69, **81; O:**221
African vine snakes **S:**211, 214
African violet (plant) **H:**267
picture(s) **H:**268
African warthogs (wild pigs) **H:**219; **P:**248
African wild asses **H:**220, 243
Afrikaans (language spoken by South Africans of Dutch descent) **A:**57; **N:**8; **S:**269
Afrika Korps (German desert force in World War II) **W:**299, 300–301
Afrikaners (South Africans of Dutch descent) **S:**269
Afro-American (newspaper) **M:**127
Afro-Americans *see* African Americans
Afro-Asian languages **A:**56
Afrocentrism (African American educational approach) **A:**80
Afterimage (optical illusion) **C:**428; **O:**175–76
Afterlife (religious belief) **D:**51; **J:**144; **R:**146, 151, 283
After the Bath (painting by Raphaelle Peale)
picture(s) **P:**110
A.G. Nova Scotia* v. *A.G. Canada (Canada, 1951) **S:**506
Agadez (Niger) **N:**252
Agam, Vaacov (Israeli painter)
Double Metamorphosis II (painting) **P:**32
picture(s)
Double Metamorphosis II (painting) **P:**31
Agamemnon (in Greek mythology) **G:**368–69; **T:**316
Iliad **I:**61
Schliemann, Heinrich, searched for his burial place **S:**59
picture(s) **W:**259
Mycenaean gold mask **A:**229; **M:**562
Agapetus I, Saint (pope) **R:**292
Agapetus II (pope) **R:**292
Agar (gum obtained from algae) **M:**278; **R:**185
Agassi, Andre (American tennis player)
picture(s) **T:**99
Agassiz, Elizabeth Cary (wife of Jean Louis Rodolphe Agassiz) **A:**81
Agassiz, Jean Louis Rodolphe (Swiss-born American geologist and naturalist) **A:81; G:**221; **I:**8–9
picture(s) **A:**81
Agassiz, Lake (ancient glacial lake) **M:**80, 328; **N:**322
Agate (chalcedony quartz) **Q:**8
Agate Fossil Beds National Monument (Nebraska) **N:**90
Agatho, Saint (pope) **R:**292
Age *see* Aging
Aged, the *see* Old age
Agee, James (American writer) **T:**86 *profile*
Agents provocateurs (spies) **S:**407
Agents (in publishing) *see* Literary agents
Age of Bronze, The (sculpture by Rodin) **R:**281
picture(s) **R:**281
Age of Exploration and Discovery **E:**403–6; **G:**105
Age of Fish (Devonian period in geology) **F:**184
Age of Innocence, The (novel by Wharton) **W:**156
Age of Kings (17th and 18th centuries in Europe) **A:**432–33
Age of Mammals (Tertiary Period) **E:**25; **F:**388
table(s) **F:**384
Age of Reason **H:**151
American literature **A:**209
Age of Reptiles **D:**164
Ageratums (flowers) **G:**46
picture(s) **G:**50
Aggravated assault (crime) **J:**167
Aggregation (process in the formation of snowflakes) **R:**95
Agha Mohammed Khan (Persian ruler) **I:**309
Aghlabids (Tunisian dynasty) **T:**336
Agincourt, Battle of (1415) **H:**109, 293
picture(s) **H:**109
Aging **A:82–87**
Alzheimer's disease **A:**196; **D:**188
blindness **B:**255
cell aging and division **C:**159
deafness **D:**49
degenerative diseases **D:**185
heart disease, risk factors for **H:**84
How long do insects live? **I:**233–34
old age **O:**98–100
organisms grow and develop **B:**196
percentages of older people in populations **P:**385–86
skeletal joints can stiffen **S:**184b
trees **T:**300
picture(s)
how to determine the age of a fish **F:**189
Aging (of wine) **W:**190a
Aging, Administration on (United States) **H:**78
Agitato (musical term) **M:**536
Aglyphous snakes **S:**211
Agnew, Spiro Theodore (American public official) **N:**262f; **U:**202; **V:**330 *profile*
picture(s) **N:**262d; **V:**330
Agnon, Shmuel Yosef (Samuel Joseph Czaczkes) (Hebrew novelist) **H:**101; **I:**374
Agnosticism (belief that it is not possible to know if God exists) **A:**476b; **R:**145
Agora (marketplace in Greek cities) **A:**368; **G:**341
Agoraphobia (anxiety disorder) **M:**222
Agoutis (rodents) **R:**278
Agra (India)
Taj Mahal **T:**12
picture(s)
boatman on Jumna River **A:**438e
Taj Mahal **I:**116
Agribusiness (agricultural industry) **A:**95
Agricola, Georgius (German mineralogist) **G:**109
Agricultural Adjustment Administration (AAA) **N:**138h; **R:**324
Agricultural engineers **E:**225
Agricultural fairs **F:**13–15, 18
picture(s) **F:**14, 15
Agricultural Index **I:**115
Agricultural machinery *see* Farm machinery
Agricultural pests *see* Plant pests
Agricultural Revolution (early discoveries in agriculture) **A:**99
Agricultural Wheel (protest organization in Arkansas history) **A:**418
Agriculture **A:88–100** *see also* Farms and farming (for specific information on how plants and animals are raised); the agriculture section of continent, country, province, and state articles; the names of domestic animals, livestock, and agricultural crops and products
agricultural engineering **E:**225
agricultural fairs **F:**13–15
Agriculture, United States Department of **A:**100a

antibiotics, uses for **A:**311
aquaculture **A:**336
Are genetically engineered crops safe? **G:**84
atmosphere, effects on **A:**482
biotechnology **G:**85; **H:**228
Burbank's experimental work **B:**452
Carver's agricultural research **C:**130
civilization, beginning of **I:**279; **S:**487
collective and state farms of the USSR **U:**38
conservation of soil **C:**524; **D:**354
controlling plant pests **P:**289–91
desert farming **D:**127
dust, source of **D:**353
Egypt, ancient **E:**107
electronics in business **E:**162
famine **F:**44, 45
farming the sea *see* Aquaculture
farms and farming **F:**48–62
feudal system **F:**99–103
FFA (Future Farmers of America) **F:**104
food supply **F:**350–51
4-H clubs **F:**395–96
Indians, American **I:**165, 166, 170, 178
irrigation **I:**339–41
kinds of industry **I:**225
Maya civilization **A:**243
migratory agriculture **J:**158
natural resources **N:**62
physical geography **G:**100
poverty caused by crop failure **P:**419
prehistoric people **F:**336; **P:**441–42
rain-forest farming **R:**100
trucks, uses of **T:**319
urban societies, beginning of **H:**191
vegetable-growing on spacecraft **S:**344
map(s)
North America **G:**102
picture(s)
aerial spraying of crops **A:**108
Chinese student working on farm **E:**74
Egypt, ancient **E:**108
Slovak farmer plowing with horses **S:**200
Soviet collective farm **U:**38
vegetable-growing on spacecraft **S:**342
Agriculture, United States Department of **A:100a; P:**447
food inspection **F:**335
food regulations and laws **F:**345
Forest Service **N:**30
4-H clubs **F:**395, 396
meat inspection **M:**198
National Agricultural Library **L:**178
nutrition **N:**428
organic foods, labeling and processing of **H:**79; **V:**288
Agrippina (Roman empress) **N:**114
Agronomy *see* Farms and farming
Aguinaldo, Emilio (Philippine hero) **P:**188
Aguiyi-Ironsi, Johnson (Nigerian political leader) **N:**258
Ahab (king of Israel) **E:**189
Ahad Ha-am (Asher Ginzberg) (Hebrew writer) **H:**101
Ahasuerus (king of Persia) **P:**549
Ahimsa (Nonviolence) (religious belief) **R:**150
Ahmadi (Kuwait) **K:**310
Ahmedabad (India) **I:**139
Ahmes (Egyptian scribe) **G:**128
Ahmes papyrus (early mathematical handbook) **M:**162
Ahuizotl (Aztec ruler) **I:**172
Ahura Mazda (Zoroastrian god) **Z:**394
Ahvenanmaa *see* Aland Islands
AI *see* Artificial intelligence
Aïda (opera by Verdi) **O:**149–50; **S:**481
picture(s) **O:**139
Aidid, Mohammed Farah (Somali leader) **S:**255
AIDS (Acquired Immune Deficiency Syndrome) **A:100b**
African death rates **A:**69; **P:**388
applied anthropologists advise African physicians **A:**301
blood donations tested for AIDS antibodies **T:**273
cancer, causes of **C:**92
hypodermic needles of drug abusers can carry the AIDS virus **D:**332
immune system, disorders of **I:**98
lymphatic system, disorders of **L:**350
medicine, history of **M:**208f
pneumonia **D:**198
public health **P:**513
Thailand **T:**152
vaccine needed **V:**261
virus *see* HIV
picture(s)
halting the spread of AIDS **D:**212
viruses emerging from infected cell **I:**98
Aid to Families with Dependent Children (AFDC) **W:**119–20
Aietes (in Greek mythology) **G:**368
Aigeus (in Greek mythology) **G:**368
Aiken, George D. (United States senator) **V:**318 *profile*
Aiken, George L. (American dramatist) **D:**304
Aiken, Howard (American mathematician) **C:**490
Aikido (martial art) **M:**116
Aikman, Troy (American football player)
picture(s) **F:**354
Ailerons (of airplanes) **A:**112
Ailey, Alvin (American choreographer) **D:**34
Ain Jalut, Battle of (1260) **B:**103f
Ainsworth, Mary (American psychologist) **P:**510
Ain't Misbehavin' (musical) **M:**555
Ainu (a people of Japan) **A:**445; **J:**26, 41; **R:**33
Ai Qing (Chinese poet) **C:**279
Air **A:**479–82
aerodynamics **A:**37–41
air conditioning **A:**101–3
ancient Greek theories of the elements **C:**206
balloons inflated with hot air **B:**34
Boyle's law **B:**354; **C:**207
buoyancy **F:**251
burping and intestinal gases **B:**301
cloud formation **C:**382–83
dust **D:**353
falling bodies, laws of **F:**34
gases **G:**56
jet streams **J:**93
liquefaction of gases **L:**253
matter, states of **M:**172
pollution *see* Air pollution
pressure *see* Air pressure
weather **W:**79–95
What makes air move? **W:**186–87
winds **W:**186–89
Aïr (region of Niger) **N:**251, 252
Air, compressed *see* Compressed air
Air, liquid *see* Liquid air
Air bags (system to protect automobile passengers from injury) **A:**544, 552; **N:**262
picture(s) **A:**552
Airborne tanks **T:**15
Air brakes **R:**84, 89
pneumatic systems **H:**314
trucks **T:**319
Westinghouse, George **W:**125
Air-breathing missiles **M:**344
Air Canada (airline) **C:**66
Air carrier airports **A:**126
Air Combat Command (of the United States Air Force) **U:**107
Air Commerce Act (United States, 1926) **A:**563
Air conditioning **A:101–3**
air cycle system of refrigeration **R:**134
heat pumps **H:**96
Legionnaires' disease can be spread through air-conditioning systems **D:**198–99
refrigeration **R:**133, 134, 135

Air conditioning (cont.)
spacecraft and space suits **S:**340h, 342–43
diagram(s) **A:**101, 103
Air-cooled engines **A:**115, 548
Aircraft *see* Airplanes; Balloons and ballooning; Gliders; Helicopters
Aircraft carriers **I:**18; **S:**154; **U:**114
picture(s) **V:**347
Air cycle cooling system **R:**134
Air defense artillery (of the United States Army) **U:**102
Air deflectors (on trucks) **T:**319
Air division (Air Force unit) **U:**109
Air Education and Training Command (of the United States Air Force) **U:**107
Airfields *see* Airports
Airfoil (surface that produces lift when air moves over it) **A:**109, 115
Air Force, Canada *see* Royal Canadian Air Force
Air Force, United States *see* United States Air Force
Air Force Cross (American award)
picture(s) **D:**66
Air Force Materiel Command (of the United States Air Force) **U:**107
Air Force Reserve **U:**107, 108, 109
Air Force Space Command **U:**107
Air Force Special Operations Command (of the United States Air Force) **U:**107
Airframe (of an airplane) **A:**110
Air guns **G:**415
Air-launched cruise missiles (ALCM) *see* ALCM
Airlift, Berlin *see* Berlin Airlift
Airline flight attendants **A:**571
Airlines **A:**126–27, 129, 563, 568 *see also* the transportation section of country, province, and state articles
Airline stewardesses *see* Airline flight attendants
Airmail **A:**563; **P:**398
Air mass (in meteorology) **W:**85
Air Mobility Command (of the United States Air Force) **U:**107
Air National Guard (of the United States) **N:**42; **U:**108
Airplane models **A:104–7**
Airplanes **A:108–21**
aerodynamics **A:**37–41
airborne observatories **O:**9–10
airports **A:**126–29
automation **A:**532
aviation **A:**561–70, 571–72
battles **B:**103f
Bermuda Triangle disappearances **B:**152
fishing industry, use in **F:**218
gliders compared to **G:**238
gyroscopes **G:**437, 438
hijacking **H:**134
hydraulic systems **H:**313
inventions in air transportation **I:**284
jet propulsion **J:**90–92
microwaves as power source **M:**288
models **A:**104–7
radio signals used by **C:**469
rocket-powered **S:**502
supersonic flight **S:**499–502
terrorist bombings **T:**114
transportation, history of **T:**287
turboprop and turbojet engines **T:**343
United States Air Force **U:**109–10
United States Army **U:**105
United States Navy **U:**115
used in farming **F:**56–57
Wright brothers **W:**328
picture(s)
Beech Starship **A:**571
Bell XV-15 **A:**121
Boeing Company plant **W:**21
early airplanes **A:**564
forest-fire fighting **A:**569
hypersonic plane **A:**121
jet fighter **M:**374; **U:**107
jet liners **A:**568; **E:**212
Kansas industry **K:**183
polluting the air **A:**125
Princess Mary, early airliner **I:**284
seaplanes **A:**151, 569
servicing of **A:**128
World War I **W:**286, 287
Air plants *see* Epiphytes
Air pollution **A:122–25** *see also* Dust; Fallout
acid rain **A:**9–10
automobiles are a cause of **A:**544
coal **E:**220
disease prevention **D:**212
diseases, environmental **D:**186
emphysema **D:**192
environment, problems of **E:**303–5
experiments and other science activities **E:**391
fire and the environment **F:**144
forest, enemies of the **F:**376
gasoline reformulation **G:**62; **P:**176
hazardous wastes **H:**72
Los Angeles **L:**303
lung diseases **L:**345
ozone is a pollutant in the lower atmosphere **O:**292
Pittsburgh, history of **P:**267
pollution controls in automobiles **A:**547; **I:**265
smog **F:**291
Taj Mahal, damage to **T:**12
Venice's stonework, destruction of **V:**301
Airports **A:126–29; H:**37 *see also* the transportation section of country, province, and state articles
automation **A:**532
buses between airports and hotels **B:**461
Denver (Colorado) **C:**439; **D:**117
deregulation causes problems **A:**568
hotels **H:**259
world's first airport in Maryland **M:**120
world's ten busiest airports, list of **A:**129
picture(s)
Dallas/Fort Worth airport **N:**304
National Guard security **N:**41
Riyadh (Saudi Arabia) **B:**439
Air (Atmospheric) pressure **A:**480
aerodynamics **A:**109
air pollution affected by **A:**123
barometer **B:**62
barometer, how to make a **W:**89
Boyle's law **B:**354; **C:**207
climate **C:**363
how heat changes matter **H:**91
hurricane, eye of **H:**303
jet streams caused mainly by differences in **J:**93
long-span roofs held up by air pressure **B:**439
modern passenger jets are pressurized **A:**111
pneumatic systems **H:**314
pumps, action of **P:**540
shown on weather maps **W:**92
sonic booms **S:**501
tunnel building **T:**338
tunnels, underwater **T:**339
vacuum formed by **V:**263, 265
Venturi tube in aerodynamics **A:**38
weather, creation of **W:**79–81, 81–82, 84–85
weather instruments to measure air pressure **W:**89
What keeps a plane up in the air? **A:**38
winds **W:**186
picture(s)
supersonic flight **S:**499
Air resistance *see* Drag

Air sacs (Alveoli) (of the lungs) **B**:283; **D**:198; **L**:343, 344, 345
emphysema **D**:192
picture(s) **B**:282; **L**:344
Airships **A**:560
aerodynamics, principles of **A**:41
World War I **A**:562
picture(s)
Goodyear blimp **H**:106
weather balloon **W**:91
Airspeed (of an airplane) **A**:118
Airspeed indicator (in airplanes) **A**:118
Air terminals *see* Airports
Air-to-air missiles (AAM) *see* AAM
Air-to-surface missiles (ASM) *see* ASM
Air traffic control **A**:128–29
picture(s) **A**:126; **R**:36
Ais (Indians native to Florida) **F**:271
Aisne, First Battle of the (1914)
picture(s) **W**:276
Aisne, Second Battle of the (1917) **W**:288
Aiún, Al (Western Sahara) **W**:124
Aix-la-Chapelle, Treaties of **F**:463
Ajanta (India) **I**:136, 139
Ajar, Emile (French novelist) *see* Gary, Romain
AK-47 (assault rifle) **G**:424
Akan (African language) **A**:78
Akan (a people of Africa) **A**:72, 74; **P**:411
Akbar (emperor of the Mogul dynasty of India) **I**:132, 137
Akeyasu, Jean-Paul (Rwandan public official) **G**:97
Akhmatova, Anna (Russian poet) **R**:384
Akhnaton (Akhenaten; Amenhotep IV) (king of ancient Egypt) **E**:104, 109, 115–16
Akiba ben Joseph (Jewish scholar) **T**:13
Akihito (Crown Prince of Japan) **J**:47
picture(s) **J**:47
Akikah (Muslim welcoming ceremony for baby) **I**:349
Akkad (ancient city in Mesopotamia) **A**:231; **M**:231; **S**:487
Akkadian language **A**:462; **C**:613
Akosombo (Ghana)
picture(s) **G**:197
Akron (Ohio) **O**:68, 69, 72; **S**:218a
Akron, University of (Ohio) **O**:72
Aksenfeld, Israel (Yiddish author) **Y**:360
Aksum (Ethiopia) **A**:65; **E**:317, 333
Akureyri (Iceland) **I**:35, 36
Al- (in Arabic names) *see* the main part of name, as Azhar University, al-
ALA *see* American Library Association
Alabama **A:130–43**
map(s) **A**:141
picture(s)
Bellingrath Gardens **A**:138
Birmingham **A**:131, 138
cotton **A**:135
county fair **A**:134
Guntersville Lake **L**:27
loblolly pine trees **A**:133
Mobile **A**:137
Montgomery **A**:139
Oakleigh Mansion **A**:131
U.S. Space and Rocket Center **A**:138
Alabama (Indians of North America) **I**:178
Alabama, University of **A**:135
football **A**:135
picture(s)
football **A**:134
Alabama Claims **A**:11; **G**:296
Alabama River **A**:132
Aladdin (animated cartoon) **A**:342
"Aladdin and the Wonderful Lamp" (story from *Arabian Nights*) **A**:339–40
Alajuela (Costa Rica) **C**:566
Alakaluf (Indians of South America) **I**:199
Alamein, El, Battle of (1942) **M**:443; **W**:307
Alamo, Battle of the (1836) **B**:347; **C**:592; **T**:139
picture(s) **T**:138
Alamo, The (San Antonio, Texas) **S**:26; **T**:132
picture(s) **T**:132
Alamogordo (New Mexico) **N**:185
Aland Islands (Finland) **I**:361
Al-Anon (program for the family and friends of alcoholics) **A**:173
Alarcón, Juan Ruiz de (Mexican-born Spanish playwright) **S**:388
Alarcón, Pedro Antonio de (Spanish writer) **S**:390
Alas, Leopoldo (Spanish writer) *see* Clarín
Alaska **A:144–58; T**:109–10; **U**:77, 81–82, 186
Aleutian Islands **I**:361
Alexander Archipelago **I**:362
discovered by Vitus Bering **B**:145
earthquake (1964) **E**:41
Eastern Orthodox churches **E**:47
Exxon Valdez oil spill **P**:176
glaciers **G**:223
gold discoveries **G**:252
Inuit **I**:190–91, 272–76
pioneers **P**:261
postal service **P**:397, 398
Pribilof Islands **I**:367
vegetation **U**:90
Wrangell-Saint Elias National Park and Preserve **N**:49
Yupik **I**:190–91
map(s) **A**:155
picture(s)
Anchorage **A**:153
blanket toss **I**:272
brown bear **A**:148
Columbia Glacier **I**:5
conservationists counting plant species **C**:527
Cook Inlet **A**:149
Dall sheep **A**:145
Denali National Park and Preserve **N**:47
Exxon Valdez oil spill **P**:175
fishing **A**:151
fur seals **A**:149
Glacier Bay National Park **E**:13; **W**:51
glaciers **G**:116; **N**:287
gold rush **A**:157
Juneau **A**:153, 154
Mendenhall Glacier **A**:148
Mount McKinley **A**:146, 557; **N**:47
people **A**:145, 150
polar climate **C**:363
robot exploring volcano **C**:485
Russian Orthodox church **A**:145
seaplanes **A**:151
totem **A**:148
Trans-Alaska Pipeline **A**:152
Wrangell-Saint Elias National Park and Preserve **N**:49
Alaska, University of **A**:150–51
Alaska Federation of Natives (Inuit political group) **I**:276
Alaska Highway (North America) **A**:152, 158; **B**:405; **Y**:372
Alaska National Interest Lands Conservation Act (United States, 1980) **A**:158
Alaska Native Claims Settlement Act (United States, 1971) **A**:156, 157, 158; **I**:276
Alaskan fur seals *see* Northern fur seals
Alaskan malamute (working dog) **D**:247, 249
Alaska Peninsula (Alaska) **A**:146
Alaska Pipeline *see* Trans-Alaska Pipeline
Alaska Railroad **A**:153
Alaska Range (Alaska) **A**:146; **N**:284–85
Alaska State Museum (Juneau) **A**:151
Alateen (program for young people who live in an alcoholic family) **A**:173
Alava, Cape (Washington)
picture(s) **W**:16
Al-Azhar University *see* Azhar University, al-
Albacore (fish) **F**:217

Albania **A:159–62**
Albanians in Macedonia **M:**4
Albanians in Yugoslavia **Y:**369
Balkans **B:**22, 23
Italian invasion of (1939) **W:**295
only nation in Europe with Muslim majority **E:**356
picture(s)
election victory celebration **A:**162
flag **F:**226
mosque **A:**160
refugees fleeing to Italy **R:**136
statue of Skanderbeg **A:**162
woman in refugee camp **P:**418
Albanian (language) **A:**160
Albany (capital of New York) **N:**220
picture(s) **N:**221
Albany Plan of Union (first formal plan for unification of the American colonies) **F:**456
Albany Regency (New York political group) **V:**272
Albatross D-III (airplane)
picture(s) **W:**287
Albatrosses (birds) **B:**231, 233; **H:**197
picture(s) **B:**235
wandering albatross **B:**244
wing **B:**218
Albee, Edward (American playwright) **A:**218; **D:**305; **W:**35 *profile*
picture(s) **W:**35
Albéniz, Isaac (Spanish composer) **S:**392b
picture(s) **S:**392b
Albert (antipope) **R:**292
Albert (prince consort of Great Britain) **A:163; E:**250; **V:**332a
first Christmas tree in England **C:**297
International Exposition of 1851 **F:**16
Albert, Carl Bert (American legislator) **O:**94 *profile*
Albert, Lake (Uganda–Democratic Republic of Congo) **L:**33; **N:**260; **U:**6
Albert I (king of Belgium) **A:163; B:**135; **W:**278–79
Albert II (king of Belgium) **A:163; B:**135
Albert I (prince of Monaco) **M:**409
Alberta (Canada) **A:164–72**
Banff National Park **B:**46; **N:**56
Edmonton **E:**73
Jasper National Park **J:**54
world's largest deposits of tar sands **E:**221
map(s) **A:**168
picture(s)
badlands **A:**166
Banff National Park **A:**167; **B:**46; **C:**56; **N:**57
Calgary Stampede **A:**170
Edmonton **A:**170
Jasper National Park **J:**54
oil sands recovery plant **A:**169
wheat farming **A:**166
Alberti, Leon Battista (Italian architect) **H:**284; **I:**395; **R:**164–65
Albertus Magnus, Saint (German philosopher, theologian, scientist, and writer) **A:**338; **S:**18d *profile*
Albigensian heresy **L:**309
Albrecht V (duke of Bavaria) **D:**261
Albright, Madeleine K. (United States secretary of state) **W:**35 *profile*
Album (for stamp collecting) **S:**421–22
Albumen (white of egg) **E:**95; **P:**211
Albumin (protein) **L:**269
Albumin glue **G:**243
Albuquerque (New Mexico) **N:**180, 183, 185, 187, 189
picture(s) **N:**189
Alcaeus (Greek lyric poet) **G:**355
picture(s) **G:**354
Alcan Highway *see* Alaska Highway
Alcatraz Island (California) **C:**28
Alcázar, The (castle, Segovia, Spain)
picture(s) **C:**131; **S:**369
Alcázar, The (castle, Seville, Spain) **S:**381
Alchemy (ancient practice of chemistry) **C:**207
aging **A:**87
distillation **D:**219
extrasensory perception **E:**427
picture(s) **C:**206
Alcibiades (Athenian statesman) **P:**120a
Alcindor, Lew (American basketball player) *see* Abdul-Jabbar, Kareem
ALCM (air-launched cruise missiles) **M:**349
Alcman (Greek poet) **G:**356
Alcmene (in Greek mythology) **G:**365
Alcohol **A:172**
Alcohol and Tobacco Tax and Trade Bureau **T:**294–95
anesthesia **A:**254
avoiding health hazards **H:**76
beer and brewing **B:**114
chemical term **C:**204
distillation process **D:**219
driving under the influence of **D:**326–27; **H:**76; **P:**364
drug abuse **D:**329, 330
family problems **F:**42
fermentation **F:**90
fuel **F:**489; **N:**294
grain, uses of **G:**284–85
juvenile crime **J:**169
liver damaged by alcohol abuse **L:**270
Maine Law (1850) **M:**50
mental illness and **M:**223
pregnant woman's use can hurt fetus **R:**190
prohibition **P:**483–85
thermometers, use in **T:**163
whiskey and other distilled beverages **W:**161
Alcohol and Tobacco Tax and Trade Bureau **T:**294–95
Alcoholics Anonymous (AA) **A:**173
Alcoholism **A:173; H:**183
Alcohol, Tobacco, Firearms, and Explosives, Bureau of **J:**165
Alcott, Amos Bronson (American educator) **A:**174
Alcott, Louisa May (American author) **A:174–75; C:**236; **F:**115
Little Women, excerpt from **A:**174–75
Aldebaran (star) **C:**531
Alden, John (Pilgrim settler) **P:**345
Alderney (one of the Channel Islands, Britain) **I:**363
Aldis, Dorothy (American poet)
"Brooms" (poem) **F:**124
Aldiss, Brian (English author) **S:**80 *profile*
Aldrich, Nelson Wilmarth (American political figure) **R:**224 *profile*
Aldrin, Edwin E., Jr. (American astronaut) **A:**467; **E:**417; **S:**340f, 340h, 340j, 347 *profile*
Armstrong, Neil A. **A:**426
picture(s) **E:**417; **M:**453; **S:**340i, 347
Aldus Manutius (Italian book publisher) *see* Manutius, Aldus
Ale (type of beer) **B:**114, 115
Alegría, Claribel (Salvadoran writer) **E:**198
Alegria, Fernando (Chilean American author) **H:**147
Aleichem, Sholem (Jewish writer and humorist) *see* Aleykhem (Aleichem), Sholem
Aleijadinho (Brazilian sculptor) *see* Lisboa, Antonio Francisco
Aleixandre, Vicente (Spanish poet) **S:**392
Alekseev, Konstantin (Russian actor) *see* Stanislavski, Konstantin
Alemán, Mateo (Spanish writer) **S:**388
Aleman Lacayo, José Arnoldo (Nicaraguan political leader) **N:**248
Alemán Valdés, Miguel (Mexican president) **M:**252
Alembert, Jean d' (French philosopher) **E:**297
Alençon lace **L:**19
Aleppo (Syria) **S:**549, 551
Alert (Nunavut) **N:**411
Alesia, Battle of (52 B.C.) **B:**103e
Alessandri Palma, Arturo (Chilean president) **C:**255
Alessandro Filipepi (Italian painter) *see* Botticelli, Sandro
Aletsch Glacier (Switzerland) **A:**194d
Aleut (Native Americans) **A:**144, 150; **I:**191, 273; **R:**31

Aleutian Islands I:361; U:82
Alaska A:146, 149, 158
World War II W:306
Aleutian Range (Alaska) A:146
Alexander, Grover Cleveland (American baseball player) B:88 *profile*
picture(s) B:88
Alexander, Harold (1st Earl Alexander of Tunis, British field marshal) W:307
Alexander, Lloyd (American writer) C:230 *profile*
Alexander V (antipope) R:293
Alexander III (king of Macedonia) *see* Alexander the Great
Alexander I, Saint (pope) R:292
Alexander II (pope) R:292
Alexander III (pope) R:292
Alexander IV (pope) R:293
Alexander VI (pope) E:405; R:160, 293
Alexander VII (pope) R:293
Alexander VIII (pope) R:293
Alexander I (emperor of Russia) **A:176;** R:370
Alexander II (emperor of Russia) **A:176–77;** R:370; U:39
Alexander III (emperor of Russia) **A:177;** R:370; U:39
picture(s) A:177
Alexander III (king of Scotland) S:88
Alexander I (king of Yugoslavia) S:126; Y:368
picture(s) Y:367
Alexander and the Terrible, Horrible, No Good, Very Bad Day (book by Viorst)
picture(s)
Cruz illustration C:244
Alexander Archipelago (island group, Alaska) A:146; I:362
Alexander Nevsky (Russian hero) R:368
Alexander Nevsky Cathedral (Sofia, Bulgaria) B:444
Alexander of Battenburg (Bulgarian prince) B:445
Alexander the Great (king of Macedonia) **A:177–78,** 453; G:344
Aristotle was teacher of A:387
diving bell legend U:26
Egypt, ancient E:109
Greek civilization extended by A:238–39
India, invasion of I:131
Jews, Greek rule over J:103
Mesopotamia, decline of M:232
Middle East M:304
Persia, ancient P:155
submarine experiment S:473
wine making, history of W:190a
picture(s)
sculpture A:177
Alexandra (Russian empress) N:249
picture(s) R:371
Alexandria (Egypt) E:103; M:302
Alexander the Great founds A:178
Greek literature, center of G:358
library E:79; L:172
mathematics, history of M:163
Pharos lighthouse was a wonder of the ancient world W:219–20
science, milestones in S:68, 69
Alexandria (Louisiana) L:323
Alexandria (Virginia)
picture(s) V:355
Alexandria, Museum of (ancient Egypt) M:527
Alexandrite (gemstone) G:73
Alexis (heir to Russian throne) N:249
picture(s) R:371
Alexis (Russian Orthodox metropolitan) I:413
Alexius I Comnenus (Byzantine emperor) C:598–99
Aleykhem (Aleichem), Sholem (Jewish writer and humorist) Y:360–61
Alfaro, Eloy (Ecuadorian political reformer) E:69
Alfieri, Vittorio (Italian poet) I:408
Al fine (musical term) M:536
Alfonsín, Raúl (Argentinian political leader) A:386d
Alfonso X, the Wise (king of Castile) S:386, 387
picture(s) M:290
Alfonso XII (Spanish king) S:378
Alfonso XIII (Spanish king) S:378, 393
Alfred the Great (king of England) **A:179;** E:237–38
English literature flourished under E:268–69
London L:298
spies S:408 *profile*
Algae (simple organisms) **A:180–81;** M:275
corals, relationships with J:77
eutrophication of water sources W:67, 70
fertilizers stimulate growth and cause pollution E:301
food for the future P:221
kingdoms of living things K:258
ocean, uses of the O:28
plankton P:283–84
red tides E:209
picture(s) K:258
Algal blooms (overgrowth of algae on a body of water) A:181
Algebra (branch of mathematics) **A:182–84;** M:157 *see also* Arithmetic
Arab achievements A:345
Boole's symbolic logic L:290
Gauss, Carl Friedrich G:64
mathematics, history of M:163, 164, 165–66, 169
science, milestones in S:69
Alger, Horatio, Jr. (American author) M:148 *profile*
Algeria **A:185–88**
France, history of F:417, 420
Organization of Petroleum Exporting Countries O:222
map(s) A:186
picture(s)
Algiers A:187
election E:130
flag F:226
natural gas processing A:187
people A:185
prehistoric art P:437
Algiers (capital of Algeria) A:187, 188
picture(s) A:187
Algonkians (Indians of North America) I:177–78
Massachusetts M:136, 146
New Brunswick N:138f
New England N:139
New York, history of N:221
Algorithm (set of simple steps for solving a problem) C:482
picture(s) C:483
Alhambra palace (Spain) I:357
fountains F:393
Spain, art and architecture of S:381
picture(s) S:381
Court of the Lions I:356
Alhazen (Arab mathematician and optical scientist) O:178
Ali (cousin and son-in-law of the prophet Mohammed) I:347, 350, 351
picture(s) I:350
Ali, Muhammad (Cassius Marcellus Clay, Jr.) (American boxer) **A:189;** B:351, 352 *profile;* O:113; P:106
picture(s) A:189; B:352; K:225
Alia, Ramiz (Albanian political leader) A:162
Alianza Federal de Mercedes (Hispanic-American organization) N:194
Ali Baba (hero of story "The Forty Thieves" from *Arabian Nights*) A:340
Alice in Wonderland (book by Carroll) C:119, 120
excerpt from C:120
picture(s)
Tenniel illustration C:232
Alice Springs (Australia) A:513
Alice Tully Hall (Lincoln Center, New York City) L:248
Alien and Sedition Acts (United States, 1798) A:14, 189; K:227; U:178

Aliens **A:189; G:**276 *see also* Citizenship; Immigration; Naturalization
compared to citizens **C:**322
naturalization **N:**61
passports and visas **P:**96
refugees **R:**136–37
Alimony (in divorce) **D:**230
Al-isra wa-l-miraj (Muslim holiday) **I:**349
Aliyev, Heydar A. (president of Azerbaijan) **A:**574
Aliyev, Ilham (president of Azerbaijan) **A:**574
Alkali metals **C:**204; **E:**167
Alkaline batteries **B:**103b
Alkaline-earth metals **E:**167
Alkaline soils **S:**238
Alkalis (strong chemical bases) **C:**204; **D:**140
Alkaloids (toxic compounds) **R:**100
Alkyd resins (types of liquid plastics) **P:**32
Allagash Wilderness Waterway (Maine) **M:**44
Allah (Arabic name for God of Islam) **I:**346; **K:**292; **M:**401; **R:**148
Allahabad (India) **G:**25
All-America Football Conference **F:**364
All American Futurity (horse race) **H:**234
All-American Soap Box Derby *see* Soap Box Derby
Allegheny Front (escarpment) **O:**269; **W:**128
Allegheny Mountains (North America) **P:**128; **W:**128, 129, 130
Allegheny Plateau (eastern North America)
Maryland **M:**122
New York **N:**213
Ohio **O:**64
Pennsylvania **P:**128
West Virginia **W:**126, 128
Allegheny River (United States) **O:**78; **P:**128, 266
Allegory (story to explain or teach something)
early English literature **E:**269
early French literature **F:**436
Everyman (greatest morality play) **E:**271
Pilgrim's Progress **E:**276
Allegretto (musical term) **M:**536
Allegri, Antonio (Italian artist) *see* Correggio, Antonio Allegri da
Allegro (musical term) **M:**536, 539
Allegro Brillante (ballet)
picture(s) **B:**33
Alleles (in genetics) **G:**79, 81
Allen, Ethan (American Revolutionary War hero) **A:190; I:**204; **R:**199; **V:**314, 318
Allen, Florence E. (American jurist and feminist) **O:**76 *profile*
Allen, H. W. (American inventor) **A:**360
Allen, Horatio (American engineer) **R:**87
Allen, Richard (American religious leader) **A:**79e; **P:**140 *profile*
Allen, Woody (American actor, writer, and filmmaker) **M:**493 *profile,* 497
Allenby, Sir Edmund H. H. (British general) **J:**84
Allende, Isabel (Chilean author) **C:**254
Allende, Pedro Humberto (Chilean composer) **L:**73
Allende Gossens, Salvador (Chilean political leader) **C:**255
Allentown (Pennsylvania) **P:**135
Allergens (allergy-causing substances) **A:**190–91
Allergic rhinitis *see* Hay fever
Allergies (immune system's abnormal responses to normally harmless substances) **A:190–91; D:**184, 187–88
antibiotics **A:**310
asthma attacks can be brought on by **A:**463
drugs, effects of **D:**335
food inspection **F:**335
food-labeling rules **F:**345
hypoallergenic cosmetics **C:**560
immune system, disorders of **I:**97
insect stings **F:**161; **S:**3
peanuts and peanut products **P:**112
pollen **F:**286
rubber **R:**345
All for Love (play by Dryden) **D:**342
All Hallows' Day (religious holiday) *see* All Saints' Day
Alliance for Progress (development program for Latin America) **G:**400; **K:**209
Alliances (of nations) **I:**269
All I Desire (motion picture, 1953) **M:**492
Allied Control Council (over Germany after World War II) **G:**164
Allied Powers (during World War I) **W:**280, 289, 290, 293–94
map(s) **W:**279
Allied Powers (during World War II) **W:**292
profiles of leaders **W:**300–301
Allies (among nations) **I:**269; **U:**103
Allies Day, May 1917 (painting by Hassam)
picture(s) **I:**106
Alligators **A:**284; **C:592–94; R:**179–80
picture(s) **R:**180; **U:**90
Alligator snapping turtle *see* Temminck's snapper
Alliteration (repetition of the same first sounds in a group of words) **B:**144a; **P:**350
Allopatric speciation (in evolution) **E:**378
Allosaurus (dinosaur) **D:**169
picture(s) **D:**164, 167, 168
Allotropes (forms of a chemical element) **C:**204
Alloys **A:192–93; C:**204; **M:**236 *see also* Brass; Brazing; Bronze; Metals and metallurgy; Soldering; Welding
aluminum **A:**195
bronze and brass **B:**409–10
chemistry, history of **C:**206
copper **C:**554
gold alloyed with other metals **G:**248
jewelry making **J:**96
kinds of steel **I:**329
magnesium alloys **M:**27
nickel **N:**249–50
silver **S:**178
standard jewelry alloys of gold **G:**248
thermocouples, use in **T:**164
tin, use of **T:**209
tungsten and steel alloys **T:**332
wire **W:**191
Alloy steels **A:**192; **I:**329
All Quiet on the Western Front (novel by Remarque) **G:**182
All Saints Cathedral (England)
picture(s)
stained-glass window **S:**417
All Saints' Day (All Hallows' Day) (religious holiday) **H:**13, 164; **R:**155
All Souls' Day (religious holiday) **R:**155
Hispanic Americans' *El Día de los Muertos* **H:**146
Latin America **L:**56
Mexico **M:**243–44
Allspice **H:**120
All-star games (in baseball) **B:**84, 91
All's Well That Ends Well (play by Shakespeare) **S:**135
All-terrain bicycles (ATB's) **B:**175, 176, 177
All the King's Men (novel by Warren) **A:**218; **W:**12
All-Union Party Congress (Soviet government) **U:**37
Alluvial deposits **G:**248–49; **R:**237
Alluvial soils **L:**318; **N:**291; **O:**207; **S:**238
Alluvium (river deposits) **R:**237
All-wheel drive (of a truck) **T:**319
Almagest (book, Ptolemy) **A:**469
Almagro, Diego de (Spanish soldier) **C:**254; **E:**409; **P:**268
Almanacs (reference books) **R:**129
Poor Richard's Almanack **F:**454
Almandite (garnet gemstone) **G:**73
Almaty (Kazakhstan) **K:**201
Almohads (Berber dynasty in Spain) **M:**461; **S:**376, 381
Almonds **N:**432
Almoravids (Berber dynasty) **M:**461; **S:**376
Almsgiving (charitable donations) **I:**348–49
Almshouses (early hospitals for the poor) **H:**253
Aloe (plant used for medicinal purposes) **H:**119
Aloha (Hawaiian word meaning "love") **H:**48

"Aloha Oe" (song) **H:**61
Aloha State (nickname for Hawaii) **H:**48, 49
Alonso, Alicia (Cuban ballerina) **C:**609
Alpacas (hoofed mammals) **H:**220; **L:**273; **S:**283
Alphabet **A:194–94c** *see also* Writing systems; individual letters of the alphabet
Braille **B:**257
Chinese in Roman alphabet **C:**258
communication advanced by **C:**463
Danish has 29 letters **D:**108
development of languages **L:**38
encyclopedias in unit and split-lettered alphabetical systems **E:**206
Greek alphabet **G:**353
Hebrew **H:**98
how to cut paper and fabric letters **B:**449
indexes, learning to use **I:**115
International Code of Signals for use at sea **F:**247
inventions **I:**280
Japanese language **J:**30
Latin language **L:**74
letter name knowledge in reading readiness **R:**109
most used letter in English **E:**1
phonics **P:**194
pronunciation **P:**486
Roman alphabet letters were once hieroglyphs **H:**131
Russian uses Cyrillic alphabet **R:**358, 368, 380
picture(s)
children learning letters **K:**246
cursive alphabet **H:**23
manual alphabet of the deaf **D:**49
manuscript alphabet **H:**22
Alpha brass (alloy) **B:**410
Alpha Centauri (star) **A:**472; **S:**353, 428, 488
Alpha particles (of radioactive atoms) **R:**67
Alpha rays (streams of alpha particles) **R:**47, 67
Alpine Club of London (mountain climbing club) **M:**499
Alpine glaciers *see* Valley glaciers
Alpine horn (musical instrument)
picture(s) **S:**542
Alpine skiing **S:**184c, 184e–184f, 185
Alpine tundra **T:**331
Alps (mountains of Europe) **A:194d**
Alpine regions of Austria **A:**520
branches named and located **E:**345
France **F:**409
Frejus tunnel **T:**339
Italy **I:**384
Liechtenstein **L:**191
mountains of the world **M:**502, 504–5
Switzerland **S:**542–43
picture(s) **M:**503
France **F:**408
Grossglockner **A:**518
ibex **G:**244
Mont Blanc **A:**194d; **G:**221
Al Qaeda (terrorist organization) *see* Qaeda, Al
ALS *see* Amyotrophic lateral sclerosis
Alsace-Lorraine (historic region of eastern France) **F:**417, 452; **W:**280–81, 291
Alsatian (dog) *see* German shepherd
Altaic languages **A:**445; **L:**40
Altair (star) **C:**531
Altamira cave paintings (Spain) **P:**15; **S:**380
picture(s) **P:**14, 436
Altekruse, William (American puzzle maker) **P:**553
Alternate arrangement (of leaves) **L:**113, 114; **P:**306
Alternating current (A.C.) (in electricity) **E:**145
electric clocks **C:**370
electric generators **E:**133–34
electric motors **E:**153–54
electric traction motors **L:**287
transformers **T:**272
Alternation of generations (in biology) **F:**94–95; **M:**473; **P:**302
Alternative medical systems (category of alternative therapy) **A:**194e
Alternative medicine **A:194e; H:**171; **M:**207, 210
Alternative rock music **R:**264
Alternators (of automobiles) **A:**547; **B:**103b, 103c
Altes ("Old") Museum (Berlin, Germany) **M:**528
Althing (Iceland's legislature) **I:**37; **L:**137; **P:**83; **V:**340
Altimeter (measures altitude) **A:**118; **B:**62
Altiplano regions (of South America) **B:**307, 308, 309; **P:**162
Altitude
boiling point of water affected by **H:**91
climatic control **C:**361, 362; **M:**507
cloud formation **C:**382
temperature of environment affected by **L:**202
Alto (musical term) **C:**282
Altocumulus clouds **C:**385; **W:**87
picture(s) **C:**384
Altostratus clouds **C:**385; **W:**87
picture(s) **C:**384
Altricial birds **B:**233
"Alturas de Machu Picchu" (poem by Neruda)
excerpt from **L:**69
Alum (chemical compound) **D:**375; **W:**57
Alumina *see* Aluminum oxide
Aluminum (Aluminium) **A:194f–195; E:**170
acid rain's effect on soils **A:**10
airplanes designed for subsonic flight **S:**501
archery equipment **A:**361
atomic number **A:**486
jewelry making **J:**96
non-ferrous alloys **A:**192, 193
table(s) **M:**235
Aluminum bronze (alloy) **B:**410
Aluminum oxide (alumina) **A:**194f; **G:**391–92; **O:**288
Alva, Walter (Peruvian archaeologist) **A:**354
Alvarado, Pedro de (Spanish soldier) **E:**198; **M:**187, 443
Alvarez, Luis Walter (American physicist) **A:195; D:**175
geology **G:**111–12
Alvarez, Walter (American geologist) **A:**195; **D:**175
Alvars (a people of India) **H:**142
Alveoli *see* Air sacs
Alvin (submersible) **U:**23, 26
picture(s) **S:**476
Always Prepared (motto of U.S. Coast Guard) *see* Semper Paratus
Alyssum, sweet (flower)
picture(s) **G:**27, 28
Alzheimer, Alois (German physician) **A:**196
Alzheimer's disease **A:196; D:**188; **M:**223
picture(s)
man with Alzheimer's disease **M:**222
AM (radio) *see* Amplitude modulation
Amado, Jorge (Brazilian novelist) **L:**70
Amager (island, Denmark) **C:**551
Amahl and the Night Visitors (opera by Menotti) **O:**150
picture(s) **O:**151
Amalgam (alloy)
gold and mercury **G:**247
silver-mercury alloys **S:**178
Amalgamation (of ores) **G:**249; **M:**233
Amalienborg Palace (Copenhagen, Denmark) **C:**551–52
Amalthea (moon of Jupiter) **J:**162
Amana colonies (Iowa) **I:**294, 298
Amanitas (poisonous mushrooms) **F:**500; **M:**529
Amaral, Antonio H. (Brazilian artist) **L:**65
Amaranth (plant) **G:**286; **I:**165
Amateur Athletic Union of the United States (AAU) **G:**433; **S:**536
Amateur guilds **G:**405
Amateur International Boxing Association (AIBA) **B:**353
Amateurism (in the Olympic Games) **O:**103, 108, 114
Amateur Radio Emergency Service **R:**63
Amateur radio *see* Radio, amateur
Amateur telescope makers (ATM's) **T:**60

Amateur theatricals P:335–38; T:157
Amati family (Italian violin makers) B:71; V:345
"Amazing Grace" (hymn) F:324
Amazing Stories (science-fiction magazine) S:80–81
Amazonite (gemstone) G:73
Amazon Pact (Treaty of Amazon Cooperation) (1978) A:198
Amazon parrot B:250
  picture(s) P:178
Amazon River (South America) **A:197–98;** S:274, 280
  Brazil B:378
  river basin S:277, 281
  tidal bore T:197
  map(s) A:197
  picture(s) A:197, 198; B:378
    aerial view S:281
    houseboat R:241
    rain forests of Amazon basin S:290
Amazons (in Greek mythology) A:198
Ambartsumian, Victor (Armenian astrophysicist) A:421
Ambassadors (highest ranking officers in embassies) F:371; I:269
  forms of address A:22
Amber (fossil resin) R:184
  discovery of static electricity E:136
  fossils preserved in F:382
  organic gems G:75
  picture(s)
    grasshopper fossil F:382
Ambergris (substance formed by whales) P:151; W:150, 154
Amboise Conspiracy (in French history) F:449
Ambrogini, Angelo (Italian poet) *see* Poliziano
Ambrose, Saint A:494; C:290; H:321; S:18d *profile*
Ambrose Offshore Light Structure (off New York Harbor)
  picture(s) L:229
Ambulances (specially equipped vehicles to transport the sick or injured to hospitals) **A:199;** E:162
Ambulatory surgery (surgery not requiring an overnight hospital stay) H:253
Amendments to the United States Constitution G:276; U:147, 155–60 *see also* Bill of Rights, American
  civil rights amendments in the Bill of Rights C:326, 328
  First Amendment freedoms F:163
  first ten are Bill of Rights B:182–83
  Fourteenth Amendment J:117
Amenemhet I (king of ancient Egypt) E:112–13
Amenhotep III (king of ancient Egypt) E:115
Amenhotep IV *see* Akhnaton
Ament, Jeff (American rock musician) R:263
America *see also* Central America; Latin America; North America; South America; the names of countries
  ancient civilizations A:243–45
  Columbus discovered C:445–48
  exploration and discovery of E:404, 405, 407–9
  prehistoric people P:441
  Vespucci, Amerigo, continents named for V:321
  Viking discovery of V:342–43
  Why was the New World named "America"? E:409
America (schooner) S:12
"America" (song by Smith) N:20, 22
American, The (book by Henry James) J:20
American Antiquarian Society (Worcester, Massachusetts) M:145
American Anti-Slavery Society A:6, 6b
American architecture *see* United States, architecture of the
American art *see* United States, art of the
American Association for Affirmative Action C:326
American Association of Family and Consumer Sciences H:180, 181
American Ballet Theatre B:33
American Bar Association (ABA) L:90
American Basketball Association (ABA) B:99
American Basketball League (ABL) B:99
American Battle Monuments Commission (ABMC) N:29
American beech trees
  picture(s) T:304
American Bill of Rights *see* Bill of Rights, American
American black bears B:104, 105–6
  picture(s) B:105
American bond (in masonry) *see* Common bond
American Bowling Congress (ABC) B:348, 350
American Boy (magazine) M:17
American buffalo *see* Bison
American bullfrog
  picture(s) A:222
American Camping Association C:49
American Cancer Society C:93, 95
American Canoe Association C:101
American Checker Federation C:192
American Civil Liberties Union (ACLU) **A:199;** C:326; L:86
American Civil War *see* Civil War, United States
American College Testing Program (ACTP) T:118
American colonies *see* Colonial life in America; Thirteen American colonies
American Colonization Society L:165, 168; S:195
American crawl (swimming stroke) S:536
American Dictionary of the English Language, An (by Webster) W:99
American drama A:216, 218; D:304–5
  Anderson, Maxwell N:334
American eagles *see* Bald eagles
American elk (Wapiti) H:218
American elm trees
  picture(s) M:137; N:323; T:302
American English S:191; W:240
American Expeditionary Force (A.E.F.) P:153; W:289
American Express credit card C:582
American Federation of Labor (AFL) G:261; L:14, 16
American Federation of Labor–Congress of Industrial Organizations (AFL-CIO) L:16–17, 18
American flag *see* United States flags
American Folklore Society F:316
American folklore *see* Folklore, American
American Football Conference F:360
American Football League F:364
American Foundation for the Blind B:258
American Friends Service Committee (AFSC) Q:4a
American Friends Society *see* Quakers
American Fur Company (of John Jacob Astor) A:464; F:521, 523, 524
American Gothic (painting by Wood) W:221
  picture(s) W:221
American Heart Association (AHA) D:212
American history *see* America; Thirteen American colonies; United States, history of the
American Holistic Medical Association (AHMA) H:171
American Holistic Nurses Association (AHNA) H:171
American holly
  picture(s) D:89
American Home Economics Association H:180
American Independent Party (in the United States) P:372
American Indian Movement (AIM) **A:199;** C:326; S:327
American Indians *see* Indians, American
Americanisms (in the English language) W:240
American Kennel Club D:248, 249
American kestrels (birds) F:32, 33
American Labor Party L:18
American League (baseball) B:80, 84, 87, 93
  World Series records B:86
American Legion (veterans' organization) **A:199;** U:121
American Library Association L:180–81
  Caldecott and Newbery Medals C:11–12
  children's book awards C:239–40
American lions *see* Mountain lions
American literature **A:201–19;** U:98–99 *see also* African American literature; Canada, literature of; Children's literature; Folklore, American; Humor; Latin America, literature of; Literary criticism; Magazines; Short stories; the names of writers
  African Americans *see* African American literature

children's book awards **C:**239–40
drama *see* American drama
essays **E:**322
Hispanic Americans **H:**147
novels **F:**115, 116; **N:**360, 361–62, 363
Pulitzer Prizes **P:**533–38
romanticism **R:**304
American Lung Association **D:**212
American Medical Association
picture(s)
symbol **M:**205
American Museum of Immigration (Liberty Island, New York) **L:**169
American Museum of Natural History (New York City) **M:**523
American Museum of Science and Energy (Oak Ridge, Tennessee) **T:**82
American music *see* Folk music; Jazz; Spirituals; United States, music of the
American National Red Cross *see* Red Cross
American Nazi Party **N:**81
American Numismatic Association **C:**399, 400
American Nurses' Association **N:**421
American Occupational Therapy Association (AOTA) **O:**15
American painting *see* United States, art of the
American Party *see* Know-Nothing Party
American Peace Society **P:**105
American Philosophical Society **F:**454; **P:**180, 181
American plan (of hotel rates) **H:**256
American Popular Revolutionary Alliance (APRA) (Peruvian political party) **P:**165
American Printing House for the Blind **B:**258
American Professional Football Association **F:**364
American Psychiatric Association **M:**221
American quarter horses *see* Quarter horses
American Radio Relay League (ARRL) **R:**62, 63
American Recorder Society **R:**121
American Red Cross *see* Red Cross
American regionalism (style of painting) **W:**221
American Revolution *see* Revolutionary War
American Samoa **P:**8, 10; **T:**112; **U:**84–85
American's Creed, The (by Page) **U:**161
American shorthair cat **C:**138
American Society for Information Science **L:**181
American Society for the Prevention of Cruelty to Animals (ASPCA) **A:**261; **D:**244
American Society of Free People of Color **A:**79f
American Society of Interior Designers (ASID) **I:**261
American Sokol Educational and Physical Culture Organization **G:**433
American Stock Exchange **S:**457
Americans with Disabilities Act (United States, 1990) **O:**15
American Telephone and Telegraph Company **P:**523
Johnson's "Chippendale Building" **A:**376; **J:**123
picture(s)
Bell Labs chemist **A:**79b
American Temperance Society **P:**484
American Tragedy, An (novel by Theodore Dreiser) **D:**322
American Upland cotton **C:**568
American Veterans (AMVETS) **U:**121
American War of Independence *see* Revolutionary War
American Water Ski Association **W:**75
American Woman Suffrage Association **W:**212a
American Youth Hostels, Inc. **H:**254
American Youth Soccer Organization **S:**222
America's Cup (yacht-racing trophy) **R:**212; **S:**12
America's Dairyland (nickname for Wisconsin) **W:**192
America's Sweetheart (nickname for Mary Pickford) **M:**491
"America the Beautiful" (song by Bates) **N:**23
Americium (element) **E:**170
Americo-Liberians (Liberian descendants of settlers from the United States) **L:**165, 168
Amerigo Vespucci (Italian navigator) *see* Vespucci, Amerigo
Amerindians *see* Indians, American
Amethyst (quartz gemstone) **G:**72, 74; **Q:**8
February's birthstone **G:**74
picture(s) **G:**74
Amharas (a people of Ethiopia) **E:**330
Amharic (language) **E:**330–31
Amherst, Lord Jeffrey (British soldier) **F:**464; **I:**203
Amiens, Treaty of (1802) **N:**11
Amiens Cathedral (France) **F:**423
Amin, Idi (Ugandan dictator) **U:**4, 7
Amine (chemical) **V:**370b
Amino acids (in body chemistry) **B:**185–86, 296–97, 298, 299
digestion **D:**162–63
enzymes **E:**307
evidence of evolution **E:**374–75
genetics **G:**78, 79, 90
hormones **H:**228
liver **L:**268–69
living things build proteins from **L:**199
phenylketonuria **D:**198
proteins in nutrition **N:**423
structure of antibodies **I:**97
sulfur as a component **S:**486
Aminopeptidase (digestive enzyme) **D:**162
Amis, Kingsley (English writer and teacher) **E:**290
Amish (conservative Protestant group) **A:220; P:**134
folk art **F:**297
traditional agriculture **A:**89
What is shunning? **A:**220
picture(s) **A:**220; **P:**127
Delaware farm **D:**90
Amistad Rebellion (slave mutiny, 1839) **A:221**
Amman (capital of Jordan) **J:**131
Ammann, Jakob (first leader of the Amish) **A:**220
Ammonia (gas) **G:**60; **N:**262
coal by-product **C:**391
liver removes from amino acids **L:**268–69
Saturn's atmosphere **P:**280; **S:**55
structural formula **C:**201
Ammonicera japonica (gastropod) **S:**150, 208
Ammonites (creatures with coiled shells) **F:**387; **S:**151
Ammonium nitrate (chemical compound) **E:**421
Ammunition **G:414–26**
explosives **E:**419–23
lead **L:**93
Amnesty (freedom from prosecution) **A:221; G:**276
illegal aliens **I:**93
Amnesty and Reconstruction, Proclamation of (1863) **R:**117
Amnesty International (human rights organization) **C:**327; **H:**287
Amniocentesis (prenatal testing) **R:**191
Amniotic fluid (surrounding the fetus before birth) **B:**2, 3
Amoebas (one-celled animals) **D:**163; **M:**276; **P:**496
picture(s) **P:**495
Amon-Re, Temple of (Karnak, Egypt) **E:**114–15
Amorites (ancient Syrian people) **S:**487
Amorphous carbon **C:**106
Amorphous materials **M:**154
Amortization (of a debt) **R:**112d
Amos (Hebrew prophet) **B:**160, 162
Amosite (mineral) **A:**438c
Amoskeag Mills (Manchester, New Hampshire) **N:**159, 162
Amperage (of electricity) **E:**139–40
Ampère, André Marie (French scientist) **E:**140, 154; **L:**218–19; **M:**30
Amperes (measure of electric current) **B:**103c; **E:**139–40; **T:**271, 272; **W:**117
Amphetamines (drugs) **D:**331
Amphibians (aircraft) **A:**115
Amphibians (land-water animals) **A:222–24,** 266–67
acid rain's effects **A:**10
dormancy **H:**128
Earth, history of **E:**27
estivation **H:**128

Amphibians (cont.)
evolution from fish **F:**185
frogs and toads **F:**476–78
locomotion **A:**278
prehistoric animals **P:**433
Amphibious assault ships **S:**154
Amphibious tanks **T:**15
Amphibious vehicles **U:**122
picture(s) **U:**111
Amphibious warfare
Normandy invasion was largest amphibious operation in history **W:**310
Okinawa was largest Pacific amphibious landing in World War II **W:**314
United States Navy **U:**114
Amphibole (form of asbestos) **A:**438c
Amphipods (shrimplike creatures) **W:**153
Amphoras (ancient Greek vases)
picture(s) **D:**73; **P:**411; **U:**19
Ampicillin (antibiotic) **A:**307
Amplifiers (in electronics)
amplified music is hazardous to hearing **S:**258
electronic music **E:**155
high-fidelity systems **H:**131, 133
modern stereo systems **S:**267b
radio **R:**54
transistors, uses for **T:**276, 277
Amplitude (in physics) **L:**219; **R:**52; **S:**258–59
Amplitude modulation (AM) (in radio) **R:**53, 54, 56
Ampullae of Lorenzini (sharks' sensors) **S:**143
Amputation (surgery) **S:**513
Amritsar (India) **I:**134
picture(s) **I:**118
Amsterdam (capital of the Netherlands) **A:225; N:**120, 120c
early stock exchange **S:**455
Olympic Games (1928) **O:**112
picture(s) **A:**225; **N:**120a, 120c
Amsterdam Island (Indian Ocean)
picture(s) **I:**362
Amtrak (operator of U.S. passenger rail service) **L:**288; **R:**81, 90; **T:**290; **U:**95
New Mexico **N:**187
Amu Darya (in ancient times called the Oxus River, in central Asia) **A:**44; **L:**32; **T:**11; **U:**258
Amulets (ornaments to ward off evil) **E:**108; **G:**72; **J:**94, 98
picture(s)
pre-Columbian amulet **D:**73
in shape of Thor's hammer **N:**279
Viking amulet **V:**343
Amun (Egyptian king of the gods) **E:**108
Amundsen, Roald (Norwegian explorer) **A:226; N:**339
first Northwest Passage by sea **A:**380; **E:**414; **N:**413
first to reach South Pole **A:**295; **E:**415
picture(s) **A:**226; **E:**414
Amur River (Asia) **R:**240, 362
Amusement and theme parks **P:**78–79
audio-animatronic figures **A:**530
Disneyland (California) **C:**28; **D:**216
Disneyland (Japan) **T:**219
Disney World (Florida) **D:**216
Holiday World (Indiana) **I:**152
Los Angeles **L:**305
midway rides at agricultural fairs **F:**14–15
narrow-gauge railways **R:**78
Opryland U.S.A. **T:**82
places of interest in Florida **F:**270
Six Flags Great Adventure (New Jersey) **N:**172
West Edmonton Mall (Alberta) **E:**73
picture(s)
centrifugal effect of rides **G:**323
Disneyland (California) **D:**215
Disney World (Florida) **M:**94
Amusements *see* Recreation
Amygdala (part of the cerebrum) **B:**365; **E:**203
Amylase (digestive enzyme) **B:**280; **D:**162
Amyotrophic lateral sclerosis
Gehrig, Lou **G:**67
Hawking, Stephen William **H:**63
Anabaptism (Protestant movement) **A:**220; **R:**131
Anacletus, Saint (pope) *see* Cletus, Saint
Anacletus II (antipope) **R:**292
Anaconda Company **M:**440
Anacondas (snakes) **S:**213, 217, 283
picture(s) **S:**283
Anacostia River (Washington, D.C.) **W:**29
Anaerobic bacteria **L:**203
Anaerobic respiration (of plants) **P:**315
Anagrams (word games) **G:**17; **W:**236
Analects (sayings of Confucius) **C:**498; **R:**151
Anal fins (of fish) **F:**188
Analgesics (substances that relieve pain) **N:**15
Analog devices **C:**491
Analogies (test questions) **T:**120
Analog mode (of transistors) **T:**276
Analog signals (in telecommunications) **T:**48–49
Analog sound storage **H:**132
Analog synthesizer **E:**156
Analog time display (in solid-state watches) **W:**45
picture(s) **W:**45
Analog transmission (of cellular telephones) **T:**56
Analog video recording **V:**332e
Anal sphincter (muscle at the end of the digestive tract) **B:**301
Analysis (in chemistry) **C:**204
Analysis (of scientific experiments) **S:**77–78
Analysis of Beauty, The (book by William Hogarth) **H:**159a
Analytical chemistry **C:**205
Analytical engine (early computer) **C:**490
Analytical method (in philosophy) **P:**189
Analytic cubism (art style) **C:**612
Analytic geometry *see* Coordinate geometry
Anansi (hero of African folktales) **A:**76b
Anapests (metrical feet in poetry) **P:**351
Anaphylaxis (extreme allergic reaction) **A:**190, 191; **D:**187
Anarchism (political theory) **A:226; G:**276
Anarchy (in English history) **H:**108
Anasazi (early Native Americans) **A:227** *see also* Cliff dwellers
Arizona **A:**400, 402
Anastasia (Russian princess)
picture(s) **R:**371
Anastasia, Albert (Italian-American mobster) **O:**224–25 *profile*
Anastasius (antipope) **R:**292
Anastasius I (pope) **R:**292
Anastasius II (pope) **R:**292
Anastasius III (pope) **R:**292
Anastasius IV (pope) **R:**292
Anatase (mineral)
picture(s) **M:**316
Anatidae (waterfowl family) **D:**343
Anatman (Buddhist teaching of selflessness) **B:**425
Anatolia (Asia Minor) (region of Turkey) **H:**155; **O:**259; **T:**345, 346, 347 *see also* Asia Minor
Anatomy, comparative **A:**276–77; **S:**66
Anatomy, human (structure of human body) **B:**272–92; **M:**208–8a; **S:**70
Anatomy Lesson of Dr. Tulp, The (painting by Rembrandt)
picture(s) **M:**208a; **W:**266
Anatosaurus (dinosaur)
picture(s) **D:**172
Anaya, Rudolfo (American writer) **A:**219
Ancestor worship **R:**147
Africa **A:**60
Africa, art of **A:**70
China, ancient **A:**240
ghosts **G:**199
Liberia **L:**165–66
Madagascar **M:**8
Rome, ancient **R:**311

Anchises (father of Aeneas) **A**:36
Anchorage (Alaska) **A**:144, 150, 151, 152, 153, 158
earthquake (1964) **E**:41
picture(s) **A**:153
"Anchors Aweigh" (song by A. H. Miles and R. Lovell) **N**:23
Anchovies (fish) **F**:200
Ancient civilizations **A:228–45; W**:259 *see also* the names of ancient races and peoples; the names of countries of ancient times
African kingdoms, early **A**:65–66
art as a record **A**:429
Asia **A**:453
Assyria **A**:462
Aztecs **A**:575–78
bread and baking **B**:388a
Celts **C**:163–64
cuneiform **C**:613
eclipse studies **E**:52
education systems **E**:77–79
Egypt **E**:106–9
European civilization, development of **E**:365
exploration and discovery **E**:398–400
fairs and expositions **F**:17
food preparation in ancient times **F**:336
furniture **F**:506–8
Heyerdahl, Thor **H**:125
historical writings **H**:150
Hittites **H**:155
homes and housing **H**:191–92
Incas **I**:107–10
Indians, American **I**:164–73
inventions **I**:279–80
law and law enforcement **L**:84
leather through the ages **L**:111
libraries **L**:171–72
masonry of brick and stone **B**:394
Maya **M**:184–87
Mediterranean Sea regions **M**:212
Mesopotamia **M**:231–32
Middle East called the cradle of civilization **M**:304
mummies **M**:512–13
Mycenaean culture **M**:562
Persia, ancient **P**:154–57
Persian art **P**:155, 157
pirates **P**:262–63
pottery **P**:409–12
prehistoric people **P**:442
Rome, ancient **R**:309–17
science, milestones in **S**:68–69
slavery **S**:192–93
Sumer **S**:487
technology **T**:40
Tiahuanaco civilization in the Andes **B**:306, 310
time line **A**:230–35
toys, history of **T**:250–51
wonders of the ancient world **W**:216–20
map(s)
sites of some ancient civilizations **A**:230, 235
picture(s)
Zimbabwe stone ruins **Z**:383
Ancient history *see* Ancient civilizations
Andalusia (Spain) **S**:370, 374, 392a
Andaman Islands (India) **I**:362
Andaman Sea **O**:43
Andante (musical term) **M**:536, 539
Andean civilizations **A**:244–45
Andean Common Market **L**:59
Andean condors **V**:394
Andean hummingbirds **H**:288
Anders, William A. (American astronaut) **S**:347 *profile*
Andersen, Hans Christian (Danish writer of fairy tales) **A:246–49; C**:232; **F**:21
Andersen Medal (book award) **C**:240
"The Emperor's New Clothes" **A**:247–49
Little Mermaid statue was inspired by his story **C**:551
"The Princess on the Pea" **F**:26
Scandinavian literature **S**:58i
picture(s) **A**:246
Anderson, Bill (American singer) **C**:573
Anderson, Edward (American author) **M**:564
Anderson, French (American scientist) **G**:91
Anderson, Kenny (American basketball player)
picture(s) **B**:95d
Anderson, Marian (American singer) **A**:79c, 79k, **249**
picture(s) **A**:249
Anderson, Maxie (American balloonist) **B**:36
Anderson, Maxwell (American playwright) **N**:334 *profile*
Anderson, Robert (American army officer) **C**:332, 336–37
Anderson, Sherwood (American writer) **A**:214b; **O**:76 *profile;* **S**:163
picture(s) **O**:76
Andersonville National Cemetery (Georgia) **N**:28
Andersonville National Historic Site (Georgia) **G**:140
Andes (mountains of South America) **A:250–51; M**:504; **S**:274, 276
ancient civilizations *see* Andean civilizations
Argentina **A**:382, 384–85
Bolivia **B**:307
climate **S**:282
Colombia **C**:404
Ecuador **E**:66
Indians, American **I**:168, 195–96
llamas used as transportation **L**:278
Peru **P**:161, 162
Venezuela **V**:296
map(s) **A**:250
picture(s) **A**: 385; **S**:275
Bolivia **B**:308
Cotopaxi **A**:250
glacier **S**:277
highlands in Colombia **C**:405
Inca trail in Peru **S**:275
plateau in Ecuador **S**:276
Andes, Army of the **S**:36
AND operation (in Boolean logic) **C**:487
Andorra **A:252–53**
map(s) **A**:253
picture(s) **A**:253
flag **F**:226
Andorra la Vella (capital of Andorra)
picture(s) **A**:253
Andrada e Silva, José Bonifácio de (Brazilian statesman) **B**:383
André, John (English spy) **A**:426; **D**:65; **R**:206; **S**:408 *profile*
picture(s) **R**:206
Andrea Chénier (opera by Giordano) **O**:150
Andrew (hurricane, 1992) **F**:275
picture(s)
Florida damage **F**:274
Andrew (prince of England) **E**:192
Andrew, Saint (one of the 12 Apostles) **A**:328–29
Andrew II (king of Hungary) **H**:298
Andrew Jackson (clipper ship) **S**:158
Andreyev, Leonid (Russian author) **R**:383
Andromeda (constellation) **C**:531
spiral galaxy in **M**:309; **U**:214, 217
picture(s)
spiral galaxy in **S**:340b
Andromeda (in Greek mythology) **G**:365
Andronicus, Lucius Livius (Greek-born Roman poet and playwright) *see* Livius Andronicus, Lucius
Andropov, Yuri Vladimirovich (Soviet political leader) **R**:372; **U**:43
Andros, Sir Edmund (English governor) **C**:521
Androscoggin River (New Hampshire–Maine) **M**:38; **N**:152
Andros Island (Bahamas) **B**:17
Anechoic chamber (room without echoes) **S**:260–61

Anemia (deficiency of red cells or hemoglobin in the blood) **B:**262; **D:**188
deficiency disease **N:**429; **V:**370c, 370d
leukemia **D:**195–96
sickle-cell anemia **D:**201
transfusion used in treatment **T:**273
Anemometers (instruments that measure the strength of the wind) **W:**88–89, 189
Anemones (flowers) **F:**282–83
picture(s) **F:**283
Anemones, sea *see* Sea anemones
Aneroid barometer **B:**62
Anesthesia **A:254–57** *see also* Drugs
hospitals **H:**248
hypnotism **H:**327, 328, 329
progress in modern surgery **M:**208a, 208b–208c
surgery **S:**513, 514, 515
picture(s)
first public demonstration **S:**512
Anesthesiologist (physician who specializes in anesthesia) **A:**255
Aneurysm (weak place in an artery) **D:**189
Angel (painting by Fra Angelico)
picture(s) **R:**166
Angel dust (drug) *see* PCP
Angel Falls (Venezuela) **S:**274, 277; **V:**296; **W:**62, 63
picture(s) **S:**280; **V:**295
Angelfish **F:**204
picture(s) **F:**204
Angelico, Fra (Italian painter) **A:257; I:**396; **P:**20; **R:**166
picture(s)
Angel (painting) **R:**166
detail from Perugia altarpiece **A:**257
Angeli Laudantes (Praising Angels) (tapestry designed by Burne-Jones)
picture(s) **T:**21
Angelou, Maya (American writer, stage performer, and composer) **A:258,** 418 *profile*
picture(s) **A:**418
Angels (spiritual beings in many religious traditions) **A:258**
Angel sharks **S:**143
Anger, feeling of (in psychology) **D:**231; **G:**380
Angerstein, John Julius (English merchant and art patron) **N:**35
Angina pectoris (chest pains) **D:**193; **H:**82
Angiogenesis (formation of blood vessels) **C:**95
Angiosperms (division of the plant kingdom) **F:**280, 374; **P:**301, 302
Angkor (ancient city in Cambodia) **A:**242; **C:**35, 37
Angkor Thom (temple in Cambodia) **A:**243
picture(s) **S:**335
Angkor Wat (temple in Cambodia) **A:**243
picture(s) **A:**234; **C:**35
Angle, Edward (American orthodontist) **O:**233
Angle bars (steel pieces joining sections of railroad track) **R:**77
Angle of incidence (in physics of light)
diagram(s) **L:**212
Angle of reflection (in physics of light)
diagram(s) **L:**212
Angler fish **A:**281; **F:**182
picture(s) **F:**183
Anglers (persons who fish for sport) **F:**209
Angles (Germanic people, invaders of Britain) **E:**236
Angles (in geometry) **G:**121
bevel gauges **T:**230
optical instruments that measure angles **O:**182–83
trigonometry **T:**312–13
diagram(s) **G:**121
Angleworms *see* Earthworms
Anglican Church (Protestant Episcopal Church) **P:**491, 492, 493, 494 *see also* England, Church of
Christianity, history of **C:**293
Cranmer's prayer books **E:**243
Reformation **R:**132
saints **S:**18c
United States **C:**294; **P:**494
Angling *see* Fishing
Anglo-Burmese wars **M:**561
Anglo-Egyptian Sudan *see* Sudan
Anglo-Norman French language **F:**434
Anglo-Saxon Chronicle **E:**268–69
Anglo-Saxon (Old English) language **E:**265
compared with Anglo-Norman French **F:**434
names **N:**4
Anglo-Saxon literature **E:**268–69
Beowulf **B:**144a–144b
Anglo-Saxons (Teutonic peoples who settled in England) **E:**237
Celtic and Anglo-Saxon art **E:**256–57
rulers of England, list of **E:**236
Angola **A:259–60; C:**610
map(s) **A:**260
picture(s)
flag **F:**226
Luanda **A:**259
Angora (now **Ankara**) (capital of Turkey) **T:**347
Angoulême kings (of France) **F:**414
Angry young men (in English literature) **D:**303; **E:**290; **O:**237
Anguilla (one of the Leeward Islands in the Caribbean Sea) **C:**114; **S:**13
Angus (breed of beef cattle) **C:**151
picture(s) **C:**152
Anhinga (bird)
picture(s) **A:**277
Anicetus, Saint (pope) **R:**292
Animal behavior *see* Animal intelligence and behavior
Animal bites **F:**161; **S:**3–4
Animal breeding *see* Breeding, animal
Animal communication **A:**284; **C:**462–63
ants **A:**318–19
bee "dances" **B:**120
birds **B:**227
cats, wild **C:**143–44
coyotes **C:**580
dogs **D:**247
elephants **E:**180
foxes **F:**396a
horses **H:**239
llamas **L:**278
whales **W:**149
Animal defenses *see* Protective coloration; Protective devices
Animal diseases *see also* Distemper
anthrax **D:**188; **K:**291
Can people get parrot fever? **B:**249
cattle **C:**154
chickens can catch many diseases **P:**414
endangered species **E:**209
fish as pets **F:**205
lung disease in penguins **P:**124
rabies **D:**199–200
treating sick animals in zoos **Z:**392–93
vectors of disease **V:**282–85
veterinarians and what they do **V:**323
Animal experimentation
animal rightists' opposition to **A:**261
cloning **L:**210
dogs **D:**243–44
drug testing **D:**335
Pavlov, Ivan **P:**103
primates **P:**457
What kinds of animals have traveled in space? **S:**350
Animal Farm (novel by Orwell) **E:**289; **O:**234
Animal feed *see* Feeding and feeds, animal
Animal husbandry (art and science of livestock raising)
aquaculture **A:**336
fish farming **F:**205–8
livestock **L:**271, 273

Animal intelligence and behavior
beetles **B:**124–25
birds **B:**224–27
conditioning experiments in learning **L:**98–99
dinosaurs tended their young **D:**171
dolphins **D:**277–78
Lorenz, Konrad **L:**302
play **P:**333, 334
Animal kingdom **A:**265–67; **K:**253, 254–55; **L:**208, 209
classes of animals **A:**264
eggs and embryos **E:**95–98
Animal locomotion **K:**255
beetles **B:**124
birds **B:**218–19
dinosaurs **D:**168, 170–71, 172, 173
dolphins **D:**275
feet **F:**81–82
fish **F:**198–99
hands **F:**83–84
how animals move from place to place **A:**278–79
mammals **M:**71–72
marsupials **M:**115
protozoans **P:**496–97
snakes **S:**209–11
spiders, ballooning of **S:**406
starfish **S:**426
turtles **T:**356–57
Animal rights **A:261; F:**504, 505
hunting, objections to **H:**301
vegetarian diet for ethical reasons **V:**293
Animals **A:262–87** *see also* Biology; Zoology; the animal life sections of continent, province, country, and state articles; the names of animal classes, as Birds, Insects; the names of animals as Elephants, etc.
acid rain's effects **A:**10
agents for dispersal of seeds **F:**286–87
Arctic region **A:**379
biological clocks **L:**203–4
bioluminescence **B:**205
biomes **B:**206, 207, 208, 210, 212
blue whales are the largest animals ever to live on Earth **W:**152–53
breeding *see* Breeding, animal
cattle **C:**151–54
cave dwellers **C:**157–58
cell structure **C:**160, 161
circus acts **C:**307, 310
cold-blooded **H:**127
color in nature **C:**427–28
color vision **C:**428
communication *see* Animal communication
conservation of **C:**525
dolphins and porpoises **D:**273–78
drugs, sources of **D:**334
Earth, history of **E:**24–29
Earth's geology affected by **G:**117
ecology **E:**53–55
ecosphere **N:**63
endangered species **E:**208–11
evolution **E:**372–79
experiments in life sciences **E:**396
extinction **E:**425–26
flower-pollination experiment **F:**286
food chain **L:**205
food sources for humans **F:**330
fossils **F:**380–89
frogs and toads **F:**476–78
genetic engineering **G:**85
genetics and heredity **G:**77–91
hair **H:**5
hibernation and estivation **H:**126–28
homing and migration **H:**197–202
hoofed mammals **H:**216–20
hormones **H:**228
Ice Age animals **I:**11–12
intelligence and behavior *see* Animal intelligence and behavior
jungle **J:**158
kingdoms of living things **K:**253, 254–55
leather **L:**109–11
life, adaptations in the world of **L:**197–98
life spans **A:**82–87
locomotion *see* Animal locomotion
mammals **M:**65–76
marsupials **M:**113–15
metamorphosis **M:**237–38
mollusks **M:**405–8
mongooses, meerkats, and their relatives **M:**419
monkeys **M:**420–22
mummies, ancient Egyptian **M:**512
nature, study of **N:**67–70
ocean life **O:**23, 24–28
oils and fats obtained from **O:**80
pets **P:**177–79
plankton **P:**283–85
plant poisoning **P:**316
pollination of flowers **F:**284–86
prehistoric animals **P:**432–34
protozoans sometimes classified as animals **P:**495
quarantine officers inspect imported animals **P:**514–15
rain forest dwellers **R:**99
reproduction **R:**176–79
reptiles **R:**179–80
rights of **A:**261
rodents **R:**274–78
seed dispersal **P:**313
social organization *see* Animal social organization
soils, animals in **S:**236
sponges **S:**411–12
starfish **S:**426–27
taxidermy **T:**26
taxonomy **T:**27–29
tundra **T:**331
ultrasonic sounds **S:**265
veterinarians **V:**323
warm-blooded **H:**127
water is essential for life **W:**50–51
wetlands **W:**145–46, 148
zoology **Z:**388
zoos **Z:**389–93
picture(s)
circus acts **C:**307
table(s)
Earth, history of **E:**25
Animals, domestic *see* Domestic animals; Livestock
Animals, extinct *see* Extinction; Fossils
Animals, poisonous and venomous
amphibians **A:**223
animals that eat meat **A:**280
ants **A:**319–20
arachnids **A:**348
centipedes **C:**168–69
coelenterates **J:**72, 75, 77
fish **F:**201
frogs and toads **F:**477
lizards **L:**276
millipedes **C:**169
mollusks **M:**406
scorpions **S:**84
shrews **S:**166
snakes **S:**216–17
spiders **S:**406
picture(s)
frogs and toads **A:**273
Animals harmful to people
centipedes **C:**169
rats and their fleas spread plague **D:**212
venomous snakes **S:**216–17

Animals in art and literature
bears **B**:107
birds **B**:216
fantasy in children's literature **C**:239
Hughes, Ted **H**:276
Islamic art **I**:355, 359
unicorns **U**:30
Animal social organization
ants **A**:318, 320–21
apes **A**:326–27
bats **B**:101
bees **B**:116, 117–21
birds **B**:226–27
cats, wild **C**:143–44
coyotes **C**:579–80
elephants **E**:182
fish, social behavior of **F**:201
horses **H**:237
insects **I**:246–47
mammals **M**:70–71
parrots **P**:86
primates **P**:456
Animals with backbones *see* Vertebrates
Animals without backbones *see* Invertebrates
Animal tales (fables) **F**:2, 3
Animal viruses **V**:366–67
Animal welfare **A**:261
Animation **A:288–91** *see also* Cartoons; Motion pictures
comic books about the same characters **C**:453
computer graphics **C**:484
Disney, Walt **D**:215–16; **M**:493
motion picture special effects **M**:484
myth in the modern world **M**:577
television cartoons **T**:70
Animato (musical term) **M**:536
Animism (religion) **A**:449; **K**:229; **T**:207
Anion (Negative ion) (in chemistry) **A**:485; **C**:204; **I**:288
Ankara (capital of Turkey) **T**:347
Anklebones
picture(s) **F**:79
Anna Christie (play by O'Neill) **O**:122
Anna Karenina (novel by Tolstoi) **N**:360; **T**:222
Annamese Cordillera (mountain range, Asia) **L**:42
Annan, Kofi (secretary-general of the United Nations) **U**:68, 70 *profile*
picture(s) **U**:66
Annapolis (capital of Maryland) **M**:129
United States Naval Academy **U**:118
picture(s)
State House **M**:130
United States Naval Academy **M**:125
Annapolis Convention (1786) **U**:146
Annapolis Royal (Nova Scotia) **N**:356
Annapolis Valley (Nova Scotia) **N**:350, 353
Ann Arbor (Michigan) **M**:264, 267, 556
Annatto (yellow dye) **B**:474; **D**:375
Anne (princess of England) **E**:192
Anne (queen of Great Britain and Ireland) **E**:248
Anne, Saint (mother of the Virgin Mary) **S**:18d *profile*
Annealing (in metallurgy) **M**:236
bronze and brass **B**:410
glass **G**:234
wire **W**:191
Anne Boleyn (2nd queen of Henry VIII of England) *see* Boleyn, Anne
Anne Frank House (Amsterdam, the Netherlands) **H**:174
Annelids (worms) **E**:42; **W**:319–20
Anne of Cleves (4th wife of Henry VIII of England) **H**:114
picture(s)
portrait by Hans Holbein the Younger **G**:167
Anne of Green Gables (novel by Montgomery) **C**:86–87; **P**:465
Annie Get Your Gun (musical by Berlin) **M**:554
Annobon (island, Equatorial Guinea) *see* Pagalu
Annual layerings (in glaciers) **I**:6
Annuals (plants) **F**:287; **P**:311
cultivated grasses **G**:317
gardens and gardening **G**:29–30, 46
Annular eclipses **E**:51
Annulment of marriage **D**:230
Annunciation (painting by Martini)
picture(s) **I**:394
Anoa (hoofed mammal) **B**:430
Anode (electric conductor) **E**:158
Anointing of the sick (Extreme unction) (Roman Catholic sacrament) **C**:287; **R**:294
Anoles (lizards) **L**:275
picture(s) **L**:277
Anonymity of sources (in journalism) **J**:137
Anopheles mosquito **D**:196; **H**:260
Anorexia nervosa (disease) **D**:188; **M**:223; **N**:426
Anorthosite (rock) **M**:453
Anouilh, Jean (French playwright) **F**:442
Año Viejo (Old Year) (holiday in Ecuador) **H**:160
Anschluss (German annexation of Austria, 1938) **H**:154
Anselm, Saint (archbishop of Canterbury) **W**:172
Ansky, S. (Yiddish author) **Y**:361
Answering machines **A**:532; **C**:468; **O**:58; **T**:56
Antananarivo (capital of Madagascar) **M**:8, 9
"Ant and the Grasshopper, The" (fable by Aesop) **F**:5
Antarctic (south polar region)
Amundsen, Roald **A**:226
icebergs **I**:17, 18
ice sheet and ice shelves **I**:5–6
map(s)
penguins: where they live **P**:121
Antarctica (continent) **A:292–95**
Argentina's claims **A**:386b
Australian Antarctic Territory **A**:496
Chile's claims **C**:251
continental ice sheet **G**:223, 224, 225
continents **C**:537, 538
exploration and discovery **E**:414–15
exploration by Byrd **B**:485
measuring the age of ice **I**:7
meteorite believed to be from Mars **M**:109
mountains **M**:506
ozone depletion over **A**:480
map(s)
explorations **E**:415
Antarctic Ocean **O**:43
Antarctic Treaty (1959) **A**:295
Ant cows *see* Aphids
Anteaters (mammals) **A:296; Z**:392
Anteaters, marsupial **M**:115
Anteaters, spiny *see* Spiny anteaters
Antelopes (hoofed mammals) **A**:284, **297–98; H**:216, 219
picture(s)
pronghorn **B**:208; **I**:47
sable antelope **A**:53
stalked by leopard **B**:198
in zoo **Z**:392
Antennae (of animals)
ants **A**:318
bees **B**:116
butterflies and moths **B**:475
crabs **C**:581
"feelers" (of insects) **I**:230–31, 234–35
shrimps **S**:167
Antennas (in electronics)
Apollo tracking antennas **S**:340L
cable television **T**:48
dish antennas **T**:48, 63, 66
radar systems **R**:37, 38
radar telescopes **R**:73
radio **R**:52, 53, 54, 57, 58
radio telescopes **R**:70–71; **T**:59
television reception **T**:63
picture(s)
radio telescopes **R**:69

Anterus, Saint (pope) **R:**292
Anthem (musical form) **E:**291; **M:**539
Anthemius of Tralles (Byzantine architect) **B:**489
Anthems, national *see* National anthems and patriotic songs
Antheridia (of mosses) **M:**473
Anthers (of flowers) **F:**282; **P:**307
Anthocyanins (plant pigments) **L:**115; **T:**308
Anthony, Kenny (prime minister of Saint Lucia) **S:**18
Anthony, Susan B. (American suffragist) **A:299; W:**212, 212a, 214
pictured on dollar coin **D:**259
Stanton, Elizabeth Cady **S:**424
picture(s) **W:**214
Anthony Island Provincial Park (British Columbia) **B:**406b
Anthony of Padua, Saint (Franciscan monk and theologian) **S:**18d *profile*
Anthophyllite (mineral) **A:**438c
Anthozoans (coelenterates) **J:**77
Anthracite (hard coal) **C:**388; **F:**488; **P:**126, 133, 135
Anthrax (disease) **D:**188; **K:**291; **P:**98
bioterrorism **H:**182; **P:**402; **T:**115
Anthropoids (group of primates) **P:**455, 456
Anthropology (study of human beings and human culture) **A:300–305** *see also* Human beings; Sociology
archaeology is a branch of **A:**350
Boas, Franz **B:**265
forensic science **F:**373
Leakey family **L:**96–97
Mead, Margaret **M:**195
mummies **M:**512–13
natural history museums **M:**523
prehistoric people **P:**438–42
races, human **R:**30–33
science, milestones in **S:**74
Anthropomorphization (attributing human qualities to non-human things) **M:**574–75, 577
Greek mythology **G:**361
Anti-aircraft guns **G:**425; **T:**14
Anti-aircraft missiles **M:**349
Antiballistic missile systems **N:**379
Antibiotics (drugs) **A:306–12; D:**332, 334
bacteria evolve resistance to **E:**378
bacterial diseases are treated with **D:**183
chemical control of pests **P:**290
Fleming's work **F:**249
made by fungi **F:**500
medicine, history of **M:**208c, 209
science, milestones in **S:**75
streptomycin **M:**206
surgery, history of **S:**513
vitamin K deficiency may occur in users **V:**370d
Antibodies **A:313**
acquired immunity **I:**96–97
allergies **A:**190, 191
autoimmune diseases **D:**184
disease prevention and treatment **D:**183, 208, 210, 211
made in blood **B:**261
monoclonal antibodies **C:**95
structure and source **I:**98
vaccination and inoculation **V:**260, 261
Anticline traps (rock formations that hold petroleum) **P:**168
Anticorrosives *see* Corrosion
Anticosti Island (Quebec) **I:**362
Anticyclones (in meteorology) **W:**81
Anti-Defamation League of B'nai B'rith **C:**326
Antidotes (remedies for effects of poisons) **P:**356
Antietam, Battle of (1862) **C:**339
Antietam National Battlefield Site (Maryland) **M:**128
Anti-federalists (in United States history) **U:**147
Antifouling paints **P:**33
Antifreeze **P:**355
Antigens **A:313; I:**95, 96, 97
blood types **B:**261
"Antigonish" (poem by Mearns) **N:**275
Antigua (Caribbean island) *see* Antigua and Barbuda
Antigua (Guatemala) **G:**397
Antigua and Barbuda **A:314; C:**114, 115
picture(s)
flag **F:**226
Antihistamines (drugs for allergic reactions) **A:**191; **D:**188, 191
Antihydrogen **A:**489
Antihypertensives (drugs) **D:**334
Anti-inflammatories (drugs) **A:**191; **D:**209
Anti-Lebanon Mountains (Syria–Lebanon) **L:**120; **S:**550
Antilles (island group dividing Caribbean Sea from Atlantic Ocean) **C:**112–15
Antilles, Greater *see* Greater Antilles
Antilles, Lesser *see* Lesser Antilles
Antilles Current **G:**413
Antilocapridae (family of hoofed mammals) **H:**219
Antimasque (comic dance preceding masque) **D:**25
Antimatter **A:**489; **R:**262
Antimicrobials (drugs) **A:**306
Anti-Monopoly (game) **G:**14
Antimony (element) **E:**170
table(s) **M:**235
Antinoüs (cult figure of ancient Rome)
picture(s)
statue **R:**319
Antioch (ancient city, now Antakya, Turkey)
tarred torches lit **L:**231
Antioch, Principality of (Crusader state) **C:**600
Antiochus IV Epiphanes (Syrian king) **H:**28; **J:**103
Antioxidants (in chemistry) **H:**211; **V:**370d
Antipopes (pretenders to the papacy of the Roman Catholic Church) **R:**292–93
Antiques and antique collecting **A:315–17**
dolls **D:**271
Antiquities, popular **F:**312
Anti-Saloon League **P:**484
Anti-Semitism (hostility toward Jews and Judaism) **J:**106, 107
Antiseptics (chemicals used to kill germs on the skin) **D:214; L:**257; **M:**208b, 208c *see also* Disinfectants
Antiserums (used to acquire passive immunity) **A:**313
Antisocial personality disorder **M:**224
Antitoxins (kind of antibody) **B:**127a; **D:**203
Antitrust laws **B:**473
Antivenin (Antivenom) (treatment for snakebite) **S:**215
Antiviral drugs **D:**183
Antlers (of animals)
deer **D:**80, 81; **H:**216, 218, 220
mammals' weapons **M:**74
reindeer and caribou **H:**219; **R:**138
picture(s) **D:**80
Antlia (constellation) **C:**529
Antonescu, Ion (Romanian political leader) **R:**300–301; **W:**313
Antoninus Pius (Roman emperor) **R:**316
Antony, Mark (Roman ruler) **A:**239, **317; R:**316
Augustus **A:**494–95
Cicero's opposition to **C:**303
Cleopatra **C:**355
Herod I (the Great) **H:**123
Antony, Saint **S:**18d *profile*
Antony and Cleopatra (play by Shakespeare) **S:**135
Antonyms (words) **S:548**
Antrodemus (dinosaur) *see Allosaurus*
Antrum (part of the stomach) **S:**460
Ants **A:318–24**
acacia plant, relationship with **P:**317
household pests **H:**261–62
leaf-cutter ants **A:**267
navigation **H:**197
strength of **I:**241
picture(s)
life cycle **A:**321

Antwerp (Belgium) **B:**133, 134
trade, early development of **S:**455
World War II **W:**312
Antz (motion picture, 1998) **A:**291
Anubis (Egyptian god of embalming) **E:**107, 108
picture(s) **E:**108
Anvil (bone in the ear) **E:**4, 6
picture(s) **E:**5
Anxiety (emotion)
mental illness **D:**186
stuttering, causes of **S:**397–98
Anxiety disorders **E:**204; **M:**221–22, 224
Anyang (early Chinese capital) **A:**241–42
Anything Goes (musical by Porter) **M:**554
Anzio (Italy)
beachhead battle (World War II) **W:**309
ANZUS Treaty (defense agreement) **A:**517; **N:**242
Ao (early Shang dynasty capital) **A:**241
Aoki, Rocky (Japanese balloonist) **B:**36
Aorta (artery carrying blood from heart) **B:**285; **C:**305; **H:**81
Aoudad (kind of wild sheep) **H:**219; **S:**147
Aoun, Michel (Lebanese political leader) **L:**123
Apache (Indians of North America) **I:**184–85 *see also* Cochise
Arizona **A:**397, 402, 404
Geronimo **G:**190
Indian Wars **I:**205
New Mexico **N:**184, 190, 193
picture(s)
plant pollen used in ceremony **P:**295
Apalachee (Indians native to Florida) **F:**271; **I:**178
Apalachicola River (Florida) **F:**263
Apartheid (racial segregation in South Africa) **S:**269–70, 273
abolition of **C:**327
racism **R:**34c
Apartment houses **H:**194–95 *see also* Condominium
ancient Rome **H:**192
elderly, housing for the **H:**190
Latin American tenements **L:**53
New York City **H:**195; **N:**230
picture(s)
solar panels **H:**195
Apatite (mineral) **F:**97; **T:**43
Apatosaurus (dinosaur) **D:**167, 170–71
picture(s) **P:**433
Apennines (mountain range of Italy) **I:**384; **S:**35
Apennines Mountains (on the moon)
picture(s) **M:**450
Aperture (camera lens opening) **P:**201
diagram(s) **P:**202
Apes **A:325–27**
animal rights **A:**261
feet and hands **F:**83–84
science, milestones in **S:**74–75
Aphelion (point in comet's or planet's orbit farthest from the sun) **S:**242
Mars **M:**105
picture(s)
Mercury's orbit **R:**144
Aphids (plant lice) **P:**289
ants live with aphids **A:**324
vectors of plant diseases **V:**282, 367
Aphotic habitat (of the ocean) **O:**23
Aphrodite (Venus) (Greek goddess) **G:**363, 367, 368
picture(s) **G:**361
Aphrodite of Melos (Greek statue) *see Venus de Milo*
Aphrodite Terra (continent on Venus) **V:**303a
Apia (capital of Samoa) **W:**124
Apical bud (of a plant) **L:**114
Apical meristem (of a plant) **L:**114
Apinaye (Native American language) **I:**197
Aplacophorans (mollusks) **M:**406
Aplastic anemia (disease) **B:**262
Aplodontia *see* Mountain beaver
Aplomado falcons (birds) **F:**33
Apo, Mount (highest peak in the Philippines) **P:**185
Apocalypse (type of writing that gives a revelation of the future) **B:**167
Norse mythology **N:**281
Apocrine sweat glands **G:**226
Apocrypha **B:**156, 157, 163–64; **C:**288
Apogee (point of a satellite's orbit farthest from Earth) **S:**53
moon's orbit **M:**446
Apollinaire, Guillaume (French poet) **F:**442
Apollo (Phoebus Apollo) (Greek and Roman god) **G:**363, 366, 367
temple at Bassae **G:**348
picture(s) **G:**361
Apollo and Daphne (sculpture by Bernini)
picture(s) **I:**400
Apollodor of Damascus (Greek engineer) **E:**228
Apollodoros (Greek author) **G:**360
Apollonius (Greek scholar-poet) **G:**358
Apollo program (to put astronauts on the moon) **M:**452, 453; **S:**340e, 355
Apollo 1 fire **S:**352
Apollo 8 **S:**345, 347
Apollo 11 (first moon landing) **E:**417; **S:**340e, 340f–340j, 347
Apollo 13 **S:**352
Apollo 14 **S:**346
Apollo 15 **S:**347
Apollo 17 **S:**342
Apollo-Soyuz mission **S:**355
Armstrong, Neil A. **A:**426
integrated circuits' first large application **T:**278
lunar lander replica at National Air and Space Museum **P:**274
moon's origin, theories about **M:**454
NASA programs **S:**338
photographs of the moon's surface **P:**216
portable life support system **S:**343
space research and technology **S:**362
tracking network **S:**340k–340L
picture(s)
Apollo 11 (first moon landing) **M:**453; **W:**275
Aponeuroses (sheets of tissue joining muscles to bones) **M:**518
Apoplexy *see* Stroke
Apostle Islands National Lakeshore (Wisconsin) **W:**200
picture(s) **W:**200
Apostles, The (12 disciples of Jesus Christ) **A:328–29; C:**288; **J:**85–89
New Testament of the Bible **B:**165
Peter, Saint **P:**166
Roman Catholic Church, history of **R:**284, 285
Apostolic succession **E:**45; **R:**284, 291
Apostrophes (punctuation marks) **P:**543
Apotheosis of George Washington, The (painting by Brumidi) **C:**104
Appalachia (region in the eastern United States)
folklore, American **F:**314
Appalachian Mountains (North America) **M:**502; **N:**285
Canada **C:**54–55; **N:**140; **Q:**10
folk music **F:**323
overland trails **O:**269–70
Pennsylvania **P:**128
United States **U:**78–79
westward movement **W:**140–41
Appalachian National Scenic Trail (hiking trail from Maine to Georgia) **H:**136; **M:**122
picture(s) **N:**49
Appalachian Plateau *see* Allegheny Plateau; Cumberland Plateau
Appaloosas (horses) **H:**240
picture(s) **H:**238
Apparent magnitude (of stars) **S:**428
Appeals (in law) **C:**576
Supreme Court of the United States **S:**509

Appellate courts C:576
state courts (the judiciary) S:438
Supreme Court, jurisdiction of the S:507
United States, government of the U:171
Appendages (jointed limbs of crustaceans) C:602
Appendicitis (infection in the appendix) D:188–89
Appendicular skeleton (of the body) S:183–84
Appendix (dead-end tube connected with the large intestine) D:188–89; E:375; S:514–15
Appert, Nicolas (French chef) F:342
Appian Way (Roman road) E:227
Apple **A:329–33**
how to sprout apple seeds A:332
Newton discovers law of gravitation N:206
storage F:52
Washington is nation's leading producer W:20
Who was Johnny Appleseed? A:333
picture(s) F:59; W:21
flower A:407; M:259
harvesting A:331
orchard A:331
popular varieties A:330
trees and their leaves T:303
Applebee, Constance M. K. (British physical education teacher) F:120
Apple Computer Corporation C:493
Applegate, Jesse (American political leader) O:277
Apples and Oranges (painting by Cézanne)
picture(s) F:430
Appleseed, Johnny (American folk hero) A:333
Appliances, electric *see* Electric appliances
Applications, computer C:483–86
Applied anthropology A:301
Applied art *see* Commercial art; Industrial arts
Applied force (in physics) F:365
Applied mathematics M:156
Applied research R:181; S:67
chemical industry C:197
Appliqué (needlecraft) N:101
Appomattox Court House (Virginia) C:347
Lee surrenders to Grant L:126
National Historical Park V:354
picture(s)
Lee surrenders to Grant C:346
National Historical Park V:354
Apportionment (of government representatives) G:276
Supreme Court rulings S:509
Appreciation, notes of L:160–60a
Apprentices (persons learning a trade) G:404
automobile manufacturing A:556
colonial America C:415
plumbers P:340
woodworkers W:233
Appropriations bills (suggested laws) U:168
APRA *see* American Popular Revolutionary Alliance
Apricots P:107–8
picture(s) P:107
April (4th month of the year) **A:334–35**
April (manuscript illustration by the Limburg brothers)
picture(s) D:355
April Fools' Day H:163
Apse (semicircular projection of a building) A:369; C:134; I:392
Aptidon, Hassan Gouled (president of Djibouti) D:233
Aptitude tests T:118, 120–23
Apuleius (Roman writer) L:76
Aqaba (Jordan) J:131
Aqaba, Gulf of (extension of the Red Sea) E:105; I:376; N:17
Aqsa, Al (Islamic shrine in Jerusalem) J:82
Aquaculture (raising animals or plants in water environments) **A:336**
bivalves O:291
fish farming F:205–8
New Brunswick N:138c
sea farming O:28, 29
shrimps S:168
table(s)
United States production F:208
Aqualung (for underwater swimming) C:577; E:416; S:187; U:22, 27
Aquamarines (gems) G:71, 73, 74
amulets G:72
picture(s) G:72, 74
Aquanauts (underwater explorers) U:24–25
Aquaplaning *see* Waterskiing
Aqua regia (hydrochloric and nitric acids) G:247
Aquariums **A:336–37**; M:523; P:179
Connecticut places of interest C:514
fish as pets F:203–4
list of A:337
looking at aquarium life through a microscope M:283
Louisiana places of interest L:322
New Jersey State Aquarium N:172
picture(s)
Monterey Bay Aquarium A:337
National Aquarium (Baltimore) M:125
New Jersey State Aquarium N:168
swim-through aquarium A:336
Vancouver Public Aquarium A:337
Aquarius (constellation) C:529; Z:386
Aquarius (lunar module) S:352
Aquarius (underwater laboratory) U:24–25
picture(s) U:24
Aquatic animals
beetles B:124
dolphins D:273–78
fish F:181–202
fur seals F:518
sea lions S:106
seals S:107–8
snails and slugs S:208
snakes S:209
walruses W:6–7
water pollution's effects W:67, 68, 71
whales W:149–53
zooplankton P:283, 284–85
Aquatic plants
ferns F:94
phytoplankton P:283–84
picture(s) P:320
ferns F:93
Aquatic sports *see* Water sports
Aquatint (etching process) E:327; G:307
Aquavit (distilled beverage) S:524; W:161
Aqueducts A:369; P:339
ancient Rome R:318; U:235
California C:23
picture(s) A:368; R:270
Pont du Gard E:228
Aqueous humor (in the eye) E:431
Aquidneck Island (Rhode Island) R:212, 214, 224, 225
Aquifers (water-bearing layers of permeable rocks) P:521; W:121–22
Arizona A:396
Florida F:262
groundwater, pollution of W:67
United States water supply U:84–85
Aquila (constellation) C:531
Aquinas, Saint Thomas (Italian monk and philosopher) **A:338**; C:291; P:190; R:289
Aquino, Benigno S., Jr. (Philippine political leader) A:338; P:188
Aquino, Corazon C. (Philippine president) **A:338**; P:188
Aquitaine (region of France) E:126
AR-15 (assault rifle) G:424
Arabesques (pattern designs) I:352
Islamic art A:370; I:355, 357, 358
ornamentation of tapestry T:20

Arabesques (cont.)
Spain, art of **S:**382
picture(s)
Islamic art **I:**354
Arabia (Arabian Peninsula) (southwestern Asia) **M:**300 *see also* Arabs
Bahrain **B:**18–19
Jewish communities of exile **J:**104
Kuwait **K:**308–11
Oman **O:**121
Qatar **Q:**3–4
Saudi Arabia **S:**58a–58e
United Arab Emirates **U:**45
Yemen **Y:**357–59
picture(s)
desert **A:**346
Arabia Felix (Roman name for an area usually restricted to Yemen) **Y:**357
Arabian camels **C:**39; **H:**220
picture(s) **C:**39
Arabian coffee plant **C:**396
Arabian Desert (Egypt) **E:**102
Arabian horses **H:**239, 244
picture(s) **H:**239
Arabian Nights **A:339–40**
Arabic literature **A:**342
Burton, Sir Richard **B:**457
early history of the short story **S:**161
Arabian Peninsula *see* Arabia
Arabian Sea **O:**43
Arabic-Hindu numerals *see* Hindu-Arabic numerals
Arabic language **A:**344; **L:**39; **M:**299
Arabic literature **A:**341–42
Islam, language of **I:**352
Israel, official language of **I:**369
Koran **K:**293
northern Africa **A:**56
Saudi Arabia, official language of **S:**58a
Spanish language, influence on **S:**386
picture(s)
alphabet **A:**194c
Arabic literature **A:341–42**
genies **F:**10
Arab-Israeli wars **A:**347; **I:**375–76; **J:**84, 107; **M:**305
Egypt **E:**105
hijacking **H:**134
Jordan **J:**132
Kissinger, Henry **K:**266a
Lebanon **L:**122
Meir, Golda **M:**212
Nasser, Gamal Abdel **N:**17
Palestine **P:**41–42
refugees **R:**136
Sadat, Anwar el- **S:**2
Suez Canal **S:**481
Syria **S:**552
Thant, U **T:**155
Arabs **A:**55, **343–47** *see also* Palestine
alchemists **C:**207
Arabic literature **A:**341–42
geography, history of **G:**105
Iraq **I:**311
Islam **I:**346–53
Libya **L:**187
mathematics, history of **M:**164
Morocco **M:**458, 461
Palestine **P:**40d–41, 42–43
preserved Greek knowledge in Middle Ages **A:**469
Saudi Arabia **S:**58a–58e
Syria **S:**549
textiles, history of **T:**144
picture(s)
Algeria **A:**185
Libya **L:**187
many faces of the Arab world **A:**345
Moroccan mother and child **M:**458
Sudan **S:**477
Arachne (in Greek mythology) **S:**404; **W:**96
Arachnids (class of animals) **A:348**
scorpions **S:**84
spiders **S:**402–6
ticks **T:**192
Arachnoid (covering of the brain) **B:**364
Arafat, Yasir (Palestinian leader) **A:349; C:**369; **I:**376; **P:**42, 43
picture(s) **A:**349; **C:**368; **P:**43
Aragats, Mount (Armenia) **A:**421
Aragon (ancient kingdom in Spain) **F:**88; **S:**376
Aragon, Louis (French poet) **F:**442
Aral Sea (central Asia) **L:**32; **W:**54
Aramaic language **H:**98
alphabets derived from its syllabary **A:**194c
in the Bible **B:**157
Dead Sea Scrolls **D:**47
Persia, ancient **P:**155
Aramid (type of nylon) **F:**111, 112; **N:**437
Aramis (one of *The Three Musketeers*) **D:**349–50
Aran Islands (Ireland) **I:**318
Aransas National Wildlife Refuge (Texas) **T:**128
Arantes do Nascimiento, Edson (Brazilian soccer player) *see* Pelé
Arapaho (Indians of North America) **C:**443; **H:**161; **I:**180; **W:**338
Ararat, Mount (Asian Turkey) **T:**345
picture(s) **T:**345
Araucanians (Indians of South America) **C:**249, 254; **I:**199
Arawak (Indians of South America) **I:**197
Cuba **C:**609
Dominican Republic **D:**283
Haiti **H:**11
Jamaica **J:**15
Puerto Rico **P:**526, 532
Saint Vincent and the Grenadines **S:**20
Suriname **S:**516
Trinidad and Tobago **T:**315
Arawanas (fish) **F:**199–200
Arbeau, Thoinot (French priest) **D:**27
Arbela, Battle of (331 B.C.) *see* Gaugamela, Battle of
Arbella (ship) **P:**550
Arbenz Guzmán, Jacobo (Guatemalan political leader) **G:**398
Arbitration **A:349**
international relations **I:**269–70
labor-management relations **L:**8
peace movements, goal of **P:**105
provided for in treaties **T:**299
Arbor Day (holiday) **H:**162
Jewish Arbor Day in Israel **R:**153–54
origin in Nebraska **N:**82, 90
Arboretums (museums of living plants) **M:**523
Arbour, Louise (Canadian Supreme Court justice)
picture(s) **S:**505
Arbuckle Mountains (Oklahoma) **O:**84
Arbus, Diane (American photographer) **P:**215 *profile*
picture(s) **P:**215
Arbutus, trailing *see* Trailing arbutus
Arcade (in architecture) **A:**371
Arcades, video
picture(s) **V:**332b
Arcade-style video games **V:**332c
Arcadian poetry **I:**408
Arc de Triomphe (Paris) *see* Arch of Triumph
Arch *see* Arches
Archaea (microscopic organisms) **K:**259; **L:**209
Archaefructus lianingensis (ancient flowering plant) **F:**280; **P:**301
Archaeology (study of how people lived in the past) **A:350–59** *see also* Ancient civilizations
aerial photography **P:**208

Anasazi **A**:227
Andean discoveries **A**:245
anthropology of ancient human societies **A**:302, 305
architecture, history of **A**:364
cave dwellers and their art **P**:435–37
Celtic tribes **C**:163–64
Guatemala **G**:397, 398
Heyerdahl, Thor **H**:125
Hittites **H**:155
humanism **H**:284
Israel, discoveries in **I**:374
mummies **M**:512–13
neoclassicism in architecture **A**:372–73
Pompeii **P**:381
pottery provides a valuable record of daily life **P**:409
prehistoric people **P**:438–42; **W**:258
Schliemann, Heinrich **S**:59
Troy rediscovered **T**:316
underwater archaeology **U**:18–20
map(s)
prehistoric people's remains **P**:439
picture(s)
cleaning a dinosaur skeleton **D**:167
Monte Verde (Chile) **L**:57
recovering dinosaur bones **D**:166
Roman ruins at Carthage **T**:336
Archaeopteryx (rare bird fossil) **B**:247; **D**:168; **E**:374; **F**:388
picture(s) **D**:164; **E**:373; **F**:388; **P**:433
Archaic Period (of Greek art) **G**:346–48; **S**:96
Archaic Period (of Greek literature) **G**:354–56
Archambault, Louis (Canadian sculptor) **C**:73
Archangel (Russia) *see* Arkhangel'sk
Arch bridges **B**:396
picture(s) **B**:397
table(s)
notable bridges of the world **B**:400
Archean Eon (in geology) **E**:26
Archegonia (of mosses) **M**:473
Archeoastronomy **A**:476b
Archer (constellation) *see* Sagittarius
Archer, Frederick Scott (English chemist) **P**:211
Archerfish
picture(s) **F**:199
Archery (sport) **A:360–62**
longbows at Battle of Crécy **H**:292–93
Arches (in architecture)
flying buttresses **A**:371; **G**:266
Gothic pointed arch **A**:371; **G**:265, 267
Greece, architecture of **G**:351
Rome, architecture of **A**:368–69; **R**:318
Visigothic horseshoe arch **S**:380, 381
picture(s) **A**:368
flying buttresses **G**:265
Gothic pointed arch **G**:264
Arches National Park (Utah) **U**:250
picture(s) **U**:245
Archetypes (in psychology) **J**:156
Archimedes (Greek inventor and mathematician) **A:363**; **M**:163
elevators, history of **E**:185
pi, calculation of **G**:128
science, milestones in **S**:69
Archimedes' principle (in physics) **A**:363; **F**:250–51
Archipenko, Alexander (Russian sculptor) **C**:612
Architectural engineers **E**:225
Architecture **A:364–77** *see also* Building construction; Building materials; Homes; the names of architects; the names of art periods, as Byzantine architecture; the names of specific countries, as English architecture or United States, architecture of the
accessibility for the disabled **O**:15
Africa **A**:76
ancient **A**:228, 230, 235, 236
architectural engineers **E**:225
automated drawing software **A**:533
blueprint **B**:263
bricks and masonry **B**:390–94
building construction **B**:433, 436, 438–39
Canada, architecture of **C**:71–73
castles **C**:131–32; **F**:378–79
cathedrals **C**:133–35
colonial American **C**:415–16
design **D**:137
environmental graphics and building design **C**:457
Finland is a center for modern design **F**:138
"high tech" **T**:40
homes of the past and of today **H**:186–95
Islamic **I**:355–57
Khmer temple complexes **A**:243
Latin America **L**:60–62, 63, 65
mathematics in careers **M**:161
Maya **M**:186
mechanical drawing **M**:200
modern *see* Modern architecture
Petronas Towers (Malaysia) are world's tallest buildings **S**:334
pyramids **P**:556–58
Archival storage (of computers) **C**:482
Archives (place in which records are preserved)
National Archives **N**:24
Arch of Triumph (Paris) **P**:74; **U**:227
picture(s) **H**:168; **P**:71
Arch-top guitars **G**:412
Arc lamps **I**:284; **L**:235
picture(s) **L**:232
Arco (Idaho) **I**:59
Arctic (north polar region) **A:378–81** *see also* Northeast Passage
Alaska's Arctic lands **A**:147, 149
Bering's explorations **B**:145
Canada **Y**:370–75
cold deserts **D**:124
exploration and discovery **E**:414
Greenland ice sheet **I**:5
icebergs **I**:17–18
Inuit **I**:272–76
Lapland **L**:44–45
Nordic countries **S**:58f
Nunavut **N**:410
Peary, Robert E. **P**:117
reindeer and caribou **R**:138
tundra **T**:331
map(s) **A**:381
explorations **E**:415
Arctic Archipelago *see* Arctic Islands
Arctic Basin (Canada) **C**:57
Arctic Bay (Nunavut) **N**:412
Arctic Circle (imaginary line around the globe) **A**:378
Arctic College (Nunavut) **N**:412
Arctic Current *see* Labrador Current
Arctic foxes **E**:377; **F**:396a, 396b, 501
picture(s) **B**:209; **E**:377
Arctic hares **R**:24
Arctic Islands (Arctic Archipelago) (landform region of Canada) **C**:56
Arctic loon (bird)
picture(s) **B**:235
Arctic National Wildlife Refuge (Alaska) **A**:158; **B**:468
Arctic Ocean **A**:378; **O**:43
some consider it part of the Atlantic **A**:478
Arctic Slope (Alaska) **A**:146
Arctic terns (birds) **A**:286; **B**:233; **H**:198
picture(s) **B**:238
migration route **H**:201
Arcturus (star) **C**:531
Arc welding **W**:118
Ardagh chalice
picture(s) **C**:163
Ardashir I (Persian king) **P**:156

Ardeidae (family of wading birds) **H:**124
Ardennes (region of Belgium) **B:**131, 132
Ardennes, Battle of the (1944–1945) *see* Bulge, Battle of the
Ardra (African kingdom) **B:**144
Area (measure of a bounded surface) **G:**124–25; **W:**112–13, 117
Area codes (for telephoning) **T:**54
Arecibo Observatory (Puerto Rico) **O:**9; **R:**72
Does life as we know it on Earth exist anywhere else in the universe? **R:**70
picture(s) **R:**71
Arena Chapel (Padua, Italy) **I:**394
Arena Football League (AFL) **F:**364
Arenas (for bullfighting) **B:**451
Arena stage (theater in the round) **T:**156
picture(s) **T:**156
Areopagitica (pamphlet by Milton) **E:**275; **M:**312
Areopagus (historic site in Athens, Greece) **A:**476c
Ares (Mars) (Greek god) **G:**362
picture(s) **G:**360
Arévalo, Juan José (Guatemalan political leader) **G:**398; **I:**194
Argali (wild sheep) **S:**147
Argall, Samuel (English navigator and colonial official in America) **D:**88
Argaña, Luís María (Paraguayan public official) **P:**66
Argand oil lamps **L:**233
Argentina **A:382–86d**
Buenos Aires **B:**428–29
fascism in **F:**64
folk dance **F:**302
food **F:**333
Islas Malvinas (Falkland Islands) **I:**365; **S:**281
Latin America **L:**48, 49, 50, 51, 55, 57
literature **L:**68
modern art **L:**65
Patagonia **S:**280
San Martín, José de **S:**36
wine **W:**190
map(s) **A:**383
picture(s)
Andes **A:**385; **S:**275, 277
Buenos Aires **A:**384, 386a; **L:**53; **S:**286
cattle on Pampas **A:**386
flag **F:**226
gaucho **S:**284
gaucho barbeque **L:**5
gaucho herding sheep on Pampas **S:**274
Iguazú Falls **A:**382
Mothers of the Plaza de Mayo **H:**285
Pampas, The **G:**314
Patagonia **A:**385
sheep ranch in Patagonia **P:**429
tango demonstration **L:**47
Argo (ship in Greek mythology) **G:**368
Argon (element) **E:**171
gases in industry **G:**61
Langmuir's use in light bulbs **L:**35
noble gases **N:**105, 106
rocket fuel **R:**262
Argonautica (epic poem by Apollonius) **G:**358
Argonauts (in Greek mythology) **G:**358, 368
Argumentation *see* Debates and debating
Arguments (in logic) **L:**289–90
Arhats (Buddhist saints) **B:**424
Århus (Aarhus) (Denmark) **D:**112
Aria (accompanied song for the single voice) **B:**70; **M:**539; **O:**140, 141
Ariadne (in Greek mythology) **G:**368
Arianism (heresy of Arius) **C:**289–90
Arias Madrid, Arnulfo (Panamanian president) **P:**48
Arias Sánchez, Oscar (Costa Rican political leader) **C:**567
Ariel (essay by Rodó) **U:**240
Ariel (moon of Uranus) **U:**233
picture(s) **U:**233
Arienspace (space technology company) **S:**339
Aries (constellation) **C:**528; **Z:**386
Arikara (Indians of North America) **I:**180; **S:**324
Ariosto, Lodovico (Italian poet) **I:**407
Aristarchus of Samos **A:**468; **S:**69
Aristide, Jean-Bertrand (Haitian president) **H:**12
Aristides (race horse) **K:**227
Aristocracy (type of government) **G:**273
Aristophanes (Greek dramatist) **D:**297; **G:**356
picture(s) **G:**356
Aristotle (Greek philosopher) **A:386d–387; P:**189–90
air, ideas about **E:**380
Alexander the Great, teacher of **A:**177
astronomy, early history of **A:**469
biologist of the ancient world **B:**200; **F:**184
classification of living things **K:**253; **L:**207; **T:**27
early encyclopedias **E:**207
education, history of **E:**78, 81
elements, theory of the **C:**206–7
ethics **E:**328
geology, history of **G:**107
government systems **G:**273
Greek literature **G:**357
library of **L:**172
logic **L:**289
oratory and rhetoric **O:**190
physics, history of **P:**233, 234, 235
psychology, history of **P:**505–6
science, milestones in **S:**69
picture(s) **B:**200; **G:**357; **L:**289; **S:**68
Roman statue **A:**387
Arithmetic **A:388–91; M:**157
abacus **A:**2–3
decimal system **D:**56
fractions and decimals **F:**397–402
graphs **G:**309–13
interest **I:**255
kindergarten activities **K:**246
numbers and number systems **N:**396–402
numerals and numeration systems **N:**403–9
percentage **P:**144–46
sets **S:**128–28a
Arithmetic mean (kind of average of a set of numbers) **S:**441
Arithmetic sequences (of numbers) **N:**383
Arius (Greek theologian) **C:**289; **R:**286
Arizona **A:392–405**
Grand Canyon National Park **G:**290–92
Phoenix **P:**192–93
Tucson **T:**329
map(s) **A:**403
picture(s)
cattle drive **A:**399
cowboy on ranch **A:**396
flood damage **F:**254
Grand Canyon National Park **A:**393, 400; **G:**291, 292; **N:**45; **W:**50, 216
Hoover Dam **A:**395
irrigated desert regions **D:**126
Kitt Peak National Observatory **A:**398; **O:**9
Meteor Crater **C:**449
Mogollon Rim **A:**394
Native American weaving **A:**393
Navajo National Monument **A:**400
Petrified Forest National Park **A:**400
Phoenix **A:**401; **P:**193; **U:**98
prickly pear cacti **U:**78
rock inscriptions **A:**393
saguaro cactus **A:**396
San Francisco Peaks **A:**394
San Xavier del Bac **A:**400
Taliesin West **W:**326
Tucson **T:**329; **W:**79
Wupatki National Monument **N:**51
Arizona, University of (Tucson) **T:**329
Arizona, USS, Memorial (Pearl Harbor, Hawaii) **H:**52
picture(s) **H:**52

Arjuna (legendary Hindu warrior) **H:**139, 140; **I:**140
Arkansas **A:406–19**
Clinton's governorship **C:**367
map(s) **A:**417
picture(s)
Blanchard Spring Caverns **A:**414
Buffalo National River **A:**414
Crater of Diamonds State Park **A:**414
Little Rock **A:**413, 415
Ozark Folk Center **A:**414
school integration (1957) **A:**419
Arkansas, University of **A:**411
traditional cheer **C:**194
Arkansas Post National Memorial (Arkansas) **A:**414
Arkansas River (United States) **A:**408, 413
Colorado **C:**432–33
Oklahoma **O:**84, 85
overland trails **O:**274
Arkhangel'sk (Archangel) (Russia) **O:**47
Ark of the Covenant (sacred chest) **J:**102, 147
Arktika (nuclear-powered Soviet icebreaker) **A:**381
Arkwright, Richard (British inventor and early industrialist) **I:**219
Arlandes, Marquis d' (French balloonist) **B:**34
Arlberg Pass (Austrian Alps) **A:**194d
Arlington House, The Robert E. Lee Memorial (formerly **Custis-Lee Mansion,** Virginia) **N:**27; **V:**354
picture(s) **N:**27
Arlington National Cemetery (Virginia) **N:**27, 29; **V:**354
Unknown Soldier **U:**227
Washington, D.C. **W:**32
picture(s)
Arlington House and Kennedy's grave **N:**27
Tomb of the Unknown Soldier **U:**227
Arm (part of the body) *see* Arms
Armada, Spanish (1588) *see* Spanish Armada
Armada Portrait (of Elizabeth I)
picture(s) **W:**265
Armadillos (mammals) **E:**98
picture(s) **A:**282; **M:**73; **T:**128
Armagh (Northern Ireland) **U:**54
Armature (framework used in clay modeling) **C:**354
Armatures (in electric motors) **E:**134, 152
Armed Forces, U.S. *see* United States, Armed Forces of the
Armed Forces Day **U:**101
Armenia **A:420–22**
Kurds **K:**307
map(s) **A:**420
picture(s)
flag **F:**226
Armenian Apostolic Church **A:**420; **U:**34
Armenian language **A:**420, 422
Armenians (a people of western Asia) **A:**420
Azerbaijan **A:**573
life in the Soviet Union **U:**34
Los Angeles **L:**304
massacre in World War I **G:**96; **H:**285
Syria **S:**549
picture(s)
traditional costume **A:**421
Armies
Alexander the Great **A:**177–78
battles **B:**103d–103f
Canada, Armed Forces of **C:**70
Egypt had first professional army in history **E:**107–8
Nightingale, Florence, and British army reform **N:**259
United States **U:**102–6
Armijo, Antonio (Mexican trader) **O:**275
Armistice Day *see* Veterans Day
Armonica (musical instrument) **F:**455
Armor **A:423–25**
battles **B:**103d
coats of arms **H:**116–18
combat arms of United States Army **U:**102, 105
early decorations **D:**75
knights, knighthood, and chivalry **K:**272–73
Metropolitan Museum of Art collection **M:**239
tanks **T:**14–15
Vikings **V:**340
picture(s)
historic suits of armor **A:**424, 425
Armored animals **A:**283
dinosaurs **D:**173–74
Armory Show (New York art show, 1913) **M:**395; **P:**30; **U:**132
Arms (parts of the body)
bones of the **F:**79; **S:**183
folk dances, movements in **F:**301
siamang gibbon's long arms **A:**325
Arms control *see* Disarmament
Arms races (between nations) **D:**180
Armstrong, Edwin H. (American engineer) **R:**56
Armstrong, Henry (American boxer) **B:**353
Armstrong, Louis Daniel ("Satchmo") (American jazz trumpeter, singer, and bandleader) **L:**326 *profile*
jazz **J:**59, 60
picture(s) **J:**59; **L:**327
jazz **U:**208
Armstrong, Neil A. (American astronaut) **A:426; S:**347 *profile*
astronauts **A:**467
exploring space **E:**417
space exploration and travel **S:**338, 340e, 340f, 340h, 340j
picture(s) **A:**426; **S:**340i
Armstrong, William H. (American author) **C:**238
Army, Canadian *see* Canada, Armed Forces of
Army, Roman **R:**310
Army, United States *see* United States Army
Army, United States Department of the
national cemeteries **N:**27
Army ants **A:**324
picture(s) **A:**318
Army Medical Department (of the United States Army) **U:**103
Army National Guard (United States) **U:**105
Army of the Andes *see* Andes, Army of
Army of the Potomac *see* Potomac, Army of the
Army worms
picture(s) **B:**483
Arnarson, Ingólfur (Norwegian Viking) **I:**36, 37
Arnaz, Desi (Cuban-American bandleader) **N:**224
Arnica (plant used for medicinal purposes) **H:**119
Arnold, Benedict (American soldier and traitor) **A:426; C:**521
Revolutionary War **R:**199, 201, 203, 204, 206
picture(s) **R:**206
Arnold, Eddy (American singer) **C:**573
Arnold, Henry Harley "Hap" (American general) **W:**300 *profile*
picture(s) **W:**300
Arnold, Matthew (English author) **E:**284
Arno River (Italy) **I:**385
Aromatic plants *see* Herbs; Spices
Aroostook County (Maine) **M:**40–41, 43
picture(s) **M:**40
Aroostook War (Maine–New Brunswick boundary dispute) **M:**50; **N:**138g
Arouet, François Marie (French writer) *see* Voltaire
Arp, Jean (Hans) (French artist) **M:**394; **S:**104
Arp220 (galaxy)
picture(s) **U:**216
Árpád (Magyar chief) **H:**298
ARPANET (forerunner to the Internet) **C:**493; **I:**286; **T:**49
Arpeggio (in music) **M:**536
Arpino, Gerald (American choreographer) **B:**33
picture(s)
Clown (ballet) **D:**33
Arrack (alcoholic beverage from coconut palm) **C:**392
Arraignment (in law) **C:**575
Arrangement in Grey and Black, No. 1, Portrait of the Artist's Mother (painting by Whistler)
picture(s) **W:**162

Arras, Battle of (1917) **W**:288
picture(s) **W**:288
Array (radio telescope that has many reflectors) **R**:72
Arrays (flat rows of solar cells) **S**:240
Arrest (for breaking the law) **C**:574–75
juvenile offenses **J**:167, 169
Arrhythmias (irregular heartbeat patterns) **H**:83–84
"Arrow and the Song, The" (poem by Longfellow) **L**:302
Arrowhead Country (area of Minnesota) **M**:326
Arrowroot (edible starch)
Saint Vincent and the Grenadines is the world's leading producer **S**:20
Arrows *see* Bows and arrows
Arrowsmith (novel by Sinclair Lewis) **L**:162
Arroyos (dry river beds) **D**:124; **R**:237
Arsenal (building for storing weapons)
Harper's Ferry (West Virginia) **W**:134, 138
Arsenal of Democracy (nickname for Michigan) **M**:273
Arsenic (element) **E**:171
Ars nova (New art) (in French music) **F**:444
Arson **F**:147
dogs trained to recognize fire-starting chemicals **D**:242
juvenile crime **J**:167
Arsphenamine (antibiotic) **M**:208c, 209
Art **A**:**427–33** *see also* the names of art forms, as Painting or Industrial design; the names of art periods, as Baroque art; the names of individual artists, such as Rembrandt; the names of specific countries, as Italy, art and architecture of
Africa, art of **A**:70–76
American *see* United States, art of the
Andean civilizations **A**:245
computers, uses of **C**:484
cubism **C**:612
decorative arts **D**:68–78
drawing **D**:306–12
drawing, history of **D**:313–16
engraving **E**:294
etching **E**:326–27
graphic arts **G**:302–8
Hispanic Americans **H**:147
Latin America **L**:60–65
mathematics in careers **M**:160
Maya **M**:186
Mesopotamia **M**:232
modern **M**:386–96b
museums *see* Art museums
Olmecs **A**:243
painting **P**:14–32
photography as an art **P**:203, 214
prehistoric art **P**:435–37, 441
preschool children **T**:249
religious *see* Religious art
restoration work **M**:527
romanticism **R**:302–3
sculpture **S**:90–105
surrealism **S**:518
Vatican contains many works of art **V**:280–81, 282
picture(s)
crop art **K**:180
Art, commercial *see* Commercial art
Artabanus (Parthian king) **P**:156
Art cabinets (to hold curios and toys) **D**:261
Art deco (style of decorative arts) **C**:73; **D**:78
furniture **F**:517
jewelry **J**:100
picture(s)
jeweled pin **J**:100
Miami architecture **F**:269
plastic radio **D**:78
Art directors
books **B**:327
commercial art **C**:457–58
magazines **M**:17
Artemis (Diana) (Greek goddess) **G**:363, 369
amethyst, legend of the **G**:72
story of the Dog Star (Sirius) **D**:243
Temple of Artemis **W**:218
picture(s) **G**:361
Artemis Chasma (valley, Venus) **V**:303b
Arteries (blood vessels) **B**:285; **C**:305, 306
cholesterol in body chemistry **B**:296
hardening of **D**:189
heart **H**:81
kidneys **K**:242
Arteriosclerosis (Hardening of the arteries) (cardiovascular disease) **C**:306; **D**:189; **H**:82
picture(s) **D**:189
Artesian wells **W**:122
Australia's Great Artesian Basin **A**:505
picture(s) **W**:121
Art galleries *see* Art museums
Art Gallery of Ontario (Toronto) **T**:244
Arthritis (disease of the joints) **D**:189; **S**:184b
occupational therapy **O**:15
Arthropods (animals) **A**:267; **P**:432 *see also* Arachnids; Crustaceans; Insects
benthic ocean life **O**:26
centipedes and millipedes **C**:168–69
vectors of disease **V**:282, 285
Arthur, Chester Alan (21st president of the United States) **A**:**434–37**; **V**:327 *profile*
picture(s) **A**:434; **P**:450
Arthur, Ellen Lewis Herndon (wife of Chester A. Arthur) **A**:437
picture(s) **A**:436
Arthur, Frederick, Lord Stanley of Preston **I**:28
Arthur, Gabriel (American trader) **T**:84
Arthur, King (legendary hero of Britain) **A**:**438–38c**; **E**:237
English literature **E**:269, 284
Geoffrey of Monmouth **M**:294
Holy Grail **H**:175
Welsh folklore **W**:3–4
picture(s)
English literature **E**:268
Artichokes (vegetable) **V**:288, 290
picture(s) **C**:26
Article (part of speech) **P**:92
Articles of Confederation (1781) **R**:203; **U**:145–46, 177
Albany Plan of Franklin **F**:456
attacked by *The Federalist* **F**:78
Continental Congress **C**:536
Ohio established as Northwest Territory **O**:75
Articulated buses **B**:460
Articulated locomotives **L**:288
Articulation (production of speech sounds) **S**:397
Artifacts (things used in the past) **A**:350, 351, 354–55
prehistoric people **P**:438, 440
underwater archaeology **U**:18, 19, 20
Artificial elements **A**:485
Artificial hand
picture(s) **D**:177
Artificial heart **D**:193; **M**:208g; **O**:227
picture(s) **I**:279; **M**:208g; **O**:227
Artificial horizon (navigation device in airplanes) **A**:118
Artificial insemination (of livestock) **L**:273
Artificial intelligence (branch of computer science) **C**:491, 494
decision-based automation **A**:530
inventions **I**:286
robots **R**:254, 255
video games **V**:332c
Will computers ever outsmart humans? **C**:492
picture(s)
Kismet (robot) **I**:286
Artificial languages **L**:40
Artificial limbs **M**:208g–208h
Artificial liver **L**:270
Artificial organs **B**:214; **O**:227
Artificial pearls **P**:116

Artificial respiration **F:**158
picture(s) **F:**158
Artificial satellites *see* Satellites, artificial
Artificial selection (selective breeding of species) **E:**379
Artificial sweeteners *see* Sweeteners, artificial
Artigas, José Gervasio (Uruguayan leader) **U:**241
picture(s)
statue **U:**237
Artillery (weaponry) **G:**415, 424–25
battles **B:**103f
United States Army **U:**102
weapons used against tanks **T:**14
Art Institute of Chicago (Illinois) **I:**67; **M:**525
picture(s) **I:**67
Artiodactyla (order of even-toed hoofed mammals) **H:**218–20
picture(s)
impala as example **M:**68
Artisan (maker of decorative art objects) **D:**68
Artisanal bakeries **B:**388a
Artistic director (of plays) **T:**157
Artist in His Museum, The (painting by Charles Willson Peale)
picture(s) **P:**110
Artist in His Studio (painting by Vermeer)
picture(s) **D:**366
Art museums **M:**523, 525–26 *see also* the names of museums
picture(s)
North Carolina **N:**311
Vermont **V:**311
Art music **F:**321, 327; **M:**540
Art nouveau (art movement) **D:**78
architecture **A:**373
furniture **F:**516
jewelry **J:**99–100
Klimt, Gustav **K:**271
picture(s) **D:**78
Art of Fugue, The (collection of fugues by Bach) **B:**6
Arts *see* Art
Arts and crafts *see* Decorative arts; Handicrafts
Arts and crafts movement (in English art) **E:**263; **F:**514
pottery **P:**413
picture(s)
Rookwood pottery **P:**413
Arts of the West (painting by Benton)
picture(s) **B:**144a
Art song (song created by a composer to a poetic text) **C:**351; **M:**542; **V:**378
Aruba (island in the Caribbean Sea) **C:**114, 115; **L:**50
Arusha (Tanzania) **T:**19
Arvon, Mount (Michigan) **M:**259, 260
Aryabhata (Indian mathematician) **M:**164
Aryan Brotherhood (prison gang) **O:**223
Aryan master race (Nazi concept) **N:**79
Aryans (a people of India) **I:**131
Hinduism, origins of **H:**141
Pakistan, history of **P:**40
Persia, ancient **P:**154, 156
Arya Samaj (Hindu movement) **H:**142
Arzú Irigoyen, Álvaro (president of Guatemala)
picture(s) **G:**398
Asad, Lake Al- (Syria) **S:**550
Asam brothers (German architects) **G:**171
Asante (a people of Africa) *see* Ashanti
Asbestos (mineral) **A:438c**
Canada **C:**61, 65
particulate pollutant **A:**123
Asbestosis (lung disease) **D:**186
Ascanius (son of Aeneas) **A:**36
Ascension Day (Ear of Wheat Thursday) (Christian holiday) **C:**288; **E:**43; **P:**492
Ascension Island (South Atlantic) **I:**362
turtle nesting grounds **H:**199; **T:**358
Ascent stage (part of spacecraft) **S:**340g–340h
Asceticism (rejection of material comforts) **H:**139, 140; **R:**150
Asch, Sholem (Polish-American Yiddish writer) **Y:**361
Ascham, Roger (English writer and scholar) **E:**271
Ascorbic acid *see* Vitamin C
ASEAN *see* Association of Southeast Asian Nations
Asen, John I and II (rulers of Bulgaria) **B:**445
Asen, Peter (ruler of Bulgaria) **B:**445
Asexual reproduction **A:**284–85; **B:**197; **R:**175–76
plants **P:**310
protozoans **P:**496
Asgard (home of the Norse gods) **N:**279, 281
Ashanti (Asante) (a people of Africa) **G:**194, 197, 198
jewelry **J:**100
sculpture **A:**72
talking drum **A:**77
Ashcan school (art group) *see* Eight, The
Ashe, Arthur Robert, Jr. (American tennis player) **T:**96 *profile*
picture(s) **T:**93, 96
Ashflow calderas (volcanoes) **V:**380–81, 383–84
Ash glaze (on pottery) **P:**408
Ashikaga (ancient rulers of Japan) **J:**42, 43; **K:**312
Ashkenazim (Jews whose ancestors lived in European lands) **I:**369; **J:**145
Ashkhabad (Ashgabat) (capital of Turkmenistan) **T:**352
Ashland (Kentucky) **K:**226
Ashlar masonry **B:**393
Ashley, James M. (American political figure) **M:**428; **W:**334
Ashley, William Henry (American pioneer) **F:**522 *profile,* 523
Ashley National Forest (Utah–Wyoming)
picture(s) **N:**34
Ashmole, Elias (English antiquarian) **M:**528
Ashmolean Museum (Oxford, England) **M:**528
Ashoka (king of Magadha, modern Bihar, India) *see* Asoka
Ashramas (ideal stages in Hindu life) **H:**140
Ashton, Frederick (English choreographer) **B:**30–31
Ashton-Warner, Sylvia (New Zealand writer) **N:**236
Ash trees
picture(s)
leaf **L:**113; **P:**305
uses of the wood and its grain **W:**223
white ash **T:**303
Ashur (god worshiped by the Assyrians) **A:**462
Ashurbanipal (king of Assyria) **A:**233, 462; **L:**171
picture(s)
stone carving of him hunting **A:**232
Ashurnasirpal II (king of Assyria) **A:**462
Ash Wednesday (religious holiday) **E:**43; **R:**154
Asia **A:438d–457** *see also* the names of countries
agriculture **A:**89, 90, 93
Alexander the Great's conquests in **A:**177–78
ancient civilizations **A:**240–43
Arctic region **A:**378–81
art and architecture *see* Asian art and architecture
boundary with Europe **C:**537
continents **C:**537, 538
emigration to the United States **I:**91, 92, 93
Europe's geographic relation to Asia **E:**340–41
exploration and discovery **E:**413
food of southern Asia **F:**331–32
immigration **I:**94
important dates in Asian history **A:**454
lakes of the world **L:**30, 31–33
Middle East **M:**298–305
mountains **M:**505
music *see* Asian music
national dances **D:**31–32
poverty **P:**418, 420
prairies **P:**426, 427–28
refugees **R:**136–37
rice diet **G:**282; **R:**228
Siberia **S:**170
Southeast Asia **S:**328–36
map(s)
physical map **A:**439
political map **A:**447

Asia (cont.)
map(s) (cont.)
population density **A:**446
prehistoric people's remains **P:**439
picture(s)
camels on steppes **A:**438g
Everest, Mount **A:**438g
folk dance **F:**301
table(s)
waterfalls **W:**63
Asia Minor (peninsula forming the western extremity of Asia)
Asian Turkey **T:**345
What and where is Asia Minor? **A:**441
Asian American Heritage Month **A:**458
Asian Americans **A:457–61**
food **F:**332–33
Los Angeles **L:**304
Oriental Exclusion Acts **O:**228
percentage of United States population **U:**74
Asian art and architecture *see also* China, art and architecture of; Japanese art and architecture
architecture **A:**366–67
art, the meanings of **A:**428
art as a record **A:**430–31
graphic arts **G:**303
India, art and architecture of **D:**72; **I:**135–39
jewelry **J:**100
Korean art **K:**302
Mongol influences on Islamic art **I:**357
pottery **P:**409–10
rugs and carpets **R:**355
picture(s)
rugs and carpets **R:**354
Asian buffalo *see* Water buffalo
Asian elephants *see* Indian elephants
Asian golden cats (animals) **C:**146
Asian Indian Americans **A:**458, 460; **O:**228
picture(s) **A:**458
Asian music **M:**543–44
India, music of **I:**143
Asian Pacific Americans **A:**457
Asia-Pacific Economic Co-operation (APEC) forum **I:**271
Asiatic Barred Zone (immigration restrictions in United States history) **O:**228
Asiatic black bears **B:**104, 107
Asimov, Isaac (Russian-American author) **S:**80 *profile*
Asir (region in Saudi Arabia) **S:**58c
Ask (first man in Norse mythology) **N:**279
ASM (air-to-surface missiles) **M:**345, 349; **U:**110
Asmara (capital of Eritrea) **E:**317
Asoka (king of Magadha, modern Bihar, India) **A:**453; **B:**426; **I:**131, 135–36
Asparagus **P:**304; **V:**289, 290
Asparagus fern (houseplant)
picture(s) **H:**268
Aspartame (artificial sweetener) **S:**484
ASPCA *see* American Society for the Prevention of Cruelty to Animals
Aspdin, Joseph (English bricklayer who invented Portland cement) **C:**165
Aspect ratio (in motion pictures) **M:**479
Aspen (tree)
picture(s) **C:**432; **T:**304
Aspen Festival (Aspen, Colorado) **M:**556
Asperger, Hans (Austrian physician) **A:**526
Asperger's disorder **A:**526; **M:**224
Aspergillus (fungus)
picture(s) **M:**276
Asphalt (tarlike substance) **P:**172, 174
climate, urbanization's effect on **C:**364
road surfaces **R:**250
Trinidad and Tobago has world's largest supply **T:**315
Aspirin (drug) **M:**208g
medicines from plants **P:**297
Reye's syndrome may be caused by **D:**200
trademarks **T:**267
treatment of rheumatoid arthritis **D:**189
Asquith, Herbert Henry (British statesman) **A:461**
Assab (Eritrea) **E:**317
Assad, Bashar al- (president of Syria) **S:**552
Assad, Hafez al- (president of Syria) **S:**552
Assam (state, India) **I:**128
Assassinations **P:**448; **V:**324
Alexander II (of Russia) **A:**177
Argaña, Luís María **P:**66
Francis Ferdinand (archduke of Austria) **S:**126
Gandhi, Indira **G:**23
Gandhi, Mohandas Karamchand **G:**24
Gandhi, Rajiv **G:**24
Garfield, James A. **G:**52, 55
George I (king of Greece) **G:**131
Kennedy, John F. **K:**210; **W:**12
Kennedy, Robert F. **K:**211
King, Martin Luther, Jr. **K:**251
Lincoln, Abraham **B:**335; **L:**246–47
Mainassara, Ibrahim Bare **N:**252
Malcolm X **M:**59
McKinley, William **M:**194
Milk and Moscone **S:**32
Nepalese royal family **N:**110
Rabin, Yitzhak **I:**376
Sadat, Anwar el- **S:**2
Sarkisian, Vazgen **A:**422
Swedish political figures **S:**529
terrorism **T:**114, 115
picture(s)
wanted poster for John Wilkes Booth **L:**247
Assassins (secret Muslim sect) **T:**114
Assateague National Seashore (Virginia) **V:**354
picture(s) **N:**55; **V:**348
Assault (crime) **J:**167
Assault rifles **G:**424
Assemblages (works of art) **N:**137
Assemblage with Rainbow (collage by Schwitters) *see Merzbild mit Regenbogen*
Assembly, freedom of *see* Freedom of assembly
Assembly edit (in motion picture production) **M:**485
Assembly language (in computer programming) **C:**483
Assembly-line method (in manufacturing) **M:**88–89
automobiles **A:**543, 553–54; **M:**272–73
Chinese porcelain **P:**410
Ford, Henry **F:**369; **T:**286
robots **R:**254
technology, major developments in **T:**40, 41
picture(s) **A:**530; **M:**272
Asses, wild *see* Wild asses
Assessed value (of property) **R:**112d
Assets (shown in bookkeeping statements) **B:**311
Assimilation (of ethnic groups) **E:**335
Jews in the Soviet Union **J:**106
Assiniboin (Indians of North America) **I:**180, 190
Assiniboine, Mount (British Columbia)
picture(s) **B:**403
Assist (in baseball) **B:**83
Assistant directors (for motion pictures) **M:**483
Assisted living (special housing with services for older people) **O:**100
Associated Press (wire service) **J:**140
Associate's degree (in education) **U:**220
Association football *see* Soccer
Associationism (in psychology) **P:**506, 507
Association of Southeast Asian Nations (ASEAN) **I:**271; **S:**336
Associative properties (of numbers) **N:**398–99
Assonance (kind of rhyme) **P:**350
Assoumani, Azali (presient of Comoros) **C:**475
Assumption of the Blessed Virgin Mary (doctrine of the Roman Catholic Church) **R:**284
Assumption of the Virgin (painting by Correggio) **I:**398
Assur (Assyria) **A:**232, 462
Assurbanipal (king of Assyria) *see* Ashurbanipal

Assur-uballit (Assyrian king) **A:**232
Assyria (ancient empire of Asia) **A:**232–33, **462; M:**232
Israel, ancient kingdom of **J:**102
libraries, history of **L:**171
sculpture **S:**93–94
map(s) **A:**462
picture(s)
hairstyling **H:**6
Nimrud **A:**228
stone relief **A:**462; **W:**259
Astaire, Fred (American dancer, singer, and actor) **D:**34; **M:**486 *profile*
Astana (capital of Kazakhstan) **K:**201
Astatine (element) **E:**171
Aster (pattern of cell division) **C:**161, 162
Asterism (star effect in gems) **G:**70
picture(s) **G:**70
Asterisms (groups of stars in constellations) **C:**529
Asteroids (Planetoids) (small planets) **A:**471; **C:449–51; P:**279; **S:**241, 244
dinosaur extinction theory **C:**449; **D:**175; **E:**29, 426; **F:**387; **G:**112
Mars' moons may have been asteroids **M:**109
Pluto may really be an asteroid **P:**341
satellites' origin **S:**52
picture(s)
dinosaur extinction theory **G:**111
Asters (flowers) **G:**49
Asthma (lung disorder) **A:463; D:**187; **L:**345
acid rain's effects **A:**10
allergies **A:**190
dust mites may trigger **A:**348
Astigmatism (eye defect) **C:**535; **E:**431; **L:**150, 151
Astley, Philip (English circus performer) **C:**309
Astor, Brooke (American socialite) **A:**464
Astor, John Jacob (British publisher; 1886–1971) **A:**464
Astor, John Jacob (German-born American merchant and fur trader; 1763–1848) **A:**464
fur trade **F:**521, 522 *profile,* 523
Oregon, history of **O:**216, 271
real estate fortune **R:**112d
picture(s) **A:**464
Astor, John Jacob IV (American millionaire; 1864–1912) **A:**464
Astor, Lady (first woman member of the British Parliament) **A:**464; **V:**358 *profile*
Astor, Vincent (American publisher) **A:**464
Astor, Waldorf (British publisher and political figure) **A:**464
Astor, William Backhouse (American millionaire) **A:**464
Astor, William Waldorf (American-born British publisher and political figure) **A:**464
Astor Column (Astoria, Oregon) **O:**210
Astor family (in American history) **A:464**
Astoria (Oregon) **A:**464; **F:**523; **O:**210, 211
Astounding Science Fiction (Astounding Stories) (magazine) **S:**81
Astrakhan fur *see* Persian lamb
Astrochemistry **C:**205
Astrodome (Houston, Texas)
picture(s) **B:**87
Astrolabes (navigation instruments) **N:**75
picture(s) **I:**352; **O:**178
Astrology (study of stars and planets for revelation of what will happen on Earth) **A:465,** 468; **B:**5; **C:**529; **Z:**386–87
Astronautical engineers **E:**225
Astronauts **A:466–67; S:**340d
Armstrong, Neil A. **A:**426
dangers of spaceflight **S:**344–45
Glenn, John H., Jr. **G:**237
Lucid, Shannon **O:**94
navigation in space **N:**77
profiles **S:**346–48
space shuttles **S:**364–65
space stations **S:**54
space tourists **S:**356
Why are astronauts weightless? **A:**467
Astronomical telescopes **O:**181
Astronomy **A:468–76b; S:**66 *see also* Comets; Constellations; Earth; Eclipses; Meteorites; Meteors; Moon; Planets; Radar astronomy; Radio astronomy; Satellites; Solar system; Space exploration and travel; Stars; Sun; Telescopes; Tides; Universe; the names of planets
black holes **B:**252–53
comets, meteorites, and asteroids **C:**449–52
constellations **C:**528–32
eclipses **E:**50–52
experiments and other science activities **E:**383, 389–91
history *see* Astronomy, history of
lasers, uses of **L:**46c–46d
masers **L:**46d
measuring the distance of galaxies **U:**216
modern natural clocks **T:**202
nebulas **N:**96
observatories **O:**7–12
photography, special uses of **P:**209
planetariums and space museums **P:**269–74
planets **P:**275–82
pulsars **P:**539
quasars **Q:**8–9
radio and radar astronomy **R:**69–76
satellites, artificial **S:**54
seasons **S:**109–11
solar system **S:**241–49
space telescopes **S:**367–68
spectrum lines, use of **L:**225–26
stars **S:**428–33
sun **S:**488–97
telescopes **T:**57–60
universe **U:**211–18
Astronomy, history of **A:**468–75
Babylonia **S:**68
Brahe, Tycho **B:**361
Cannon, Annie Jump **D:**100
Copernicus was father of modern astronomy **C:**552–53
Galileo's discoveries **G:**6
Gauss, Carl Friedrich **G:**64
Huygens, Christiaan **H:**310
Kepler, Johannes **K:**234
Maya **M:**186
physics, history of **P:**233–34
Renaissance **R:**162
Sagan, Carl Edward **N:**233
science, milestones in **S:**70, 74
science, modern **S:**70
Stonehenge **S:**462
Astrophotography **P:**208
Asturias, Miguel Ángel (Guatemalan writer) **G:**397
Asunción (capital of Paraguay) **P:**62, 63, 65
picture(s) **P:**65
Aswan High Dam (Egypt) **D:**20–21; **E:**102; **M:**302; **N:**261
Asymmetrical balance (in design) **D:**133
As You Like It (play by Shakespeare) **S:**135
Atacama Desert (Chile) **C:**251, 252; **L:**47; **S:**274
picture(s) **C:**252; **D:**126; **S:**277; **W:**95
Atahualpa (Inca ruler) **I:**110, 173; **P:**164, 268
picture(s) **S:**292
Atakora Mountains (Togo) **T:**216
Atatürk, Mustafa Kemal (president of Turkey) **T:**347, 348–49; **W:**284 *profile*
picture(s) **T:**349; **W:**284
Ataturk Dam (Turkey) **M:**302
Atauro (island, East Timor) **T:**207
Atbara River (tributary of the Nile) **N:**260
ATB's *see* All-terrain bicycles
Atchafalaya Basin Floodway (Louisiana) **L:**316
Atchison, Topeka, and Santa Fe Railway **N:**187, 189
Atelectasis (collapse of the alveoli) **L:**345
A tempo (in music) **M:**536

Aten (Aton) (Egyptian sun god) **E**:108, 109, 115
picture(s) **E**:109
Athabasca, Lake (Canada) **A**:165
Athabasca River (Canada) **A**:171; **J**:54
Athabasca tar sands (Alberta) **A**:166, 167; **C**:61–62
Athanasius, Saint (Bishop of Alexandria) **C**:290
Athapascan language family (of North American Indians) **A**:150; **I**:184, 188
Atheism (belief that there is no God) **A:476b; C**:258; **R**:145, 294
Athena (Minerva) (Greek goddess) **G**:362, 369; **W**:96
picture(s) **G**:360
Roman statue **A**:238
statue **M**:569
Athena, Temple of (Delphi, Greece)
picture(s) **A**:229
Athens (Georgia) **G**:141
Athens (capital of Greece) **A:476c–476d; G**:335, 336
amnesty, early example of **A**:221
ancient civilization in Athens **A**:238; **C**:315; **G**:341
citizenship **C**:324
early form of democracy **D**:105; **G**:273
education in early Athens **E**:77–78
Greek art, center of **G**:348
Olympic Games (1896) **O**:105, 112
oratory **O**:190
Parthenon **A**:368
Peloponnesian War **P**:120a
Pericles was its greatest statesman **P**:152
physical education program **P**:223
Solon was the founder of democracy in ancient Athens **S**:253
picture(s) **A**:476c; **C**:314
Little Metropole church **B**:491
Parthenon **A**:364; **E**:340; **G**:339, 348
Athens of the South (nickname for Nashville, Tennessee) **N**:16
Athens State College (Alabama) **A**:135
Atherosclerosis (cardiovascular disease) **H**:82; **N**:430
Athlete's foot (skin infection) **D**:200; **F**:498; **M**:276
Athletics *see* Gymnastics; Olympic Games; Sports
Athos (one of *The Three Musketeers*) **D**:349–50
Athos, Mount (religious state in Greece) **G**:332
Atikal, Ilanko (Indian poet) **I**:141
Atitlán, Lake (Guatemala) **L**:29
picture(s) **G**:394
Atkins, Chet (American singer, musician, and record producer) **C**:573
Atlanta (capital of Georgia) **A:477; G**:132, 139, 141
Civil War **C**:343; **S**:152
Olympic Games (1996) **O**:113
picture(s) **A**:477; **G**:141
capitol building **G**:142
Civil War **C**:342
Georgia State University **G**:136
High Museum of Art **G**:133
Atlanta Memorial Arts Center *see* Robert W. Woodruff Arts Center
Atlantic, Battle of the (1940–1941) **W**:301
Atlantic Basin (Canada) **C**:56
Atlantic City (New Jersey) **N**:172
picture(s) **N**:165
Atlantic Coastal Plain (United States) *see* Coastal Plain
Atlantic Fleet (of the United States Navy) **U**:111
Atlantic Intracoastal Waterway *see* Intracoastal Waterway
Atlantic Monthly (magazine) **H**:172
Atlantic Ocean A:478–79
Bermuda Triangle **B**:152
cables, submarine **T**:51
Gulf Stream **G**:413
icebergs in the North Atlantic **I**:17, 18
Mid-Atlantic Ridge **M**:504
ocean liner crossings **O**:30–31, 32–33
rivers flowing into **U**:82
map(s)
iceberg route **I**:18
Atlantic Provinces (of Canada) *see* New Brunswick; Newfoundland and Labrador; Nova Scotia; Prince Edward Island
Atlantis (legendary island) **A**:478
Atlantis (United States space shuttle) **S**:340j, 348, 364
picture(s) **S**:340b
approaching *Mir* **S**:355
crew eating in microgravity **S**:341
Atlas (in Greek mythology) **A**:478; **G**:362; **W**:243
picture(s) **G**:362
Atlas Buoy (automated weather instrument)
picture(s) **W**:90
Atlases (bound volumes of maps) **R**:129
Atlas Mountains (northern Africa) **A**:47–48, 185; **M**:459–60, 505
picture(s) **A**:48; **M**:459
Atlatl (weapon) **I**:166
Atman (Hindu spiritual principle) **H**:140
Atmosphere (gases enveloping planets) **A:479–82; E**:20–21
see also Air; Meteorology
acid rain **A**:9–10
air pollution **A**:122–25; **E**:303–5
climatic changes, sources of **C**:364
clouds **C**:382–85
cosmic rays **C**:562–63
dust **D**:353
early Earth atmosphere **F**:383, 385
Earth, history of **E**:23, 26
Earth's atmosphere **P**:278
Earth's atmosphere interferes with radiation from space **S**:367
Earth's atmosphere supports life **L**:202
ecosphere **N**:63
Is Earth's atmosphere warming? **A**:482
Jupiter **J**:159; **P**:279
Mars **M**:105, 106, 108; **P**:279
Mercury **M**:230; **P**:276
meteorites **C**:450, 451
moon lacks **M**:451, 453–54, 455
Neptune **N**:111–12; **P**:282
ozone layer **O**:292
plants' release of oxygen **L**:118
Pluto **P**:282, 343
pressure centers are a climatic control **C**:363
research with balloons **B**:36, 37
Saturn **P**:280; **S**:55
scattered light **L**:215
sun's atmosphere **E**:52; **S**:494–97
Titan **P**:280; **S**:58
Triton **N**:113; **P**:282
twinkling layer of air **S**:432
Uranus **P**:281; **U**:231–32
Venus **P**:276; **V**:303a, 303b
weather **W**:79–95
Atmospheric pressure *see* Air pressure
ATM's *see* Amateur telescope makers; Automatic teller machines
Atolls (coral islands) **C**:556; **P**:3
picture(s)
Palau **P**:2
Atomic bomb *see* Atomic weapons
Atomic clocks (devices for measuring time with great accuracy) **C**:371, 372; **L**:46d; **T**:201
Atomic Energy Commission T:326
Atomic energy *see* Nuclear energy
Atomic force microscopes A:484; **M**:285
Atomic numbers A:485–86; **C**:202, 204; **E**:166 *see also* Periodic table
Atomic physics *see* Nuclear physics
Atomic power *see* Nuclear energy
Atomic second (basic unit of time measurement) **C**:371
Atomic weapons N:373, 374–75, 377–78; **W**:272–73
aviation in World War II **A**:566
battles **B**:103f

Chicago, research in **I**:76
Einstein and **E**:120
fission **F**:223
Hiroshima and Nagasaki (Japan) **J**:47
Manhattan Project **W**:318
Marshall Islands used for testing **M**:113
New Mexico **N**:194
Oppenheimer, J. Robert **N**:232–33
Truman, Harry S., and bombing Japan **T**:325
World War II **W**:317–18
picture(s) **N**:194; **S**:74; **U**:196
bombing of Hiroshima **A**:456
Atomic weight **A**:486–87; **C**:204
Dalton's theory **D**:15
elements **E**:166, 168–69, 170–78
experimental measurements **C**:209
isotopes **C**:205
Atomium (landmark in Brussels, Belgium) **B**:134
Atom-probe field ion microscopes **M**:285
Atoms **A:483–89**
alloy structures **A**:192, 193
atomic theory **C**:198, 207, 209
Bohr, Niels **B**:304; **L**:224
bonding **M**:151–52
carbon chains and rings **C**:106
chemical structure **C**:198, 201–3, 204
chemistry, history of **C**:207, 209, 211
chemistry of life **L**:198–99
cosmic rays **C**:562–63
crystals **C**:603–4; **M**:151
Dalton's theory **D**:15; **S**:73
Democritus' theory **S**:68
electricity **E**:135–36
elements, chemical **E**:166–70
fission **F**:222–23
ions and ionization **I**:287–89
lightning, causes of **T**:185
magnetism **M**:31
materials science **M**:151–55
matter and atoms **M**:176–78
nuclear energy **N**:366–73
physics, history of **P**:234, 235
quantum theory **P**:231–32
radiation **R**:42
radioactive elements **R**:67
radiometric dating **R**:64–66
Rutherford's theory **R**:387
scanning tunneling microscope can examine **E**:164
subatomic particles **P**:232
water molecule **W**:47
Where does fission take place? **F**:223
diagram(s)
carbon-12 atom **A**:486
structure **A**:484
water molecule **W**:48
picture(s)
scanning tunneling microscope view **A**:489
tracks seen in bubble chamber **A**:483
Atoms for Peace Plan (1953) **D**:179; **E**:125
Atom smashers *see* Particle accelerators
Aton(Egyptian god) *see* Aten
Atonality (in music) **M**:397, 536
Germany **G**:189
Schoenberg, Arnold **S**:60
Atonement (in religion) **J**:144, 146a
Atonement, Day of *see* Yom Kippur
ATP (adenosine triphosphate) **B**:298
bioluminescence **B**:205
muscle contraction **M**:521
photosynthesis forms **P**:220, 315
Atrioventricular node (AV node) (heart structure that regulates heartbeat) **H**:81, 82
Atrioventricular valves (of the heart) **H**:80, 82
Atrium (plural: **atria**) (chamber of the heart) **B**:284; **C**:305; **D**:193; **H**:80, 81, 82
Atrophy (wasting away of muscle fibers) **M**:521
Attachés (embassy employees) **F**:371
Attar of roses
Bulgaria is a major producer **B**:443
Attention-Deficit Hyperactivity Disorder *see* ADHD
Atterbom, Per Daniel Amadeus (Swedish poet) **S**:58i
Attica (region around Athens)
Attic dialect became the language of Greece **G**:353
Attic system (of numeration) *see* Herodianic system
Attila (king of the Huns) **A:490; B**:103d *see also* Huns
Attitude (of aircraft) **A**:117, 118
rockets **R**:260
space terms **S**:340d
Attitude control system (of spacecraft) **S**:340k
Attitude scales (personality tests) **T**:119
Attlee, Clement (British prime minister) **A:490**
picture(s)
with Stalin at Potsdam Conference **S**:419
Attorney General (head of the United States Department of Justice) **C**:2; **J**:164; **P**:447
list of **J**:165
powers of **W**:65
Attorneys *see* Lawyers
Attractants *see* Pheromones
Attucks, Crispus (American revolutionary patriot) **A**:79c; **R**:196, 208 *profile*
Attu Island (Alaska) **A**:158
Atwood, Margaret (Canadian poet and novelist) **C**:87
picture(s) **C**:86
Atzerodt, George (American conspirator in Lincoln's assassination) **B**:335
Aubrey, John (English scholar) **S**:462
Auburn (Maine) **M**:48
Auburn system (of punishment) **P**:482
Auburn University (Alabama) **A**:135
Auckland (New Zealand) **N**:240
Auctions
cattle **C**:154
furs **F**:502–3
tobacco **T**:215
Audemars, Georges (Swiss scientist) **F**:109–10; **N**:439
Auden, W. H. (English-born American poet) **E**:288; **O**:52
Audhumla (cow in Norse mythology) **N**:279
Audible sounds **S**:258
Audio-animatronic figures **A**:530
picture(s) **A**:530
Audio signal (television) **T**:62, 63
Audiotape **C**:467
Audiovisual materials and equipment **E**:86; **L**:177, 182
Auditions (of actors) **P**:337
Auditorium (part of a theater where the audience sits) **T**:157
Auditorium Building (Chicago, Illinois)
picture(s) **S**:486
Auditory memory (for things you hear) **S**:399
Audits (in bookkeeping) **B**:313
Audubon, John James (American naturalist and painter) **A:491; U**:129
Kentucky memorial **K**:220
watercolor painting **W**:60
Audubon Park Zoo (New Orleans, Louisiana) **Z**:390
Audubon Society, National (NAS) **C**:526
Aue, Hartmann von (German poet) *see* Hartmann von Aue
Auerbach, "Red" (American basketball coach) **B**:95b
Augean stables (in Greek mythology) **G**:366
Augers (tools) **T**:234, 235
Augier, Emile (French dramatist) **D**:301
Augmented interval (in music) **M**:536
Augsburg, Peace of (1555) **G**:160
Augsburg Confession (1530) **R**:131
August (8th month of the year) **A:492–93**
Augusta (Georgia) **G**:141
Augusta (capital of Maine) **M**:42, 46
picture(s) **M**:46
Auguste clown **C**:387
Augustin I *see* Iturbide, Agustín de

Augustine, Saint (?–604, archbishop of Canterbury) **R:**287
Anglo-Saxons converted to Christianity **E:**237
Augustine, Saint (354–430, early Christian thinker and Bishop of Hippo) **A:494; C:**290
father of Latin theology **R:**287
Petrarch, imaginary conversation with **R:**159
philosophy, history of **P:**190
picture(s) **R:**287
Augustus (emperor of Rome) **A:**239, **494–95; R:**316
Aeneid written in honor of Augustus **A:**36
Antony, Mark **A:**317
Latin literature, golden age of **L:**75–76
picture(s) **A:**494
marble bust **A:**234
statue **R:**316; **S:**96; **W:**260
"Auld Lang Syne" (song by Burns) **B:**455
Aung San (Burmese political leader) **M:**561
Aung San Suu Kyi (political leader in Myanmar) **M:**561
picture(s) **M:**561
Aurangzeb (emperor of Mogul dynasty of India) **I:**132
Aurelian (Roman emperor) **R:**317
Auricle (part of the outer ear) *see* Pinna
Aurochs (extinct wild oxen) **H:**219; **O:**286
Aurora australis (Southern lights) (in the Antarctic) **I:**289
Aurora borealis (Northern lights) (in the Arctic) **I:**289
picture(s) **I:**288; **M:**30; **S:**496
Auroras (polar lights) **I:**289
magnetism **M:**29
radiation belts **R:**49
solar flares **S:**497
solar wind **S:**475, 497
Auschwitz concentration camp (Poland) **H:**174
Ausculum, Battle of (279 B.C.) **P:**559
Ausonius, Decimus Magnus (Roman writer) **L:**76
Austen, Jane (English novelist) **A:495; E:**283; **F:**115
style and themes of her novels **N:**359
Austerlitz, Battle of (1805) **N:**12
Austin (capital of Texas) **T:**134
"outlaw" country music **C:**573
picture(s) **T:**137
Austin, Moses (American pioneer miner) **N:**366
Austin, Stephen Fuller (American pioneer) **T:**138 *profile*
Australia **A:496–517**
Aborigines **A:**7
aquarium (Sydney) **A:**337
Australia Day **H:**167
brumbies (wild horses) **H:**242
Canberra (capital of Australia) **C:**91
continents **C:**537, 538
dependencies **C:**461
education **E:**74
endangered species **E:**209
exploration and discovery **E:**411
explored by Captain Cook **C:**539
food **F:**331
gold discoveries **G:**252; **M:**324
humans migrated by land during Ice Age **I:**13
immigration **I:**94
kangaroos **K:**174–75
Kelly, Ned, legend of **L:**130; **O:**264
koalas **K:**290
lakes **L:**34
lumber and lumbering **L:**342
Melbourne **M:**213
mountains **M:**506
national parks **N:**56
New Guinea **N:**149; **P:**59
prairies **P:**426, 427, 428–29
rabbit plague **R:**24
Sydney **S:**547–48
theater **T:**162
What is the Great Barrier Reef? **P:**5
wine **W:**190
Wollomombi waterfall **W:**63
World War II **W:**306–7
map(s) **A:**502, 508
population **A:**509
precipitation **A:**503
wildlife **A:**507
picture(s)
Aborigines **A:**7
Ayers Rock **A:**505
coat of arms **A:**514
farmland **A:**504–5
flag **F:**226
flying doctor service **A:**499
gold mining **A:**511
Great Barrier Reef **A:**504; **J:**75
history **A:**515, 516
kangaroo-crossing sign **A:**506
Melbourne **A:**513
people **A:**496, 497, 498
prehistoric art **P:**435
Queensland **A:**512
rain forest **A:**505
School of the Air **A:**499
sheep industry **A:**510–11
surfboat team **A:**500
Sydney **A:**496, 513, 517; **M:**33; **O:**102; **S:**547
western desert area **D:**125
wheat farming **A:**510
Australia Day **H:**167
Australian Alps **A:**504; **M:**506
Australian-American Memorial (Canberra, Australia) **C:**91
Australian Antarctic Territory **A:**496
Australian ballot **V:**393
Australian Capital Territory **A:**513; **C:**91
Australian cassowaries (flightless birds) **O:**245
Australian crawl (swimming stroke) **S:**536
Australian death adders **S:**212
Australian Elizabethan Theatre Trust **T:**162
Australian National Gallery (Canberra)
picture(s) **C:**91
Australian Open (tennis tournament) **T:**98, 99
Australian Rules (of football) **M:**213
Australian trumpet snails **S:**208
Australopithecus (early humanlike creature) **E:**379; **K:**233; **L:**96, 97; **P:**440
map(s)
where remains have been found **P:**439
picture(s) **P:**438
fossil skull **F:**386
Austria **A:518–25**
annexation by Hitler (1938) **H:**154; **W:**295
Czech way of life influenced by **C:**618–19
folk dance **D:**30
food **F:**331
German and Austrian literature **G:**176–82
German and Austrian music **G:**183–89
German language **G:**174–75
Habsburgs **H:**2–4
Hallstatt culture **C:**163–64
Vienna **V:**332j–333
World War II **W:**313, 315, 318
map(s) **A:**521
picture(s)
flag **F:**226
Grossglockner **A:**518
Vienna **A:**519; **V:**332j
Austria-Hungary **A:**524–25; **H:**299
Ukraine, history of **U:**11–12
World War I **W:**277, 278, 283, 285, 288, 290, 291
map(s) **A:**525
Austrian music **G:**183–89 *see also* the names of Austrian composers
Austrian Succession, War of the (1740–1748) **A:**524; **F:**459
Authentic assessments (of reading skills) **R:**111
Authoring languages (in computer programming) **C:**483
Authoritarian family **F:**42

Authoritarian government **G:**274
Latin America **L:**59
Authorization bills (suggested laws) **U:**168
Authors (game)
picture(s)
box **G:**16
Authorship *see* Writing (authorship)
Autism (neurological disorder) **A:526–27; E:**204; **M:**224
Autobiography (story of a person's own life) **B:192**
Confessions of Saint Augustine **A:**494
Franklin, Benjamin **A:**204
Irish memoirs **I:**328
library arrangement **L:**183
literature, types of **L:**258
Pulitzer Prizes **P:**535–36
Rousseau's *Confessions* **R:**339
Wright's *Black Boy* **W:**327
Autobiography of Alice B. Toklas, The (book by Gertrude Stein) **S:**446
Autoclave (machine)
picture(s) **S:**343
Autocracy (absolute government by a power-seeking individual) **G:**273
Autocrat of the Breakfast Table, The (essays by Holmes) **H:**172
Auto-exposure (in cameras) **P:**202
Autofocus cameras **P:**200, 213
Autogiro (flying machine) **H:**103
Autographs **A:527–28**
Autoharp (musical instrument)
picture(s) **W:**130
Auto-hypnosis *see* Self-hypnosis
Autoimmune (Self-immune) diseases **D:**184; **I:**98
multiple sclerosis **D:**196
Automated Guided Vehicles (mobile robots) **R:**254
Automated instruction *see* Programmed instruction
Automated Surface Observing Systems (ASOS) **W:**90
Automatic pilot (in airplanes) **A:**120; **G:**437
Automatic teller machines (ATM's) (in banking) **A:**532; **B:**58
Automatic transmissions (in motor vehicles) **A:**549; **T:**279–80
Automatic typewriters **T:**373
Automatic weapons **G:**422–24
picture(s) **G:**425
Automation **A:529–33**
bottling industry **B:**346–47
candy and candy making **C:**99
computers **C:**480–94
dairy farming **C:**154
effect on labor **L:**9
elevators **E:**186
manufacturing **M:**89
modern librarianship **L:**180, 186
modern tool use **T:**235
power plants **P:**422
robots **R:**252–56
rug-weaving looms **R:**353, 354
technology advances **T:**40–41
weather measurements **W:**90
picture(s)
chemical industry **C:**197
robots **A:**531, 554; **M:**89, 266
Automatism (in modern art) **M:**393, 394
Automatistes (group of Canadian artists) **C:**73
Automobile industry **A:**542–43, 554–56 *see also* Automobiles
air pollution standards **A:**125
Chrysler, Walter Percy **K:**188
Detroit (Michigan) is home of **D:**142
Ford, Henry **F:**369
Japan **A:**451; **J:**38
Michigan **M:**263, 265–66, 272–73
Missouri **M:**373
Rhode Island, history of **R:**226
robot technology **A:**531–32; **R:**253, 254
Tennessee **N:**16; **T:**80
United States **U:**93
picture(s)
assembly line **M:**272
Brazil **S:**291
Canada **C:**65
Czech Republic **C:**620
Europe **E:**358
factory in Germany **G:**155
Ferrari factory **I:**386
Ford, Henry **I:**281
Kentucky **K:**218
Korea, South **K:**301
robot technology **A:**531, 554; **M:**89, 266; **N:**301
South Carolina BMW plant **S:**303
South Korean plant **A:**451
Tennessee **T:**81
Yugoslavia **Y:**366
Automobile insurance *see* Insurance, automobile
Automobile models **A:534–35**
Automobile racing **A:536–38**
automobile models **A:**534–35
early competition **A:**542
karting **K:**196
picture(s)
car with inverted wing design **A:**41
Indianapolis 500 **I:**145
Automobiles **A:539–56** *see also* Buses; Internal-combustion engines; Trucks and trucking
acid rain **A:**9, 10
air pollution **A:**123, 125; **E:**304
automated production lines **A:**531–32
avoiding health hazards **H:**76
batteries **B:**103b, 103c
carbon monoxide poisoning **P:**355
carried on pure car truck carrier ships **S:**154–55
consumer protection **C:**534
cruise control **A:**532
driver education **D:**324–27
drunk driving *see* Drunk driving
electric *see* Electric automobiles
electronics **E:**162
environment, effect on **E:**304
gasoline as fuel **G:**62
gears in transmissions **G:**66
Global Positioning System (GPS) receivers **N:**77
headlights **L:**235
hydraulic brakes **H:**313
internal-combustion engines **I:**262–65
inventions **I:**281
juvenile thefts **J:**167, 168
models *see* Automobile models
motels created to serve automobile travelers **H:**259
motor vehicle safety **S:**3
natural gas vehicles **N:**59
passenger-side mirrors **L:**214
plastic parts **P:**323
racing *see* Automobile racing
roads to fit high-speed vehicles **R:**249–50
tires **T:**210–12
traffic control **T:**269–70
transmissions **T:**279–80
transportation, history of **T:**286–87
United States use in transportation **U:**76, 95
picture(s)
battery **B:**103a
car models **A:**534, 535
development of the automobile **A:**541, 542, 544, 545
electronic map display **E:**160
hybrid electric-gasoline car **C:**526
plastic car bodies **P:**322
Automobile State (nickname for Michigan) **M:**258, 259
Automobile trucks *see* Trucks and trucking
Autonomic nervous system **N:**117
Autonomous communities (in Spanish local government) **S:**375

Autonomous underwater vehicles (AUV's) U:27
Autonomous University of Honduras H:205
Autonomous University of Santo Domingo (Dominican Republic) D:280; N:298; U:226
Autonomy (self-government) G:276
Autonomy (stage of child development) C:226
Auto pilot *see* Automatic pilot
Autopsy (pathologist's examination of a dead body) F:373
Autoradiograms (patterns of lines in DNA) F:373
Autos sacramentales (Spanish religious plays) D:299
Autotrophic bacteria B:12
Autry, Gene (American actor and singer) C:572
Autumn (season) S:109, 111 *see also* the names of months
- constellations C:531–32
- flowers for fall G:49
- leaves' color change L:114–15
- Why do leaves change color in the autumn? P:306
- *picture(s)*
  - constellations C:531
  - deciduous trees L:115
  - foliage in Vermont V:307

Autumn and Spring Annals (book by Confucius) R:151
Autun (France) F:422
AUV's *see* Autonomous underwater vehicles
Auxiliaries (in grammar) G:289
Auxiliary personnel (in hospitals) H:249
Auxins (plant hormones) P:312
Auyuittuq National Park (Canada) N:412
Available-light photography P:214
Avalanches (masses of snow or ice that slide rapidly down mountain slopes) **A:557–58**
- Austrian Alps A:520
- caused by sympathetic vibrations of sound S:261
- volcanoes: glowing avalanches V:383
- *picture(s)* A:557

Avalon Peninsula (Newfoundland and Labrador) C:54
Avenida 9 de Julio (Buenos Aires, Argentina)
- *picture(s)* B:429

Avenida de José Antonio (Gran Via) (Madrid, Spain)
- *picture(s)* M:15

Aventurescence (reflections inside gems) G:70
- *picture(s)* G:70

Aventurine (quartz) Q:8
Avenue, Middelharnis, Holland, The (painting by Hobbema)
- *picture(s)* D:367

Averages (values of sets of numbers) S:441–42
Avery, Oswald (American biologist) B:187
Avery Fisher Hall (Lincoln Center for the Performing Arts, New York City) L:248
Avery Island (Louisiana) L:322
Aves (class name for birds) B:215
Avesta (holy book of Zoroastrianism) Z:394
Aviaries (bird exhibits in zoos) Z:390
Aviation **A:559–72**
- aerodynamics A:37–41
- aerospace engineers E:225
- airplane models A:104–7
- airplanes A:108–21
- airports A:126–29
- balloons and ballooning B:34–38
- Berlin airlift B:149; G:164
- computers used in flight simulation C:486
- Doolittle, James Harold W:300
- Earhart, Amelia E:7
- early attempts to fly A:559
- Federal Aviation Administration T:293
- gliders G:238–40
- ground-controlled approach (GCA) radar R:39
- helicopters H:103–5
- inventions I:284
- jet propulsion J:90–92
- Lindbergh's New York-Paris flight L:249
- mail service P:398
- mathematics in careers M:161
- National Air and Space Museum P:273–74
- navigation N:73, 76
- North Carolina called "first in flight" N:320
- parachutes P:60
- record flights A:563, 567
- supersonic flight S:499–502; U:57
- transportation, history of T:287–88
- United States Air Force U:107–10
- United States air transportation U:95
- United States Army U:102, 105
- United States Marine Corps U:120
- United States Navy U:115
- World War I W:286
- Wright, Wilbur and Orville W:328
- Yeager, Charles Elwood W:139
- *picture(s)*
  - Berlin airlift B:148

Aviation Challenge (science education program) S:340a
Avicenna (Persian philosopher) G:109
Avignon (France) R:290
Ávila, Pedro Arias de (Spanish colonial governor) *see* Pedrarias Dávila
Ávila Camacho, Manuel (Mexican president) M:252
Avilés, Pedro Menéndez de (Spanish naval officer) *see* Menéndez de Avilés, Pedro
AV node (in the heart) *see* Atrioventricular node
Avocado (fruit) T:317
- *picture(s)* T:317

Avocations *see* Hobbies
Avodire (tree)
- *picture(s)*
  - uses of the wood and its grain W:223

Avogadro, Count Amedeo (Italian scientist) P:234
Avoirdupois (weight) W:115
Avvakum, Archpriest (Russian religious leader) R:380
Awards (in arbitration) A:349
Awards, literary
- Caldecott and Newbery Medals C:11–12
- children's book awards C:239–40
- Laura Ingalls Wilder Award W:170
- Nobel prizes N:265–66
- O. Henry Awards H:112
- Pulitzer Prizes P:533–38

Awls (tools for piercing holes) S:160; T:233
- needles probably developed from N:102

A.W.S.A. *see* American Water Ski Association
Axe (tool) T:227, 234; W:250
- *picture(s)* A:232; T:228

Axial skeleton (of the body) S:183
Axioms (mathematical assumptions) G:120; M:157
Axis (in coordinate geometry) A:184
Axis (of a bar graph) G:309, 311
Axis (of a lens) L:144–45
Axis (of celestial bodies)
- Earth E:9
- Mars M:105
- moon M:446
- Uranus U:231

"Axis of evil" (George W. Bush's term for countries supporting terrorism and trying to build weapons of mass destruction) B:468; I:316a
Axis Powers (alliance of Italy, Germany, and Japan during World War II) W:292
- profiles of leaders W:302–3

Axles (of wheels) W:159, 160, 250–51
- *picture(s)* W:243

Axminster carpets R:354–55
Axons (of neurons) B:362, 363; N:117, 118
Axum (Ethiopia) *see* Aksum
Ayahs (verses of the Koran) K:293
Ayatollahs (Shi'ite Muslim leaders) I:308, 347
Aycock, Charles Brantley (American statesman) N:320
Aye-ayes (lemurs) P:456
Ayer Directory of Publications M:19

Ayers Rock (Australia)
picture(s) **A**:505
Ayllón, Lucas Vázquez de (Spanish explorer) **S**:308
Aylwin Azócar, Patricio (Chilean president) **C**:255
Aymara (Indian language of South America) **P**:159; **S**:285, 288
Aymara (Indians of South America) **I**:173, 196; **L**:30
Bolivia **B**:306–7
Peru **P**:162
Ayres (songs) **E**:292; **R**:173
Ayrshire (breed of dairy cattle) **C**:154
picture(s) **C**:153; **D**:5
Ayub Khan, Mohammed (Pakistani political leader) **P**:40a
Ayurveda (ancient Hindu medicine) **M**:207
Ayutthaya (early kings of Thailand) **T**:152
Ayyubid Dynasty (of Egypt and the Holy Land) **I**:352
Azad ("Free") Kashmir (Pakistani-controlled section of Kashmir) **K**:198
Azaleas (shrubs)
picture(s) **G**:28, 36; **S**:299
Azerbaijan **A:573–74**
Commonwealth of Independent States **C**:460
Kurds **K**:307
picture(s)
flag **F**:227
Azeri (Azerbaijani) (Turkic people) **A**:573; **U**:34
Azhar University, al- (Cairo, Egypt) **C**:8; **E**:100; **U**:219
Azimuthal equidistant projection (of maps) **M**:97
Azizia (Libya) **A**:49; **S**:7
Azobe (dense African wood) **R**:78
Azores (islands off Portugal) **I**:362; **P**:393
Azorín (Spanish writer) *see* Martínez Ruiz, José
Azov, Sea of **O**:43
AZT (Azidothymidine) (drug) **I**:282
Aztecs (Indians of Mexico) **A**:244, **575–78**; **I**:172–73
archaeological sites uncovered by subway excavation **A**:351
cacao beans used to make chocolate **C**:280
cigarette smoking started by **S**:207
Cortés conquered **C**:559
dragons in mythology **D**:293
factors important in helping Cortés conquer Mexico **M**:248
hieroglyphic writing systems **H**:131
Mexico City **M**:253
Montezuma II **M**:443
postal service, history of **P**:397
picture(s)
conquest by Spanish forces **I**:173; **W**:264
manuscript **L**:66
Quetzalcoatl **M**:568
sculpture **I**:173
turquoise sculpture **E**:409

PHOTO CREDITS

The following list credits the sources of photos used in THE NEW BOOK OF KNOWLEDGE. Credits are listed, by page, photo by photo—left to right, top to bottom. Wherever appropriate, the name of the photographer has been listed with the source, the two being separated by a dash. When two or more photos by different photographers appear on one page, their credits are separated by semicolons.

A

Cover © Dan Lim—Masterfile
2 © Terry Madison—The Image Bank
6 The Granger Collection (all photos on page).
6a The Bettmann Archive; The Granger Collection; The Granger Collection; The Granger Collection.
6b The Bettmann Archive
7 © Jack S. Grove—Liaison Agency
8 Giraudon/Art Resource
10 © John Elk III—Bruce Coleman Inc.; © Fletcher & Baylis—Photo Researchers.
11 The Granger Collection
12 The White House Collection, © copyright White House Historical Association; The Granger Collection.
13 National Gallery of Art, Washington; Gift of Mrs. Robert Homans.
14 Courtesy of Maryland Historical Society
15 Yale University Art Gallery
16 Corcoran Gallery of Art; The Granger Collection; The Bettmann Archive.
18 The Bettmann Archive; The Granger Collection.
19 The Bettmann Archive
20 The Granger Collection
21 Historical Pictures Service
24 © Jeff Isaac Greenberg—Photo Researchers
29 Courtesy of Binney & Smith Inc.
30 Courtesy of Young & Rubicam, New York
31 © Danilo Boschung—Leo de Wys; Courtesy of the American Cancer Society.
32 Courtesy of Grolier Enterprises Corp.
35 Warshaw Collection of Business Americana
37 British Aerospace
41 © Steve Swope—Indy 500 Photos; © Yogi, Inc.
42 © Jackie Foryst—Bruce Coleman Inc.; © Reuters/Oleg Popov—TimePix.
43 © Emil Muench—Photo Researchers
44 © Arthur C. Twomey—Photo Researchers; © Peter Knapp—The Image Bank.
45 © Laura Rauch—AP/Wide World Photos
46 © Sally Mayman—Stone; © R.I.M. Campbell—Bruce Coleman Limited; © Gerald Cubitt; © Fridmar Damm—Leo de Wys; © Gerald Cubitt.
47 © Hiroyuki Matsumoto—Black Star; © Pedro Coll—The Stock Market; © Michael J. Howell—Leo de Wys.
48 © Robert Everts—Stone; © Hiroyuki Matsumoto—Black Star.
49 © Carl Frank—Photo Researchers
50 © Robert Frerck—Stone
52 © James P. Rowan—Stone
53 © M. Philip Kahl—Black Star; © Alan Binks—Anthony Bannister Picture Library; © Mitch Kezar—Stone.
54 © Gerald Cubitt; © Betty Press—Woodfin Camp & Associates; © Nicholas DeVore—Stone; © Pedro Coll—The Stock Market.
55 © Kerstin Beier—Anthony Bannister Picture Library; © Stone; © Martin Rogers—Stone.
56 © Marc & Evelyne Bernheim—Woodfin Camp & Associates; © Paul Stepan—Photo Researchers.
57 © Michael Coyne—Black Star; © Gerald Cubitt; © Marc & Evelyne Bernheim—Woodfin Camp & Associates.
58 © J. Bertrand—Leo de Wys
60 © Betty Press—Woodfin Camp & Associates; © Kerstin Beier—Anthony Bannister Picture Library.
61 © Betty Press—Woodfin Camp & Associates
62 © Hubertus Kanus—Photo Researchers (all photos on page).
63 © Victor Englebert—Photo Researchers
64 © Pierre Boulat/Cosmos—Woodfin Camp & Associates; © Jason Laure—Woodfin Camp & Associates.
65 The Granger Collection
66 The Granger Collection (all photos on page).
69 © Brooks Kraft—Corbis-Sygma
70 © Richard Saunders—Leo de Wys
71 © George Holton—Photo Researchers; Photographed by Kathy Corday. National Museum of African Art, Eliot Elisofon Photographic Archives, Smithsonian Institution.
72 Photographed by Franko Khoury. National Museum of African Art, Eliot Elisofon Photographic Archives, Smithsonian Institution (all photos on page).
73 Photographed by Dick Beaulieux. Ethnographic Museum, Antwerp; © Lee Boltin; © Lee Boltin.
74 Photographed by Franko Khoury. National Museum of African Art, Eliot Elisofon Photographic Archives, Smithsonian Institution. Gift of Dr. Ernst Anspach and museum purchase; © Lee Boltin; © Lee Boltin.
75 Photographed by Franko Khoury. National Museum of African Art and National Museum of Natural History, Eliot Elisofon Photographic Archives, Smithsonian Institution; Photographed by Jim Young. National Museum of African Art, Eliot Elisofon Photographic Archives, Smithsonian Institution.
76 © Strauss—Curtis—The Stock Market
76a © Marc & Evelyne Bernheim—Woodfin Camp & Associates
77 © Paul Funston—Anthony Bannister Picture Library; © Bill Kaufman—Leo de Wys; © Marc & Evelyne Bernheim—Woodfin Camp & Associates.
79a © Jeffrey Henson Scales; © George Olson—Woodfin Camp & Associates.
79b © Nick Kelsh—Kelsh Wilson Design Inc.; © Yva Momatiuk/John Eastcott—Woodfin Camp & Associates.
79c © Tom Raymond—Stone/Getty Images
79d The Granger Collection
79e Peter Newark's American Pictures; Schomburg Center for Research in Black Culture—The New York Public Library—Astor, Lenox and Tilden Foundations.
79f The Granger Collection
79g The Granger Collection; Peter Newark's American Pictures.
79h Schomburg Center for Research in Black Culture—The New York Public Library—Astor, Lenox and Tilden Foundations
79i Peter Newark's American Pictures; The Bettmann Archive.
79j The Granger Collection; Peter Newark's American Pictures.
79k UPI/Bettmann Newsphotos; The Bettmann Archive.
79l © Driggs Collection—Magnum Photos; © David Diaz, courtesy of HarperCollins Publisher; The Bettmann Archive; National Museum of American Art, Smithsonian Insti-

tution, Washington, DC. Gift of the Harmon Foundation—Art Resource; Schomburg Center for Research in Black Culture—The New York Public Library—Astor, Lenox and Tilden Foundations.
79m Philadelphia Museum of Art: Gift of Dr. and Mrs. Mathew T. Moore; Peter Newark's American Pictures.
79n UPI/Bettmann Newsphotos; © Topham—The Image Works.
79o © Ted Russell—Corbis-Sygma; © Charles Moore—Black Star.
79p © Kenneth Jarecke—Contact Press Images; Peter Newark's American Pictures.
80 © Jonathan Barth—Getty Images; © Ulf Andersen/Newsmakers/Getty Images; © Jamal A. Wilson/Newsmakers/Getty Images; © Chris Kasson—AP/Wide World Photos; Albert Trotman—Allford Trotman Associates.
81 Hulton/Archive by Getty Images
82 © Dugald Stermer
84 © William Hubbell—Woodfin Camp & Associates
85 © Phil Huber—Black Star; © Ira Wyman—Corbis-Sygma.
86 Gerald Davis—Contact
87 The Bettmann Archive
88 © Earl Roberge—Photo Researchers
89 © Jules Bucher—Photo Researchers
90 © Andrew Holbrooke—Wheeler Pictures; © Ronny Jacques—Photo Researchers.
91 © Andrew Holbrooke—Wheeler Pictures
92 © Bill Backman—Photo Researchers; © George Holton—Photo Researchers.
93 © Louis Goldman—Photo Researchers; © Ulrike Welsch—Stock, Boston.
94 © Joe Munroe—Photo Researchers
95 © Photo Action Press—Photo Researchers
96 © Grant Heilman Photography
98 The Pierpont Morgan Library
99 National Gallery of Art, Washington, DC, Garbisch Collection
100 © Liane Enkelis—Stock, Boston
100a U.S. Department of Agriculture
104 Model Airplane News
106 Robert Schleicher
107 Courtesy of Byron Originals
108 © James A. Anderson—Unicorn Stock Photos; PhotoEdit; Courtesy, Cessna; Brent Jones.
110 © R. Caton—H. Armstrong Roberts, Inc.
111 © Ingrid Johnsson—Journalism Services
112 Courtesy, British Aerospace
113 © Dennis Barnes; © David Brownell.
114 © Heinz Steenmans—Wheeler Pictures; Leonard Lee Rue III—Bruce Coleman Inc.
115 © Joseph Jacobson—Journalism Services
116 © Lepper & Miller—H. Armstrong Roberts; NASA.
117 © Randa Bishop
119 Courtesy, Boeing Aircraft Co.
120 Courtesy, McDonnell Douglas Corporation; © PhotoEdit.
121 NASA; Courtesy, Bell Helicopter Textron.
122 © John V. A. F. Neal—Photo Researchers
124 © Peggy Kahana—Peter Arnold, Inc.; © Dave Davidson—Tom Stack & Associates.
125 © DeSazo—Rapho Guillumette; © George Hall—Woodfin Camp & Associates.
126 © Ruud Taal—Capital Press
128 Courtesy, Airports Commission, City & County of San Francisco; © Martin Rogers—Stock, Boston.
129 © Ruud Taal—Capital Press
131 © F. Sieb—H. Armstrong Roberts; © Marc Bondarenko; © Wally Argus.
133 © Rob Outlaw—Root Resources; © David Haynes—Photo Options.
134 © University of Alabama; © Ed Malles—Pic's.
135 © Sonja Reiger—Photo Options
136 © Marc Bondarenko
137 © William H. Allen, Jr.
138 © R. Krubner—H. Armstrong Roberts; © Richard T. Nowitz; © David Haynes—Photo Options.
139 © Leo de Wys
140 The Granger Collection
142 The Bettmann Archive; © Charles Phelps Cushing—H. Armstong Roberts; The Bettmann Archive.
143 UPI/Bettmann Newsphotos
145 © James Balog—Photo Researchers; © Bob & Ira Spring; © Sullivan & Rogers—Bruce Coleman Inc.
146 © Ken Graham—Bruce Coleman Inc.
147 © James Balog—Bruce Coleman Inc.
148 © Thomas Kitchin—Tom Stack & Associates; © John Shaw—Bruce Coleman Inc.; © Mark Kelley.
149 © Rod Planck—Photo Researchers; © Ken Graham—Bruce Coleman Inc.
150 © Bob & Ira Spring (all photos on page).
151 © Jim Nilsen—Tom Stack & Associates; © Lael Morgan—Stone.
152 © Thomas Kitchin—Tom Stack & Associates
153 © Ken Graham—Bruce Coleman Inc. (all photos on page).
154 © Thomas Kitchin—Tom Stack & Associates
156 Alaska State Library—Early Prints Collection; The Granger Collection; Alaska State Library—Centennial Commission.
157 © Michael Penn—Liaison Agency; Alaska State Library—Eric A. Hegg Collection.
159 © Soren Rasmussen—Sipa Press; © Filip Horvat—SABA.
160 © Facelly—Sipa Press
161 © Chris Niedenthal—Black Star
162 © Tom Stoddart/Katz—SABA; © Paolo Koch—Photo Researchers.
163 The Granger Collection; The Bettmann Archive.
165 © Von Rhijn—Miller Comstock, Inc.
166 © E. Otto—Miller Comstock, Inc.; © Malak—Miller Comstock, Inc.
167 © Thomas Kitchin—Tom Stack & Associates
169 © George Hunter—Miller Comstock, Inc.
170 © Paolo Koch—Photo Researchers; © E. Otto—Miller Comstock, Inc.
174 Orchard House
175 Concord Free Public Library
176 Giraudon/Art Resource; The Granger Collection.
177 The Granger Collection; Pella Museum—Courtesy, The Art Institute of Chicago.
179 The Granger Collection
180 © Bob Evans—Peter Arnold Inc.; © Walter H. Hodge—Peter Arnold, Inc.; © Michael P. Gadomski—Photo Researchers; © James Bell—Photo Researchers.
181 © Biophoto Associates/Science Source—Photo Researchers; © Manfred Kage—Peter Arnold, Inc.; © Manfred Kage—Peter Arnold, Inc.; © Walter H. Hodge—Peter Arnold, Inc.
182 © Scott Barrow
185 © F. Jackson—Bruce Coleman Inc.; © Jean du Boisberranger—The Image Bank/Getty Images.
187 © Brian Rybolt—Art Directors etc.; © Bruce Stanley—AP/Wide World Photos.
188 © Hulton/Archive by Getty Images
189 © John Rooney—AP/Wide World Photos
191 © Suzanne & Nick Geary—Stone/Getty Images
193 © Manfred Kage—Peter Arnold, Inc.
194–194a Art Resource
194d © Ray Manley—SuperStock
194e © Will and Deni McIntyre—Photo Researchers
195 University of California, Lawrence Livermore Berkeley Laboratory
197 © Chislaine Morel—Liaison Agency
198 © Malcolm S. Kirk—Peter Arnold, Inc; © Chislaine Morel—Liaison Agency.
202 The Granger Collection; The Granger Collection; The Bettmann Archive.
203 The Granger Collection
204 The Granger Collection; Culver Pictures; The Granger Collection; North Wind Picture Archives; Culver Pictures.
205 The Free Library of Philadelphia; The Granger Collection; The Granger Collection; The Bettmann Archive; The Granger Collection.
206 Culver Pictures; The Granger Collection; Culver Pictures; North Wind Picture Archives; The Granger Collection.
207 The Granger Collection; The Granger Collection; Culver Pictures; The Granger Collection; Culver Pictures.
212 Culver Pictures
214a The Bettmann Archive (all photos on page).
214b The Granger Collection
218 The Everett Collection
220 © Sylvain Grandadam—Stone/Getty Images
221 © New Haven Colony Historical Society/AP/Wide World Photos
222 © E. S. Ross—California Academy of Sciences
224 © Joe McDonald—Animals Animals
225 © Johan Elzenga—Stone/Getty Images
226 AP/Wide World Photos
227 © J. C. Leacock—Network Aspen
228 SuperStock
229 © Dagli Orti—The Art Archive; © F. Damm—Zefa Collection/Masterfile; © Erich Lessing—National Archaeological Museum, Athens, Greece/Art Resource, NY; © Giraudon/Art Resource.
230 © British Museum/Topham/The Image Works
231 © Dagli Orti—Archaeological Museum, Baghdad/The Art Archive; © Scala/Art Resource, NY; © Borromeo/Art Resource, NY; © Scala/Art Resource, NY; © Genius of China Exhibition/The Art Archive.
232 © Ancient Art & Architecture/Danita Delimont, Agent; © Dagli Orti—Heraklion Museum/The Art Archive; © Erich Lessing—Art Resource, NY; © Werner Forman—Art Resource, NY.
233 © Klaus Goeken—Bildarchiv Preussischer Kulturbesitz/Art Resource, NY; Walters Art Museum, Baltimore, MD/The Bridgeman Art Library; The Granger Collection; © Dagli Orti—National Anthropological Museum, Mexico/The Art Archive.
234–235 © Jason Edwards—NGS Image Collection
234 © Charles Graham—eStock Photo; © Dagli Orti—Museo Capitolino, Rome/The Art Archive; © Courtney Milne—Masterfile.
235 The Granger Collection
236 National Archaeological Museum, Athens, Greece/The Bridgeman Art Library
237 British Museum, London, UK/The Bridgeman Art Library
238 © Miles Ertman—Masterfile; © Dagli Orti—The Art Archive.
239 © Dave G. Houser—Houserstock
240 © Borromeo/Art Resource, NY
241 Masterfile
242 © Dagli Orti—The Art Archive
243 © Martha Cooper—Peter Arnold, Inc.
244 © Eileen Tweedy—Museum of Mankind, London/The Art Archive
244–245 © Steve Vidler—SuperStock
245 © Lee Boltin
246 The Granger Collection
247 © Jack Delano
249 Courtesy of Marian Anderson, RCA Records
250 © Maurice and Sally Landre—FPG
251 Lisl Steiner—Grolier Inc.; © Jerry Frank.
253 © Tom Hollyman—Photo Researchers; © Peter Wichman—Birnback.
254 Boston Medical Library, Massachusetts Medical Society
257 Art Resource
258 © Dagli Orti—Museo Civico, Padua/The Art Archive
259 © Joao Silva—Black Star
261 © Marilyn Kazmers—Peter Arnold, Inc.
264 © Michel Viard—Peter Arnold, Inc.; © Matt Meadows—Peter Arnold, Inc.; © Science Photo Library—Photo Researchers.
265 © Tom McHugh—Photo Researchers; © Bob Winsett—ProFiles West/Index Stock; © Nicole Duplaix—Peter Arnold, Inc.; © Manfred Kage—Peter Arnold, Inc.
266 © M. P. Kahl—Photo Researchers; © R. Andrew Odum—Peter Arnold, Inc.; © E. R. Degginger—Animals Animals; © Joe McDonald—Tom Stack & Associates.
267 © Gregory G. Dimijian—Photo Researchers; © Carl Roessler—Animals Animals; © Jeff Foott.
268 © Richard R. Hansen—Photo Researchers; © M. P. Kahl—Photo Researchers; © Nigel Dennis—Photo Researchers.
270 © Joseph T. Collins—Photo Researchers; © Kathie Atkinson—Animals Animals; © Toni Angermayer—Photo Researchers; © Robert A. Tyrrell—Animals Animals.
271 © Tom McHugh—Photo Researchers; © Kevin Schafer—Tom Stack & Associates.
272 © Stephen J. Krasemann—Photo Researchers
273 © Zig Leszczynski—Animals Animals
274 © Thomas Kitchin—Tom Stack & Associates
275 © Breck P. Kent—Animals Animals
276 © Tom Stack—Tom Stack & Associates; © Chlaus Lotscher—Peter Arnold, Inc.
277 © Jeff Foott; © Richard Kolar—Animals Animals; © Dave Watts—Tom Stack & Associates.
278 © Fred Bavendam—Peter Arnold, Inc.
279 © Anup & Manoj Shah—Animals Animals; © Mark Chappell—Animals Animals.
280 © Bruce Davidson—Animals Animals; © Jany Sauvanet—Photo Researchers.
281 © J. H. Robinson—Animals Animals; © Allen Russell—ProFiles West/Index Stock.
282 © Jeff Lepore—Photo Researchers; © Jeff Foott.
283 © Stan Wayman—Photo Researchers
284 © Jeff Foott
285 © Nancy Sefton—Photo Researchers; © William J. Jahoda—Photo Researchers; © Brian Parker—Tom Stack & Associates.

286 © S. R. Maglione—Photo Researchers
287 © Bradley Smith—Animals Animals
288 Photofest
289 © 1951 Warner Bros. Inc.; © Will Vinton Productions, The California Raisins, © CALRAB; © Touchstone Pictures—Amblin Entertainment, Inc.
290 © 1988 Pixar
291 © 1937 The Walt Disney Company; © The Walt Disney Company.
292 © Douglas T. Cheeseman, Jr.—Peter Arnold, Inc.; © Russ Kinne—Photo Researchers.
293 © Schoeck—Leo de Wys
296 © François Gohier—Photo Researchers
297 © Bruce Davidson—Animals Animals; © Stephen J. Krasemann—Photo Researchers.
298 © Arthur Gloor—Animals Animals
299 The Bettmann Archive
300 © Dave G. Houser—Houserstock; © Kevin Frayer—Canadian Press/AP/Wide World Photos; © David Young-Wolff—PhotoEdit.
301 © David R. Austen—Stock, Boston/PictureQuest
302 © Peggy & Yoram Kahana—Peter Arnold, Inc.; C. C. Lockwood—Bruce Coleman Inc.
303 © Ken Heyman
304 © Thomas Hoepker—Magnum Photos
305 © Bill Foley—Bruce Coleman Inc.
306 The Granger Collection; Courtesy, Stuart B. Levy, M.D. from *The Antibiotic Paradox: How Antibiotic Drugs Are Destroying the Miracle*, © Plenum Press, 1992.
307 The Bettmann Archive (all photos on page).
308 Courtesy, Professor Greenwood—University Hospital Queen's Medical Centre—Nottingham (all photos on page).
309 Raymond T. Testa—Lederle Laboratories
311 © Dennis Kunkel, University of Hawaii
312 © James Holmes—Celltech Ltd/Science Photo Library—Photo Researchers
315 Yale University Art Gallery, Mabel Brady Garvan and C. Sanford Bull, B.A. 1893, Collections (by exchange); © SuperStock; © SuperStock.
316 Cooper-Hewitt Museum; Sandwich Glass Museum; National Museum of American History, John Paul Remansnyder Collection.
316a Buten Museum of Wedgwood; Abby Aldrich Rockefeller Folk Art Center; Yale University Art Gallery, William Inglis Morse Collection, Gift of his daughter, Mrs. Frederick W. Hilles.
316b © Stan Aggie—Picture Group; Cooper-Hewitt Museum.
317 Art Resource
318 © Satoshi Kuribayashi—Nature Production; © Satoshi Kuribayashi—Nature Production.
322 © Michael Fogden—DRK Photo
323 © Varin—Jacana—Photo Researchers; © Mark Moffett—Minden Pictures; © Mark Moffett—Minden Pictures.
324 © Dwight Kuhn—DRK Photo
325 © Gerry Ellis Nature Photography; © Gerry Ellis—Bruce Coleman Inc.
326 © BIOS—Peter Arnold, Inc.; © Gerry Ellis Nature Photography.
327 © Peter Davey—Bruce Coleman Inc.; © Gerry Ellis Nature Photography
328 © Roberto Hoesch
330 Photo courtesy of NY Apple Association; © Alan L. Detrick—Photo Researchers; © Alan L. Detrick—Photo Researchers; © Alan L. Detrick—Photo Researchers; © Alan L. Detrick—Photo Researchers; Photo courtesy of NY Apple Association.
331 © Eric Crichton—Bruce Coleman Inc.; © Martha McBride—Unicorn Stock Photos.
333 The Granger Collection
336 © Michael Yamashita
337 © Phyllis Picardi—Photo Network; © Gerd Ludwig—Woodfin Camp & Associates.
340 *Stories From Arabian Nights* retold by Lawrence Housman. Illustrated by Edmund Dulac. Charles Scribner's Sons, 1907.
341 The Granger Collection (all photos on page).
342 The Granger Collection
343 © K. Scholz—H. Armstrong Roberts, Inc.; © Bernard Gerard—The Viesti Collection, Inc..
344 © Wendy Chan—The Image Bank; The Granger Collection.
345 © Marge George—Spectrum Stock; Brannan Linsley—AP/Wide World Photos; Jeremy Ferguson—Spectrum Stock; © Jeremy Ferguson—Spectrum Stock.
347 © Peter Paz—The Image Bank
348 © Anthony Mercieca—Root Resources; © Patti Murray—Animals Animals; © J. H. Robinson—Photo Researchers.
349 © Husanne Husanne—PPO/Getty Images
350 © Dennis Cox—Time Life Pictures/Getty Images; © Steve Helber—AP/Wide World Photos; © Kenneth Garrett—NGS Image Collection.
351 Art Resource, NY
352 Art Resource, NY; © Richard A. Cooke III—Stone/Getty Images.
353 © David Ortiz—Bruce Coleman Inc.; © Scala/Art Resource, NY.
354 © Heinz Plenge—Peter Arnold, Inc.
355 © Volker Steger—Science Photo Library/Photo Researchers; © Eduardo Verdugo—AP/Wide World Photos.
356 © Kenneth Garrett—NGS Image Collection; © Dennis Cox—Time Life Pictures/Getty Images.
357 AP/Wide World Photos
358 Mary Evans Picture Library
359 © E. R. Degginger—Bruce Coleman Inc.
360 © Douglas Mazonowicz—Bruce Coleman Inc.; © Jock Montgomery—Bruce Coleman Inc.
362 © Focus on Sports
364 © Picture Colour Library Ltd./eStock Photo
365 © John Elk III—Bruce Coleman Inc.
366 © Steve Vidler—eStock Photo
367 © Jason Edwards—NGS Image Collection
368 © Steve Vidler—eStock Photo
369 © Michele Burgess—Index Stock Imagery/PictureQuest
370 © Anthony Scibilia—Art Resource, NY
371 © Robert Frerck—Woodfin Camp & Associates
372 © Scala/Art Resource, NY
373 © Vladpans—eStock Photo
374 © Rankin Harvey—Houserstock; © Bernard Boutrit—Woodfin Camp & Associates.
375 © Paul Maeyaert—The Bridgeman Art Library; © Spencer Grant—PhotoEdit.
376 © Lower Manhattan Development Corporation/AP/Wide World Photos
377 © Morry Gash—AP/Wide World Photos; © Neil Setchfield—Travelsite.
378 © SuperStock; © Ted Spiegel—Black Star.
379 © Stephen J. Krasemann—Peter Arnold, Inc.
382 © Loren McIntyre
384 © Allen Green—Photo Researchers
385 © Victor Englebert—Photo Researchers; © David Barnes—Stone.
386 © J. Zeister—Z.E.F.A./Leo de Wys
386a © Loren McIntyre
386b The Bettmann Archive
386c UPI Bettmann Newsphotos
386d © Diego Goldberg—Corbis-Sygma
387 Alinari—Art Reference Bureau
393 © Larry Ulrich; © Tom Bean—The Stock Market; © Jerry Jacka.
394 © Willard Clay; © Bob Clemenz.
395 © Bob Clemenz
396 © Bob Clemenz; © Jerry Jacka.
397 © Bob Clemenz
398 © Joe Bator—The Stock Market; © Cameramann International Ltd.
399 © Jane R. Kriete—Root Resources
400 © Larry Ulrich; © M. Schneiders—H. Armstrong Roberts; © Willard Clay; © Larry Ulrich.
401 © Jerry Jacka; © George Hunter—H. Armstrong Roberts.
404 © Steve Leonard—Black Star
405 Arizona Historical Foundation; © Everett Collection.
407 © Matt Bradley; © Matt Bradley; © Bob Firth.
408 © Terry Donnelley—Stone; © Bill Barksdale—Root Resources.
409 © Matt Bradley
410 © Matt Bradley (all photos on page).
411 © Matt Bradley
412 © Garry D. McMichael—Root Resources; © Don Smetzer—Stone.
413 © H. Abernathy—H. Armstrong Roberts
414 © Garry D. McMichael—Root Resources; © John Elk III; © Terry Donnelley—Stone; © Matt Bradley.
415 © John Elk III
416 1993 National Gallery of Art, Washington, Paul Mellon Collection
418 © Wide World; © Karl Gehring—Liaison Agency.
419 UPI/Bettmann Newsphotos; Historical Pictures—Stock Montage, Inc.
421 © Alex Borodulin—Leo de Wys; © Eugene G. Schulz.
423 The Metropolitan Museum of Art
424 Photographie Giraudon—Musee de l'Armee; The Bettmann Archive; The Metropolitan Museum of Art; The Metropolitan Museum of Art; The Granger Collection.
425 The Metropolitan Museum of Art (all photos on page).
426 Archive Photos
427 The Bridgeman/Art Resource; Giraudon/Art Resource; The Metropolitan Museum of Art, Gift of Renate Hofmann, 1975; © Lee Boltin.
428 Scala/Art Resource; Musee des Antiquities Nationales, St. Germaine-en-Laye, France.
429 Scala/Art Resource
430 Giraudon/Art Resource
431 The Metropolitan Museum of Art, Bequest of Mrs. H. O. Havemeyer, 1929. The H. O. Havemeyer Collection; General Egyptian Book Organization, Cairo.
432 Art Resource; Scala/Art Resource.
433 Collection, The Museum of Modern Art, New York. Gift of Mrs. Simon Guggenheim; The Metropolitan Museum of Art, Purchase, 1983.
434 The White House Collection, © copyright White House Historical Association; The Bettmann Archive; The Granger Collection.
435 The Bettmann Archive; The Granger Collection.
436 © The White House Collection, © copyright White House Historical Association
438d © Bill Holden—Leo de Wys; © Roland Seitre—Peter Arnold, Inc.; © Charles Gupton—Stone; © Charles Gupton—Stone.
438e © Dian Duchin—Bruce Coleman Inc.; © Steve Vidler—Leo de Wys; © David Ball—The Stock Market.
438f © Robert Azzi—Woodfin Camp & Associates; © Nigel Dickinson—Stone.
438g © Colin Prior—Stone; © George Holton—Photo Researchers.
440 © Bryan Alexander—Black Star; © Jeffrey Aaronson—Network Aspen.
441 © Jeffrey Aaronson—Network Aspen; © Norman Meyers—Bruce Coleman Inc.
442 © Norman Owen Tomalin—Bruce Coleman Inc.
443 © Wardene Weisser—Bruce Coleman Inc.; © Manoj Shah—Stone.
444 © Alain Nogues—Corbis-Sygma; © Ned Gillette—The Stock Market; © Clark James Mishler—The Stock Market; © Anthony Cassidy—Stone; © Zviki-Eshet—The Stock Market.
445 © Catalyst—The Stock Market; © Ian Lloyd—The Stock Market; © Anthony Cassidy—Stone; © Paul Steel—The Stock Market.
448 © Benjamin Rondell—The Stock Market; © Gerd Ludwig—Woodfin Camp & Associates; © Steve Vidler—Leo de Wys; © Luis Villota—The Stock Market.
449 © Paolo Koch—Photo Researchers; © D & J Heaton—First Light.
450 © Lawrence Manning—First Light; © Steve Vidler—Leo de Wys.
451 © Bruno Barbey—Magnum Photos; © Phillip Jones Griffiths—Magnum Photos.
452 © Jacques Langevin—Corbis-Sygma; © Stone.
453 © Jon Hicks—Leo de Wys; National Museum of Pakistan, Karachi; The Granger Collection.
455 The Granger Collection (all photos on page).
456 Mansell/Time*Life*/Getty Images; National Archives.
457 ©Ariel Skelley—Masterfile
458 © A. Ramey—Woodfin Camp & Associates; © Tomas del Amo—The Viesti Collection, Inc.; © John & Lisa Merrill—Danita Delimont, Agent; © David Young-Wolff—PhotoEdit.
459 © Susan Sterner—AP/Wide World Photos; © A. Reininger—Woodfin Camp & Associates.
460 AP/Wide World Photos
462 Archaeological Museum, Baghdad/The Art Archive
463 © Damien Lovegrove—Science Photo Library/Photo Researchers
464 © National Portrait Gallery/Smithsonian Institute/Art Resource, NY
465 The Granger Collection
466 Lyndon B. Johnson Space Center/NASA
468 © Brian Seed—Stone
469 The Rohss Museum of Arts and Crafts, Gothenburg
471 © 1986 Australian National University/California Institute of Technology; NASA.
472 © Fred Espenak—Science Photo Library—Photo Researchers
474 The Granger Collection; UPI/Bettmann Newsphotos.
475 NOAO; The Granger Collection; North Wind Picture Archives.
476 The Granger Collection; UPI/Bettmann Newsphotos.
476c Digital Vision/Getty Images
476d © Nimatallah/Art Resource, NY
477 © Greg Probst—Stone
480 NASA

483 © Omikron—Photo Researchers
484 The Granger Collection
486 Brown Brothers
489 © Phototake
490 North Wind Picture Archives
491 National Audubon Society
494 The Bettmann Archive
496 © Harvey Lloyd—The Stock Market; © John Carnemolla—Australian Picture Library; © Michael Coyne—Black Star.
497 © Luis Villota—The Stock Market; © Bill Bachman—Photo Researchers; © Michael Coyne—Black Star; © David Austin—Stone.
498 © David Austen—Stone; © Nick Rains—Australian Picture Library.
499 © Ulrike Welsch; © Denis O'Byrne—Stock Photos Pty Ltd.
500 © Robert Garvey—Black Star; © David Davies—Stone
501 The Art Gallery of New South Wales; © Jack Vartoogian; The Bettmann Archive; © AP/Wide World Photos; © Rick Maiman—Corbis-Sygma.
504 © Paul Chesley—Stone
505 © SuperStock; © Robin Smith—Stone; © Kevin Schafer—Stone
506 © Paul McKelvey—Stone
507 © Ben Simmons—The Stock Market
510 © Robert Frerck—Woodfin Camp & Associates; © J. Burry—Australian Picture Library.
511 © J. Burry—Australian Picture Library; © Patrick Ward—Stone
512 © John Carnemolla—Australian Picture Library; © Hideo Kurihara—Stone
513 © Raga—The Stock Market; © Noeline Kelly—Australian Picture Library.
514 © John Carnemolla—Australian Picture Library
515 The Tate Gallery, London—Art Resource
516 The Granger Collection; Image Library.
517 © Robert Garvey—Black Star
518 © Joachim Messerschmidt—Bruce Coleman Inc.
519 © Stone; © Herlinde Koelbl—Leo de Wys; Austrian Information Service.
522 The Granger Collection; Scala/Art Resource, NY; The Granger Collection; The Granger Collection; The Granger Collection; The Bettmann Archive.
523 Giraudon/Art Resource
524 © Dagli Orti—Museum der Stadt Wien/The Art Archive
530 © SuperStock; © Tim Boyle—Getty Images.
531 © Adam Lubroth—Stone
532 © Paul Shambroom—Photo Researchers
533 © David Young-Wolff—Stone
534 © Robert Schleicher
535 © Robert Schleicher; Aurora Plastics Corp.
536 UPI; © Diana Burnett—Focus on Sports.
537 © J. DiMaggio—Focus on Sports; © Jeffry W. Meyers—Alpha.
538 © SuperStock
539 Ford Motor Company
541 The Bettmann Archive; © Cindy Lewis—All Rights Reserved; © 1981 Henry Austin Clark, Jr.—Mr. Donald M. Scott, Penfield, New York; © 1970 Henry Austin Clark, Jr.—Mr. Frank H. Gardner, West Newton, Massachusetts; © 1972 Henry Austin Clark, Jr.—Mr. Willard W. Newman, Tampa, Florida; © 1980 Henry Austin Clark, Jr.—Mrs. William C. Donze, Strongsville, Ohio.
542 © Cindy Lewis—All Rights Reserved; © 1981 Henry Austin Clark, Jr.—Mr. Morris Stone; © Henry Austin Clark, Jr.; © Cindy Lewis—All Rights Reserved; From the collections of Henry Ford Museum & Greenfield Village.
543 From the collections of Henry Ford Museum & Greenfield Village
544 © Henry Austin Clark, Jr.; © Chet Bahn—Volkswagen Corp.; From the collections of Henry Ford Museum & Greenfield Village; © Ron Kimball; From the collections of Henry Ford Museum & Greenfield Village.
545 © Cindy Lewis—All Rights Reserved; Acura; Toyota Motor Sales; 1998 GM Corp.—Used with Permission of GM Media Archives. All Rights Reserved; Mercedes Benz; Ford Corporation; Honda Automobile News Bureau; Reprinted with permission of Chrysler Historical Foundation; Volvo Corporation; 1996, 1997 GM Corp.—Used with Permission of GM Media Archives.
552 Ford Motor Company; General Motors.
553 © John Zoiner—Nawrocki Stock Photos; Chrysler Corporation; Chrysler Corporation.
554 Ford Motor Company.
555 © Ovak Arslanian; © Cameramann International Ltd.
556 Ford Motor Company.
557 © William Bacon—Photo Researchers
558 © Spencer Grant—Photo Researchers
559 © Jim Sugar—Black Star
560 The Bettmann Archive; Science Museum, London.
561 National Air & Space Museum—Smithsonian Institution
563 The Granger Collection; Culver Pictures, Inc.
565 Photo by Ed Castle from the *Smithsonian Book of Flight* by Walter J. Boyne © 1987, Smithsonian Institution; The Bettmann Archive.
566 © David Falconer—Bruce Coleman Inc.
567 © James Sugar—Black Star
568 © David O. Hill—Photo Researchers; © Mel M. Boughman—Bruce Coleman Inc.
569 © Journalism Services; © Matt Bradley—Bruce Coleman Inc.; © Jean-Claude Carton—Bruce Coleman Inc.
570 © Mike Smith—MIT
571 © Michael Melford—Wheeler Pictures
573 © Serguei Fedorov—Woodfin Camp & Associates
575 Courtesy Department of Library Services—American Museum of Natural History
577 © Buddy Mays; © Comstock.
578 © George H. Harrison—Grant Heilman Photography